The European Powers
in the First World War

GARLAND REFERENCE LIBRARY OF THE HUMANITIES
VOLUME 1483

The European Powers
in the First World War
An Encyclopedia

Edited by
Spencer C. Tucker

Associate Editors
Laura Matysek Wood
Justin D. Murphy

GARLAND PUBLISHING, INC.
New York & London
1996

Library of Congress Cataloging-in-Publication Data

The European powers in the First World War : an encyclopedia / edited
    by Spencer C. Tucker ; associate editors, Laura Matysek Wood,
    Justin D. Murphy.
           p.   cm. — (Garland reference library of the humanities ;
    v. 1483)
        Includes bibliographical references and index.
        ISBN 0-8153-0399-8 (acid-free paper)
        1. World War, 1914–1918—Encyclopedias. 2. World War, 1914–1918—
Europe—Encyclopedias. I. Tucker, Spencer, 1937–   . II. Wood, Laura
Matysek. III. Murphy, Justin D. IV. Series: Garland reference library of the
humanities ; vol. 1483.
    D510.E97   1996
    940.3'03—dc20   95-41418
                                             CIP

Cover design by Lawrence Wolfson Design, New York. Photograph research by
Margery Trenk. Cover photograph courtesy of the Bettmann Archive.

Printed on acid-free, 250-year-life paper
Manufactured in the United States of America

Contents

Introduction

The First World War was the single most important event of the twentieth century. Designed as a companion to Garland's *The United States in the First World War*, this volume concentrates on non-U.S. aspects of the conflict. Organized alphabetically, its more than 600 detailed entries offer information and insight on such subjects as the causes of the conflict, major battles and campaigns, weapons systems (including military aviation, chemical warfare, the submarine, and the tank), and the terms of the peace. Some 350 biographies provide information on the roles played in the conflict by generals, admirals, and civilian leaders. There are also biographies of individuals who were shaped by the war, such as Charles De Gaulle, Adolf Hitler, Benito Mussolini, and Joseph Stalin; essays on each of the countries involved in the conflict; new appraisals of such subjects as military medicine and artillery tactics; and essays on such diverse subjects as art, literature, and music in the war. Each entry has references for additional reading, and a subject index provides easy access. The volume is an excellent reference source for scholar and neophyte alike.

All dates in this encyclopedia, unless otherwise noted, are according to the Western calendar. For Slavic names we have opted for the Library of Congress transliterations. Exceptions are in rendering into English names of some persons or places. For the convenience of the reader we have retained those names and places that have become anglicized: Moscow (for Moskva) and Nicholas II (for Nikolai II), for example. Times are all on a military, twenty-four-hour clock. Thus 6:00 A.M. is 06:00, and 6:00 P.M. is 18:00. In entries on individuals, the military rank listed is the highest earned during the war.

Perhaps not surprisingly, this book has turned into a much larger undertaking than I had anticipated. Simply arranging for the 620 entries was in itself a daunting task. Bringing all of it to completion would not have been possible without the great assistance of my two associate editors: Justin D. Murphy, professor at Howard Payne University, and Laura Matysek Wood, professor at Tarrant County Junior College. They are two of my doctoral students, and I am most proud of them. Their knowledge of this period and editing skills have proven invaluable.

I am, of course, particularly grateful to the ninety-four individuals who contributed entries to the encyclopedia. Some did only one entry; others wrote a great many. Without their assistance there would have been no encyclopedia.

I would also like to thank my wife, Beverly, for her patience and understanding in what has been a long and very time-consuming task. Her editorial skills have also been very helpful. I would also like to thank my graduate assistant, Mark Beasley. He has been of great assistance in looking up numerous small details, checking dates, and obtaining full citations. I am also grateful to Bill Pohl of the Department of Modern Languages at Texas Christian University for translations from the German. Don Frazier of McMurry University did a superb job on the maps. As always, the assistance of History Department office manager Barbara Pierce has been invaluable. She retyped many of the entries that had to be scanned and assisted in many other tasks.

I have tried to ensure consistency throughout the volume and to catch errors. In any work of this magnitude there are bound to be some of the latter. I hope they are few and take full responsibility for any that may appear.

Spencer C. Tucker

Maps

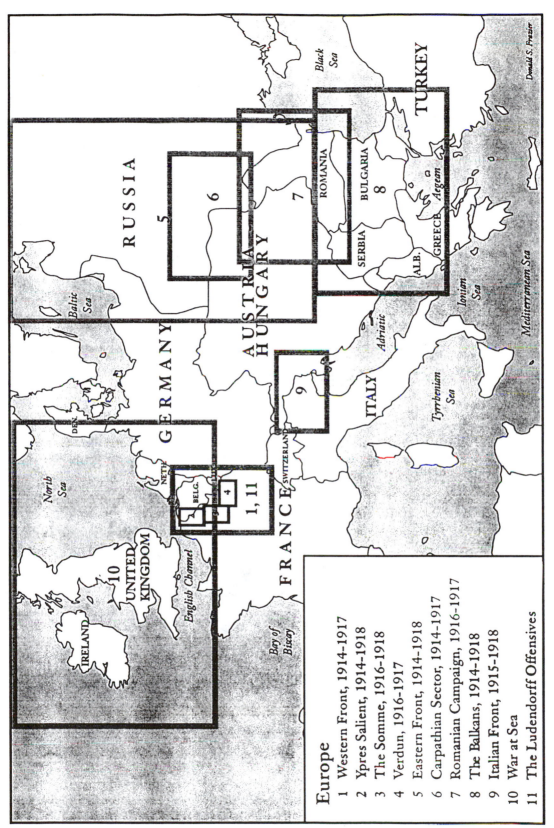

Europe

1 Western Front, 1914–1917
2 Ypres Salient, 1914–1918
3 The Somme, 1916–1918
4 Verdun, 1916–1917
5 Eastern Front, 1914–1918
6 Carpathian Sector, 1914–1917
7 Romanian Campaign, 1916–1917
8 The Balkans, 1914–1918
9 Italian Front, 1915–1918
10 War at Sea
11 The Ludendorff Offensives

Donald S. Frazier

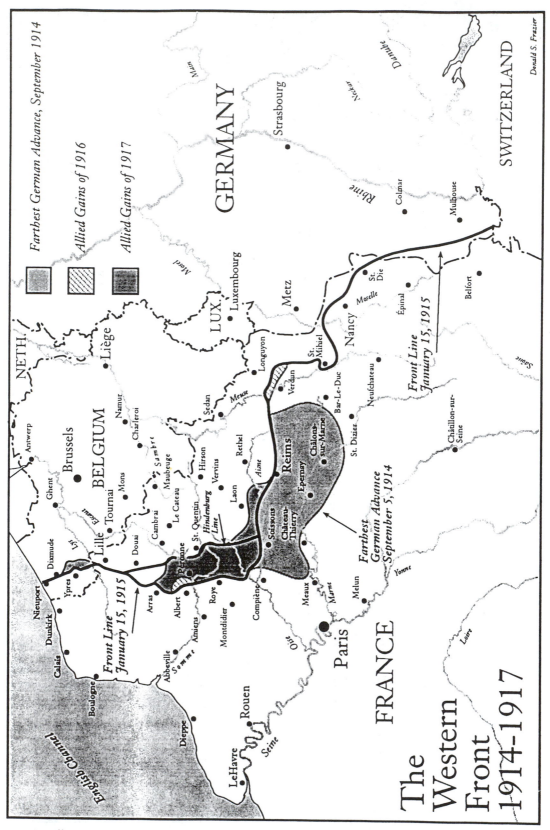

The
Western
Front
1914–1917

FRANCE

GERMANY

SWITZERLAND

NETH.

BELGIUM

LUX.

Farthest German Advance, September 1914

Allied Gains of 1916

Allied Gains of 1917

Donald S. Frazier

Front Line January 15, 1915

Front Line January 15, 1915

Farthest German Advance September 5, 1914

English Channel

Calais
Boulogne
Dunkirk
Neuport
Dixmude
Ypres
Lille
Tournai
Ghent
Brussels
Antwerp
Liège
Namur
Charleroi
Mons
Maubeuge
Le Cateau
Cambrai
Douai
Arras
Albert
Péronne
St. Quentin
Hindenburg Line
Roye
Montdidier
Compiègne
Amiens
Abbeville
Somme
LeHavre
Rouen
Dieppe
Seine
Hirson
Vervins
Laon
Soissons
Château-Thierry
Reims
Épernay
Châlons-sur-Marne
Meaux
Melun
Paris
Sedan
Rethel
Aisne
Verdun
St. Mihiel
Longuyon
Bar-Le-Duc
St. Dizier
Neufchateau
Nancy
Metz
Luxembourg
St. Die
Épinal
Belfort
Strasbourg
Colmar
Mulhouse
Châtillon-sur-Seine
Meuse
Moselle
Oise
Marne
Yonne
Loire
Saône
Rhine
Moselle
Main
Neckar
Danube
Scheldt
Sambre
Lys

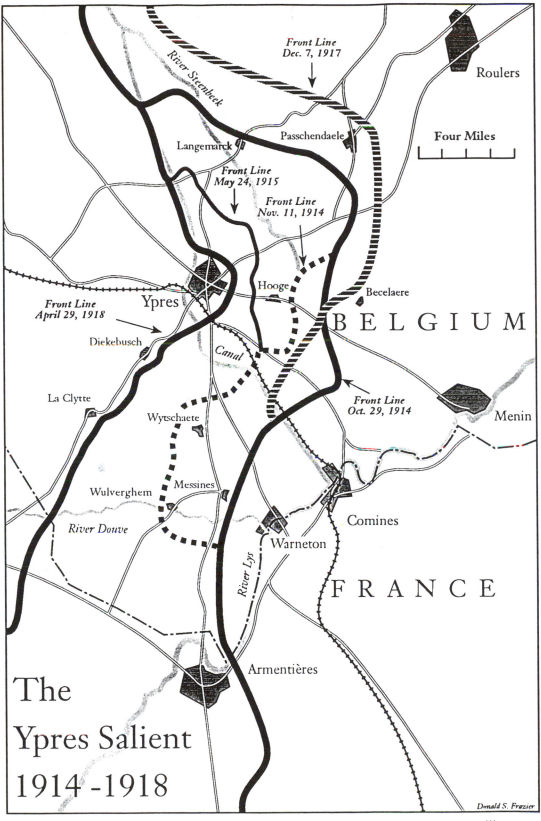

The Ypres Salient
1914-1918

MAPS xiii

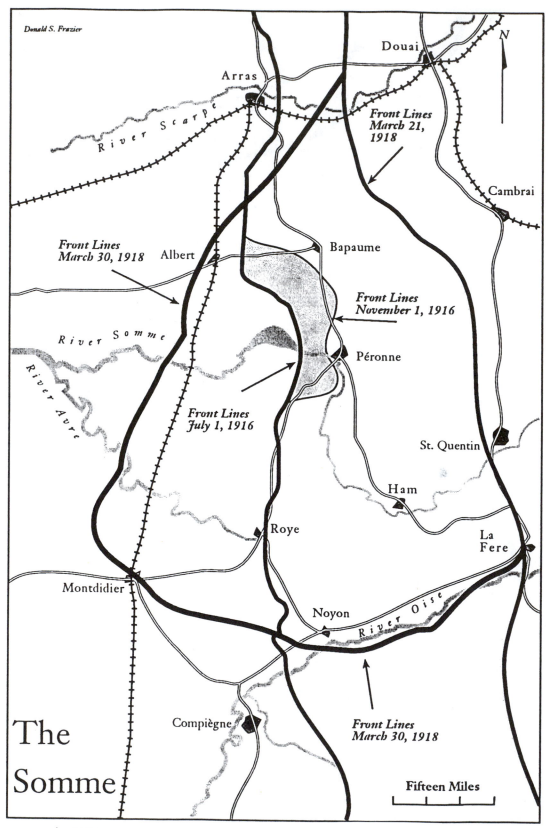

Donald S. Frazier

Douai

Arras

River Scarpe

N

*Front Lines
March 21,
1918*

Cambrai

*Front Lines
March 30, 1918*

Albert

Bapaume

*Front Lines
November 1, 1916*

Péronne

River Somme

River Avre

*Front Lines
July 1, 1916*

St. Quentin

Ham

Roye

La
Fere

Montdidier

Noyon

River Oise

*Front Lines
March 30, 1918*

Compiègne

The
Somme

Fifteen Miles

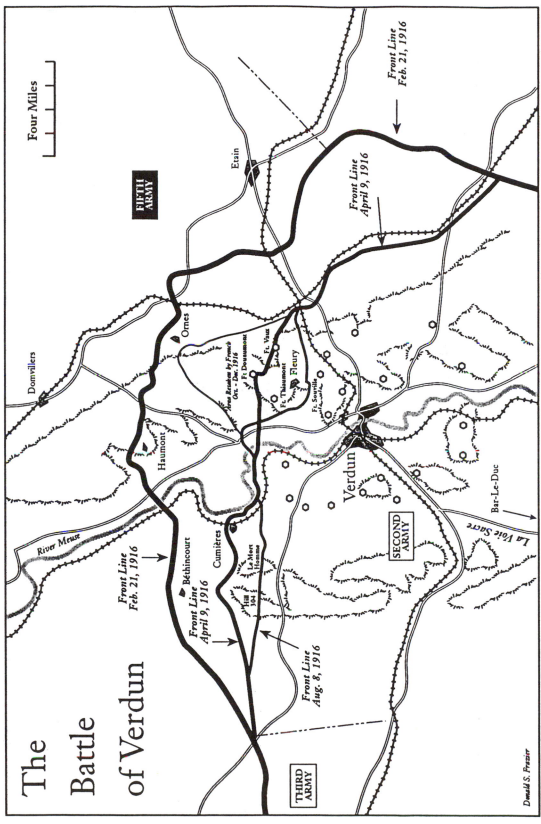

The
Battle
of Verdun

Four Miles

Front Line
Feb. 21, 1916

Front Line
April 9, 1916

Front Line
Feb. 21, 1916

FIFTH
ARMY

Etain

Ornes

Domvillers

Ft. Vaux

Ft. Douaumont

Area Retaken by French
Oct. – Dec. 1916

Fleury

Ft. Thiaumont

Ft. Souville

Haumont

Verdun

SECOND
ARMY

Bar-Le-Duc

La Voie Sacrée

River Meuse

Béthincourt

Cumières

Front Line
April 9, 1916

Front Line
Feb. 21, 1916

Le Mort
Homme

Hill
304

Front Line
Aug. 8, 1916

THIRD
ARMY

Donald S. Frazier

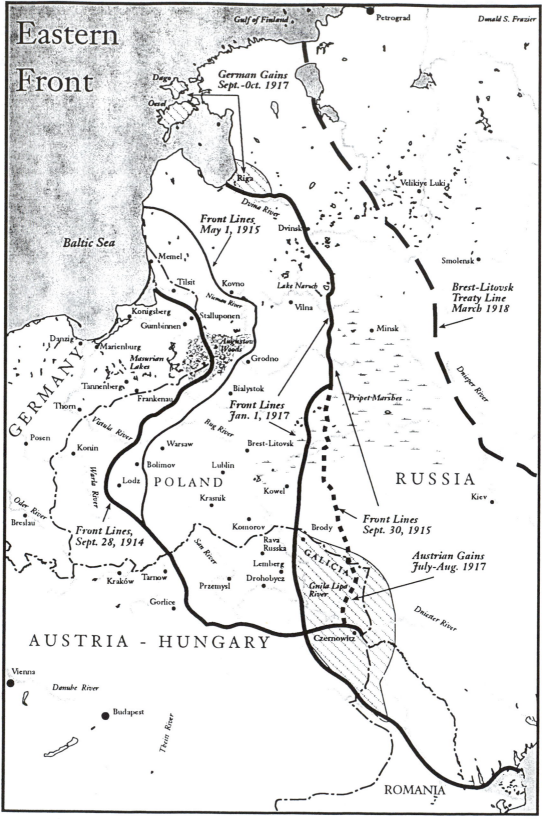

Eastern Front

Donald S. Frazier

Gulf of Finland

*German Gains
Sept.–Oct. 1917*

Petrograd

Velikiye Luki

Baltic Sea

Riga

Dvina River

Dvinsk

Smolensk

*Front Lines
May 1, 1915*

*Brest-Litovsk
Treaty Line
March 1918*

Memel

Tilsit

Kovno

Niemen River

Lake Narnch

Vilna

Minsk

Königsberg

Stalluponen

Gumbinnen

*Augustow
Woods*

Danzig

Marienburg

*Masurian
Lakes*

Grodno

Dnieper River

GERMANY

Tannenberg

Frankenau

Bialystok

Bug River

Pripet-Marshes

Thorn

*Front Lines
Jan. 1, 1917*

Posen

Konin

Warsaw

Brest-Litovsk

RUSSIA

Vistula River

Bolimov

Lublin

Lodz

POLAND

Kowel

Kiev

Warta River

Krasnik

Oder River

Breslau

*Front Lines,
Sept. 28, 1914*

Komorov

Brody

*Front Lines
Sept. 30, 1915*

San River

Rava
Russka

GALICIA

*Austrian Gains
July–Aug. 1917*

Lemberg

Kraków

Tarnow

Przemysl

Drohobycz

*Gnila Lipa
River*

Gorlice

Dniester River

AUSTRIA - HUNGARY

Czernowitz

Vienna

Danube River

Budapest

Theiss River

ROMANIA

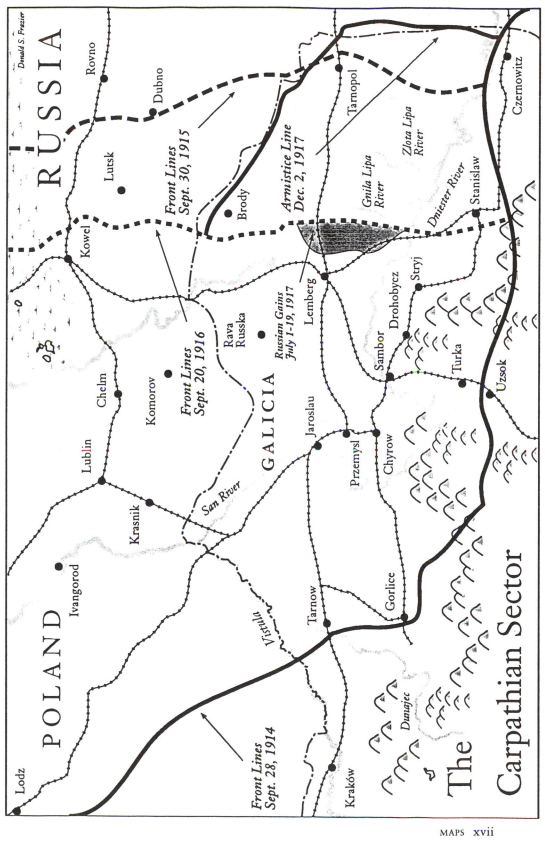

Donald S. Frazier

RUSSIA

Rovno
Dubno
Lutsk
Kowel
Chelm
Lublin
Krasnik
Ivangorod
Lodz

POLAND

Komorov
Rava Russka
San River
Vistula

Front Lines Sept. 30, 1915

Front Lines Sept. 20, 1916

GALICIA

Russian Gains July 1-19, 1917

Jaroslau
Przemysl
Chyrow
Tarnow
Gorlice
Kraków
Dunajec

Front Lines Sept. 28, 1914

Tarnopol

Armistice Line Dec. 2, 1917

Lemberg
Brody
Stryj
Drohobycz
Sambor
Turka
Uzsok
Stanislaw
Czernowitz

Zlota Lipa River
Gnila Lipa River
Dniester River

The Carpathian Sector

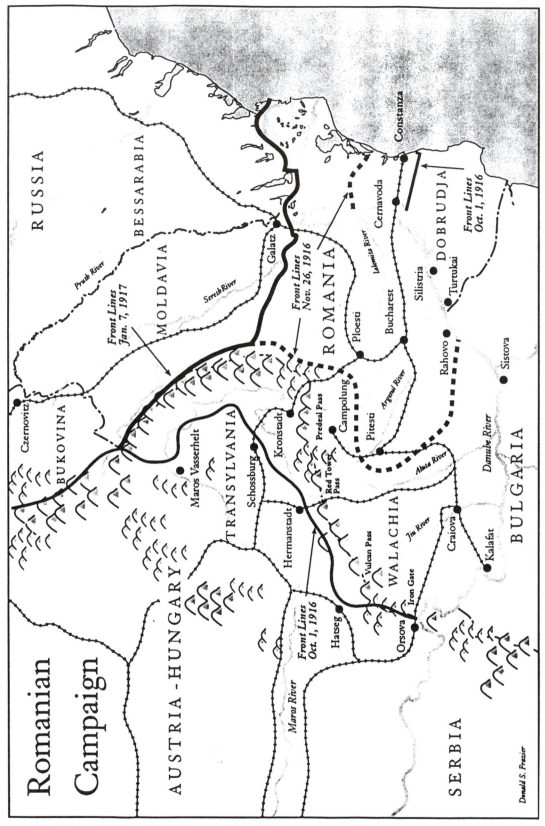

Romanian Campaign

RUSSIA

BESSARABIA

MOLDAVIA

Pruth River

Sereth River

Galaz

*Front Lines
Jan. 7, 1917*

*Front Lines
Nov. 26, 1916*

ROMANIA

Czernovitz

BUKOVINA

TRANSYLVANIA

Maros Vasserhelt

Schossburg

Kronstadt

Predeal Pass

Campolung

Pitesti

Argeul River

Ploesti

Bucharest

Silistria

Ialomita River

Cernavoda

Constanza

DOBRUDJA

*Front Lines
Oct. 1, 1916*

Turtukai

Rahovo

Sistova

Danube River

AUSTRIA - HUNGARY

Hermanstadt

Red Tower
Pass

Vulcan Pass

WALACHIA

Iron Gate

Orsova

Haseg

*Front Lines
Oct. 1, 1916*

Maros River

Jiu River

Craiova

Kalafat

Aluta River

BULGARIA

SERBIA

Donald S. Frazier

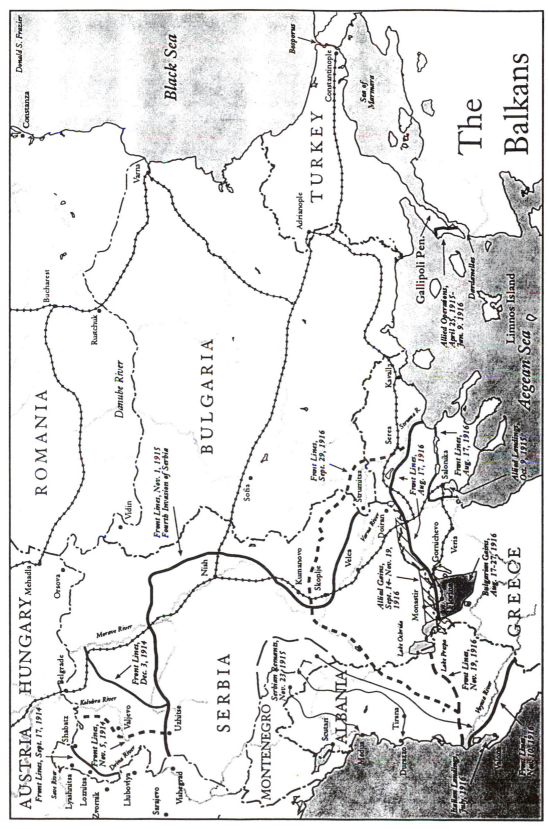

The Balkans

Donald S. Frazier

Black Sea

Constanza

TURKEY

Bosporus

Constantinople

Sea of Marmara

Adrianople

Gallipoli Pen.

Allied Operations, April 25, 1915– Jan. 9, 1916

Dardanelles

Limnos Island

Aegean Sea

BULGARIA

Varna

Bucharest

Rustchuk

Danube River

ROMANIA

Mehadia

Orsova

Vidin

Sofia

Front Lines, Nov. 1, 1915 Fourth Invasion of Serbia

Kavala

Strma R.

Serca

Front Lines, Sept. 29, 1916

Strumitsa

Front Lines, Aug. 17, 1916

Salonika

Front Lines, Aug. 17, 1916

Allied Landing, Oct. 9, 1915

AUSTRIA HUNGARY

Front Lines, Sept. 17, 1914

Belgrade

Morava River

Nish

Kumanovo

Skopjle

Velca River

Doiran

Velca

Gornichevo

Veria

GREECE

Sava River

Lyashnitsa

Loznitsa

Shabatz

Kolubra River

Front Lines, Nov. 5, 1914

Valjevo

Uzhitse

Front Lines, Dec. 3, 1914

Allied Gains, Sept. 14–Nov. 19, 1916

Bulgarian Gains, Aug. 17–27, 1916

Monastir

Lake Ochrida

Lake Prespa

Zvornik

Lhubovija

Drina River

SERBIA

Serbian Remnants, Nov. 23, 1915

Vojusa River

Front Lines, Nov. 19, 1916

Sarajevo

Visebrad

MONTENEGRO

Scutari

Medua

ALBANIA

Tirana

Durazzo

Valona

Italian Landing, July 1916

Front Lines, Nov. 10, 1916

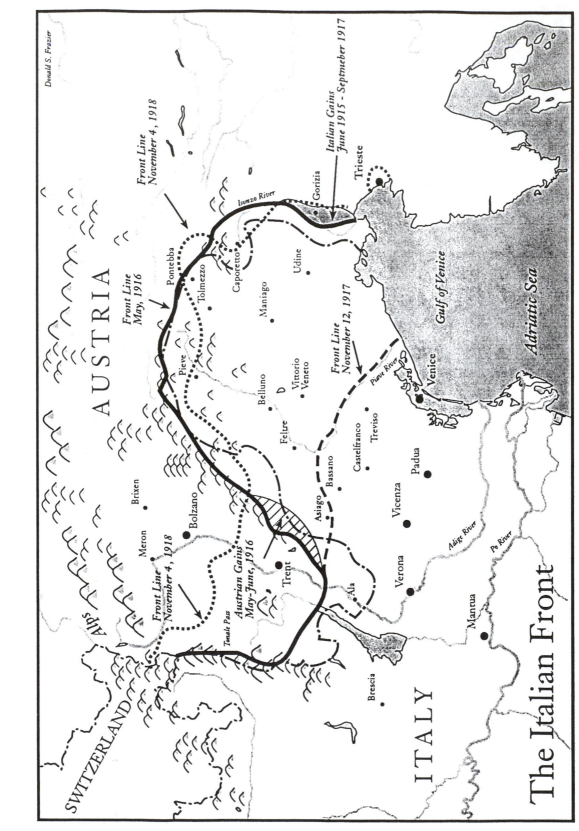

Donald S. Frazier

SWITZERLAND

AUSTRIA

ITALY

Alps

Front Line
November 4, 1918

Front Line
May, 1916

Austrian Gains
May–June, 1916

Front Line
November 4, 1918

Tonale Pass

Meron

Brixen

Bolzano

Trent

Ala

Pontebba

Tolmezzo

Pieve

Caporetto

Maniago

Udine

Belluno

Vittorio
Veneto

Felre

Asiago

Bassano

Castelfranco

Treviso

Vicenza

Padua

Verona

Mantua

Brescia

Isonzo River

Gorizia

Trieste

Italian Gains
June 1915 – Septmeber 1917

Front Line
November 12, 1917

Piave River

Venice

Gulf of Venice

Adriatic Sea

Adige River

Po River

The Italian Front

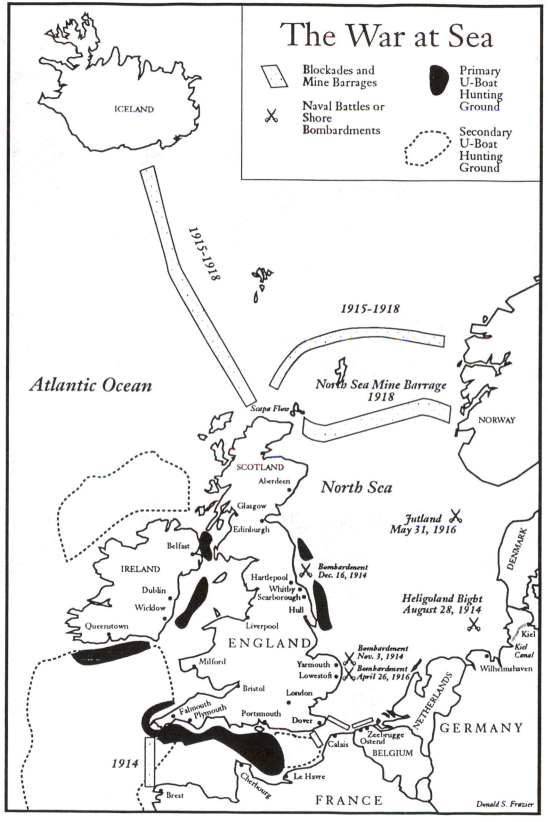

The War at Sea

Blockades and Mine Barrages

Naval Battles or Shore Bombardments

Primary U-Boat Hunting Ground

Secondary U-Boat Hunting Ground

ICELAND

Atlantic Ocean

1915-1918

1915-1918

North Sea Mine Barrage 1918

NORWAY

Scapa Flow

SCOTLAND

Aberdeen

North Sea

Glasgow

Edinburgh

Jutland May 31, 1916

Belfast

IRELAND

Dublin

Hartlepool

Whitby
Scarborough

Bombardment Dec. 16, 1914

DENMARK

Wicklow

Hull

Heligoland Bight August 28, 1914

Queenstown

Liverpool

ENGLAND

Kiel
Kiel Canal

Milford

Yarmouth
Lowestoft

Bombardment Nov. 3, 1914

Bombardment April 26, 1916

Wilhelmshaven

NETHERLANDS

Bristol

London

GERMANY

Falmouth
Plymouth

Portsmouth

Dover

Calais

Zeebrugge
Ostend

BELGIUM

1914

Cherbourg

Le Havre

Brest

FRANCE

Donald S. Frazier

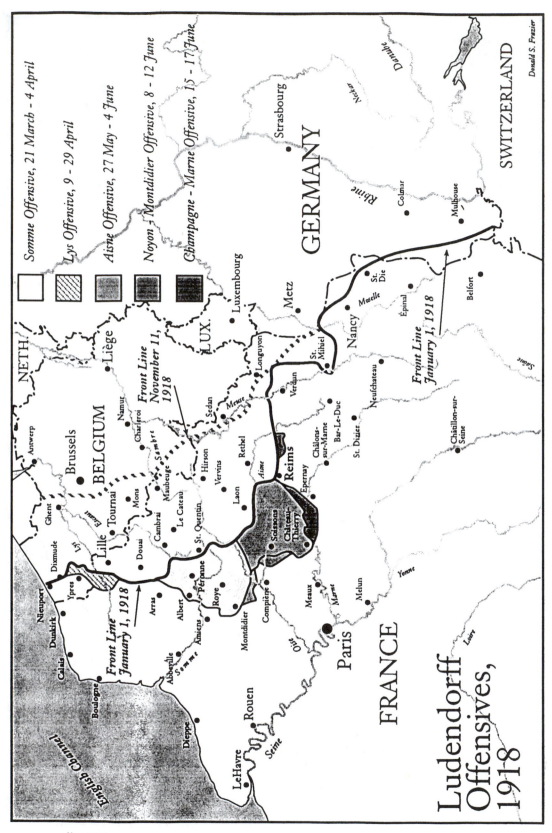

Ludendorff Offensives, 1918

Somme Offensive, 21 March - 4 April

Lys Offensive, 9 - 29 April

Aisne Offensive, 27 May - 4 June

Noyon - Montdidier Offensive, 8 - 12 June

Champagne - Marne Offensive, 15 - 17 June

GERMANY

SWITZERLAND

NETH.

BELGIUM

FRANCE

LUX.

Front Line November 11, 1918

Front Line January 1, 1918

Front Line January 1, 1918

Donald S. Frazier

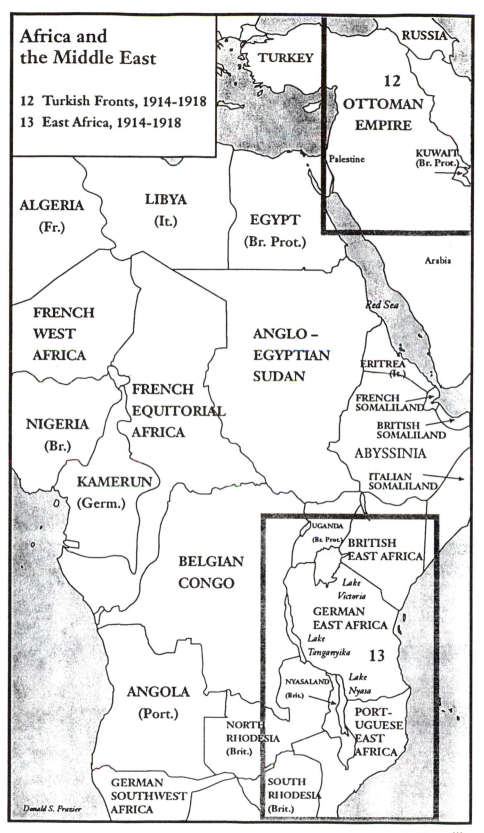

Africa and the Middle East

12 Turkish Fronts, 1914-1918
13 East Africa, 1914-1918

TURKEY

RUSSIA

**12
OTTOMAN
EMPIRE**

Palestine

KUWAIT
(Br. Prot.)

ALGERIA
(Fr.)

LIBYA
(It.)

EGYPT
(Br. Prot.)

Arabia

Red Sea

FRENCH
WEST
AFRICA

ANGLO –
EGYPTIAN
SUDAN

ERITREA
(It.)

FRENCH
SOMALILAND

FRENCH
EQUITORIAL
AFRICA

NIGERIA
(Br.)

BRITISH
SOMALILAND

ABYSSINIA

ITALIAN
SOMALILAND

KAMERUN
(Germ.)

BELGIAN
CONGO

UGANDA
(Br. Prot.)

BRITISH
EAST AFRICA

Lake
Victoria

GERMAN
EAST AFRICA

Lake
Tanganyika

13

NYASALAND
(Brit.)

Lake
Nyasa

ANGOLA
(Port.)

NORTH
RHODESIA
(Brit.)

PORT-
UGUESE
EAST
AFRICA

GERMAN
SOUTHWEST
AFRICA

SOUTH
RHODESIA
(Brit.)

Donald S. Frazier

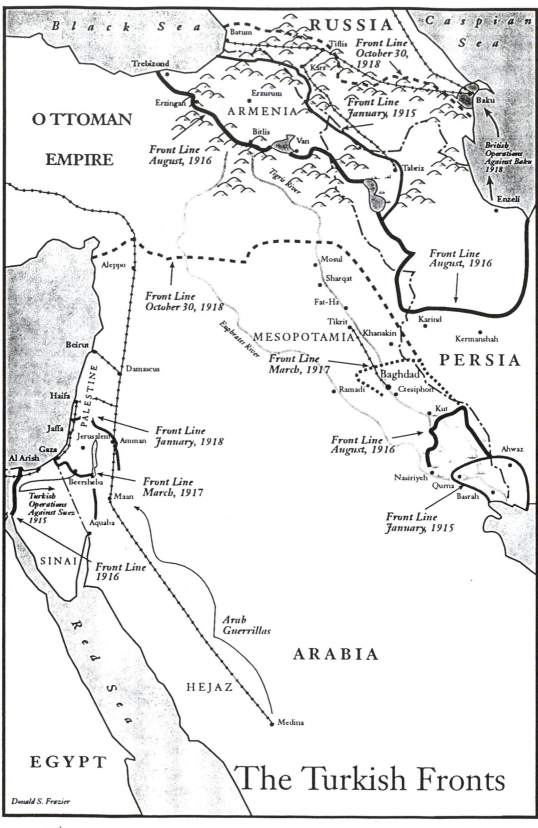

Black Sea

RUSSIA

Caspian Sea

Batum

Front Line October 30, 1918

Tiflis

Trebizond

Kars

Baku

Erzingan

Erzurum

ARMENIA

Front Line January, 1915

OTTOMAN

EMPIRE

Bitlis

Van

Tabriz

Enzeli

Front Line August, 1916

Tigris River

British Operations Against Baku 1918

Front Line August, 1916

Mosul

Aleppo

Front Line October 30, 1918

Sharqat

Fat-Ha

Karind

Kermanshah

Euphrates River

MESOPOTAMIA

Tikrit

Khanakin

Beirut

Front Line March, 1917

PERSIA

Damascus

Baghdad

Haifa

Ctesiphon

Ramadi

PALESTINE

Jaffa

Jerusalem

Amman

Kut

Ahwaz

Front Line January, 1918

Gaza

Front Line August, 1916

Al Arish

Beersheba

Front Line March, 1917

Nasiriyeh

Maan

Qurna

Turkish Operations Against Suez 1915

Basrah

Aquaba

Front Line January, 1915

SINAI

Front Line 1916

Red Sea

Arab Guerrillas

ARABIA

HEJAZ

EGYPT

Medina

The Turkish Fronts

Donald S. Frazier

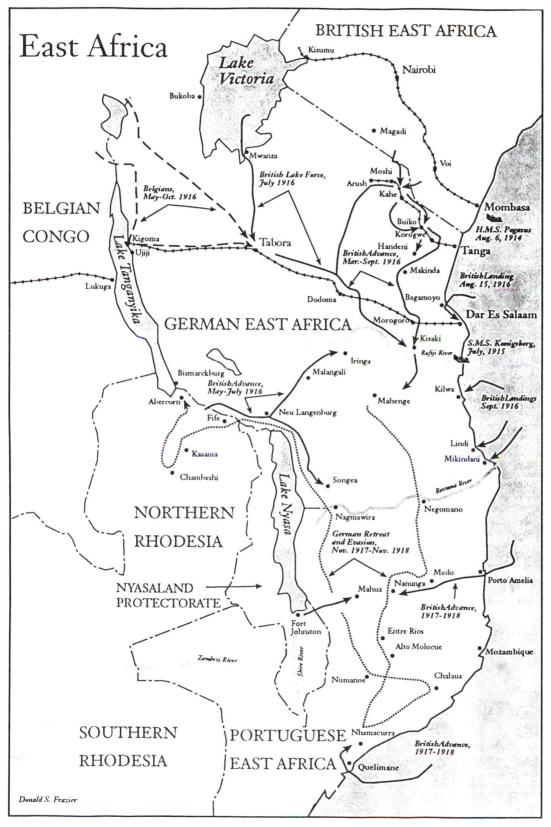

East Africa

BRITISH EAST AFRICA

Lake Victoria

BELGIAN

CONGO

Bukoba

Kisumu

Nairobi

Magadi

Voi

Mwanza

Moshi

Arush

Kahe

Belgians, May–Oct. 1916

British Lake Force, July 1916

Kigoma

Ujiji

Tabora

Lake Tanganyika

Lukuga

GERMAN EAST AFRICA

Buiko

Korogwe

Handeni

Makinda

British Advance, Mar.–Sept. 1916

Dodoma

Morogoro

Kisaki

Rufiji River

Mombasa

H.M.S. Pegasus Aug. 6, 1914

Tanga

British Landing Aug. 15, 1916

Bagamoyo

Dar Es Salaam

S.M.S. Koenigsberg, July, 1915

Bismarckburg

Abercorn

Fife

British Advance, May–July 1916

Neu Langenburg

Iringa

Malangali

Mahenge

Kilwa

British Landings Sept. 1916

Lindi

Mikindani

Kasama

Chambeshi

Lake Nyasa

Songea

Nagmawira

NORTHERN

RHODESIA

German Retreat and Evasion, Nov. 1917–Nov. 1918

Rovuma River

Negomano

Medo

Porto Amelia

NYASALAND

PROTECTORATE

Mahua

Nanunga

British Advance, 1917–1918

Fort Johnston

Zambezi River

Shire River

Entre Rios

Alto Molocue

Mozambique

Numanoe

Chalaua

SOUTHERN

RHODESIA

PORTUGUESE

EAST AFRICA

Nhamacurra

British Advance, 1917–1918

Quelimane

Donald S. Frazier

Contributors

Jose E. Alvarez
Tallahassee, FL

Donald F. Bittner
United States Marine Corps,
Command and Staff College

James J. Bloom
Silver Spring, MD

George P. Blum
University of the Pacific

Charles H. Bogart
Frankfurt, KY

John W. Bohon
Texas Christian University

Carl Boyd
Old Dominion University

Meredith L. Bragg
Texas Christian University

Ian M. Brown
Calgary, Alberta, Canada

Blaine T. Browne
Broward Community College North

David L. Bullock
United States Air Force Reserves

Edward L. Byrd, Jr.
Southeastern Oklahoma State University

Tom Cagley
Austin, TX

Craig Cameron
Old Dominion University

Susan N. Carter
Shalimar, FL

Bernard A. Cook
Loyola University

Gary P. Cox
Barnesville, GA

Stephen M. Cullen
Edinburgh, Scotland

Thomas W. Davis
Virginia Military Institute

Corie Delashaw
Southeastern Oklahoma State University

Timothy C. Dowling
Tulane University

William Christian Dughi
Old Dominion University

John P. Dunn
Valdosta, GA

M.K. Dziewanowski
Milwaukee, WI

Steven Eden
United States Military Academy

Peter R. Faber
United States Air Force Academy

Steven D. Fisher
Indianapolis, IN

Suzanne Hayes Fisher
Indianapolis, IN

Donald S. Frazier
McMurry University

A. Harding Ganz
Ohio State University

N.H. Gaworek
University of Wisconsin-Green Bay

Mark P. Gingerich
Ohio Wesleyan University

Philip J. Green
Great Britain

Ekkehart P. Guth
Fuehrungsakademie der Bundeswehr

Richard C. Hall
Mankato State University

Paul G. Halpern
Florida State University

Paul B. Hatley
Kansas State University

Gerhard Hümmelchen
Winnenden, Germany

Jeff Kinard
Texas Christian University

Meredeth Kulp
Texas Christian University

T.M. Lansford
Virginia Beach, VA

Roger D. Launius
National Aeronautics and Space Administration

Clayton D. Laurie
United States Army Center of Military History

Van Michael Leslie
Union College in Kentucky

E. Ray Lewis
Washington, DC

David L. Longfellow
Baylor University

Montecue J. Lowry
Houston, TX

Mark A. Macina
Texas Christian University

Karl P. Magyar
Air Command and Staff College

William L. Mathes
Seton Hall University

Thomas D. Mays
Texas Christian University

Jack McCallum
Texas Christian University

Julius A. Menzoff
Texas Christian University

Randall J. Metscher
Texas Christian University

Dennis J. Mitchell
Jackson State University

Malcolm Muir, Jr.
Austin Peay State University

Richard R. Muller
Air Command and Staff College

Justin D. Murphy
Howard Payne University

James Newcomer
Texas Christian University

Thomas G. Oakes
Texas Christian University

Stephan C. Palmer
Texas Christian University

Clayton Perkins
Houston, TX

A

Abbeville Conference (1–2 May 1918)

The fifth meeting of the Allied Supreme War Council, held 1–2 May 1918, at Abbeville, France, dealt mostly with questions of manpower. The essential issue was the deployment of newly arrived and arriving American troops.

Initially, U.S. troops had been amalgamated with British and French units out of necessity. The American commander, General John J. Pershing, wanted to wait until an American army could be formed, however, before committing U.S. troops in force. Pershing believed that this was the "truest desire of the American people and their government." Further, he claimed that there was an Allied agreement not to undertake any offensive action in 1918, allowing the American army time to train for action in 1919.

The German offensives in the spring of 1918, however, created an immediate need for Allied manpower that neither the British nor the French could fulfill. According to the Allied commander in chief, General Ferdinand Foch, Allied losses in those offensives equaled those of the previous three years combined. If reinforcements did not arrive soon, he argued, the Allies risked a breach in their lines.

The French were particularly nettled because, while Pershing had refused to place U.S. troops under Foch's command, he had earlier agreed to provide troops to the British. Worse, he had done so without consulting either Washington or the Allied command. The French, who already believed that the British were not contributing the number of troops of which they were capable, wanted at least equal relief. "Give me some of that American meat," French Premier Georges Clemenceau reportedly said at one point. Supported by Lord Balfour and British Prime Minister David Lloyd George, Clemenceau and Foch got what they wanted at Abbeville.

The final agreement was that 130,000 American troops would serve with British and French units in May, with the first six divisions allotted to the British. If the British were able to provide transport, another 150,000 U.S. troops would be put into the line in June, as Foch determined necessary. Priority was to be placed on training and transporting machine-gun and infantry units, which were to consist of at least six American divisions.

Having met the crisis, Pershing remained firm with regard to the creation of an American army. He refused to commit any troops after June, agreeing only to review the situation later. He also forced the Allies to agree that U.S. troops serving with Allied armies would eventually join their own national force.

To alleviate French doubts about British resolve, Lloyd George agreed that if the Germans broke the Allied line, the British army would retreat south to keep contact with the French army. He also agreed to allow a French military planner to visit London and, essentially, check on the British recruitment and war effort. While many British politicians viewed that as an insult, the gesture, as with the rest of the Abbeville agreements, went a long way in establishing trust and cooperation between the Allies as the end of the war approached.

Timothy C. Dowling

References

Clemenceau, Georges. *Grandeur and Misery of Victory*. Translated by F.M. Atkinson. New York: Harcourt, Brace, 1930.

Horne, Charles F., ed. *The Great Events of the Great War.* Vol. 6. New York: National Alumni, 1920.

Watson, David Robin. *Georges Clemenceau: A Political Biography.* New York: David McKay, 1974.

See also CLEMENCEAU, GEORGES; FOCH, FERDINAND; LLOYD GEORGE, DAVID

Abdullah ibn-Hussein, Emir (1882–1951)

A controversial Arab diplomat, soldier, and founder of the Hashemite Kingdom of Jordan. Born at Mecca on 12 September 1882, second son of Sharif Hussein ibn-Ali of Mecca, Abdullah was educated at Constantinople and served as Mecca's representative to the Ottoman parliament.

While Abdullah was returning home via Cairo in 1914, a "chance meeting" with Lord Kitchener initiated the famous Hussein-MacMahon Correspondence between his father and Britain's High Commissioner for Egypt. From this evolved the Arab Revolt (1916) and Abdullah's elevation to foreign minister (1917).

While a first-rate diplomat, Abdullah had mixed luck as a general. He led successful forays into Syria and the siege of Taif. A 1919 campaign against ibn-Sa'ud, however, ended disastrously at Turaba. Still, Abdullah's wartime record, combined with his considerable political savvy, resulted in his elevation to *Emir*, or prince, of Trans-Jordan in 1921. Made king in 1946, he was assassinated at Jerusalem on 20 July 1951.

John P. Dunn

References

Abdullah, King of Jordan. *Memoirs of King Abdullah of TransJordan.* Philip Graves, ed. London: Jonathan Cape, 1950.

el-Edros, Brigadier Syed Ali. *The Hashemite Arab Army, 1908–1979.* Amman, Jordan: The Publishing Co., 1980.

Nevakivi, Jukka. *Britain, France and the Arab Middle East, 1914–1920.* London: Athlone, 1969.

Wilson, Marcy C. *King Abdullah, Britain and the Making of Jordan.* Cambridge: Cambridge University Press, 1987.

See also ARAB REVOLT; IBN SA'UD, KING; KITCHENER, HORATIO; PALESTINE AND SYRIA; SYKES-PICOT AGREEMENT

Abruzzi, Amedeo di Savoia-Aosta (1837–1933)

Italian admiral and commander in chief of the fleet, 1914–1917. Born in Madrid on 29 January 1873 and better known by his title, the Duke of the Abruzzi, he was the third son of Amedeo, Duke of Aosta and one-time King of Spain (1870–73) and cousin of King Victor Emmanuel III. The duke chose a naval career but was probably best known before the war for his well-publicized geographical and scientific expeditions.

At the beginning of the war Abruzzi commanded Italian battle squadrons concentrated at Taranto and had, initially, a bold offensive strategy for the Adriatic. Changed conditions of naval warfare made those plans too dangerous to implement. The army was reluctant to provide troops for amphibious landings, and the Austrians refused to commit their battleships to a classic naval encounter. Abruzzi was reduced to carrying on a form of naval guerrilla war, one of raids and counterraids. He won praise for his handling of the disparate forces involved in the evacuation of the Serbian army at the beginning of 1916 but increasingly became the target for criticism generated by the frustrating and indecisive nature of the war. He finally resigned "for reasons of health" in February of 1917. After the war he became president of a colonial agricultural society that obtained a large concession in Italian Somaliland, where he spent most of his time. Abruzzi died at Jowhar, Somalia, on 18 March 1933.

Paul G. Halpern

References

Dainelli, Giotti. *Il Duca degli Abruzzi.* Turin: Union Tipografico, 1967.

Ferrante, Ezio. *La Grande Guerra in Adriatico.* Rome: Ufficio Storico della Marina Militare, 1987.

Halpern, Paul G. *The Naval War in the Mediterranean, 1914–1918.* London and Annapolis, Md.: Allen & Unwin and Naval Institute Press, 1987.

Ufficio Storico della R. *La Marina Italiana nella Grande Guerra.* 8 vols. Florence: Vallecchi, 1935–42.

See also ITALY, NAVY; MEDITERRANEAN NAVAL OPERATIONS

Abyssinia

Africa's oldest nation faced significant challenges during World War I. In December of 1913 Emperor Menelik died and was succeeded by his grandson, Lidj Iyasu. The latter shocked his nation's Christian ruling class by deciding to embrace Islam. He also worried Allied diplomats with an erratic foreign policy that favored Germany and the Ottoman Empire.

The new emperor desired to profit from the Great War. At its start, in the hope that Italy would join the Central Powers, he mobilized Abyssinian forces for an invasion of Eritrea. Foiled in this venture, Lidj Iyasu opened negotiations with German and Ottoman consular officials. In return for vague promises, he agreed to support several covert operations directed against Allied colonies. These operations were centered in the Sudan and particularly Somalia. Under the leadership of Sayyid Muhammad 'Abdille Hassan, Somalis were fighting a successful guerrilla war against British invaders. Lidj Iyasu's job was to expedite the shipment of arms and munitions to the forces of Sayyid Muhammad. German-Ottoman officials hoped this would tie down Allied soldiers, while Lidj Iyasu foresaw the possibility of uniting these lands with his own.

At home, the young emperor further alienated local power blocs by granting government positions to Muslim Oromo, Somali, and Arab minority leaders. By 1916 these actions, plus pressure from Allied diplomats, sparked an Abyssinian civil war. Despite an initial setback, rebel forces, under the overall command of Ras Tafari, decisively defeated government troops at Segale on 27 October 1916. This battle marked the beginning of Tafari's rise to power and placed Abyssinia firmly in the Allied camp for the rest of World War I.

John P. Dunn

References

Labrousse, Henri. "L'Ethiopie et le Traité de Versailles." In *Modern Ethiopia,* edited by Joseph Tubiana. Rotterdam: A.A. Balkena, 1980.

Marcus, Harold. *Haile Selassie I: The Formative Years, 1892–1936.* Berkeley: University of California Press, 1986.

Scholler, Heinrich. "German World War I Aims in Ethiopia—The Frobenius-Hall Mission." In *Modern Ethiopia*, edited by Joseph Tubiana. Rotterdam: A.A. Balkena, 1980.

See also AFRICA; SOMALIA

Aces

The best of the aerial warriors were known as "aces," that is, pilots who each had a minimum of five confirmed victories. By May of 1917 the required number of kills had been raised to ten. Of all the technological developments first employed on a large scale in World War I, aircraft had most captured the popular imagination. Paradoxically, while airplanes represented the utmost advance in the machinery of war, their pilots seemed to be throwbacks to the days of chivalry and jousting. To soldiers enduring the muck, mire, and misery of the trenches, aerial combat seemed remote and clean. But the hazards and the horrors of air warfare were just as real and terrifying. By 1917 the average life expectancy of a pilot on the Western Front was three weeks, and few, if any, were immune to the obsessive fear of a fiery death. Survival was a significant accomplishment.

For those who did survive, at least for a while, and whose proficiency in combat brought success, popular acclaim and official recognition were the rewards.

The French introduced the system of recognition for aces. Roland Garros (six victories), a stunt pilot before the war, was one of the early aerial warriors. He devised the tactic of using the plane to aim the machine gun and firing straight ahead. To avoid shooting off the propeller, Garros attached steel wedges to the blades to deflect the bullets. Another early hero was Jean Navarre (twelve kills), who recorded the first double victory of the war and was the first pilot recognized in the daily army communiqué.

Probably the most worshiped French ace was Georges Guynemer (fifty-four victories), a member of the Storks (*Les Cicognes*), the formidable elite fighter formation. He fought with great skill and passionate devotion to duty, but the strain of prolonged combat eroded his capabilities. On 11 September 1917 Guynemer disappeared into a cloud bank while engaged in combat and was never seen again.

Other notable French aces were Charles Nungesser and René Fonck. Nungesser (forty-five victories), a former boxer and among the most flamboyant of aces, helped build the image of the swashbuckling cavalier of the air. He enjoyed Parisian society and its nightlife; he adorned every airplane he flew with a black heart enclosing a skull, crossbones, coffin, and candlesticks; and he fought with skill and flair. Nungesser survived the war only to die while trying to fly westward across the Atlantic in May of 1927.

René Fonck (seventy-five victories) was the Allied "Ace of Aces." He avenged Guynemer by shooting down Kurt Wisseman, the German pilot who claimed to have shot down Guynemer. Twice, on 9 May and 26 September 1918, Fonck recorded six victories in one day against German aviators. He was a cool, calculating ace who scored his victories by means of careful tactics, extraordinary marksmanship, and knowledge of his opponents. He died in Paris in June of 1953.

Great Britain also had its contingent of heroic aviators. The first fighter ace of the Royal Flying Corps was Lanoe George Hawker (nine victories), also the first to receive the Victoria Cross (VC) for aerial combat. Although a skillful pilot, Hawker fell victim on 23 November 1916 to another ace, Manfred von Richthofen, who was not only skillful but also blessed with a superior airplane.

Youthful and shy, Albert Ball (forty-four victories) was the first British pilot to become a national hero. Ball preferred fighting alone, so that he could attack and escape quickly. He died in combat on 7 May 1917, posthumously receiving the Victoria Cross from King George V.

James McCudden (fifty-seven victories) became Great Britain's most decorated combat pilot. His meticulous preparation and courage in action brought him the VC, DSO and Bar, MC (Military Cross) and Bar, MM (*Médaille Militaire*), and *Croix de Guerre*. He died on 9 July 1918 as a result of a mechanical failure on takeoff.

Edward "Mick" Mannock (seventy-three victories) was an implacable fighter and intense patriot who rose from the ranks to become the highest-scoring British ace. Mannock was ruthless in battle but also gained a reputation as a great patrol leader and mentor to novices. In June of 1918, while following too low after a downed plane, Mannock was killed by ground fire.

The British air effort benefited considerably by infusions of talent from the dominions. Canada made a major contribution, particularly the three pilots William Avery Bishop, Raymond Collishaw, and William George Barker. "Billy" Bishop (seventy-two victories) was the leading Canadian ace and second on the list of British aces; an aversion to mud had changed this cavalry officer into an aviator. Bishop attacked recklessly and was an excellent marksman. He survived the war, helped found the Royal Canadian Air Force, and served as its director during World War II. Collishaw (sixty-two victories) was the top naval ace of World War I and leader of one of the most famous and successful Allied fighter units—the "Black Flight" of Sopwith airplanes. He, too, survived the war and helped start the Royal Canadian Air Force. Barker (fifty-two victories) received his wings in January of 1917 and was transferred to the Italian front in September of 1917. Major Barker earned the Victoria Cross in October of 1918. Australia made its contribution, too, with Robert Alexander Little (thirty-seven victories), who flew with the Royal Naval Air Service No. 8 Squadron. He was killed on 28 May 1918 after intercepting German Gotha bombers during a night raid.

Other Allied nations also had aerial aces. Willy Coppens, with thirty-seven victories, was Belgium's leading ace. Francesco Baracca led Italian pilots with thirty-four until his death on 19 June 1918. Alexander Kazakov (seventeen victories) commanded the XIX Corps Air Squadron and was Russia's leading ace. Although the United States did not enter the war until April of 1917, some American pilots had already become combatants. Raoul Lufbery joined the *Lafayette Escadrille* on 24 May 1916 and scored seventeen victories. He won the British Military Cross, the French *Croix de Guerre*, and the Médaille Militaire, and on 7 November 1917, he was commissioned a major in the United States Army Air Service. Edward Vernon Rickenbacker, America's foremost ace, scored his twenty-six victories between March and October of 1918. For his actions he received the Congressional Medal of Honor.

The Central Powers, particularly Germany, added greatly to the legend, lore, and technological development of the war in the air. Germany had many notable warriors in the air: Oswald Boelcke (forty victories), who developed a set of rules for aerial combat and also an outline of fighter squadron organization; Hermann Göring, who would achieve greater fame but earn less respect in World War II; and Manfred Freiherr von Richthofen (eighty victories), the most prolific ace of them all, known worldwide as the "Red Baron." Max Immelmann (fifteen victories) helped establish the idea of hunter groups composed of fast, single-seat fighters; he developed the acrobatic rolling turn named for him. Immelmann, the "Eagle of Lille," died on 8 June 1916 after his plane broke apart in mid air.

Werner Voss (forty-eight victories) was one of the most talented of German pilots. He was Richthofen's closest rival until he met death on 23 September 1917 when he battled seven planes of the No. 56 Squadron of the RFC led by James McCudden. He was killed by a burst of machine-gun fire. McCudden later stated that Voss was "the bravest German airman whom it has been my privilege to fight."

One other German ace demanding mention is Ernst Udet (sixty-two victories). The second leading German ace of the war, he later became chief of the Technical Office of the *Luftwaffe* and was responsible for developing the dive-bomber.

The highest-scoring pilot of the Austro-Hungarian Empire was Godwin Brumowski (thirty-five victories), an intrepid and reliable flyer who survived the war only to die as a passenger in an aircraft crash in 1936.

LEADING ACES

Name	Number of kills	Country
Allied Powers		
René Fonck	75	France
Edward Mannock	73	Great Britain
William Bishop	72	Canada
Raymond Collishaw	62	Canada
James McCudden	57	Great Britain
Georges Guynemer	54	France
William Barker	52	Canada
Charles Nungesser	45	France
Albert Ball	44	Great Britain
Robert Little	37	Australia
Willy Coppens	37	Belgium
Francesco Baracca	34	Italy
Edward Rickenbacker	26	U.S.A.
Central Powers		
Manfred von Richthofen	80	Germany
Ernst Udet	62	Germany
Werner Voss	48	Germany
Oswald Boelcke	40	Germany
Godwin Brumowski	35	Austria-Hungary

There were hundreds of other aces in World War I, each worthy of mention. All of them, regardless of differences in personality and purpose, were men of valor. Many were innovative, and together they paved the way for subsequent developments in aviation. They were a rare breed of fighting men who provided their war-weary nations with heroes in a most unglamorous war.

Edward L. Byrd, Jr.
Ingrid P. Westmoreland

References

Campbell, Christopher. *Aces and Aircraft of World War I*. Poole, Dorsett: Blandford, 1981.

Clark, Alan. *Aces High*. London: Weidenfeld & Nicolson, 1973.

Reynolds, Quentin J. *They Fought for the Sky*. New York: Bantam, 1957.

See also AIRCRAFT, FIGHTERS; BOELCKE, OSWALD; FOKKER, ANTHONY; GÖRING, HERMANN; RICHTHOFEN, MANFRED

Africa, 1914–18

The Great War was also waged in Africa, although just why is somewhat perplexing, for political objectives in Germany's distant outposts in Africa were certainly peripheral to core concerns in Europe. Some large territories were lost quickly; other campaigns lasted until the end of the war under circumstances more scripted for the movies or for comic relief. Soldiers faced an assorted array of vintage weapons and at times had to fend off attacks by wild animals that owed allegiance to neither side. Indeed, one Indian contingent in Tanganyika was routed by a swarm of bees. No wonder that one book on this theater of the war is subtitled *The Bizarre Story of the First World War in East Africa*.

No matter the reason Europeans chose to expend men and matériel in pursuit of peripheral objectives, those objectives were pursued with vigor and not inconsiderable expense. Strategic objectives included wireless stations and coal stores for the war effort. The considerable number of natives who could be pressed into military service was another attraction. Another motive was colonial expansion. Britain and France quickly carved up the German colonies of Togoland and Cameroon between themselves once the war started, while Germany had the fuzzy ambition of creating a large colony through the middle of Africa that would link her possessions on the Atlantic coast to the Indian Ocean. Tying up the other side's troops to prevent their use in Europe was yet another objective for the European powers fighting in Africa.

In reality, neither side committed many soldiers in Africa. Most military personnel were Africans, and tropical diseases proved a much more formidable enemy than soldiers. White officers died in great numbers not on the battlefield but on hospital cots. Another irony was that the contested African territories were often much larger than the European countries themselves, yet only a small fraction of military resources was expended for them. The fighting in Africa was prosecuted in an environment radically different from that in Europe. Overall, it remained a sideshow to the real war.

Although battles in Africa were not pivotal in the Great War, fighting there was an integral part of the war. There were contests over Togoland, Cameroon, South West Africa, and German East Africa. Parts of North Africa were also involved, as in the need to defend the Suez Canal against Turkish threats, but those were integral to the Mediterranean or Middle Eastern theaters and hence will not be considered here.

Togoland's Rapid Defeat

Perhaps because German Togoland was the best-managed colony in West Africa, the territory required virtually no German military presence. It was a model colony, exporting agricultural goods. The fact that Togoland was surrounded by areas under British and French control worked against Germany's interest, as it made the colony attractive to possess and easy to conquer.

No sooner had Britain declared war on Germany than London undertook preparations to take Togoland. The attractions were not only its profitability but also an important wireless station some 100 miles inland at Kamina. The attack was greatly expedited by the personal ambitions of a young officer in temporary charge of the neighboring Gold Coast Regiment, Captain F.C. Bryant. Major von Doering, Togoland's acting governor, somewhat naively called for a state of neutrality for the colony, but Bryant was not to be thwarted. Besides, there was the matter of the wireless station.

The German coastal station of Lome surrendered without a fight to the presence of a British cruiser, its three hundred German and twelve hundred native troops retreating inland toward Kamina. During the next few days more British forces invaded Togoland from the west, joined by French contingents from Dahomey. These forces took over uncontested control of the south. This accomplished, the Allies began an advance on Kamina (at Atakpane). The Germans tried to slow this northward movement without success. Although they suffered major casualties, on 21 August 1914 the larger and better equipped Allied force defeated the Germans. A few days later the Germans destroyed the wireless station, and on 26 August Captain Bryant accepted the German surrender. Togoland was quickly carved up between Britain and France, normal commerce was restored, and Captain Bryant was promoted.

Cameroon

It took longer to conquer Cameroon, but the important region of the colony, the coast, fell quickly. Thereafter, the hinterland offered the Germans opportunities to delay further conquest before they escaped into neighboring Spanish-held territory. British and French objectives were much the same as in Togoland: to capture an important German wireless station servicing German ships in the South Atlantic and to divide the colony between them. France also wanted to regain a portion of its adjacent Congo colony, which had been ceded to Germany after the Second Moroccan crisis. The port at Douala was a special prize. Much of Cameroon was inhospitable to European settlement and the Germans had the advantage of their knowledge of the interior. They had also built a railway that would serve them well in prolonging the war.

The Allied war effort in Cameroon required considerable manpower, and troops and support personnel were brought in from other colonies in west and central Africa. At the end of August 1914 British-led Nigerian troops invaded Cameroon but were defeated by well-equipped German forces, who had the advantage of mobility by railway. The Germans had forces in various parts of Cameroon as well as at an important base in the north, at Mora, which never fell in battle and was yielded only after the Germans abandoned the rest of the colony.

Initial Allied offensives in Cameroon met with no success but consumed great quantities of manpower and resources. This led London to send General C.M. Dobell to take command. He assembled troops, supported by warships, from the garrison at Sierra Leone for an offensive against Douala. The attack would be made by sea because the Germans were too strong on land.

The British attack was mounted in mid-September 1914 and included the cruiser *Challenger*. The Germans attempted to blockade the harbor at Douala and mine its approaches, but the British overcame these obstacles and landed forces on 26 September. The Germans surrendered Douala the next day after destroying its wireless station.

British and French forces then moved inland from Douala and from other points along their borders with Cameroon. There were some major engagements during the next few months, but the Allies achieved their major strategic objective in taking the coast. In January of 1916 the Allies took their next major objective, the new capital of Yaounde. Its fall served to send the Germans scurrying to Spanish Rio Muni. Fighting in the north lasted a bit longer; several times the Germans attacked across the Nigerian border. Finally, on 18 February Mora surrendered on generous terms, ending German control of Cameroon. The interior of the country offered no immediate strategic advantage to the Allies, and the Germans had managed to tie up a large amount of Allied resources. Nearly 2,000 British and well over 2,000 French troops, most of whom were Africans, were killed in the Cameroon fighting.

South West Africa

German South West Africa's major strategic importance to the Allies was a third set of wireless stations located in this vast but remote German colony at Luederitz Bay, Swakopmund, and Windhoek, the inland colonial capital. To South Africa, cooperation with Britain in immobilizing those stations held the prospect that it might then absorb the territory at modest cost. Another motive for South Africa's taking the initiative was that Britain would introduce other Commonwealth troops there if South Africa did not.

South West Africa had 140 German officers and 3,000 trained troops. In addition, the Germans could call into service several thousand able-bodied men from among the European population. Against significant British naval assets and vastly superior numbers of South Africans, many of whom had had lead-

ership experience in the Boer War, the Germans could hope for little more than a defensive holding action. That is, in fact, what happened.

In September of 1914 British naval forces, acting in concert with South African troops, took coastal Luederitz Bay and Swakopmund without a fight. A small advance party then crossed the frontier into South West Africa, where it encountered a German force. A battle ensued that was lost by the South Africans, who suffered sixteen men killed in action.

Thereafter, the South African government, led by Prime Minister Louis Botha, had to concentrate on deep divisions within its own Afrikaner ranks. Many of the South African troops did not want to fight the Germans. During the Boer War the Germans had extended limited support to the Boer side and now they offered to help the Orange Free State and the Transvaal regain their independence if the Boers would aid them against Britain. In late 1914 there was a rebellion in several Afrikaner contingents. Led by respected Boer War leaders such as Christiaan de Wet, Christiaan Beyers, Jan Kemp, and Solomon Maritz, the revolt, however, was decisively put down within a few months by government forces. Thereafter, Botha, as commanding general, and Defense Minister General Jan Smuts were able to prosecute the land war into South West Africa. Botha and Smuts overrode continued resentment regarding the government's hostile stance toward Germany, which continued to cloud South Africa's domestic political climate.

Having quelled the rebellion, South Africa's leaders could now undertake full-scale military action against the main German forces. Botha commanded four columns, which were to advance from Luederitz Bay, Swakopmund, and from northwestern South Africa. The offensives began in April of 1915 with the Germans moving inland and northward. The Germans lost a number of small battles and in mid-May Botha's column entered Windhoek without resistance. With the surrender of Windhoek, German forces regrouped in the north around Grootfontein. The Allies rejected an offer by the German governor to partition the colony. Having brought the south of the colony under their control, they prepared to send three columns north.

The South Africans won a major battle at Otavifontein in June of 1915. The action then shifted northward to Tsumeb where the numerically vastly superior South Africans moved to surround German forces and prevent their escape. On 9 July 1915 the German governor at Tsumeb surrendered unconditionally. The South African government's war against rebellious Afrikaners was more costly and had lasted longer than the campaign in South West Africa. Three times as many government troops died fighting their fellow Afrikaners as died fighting the Germans.

German East Africa

Germany's longest stand in Africa was in its East African colony, the result of the military abilities and tenacity of General Paul von Lettow-Vorbeck. He possessed extensive colonial experience, including military service in South West Africa, a solid military background, and considerable arrogance, all of which led him to exercise his ambition and initiative. On his arrival in East Africa in early 1914, Lettow-Vorbeck set about building an appropriate military organization. The vast majority of his soldiers were Africans from tribes with warlike reputations. With these troops and a generous supply of machine guns he soon tied down thousands of British troops in Tangan-yika, thereby preventing their deployment in Europe. Lettow-Vorbeck surrendered only after the armistice in Europe.

Hostilities began in early August of 1914 when the Royal Navy bombarded the coastal town of Bagamoyo, capital of Dar-es-Salaam, destroying a wireless station. Although the British dominated the seas, it was not until land reinforcements arrived from India that they could undertake a land campaign. Initially, Lettow-Vorbeck had superior numbers: 250 European officers, some 5,000 native troops—Askaris—and thousands of native bearers. German settlers could also be pressed into service. British forces included roughly the same number of European officers and some 2,300 natives organized in the King's African Rifles. Although these forces were trained and equipped more for police activities than for war, they fought the Germans effectively.

Lettow-Vorbeck's strategy was to disrupt British supplies by striking at the Mombasa-to-Uganda railway. These early and persistent German forays into Kenya were repulsed by the British. After the arrival of two brigades from India, in November the British made an attempt to take Tanga on the coast of Tanganyika and close to the common border. Their goal was to interdict the vital railway line into the interior.

The Germans repulsed the attack and inflicted a major defeat on the British force. They also secured substantial quantities of arms and ammunition, which the British forces had abandoned in their hasty retreat. In January of 1915 the British suffered defeat at Jassin. All the while, Lettow-Vorbeck sought to keep his forces close to the border so that he could defend German East Africa and at the same time be able to enter Kenya. Both sides recognized the importance of their railways, which ran parallel to the common border.

The British had the considerable advantage of being able to augment their forces. They did this with British troops as well as Indians, Nigerians, South Africans, the Mounted Rifles (composed of white settlers from Kenya), Rhodesians, and thousands of native troops and carriers. They also concluded an alliance with Belgium and Portugal. As a result, troops from the Belgian Congo attacked German East Africa from the west while Portuguese forces from Mozambique lent their support.

Lettow-Vorbeck was reduced to trying to hold as much of Tanganyika as possible. No Europeans could be added to his forces except those residing in the colony. That he managed to remain in the field against such large opposing forces speaks volumes for his military skill. Although the Germans fought numerous battles they came to avoid conventional encounters whenever possible, Lettow-Vorbeck's adopting a highly evasive mobile guerrilla strategy.

Beginning in February of 1916, Smuts, the new commander of British forces, slowly brought the Germans under control. In Smuts the British side had a leader equally experienced in bush warfare. He devised new plans that centered on clearing the north around Kilimanjaro and then bringing the railways under control. His main forces were two South African and one British/Indian division. The South Africans were led by officers seasoned in the successful campaign in South West Africa. Smuts slowly wore down his enemy, who felt the effects of superior opposing numbers, diminishing stocks of weapons, and the ravages of nature. Lettow-Vorbeck was forced southeast and eventually into northern Mozambique. By now the Germans were fighting a defensive war of survival. From Mozambique, the diminishing German force reentered Tanganyika and made its way into northern Rhodesia. There Lettow-Vorbeck finally surrendered after the formal end of the war in Europe and returned to Germany a hero.

The First World War in Africa was largely a European concern, although most of those who died in it were native Africans. Within a half century, however, those territories all became independent, which rendered the war's extension from Europe to Africa all the more absurd.

Karl P. Magyar

References

Farwell, Byron. *The Great War in Africa.* New York: W.W. Norton, 1986.

Gardner, Brian. *On to Kilimanjaro: The Bizarre Story of the First World War in East Africa.* Philadelphia: Macrae Smith, 1963.

Hoyt, Edwin P. *Guerrilla: Colonel von Lettow-Vorbeck and Germany's East Africa Empire.* New York: Macmillan, 1981.

Lettow-Vorbeck, Paul von. *East Africa Campaigns.* New York: Robert Speller & Sons, 1957.

Miller, Charles. *Battle for the Bandu: The First World War in East Africa.* New York: Macmillan, 1974.

See also BOTHA, LOUIS; LETTOW-VORBECK, PAUL; SMUTS, JAN; SOUTH AFRICA, UNION OF

Air Warfare: Fighter Tactics

German air ace Manfred von Richthofen thought that the best fighter tactics were the simplest ones. He wrote to his squadron commanders: "With one sentence, one can settle the topic: 'Aerial Combat Tactics,' namely: 'I get within 50 meters of the enemy from behind, aim neatly, then the opponent falls.' Those are the words Boelcke spoke when I asked him his trick. Now I know that this is the whole mystery of shooting them down."

At the beginning of World War I both sides used aircraft as airborne cavalry, primarily relegated to observation and artillery spotting duties. Pilots regarded each other as kindred spirits of the air rather than enemies. But once military commanders realized the value of aerial reconnaissance, they also realized the value of keeping that information from the enemy: airmen began to arm themselves with rifles, then machine guns. Pusher aircraft, having the engine in the rear, could carry forward-firing machine guns, as could machines with a gun mounted on the upper wing. But it was not until

the invention of a machine gun that could be synchronized to fire through the propeller that fighter aircraft became deadly.

The problem of synchronized machine guns had occupied engineers in several countries before the war, but the Dutch manufacturer Anthony Fokker was the first to install a successful synchronizing mechanism, utilizing a single forward-firing machine gun, on his monoplane (*Eindekker*). German pilots shot down a number of unsuspecting opponents with the *Eindekker* before the Allies developed their own synchronized gun and put an end to the "Fokker scourge." Fokker scouts were not necessarily better than Allied planes; their advantage was in combining agility with the synchronized gun. In spite of their relatively slow and awkward aircraft, Fokker pilots of 1915 developed some basic fighter tactics that are still valid today.

In the summer of 1916 the German High Command charged German ace Oswald Boelcke with the formation of a *Jagdstaffel*, the first squadron developed not for reconnaissance, bombing, or artillery spotting duties but strictly for shooting down the enemy. Boelcke's handpicked unit, *Jasta* 2, became operational on 1 September 1916 and included future aces Manfred von Richthofen and Erwin Böhme. Boelcke believed in giving his men a firm grounding in combat flying and marksmanship before turning them loose on the enemy, and during a two-week training session he taught all of his new pilots—his "cubs"—these eight basic principles of aerial combat:

1. Always try to secure advantages before attacking. If possible, keep the sun behind you.
2. Always carry through an attack when you have started it.
3. Fire only at close range and only when your opponent is properly in your sights.
4. Always keep your eye on your opponent and never let yourself be deceived by ruses.
5. In any form of attack it is essential to fight your opponent from behind.
6. If your opponent dives on you, do not try to evade his onslaught but fly to meet it.
7. When over the enemy's lines, never forget your own line of retreat.
8. For the Staffel: Attack on principle in groups of four or six. When the fight

breaks up into a series of single combats, take care that several pilots do not go for one opponent.

Allied pilots followed the same general rules. British Squadron Commander Mick Mannock instructed his men to hide in clouds or the sun and to attack the enemy with superior numbers from a position of advantage. He knew how difficult it was to see and identify enemy aircraft, so he warned his pilots to shoot first and ask questions later. It was better to accidentally attack friendly aircraft than to be caught off guard by a German patrol. Mannock demanded that his men keep their aircraft in close formation at all costs, realizing that they were easy prey for the Germans as soon as they separated from the pack; the primary purpose of a formation was to ensure safety with numbers. Squadron leaders grouped their aircraft into formations both for offensive and defensive reasons. Most fighter pilots would hesitate to attack a large formation but considered single enemy machines easy prey. Enemy pilots attacked lone aircraft carefully in case they were bait for a larger formation hiding in the clouds. A formation attack usually succeeded because its victims would scatter under a mass onslaught and individual aircraft would then fall prey to the attackers. Boelcke divided his squadron into two flights of five or six aircraft, a number that he could control easily during a battle, but the British preferred to use combinations of only four machines.

Commanders developed five basic formations: line abreast, diamond, line astern, vee, and echelon. In the line abreast formation all aircraft were at the same altitude, with their wingtips in a line. In the latter four formations, machines were staggered at fifty-meter vertical intervals, with the leader in the front and lowest position and planes at the rear at the highest. A staggered formation enabled pilots at the back to watch over the rest of their comrades, protected the rear aircraft from the slipstreams of those in front, and helped guard against the possibility that a burst of antiaircraft fire would disable the whole patrol; unfortunately, enemy pilots could pick off the aircraft furthest from the leader without being seen by the rest of the formation.

In the summer of 1917 the German High Command ordered the formation of *Jagdgeschwader* 1 (JG 1), a larger unit that combined four Jastas, numbers 4, 6, 10, and 11, for an effective strength of forty-eight aircraft. Each Jasta flew as a unit under its own leader but under the overall command of one man. JG 1 was under the leadership of Manfred von Richthofen, who wrote down his thoughts on formation tactics and single combat in a document that was issued to all flight commanders and aviation staff officers shortly before his death in April of 1918. His brief treatise remains one of the few contemporary written records of combat tactics available today. Many of his ideas were elaborations on Boelcke's dicta, but he offered more explicit instructions for commanders on formation tactics and the training of beginners. In this document Richthofen also described his use of fighters as interceptors, a practice used successfully by the British during the Battle of Britain in 1940. As Richthofen phrased it, "We can just wait for the customers to come to the shop."

Rather than waste time and precious fuel patrolling a quiet sector, Richthofen's men went up only when the enemy was sighted near the German lines. Observers at the Front telephoned *Jagdgeschwader* headquarters and reported on enemy strength, and the necessary number of fighters would scramble to intercept. After all of his men were airborne, Richthofen would then take off and assemble his flock at low altitude, gearing his speed to that of the slowest aircraft. The formation would then head for the Front. Richthofen maintained that the sole purpose of a fighter group was to destroy enemy squadrons. The best way to accomplish that objective, he wrote, was to wait in a spot between the front lines and the point where the enemy had penetrated the defenders' territory, cut off the returning squadron's escape route, and force a confrontation. But the formation had to reach the Front intact. Richthofen advised his commanders to acquaint themselves with all aerial activity in the vicinity—German and Allied—and to watch their own squadrons for stragglers.

Most fighter attacks began with a dive on the enemy. One of the simplest maneuvers was to swoop down out of the sun, waiting to fire until the enemy was at close range. The attacker's dive would carry him below his victim's line of flight, but, using his momentum, he could easily climb high enough for a repeat onslaught. When attacking two-seaters, the aggressor might shoot from below, where the defender's machine gun could not hit the attacker without endangering his own aircraft.

One of the most famous defensive maneuvers was the so-called "Immelmann turn," commonly described as a half loop with a half roll on top. In practice, the Immelmann turn was most likely a quick dive to gain speed followed by a steep climbing turn, or *chandelle*.

Every formation battle eventually dissolved into a series of single combats. In the confusion of a dogfight, it was easy for pilots to forget how many aircraft were involved and to leave themselves vulnerable to attack from an unanticipated quarter. When beginning the attack each pilot needed to count the number of opponents, and when the fight broke into a free-for-all everyone had to keep track of the positions of all of the hostile aircraft—in order to avoid unpleasant surprises.

The greatest danger for a single-seater pilot was the surprise attack from the rear. Many experienced fighter pilots were surprised and shot down from behind. Richthofen told his men, "Everyone must direct his main attention to the rear. A surprise has never come from the front." Even in the heat of battle, pilots had to be especially careful not to come under attack from behind. Richthofen counseled his new pilots not to attempt to escape an unexpected attack from the rear by pushing the stick forward and diving away from the assailant, because the enemy could easily follow him down. Instead, the best defense was a sudden very tight turn and then a follow-up attack as quickly as possible.

Two-seaters were often more difficult to shoot down than faster, more agile single-seat fighter planes. The attacker had to contend not only with a forward-firing gun on the front but also with the observer's moveable gun in the rear. The only way to avoid both of the guns was to attack quickly and directly in the machine's line of flight from behind and to disable the observer with the first few shots. The two-seater was especially vulnerable if it was flying straight ahead or just beginning to turn, but when it was attacked from the side or while banking, its observer had a clear shot at the enemy.

Most pilots considered a frontal attack on a two-seater to be dangerous, if not suicidal. If the attacker did not destroy his victim with the first shots he first came under fire from the pilot's fixed guns and then from the observer's moveable one. When the pursuit pilot turned around to get on his opponent's tail for a second pass, he left himself completely open to the observer's fire. If a pilot found himself on a collision course with a two-seater, he did not necessarily have to break off the attack but could try to make his U-turn directly under the enemy aircraft at the exact moment it flew overhead. He could then shoot it down from below, screened from the observer's fire by the fuselage.

A head-on attack was not nearly as hazardous with single-seaters as with two-seaters, but neither was it likely to be successful, because the two aircraft were within combat range only for moments. Experienced pilots found it simple to surprise a single-seater from behind. If the enemy pilot had been watchful, he immediately began to turn tightly and climb above his opponent. The attacker had to turn and dive with full throttle so as not to lose altitude to his enemy. Most important, he could never let the opponent get on his tail.

Slow, lumbering two-seaters might have appeared easy prey for fighter pilots in their fast, maneuverable scout planes, but single combat against single-seaters was by far the easiest, according to Richthofen. He wrote confidently, "If I am alone with an opponent and on this side of the lines, only a jammed gun or an engine problem can prevent me from shooting him down." Dismissing any special skills, Richthofen reduced fight r tactics to one sentence: "One does not need to be a crack pilot or marksman, but only to have the courage to fly within the closest proximity of the opponent."

Suzanne Hayes Fisher

References

Hallion, Richard P. *Rise of the Fighter Aircraft 1914–1918*. Annapolis, Md.: Nautical and Aviation Publishing Company of America, 1984.

Richthofen, Manfred Albrecht von. "Treatise on Aerial Combat Tactics, 1918." Tms [photocopy]. Author's collection via estate of Kimbrough S. Brown.

Werner, Johannes. *Knight of Germany: Oswald Boelcke, German Ace*. Translated by Claude W. Sykes. London: John Hamilton, 1933.

Winter, Denis. *The First of the Few: Fighter Pilots of the First World War*. Athens: University of Georgia Press, 1983.

See also ACES; AIRCRAFT, FIGHTERS; BOELCKE, OSWALD; FOKKER, ANTHONY; RICHTHOFEN, MANFRED VON

Air Warfare: Ground-Support Aviation

World War I saw the creation of specialized units and aircraft designed for direct participation in ground operations. Great Britain and Germany took the lead in developing close support and interdiction aviation, although all of the major powers employed aircraft in this fashion by 1917–18. Along with air superiority and bombardment, tactical air support was one of the most significant air-power legacies of the conflict.

The Royal Flying Corps (RFC) generally receives credit for the first use of aircraft in a direct support role, although, as was the case with most military innovations, the concept evolved independently elsewhere. The RFC took steps to integrate air and ground operations through expanded use of its artillery spotting and infantry contact aircraft in the spring of 1916. Ground and air commands developed simple recognition procedures for liaison between ground forces and their supporting aircraft.

Actual direct support combat missions, however, occurred only sporadically until the Passchendaele Campaign of 1917. British fighter squadrons began attacking ground targets with small twenty-five-pound Cooper bombs carried in racks of four beneath Sopwith and SE 5 fighters. Initially, target selection was left to the discretion of individual pilots. General Hugh Trenchard lamented the resulting haphazard character of the attacks. By the time of the Battle of Cambrai in November of 1917, British ground-support procedures had matured. British fighters operating as "ground strafers" cooperated with advancing tanks, suppressing German artillery positions in the path of the British armor.

British close support operations were effective. The memoirs of German General Erich Ludendorff are filled with testimonials to the impact of air attacks on the morale of his troops. One German unit reported the death in action of one of its battalion commanders, who was "run over by an SE 5." On some occasions, notably during the "Michael" offensive of March 1918, British close-support aircraft were instrumental in slowing the pace of the German advance.

The most successful application of British tactical air power occurred not on the Western Front but in one of the war's outlying theaters. In September of 1918 British and Australian flying units supporting the Palestine campaign of General Sir Edmund H.H. Allenby destroyed the Turkish Eighth Army at Wadi al Far'a. That was the first time in history that a major ground unit was defeated entirely by air action.

Although the RFC/RAF developed close support into an effective military instrument, the cost of such operations was extraordinarily high. Ground strafing was a high-risk undertaking, and the British official history recorded that a squadron of fighter aircraft employed on such operations would be unfit for action after only four days' combat. "Only in exceptional cases, or in extreme emergencies, would such a rate of wastage be justified." This high cost was one of the reasons for the neglect of tactical aviation in the postwar RAF.

The German Air Service pursued a somewhat different approach to the problem of direct support, and it created the war's most effective tactical air arm. Unlike the RFC, which viewed close support as a secondary mission for fighter aircraft, the Germans developed a specialized class of two-seat aircraft, originally intended as escorts for observation planes, as "pure" ground attack machines. They included the Halberstadt CL. II and IV, the Hannover CL. II, and the armored, all-metal Junkers J. 1 and CL. II.

The Germans grouped these aircraft into units known as *Schlachtstaffeln*, or "battle flights." Working in conjunction with squads of infiltrating infantry "storm troop detachments," the battle flights would attack enemy trenches with machine-gun fire, light fragmentation bombs, and hand grenades. Unlike the earlier British efforts, those by the German units were employed within the framework of an overall concept for breaking the trench stalemate.

The German Air Service amassed no fewer than thirty-eight battle flights for the great offensive of March 1918. General Ernst von Höppner, the German air commander, reportedly told Ludendorff, "Our aircraft will guarantee you success." Ludendorff replied, "Don't you think, Herr General, that our six million riflemen will be useful also?" In many cases during the spring 1918 battles, the intervention of the ground-attack aircraft transformed an assault into a breakthrough. As the advance progressed, however, German air units took increasingly heavy losses. In the final months of the war, the high command employed the battle flights as a mobile reserve, assisting in the German defensive effort.

Tactical air power came of age in the First World War. Many of the problems associated with the mission, such as rapid identification of targets, coordination of air and ground action, the avoidance of friendly-fire incidents, and the creation of specialized aircraft designs, were first addressed by the major powers. The Germans would incorporate these lessons into their Blitzkrieg tactics, which relied heavily upon air-to-ground support.

Richard R. Muller

References

Hallion, Richard P. *Strike from the Sky: A History of Battlefield Air Attack, 1911–1945*. Washington, D.C.: Smithsonian Institution, 1989.

Morrow, John H., Jr. *The Great War in the Air: Military Aviation from 1909 to 1921*. Washington, D.C.: Smithsonian Institution, 1993.

Norman, Aaron. *The Great Air War*. New York: Macmillan, 1968.

Raleigh, Sir Walter A., and Henry A. Jones. *The War in the Air*. Vols. 1–6. Oxford: Clarendon, 1922–37.

See also AIRCRAFT, BOMBERS; AIRCRAFT, FIGHTERS; CAMBRAI, BATTLE OF; LUDENDORFF OFFENSIVES; PALESTINE AND SYRIA; PASSCHENDAELE; TRENCHARD, HUGH

Air Warfare: Strategic Bombing

The objectives of strategic warfare are to attack an enemy's warmaking capability at its most vulnerable points and to cripple the enemy's will. That is no less true of aerial warfare, although the concept significantly antedates it. Carl von Clausewitz had articulated the idea when he defined the enemy's center of gravity as that point at which the enemy is most vulnerable.

Although it was World War I that gave birth to strategic aerial warfare, the idea of using the air for attacking the enemy's center of gravity was conceived in the middle of the nineteenth century. During the Mexican War of 1846–48 an American balloonist named John Wise proposed using balloons to drop explosives on the Mexican fort of San Juan de Ulloa. The following year, Austrians attempted to use balloon-borne explosives to attack Venice. Balloons, as a means of delivering explosives, had

the great drawback of being at the mercy of the winds.

Realistic approaches to strategic bombing became possible in 1884 when two French army officers flew a cigar-shaped balloon over a 4.2-mile course. The balloon was controlled and directed by a propeller powered by one thousand pounds of electrical batteries. The weight of the batteries and the slowness of the vehicle made that particular innovation an unlikely means for conducting military operations. Count Ferdi-nand von Zeppelin further developed the concept to achieve a workable delivery vehicle by coupling the oblong balloon with the internal combustion engine. The dirigible was thus born, and in 1893 Zeppelin proposed to the German army that it would be possible to construct an airship useful for bombing enemy fortifications and troop concentrations.

In August of 1914, when war broke out on the continent, the possibility of aerial warfare had already been popularized in stories and novels. Indeed, many Europeans feared widespread destruction from the air. The Germans had developed more dirigibles than any other European power. During the first months of the war, Germany cobbled together a force, dubbed the "Ostend Carrier Pigeon Detachment," an innocuous name for a unit assigned to bomb English ports.

The first strategic raids were hardly awesome. In fact, the actual destruction and scope of strategic bombing in the Great War were limited. The impact on air-power thinking in the period after the war far exceeded any tangible manifestation of the actual bombing, thus setting a trend followed by adherents of strategic bombing through a subsequent world war and beyond.

The British Royal Naval Air Service (RNAS) conducted the first effective "strategic" raids of the war when, on 22 September and then again on 8 October 1914, a tiny force of airplanes carrying twenty-pound bombs flew from Antwerp to strike at zeppelin sheds at Dusseldorf, destroying one airship. On 21 November RNAS seaplanes flew across Lake Constance to bomb the zeppelin factory at Friedrichshafen and the sheds at Ludwigshafen, with modest results.

Germany was in the best position to engage in strategic bombing, from 1915 on, because of the large fleet of dirigibles it possessed at the beginning of the war. Although these airships soon proved to be more vulnerable than airplanes, they possessed a greater bomb-carrying capacity. Following the RNAS raids, Kaiser Wilhelm II on 7 January 1915 authorized zeppelin raids on England. The first raid occurred two days later, when a pair of airships spread bombs around Yarmouth and King's Lynn with little effect except to outrage English citizens. Before the war was over German airships had raided England some fifty-one times, with the last raid taking place in 1918 and the year of greatest intensity being 1916.

While airships could carry considerable bomb loads over long distances, they possessed a number of disadvantages. Compared with airplanes they were expensive to build and maintain. As a result Germany used only 125. Dirigibles were large and comparatively slow. Their large size made them both vulnerable to antiaircraft fire and difficult to handle in stormy weather. Their slow speed made them easy prey for airplane interceptors. Below 5,000 feet they were susceptible to antiaircraft artillery, and up to 10,000 feet they were vulnerable to interceptors using incendiary bullets. Over half of Germany's airships were either shot down, lost in storms, or accidentally destroyed as a result of the explosive nature of the hydrogen gas used to float them. German airship crews suffered a 40 percent attrition rate during the war, the highest of all units in the German army.

Before zeppelins raided England, airplanes had been used in strategic bombing. During the Battle of the Marne in late 1914, a lone German single-engine Taube monoplane dropped five small bombs on Paris along with a note from the pilot demanding the city's—indeed the French nation's—immediate surrender. Before the front stabilized, Taubes had dropped over fifty bombs on Paris, with little result other than to outrage Parisians when Notre Dame Cathedral was slightly damaged.

In 1917 Germany undertook raids against England with twin-engine Gotha and multi-engine *Risenflugzeug* or "R" series, bombers. These planes flew at about 80 to 100 miles per hour and could fly at upwards of 14,000 feet. Some could haul up to a ton of high explosives. The first Gotha/R-plane raids took place on 25 May 1917. The last took place on 20 May 1918. Eighteen of the twenty-seven raids conducted during this period took place at night. London was the target of seventeen raids. The targets were legitimately "strategic": industries, port facilities, and defense ministry buildings. Very few of the intended targets were actually hit, however. Schools, hospitals, homes, hotels, and private businesses bore the brunt of the destruction and innocent civilians the bulk of the casualties. Throughout the war, Germany dropped just under three hundred tons of bombs on England, injuring slightly fewer than five thousand people and killing about 1,400.

Virtually all the belligerent air forces engaged in strategic bombing during the Great War, and every capital, except Rome, was struck. In 1914 the Russians outdistanced everyone else in advanced multiengine aircraft. The *Ilya Murometz* (IM), Igor Sikorsky's four-engine biplane, had an enclosed cabin large enough to accommodate (on one occasion) sixteen people and a dog, and a range of more than three hundred miles.

In August of 1914 there were four IMs in the Russian inventory. In December they were sent to a base near Warsaw to conduct bombing and reconnaissance missions. Before Russia left the war, in March of 1918, some seventy IMs had been built. They flew 350 bombing and reconnaissance missions all along a front stretching from the Balkans to the Baltic. The IMs had a combat radius of over 150 miles, which allowed for relatively deep penetration behind German lines to bomb railroad marshaling yards, depots, and stations, as well as supply dumps and troop concentrations.

For the Allies, geography and the prevailing winds were a distinct disadvantage. London was within range of German bombers stationed along the coasts of occupied France and Belgium. Furthermore, on the outbound portion of their missions, while still heavy with bombs and fuel, the German bombers had the advantage of tailwinds. On the homeward leg they were lighter, meaning improved handling and less fuel consumption in the face of headwinds. Berlin, on the other hand, was beyond the range of Allied aircraft until near war's end. One French airman, however, flew a modified Nieuport from France over Berlin in 1916 to drop leaflets announcing that, while these sheets of paper could have been bombs, Paris did not make war on women and children. His ultimate destination was the Russian front, but engine trouble forced him down sixty miles short of his goal.

By 1918 strategic bombing was a reality. Thousands of men and hundreds of machines were dedicated to—and devised for—the purpose of striking at the enemy's industrial, political and moral centers of gravity. Spotting targets from altitudes of up to ten thousand feet (much less hitting them, given the primitive bomb sights of the period) was not easy. By 1918 most of the warring powers possessed aircraft with sufficient range to haul significant bomb loads to specified targets, but no air force had the ability to hit their targets with any degree of accuracy. According to Lee Kennett, a scholar on strategic bombing, British Air Minister Lord Weir told Sir Hugh Trenchard, commander of the Independent Air Force (IAF), in 1918 that he did not have to worry about bombing accuracy. Trenchard's reply was, "All the pilots drop their eggs into the center of town generally."

Ironically, while the Italian Giulio Douhet was to become the most prominent advocate of air power of the post-war period, Italy's contribution to strategic bombing during the war was slight. In August of 1915, three months after Italy entered the war on the side of England, France, and Russia, Giovanni Caproni's three-engine biplane's Ca.1s, joined the Twenty-first Squadriglia of the Italian Air Service. While the rest of the Italian Air Force languished with a motley assortment of mostly obsolete French machines, the Caproni Ca.1 was the only bomber in service at the time specifically designed to conduct strategic missions. During October and November of 1915, Italy's Ca.1s flew long-range reconnaissance and bombing missions to strike at railroad junctions and depots behind the Austrian lines. Meanwhile, Giulio Douhet was in "exile," as chief of staff for an infantry division stationed in Lombardy, as punishment for ordering the Capronis without the proper authorization.

Although English RNAS planes conducted some of the first strategic raids of the war by striking Zeppelin sheds and factories at Dusseldorf and on Lake Constance, the British did not get deeply involved in strategic bombing until late in the war. In the spring of 1918, the RNAS and the Royal Flying Corps merged to form the Royal Air Force, with Hugh Trenchard as its chief of staff. By then, over 4,000 English civilians had been injured and nearly 1,400 killed by German bombs. Prime Minister David Lloyd George had promised to repay Germany "with compound interest." In 1918 the RAF had a new command, the Independent Air Force, designed specifically to attack the German industrial system. When the war ended there were grandiose plans for a British, French, American, and Italian multinational Allied air campaign to attack German industry and un-dermine civilian morale. Although the campaign never materialized, the IAF did deliver 660 tons of bombs to German targets—roughly twice the tonnage dropped on England by the Gothas, R-planes, and zeppelins combined. Berlin, however, was still beyond the range of English planes.

Aviation came of age during the Great War, but strategic bombing emerged more full of sound and fury than tangible military substance. The legacy of strategic bombing, however, was immense. That legacy drove air-power enthusiasts, particularly Douhet in Italy and Brigadier General William Mitchell in the United States, to devise elaborate prophecies concerning the potential decisiveness of strategic bombing. Whether or not those prophecies have been fulfilled remains a matter of contention among military theorists examining the historical record of subsequent wars.

Earl H. Tilford, Jr.

References

Fredette, Raymond H. *The Sky on Fire: The First Battle of Britain, 1917–1918 and the Birth of the Royal Air Force*. New York: Holt, Rinehart and Winston, 1966.

Kennett, Lee. *The First Air War: 1914–1918*. New York: Free Press, 1991.

———. *A History of Strategic Bombing*. New York: Charles Scribner's Sons, 1982.

Morrow, John H., Jr. *The Great War in the Air: Military Aviation from 1909 to 1921*. Washington, D.C.: Smithsonian Institution, 1993.

See also AIRCRAFT, BOMBERS; ZEPPELINS

Aircraft, Bombers

It is uncertain exactly by whom or when explosive devices were first dropped from airplanes. Certainly, the concept of the manned bomber predated the rise of fighter aircraft by several years. Before the outbreak of World War I in 1914, the French, Germans, Russians, and Austro-Hungarians were developing aircraft specifically designed to carry and release bombs on a target. Great Britain also experimented with the possibility of dropping bombs from aircraft before the war but did not start building aircraft specifically for the task until after the beginning of hostilities. In addition, the Central Powers built a fearsome bombing force around zeppelin airships before 1914 and used them extensively early in the war.

Virtually all types of aircraft were used for bombing operations at some time during the war. Observation and fighter planes often carried small amounts of ordnance for dropping on enemy troops and installations. The British De Havilland 6, for example, could carry either an observer or bombs, but not both. The technological choice, however, was to develop large aircraft that were capable of penetrating enemy defenses, defending themselves from aerial attack, and delivering massive amounts of bombs on a target far behind the front.

The first genuine bomber to be employed in combat was the French *Voisin,* which bombed the Zeppelin hangars at Metz-Frascaty on 14 August 1914. A pusher biplane, the *Voisin* was rugged and weather-worthy because of its steel airframe. Throughout the war it took advantage of advancing technology to incorporate increasingly more powerful engines into its system, moving successively through engines that generated from 70 to 155 horsepower. The early versions of the *Voisin* could deliver about 132 pounds of ordnance, but by late in the war its bomb load had risen to 661 pounds. The later versions also incorporated a 37mm cannon into the plane. Recognition of the effectiveness of the *Voisin* bomber in the French army came in September of 1914 when the *Aviation Militaire* began reorganizing its *Voisins* into bombardment squadrons. The *Voisin* force, eventually numbering more than 600 aircraft and being effectively flown until the end of the war, was used by France after May of 1915 to conduct a sustained bombing campaign along the Western Front.

The French efforts toward building a bombing force were quickly followed by the Imperial Russian Air Service equipped with Igor I. Sikorsky's huge *Ilya Mourometz* aircraft. The world's first four-engine airplane, the *Ilya Mourometz* first flew on 13 May 1913. Its four engines each generated from 100 to 220 horsepower. Its crew of five had sleeping compartments in the rear fuselage, and it was protected from air attack by either three or four machine guns. The most advanced variant of the *Ilya Mourometz* could remain aloft for five hours at an altitude of about 9,000 feet at a speed of eighty-five miles per hour. It could carry a bomb load of between 992 and 1,543 pounds, depending on other operational factors. It also enjoyed a 60 percent bombs-on-target rating because of its precise bombsights and the excellent training of its bombardiers.

Russian Major General M.V. Shidlovski, commanding the *Eskadra Vozdushnykh Korablei* (Squadron of Flying Ships), equipped his unit with the *Ilya Mourometz.* Formed specifically to exploit the air weakness of the Central Powers on the Eastern Front, Shidlovski's squadron was a self-contained force with its own test operations and training. It was first employed in combat on 15 February 1915, when the squadron left from its base at Jablonna, Poland, to raid a German base in East Prussia. Between that time and the November 1917 Russian Revolution, Shidlovski's unit made more than 400 bombing raids over Germany and the Baltic states. The *Ilya Mourometz* was a rugged airplane. Its only casualty from air attack occurred on 12 September 1916—and only after the aircraft's gunners had shot down three German fighters. Two other bombers were lost in crashes, but the force was not crippled until February of 1918, when thirty planes were destroyed by the Russians at Vinnitza to prevent their capture by an advancing German army.

On 23 May 1915 Italy entered World War I on the side of the Allies, and, while overall poorly prepared for the conflict, it had a competent bombing force. A family of *Caproni* bombers, almost all of which were trimotors, had been first incorporated into the Italian military just before the war. The Ca 2, which had the range and reliability to cross the Alps and attack Austro-Hungary, flew the first Italian bombing mission of the war on 20 August 1915. A total of 174 Ca 2s were built between 1914 and 1916 and served as Italy's principal daylight bomber until the appearance of the Ca 3 in 1917. The *Caproni* Ca 5 series of bombers was the most advanced produced in Italy during the war. A biplane with one pusher and two tractor engines, each generating 200–300 horsepower, it could carry a bomb load of 1,190 pounds for four hours at 94.4 miles per hour. It was susceptible to aerial attack, however, since it mounted only two defensive machine guns. A total of 255 Ca 5 aircraft were built, some of which were torpedo bombers for use against naval forces. The *Caproni* bombers were used throughout the war. Characterized by exceptional range and moderate bomb-carrying capabilities, many were converted to cargo and passenger operations after the war.

The British also entered the sweepstakes to build an effective bomber force early in the war. In December of 1914 Commodore Murray F. Sueter of the British Admiralty's Air Department began the process by mandating the development of a "bloody paralyzer of an aeroplane" to bomb Germany. He asked for a two-seat, twin-engine aircraft with a speed of at least seventy-five miles per hour and a carrying capacity of at least six 112-pound bombs. The result was the Handley Page O/100, and by March of 1915 forty aircraft had been ordered, although the prototype did not fly until December. It exceeded Sueter's payload requirements, used a crew of four, mounted machine guns in the nose, dorsal, and downward from the lower fuselage, and could have its wings folded to fit into standard hangars. The O/100 went into service with the Royal Navy Air Service in November of 1916 and was used at first for daylight sea patrols near Flanders. Beginning in March of 1917, however, the planes were concentrated for night bombing of German U-boat bases, railway stations, and industrial sites. They served effectively until the end of the war.

A more advanced version of the Handley Page, designated the O/400, mounted more powerful engines and possessed superior bomb-carrying, altitude, and speed characteristics. The British ordered 800 of these bombers, building about 550 themselves. Another 150 were assembled from parts manufactured in the United States by the Standard Aircraft Corporation, while the rest of the order was eventually cancelled. At about the same time that the O/100 was being assigned night-bombardment responsibilities, the O/400 became the standard British day bomber. At the time of the Armistice, 258 O/400s were still in service in France, carrying the new 1,650-pound blockbuster bombs. The aircraft remained in British military service until 1920.

The final Handley Page bomber, the V/1500, came too late in the war to see combat. A four-engine aircraft, the V/1500 first flew in May of 1918. It had a range of 600 miles, excellent defensive gun placement, and a bomb capacity of thirty 250-pounders. The first three operational V/1500s were assigned to No. 166 Squadron of the Royal Air Force on 8 November 1918 and were waiting with a bomb load on the flightline when the Armistice was signed. Only thirty-six of these strategic bombers were built and only one saw combat, a May 1919 mission to Kobul, then in northwestern India,

to expedite the settling of a rebellion against the British.

Germany had long been enamored with the possibility of using lighter-than-air zeppelins for bombing purposes and early in the war employed them with great success against Allied targets. Coasting high above the enemy, out of reach of enemy fighters until newer versions entered service in the spring of 1917, they could place tons of ordnance on such far-off targets as London. John Slessor, a Royal Flying Corps pilot, described his experience of trying to catch a zeppelin on the night of 13 October 1915 near London. Slessor tried to climb to the zeppelin's altitude, but as he slowly pulled closer he saw the crew drop ballast and the *Zeppelin 15* "cocked its nose up at an incredible angle and climbed far above me." Slessor gave up his chase soon thereafter. Later fighters could reach the zeppelins, however, and had a field day against them because of their large size and explosive gases. To counteract this threat, in 1917 Germany developed some new high-altitude zeppelins that could bomb from 20,000 feet, but they were subject to all manner of accuracy, navigation, and equipment failures that hastened their abandonment by the military. Thereafter, zeppelins were used by the German Naval Air Service principally for sea patrol.

Germany produced two principal types of bombers during the war. The earliest was the *Friedrichshafen G* twin-engine pusher biplane, which first went into operational service in 1916. Mounted with a Parabellum machine gun in both the nose and rear cockpits, it could carry a moderate bomb load of 1,102 pounds against night targets in Belgium and France. Far more significant was the *Gotha*, the *Grossflufgzeng* (large airplane), the first version of which was a twin-engine biplane intended for ground-attack and general tactical duties. The prototype was built in January of 1915 and found service both in France and the Eastern Front. The *Gotha* G.II version was an entirely new design executed by Hans Burchard that had emerged from requirements established by the German army for its attacks against England. Carrying a crew of three and a defensive armament of only two machine guns, it first flew in April of 1916. It entered service in the Balkans that fall but was soon withdrawn because of engine crankshaft failures and was replaced by the G.III, which had 260-horsepower Mercedes engines and an extra machine gun. By December of 1916 fourteen were already in operation, and they continued to be used until near the end of the war.

The first important production *Gotha* was the G.IV, going into operation in March of 1917. Chosen to lead the bombing raids against Britain, the G.IV had more powerful engines, four defensive machine guns, ailerons on both wings of the biplane, and a maximum bomb load of about 1,000 pounds. In about September of 1917 the G.V was introduced, with a somewhat greater capacity and a relatively good cross-channel range. By April of 1918, thirty-six *Gotha* G.Vs were in service.

The cycle of bombing was consistent throughout the war. The first attacks came in the daylight, then, facing better defenses, the bombers switched to night campaigns against London. The Germans eventually abandoned bombardment altogether when it became too costly. None of the raids contributed to the overall outcome of the war.

Throughout the war, technological development of the bombing force was continuous but not as dramatic as that of the fighter aircraft. The range, altitude, and bomb load of the aircraft involved in these missions grew throughout the conflict. For instance, at the beginning of the war, the standard bomb was a 20-pounder, supplanted by 1,650-pound block-busters by the time of the Armistice. The Handley Page V/1500 could carry two 3,300-pound bombs. Smaller bombs, carried by all manner of aircraft, were good mostly for their nuisance value but occasionally served a tacti-cal purpose, as when in 1915 a zeppelin that flew too low was bombed by a fighter and brought down in flames.

Two major variations on World War I bombers emerged for help in sea combat. The first was the torpedo bomber, which carried torpedoes instead of bombs for use against enemy ships. Many bomber types were also modified for sea landings and takeoffs, and these amphibians patrolled the seas and defended naval installations. They usually carried machine guns and a small bomb load and proved their value in a large amount of routine but critical work. A prime example was a seaplane version of the *Gotha* that entered service in January of 1916 with the German navy, being used in patrol and logistics duties.

Although bombing operations did not affect in any significant way the outcome of the conflict, they did set the stage for the development of the strategic bombardment doctrine and air campaigns of World War II. For example, the Germans dropped 9,000 bombs totaling about 280 tons on Britain in fifty-one airship and fifty-two airplane raids. In the process they killed 1,413 people and wounded another 3,408. That was not a particularly significant figure when placed in juxtaposition to British war dead of over 300,000 and more than a million wounded. Nor did the raids destroy a lot of property—about £3 million worth over the course of the war. By contrast, it has been estimated that rats in England destroyed about £70 million worth of property annually

REPRESENTATIVE WORLD WAR I BOMBERS

Airplane	Country	Service	Speed (mph)	Bomb Load (lbs)	Horsepower/ Engine
Voisin	France	9/14–11/18	85	132–661	155 (1 engine)
Ilya Mourometz	Russia	5/13–2/18	75	992–1,543	150 (4 engines)
Caproni	Italy	8/15–11/18	94.4	1,190	300 (3 engines)
Handley Page O/100	G.B.	11/16–11/18	90	1792	275 (2 engines)
Handley Page O/400	G.B.	3/17–11/18	97.5	1,792	322 (2 engines)
Handley Page V/1500	G.B.	11/18	90.5	7,500	375 (4 engines)
De Havilland 4	G.B.	1/17–1/18	120	4 bombs	200 (1 engine)
De Havilland 5	G.B.	5/17–3/18	104	4 bombs	110 (1 engine)
Bristol F.2A/B	G.B.	3/17–11/18	123	12 bombs	275 (1 engine)
S.E. 5a	G.B.	4/17–11/18	121	4 bombs	200 (1 engine)
Sopwith Camel	G.B.	6/17–11/18	104.5	4 bombs	130 (1 engine)
Friedrichshafen	Germany	5/16–11/18	87.6	1,102	200 (2 engines)
Gotha	Germany	12/16–11/18	87	1,000	260 (2 engines)

during that same period. What bombing did, at least at first, however, was to create terror in the populace. The casualties resulting from a German raid on Oldham on 28 January 1918, where one bomb hit a printing plant, killing thirty-eight and wounding eighty-five, were cited for years as evidence of the horrible power of strategic bombardment. That fact became the principal lesson to military leaders interested in aviation during the 1920s and 1930s. While an imperfect lesson—studies confirmed that the terror was quickly replaced by a sense of camaraderie and resistance against the worst that could be delivered by the enemy—it served to influence the direction of the bombing campaigns of later years.

Roger D. Launius

References

Bruce, John M. *British Aeroplanes, 1914–1918.* New York: Funk & Wagnalls, 1969.

Douhet, Giulio. *The Command of the Air.* New York: Coward-McCann, 1942. Originally published in Italian in 1921.

Fredette, Raymond H. *The Sky on Fire: The First Battle of Britain, 1917–1918.* New York: Harcourt Brace Jovanovich, 1976.

Higham, Robin. *Air Power: A Concise History.* New York: St. Martin's, 1973.

Kennett, Lee B. *The First Air War, 1914–1918.* New York: Free Press, 1991.

Morrow, John H. *German Air Power in World War I.* Lincoln: University of Nebraska Press, 1982.

Munson, Kenneth. *Bombers, Patrol and Reconnaissance Aircraft, 1914–19.* New York: Macmillan, 1968.

See also AIRCRAFT, PRODUCTION; ZEPPELINS

Aircraft, Fighters

As a result of the First World War, the small, fast, maneuverable, and heavily armed fighter emerged as a major component of modern warfare. Although powered flight had been possible since 1903, as late as 1914 there was little understanding of its possibility to extend warfare into a three-dimensional battlefield. Accordingly, the few military leaders who thought about employing it viewed aviation essentially as an adjunct of the artillery—a superior perch from which to spot—and as an aerial observer of enemy troop dispositions and movements.

Indicative of this view was the comment of American army Lieutenant Fred Humpheries in 1910:

> From a military standpoint, the first and probably the greatest use will be found in reconnaissance. A flyer carrying two men can rise in the air out of range of the enemy, and passing over his head out of effective target range, can make a complete reconnaissance and return, bringing more valuable information than could possibly be secured by a reconnaissance in force. This method would endanger the lives of two men; the other would detach several thousand men for a length of time and endanger the lives of all.

When the war began, therefore, the air doctrine of all combatants involved using the airplane for observation and message carrying, not for combat.

Most aircraft were not even armed during the first months of the war. Pilots of the various nations, moreover, had been prewar flying enthusiasts and many knew each other from European air meets. It was a little like old home week as the opposing pilots hailed each other in the air. This did not last long, however, for by the fall of 1914 the airplane had proven its worth as a reconnaissance vehicle. Field commanders recognized that it was important to keep opposing observation planes from accomplishing their missions, because of the massive ground attacks that were sure to head for a weak sector discovered from the air. Antiaircraft fire quickly became coordinated and deadly, but opposing pilots also began taking weapons up with them to take occasional pot shots at enemy planes. Within a very short period, machine guns had been mounted on aircraft, either for the observer to fire or fixed straight ahead so that the pilot could aim the plane like a weapon. The machine gun, as had been the case on the ground, became the master of the aerial battlefield. For the rest of the war the legendary "Knights of the Air" dueled for control of the skies over the European battlefields and later employed aircraft as a ground-attack weapon.

Once airplanes were transformed into "warplanes" they evolved through five essential generations during the remainder of the Great War (see table on page 24). Each stage represented a major technological breakthrough and was dominated by one side in the conflict. It also forced the development of fighter tactics to make aerial combat more effective. In turn, each stage was made obsolete by its successor, and while vestiges of outdated aircraft and tactics might remain throughout the rest of the war, they became less significant as they were superseded by later developments.

The first generation of armed fighters, in all combatant nations, was modified from prewar designs, usually quite hastily and with varying degrees of success. These aircraft lacked the maneuverability, range, altitude ceiling, speed, payload, and sophisticated control equipment that showed up in successive generations. For example, most used the wing-warping technique for lateral control that had been developed by the Wright brothers and that would soon become obsolete with the innovation of movable ailerons. For the first year of the war, however, aircraft of this generation ruled the skies over the Western Front.

The addition of the machine gun to these airplanes, a fundamental modification, took a twisted course during the latter half of 1914. The first recorded instance of a forward-firing fixed machine gun was on 22 August 1914, when British pilot Louis Strange made a field modification to his B.E. 2—adding a Lewis machine gun—and ventured aloft to stalk a German observation plane. His aircraft was underpowered, however, and the Lewis was a heavy weapon; he failed to come close to the enemy plane. When Strange returned to his airfield, his commander made him remove the Lewis and stick to carrying rifles aloft. The commander might have been more favorably disposed to Strange's efforts, however, if they had been successful.

Other machine-gun adaptations met with more success. More powerful two-seater aircraft soon added machine guns, usually on some type of swivel mount, for firing by the observer. The first casualty of this new weapon came on 5 October 1914, when a French crew (Sergeant Joseph Frantz, pilot, and Corporal Louis Quenault, observer) with their *Voisin* fighter and Hotchkiss machine gun engaged a German *Aviatik* biplane over Rheims. The *Voisin* attacked and destroyed the unarmed German plane. For most of the next six months fights between the first generation of fighter airplanes involved observers with machine guns blasting away at each other while the pilots tried to fly along essentially parallel courses above the trenches of the Western Front.

The most logical means of using the machine gun, however, was for it to be mounted to fire forward. This allowed the pilot to point his airplane toward the enemy, using the whole vehicle as a weapon. Unfortunately, the propeller got in the way of any gun mounted on the fuselage. To avoid that difficulty, machine guns were sometimes mounted on the upper wings of biplanes, but that created a different set of problems. Aiming and reloading the weapon were tedious, and when it jammed, as early machine guns frequently did, clearing by hand was both difficult and dangerous.

Indicative of one type of problem associated with wing-mounted guns was the mission of Lewis Strange on 10 May 1915. He was flying a Martynside S.1 Scout equipped with an upper wing-mounted Lewis machine gun, and after exhausting his ammunition during a dogfight he stood up to replace the ammunition drum. Clenching the control stick between his legs, he tugged at the drum but it failed to budge. While he was working on the gun, he lost control of the stick, and the Martynside flipped upside down. Strange was tossed outside the cockpit but managed to hang on to the machine-gun drum, which should have slipped easily out of its mount but, as luck would have it, had jammed. Quickly the plane righted itself, more or less, allowing Strange to climb back into the cockpit and return to his airfield only a little worse for wear. While an extreme case, the incident points up the uncommon hazards of this type of aerial warfare.

A major breakthrough in aerial combat came in 1915 when French pilot Roland Garros first installed a propeller synchronizer on his aircraft, so that he could install a forward-facing fixed machine gun and thereby turn his fighter into a truly lethal weapon. The synchronizer allowed him to fire through the spinning propeller without damaging it. Inasmuch as machine-gun rounds sometimes misfired, he also sheathed the prop blades in metal to protect them. Garros successfully flew his fighter in combat for several weeks, but on 18 April he was forced down behind German lines and his aircraft was captured intact. The Germans copied the armored propeller, but without the synchronizer they still damaged props and sent bullets flying dangerously in all directions. They soon developed their own propeller synchronizer.

That represented the state of technology in the first generation of fighters in the spring of 1915. Several moderately successful fighters emerged from the modification effort. Perhaps the most successful was the German *Eindecker* monoplane, which was a small single-seater that mounted a forward-firing Spandau or Parabellum machine gun. Dutchman Anthony Fokker, who built aircraft for the Germans, developed his own cam-operated machine gun synchronizer and installed it on the *Eindecker*. Employing a 100-horsepower rotary engine it could manage a speed of only 87.5 miles per hour, but it was a match for anything the Allies flew. The *Eindecker*/forward-firing machine gun combination proved itself in combat on 1 August 1915, when a flight attacked a formation of British airplanes trying to bomb the Douai airfield in France. This inaugurated what has been called the "*Fokker* Scourge," about eight months during which the *Eindecker* ruled the skies over the Western Front.

The *Eindecker* became such a significant force in the air war over France that the British air commander, Hugh Trenchard, took action to reduce the likelihood of single dogfights. He directed the Royal Flying Corps on 14 January 1916 to refrain from fighting the *Eindeckers* unless they had numerical superiority. In the official British history of air combat in World War I, Trenchard wrote that:

> a machine proceeding on a reconnaissance must be escorted by at least three other fighting machines. These machines must fly in close formation and a reconnaissance should not be continued if any of the machines becomes detached. . . . From recent experience it seems that the Germans are now employing their aeroplanes in groups of three or four, and these numbers are frequently encountered by our aeroplanes. Flying in close formation must be practised by all pilots.

The *Eindeckers* forced the Allies to expend large numbers of aircraft on escort duty and kept them from fighting for air superiority.

More positively for the Allies, Germany's control of the skies prompted the rapid development of innovative fighter tactics to help equalize the disparity between their machines.

The British adopted a basic formation of four aircraft. The Germans and most other combatants used aircraft in pairs, with three standard configurations: line abreast, line astern with different altitudes for each plane, and echelon. These patterns were helpful in Allied defense against the *Eindeckers*, but they did not tip the balance of air power in the Allies' favor. What accomplished that were new Allied aircraft, designs successfully incorporating the machine gun into its system. One of those was the French *Morane-Saulner* Type L fighter, an aircraft comparable to the *Eindecker*. It was employed by the Allies during the early stages of the war and represented the first generation of aircraft to be flown in combat. The first generation of fighters remained in service as late as September of 1916, but most were quickly retired during the middle of 1916 and thereafter could infrequently be found outside of training units.

The second generation of fighters was a more diverse collection of aircraft. Their designs had been intended from the outset to incorporate armaments. First appearing in the theater in the spring of 1915, this generation of aircraft may have been on the drawing boards before the outbreak of hostilities, but they incorporated the lessons of early combat experience into their features. The first of this new generation was the British Vickers F.B. 5 "Gunbus," a two-man biplane with the engine propeller facing the rear in a "pusher" configuration that allowed the swiveling machine gun on the front seat a remarkably wide field of fire. Most of the other aircraft in this generation had fixed forward-firing machine guns utilizing a propeller synchronizer. These aircraft represented the first attempt to integrate weapon and vehicle into a single system.

Other aircraft in the second generation of fights were the French *Nieuport* 11, the British De Havilland 2, and the German *Fokker* D biplanes, which appeared in 1916. These were all effective matches for the first-generation fighters. The *Nieuports*, for instance, effectively swept the *Eindeckers* from the sky in 1916. While these fighters remained in operation at least until August of 1917, they were superseded by a third generation within less than a year of their first appearance.

The third generation of fighters emerged in the spring and summer of 1916 and were unique for being the first machines designed to incorporate the lessons learned in air combat over France during the early stages of the war. Historian Richard P. Hallion described them as "much more powerful than either of the first- or second-generation aircraft, with more efficient armament systems (as exemplified by a trend toward twin synchronized machine guns firing forwards and rotating and traversing "ring"-type gun mounts for an observer), improved structural design, and great attention to reducing aerodynamic drag and streamlining." Some of these aircraft remained in combat service through the end of the war.

There were several distinct families of fighters in this third generation. The French *Nieuport* 17–27 aircraft, the *Albatros* series of fighters built by the Germans (modeled after captured *Nieuports*), and the British Sopwith planes were all examples of this type. These airplanes dominated the airspace over their particular sectors during much of 1916 and the first part of 1917. The deadliest of these new warplanes was the *Albatros* D III, made of a monocoque wooden shell rather than doped cloth and powered by a 160-horsepower Mercedes engine that could generate a speed of 103 miles per hour. That was fifteen miles per hour faster than the *Eindecker* it replaced. Mounting twin-synchronized Spandau machine guns and possessing excellent handling qualities, the *Albatros* D III posed a major threat to Allied aviation at the midpoint of the war.

German fighter power was apparent during this stage of the air war. In 1916 and the first three months of 1917, Germany's fine *Albatros* fighters were employed in sufficient numbers to achieve local air superiority. The combination of technically advanced fighters, outstanding training, and tactical employment by Oswald Boelcke marked a significant increase in Germany's mastery of the air. The high point of German success was in March of 1917 when the *Luftstreitkrafte* (German air corps) shot down 120 British aircraft. The *Albatros* maintained a central place in the air war until that time, when a newer generation of more advanced Allied aircraft appeared.

German air superiority was certainly not total, however, during the middle part of the war. The Allies' third generation of fighters came into the war by the fall of 1916 in sufficient numbers to make a difference. Newer *Nieuports* and British Sopwith and Bristol fighters were a match for the German warplanes, and the Allied industrial base out-produced Germany's. By April of 1917, the British Royal Flying Corps could muster 754 aircraft on the Western Front, of which 385 were fighters. The German force was approximately 264 airplanes (only 114 of which were fighters).

Ironically, the success of the *Albatros* helped ensure the loss of German air superiority over France in 1917. In the early months of 1917 a fourth generation of fighters began to appear among the Allied forces over the Front, and with their emergence the Central Powers lost what semblance of equality in the air had been left them. "After April 1917," wrote Richard Hallion, "Germany was never again in a position to contest seriously for control of the air because British fighter technology caught up with and eventually surpassed that of Germany."

Germany had made several bad production decisions. Its air leaders decided to standardize most production on the successful third generation *Albatros* D III fighter design, causing research and development work to stagnate. They also decided to build a *Fokker* version of a British Sopwith triplane whose ability to challenge modern designs was transitory at best. Finally, Boelcke had been killed in combat on 28 October 1916, and with his death many of his air tactics were abandoned—or at least did not continue to evolve in response to new conditions.

In the meantime, Great Britain introduced a fourth generation of fighters in March of 1917, with the Bristol F.2B. This was quickly followed by the Royal Aircraft Factory S.E. 5a and the Sopwith Camel, the latter so named because of the distinctive hump where the machine guns were mounted. This new generation was characterized by an explicit response to combat experience in the first years of the war and by air-crew preferences based on extensive operations. These British planes, along with the French *Spad* 13, were the fighters that turned back the German challenge and won the air war. Not until nearly a year later did Germany have comparable fighters with which to contest Allied air power.

Indicative of the improvement in Allied fighters was a private communication from Baron Manfred von Richthofen, an air ace and student of Boelcke's, to a close friend serving on the staff of Ernst von Hoeppner. Written while convalescing from a head wound suffered in a dogfight, von Richthofen's letter described British air superiority:

The English . . . can fly whither they wish, with absolute command of the air not only over their own lines, but over the entire countryside. . . .

Our aircraft are inferior to the English in an absolutely laughable fashion. . . . And in addition to better quality of aircraft, they have greater numbers. . . . And the people at home, for nearly a year, have developed nothing better than this lousy Albatros, remaining with the Albatros D III with which I fought last fall. . . .

English single-seaters climb better and are faster than us, and the English even have already [the Bristol fighter], a two-seater, that can overhaul an Albatros, easily overpowering us in turns, against which one is virtually powerless.

Low morale was taking its toll along with the enemy, and Richthofen demanded change.

Richthofen's forceful intervention led directly to two crucial decisions by the German high command. The first was the development of the *Fokker* Dr I triplane, modeled on a British Sopwith design. The greater lift-to-drag ratio of the triplane gave it exceptional climbing capabilities and suited it well to the defensive air war then being fought by the *Luftstreitkrafte* against the more advanced and more numerous Allied air forces. While a capable fighter, the *Fokker* triplane, made famous in Richthofen's Flying Circus in 1917, had limitations in combat and suffered from in-flight structural deficiencies that killed several fliers. The *Fokker* triplane, therefore, was not a fully successful design, and Richthofen soon abandoned it as the machine of choice for challenging the Allies.

Richthofen also championed the procurement of a new *Fokker* aircraft in January of 1918, the D VII, arguably the finest single-seat fighter of the war. A biplane with a clear line of inheritance from earlier *Fokker* designs, it had a powerful 160-horsepower in-line Mercedes engine. The *Fokker* D VII first arrived at the front in April of 1918, a few days after Richthofen was shot down and too late to make any real difference in the outcome of the war. Historian John H. Morrow concluded: "To Richthofen's sponsorship of the *Fokker* D VII, which appeared too late to save him, many a German combat pilot of 1918 owed his life."

The *Fokker* D VII was faster, safer, more lethal, and more rugged than even the best all-around Allied fighter of this generation, the Sopwith Camel. Everyone was impressed with the D VII's ability to place enormous firepower on a target through its combination of outstanding flying characteristics and weaponry. An Allied pilot reported that in a dogfight a *Fokker* D VII "just hung right there and sprayed me with lead like he had a hose. All I could do was to watch his tracer and kick my rudder from one side to the other to throw his aim off. This war isn't what it used to be." The D VII was a gritty opponent: small wonder that the armistice terms agreed to in the fall of 1918 specifically ordered the surrender of all *Fokker* D VII aircraft in service by Germany.

With the advent of the fourth generation of fighters, and the heightened capabilities and armaments they gave their pilots, the uses of these aircraft also changed. Until the spring of 1917 fighters had been used principally to achieve air superiority over the battlefield, so that observation aircraft could operate without hindrance. An exception was the effort of fighters to defend against bombers and Germany's large fleet of lighter-than-air zeppelins, used for bombing Allied targets. But, until the newer aircraft appeared in the spring of 1917, that was mostly a futile effort. With the advent of the new fighters, their expanded capabilities made it possible to defend effectively against day or night long-range bombers and zeppelins. The new planes could also function as fighter-bombers on the front.

The effectiveness of the new fighters was especially evident in combat against zeppelins. Although zeppelins made huge targets and the hydrogen that kept them aloft was highly explosive and could be ignited with machine-gun fire, in the early years the zeppelins, with a bombing altitude of 10,000 feet, were almost invulnerable because of the low effective ceiling of the fighters. British flyer John Slessor commented that on the night of 13 October 1915 he was flying an antizeppelin patrol near London when he encountered the *Zeppelin* L 15 high above him. He likened his view of the L 15 to "a cod's eye view of the *Queen Mary*." Slessor tried to climb to the zeppelin's altitude but, as he slowly pulled closer, he saw the crew drop ballast. The L 15 "cocked its nose up at an incredible angle and climbed far above me." Slessor gave up his chase soon thereafter. Later fighters could reach the zeppelins, however, and had a field day. To counteract that threat, in 1917 Germany developed some new high-alti-

A

tude zeppelins that could bomb from 20,000 feet. They were subject to all manner of accuracy, navigation, and equipment failures, however, which hastened their abandonment by the military.

The Allies also began to develop an integrated doctrine of air power. As early as the battle of the Somme in the summer of 1916, German army leaders had recognized that Allied fighters occasionally strafed or bombed infantry in trenches at the Front. In early 1917 a decision was made to use artillery fire to pin down German troops in their trenches while low-flying fighters swarmed over the battle line

to hit balloons or ground targets and return unmolested. The approach was implemented on 2 May 1917, when six *Nieuports* hopped over the trenches, quickly climbed to 2,000 feet, and destroyed four observation balloons before returning without loss. The next day five Sopwith airplanes broke up German troop movements using the same tactic. On 11 May 1917, Allied fighters supported a ground attack by pounding dug-in troops in advance of the Allied army. Another new wrinkle was added to the ground interdiction campaign in July of 1917 when British fighters were equipped with 25-pound Cooper bombs fitted to racks beneath the

REPRESENTATIVE WORLD WAR I FIGHTERS

Airplane	Country	Service	Speed (mph)	Armament	Horsepower	Weight (lbs.)
First Generation						
Bristol Scout D	G.B.	9/14–9/16	70	1 Vickers	100	1,440
Morane Type N	France	6/15–9/16	102	1 Hotchkiss	80	981
Fokker E III	Germany	7/15–9/16	87.5	2 Spandau	100	1,342
Second Generation						
Vickers F.B. 5	G.B.	2/15–6/16	70	1 Lewis	110	2,050
Nieuport 11	France	1/16–8/17	97	1 Lewis	80	1,210
De Havilland 2	G.B.	12/15–6/17	93	1 Lewis	100	1,441
Fokker D II	Germany	7/16–12/16	93	1 Spandau	100	1,267
Third Generation						
Sopwith Pup	G.B.	4/16–10/17	111	1 Lewis, 8 Rockets	80	1,225
Halberstadt D	Germany	6/16–12/17	95	2 Spandau	95	1,606
Albatros D I/II	Germany	8/16–9/17	109.4	2 Spandau	160	1,976
Spad 7	France	8/16–11/18	119.5	1 Vickers	180	1,550
Albatros D III	Germany	1/17–9/18	103	2 Spandau	160	1,949
Sopwith Triplane	G.B.	2/17–11/17	113	2 Vickers	130	1,541
De Havilland 5	G.B.	5/17–3/18	104	1 Vickers, 4 bombs	110	1,492
Albatros D Va	Germany	6/17–11/18	106.9	2 Spandau	185	2,013
Fokker Dr I	Germany	9/17–8/18	97	2 Spandau	110	1,290
Fourth Generation						
Bristol F.2A/B	G.B.	3/17–11/18	123	1 Vickers, 1 Lewis, Free, 12 bombs	275	2,848
S.E. 5a	G.B.	4/17–11/18	121	1 Vickers, 1 Lewis, 4 bombs	200	1,953
Spad 13	France	4/17–11/18	130	2 Vickers	200	815
Sopwith Camel	G.B.	6/17–11/18	104.5	2 Vickers, 4 bombs	130	1,482
Fokker D VII	Germany	4/18–11/18	125	2 Spandau	185	2,112
Pfalz D XII	Germany	9/18–11/18	120	2 Spandau	180	1,962
Fifth Generation						
Junkers D I	Germany	9/18–11/18	115.5	2 Spandau	180	1,841

wings, for use against infantry targets. At one point in this campaign, Trenchard ordered his air forces to "cross the line at Armentières very low and then shoot at everything." The result was the emergence, with these newer and more capable fighters, of a new role for airplanes in combat.

The German *Luftstreitkrafte* was quick to learn from these new tactics. It began to operate in much the same way with the *Fokker* D VII. It explicitly adopted a doctrine of inflicting demoralizing attacks on enemy troops in the trenches. Issued in February of 1918, German air doctrine emphasized large formations of aircraft hitting a small selection of targets at the forward line of the infantry along with its supporting artillery emplacements. On both sides the casualties inflicted on the ground by air attack from these new fighters were significant. But it was also costly to the air forces. About 30 percent of the fliers engaged in ground-attack at the battle of Cambrai, for example, became casualties. Arthur Gould Lee was one of only three flight commanders left in the British 46 Squadron after a week of low-level attacks at Cambrai. This type of flying, Lee believed, was "a wasteful employment of highly trained pilots and expensive aeroplanes." Even so, these attacks served their purpose and were extended through the last great battles of World War I in 1918.

A final generation of fighters appeared just before the end of World War I. They were characterized by all-metal construction and single wings mounted on the lower part of the fuselage. The single-seat *Junkers* D I, and its two-seat variant, the C1 I, could outfly and outgun any aircraft operated by the Allies. With a speed of 115 miles per hour, the *Junkers* D I was ten miles per hour faster than the next best Allied fighter, the Sopwith Camel. Unfortunately for the *Luftstreitkrafte,* these planes were inserted into the war too late and in too small a number to make much of a difference.

The large and capable Allied air forces, to which the Americans were added in 1917 and 1918 although no American-designed aircraft made it into combat, were too much for German fliers. The full power of the Allies was felt by Germany in the massive St. Mihiel aerial offensive late in the war. No fewer than 1,481 Allied airplanes were used, over 700 of which were fighters. Under the command of American Colonel Billy Mitchell, the Allied air forces flew the trench-strafing, close-air-support, interdiction, and air-superiority missions that had been pioneered by the British. Everywhere the German fliers were shot out of the sky. In this campaign some of the promise of air power began to be realized, employed to meet the needs of the American ground commander John J. Pershing and his troops.

By the end of the war, fighter technology and air doctrine had both evolved considerably. Most of the evolution had emerged from the crucible of combat, and without that practical experience the process might have taken a far different course—certainly it would have been slower. Most important, military leaders of all countries involved in the conflict recognized that never again could war planning take place without considering the role, both positive and negative, of fighter aircraft.

Roger D. Launius

References

Bruce, John M. *British Aeroplanes, 1914–1918.* New York: Funk & Wagnalls, 1969.

Grey, Peter L., and Owen Thetford. *German Aircraft of the First World War.* London: Putnam, 1962.

Hallion, Richard P. *Rise of the Fighter Aircraft, 1914–1918.* Baltimore, Md.: Nautical and Aviation Press, 1984.

Kennett, Lee B. *The First Air War, 1914–1918.* New York: Free Press, 1991.

Lamberton, W.M. *Fighter Aircraft of the 1914–1918 War.* Fallbrook, Calif.: Aero, 1964.

Lewis, Gwilym H. *Wings Over the Somme, 1916–1918.* London: William Kimber, 1976.

Morrow, John H. *German Air Power in World War I.* Lincoln: University of Nebraska Press, 1982.

Munson, Kenneth. *Fighters, Attack, and Training Aircraft, 1914–19.* New York: Macmillan, 1968.

Weyl, A.R. *Fokker: The Creative Years.* London: Putnam, 1965.

Winter, Denis. *The First of the Few: Fighter Pilots of the First World War.* London: Allen Lane, 1982.

See also AIR WARFARE, FIGHTER TACTICS; AIR WARFARE: GROUND-SUPPORT AVIATION; AIRCRAFT, PRODUCTION; BOELCKE, OSWALD; FOKKER, ANTHONY; TRENCHARD, HUGH

Aircraft, Production during the War

At the beginning of World War I, aviation was still in its infancy, and the strategic uses of aircraft had barely been explored by the world's military leaders. Although the armies of several nations had awarded contracts for military aircraft between 1908 and 1911, the number of machines actually available for wartime purposes remained extremely small. France, a major force before the war in aircraft production and aviation technology, had 268 combat-ready aircraft at mobilization and approximately another 330 unfit for service. Germany claimed 246 serviceable aircraft out of a total of 450, but Britain could mobilize only sixty-three planes to cross the Channel, leaving a reserve of 116 machines at home that were mostly obsolete or useless. Russia's aircraft strength was comparable to that of Germany on paper, but in reality the machines were unfit for military service and had few spare parts in reserve.

When war began, military leaders were convinced that the conflict would last but a few weeks. The first officials in charge of aircraft procurement for the armies handled the needs of aviation units in different ways. While German aircraft manufacturers were negotiating contracts with the War Ministry, and the British War Office was demanding maximum output from its few engine and airframe factories, the French director of military aeronautics, General Bernard, cut back factory production and canceled new aircraft orders in order to release the maximum number of workers for combat duty. The French thus lost their former lead in aircraft production at the beginning of the war and had to struggle to regain manufacturing capacity once the military realized the need for aircraft in a protracted war.

The primary limiting factor in aircraft production was the availability of suitable engines. A factory could produce many more airframes than there were powerplants, so manufacturers fought for a reliable supply of engines. An aircraft engine had to be both light and powerful, and most gasoline engines of the period were still too heavy for aircraft. Three types of engines were common at the beginning of the war: the in-line (cylinders in a straight line), usually water-cooled and therefore relatively heavy because of the need for a radiator and its associated tubing; the radial (cylinders grouped around the crankshaft in star formation), which was lighter than an in-line engine and could be either air or water cooled; and the rotary (which itself spun around its stationary crankshaft). The latter incorporated both power and light weight, but its torque caused some potentially dangerous handling characteristics, especially for new pilots.

The most popular rotary engines were French: the *Clerget*, Gnôme, and the Rhône. The Gnôme's machined nickel-steel cylinders each had a single valve, which was operated automatically as the piston moved. A combined fuel-lubricating oil mixture (employing castor oil, because it is not soluble in gasoline) passed through the cylinder from a valve in the piston head, and the centrifugal force of the spinning engine flung the unburned oil out of the exhaust and all over the aircraft and pilot. The Gnôme was a reliable engine, but it consumed enormous quantities of fuel and oil and, more important, had only two speeds—off and on. The pilot had some degree of control over engine speed by means of a switch that cut the ignition to one, three, or five cylinders at a time, but fuel could build up in the unused cylinders with explosive results when full ignition was restored.

The Rhône engine worked on the same general principle as did the Gnôme, but it had a more conventional valve system and so the speed could be controlled by a throttle rather than an ignition cutout switch, although a switch was usually installed that could run all or none of the cylinders. The Rhône used less fuel and oil than the Gnôme, an important factor in the range and endurance of military aircraft. Gnôme quickly saw the advantages of its rival's engines, and the two companies merged just a few weeks before war began. But French aircraft were not the only ones that carried Gnôme and Rhône engines; the factory also had licensees and distributors in England, Italy, Russia, and the United States. Some German aircraft manufacturers bought Rhône engines from Thulin in Sweden, and Anthony Fokker's Oberusel engine factory produced a licensed copy of the Gnôme (and later copied the Rhône). Allied aircraft production relied on French engines throughout the war; France produced twice as many engines as did either Britain or Germany, and many British engines were built under French license.

Radial engines were not produced in great quantities at the beginning of the war, but by 1918 rotaries had lost some of their earlier favor. Radials still had not caught up to rotaries, but stationary engines (V- or in-line) now accounted for nearly three-quarters of all engines produced in France. The European auto manufacturers Renault, Hispano-Suiza, Daimler, Benz, BMW, and Mercedes all produced in-line or V-8 and V-12 engines. In 1914 Daimler produced the majority of German aircraft engines and the army's machines all carried the same 100-hp Daimler motor. In-line engines were considered by both pilots and manufacturers to be superior to the Oberusel, but factory output was controlled by the high command, which favored the *Albatros* factory, limiting the number of in-line engines available to other aircraft manufacturers.

At the start of the war, French aviation was in a disastrous state. With all factory orders canceled, no replacements or spare parts were available for squadrons at the Front. The high command finally took notice, replaced General Bernard, and released aircraft manufacturers Blériot, Caudron, and Bréguet from military service with orders for over two thousand new machines. Unfortunately, many of the factories supplying materials for airframes and engines were in enemy hands or war-torn areas, and electrical components such as spark plugs, magnetos, and switches had been furnished by Bosch of Germany. Aircraft production would have to wait until French industry could adapt to wartime conditions.

The French Air Service decided to reduce the number of aircraft types produced, hoping that standardization would alleviate problems of supply and maintenance. Four models went into production: *Caudron* GIIIs, *Farmans*, *Voisins*, and *Morane-Saulnier Parasols*, with other manufacturers constructing these types under license. By the end of 1915 fast and agile fighter aircraft were needed, and the *Nieuport "Bebé"* went into production. At that time, France also sought a feasible heavy bomber design but lacked engines powerful enough to lift a plane that could carry a sufficient bomb load.

Another factor influencing French aircraft production was the decentralization of the Procurement Service in November of 1915. Instead of a central inspectorate, manufacturers now had to go through dozens of regional offices. Supply procedures were equally convoluted, resulting in enormous amounts of paperwork and red tape.

By the end of 1916 the aircraft situation had not improved significantly. The new *Spad* fighter had been in production for three months, but, as a result of problems with the Hispano-Suiza engine, the factory had delivered only twenty-five out of a total order of 630. Only 328 fighters were in service, and one-quarter of those were obsolete. The 253 bombers, rotary-engine pushers, had to fly night missions because they were too slow and lumbering to function against enemy fighters. Nearly all reconnaissance and observation machines were antiquated. The treasury official responsible for aviation suggested that aircraft manufacturers had exercised "undue influence" on military officials to continue ordering outmoded machines instead of developing and producing new designs.

Finally, in March of 1917, the government began to concentrate on producing the latest aircraft and phasing out those that were obsolete. French factories were ordered to construct *Spads*, *Bréguets*, and British Sopwith 1½ Strutters, but engine problems and lack of adequate supplies kept French aircraft from fulfilling expectations. The new undersecretary for aviation, Daniel Vincent, tried to speed production by subcontracting airframes and engines and threatening uncooperative manufacturers with the reassignment to combat duty of their workers. It was essential for France to increase aircraft production in the spring of 1917; America had just entered the war and France had promised to equip the U.S. Army Air Corps with five thousand aircraft and 8,500 engines.

Political maneuvering and frequent changes in governmental appointments kept the industry and the Air Service in a state of confusion. Each new minister had his own idea of how aircraft should be built and utilized. To add to the problems of aircraft procurement, labor strikes sporadically curtailed production throughout 1917. Advances in technology in the last two years of the war brought about improved engines, but factories needed time in which to adapt their procedures and machinery. The poor quality of French engines caused problems with aircraft at the Front.

In anticipation of the German spring offensive in 1918, the French army commander General Henri-Philippe Pétain called for an all-out effort to improve the French Air Service's organization, production, and implementation. Production increased between November of 1917 and March of 1918, and the number of new fighter types arriving at the Front was further simplified to three: the *Spad* 7, *Spad* 13, and the *Bréguet*. Aircraft quality also improved in 1918, and obsolete machines were quickly replaced with modern types as factories became more efficient. By the end of the war, France had the most aircraft of any air force in the world.

When Britain entered the war, the BEF took just sixty-three aircraft—almost her entire supply of serviceable machines. After five months, Britain had no more aircraft than when the war began; the aviation industry was simply too small to supply the quantity of machines necessary to support an air force. One problem that British aircraft manufacturers faced was the lack of domestic engines. Most aircraft produced in Britain were fitted with French Renault or Gnôme engines or derivatives, while other engine makers attempted to design motors light enough for aircraft use.

Unlike France or Germany, Britain had a state-supported manufacturer, the Royal Aircraft Factory (RAF). At the beginning of the war, RAF concentrated its effort on building large numbers of the B.E. 2c, a stable reconnaissance machine. The factory could not turn out enough aircraft to equip the Royal Flying Corps (RFC), so the British government allowed other firms to produce aircraft under license and to design new models. Still, there were not enough machines to supply both the RFC and the Royal Naval Air Service (RNAS). The navy, as senior service, demanded priority on new aircraft, but the army claimed that the RFC was essential to support the BEF in the field while the RNAS was merely responsible for home defense. The RFC and RNAS competed with each other for French engines and aircraft parts, causing friction between the services and between the British and French, who delayed shipping orders until each other's bargains were kept. Finally, in 1916, the British began to deal directly with the French government instead of the factories, allowing both governments to control the flow of raw materials and finished products between their countries.

As the quality of German fighter aircraft improved in 1916, the British were pressed to develop better machines than the D.H. 2, the "spinning incinerator," and the B.E. 2c. The Bristol fighter, Sopwith Pup (and later in 1917, the Camel), and S.E. 5 (a product of the RAF) were all developed during 1916. At the end of the year, the RFC began to revise its training procedures in hopes of saving both men and machines. At times, as many as two-thirds of total aircraft losses resulted from takeoff and landing accidents. The RNAS, with less urgent demands for aircraft and men than the RFC,

had the time and money to train its pilots more thoroughly and provide them with more modern aircraft, such as the French *Nieuport*. Several successful aircraft were initially produced for the RNAS: the Sopwith 1^1/$_2$ Strutter, the Handley Page bomber, and the Sopwith Triplane.

In 1917 the RAF ceased building machines and concentrated on testing prototypes, while other factories produced its designs. Manufacturers reduced the number of types being built from fifty-five to thirty in an effort to simplify production, but added seven thousand additional workers as demand for aircraft grew. The supply of new machines did not meet expectations, for labor strikes late in 1917 slowed construction of airframes, and serious design and quality-control problems nearly halted engine manufacturing.

Despite these difficulties, the new Bentley and Rolls Royce engines, along with imported French Hispano-Suiza and Rhône motors, improved the 1917-model aircraft so that few design changes for airframes were necessary in 1918. Both airframe and engine production figures more than doubled from 1917 to 1918, but imported engines still accounted for nearly 40 percent of the aircraft produced in Britain. Nevertheless, by the end of the war, Britain's aircraft industry had grown larger than that of France.

Like the other major powers, Germany experienced problems with both quantity and quality of aircraft delivered to the Front, partially because of the influx of inexperienced labor taking the place of skilled workers who were called up for army service. Like the British, the German army and navy fought over the machines coming out of the factories, but Germany's war ministry had much more control over industry than did the Allies, and the army maintained strict authority over aircraft design, production, and distribution.

Germany started the war with an obsolete monoplane, the *Taube*, and several unarmed biplane types superior to most of the French and British reconnaissance aircraft. By the spring of 1915, C-planes, two-seat biplanes armed with a machine gun in the observer's cockpit, became primary machines for reconnaissance and day bombing missions. Giant bombers were developed to attack England, but they lacked sufficient range for the flight and were reduced to bombing Allied installations on the continent. The *Fokker Eindekker* appeared at the Front in June, but pilots found the light, rotary-engine machine difficult to fly, and after several crashes it was banned. Aces Boelcke and Immelmann interceded with the High Command, however; their aggressive and successful use of the *Eindekker* ensured its continued production. By the Battle of the Somme, French and British aircraft had surpassed the *Eindekker* in quantity and quality and controlled the skies. German aviation units reorganized during the summer of 1916 in an attempt to regain aerial superiority, but it was not until the introduction of the *Albatros* D-I in September that the new fighter squadrons began to demonstrate success. The *Albatros* utilized a plywood fuselage that resulted in a stronger and faster machine, and it consumed less of the hard-to-find spruce than did conventional fabric-covered structures. It was superior to most of the Allied aircraft that opposed it.

By the end of 1916 German industry was hindered by the scarcity of raw materials because of the British blockade and by a lack of skilled labor. The Hindenburg program, instituted in October, called for total mobilization for the war effort, and aircraft factories expanded under its auspices. During the winter of 1916–17 (and again in the following winter), shortages of coal and other materials prevented aircraft manufacturers from delivering their promised numbers of machines. The Hindenburg program would in theory make raw materials available to essential industries, but delivery dates were unreliable and prices rose drastically. Manufacturers could no longer guarantee the quality of their aircraft and engines, because raw materials were substandard.

After America entered the war in April of 1917, Germany began another program of expansion (the America program) designed to defeat the Allies before American industry could be mobilized against Germany. This increased effort led to even more shortages of materials and more frequent strikes from already exhausted workers. Nevertheless, German designers continued to produce new aircraft and to improve their engines. The *Fokker* Triplane was patterned after the successful Sopwith Triplane, but production paused after several crashes caused by faulty workmanship, so that the number of Triplanes arriving at the Front was never as high as planned. The Triplane was rendered obsolete shortly after it entered service because the lubricant for its rotary engine, castor oil, was no longer available in Germany, and ersatz lubricants caused the engines to seize up. Fokker continued development of a rotary-engine unbraced monoplane, but although the design had great potential, the rotary engines proved unserviceable.

The *Albatros* continued in service, even though it had not changed significantly since its inception, because the high command favored the factory and kept it supplied with the powerful and reliable Mercedes engine. Pilots, led by Manfred von Richthofen, advocated an open competition for a new aircraft design among manufacturers, with each entrant to have access to the 160-horsepower Mercedes engine. In January of 1918 the competition was won by *Fokker*'s D VII, the mainstay of the German Air Service until the Armistice and considered by most historians to be the best fighter of the war.

All of the major powers suffered from labor strikes, shortages of raw materials, and lack of sufficient engines for the number of available airframes. The balance between quantity and quality of aircraft was delicate. Because of the blockade Germany had more difficulty in obtaining materials than did the Allies, so, although German technology might have been superior, the Allies were able to produce more aircraft without recourse to inadequate or ersatz materials. In the nearly five years of war, aviation technology had made considerable progress, from producing mere toys to machines capable of crossing the Atlantic.

Suzanne Hayes Fisher

References

Hallion, Richard P. *Rise of the Fighter Aircraft, 1914–1918*. Annapolis, Md.: Nautical & Aviation Publishing Company, 1984.

Morrow, John H., Jr. *German Air Power in World War I*. Lincoln: University of Nebraska Press, 1982.

———. *The Great War in the Air: Military Aviation from 1909 to 1921*. Washington, D.C.: Smithsonian Institution, 1993.

See also AIRCRAFT, BOMBERS; AIRCRAFT, FIGHTERS; AIRCRAFT, SPOTTER AND AUXILIARY; FOKKER, ANTHONY

Aircraft, Spotter and Auxiliary

Some of the least glamorized but most useful aircraft of World War I were spotter and auxiliary planes that carried out a wide range of routine operations. Most military leaders who thought about employing airplanes in military roles before the war viewed them as useful mainly as an adjunct to the artillery—a great perch for observation—and as an aerial observer of enemy troop dispositions and movements.

Indicative of this view was the comment of American army Lieutenant Fred Humpheries in 1910:

> From a military standpoint, the first and probably the greatest use will be found in reconnaissance. A flyer carrying two men can rise in the air out of range of the enemy, and passing over his head out of effective target range, can make a complete reconnaissance and return, bringing more valuable information than could possibly be secured by a reconnaissance in force. This method would endanger the lives of two men; the other would detach several thousand men for a length of time and endanger the lives of all.

When the war began, therefore, the air doctrine of all combatants involved using the airplane for observation and message carrying. While aircraft were used in other important capacities, the spotter and auxiliary roles believed critical at the outset remained so throughout World War I.

While fighters and bombers grabbed what glory was to be had in the air war, the real workhorses for every air service were the two-seat observation and reconnaissance aircraft. The small, light, flimsy, highly maneuverable, and fast airplanes were employed on both sides

to fly over enemy lines and report on troop movements, spot for the artillery, or search for weak spots in the enemy's fortifications. Most of these aircraft were not armed at first, but by the fall of 1914 field commanders recognized that it was important to keep opposing observation planes from accomplishing their missions; they took action to bring them down. Within a short period, machine guns had been mounted on aircraft, either for the observer to fire or fixed so that the pilot could aim the plane like a weapon. The machine gun, as had been the case on the ground, became the master of the aerial battlefield, and the fighter aircraft began to emerge.

The earliest spotter aircraft had placed the observer in the forward seat, but all air services soon learned that the engine block on a tractor propeller configuration (in front), the wings and struts (on either side), and the pilot behind blocked his view. These same impediments also prohibited a clear field of fire. The German *Deutsche Flugzeug-Werke's* (DFW) C type of armed two-seater solved this problem. It placed the spotter in the rear seat to permit better observation and defense against enemy attack. Brought out in the spring of 1915, the DFW was one of the finest lines of spotter aircraft of the war, with more than 2,340 of them seeing service. About 600 were still in use at the end of the war. Somewhat less capable was the Austrian-built *Aviatik* series of reconnaissance planes that first appeared early in the war. These two-seater biplanes had excellent range and altitude, but by 1916 most were retired to training squadrons in favor of the DFWs. Principal uses of all these aircraft included artillery coop-

REPRESENTATIVE WORLD WAR I SPOTTER AIRCRAFT

Airplane	Country	Service	Speed (mph)	Armament	Horsepower	Weight (lbs.)
B.E. 2	G.B.	2/12–11/18	82	None	90	2,100
Bristol Scout D	G.B.	9/14–9/16	70	1 Vickers	100	1,440
Aviatik	Austria	9/14–12/16	67.7	1 Schwarlose	120	1,918
DFW C	Germany	3/15–11/18	87	1 Spandau	100	1,300
SAML	Italy	5/15–11/18	100.7	1 Revelli	300	3,075
Ansaldo	Italy	3/17–11/18	142.9	1 Vickers	220	2,315
Nieuport 11	France	1/16–8/17	97	1 Lewis	80	1,210
Sopwith Scout	G.B.	4/16–10/17	111	1 Lewis, 8 Rockets	80	1,225
Spad 7	France	8/16–11/18	119.5	1 Vickers	180	1,550
Spad 13	France	4/17–11/18	130	2 Vickers	200	1,815

eration, infantry direction, and visual and photographic reconnaissance.

The Allies also developed specialized spotter aircraft. The Italian *Societa Aeronautica Meccanica Lombarda* (SAML) spotter was based on the *Aviatik* design. This was a strong, reliable aircraft, 657 of which were built. They found service in the war with sixteen Italian *Squadriglie da Ricognizione* in Italy, Albania, and Macedonia. The Italian *Ansaldo* single-seater scout plane was also an excellent design; it was probably the fastest reconnaissance airplane used by any combatant in the war. These were the two best spotter aircraft employed by the Allies. France relied largely on *Spad* and *Nieuport* fighter variants for observation, while the British used the B.E. 2, an unsuccessful fighter, for reconnaissance duties before employing Sopwith Scouts and other fighter variants.

Waterborne aircraft were also operated in the war for spotter work. Several flying boats flown by the Allies found exceptional service in the war. Probably the most important was the British Felixstowe F.2A flying boat operated by the Royal Navy Aviation Service, an efficient long-haul patrol craft. The brainchild of Squadron Commander John Porte, the Felixstowe had taken as its basis an American Curtiss Aircraft Company design and modified it into a truly exceptional aircraft. The Felixstowe set the course for British amphibians for the next two decades. The Germans refrained from using amphibians, but many of their naval vessels were fitted with floatplanes for observation and other duties.

Throughout the war, spotter aircraft proved to be every bit as useful as Humpheries and other prewar fliers had believed they would. During the conflict there was a persistent, though not spectacular, advance of technology associated with the aircraft. Equally important, the equipment used for reconnaissance also improved. Photographic equipment, rarely used at the outset, became the norm by the time of the Armistice. Communication with artillery and other organizations requiring reconnaissance information also improved through the use of radio and signal equipment.
Roger D. Launius

References

Bruce, John M. *British Aeroplanes, 1914–1918*. New York: Funk & Wagnalls, 1969.

Higham, Robin. *Air Power: A Concise History*. New York: St. Martin's, 1973.

Kennett, Lee B. *The First Air War, 1914–1918*. New York: Free Press, 1991.

Morrow, John H. *German Air Power in World War I*. Lincoln: University of Nebraska Press, 1982.

Munson, Kenneth. *Bombers, Patrol and Reconnaissance Aircraft,1914–19*. New York: Macmillan, 1968.

Aircraft Carriers

See WARSHIPS: AIRCRAFT CARRIERS

Airships

See ZEPPELINS

Albania

Albania was a victim of the Great War. After more than five centuries of domination and oppression under the Turks, Albania proclaimed its independence on 28 November 1912. Albanian sovereignty was confirmed by the London Conference in 1913 and a German aristocrat, Prince Wilhelm zu Wied, was designated to rule Albania as an independent principality.

Wilhelm zu Wied assumed his position in March of 1914 but fled shortly after war erupted in August. Albania's newfound independence was soon swept away. Greek troops occupied the south, and in November of 1914 Italy, although officially a neutral, sent troops into the port of Vlonë (Valona). In the summer of 1915, Serbian and Montenegrin forces moved into the northern and central provinces, to be attacked by an Austro-Hungarian army invading from the north. Throughout the war Albania had no government and served only as a battleground for powers great and small.

According to the secret Treaty of London of 1915, by which Britain, Russia, and France bribed Rome into joining the Entente, Italy was to receive the Port of Vlonë and a protectorate over much of the rest of Albania. The same agreement allowed Greece and Serbia to carve up what remained. During the war, Austria-Hungary was seen by most Albanians as their only champion.

At the Versailles Peace Conference, the United States, England, and, ironically, Yugoslavia supported Albanian independence. Italian troops, however, continued to occupy most of the country until an armed rebellion, coupled with unrest in Italy, compelled Rome to agree to remove its forces in August of 1920. In December the League of Nations admitted Albania to membership and reaffirmed the borders established by the London Conference of 1913.

Earl H. Tilford, Jr.

References

Logoreci, Anton. *The Albanians: Europe's Forgotten Survivors*. Boulder, Colo.: Westview, 1977.

Marmullaku, Ramadan. *Albania and the Albanians*. Hamden, Conn.: Archon, 1975.

See also BALKAN WARS; LONDON, TREATY OF

Alberich, Operation of (Siegfried Line)

In September of 1916 the OHL (German Supreme Command of the Army) began the secret planning and construction of a heavily fortified defensive line behind its then-current front line positions on the Western Front. The Germans called this new line the Siegfried Line (*Siegfriedstellung*) after Wagner's hero; the Allies called it the Hindenburg Line after the German army commander. Its planners intended the position to consist of five sections running from the Belgian coast to Pont-à-Mousson on the Moselle River. The most important section of the line was the one that ran from Arras to Soissons and was supposed to eliminate the Noyon salient held by Bavarian Crown Prince Rupprecht's army group. This section was the first completed and would shorten the German line by twenty-five miles and free thirteen German divisions for redeployment in the East.

The mastermind behind the *Siegfriedstellung* was Colonel Fritz von Loßberg of the Second Army. Loßberg was a true genius of defensive warfare. In 1915 he had been called upon to reorganize and direct the defense of the Western Front when the Allied armies seemed on the verge of breaking the German lines. In 1916 he repeated his role of defensive coordinator during the Somme battle. Loßberg drew from previous experience as well as the suggestions of frontline officers in the development of his defensive ideas, a novel approach in 1916.

One of Loßberg's key ideas for the *Siegfriedstellung* was to locate the front line on the reverse slope of a hill rather than on the forward one, as was customary. On the reverse slope, the enemy artillery would not be able to observe the German infantry; the crest would be held only by scattered outposts, which would give warning of an enemy attack. This arrangement caused attacking infantry to become silhouetted when reaching the crest of the hill, presenting a more favorable target to the defenders. A further idea was the elastic defense, or defense in depth, in which the enemy was forced to penetrate a series of defensive lines until he was exhausted. At that time, the defenders would launch a vigorous counterattack and drive the enemy back to his own lines.

In addition to its new defensive layout, the *Siegfriedstellung* also incorporated many features for the comfort and protection of the troops. These included reinforced concrete bunkers, tunnels, electric lighting, and concrete machine-gun positions. The effort required to prepare the new positions was monumental. The line was already ninety miles long and could accommodate about twenty divisions. German soldiers, Russian prisoners of war, and Belgian workers were employed on the project, which took five months to complete. The construction of a fortification of this magnitude in such a short time was a tremendous feat of organizational and industrial skill, especially considering the material and manpower shortages faced by the Germans in the later stages of the war.

The first part of the position consisted of a forward observation zone (*Vorpostenfeld*), on the crest of the hill overlooking the enemy trenches. Between this line and the entrenchments on the reverse slope lay masses of barbed wire entanglements. The front trench was occupied by small storm squads (*Stoßtruppen*) in concrete bunkers. Behind the storm squads were the actual garrisons, housed in reinforced-concrete bunkers and equipped with machine guns, trench mortars, and artillery. Placed in checkerboard fashion across the battle zone were miniature fortresses (*Widas*) that harbored reinforced concrete machine-gun emplacements and contained enough men and ammunition to maintain a defense while the enemy tried to attack between them. The artillery took a position behind the *Widas*. In mid-1917 two additional zones were added, increasing the depth of the *Siegfriedstellung* to between six thousand and eight thousand yards.

Troops garrisoned within the battle zone lived in large reinforced-concrete bunkers deep under the ground, equipped with electric lights, aid posts, and command bunkers, as well as an intricate tunnel system that reduced the troops' exposure to shell fire. The *Siegfriedstellung* was luxurious compared with the old front lines, which were mired in mud and badly in need of repair. Conditions there steadily lowered the morale of the German troops, who required a respite from the trenches.

The decision to withdraw into the *Siegfriedstellung* was taken only reluctantly by the German High Command, which feared a drop in troop morale in giving up ground to the enemy. The high command also worried about the effect of such news on the home front. Hindenburg and Ludendorff, however, believed that Russia was on the verge of collapse and wanted to drive her out of the war. Falling back to the *Siegfriedstellung* would release troops from the Western Front who could deliver the knockout blow to the Russians. Finally, on 4 February 1917, permission was given for Crown Prince Rupprecht's army group to fall back to the *Siegfriedstellung*. The withdrawal was code named "Alberich," after the destructive dwarf in Teutonic mythology, and was scheduled to begin on 16 March. All material of use to the enemy was to be removed or destroyed before the salient was abandoned.

Although preparations for the withdrawal were carried out, the Allies did not realize what was happening until just a few days before the pullout—not enough time to take advantage of the situation. The Germans' greatest fear was of a vigorous Allied attack while the troops were on the move. Small squads remained behind to delay the enemy with machine guns and booby traps. The Noyon salient lay between the French and English armies. The French pursuit was quicker than that of the British, but it was ineffective.

The Germans left behind a wasteland: Houses were destroyed, bridges dynamited, railroad tracks uprooted, wells poisoned, and trees felled. Everywhere lay booby traps for unwary Allied soldiers. Everything of any use was removed; only a few aged French civilians were left behind, without shelter. Crown Prince Rupprecht had opposed some of these harsh measures but had been overruled by Hindenburg and Ludendorff.

Alberich went off like clockwork. The German line was shortened and the Allies were left with ruins and scorched earth. Not a single German soldier was lost in the pullout. The withdrawal also had the effect of disrupting Allied, particularly French, plans for an offensive in 1917. Operation Alberich contributed to the disastrous defeat of the Nivelle Offensive and the resulting French army mutinies.

Steven D. Fisher

References

Wynne, G.C. *If Germany Attacks*. London: Faber and Faber, 1940.

See also HINDENBURG, PAUL VON; INFANTRY TACTICS; LUDENDORFF, ERICH; LOßBERG, FRIEDRICH VON; TRENCH WARFARE

Albert I, King of Belgium (1875–1934)

Albert, heir apparent to his uncle King Leopold II, was born in Brussels on 8 April 1875. An army officer since 1892, Albert was crowned king of Belgium in December of 1909. In 1913, while he was on a visit to Germany, Albert heard his cousin Emperor Wilhelm II warn of a future war with France. Although Belgium was traditionally neutral and its territorial integrity had been guaranteed by the great powers (including Prussia) in 1839, the Belgian government prepared militarily for a German invasion.

Albert unsuccessfully appealed an ultimatum by the Kaiser that his army traverse Belgium, and the German army invaded on 4 August. Albert told the Belgian parliament that the country would fight to defend its territory and that he himself would command Belgium's army. At Liège on 5 August Albert ordered his forces to "hold to the end," but the fortress was eventually captured. Albert withdrew the remainder of the army to Antwerp on 20 August.

In early October the Germans assaulted Antwerp. Winston Churchill, who observed Albert during the siege, described him as a "grave, calm soldier King . . . preserving an unconquerable majesty amid the ruins of his kingdom." Albert evacuated his forces from Antwerp on 6 October.

Albert and the Belgian army defended coastal areas near the Yser River from 13 to 30 October. Because he disagreed with Allied war goals, Albert insisted that Belgium's army be independent and stay in Belgium. He refused to allow Field Marshal Sir Douglas Haig to utilize the Belgian army to strengthen the British offensive at Ypres in 1917. Unlike the Allies, Albert did not want to defeat Germany and instead hoped to negotiate a compromise peace.

In protest of Albert's position, in 1918 opposition leaders ousted several of his cabinet members and usurped their positions. As the war waned, Albert acquiesced and allowed Belgian forces to join the Allies, and Foch appointed him to command the Flanders Army Group in the autumn of 1918. Albert led these troops in the final Allied offense and entered Brussels a hero on 22 November 1918. He then terminated Belgium's neutrality. Albert ruled Belgium until he died while mountain climbing near Namur on 17 February 1934.

Elizabeth D. Schafer

References

Albert I, King of the Belgians. *The War Diaries of Albert I, King of the Belgians.* Edited and translated by R. Van Overstraeten. London: William Kimber, 1954.

Cammaerts, Emile. *Albert of Belgium: Defender of Right.* London: Ivor Nicolson & Watson, 1935.

D'Ydewalle, C. *Albert and the Belgians.* London: Methuen, 1935.

De Flemalle, G. de Libert. *Fighting with King Albert.* London: Hodder & Stoughton, 1915.

Galet, E.J. *Albert, King of the Belgians in the Great War.* London: Putnam, 1931.

See also BELGIUM, ARMY, AND NEUTRALITY OF

Albrecht, Duke of Württemberg (1865–1939)

German field marshal and one of the more capable royal personages in Germany who held senior command positions during the First World War. Born on 23 December 1865 in Vienna, Albrecht was the son of a Württemberg prince and a Habsburg archduchess. Albrecht entered the (German or Württemberg) army in 1883 and thereafter rose rapidly in its hierarchy. He married Archduchess Margarete Sophie of Austria in 1893 and ten years later became heir to the Württemberg throne. In 1913 he was named head of the Sixth Army Inspectorate at Stuttgart and promoted to colonel-general.

Upon mobilization in August of 1914, Duke Albrecht became the commander of the Fourth Army, initially composed of five Prussian corps. He led his troops through Luxembourg and southern Belgium into Champagne during the German sweep into northeastern France. After the Battle of the Marne, he was assigned to Flanders, where a totally new Fourth Army was being formed. Made up of one seasoned and four newly raised reserve corps, this ill-trained and underequipped force launched the costly offensive of First Ypres against Belgian, British, and French troops that soon bogged down in mud and mire. The following spring, Albrecht's army participated in the first chlorine gas attacks against Allied troops at Second Ypres.

Promoted to field marshal in 1916, Albrecht remained in charge of the crucial Flanders sector until February of 1917. He then was sent to Strasbourg to command an army group holding the southern portions of the Western Front. He successfully defended his sectors in Alsace and Lorraine until the end of the war. Because Albrecht was Roman Catholic, he was considered suitable to become the regent of a new, German-sponsored Polish kingdom in 1917, but he declined the offer. He died on 29 October 1939 in Altshausen, Upper Swabia.

Ulrich Trumpener

References

Janssen, Karl-Heinz. *Macht und Verblendung: Kriegszielpolitik der deutschen Bundesstaaten 1914–1918.* Göttingen: Musterschmidt, 1963.

Reichsarchiv. *Der Weltkrieg 1914 bis 1918: Die militärischen Operationen zu Lande.* 14 vols. Berlin: Mittler & Sohn, 1925–1944.

Trumpener, Ulrich. "The Road to Ypres: The Beginnings of Gas Warfare in World War I." *Journal of Modern History* 47 (1975): 60–80.

Unruh, Karl. *Langemarck: Legende und Wirklichkeit.* Koblenz: Bernard & Graefe, 1986.

See also POLAND; YPRES, 1ST AND 2ND BATTLES OF

Alekseev, Mikhail Vasilevich (1857–1918)

Russian general and chief of staff of the army, born in Tver Province on 15 November 1857. Alekseev is generally recognized as Russia's most able strategist of World War I. Unfortunately, there were very few others who matched his capabilities. From humble origins Alekseev rose, by sheer talent, to the post of commander in chief of the army. His first ten years in the army were spent as a junior officer in an infantry regiment posted at Mogilev in the Ukraine. During the Russo-Turkish War of 1877–78 he saw combat on the Danube, and during the Russo-Japanese War he served as chief operations officer of the Third Army in Manchuria. It was there that he gained invaluable administrative experience that was to serve him so well in 1914. If General Alekseev had professional faults they were in protecting incompetent but loyal subordinates and a refusal to delegate authority, which caused him to become overwhelmed by details and eventually resulted in the breakdown of his health.

Between 1905 and 1914, attempts to reform the Russian army after the disaster against the Japanese failed largely for political reasons. During that time Alekseev was posted to the Kiev Military District, where he joined the ablest and most innovative Russian general officers: Nikolai Ruzsky, Aleksei Brusilov, Nikolai Dukhonin, and Lavr Kornilov. By the end of the war all of these men had been promoted to high commands, but too late to save Russia. Most of them were also political liberals who had, prior to 1914, expressed the need to bring Russia into the twentieth century by modifying or ending the monarchy. This of course resulted in their disfavor at court. In the years before 1914, however, these officers attempted to lay plans to prepare Russia for war. They correctly foresaw that Austria was the weak link among the Central Powers.

The outbreak of the war in 1914 saw Grand Duke Nikolai Nikolaevich appointed commander in chief of the Russian army. He asked that Alekseev be his chief of staff, but the incompetent minister of war, Vladimir Sukhomlinov, wanted his equally incompetent friend General Nikolai Yanushkevich in that position, and asked the czar to block Alekseev's appointment. Instead, Alekseev became chief of staff of the southwestern Front, where he was instrumental in planning the Galician offensive that nearly drove Austria from the war. For his work in this campaign Alekseev received the Order of St. George Second Class (for the conquest of a province).

During his time on the southwestern Front, Alekseev made numerous reports back to St. Petersburg (Petrograd) concerning supply shortages. These reports were as quickly ignored by Sukhomlinov, however. As a result, when the

Germans launched their counter-offensive on 5 May 1915 the Russian regular army, defenseless in the face of German artillery, was all but destroyed. It was Alekseev who, by vigorous defensive actions, planned the strategic retreat that saved what was left of the army.

In September of 1915 czar Nicholas II removed his uncle, Grand Duke Nikolai Nikolaevich, as commander in chief and assumed personal command of the army himself. Alekseev became the czar's chief of staff, and in that position he was allowed to plan and conduct military operations while the czar remained in the background. In the ensuing months Alekseev, along with General Aleksei A. Polivanov, who had replaced Sukhomlinov as minister of war, succeeded in restoring the fighting capacity of the Russian army. They worked with the zemstvos and the War Industries Committee, and supplies of munitions and other war materials began to reach the front. Brusilov, Ruzsky, and other capable generals were given command of the major fronts, and rigorous training programs were established behind the lines. Russia's political problems were insurmountable, however. While the czar was away Empress Alexandra and her advisor, Rasputin, replaced the cabinet, including Polivanov, with aged reactionaries who aborted many of the military reforms. What is more, there is ample evidence that the Germans had access to information on Russian military operations through Rasputin and the Empress, who told everything contained in letters from her husband at the front.

Just as the Russian army began to recoup its fighting capacity, Russia's allies once again appealed for help. In 1916, to relieve pressure on Verdun, a Russian army attacked in the Vilna sector with huge losses. And in June, to aid the Italians, General Brusilov launched an offensive against the Austrians. He actually broke the enemy lines but lacked the reserves to follow through. When the Germans counterattacked, the Russians suffered another 500,000 casualties. At the end of 1916 Alekseev's health broke down, and he took a six-week medical leave in the Crimea. He returned to headquarters just in time to be confronted with the political upheaval in Petrograd in March of 1917. At the request of the Provisional Committee, Alekseev polled senior Russian generals as to their opinion on the abdication of the czar. Their unanimous agreement that he should step down most likely caused the czar to go quietly.

After the Bolshevik takeover, Generals Kornilov and Alekseev attempted to form an anti-Bolshevik army, but in 1918 Kornilov was killed by a stray shell, and Alekseev died in Ekaterinodar on 8 October 1918.

John W. Bohon

References

Golovin, General N.N. *The Russian Army in the World War*. New Haven: Yale University Press, 1931.

Gurko, General Basil. *War and Revolution in Russia, 1914–1917*. New York: Macmillan, 1919.

Pares, Sir Barnard. *The Fall of the Russian Monarchy*. New York: Vintage, 1961.

See also BRUSILOV, ALEKSEI; EAST GALICIA, 1914 CAMPAIGN; KORNILOV, LAVR; NICHOLAS II; NIKOLAI NIKOLAEVICH; POLIVANOV, ALEKSEI; RUSSIA, HOME FRONT, AND ARMY; RUZSKY, NIKOLAI; SUKHOMLINOV, VLADIMIR; YANUSHKEVICH, NIKOLAI

Alexander, Prince (1888–1934)

Prince regent, later king, of Serbia. Born at Cetinje, Montenegro, on 16 December 1888, Alexander Karađorđević was the second son of the future King Peter I of Serbia, a hero of Bosnia-Herzegovina's 1875 rebellion against Turkish rule. Alexander's early years were spent with his father in exile in Geneva and later (1899–1904) at the Russian Imperial court.

Alexander's father became king in 1903 upon the assassination of his predecessor, Alexander I of the rival house of Obrenovich. When his elder brother George renounced his right of succession in 1909, Alexander became heir apparent. He distinguished himself in the 1912 and 1913 Balkan wars. In 1914, only fourteen days before Franz Ferdinand was assassinated at Sarajevo, his father's ill health led Alexander to become regent—a responsibility he held throughout World War I and up to his father's death in 1921.

As commander in chief, Alexander accompanied the Serbian army on its retreat through the Albanian mountains in the bitter winter of 1915–16 (as did his father at age seventy-one) and supervised its subsequent reorganization on Corfu. In June of 1917 he escaped an assassination attempt at Salonika by Black Hand terrorists. He visited many Western capitals during the war, pressing the case for a new

Kingdom of the South Slavs—in effect, a Greater Serbia—as a reward for Serbia's efforts on the Allied side. As the war ended, he saw this dream come true, entering Belgrade in triumph on 31 October 1918 to proclaim the Kingdom of the Serbs, Croats, and Slovenes, with his father as king and himself regent.

Upon his father's death in 1921 he became King Alexander I. His efforts to build a united and democratic country were beset with difficulties. After the murder of the Croatian leader Stjepan Radic in 1928, he suspended the constitution, banned ethnically based parties, renamed his country Yugoslavia, and became a royal dictator. He was assassinated by members of the Ustase, the Croatian separatist movement, at Marseilles on 9 October 1934, along with French Foreign Minister Louis Barthou.

Philip J. Green

References

Graham, Stephen. *Alexander of Jugoslavia*. London: Cassell, 1938.

See also YUGOSLAVIA, CREATION OF

Alexandra Feodorovna (1872–1918)

Russian empress, born in the German city of Darmstadt on 6 June 1872. The full maiden name of the future Empress of Russia was Alix Victoria Louise Beatrice, Princess of Hesse-Darmstadt. Her father was Grand Duke Louis of Hesse, and her mother, Princess Alice, was the youngest of Queen Victoria's nine children. At the age of six, after the death of her mother, Alexandra went to live with her grandmother in Windsor Castle in England. Alex, as she was called, was a shy and introverted child. On the advice of Queen Victoria she accepted without question the marriage proposal of Grand Duke Nicholas, heir to the Russian throne, who had fallen in love with her. After she converted from Lutheranism to the Russian Orthodox Church, they were married in 1894, just a few weeks before the death of Czar Alexander III.

As the wife of Czar Nicholas II, the Empress Alexandra Feodorovna (her Orthodox name) can only be described as tragic. Her aversion to Russian society resulted in her unpopularity among court circles. She sought diversion in religion, into which she plunged with a near-obsessive zeal. As for her family, after giving birth to four daughters she gave birth to a son on 12 August 1904, the Tsarevich Alexei. Unfortunately, he was born with severe hemophilia, which led the empress to succumb to the influence of Rasputin, the mysterious peasant monk who was somehow able to control the boy's illness.

With the outbreak of the war in 1914, the empress plunged into charitable work, financing hospitals and working as a nurse. In mid-1915 after the Carpathian disaster, ever jealous of the popular army commander Grand Duke Nikolai Nikolaevich, she persuaded her husband to take personal command of the army and to go to the front. This left her in charge of the government, and she endeavored to run it in the spirit of Catherine the Great. Taking Rasputin as her personal advisor, she proceeded to dismantle the administration by dismissing all capable ministers who had dared to criticize the czar's assumption of military command or the personal behavior of Rasputin. Among the first to be ousted was Minister of War Aleksei A. Polivanov, who had done so much to rebuild the army. The contemptible Boris Sturmer was appointed prime minister, and the mentally unstable Aleksander Protopopov minister of interior.

By late 1916 both the empress and Rasputin were being openly attacked from the Duma floor. She suffered a further loss in December of 1916 when Rasputin was murdered, not by left-wing radicals but by conservative political leaders who saw him as a dark force controlling the empress. After the revolution in March of 1917 and the abdication of her husband, the Imperial Family was placed under arrest by order of the provisional government. Subsequently, after Russia had passed under Bolshevik control, the empress and her family were murdered at Ekaterinburg on 16 July 1918. The empress Alexandra Feodorovna, though a tragic figure, did much to weaken the Russian government at a critical time, which in turn hastened the end of the monarchy.

John W. Bohon

References

Florinsky, Michael. *Russia, A History and Interpretation*. New York: Macmillan, 1958.

Massie, Robert K. *Nicholas and Alexandra*. New York: Atheneum, 1967.

Pares, Sir Bernard. *The Fall of the Russian Monarchy*. New York: Vintage, 1939.

See also NICHOLAS II; RASPUTIN, GRIGORII; RUSSIA, HOME FRONT AND REVOLUTIONS OF 1917

A

Allenby, Edmund Henry Hynman (1861–1936)

British field marshal who led British forces in the conquest of Palestine. Born on 23 April 1861 at Brackenhurst, near Southwell, Nottinghamshire, into a respected gentry family, Allenby received a classical education in public schools and graduated a cavalry officer from Sandhurst in 1882. He served with the Dragoons in Bechuanaland in 1884–85 and Zululand in 1888. Allenby returned to South Africa during the Boer War as a cavalry commander and was promoted to colonel in 1902. By 1905 he was a brigadier general. In 1910, as a major general, he was appointed inspector general of cavalry, and it is said he organized one of the best cavalry forces of the time, which, in 1914, he was to command in France.

During the war he commanded V Corps and later the Third Army during the Battle of Arras. There he had differences with General Herbert Gough and Field Marshal Douglas Haig, which might have contributed to his being posted as commander of the Egyptian Expeditionary Force in June of 1917. The mission of this force was to clear the Turks from the Palestine/Syria region. That effort had been stalled by a series of reverses for the British at Gaza, and the decision in London was to provide a new commander and to reinforce the seasoned troops.

Allenby's first decision was to move his headquarters from Cairo to the front. That act, coupled with his strong personality and leadership ability, gave a new determination to the command and the troops. He was faced by a formidable Turkish force assisted by the Germans, first under General Erich von Falkenhayn and then General Otto Liman von Sanders. Through brilliant planning and the use of surprise, ruse, and maneuver, Allenby's forces broke the front at Beersheba, Gaza, and then captured Jerusalem on 9 December 1917 in what is often viewed as a classic military operation. Allenby's forces had a stunning victory at Megiddo in September of 1918 and went on to reach Damascus on 30 September 1918. Turkey ceased hostilities on 31 October 1918.

In 1919 Allenby was promoted to field marshal and named Viscount of Megiddo and

Felixtowe. He received many other honors from his grateful country and high decorations from foreign states. In 1919 Allenby was named British high commissioner to Egypt, a trying post that he held for six years. Allenby died in London on 14 May 1936.

Raymond L. Proctor

References

Lawrence, T.E. *Seven Pillars Of Wisdom.* New York: Garden City, 1938.

Liddell Hart, B.H. *The Real War 1914–1918.* Boston: Little Brown, 1964.

Preston, R.M.P. *The Desert Mounted Corps.* Boston: Houghton Mifflin, 1921.

Wavell, Field Marshal Archibald P. *The Palestine Campaigns.* London: Constable, 1928.

———. *Allenby, Soldier And Statesman.* London: Harrap, 1946.

See also EGYPT; PALESTINE AND SYRIA; SINAI CAMPAIGN; VIMY RIDGE

Alliances, Prewar

By 1914 the European great powers were divided into two hostile alliance systems: the Triple Alliance of Germany, Austria-Hungary, and Italy; and the Triple Entente of France, Russia, and Great Britain. Lesser European states were either attached to one or more of the great powers, such as Romania's alliance with Germany and Austria-Hungary, or considered vital to a great power's national interests, such as was Serbia to Russia in the Balkans. Because the prewar alliances were brought into play during the crisis that followed Archduke Franz Ferdinand's assassination, some contemporaries (such as U.S. president Woodrow Wilson) and postwar historians (such as Bernadotte E. Schmitt) blamed them for causing the First World War. While that is a great oversimplification, no study of the origins of the First World War would be complete without an examination of the prewar alliance system.

The unification of Germany, and to a lesser extent that of Italy, dramatically altered the European balance of power that had existed since the days of Louis XIV. Germany emerged from its decisive victories over Austria in the Seven Weeks War (1866) and France in the Franco-Prussian War (1870–71) as the dominant military power in Europe. Under Otto von Bismarck, minister-president of Prussia since 1862 and later imperial chancellor until 1890, Germany dominated European diplomacy.

Inasmuch as Bismarck was satisfied with Germany's gains from unification, his chief interest after 1871 was to protect the status quo. Bismarck realized that Germany's seizure of Alsace-Lorraine had created lasting enmity with France, but he was confident that Germany could defeat France in any one-on-one conflict. The key, therefore, was to keep France diplomatically isolated. With Britain committed to a policy of "splendid isolation," Bismarck moved to tie Russia and Austria-Hungary to Germany. Negotiations conducted between 1872 and 1873 produced the *Dreikaiserbund* (Three Emperor's League). The three powers agreed to assist each other if attacked by another power and to coordinate their policies. In 1878, however, Russia angrily withdrew from the *Dreikaiserbund* after Germany and Austria-Hungary failed to support it at the Congress of Berlin.

Forced to choose between Russia and Austria-Hungary, Bismarck chose the latter because of common cultural ties and because Germany could be the dominant partner. Germany and Austria-Hungary signed the Dual Alliance on 7 October 1879. Under its terms, if either party were attacked by Russia, the other would support it with all its forces and not make a separate peace. If either party should be attacked by another power (that is, Germany by France or Austria-Hungary by Italy), the other would maintain at least benevolent neutrality. If some other power supported by Russia were to attack one of them, each would aid the other. Although originally scheduled to run for five years, the Dual Alliance was extended to 1918. Of all of Bismarck's diplomatic arrangements, it was the most lasting and remained the foundation of German foreign policy.

Despite the Dual Alliance, Bismarck still left the door open for Russia. Indeed, Russian fear of being isolated led to the second Dreikaiserbund, signed on 18 June 1881. It guaranteed that if any of the three parties became involved in a war with another power, other than the Ottoman Empire, the others would maintain a benevolent neutrality. It acknowledged Austria-Hungary's special interests in Bosnia-Herzegovina and Russia's in Bulgaria. All three powers also agreed to consult each other in the event of a conflict with the Turks and there would be no modification of the territorial status quo in southeastern Europe without agreement among the three.

Bismarck next turned his attention to Italy. Italians had been upset by the French acquisition of Tunis in May of 1881. Negotiations between Germany, Italy, and Austria-Hungary led to the signing of the Triple Alliance on 20 May 1882. Under its terms, Germany and Austria-Hungary agreed to aid Italy if France attacked it without provocation, while Italy would support Germany if it were attacked by France. If one of the allies became involved in a war with two or more powers, the others would come to its aid. Finally, if one of the allies had to launch a preventive attack on a great power, the others would preserve a benevolent neutrality. Originally concluded for five years, the alliance continued to be renewed until 1915. At each renewal, however, Italy extracted greater promises from Germany, especially in support for its colonial ambitions in northern Africa. The great weakness of the alliance was that Italy's territorial aims in the Tyrol and Dalmatia, where a large number of Italians lived, could be achieved only at the expense of Austria-Hungary.

In 1883 Bismarck added a new member to his alliance system by negotiating an alliance between Austria-Hungary and Romania, to which Germany adhered. As a member of the Hohenzollern family, King Carol I of Romania had long leaned toward Germany anyway, but fear of Russia's support of a larger Bulgaria provided the impetus behind the alliance. (Russia supported Bulgarian aspirations for a large state at the expense of its neighbors.) Under its terms none of the three states would enter an alliance against the other, and Austria-Hungary and Romania would aid each other if either were attacked by Russia. Although the alliance was renewed every five years until 1916 and Italy adhered to it in 1888, it was fatally flawed because the Austro-Hungarian province of Transylvania contained a large population of ethnic Romanians. The lure of Transylvania ultimately led Romania to abandon the alliance during World War I and declare war on Austria-Hungary.

Although the second Dreikaiserbund was renewed in 1884, in 1887 Russia refused to do so again, because during the Bulgarian Crisis of 1885–86 Austria had threatened to intervene if Russia occupied Bulgaria. Since Russia did not wish to be diplomatically isolated and Bismarck hoped to prevent a two-front war

against France and Russia, the two powers signed a secret Reinsurance Treaty on 18 June 1887. Although Germany and Russia promised to remain neutral if either became involved in a war with a third power, this would not apply if Germany attacked France or Russia attacked Austria-Hungary. In addition, they agreed to work for the status-quo in the Balkans and reaffirmed the closure of the Straits in wartime. Germany also recognized Russia's special interests in Bulgaria and pledged to support Russian efforts to gain control of the Straits.

Although Russia desired a renewal of the Reinsurance Treaty in 1890, Kaiser Wilhelm II's dismissal of Bismarck on 18 March 1890 brought an end to the alliance. At a ministerial conference held on 23 March, Baron Fritz von Holstein, who had broken with Bismarck, urged the young kaiser not to renew the alliance because it was incompatible with the Dual Alliance. Despite repeated Russian overtures, the treaty was allowed to lapse on 18 June 1890. While it is true that perhaps only Bismarck could manage the tangled web of alliances, the decision not to renew the Reinsurance Treaty was a monumental blunder. Bismarck's nightmare of a Franco-Russian rapprochement was soon to be fulfilled.

Although Wilhelm II and Holstein had believed that an autocratic Russia and republican France would never work together, international diplomacy often makes strange bedfellows. Despite the vast differences between their political systems, Russia and France were drawn together because they both were diplomatically isolated and they shared a common fear of Germany, whose alliance system was aimed at the two countries. Sensing the opportunity to gain an alliance with Russia, France greased the wheels of diplomacy by extending loans to help Russia's industrialization and by opening French markets to Russian grain. Germany had halted the sale of Russian securities and placed high tariffs on Russian produce, and the French initiative was soon parlayed into closer diplomatic relations.

The first step toward an alliance was taken on 24 July 1891, when a French naval squadron visited the Russian naval base at Kronstadt and was personally welcomed by Czar Alexander III. Negotiations conducted between 21 and 27 August produced the August Convention, by which France and Russia agreed to consult each other for a joint response if either

A

were threatened by an act of aggression or if peace in Europe were endangered. Although France had desired a stronger commitment, the August Convention had finally broken its diplomatic isolation.

The Russians were clearly reluctant allies, and the French wasted no time in trying to add to the August Convention. On 1 August 1892, Chief of the General Staff General Raoul le Mounton de Boisdeffre arrived in St. Petersburg bearing a draft military convention. Although the Russians continued to drag their feet for two more years, the passage of an 1893 German military bill, which increased the size of its army, provided the French with the leverage they needed. After a Russian naval squadron visited the French naval base at Toulon on 13 October the two governments exchanged notes (27 December 1893 and 4 January 1894) that sealed their alliance.

Under the terms of the Franco-Russian Military Convention, which was to remain in effect as long as the Triple Alliance, Russia promised to aid France with all its forces if France were attacked by Germany or by Italy supported by Germany. In return, France was to support Russia with all its resources in the event Russia were attacked by Germany or by Austria-Hungary supported by Germany. In addition, if the Triple Alliance or one of its members mobilized, France and Russia would mobilize immediately. It also provided for regular consultation and military planning. It is important to note that the alliance was classed as a convention, rather than a treaty, so that it would not have to be submitted to the French Chamber of Deputies for ratification. This was done to thwart opposition from socialist deputies, as well as to keep the terms of the alliance secret.

The Franco-Russian Military Convention marked the first step in what some historians have termed the "diplomatic revolution." Although Germany remained the dominant military power in Europe, it was losing the diplomatic hegemony it had enjoyed under Bismarck. Indeed, France's next diplomatic coup came with Italy. Playing on Italian colonial ambitions, French Foreign Minister Théophile Delcassé reached an agreement on 14 December 1900 with Italy in which France recognized Italy's interests in Tripoli while Italy recognized those of France in Morocco. Building upon this, Delcassé won a secret agreement with Italy on 1 November 1902 by which Italy promised to remain neutral in the event Germany attacked France or if France—in order to protect her national honor—felt obligated to attack Germany. France had effectively drawn Italy out of the Triple Alliance, although on paper she remained a member. Germany could no longer count on Italian participation in a Franco-German conflict, while France could concentrate all of its resources against Germany.

Even more significant in the so-called "diplomatic revolution" was Great Britain's abandonment of its "splendid isolation," which the British had consistently followed since the end of the Napoleonic Wars. While Wilhelm II's pursuit of colonies to secure "Germany's place under the sun" and his propensity for bombastic saber-rattling had raised British concerns, it was Wilhelm's attempt to challenge British naval power that drove the British into the arms of France and Russia. As an island nation that imported the bulk of its food and much of its raw materials, Britain understood that its security rested on its navy. Indeed, under the Naval Defense Act of 1889 the British had adopted a two-power standard (a navy as large as that of the next two naval powers combined). The massive German naval buildup therefore placed profound stress upon the British naval commitment.

On 30 January 1902 the British concluded an alliance with Japan, which they hoped would strengthen their position in the Pacific. According to this agreement, if one of the allies became involved in a war with a third party, the other would remain neutral, unless one or more powers should join in the war, at which point the allies would assist each other. While originally aimed at Russia, the treaty would bring Japan into the First World War on the side of the Allies.

Much more significant than the alliance with Japan, however, was the rapprochement between France and Britain. France had long been Britain's traditional opponent in Europe, and the two countries had barely avoided conflict in 1898 during the Fashoda Crisis over the Sudan. With the German naval buildup, and especially the passage of the second German Naval Law in 1900, Britain came to see Germany as the greater threat. Negotiations, speeded up by the outbreak of the Russo-Japanese War, led to the Entente Cordiale.

Concluded on 8 April 1904, the Entente Cordiale consisted of three separate agreements that resolved all outstanding colonial differences between Britain and France in order to prevent another misunderstanding similar to that of Fashoda. France recognized the British occupation of Egypt, in return for which Britain guaranteed free navigation of the Suez Canal and promised diplomatic support in helping France gain Morocco. While France agreed to surrender its rights on the shores of Newfoundland, it retained the right to fish offshore and received territory near French Gambia and east of Niger. The two countries also divided Siam into spheres of influence and settled disputes over Madagascar and the New Hebrides. Although the Entente Cordiale did not contain any military commitments, Britain and France began to cooperate closely in foreign policy. Indeed, after Wilhelm II provoked the First Moroccan Crisis in 1905, the two countries began to hold annual military and naval conversations.

Having settled colonial differences with France, the British next moved to do the same with Russia, whose defeat in the Russo-Japanese War no longer made it as great a threat to British interests in Asia and the Far East. Negotiations began in October of 1905 and were concluded on 31 August 1907 with the signing of the Anglo-Russian Entente. Like the French, the British had prepared the way by extending much-needed loans to Russia. The entente resolved differences in Persia by acknowledging a Russian sphere of influence in northern Persia, a neutral sphere in the center, and British control of southern Persia. The Russians also recognized Britain's special interests in the Persian Gulf and in Afghanistan. Both countries promised to respect the territorial integrity of China and its suzerainty over Tibet. Finally, Britain expressed a willingness to modify the Straits Agreement in the favor of Russia.

Although the conclusion of the Anglo-Russian Entente linked Britain, Russia, and France together in a Triple Entente, it is important to note that the Franco-Russian Military Convention provided the only military commitment against the Triple Alliance. Britain might have settled its differences with France and Russia, but it was still reluctant to make a firm commitment in Europe. Indeed, between 1908 and 1912 the British made several attempts to settle differences with Germany. The most important attempt followed the Second Moroccan Crisis of 1911, when the British minister of war, Lord Richard Burdon Haldane, traveled to Berlin on 8 February 1912 to try to bring an end to the naval arms race. Passage of a new German Naval Law on 8 March, however, torpedoed the discussions.

The failure of the Haldane mission brought Britain closer to France and secured the military cooperation the French had long desired. Discussions between the British and French governments resulted in the Anglo-French Naval Convention of 1912, by which Britain was able to withdraw the bulk of its fleet from the Mediterranean in order to concentrate its forces in the North Sea. France did the reverse, restationing the bulk of its North Sea fleet in the Mediterranean. More important, Britain promised to protect the French coast from German naval attack, while France promised to protect the Suez Canal. They also agreed to consult one another if either were threatened by attack. While the British were not necessarily legally obligated to support France militarily in the event of a German attack, the British had in fact placed themselves under a moral obligation to aid France.

With the conclusion of the Anglo-French Naval Convention, Europe was divided into two armed camps. While the alliance system was largely a result of the factors that contributed to the First World War (such as nationalism, imperialism, and the arms race), it played an important role in the July Crisis that followed the assassination of Archduke Franz Ferdinand. The Austrian ultimatum to Serbia set the alliances into motion. Austrian mobilization was followed by Russian mobilization, which in turn was followed by German and French mobilization. Like falling dominoes, the alliance system prescribed actions that, as British Foreign Minister Sir Edward Grey put it, caused the lamps to go out across Europe.

Justin D. Murphy

References

Hale, Oron J. *The Great Illusion, 1900–1914.* New York: Harper and Row, 1971.

Kennan, George F. *The Fateful Alliance: France, Russia, and the Coming of the First World War.* New York: Pantheon, 1984.

Langer, William L. *European Alliances and Alignments.* 2nd ed. New York: Alfred A. Knopf, 1950.

Remak, Joachim. *The Origins of World War I, 1871–1914.* New York: Holt, Reinhart, and Winston, 1967.

Schmitt, Bernadotte E. *Triple Alliance and Triple Entente*. New York: Henry Holt, 1934.

See also HISTORIOGRAPHY OF THE OUTBREAK OF THE WAR; NAVAL ARMS RACE, ANGLO-GERMAN; ORIGINS OF THE FIRST WORLD WAR; OUTBREAK OF THE FIRST WORLD WAR

Allied Counteroffensive (18 July to 11 November 1918)

Early in 1918, although the Allies were absorbed in preparations to deal with an expected German offensive in France, General Ferdinand Foch, chief of staff of the French army, nevertheless argued that the Western powers should plan offensives to exploit opportunities that might develop during the coming campaign year. When he became generalissimo after the great German strike of 21 March, Foch was forced to concentrate on measures designed to contain the German tide. General Erich Ludendorff and his nominal superior, Field Marshal Paul von Hindenburg, launched five distinct attacks along the Western Front in a desperate effort to force a decision before the arrival of the American army tipped the balance in favor of the Allies. The German High Command had hoped to take advantage of a temporary bulge in manpower made possible by the transfer of veteran divisions from the Eastern Front after Russia left the war.

Despite the primacy of defensive operations during the crisis of March–July, Foch retained his interest in regaining the initiative in France. As early as 20 May, before three of the five enemy assaults took place, he began to plan attacks designed to restore communications between the Somme and Oise rivers in Picardy and along the Lys River in Belgium, where the German army had made its advances. When the German attacks on the Marne salient were contained, he discerned an opportunity to attack that position, an area of about forty miles in width and thirty in depth. At the beginning, Foch's thoughts centered on the restoration of Allied communications, which had been disrupted by the German advances, so that he could maneuver reserves effectively. General Charles Mangin of the French Tenth Army produced the first plan for the reduction of the Marne salient as early as 20 June.

After French intelligence had begun to gain information about Ludendorff's fifth offensive, this one aimed at Reims, Foch finalized his plans for the counterattack on the Marne salient. He envisioned strikes on both sides of the salient, seeking to free the Paris-Chalons railway running through the valley. The attack on the right would halt the German offensive against Reims, which was scheduled to begin on 15 July, and the attack on the left would recover the Tardenois region. For this effort Foch concentrated forty-four divisions, including several fresh American divisions, between the Oise River and the Argonne Forest. Foch later wrote that, because of the American reinforcement of twenty-five double-sized divisions, the opposing armies were now at approximately equal strength. "If the enemy did not attack, the hour had come for us to take the offensive; if he did attack, to accompany our parry with a powerful counter-stroke." General Henri Philippe Pétain, commander in chief of the French army, became alarmed by the German preparations and attempted to cancel the strike on the left, but Foch learned of this move in time to head it off.

The German attack of 15 July ran into an effective defense-in-depth that soon brought it to a halt, a result that allowed Mangin on 18 July to launch his surprise attack on the left from the forest of Villers-Cotteret. Immediate success attended this operation. The railway between Soissons and Reims, on which the Germans depended to supply the salient, was quickly interdicted. Ludendorff soon recognized that he must suspend another attack scheduled in Flanders and withdraw to the Vesle River. This bitter decision served as a prelude to further Allied initiatives.

On 24 July Foch convened the three Allied commanders in chief—Pétain for France, Field Marshal Sir Douglas Haig for Great Britain, and General John J. Pershing for the United States—to make known his future plans. He envisioned a series of limited offensives, employing all available force in "a series of well ordered actions . . . to prevent the enemy from recovering before we could effect his definite destruction." These coordinated attacks, beginning with the reduction of the Marne salient already underway, were intended to accomplish several purposes: to restore the morale of the Allied armies; to prevent Ludendorff from organizing his defense properly; to impose attrition on the enemy, depriving him of irreplaceable troops; to regain important territory that contained economic resources; and to restore lateral communications needed to support later operations. Foch did not yet envision victory in 1918, but he sought to place his forces in position to secure the earliest possible triumph.

Central to Foch's plans was recognition that he could not expect to achieve a breakthrough or envelopment along classic lines. He hoped instead to impose extensive attrition on the enemy, leading to his eventual collapse for lack of the human and material resources needed to continue the struggle. He would move, he wrote, "at brief intervals, so as to embarrass the enemy in the utilization of his reserves and not allow him sufficient time to fill up his units." The principal tactical requirement was surprise. "Recent operations show that this is a condition indispensable to success."

In addition to the reduction of the Marne salient, an operation well on its way, the generalissimo contemplated three other limited operations. One was an attack on the Amiens salient, the bulge in the Western Front created by the German success in March. Another was a move along the Lys River in Flanders to recover the positions lost in the German attacks of April. The last was still another attack on the German salient at St. Mihiel near the Verdun battlefield. Each of the national commanders noted difficulties with their commands, but Foch obtained their agreement to his proposal, arguing that effective coordination of the several armies would ensure success. He would move according to developments; he would adjust operations "according to the success obtained as we went long."

General Henry Rawlinson, commander of the British Fourth Army, had already started to plan an attack to the east of Amiens to open the Paris-Chalons railway. Central to the design of the operation were certain tactical principles that had been developed by stages, notably at Cambrai in November of 1917 and most recently at Hamel early in July. Australian General John Monash, the chief planner for the Hamel attack, emphasized above all the element of surprise along with close cooperation between armor, artillery, infantry, and aircraft. Here was an advanced version of the combined-arms doctrine. Tanks and infantry would lead the assault, advancing behind a moving artillery barrage. Air support would come in the form of attacks on antitank weapons and replenishment of ammunition.

The battle of Amiens began on 8 August. Two thousand guns participated in an artillery barrage that supported the assault of over 450 tanks and the infantry of the British Fourth Army. Surprise was complete; Rawlinson gained over six miles on the first day. French units on his right and other British troops on his left also made progress. Another four days of fighting brought the Allies to the desolate ground of the Somme battlefield, where the bloodiest battle of the war had been fought in 1916. Haig then suspended operations, arguing that further fighting would produce unacceptable losses.

The victory at Amiens began the process that led to the eventual collapse of Germany. Ludendorff now recognized that his grand design for 1918 had failed. Massive American reinforcements had given Foch the manpower advantage necessary to gain success. Ludendorff decided that Germany must now seek a diplomatic solution to the war, moving while his army was still sufficiently effective to force an acceptable settlement. On 14 August Kaiser Wilhelm II authorized German Foreign Minister Admiral Paul von Hintze to initiate peace negotiations through Queen Wilhelmina of the Netherlands.

Ludendorff now began a series of retreats that would eventually place his army within the extensive fortifications known as the Hindenburg Line. While doing so he moved quickly to adapt to the new tactics of the Allies, calling for defense-in-depth and improved intelligence to avoid future surprises. These measures, however, were not sufficient to counter the growing strength of Foch's forces. The arrival of many American divisions meant that Foch could replace his losses, but Ludendorff had few reserves left with which to shore up his depleted units. The American divisions had so far contributed to the offensive mostly by relieving experienced British and French units in quiet sectors and making them available for combat service.

This success confirmed Foch's belief that sustained attrition rather than a dramatic breakthrough would lead to victory on the Western Front. Haig's acceptance of this premise gave Foch the ascendancy he needed to continue his series of limited counteroffensives.

The grinding Allied attack resumed on 18 August, when the French army, this time with the assistance of several American divisions, began the Oise-Aisne offensive. That effort broke the German positions on the Vesle River, which had been occupied after the defeat on the

Marne River, and brought the French close to the Hindenburg Line.

The next Allied operation was to take place in Belgium in the Ypres-Lys area to solidify the position of the British and Belgian forces in the region. Ludendorff recognized the likelihood of this attack as well as his inability to contain it. On 26 August, therefore, he ordered a withdrawal eastward that allowed the Allied troops organized for the offensive to occupy the evacuated area by 4 September, securing their objectives without undue losses.

The last limited counteroffensive, the reduction of the St. Mihiel salient, was assigned to the American First Army, newly formed to conduct General Pershing's initial independent operation. Hitherto the few American divisions committed to combat had served under British and French commanders and staffs, mostly during the recent Aisne-Marne and Oise-Aisne offensives. Pershing refused to condone more than temporary brigading of a few American divisions with European divisions for combat service, adhering to the desire of the American government to form an independent army under its own commanders and staffs with its own services of supply to operate in its own theater on the Western Front, much as had the French, British, Belgian, and Italian armies. President Wilson's motive in mandating this approach, which meant that the American army would not make significant combat contributions until 1919 because of the time needed to complete a great mobilization, was to allow the American Expeditionary Forces (AEF) to make a decisive contribution to the victory. That outcome would strengthen his hand immeasurably at the postwar peace negotiations, where he intended to arrange a peace settlement based on his Fourteen Points, many of which would require the Allies, particularly the French, to retreat from advanced war aims.

The American assault on the St. Mihiel salient, which began on 12 September, was a scaled-down version of the original plan. From the early days of the American presence in France, Pershing's staff had planned to conduct a decisive operation in Lorraine aimed at Metz, located east of the St. Mihiel district. This achievement, the Americans believed, would cut the lateral railroads behind the German front, essential to the supply of Ludendorff's massive armies, and force a general withdrawal to the German border and perhaps even farther to the Rhine River. The idea was a misconception because alternative communications east of Metz would allow the Germans to continue to support their forces.

Pershing's wish to reduce the St. Mihiel salient and to continue eastward ran afoul of Foch's developing plans to move beyond his limited operations to a general move against the great German salient in France and Belgium known as the Laon bulge. By late August, Foch, now marshal of France, had decided to conduct a great converging attack on the Hindenburg Line. Successful penetration of these extensive fortifications would allow his armies to sever the lateral communications of the German army in France and Belgium, forcing a withdrawal of the type that Pershing had envisioned after the proposed seizure of Metz. When Field Marshal Sir Douglas Haig suggested a similar endeavor, Foch felt able to proceed. The plan entailed extensive use of the American First Army in an attack on the south face of the great German salient, in combination with the French Fourth Army, an assignment that precluded exploitation of any gains made at St. Mihiel. Pershing fiercely resisted Foch's desires but was ultimately forced to agree to halt his forward movement at the base line of the salient and transfer his First Army to the Meuse-Argonne sector just to the west.

The American attack of 12 September with fourteen divisions achieved immediate success. By 16 September Pershing had occupied the salient. He had planned the operation to demonstrate the feasibility of an independent American army, to which the Allies were generally opposed, at least until 1919. Haig, Pétain, and Foch all believed that the inexperienced American forces, lacking adequate commanders and staffs and logistical efficiency, despite the élan of the troops, would encounter significant difficulties in initial independent operations unless they were better trained and equipped than was the case in 1918. They desired temporary "amalgamation" of American units into their armies to cope with the emergency of 1918. The elated Pershing argued that his success at St. Mihiel proved his critics wrong. He ignored two important realities: Despite the American achievement, the operations revealed many weaknesses in the First Army; and, more important, the German troops in the salient had been ordered to withdraw from it and were in the process of doing so when Pershing struck. His attack accelerated and confused the German withdrawal.

On 3 September Foch made known his plan for a general counteroffensive intended to break through the Hindenburg fortifications. The British army was assigned the task of assaulting the left face of the great salient, driving toward Cambrai and St. Quentin. The French armies in the center would push the Germans past the Aisne and Ailette rivers. On the right, the American First Army and the French Fourth Army would drive northward against the south face of the great salient toward Mezières. The basic objective was the railway, located behind the Hindenburg Line, that ran between the Maubeuge-Aulnoye area to the north and the Mezières-Sedan area to the south. Interdiction of this railway, a critical link in the long line of communications between Lille and Strasbourg, would force a broad German retreat.

The final element of the plan was an attack by an inter-Allied force made up of British, Belgian, French, and American troops known as the Flanders Group of Armies, commanded by King Albert of Belgium with the assistance of French General Jean Degoutte. The operation was designed to regain control of the Belgian ports and to threaten enemy communications in the north. This attack, like that of the French in the center, was part and parcel of Foch's intention to maintain pressure on the entire Western Front so that Ludendorff could not maneuver his dwindling reserves to counter the most crucial Allied operations, the British attack toward Aulnoye and the Franco-American attack toward Mezières.

At length, Foch decided the timing of the coordinated attacks. The Franco-American attack between the Meuse and Suippe rivers on a front of forty-four miles, set for 26 September, would engage fifteen double-size divisions of the American First Army and twenty-two divisions of the French Fourth Army. The principal British attack, toward Cambrai on 27 September, would employ the twenty-seven divisions of the British First and Third armies. On 28 September the Flanders Group of Armies, including twenty-eight divisions, would strike toward Ghent between the English Channel and the Lys River. On 29 September a Franco-British force of thirty-one divisions would attack between Peronne and La Fère toward Busigny. Foch's final injunctions to the various Allied commanders emphasized the need to sustain unremitting pressure on the German army. "Shock power" would disorganize the enemy and preclude the organization of effective defenses. Foch sought to prevent the Germans from accomplishing what he had done earlier in the face of the great German offensives of March–July, the establishment of viable defensive lines after initial defeats.

On 26 September the American First Army attacked the Hindenburg fortifications between the Meuse River and the Argonne Forest, while the French Fourth Army attacked to the west. Pershing faced difficult terrain that gave the German defenders strong defensive positions on high ground from which to direct machine-gun and artillery fire. Four lines of fortifications made up the German defenses in this area. The first of these was primarily a screen for the three main fortifications, which took advantage of terrain features. The principal barrier was the third of these, the Kriemhilde Stellung, built across the heights of Cunel and Romagne. German positions on the heights of the Meuse on that river's east bank and in the Argonne Forest supported this formidable bastion. Only the German Fifth Army, of five understrength divisions, manned the German lines. Reserve divisions were located nearby to reinforce the Fifth Army if necessary. Pershing's ambitious plan required the use of three corps attacking abreast to overrun the first three lines of fortifications in two days. He had to use inexperienced divisions for the initial attack, because his veterans had been committed at St. Mihiel. Pershing assumed that the First Army could exploit its manpower superiority, its élan, and the weak German divisions in the Meuse-Argonne sector sufficiently to achieve a major breakthrough in a short period of time.

The Franco-American attack gained initial success, but it soon bogged down, especially in the Meuse-Argonne sector. The First Army lacked the doctrine, the experienced commanders, the staffs, the logistical efficiency, and the training necessary to counter the strong defensive positions taken up by the German defenders. Artillery and machine-gun fire halted the attackers before they could break through the Kriemhilde Stellung. The attack in the Meuse-Argonne sector was suspended on 30 September. It was renewed on several occasions during October, but the American First Army had sustained what amounted to a check lasting a month. The French Fourth Army on the left was not prepared to move a significant distance ahead of the First Army. Despite slow progress, the Franco-American attack managed to force

A

deployment of some German reserves in the Meuse-Argonne sector, and it imposed severe attrition on the tired but stubborn German defenders.

The developments on the south face of the salient did not prove devastating because of the great successes gained on the west face of the Laon bulge. On 27 September the British First and Third armies attacked the Hindenburg Line, moving between the Sensee River and Villers-Guilain across the Canal du Nord to the outskirts of Cambrai, a victory comparable to that at Amiens in August. The Hindenburg line was strongest in this region, but it was designed primarily to resist bombardment, not tanks. Effective artillery-armor-infantry coordination accounted for Haig's great triumph.

On 28 September the Fourth British Army and the French First Army attacked across the St. Quentin canal and also succeeded in breaching the Hindenburg line. This significant victory added to the general panic that overran German headquarters at Spa, as did the successful operations of the Flanders Group of Armies, which also attained immediate success. Once again the experience of the British and French armies and their use of sound operational doctrine led to unprecedented victories on the west face of the Laon bulge.

Foch's final blow fell on 29 September when the Franco-British attack between La Fère and Peronne against the nose of the great salient began successfully, extending Allied operations to the entire front between the North Sea and Champagne. Ludendorff encountered general defeat everywhere except on the fronts of the American First and Fourth Armies between the Suippe and Meuse rivers.

The terrible defeats of 26–29 September, especially the breakthrough toward the Maubeuge-Aulnoye area, convinced Ludendorff that Germany must seek an immediate armistice and arrange for postwar peace negotiations. He tried to place the blame on the collapse of the Bulgarian army on the Salonika front, a means of shifting responsibility for the defeat to a lesser ally, but his insistent demands on the civil government to take immediate action stemmed principally from his own difficulties. At this juncture a change of government in Berlin led to several exchanges of diplomatic notes between President Wilson and the new chancellor of Germany, Prince Maximilian of Baden. By 23 October these bilateral negotiations led to an agreement between the United States and Germany that an armistice should be arranged and a peace conference conducted later on the basis of the American Fourteen Points and associated pronouncements. The Allied leaders were excluded from this process, a measure of the extent to which the Entente had come to rely on American assistance. It remained only for the Allied governments to accept the German-American agreement. The Allies did so reluctantly during multilateral discussions in Paris (29 October–4 November). These parleys formulated the military, naval, and air terms of armistice and a separate political document of overriding significance, the pre-armistice agreement of 4 November that established the American peace program as the basis of the world settlement to come.

Meanwhile, the battle continued along the Western Front. Foch was suspicious of Germany's intentions, and in any event recognized that relentless pressure remained his principal means of destroying the will of the German army and people. After the initial successes late in September, Foch required time to organize further attacks. Meanwhile, the American First Army, bogged down in the Meuse-Argonne sector, continued its dogged attempts to penetrate the Kriemhilde Stellung. The shaken Ludendorff recovered his balance, planning to conduct an orderly withdrawal to a new line of defense reaching from Antwerp to the Meuse. Ludendorff's attempts to halt the Allies were frustrated when the British Expeditionary Force resumed its advance and penetrated the Hermann positions, the last barrier in the Hindenburg line. Prince Max's government in Berlin did not share Ludendorff's optimism. The defeated leader was finally forced to resign on 26 October.

Foch now prepared another concerted attack to take place on 1 November. On 19 October he ordered resumption of the offensives in Flanders against Ghent and on the British front toward Maubeuge. In the south he envisioned "the fall of the line of the Aisne by a maneuver of two wings." The French Fifth Army on the left would move toward Chaumont-Porcien. The French Fourth Army and the American First Army would resume their movement toward Buzancy and Le Chesne. These operations were intended to complete the interdiction of rail communications between Aulnoye and Mezières.

The attacks of 1 November gained immediate success. The Flanders Group of Armies spanned the Scheldt River and threatened Ghent. Haig's troops occupied the fortress of Maubeuge on 8 November. At long last the Franco-American operations aimed at the Mezières-Sedan area gained significant momentum. The depleted and discouraged Germans were driven out of their last remaining fortifications on the Hindenburg Line and forced to begin a precipitous retreat toward the Antwerp-Meuse Line.

Meanwhile, Foch entered into armistice negotiations with the defeated enemy, insisting upon the stringent terms agreed to at the pre-armistice conference. When the Kiel Naval Mutinies sparked revolution in Germany, forcing the abdication of the Kaiser and his flight to the Netherlands on 9 November, a new socialist government in Berlin agreed to Foch's demands, and an armistice took effect at 11:00 on 11 November.

German generals and historians later attempted to place the blame for the defeat of 1918 on the civil government, claiming that it had "stabbed the army in the back," but in reality it was Foch's brilliant campaign of July–November that brought the German army to its knees. He had discerned the impossibility of anything approaching a Napoleonic breakthrough and envelopment, turning instead to sustained attrition inflicted by means of a series of unrelenting and coordinated attacks designed to preclude Ludendorff's organizing an effective defense at any point on the Western Front. This plan took full advantage of the edge in manpower and matériel enjoyed by the Western powers. Specific operations succeeded in great part because of effective tactical modifications based on effective infantry-artillery-armor cooperation. These innovations proved sufficient to cause the necessary attrition; they were not yet enough to restore maneuver to the battlefield. Foch's campaign, reminiscent of General Ulysses S. Grant's operations in Virginia in 1864–65, ranks among the most remarkable in the history of arms.

David F. Trask

References

Asprey, Robert B. *The German High Command at War: Hindenburg and Ludendorff Conduct World War I.* New York: William Morrow, 1991.

Foch, Ferdinand. *The Memoirs of Marshal Foch.* Translated by T. Bentley Mott. Garden City, N.Y.: Doubleday, Doran, 1931.

Ludendorff, Erich. *Ludendorff's Own Story: August 1914–November 1918.* Vol. 2. New York & London: Harper & Brothers, 1919.

Paschall, Rod. *The Defeat of Imperial Germany, 1917–1918.* Chapel Hill, N.C.: Algonquin, 1989.

Trask, David F. *The AEF and Coalition Warmaking, 1917–1918.* Lawrence: University Press of Kansas, 1993.

Wilson, Trevor. *The Myriad Faces of War: Britain and the Great War, 1914–1918.* New York: B. Blackwell, 1986.

See also ARMISTICE; CAMBRAI, BATTLE OF; FOCH, FERDINAND; HAIG, DOUGLAS; HINDENBURG, PAUL VON; HINTZE, PAUL VON; LUDENDORFF, ERICH; LUDENDORFF OFFENSIVES; MANGIN, CHARLES; RAWLINSON, HENRY

Alpine Warfare

Alpine warfare is battle between specialized troops in the snow above 2,000 to 3,000 meters, most memorably exemplified in the campaign between the Hapsburg Austro-Hungarians and the Italians in the Trentino/Tyrol, 1915–18.

Alpine warfare has three defining components: *Alpinimus* (the mystique and techniques of alpine mountaineering as sport), downhill skiing, and the aerial cable car (*Seilbahn*). All three were pioneered and developed by the Hapsburg army. The famous alpine military exploits of the past—those of Hannibal, Suvorov, and Napoleon—were alpine crossings undertaken during the summer. The intention of twentieth-century alpine warfare was to maintain large forces in the mountains year-round.

After 1870, as the new mass armies were tied increasingly to railheads, all the great powers developed formations of mountain troops—light, independent brigades with supply and mountain-gun artillery on pack animals, capable of fighting in roadless terrain. These so-called mountain troops had no alpine training and were always being drawn off into colonial campaigns. The Hapsburgs had fourteen such mountain brigades in Bosnia in the prewar period. During the 1880s the Italian *Alpini* and the French *Chasseurs Alpin* made the first steps toward establishing true alpine troops. The elite *Tirolean Kaiserjäger* of the Hapsburgs did some limited alpine work on the initiative of junior officers who experimented with new downhill skiing and winter maneuvers.

Only after 1906 did the Austro-Hungarians, under General Franz Conrad von Hötzendorf, begin to consider that war with Italy would mean an alpine campaign. As the Italians shifted their *Alpini* from the French border to the Tyrolean frontier, the Hapsburgs converted the second-line Tyrolean National Guard (*Landwehr*) to an elite alpine force. With a general staff alpine command course, an army ski factory in Salzburg, and thousands of skiers trained in the new Zdarsky technique, the five regiments of the Hapsburgs were the best alpine troops in the world.

In 1914 this original cadre was lost in the Russian campaign. Skilled alpine warfare techniques were not in evidence during the terrible winter fighting in the Carpathians. For example, aerial cable cars bringing supplies might have prevented thousands of casualties.

It was during the Hapsburg war with Italy, starting in 1915, that alpine warfare came into its own. The main conventional armies were drawn up along the Isonzo River, but the long mountain border allowed ample opportunity for alpine warfare. The Hapsburgs transferred decimated alpine troops, returned from Russia, to face the Italian *Alpini*. Alpine technical advisors and civilian mountaineers were assigned to nonalpine units that were also transferred in as the campaign developed. New schools for downhill skiing and mountain climbing were opened.

In the infancy of aerial reconnaissance and artillery spotting, every peak became an observation point or gun position. The Hapsburgs had the highest gun position in history on the Ortler, at about 13,000 feet. With thousands of trained mountaineers and skiers on both sides the front quickly stabilized and became a form of siege warfare, just as on the Western Front. Unlike in France, small-unit heroic actions could still succeed. Alpine troops could do a blind-face technical climb above an enemy position or counterattack during a blizzard to capture a key post.

Although cases of ski attacks were limited, fire intensity forced troops underground for shelter as it did in France and on the Isonzo. Caverns were blasted in the rock and tunnels were dug in glacier positions and deep snowfields. On the Marmalada Glacier, both sides had miles of tunnels in their forward positions. When enemy tunnels could be detected through the ice, raids were mounted into these systems and encounters took place in the natural caverns of the glacier. Tunneling led to mining, the most famous instance of which was the Italian mine tunneled under the peak of Col di Lana. The Hapsburgs lost a battalion there when the mine was detonated in April of 1916. More dangerous than the enemy were natural hazards, encountered whenever generals ignored their alpine technical advisors. In the winter of 1916–17 most Hapsburg casualties were caused by avalanches, the "white death," which crashed into valley positions. In the summer, lightning presented a key danger on peak positions.

The large alpine formations were supplied by their system of aerial cable cars totaling over 3,000 kilometers. With cable stations built into caverns, they provided only minimal targets and did not require digging out in areas with 10–20 meters of snow.

Alpine warfare had little impact on the war in general. Technical mountaineering skills on both sides caused a stalemate. After the war, alpine formations and skills were maintained, but saw little use in World War II. The main legacy of alpine warfare was *Alpinimus* downhill skiing and the development of the aerial cable car.

R.D. Zehnder

References
Czant, Colonel Herman. *Alpinimus*. Berlin: Verlag für Kulturpolitik, 1926.
Schaumann, Walter. *Führer zu den Schauplätzen des Dolomitenkrieges*. Cortina d'Ampezzo: Foto Ghedina, 1973.

See also AUSTRIA-HUNGARY, ARMY; ITALY, ARMY

Alsace and Lorraine

The French frontier provinces of Alsace and a large part of Lorraine (to a line west of the Moselle River) had been annexed by the German Empire after the Franco-Prussian War. Much contested in European history, these territories had been added to France during the seventeenth and eighteenth centuries. Although many inhabitants spoke German as late as 1871, most considered themselves French citizens.

Germany ruled Alsace and Lorraine as an imperial territory (*Reichsland*), administered directly from Berlin through Prussian bureaucrats and an appointed governor. The inhabitants were permitted to elect deputies to the Reichstag and were thus able to petition for local autonomy and self-rule. Despite grants of limited rights in 1874, 1879, and 1911 (the last of which authorized the election of a weak regional assembly), the imperial government was so annoyed by pro-French sentiment in the region that it repeatedly threatened to annex Alsace and Lorraine to Prussia or partition them among the neighboring German states.

Within the provinces, the Germans worked to develop industry, mines, and railroads, while discouraging the use of French—by 1910, 87 percent of the population spoke German as their primary language. Inhabitants found it hard to enter the German military and civil service, and many moved into Germany proper to find work. Between 1871 and 1910 the population of the territory grew from 1.5 to 1.8 million, but this change included the departure of more than 400,000 Alsatians and Lorrainers and the settlement in the two provinces of 300,000 native Germans.

Although it had ceded the provinces in the 1871 Treaty of Frankfurt, the French republic consistently maintained that they should be returned and opposed intermittent suggestions that a plebiscite be held to determine their fate. In 1914 recovery of the lost provinces was the nation's only clear war aim, but French offensives in the area failed. Liberation had to await Germany's capitulation. The Armistice mandated German military evacuation of Alsace/Lorraine within two weeks. The Socialist party (SFIO) argued that a referendum was advisable to uphold the principle of self-determination, but President Raymond Poincaré proclaimed the restoration of French rule in Strasbourg city hall on 9 December 1918. While France rejoiced, the government moved quickly to remove German influence, dismissing German-speaking judges, teachers, and civil servants.

Many Alsatians and Lorrainers had mixed feelings about the changes they faced. The limited autonomy granted by the Germans disappeared and was replaced by prefects and Parisian administrators, and French social services were markedly inferior to those of Germany. Alsace's many Catholics bitterly opposed the introduction of the French republic's secular school legislation and the church/state separation law of 1905. Troublesome autonomist and separatist movements in the interwar years led to repeated clashes with the national government. No satisfactory political settlement was reached before the French defeat in 1940.

David L. Longfellow

References

Silverman, Dan P. *Reluctant Union*. University Park: Pennsylvania State University Press, 1972.

Young, Peter, ed. *The Marshall Cavendish Illustrated Encyclopedia of World War I*. New York: Marshall Cavendish, 1984.

Altvater, Vasilij Michaijlovic (1883–1919)

Russian admiral, born in 1883. Altvater rose through the ranks to the position of rear admiral and held important posts. Active in the Russian revolutionary movement in 1917–18, Altvater led the naval contingent of the Soviet delegation to the Brest-Litovsk Peace Conference. He also served as a member of the Collegium of the Narkomvoen, the Council of People's Commissorial and the Military Revolutionary Council of the Republic.

As a leader of a special military advisory group, Altvater directed Soviet forces on the western frontier. In March he approved the campaign plan of 1918. The plan called for a Soviet withdrawal to the eastern bank of the Volkhov River if threatened by continued German and Finnish offensives.

Appointed commander in chief of the navy in autumn of 1918, Altvater instilled a more professional attitude in naval leadership. Under his leadership, the Soviet navy shifted its focus from deep-water to river flotilla ground-support operations. Altvater died in April of 1919.

Jeff Kinard

References

Bunyan, James, and H.H. Fisher. *The Bolshevik Revolution, 1917–1918, Documents and Materials*. Stanford: Stanford University Press, 1961.

Meijer, Jan M., ed. *The Trotsky Papers, 1917–1922*. London: Morton and Company, 1964.

Pipes, Richard. *Revolutionary Russia*. Cambridge: Harvard University Press, 1968.

Shukman, Harold, ed. *The Blackwell Encyclopedia of the Russian Revolution.* Oxford: Basil Blackwell, 1988.

See also BREST-LITOVSK, TREATY OF; RUSSIA, NAVY

Amphibious Warfare

Amphibious warfare, the military art of deploying ground troops from the sea onto or from a hostile shore, underwent momentous changes in World War I. The advent of naval mines, long-range artillery, and the machine gun had altered the correlation of power between the landing fleets and their opponents ashore in favor of the latter. Revolutionary advances in land communications and transportation, moreover, had eroded traditional naval superiority in strategic and operational mobility. The British learned this lesson the hard way at Gallipoli—the first and largest amphibious operation of the war. The last was the German seizure of the Baltic Islands off Russia's western Baltic Coast. The former was a disastrous failure, mostly because of faulty planning and execution, while the latter was a great success, primarily because of poor Russian morale. In between these two extremes were many smaller-scale amphibious assaults, raids, and evacuations. In fact, every major power that participated in World War I, except the United States, conducted amphibious operations. The lessons learned from these operations established the principles that govern amphibious warfare today.

Prewar army and naval theorists did not recognize the influence that the newly emerging technologies would have on amphibious operations, that is, the importance and impact of the rapidly accelerating pace of ground operations, at least at the strategic and operational level. In fact, most navies saw little reason to change their approach to amphibious warfare. The growing power of naval gunnery seemed to ensure, indeed increase, the supremacy of naval firepower over that of ground forces ashore. Experience in gunboat diplomacy and colonial wars appeared to bear this out. Naval gunfire drove the defenders away from the beach, thereby enabling naval landing parties to get ashore and perform their missions at little cost. The fleet's superior strategic mobility ensured that it could choose landing areas at will and establish forces ashore—or evacuate them from the beach if required—long before any defender could bring significant forces to bear.

It was this perspective that led many naval leaders to underestimate the impact that naval mines would have on landing operations, even though they recognized their effectiveness as a weapon. Few military thinkers of the period believed that any opponent could mine its entire coastline, so most admirals felt that they could simply choose a landing area devoid of mines. They did not realize how much the telegraph and railroad had narrowed their hitherto almost unlimited options. More significant, they failed to appreciate the impact that air power would have on their operations. Thus, the Royal Navy's failure at Gallipoli came as a rude shock to virtually all naval leaders.

There was a parochial aspect to this problem as well. Amphibious operations were generally seen as a purely naval matter conducted by navies as dictated by "naval strategic needs." Admirals saw no need to complicate matters by including the army, unless additional troops were required for any follow-on operations that might be warranted. Even then, army troops were not to participate in the assault. Only the Austro-Hungarian and Russian navies cooperated with their respective armies in anything other than troop transport missions. Gallipoli changed all that.

The British suffered for being the first to conduct an amphibious operation in the war. Despite the setback at Gallipoli, however, the Allies exploited their naval supremacy throughout the war. The combined Anglo-French fleet of the Mediterranean conducted many successful raids against Ottoman forces along the Levant and Eastern Aegean Coasts. More significant, it reopened the Balkan front against the Central Powers by evacuating the defeated Serbian army from Montenegro and landing it, along with a combined Allied army, in Greece. Also, the Russians enjoyed great success in their landings on the Turkish coast. In fact, the Russians, as well as the Germans, applied the lessons of Gallipoli to their own operations.

Among those lessons was an appreciation of the importance of air power. After 1915 every Russian amphibious operation in the Black Sea was supported by at least one seaplane carrier. Germany did the same during its assault on the Baltic Islands during Operation Albion in 1917. The Germans, moreover, made the capture of the Islands' airfields a primary objective: a first in military planning and operations.

One of the main lessons derived from Gallipoli was the need to develop specialized landing craft. For Russia that meant improving prewar prototypes, while the Germans employed a modified river ferry. An even more important lesson was that special care must be taken in the distribution of units, equipment, and supplies among the ships. The first units and equipment required ashore had to be loaded last. More important, critical elements had to be distributed among the ships so that the loss of a single vessel would not prove catastrophic. This meant that an amphibious task force required 50 percent more ships to carry a given unit than a standard troop convoy. Another lesson of Gallipoli was the need to integrate all elements of an amphibious operation under a single commander. No single service or weapon system could, by itself, ensure success. For example, procedures had to be developed so that the ground-force commander could direct naval gunfire against land targets that could not be seen from the ships.

These lessons were applied in only two operations during the war, the aforementioned Operation Albion and the Russian multidivisional assault at Rize in 1916. Since neither Germany nor Russia was among the victors of 1918, their operations did not enjoy widespread examination. As a result, the "new" principles of amphibious warfare were understood by only a small cadre of U.S., German, and Soviet military officers during the postwar period. Their studies, however, have guided their respective national amphibious warfare doctrines well into recent times.

Carl O. Schuster

References

Cruttwell, C.R.M.F. *A History of the Great War, 1914–1918.* London: Paladin, 1986.

Greger, Rene. *The Russian Fleet 1914–1917.* London: Ian Allan, 1972.

James, Robert H. *Gallipoli.* London: Papermac, 1965.

Moorehead, Alan. *Gallipoli.* New York: Ballantine, 1956.

Tschischwitz, Lieutenant General (Ret.) von. *The Army and Navy during the Conquest of the Baltic Islands.* Fort Leavenworth, Kansas: Command and General Staff College Press, 1931.

See also BALTIC NAVAL OPERATIONS

A

Andrássy, Count Gyula the Younger (1860–1929)

Politician and Austro-Hungarian foreign minister (1918). Born on 30 June 1860 in Gomor-Kishont County, he was the son of Count Gyula Andrássy the Elder (1823–90), Hungarian minister-president and Austro-Hungarian foreign minister. In 1885 the younger Andrássy was elected to the Hungarian parliament and became one of the more influential Hungarian politicians in the early twentieth century. A liberal, he was a staunch opponent of Count István Tisza. From 1906 to 1910 Andrássy was minister of the interior and worked to reform the suffrage and create a national army.

Andrássy supported Hungary's entrance into the war. He emphasized Hungarian reliance on Germany to win the war in order that Hungary might preserve its territorial integrity. On 24 October 1918 Andrássy succeeded Count István Burián as the last Austro-Hungarian foreign minister. It was his task to end the Dual Alliance with Germany that his father had helped forge in 1879. On 27 October he communicated to President Wilson that the Dual Monarchy was willing to recognize the rights of its subject nationalities and conclude a separate peace. This led to his resignation on 2 November. He was elected to the new national Hungarian parliament and in 1921 became leader of the Christian Democratic party. Andrássy, as a leading legitimist, was involved in attempts in 1921 to restore former king Charles IV to the Hungarian throne. He retired from parliament in 1926 and died in Budapest on 11 June 1929.

Spencer C. Tucker

References

Andrássy, Gyula. *Diplomacy and the War.* London: Bale and Danielson, 1921.

Hoensch, J. *A History of Modern Hungary.* New York: Longman, 1988.

Kann, Robert A. *A History of the Hapsburg Empire 1526–1918.* Berkeley: University of California Press, 1974.

Károlyi, Mihály. *Memoirs. Faith without Illusion.* London: Jonathan Cape, 1956.

Vermes, Gabor. *István Tisza. The Liberal Vision and Conservative Statecraft of a Magyar Nationalist.* New York: East European Monographs, 1985.

See also AUSTRIA-HUNGARY, HOME FRONT; KARL I, EMPEROR OF AUSTRIA; TISZA, COUNT ISTVÁN

Angell, Norman (1873–1967)

Immensely influential British economist, journalist, and antiwar activist. Norman Angell is the *nom de plume* of Ralph Norman Angell-Lane. Born on 26 December 1873 in Holbeach, England, Lane was educated in France and Geneva and spent his youth in the United States as a rancher, prospector, and newspaperman. A successful editor, Angell is best known for his book *The Great Illusion*, published in 1910.

Angell-Lane wrote *The Great Illusion* as a response to the growing militarism of British society, which reached a crisis point in the naval panic of 1909. Those who fueled the panic saw Imperial Germany as Great Britain's greatest political and commercial rival and as a predator that would rob Britain of its riches if it gained command of the sea. The only option, navalists argued, was to expand the Royal Navy. Reginald Viscount Esher, elder statesman of the British defense establishment, worried that such navalist propaganda would undermine the implementation of a balanced defense policy. He seized upon *The Great Illusion* as a possible check to British militarists. Esher convinced Sir Richard Garton, a civic-minded industrialist, to set up the Foundation for the Study of International Policy. The foundation's actual objective, however, was to propagate "Norman Angellism," as it appeared in *The Great Illusion* and the monthly journal *War and Peace*. But Norman Angellism was not a comprehensive theory. It merely restated a cluster of beliefs first introduced by Adam Smith and later codified by nineteenth-century liberals such as Richard Cobden and John Bright.

A man of Cobdenite convictions, Angell thought that war was outdated and irrational. Because of the interdependence of credit-built finance and industry throughout Europe, any nation that attacked another was actually committing economic suicide. As a result, the problem was not whether war enhanced or detracted from a nation's well-being, but that people thought it did so. According to Angell, it was the idea of war that was outdated, and the only solution was public reeducation. If people understood that free trade was the surest path to peace and that the basic economic interests of all nations were the same, they would turn their backs on war. Such themes made *The Great Illusion* a popular antimilitarist work on the eve of war, despite its narrow economic focus and naive faith in political rationalism. After the war his book was widely quoted, particularly in the Western democracies. Angell was awarded the Nobel Prize for Peace in 1933. Angell-Lane died on 7 October 1967 at Croydon, England.

Peter R. Faber

References

Angell, Norman. *The Great Illusion*. London: William Heinemann, 1910.
Mahan, Alfred T. *Armaments and Arbitration*. New York: Harper and Brothers, 1912.
Miller, J.D.B. *Norman Angell and the Futility of War*. London: St. Martin's, 1986.

Animals, Use of

Animals served myriad roles in World War I. Most shared a close working partnership with servicemen, continuing a prewar bond in which animals worked side by side with humans on farms, in mines, and at other tasks. A variety of animals were used in the war effort: Mules pulled ammunition wagons, gunner teams of horses drew artillery, and stray dogs and cats were adopted as pets and mascots. The servicemen's affection for these war animals bolstered morale at the front.

The primary animal associated with World War I is the horse. The war memorial to horses at St. Jude on the Hill, Hampstead, commemorates their service in this inscription: "Most obediently and often most painfully they died—faithful unto death." The Horse Memorial in Port Elizabeth, South Africa, also commemorates the role of horses in World War I.

Millions of horses pulled artillery and ambulances, carried ordnance and supplies, and served as cavalry mounts. Artillery effectiveness depended on their steadiness. The Royal Corps of Signals utilized horse-drawn cable wagons, and despatch riders were crucial to prompt messenger services.

In October of 1914 the Germans established the Commission for the Purchase of Horses to raid for Belgian horses, especially those of the Brabançonne and Ardennes draft horse breeds, which Belgian breeders had spent years genetically perfecting. The Germans shipped these to Germany where they were sold at auctions of "booty horses." Belgians were able to evacuate the Belgian royal horses, preventing their capture by the Germans. German requisitions created a gap in labor for Belgian agriculture as well as interrupting breeding programs. A transportation crisis occurred because there were no horses to pull wagons, and a fuel crisis existed by winter because without horses there was no means of transporting coal.

There were relatively few horses in England when the war began because of the increase in automobiles and bicycles for transport. To meet the war need, the British imported horses from America, Australia, Canada, and Argentina and requisitioned them from civilians—much to the chagrin of many horse owners. Children wrote Lord Kitchener to spare their ponies, and he responded with an order that no horses under fifteen hands in height would be confiscated. The Remount Service provided high-quality stallions to local farmers with broodmares to improve the supply of horses for potential military uses.

Horses and mules were vital on the Front because of the deep mud that prevented trucks and wagons from securing solid traction. Shells opened drainage systems, flooding the Front, and only horses and mules could get to trenches to deliver rations and supplies, as well as to move guns to new positions. Thousands of draft animals moved guns in France and Flanders. Each field gun required six to twelve horses to pull it.

Horses endured terrible conditions on the Front. They broke down carrying extreme loads of ammunition and supplies, and died of exhaustion. Frequently they were stolen when their riders were killed. Mud was deadly, as horses fell in shell holes, collapsed, or became impossibly mired. Some horses drowned.

Horses were clipped to prevent mange, but this left them vulnerable in cold weather. Many soldiers refused to shear their horses, realizing that a thick winter coat would protect them. Horses often went without adequate rations and water, and many were so hungry that they ate blankets and uniforms, including the buckles. Medical supplies were often scarce, and servicemen used bacon fat to soothe saddle sores. Mustard gas blistered horses' hides, and they suffered when they ate poisoned grass. At first, makeshift gauze nose plugs, safety-pinned in nostrils, were devised to help horses breathe during gas attacks. These were then replaced with gas masks, but the horses confused them with feedbags and quickly tore them apart.

Soldiers realized that the better-bred horses tended to suffer more from shellshock, bolting, stampeding, and going berserk at the sounds and smells of war, while less pedigreed but sturdier mounts were wise, often lying down and taking cover as bombs and shells peppered the trenches around them. At first horses shied at airplanes, but most adjusted to the whining engines as more and more planes flew above the Western Front.

The bond between soldier and horse was often close. A World War I recruiting poster pictured the partnership of servicemen with their horses.

War horses averaged ten thousand miles of travel on fronts during the Great War. Convalescent hospitals helped horses recover from war wounds and shock. Thousands of horses' corpses lined ditches on the Western Front, and older horses were destroyed rather than returned to their homes when the war concluded. Younger horses were designated for sale to slaughterhouses or employers, upsetting soldiers who wanted to see their devoted mounts peacefully destroyed rather than at the mercy of local residents.

One interesting development during the war was the use of dummy horses to deceive the enemy into thinking that troops were in one place when they actually had relocated. One of the reasons the Germans lost the war was that they ran out of horses. The Allies blocked the importation of remounts to Germany.

Dogs were also vital on the Western Front, especially because they could maneuver difficult, shell-pocked terrain that soldiers were unable to traverse. Their sense of hearing and smell is especially keen, and they could move faster than humans in inclement weather. Dogs trained at the war dog school at Shoeburyness to serve as sentinels in camps and factories. They also guarded prisoners, located casualties, carried ammunition and supplies, delivered first aid to the wounded, tracked escaped prisoners, and guided blinded soldiers.

Two dogs pulled each mitrailleuse (mounted machine gun) to the Front. Communication dogs carried field-telephone wires, messages, and pigeons. Gas masks were designed for war dogs. Dogs, wearing Red Cross coats, pulled miniature ambulances to retrieve the wounded.

Two thousand dogs trained in Britain for war service. Airedales, bloodhounds, and retrievers proved the best candidates. The War Office asked for more dogs to train, and citizens who found it difficult to feed themselves, let alone their dogs, donated animals. Other countries in Europe, especially Germany and France, had already trained war dogs during peacetime. Prisoners also helped care for and train dogs.

Many dogs died in World War I duty, but regulations prohibited decorating them for bravery. Servicemen made collar sacks in which accounts of each dog's deeds were publicized. Some famous dogs, such as Stubby, the only American dog smuggled to the European front, were honored. Not only did Stubby receive a chamois blanket from French villagers, but General John J. Pershing awarded him medals and Woodrow Wilson asked to shake his paw. The War Dog Memorial at Hartsdale canine cemetery commemorates war dogs' service.

A variety of other animals served various roles in the war. Jane was the mascot cat who liked to walk on the guns on the turret of HMS *Queen Elizabeth*. A pigeon named Cher Ami, who carried the message of the Lost Battalion trapped at Argonne, was stuffed and mounted after his death. On the other hand, the Germans massacred carrier pigeons at Bruges and Ostend to prevent espionage. The Imperial Camel Corps navigated desert sands.

A variety of humane organizations, such as the Blue Cross Society, provided relief services including knitted pads to put under saddles to prevent sores. Food shortages necessitated that war animals be slaughtered, and starving soldiers often had to resort to stripping meat from their beloved horses killed by shellfire. Without proper inspection of such meat sources, however, disease abounded and was transmitted by flies that hovered over meat stalls and carcasses.

When the war ended, service animals seemed to realize that their service was concluded. They paraded into liberated towns, flowers fastened to bridles and collars. The War Office did not honor war animals so positively. Most horses were either slaughtered or sold. Many dogs and cats returned home with their soldiers, but others were abandoned to scavenge for themselves.

Elizabeth D. Schafer

References

Baynes, E.H. *Animal Heroes of the Great War*. New York: Macmillan, 1927.

Cooper, Jilly. *Animals in War*. London: Imperial War Museum, 1983.

Osman, A.H. *Pigeons in the Great War: A Complete History of the Carrier Pigeon Service*. London: Racing Pigeon, 1929.

Richardson, Colonel Edwin H., and Blanche Richardson. *Fifty Years With Dogs*. London: Hutchinson, 1950.

Rohan, J. Rags: *The Story of a Dog Who Went to War*. New York: Harper, 1930.

Schwartzkopf, Olaf. "The Horse in the Present War," *American Veterinary Review* 47 (June 1915): 368.

Antiaircraft Weapons

World War I was the first true test of the value of antiaircraft artillery. In earlier wars it had been extremely rare for ground-based air defenses to shoot down aircraft. For example, only one airplane was brought down in this manner in the Italo-Turkish War of 1912. It was advances made after 1914 that made it possible for antiaircraft guns to form permanent units within armies of the warring nations. The essential point about antiaircraft artillery in the First World War is that its effectiveness rose steadily throughout the war. That was made possible by advances in sound location, searchlights, and crew training.

In the early years of the war, most antiaircraft weapons were improvised and ineffective. For instance, infantrymen would often fire their rifles at strafing planes. That was largely ineffective and served principally as a morale boost for the soldiers. Later, .30- and .50-caliber machine guns provided a fixed defense against attacking aircraft. These relied on rudimentary sighting devices to allow those firing the guns to lead the planes.

Three-inch artillery pieces dominated what little antiaircraft artillery existed in World War I. The main problem for antiaircraft gunners during the war rested with the shells rather than the guns. For the gunners the problem was that of hitting an aerial target capable of performing rapid three-dimensional maneuvers. As a result, time-fused shells were the main focus of antiaircraft research. They could be fired in large quantities, providing a screen of flying shrapnel and improving the likelihood of damaging enemy planes.

The main thrust of research on time-fused explosive shells took place in Britain. German zeppelin raids on British and French cities prompted this undertaking. What was needed was a form of incendiary shell that would ignite the hydrogen contained in the airships.

This exposed another problem. British researchers believed erroneously that there was a layer of inert gas between the outer cover of the airships and the gas bags, produced by rerouting exhaust gases from the engines. Researchers believed that antiaircraft shells should have delicate fuses that would detonate upon penetrating the outer fabric envelope. Otherwise, the shrapnel would merely pass through the airship without causing a fire.

W.R. Hodgkinson conducted research into the problem at Woolwich. The result was an incendiary filled with thermit (ferric oxide and aluminum). The shell met with minimal success in the London raids of 1915 and 1916, when it was discovered that the zeppelins could rapidly climb out of antiaircraft range.

The introduction of the German Gotha bomber in 1917 led the Allies to make strides in antiaircraft techniques and training. New powerful searchlights were introduced as well as acoustic devices to aid in locating enemy planes prior to the beginning of an air raid. The Allies also made advances in wireless communication between antiaircraft batteries, compensation tables for wind speed, separate fuses for different barometric pressures, and fuses that were more resilient in extreme weather conditions.

Better training of antiaircraft crews was another Allied advancement. In 1918 the British formed the "Traveling Ballistic Party" to tour the Western Front and instruct battery crews on proper techniques and to report back to Britain on conditions. It was so successful that it was made a permanent scientific party in France and became the forerunner of the operational research sections used successfully by the United States and Great Britain during World War II.

There were few advances made in antiaircraft guns during World War I. Advances rested principally in the shells and the methods by which the guns were operated. One can see the results of these advances in the statistics. British rounds per aircraft shot down fell from 8,000 in 1917 to 4,550 in 1918. French rounds per claim dropped from 11,000 in 1916 to 7,000 in 1918, and German figures dropped from 11,558 in 1915 to 5,040 in 1918. These are impressive improvements, which led to successful widespread use of antiaircraft artillery in later wars.

Mark A. Macina

References

Dupuy, Trevor N. *The Evolution of Weapons and Warfare.* Fairfax, Va.: Hero, 1984.

Hartcup, Guy. *The War of Invention—Scientific Developments, 1914–1918.* New York: Brassey's Defense Publishers, 1988.

Werrell, Kenneth P. *Archie, Flak, AAA and SAM—A Short Operational History of Ground-Based Air Defense.* Maxwell Air Force Base, Ala.: Air University Press, 1988.

Anzac

Acronym for the Australian and New Zealand Army Corps. During the Great War Australia formed six infantry divisions and five light horse brigades for the Australian Imperial Force (AIF), which served on three continents in defense of British imperial interests. Likewise, New Zealand dispatched an infantry division and a brigade of mounted rifles that fought alongside the Australians in the Middle East, at Gallipoli, and in the trenches of the Western Front. By the end of the war, the AIF had grown to the size of a regular army, with its own medical system, veterinary detachments, flying corps, cyclist battalions, and even armored-car batteries.

Shortly after the outbreak of war, both Australia and New Zealand offered to raise troops for service overseas. A grateful British government quickly accepted, and the first contingents began mobilization before the end of August. The New Zealand Expeditionary Force, numbering 8,000 troops, arrived in Australia in October of 1914, where it joined the Australian Imperial Force. The AIF at this point consisted of the 1st Australian Infantry Division, three light horse brigades, plus assorted engineer, artillery, signal, transport, and medical units. The organizer of the AIF, and commander of its 1st Division, was the former chief of the Australian general staff, Major General Sir William Throsby Bridges. Academic, awkward, and highly unpopular, Bridges nevertheless performed well in transforming eager but ill-disciplined recruits and inexperienced officers into a modern, albeit rudimentarily trained, fighting force.

On 1 November 1914 the first contingents sailed from Western Australia bound for Great Britain through the Suez Canal. A day later news arrived that Turkey had entered the war, opening the possibility that the force might be diverted to duty in the Middle East. Shortly after passing Aden, Bridges was ordered to debark his men at Port Said, and by early December the entire force was ensconced in training camps around Cairo.

At the same time Lord Kitchener assigned Major General Sir William R. Birdwood to organize the newly arrived units into the Australian and New Zealand Army Corps. The corps headquarters was a British formation and would remain so throughout the war, even though virtually all of its subordinate units were Australasian. Birdwood himself was a British officer who had served most of his career in India. A tactician of middling skill, Birdwood was able, through sheer affability, forthrightness, and personal bravery, to overcome the natural distrust of his "Diggers" and "Kiwis" for aristocratic English officers.

For the next several months, Birdwood put his charges through an intensive training program, enlivened by the Anzacs' minor role in repelling a Turkish attack against the Suez Canal in February of 1915.

The corps' first major action took place in April of 1915, when elements of the 1st Australian and New Zealand Divisions splashed ashore on the Gallipoli Peninsula at what came to be known as Anzac Cove. The exuberant Anzacs pushed up onto the ridges surrounding the landing site, but the competence of their leaders did not match the spirit of the men. Difficulties in controlling the assault, logistical muddles on the beach, and an unexpectedly tenacious Turkish defense doomed the corps to a miserable and ultimately fruitless campaign, clinging to a shallow beachhead, until they were evacuated in January of 1916. The attack on the Dardanelles cost the Anzacs over 35,000 casualties: one in every hundred New Zealand males of military age died among the ridges above Anzac Cove.

In Egypt some 40,000 replacements were on hand, with an additional 50,000 scheduled to arrive soon. From this manpower pool three new Australian divisions were formed, along with a second Anzac corps. With no immediate prospect for their employment in the Middle East, the Anzacs were slated for duty on the Western Front. In March of 1916 the 1st Anzac Corps began arriving in France, followed three months later by its sister corps. At first, as the Anzacs were acclimatized to France through short stints in the trenches of peaceful sectors, it seemed to the veterans of Gallipoli a far more pleasant sort of war.

By late summer that illusion had been shattered. The sanguinary battles along the Somme

drew in both Anzac corps. 1st Anzac lost 23,000 men along Pozières Ridge in late July and early August of 1916, while the 5th Australian Division suffered over 5,000 casualties in just twenty-four hours around Fromelles. This brutal initiation foreshadowed two more long years of fighting in northern France. Australians and New Zealanders fought along the Hindenburg Line, at Bullecourt, Messines, Ypres, and in the desperate effort to stem the tide of Germany's spring 1918 offensive. The strain of supporting two full corps in the meat grinder of the trenches became nearly intolerable for the two island nations, but both governments declined to break up any of the existing formations to provide replacements for the others. By the end of the war, the AIF in France had reached the end of its manpower tether.

In contrast to the deadlocked infantry fighting in France, the mounted arm of the AIF participated in the war of maneuver taking place in the Middle East. Anzac horsemen fought through the Sinai and Palestine under General Edmund Allenby, a campaign featuring the near-legendary charge of the Light Horse at Beersheba in October of 1917 and culminating in the capture of Damascus, which troopers of the 3rd Australian Light Horse Brigade entered on 30 September 1918.

Steven Eden

References

Bean, C.E.W., et al. *The Official History of Australia in the War of 1914–1918.* Edited by Robert O'Neill. 12 Vols. St. Lucia, Queensland: University of Queensland Press, 1984.
Laffin, John. *Anzacs at War.* New York: Abelard-Schuman, 1965.

See also GALLIPOLI CAMPAIGN; PALESTINE AND SYRIA

Arab Revolt, 1916–18

The Arab Revolt, expressing Arab nationalism and desire for independence, erupted in the Hejaz in 1916. Prior to World War I Arab leaders had become disillusioned with the new Turkish regime of the Young Turks, which opposed and suppressed Arab nationalism and culture. Under the Turkish constitution of 1909 the Arabs sent representatives to the imperial parliament in Constantinople where they sought Arab rights. Arab newspapers and journals also propagated nationalism, and new political organizations, some of which were secret, sought Arab freedom. General strikes in Beirut and Damascus stopped all communications and precipitated demonstrations of Arab nationalism. Recognizing the Arab movement, the Turkish government sent a representative to negotiate with Arab leaders in Paris in 1913 at the first General Arab Congress. The resulting pact authorized Arab seats in parliament and Arabic as the language of instruction in public schools. The Arabs welcomed the pact, but it was never implemented.

In 1914 the Arabs of Syria, Palestine, Iraq, the western provinces of Arabia, and some of the Arabs in Yemen were under direct Ottoman rule. Ibn-Ali Hussein was sharif of Mecca. He had been named sharif in 1908 over the objections of Caliph and Sultan Abdul Hamid. Although nominal head of the Hejaz, one of the western provinces of Arabia under Turkish control, Hussein was expected to obey orders from Constantinople. Immediately before the war, Turkey tightened control over the Arabs by sending troops into Arab lands and instructing Hussein to introduce conscription in the Hejaz. Hussein's sons, Faisal and Abdullah, knew the Arab leaders in Turkish territory and were sympathetic to the Arab national movement. Accordingly, Hussein became the spokesman for this movement, which by 1914 involved all Arab countries.

The Turks had made concessions to certain foreign powers, including extraterritorial rights to the Christian states in Palestine. By 1914 Germany was gaining prestige among the Arabs. Although British influence in Arab lands was significant, the Turks were not favorably disposed toward the British.

The Turkish sultan was also the caliph. These were two separate offices, but Abdul Hamid's predecessor had usurped the religious title. The caliph was the nominal head of orthodox Islam, but Great Britain dominated the Moslem world. British Indian Moslem subjects outnumbered all Turks and Arabs worldwide. At the outbreak of World War I Lord Kitchener was high commissioner in Egypt. Although Kitchener failed to grasp the difference between the secular office of sultan and the religious office of caliph, he foresaw a Turko-German alliance as a probable cause of unrest among Indian Moslems (in fact, a total misreading of the situation). Accordingly, Kitchener sought to assist the Arab movement for independence by communicating with Hussein before the Turko-German alliance.

Hussein knew that British support was contingent on a Turkish declaration of war against the Allies. Nevertheless, when Turkey entered the war, Hussein hesitated. Unsure about who would win, he did not want to jeopardize his position.

With the declaration of war in 1914, relations between the Arabs and the Turks deteriorated. When Turkey entered the war, Kitchener, now secretary of state for war, sent a message to Hussein on 31 October 1914, pledging British support for Arab independence should the Arabs enter the war on the British side. Hussein's principal communication with the British was with Sir Henry McMahon, who succeeded Kitchener as British high commissioner in Egypt. Subsequent British encouragement for the Arab movement came more from Cairo than from London.

Hussein's second son, Abdullah, favored a British alliance; Faisal, however, was suspicious of Allied intentions. In January of 1915 Hussein received a message from Arab leaders in Syria and Iraq stating that political leaders and senior Arab officers in the Turkish army favored an Arab revolt. In the spring Faisal visited Damascus, was initiated into the secret Arab societies, and discovered that their members had the same apprehensions as he about European intentions. These Arab leaders, and those in Egypt, expressed approval of an Arab revolt provided they could obtain a guarantee of Arab independence. Thus, they drew up the Damascus Protocol as a basis for an alliance with Great Britain. In a letter to the British dated 14 July 1915, Hussein declared himself for the revolt by presenting the Damascus Protocol as the condition for Arab entry into the war. On 15 October 1915 MacMahon sent a letter to Hussein in which the British agreed to recognize and support Arab independence.

In the Ottoman army, Arabs served with other Ottoman subjects. Arab officers served in military and civilian capacities on the same basis as the Turks, and, as with officers in other armies, they took an oath of allegiance to their sovereign. With the outbreak of World War I, they fought with the Turks against the Allies in Gallipoli, Mesopotamia, and Palestine. Nevertheless, many Arabs considered themselves Arab patriots rather than Ottoman subjects, and they joined the secret societies. Once the war began, these Arabs could expect to achieve their objectives only if Turkey were defeated.

Attempting to obliterate the roots of Arab nationalism, the Turks inaugurated a reign of terror in Syria, where they hanged Arab patriots as traitors. A loathing of the Turks, fear, and a desire for revenge permeated the Arabs, and Arab refugees thronged to Mecca to persuade Hussein to join the Allies. To insure his position with the Allies, Hussein hesitated until early 1916, when he believed he had achieved the desired agreement. The Arab Revolt was precipitated by the arrival of Turkish troops, via the Pilgrim Railway, to reinforce the garrison of Medina. Being impatient, Faisal and Abdullah cut the railroad north of Medina. Following negotiations, the Arabs entered the war on the Allied side and initiated the Arab revolt. Fighting began on 5 June 1916. Although Hussein had joined the Allies, he did not have guarantees from France.

The exact significance of the Arab Revolt to the Allied cause in World War I has been much debated. It certainly did frustrate a Turko-German expedition to Arabia and the possible seizure of Aden. The Arabs bore a large share of the fighting, especially on the eastern flank of the British forces, as they fought north from Egypt and drove toward Damascus. In the spring of 1917 General Sir Archibald Murray realized that the Turks had more troops committed against the Arabs than against the British in Palestine. During General Sir Edmund Allenby's campaign in Palestine, Faisal's army was fighting almost the same number of Turkish troops east of the Jordan River as the British faced west of the river. Although T.E. Lawrence has received considerable credit for Arab successes against the Turks, the real leader of the revolt was Faisal, who did much to bring it about before Lawrence arrived on the scene. The climax of the Arab Revolt came in October of 1918 when Faisal entered Damascus at the head of his army. This event had reverberations throughout the Arab world; it freed the Arabs from Turkish domination and returned Arab land to Arab rule.

Montecue J. Lowry

References

Aldington, Richard. *Lawrence of Arabia.* London: Collins, 1955.
Izzeddin, Nejla. *The Arab World: Past, Present, and Future.* Chicago: Henry Regnery, 1953.
Pears, Edwin. "The Arab Revolt." *Living Age* 290 (July–September 1916): 437–40.
Thomas, Bertram. *The Arabs.* Garden City, N.Y.: Doubleday, Doran, 1937.
Thomas, Lowell. *With Lawrence in Arabia.* New York: Garden City, 1924.

See also ABDULLAH, IBN-HUSSEIN, EMIR; ALLENBY, EDMUND; EGYPT; FAISAL, PRINCE; HUSSEIN, IBN-ALI; IBN SA'UD, KING; LAWRENCE, T.E.; MESOPOTAMIA; PALESTINE AND SYRIA

Armaments Production

It was widely held before the outbreak of World War I that modern nations could not stand the strain of a protracted struggle. Available stocks of munitions and war matériel, supplemented by peacetime systems of armaments production, were deemed sufficient to meet military needs in case of war. No prewar plans were made to deal with the issues of industrial manpower, resources, or mobilization of the civilian economy. These prewar assumptions were quickly shattered by the initial campaigns of the war. Within months of the beginning of the conflict, available stocks of ammunition were all but depleted, and current production levels, based on peacetime organization, fell well short of the demands of the battlefield. The great matériel requirements of the armies engaged in the war forced the European powers to convert from peacetime to wartime economic conditions.

Britain and France were the most successful among the Allied powers in mobilizing manpower and resources for armaments production. Prior to 1914, Britain's system of munitions supply was designed chiefly to meet the needs of the navy and a small six-division army. Army requirements were expected to be met by Woolwich Arsenal and a number of smaller government-operated arms and gunpowder factories, rounded out by contracts issued to private firms and foreign sources. Once war began, the BEF was short on heavy artillery, machine guns, and high-explosive shells. Shell output ran at less than thirty-five rounds a day. The situation was further complicated by a shortage of machine tools and by out-of-date production methods.

By October of 1914, however, over three thousand firms were employed in armaments production. Labor shortages hampered production, as many skilled workers enlisted in the army. During the first four months of 1915 alone, more than 10,000 men in the engineering trades joined the colors. Efforts to rapidly increase production rates served in the short run only to delay critically needed guns and shells for the front. At the start of the war a cabinet committee on munitions was formed. Expert advice was sought from knowledgeable civilians on how to improve production levels. Britain was divided into manufacturing districts under the supervision of local authorities coordinated by the War Office Armaments Output Committee, formed in 1915. To compensate for the loss of skilled men to the army, women were increasingly used in factory work. It took more than a year to establish a workable system of exemptions for skilled men. Badges and certificates were issued to recall industrial workers from army service. As Britain experienced an unprecedented expansion of its war industries, greater reliance was placed on the use of unskilled labor and mass production machines.

Since the start of the war, BEF Commander General Sir John French had complained about the chronic shortage of shells. This complaint was picked up by the press and led to a debate in the House of Commons. By June of 1915 the Ministry of Munitions had been created under the dynamic leadership of David Lloyd George. The ministry had wide authority over all aspects of munitions production, from labor to raw materials. Nevertheless, problems of shell reliability and output were not fully resolved until 1917. By the end of the war, British armaments production proved sufficient to supply a sixty-division army as well as other Allied requirements.

Across the Channel, France experienced many of the same problems as Britain in shifting from a peacetime to a wartime economy. Heavy fighting in the initial phases of the war had rapidly depleted prewar stocks. Shortages of shells, explosives, and skilled workers were widespread. During the opening months of the war the French army expended an average of thirty thousand 75mm rounds per day, but only ten thousand rounds were produced daily. The German invasion and occupation of northeastern provinces deprived France of valuable raw materials and factories. By early 1915 the French government had moved to centralize control over armaments production. Skilled workers were recalled from military service and mass-production machinery introduced. In ad-

dition, both Britain and France turned to the United States to make up shortages in munitions and other war matériel. Washington took the position that the sale of munitions to the Allies did not violate U.S. neutrality.

Among the major Allied powers, Russia was the least prepared to meet the demands of modern war. Russia's industrial establishment was backward and inefficient by Western standards. Heavy reliance was placed on manufactured goods and machinery imported from Germany. With the outbreak of war Russia's limited supply of skilled manpower was absorbed into the vast Russian army. Increasingly, women, refugees, and prisoners of war were used to replace these men, with limited results. Russian shell production ran at 360,000 shells a month, but the army demanded 1.5 million. Artillery batteries received orders to economize on shells, with some units allowed fewer than four rounds a day. Russian infantry faced the confusion of using rifles of different calibers. Efforts to purchase rifles outside the country proved futile. The Russian predicament was made worse by the country's woefully inadequate transportation system and its isolation from the Allies. Any supplies shipped into Russia had to go to Vladivostok in Asia, thousands of miles from the front, or to the isolated northern ports of Archangel and Murmansk. The railway system was not able to cope with the demands placed on it. Large quantities of supplies shipped to the ports simply sat unused on the docks. The strain of the war was to push Russia into revolution.

Germany entered the conflict with no preparations for a long war. The general staff had concentrated on preparing the Schlieffen Plan, which was designed to deliver an early knockout blow to France and Russia, but by November of 1914 the plan had failed to win a quick victory. The war settled into a pattern of attrition and stalemate that stretched along the trenches that ran from Switzerland to the sea. German stocks of munitions were down to four days' worth, and by late 1914 there were less than six months' worth of the raw materials needed for war production. While the prewar German economy was among the strongest in Europe, leading in steel production and chemicals, it was short of many critical raw materials needed to wage a modern war. Copper, mercury, tin, nickel, bauxite, saltpetre, petroleum, lubricants, and metals for making high-quality steel—all had to be imported into

Germany before the war. With the imposition of the Allied naval blockade, Germany's industrial effort concentrated on finding substitute materials and utilizing new processes to overcome shortages.

The key figure in the mobilization of Germany for war was the experienced industrialist Walther Rathenau. Early in the war he approached the war ministry with plans for centralizing government control over raw materials and production. Rathenau gained the support of the Prussian minister of war Erich von Falkenhayn. This led to the creation of the War Raw Materials Department (*Kriegsrohstoff-abteilung*), or KRA. After Rathenau compiled a list of available German resources, the KRA was given authority to mobilize the resources for war production. A system of war raw materials corporations, private companies under government auspices, was created. These companies covered everything from metals to chemicals.

Plans for the distribution of valuable industrial manpower were nonexistent before the war. Skilled labor was drawn into the army in great numbers without regard for the impact on industrial production. In an effort to set some guidelines for exemptions of skilled men from military service, the Exports and Exemptions Office was created. German industrialists were encouraged to make up for labor shortages by shifting to unskilled labor.

The greatest success story of Germany's wartime armaments industry was in the area of munitions production. With the Allied blockade in place, Germany was cut off from foreign sources of the nitrates, chiefly saltpetre from Chile, essential for the production of explosives. The solution came with the adoption of the prewar Haber-Bosch process, which extracted nitrates from the atmosphere. Too expensive in peacetime, the process kept the German army in the war with an adequate supply of munitions. More and more plants were given over to the Haber-Bosch process in order to keep up with the ever-rising demands of the army. Yet, in a country with growing food shortages, the focus on the production of nitrates for military needs deprived German agriculture of essential fertilizers.

Less successful in meeting the demands of war was Germany's Austro-Hungarian ally. Lacking a large industrial base, the Austro-Hungarian industry was mostly restricted to small firms. The war ministry and the ministry of commerce adopted a cooperative approach to the issues of industrial mobilization. Suffi-

cient levels of economic centralization were never achieved. The efficiency of the Austro-Hungarian economic system was further hampered by the policy of splitting war production between Austria and Hungary.

The ability of the European powers to meet the challenges of armaments production varied. Britain, France, and Germany, Europe's most industrialized states, were the most successful in meeting the demands of the war, with the Western Allies having the great advantage of access to imported war supplies and raw materials. The Austro-Hungarian Empire and Russia proved much less successful. World War I demonstrated that manpower is not sufficient to win a great war; industrial mobilization is equally important.

Van Michael Leslie

References

Bourne, J.M. *Britain and the Great War 1914–1918*. London: Edward Arnold, 1989.

Chambers, Frank. *The War Behind the War 1914–1919*. New York: Harcourt, Brace, 1939.

Craig, Gordon A. *Germany 1866–1945*. New York: Oxford University Press, 1978.

Edmonds, Sir James E. *A Short History of World War I*. London: Oxford University Press, 1951.

See also LLOYD GEORGE, DAVID; RATHENAU, WALTHER

Armenia (1914–22)

The state of Armenia has existed in one form or another since the sixth century B.C. Armenia has been controlled by numerous empires, including the Median, Persian, Roman, and Byzantine. In 300 A.D. Armenians broke with Persia and the East by adopting Christianity as their national religion. In 1405, however, Armenia was divided between the Ottoman Empire and Persia. Russian eighteenth-century expansion annexed territory in the Transcaucasian area, including the northern section of the Armenian plateau. This led to the development of a Russian Armenia and a Turkish Armenia.

During World War I, Russia conquered parts of Turkish Armenia. Many Armenians favored a Russian victory and, early in 1915, volunteers from the Caucasus region formed battalions to fight on the Russian side. In

1915, in reprisal for this and for partisan attacks by Armenians on Turkish forces, Constantinople ordered some 1,750,000 Armenians deported to the deserts of Syria and Mesopotamia. At least 800,000 perished in the desert en route to their destinations. Meanwhile, in 1916 the Russians conquered large parts of Turkish Armenia, Georgia, and Azerbaijan, and formed a Transcaucasian alliance with these nations. This alliance dissolved during the 1917 Russian revolution. The Bolsheviks recalled troops from Armenia, leaving the country unprotected. Thus Armenia came under Ottoman rule again.

Turkish defeat and the end of World War I on 11 November 1918 did not put an end to the Armenian question. Allied leaders had promised to reestablish an independent Armenia that would embrace its historic boundaries and provinces. Although the Allied forces supported an Armenian state, they were reluctant to take specific steps to make this reality. The problem was that Armenians were widely scattered and did not constitute a distinct majority of the population where they were living. The Treaty of Sèvres of 10 August 1920 proclaimed Armenia an independent state; the Turkish leadership, however, refused to recognize the treaty. They did not want Armenia to be independent of Turkey, fearing that Russia would soon conquer it.

By 1922 Armenia, Georgia, and Azerbaijan were united as the Transcaucasian Soviet Federated Socialist Republic. The Soviet constitution of 1936 accorded Armenia the status of a Republic of the USSR.

Meredith L. Bragg

References

Helmreich, Paul Christian. *From Paris to Sèvres: The Partition of the Ottoman Empire at the Peace Conference of 1919–1920.* Columbus: Ohio State University Press, 1974.

Hovannisian, Richard G. *Armenia on the Road to Independence 1918.* Berkeley: University of California Press, 1967.

Kurkjian, Vahan M. *A History of Armenia.* New York: Armenian General Benevolent Union of America, 1959.

Toynbee, Arnold J. *Armenian Atrocities: The Murder of a Nation.* New York: Hodder and Stoughton, 1915.

———. *The Treatment of Armenians in the Ottoman Empire, 1915–1916.* London: Sir Joseph Causton and Sons, 1916.

See also ATROCITIES; CAUCASUS FRONT, 1914–18; SÈVRES, TREATY OF

Armistice, at Compiègne (11 November 1918)

By late summer 1918, after four years of war, German armed forces neared exhaustion on the Western Front. The Allied naval blockade was slowly starving the German civilian population. Increased Allied military pressure, caused by a fourteen-mile deep British breakthrough on the Somme River near Amiens on 8 August ("the black day of the German Army"), had produced a crisis within the German high command. During a conference at Spa, Belgium, on 13–14 August, Field Marshal Paul von Hindenburg and General Erich Ludendorff informed Chancellor Count Georg von Hertling, Secretary of State Paul von Hintze, and Kaiser Wilhelm II that the German army could no longer force an enemy surrender through offensive action. Because German forces could not hope to win a victory by stalemate or through a defensive strategy, the war would have to be ended by diplomacy.

Following their shocking announcement, Hindenburg and Ludendorff returned to France to attempt to stabilize the front and to await German diplomatic moves. Both officers hoped that some action would be taken while the Hindenburg Line was still intact, thereby allowing the Germans a stronger bargaining position, but the government equivocated until 8 September. German officials continued to hesitate, even after Austria-Hungary informed Germany that it could hold its front against the Italians only until the start of winter.

The crisis deepened on 26 September 1918 when American troops under General John J. Pershing broke the Hindenburg Line in the Argonne, followed by further British advances in Picardy and Flanders. Two days later, as the Allied offensive on the Western Front continued unabated, the Hertling government fell. These two events convinced Ludendorff and Hindenburg that the time was again right to push the government to open peace negotiations. As a preparatory step, on 2 October Ludendorff, with Kaiser Wilhelm's consent, sent Major Freiherr von dem Busche-Ippenburg to the Reichstag to explain the deteriorating military situation. The news that Germany could not hope to win the war shocked Reichstag members, who had been kept in ignorance of the true military situation of the Central Powers. It also came amid news of the unconditional surrender of Bulgaria three days earlier. These revelations coupled with the unauthorized public release of Ludendorff's dire estimate of the military situation and the smashing of the Hindenburg Line, panicked the members of the Reichstag. A new "peace" government was formed by Prince Maximilian von Baden the next day.

On 5 October 1918, representatives of the new German government sent the first of several notes through Swiss envoys to American President Woodrow Wilson indicating a desire to begin negotiations leading to an armistice. The note began a flurry of exchanges between Berlin and Washington over the next several weeks.

In the first note, Chancellor Max asked Wilson for help in restoring the peace and encouraged him to inform the other Allies of his request and to send representatives to open negotiations. At the same time, Max signified German acceptance of the president's Fourteen Points (announced to Congress in January of 1918) and Five Points (in his Fourth Liberty Loan speech, delivered in New York City on 27 September 1918) as a basis for peace.

President Wilson replied on 8 October that no compromise could be made with an autocracy, and he demanded to know if Germany would accept in unequivocal language terms laid down by him. Wilson also asked whether Max was speaking for the German people or merely acting for the kaiser and his military advisors. The president then indicated that he could not propose the cessation of hostilities while the armies of the Central Powers still held Allied soil, but he did offer to handle future communications for the Allied side.

German Foreign Minister Dr. Wilhelm Solf replied for Max on 12 October, stating that if the powers associated with the United States also accepted the Fourteen Points and the Five Points as the basis for peace, then Germany would be willing to begin discussions. Solf added that the government for which Max spoke had been appointed in agreement with the Reichstag, and that the chancellor was acting for that body and the German people, not the kaiser. The German government, according to Max, would evacuate occupied territory as Wilson requested, and the chancellor suggested the creation of a mixed commission to make the necessary arrangements.

When news of the German notes became public, many Allied representatives were alarmed by the implication that the German armies were seeking to withdraw unmolested within their own borders, where they could continue the war under more favorable conditions. Many feared a "peace trap" and found the idea of continued negotiations about terms, as opposed to a simple unconditional German surrender, repugnant. Wilson, who saw himself as the Entente's spokesman, had put the chancellor on record and sent a reply to Germany on 18 October. Wilson stated that the conditions of the armistice, especially concerning reparations and the evacuation of occupied territories, were questions to be resolved by Allied military leaders. Wilson could not recommend any arrangement that did not safeguard the military supremacy of the Allies, or any armistice at all while German U-boats persisted in sinking passenger ships at sea and while the retreating German army looted villages, harassed civilians, and sought to inflict further Allied casualties. Wilson reminded the German government that the destruction of autocracy and arbitrary power was one of the conditions of peace, and the Germans needed to provide some form of proof that such reforms were being made.

Following the receipt of Wilson's statement, a hurried council was held in Berlin between the kaiser and his military chiefs. Since the August meeting at Spa, the military situation had temporarily stabilized. Pershing's drive was being contained, the German armies were retreating in good order elsewhere, and the general Allied pursuit was slowing under difficult conditions. Both Ludendorff, who was angered by Wilson's latest note, and the German admiralty—in a complete about face—expressed their desire to fight on while continuing to negotiate for better terms.

On 20 October the German government sent a third note, agreeing to Wilson's conditions and offering assurances that the autocracy would be overthrown with the peace and that the German negotiators were speaking for the German people and not the kaiser. The Germans denied, however, that their armies were committing atrocities in the occupied territories as part of official policy, but they did agree to stop unrestricted submarine warfare against passenger ships.

Wilson's reply of 23 October was harsh and closed the door to any further discussion without an explicit German guarantee that they were willing to surrender on Allied terms. The note emphasized that the German military was to be rendered incapable of further effort before an armistice was considered. While Wilson indicated his willingness to transmit the latest German correspondence to the Allies, he stated that they would not deal with the Hohenzollern dynasty or with any cabinet representing them. No armistice could take place until the kaiser had left the throne and the general staff had surrendered its governing power.

On receiving word of Wilson's reply and with the military forces of the Central Powers in full retreat on all fronts, Ludendorff and Hindenburg traveled to Berlin on 24 October to insist that the government fight on and to tell the troops that Wilson's latest communication consisted of a virtually unacceptable demand for unconditional surrender. Their actions, now completely contrary to the peace policy being pursued by Chancellor Max, Secretary of State Matthias Erzberger, Foreign Secretary Solf, and Philip Scheidemann, forced the civilian leaders to supersede the Army High Command and demand Ludendorff's resignation on 26 October, an act that in effect stripped the military of its last hold over the German government. Ludendorff resigned that same day, with the kaiser's approval, and went into hiding in Berlin. He was replaced as quartermaster general by Wilhelm Groener. This change of events helped the German army escape responsibility for defeat (the "Stab in the Back" myth).

Fearing that the Allies would no longer tolerate delays, another note was delivered on 27 October, informing Wilson that massive reforms were taking place in Germany. In addition, Max now made a direct request for an armistice and for Allied proposals to bring it about. The note declared that peace negotiations were being requested by a government of the people, who had the constitutional authority to make the necessary decisions, and that the military was also responsible to this authority.

The next day the Germany admiralty ordered the High Seas Fleet to sea for a last suicidal clash with the Allied navies. Instead of obeying as ordered, sailors in the fleet mutinied, sparking other challenges to authority throughout Germany. Sensing the total breakdown of law and order in the empire, Kaiser Wilhelm II left Berlin for Spa to wait out events. At the same time, the Inter-Allied War Council of Pre-mier Georges Clemenceau, Prime Minister David Lloyd George, Marshal Ferdinand Foch, and Colonel Edward House mulled over the contents of the latest German note at Versailles and began to frame armistice terms. In the meantime, on 31 October the Ottoman Empire surrendered unconditionally, and, after suffering a tremendous defeat at Italian hands in the Battle of Vittorio-Veneto on the Piave River, the Austro-Hungarian Empire surrendered unconditionally on 4 November 1918.

Diplomatic correspondence closed on 1 November, when President Wilson informed the German government that the Allied powers were willing to make peace on the basis of the Fourteen Points, although Great Britain reserved freedom of action in regard to freedom of the seas as did France in the matter of reparations. Terms, Wilson continued, could be had by applying to the Allied commander in the field, Marshal Foch, who was fully authorized to communicate the Allied demands. On 6 November the German government sent word that an armistice delegation was leaving Berlin and would seek to enter the lines to confer with Foch. The delegation traveled to Spa, where they were informed by wire of the route to be followed and the point in the French lines where they would be received. The following day was spent in making slow progress through the picket lines south, through the Hindenburg Line, to the chateau of the Marquis de l'Aigle at Francport. Firing was stopped at the point in the lines where the commission was to arrive on 7 November, and, on the next day, Friday, a special train brought them to a siding in the Forest of Compiègne, near the village of Rethondes, where Marshal Foch and General Weygand waited in Foch's rail car with the British representative, First Sea Lord of the Admiralty Sir Rosslyn E. Wemyss. No American, Italian, or Belgian representatives were present.

The German delegation consisted of its leader, Secretary of State Matthias Erzberger, Major General Detlev von Winterfeldt, Naval Captain Ernst Vanselow, and Minister Plenipotentiary Count Alfred von Oberndorff. When the delegation had been seated in the rail car, the Allied terms were read, a process that took two hours because of frequent pauses for translations. The terms demanded that the German army evacuate all occupied areas in Belgium, France, Alsace-Lorraine, and Luxembourg by 25 November and retreat to points twenty miles east of the Rhine River. Germany was to surrender territory on the left bank of the Rhine river, including river crossings at Mainz, Coblenz, and Cologne, while turning over bridgeheads of at least a thirty-kilometer radius to the Allies. In addition, Germany was required to create a neutral zone on the west bank of the Rhine River running from the Netherlands to the Swiss frontier, no later than 11 December. Germany was to pay all costs associated with the Allied occupation.

Vast quantities of war matériel were to be turned over to the Allies, including all U-boats, five thousand trucks, two thousand aircraft, and the German navy, which was to be disarmed and interned in neutral or Allied-controlled ports. Germany was also to surrender all rail lines in Belgium, Luxembourg, and Alsace-Lorraine, as well as five thousand locomotives and 150,000 railroad cars. In the east, Germany was required to abrogate the treaties of Bucharest and Brest-Litovsk and withdraw all troops and German agents in Russia, Austria-Hungary, Rumania, and Turkey. The Baltic was to be opened to Allied shipping; Black Sea ports were to be evacuated; food shipments were to be permitted to enter Danzig for delivery to starving peoples in Russia and Poland; and the former Russian fleet, seized by Germany earlier in the year, was to be surrendered to the Allies. To ensure compliance, the Allied blockade would remain in place, and German prisoners of war and captured shipping would remain in Allied hands. The Germans, however, were required to remove immediately any and all trade restrictions they had imposed in Europe as well as release all Allied prisoners of war and captured shipping.

After the armistice document was read, Foch informed the Germans that its terms were nonnegotiable and had to be accepted or rejected within seventy-two hours. A request for a cease-fire while the terms were considered was denied. The German delegation then withdrew to communicate via courier with Berlin and the Council at Spa. They waited all of Saturday without result. The next day, Sunday, 9 November, the Berlin government proclaimed the kaiser's abdication, although he had done nothing of the sort. The next day he fled to Holland, followed by Crown Prince Rupprecht of Bavaria. Amid the chaos, Chancellor Max resigned, and a republic was declared by the Social Democrats with Friedrich Ebert as the chancellor of a new provisional government. Following an impromptu conference of a rapidly formed cabinet in Berlin and without any hope of tempering the Allied terms, word was sent via courier to the delegation at Compiègne to accept the Allied terms.

At 05:00 on Monday, 11 November 1918, the Armistice was signed by the German representatives. Marshal Foch immediately telegraphed all Allied military leaders that hostilities were to cease on the whole front as of 11:00, 11 November, and that Allied troops would not go beyond the line reached at that time until further orders were given. Hostilities continued to within a few minutes of 11:00, when the order to cease fire went up and down the line. Scattered fighting continued past 11:00, however, in remote areas where the news of the end of the war was slow to arrive.

The German army, consisting of seventeen armies of three million men, immediately began their retreat and demobilization in compliance with the terms of the Armistice. On the home front, the German people—who had been told up until virtually its conclusion that the war was being won—were totally unprepared for the news of the capitulation. The Allied advance to begin the occupation of enemy and enemy-occupied territory began on 17 November, and all Allied occupation forces had settled into their positions along the west bank of the Rhine and in western Germany by 13 December 1918.

The war was over; winning a lasting peace would be more difficult.

Clayton D. Laurie

References

Rudin, Harry R. *Armistice 1918*. New Haven: Yale University Press, 1944.
Simonds, Frank H. *History of the World War*. 5 vols. New York: Doubleday, 1920.
Weintraub, Stanley. *A Stillness Heard Round the World: The End of the Great War, November 1918*. New York: Oxford University Press, 1985.

See also ALLIED COUNTEROFFENSIVE, 1918; FOCH, FERDINAND; GERMANY, REVOLUTION OF 1918; MAX OF BADEN, PRINCE; PEACE OVERTURES DURING WAR; STAB-IN-THE-BACK MYTH

Armored Cars

Armored cars appeared on all fronts and were used by all the major powers from the earliest battles on the Western Front to the final days of the Allied victory. If the tactical problem of trench warfare was eventually solved by the tank, armored cars provided an earlier, and often more flexible, application of the principles of mobility, protection, and firepower. By the 1918 Battle of Amiens, armored cars had established themselves as a vital element in the armory of combatant nations.

Even before 1914, armored cars had been experimented with and used in combat. The first vehicle to fully qualify as an armored car appeared in Britain in 1902. The Simms Motor War Car was a cumbersome machine, armed with two machine guns and a one-pounder pom-pom. The Italians were the first to use armored cars in action, however, during the Italo-Turkish war of 1911. Several makes of car were used, the most common being the Isotta Fraschini, which was a large, boxlike vehicle carrying a single machine gun in a revolving turret. Its employment marked the beginning of Italy's widespread use of armored cars.

Other nations experimented with various designs and tactics. Most notable among innovators was an American, Colonel R.P. Davidson, who first experimented with a weapons carrier in 1898, but his foresight found little attention in U.S. military circles.

The Belgians were the first to use armored cars in World War I. Lieutenant Charles Henkart armored two of his Minerva tourers and used them for scouting and reconnaissance, the role that armored cars would eventually inherit from the cavalry. The success of Henkart's Minervas encouraged the Belgians to armor more of this type, along with some Mors tourers and two Peugeots. The Minervas had 4mm armor plate and were armed with a single Hotchkiss machine gun or a 37mm cannon. The great drawback of the design was that the crew was partially exposed to enemy fire, as the cars was open-topped. This defect cost Henkart his life in September of 1914, when he was caught in a German ambush.

The success of the Belgian armored cars inspired British naval commander Charles Samson to armor two Royal Naval Air Service cars, a Mercedes and a Rolls-Royce. These two crudely armored vehicles, with only partial protection and a single machine gun firing rearward, were the first British cars to see action. Samson led the way in arming and armoring a variety of vehicles, from former London buses to a Mercedes-Daimler lorry. These Royal Navy vehicles were used for many tasks in Belgium and France in 1914, such as for convoy protection and as mobile strongpoints. They were also involved in support operations, as on 17 October 1914, when a lorry armed with a 3-pounder assisted Life Guards near Westroosebeke.

The Royal Navy continued to lead the way in the development of British armored cars. The Royal Naval Armoured Car Division was formed in October of 1914 under Commander E.L. Boothby. By the following March it possessed seventy-eight Rolls-Royce armored cars, thirty-six Lanchesters, three Talbots, three Delaunay-Bellevilles, and thirty Seabrook armored lorries. The Rolls-Royces were the famous Admiralty pattern, destined to serve the British for another three decades. David Fletcher has justly commented that "the Admiralty design for a turreted armoured car was one of the most successful and influential ever produced; it was copied, in principle, all over the world." The armored lorries provided heavy support for the machine-gun-armed cars. Each Seabrook lorry carried a crew of nine, who manned the Maxim machine gun and the 3-pounder Hotchkiss with a 360-degree traverse once the lorry's armored side panels were folded down.

With the trench warfare on the Western Front, opportunities for the use of armored cars almost disappeared. That was not the case on the Eastern Front, however. The Russians had been interested in armored cars since 1904, initially buying them from France and Britain and later producing their own design, the Russo-Baltique, in 1912. Eventually the Russians had over five hundred armored cars of some thirty different types in their Automobile Corps. The most successful type used by Russia was the British Austin. This car could manage a top speed of 45 MPH and was armed with two machine guns in twin side-by-side turrets, a design feature typical of Russian vehicles. Many Austin chassis were delivered without armor, as the Russians preferred thicker plate to that fitted by the British. These Russian-bodied Austins were known as Putilov-Austins and had a long service life. Other Russian modifications included hooks fitted to cars that could be used in assaults on trenches to drag away barbed wire. The Russians also fielded one of the most powerful armored cars of the war, the Putilov-Garford. This 11-ton vehicle had armor 9 mm thick, and a turret-mounted 75mm gun and machine gun, along with two other machine guns in side sponsors. Although slow—its top speed was only 12 MPH—it was effective and remained in service until the 1930s. Despite the large number of vehicles in the Automobile Corps, Russian armored cars were never as effective as they might have been. Maintenance problems associated with poor roads and extreme conditions handicapped this arm of the Russian service.

The greater scope for action on the Eastern Front caused a shift in location for Allied armored cars. The Belgians, French, and British all sent armored-car units to help their Russian allies. The British initially sent thirty-six Lanchester armored cars and three Pierce-Arrow armored lorries, known as the "Russian Armoured Car Division, RNAS." Arriving in Russia in January of 1916, this unit fought its way along thousands of miles of front against Russia's enemies up until the Bolshevik Revolution. Their epic tale is recounted in fascinating detail in Perrett and Lord's *The Czar's British Squadron.*

Armored cars were used in virtually every sphere of operations during the war and by most combatant countries. No armored cars in American service saw action in Europe; several private-initiative and experimental vehicles, however, were used to patrol the Mexican border in 1916 and 1917. The mobility of armored cars ensured that they were used for similar security functions in India. Rolls-Royces, Cadillacs, Willys, Wolseleys, Jeffery Quads, and Fiats were all converted in India. Similar security considerations led to the use of Jeffery Quads in Ireland after the 1916 Easter Rebellion in Dublin, along with local improvisations used as infantry fighting vehicles. The British used armored cars in South-West Africa to great effect in 1915. Armored cars also proved useful in the East African campaign. The British used a variety of vehicles in their four-year pursuit of General Paul von Lettow Vorbeck. At Lukigura in June of 1916 armored cars played a key role in inflicting a local defeat on the Germans, pinning the Germans down frontally while a flying column outflanked them.

The Canadians were also quick to use armored vehicles, primarily armored machine-gun carriers built by the Autocar Company of Pennsylvania. The Autocars served with the Machine Gun Corps and were designed to act as mobile machine-gun posts. They were of little use until the German offensive of 1918; there, David Fletcher notes, "they came into their own, dashing all over the front to bring their firepower to bear and seal up dangerous breakthroughs." Unfortunately, the Canadian cars were open-topped, and their crews suffered accordingly.

The British and French came to see that the answer to the stalemate of the Western Front lay with armor, particularly the tank. The Germans, however, attempted to solve the tactical problem of trench warfare by the large-scale use of storm troops. In consequence, German armor development was slow. Not until 1916 did the Germans build their first armored cars, three experimental models built by Büssing, Daimler, and Ehrhardt. The Ehrhardt model was selected by the German army, and thirty-two were delivered in 1917. These vehicles, plus some captured from the Allies, served mainly on the Eastern Front and thereafter with various army and *Freikorps* units.

Although armored cars never played a central part in any of the campaigns of the war, by 1918 there were clear signs that they represented a vital part of the all-arms combination that would win future wars. At the important Battle of Amiens in August of 1918, the British used their tanks to break the back of the German army and open the front. Armored cars finally had an opportunity. Ranging freely in the German rear areas, the cars disrupted concentrations of enemy troops, spread panic among reserves, destroyed transports (including a train), and forced the evacuation of the German headquarters at Framerville. It was a portent of things to come.

Stephen M. Cullen

References
Bartholomew, E. *Early Armoured Cars.* Aylesbury: Shire, 1988.
Crow, D., ed. *Armoured Fighting Vehicles of World War One.* Windsor: Profile, 1970.
Fletcher, D. *War Cars.* London: HMSO, 1987.
Perrett, B., and A. Lord. *The Czar's British Squadron.* London: William Kimber, 1981.
White, B. *Tanks and Other Armoured Fighting Vehicles, 1900 to 1918.* Poole, Dorset: Blandford, 1970.

Arnauld de la Perlère, Lothar von (1886–1941)

German *Kapitänleutnant* and the most successful U-boat commander of the First World War.

Born at Posen, 18 March 1886, Arnauld de la Perière entered the navy in 1903 and specialized in torpedoes, but it was not until April of 1915 that he was ordered to attend the U-boat commander's course. Arnauld made fourteen cruises while in command of *U-35* of the Pola flotilla between November of 1915 and March of 1918. His record cruise took place from 26 July to 20 August 1916, when he sank fifty-four steamers and sailing craft in the western Mediterranean, which totaled over 90,150 tons of shipping. It was a striking demonstration of the ineffectiveness of the countermeasures introduced by the Allies after the Malta Conference the preceding March. In recognition of his success, Arnauld received the *Pour le Mérite*, his nation's highest honor.

The introduction of convoys reduced these spectacular scores, and in 1917 the well-worn *U-35* was under repair for four months. In May of 1918 Arnauld left the Mediterranean to take command of the large U-cruiser *U-139*, but before the Armistice he made only one cruise in the Atlantic in this rather unhandy boat and had disappointing results (five ships). Arnauld's score for the war was a staggering 189 merchant ships (453,718 tons) plus two small warships—a record for both world wars.

Discharged from the navy in 1931 with the rank of captain, Arnauld entered Turkish service and taught at the Turkish naval academy from 1932 to 1938. Recalled to service in the Second World War, he eventually reached the rank of vice admiral and served successively as naval commander in Belgium and the Netherlands, Brittany, and western France. He was proceeding to assume his new command as admiral southeast when he was killed in a plane crash near Le Bourget Airport, Paris, 24 February 1941.

Paul G. Halpern

References

Herzog, Bodo and Gunter Schomaekers. *Ritter der Tiefe. Graue Wölfe: Die erfolgreichsten U-Boot-Kommandanten der Welt des Esten nd Zweiten Weltkrieges.* Munich-Wels: Verlag Welsermühl, 1965.

Spindler, Arno. *Der Handelskrieg mit U-Booten.* 5 vols. Berlin [Vol. 5, Frankfurt-on-Main]: E.S. Mittler, 1932–66.

Tarrant, V.E. *The U-Boat Offensive, 1914–1918.* Annapolis, Md.: Naval Institute Press, 1989.

See also GERMANY, NAVY

Art during the War

The historian J.M. Winter has described the graphic arts in the Great War as a "dialectic between, on the one hand, experimentation in form and content, and on the other hand, a retreat into and reiteration of profoundly traditional themes and images." While the war might very well have marked the psychological turning point in the emergence of modernism, some of the art that the war provoked remained profoundly backward-looking.

The poet and artist Jean Cocteau, later associated with surrealism, in an apparent outburst of patriotic enthusiasm in 1914 wanted to cleanse what he considered to be dangerous Germanic elements from art. In the journal *Le Mot,* Cocteau praised the Gallic, versus the Germanic, elements found in art. He also had the notion that cubism was a German invention, until Pablo Picasso enlightened him. Cocteau, like other intellectuals, artists, and writers, tried to place the war in the grand sweep and design of history. When Italy joined the Allied cause in 1915, Cocteau exuberantly announced that "Dante is with us."

In a more popular vein, the French comic strip *Images d'Epinal,* which started in the 1830s as folk art, during the war became a vehicle for creating a simple, sentimental, and childlike version of some imaginary, heroic, and martial French past. Poster artist Jean Jacques Hansi used all manner of visual propaganda to attack the German occupation of Alsace and Lorraine by presenting an idealized, innocent, and almost fairyland image of life there under the French. In one poster, three French soldiers stare at Strasbourg Cathedral, which seems to shimmer in the sky above an enchanted landscape. Victor Hugo had written: "This heaven is our blue sky, this field is our land. This Alsace and this Lorraine are ours."

Other traditional themes and images from the past can be found in the omnipresent propaganda poster, utilized by all sides to sell the war. Sentimental depictions of angelic nurses caring for the wounded abounded in this genre. One Belgian poster soliciting funds actually depicted a nurse treating a soldier while sporting the wings of an angel. In an interesting British poster entitled *Women of Britain say— "Go!,"* two women and a child cling to each other as they stare out the window at the troops marching off to war. The poster contained two messages: Protecting home and family was a good reason to enlist, but women seemed to have the responsibility for ordering men into the fight.

Appeals to serve drew on historic iconography. World War I poster art contained many variations on the medieval knight-in-armor theme. The image of St. George vanquishing the dragon was particularly popular in Britain, but it served as the symbol of the nation in other countries as well. Old masters, such as Durer, Cranach, Schongauer, Mantegna, and Donatello, greatly influenced the work of the German poster artist Fritz Friedrich Boehle. One work called *In Deo Gratia* drew almost directly on a woodcut of a knight by Dürer. Boehle blatantly attempted to exploit Germany's medieval religious traditions in this request for money to support the war effort.

While much poster art reiterated traditional themes and images, some captured the spirit of modernity. Pal Suján of Budapest created one of the most striking and compassionate posters to come out of the war. Suján had attended a school of design in Budapest and had been influenced by the work of Vincent Van Gogh. In a 1917 poster entitled *Landes-Kriegsfürsorge-Ausstellung* (National Exhibition for War Relief), a soldier stands in a Van Goghesque landscape holding a farm tool with the aid of a hideous looking, machine-creature prosthesis that has replaced his missing shoulder and arm. The poignancy and brutal simplicity of this image of World War I cannot be denied.

Because mass conscription took men from all walks of life into the service, many artists also served in the armed forces, and, lest one forget, many promising young artists died in the war. Umberto Boccioni, Raymond Duchamp-Villon, Antonio Sant'Elia, and Franz Marc were all killed, while others, such as Marinetti, Russolo, and Braque, received severe wounds.

Most governments also formally commissioned the creation of war art for both propaganda and historic record. The first British war artists were selected in 1916. Very early in the war, Austria-Hungary established an independent *Kunstgruppe,* while in Germany artists frequently received releases from regular army duty. The state of Bavaria actually demanded special protection for many Munich artists following the death of Franz Marc. By early 1917, French war artists were being sent to cover specific war zones. Britain, and especially France, employed artists in special camouflage units. The British painter Norman Wilkinson was one of the first designers of dazzle naval camouflage.

Among these artists in uniform one still finds the conflict between tradition and experimentation, between the past and the future. Both Guirand de Scévola, the head of the very first camouflage section, and one of his artists, Luc-Albert Moreau, flirted with cubist techniques. British war artists like C.R.W. Nevinson, Wyndham Lewis, and Paul Nash all adopted unconventional approaches to their subject matter. Nevinson had studied in Paris before the war and was introduced to cubism. He also developed a particular fascination for the Futurists' ability to express force, motion, and speed. In the 1916 painting *Troops Resting*, Nevinson displayed this early vorticist style. Wyndham Lewis had traveled for years throughout Europe and was in Paris from 1906–08, right at the very moment of the birth of cubism. Lewis's war paintings showed an insistence on force and a fascination with mechanical forms. His aggressive visual style and metallic imagination came out in *A Battery Shelled* (1918), a large painting originally commissioned as one of a series of paintings for a proposed Hall of Remembrance that was never constructed. Paul Nash actually served at the Ypres front, was wounded and sent home. He later returned as a war artist, and his eerie, surreal paintings of the devastated landscape around Passchendaele, especially *We Are Making a New World* (1918), visually depict a world where, in Nash's own words, "the roads and tracks are covered in inches of slime, the black dying trees ooze and sweat and the shells never cease. . . . They plunge into the grave which is this land. . . . It is unspeakable, godless, hopeless." Max Slevogt worked hard to get an appointment as a German war artist but lasted only two weeks at the front before breaking down completely in the face of the slaughter that he witnessed. Some war artists, however, such as Muirhead Bone, Phillip Connard, and Eric Kennington, continued to paint in a traditional style that emphasized the ancient military virtues of courage, duty, honor, sacrifice, camaraderie, and heroism, ignoring the larger horror they did not want to face.

When the writer Gertrude Stein looked back at the experience of World War I, she saw a war that was totally different in composition from previous wars. The war of 1914–18 had "neither a beginning nor an end, a composition of which one corner was as important as another corner, in fact the composition of cubism." Cultural historian Stephen Kern adventurously found Stein's "bold metaphor" apt, for he argued that the "war embodied most of the transformation in time and space of the prewar period." Another historian, Modris Eksteins, wrote, "The Great War was the psychological turning point for modernism as a whole. The urge to create and the urge to destroy had changed places." For Eksteins, the spirit of the pre-1914 avant garde in the arts had been confirmed, or valorized, by the experience of the war itself, causing a strange alternation in human consciousness. These bold assertions may not be entirely convincing, but there can be no doubt that some artists, in particular the German Expressionists and the Dadaists, chose radical, violent, shocking, and emotional ways to respond visually to the war.

The German sculptor Ernest Barlach created a mystical memorial to the war. His *War Monument*, a single human form dressed in flowing robes, hangs, as if floating, from the ceiling in Gustrow Cathedral in Cologne, Germany. Unlike traditional war memorials that often portray military figures in heroic poses, Barlach created this hauntingly symbolic figure that spoke of the spiritual anguish left by the devastation of war. The brutality and bestiality of human beings now became a common theme among German artists, such as Max Beckmann, who was permanently affected by his wartime experiences as a medical orderly. After 1918 he produced a series of paintings in which mankind, exposed to mysterious powers, threatened by the environment, is reduced to a puppet in the hands of evil demons. Beckmann's paintings are filled with figures and objects stripped to a basic, almost sculpturelike simplicity. His own personal despair might be reflected in *The Dream* (1921), a tilted, zigzag work that resembles a nightmare more than a dream. Beckmann once said of his work that it reflects "the true nature of modern humanity—how weak we are, how helpless we are against ourselves in this proud era of so called progress."

The war was decisive in molding the attitudes of all the artists of Beckmann's generation, especially Otto Dix and Georg Grosz. Dix served in the German army from 1914 to 1918, but from 1916 onward he became a fanatical opponent of war. In the years immediately after the war, Dix's paintings had a strong emotional and social content—crippled ex-soldiers, swinish war profiteers, and sickly prostitutes on the street of German cities. Georg Grosz volunteered for service in 1914 but received a medical discharge in 1915. By the time he was drafted into the army in 1917, his hatred for German bourgeois society knew no bounds. His savage caricatures of everything held sacred in bourgeois society—the military, the church, and businessmen—caused him to be frequently prosecuted for "blasphemy" and "insulting public morals." In 1916 he helped to found *Neue Jugend,* the first journal of the Dada movement, and in 1920 he was represented in the 1st International Dada Fair in Berlin.

Dada got its start in the Cabaret Voltaire in Zurich in 1916. Zurich had became a haven for the war-fatigued, the objectors, shirkers, anarchists, and intellectuals like Tristan Tzara, Richard Hülsenbeck, Hugo Ball, and Jean Hans Arp, the founders of Dadaism. This movement reflected the nihilism of the war. Since there seemed to be no meaning, reason, or sanity in the world around them, the Dadaists consciously rejected any meaning. The only meaning was nonsense. The Dadaists attacked every cultural standard and any type of artistic activity. They were antiart and antitradition. Even their name was chosen as a lark from a randomly opened page of the dictionary. Dada means hobbyhorse in French. Dada sought the destruction of every current meaning of expression and demanded the spontaneous. Poetry would be read at the same time in different languages, or words would simply be made up, having no apparent meaning. Marcel Duchamp shocked and outraged the public by drawing a moustache on a photograph of the *Mona Lisa* with the intention of deflating the entire concept of art. Duchamp entered a men's urinal in an art exhibit in New York, declaring it to be a genuine work of art since he, the artist, had blessed it. Richard Hülsenbeck encouraged the "aimless of the world to unite," while Hugo Ball declared that "the war is our brothel." Dadaism became the most radical cultural response to the senseless destruction and horrors of the Great War. Maybe there existed artists in 1918 who believed that the war had done nothing to change the past meanings of words like glorious, sacrifice, and sacred duty, but for many nihilism breeds only nihilism, or, as F. Scott Fitzgerald put it, "All gods dead, all wars fought, all faiths in man shaken."

Richard A. Voeltz

References

Eksteins, Modris. *Rites of Spring, The Great War and the Birth of the Modern Age.* Boston: Houghton Mifflin, 1989.

Kahn, Elizabeth Louise. *The Neglected Majority: "Les Camoufleurs," Art History, and World War I.* New York and London: University Press of America, 1984.

Kern, Stephen. *The Culture of Time and Space, 1880–1918.* Cambridge: Harvard University Press, 1983.

Paret, Peter, Beth Irwin Lewis, and Paul Paret. *Persuasive Images, Posters of War and Revolution.* Princeton: Princeton University Press, 1992.

Silver, Kenneth E. *Espirt De Corps: The Art of the Parisian Avant Garde and the First World War.* Princeton: Princeton University Press, 1989.

Winter, J.M. *The Experience of World War I.* New York: Oxford University Press, 1989.

Artillery

In the years prior to the start of World War I, field artillery on both sides focused on mobility to the exclusion of almost everything else. Horse-drawn batteries were trained to charge into action at some critical moment, pop off a few rounds over open sights, and then rush off to do the same thing at some other point on the battlefield. Primitive forms of indirect fire, counterbattery work, and meteorological corrections were possible in the years just prior to World War I, but the actual techniques were cumbersome and thus largely ignored as being incompatible with a fast-moving war of maneuver.

Things did not quite work out the way they had been planned. Once the war started, all forms of firepower quickly gained the upper hand over maneuver, and trench warfare resulted. With two huge armies dug into the ground and facing each other across the barbed wire of No Man's Land, artillery quickly became the primary means of prosecuting the war. As Ian V. Hogg noted, "The war of 1914–1918 became an artillery duel of vast proportions." In his 1989 book *Field Artillery and Firepower*, J.B.A. Bailey described four general phases of

artillery employment experienced to varying degrees by all sides in the Great War: 1) Inadequacy, 2) Experimentation and Buildup, 3) Destruction, and 4) Neutralization.

Inadequacy, 1914

Most armies entered the war regarding artillery as strictly an auxiliary arm, the job of which was to assist the infantry in the attack. Among military leaders there always had been a great deal of interest in coordinating infantry and artillery actions, but very little real effort was ever made. During the early months of the war the results were dismal, and too often artillery fired on its own infantry. Some units in the French army even resorted to sewing large white patches on the backs of their uniforms in the hope it would prevent their own guns from firing on them.

Napoleon had taught the world the benefits of massing artillery, but in 1914 most armies continued to believe that mass firepower could be achieved only by physically massing guns well forward on the ground. The experiences of the Russo-Japanese War had proved both the value and the practicality of indirect fire to many artillerymen, but the idea was strongly resisted by the maneuver branches of most armies, which believed infantrymen needed the psychological reinforcement of seeing their own artillery right on the front line with them, instead of hiding behind a hill somewhere in the rear. When World War I started, artillery turned out to be all too vulnerable to the new forms of small arms, especially the machine gun. As the Russian army learned in Manchuria, the firepower of these new weapons quickly drove artillery off the front line, increasing the distance between the gun and the target. Gunners were forced to resort to indirect fire.

Aside from the nebulous concept of the "artillery duel," there was very little systematic counterbattery doctrine before the war. The French high command, and especially the French infantry, were hostile to the very idea of a set-piece artillery duel, seeing it as a waste of firepower better spent in support of the infantry's attack. French Field Service Regulations of 1913 specifically forbade their artillery from engaging in duels.

In 1914 there was very little real centralized command and control (C2) of artillery. In many armies the division was the highest level of artillery C2. The British army did not introduce a divisional-level artillery commander until 1912. Thus, the Royal Artillery entered the war with no experience in coordinating and controlling fires above the level of the artillery battalion, which the British at the time called artillery "brigades." In most armies of 1914, corps-level artillery existed only as a pool of assets to be divided among the divisions as needed. The senior artillery officers at corps-levels and above were merely advisors, rather than commanders.

The prewar doctrine of high mobility required that the guns used by field artillery be mobile, that is, light. All nations were armed primarily with light, flat-firing field guns. The German 77mm, the Russian 76.2mm, the American 3-inch, the British 18-pounder, and the famous French 75mm were all too light, however, to have any real effect against well-prepared field fortifications. Once these guns were forced to move back off the front lines, they lacked the higher trajectories necessary for indirect fire, especially in rough terrain.

Experimentation and Buildup, 1915

As the stalemate on the Western Front set in, the combatants spent most of 1915 scrambling to develop new ordnance and new fire-support techniques. Before those issues could even be addressed, all the belligerents ran into the more immediate and critical problem of ammunition.

Despite the evidence from recent conflicts, all armies entered World War I with far too little artillery ammo. During the Russo-Japanese War, the Russian army averaged 87,000 rounds for each month of combat in 1904. By the First Balkan War in 1912, the Bulgarian army was shooting 254,000 rounds per month. Yet the French army started World War I with less than five million rounds on hand. The Russians were in a little better position, with about twelve million rounds. The Germans seemed to have been in the best shape, with slightly more than twenty million rounds, but even that had to be split between the two fronts.

French plans called for an average consumption of 100,000 rounds per month, but the actual monthly average for 1914 was close to 900,000 rounds. By 1916 the French were shooting 4.5 million rounds per month, and by 1918 the Germans were averaging eight million rounds. Industry could not keep up with the ever-growing demand, and the ammunition crisis caused political scandals in Britain, Russia, and France. Throughout most of 1914 and 1915 tactical plans were held hostage to the supply of artillery ammunition.

Shrapnel was the standard round for the light field gun in 1914. Howitzers and heavier guns primarily fired high explosive (HE). Up until nearly the end of World War I, the HE round produced very little fragmentation and was used principally for its blast effect. The shrapnel round was packed with steel balls and a bursting charge that was triggered by a hand-set, powder-burning time fuse. When the round went off in the air, the bursting charge blew the nose cap off the front of the round and shot the balls forward—something like a huge, airborne shotgun.

Shrapnel could be deadly against troops in the open, but it was ineffective against dug-in troops and virtually worthless against fortifications. Thus, HE increasingly became the round of choice. By the end of the war the fragmentation effect had been improved to the point that an air burst of HE was almost as effective as properly adjusted shrapnel. After World War I, the shrapnel round passed from the scene.

Another source of early problems was the distinction that existed in most armies between the different branches of artillery. The U.S. Army, for example, had field artillery and coast artillery; British artillery was divided into the Royal Field Artillery and the Royal Garrison Artillery. The German army had a similar distinction between the field artillery and the foot artillery. German field artillery was mounted, armed with light field guns, and supported maneuver forces. Foot (heavy) artillery units had little mobility and used heavy howitzers and siege mortars. Like the U.S. Coast Artillery and the Royal Garrison Artillery, German foot artillery manned coastal defenses. They also manned the guns of interior fortifications and were responsible for conducting set-piece sieges in the field should such operations become necessary. The reduction of the Belgian forts along the Meuse River in 1914 was primarily a foot artillery operation.

Although the difference between these two categories of artillery seemed logical enough on paper, the distinctions started to blur during World War I as the heavier guns of the foot and garrison branches were called upon increasingly to give direct support to combat operations. In most armies, the two branches were barely on speaking terms.

Field artillery emphasized speed and mobility, while heavy artillery stressed precision and technical applications. Up until the end of 1916 in the German army, the foot and field branches even had gunsights calibrated in different units of angular measurement. Field gunners in all armies tended to look down upon their garrison and foot colleagues as "dugout artillerymen."

The French started the war with almost no heavy artillery. Their pre–World War I doctrine rejected the howitzer entirely. They put all their faith in the M1897 75mm field gun. This remarkable weapon was the world's first truly modern artillery piece. The French believed it could accomplish any artillery mission on the battlefield. Whatever the gun lacked in hitting power could be more than compensated for by its high rate of fire of twenty to thirty rounds per minute. This notion that the 75mm gun could accomplish any task seemed to be contradicted by the fact that the French entered the war with only 1,300 rounds for each of their 75mm guns—almost all of it shrapnel.

By the end of the war, the French view of heavy guns had changed drastically. In August of 1914 they had 3,840 75mm guns, but they had a grand total of only 308 guns larger than 75mm. By November of 1918 the French artillery had 4,968 field guns and 5,128 guns and howitzers above 75mm. Although the total size of the French artillery increased two and a half times during the war, the increase in heavier guns was approximately 1,700 percent.

French production figures are even more impressive considering the large number of guns they supplied to the rapidly expanded American army in 1917 and 1918. The United States entered World War I with only 604 field guns and 209 heavier guns, enough to equip about 11 divisions. Wartime expansion plans called for forty-two divisions, but the maximum U.S. production capacity was only about three hundred guns per month. Under an agreement with the French, the United States supplied the steel and other raw materials and the French manufactured 75mm and 155mm guns for the American Expeditionary Force. When the war ended, the AEF had 3,311 guns on hand; only 477 of the total were of American manufacture.

The Germans had paid closer attention to the results of the Russo-Japanese War and entered World War I in a much better position with regard to howitzers and heavy guns. The famed gun works of central Europe, including Krupp and Skoda, conducted aggressive research and development programs in heavy artillery prior to the war. By 1914 Germany had 5,086 77mm field guns and 2,280 howitzers and larger pieces—outnumbering the French heavy hitters by more than seven to one. But even German heavy artillery grew during the war at a faster rate than the light field guns. By 1918 the German artillery had 6,764 field guns and 12,286 artillery pieces above 77mm—still outnumbering the French heavies by more than five to one.

The British had learned the value of the howitzer in their relatively recent Boer War. As a result, they had a higher proportion of howitzers and heavier guns than almost any other army. Throughout the war their ratio of light guns to howitzer and heavier guns hardly changed. In 1914 the British army as a whole had 1,608 light guns and 1,248 howitzers and heavies. Unfortunately, the ill-equipped British Expeditionary Force landed in France with a total of only eighty-nine mediums and heavies, which included twenty-four old siege guns. By 1918 the British army in France had 3,242 light guns and 3,195 howitzers and heavies.

In the early part of the war, fire direction procedures for indirect fire were cumbersome and slow. As the various armies expanded, their pools of trained manpower also shrank through attrition. The gunnery problem grew technically more complex, but the large numbers of poorly and hastily trained replacements required even simpler methods. One solution to the problem was the establishment of phase lines on the ground to control the shifting of fires. The system was slow and rigid, but it worked. Requests to lift fires from one phase line to another often had to be carried by runner and sometimes took hours to accomplish.

Fire on the objective took the form of standing barrages along the enemy's trench lines. As the attackers overtook the leading trench line, the standing barrage would shift onto the next trench line. The Germans quickly learned to counter the standing barrages by taking some of their machine guns out of the trenches and placing them on the ground between the trench lines. This led to the requirement for the artillery to sweep the intervening ground with fire as it moved from one standing barrage to the next.

By 1916 on the Western Front (and most likely earlier on the Eastern Front), the standing barrages and the sweeping fire between them evolved into the creeping barrage (also called a rolling barrage), with the advancing infantry following closely behind a steadily moving wall of friendly artillery fire. But over-reliance on artillery phase lines and creeping barrages had an adverse effect on maneuver tactics. Troops were trained to follow in straight lines behind the barrage. Infantry commanders at all levels began to ignore terrain, and the old linear tactics returned in a new guise.

Destruction, 1916–17

As the war moved into its third year, rigor mortis set in on the Western Front. During this phase of the war artillery on both sides became a blunt instrument for indiscriminately pounding entire patches of ground. The main functions of artillery on the battlefield had become destruction and annihilation—destroy attacking enemy troops before they reached friendly lines and destroy the defending enemy before attacking friendly troops reached the hostile positions. Special emphasis was placed on obliterating the enemy's fortifications, with artillery even expected to cut his barbed wire. This only added to the steadily increasing rate of ammunition consumption. The prevailing philosophy of this third period became "Artillery conquers, infantry occupies."

The dominance of artillery on the battlefield naturally gave rise to counterbattery (CB) operations. Here the destruction philosophy dominated too, and CB work became almost the exclusive domain of the heavier guns. Counterbattery planning was carried out according to rigid mathematical formulas.

The key offensive fire support technique during this period became the artillery preparation. The first large-scale preparatory attack of the war took place during the British attack at Neuve Chapelle on 10 March 1915. In what was the greatest artillery bombardment in military history to that time, 363 British guns fired on the German positions for thirty-five minutes. The howitzers and heavy guns shot indirect fire against the German trenches, while the field guns concentrated on the barbed-wire with direct fire. The attack was successful initially because the field guns did an adequate job against the wire. The fire of the howitzers, however, was wildly inaccurate, and the German trenches remained largely untouched. In the end the attack failed. Unfortunately, the wrong lessons were drawn. Focusing on the destruction of obstacles, the conclusion was that the artillery needed to destroy everything in the infantry's path. This meant larger and longer preps.

As the war progressed through 1916 and 1917, artillery preps grew longer and longer, lasting days and even weeks. Military leaders on both sides convinced themselves that the more HE shells they dumped on an objective the easier the infantry's job would be. In truth, however, the long preparations accomplished very little and actually caused more problems for the attacker. In the first place, a long prep sacrificed surprise; it told the defender exactly where the attack was coming. The longer the preparation, the longer the defender had to take countermeasures. Quite often a defender was able to withdraw his frontline infantry entirely from the area being shelled, reinforce it, and reinsert it when the fire lifted.

The long preps generally did a poor job of cutting the defender's barbed wire; but they did a great job of tearing up the terrain, making it more difficult for the infantry to cross and for the artillery to follow in support. That, in turn, virtually guaranteed that an attack would falter as soon as the infantry advanced beyond the range of their own stalled artillery. Destroyed road networks to the front also made it more difficult to bring up logistical support for any advance that might be made. The long destructive preparations, then, actually created more obstacles for the attacker than they cleared.

The massive preparations also caused an enormous logistical drain that slowly bled the national economies of belligerents. By mid-1916 the Great War had degenerated into a dull, grinding war of attrition—what the Germans called *Materialschlacht*. The destruction by artillery doctrine reached its zenith (and finally demonstrated its own bankruptcy) during the apocalyptic battles of later 1916 and 1917 on the Western Front.

In July of 1916 the British army started its attack at the Somme with a seven-day preparation, during which 1,537 guns fired 1,627,824 rounds. When the British Tommies climbed out of their trenches to attack on 1 July, they moved forward in the traditional linear formations. The British military leaders believed that nothing could have survived the awesome shelling. The German *Landser,* however, were far from eliminated. They swarmed out from beneath the rubble covering their deep bunkers, set up their machine guns in the convenient new shell holes the British had just provided, and proceeded to massacre the attackers. The British army took

57,470 casualties that first day, including 19,240 killed.

After fighting five months on the Somme, the Allies had taken only about 125 square kilometers of territory. The campaign had cost the British 420,000 casualties and the French 195,000. Although the German defenders actually suffered slightly higher total losses, with 650,000 casualties, they had stopped the attackers. The Allied offensive tactics (both infantry and artillery) were a dismal failure. Unfortunately, the British tried the same sort of attack on a large-scale again at Passchendaele in July of 1917. The basic difference this time was that the size of the artillery prep was doubled. Over the course of thirteen days, 3,168 guns of the Royal Artillery threw 4.3 million rounds at the German positions. The results were no better, and British losses for that five-month-long campaign ran to nearly 400,000.

Neutralization, 1917–18

Throughout the course of the war leaders on both sides and at all levels searched for ways to improve tactics and break the deadlock. For artillery tactics, the most aggressive experimentation took place first on the Eastern Front. The key to the new fire-support thinking was a belief that artillery fire was more effective when its purpose was to neutralize rather than destroy. This idea, which meshed nicely with the evolving infantry doctrine, was actually a return to prewar tactical concepts.

The most influential artillery tactician of the war was German Colonel Georg Bruchmüller, who orchestrated fire support for all five of Ludendorff's great offensives in 1918. Starting on the Eastern Front as early as 1915, Bruchmüller experimented with various fire-support methods that were radical departures from convention. Bruchmüller was one of the first to advocate a return to the principles of neutralization. He understood the counterproductive nature of the long, destruction-oriented preparations. Thus, while the preps in the west were lasting weeks, Bruchmüller planned and executed preps in the east lasting only a few hours and with better effect. His preps may not have been long, but they were incredibly violent—designed not to obliterate a defending enemy but to stun him senseless.

Bruchmüller was one of the first to organize artillery preps into distinct phases with each phase intended to accomplish a specific tactical effect. The typical Bruchmüller prep had three main phases: a short surprise strike on command and control and communications targets; a period of reinforced fire against the enemy artillery; and a final phase against the leading enemy infantry positions. Both the U.S. and Russian armies still use this technique today.

Bruchmüller was noted for his use of gas, which was the perfect neutralization weapon. He was one of the first to match the effects of various types of gas against specific types of targets to get specific results. He used persistent mustard gas (marked with a yellow cross on German shells) to screen the flanks of attacks and contaminate enemy artillery positions, thus taking the guns out of action for the duration of the fight. Most gas masks of World War I were effective against lethal (green cross) choking gas but ineffective against nonlethal blue cross gas, which induced vomiting. Bruchmüller's technique was to fire a mixture of both, which he called *Buntkreuz* (mixed-color cross), against the same target. The blue cross gas would penetrate the mask, forcing the wearer to remove it in the presence of the lethal green cross gas.

One of Bruchmüller's greatest innovations was a system of task-tailored artillery groups, each with a specific mission to perform on the battlefield. The main mission of the counterartillery groups (called AKA) was to neutralize the enemy's artillery. While almost everyone else was using howitzers and heavy guns for counterbattery work, Bruchmüller used mostly light field guns because of their high rates of fire and the plentiful supply of gas ammunition for them. The counterinfantry groups (IKA) struck at the enemy infantry positions. During the reinforced counterbattery phase of the prep, however, the IKA guns joined with the AKA guns to overwhelm the enemy batteries.

Bruchmüller was one of the earliest advocates of centralized fire planning and C2. The IKA units were controlled by the divisions; the AKA units were controlled by corps. At the field army level, Bruchmüller created special heavy artillery groups (SCHWEFLA). These units had destruction missions against critical targets such as rail centers, bridges, and concrete-reinforced command posts. Also at the corps level, Bruchmüller set up long-range artillery groups (FEKA) whose mission was interdiction against reserves and other deep targets. Bruchmüller's FEKA groups were among the first units to appear on the modern battlefield with a specific deep-battle mission. Deep-battle has become one of the major points of focus for modern combat operations.

Accuracy in artillery fire was, and still is, a problem. The easiest way to achieve accuracy is to fire what is called a registration against a target with a precisely known location. By comparing the "should-hit" firing data to the "did-hit" data, a set of corrections can be derived and applied against future targets. The system is something like zeroing a rifle. The only problem is that, in registering, an artillery battery gives away its position and usually becomes an instant counterbattery target in the process. Also, hundreds of batteries suddenly registering in a certain area is a sure tip-off that a major attack is in the works.

On the Eastern Front, Bruchmüller experimented with various methods of eliminating or abbreviating the registration, and thereby avoiding telegraphing the attack. When he came to the Western Front in late 1917, Bruchmüller became the principal champion of a newly developed technique of predicting registration corrections from careful measurement of weather conditions and muzzle-velocity characteristics of each gun tube. The system had been developed by Captain Erich Pulkowski. The Germans used the Pulkowski method in all five of their 1918 offensives and achieved stunning tactical surprise in the process. The basic mechanics of the Pulkowski method are still used by all NATO armies today.

Bruchmüller was a pioneer in the uses of artillery and the first to make them all work in a comprehensive system. French artillerymen, for the most part, were always several steps behind the Germans. They were slow to accept a return to neutralization and to understand the value of surprise. Several British gunners, on the other hand, had been advocating many of the same principles as the war progressed. Foremost among them were Lieutenant General Sir Noel Birch, Major General Sir Herbert Uniacke (known in Royal Artillery circles as the British

Typical Artillery of World War I

Type	Caliber	Maximum Muzzle Velocity (m/sec)	HE Round Weight (kg)	Gun Weight (kg)	Maximum Range (m)
Germany					
F.K.96n/A field gun	77mm	465	6.9	1,020	7,800
F.K.16 field gun	77mm	602	7.2	1,325	10,700
l.F.H.98/09 light howitzer	105mm	302	15.7	1,225	6,300
lg.K.16 long gun	150mm	757	51.4	10,870	22,000
Mrs.10 heavy howitzer	210mm	365	113.0	3,900	9,250
Austria-Hungary					
M1911 Skoda howitzer	305mm	——	385.0	25,450	11,800
Britain					
13-pounder gun	3.0 in.	515	5.9	1,016	5,300
18-pounder Mk IV gun	3.3 in.	492	8.2	1,594	9,990
4.5-inch howitzer	4.5 in.	306	15.9	1,832	7,800
9.2-inch Mk 2 howitzer	9.2 in.	485	131.8	14,727	12,540
60-pounder Mk 2 gun	5.0 in.	644	27.3	5,477	14,760
France					
M1897 gun	75mm	527	7.3	1,141	6,750
M1917 howitzer	155mm	447	43.6	3,307	11,300
GPF gun	155mm	730	44.5	10,773	18,500
Russia					
M1902 field gun	76.2mm	586	5.9	1,182	6,420
M1909 field howitzer	122mm	——	23.0	——	7,500

Bruchmüller), and Brigadier General H.H. Tudor. For the most part, they were held back by Field Marshal Sir Douglas Haig's prejudices on artillery and the more rigid British staff system. The British attack at Cambrai actually predated the Germans in the use of a system to predict artillery corrections without registering. Some technical errors in the application produced mixed results.

After Ludendorff's 1918 offensives all three of the Western Allies, especially the Americans, quickly adopted the German artillery techniques and used them through the rest of the war. After World War I Bruchmüller wrote several books, which were translated into French, English, and Russian and intensely studied.

David T. Zabecki

References

Bailey, Jonathan B.A. *Field Artillery and Fire-power.* Oxford: Military Press, 1989.

Bidwell, Shelford, and Dominick Graham. *Fire-power: British Army Weapons and Theories of War 1904–1945.* London: Allen and Unwin, 1982.

Hogg, Ian V. *Gas.* New York: Ballantine, 1975.

———. *The Guns 1914–1918.* London: Pan Brooks, 1971.

Zabecki, David T. *Steel Wind: Georg Bruchmueller and the Birth of Modern Artillery.* Westport, Conn.: Praeger, 1994.

See also BRUCHMÜLLER, GEORG; CHEMICAL WARFARE; FRENCH 75MM FIELD GUN; LUDENDORFF OFFENSIVES, 1918; PARIS GUN; PULKOWSKI, ERICH; UNIACKE, SIR HERBERT

Artois, First Battle of (27 September to 10 October 1914)

See RACE TO SEA, 1914

Artois, Second Battle of (9 May to 18 June 1915)

After the failure of the First Battle of Champagne in March of 1915, the French high command immediately began planning to renew the offensive. With the Germans concentrating their forces against Russia in 1915, French Commander in Chief General Joseph Joffre and Ferdinand Foch, commander of the Northern Group of Armies, sought to exploit the Western Allies' estimated six-hundred-battalion advantage by seeking a breakthrough in Artois. By capturing Vimy Ridge, Artois's dominant geographic feature, French troops could command the Douai plain, sever the crucial German railborne supply net in the Douai-Lille area, and force a German withdrawal from northern France, thereby providing some relief to the hard-pressed Russians. To maximize this operation's chances of success, Joffre convinced reluctant BEF commander Field Marshal Sir John French, who lacked adequate heavy artillery, ammunition, and reserves, to contribute to the offensive by relieving two French corps in the Ypres salient and by attacking at Aubers Ridge. This BEF operation would be the largest of a series of supporting assaults all along the Western Front.

Opposing the Allies in Artois were the thirteen divisions of Bavarian Crown Prince Rupprecht's thinly spread but well-entrenched Sixth Army. This army's front consisted of up to eight interconnected trenches with strong points at Carency and the "Labyrinth" (south of the village of Neuville St. Vaast), backed by a partially finished alternate position anchored by the fortified villages of Souchez and Neuville St. Vaast.

In preparing the assault on these formidable defenses, Foch and Tenth Army commander General Victor d'Urbal incorporated the lessons of earlier offensives. To secure the flanks of the main thrust at Vimy Ridge, Foch and d'Urbal planned a five-corps assault (XXI, XXXIII, XX, XVII, and X from north to south) on a broad twenty-four-mile front between Notre Dame de Lorette and Arras. In reserve were five infantry and six cavalry divisions. To weaken German defenses, the French carefully prepared a 1,200-gun, 700,000-round bombardment with targets carefully selected through intensive aerial reconnaissance. Preparations for the assault were temporarily disrupted on 22 April when the German attack on the BEF in the Second Battle of Ypres briefly diverted one French corps from Tenth Army reserve to Ypres. Although the Germans reduced the BEF's meager artillery ammunition stockpiles, they lacked the reserves to follow up their initial successes.

With the Ypres front adequately stabilized, the French Tenth Army opened its offensive on 4 May with a five-day artillery bombardment. On 9 May the French infantry attacked and within ninety minutes General Henri-Philippe

Pétain's well-prepared XXXIII Corps had reached the crest of Vimy Ridge and enveloped Carency, the fortified village upon which the First Artois Offensive had stalled. On Pétain's right, the XX Corps advanced to the fiercely defended village of Neuville St. Vaast. This deep, critical penetration did not result in a general breakthrough, however, because French reserves, placed too far rearward and out of contact with the advancing troops, failed to reach Pétain's corps for eight hours. This delay allowed the Germans, aided by gathering darkness, to recover, counterattack, and push Pétain's exhausted units off the crest of Vimy Ridge. None of the Tenth Army's other corps made appreciable gains; the Germans restricted the French advance to only four miles of the twenty-four-mile front. Heavy fighting continued, but the chance for a quick breakthrough evaporated as German reserves began arriving on 11 May.

The BEF's I, IV, and Indian Corps operation at Aubers Ridge also began on 9 May. With the Germans distracted by the French Tenth Army, British commanders—as at Neuve Chapelle—hoped to achieve surprise by attacking after only thirty minutes of intensive artillery preparation, the brevity of which was partially necessitated by the lack of shells. This plan miscarried as the British barrage was inaccurate, plagued by defective rounds, and largely ineffective against the strong, imaginatively constructed German positions. The British suffered some 12,000 casualties and failed even to prevent Rupprecht from shifting units from this sector to Vimy Ridge.

On 16 May d'Urbal renewed his offensive in an effort to widen Pétain's constricted salient, but gains were incremental and fighting intense at Carency, Souchez, and the Labyrinth during the following month. The British First Army's two-division supporting assault at Festubert, an effort to combine the surprise of a night attack with the firepower of a massive artillery bombardment, failed despite some initial gains because of the British artillery's continued ineffectiveness and stiff German counterattacks. The BEF's commitment of three additional divisions on 16–18 May reportedly worried German commanders but ultimately gained little. By 27 May the BEF halted its attacks with nothing to show for their efforts except 17,000 additional casualties. In fact, the BEF did more to assist the French Tenth Army by taking over responsibility for about 5,500 yards of trenches south of the La Bassée Canal than by launching the Festubert operation.

The final French effort to salvage the offensive came on 16 June when d'Urbal launched an eighteen-division push all along the Artois front. Hoping to correct the fatal mistakes of 9 May, d'Urbal opted for a brief, intensive bombardment of known German positions, while concentrating his reserve formations immediately behind the first wave. This tactical combination proved disastrous. Because of the inadequate barrage, German artillery and machine guns slaughtered the densely concentrated French infantry. German counterattacks quickly eliminated all French gains, while British diversionary attacks at Givenchy, Bellewaarde Ridge, and Hooge (the latter two near Ypres) proved futile. With the offensive stalled, d'Urbal and French suspended offensive operations on 18 June.

The Second Artois Offensive, which had opened so promisingly, ended in complete failure. The Allies gained about five square miles of territory but achieved neither the tactical success of seizing Vimy Ridge nor the strategic victory of forcing the Germans to retreat in France or divert units from Russia. The failure of the offensive also increased tensions between British and French commanders and embarrassingly exposed, in the *London Times*, the BEF's artillery and ammunition shortages. While German losses numbered some 73,000 men, Allied casualties surpassed 102,000 French and 37,000 British. In spite of this, French commanders believed that Pétain's operations confirmed their belief that a breakthrough required only a heavy and well-targeted preparatory barrage, penetration on a broad front, reserves advancing close behind the first wave, and, most of all, a thoroughly detailed plan of attack to compensate for the lack of battlefield communications. Confident that correct lessons had been learned, Joffre began to plot a renewal of the offensive in Artois and Champagne for the autumn of 1915. The Germans, however, would be quite ready, as Second Artois merely heightened their confidence that a strong defense in depth, backed by sufficient reserves, could defeat any offensive.

David K. Yelton

References

Edmonds, James E., and G.C. Wynne. *Military Operations: France and Belgium,*

1915, Vol. 1. In *Great Britain, Historical Section of the Committee of Imperial Defence, History of the Great War Based on Official Documents.* London: Macmillan, 1927.

Falls, Cyril. *The Great War.* New York: Putnam, 1959.

Marshall-Cornwall, Sir James. *Foch as Military Commander.* New York: Crane, Russals and Co., 1972.

Ministère de la Guerre. *Etat-Major de l'Armée Service Historique. Les Armées Française dans la Grande Guerre, vol. II.* Paris: Imprimerie Nationale, 1931.

Reichsarchiv. *Der Weltkrieg 1914–1918, vol. 8.* Berlin: E.S. Mittler und Sohn, 1932.

See also FOCH, FERDINAND; FRENCH, JOHN; JOFFRE, JOSEPH; PÉTAIN, HENRI-PHILIPPE; RUPPRECHT, CROWN PRINCE; YPRES, SECOND BATTLE OF

Artois, Third Battle of (25 September to 16 October 1915)

The Third Battle of Artois, coupled with the Second Battle of Champagne, marked French commander General Joseph Joffre's final attempt to exploit the numerical advantage afforded the Allies by the German decision to concentrate against the Russians in 1915. Joffre planned once again to implement his General Instructions Number 8 of 8 December 1914 by launching simultaneous offensives in Champagne (the Second and Fourth armies) and Artois (the Tenth Army) aimed at rupturing the German front, severing their railborne supply lines around Attigny and Douai, and thereby forcing a German withdrawal from the Noyon salient. At the very least, Joffre expected that these attacks would relieve the hard-pressed Russians.

Complementing the Champagne-Artois Offensive, Joffre planned a whole series of assaults along the Western Front, including an Italian push along the Isonzo River. Foremost among these efforts would be a BEF attack near Loos to support the Tenth Army's left flank in Artois. Initially, BEF commander Field Marshal Sir John French and British First Army commander General Sir Douglas Haig opposed Joffre's proposal, arguing that their forces lacked the heavy artillery, ammunition, and reserves necessary to attack in this coal mining region—open ground broken by slag heaps, pit heads, and villages. Under pressure from British minister of war Lord Horatio Kitchener to cooperate with their allies, however, French and Haig reluctantly agreed to Joffre's plan in mid summer.

Although Third Artois followed the basic outline of its two predecessors—a main thrust on Vimy Ridge supported by French attacks on both flanks—the fall offensive incorporated lessons learned from the Tenth Army's earlier failures. To tax the Germans' meager reserves, Joffre planned simultaneous major attacks in Champagne and Artois/Loos, plus a series of diversionary assaults. To improve the chances for a breakthrough in Artois, General Ferdinand Foch, commander of the Northern Group of Armies and General Victor d'Urbal, commander of the Tenth Army, massed some 420 heavy guns (130 more than in May), sought close infantry-artillery coordination, and broadened the Tenth Army's attack frontage. Finally, to overcome the lack of reliable battlefield communications, Allied commanders sought to plan every strategic and tactical detail and schedule everything to the minute. French commanders continued to insist that, if all went according to plan, the morale of their infantry would bring victory.

Despite Joffre's emphasis on careful preparation and coordination, Anglo-French liaison proved poor. Sir John French even remarked that "it was easier to gain information about the strength and composition of the enemy's forces than about the French." Left to his own resources, Haig, whose First Army would make the Loos assault, concluded from the initial German success at Second Ypres that he could overcome his weakness in artillery (110 heavy guns with minimal ammunition) with a surprise gas attack. Haig reckoned that nearly 5,500 cylinders (150 tons) of chlorine gas, quickly followed by a six-division assault (I and IV Corps) against only two German divisions (14th and 117th) would rupture the enemy front near Loos. If the I and IV Corps could seize Hill 70, just east-southeast of Loos, then the I Cavalry Corps and the green XI Corps could advance to exploit the penetration. To tie down German reserves, other BEF formations would launch lesser attacks north of the La Bassée Canal and east of Ypres.

Opposing the Allied forces was Bavarian Crown Prince Rupprecht's Sixth army, seventeen and a half divisions stretched over a thirty-five-mile front. Rupprecht's men were thinly spread but well entrenched, thickly supported by cleverly emplaced machine guns and backed by a completed second line of defense that was generally out of Allied artillery range. The Germans' primary problems were scarce reserves (no more than six divisions and four brigades for the entire Western Front) and the overconfidence of German General Erich von Falkenhayn, who was so certain that the Allies would not attack in the fall of 1915 that he refused to believe intelligence reports of an Allied buildup in Artois or Champagne until early September.

With both sides anticipating success, Joffre, choosing firepower and élan over surprise, began a four-day artillery preparation on 21 September. On 25 September the French infantry went over the top at 09:15 in Champagne and at 12:45 in Artois. Within twenty-four hours, the Tenth Army's XXXIII and XXI corps had seized the fortified town of Souchez in heavy fighting, while the III and XII corps made some minor progress (less than a mile) east and southeast of Neuville St. Vaast. Although there were false reports of a breakthrough by XII Corps, nowhere did the French breach the German's second line of defense. With the attack stalled, Joffre and Foch opted to focus upon the more promising Champagne push, and d'Urbal temporarily suspended offensive operations on 29 September.

Meanwhile, in the early morning of 25 September, Haig's British First Army had attacked at Loos, just north of the French Tenth Army's left flank. Haig had almost postponed the British offensive because of lack of wind, but a slight breeze stirred about 1730 and carried the all-important gas barrage toward the Germans. Much of the gas dissipated harmlessly, some even came back on the British themselves, but a portion reached the German trenches. Exploiting the surprise of the gas barrage, IV Corps overran the German front lines. The 15th Scottish Division reached Hill 70, the green 47th Territorial Division (part of which confidently went over the top kicking soccer balls) seized Loos, and the 1st Division penetrated into the Germans' second line of defense near Hulluch. Further north, the I Corps' 7th and 9th divisions successfully breached the German front lines but stalled at the fallback position at Haisnes. The I Corps' northernmost division, the 2nd, failed miserably because of ineffective artillery and gas barrages. Nonetheless, the BEF successfully carried four to five miles of German trenches and penetrated to a maximum depth of about 4,000–5,000 yards.

Initial British gains were impressive, but an alarming gap had developed between the 1st and 15th divisions, and units of the first wave had suffered heavy losses and were exhausted. A British breakthrough was possible, given the prompt arrival of reserves. Unfortunately, Sir John French had stationed the inexperienced XI Corps (21st and 24th divisions), the first of the new "Kitchener" units to see offensive action in France, well to the rear and under his, rather than Haig's, command. Forced to make an exhausting and disorganizing seven- to ten-mile march forward, the XI Corps did not enter action until the 26th. Thrown into battle between Hill 70 and Hulluch without artillery support, the 21st and 24th divisions were met by fresh German troops who inflicted 8,229 casualties on the green "Kitchener" units. Shattered, these units had to be relieved by the last available infantry division, the Guards, and the Third Cavalry Division. Although the Guards renewed the push on the 27th and 28th, the BEF's chances for success at Loos had slipped away.

In hopes of reinvigorating the stalled offensive, Joffre sent the French IX Corps to the Loos area for a joint assault with the British I Corps, while the Tenth Army prepared a push on the northern end of Vimy Ridge. Rupprecht's Sixth Army, heavily reinforced, delayed these assaults until 10 and 13 October by launching bitter counterattacks. Only near the apex of Vimy Ridge, at Givenchy, did the renewed Allied assaults make even temporary gains. With their troops stalled and exhausted, Sir John French suspended BEF offensive actions on the 14th, while d'Urbal followed suit on the 16th.

Although British communiqués referred to Loos as a tactical success, the streams of returning dead and wounded told otherwise. Public debate concerning Sir John French's handling of the battle focused upon his disastrous employment of the XI Corps. Haig, and even General William Robertson, French's own chief of staff, urged King George V to sack the BEF commander. In a desperate effort to silence his critics, French altered the orders, releasing XI Corps to Haig's control, in an effort to show that he had released them earlier than was actually the case. This unethical and unprofessional act seems to have confirmed all suspicions about French's competence and was the final straw leading to his replacement by Haig on 17 December.

The Third Battle of Artois/Loos Offensive yielded only minor gains. The British seized about 8,000 yards of German trench frontage and penetrated to a depth of about two miles, but they failed to achieve a breakthrough, and they suffered some 62,000 casualties. The French Tenth Army's efforts posted some minor tactical gains, including seizure of the fortified town of Souchez, but at a cost of over 48,000 men. The German Sixth Army reported just over 51,000 casualties during the Third Artois/Loos Offensive. Although official reports continued to strike an optimistic note, Joffre tacitly admitted Allied defeat in Artois by surrendering the initiative there to focus upon the final phases of the Second Battle of Champagne and to prepare for the Salonika Expedition.

David K. Yelton

References

Edmonds, James E., and Wynne, G.C. *Military Operations: France and Belgium, 1915, vol. 2.* In Great Britain, Historical Section of the Committee of Imperial Defence, *History of the Great War Based on Official Documents*. London: Macmillan, 1927.

Ministère de la Guerre. *Etat-Major de l'Armée Service Historique. Les Armées Française dans la Grande Guerre, vol. III.* Paris: Imprimerie Nationale, 1923.

Reichsarchiv. *Der Weltkrieg 1914–1918, vol. 9.* Berlin: E.S. Mittler und Sohn, 1933.

Sixsmith, E.K.G. *British Generalship in the Twentieth Century.* London: Arms and Armour, 1970.

Warner, Philip. *The Battle of Loos.* London: William Kimber, 1976.

See also CHAMPAGNE, SECOND BATTLE OF; FRENCH, JOHN; HAIG, DOUGLAS; JOFFRE, JOSEPH; PÉTAIN, HENRI-PHILIPPE; RUPPRECHT, CROWN PRINCE

Arz von Straussenberg, Baron Arthur (1857–1935)

Chief of the Austro-Hungarian Imperial and Royal General Staff from 1917 to 1918. Born on 11 June 1857 at Hermannstadt, Transylvania, Arz entered the army in 1878 and rose to the rank of major general by 1908. He first achieved prominence while commanding an Austrian corps in the 1915 spring and summer offensives in Poland and distinguished himself in fighting around Gorlice, Przemsyl, and Brest-Litovsk. In 1916 he skillfully handled a scratch force of doubtful quality defending his native Transylvania against the August Romanian offensive, buying enough time to allow Austro-German reinforcements to turn the tide in early October. Thereafter, he led the First Austro-Hungarian Army into Moldavia and battled Russian troops in northern Romania. Because of his outstanding record as a field general and his influential friends at court, Arz von Straussenberg became chief of the Imperial General Staff in March of 1917.

While the even-tempered, bespectacled Arz was a sterling tactician, he proved unequal to the tremendous challenges facing the Austro-Hungarian army in the last half of the war. His influence on the youthful but indecisive Emperor Karl was uncertain, and he only dimly understood the political forces rending the Empire. He also displayed questionable strategic judgment, as in his support for the ill-fated 1918 Piave Offensive, which wasted the last precious reserves of Imperial manpower. By August of 1918, while privately admitting that prolonged resistance was impossible, he nevertheless strove to hold together army and empire. Arz, however, simply lacked the talent and resoluteness necessary to stem the progressive disintegration of the army in the last months of the war. His final act came on 3 November when he assumed the title of supreme commander of the imperial armies an hour before dispatching the order to cease fighting. He died at Budapest on 1 July 1935.

Steven Eden

References

Arz von Straussenberg, Arthur. *Zur Geschichte des Grossen Krieges 1914 bis 1918.* Vienna-Leipzig-Munich, 1924.

Kann, Robert A., Bela K. Kiraly, and Paul S. Fichtner, eds. *The Hapsburg Empire in World War I.* New York: Colombia University Press, 1977.

Rothenberg, Gunther E. *The Army of Francis Joseph.* West Lafayette, Ind.: Purdue University Press, 1976.

See also EAST GALICIA, 1914 CAMPAIGN; ROMANIAN CAMPAIGN, 1916

Asdic

Asdic evolved as a form of antisubmarine warfare during World War I. Unprepared for countering submarines when the war began, the Allied navies finally determined that underwater acoustics were the most efficient method of detecting submerged craft. Previous techniques to deter enemy submarines during the Great War ranged from nets and depth charges to the convoy system.

The British Admiralty established an Anti-Submarine Division in December of 1916. It installed hydrophones, which detected engine noise, in ships at sea. By July of 1917, the Nash Fish hydrophone, towed from British ships, could determine the direction of submarines. From 1915 to 1917 the British also erected twenty-one fixed hydrophone stations along their coasts. While these were of some assistance in defending the island's perimeter, they could not assist vessels in the ocean, where submarine attacks were concentrated. In any case, hydrophones did not work well, and researchers focused on exploring how to utilize ultrasonic waves.

In 1917 French scientist Paul Langevin researched the piezoelectricity of quartz crystals. He used alternating currents to vibrate them so that sound waves pulsed through water were reflected by objects and echoed back to the quartz. The echo created a weak pulse of alternating current that could be detected by electrical instruments. Langevin used an amplifier to increase charges and was able to detect submerged submarines. Tests resulted in clear echoes from as far away as eight kilometers.

Aware of Langevin's work, in 1918 British scientists modeled it and began their own experiments in ultrasonic wave detectors. The term "asdic" was first used to describe supersonic experiments in the 6 July 1918 weekly report of the research facility at Parkeston Quay. It was an abbreviation for Admiralty's Anti-Submarine Divisionic but is often falsely attributed as an acronym of the Allied Submarine Detection Investigation Committee; no such committee is noted in Admiralty archival records.

By the armistice, R.W. Boyle and W.H. Eccles had succeeded in discovering the principles of ultrasonic detection, but their research did not fundamentally affect the war's outcome. If the conflict had continued, however, the Royal Navy would have been the first Allied power to employ ultrasonic sound ranging equipment at sea.

Asdic sent out sound that bounced back to the receiver as a pinging noise. The frequency and loudness of these pings indicated where the sound waves encountered submarines. Because the speed of sound waves was a known quantity, the distance of the submarine could be determined. Asdic operators were trained to interpret the pinging noises.

The first operational asdic transducer, which could transmit and receive signals from distances of 3,000 yards, was manufactured in late 1919. Asdic sets were first installed in patrol boats in 1919 and in destroyers the next year. Asdic estimates were occasionally inaccurate, did not determine depth well, and did not warn of the surface attacks that dominated U-boat offensive maneuvers. Despite these drawbacks, asdic certainly performed better than hydrophones.

British researchers refined asdic between the world wars, enhancing its abilities. Thousands of vessels employed asdic in World War II, when asdic's ability to measure depth was enhanced to detect the deeper-diving, newer submarines. In 1943 the technologically advanced asdic was renamed sonar (sound navigation and ranging), a standard feature of today's anti-submarine warfare.

Elizabeth D. Schafer

References

Hackmann, Willem. *Seek and Strike: Sonar, Anti-Submarine Warfare and the Royal Navy 1914–54*. London: Her Majesty's Stationery Office, 1984.

Hartcup, Guy. *The War of Invention: Scientific Developments, 1914–18*. London: Brassey's Defence Publishers, 1988.

Hill, J.R. *Anti-Submarine Warfare*. 2nd ed. Annapolis, Md.: Naval Institute Press, 1989.

Asquith, Herbert Henry (1852–1928)

Liberal politician in Britain and prime minister from 1908 to 1916. Born in Yorkshire on 12 September 1852, he was educated at Balliol College, Oxford, and studied law at Lincoln's Inn. He entered the House of Commons as a Liberal for East Fife (Scotland) in 1886, a seat he held for the next thirty-two years. He was Gladstone's home secretary from 1892 to 1894 and became chancellor of the exchequer in 1905 after the Liberals' surprising election victory. Following Campbell-Bannerman's resignation in April of 1908, Asquith accepted George V's invitation to form a new government.

From 1908 to 1914 Asquith dealt primarily with major domestic issues—including David Lloyd George's People's Budget in 1909, the Parliament Act of 1911, Irish home rule, and the suffragettes—as menacing war clouds formed over Europe. He believed that England could stay on the sidelines in any European conflict, stating as late as 24 July 1914, "Happily there seems to be no reason why we should be anything more than spectators."

With Germany's invasion of Belgium in early August, Asquith recognized the need for war and so informed the Commons. Personally regretting England's involvement, he nevertheless harbored no doubts about his ability to continue as prime minister and organized his War Council accordingly, relying heavily on Winston Churchill, Edward Grey, Lloyd George, and Lord Kitchener. Partial to his military chiefs, especially Kitchener, and not willing to override their strategic views, Asquith came to favor the concentrated effort on the Western Front. He lamented the split within the Admiralty, particularly between Churchill and Lord John Fisher, but saw no reason to oppose the Dardanelles campaign, especially once Kitchener apparently agreed to it.

In the wake of forming a coalition government in May of 1915, Asquith made two important personnel decisions. First, he named Lloyd George to head the new ministry of munitions. Six months later he replaced General Sir John French as commander in chief of British forces in France with General Sir Douglas Haig, who had been commander of the First Army.

In 1916 Asquith faced a number of governmental crises. Opposing conscription as long as possible, he yielded to the obvious manpower needs and the wishes of the Commons. More alarming still was the Easter Rebellion in Dublin, a crisis that prompted him to make a personal visit to Ireland; in search of a political solution, he managed mainly to alienate the unionists. Then came Kitchener's death at sea in May and the resulting void left at the War Office. Increased shipping losses from U-boat actions and mounting casualties at the Somme led to heated criticism of Asquith as a war leader, a severe cleavage within the Liberal party, and his forced resignation in December. Lloyd George was his successor.

In the 1920s Asquith returned to the Commons (for Paisley, 1920–24), wrote three volumes of memoirs, and accepted such honors as Knight of the Garter and chancellor of Oxford University. He went to the House of Lords as 1st Earl of Oxford and Asquith in 1925, three years before his death on 15 February 1928 in Berkshire at the age of seventy-five.

Thomas W. Davis

References

Jenkins, Roy. *Asquith*. Revised edition. London: Collins, 1978.
Koss, Stephen E. *Asquith*. New York: St. Martin's, 1976.
Spender, John A., and Cyril Asquith. *Life of Herbert Henry Asquith*. 2 vols. London: Hutchinson, 1932.

See also GREAT BRITAIN, HOME FRONT

Atrocities (1914–19)

World War I and the birth of total industrial warfare saw new weapons, new tactics, and new attitudes toward civilians. In total warfare, war is waged against civilians as well as an enemy army. Nonetheless the world was shocked and outraged by acts during the war that have been labeled atrocities. In many cases exactly what happened will never be known, because both sides exploited atrocity stories for propaganda purposes.

Belgium was the first focus of atrocity reports. In August of 1914 Germany disregarded both the Hague and Geneva conventions by violating the neutrality of Belgium and Luxembourg in order to invade France. As the Germans crossed Belgian territory, the Allies accused them of massacring people, looting homes, and burning towns and villages. There were accounts of German soldiers bayoneting babies to doors, violating women and young girls, mutilating bodies, and torturing and killing men found in the towns. The Germans executed nurse Edith Cavell for assisting Allied soldiers in Brussels. Once the Germans settled in Belgium, they reportedly deported between 80,000 and 120,000 Belgians to work in Germany. Some testified that items such as food and clothing sent to Belgians by relief agencies were used by the Germans instead. The Allies also accused the Germans of providing inadequate care for Allied prisoners of war.

The Germans replied to these charges with their own accusations. They reported that the citizens of Belgium were attacking the German soldiers and aiding the enemy. Under these circumstances, the Germans felt it necessary to use force to control the territory they occupied. According to the Hague conventions of 1899 and 1907, resistance on the part of civilians in occupied territory warranted the death penalty. The Germans also alleged that French and Belgian civilians had mutilated dead German soldiers by gouging out their eyes.

There were also cultural atrocities. Between 25 and 30 August 1914, the Germans ransacked and burned the medieval town of Louvain, Belgium. They destroyed the university library, churches, shrines, cemeteries, priceless artwork, and medieval manuscript collections. The Germans carried this out as an act of reprisal against the Belgians for firing on German troops, thereby breaking international law by destroying cultural sites not directly involved in the war. The Germans responded to these charges by asserting that the Belgians had broken international law first by firing on German troops.

At the same time that these actions were taking place in Belgium, Britain began enforcing the Aliens Restriction Act of 1914. This act restricted areas in which people of German and Austrian heritage could live and work. Between August of 1914 and May of 1915, the government selectively arrested and interned German and Austrian males of military age; by late 1914, 10,000 were in captivity. German and Austrian women and children were encouraged to return to their homelands. In May of 1915, after news reached London of the sinking of the *Lusitania,* the government began interning all alien males and deporting women and children. Only those who could secure a tribunal exemption were spared. In the next two years the number of those in captivity rose to 32,000, while 10,000 were forcibly deported. Fathers and husbands were interned, leaving no breadwinner for these families. Anti-German and anti-Austrian sentiment made it hard for the women to find jobs. Even though many of these families had lived in Britain for generations, Germany bitterly protested their treatment.

The German government also deported civilians in occupied France. Pretending to be concerned about the lack of work in Lillie, Tourcoing, and Roubaix, the Germans forcibly removed and relocated French citizens. These people were made to work in labor camps for the Germans. Women made up a large number of these workers, although the Germans made it clear that women between the ages of fourteen and twenty would not be removed without another member of their family. The Germans deported approximately 20,000 French citizens to work but later returned five thousand women and children to their homes. The French government protested the treatment of its citizens in occupied territory but was unable to prevent it.

The Allies labeled German submarine warfare an atrocity because the Germans ultimately resorted to sinking unarmed merchant ships without warning. The Germans justified their action, saying that in order to warn a ship a submarine was forced to surface, making it an easy target for its adversary. In some cases Britain used decoy Q-ships with hidden armament to attack U-boats. When submarines surfaced to warn the ship that they were going to sink it, in order to spare lives, the Q-ship would fire on the U-boat. The Q-ships encouraged German submarines to discontinue these warnings. One of the most controversial acts occurred when a German submarine sank the *Lusitania* on 7 May 1915, killing 1,198 passengers, including 128 Americans. The Allies neglected to mention in their propaganda that the *Lusitania* was carrying munitions. Americans were infuriated by the incident. President Wilson secured a German promise not to sink passenger ships and to adequately warn others. The Germans did not keep their promise; in February of 1917 the Germans began a policy of unrestricted submarine warfare.

The Allied blockade of Germany was also seen as a great atrocity, particularly its continuation after the armistice. The Allied Powers initiated the blockade at the end of 1914. The Allies hoped to weaken Germany by blocking the shipment of contraband. German civilians suffered terribly from lack of food and other supplies, and the German government was unable to obtain needed supplies with which to sustain its military. The Allies continued to search and seize ships destined for Germany until the German government signed the Treaty of Versailles on 28 June 1919. The German government claimed that the blockade was the worst atrocity of the war, because it caused German women and children to starve to death.

German chemical warfare also became a target of Allied atrocity propaganda, because it directly violated the Hague agreement. Once the Germans initiated it, however, the British and French did not hesitate to develop and use chemical weapons of their own. By the end of the war neither side considered chemical warfare unlawful.

Perhaps the best documented World War I atrocity was Turkey's systematic attempt to exterminate the Armenians, between 1914 and 1918. The Armenians had long been the target of massacres and persecution. Turkey may have been motivated by jealousy of Armenian economic success. The Turks conducted house-to-house searches in each town or village known to have an Armenian population. These people were then marched out of town. The men were separated and killed, many children under twelve were sold into slavery, and the most attractive young girls and women were sold to harems. The remaining women and children were subjected to continual torture, rape, and other harassment. From 1915 to 1918 an estimated 800,000 to 1,000,000 Armenians were killed. While the Allies blamed the Germans for the atrocity, there is no evidence to prove their complicity.

In the years following World War I it became apparent that some of the atrocities never occurred, and those that did were exploited by governments for propaganda purposes. Citizens lost faith in their governments. World War I propaganda concerning atrocities was responsible in some degree for widespread disbelief concerning stories of German atrocities against Jews and other minorities in World War II.

Meredith L. Bragg

References

Bland, J.O.P. *Germany's Violations of the Laws of War 1914–15*. New York: G.P. Putnam's Sons, 1915.

Cesarani, D., and Tony Kushner, eds. *The Internment of Aliens in Twentieth Century Britain*. Portland, Oreg.: Frank Cass, 1993.

Read, James Morgan. *Atrocity Propaganda, 1914–1919*. New Haven: Yale University Press, 1941.

Siney, Marion C. *The Allied Blockade of Germany 1914–1916*. Ann Arbor: University of Michigan Press, 1957.

Stokesbury, James L. *A Short History of World War I*. New York: William Morrow, 1981.

Toynbee, Arnold J. *Armenian Atrocities: The Murder of a Nation*. New York: Hodder and Stoughton, 1915.

———. *The German Terror in France*. New York: Hodder and Stoughton, 1917.

———. *The Treatment of Armenians in the Ottoman Empire, 1915–16*. London: Sir Joseph Causton and Sons, 1916.

See also BELGIUM, OCCUPATION OF; CAVELL, EDITH; PROPAGANDA, USE IN WAR.

Auffenberg-Komarów, Baron Moritz von (1852–1928)

Austro-Hungarian politician and general. Born in Troppau (Opava) on 22 May 1852, Moritz von Auffenberg was a controversial figure who made numerous political and professional enemies while trying to modernize the Hapsburg army. Through the influence of Archduke Franz Ferdinand he became minister of war in September of 1911, a post he held until December of 1912. In that position he increased both the size of the Hapsburg army and the level of military spending. His antipathy toward the Hungarians made him a political liability and, in December of 1912, Emperor Franz Josef forced him to resign.

In August of 1914, Auffenberg commanded the Fourth Army on the Galician front. In carrying out the plan of Commander in Chief Franz Conrad von Hötzendorf to drive the Russians out of Galicia, Auffenberg's Fourth Army advanced 100 miles northward, capturing Komarów and nearly outflanking the Russian Fifth Army. Austro-Hungarian defeats to the south, where the Russian Third and Eighth armies had pushed back the heavily outnumbered Austro-Hungarian Third Army, forced Conrad to order Auffenberg to disengage and go to the aid of the Third Army. In shifting his axis of attack from northeast to south, to comply with Conrad's order, Auffenberg opened a gap with the Austrian First Army to the north that Conrad failed to cover with sufficient troops. As a result, the Russian Fifth Army penetrated the gap, threatening to roll up both the First and Fourth armies. This led to the disastrous battle of Rawa Ruska (5 to 11 September 1914), which forced an Austro-Hungarian retreat of over 200 miles, with high losses of both men and equipment. The line was stabilized some 100 miles inside Austrian territory, after the fall of Lemberg and most of East Galicia to the Russians.

Although Auffenberg had merely carried out Conrad's orders, he was made the scapegoat for the defeat and was forced to resign his command. In April of 1915 he was arrested for alleged irregularities with army accounts during his tenure as minister of war. The subsequent trial led to his acquittal and release. His reputation, however, was so damaged that he held no further military or political positions. He devoted his remaining years to writing, producing two volumes of memoirs and numerous articles after the war. He died in Vienna on 18 May 1928.

Charles H. Bogart

References

Auffenberg-Komarów, Moritz von. *Aus Österreichs Höhe und Niedergang, Eine Lebensschilderung.* Munich: Drei-Masken-Verlag, 1921.
————. *Aus Österreichs Teilnahme am Weltkrieg.* Berlin: Ullstein, 1920.
Stone, Norman. *The Eastern Front, 1914–1917.* New York: Scribner, 1975.

See also EAST GALICIA, 1914 CAMPAIGN

Augagneur, Jean Victor (1855–1931)

French politician. Born 16 May 1855 in Lyon, Augagneur was trained as a physician and was an advocate of an enlightened public-health policy. His immediate prewar years were spent as mayor of Lyon, deputy from the Rhône, and colonial governor of Madagascar.

When World War I began, Augagneur was minister of the navy in the René Viviani government (1914–15). His significance rests, unfortunately, on the fact that he committed France to one of the war's biggest fiascos: the 1915 Dardanelles campaign. In response to Russia's pleas in January of 1915 for an Allied demonstration against Turkey, Britain's first lord of the admiralty, Winston Churchill, proposed to Augagneur that the Allies smash through the Dardanelles by ships alone. In addition, Churchill informed Augagneur that, in order to support the attack on the Dardanelles, Britain intended to occupy Alexandretta, a seaport in southwestern Turkey. Augagneur rejected any British plan to land at Alexandretta. He was afraid that a British landing there would prevent France from fulfilling her imperial goal of taking Syria and Lebanon. Churchill understood France's concerns and abandoned the idea of a landing at Alexandretta. In return, Augagneur, despite the warning of French naval authorities that an attempt to force the Dardanelles by ships alone would fail, agreed to place a French squadron under British command for the forthcoming disastrous Dardanelles campaign. Augagneur's acceptance of the campaign was based not on military but imperial considerations. He feared that if the Dardanelles were forced and Britain were to gain control of Constantinople without French participation, Britain would be in total control of the Middle East. To allow Asiatic Turkey to be incorporated into the British empire with no share for France would be a threat to France's national prestige and her standing as a great power.

When the Viviani government resigned in October of 1915, Augagneur returned to the Chamber of Deputies. Defeated for reelection in 1919, Augagneur later served as governor of French Equatorial Africa. He died at Vésinet on 23 April 1931.

Jan Karl Tanenbaum

References

Cassar, George H. *The French and the Dardanelles: A Study in Failure in the Conduct of War.* London: George Allen and Unwin, 1971.
Halpern, Paul G. *The Naval War in the Mediterranean 1914–1918.* Annapolis, Md.: Naval Institute Press, 1987.

See also DARDANELLES CAMPAIGN

Austria-Hungary, Army, 1914–18

Since the *Ausgleich* of 1867, the Dual Monarchy of Austria-Hungary had been a union of the Empire of Austria and the Kingdom of Hungary. The two countries conducted their own domestic affairs and were united only for defense and foreign affairs and in the person of the emperor. Military affairs reflected this arrangement. There were three armies, Imperial, Austrian, and Hungarian, each with its own minister, general staff, and annual budget.

The Imperial, or Common, Army recruited in both countries. Its units were entitled Imperial and Royal (*Kaiserlich und Königlich*, or *KuK*). Austria and Hungary also recruited armies in their own territories; these were called *Landwehr*, though the Hungarian *Landwehr* was known unofficially as the *Honved*. Under the 1867 arrangement, the Imperial Army was to provide an expeditionary force of fifty-five divisions, leaving the two *Landwehr* responsible for home defense. This proved impracticable, and in 1890 the *Landwehr* were upgraded to first-class status. The three armies were to come together in time of war to form one Austro-Hungarian army. Equipment, weapons, training doctrines, and organizations were to be common, though this had not been entirely achieved by 1914. At the same time, the *Landsturm* (reserve army) of each country was modernized to undertake home defense in the absence of the *Landwehr*.

Most recruits were conscripts, with every fit man liable for service at age twenty-one. Recruiting districts had to select enough men every year to meet the needs of the Imperial Army and its own country's *Landwehr*. Those selected served three years on active duty and ten in the reserves (infantry), or four and seven years (in cavalry and artillery). On completion of his commitment a reservist was transferred to the *Landsturm*.

There were three ways to avoid conscription. Men in key occupations or a family's sole breadwinner served for ten weeks only and were then placed on the *Ersatz* Reserve, which was called on only upon full mobilization. Those who could afford to maintain themselves without pay had to serve for only one year. This option was attractive to educated men wanting to avoid a long disruption in their university studies and was regarded by the authorities as providing a pool of potential officers in the event of war. Lastly, a man could become a regular, serving three years on active duty and seven in the reserves. Only about one-third of the Imperial Army and a mere 5 percent of the *Landwehr* were regular soldiers.

Over the centuries officers had been mainly aristocrats, but in the fifty or so years before 1914 there had been great change. By World War I they were predominately from the middle class. The German states were another source of officer recruitment that had dried up. Prior to 1870 many ambitious Germans made their careers in the Austro-Hungarian army, but the proclamation of the German Empire provided them an expanding army of their own to serve. This loss of military talent was a sore blow to Austria-Hungary.

Officers for both the Imperial Army and the *Landwehr* came from two sources. A pupil could enter a military preparatory school at age twelve and then pass into a military academy at eighteen. The Imperial Army ran two such academies, one for infantry and cavalry, and one for artillery and engineers. Each *Landwehr* had one as well. Alternatively, at age eighteen a young man could enter one of the eleven cadet schools of the Imperial Army or one of the three run by the *Landwehr*. Some 40 percent followed the first route and 60 percent the second. Either way, the young man would be commissioned at age twenty-two after a four-year course.

One problem faced by the Austro-Hungarian officers was language. The empire was multinational. In 1914 its population consisted of approximately 23 percent Germans, 19 percent Magyars, 13 percent Czechs, 10 percent Poles, 8 percent Ruthenians, 6 percent Rumanians, 6 percent Croats, 4 percent Serbs, 4 percent Slovaks, 3 percent Slovenes, and others (Italians, Bosnians, gypsies, and so forth). The three armies reflected this mix, though the Slavs, with 44 percent of the armies' strength, supplied 67 percent of the infantry. Although the official language of command in the Imperial Army and *Landwehr* was German, officers were expected to learn the language of their men, each regiment having one or more official languages. It has been estimated that, in the Imperial Army, 142 units had one regimental language, 163 had two, 24 had three, and a few four or even five languages. A similar problem existed in the Austrian *Landwehr*. Hungary had to cope with Magyar, Croat, and Slovak.

When these armies, composed mainly of conscripts and reservists, mobilized in July of 1914, they mustered forty-nine infantry and eleven cavalry divisions, organized into sixteen corps and six armies. Before the war the three armies had been starved of money, and these formations, although strong in numbers, were poorly equipped compared with the armies of the other major powers. By 1918 this force had expanded to seventy-eight divisions, twenty-six corps, and nine armies.

The Austro-Hungarian army fought the entire war on a variety of fronts. Losses in the first year were 42 percent of mobilization strength. Replacing these losses, while at the same time expanding from sixty to seventy-eight divisions and also keeping factories and farms running, placed a severe strain on manpower, a problem never solved by the imperial government. In all, 7.8 million men served in the army (the 1910 population of the empire was 51 million), of whom 922,000 (11.8 percent) were killed and 3.6 million (46.2 percent) wounded.

Imperial officials had always hoped that this multiracial army, bound together by its oath of loyalty to the emperor, would rise above the petty national squabbles that disturbed the empire. Under the pressures of such a long and bloody war, however, this proved impossible. Not all the nationalities were enthusiastic members of the empire, a fact reflected in high rates of surrender and desertion. In the first year of the war the Allies took almost half a million Austro-Hungarian prisoners. In one case a complete regiment, the 218th Infantry, made up entirely of Czechs, gave itself up to the Russians. Despite these nationalistic pressures and the lack of attention and funds for the prewar military, the Austro-Hungarian army remained an effective fighting force until a few weeks before the 1918 armistice.

Another problem was lack of ability at the highest level. In Serbia, Russia, and Italy, Austro-Hungarian formations were placed under German command after mistakes by their own generals, and Austria-Hungary's two greatest triumphs, against Serbia in 1915 and Italy in 1917, were achieved alongside German troops and under German direction.

An Austro-Hungarian corps usually contained three divisions. Infantry divisions had one cavalry, one artillery, and two infantry brigades; cavalry divisions had two cavalry brigades and three horse artillery batteries. Brigades of all three arms usually had two regiments. These regiments were the building blocks of the army in peace and war and the repository of its history and traditions. Although commanded by professional officers, each had an honorary colonel-in-chief (*Inhaber*), usually a member of the royal family or a distinguished retired senior officer, whose name was incorporated into the regiment's title along with its permanent number during his period in office (for example, 1st [Kaiser Franz Josef] Infantry Regiment, or 14th [General von Kolossvary] Hussars). A regiment had its own recruiting area, where it maintained a depot responsible for recruitment, training, mobilization, and reinforcements.

Infantry was recognized as the paramount arm. A 1911 manual stated that "the infantry is the main arm and decides the outcome of battle." On mobilization, the Imperial Army provided 102 infantry regiments, the Austrian *Landwehr* 38, and the Hungarian *Landwehr* 32. Each consisted of a machine-gun company (eight weapons) and four battalions (or three in the *Landwehr*) of four companies. At full strength an imperial battalion numbered 1,000 men and a *Landwehr* battalion 800. Every regiment had to supply a company for the divisional HQ defense unit. In addition to these standard infantry regiments, there was one Jäger (light infantry) battalion per division and also a number of specialist mountain units.

In the middle of the First World War, Austrian gray uniforms were replaced by German field-gray; by 1918 all Austro-Hungarian infantrymen wore German-style steel helmets. Each infantryman carried 100 rounds of ammunition, a greatcoat, water, and one day's rations. The standard rifle was the 1895 Mannlichen; mountain troops were armed with the 1890 Stutzen carbine. Machine-gun companies were armed with the Schwarzlose. All these weapons were 8mm.

As in other armies, the firepower of the Austro-Hungarian infantry increased as the war progressed. Its equipment also became more sophisticated. In 1916 a technical company, with mortar, grenadier, telephone, and searchlight sections, was added to each battalion. In the same year regimental machine-gun companies were increased from eight to sixteen weapons; a year later they grew to twenty-four, and each battalion was given a platoon of eight light machine guns. The only major organizational change came in October of 1917 when four battalion regiments were reduced to three battalions, the fourth battalions being used to form new regiments.

All armies entered World War I with large cavalry forces, only to find little use for them under modern conditions. Austria-Hungary was no exception, and it mobilized sixty-four regiments, each split into "half-regiments" of three squadrons. A squadron contained about 150 men, a complete regiment 1,000. Apart from its three-horse artillery batteries, four machine guns constituted the only other modern weapons in a cavalry division. It was soon realized that such formations had no place on a World War I battlefield, and as early as 1915 some regiments were dismounted.

By the end of 1917 there was but one mounted squadron to a division, infantry, or cavalry. Cavalry divisions now had four dismounted regiments, each half-regiment containing four squadrons; in addition a regiment had sixteen machine guns, sixteen light machine guns, and a technical company organized on infantry lines.

In 1914 the artillery had three major defects, the result of earlier financial restraints and poor planning by the general staff. Most of its weapons were out of date and outranged by its enemies; divisions had less artillery than in other major armies; and the proportion of guns to howitzers was too high. On mobilization there were fifty field-gun regiments (each with five batteries of eight guns), fourteen field-howitzer regiments (four batteries of six howitzers), five horse-artillery regiments (six batteries of four guns), seven heavy regiments (four batteries of four guns), and ten mountain regiments (seven batteries of six guns). All were capable of splitting into "half-regiments" for tactical purposes. They manned 2,562 weapons, about 82 percent of the planned mobilization figure. There were also twenty-eight fortress battalions of various sizes, mainly manning forts on the Alpine frontier with Italy.

Each infantry division contained a brigade composed of a field-gun regiment and a field-howitzer regiment or "half regiment." Cavalry regiments had their "half-regiment" of horse artillery. Heavy and mountain artillery was deployed at corps level.

In 1914 most guns and howitzers were obsolescent, particularly the 90mm gun and 105mm howitzer, the artillery pieces of the infantry divisions. The exceptions were twenty-four 305mm howitzers, introduced in 1912, some of which supported the Germans in France. New weapons—a 75mm mountain gun, 100mm and 105mm field guns and howitzers—came into service in 1915 and 1916. Many of these had been originally destined for the Chinese and Turkish armies.

During the First World War artillery in the Austro-Hungarian army expanded greatly; both organizations and weapons underwent change. The numbers of heavy, field, and mountain batteries increased by factors of 11, 2.25, and 4.5 respectively. The ratio of guns to howitzers fell from 4.5/1 to 0.33/1. These changes are reflected in the February 1918 reorganization. Henceforth, each infantry division had two field regiments (each of two gun batteries, three howitzer batteries, and one AA battery), a heavy regiment (of one gun battery and four howitzer batteries), and a mountain "half-regiment" (of one howitzer battery and two gun batteries). Horse artillery regiments supporting the dis-

mounted cavalry divisions contained two gun batteries, four howitzer batteries, and one AA battery.

Fortress artillery was even more obsolete at the start of the war. Some of it dated back to 1861, and the only modern pieces, a few 240mm guns, were soon dispatched to the Eastern Front. The old weapons were slowly replaced by 100mm turreted guns, 240mm and 350mm guns, and 210mm, 380mm and 420mm mortars.

The Austro-Hungarian Engineer Corps in 1914 was made up of one pontoon, eight pioneer, and fourteen sapper battalions. In 1917 it was reorganized into composite battalions, one per division. Flamethrower units, developed during the war, became an engineer responsibility. The Signal Corps increased from 16 to 249 companies, the Railway Corps from 34 to 71. Motorized transport units were introduced during the war.

The Flying Corps (*Luftfahrttruppen*) grew dramatically. It started the war with one company of six aircraft and a number of balloons and ended the war with eighty-two aircraft and thirty-two balloon companies. Despite this expansion, capabilities always lagged behind requirements. Priority was given to reconnaissance, though a small number of fighter and bomber companies were formed. Most aircraft models were Austrian-designed, but a few were German manufactured under license.

The Austro-Hungarian army ceased to exist when the empire it had served for three centuries collapsed at the end of the war. Its history is commemorated in the Heersgeschichtliches Museum in Vienna.

Philip J. Green

References

Haythornthwaite, Philip J. *The World War One Source Book*. London: Arms and Armour, 1992.

Lucas, James. *Fighting Troops of the Austro-Hungarian Army, 1868–1914*. New York: Hippocrene Books, 1987.

Taylor, A.J.P. *The Hapsburg Monarchy, 1915–18*. London: Hamish Hamilton, 1944.

Zeman, Z.A.B. *The Break-up of the Hapsburg Empire, 1914–1918*. London: Oxford University Press, 1961.

See also AUSTRIA-HUNGARY, HOME FRONT

Austria-Hungary, Home Front

The Austro-Hungarian Empire entered the twentieth century in a state of almost constant indebtedness and political turmoil. Riven by ethnic tensions as its Slavic residents agitated for greater participation in the government, the empire's divided and cumbersome bureaucracy found it could neither reform itself nor control the dissent. Indeed, Austria-Hungary's disparate ethnic groups were united only by their veneration for a respected leader and fear of being dominated by a powerful neighboring state. Aging Emperor Franz Josef was the leader to whom all felt a sympathetic if not passionate loyalty. Russia and Germany were the powerful, domineering, and feared neighbors, the latter resented by a growing proportion of the empire's population. As a result, many of the emperor's advisors welcomed the war (although he did not), believing it would be a short-lived affair that would divert the empire's restive Slavs away from political agitation. The government's disastrous military and economic performance, however, gradually wore away at its credibility and the population's support waned as the war progressed. The empire's disintegration accelerated after the emperor's death in December of 1916. Yet despite its problems and failures, the empire retained the loyalty of the majority of its inhabitants until early 1918.

Ironically, the majority of the empire's subjects felt sympathy for the emperor at the death of his heir, Archduke Franz Ferdinand, assassinated at Sarajevo on 28 July 1914. In fact, all but the empire's ethnic Serbs supported the government's declaration of war against Serbia. Even its most vocal Czech and Croat political dissidents agreed to cease political agitation for the duration of what most observers felt was going to be a very short war. Both they and the emperor's advisors were to be sadly disappointed. More significantly, belief in a conflict of limited duration led the government to neglect long-term economic considerations, which severely damaged the empire's ability to sustain its war effort. Despite the abysmal performance of its army in the field, it was the empire's political and economic failings that brought it down.

The empire's political problems can be traced to the diverse makeup of its population and cumbersome governmental structure. Austria-Hungary was a dual monarchy, consisting, officially at least, of two equal, semiautonomous kingdoms, Austria and Hungary. The emperor served as sovereign of both, and in theory the kingdoms had domestic autonomy, while the imperial (central) government in Vienna was responsible for foreign policy, the military, the postal system, and internal security. One exception was a type of national guard known as the *Landwehr* in Austria and *Honved* in Hungary, which served under the two kingdoms in peacetime but came under the central government during war. As a practical matter, however, the central government could impose its will on Hungary only with difficulty, particularly with respect to economic and political policies. The two kingdoms conducted their affairs in their respective official languages: German in Austria and Magyar in Hungary. By 1906 Hungary had gained the right to raise and train its own units for the army.

This divided government structure led to duplication and inefficiency, which was aggravated further by the competing interests of the two states, both of which contained significant Slavic populations. Many in the Austrian and central governments favored a triple monarchy, which would give the Slavs their own kingdom within the empire, drawing territory from the Slavic lands of both of the current kingdoms. The Hungarians vehemently opposed such reforms, preferring to whittle away at the Austrian dominance of the central government in hopes of gaining eventual control of it for themselves. This competition manifested itself most often during the central government's annual budgetary deliberations.

The central government's budget was funded by contributions negotiated between it and the two kingdoms. This lack of direct taxing authority inhibited its ability to raise operating funds. The nature of the process, moreover, precluded the central government from formulating any consistent or long-term budget planning. Hungary exploited the budget process to gain political concessions from the emperor, who of course resisted strenuously. The resulting struggle, which continued throughout the war, undermined public confidence and led both to a shortfall in government funding and disparity in tax burden between the two kingdoms. The former was dealt with by a combination of borrowing and printing money, which ultimately led to inflation. The latter problem was never adequately addressed and became an increasingly divisive issue as the war progressed.

This uncertain budgetary process, coupled with the empire's deep indebtedness, also affected the empire's internal development. The government lacked funds to develop the empire's infrastructure or to sponsor technological developments. As a result, industrialization lagged behind that of the other great powers. Even Imperial Russia had a more highly developed industrial sector than Austria-Hungary. Thus, Austria-Hungary entered a modern war with an army smaller than the one it had had in 1866 and one less well equipped than those of its likely opponents. More significant was that it lacked the industrial capacity to sustain military operations in a modern war. Finally, the empire was neither self-sufficient in food production, nor did its transportation network have the surplus capacity to sustain both the war effort and domestic economic production and distribution.

The central government exacerbated this situation by mobilizing all reserves at war's start, including critical skilled laborers. Thus production fell at a time when ordnance and armaments were needed most. Nor did the government implement rationing of critical materials until well into 1915. Worse, it lacked the authority to impose a consistent rationing program throughout its territories. As the war progressed, inflation and problems of food distribution eroded support for the government. The central government's efforts to resolve these problems only deepened the empire's other problems or created new ones.

In 1915, for example, the central government belatedly recognized the shortsightedness of its mobilization policies and exempted certain industrial workers from military duties. The Hungarian leadership protested almost immediately. Because most industry was located in the Austrian half of the empire, this exemption led to a disproportionate number of Hungarians serving in the military. The Hungarians were then allowed to exempt some categories of farm workers. Naturally, the disenfranchised Slavs did not benefit from either policy.

This situation worsened as the war went on and supplies of even the most basic foods and domestic materials declined. The emperor's death on 21 November 1916 removed the empire's one remaining unifying factor. His successor, emperor Karl, lacked Franz Josef's familiarity or credibility with the people. This led him to cede greater autonomy to the Hungarian government in exchange for their loyalty to the crown. Coming at a time when the central government needed more

authority and other reforms to stabilize the country's economy, his actions further reduced his support and effectiveness. The Slavs remained disenfranchised in the Hungarian half of the empire and the Hungarian government continued to withhold food supplies from the Austrian half of the empire. This led to growing dissatisfaction and political agitation within both parts of the empire.

The central government also inhibited its ability to mobilize public support by not convening parliament until 1917. The emperor belatedly urged his ministers to convene the body in May of that year, in an effort to garner support for his governmental and political reforms. By then, it was too late. The Austrian socialists and Slavic parties, in particular, let it be known that they had little loyalty left for either the monarchy or the empire. Radical German nationalists openly argued for union with Germany. Yet surprisingly, the majority of the parliament and the empire's population remained loyal. Every anti-Hapsburg statement and gesture from Slavic independence groups, including those in exile, was condemned by local Slavic authorities, including Czech authorities, and followed by statements of loyalty and solidarity with the crown. Some of this was coerced, and those who supported independence had been arrested. Still, the new emperor recognized that the empire's survival, at least over the near term, depended on a quick end to the war. Tied ever too tightly to Germany, he could not bring it about.

As the war continued, the population's expanding economic deprivation and political frustration ate away the remaining fabric of the empire. Inflation eroded the living standards of the working class within the Austrian half of the empire, which led to growing labor and political unrest as 1917 wore on. Meanwhile the Hungarian government, under Prime Minister Count István Tisza, grew increasingly oppressive in its efforts to control the Slavic elements of its population. Employing Hungary's control of the empire's food supplies to gain political concessions from the new emperor, Tisza unwittingly destroyed the fabric of the very empire he was trying to dominate. Frustrated with the emperor's inability or unwillingness to control Hungarian excesses, the empire's Slavs began to lose faith in the central government. This was exacerbated by a deepening resentment of Germany's increasing dominance over the policies of the central and Austrian governments.

The final straw came in January of 1918 with the publication of President Wilson's Fourteen Points. Promising "autonomy for all the peoples of the Austrian Empire," this proclamation was believed to be an offer of both political freedom and security from German, Russian, and Hungarian domination. In the eyes of its Slavic subjects, this perception undercut the empire's last justification for existence. Germany's failure to win the war with its "final offensives" of March 1918 accelerated the process. An Entente victory seemed all but inevitable, and with it would go the empire's ability to protect its subjects.

In June of 1918 the Czech National Council was formally recognized by the Entente powers, while south Slav nationalists, albeit still a minority among the monarchy's Slavs, declared an independent state in Zagreb. The emperor's advisors urged him to declare the empire a confederacy of independent states but, as always, the plan foundered in the face of Hungarian intransigence. Faced with a restive Slavic population in its territories, the Hungarian government recalled Hungarian forces from all fronts in August of 1918. By October, the emperor controlled only selective units of the army and the German areas of the Austrian half of the empire. Emperor Karl formally abdicated on 3 November 1918, but his empire had ended some weeks before. The five-hundred-year reign of the Hapsburgs in central Europe was over.

Contrary to popular myth, the majority of the empire's subjects remained loyal until the war's final months. As with modern Yugoslavia, Austria-Hungary's disparate ethnic nationalities were united only by their common fear of their neighbors. That unity ended with the removal of the threat posed by those neighbors, particularly Imperial Germany and Russia. Denied that unifying external threat, the empire could have survived only through political reforms establishing a confederal governmental system. Unfortunately, neither Franz Josef nor his successor, Karl, ever found the means to overcome Hungarian resistance or accommodate the political aspirations of their Slavic subjects. It was that failure, and not the war, that ultimately destroyed their empire.

Carl O. Schuster

References

Crankshaw, Edward. *The Fall of the House of Habsburg.* London: Macmillan, 1981.
Czernin, Ottokar. *Im Weltkrieg.* Berlin: Verlegt bei Ullstein, 1919.
Michel, Bernard. *La Chute de L'Empire Austro-Hongrois, 1916–1918.* Paris: Robert Laffont, 1991.
Stone, Norman. *The Eastern Front, 1914–1917.* London: Houghton and Stoddart, 1975.

See also CZECHS; FRANZ FERDINAND; FRANZ JOSEF; KARL I, EMPEROR OF AUSTRIA; SLOVAKS; TISZA, ISTVÁN; YUGOSLAVIA, CREATION OF

Austria-Hungary, Navy, 1914–18

The Austro-Hungarian navy (*Kaiserlich und Königlich Kriegsmarine*) was a significant factor in the Mediterranean until it disappeared along with the empire and dynasty it served. The Austrian decision before the war to build dreadnought-type battleships and transform the navy from a purely coastal defense force to one capable of fighting on the high seas revolutionized the Mediterranean naval situation. If the Austrians were to join with the naval forces of Italy, the Triple Alliance might be able to win control of the Mediterranean. The Austrians were actually building *against* the Italians, but both were allied to Germany in the Triple Alliance, and in 1913 a Triple Alliance Naval Convention was concluded foreshadowing exactly such a combination. It proved to be an illusion once Italy declared its neutrality in August of 1914.

At the beginning of the war the Austrians had three Tegetthoff-class dreadnoughts (a fourth was completed in 1915), three semidreadnought Radetzky class, six predreadnoughts, three coast-defense ships, two armored cruisers, three protected cruisers, two fast light cruisers (another pair were completed within a few months), eighteen destroyers, twenty-one to thirty high-seas torpedo boats, approximately forty coastal torpedo boats, six monitors and five to six patrol boats for service on the Danube, and three submarines (another two were useful only for training and local defense).

Inasmuch as the Austrian fleet alone was far inferior to that of the French, it is not surprising that its commander, Admiral Anton Haus, followed a basically defensive strategy. At the beginning of the war the Germans wanted the Austrians to sail to Messina to support Admiral Wilhelm Souchon's *Goeben* and *Breslau,* which were blockaded by British forces. The Austrian fleet was not fully mobilized and Haus refused, for he did not know the location of the French fleet, which he incorrectly assumed was rushing to the scene. The most he eventually agreed to do was to cover the Germans when they reached Austrian waters in an attempt to reach Pola. The Austrians sailed and were about halfway down the Adriatic when Haus learned that Souchon was heading to Constantinople, and he immediately returned to Pola.

The Austrian fleet would remain the classic "fleet-in-bèing," secure in its anchorage at Pola. Haus resisted pressure from the Germans—and some from his own countrymen—to send the fleet to Constantinople for operations against the Russians in the Black Sea. He considered the scheme impracticable, if only because Constantinople lacked sufficient coal and docking facilities. The main reasons, however, were his desire to keep the fleet intact in the face of the uncertain attitude of the Italians and his understandable reluctance to leave the Austrian coast exposed. That concern was justified when Italy concluded the Treaty of London with the Entente on 26 April 1915 and entered the war within a month. Within hours of the Italian declaration of war Haus took the fleet to sea on 23 May and bombarded various points on the Italian coast. It was the first and only time the entire fleet would be at sea for a military operation during the war. Nevertheless, the fact that there was a nucleus of six to seven modern and powerful Austrian battleships meant that the French or Italians could venture far into the Adriatic only if they were prepared to meet them. This meant employing similar heavy ships, which was dangerous under the altered conditions of war in which submarines came to play an increasing role. The French and Italians chose not to take this risk, and the Austrian fleet by its very existence raised the potential price of any offensive, and thereby fulfilled a useful function preserving the Austrian coast from attack.

The handful of Austrian submarines had an effect far out of proportion to their numbers by making the Adriatic too dangerous for the big ships of the French navy. On 21 December 1914, *U.12* torpedoed (but did not sink) the French flagship *Jean Bart*, and on the night of 26–27 April 1915 *U.5* torpedoed and sank the French armored cruiser *Léon Gambetta*. Soon after joining the war, the Italians also lost two armored cruisers to submarines, *Amalfi* to a German and *Garibaldi* to an Austrian. The Austrians lacked the capacity to build large numbers of submarines themselves. They were able to commission only four of the obsolete Havmanden design and eight of the German UB.II design before the end of the war, plus a salvaged French submarine and two UB.IIs transferred from the German navy. On the whole, Austrian submarines were confined to defensive tasks in the Adriatic, although in 1917 and 1918 they joined the German submarine campaign, usually operating against shipping lanes between Malta and Cerigotto. The greatest Austrian contribution to the submarine war was to provide bases for the German Mediterranean U-boat flotillas at Pola and in the Gulf of Cattaro.

Austrian light cruisers, destroyers, and high-seas torpedo boats had a more active war, with raids on the Italian and Montenegrin coast and against Allied forces blockading the Straits of Otranto. This led to clashes with Allied light forces on 29 December 1915 and 15 May 1917 in which the Austrians emerged from encounters with superior forces with relatively light losses. The fleet was not immune to the nationality problems that plagued the Hapsburg Monarchy, however, and in February of 1918 a serious mutiny broke out among the naval units stationed at Cattaro. It was quelled with relatively little bloodshed and probably resulted more from poor conditions in the service and a desire for peace than from the nationality conflict. In the aftermath there was a rejuvenation of the high command and new *Flottenkommandant* Rear Admiral Miklós Horthy decided on a more offensive strategy that would employ the battleships in a raid on the Allies in the Straits of Otranto. This led to a disaster when a division of the Austrian force had a chance encounter at night with two Italian MAS boats (motor torpedo-boats) off Premuda, and the dreadnought *Szent Istvan* was torpedoed and sunk. The operation was then aborted.

The Austrian navy succeeded in maintaining lines of communication with Austrian forces in Albania and on the whole remained loyal and effective until the end of the war. It remains the classic case of a "fleet-in-being," and because the French and Italians could never agree on a joint commander in the Adriatic, the Austrians actually tied down the battle squadrons of two navies in watching them.

On 30 October 1918 Kaiser Karl transferred remaining units of the Austro-Hungarian navy to the new state of Yugoslavia.

Paul G. Halpern

References

Aichelburg, Wladimir. *Die Unterseeboote Österreich-Ungarns.* 2 vols. Graz: Akademische Druck und Verlagsanstalt, 1981.

Halpern, Paul G. *The Naval War in the Mediterranean, 1914–1918.* London and Annapolis, Md.: Allen and Unwin/ Naval Institute Press, 1987.

Plaschka, Richard Georg. *Cattaro-Prag: Revolte und Revolution.* Graz and Cologne: Böhlau, 1963.

Sokol, Hans Hugo. *Österreich-Ungarns Seekrieg.* 2 vols. Vienna: Amalthea Verlag, 1933. Reprint. Graz: Akademische Druck und Verlagsanstalt, 1967.

Wulff, Vize Admiral Olaf Richard. *Die Österreichisch-ungarische Donauflottille im Weltkriege 1914–1918.* Vienna and Leipzig: Wilhelm Braumüller, 1934.

See also HAUS, ANTON; MEDITERRANEAN NAVAL OPERATIONS, 1914–18

Austro-Hungarian War Plan, 1914

Austria-Hungary entered World War I with a war plan every bit as complex and daring as the German Schlieffen Plan. Unfortunately the country lacked the ability to carry the plan out successfully. The frugal Austro-Hungarian army maintained a smaller peacetime cadre force than did either France or Germany and would have to triple in size to reach a comparable level of fifty divisions. During the mobilization phase, companies would grow in size from 93 men to 270. Although the empire had an extensive rail system, the Carpathian border with Russia and the Balkans had only a limited rail capacity and required extra engines in the mountains. For these reasons the Austro-Hungarian army would have to be concentrated in several successive rail echelons. The A echelon was the main striking force, consisting of thirty divisions formed into the First, Fourth, and Third armies; it was destined for fighting against Russia or Italy, depending on circumstances. The B echelon, the Second Army of twelve divisions, could then be directed at any foe. The C echelon consisted of replacements, supply troops, and third-line *Landsturm* forces.

The war plan was developed by Chief of the General Staff General Franz Conrad von Hötzendorf. During the Bosnia-Herzegovina annexation crisis of 1907–9 Conrad faced the prospect of a multifront war with an army that was too small. Although Austria-Hungary had a population of fifty-five million, her army remained the size it had been in the 1880s. Conrad hoped to use the railway system and interior lines to multiply his inadequate force. This was called *Bahnrockade* after the "castling move" in chess. The B echelon would move off first and attempt to appear in both theaters of operation. Although this would have succeeded against Serbia and Italy in 1909, transferring the idea to war against Russia in 1914 was a gamble.

Conrad's plan provided that in a war with Italy A echelon would hold its own, while B echelon and a minimum Balkan group of eight divisions, along with Fifth and Sixth armies, defeated Serbia. B echelon could then make the *Bahnrockade* move to Italy as a general reserve. In a war against Russia, however, the three Hapsburg armies of A echelon would be dangerously outnumbered by four or five Russian armies. Thus, B echelon would have to be in the basic deployment.

In July of 1914 Austria-Hungary carried out a partial mobilization of minimum its Balkan forces and B echelon in the hopes of fighting a localized war with Serbia. After it became clear that Russia and Germany would join the conflict, A echelon was mobilized and concentrated in eastern Galicia. In a very risky and controversial move, Conrad allowed B echelon to attempt the *Bahnrockade*.

The planned deployment was not an ambitious attempt to win the war at one stroke. Rather, it focused on defeating Russian forces in the Polish salient with a double envelopment at Siedlce, east of Warsaw. The plan called for the German Eighth Army to strike south while the Austro-Hungarian First and Fourth armies moved north from Galicia. Meanwhile, the Third and late-arriving Second armies would cover the open east flank. The plan almost succeeded. It failed because the Serbs held up B echelon, and the Germans did not support initial Austro-Hungarian successes with the Siedlce attack. Although the Austro-Hungarians contained the Russians on the border, it was at irreparable cost.

R.D. Zehnder

References

Rothenberg, Gunther. *The Army of Francis Joseph*. West Lafayette, Ind.: Purdue University Press, 1976.

Stone, Norman. *The Eastern Front 1914–17*. New York: Scribners, 1975.

See also BALKAN FRONT, 1914; EAST GALICIA, 1914 CAMPAIGN; POLAND: GERMAN OFFENSIVE OF SEPTEMBER–NOVEMBER 1914

Authors

See LITERATURE

Averescu, Alexandru (1859–1938)

Romanian general. Born in Bessarabia to a peasant family on 9 March 1859, Averescu was perhaps Romania's greatest soldier of the war. He fought in the 1877–78 war of independence against Turkey and afterward obtained a regular commission and studied military theory in Italy. He returned to Romania to serve as minister of war and in March of 1907 directed 140,000 troops in suppressing an agrarian insurrection. In 1913 he was chief of staff in the Second Balkan War, in which Romania gained the Dobrudja region from Bulgaria. In August of 1916, when Romania declared war on the Central Powers, Averescu commanded the Third Army, defending the Danube region from an attack from Bulgaria and covering the rear of the First, Second, and Fourth armies, attacking into Transylvania. Instead of forcing the Danube, the Bulgarian-Turkish force attacked up the south bank of the river to recapture the Dobrudja. The defending Romanian troops were pushed back, as the Third Army was unable to intervene. On 15 September Averescu was given command of Army Unit South, which contained both the Third Army and the Dobrudja forces. He planned to trap the Bulgarian-Turkish troops by holding them in place at Constanta-Cernavoda, while having his main force cross the river downstream and attack from the rear. The attack across the Danube failed in the face of strong Bulgarian resistance, the destruction of a pontoon bridge in a storm, and the poor performance of supporting forces. A few weeks later, Bulgarian-Turkish forces used the same plan to rout the Romanians.

Averescu restored his military reputation by directing defensive operations in the Carpathian Mountains. The Second Army, the only effective remaining Romanian military force, was soon obliged, however, to retire northeastward. Averescu distinguished himself by his defense of Marasesti in August of 1917 against a strong Central Powers offensive aimed at driving Romania from the war. The collapse of Russian forces and shortages of equipment forced Romania to sue for peace by 1918.

In February of 1918 King Ferdinand I designated Averescu prime minister to negotiate a peace treaty. The king, dissatisfied with concessions in the treaty, forced Averescu from office, but he returned as prime minister in the fall. On 10 November 1918, Romania redeclared war on the Central Powers.

After World War I Averescu founded the Peoples League, later renamed the Peoples party. It was victorious in the March 1920 elections, and Averescu served as prime minister until December of 1921 when he resigned, although he continued as head of the Peoples party. In March of 1926, with the resignation of Ion Bratianu, Averescu again became prime minister. His domestic policy did not differ from that of his predecessor, but in foreign policy he initiated a rapprochement with France and Italy to counter the menace of the USSR. This resulted in treaties of friendship and a loan from Italy in exchange for Romanian oil. He resigned as prime minister in 1928. He continued to hold prominent positions in the Peoples party but his involvement in government was indirect. In 1930 he was made a field marshal in the Romanian army. In 1937 King Carol II appointed him a member of the permanent Crown Council. Averescu died on 2 October 1938 and was buried on the battlefield at Marasesti.

Charles H. Bogart

References

Seton-Watson, R.W. *A History of the Roumanians*. Hamden, Conn.: Shoe String Press, 1934.

Spector, Sherman David. *Rumania at the Paris Peace Conference: A Study of the Diplomacy of Ioan Bratianu*. New York: Bookman, 1962.

Vinogradov, V.N. *Romania in the Period of the First World War*. Moscow: Academy Press, 1969.

See also ROMANIA; ROMANIAN CAMPAIGN, 1916

Avesnes Conference, 13–14 August 1918

At Avesnes the German Supreme Army Command, faced with demoralizing losses, first admitted to the country's political leaders that military victory was no longer possible. Confronted by that reality, the German government began to prepare peace overtures. The military, however, clung to and published the notion that Germany's earlier territorial gains would win the peace. These conflicting aims set the stage for the "stab-in-the-back" myth.

There were those in the German government who recognized the need for peace as early as the spring of 1918, when German offensives failed to break the Allies at Amiens. In May of 1918 Kaiser Wilhelm II told General Erich Ludendorff: "We have reached the limits of our physical endurance; the war must be ended." Ludendorff approved the preparation of a "peace offensive" but reneged when the imperial chancellor announced the move in the Diet.

The German high command essentially dictated policy and, led by Ludendorff and Field Marshal Paul von Hindenburg, refused publicly to admit that they could not decisively defeat the Allies. Asked in mid-July if he was certain of defeating the enemy, Ludendorff said, "I can reply to that with a decided 'yes.'"

That notion was shattered by the failure to break the Allied line at Chemin des Dames, the demoralizing surrender of the German army at Amiens on 8 August—"Germany's Black Day"—and the subsequent success of the British counterattacks of 9–11 August. Ludendorff summoned Germany's political leaders to the army's advanced headquarters in Avesnes, France, to break the news.

On 13 August Ludendorff and Hindenburg met with Foreign Secretary Paul von Hintze and Imperial Chancellor Count Georg von Hertling to review the situation. Ludendorff decided to "tell the whole truth" and laid out a realistic overview of the military situation. "Four weeks ago I told you I still hoped to conquer the enemy," Ludendorff told Hintze, "I am no longer sustained by that hope."

Ludendorff proposed a strategic defensive, believing the German army could demoralize the enemy and that Germany's continued presence on French soil would bring the enemy to terms. He agreed, however, that Hintze should prepare a peace offensive.

The next day's conference, attended by the Kaiser, Crown Prince Wilhelm, Chief of the Civil Cabinet Friedrich von Berg, Chief of the Military Cabinet General Ulrich Baron von Marschall, the adjutant-general, Colonel General Hans von Plessen, Ludendorff, Hertling, Hindenburg, and Hintze, followed similar lines. Hintze described the international situation: Germany's allies were on the verge of surrender; time was working against Germany, and a military victory was no longer possible. He concluded that it was also politically impossible to break the enemy at this point and bowed to Ludendorff's proposal for a strategic defensive. The politicians would wait for military approval before making any peace overtures. Such a moment, Hertling added, "might present itself after the next successes in the west." Hindenburg then added the military's position, which Ludendorff altered in the minutes to read that "it would be possible to remain fixed on French territory, and thereby in the end enforce our will upon the enemy," a much firmer statement than Hindenburg actually made. The civilian government was now prepared for peace, while the military still hoped to dictate terms.

Timothy C. Dowling

References

Ludendorff, General Paul. *The General Staff and its Problems; the History of Relations between the High Command and the German Imperial Government as Revealed by Official Documents.* 2 vols. Translated by F.A. Holt, O.B.E. London: Hutchinson and Co., 1920.

Ludwig, Emil. *Hindenburg.* Translated by Eden and Cedar Paul. Philadelphia: John C. Winston Co., 1935.

Lutz, Ralph, ed. *Fall of the German Empire 1914–1918.* 2 vols. Hoover War Library Publications #1. Stanford, Calif.: Stanford University Press, 1932.

Wheeler-Bennett, John W. *Wooden Titan: Hindenburg in 20 Years of German History.* London: Archon, 1936.

See also ALLIED COUNTEROFFENSIVE, 1918; ARMISTICE, AT COMPIÈGNE

Azerbaijan

Azerbaijan is bordered by the Caucasus Mountains to the north, Armenia to the west, Persia to the south, and the Caspian Sea to the east. Its location and abundant mineral wealth attracted much attention during World War I. The territory belonged to Russia, but Turkey, Germany, and Great Britain were interested in the rich oil deposits near the Caspian Sea city of Baku.

Prior to and during the war, pan-Turkic and pan-Islamic movements had considerable impact in the area. Several political parties competed for support. The most important of these was the Musavat, which emphasized Muslim unification. When Russia entered the war it counted on support from Azerbaijan. Shortly thereafter, however, Turkey joined the Central Powers, dividing the loyalties of the Muslim community.

After the failed attempt to create a Transcaucasian union of Georgia, Armenia, and Azerbaijan, the Azerbaijanian independence movement gained momentum. On 28 May 1918 the Azerbaijan National Council proclaimed its independence from Russia and named Khan Khosiki premier. The council enacted a charter granting full citizenship rights to all, regardless of religion, class, or sex.

Britain recognized Azerbaijan, except for the oil-rich city of Baku, which Britain seized and occupied until 1919. On 15 January 1920 the Allied Powers recognized Azerbaijani independence, but in April the Red Army invaded the country. It became a Soviet satellite, the Azerbaijan Soviet Socialist Republic, and in March of 1922 was combined with Georgia and Armenia to form the Transcaucasian Soviet Socialist Republic.

Corie Delashaw

References

Rezul-Zade, Emin. "The Republic of Azerbaijan." *Ukrainian Quarterly* 7 (1951): 237–41.

Scheltema, J.F. "The Caucasus and the World War." *Current History* 12 (1915): 99–102.

Swietochowski, Tadeusz. *Russian Azerbaijan, 1905–1920. The Shaping of National Identity in a Muslim Community.* London: Cambridge University Press, 1985.

See also CAUCASUS FRONT

B

Bachmann, Gustav (1860–1943)

German admiral and chief of the admiralty staff in 1915. Born on 13 July 1860 in Cammin, Bachmann joined the German navy in 1877 and held line and staff positions overseas and at home, where he impressed superiors with his intelligence and competent leadership of large fleet units. As chief of the Central Department of the Navy Office (1907–10) and later, Bachmann associated himself closely with Admiral Alfred von Tirpitz.

In February of 1915 Bachmann replaced Hugo von Pohl as chief of the admiralty staff and was promoted to full admiral. He strongly advocated operational freedom for the surface fleet and more aggressive submarine warfare. Following the *Lusitania* and *Arabic* incidents, Bachmann objected to the government's restrictions on U-boat activities. He resigned in September of 1915, resuming his previous command as chief of the Baltic Station until his retirement from the navy in October of 1918. During the naval mutinies in Kiel, Bachmann sought to suppress pacifist-leftist movements in the fleet, pushing instead for patriotic indoctrination. Bachmann died at Kiel on 30 August 1943.

Eric C. Rust

References

Görlitz, Walter, ed. *The Kaiser and His Court: The Diaries, Note Books and Letters of Admiral Georg Alexander von Müller, Chief of The Naval Cabinet, 1914–1918.* New York: Harcourt, Brace, World, 1964.

Herwig, Holger H. *The German Naval Officer Corps: A Social and Political History, 1890–1918.* Oxford: Oxford University Press, 1973.

Horn, Daniel. *The German Naval Mutinies of World War I.* New Brunswick, N.J.: Rutgers University Press, 1969.

Hubatsch, Walther. *Der Admiralstab und die obersten Marinebehörden in Deutschland. 1848–1945.* Frankfurt: Bernard, Graefe, 1958.

Bacon, Sir Reginald Hugh Spencer (1863–1947)

Royal Navy admiral and historian. Born on 6 September 1863 at Wiggonholt Rectory, Sussex, Bacon entered the Royal Navy in 1878. Between 1899 and 1909 he specialized in submarines, mines, torpedoes, electricity, and ship design. Promoted to rear admiral in July of 1909, Bacon retired that November to become managing director of the Conventry Ordnance Works.

Upon the outbreak of World War I, Bacon returned to active service. In April of 1915 he assumed command of the Dover Patrol, which had the tasks of denying German U-boats access to the Channel and ensuring uninterrupted passage to France of men and supplies. The Dover Patrol also made preparations for operations against the Belgian coast and attacked enemy shore positions and surface forces.

In 1917 government confidence in Bacon declined, primarily because of the high transient rate of German U-boats through his area of responsibility (although few sinkings of Allied vessels occurred there). On 28 December 1917 Bacon was relieved of command, but Winston Churchill appointed him controller of the Inventions Department at the Ministry of Munitions.

Promoted to admiral in September of 1918, Bacon retired in March of 1919. In retirement Bacon became a naval historian. He defended Admiral John Jellicoe's handling of the Grand Fleet at the Battle of Jutland (*The Jutland Scandal, 1926*), and then wrote, among other books, biographies of Lord John Fisher (1929) and Jellicoe (1936), and two books on the Dover Patrol. He also wrote his autobiography: *A Naval Scrap-Book, 1877–1900* (1925) and *From 1900 Onward* (1940). He died on 9 June 1947 at Romsey, Hampshire.

Donald F. Bittner

References

Baddeley, Vincent W. "Bacon, Sir Reginald Hugh Spencer," *Dictionary of National Biography, 1941–1950.* Oxford: Oxford University Press, 1959, pp. 32–34.

Kemp, Peter. "Bacon, Sir Reginald Hugh Spencer," *The Oxford Companion to Ships and the Sea.* Oxford: Oxford University Press, 1988.

Marder, Arthur J. *From the Dreadnought to Scapa Flow.* Vols. 1–5. Oxford: Oxford University Press, 1961–70.

The Times (London), 10 June 1947.

Badoglio, Pietro (1871–1956)

Italian general. Born in Grazzano (Asti) on 28 September 1871 Badoglio entered the Italian military as an artillery officer and participated in the campaigns in Abyssinia (1896) and in Libya (1911–12). He commanded the XXVII Army Corps at Caporetto in 1917, and many felt that his faulty deployment and poor handling of his corps opened a gap in the Italian lines and facilitated the advance of the 12th Silesian Division. Orlando's suppression of several pages of damaging testimony in the parliamentary inquest of the defeat at Caporetto, however, helped Badoglio to escape disciplinary action for his failures. Indeed, he became deputy to chief of staff of the Italian army General Armando Diaz.

After the war Badoglio continued his rise in the army. In 1920 he forced D'Annunzio out of Fiume, and in 1921 he succeeded Diaz as chief of staff and became chief of the general staff in 1925. After a tour of duty as governor of North Africa (September of 1928 to December of 1933), where he oversaw the suppression of the Senussi rebellion, Badoglio succeeded Emilio De Bono as supreme commander in Ethiopia, where he was named viceroy in May of 1936. Promoted field marshal and awarded the

title of Duke of Addis Ababa in July of 1936, he served as chief of staff for the Italian Armed Forces until forced to resign in December of 1940 after the Italian failure in Greece. Following Mussolini's arrest in July of 1943 he was appointed head of government by the king. Forced to resign in June of 1944, he died at Grazzano on 1 November 1956. An eminently political general, who has justified his actions in print, Badoglio has been blamed for Caporetto and the failure of the Italian armed forces to prepare for World War II.

James J. Sadkovich

References

Badoglio, Pietro. *Italy in the Second World War: Memoirs and Documents.* London: Oxford, 1948.

———. *Rivelazioni su Fiume.* Rome: Donatello de Luigi, 1946.

———. *The War in Abyssinia.* New York: G.P. Putnam's Sons, 1947.

De Biase, Carlo. *L'aquila d'oro. Storia dello stato maggiore italiano (1861–1945).* Milan: Il Borghese, 1969.

Pieri, Piero, and Giorgio Rochat. *Badoglio.* Turin: UTET, 1974.

See also CAPORETTO

Balfour, Arthur James (1848–1930)

British political leader. Born 25 July 1848 in Edinburgh, Scotland, James Balfour, first Earl Balfour and Viscount Traprain, was a member of the politically powerful Cecil family. Balfour inherited a fortune, including the family estate, Whittingehame, East Lothian, Scotland. He attended Cambridge, where he demonstrated an interest in philosophy, but he soon entered politics, accelerating to the top rapidly in the Conservative-Unionist party.

In 1902 Balfour succeeded his uncle, Lord Salisbury, as prime minister, serving until 1905. He remained as leader of the opposition until 1911 and returned as a member of a coalition cabinet: first lord of the admiralty and foreign secretary during and after World War I. He was first lord during the battle of Jutland and is generally blamed for the depressing, uninformative public announcement of the battle and its results. As foreign secretary in 1917, he issued the Balfour Declaration, for which he is best known, recognizing the right of the Jews to a homeland in Palestine. He played a major role in the peacemaking process and the Washington Naval Conference.

As early as 1902, Balfour initiated action that would have a profound impact on plans and organizational structure for war. He established the Committee of Imperial Defence (CID), the basis for a future strategic planning structure for the British imperial armed forces.

Balfour died on 19 March 1930 at Woking, outside London.

Eugene L. Rasor

References

Egremont, Lord Max. *Balfour: A Life of Arthur James Balfour*. London: Collins, 1980.

Mackay, Ruddock F. *Balfour: Intellectual Statesman*. London: Oxford University Press, 1985.

Young, Kenneth. *Arthur James Balfour: The Happy Life of the Politician, Prime Minister, Statesman, and Philosopher, 1848–1930*. London: Bell, 1963.

Williams, Rhodri. *Defending the Empire: The Conservative Party and British Defence Policy, 1899–1915*. New Haven: Yale University Press, 1991.

See also BALFOUR DECLARATION

Balfour Declaration

The Balfour Declaration of November 1917 was an attempt by the British government to secure support from Jews worldwide for the war effort. It was the result of prolonged Zionist efforts in the United States and Britain to obtain a guarantee that in the event of the defeat of Turkey, Palestine would be recognized as a Jewish commonwealth.

Dr. Chaim Weizmann was leader of the Zionists. He was a chemistry professor at Manchester University who had discovered a new way of producing acetone. The British Palestine Committee included journalists, prominent Jews such as Sir Herbert Samuel and the Rothschilds, and Foreign Secretary Lord Arthur J. Balfour.

Weizmann had been campaigning for Allied support for a Jewish state since the start of the war without much success. Two events in the spring of 1917 significantly aided his cause. The first was the March revolution in Russia.

Prime Minister David Lloyd George and Balfour viewed support for Zionism as a means of maintaining the support of Jews who were prominent among leaders in the revolution. The other event was the entry into the war of the United States, with its large Jewish population. In addition, Weizmann thought that Allied advocacy of a homeland for the Jews would cause disaffection on the part of German Jews toward their government. The Judeao-Christian tradition and politics in the United States were also factors.

In May of 1917 Lord Balfour visited the United States, where he talked to Justice Louis Brandeis, a Zionist and close advisor to President Wilson. A number of prominent American officials, including former Secretary of State William Jennings Bryan, openly endorsed Zionist proposals. Wilson supported the idea of a Jewish state in Palestine but was unwilling to commit to it publicly because the U.S. was not at war with Turkey. He did, however, authorize Colonel House to approve the pro-Zionist draft prepared by the British cabinet.

Zionists had a harder time in Britain than in the United States; two prominent Jewish groups in Britain announced their opposition to Zionism. This did not include powerful members of the government, such as Lloyd George. After discussing the Zionist draft proposal, the British cabinet accepted its major points. On 2 November 1917 Lord Balfour sent the following letter to Lord Rothschild:

Dear Lord Rothschild,

I have much pleasure in conveying to you, on behalf of His Majesty's Government, the following declaration of sympathy with Jewish Zionist aspirations which has been submitted to, and approved by, the Cabinet.

His Majesty's Government view with favour the establishment in Palestine of a national home for the Jewish people, and will use their best endeavours to facilitate the achievement of this object, it being clearly understood that nothing shall be done which may prejudice the civil and religious rights of existing non-Jewish communities in Palestine, or the rights and political status enjoyed by Jews in any other country.

I should be grateful if you would bring this declaration to the knowledge of the Zionist Federation.

Yours sincerely,

Arthur James Balfour

The French government expressed support for the declaration on 11 February 1918, and Wilson gave his open support in a letter to Rabbi Stephen Wise on 29 October 1918.

The declaration was undoubtedly successful in winning full support of Zionists to the Allied cause, but it had other consequences. It violated the earlier Sykes-Picot agreement that provided for the internationalization of the Holy Land, and it alienated Arabs.

At the end of the war Britain accepted a mandate over Palestine, where Arabs made up 80 percent of the population. Violence soon flared between the Arab and Jewish communities as increasing numbers of Jews immigrated to Palestine, although without British government support. The British found themselves caught in the impossible situation of trying to please both Jews and Arabs and ultimately, in 1948, they terminated their mandate, an event that led to the proclamation of modern Israel.

Spencer C. Tucker

References

Lenczowski, George. *The Middle East in World Affairs*. Ithaca: Cornell University Press, 1952.

Sanders, Ronald. *The High Walls of Jerusalem. A History of the Balfour Declaration and the Birth of the British Mandate for Palestine*. New York: Holt, Rinehart and Winston, 1983.

See also BALFOUR, ARTHUR JAMES; SYKES-PICOT AGREEMENT; ZIONISM

Balkan Front, 1914

It is doubtful if those responsible for the assassination of Franz Ferdinand foresaw that their actions would plunge Europe and much of the rest of the world into war. Despite the intervention of British, French, German, and Italian forces in the Balkans, World War I operations there were as much a continuation of earlier Balkan disputes as part of the overall Great Power conflict. One key factor of prewar Balkan politics had been the final collapse of Ottoman power, leading to the Balkan wars of 1912 and 1913 in which Bulgaria, Greece, Montenegro, and Serbia first combined to expel the Turks and then fell out over the spoils of victory. Another factor had been Serbia's aim of expanding at the expense of Austria-Hungary.

On 28 July, following Serbia's rejection of the post-Sarajevo ultimatum, Austria-Hungary declared war. Serbia's army of 350,000 under General Radomir Putnick faced an enemy three times as big. Her only immediate help came from Montenegro, with a population of 500,000, which entered the war on 3 August. A major disadvantage for Serbia was the position of its capital on the Danube, across from Austria-Hungary. Austrian plans, like those of Germany in the west, were based on speed. The intention was to occupy Belgrade and Valyevo, key cities of northern and western Serbia, before the Serbian army could be fully mobilized.

Initially, all went according to plan. On 12 August the Austrian army crossed the Save River and quickly captured Shabatz and Lesnica. But the battle of the Tser Mountains, a bloody conflict lasting from 16 to 25 August and involving a quarter million men on each side, ended in complete defeat for the Austrians. The Serbs recaptured both towns and forced the Austrians back across the Drina and Save into their own territory. It was now the Serb turn to advance. In early September they crossed the Danube and captured Semlin, a fort on the left bank of the river immediately opposite Belgrade, and on 10 September they cut railway links between Hungary and Romania at Orsard.

Further west, with Montenegrin support, they captured Visegrad and by early October were besieging Sarajevo. Two relief attempts by the Austrians were decisively beaten back by Serbian and Montenegrin forces under General Vakovitch at the two battles of Moukine. During this period Austria attempted diversions by a naval bombardment of the port of Antivari and an incursion into the Jakova region of Montenegro by an Albanian irregular force under Austrian officers, but both proved fruitless.

Despite their successes the Serbs were running out of ammunition and were slowly but surely forced to yield their gains. The Austrians regained Senlin on 22 October and then concentrated their efforts on Belgrade. Three attempts to outflank the city by crossing the Drina some fifty miles to the west were bloodily repelled, even though the Austrians had a five-to-one local superiority. On one occasion nature came to the help of the Serbs, when a winter flood washed away an enemy column of at least one thousand men. On 10 November the Austrian effort switched to Semendria, twenty-five miles east of Belgrade. Aided by river monitors, the Austrians came close to success; they gained a foothold on the Serbian side of the Danube, only to be forced back by a determined counterattack.

The third Austrian attempt was successful. Four divisions under General Pohorek crossed the Save some ten miles to the southwest and, after two weeks of hard fighting, advanced along the south bank to capture the deserted city on 2 December. Belgrade had been under constant artillery bombardment since the start of the war, even when Semlin had been in Serbian hands; its civilian population had long since fled, and the Serbian government had retired to Nish.

The fall of Belgrade marked a low point in Serbia's 1914 fortunes. Death, disease, and desertion had reduced her army to 100,000 men, and there was a desperate shortage of ammunition and other supplies. While Serbian attention had been focused on the capital, another large Austrian formation had forced its way across the River Koloubara and, advancing into Serbian territory, had captured Valyevo. Four months after the start of the campaign the Austrians had at last achieved their initial aims—the capture of Belgrade and Valyevo.

The Austrian advance continued southwestward from Valyevo in the general direction of Nish, the new seat of government. But French ammunition finally reached the Serbs in decisive quantities, and under the command of aged Field Marshal Mischitch they made one last supreme effort. At the battle of Rudnizk-Souvoba (5–8 December) they inflicted a serious defeat on the Austrians and recaptured Valyevo. The Austrians attempted to stand north of the city but were again defeated on 11 December. They now attempted to withdraw in an orderly fashion along two axes, to Belgrade and to Visegrad and Sarajevo. Their withdrawal soon turned into a rout, particularly near Belgrade, where, when forced up against the Danube, whole units abandoned their equipment and surrendered. On 15 December the Serbs recaptured Belgrade. King Peter, accompanied by his sons Crown Prince Alexander and Prince George, rode at the head of his troops as they entered the capital. By the end of the year there were no Austro-Hungarian soldiers on Serbian soil, and Serbia even held a strip of enemy territory near Visegrad.

Between 12 August and mid-December 1914, Austria had lost 273,000 men in the Serbian campaign. This was one fifth of her entire field army. The Serbs had taken 50,000 prisoners; 300 guns and 100 machine guns; 140,000 rifles; 4,000 vehicles; 3,000 horses; and two planes. At this stage they could proudly claim that, despite the great numerical and technological superiority of their enemy, they were the only victorious nation among the Allies. At the same time, the inability of the Austro-Hungarian Empire to defeat such a small state as Serbia cast grave doubts on her ability to perform as a "Great Power," even when her commitments on other fronts were taken into account.

Philip J. Green

References
Falls, Cyril. *Military Operations: Macedonia.* 2 vols. London: HMSO, 1933 and 1935.
Graham, Stephen. *Alexander of Yugoslavia.* London: Cassell, 1938.
Knight, W. Stanley Macbean. *The History of the Great European War.* Vol. 6. London: Caxton, 1923.

See also BALKAN WARS, 1912–13; PUTNICK, RADOMIR; SERBIA

Balkan Front, 1915

The year 1914 had been a triumph for Serbia, with the Austro-Hungarian invasion being decisively defeated. In complete contrast, 1915 brought nothing but disaster; the year began with an appalling epidemic, and by February of 1916 Serbia and Montenegro had been completely occupied by the enemy, with the remnants of the Serbian army sheltering on the Greek island of Corfu.

Typhus had broken out at the end of 1914 among Austrian troops in Valyevo. It spread to the civilian population and ultimately to the Serbian army when the town was recaptured in December. The movement of refugees and soldiers on leave ensured the wide spread of the epidemic, which was soon beyond Serbian ability to control. By May, Allied medical units and the American Red Cross had stamped the disease out, but not before some 100,000 people had died. To add to Serbia's troubles, a rebellion broke out in Macedonia, which had come unwillingly under Serbian rule as a result of the Balkan Wars. Fomented by Bulgaria, it was suppressed with difficulty and only after political concessions had been made.

Bulgaria played a key role on the Balkan stage in 1915, and what followed was as much a part of Balkan politics—in which Serbia and Bulgaria competed for regional hegemony—as of the wider world conflict. It was in the Allied interest for Bulgaria to enter the war on their side, but she would do so only if promised Macedonia. The Allies regarded this as reasonable on ethnic grounds, but not unnaturally the Serbs refused to consider it. The result was that Bulgaria, encouraged by Germany, made an alliance with Turkey and on 19 September mobilized "to protect her neutrality," as she put it. On 6 October Russia declared war on Bulgaria, and on the same day German and Austrian troops crossed the Danube and Save on a 100-mile front to invade northern Serbia. A week later the Bulgarian Army launched its attack on southwestern Serbia.

The Serbian situation was now desperate. With a small population, she had been severely weakened by her efforts the previous year and by the typhus epidemic. She now faced not just the Austrians, but German and Bulgarian troops as well; moreover, the northern invasion was led by German General August von Mackensen—there was going to be no repeat of the Austrian incompetence of 1914. Little help could be expected from either the Allies or Russia. Serbia was on her own.

Mackensen's northern offensive was carried out with ruthless efficiency. Belgrade fell on 10 October and Kruguivatz, some fifty miles south of the Danube and Serbia's principal arsenal, on 21 October. By the end of the month, Mackensen's divisions had linked up with the Bulgarians at Lubiskevatz on the Danube and occupied a Valyevo-Kruguivatz-Pirot-Ushub line.

The Bulgarian invasion took the Serbs by surprise and was at first virtually unopposed. The attack was two-pronged: The northern one under General F.N. Todoroff was aimed at Nish, the Serbian capital since the previous November; the southern one, under General F.N. Bojadjeff, was intended to cut Serbia off from any help that might come via Salonika. Nish was captured on 5 November while the Serbian army in the south, together with a small French force, had to fall back on Monastir. By now, half of Serbia was in enemy hands and the army was disintegrating.

In September, Serbia had appealed to Britain, France, and Greece for help. Britain and France sent thirteen thousand men, all that could be spared, to Salonika. Greece was bound by treaty to help Serbia, and Premier Eleutherios Venizelos mobilized its army. It was proposed that a joint force should move through Greece into southern Serbia, but at this stage a remarkable situation arose. Pro-German King Con-stantine overruled his premier, refused to allow the British and French to move through Greece, and announced that, despite treaty obligations, his country would remain neutral. The Greek army did everything possible, short of actual fighting, to obstruct the Allied force in Salonika, and the only practical intervention the Allies could make was a bombardment of the Bulgarian port of Dedeagatch on 21 November, which had no effect on land operations.

Clearly, Britain and France could not allow the situation to continue, and economic pressure was brought to bear. After a blockade of Greek ports, Constantine agreed that the Allies could use Greek territory as a base for their advance into Serbia, and, if need be, Serbian troops could withdraw into Greek territory. Greece, however, remained neutral, and without her army there was little the small Anglo-French force could do to help. In mid-October they advanced into Serbia, but they were too few and too late. Some French units did make contact with the Serbs and helped them to delay Todoroff's advancing Bulgarians near Valandovo, but otherwise the Allies' main preoccupation, weak as they were, was self-defense, the British to the north of Lake Doiran and the French along the line of the River Vhrdar.

There was nothing now left for the Serbs—the government, remnants of the army, or refugees—to do except retreat into Albania, which had by now declared war on the Central Powers. The two main routes were through Mitrovitza and Prisrend. When these two towns fell Serbia was effectively lost, although Monastir held out until early December. The flight into Albania was carried out under appalling conditions, by starving, weak, and inadequately clothed people over icebound mountain passes in the depths of winter. Although Albanian troops were sent to escort the aged

King Peter, Albania was too poor and primitive to help the Serbians. Allied and United States medical teams, which had originally gone to Serbia to fight the typhus epidemic, marched with the Serbs, but what little medical supplies they still had were soon exhausted. There are no accurate figures on the number of people who died, but the loss of 90 percent of the fifty thousand Austrian POWs who took part is an indication of the scale of the disaster.

Nor was there any relief on arrival at Seutari. The Albanians could not feed this mass of people, the Austrians launched air attacks on the town, and the victorious Bulgarians were not far behind. After a short rest, the exodus had to continue another sixty miles south to Durazzo. From there, under the protection of an Italian garrison, British, French, and Italian ships evacuated the survivors to Corfu. By 10 February 1916 the evacuation was complete. The whole of Serbia, Montenegro, and Albania was now in enemy hands. The Serbian army, 300,000 strong at the start of the war, now mustered but 75,000 men. That these men were in action again in Salonika two months later after being reequipped and retrained speaks volumes for their courage and patriotism. But it cannot hide the extent of the disaster, not just for Serbia but for the Allied cause as a whole. The Central Powers, with Bulgaria now on their side and Serbia occupied, had obtained an overland link with their Turkish allies that canceled out the Allies' command of the Mediterranean.

Philip J. Green

References

Falls, Cyril. *Military Operations: Macedonia.* 2 vols. London: HMSO, 1933 and 1935.
Graham, Stephen. *Alexander of Yugoslavia.* London: Cassell, 1938.
Knight, W. Stanley Macbean. *The History of the Great European War.* Vol. 6. London: Caxton, 1923.

See also ALBANIA; BULGARIA; CONSTANTINE I; GREECE; MACKENSEN, AUGUST VON; MONTENEGRO; SALONIKA CAMPAIGN; SERBIA; VENIZELOS, ELEUTHERIOS

Balkan Front, 1916

The Central Powers' successes in 1915 had left them in possession of the whole of Albania, Montenegro, and Serbia. By February of 1916 the Bulgarian army has assumed positions along the length of the border between Serbia and neutral Greece, while the small Anglo-French force had withdrawn to its Salonika base after its belated and unsuccessful attempt to help the Serbs. The Balkan Front was of secondary importance to both sides in the war, but the immediate Allied aim was to stop the Central Powers' gaining a Mediterranean foothold at Salonika. The long-term Allied aim was to reconquer Serbia from the south and reinstate the country's legitimate government. Success in this area might encourage Romania to enter the war on their side.

Allied forces at Salonika, commanded by French General Maurice Sarrail, spent the first half of 1916 fortifying Salonika and building it up as a logistics base for future operations. A 130,000–man Serbian army—survivors of the 1915 retreat augmented by new recruits—clothed and equipped by France, arrived in May from the island of Corfu. It went into action in July. The Serbian force was followed in July and August by small Italian and Russian contingents. Britain, which feared a Turkish attack on the Suez Canal, felt it could not spare any further troops, and henceforth the main Balkan effort fell to France and Serbia.

Throughout 1916 the Allied position was complicated and endangered by the political situation in Greece. King Constantine and the bulk of his army were pro-German, while another party, headed by Premier Eleutherios Venizelos, wanted to enter the war on the Allied side. Early in the year Constantine dismissed Venizelos and replaced him with Stephanos Skouloulis, a politician sympathetic to his views. On grounds of military necessity the British and French had already occupied Salonika and Corfu; in April of 1916 they took over Kara Burun, which commanded the approaches to Salonika, and set up naval bases in a number of Ionian and Aegean islands. Constantine retaliated by allowing a Bulgarian-German force to enter northeastern Greece and occupy Fort Rupel in Greek Macedonia; French attempts to recapture Rupel proved fruitless.

This brought matters to a head, and on 21 June the Allies demanded the dismissal of pro-German ministers and officials and the partial demobilization of the Greek army. This ultimatum was backed up by an Allied naval blockade of Greek ports. As the population depended on imported food, this soon brought compliance. The Greek cabinet was reorganized and the army put on a peacetime footing. All remained well until August when, with the Venizelos party heartened by the arrival of more French troops, the two rival Greek factions clashed on the streets of Athens. The French restored order, and on 9 October, in a move fostered by General Sarrail, Venizelos set up his provisional government in Salonika, where it declared war on Germany and Bulgaria on 23 November.

The situation was further complicated when the Bulgarians and Germans counterattacked the Salonika forces, pushing them back. The Central Powers took Seres (19 August), Drama, and Kavalla (18 September), where the Fourth Corps of the Greek army surrendered without a fight. Further street fighting took place in Athens in early December, resulting in the deaths of two hundred Venizelists and one hundred British and French troops, disembarked from warships in the harbor.

The Allies could obviously not tolerate this chaotic and insecure situation in the rear of their Balkan operations, and they were incensed by the Greek surrender at Kavalla, a port on the Aegean coast thirty miles west of the Bulgarian-Greek border. The Allies now issued the Athens government a final ultimatum, enforced by a naval blockade. Greece was ordered to withdraw its army south of the Corinth canal into the Peloponnesus. The Allies recognized both Greek governments and established and policed a neutral zone between their respective territories.

While all this was taking place there were no military operations north of Salonika until late July. The Bulgarians, aware of Allied reinforcements, expected an attack up the Vardar valley. Deciding to strike first, they launched their own attack farther west. Taking the new Serbian army by surprise, they forced it back ten miles to the shores of Lake Ostrovo. The Serbs quickly recovered and with some French and Russian help regained the lost ground within a month.

The long-awaited Allied offensive started on 12 September. While the small British force conducted a defensive operation against German units on the east bank of the Vardar, and later launched an attack up the Strama valley toward Fort Rupel, the main Allied thrust was directed along the Florina-Monastir-Prilep railway. Conducted by Serbian, French, and Russian units, its aim was to capture Prilep and there set up a Serbian government on Serbian soil. The fighting lasted for the rest of the year and was as bloody as any in World War I, es-

pecially at Florina, Cenna, and on Mount Kaimakchalan. The Serbs and Bulgarians, in particular, showed each other little mercy, and the approach of the Balkan winter made conditions atrocious. Little artillery was used by either side, and much of the fighting was at close quarters.

After two months of such fighting the Bulgarians evacuated Monastir on 19 November. A few days later Crown Prince Alexander of Serbia arrived, expecting to be able to move on to Prilep. But it was not to be—the Allies were too exhausted to advance the last twenty-five miles. General Maurice Sarrail feared denuding his Salonika base of troops while Greek intentions were so uncertain, and he had no other reserves. The Germans and Bulgarians, on the other hand, were able to send reinforcements and halt the Allied advance a few miles north of Monastir. Prilep, its civilian population evacuated, spent the winter virtually under siege and well within range of enemy artillery. The establishment of a Serbian government at Prilep would have to wait until 1917.

The minor British offensive in the Struma valley similarly resulted in limited gains, its advance halting short of the main objective of Rupel. But the small gains here and in the Vardar valley had improved the security of the Salonika base.

After the disaster in Serbia the previous year, 1916 had proved relatively successful for the Allied cause on the Balkan front. The Allies had stabilized the political situation in Greece, established a secure base at Salonika, and in the last four months of the year made a start to the reconquest of Serbia. They had not, however, been able to exert enough pressure to prevent the Central Powers from attacking Romania from Bulgaria and Hungary. Romania, which had finally entered the war on 28 August, was invaded in November and completely overrun by the end of the year. Its valuable wheat and oil fields thus fell into German hands.

Philip J. Green

References

Falls, Cyril. *Military Operations: Macedonia.* 2 vols. London: HMSO, 1933 and 1935.

Graham, Stephen. *Alexander of Yugoslavia.* London: Cassell, 1938.

Knight, W. Stanley Macbean. *The History of the Great European War.* Vol. 8. London: Caxton, 1923.

See also BULGARIA; CONSTANTINE I; GREECE; ROMANIA; SARRAIL, MAURICE; VENIZELOS, ELEUTHERIOS

Balkan Front, 1917

Despite heavy fighting in the first half of the year, the situation on the Balkan Front in 1917 was a stalemate. In Greece, on the other hand, the Allies acted decisively to end political turmoil, which had threatened the security of their Salonika base since 1915.

The front line ran from Valna, on the Adriatic, eastward through Albania and Macedonia almost to the southwestern tip of Bulgaria, thence southeast to the Aegean, some fifty miles east of Salonika. Conflict on this front was as fierce, and casualty rates as high, as any on the Eastern or Western fronts, though the numbers involved were much smaller. The two sides were equal in men and equipment, and the rugged terrain, Balkan winter, and primitive communications afforded a tremendous advantage to the defenders: Hence the stalemate. Macbean Knight described the problem in these words:

> The mountains were themselves a range of natural fortresses in outline their giant towers and parapets suggestive of superhuman construction; in height, perpendicular at places, piercing the skies, savage, impregnable, grand and imposing beyond description. Of these the Bulgars . . . had supplemented nature with a perfect system, three lines of trenches, gun emplacements, and all the latest aids of modern warfare.

Between 1 January and 19 May four battles took place. Throughout the winter the Bulgarians made constant efforts to recapture Monastir, but all their attacks were beaten off by the French garrison. The French were, however, unable to push the Bulgarians further from the city; their nearest positions were on hills no more than two miles distant, from which they were able to shell Monastir at will to add to the miseries caused by the climate.

On 11 March the French attempted to relieve the pressure on Monastir with a local offensive in the area of Lake Prespa, twenty miles to the southwest and close to the Albanian border. Although they captured a few objectives, their gains were minimal, and on 17 March they called off the attack. The week's fighting had occurred in blinding blizzards, and the French had been defeated as much by the weather as by the enemy.

In April and May it was the turn of the British, who attempted to advance up the Vardar valley in the region of Lake Dovian. On 24 April, after a two-day artillery bombardment, they launched a night attack in the mountains. Three days of close quarter fighting ensued, but, like the French, the British made little progress, and on 26 April they withdrew to their starting positions. Two weeks later they tried again, with another night attack on 5 May. At one point they broke through the enemy lines, but the Bulgarians counterattacked to restore their position, and on 19 May the British had to admit failure.

While these land battles had been taking place, the Salonika base came under air attack from modern German three-engine bombers, a threat that was not countered until the arrival of British and French fighters from France.

If the Allies were unable to advance further into Serbia, they nonetheless found the will to end the political crisis in Greece, which by now was partitioned into four zones. The royal pro-German government controlled the southern part of the country only; Eleutherios Venizelos's pro-Allied provisional government, based in Salonika, governed the north. There was a neutral zone between the two, while the northeastern area was under Bulgarian occupation. Despite this chaotic situation, King Constantine still firmly believed that Germany would win the war, and his intransigence was increased by the collapse of the Russian army.

Britain and France finally ran out of patience. First, at the beginning of June, they entered Thessaly, a province under royalist control and the granary of Greece. They seized corn supplies withheld from the provisional government zone as a bargaining counter. On 11 June they took the ultimate step and forced Constantine to abdicate. He was permitted to go to Germany via neutral Switzerland and was replaced by his second son, the twenty-three-year-old Alexander. The country was reunited with Venizelos as premier and formally joined the Allies, contributing 100,000 soldiers to their cause.

Although their strength was now more than half a million men, all was not well in the Allied camp. A mutiny among French troops, a severe outbreak of malaria, and the lack of training of the Greek reinforcements precluded any resumption of offensive operations for the rest of 1917. Another problem was friction among the various national contingents. The Allied commander in chief, General Maurice Sarrail, was an abrasive man, and his task was not made easy by the British habit of requesting instructions direct from London. Sarrail was replaced in December of 1917 by another Frenchman, General Marie Guillaumat, who reorganized the multinational force and took particular pains to integrate the Greek units into his plans.

If 1917 was a frustrating year for the Allies, in that they were unable to proceed with the reconquest of Serbia, the major problem of the Greek menace in their rear had been resolved and a firm foundation had been laid for the successes that were to follow in 1918.

Philip J. Green

References

Falls, Cyril. *Military Operations: Macedonia.* 2 vols. London: HMSO, 1933 and 1935.

Graham, Stephen. *Alexander of Yugoslavia.* London: Cassell, 1938.

Knight, W. Stanley Macbean. *The History of the Great European War.* Vol. 8. London: Caxton, 1923.

See also ALEXANDER, PRINCE; CONSTANTINE I; GUILLAUMAT, MARIE; SARRAIL, MAURICE; VENIZELOS, ELEUTHERIOS

Balkan Wars, 1912–13

The Balkan Wars of 1912 and 1913 were a series of bloody conflicts in southeastern Europe that led into the First World War. The Balkan peninsula came under Ottoman domination at the end of the fourteenth century. By the end of the nineteenth century nation states had emerged in the peninsula from the weakened structure of the Ottoman Empire. These states included Bulgaria, Greece, Montenegro, Romania, and Serbia. All these states sought means to unite with their fellow nationals and obtain the territory they desired.

An opportunity for the realization of their nationalist objectives arose in 1911 and 1912 when the weakness of the Ottoman Empire became apparent during the Tripolitanian War. With the support of Russia, Bulgaria and Serbia signed an alliance in March of 1912. The Serbs and Bulgarians agreed to a rough division of Ottoman territory, partitioning Macedonia into a Bulgarian zone and a contested zone to be arbitrated by the Russian czar. Bulgaria signed subsequent agreements in the spring and summer of 1912 with Greece and Montenegro. Serbia concluded a written agreement with Montenegro. The Balkan allies made little further effort to arrange for a division of any territory conquered from the Ottomans. The Bulgarians also signed military agreements with Serbia and Greece.

When the First Balkan War erupted in October of 1912, the Balkan allies separately confronted the common enemy. To the surprise of Europe, the Balkan allies triumphed against their ancient enemy. The Serbs easily defeated the Ottomans at Kumanovo in Macedonia and advanced into Albania. On land the Greeks advanced against slight opposition in Thessaly and Epirus and besieged Janina. At sea the Greeks, the only Balkan ally with an appreciable navy, seized the Aegean Islands and held the Ottoman fleet at bay. The Montenegrins moved into northern Albania and brought the northern Albanian town of Shkodër (Scutari) under siege. The most important theater was in Thrace, where a strong Bulgarian offensive overcame the Ottoman forces in major battles at Kirk Killise and Buni Hisar/Lule Burgas; the Bulgarians surrounded Adrianople. The Bulgarians then thrust the Ottomans back to defensive positions at Chataldzha, only twenty-five miles from Constantinople. On 16–17 November the Ottomans did rally to defeat a Bulgarian attempt to breach the Chataldzha fortifications and seize Constantinople. By the time the warring parties agreed to an armistice on 3 December 1912, the only territory the Ottomans controlled in Europe was Shkodër, Janina, Adrianople, the area behind the Chataldzha lines, and the Gallipoli peninsula.

The Balkan allies and the Ottomans met in London later in December for peace talks. At the same time the ambassadors of the great powers in London met to direct the course of the peace settlement in the Balkans and to protect their own interests. The Ambassadors Conference, on the insistence of Austria-Hungary and Italy, established an independent Albanian state. This state blocked Serbian and Montenegrin claims to territories on the eastern shore of the Adriatic Sea. The talks between the Balkan allies and the Ottomans stalled mainly over the issue of Adrianople. On 3 February 1913, hostilities resumed.

In March of 1913 the Ottoman cities of Janina and Adrianople fell. The Montenegrins, however, bogged down in front of Shkodër.

With Serbian military help and bribery they succeeded in entering Shkodër on 23 April 1913. The great powers of Europe refused to sanction a Montenegrin occupation of this Albanian city because they had assigned it to the new Albanian state. Finally, the great powers induced the Montenegrins to evacuate their prize by the promise of generous subsidies. The Ottomans and the Balkan allies signed a peace treaty in London on 30 May 1913.

By the time of the signing of the London peace treaty the Balkan alliance was collapsing because of disagreements over Macedonia. The Serbs felt they deserved compensation in Macedonia because the great powers had thwarted their claims in Albania. On 5 May 1913 Greece and Serbia signed an agreement directed against Bulgaria. A feeble attempt at Russian arbitration failed. On 29–30 June 1913 Bulgarian forces launched a probing attack against Serb positions in Macedonia. The Second Balkan War ensued.

The Bulgarian attacks failed, and Bulgaria came under counterattack from Serb and Greek forces. Taking advantage of the situation, Romanian and Ottoman troops joined in the attack on Bulgaria. The Romanians objected to the establishment of a Greater Bulgaria, and the Ottomans perceived an opportunity to recover Adrianople. The result was a Bulgarian catastrophe. Bulgarian forces retreated on all fronts, and within a month Bulgarian resistance ceased. In the Treaty of Bucharest (10 August 1913) and the Treaty of Constantinople (30 September 1913) Bulgaria acknowledged complete defeat and the loss of much of its gains in the First Balkan War.

The Balkan Wars changed the map of south-eastern Europe. Serbia and Greece divided most of Macedonia. Serbia and Montenegro divided Novibazar. Greece also acquired Epirus (with the city of Janina), a large share of western and southern Macedonia (with the ports of Salonika and Kavalla), Crete, and most of the Aegean Islands. Montenegro almost doubled in size. An independent Albania appeared. Bulgaria obtained a bit of Macedonia in the vicinity of Strumitsa and central Thrace (including the insufficient port of Dedeagach). Romania received part of the Dobrudja. Only eastern Thrace remained to the Ottoman Empire.

The Balkan Wars were the first conflicts in Europe in the twentieth century and presaged the First World War. Mass attacks against entrenched positions, concentrated artillery bombardments, and airplanes made their first appearance in European warfare. The two wars resulted in at least 70,000 dead, with the Bulgarians suffering the greatest losses. Many more soldiers were wounded and missing, and hundreds of thousands of civilians were displaced. These wars left a legacy of national frustration among the Bulgarians and Ottomans, providing a basis for continued conflict. They also imparted a sense of inflated success among the Serbs, Greeks, and Romanians. Less than a year after the signing of the Treaty of Bucharest, war again erupted in the Balkans. Within the next five years all of the participants in the Balkan Wars would become involved in further disastrous conflicts.

Richard C. Hall

References

Helmreich, E.C. *The Diplomacy of the Balkan Wars, 1912–1913*. New York: Russell and Russell, 1972.

Kiraly, Bela K., and Dimitrije Djordjevic, eds. *East Central European Society and the Balkan Wars*. Boulder, Colo.: Social Science Monographs, 1987.

Rossos, Andrew. *Russia and the Balkans 1908–1914*. Toronto: University of Toronto Press, 1981.

See also ORIGINS OF THE FIRST WORLD WAR; OUTBREAK OF THE FIRST WORLD WAR

Balloons

Balloons were used in isolated incidents for aerial reconnaissance during eighteenth- and nineteenth-century conflicts, but their military role expanded during World War I. In addition to acting as protective barrages, stationary balloons served as observation platforms for artillery spotting; powered German zeppelins conducted bombing raids over England. Balloons participated in offensive maneuvers for both the Allies and Central Powers.

Germany in the late nineteenth century developed a kite balloon. Utilizing both kite and balloon principles, it resembled a giant sausage with a smaller balloon curved underneath, acting as a rudder. Streamlined, it could tolerate strong winds and high altitudes. Constructed in two parts—the front filled with gas and the rear inflated with air—kite balloons had wind sails attached at right angles to keep the rear aloft.

The Allies appropriated early Germany military balloon tactics and designs. French and Belgian agents secured German military balloon plans and crew manuals, and French inventor Albert Caquot adapted the German kite balloon design. German, French, and British balloons were deployed, as the war began, for scouting and artillery spotting duty.

Tethered to the ground to provide stability, these captive kite balloons had gondolas. Balloon crews transported balloons to ascension sites and inflated them using portable gas wagons. Elevated by winches to altitudes as high as 6,000 feet, observers used the balloons as platforms for surveillance and photography of enemy artillery. For that purpose the balloons were equipped with maps, binoculars, a telephone, and aerial reconnaissance cameras. Photographic results from the balloons were mixed, because balloons had to be tethered and manned by crews far enough away from enemy lines to reduce their vulnerability to attack.

Using the telephone, observers could call directly from the balloon basket to artillery positions. From their position thousands of feet above the earth, spotters could observe enemy camps and supply trains. This intelligence was useful both in preparing offensive attacks and also in plotting defensive positions. Spotters also directed artillery fire by means of signal flags. During battle, balloon observers described ground action and enemy responses, and they communicated field conditions. Balloons over fortifications were useful in adjusting artillery fire and in observation.

Balloon deployment in the Great War encountered natural obstacles that hindered performance, such as limited horizons and poor weather conditions. Fog, rain, and snow prevented balloons from being sent aloft. The terrain also determined balloon use, and their large size reduced their maneuverability.

Because these observation stations were tethered, balloons were a prime target for enemy aviators. Occasionally they were mistaken as enemy craft and attacked by planes of their own side. Although they were guarded by antiaircraft batteries, balloons were easy targets for what were termed balloon busters. American Frank Luke was one pilot famed for his prowess at crippling balloons on the Western Front.

Although on occasion machine guns were sent aloft in balloons, using those guns to defend against airplanes was impractical. Observers did not carry weapons aloft because they risked igniting the inflammable hydrogen gas that kept the balloon afloat. Tracer bullets not only pierced balloons, deflating them, but also turned them into fireballs. Balloons were easily set afire, and frictional sparks during deflation could set them ablaze within seconds. Tethered balloons then collapsed to the ground or exploded.

Serving as a balloon observer was very risky. Spotters wore harnesses attached to silk parachutes packed in aluminum containers that were secured to the gondolas. When the observer jumped, his weight released the chute. As the observer floated to the ground, he hoped that he would not be hit by burning debris from the flaming balloon and that the parachute would not catch fire.

Observers realized that they might have to escape disabled craft more than once, and they devised a system of tallying individual jump survivals. Considered the American balloon ace, Lieutenant Glenn Phelps jumped five times from July to November of 1918. During fifteen days of the 1918 Meuse-Argonne offensive, American balloonists jumped thirty times and ninety-one balloons were destroyed by enemy air and ground fire. Of a total of 1,870 German observation balloons in World War I, 655 were crippled by enemy planes, artillery, and inclement weather.

By January of 1915 Germany used powered balloons—zeppelins—to raid England, and both U.S. and British forces experimented with launching planes from dirigibles to increase their range. Powered balloons were also used to escort convoys and to scout for enemy submarines.

In February of 1918 the British used balloons to release propaganda. Balloons were selected instead of airplanes because international military dictates were ambiguous about whether downed pilots could be lawfully tried by warring nations for the war crime of distributing propaganda. Balloons carried pamphlets packaged in bundles along wires suspended from underneath. Carried into enemy territory according to wind patterns, the balloons released their cargo at intervals when cotton wicks attaching the leaflets to the wire burned.

Balloons also defended military targets. Some were used by the Royal Navy to protect ships from air attack. In 1917 both the Allies and Central Powers devised balloon barrages around crucial cities and industrial sites to protect them from bombing raids. The concept of barrage balloons originated before the war with military thinkers and civilians such as engineer Edgar Booth, who wrote a pamphlet outlining his ideas on the subject.

Booth's balloon barrage included electrically detonated charges on suspended wires and a warning system. When he sent it to the British Ministry of Munitions in 1916, officials rejected it because they said enemy aircraft would be able to see and avoid the balloons. Booth defended his idea, believing that "aerial nets" would protect London at night.

After an especially deadly German raid in September of 1916, Jan Smuts, a member of the British War Cabinet, demanded a balloon barrage for London. Major General Edward B. Ashmore, commander of the London Air Defence Area, supported Smuts. British officials traveled to Venice to see the barrage bobbing over the city, and on their return to London they planned a series of barrage balloons, called aprons.

Barrage balloons were sausage-shaped with fins. Made of rubberized cotton and as large as 70,000 cubic feet when filled with hydrogen, the balloons could withstand being tethered in strong winds. An apron consisted of three balloons anchored to the ground and linked by 500-foot-long cables. Every twenty-five yards, 1,000-foot-long steel wires hung vertically from these adjoining cables.

In early October the first of twenty authorized aprons were put in place, forming a fifty-one-mile-long barrage east of Lewisham, Plumstead, Barking, Ilford, and Wanstead, and north of Tottenham. Three Balloon Apron Squadrons were headquartered at Barking and Woodford in Essex and Shooters Hill in southeast London.

Barrage balloons hovered from 7,000 to 10,000 feet high, stressing the limits of German aircraft. Barrage balloons were most effective in forcing squadrons to fly at predictable and uniform heights. Antiaircraft artillery could concentrate fire on enemy planes above the balloons. The presence of balloons also prevented accurate bombing. Coinciding with the introduction of German Gotha bombers in the air war, the balloon barrages prevented these planes from inflicting as much damage as they would have without the defense measures.

Lack of proper construction material limited the balloons' maximum effect. Although some people ridiculed the balloons, the British public gained confidence, thinking that Gothas would fly into them and crash. Actual damage to German planes, though, was limited. The barrage at Chingford had two wires torn away when hit by a German plane, and, on his way into London in February of 1918, German pilot Lieutenant Götte struck the barrage at Woolwich. His plane twisted and plummeted before he regained control. The plane suffered only minor damage, and Götte was able to continue his bombing mission.

After the tenth apron was completed on 4 June 1918—half of the original plan—the Ministry of War decided to abandon balloon barrages. General Ashmore argued that without them London would be bombed from low altitudes and that balloons should continue to be built, but officials deemed the aprons unworthy of further use as the war waned. Similar barrage balloons were used in World War II in increased numbers and over prominent sites such as factories.

Balloons performed varied roles during World War I for both sides. The Great War witnessed the last extensive military use of balloons, although during World War II the Japanese armed balloons to deliver firebombs to the American West Coast. Twentieth-century conflicts relied upon technological advances in high-speed, high-altitude jet airplanes, satellite imagery, and computer modeling to provide reconnaissance data.

Elizabeth D. Schafer

References

Ashmore, Major General Edward Bailey. *Air Defense*. London: Longmans, Green, 1929.

Castle, H.G. *Fire Over England: The German Air Raids of World War I*. London: Secker and Warburg, 1982.

Cole, Christopher, and E.F. Cheesman. *The Air Defence of Britain 1914–1918*. London: Putnam, 1984.

Jackson, Donald Dale. *The Aeronauts*. Alexandria, Va.: Time-Life Books, 1980.

Livesey, Anthony. *Great Battles of World War I*. New York: Macmillan, 1989.

Mason, Francis K. *Battle Over Britain*. Bourne End: Aston, 1990.

Rawlinson, Alfred. *The Defence of London 1915–1918*. 3rd ed. London: Andrew Melrose, 1924.

Waligunda, Bob, and Larry Sheehan. *The Great American Balloon Book: An In-*

troduction to Hot Air Ballooning.
Englewood Cliffs, N.J.: Prentice-Hall, 1962.

Widmer, Emil J. *Military Observation Balloons (Captive and Free): A Complete Treatise on Their Manufacture, Equipment, Inspection, and Handling, with Special Instructions for the Training of a Field Balloon Company.* New York: D. Van Nostrand, 1917.

See also ANTIAIRCRAFT WEAPONS

Baltic Naval Operations, 1914–18

Although often perfunctorily treated in Anglo-American works, German naval control of the Baltic Sea ensured continued importation of high-grade Swedish iron ore and helped deny succor to Russia, contributing to her collapse in 1917.

While Russia had been the leading Baltic naval power in 1900, her Baltic fleet had been destroyed in the 1905 Battle of Tsushima Straits during the Russo-Japanese War. As a result, in August of 1914 Vice Admiral Nikolai von Essen's Baltic fleet included only four battleships. The German High Seas Fleet was concentrated against the British Grand Fleet in the North Sea, allowing the Russians to complete their four *Gangut*-class dreadnoughts. Nonetheless, German Commander in Chief Baltic Sea, Admiral Prince Henry undertook aggressive operations with what forces he had. His light cruisers laid mines off the Gulf of Finland on 17 August, and a week later Rear Admiral Behring took them into the gulf itself under the cover of fog. On 26 August, however, the light cruiser *Magdeburg* was stranded on Oldensholm Island during a clash with Russian cruisers and was lost. Russian divers recovered the German naval code books and presented them to the British, giving admiralty cryptanalysts (Room 40) a tremendous advantage in decoding German wireless signals.

The strategic shifting of the German battle fleet between the North Sea and the Baltic was greatly facilitated by the Kaiser Wilhelm (Kiel) Canal, cutting sixty-one miles across the neck of the Jutland peninsula. In September of 1914 Prince Henry, with his flag in the armored cruiser *Blücher,* took seven older battleships and forayed to the Gulf of Finland. On the 6th these clashed with Russian cruisers off the Aland Islands. German submarines were also active, and

on 11 October *U26* sank the armored cruiser *Pallada.*

As the world war stalemated to a struggle of attrition, Russia's industrial weakness was of increasing concern to her Western allies. A major concern was how to ship her the vital munitions of war. The German navy barred the Baltic, closing Peter the Great's "Window to the West"; the Turks and their German advisers and ordnance denied the Black Sea Straits; Murmansk on the Arctic Ocean lacked a railroad south; Archangel was blocked by ice half the year; and Vladivostok on the Pacific was too distant. British First Sea Lord Admiral Sir John Fisher favored a Baltic attack, and was building three fast shallow-draft battle cruisers, the *Courageous* class, to carry it out. But German torpedo boats in the Danish isles gave him pause, and the neutral Danes, recalling Nelson's attack on Copenhagen in 1801, mined the Great Belt from the Kattegat. First Lord of the Admiralty Winston Churchill insisted on forcing the Dardanelles in 1915, though Krupp cannon and Turkish mine-fields blocked the battleships, and the agony of Gallipoli meant failure.

British submarines were dispatched to the Baltic, however; by October of 1914 *E1* and *E9* had made the hazardous transit. They were to operate from Libau in Courland, but the Russians, fearing a German attack, destroyed the facilities and mined the approaches. The British E-boats had to base off Finland. When Behring swept in to bombard Libau on 17 November, he lost his flagship, the armored cruiser *Fredrich Karl,* to the mines. Although other sinkings would be attributed to the English submarines that winter, most were caused by Russian mines, which were the primary threat.

In the spring of 1915 the German armies defeated the Russians and drove them from Poland and the Courland peninsula. German naval units assisted in the capture of Libau and Windau, while the Russians were unwilling to risk their four dreadnoughts. Ready to facilitate a further army advance that might drive on Riga and then Petrograd itself, the German navy redeployed major elements of the High Seas Fleet to the Baltic. On 8 August, Vice Admiral Erhard Schmidt, commanding seven predreadnought battleships, attempted to break into the Gulf of Riga, covered by Vice Admiral Franz Hipper's three battle cruisers and eight dreadnoughts which swept to the Gulf of Finland. The minefields proved too thick. The addition of more minesweepers enabled dreadnoughts, *Nassau* and *Posen,* after trading broadsides with the old battleship *Slava* and smashing gunboats *Sivuch* and *Korejetz,* to break into the gulf on the 19th. This operation cost the Germans two torpedo boats and three minesweepers. Battlecruiser *Moltke* was damaged in a torpedo hit from *E1.*

Admiral Gustav Bachmann, head of the admiralty staff, had asked General Erich von Falkenhayn of the army's high command if the army intended to capture Riga, but Falkenhayn was more concerned with seeking a decision on the Western Front. When the navy raised the question in December about an invasion of the Baltic Islands off the Gulf of Riga, Falkenhayn bluntly said no forces were available.

In 1916, the stalemate continued on land and sea. That year the major German naval effort was at Jutland (Skagerrak). The focus shifted to the Baltic early in 1917, when the February Revolution in Petrograd raised the possibility of a Russian collapse. The Germans contemplated a combined operation against the Baltic Islands to open Estonia and Livonia for a drive against the Russian capital. Field Marshal Paul von Hindenburg, who had succeeded Falkenhayn, expressed interest, though his chief of staff, General Erich Ludendorff, felt that Russia was disintegrating anyway.

By the autumn, however, the new Russian parliamentary regime was still continuing the war effort, and the German high command determined on a *coup de grace* before winter. The navy was especially eager for action, for idleness and political agitation in the capital ships had already generated mutinous unrest in August. The German Eighth Army launched an offensive that captured Riga on 3 September, but the forest and swamp terrain beyond was forbidding. Hindenburg and Ludendorff, therefore, planned an amphibious operation with the navy to invade the Baltic Islands, code-named Operation Albion.

In the predawn darkness on 12 October, broadsides from Schmidt's eleven dreadnoughts smashed Russian gun batteries on Oesel Island. Torpedo boats and motorized barges then sped in with the first waves of Major General von Estorff's veteran 42nd (Alsace-Lorraine) Infantry Division (reinforced), to land at Tagga Bay on the northwest side. The defending Russian 107th Division was already politically demoralized, though the Germans encountered pockets of resistance.

The dreadnoughts *König* and *Kronprinz* negotiated the minefields and entered the Gulf of Riga. On the 17th they engaged Russian warships behind their Moon Sound minefields, wrecking the old battleship *Slava,* and putting battleship *Grazhdanin* (formerly the *Tsetsarevich*) and the armored cruiser *Bayan* to flight. By the 21st Dagö Island had been secured, completing Operation Albion. Petrograd itself was now vulnerable to attack by land and sea, and the Kerensky government was impotent to prevent it. Two weeks later the Bolsheviks overthrew the Kerensky regime and ended Russia's participation in the war. The continuing German military threat finally brought the Treaty of Brest-Litovsk on 3 March 1918, by which six countries gained their independence from Russia.

The German Baltic fleet also played an important role in assisting the Finns against Red Bolshevik forces. In February the German navy transported German-trained Finnish volunteers and then in April the "Baltic Division" under Brigadier General Count Rüdiger von der Goltz, to assist the Finnish government of Pehr Svinhufvud against the Finnish and Russian Reds. These operations, covered by dreadnoughts *Rheinland* and *Posen,* proved decisive, and Helsingfors (Helsinki) was liberated by 14 April. But Germany herself was defeated by November of 1918, and the new Baltic nations faced an uncertain future.

A. Harding Ganz

References

Ganz, A. Harding. "'ALBION'—The Baltic Islands Operation." *Military Affairs* 42 (April 1978): 91–97.

———. "The German Expedition to Finland, 1918." *Military Affairs* 44 (April 1980): 84–89.

Greger, René. *Die russische Flotte im Ersten Weltkrieg 1914–1917.* München: J.F. Lehmanns Verlag, 1970.

Krieg in der Ostsee. 3 vols. Der Kriegzur See Series. Berlin: E.S. Mittler und Sohn, 1929–1964.

Tomitch, V.M. *Warships of the Imperial Russian Navy.* Vol. 1, *Battleships.* San Francisco: B.T. Publishers, 1968.

See also BALTIC STATES; FINLAND, ROLE IN WAR; GERMANY, NAVY; GOLTZ, RÜDIGER VON DER; HENRY, PRINCE; HIPPER, FRANZ VON; MAGDEBURG; RIGA,

Baltic States

When war began in 1914, the Lithuanian, Latvian, and Estonian inhabitants of the Russian Baltic provinces were initially supportive of Russia. Latvia and Estonia came out openly in support of the czarist forces, while Lithuania adopted some Russian war aims, particularly territorial claims. Only as the war turned against Russia and conditions worsened did the Baltic states recognize the potential for national independence.

Although initially far from the field of battle, the Baltic states quickly experienced fighting on their territories. Beginning in March of 1915, German forces advanced into Lithuania and by the following September had occupied the entire region. With the German advance and Russian retreat, local administration collapsed, and large segments of the population abandoned their homes. German troops next advanced into Latvia, taking Liepaja on 8 May 1915. Two Latvian Home Guard battalions held off the initial German assault on Jelgava, but the city fell on 1 August. About 500,000 Latvians fled to Russia, and at the same time most of the industry in this area, the Courland, was dismantled and moved to Russia. The Latvians did petition Grand Duke Nikolai to form their own volunteer units, and this was granted. The establishment of the eight Latvian Rifle battalions was a victory for the nationalists. The German advance halted only on the Daugava River outside of Riga, and by early 1916 the front in Latvia had stabilized. In February of 1916, as part of the Russian assault designed to relieve some of the pressure on the Western Front, two Latvian rifle battalions broke through the German lines at Riga, but they were quickly forced to withdraw. The Germans kept up pressure along the Daugava River, and on 19 August 1917, they crossed the river. Three days later Riga fell.

While much Baltic territory remained unconquered by the Germans, the war nevertheless had a powerful impact on the region. Refugees fled to areas of Latvia, especially Livonia, and to Estonia. Nationalist sentiment mounted, such as Latvia's request for the formation of national forces to fight for the czar. Nationalist activity also grew in Estonia, though slowly. Delegates to the Duma from Latvia and Estonia began to recognize that the war would weaken the czarist regime and lead to the formation of a federation. The overthrow of the czar in February of 1917 was welcomed in the Baltic region, as nationalist and revolutionary sentiment surged forward. Nationalists formed political parties that called for autonomy, and the Latvians openly sought national independence. The Russian provisional government made only slight concessions, but Estonia did gain autonomy by June of 1917.

Political life in Latvia and Estonia was increasingly shaped by radical leftist groups, much as in Russia. In the Baltic region the Bolsheviks gained importance both in the councils and through local elections. After the October Revolution and the Bolshevik takeover, sailors and soldiers stationed in this area were among the first to recognize the revolutionary leaders. With the collapse of the Russian monarchy, the Iskolat Republic was established in that part of Latvia not occupied by German forces. This new revolutionary government ensured the takeover of power by the local Soviets. Its rule was firm and it successfully managed the economy, resolved the agrarian question, and organized schools. While taking over control from the local councils, the Iskolat also guaranteed that the transition was gradual. The Iskolat Republic ended, however, when German forces overthrew it in February of 1918. In Estonia, moderates pushed for independence, but the Bolsheviks canceled elections scheduled for 9–10 February and strengthened their control, often through terror.

On the military front German forces pushed northward, and by early 1918 they occupied the whole region (Lithuania had been occupied in March of 1915, Latvia in May of 1915, and Estonia in September of 1917). The territory was administered as *Land Ober-Ost* under Major General Max Hoffmann, whose occupation policy was thorough and far-reaching. In Lithuania, for example, the Germans reorganized the judicial and education systems, strengthened the economy, and conscripted local workers to provide food and timber to the occupation force. In planning for the postwar era, German authorities made concessions to Lithuanian nationalists (to counter Polish and Russian ambitions) and later, in June of 1917, permitted the establishment of a Lithuanian Council. By late 1917 the drive for recognition of an independent Lithuania gathered momentum. In a 13 November speech, a nationalist called for a new Lithuanian state based not on the historical boundaries but ethnological community. The German chancellor proposed recognizing Lithuanian sovereignty, and Kaiser Wilhelm II signed the authorization on 23 March 1918. The new president was Augustinas Voldemaras.

The situation in Latvia and Estonia differed; there the Germans dealt not with indigenous representatives but Baltic Germans, longtime and well-established residents. German policy also included the use of Courland as an area for future colonization by demobilized soldiers. Other aspects of German policy, however, aided its efforts. After the Bolshevik Revolution in Russia and the rise of pro-Bolshevik councils in Latvia and Estonia, German troops took on the appearance of liberators from a worse fate. A declaration of their independence was handed to Russian representatives in Stockholm in early 1918, but Communist authorities in Tallinn moved swiftly against leading Baltic-German politicians. The advance of German forces into Estonia forced the Communists to flee, and local nationalists published a manifesto proclaiming Estonian independence on 24–25 February 1918. German military leaders refused to recognize the declaration. Nevertheless, the Germans did liberate the Baltic region from Bolshevik rule, but only by occupying it.

With German occupation, Baltic nationalists and political leaders had little impact on events. Nevertheless, efforts to obtain support for independence from the Western Allies intensified in the spring of 1918. Within a few months, both the Allies and Germans were too preoccupied with hostilities on the Western Front to pay much attention to the Baltic region, and by the later summer it was clear that Germany would have to sue for peace.

The collapse of German rule in the Baltic states had far-reaching consequences. With local troops scarcely existent, the area was vulnerable to Bolshevik invasion. Already on 11 November the 6th Soviet Russian Division took up position on the Estonian border. It invaded on the 22nd, and Narva fell to the Red army on the 29th, the same day that a Soviet Republic of Estonia was declared. Latvian and Red army forces invaded Livonia and pushed on toward Riga, which fell on 3 January 1919. By the end of the month most of the territory had been conquered. Bolshevik troops also moved against Lithuania and entered Vilnius on 5–6 January. Soviet rule was particularly severe, and terror prevailed.

Although 1919 began with the nationalist movements in the Baltics appearing defeated, local forces, aided by Finnish and in some instances German troops, soon turned the tide. By the end of January 1919 they had successfully pushed the Bolsheviks out of Estonia and by the late summer of 1919 out of Lithuania. Some German troops remained active in the fight against the Bolsheviks. The situation in Latvia proved more difficult for the nationalists, and Germany, worried about the spread of revolution, sent forces in from East Prussia in February. These troops occupied Riga on 22 May but evacuated it on 3 July in accordance with an armistice.

The victorious Allies showed some interest in the Baltic states, but their policy was shaped mainly by events in Russia. In intervening in the Russian Civil War, the British were primarily concerned with preventing the reassertion of Russian or German dominance in the Baltic region. France focused on the establishment of an independent Poland, while the United States withdrew. With the changing military situation, Russian forces pressured the Baltic states. Only in the summer of 1919 did peace negotiations between Russia and Estonia, Latvia, and Lithuania begin. A peace treaty with Estonia was concluded at Tartu on 2 February 1920, recognizing Estonian independence. Discussions with Latvian leaders began in April and resulted in the Treaty of Riga and similar recognition on 11 August 1920. A Latvian-Germany treaty was concluded on 5 July 1920; it recognized the Latvian republic and set German reparations. The Treaty of Moscow, concluding hostilities between Lithuania and Russia, was signed on 12 July. These treaties launched independence for the Baltic states.

Robert G. Waite

References

Ezergailis, Andrew. *The Russian Baltic Provinces between the 1905/1917 Revolutions*. Cologne: Böhlau Verlag, 1982.

Mangulis, Visvaldis. *Latvia in the Wars of the 20th Century*. Princeton Junction, N.J.: Cognition Books, 1983.

Nodel, Emanuel. *Nation on the Anvil*. New York: Bookman, 1963.

Rauch, Georg von. *The Baltic States: The Years of Independence, Lithuania, Latvia, Estonia, 1917–1940*. London: C. Hurst, 1974.

B

See also EASTERN FRONT, 1915 CAMPAIGNS; FINLAND, ROLE IN WAR; HOFFMANN, MAX; RIGA, BATTLE OF; RUSSIA, HOME FRONT AND REVOLUTIONS OF 1917

Beatty, David, 1st Earl (1871–1936)

British admiral and commander of the Grand Fleet. Born 17 January 1871 in Stapeley, Cheshire, David Beatty was the son of an army officer. He entered the Royal Navy in 1884 at age thirteen. At the turn of the century he served abroad in Africa (Egypt-Sudan) and China. Beatty was the epitome of the dashing, charismatic, flamboyant, courageous, young naval officer—captain at age twenty-nine, rear admiral at forty-three. Some compare him to Lord Horatio Nelson a century earlier. Also like Nelson he was implicated in scandals, involving his marriage to the divorced heiress of Marshall Field and a long-time and open relationship with the wife of another naval officer.

Winston Churchill drafted Beatty to be his naval secretary when he became first lord of the admiralty in 1911. Soon Beatty was named commander of the battlecruiser squadron, the advanced guard of the Grand Fleet. He served in that key capacity during three significant battles in the Channel/North Sea area: Heligoland Bight (August of 1914), Dogger Bank (January of 1915), and Jutland (May of 1916). After Jutland, Commander of the Grand Fleet Admiral John Jellicoe praised Beatty in his official dispatches for locating the enemy and leading them to the Grand Fleet. Yet in all three of these battles there were critical problems of communication, confusion over targets, and poor staff coordination linked to Beatty.

Nevertheless, after Jutland Beatty was made commander of the Grand Fleet. In January of 1919 he was promoted to admiral and, in April of 1919, to admiral of the fleet. He was first sea lord from 1919 to 1927 and is credited with restoration of the morale of the Royal Navy. During the early 1920s a controversy developed over various accounts of the battle of Jutland and, especially, the official naval history of the war written by Sir Julian Corbett. There were pro-Jellicoe and pro-Beatty factions. The Beatty admiralty actually added a disclaimer at the beginning of volume 3, the Jutland account; Arthur Marder's account of the battle, also in volume 3, was generally pro-Jellicoe. Stephen

Roskill, in the best biography of Beatty, became the primary apologist for Beatty.

Beatty is also faulted by many because the Fleet Air Arm (FAA) was shifted from the navy to the newly formed Royal Air Force "on Beatty's watch." This was a serious blow to potential naval capabilities and funding during the interwar period. The navy was seriously deficient in air capabilities at the beginning of World War II, shortly after FAA was returned.

Beatty insisted on being pallbearer both at the funerals of Lord Jellicoe and King George V. He died shortly thereafter, on 11 March 1936, in London. He is buried in St. Paul's Cathedral.

Eugene L. Rasor

References

Beatty Papers, National Maritime Museum, Greenwich and Churchill College, Cambridge.

Beatty, Charles. *Our Admiral: A Biography of Admiral of the Fleet.* London: Allen, 1980.

Chalmers, William S. *The Life and Letters of David, Earl Beatty, Admiral of the Fleet.* London: Hodder, 1951.

Dictionary of National Biography, 1931–1940 Supplement. "David Beatty, First Earl Beatty." London: Oxford University Press, 1949.

Roskill, Stephen W. *Admiral of the Fleet Earl Beatty: The Last Naval Hero.* London: Collins, 1980.

See also DOGGER BANK, NAVAL BATTLE OF; HELIGOLAND BIGHT, BATTLE OF; JELLICOE, JOHN; JUTLAND, BATTLE OF

Belgium, Army, 1914–18

When Belgium's army mobilized for World War I in August of 1914, it was small and inexperienced compared with its European counterparts. Because of Belgium's neutrality, the Belgian officer corps, trained at the Ecole de Guerre, did not attract superior candidates.

The Belgian army had evolved from the Belgian Civic Guard, established in 1831. That force maintained order and provided wartime auxiliary services such as supply. It was not until 1913, when threatened by German military expansion, that Belgium established compulsory military service. By August of 1914, 117,000 men served in six infantry divisions and one cavalry division of the Belgian army. Supplies were minimal: Only one bullet per man was available for training at weekly range practice. Soldiers had to improvise or borrow equipment. Few machine guns were distributed, and the Belgian army had no heavy field artillery. The parliament refused to purchase more sophisticated weapons equivalent in quality to those used by German troops.

The Belgian army also encountered difficulties in administration. General Selliers de Moranville, chief of the Belgian army's general staff, did not want King Albert to devise strategy, and disagreements between the two men caused conflicting orders to be dispatched; King Albert wanted to strengthen forts, and Selliers wanted to concentrate troops in Belgium's center.

General mobilization orders were issued in August of 1914, and the Belgian army declared that it would resist invading German troops in response to the German ultimatum for passage. The Belgian army, commanded by King Albert, was in active service by the 4th, defending its territory when German troops crossed the border.

German forces enjoyed quick successes as they advanced toward the fortress at Liège. The weak Belgian army, lacking assistance from French or British forces, proved unable to repulse the invaders. Some troops managed to destroy bridges over the Meuse River before the Germans arrived, but that only temporarily delayed the invasion. German cavalry and infantry forces of 320,000 overwhelmed the 70,000 Belgians defending border forts at Liège.

General Gérard Mathieu Leman, commander of the 3rd Division, initially repulsed the Germans at Liège on 5 August, but, because of disagreement between Selliers and Albert, he was not allowed to counterattack. In the first land operation of the war, the Belgian soldiers inflicted heavy casualties, especially to German troops crossing the river on pontoons, but the Germans rallied, bombarding the resisting Belgians, and captured the fortress within days. Leman ordered his men to join the main body of the Belgian army, which Albert was steering toward Antwerp.

The Belgian army barely resisted the German armies moving toward the French frontier, except at Haelen, where the Belgian army was victorious on 12 August 1914. At the siege of Namur from 20 to 25 August, 37,000 Belgians of the 14th Division, commanded by General Michel, attempted to outlast 100,000 Germans

but were forced to surrender under constant mortar attack. After Namur fell, several thousand Belgian soldiers circuited through Ostend, where army supplies were stored, to Antwerp to rejoin the army. Others who refused to surrender were interned in German camps in Holland until the war ended.

German forces occupied Brussels on 20 August and Albert withdrew 65,000 men to Antwerp, which was more secure. The Antwerp fortress had 80,000 troops to reinforce the army. From Antwerp the Belgian army abandoned defensive measures and, in an offensive campaign to liberate Belgium, harassed rear units of the German force engaged in the Battle of the Marne, destroying petroleum supplies and communications and seizing German vessels.

The Germans responded with artillery attacks on the outer fortifications of Antwerp, and a siege there began on 28 September. Because he had only 150,000 men with which to defend Antwerp, Albert evacuated the city on 6 October. The Belgian army escaped southwest along the Flanders coast and dug fortifications behind the Yser River.

A German assault against the Belgian forces at the Yser was repulsed by a weak but determined army. The Belgians lost a quarter of their 60,000-man force, but German casualties were greater than the size of the Belgian army. During the First Battle of Ypres, the German Fourth and Sixth armies pushed Belgian forces back to Nieuport, where they opened the sea dike sluices, flooding a two-mile-wide area between them and the Germans, thereby saving the Belgian army.

Digging into a stationary front of trenches, Belgian artillery defended its sliver of the Western front. The remainder of Belgium was occupied by the German army. Albert declared, "the Army was practically the only remaining emblem of Belgian nationality."

The Belgian army attempted to rebuild its battered forces by recruiting refugees, with enlistment offices in England. In a decree of 1 March 1915, the Belgium government stated that all males between eighteen and twenty-five had to enlist in the military or be deported. The army had begun the war with over 100,000 men, and in January of 1915 only approximately half that number remained. By 1915 an additional cavalry division was created. This was possible because 40,000 men crossed the Dutch border, escaping from occupied Belgium.

The arsenal at Le Havre was restocked, and Belgian gunsmiths traveled to Russia to make weapons. The standard Belgian rifle was the Fusil D'Infanterie Modèle 1889, which arms manufacturer Fabrique National designed especially for World War I. Belgian manufacturers also produced automatic pistols and machine guns for the Belgian army. The Belgians had initially used private cars in raids against invading German forces. The Minerva factory in Antwerp produced the first armored cars. These were used by the Belgian army until the 1930s. A Belgian armored car unit also supported Russian forces on the Eastern Front until August of 1917.

At the beginning of the war, the Compagnie des Aviateurs had four squadrons, each supporting an army division, but so few pilots were available that the air force was not immediately effective. A revamped force of fighter and bomber squadrons renamed Aviation Militaire was successful on the Western Front in 1915 and produced three aces.

Albert rejected participating in Allied offensive operations during most of the war because of his disagreement with Allied war aims. He urged a compromise peace. For four years the Belgian army remained on the Yser. Finally, in the climactic battles of the war, Albert agreed to let the Belgian army go on the offensive; in return, in the fall of 1918 Marshal Ferdinand Foch named him commander of the Flanders Army Group, which included French and British units.

The Belgian army participated in the final Allied advance. Belgian troops also helped British forces capture Germany's African colonies and defended the Belgian Congo. The Belgian army had increased to 200,000 men by the time the Armistice was signed.

Elizabeth D. Schafer

References
Buffin, Baron C. *Brave Belgians*. Translated by Alys Hallard. New York: G.P. Putnam's Sons, 1918.
de Gomery, Commandant de Gerlache. *Belgium in War Time*. London: Hodder and Stoughton, 1917.
Tuchman, Barbara W. *The Guns of August*. New York: Macmillan, 1962.

See also ALBERT I, KING OF BELGIUM; BELGIUM INVASION OF; RACE TO THE SEA; YPRES, FIRST BATTLE OF

Belgium, Invasion of (August 1914)

Acting under the Schlieffen Plan, the German army overran Belgium in August of 1914. Within three weeks, 1.5 million German troops in seven armies had passed through Belgium and established an occupation force, violating Belgian neutrality and forcing the Belgian government into exile.

Although Belgium had begun general military training in 1913, the Belgian army in 1914 was still small and ineffective. It was also woefully short of artillery, which had been ordered from Krupp; the Germans, understandably, had delayed shipping it. The Belgian air service in 1914 was also woefully inadequate, consisting of only four squadrons, each supporting one army. Trained pilots were also in short supply.

On 2 August 1914, German minister in Brussels Herr von Below-Saleske delivered an ultimatum to Belgian Minister of Foreign Affairs M. Davignon demanding free passage of German troops through Belgium and warning that if Belgium did not agree to German demands she would be treated as an enemy. The Belgian government was given only twelve hours to respond, and King Albert's appeal to the Germans that they reconsider was unsuccessful. The Belgians then began a general mobilization of their army and national guard units, but most Belgians refused to believe the war would come to them.

On 3 August Albert asked British King George V for diplomatic support of Belgian neutrality, hoping that this would cause Germany to reconsider. Albert also sought aid from France. Neither country offered immediate assistance, and Below-Saleske predicted, "The Belgians will line up to see us pass."

At dawn on the 4th, the German army crossed the Belgium border at Gemmenich, fifty kilometers from Liège. The British government issued an ultimatum to Germany to halt the invasion by midnight, but the German army continued its advance. This refusal produced a British declaration of war against Germany.

The Germans converged along four roads to Liège, the gateway to the country. It had a strong fortress with a ring of smaller forts—six on each side of the river—surrounding it. At Warsage, the first village encountered, the Germans distributed a proclamation from General Otto von Emmich, commander of the Special Army of the Meuse, promising no atrocities would be committed. When a German soldier was killed on the outskirts of town, however, the Germans executed hostages and plundered and burned buildings, including churches. This pattern would be repeated elsewhere.

One hour after the German invasion began, Albert informed parliament that Belgium would resist, to defend its territory, and that he would be military commander in chief. Neither French nor British forces were deployed in time to help the Belgians. Belgian civilians assisted the military effort by blowing up railroads and tunnels. They destroyed bridges over the Meuse River before the Germans arrived and razed farms and homes near Liège to provide clear fields for defensive fire. Private cars were used in raids against the Germans, and the Minerva factory undertook the production of armored cars. Belgians also utilized wireless radios to spy on advancing troops, and guerrillas conducted raids against the invaders.

Twelve German cavalry regiments and battalions of chasseurs in automobiles on the German right wing tried to seize Visé bridge. They were unsuccessful but moved north and crossed the Meuse at Lexhe ford, for Liège. As General von Emmich's 60,000 troops crossed the Meuse on pontoons, they were fired on by 25,000 Belgians. They continued toward Liège, the capture of which was necessary for the Germans to continue their advance toward northern France. By the night of 4 August a cavalry advance guard and six German infantry brigades of General Karl von Bülow's Second Army of the German right wing had penetrated the resistance of Liège's outer forts.

By 5 August the Liège forts were under full attack by a German force of 320,000 men. Commander of the 3rd Division General Gérard Mathieu Leman led 70,000 Belgians in this first land operation of the war. German troops were pounded by Belgian artillery and mowed down by machine guns as they charged up the slope toward the fort. Belgian opposition inflicted heavy casualties, and Emmich called a halt to the offensive until he could maneuver cavalry behind the Belgian positions.

With reinforcements, the Germans soon captured the smaller forts. As Belgian supplies dwindled, German Major General Erich Ludendorff of the Second Army led a brigade between the decimated forts, entered the town of Liège, and forced its surrender by 7 August. The Belgians were stunned by the German use of heavy 305mm and 420mm siege howitzers, weapons the Allies had not anticipated.

Belgian resistance at Liège ceased on 16 August after eleven days of bombardment, but Leman ordered the final outpost, Fort Loncin, destroyed to defy the invaders. The Germans carried Leman, unconscious, from its rubble and made him a prisoner. While the Germans were fighting at Liège, the French and British at last deployed forces.

On 17 August the Germans renewed their advance, beginning the next phase of the Schlieffen Plan with the First, Second, and Third armies making a turning movement through Belgium. The Belgian army moved toward Antwerp so as not to be cut off by the Germans.

Beyond Liège the German invaders dispersed. The right advance group headed northwest to outflank the Belgian army protecting Brussels. The Germans encountered defeat at Haelen on 12 August but regrouped and entered Hasselt that day and took Aerschot and Louvain on the 19th. They entered Malines but were driven out by a Belgian sortie from Antwerp on the 25th. They recaptured Malines by the end of August.

At the siege at Namur, considered the "cornerstone of the frontier," from 20 to 25 August, General Michel's 14th Division of 37,000 Belgians fought 100,000 Germans of Bülow's Second Army. Meanwhile, the main German force battled the French Fifth Army led by General Charles Lanrezac at Sambre.

Namur consisted of ten forts, minefields, and trenches, and the Belgians believed it could hold out for at least a month. They defended their city and forts, but the defenders were at low strength because the main Belgian force had marched toward Antwerp, and five forts fell on the first day. The Belgians sustained heavy casualties from concentrated German artillery and mortar fire and surrendered on 25 August. The Germans took 50,000 prisoners. With the loss of Namur, the French and British were unable to make a defensive stand against the Germans until the Battle of the Marne.

While the Belgians were attempting to hold on to Namur, on 20 August General Alexander von Kluck and the German First Army occupied Brussels. As both British and French troops retreated south, the German forces chased them into France, reaching Mons by the 23rd and Tournai the next day.

The main Belgian force of 65,000 men led, by Albert, had meanwhile been forced to withdraw to Antwerp to secure that vital channel port while the Germans advanced on Brussels after the fall of Liège. From Antwerp, the Belgians staged sorties against the flank of German forces now massing to invade France.

On 28 September the Germans began a siege of Antwerp. General Hans von Beseler led five divisions, supported by artillery, against the outer forts. With only 150,000 defenders, Albert appealed to London for assistance. The British were concerned about the loss of Antwerp because it was a crucial channel port. Churchill send Royal Navy troops to Belgium but they were insufficient to repel the Germans. As morale and supplies dwindled, the Belgian Council of War decided to evacuate Antwerp.

Much of the Belgian army escaped down the Flanders coast, guarded by British troops commanded by General Sir Henry Rawlinson. The Germans occupied Antwerp on 9 October. Although the Belgians suffered heavy casualties at Antwerp, its siege slowed the German advance to the coast and enabled both Belgian and British troops to improve their defensive positions and prepare for future fighting on the Yser River as the Germans raced to the sea. Additional towns in Flanders fell in this German offensive: Ghent on 12 October, Bruges on the 14th, and Ostend on the 15th.

The Belgian army dug in fortifications behind the Yser. The German Sixth Army, commanded by Bavarian Crown Prince Rupprecht, and the Fourth Army attacked in mid-October, attempting to cross the Yser and smash the Allied northern flank. The weakened Belgians resisted for a time, before falling back to the Dixmunde-Nieuport railway when the Germans crossed the river on 24 October. On 29 October the Belgian army opened the sea dike sluices at Nieuport, flooding fields between them and the Germans. The Germans renewed their attack on 30 October five miles east of Ypres and temporarily broke through at Gheluvel. The third German assault began on 11 November with Ypres the primary objective. When the Germans broke through the northern line, they hesitated. This allowed the Allies to launch a counterattack that preserved Ypres. Total casualties in this fighting mounted to 50,000 Belgians and greater numbers of French and German forces. The Belgian army held the line from Ypres to Nieuport, and a stationary front of trenches emerged. They continued to hold this territory for four years till the end of the war.

The German invasion of Belgium from August to November 1914 was quick and decisive and provided the Germans access to France. Belgium overrun soon became Belgium occupied. Germany's invasion of Belgium helped produce the Allied resolve that ultimately won the war.

Elizabeth D. Schafer

References

de Gomery, Commandant de Gerlache. *Belgium in War Time.* London: Hodder and Stoughton, 1917.

Keegan, J. *Opening Moves: August 1914.* New York: Ballantine, 1971.

Meeüs, Adrien de. *History of the Belgians.* Translated by G. Gordon. New York: Frederick A. Praeger, 1962.

Tuchman, Barbara W. *The Guns of August.* New York: Macmillan, 1962.

Belgium, Neutrality of to 1914

Following the Belgian Revolution of 1830, the British and French worked out a compromise establishing an independent and perpetually neutral Belgian state. The British did not wish to see Belgium, strategically located across from the mouth of the Thames and a conduit for British trade with the Continent, come under the control of France. The conservative eastern powers of Russia, Prussia, and Austria were persuaded to accept this alteration of the Vienna settlement, and Dutch King William I, after futile resistance, bowed to the inevitable and assented to the Five Power Treaty on 19 April 1839. In the 1860s Napoleon III of France hoped to expand French territory along the Rhine; in order to forestall this, Britain, at the outbreak of the Franco-Prussian War, successfully pressed Prussia and France to sign treaties guaranteeing Belgian neutrality.

Belgium fared less well in 1914. It played a key role in the German Schlieffen Plan, which called for a massive maneuver of encirclement to drive through Belgium into France. Chief of the German General Staff General Alfred von Schlieffen was not troubled about the prospective violation of Belgian neutrality; he believed that the war would be won so quickly that adverse international reaction would make no difference. He also questioned the neutrality of Belgium, which had fortified its frontier with Germany but not with France. Friedrich von Holstein of the German Foreign Office responded to a query from Schlieffen in 1900 that German diplomacy would have to acquiesce to strategy and justify the proposed violation. Chancellor Theobald von Bethmann Hollweg knew about the planned violation, but lamely asserted that he never had an opportunity to discuss it with the military.

In an effort to gain Belgian neutrality, on 29 July 1914, Bethmann Hollweg hinted that Belgian neutrality would have to be violated. Edward Grey called this a "disgrace" and on 31 July asked France and Germany to agree to respect the neutrality of Belgium unless it were first violated by the other. Early on 1 August France gave a definitive assent, but the German government refused. On 2 August, after its declaration of war on Russia, Germany presented an ultimatum to Belgium demanding the right of passage for German troops. The German government promised that if Belgium acquiesced its integrity would be ensured, and it would be compensated at the expense of France after the war. On 3 August, anticipating an invasion of Belgium, the British cabinet sent Grey to speak to the House of Commons; after a rousing speech, he won its support for war if Belgium were violated. Early on 4 August Grey demanded an immediate affirmation from Germany of Belgian neutrality, but Bethmann Hollweg told the British ambassador that he was confident Britain would not go to war over "a scrap of paper." At 14:00 Grey was informed that Belgium had been invaded. At midnight, when the British ultimatum deadline passed, she entered the war.

In a speech before the Reichstag on the day of the invasion, Bethmann Hollweg, insisting that Germany had been forced by Russia into a defensive war, claimed that the threat of a French attack had compelled it to violate Belgian neutrality. He accepted, however, the protests of the Belgian government as "legitimate" and added, "We shall try to make up for this injustice—I speak openly—this injustice we are committing, once our military aims have been accomplished."

Bernard A. Cook

References

Davignon, Henry. *Belgium and Germany: Texts and Documents*. Edinburgh and New York: Thomas Nelson, 1915.

Fuehr, Alexander. *The Neutrality of Belgium: A Study of the Belgian Case under Its Aspects in Political History and International Law*. New York and London: Funk and Wagnalls, 1915.

Thomas, Daniel H. *The Guarantee of Belgian Independence and Neutrality in European Diplomacy, 1830's-1930's*. Kingston, R.I.: D.H. Thomas, 1983.

Waxweiler, Emile. *Belgium and the Great Powers: Her Neutrality Explained and Vindicated*. New York and London: Putnam, 1916.

See also SCHLIEFFEN PLAN

Belgium, Occupation of, 1914–18

The Germans responded brutally to the August 1914 Belgian resistance. Hostages were used as human shields; individuals suspected of being guerrillas, of performing acts of sabotage, or of giving active support to Belgian soldiers were summarily executed; and houses, towns, and parts of cities were put to the torch. Among those executed were priests and women. Belgian officials were forced to stay at their posts and take orders from the Germans, and individuals, such as Burgomaster Adolphe Max of Brussels, were imprisoned and deported for acts of independence. Although a few Flemish nationalists cooperated with the Germans, the vast majority of the Belgians remained loyal to King Albert and to the government-in-exile, headquartered at Sainte-Adresse near Le Havre, France.

On 26 August Field Marshal Colmar von der Goltz became governor general of occupied Belgium with Dr. von Sandt as chief of civil administration. The whole country was placed under martial law. After Goltz was transferred to Constantinople in November, General von Bissing held the post until his death on 18 April 1917. General Ludwig von Falkenhausen served as the final governor general.

The Germans sought to keep the Belgians isolated and uninformed. They forbade the use of telephone and telegraph and permitted communication with the outside world only through letters censored by the Germans. Censorship and information control were pervasive, but clandestine newspapers, such as *Libre Belgique* and *Flambeau*, were printed and circulated. The four Belgian universities refused to open for class in the fall of 1914. Three remained closed for the duration, but the Germans, in an effort to court the Flemish, transformed the University of Ghent into a Flemish-language university and reopened it. In addition, on 4 June 1918 Flemish was proclaimed the language of instruction in all state-supported schools in the Flemish section of Belgium. Belgians were required to obtain passports to travel from one town to another. Although the Germans attempted to close off the Dutch border with an electrified, barbed-wire barrier, forty thousand Belgians crossed it to join the Belgian army on the Yser front.

The stoppage of transportation, communication, and credit brought commerce and industry to a complete standstill. Cash reserves and a large part of the negotiable securities had been removed from banks at the end of July and the beginning of August. Subsequently, banks, placed under German control, stopped payment or limited them to very small sums, and businesses and wealthy Belgians were unable to negotiate their investments at will. Since the Belgian National Bank had shipped its assets and plates to London, the Germans denied its right to issue bank notes. Instead, on 22 December 1914, the Germans empowered the Société Général de Belgique to resume the issuance of currency. In the meantime a number of towns issued vouchers payable within the limits of their own territory.

In October of 1915 the Germans began conscripting Belgians for military work within Belgium. On 2 May 1916 they forbade the continuation of relief work, which had been implemented by the Belgian National Committee for Relief and Alimentation, to combat unemployment. To the Germans such work was unproductive and inhibited their effort to draw Belgian workers to Germany to supplement the depleted German labor force. Between June of 1915 and March of 1916 the Germans had been able to recruit only 12,000 Belgian workers. Although voluntary recruits increased after May, they still fell short of German needs. In October of 1916 the Germans resorted to forced deportation, and by the end of their occupation they had deported 120,000 workers.

The Germans imposed war contributions on the Belgians that far exceeded the cost of military administration. They also systematically stripped Belgium of machinery and raw materials. Much of the requisitioning was done without compensation or with totally inadequate compensation. In addition, there was rampant pillaging by German officers and men. In the interest of increasing the food supply, the Germans did agree not to requisition food imported by the Belgian National Committee and the American Commission for Relief in Belgium. By the end of the war the number of cattle

in the country had been cut in half. Fifteen hundred of the former twenty-five hundred coke ovens had been destroyed or dismantled, and only eleven of the country's fifty-seven prewar blast furnaces remained.

Belgium paid a heavy cost in World War I for her geographical location. One result was that at the end of the war King Albert advocated abandonment of the country's traditional neutrality. In September of 1920 Belgium signed a military convention with France and, when the Germans halted reparations payments, her forces participated in the 1923 occupation of the Ruhr.

Bernard A. Cook

References

de Gomery, Commandant de Gerlache. *Belgium in War Time*. Translated by Bernard Miall. New York: George H. Doran, 1918.

Köhler, Ludwig von. *The Administration of the Occupied Territories: Belgium*. Washington: Carnegie Endowment for International Peace, 1942.

Whitlock, Brand. *Belgium: A Personal Narrative*. New York: D. Appleton, 1919.

See also ATROCITIES; PROPAGANDA, USE IN WAR

Below, Fritz von (1853–1918)

German general and army commander. The son of a Prussian army officer, Below was born at Danzig on 23 September 1853. Commissioned in 1873, he attended the Prussian *Kriegsakademie* and thereafter rose rapidly through a variety of staff and command postings. In October of 1912, he was made commanding general of the newly formed XXI Corps (at Saarbrücken). In World War I, after leading his corps during the first eight months, particularly at the Second Battle of the Masurian Lakes, Below was chosen to replace the ailing Field Marshal Karl von Bülow as commander of the Second Army (4 April 1915).

Deployed in the Somme region and holding a front over fifty miles long, the Second Army was badly mauled during the opening day of the great Anglo-French Somme Offensive (1 July 1916). The next day, the OHL recalled Below's chief of staff, Major General Paul Grünert, and replaced him with the highly reputed Colonel Fritz von Lossberg. On 19 July Below and his new chief of staff were reassigned to the newly created headquarters of First Army, which would henceforth be responsible only for the northern sections of the Somme region.

In April of 1917 Below's First Army was moved to the Reims area where, inserted between the German Third and Seventh armies, it helped to repel the ill-fated Nivelle Offensive. During the ensuing fourteen months, Below, now assisted by Lieutenant Colonel Robert von Klüber, remained in charge of the Reims sector. Afflicted with pneumonia and other health problems, Below went on leave in June of 1918 and was placed on the standby list two months later. He died at Weimar on 23 November 1918.

Ulrich Trumpener

References

Möller, Hanns. *Fritz von Below*. Berlin: Bernard & Graefe, 1939.

Reichsarchiv. *Der Weltkrieg 1914 bis 1918: Die militärischen Operationen zu Lande*. Vols. 1, 3–14. Berlin: E.S. Mittler und Sohn, 1925–1942.

Zipfel, E. "Fritz von Below." *Deutsches Biographisches Jahrbuch*. Vol. 2. Stuttgart: Deutsche Verlagsanstalt, 1928.

See also NIVELLE OFFENSIVE; SOMME, BATTLE OF

Below, Otto von (1857–1944)

German general widely regarded as one of the best German field commanders in World War I. Born on 18 January 1857 at Danzig, he joined the Prussian army in 1875 and attended the *Kriegsakademie* in the mid-1880s. By April of 1912 he had worked his way up to a divisional command in East Prussia.

In mobilization for World War I, Below took over the I Reserve Corps and led it with distinction through the opening campaigns in East Prussia and Poland. On 7 November 1914 he succeeded General Hermann von François as commander of the Eighth Army and played a major role in that capacity (and later as the commander of the so-called Niemen Army) in defensive and offensive operations against the Russian armies in the Northwestern and Northern fronts.

In October of 1916 Below was sent to Macedonia to take charge of the German and Bulgarian divisions deployed in that theater. Six months later he was transferred to France as commander of the Sixth Army, but he was

moved again in September of 1917, this time to the Italian front. Appointed head of a newly formed Austro-German formation (the Fourteenth Army), Below launched the highly successful offensive in the Isonzo region ("Caporetto"), which earned him much public acclaim but no promotion.

On 1 February 1918 Below resumed his service in France. As commander of the new Seventeenth Army in the Arras-Cambrai region he participated in the German Spring Offensive and, later, in the defensive battles against the Allies. In the final weeks of the war, he and the commander of the First Army, Bruno von Mudra, switched places.

After the Armistice, Below was sent to eastern Germany as a corps commander. He was dismissed in late June of 1919 after vowing that he would lead an "uprising" against the Versailles Treaty, if necessary. He died at Besenhausen, near Göttingen, on 9 March 1944.

Ulrich Trumpener

References

Einem, Günter von. *Otto von Below: Ein deutscher Heerführer*. Munich: Lehmann, 1929.

Krafft von Dellmensingen, Konrad. *Der Durchbruch am Isonzo*. 2 vols. Oldenburg and Berlin: Stalling, 1926.

Möller, Hanns. *Geschichte der Ritter des Ordens "pour le merite" im Weltkrieg*. 2 vols. Berlin: Bernard & Graefe, 1935.

Reichsarchiv. *Der Weltkrieg 1914 bis 1918: Die militärischen Operationen zu Lande*. Vols. 2, 5–14. Berlin: E.S. Mittler und Sohn, 1925–1942.

Showalter, Dennis E. *Tannenberg: Clash of Empires*. Hamden, Conn.: Archon, 1991.

See also CAPORETTO; EAST PRUSSIA CAMPAIGN; EASTERN FRONT, 1915

Benedict XV (1854–1922), Pope (1914–22)

Roman Catholic pontiff during World War I. Born Giacoo Della Chiesa on 21 November 1854 in Pegli, he was elected pope on 3 September 1914.

As pope, Benedict devoted much energy to end what he characterized as "the suicide of Europe." He was particularly eager to prevent the destruction of the Dual Monarchy, a leading Catholic state. Benedict XV also sought to prevent Italy from joining the belligerents. His encyclical of 1 November 1914, *Ad Beatissimi,* appealed to the belligerents to negotiate a peaceful settlement. In early 1915 he appealed for an exchange of crippled prisoners of war. On 28 July 1915 he wrote a plea for a just and rational solution to international problems, a solution that would respect the rights and lawful aspirations of peoples. He frequently made specific protests against violations of human rights and morality, and he personally directed Vatican relief agencies.

Benedict XV's greatest effort to end the war came in his seven-point peace note of 1 August 1917, which he sent to the leaders of the Allied and Central powers. The timing of this was directly related to the fall of Theobald von Bethmann Hollweg in Germany, which seemed to presage a hardening in the German position. Benedict called for the substitution of right for force, simultaneous reduction of military might, evacuation of all occupied territory, arbitration, renunciation of war indemnities, a conciliatory examination of territorial claims, and freedom of the seas. Benedict XV was deeply disappointed at the response by the major powers; only Austria expressed support. The peace note may also have served to undermine morale in the Italian army. Italian interventionists regarded his reference to the "useless carnage" as an affront.

After the war, Benedict XV sought to assuage the wounds caused by the conflict. On 23 May 1920 he issued an encyclical, *Pacem Dei Munus,* that appealed for mutual charity and justice to replace the hatred generated by the war, and he expressed support for the League of Nations. He died on 22 January 1922.

Bernard A. Cook

References

Hughes, Philip. *The Pope's New Order.* New York: Macmillan, 1944.

Peters, Walter H. *The Life of Benedict XV.* Milwaukee, Wis.: Bruce, 1959.

Rope, H.E.G. *Benedict XV: The Pope of Peace.* London: J. Gifford, 1941.

See also PEACE OVERTURES DURING THE WAR

Beneš, Edvard (1884–1948)

Austro-Hungarian politician. Born 28 May 1884 at Kozlany, Bohemia, Beneš rose from a modest background to become a founder and statesman of Czechoslovakia. One of ten children of a successful farmer in Bohemia, Beneš graduated from the Imperial and Royal Czech College at Vinahrody. He received a doctorate from Charles University in Prague, where he first met Tomáš Masaryk. He went on to graduate work at the Sorbonne in Paris, where he earned a doctorate and wrote for the Social Democratic Press. He also received a doctorate of laws in 1908 from the School of Political Science at Dijon. In 1909 he married Anna Vlcek and returned home. At the age of twenty-five he began teaching at the Prague Commercial Academy and Charles University. He wrote extensively and, having dumped Marxism, joined Masaryk's Progressive party and wrote for the party newspaper, *Cas.*

When World War I began, Beneš was excused from military service because of an old leg injury. Instead, he helped Masaryk train the Czech Mafia, which pushed for Czech rights. He acted as the Mafia's contact with a top informant, the valet of Austrian Home Secretary Baron Reinhold Kovanda. When Masaryk was forced to leave the empire in 1915, Beneš met him in Switzerland to discuss their plans and then went on to France to form a propaganda organization and national committee for Czech independence. This committee was recognized as the voice of the Czechs by the Allied governments in May of 1918.

As the end of the war approached, the National Committee received recognition as the provisional government of Czechoslovakia on 14 October 1918, and upon the end of the war in November became the acting government of the new Czechoslovakia. The thirty-four-year-old Beneš became foreign minister, a post he held until 1935. In 1919 he headed the Czech delegation to Paris and fought hard for Czech rights. He believed strongly in the League of Nations and served as its council chairman six times in the interwar period; he was president of the assembly in 1935. He adamantly opposed the union of Austria and Germany, viewing it as a threat to the fledgling Czech state. To protect his new state, Beneš created the Little Entente in 1921 in Eastern Europe through treaties with Romania and Yugoslavia; France joined in 1924. Beneš, who understood the possible threat from the Soviet Union, tried to cultivate good relations, culminating in a 1935 mutual assistance pact.

When Tomáš Masaryk resigned as president of Czechoslovakia, Beneš was easily elected. While president he repeatedly warned of possible war in Europe and urged the League to take collective action to prevent it. Unfortunately for Beneš and the Czechs, the West paid little heed. In September of 1938, when Hitler demanded the Sudetenland, Great Britain and France abandoned Czechoslovakia at the Munich Conference and forced Beneš to capitulate. He resigned on 5 October and went into exile.

During World War II, Beneš established a Czech national committee in France, which subsequently moved to London in 1940 and became the Czech government-in-exile with Beneš as its president. The Beneš government was recognized by Britain, America, and the Soviets. In April of 1945 Beneš helped reestablish the government in Czechoslovakia, and he reentered Prague triumphantly in May. The Czech government was the only East European exile government to be allowed to return at the end of the war, because Beneš had worked hard to cultivate Soviet friendship and realized the need to cooperate with the USSR.

In 1947 Beneš's health faltered and he suffered two strokes. His effectiveness as the Czech leader also suffered. On 25 February 1948 Communist Prime Minister Klement Gottwald demanded that he accept a Communist-dominated cabinet. Beneš capitulated but refused to sign the new constitution and, instead, resigned. He died on 3 September.

Laura Matysek Wood

References

Beneš, Edvard. *Memoirs: From Munich to New War and New Victory*. Boston: Houghton Mifflin, 1954.
———. *My Fears and Hopes*. Cardiff: Western Mail & Echo, 1940.
Hitchcock, Edward B. *I Built a Temple for Peace: The Life of Eduard Beneš*. 3rd ed. New York: Harper, 1940.

See also CZECHS; MASARYK, TOMÁŠ

Berchtold von und zu Ungarschitz, Fratting und Pullitz, Leopold Count von (1863–1942)

Austro-Hungarian diplomat and foreign minister. Born in Vienna on 18 April 1863 into a wealthy noble family, Berchtold was tutored at home and later studied law. He entered the diplomatic corps in 1893 and served in Paris, London, and St. Petersburg, where he was named Austro-Hungarian ambassador in 1906. At the death of Count Alois von Aehrenthal in 1912, he reluctantly became Austria-Hungary's foreign minister. Berchtold, who was well received at court, lacked the strong character and broad experience to meet his government's challenges during the Balkan Wars and in the early months of the First World War. Under the sometimes contradictory influence of Austro-Hungarian chief of staff Conrad von Hötzendorf and Archduke Franz Ferdinand, the heir to the throne, he attempted to shore up the position of the empire by pursuing a hard-line policy that was frequently compromised by vacillation.

The assassination of Franz Ferdinand at Sarajevo on 28 June 1914 was a product of the heightened tension between Austria-Hungary and Serbia following the Balkan Wars and earlier conflicts. For Berchtold, who had failed to contain the rising Russian influence in the Balkans and thwart Serbian ambition for a south Slav state, it became the occasion for punitive action against Serbia. Although he knew that a preventive strike against the little Slav brother of Russia carried the risk of a major war, he sided with Conrad von Hötzendorf, who advocated military action once assured of German backing. In contrast, Count István Tisza, prime minister of Hungary, had reservations on the use of force against Serbia. His influence prompted the council of ministers to present Serbia with an ultimatum. Berchtold worked out the ultimatum procedure, which avoided the "odium of attacking Serbia without warning" but was designed to humiliate her. When the ultimatum was presented on 23 July, Serbia accepted all demands except one—that Austrian officials be permitted to conduct an investigation on Serbian territory. That refusal was sufficient cause for the Austro-Hungarian government to declare war against Serbia.

Berchtold's downfall came in January of 1915 over the issue of Italy's participation in the war. When Italy demanded territorial compensations from Austria-Hungary in return for remaining in the Triple Alliance, Berchtold demurred, but, under German pressure, he indicated he was ready to cede the Trentino and parts of the Albanian coastline. Once Count Tisza and Conrad von Hötzendorf learned of the concessions from Berchtold, they forced him to resign from the foreign ministry. He was replaced by Count Stefan Burian. After several high court appointments, Berchtold retired to his estate at Peresnye near Csepreg in Hungary, where he died on 21 November 1942.

George P. Blum

References

Fischer, Fritz. *Germany's Aims in the First World War.* New York: W.W. Norton, 1967.

Hantsch, Hugo. *Leopold Graf Berchtold: Grandseigneur und Staatsmann.* 2 vols. Graz: Styria Verlag, 1963.

Kann, Robert A. *A History of the Hapsburg Empire, 1526–1918.* Berkeley: University of California Press, 1974.

See also ORIGINS OF THE FIRST WORLD WAR; OUTBREAK OF THE FIRST WORLD WAR

Bergson, Henri (1859–1941)

French philosopher. Born in Paris, 18 October 1859, of Jewish parentage, Bergson received his education at the Lycée Condorcet in Paris and later studied at the Ecole Normale Supérieure for a teaching career. In 1900 he was awarded a chair at the Collège de France, where his lectures on "Creative Evolution" were packed with eager students, including symbolist poet Charles Péguy.

The publication of Bergson's book *Creative Evolution* (1907) enhanced Bergson's popularity in France. In his theory of "Creative Evolution" a single spiritual force, the *élan vital* —vital impulse—constitutes ultimate reality. To grasp one's impulse pure intellect is left behind: "You must take things by storm; you must thrust intelligence outside itself by act of will." Action, instinct, will, and force, all take precedence over reason. This concept of the *élan vital* appealed not only to intellectuals, students, and romantics like Péguy (who died in the first few weeks of World War I), but it also helped create a cult of the offensive in the French military and society. A member of the French Chamber of Deputies declared, "The idea of the offensive must penetrate the spirit of the nation." Marshal Foch also spoke of "the decisive power of offensive action undertaken with resolute determination to march on the enemy, reach, and destroy him."

When war began in 1914, Bergson thought it would bring the "moral regeneration of Europe" because "there is at present a conflict of two forces, one that will be worn down, because it is not based on an ideal, and one that cannot be defeated, because it is based on an ideal of justice and liberty." Bergson also accused the Germans of making their barbarism "scientific." Ultimately, the popular concept of the *élan vital* led to the slaughter of millions of young men in a war where the defensive, and new technology, proved decisive.

After World War I Bergson retired from teaching and became an advocate of postwar international cooperation. In 1927 he received the Nobel Prize for Literature. When Germany occupied France during World War II, Bergson, who had earlier declared himself philosophically close to Catholicism, declined special exemption from German "Jewish laws." He died in Paris on 4 January 1941.

Richard A. Voeltz

References

Chevalier, Jacques. *Henri Bergson.* Translated by Lilian A. Clare. New York: Macmillan, 1928.

Hanna, Thomas, ed. *The Bergsonian Heritage.* New York: Columbia University Press, 1962.

Ruhe, Algot, and Nancy Margaret Paul. *Henri Bergson—An Account of His Life and Philosophy.* London: Macmillan, 1914.

Slosson, Edwin E. *Major Prophets of Today.* Boston: Little Brown, 1914.

Stromberg, Roland N. *Redemption By War: The Intellectuals and 1914.* Lawrence: Regents Press of Kansas, 1982.

Bernstorff, Count Johann Heinrich von (1862–1939)

German diplomat and statesman. Born on 14 November 1862 in London into an ancient Mecklenburg family of diplomats, Bernstorff was at first a military officer. He joined the diplomatic corps in 1889 and served in Belgrade, St. Petersburg, London, and Cairo prior to 1906.

In 1908 Kaiser Wilhelm II personally selected him as German ambassador to the United States. Bernstorff was well received in Washington, where he was considered intelligent, debonair, charming, and candid. He sought to improve German-American relations after 1914 and discouraged any actions that threatened this friendship or American neutrality. Bernstorff opposed the plans for sabotage attacks against the United States that caused the expulsions of Franz von Papen and Karl Boy-Ed in December of 1915, and he advised against unrestricted submarine warfare. He repeatedly warned Theobald von Bethmann Hollweg and the foreign office that U-boat attacks on neutral vessels plying the high seas would bring the United States into the war on the Entente side, but these warnings were overridden by the high command. Bernstorff played only a minor role in the German peace offer of December 1916 and in the Pless decision to resume unrestricted submarine warfare. In March of 1917, as German-American relations deteriorated over the Zimmermann Telegram incident, he returned to Germany and was posted to Turkey. He served as German ambassador there from September of 1917 until November of 1918. Pessimistic about the possibility of a German victory, Bernstorff endorsed the idea of a compromise peace negotiated with Woodrow Wilson.

Bernstorff supported Prince Maximilian von Baden during the November 1918 revolution and favored a reconciliation with the Social Democrats, but he refused the foreign minister's post when it was offered him by Friedrich Ebert in 1919. Retiring briefly, Bernstorff returned to public life as a Democratic party Reichstag member between 1921 and 1928, where he supported the League of Nations and advocated disarmament. Bernstorff was shunned by the former Kaiser and was frequently denounced by Pan-Germans, Ludendorff, and militarists for his views. Appalled by the Nazis, Bernstorff left Germany and lived in Swiss exile until his death in Geneva on 6 October 1939.

Clayton D. Laurie

References

Bernstorff, Johann H. von. *Memoirs of Count Bernstorff*. Translated by Eric Sutton. New York: Random House, 1936.

————. *My Three Years in America*. London: Skeffington, 1920.

Dorries, Reinhard R. *Imperial Challenge: Ambassador Bernstorff and German-American Relations, 1908–1917*. Translated by Christa D. Shannon. Chapel Hill: University of North Carolina Press, 1989.

See also ZIMMERMANN TELEGRAM

B

Berthelot, Henri Mathias (1861–1931)

French army general. Born at Feurs (Loire) in December of 1861, Berthelot graduated from St. Cyr and received his commission in 1883. He served in Algeria, Tonkin, and Annam before becoming secretary to the general staff in 1907. He held that position until 1913, when he was promoted to command a brigade. Upon the outbreak of the war Berthelot became chief of staff to General Joseph Joffre. In November he took over command of reserves in the Soissons area. In 1915 he was given command of the 53rd Division and then XXXIII Corps. After taking part in the Battle of Verdun, he was sent to Romania in September of 1916 to head the French military mission there. After the Romanian defeat he returned to the Western Front to command the Fifth Army, which held the line west of Reims in the Second Battle of the Marne in 1918. The Fifth Army fared poorly in the 15 July German offensive; it was pushed back in disorder largely because Berthelot ignored General Henri-Philippe Pétain's elastic defense scheme, which General Henri Gouraud had adopted for the Fourth Army. The Germans were halted on the Marne only by determined American resistance and because French reserves were made available by Gouraud's success east of Reims.

Berthelot then returned to the Balkans as commander in chief of the Danube Army. After the war he was governor of Metz and a member of the French Supreme War Council. Known as a steady but not brilliant soldier, he died in Paris on 28 January 1931.

Spencer C. Tucker

References

Ryan, Stephen. *Pétain the Soldier*. New York: A.S. Barnes, 1969.

The Times (London), 29 January 1931.

See also LUDENDORFF OFFENSIVES; PÉTAIN, HENRI-PHILIPPE

Bethmann Hollweg, Theobald von (1856–1921)

German politician and chancellor. Born on 28 November 1856 at Hohenfinow, the son of a prominent land owner and district official, Bethmann Hollweg studied law and rose through the Prussian bureaucracy. In 1906 he was appointed Prussian minister of interior and unsuccessfully attempted to promote a basic change in the inequitable Prussian class-based franchise system.

In 1907 Bethmann Hollweg became state secretary of the interior for the German Empire. His ability to work with the Center party as well as the Conservatives led to his appointment as chancellor in 1909, after the failure of Chancellor Bernard von Bülow's proposal for an inheritance tax.

In 1911 Bethmann Hollweg won approval for the standardization and extension of the social insurance program and a liberal constitution for Alsace-Lorraine, but he was ultimately faced with a political impasse. He was unable to effect a dependable majority in the Reichstag. His difficulties were compounded by the growing strength of the Social Democratic party, Germany's largest political party, supported by approximately 35 percent of the electorate. Bethmann Hollweg's dependence upon the Kaiser, the bureaucracy, and the army heightened the militarization of Wilhelmine Germany. He received a vote of no confidence in December of 1912 when he was forced to stand with Kaiser Wilhelm II and the military at the time of the Zabern Affair. In January of 1914 the Prussian upper house (*Herrenhaus*) censured him for "failing" to uphold conservative principles.

The influence of the military affected diplomacy as well. Bethmann Hollweg was no more successful in dealing with the diplomatic impasse that he had inherited. Despite his efforts, Admiral Alfred von Tirpitz successfully scuttled the 1912 Haldane mission and forced a new naval bill through the Reichstag. Bethmann Hollweg's performance during the July Crisis has been much debated. He feared that unless Germany pushed the Austro-Hungarians to respond vigorously toward Serbia, they would ultimately seek a rapprochement with the Western powers, causing Germany to lose its last ally. He took steps that he knew could lead to war, but he felt that Germany's internal and external security required him to take the risk, the consequences of which he was fully aware. The crux of the debate is whether, as Fritz Fischer asserts, Bethmann Hollweg's actions were designed to achieve the most favorable conditions for a major war, or whether, as Volker Berghahn argues, the chancellor genuinely hoped for a German victory short of a great war.

Bethmann Hollweg's reference at the outbreak of the war to the 1839 guarantee of Belgian neutrality as "a scrap of paper" and his acknowledgement before the Reichstag of German injustices toward Belgium further cloud his reputation. He also espoused an expansionist program, detailed on 9 September 1914, which would have established complete German dominance in Europe. His espousal of expansionism (the creation of Congress Poland) and deference to the military precluded compromise with Russia and ultimately brought the United States into the war. Despite his grave misgivings about the resumption of unrestricted submarine warfare, on 9 January 1917 he acquiesced to the demands of Generals Paul von Hindenburg and Erich Ludendorff and Admiral Henning von Holtzendorff.

Bethmann Hollweg ultimately aroused the ire of Hindenburg and Ludendorff by persuading the Kaiser to agree to the eventual abolition of the three-class system of voting in Prussia and by his inability to derail the Reichstag Peace Resolution of 7 July 1917. Hindenburg and Ludendorff threatened to resign if the chancellor was not removed, and Bethmann Hollweg resigned on 13 July 1917 and was replaced by Prussian Food Commissioner Dr. Georg Michaelis, whose chancellorship signaled the political dominance of Hindenburg and Ludendorff. Bethmann Hollweg withdrew to his estate of Hohenfinow, where he died on 1 January 1921.

Bernard A. Cook

References

Berghahn, Volker R. *Germany and the Approach of War in 1914*. New York: St. Martin's, 1973.

Bethmann Hollweg, Theobald von. *Reflections on the World War*. London: Butterworth, 1920.

———. *Seven War Speeches*. Zurich, 1916.

Fischer, Fritz. *Germany's Aims in the First World War*. New York: Norton, 1967.

Jarausch, Konrad H. *The Enigmatic Chancellor: Bethmann Hollweg and the Hubris of Imperial Germany*. New Haven: Yale University Press, 1973.

See also ORIGINS OF THE FIRST WORLD WAR; OUTBREAK OF THE FIRST WORLD WAR; GERMANY, HOME FRONT; WILHELM II, GERMAN KAISER

Birch, Sir James Frederick Noel (1865–1939)

British general. Born at Llanrhaiadr, Denbighshire, on 29 December 1865, Birch graduated from the Royal Military Academy and was commissioned in the artillery in 1885. He spent most of his early career in the Royal Horse Artillery, commanding a battery in the cavalry division under General John French during the Ashanti Expedition.

In 1914 Birch commanded a brigade of the Royal Horse Artillery and took it to France. In July of 1915 he became artillery commander of I Corps, then commanded by General Douglas Haig. In March of 1916 Birch was a major general commanding Fourth Army's artillery under General Henry Rawlinson. As such, he began initial artillery planning for the Somme offensive.

In May of 1916 Haig brought Birch to British general headquarters, making him the top ranking British artillery commander in France. Strictly speaking, the British army had no artillery commanders above the division level. Senior artillerymen at corps level and above were merely advisors to the commander. Birch, however, came to exercise considerable actual control over artillery matters, and under him the positions of the artillery advisors at army and corps level were strengthened. In May of 1918 Birch was given the added responsibility of supervising the gunnery of the Royal Tank Corps, and that June he also assumed the supervision of chemical warfare.

Birch's ideas on the use of artillery were innovative. But he and other progressive British gunners, such as Major General Herbert Uniacke, often were overruled by the more conservative general staffs and commanders, particularly Haig. Birch was among the first Allied artillery commanders to criticize infantry commanders who expected the artillery preparation and creeping barrage to take them to the objective unscathed.

Birch remained in the army until 1927, reaching the rank of full general in 1926. In 1921 he became director-general of the Territorial Army, and in 1923 he was appointed master-general of ordnance. In this latter position he sponsored the development of Britain's first self-propelled artillery gun, known as the Birch Gun. After his retirement he became a director of Vickers-Armstrong, an armament manufacturer. He died in London on 3 February 1939.

David T. Zabecki

References

Bidwell, Shelford, and Dominick Graham. *Fire-Power: British Army Weapons and Theories of War, 1904–1945*. London: Allen and Unwin, 1982.

Farndale, Sir Martin. *History of the Royal Regiment of Artillery: Western Front, 1914–1918*. London: Royal Artillery Institution, 1986.

Royal Artillery. *The Royal Artillery War Commemoration Book*. London: G. Bell and Sons, 1920.

See also Artillery; Somme, Battle of; Uniacke, Herbert

Birdwood, Lord William Riddell (1865–1951)

British field marshal and Anzac commander. Born on 13 September 1865 at Kirkee, India, Birdwood served with distinction in the Boer War (1899–1902) and returned to India in 1902 as military secretary to Lord Kitchener. Promoted to brigadier general in 1909 and major general two years later, from 1914 to 1918 he was commander of Australian and New Zealand troops (Anzac) and led them at Gallipoli in 1915.

In February of 1915 Kitchener sent Birdwood to the Dardanelles to report on the situation. He returned to Egypt convinced that the passage could not be forced by the navy alone. Birdwood drew up detailed landing plans, believing he would be appointed overall commander at Gallipoli. Superseded by Sir Ian Hamilton, his plans were rejected. His Anzac Corps of 17,000 men, which was to have landed on a 2,000-yard stretch, landed at Ari Burnu (renamed Anzac Bay) on 25 April 1915. On the night of 2–3 May 1915, Birdwood launched a poorly prepared major assault, resulting in a series of individual attacks instead of a concerted effort. Forced onto the defensive, Birdwood maintained a policy of "cautious aggression," keeping the Turks continuously apprehensive without taking unnecessary risks. His attention to detail and regular tours of the trenches earned him the sobriquet "the Soul of Anzac." During the August 1915 assault, Birdwood insisted on a frontal attack on Lone Point by the 1st Australian Division. A stout opponent of withdrawal, he was appointed commander in chief of the Mediterranean Expeditionary Force in November of 1915 to oversee the final evacuations.

In 1916 Birdwood was sent with the I Anzac Corps to the Western Front, where he went on to participate in the battles of the Somme, Arras, Third Ypres (which he opposed), Amiens, and St. Quentin, which his forces captured on 2 September 1918. In May of 1918, Birdwood replaced Sir Hubert Gough as commander of the Fifth Army. Promoted to field marshal in 1925, he was commander in chief in India from 1925 to 1930. Elevated to the peerage as First Baron Birdwood of Anzac and Totnes in 1938, Birdwood died in London on 17 May 1951.

Andrzej Suchcitz

References
Birdwood, Sir William R. *In My Time*. London, 1946.
James, Robert Rhodes. *Gallipoli*. London: B.T. Batsford, 1965.
Moorehead, Alan. *Gallipoli*. New York: Harper and Row, 1958.

See also ANZAC; GALLIPOLI CAMPAIGN

Black Hand

Serbian terrorist organization responsible for the assassination of Franz Ferdinand on 28 June 1914. Union or Death (*Ujedinjenje ili Smrt*), popularly known as the Black Hand, was formed in 1911 by radical Serb nationalists. Its aim was the unification of all South Slav territories in Europe in a single Serbian national state. This goal was to be achieved by destabilizing the neighboring states of Austria-Hungary and the Turkish Empire through espionage, sabotage, and assassination. Organization was through small cells at the local level controlled by a central committee in Belgrade, and total membership probably never numbered more than a few thousand. As cover for its own actions, the Black Hand also attempted to infiltrate other groups.

The Black Hand was linked with a tradition of military violence in Serbia. In 1903 Serbian officers murdered the reigning monarch and his wife in their own bedchambers, replacing the Austrophile Obrenović dynasty on the throne with the rival Karađorđević family. Many of the founding members of the Black Hand were former regicides from 1903, including the leader of the organization, Colonel Dragutin Dimitrijević, also known as Apis. Since 1913 Dimitrijević was chief of intelligence

of the Serbian general staff, a position that not only gave him insight into the innermost workings of the Serb power structure but also the authority to penetrate it with his own agents.

Much about the Black Hand organization has never been fully clarified, especially its role in the assassination of the Archduke Franz Ferdinand, heir to the Austro-Hungarian throne. Dimitrijević may have authorized the killing in part because he feared that the archduke's reform plans would undermine South Slav disaffection with the monarchy and so make a pro-Serbian revolutionary movement there impossible. He may also have hoped to create a foreign crisis that would put pressure on his domestic opponents: The Black Hand was locked in a bitter power struggle with the civilian authorities in 1914 over ultimate control of the Serb political system. Serb Prime Minister Nikola Pašić actually knew of the plot; his inadequate efforts to stop it remain a major area of controversy.

The immediate perpetrators of the murder were a group of revolutionary youths from Bosnia, an Austro-Hungarian province claimed by Serbia. Dimitrijević's agents provided them weapons and rudimentary training. The assassins gathered in Sarajevo, the Bosnian capital, for an announced visit by the archduke on 28 June 1914. One conspirator threw a bomb at his car as it passed, but without effect. Later in the day, however, Gavrilo Princip shot and killed both Franz Ferdinand and his wife as they drove from city hall.

The Black Hand failed to survive the ensuing world war. In 1917 the Serbian government-in-exile tried the leaders of the organization on trumped-up charges of plotting to kill Serb Prince Regent Alexander. Dimitrijević and his closest associates were found guilty and shot.

Gary W. Shanafelt

References
Cassels, Lavender. *The Archduke and the Assassin: Sarajevo, June 28th 1914*. London: Frederick Muller, 1984.
Dedijer, Vladimir. *The Road to Sarajevo*. New York: Simon and Schuster, 1966.
Remak, Joachim. *Sarajevo, The Story of a Political Murder*. London: Weidenfeld and Nicolson, 1959.
Würthle, Friedrich. *Die Spur Führt Nach Belgrad, Die Hintergründe des Dramas von Sarajevo, 1914*. Vienna-Munich-Zurich: Molden, 1975.

See also DIMITRIJEVIĆ, DRAGUTIN; FRANZ
FERDINAND; PRINCIP, GAVRILO; SERBIA

Black Sea, Naval War in

The Black Sea was an important and active theater of World War I naval operations. A longstanding Russian aspiration had been to gain control of the Straits and thus secure an exit from the Black Sea to the Mediterranean. Russian war planners anticipated with some anxiety the possibility of German/Austro-Hungarian naval support of Turkey. The 1909 Russian plan therefore envisaged blocking the exit from the Bosphorus of a Turkish-Austrian fleet with three barrages of some 2,300 mines. Also, in 1911 the Russian Duma agreed to the construction of three dreadnoughts, nine large destroyers, and six submarines for the Black Sea Fleet to counter Turkish purchases and orders.

In Turkey the 1908–09 revolution of the Young Turks did not result in reform of the government and modernization of the long-neglected army and navy in time to prevent extensive territorial losses in the Italo-Turkish war of 1912 and the two Balkan wars of 1912–13. Afterward, Minister of War Enver Pasha invited a German military mission to reorganize and train the army. Naval reform had been supervised by a British mission in Turkey since 1908. At the same time the Turks in 1911 ordered two dreadnoughts from a British yard to counter increases in the Greek navy; one was to be ready in the autumn of 1914, as was a second dreadnought, constructed for Brazil and purchased in January of 1914 by Turkey as a replacement for the canceled second ship. In 1914, now regarding Russia as their most dangerous possible antagonist in war, the Turks ordered a third battleship, two cruisers, four destroyers and two submarines in England, and six destroyers and two submarines in France. The Russians countered in 1912–14 with new orders for a fourth battleship, four cruisers, eight destroyers and six submarines.

When war began in August of 1914, the Russian Black Sea fleet was in good shape, but only four destroyers of the 1909–14 program were operational. The main Russian base on the Black Sea was Sevastopol. Vice Admiral Andrei Eberhardt commanded five predreadnought battleships, two cruisers, thirteen destroyers, four torpedo boats, four submarines, three gunboats, and eight minelayers. They had been modernized and their crews were well trained.

In August of 1914 the Turkish fleet was in an unfortunate situation. The two almost finished dreadnoughts, *Reshadije* and *Sultan Osman I*, were taken by the Royal Navy, as were the other ships ordered. That left the Turks with two old German-built pre-dreadnought battleships, two cruisers, eight torpedo boats, and two gunboats, as well as some old ships not usable at sea. To counter Russian ambitions, on 2 August Enver Pasha concluded a secret alliance with Germany. When the British took over the two new battleships, the Turkish public was shocked; this strengthened the pro-German faction in the government. The subsequent arrival of the German battlecruiser *Goeben* and light cruiser *Breslau,* their official transfer to the Turkish flag, and installment of German Rear Admiral Wilhelm Souchon as commander of the Turkish fleet led to the dismissal of the British naval mission. The Germans sent experts and personnel to help the Turks train the fleet and to prepare the defense of the narrows.

When efforts by Admiral Souchon to force incidents with British or Russian vessels during training cruises outside the Dardanelles or the Bosphorus failed, he secured the secret approval of Enver Pasha to commence the war with Russia by attacking Russian ports. On 29 October 1914 the Turkish torpedo boats *Muavenet* and *Gairet* entered Odessa harbor and sank the Russian gunboat *Donets* and damaged its sister, *Kubanets.* The *Goeben* also bombarded Sevastopol but had to break off the attack when she came under fire from shore batteries. A Turkish minelayer, the *Nilufer,* did lay some mines, however. Also, the cruisers *Hamidije* and *Breslau* bombarded the harbors of Feodosiya and Novorossijsk.

The Russian fleet reacted as planned, first by laying defensive minefields off their harbors and then, on 4–5 November, by commencing minelaying operations off the Bosphorus with four modern destroyers covered by the whole fleet. The following day the Russians bombarded the coal port of Zonguldak with two battleships. Then, from 15 to 18 November, the fleet covered minelaying operations off the Turkish harbors of the northeastern Anatolian coast, harbors that were used to supply the Turkish Third Army, preparing to attack the Russian Transcaucasian Army. In addition, the Russians shelled the main port of Trapezunt. When on 18 November the *Goeben* and *Breslau* attempted to intercept the Russian squadron, there occurred the first of many inconclusive actions south of the Crimea.

Similar operations by both fleets continued to the end of the year. To stop supplies from reaching the Turkish Third Army by sea, on 20–25 December four Russian minelayers, again covered by the fleet, laid a large minefield off the Bosphorus. The returning *Goeben* was heavily damaged by a mine in this field on 26 December, as was the gunboat *Berk* on 2 January and the cruiser *Breslau* on 18 July 1915. While the Turks used remaining ships to try to continue supplying the Third Army, heavily defeated in its attack in the battle of Sarikarmish in early January, and to defend the coal transports off the Anatolian north coast, the Russians continued their offensive sweeps and sank a number of supply vessels and small sailing supply ships. On the Russian side, a shortage of mines forced a postponement of mining operations from the spring of 1915.

The most important event in 1915 was the British/French attack against the Dardanelles, initiated on the one side by Russian requests to reduce the Turkish threat on the Armenian border, and on the other side by the British desire to open up another front against Germany's allies. Beginning in February, French and British warships bombarded Turkish forts at the southern entrance of the narrows. The 18–19 March attempt to force the Dardanelles with the British/French fleet failed, however, with heavy losses to the ships from a small Turkish mine barrage. The Russian plan, to land an army corps at the Bosphorus in order to capture Constantinople in case of an Allied success in the Dardanelles, had to be canceled after the major German victories on land in East Prussia and the German/Austrian breakthrough at Tarnów-Gorlice. The Russians were reduced to supporting the Allied operations by shelling forts at the entrance of the Bosphorus and the coal ports of Zonguldak and Eregli with their old battleships and, for the first time, using seaplane carriers for air attacks against observation posts and installations. One of these operations was undertaken on 25 April when the Allies began their landing operation at Gallipoli; several times in May two of the Russian battleships, covered by the other three battleships, shelled the Bosphorus entrance.

German-Turkish ships, meanwhile, covered supply transports to the Anatolian front or coal transports, and cruisers shelled Russian ports. During one of these operations, on 3 April, the cruiser *Medjidije* sank after hitting a mine off Odessa. The ship was raised by the Russians and commissioned in the Russian navy as the *Prut*. During such operations, which continued into the autumn, there were several short but inconclusive clashes of Russian ships with the cruisers *Breslau* and *Hamidije* and the repaired *Goeben*.

New factors appeared in the second half of 1915. The first new Russian submarines became operational and started to cruise off the Bosphorus and the coal ports, where they sank a number of transports and sailing vessels. They were unsuccessful in attacks against warships, however. Also, on 14 July the first purpose-built minelaying submarine, *Krab,* laid the first mine barrage close to the Bosphorus entrance. On the other side, the Germans sent some small *UB-I* U-boats, and later bigger ones, into the Black Sea, but they too sank only some small vessels, failing in attempts to attack the Russian fleet.

In September and November of 1915 the first two new Russian battleships, *Imperatritsa Mariya* and *Yekaterina II,* became operational, and Admiral Eberhardt organized two task groups of one battleship, one cruiser, and up to four destroyers each. A third task group was composed of the three more modern predreadnought battleships and some torpedo-boat-destroyers. When the last group was used for shore bombardment, one of the other two took a covering position. After the entry of Bulgaria into the war on the side of Germany and Turkey on 14 October, the Russian fleet demonstrated several times off the Bulgarian coast.

On 10 January 1916, Russian Transcaucasian forces began an offensive against the Turkish Third Army in eastern Anatolia, securing only limited gains. The old battleship *Rostislav* and some old gunboats and torpedo boats supported the attack, while the other side used the *Goeben* and *Breslau* to transport reinforcements to Trapezunt. On 4 March the Russians started to land troops just behind the Turkish lines, forcing their retreat.

In April the Russian fleet, using transports and specially built *El'pidifor* landing vessels, landed two army brigades, totaling 14,000 men, at Rize. On the 14th the Russians opened a new offensive, supported by the battleship *Pantelejmon,* which on 18 April led to the capture of Trapezunt. In May the Russians landed two divisions of 16,838 and 17,647 men just behind the front. These were covered in turns by the First and Second Task Groups against German-Turkish ships trying to shell Russians ashore.

In June Admiral Eberhardt was replaced as commander by Rear Admiral Aleksandr Kolchak, an experienced and forceful commander of destroyer forces in the Baltic. In July he renewed mine operations against the Bosphorus, using the *Krab* and the modern destroyers. By 21 August they had laid 1,200 mines in an effort to stop the *Goeben* and *Breslau* from operating against the Romanian coast, after that country's entry into the war on the Allied side. But the Romanian offensive against Dobrudja failed, and on 9 October a German-Bulgarian-Austrian army under General August von Mackensen started a counterattack that reached Konstanza on 23 October and the Danube estuary a few days later. Efforts by the Russian fleet to support the flank of the retreating army by minelaying operations and coastal bombardment, could not prevent the defeat of the Romanian-Russian army on the shore. During this time Russian minelaying operations continued. Mines were laid off the Bosphorus, utilizing shallow-draft minelayers, and against the supply traffic along the Anatolian coast. This led to the destruction of a great many small sailing vessels used to transport supplies and coal.

In October of 1916 the Russian fleet lost one of its modern battleships when the *Imperatirca Mariya* blew up in an internal explosion in Sevastopol harbor. After the March Russian revolution, Admiral Kolchak was able to continue operations, up to May of 1917, against the Bosphorus and Turkish supply traffic. The Russians used small motor launches, carried by the cruiser *Pamjat' Merkuriya*, to lay mines in the Bosphorus entry. But a newly arrived German minesweeping group continually cleared a path for German-Turkish ships.

On 19 June Kolchak was forced to resign by the fleet's revolutionary committees. He was replaced by Vice Admiral Lukin, who was himself replaced by Rear Admiral A.V. Nemits in August. Notwithstanding deterioration of discipline in the fleet, the Russians continued naval operations with their remaining dreadnought, now renamed the *Svobodnaya Rossiya,* their cruisers, the modern destroyers and submarines, seaplane carriers, shallow-draft minelayers, and landing vessels for coastal bombardment, minelaying, and commando raids.

But on 1 November 1917, during an operation by the entire fleet to intercept the *Breslau,* mutinies broke out. When reports came in on 8 November about the Bolshevik Revolution in Petrograd, Admiral Nemits was forced to obey orders of the sailors' council, the *Centroflot,* and offensive operations ceased. On 15–16 December 1917 the new Soviet government concluded a truce with Germany. On 9 February 1918 the new Ukrainian government concluded peace with Germany, and on 3 March Russia and Germany signed the Treaty of Brest-Litovsk.

The German high command then decided to occupy southern Russia and the Ukraine. On 13 March the Germans occupied Odessa, on 17 March Nikolayev, and on 25 April Simferopol. The new Russian commander on the Black Sea, Rear Admiral M.P. Sablin, wanted to disarm his ships at Sevastopol, but a misunderstanding prevented talks with the Germans, and he transferred his two new battleships (the *Imperator Aleksandr III,* renamed *Volja,* was just becoming operational) and fifteen destroyers to Novorossijsk. On 1 May the Germans occupied Sevastopol, where the superficially repaired *Goeben* put in. She had been heavily damaged on 20 January 1918 by three mines off Imbros in the Aegean, where the *Breslau* was sunk.

During negotiations between Germany and the Soviets about decommissioning the fleet, the Soviets feared that their warships might come under control of the White counterrevolutionaries. As a result, on 13 June the Soviets formally agreed to return the fleet to Sevastopol while at the same time Admiral Sablin was given secret orders to scuttle his ships outside Novorossijsk. Officers and sailors on some ships obeyed the order to scuttle, but others decided to save the vessels for future service. Thus the *Volja* and five destroyers returned to Sevastopol and came under German control, while the *Svobodnaya Rossiya* and nine destroyers were scuttled. The Germans tried to return some of the scuttled ships captured in Sevastopol to service, but the war ended before they became operational.

Jürgen Rohwer

References

Grechanyuk, G.M., A.A. Lyakhovich, and V.S. Shlomin. "Dejstviya Flotov v Chernom More. " *Flot v Pervoj Mirovoj vojne.* Vol. 1. Moscow: Voenizdat, 1964.

Greger, René. *The Russian Fleet, 1914–1917.* London: Ian Allan, 1972.

Mitchell, Donald W. *A History of Russian and Soviet Sea Power.* London: André Deutsch, 1974.

Nekrasov, G. *North of Gallipoli. The Black Sea Fleet at War 1914–1917.* New York: Columbia University Press, 1992.

Novikov, N. *Operacii na Chernom More i sormestuye dejstviya armii i flota na poberezhe Lazistana.* Leningrad: VMA RKKA, 1927.

Rohwer, Jürgen. "Der Seekrieg in der Ostsee und im Schwarzen Mer," *Seemacht. Eine Seekriegsgeschichte von der Antike nis zur Gegenwart.* 3rd ed. Edited by E.B. Potter, C.W. Nimitz, and J. Rohwer, 400–425. Herrsching: Pawlak, 1982.

See also CAUCASUS FRONT; DARDANELLES CAMPAIGN; EBERHARDT, ANDREI; ENVER PASHA; *GOEBEN* AND *BRESLAU;* KOLCHAK, ALEKSANDR; OTTOMAN EMPIRE, NAVY; RUSSIA, NAVY; SOUCHON, WILHELM

Blank Check

See OUTBREAK OF THE FIRST WORLD WAR

Blockade, Naval, of Germany

A naval blockade is essentially economic warfare. At the time of World War I, a blockade was defined as a declaration published by a belligerent power forbidding seaborne trade with a designated enemy. Questions in contention concerned maritime rights, freedom of the seas, the rights of neutrals, designations of contraband, international legal implications, and enforcement procedures. Blockade was governed by international convention. Such concepts as the doctrine of continuous voyage meant that any goods needed by the designated enemy were assumed to be headed for that destination. The rule was that a blockade must be effective, that is, must be enforced by the declaring country, to be binding.

Blockade during World War I was a unified policy of the Allies against the Central Powers. All Allied Powers participated in the blockade, but the British consistently took the initiatives and contributed the largest contingent of ships and administration. At first the British Foreign Office was the responsible agency, but soon a cabinet-level organization, the Ministry of Blockade, was created.

Previous implementation of blockades, particularly by the British, had created much controversy, diplomatic agitation, and even war. The latest international statements prior to World War I had been the Declaration of Paris of 1856 and the Declaration of London of 1909. Although the British had never ratified the latter, in 1914 they implemented a variation of it. The British anticipated the most opposition to a blockade from the United States, as had been the case on this issue since the late eighteenth century. The British recalled the War of 1812 and the Alabama Claims settlement. In the instance of World War I, however, the Americans led by President Wilson became increasingly compliant and eventually joined in enforcing the blockade after entering the war as a belligerent.

On the outbreak of World War I the Germans expected a traditional close blockade. Indeed, German naval war plans were primarily based upon the assumption that the Grand Fleet would immediately seek battle en masse. Leaders of the High Seas Fleet were to be surprised and disappointed.

British strategic thinking underwent a transformation during the late nineteenth century. After simulation exercises in the 1880s, British naval authorities concluded that close blockade was impossible. An interim concept, called "observational blockade," was considered. Finally, the admiralty formally changed its war plan to implement a far blockade using patrolling cruisers. The Grand Fleet was to steam away from the enemy and anchor in a faraway base, Scapa Flow, in the Orkney Islands north of Scotland. The reasons for the change involved technological advances such as the steam engine, the submarine, improved guns, mines, and the torpedo. Geography also favored the British. Germany could be isolated by closing sea entrances in the Channel, North Sea, and relatively narrow straits north of the British Isles. Trade would be intercepted far out at sea by blockading squadrons of cruisers, while the British battle fleet would be based in remote safety.

Later during the war, cruisers, first-line warships, were replaced by auxiliary, armed merchant cruisers that patrolled the entrance spaces. Conditions on board were generally horrendous: boredom, devastating storms, extreme cold, and occasional attacks from U-boats. Nonetheless, these operations were crucial. As an indication of their extent, the 10th Cruiser Squadron, based at Scapa Flow, intercepted 12,979 vessels during the war.

The blockade developed into a complex series of activities: economic duress, naval encirclement, diplomatic machinations, and an elaborate organizational structure (for example, Prize Courts, a Contraband Department, a Black List, and the Ministry of Blockade). The British also established the Navicert system, involving complex prior arrangements of consignment from and to neutral countries.

Because the Germans were unable to attack the blockading forces of the British directly with their surface warships, they vowed to retaliate against the Allied blockade by resort to a form of maritime warfare that the French called *guerre de course,* a kind of indirect war against the trade of the enemy. The Germans introduced the practice of unrestricted submarine warfare.

Unique to the Allied blockade during World War I was the extension of the blockade after the armistice as a device to force the Germans to sign the peace treaty. This hardened stance by the Allies has been seen as an innovative and ominous aspect of total war in the twentieth century. Consequences of this duress have been assessed: serious malnutrition, extensive starvation, and what C. Paul Vincent called "psychological impact," making young Germans more vulnerable to the machinations of the Nazis later. John Maynard Keynes was also critical in his assessment of the peace settlement, *The Economic Consequences of the Peace* (1920).

Although some historians now play down the importance of the blockade in World War I, in his history of the naval war, Richard Hough concluded: "The Royal Navy provided the greatest contribution to victory. . . . It was the blockade that finally drove the Central Powers to accept defeat." And Marion Siney concluded: "The system of coercion was ultimately a decisive factor in the downfall of the Central Powers."

Eugene L. Rasor

References

Bane, Suda L., and Ralph H. Lutz. *The Blockade of Germany after the Armistice, 1918–1919.* Stanford: Stanford University Press, 1942.

Bell, Archibald C. *A History of the Blockade of Germany, 1914–1918.* London: HMSO, 1937, 1961.

Coogan, John W. *The End of Neutrality: The U.S., Britain, and Maritime Rights, 1899–1915.* Ithaca: Cornell University Press, 1981.

Hampshire, A. Cecil. *The Blockaders.* London: Kimber, 1980.

Hough, Richard. *The Great War at Sea, 1914–1918.* New York: Oxford University Press, 1983.

Keynes, John Maynard. *The Economic Consequences of the Peace.* New York: Harper, 1920.

Siney, Marion C. *The Allied Blockade.* Ann Arbor: University of Michigan Press, 1957.

Vincent, C. Paul. *The Politics of Hunger: The Allied Blockade of Germany, 1915–1919.* Athens: Ohio University Press, 1985.

See also GERMANY, HOME FRONT; GREAT BRITAIN, NAVY; SCANDINAVIA

Boelcke, Oswald (1891–1916)

One of the first German air aces, considered to be the father of air combat. Born 19 May 1891 in Saxony, Oswald Boelcke began his military career in a telegraphers unit in 1911, but he was interested in flying and became a pilot in 1914. For his efforts in the early months of the war, Boelcke received the Iron Cross (Second Class) in October of 1914 and the First Class award in February of 1915. In early 1915 Boelcke began flying the new Fokker *Eindekker* single-seat monoplane fighters, and in April he was transferred to a fighter unit. There, he and other young German fighter pilots, such as Max Immelmann, realized the need to inhibit enemy observation planes. Air-to-air combat now began in earnest. Boelcke notched the first of his forty kills on 4 July 1915. He recorded his eighth victory in January of 1916, at which time he received Germany's highest decoration, the *Pour le Mérite,* or Blue Max. After Immelmann's death in June of 1916, the German high command sought to protect Boelcke by removing him from combat and sending him on an inspection tour in the southeast.

He returned to combat in July, at the head of a new air fighting unit on the Somme battlefront. His unit included some of Germany's best fighter pilots, such as Manfred von Richthofen, and some of Germany's best new planes. Boelcke's death came all too soon, on 28 October 1916, in a midair collision with a fellow pilot.

Boelcke's impact, however, continues. He was more than a fighter pilot, inspirational young leader, and the leading air ace of the first half of the war; Boelcke was one of the first air tacticians. He developed strategies for air combat that are still followed today; these "Dicta Boelcke" include such accepted basics as surprising the enemy from above and behind, using the sun, and working together as a unit. Because he saw the importance of airplanes in the overall war strategy, Boelcke helped raise air combat to a science, based on the use of formations rather than single airplanes. His combat success and congenial personality made him a national hero and a revered figure in Germany; the entire nation mourned his loss. In tribute, his old unit was renamed "Jasta Boelcke," and one of his pupils, Richthofen, became the leading ace of the war.

Laura Matysek Wood

References

Spick, Michael. *The Ace Factor.* Annapolis, Md.: Naval Institute Press, 1989.

Werner, Johannes. *Knight of Germany: Oswald Boelcke German Air Ace.* Translated by Claud W. Sykes. London: Greenhill, 1985.

See also ACES; AIR WARFARE: FIGHTER TACTICS; RICHTHOFEN, MANFRED VON

Bohm-Ermolli, Eduard (1856–1941)

Austro-Hungarian field marshal. Born in Ancona, Italy, on 21 February 1856 Bohm-Ermolli entered military service at age fourteen. He spent the next forty-four years as a cavalry commander and general staff officer. The dapper Tyrolean began the First World War as commander of the Second Army, supporting the Austrian offensive against Serbia. In August, Russian pressure in Galicia forced the reassignment of his command to the eastern front. Characteristically, mediocre planning scattered his army among various railheads and prevented it from operating as a whole until November, when it entered the fight in Silesia.

In February of 1915, Bohm-Ermolli took part in the offensive to relieve Przemysl. Most Austrian commanders doubted the feasibility of forcing the Carpathian passes, but Bohm-

Ermolli expressed confidence born of ambition and a consistently poor grasp of reality, two of his trademarks throughout the war. Cold, sickness, and violent Russian counterattacks stymied the attack. A renewed assault in April culminated in the high point of Bohm-Ermolli's career, the capture of Lemberg in June of 1915. Bohm-Ermolli's forces continued to drive eastward, and by October he had assumed command of an army group entrenched just south of the Pripet Marshes.

In July of 1916 the Brusilov Offensive shattered Bohm-Ermolli's line, in part because of his slow and uncertain reaction. Bohm-Ermolli was temporarily relieved of command but managed to reemerge in command of the three southernmost Austrian armies in Russia. His final campaign of any consequence was in the summer of 1917, when his troops turned back part of the last desperate offensive by Kerensky's rapidly disintegrating armies. He died at Troppau on 9 December 1941.

Steven Eden

References

Rothenberg, Gunther. *The Army of Francis Joseph.* West Lafayette, Ind.: Purdue University Press, 1976.

Stone, Norman. *The Eastern Front, 1914–1917.* New York: Charles Scribner's Sons, 1975.

See also BRUSILOV OFFENSIVE; EAST GALICIA, 1914 CAMPAIGN

Bonar Law, Andrew (1858–1923)

British Conservative politician. Born 16 September 1858 in Canada, Andrew Bonar Law had enjoyed a successful career as a Scottish iron merchant prior to entering politics. He was elected to Parliament in 1900 and two years later was appointed to the post of parliamentary secretary to the board of trade. He gained the leadership of the Conservative party by 1911. After the outbreak of war, he was named to the minor office of colonial secretary in Herbert Asquith's coalition government formed in 1915. Dissatisfied with the conduct of the war, Bonar Law joined with the dynamic Liberal politician David Lloyd George to topple Asquith from power. Bonar Law went on to serve as chancellor of the exchequer and hold a seat in the war cabinet. His support was essential for the survival of Lloyd George's coalition government.

Following the war, he was prime minister after the fall of Lloyd George and the collapse of the wartime coalition in 1922. Bonar Law died in London on 30 October 1923.

Van Michael Leslie

References

Blake, Robert. *The Unknown Prime Minister: The Life and Times of Andrew Bonar Law.* London: Eyre & Spottiswoode, 1955.

Bourne, J.M. *Britain and the Great War 1914–1918.* London: Edward Arnold, 1989.

Pugh, M.D. "Asquith, Bonar Law and the First Coalition," *Historical Journal* 17 (1974); 813–836.

Taylor, A.J.P. *English History 1914–1915.* Oxford: Clarendon, 1965.

See also Asquith, Herbert; Great Britain, Home Front; Lloyd George, David

Borden, Sir Robert Laird (1854–1937)

Canadian prime minister. Born in Grand Pré, Nova Scotia, on 26 June 1854, Borden entered politics in 1896 and became leader of the Conservative party in 1901 and Canadian prime minister on 15 October 1911. Borden oversaw one of the most tumultuous periods in Canadian history.

Borden's policies led to an impressive commitment by the Dominion of Canada in the war effort. The success of the Canadian Corps in battle in France led the Borden government to demand more say in Imperial affairs. This helped lead to the inclusion of the dominions in a new imperial cabinet—the imperial War Cabinet, which first met in 1917. As a member, Borden helped exert influence that gained the dominions representation at the Paris Peace Conference. By the end of the war, Canada and the other dominions were exerting themselves as semiautonomous states, not merely the adjuncts of Britain.

The support of Borden's government for the war and the drive for greater representation in imperial councils because of military success in France led to a conscription crisis in 1917. The crisis had been brought on by a dwindling number of volunteers, and the belief in English Canada that the French part of the country was not pulling its weight. In a rigged election in 1917, Borden was reelected as a proconscription Unionist member of parliament, rather than as a Conservative as in 1911. Riots in Quebec led to as grave a crisis as Canada has ever faced; before more than a token number of conscripts saw action, however, the war ended.

Borden retired to Ottawa and died on 10 June 1937. His legacy was a Canada far more industrialized than in 1914 and with greater recognition abroad, a Canada on the road to true independence from Britain, but a divided country with the wounds from the conscription crisis only partially healed.

Ian M. Brown

References

Borden, Henry, ed. *Robert Laird Borden: His Memoirs.* Toronto: Macmillan, 1938.

Brown, R.C. *Robert Laird Borden.* Toronto: Macmillan, 1975.

English, John. *Borden, His Life and World.* Toronto: McGraw-Hill Ryerson, 1977.

See also Canada, Role in War

Boroević von Bojna, Svetozar (1856–1920)

Austro-Hungarian field marshal. Born in Umetic, Croatia, on 13 December 1856, Boroević was as fine a commander as the Hapsburg Empire produced during the war. His distinguished prewar career as an infantry and staff officer led to his appointment in September of 1914 to command of the Third Austro-Hungarian Army in Galicia. He immediately conducted a fighting withdrawal and tough defensive stand in the Carpathians against a Russian force three times larger than his own, preventing Russian penetration of the mountains and ultimately allowing the Austrians to turn back the enemy advance on Cracow.

In January of 1915, the Third Army took part in an abortive attempt to relieve the fortress of Przemysl. Boroević recognized the futility of the relief effort in the face of bitter winter weather, tenuous supply lines, and fierce Russian resistance. After minor gains the offensive was called off, but almost immediately the Austro-Hungarian high command (AOK) issued plans for renewing the attack in February. Boroević, quarrelsome at the best of times, protested vigorously over what he considered to be wasteful attacks for an objective of limited value. Austrian Chief of Staff General Franz

Conrad von Hötzendorf mistook Boroević's realism for a loss of nerve and transferred most of his part of the front to the more pliable General Eduard Bohm-Ermolli.

Out of favor, Boroević soon received a second chance. As war with Italy became imminent, Boroević took over the hastily formed Fifth Army, defending the approaches to Trieste. From June until December of 1915, he displayed his mastery of defensive warfare. During the First through Fourth Battles of the Isonzo, Boroević resolutely turned back the Italians despite desperate shortages of munitions and manpower.

For the next two years, Boroević maintained a defensive posture along the Isonzo. In October of 1917 his command played a minor role in the Battle of Caporetto, relegated to pursuing the Italians as they fled westward. The bit part rankled Boroević, who felt with some justification that he had been excluded from planning for the offensive. Even worse, he bungled the pursuit, allowing the Italians to escape to new defensive positions along the Piave.

By the end of 1917 the front had once more congealed along the Piave River. Boroević favored remaining on the defensive throughout 1918, but he was overruled by AOK. His Piave Army Group was ordered to attack in May of 1918 as part of an offensive all along the Italian front. Temperamentally better suited to the role of defender, his plan was technically sound but unimaginative, amounting to little more than frontal attacks at several points along the Piave. Fierce fighting and ruinous casualties secured only a few isolated bridgeheads. Boroević managed to pull his troops back from their exposed bridgeheads in the face of heavy pressure, thereby saving a portion of his force.

By October of 1918, Boroević faced widespread disaffection among his half-starved troops. The Vittorio Veneto Offensive precipitated the collapse of Boroević's Army Group, but the stubborn commander still managed to conduct a fighting retreat from Italy, perhaps his most brilliant achievement of the war. Boroević briefly considered launching a coup with the remnant of his force to restore the monarchy, but he abandoned the idea when the emperor himself offered no encouragement. Shortly after avoiding extradition to face charges of war crimes, the old soldier died in Klagenfurt on 23 May 1920.

Steven Eden

References

Rothenberg, Gunther. *The Army of Francis Joseph*. Princeton: Princeton University Press, 1976.

Stone, Norman. *The Eastern Front, 1914–1917.* New York: Charles Scribner's Sons, 1975.

Villari, Luigi. *The War on the Italian Front.* London: Cobden-Sanderson, 1932.

Young, Peter. *History of the First World War.* 8 vols. London: BPC Publishing, 1971.

See also CAPORETTO; EAST GALICIA, 1914 CAMPAIGN; ISONZO, BATTLES OF, NUMBERS I–II; VITTORIO VENETO CAMPAIGN, 1918

Boselli, Paolo (1838–1932)

Italian politician and premier. Born in Savona on 8 June 1838, Boselli taught university-level economics before entering parliament in 1870. He served in a number of government cabinets before World War I.

Italy entered the war on the side of the Entente in May of 1915, but the unsuccessful battles of the Isonzo and the Austrian offensive from the Trentino brought the fall of the Antonio Salandra government. A national coalition cabinet was formed under the seventy-eight-year-old Boselli on 19 June 1916, although policy continued to be driven by Foreign Minister Giorgio Sonnino, who was determined to secure territorial gains across the Adriatic.

With the Italian collapse at Caporetto (Karfreit) in October of 1917, the Boselli government resigned on the 26th in favor of Vittorio Orlando, though Sonnino remained as foreign minister. After the war the aged senator supported Benito Mussolini's Fascists. He died in Rome on 10 March 1932.

A. Harding Ganz

References

Herwig, Holger H., and Neil M. Heyman. *Biographical Dictionary of World War I.* Westport, Conn.: Greenwood, 1982.

Villari, Luiji. "Italy." *Encyclopaedia Britannica,* 12th ed., 1922. Vol. 31: 615–38.

See also ITALY, HOME FRONT; SONNINO, GIORGIO

Bosnia-Herzegovina

Bosnia-Herzegovina, one of six republics belonging to the former Yugoslavia, is shaped like a triangle and surrounded by Serbia and Montenegro to the east and southeast and Croatia to the north and west. It consists of 19,741 square miles of mountainous terrain and a thirteen-mile coastline along the Adriatic Sea. The Bosna, Una, and Vrbas rivers empty into the Sava, forming the northern boundary with Croatia. The Drina River forms the eastern boundary with Serbia and the Neretva flows to the Adriatic.

Bosnia-Herzegovina fell under Ottoman rule when it became a Turkish province in 1463, resulting in the conversion of many local Slavs to Islam. Following the Russo-Turkish War of 1877–78, Austria-Hungary occupied Bosnia-Herzegovina (1878), joining both provinces into one administrative district. In 1881 the Bosnians revolted against Hapsburg attempts to impose military conscription. During the governorship of Benjámin Kállay (1883 to 1903) the Austrians attempted to modernize the area by establishing a bureaucracy similar to their own and bringing in Slavs from other areas to serve as administrators.

In September of 1908 Russian Foreign Minister Aleksandr Izvolsky and his Austrian counterpart, Alois von Aehrenthal, met in Buchlau to discuss the future of the Ottoman territories. Russia agreed to support Austrian annexation of Bosnia in return for Hapsburg aid in opening the Straits to Russian warships. Austro-Hungarian annexation of Bosnia on 7 October resulted in Russian anger over terms not previously clarified. A crisis developed between the monarchy and the Serbs over Bosnian annexation after the Serbs publicized their intent to acquire part of Bosnia. An Austrian ultimatum forced the Serbs to back down, denying them access to the sea. This humiliated the Serbs and the Russians, who did not have the resources in 1908 to confront the Austrians. Russia responded by reopening the Eastern question and encouraging Balkan states to form alliances among themselves.

The growth of national organizations, many having ties to Serbia, increased tensions in the Balkans. On 28 June 1914 Archduke Franz Ferdinand of Austria-Hungary traveled to Sarajevo. The archduke promoted joining Bosnia with other South Slav lands to form an autonomous state within the Hapsburg Empire. When Franz Ferdinand visited Sarajevo, he was assassinated by Gavrilo Princip, a Bosnian revolutionary and member of the Black Hand. The Austrians delivered an ultimatum to the Serbs when they discovered that Serbian members of the Black Hand had assisted Princip into Bosnia and that the gun used in the assassination had been illegally obtained from a Serbian state arsenal. Vienna was not interested in a peaceful resolution to the crisis; it declared the Serbian reply unsatisfactory. Austria-Hungary declared war on Serbia, which in turn led to World War I.

In November of 1918 Serbian troops moved into Bosnia-Herzegovina, unofficially occupying the lands which they hoped to include in a Serbian state. The Declaration of Corfu (1917), which had stated South Slav intentions of forming a Yugoslav state, categorized Bosnian Muslims, Albanians, Montenegrins, and Macedonians under the heading of Serbs, Croats, or Slovenes.

After the war, Bosnia-Herzegovina became a province of the Kingdom of Serbs, Croats, and Slovenes. It remained a province of Yugoslavia until the Bosnian parliament declared its sovereignty on 15 October 1991.

Susan N. Carter

References

Hoffman, Mark S., et al., eds. *The World Almanac and Book of Facts 1993*. New York: Pharos, 1992.

Jelavich, Barbara. *History of the Balkans*. Vol. 2, *Twentieth Century*. New York: Cambridge University Press, 1983; Reprint. New York: Cambridge University Press, 1989.

Jelavich, Charles. *Tsarist Russia and Balkan Nationalism: Russian Influence in the Internal Affairs of Bulgaria and Serbia, 1879–1886*. Berkeley: University of California Press, 1958.

Jelavich, Charles, and Barbara Jelavich. *The Balkans*. Englewood Cliffs, N.J.: Prentice-Hall, 1965.

———. *The Establishment of the Balkan National States, 1804–1920*. Vol. 8 of *A History of East Central Europe*, edited by Peter F. Sugar and Donald Treadgold. Seattle: University of Washington Press, 1977.

See also BLACK HAND; CORFU, DECLARATION OF; FRANZ FERDINAND; OUTBREAK OF THE FIRST WORLD WAR

Botha, Louis (1862–1919)

South African soldier and statesman. Born on 27 September 1862, near Greytown, Natal,

Botha was the son of a Voortrekker. Educated at a German Orange Free State mission school, Botha joined the Transvaal commandos during the Boer War and helped defeat the British at Colenso, Spion Kop, and Vaal Kranz. He commanded Transvaal forces after P.J. Joubert died in March of 1900 and proved himself a talented leader whose strong will, charm, and personality created unity among the Boers. He lost Johannesburg and Pretoria in late 1900 but skillfully directed a guerrilla war for two years. Botha played a major role in the May 1902 Vereeniging Conference and signed the peace treaty with Britain. His efforts at reconciliation enraged many of his countrymen, but Botha was elected first prime minister of the Transvaal under British rule in 1907 and was also first prime minister of the Union of South Africa, a post he held between 1910 and 1919.

Botha supported Britain in 1914 and suppressed an anti-British insurrection in South Africa in 1914–15. Between March and July of 1915 he attacked German Southwest Africa with motorized troops and forced the unconditional surrender of the colony. Although in failing health, he attended the 1919 Paris Peace Conference with Jan Smuts and signed the Versailles Treaty. Botha died on 27 August 1919 at Pretoria.

Clayton D. Laurie

References

Malesan, Jacques, and Tom Hennings. *General Louis Botha*. Pretoria: National Cultural History and Open-Air Museum, 1979.

Meintjes, Johannes. *General Louis Botha: A Biography*. London: Cassell, 1970.

Morris, K. *A Great Soldier of the Empire: Botha's Wonderful Conquests*. London: Stevens, 1917.

Ritchie, M. *With Botha in the Field*. London: Longmans, 1915.

Trew, H.F. *Botha Treks*. London: Blackie, 1936.

See also AFRICA; SOUTH AFRICA, UNION OF

Bothmer, Felix Count von (1852–1937)

Bavarian colonel general and army commander. Born in Munich on 10 December 1852 the son of a Bavarian army officer, Felix von Bothmer was commissioned during the Franco-Prussian War. He attended the Bavar-

ian War Academy and thereafter rose rapidly through a broad range of staff and command positions.

Promoted to general of infantry in 1910, Bothmer was recuperating from a leg fracture when the First World War began and therefore had to wait until December of 1914 before receiving a field command. After serving a few weeks as commander of a Bavarian reserve division, he was entrusted with a corps command on the Eastern Front. Seven months later he succeeded General Alexander von Linsingen as head of the *Südarmee* (South Army), a mixed force of German and Austro-Hungarian (and later also of Turkish) units that was deployed in the southern sector of the Eastern Front. Under his direction the *Südarmee* fought with considerable success against numerically superior Russian forces during the next two years, particularly in connection with the Brusilov Offensive of 1916 and the Kerensky Offensive in 1917.

Following the armistice on the Eastern Front the *Südarmee* was dissolved (January of 1918), and Bothmer was sent to the Western Front. Appointed commander of the newly formed Nineteenth Army, he was placed in charge of a relatively quiet sector in Lorraine and remained in that position until the end of the war. Promoted to colonel general in April of 1918, Bothmer retired from active service a month after the armistice. He died in Munich on 18 March 1937.

Ulrich Trumpener

References

Glaise-Horstenau, Edmund, and Rudolf Kiszling, eds. *Oesterreich-Ungarns letzter Krieg 1914–1918*. Vols. 2–7. Vienna: Verlag der Militärwissenschaftlichen Mitteilungen, 1931–38.

Möller, Hanns. *Geschichte der Ritter des Ordens "pour le mérite" im Weltkrieg*. 2 vols. Berlin: Bernard & Graefe, 1935.

Schlotheim, Ludwig Eberhard Freiherr von. *Die Kaiserlich Deutsche Südarmee in den Kämpfen während der Brussilow-Offensive vom 4. Juni bis 14. August 1916*. Munich: C.H. Beck'sche Verlagsbuchhandlung, 1936.

Stone, Norman. *The Eastern Front 1914–1917*. New York: Charles Scribner's Sons, 1975.

Boué de Lapeyrère, Augustin Emmanuel Hubert Gaston (1852–1924)

French vice admiral and commander of the Mediterranean fleet at the beginning of World War I. Born on 18 January 1852 at Castera-Lectourois (Gers), Boué de Lapeyrère entered the Ecole Navale in 1869 and earned a reputation for outstanding bravery and initiative during Admiral Amédéé Anatole Prosper Courbet's operations against the Chinese (1883–85). As Minister of Marine from July of 1909 to March of 1911, he was responsible for laying down the first two French dreadnoughts and preparing the groundwork for the Naval Law of 1912. In August of 1911 Lapeyrère became commander of the French Mediterranean fleet (1ère Armée navale) and served in that capacity until October of 1915. Lapeyrère had trained intensively for what he assumed would be a classic encounter with the fleets of Italy and Austria. Italian neutrality left him without a role. In the early days of the war he concentrated on protecting troop transports between North Africa and France and was subsequently accused of having permitted the *Goeben* to escape. Lapeyrère was unable to draw the Austrian fleet, secure in its Adriatic bases, into battle and, hampered by the lack of a base, had to content himself with a blockade of the Straits of Otranto. Although Lapeyrère was titular head of Allied naval forces in the Mediterranean, British forces at the Dardanelles were not under his control. The German submarine campaign in the Mediterranean found him ill prepared both materially and psychologically. Lapeyrère's force lacked sufficient escort vessels, and he much preferred "offensive" action such as hunting submarines to "defensive" measures such as escorting transports. Exhausted, he resigned his command in October of 1915 and retired the next year. He died at Pau on 17 February 1924.

Paul G. Halpern

References

Halpern, Paul G. *The Naval War in the Mediterranean, 1914–1918*. London and Annapolis, Md.: Allen & Unwin and Naval Institute Press, 1987.

Laurens, Adolphe. *Le Commandement Naval en Méditerranée, 1914–1918*. Paris: Payot, 1931.

Taillemite, Etienne. *Dictionnaire des Marins Français*. Paris: Editions Maritimes et d'Outre-Mer, 1982.

Thomazi, A. *La Guerre navale dans l'Adriatique*. Paris: Payot, 1925.

———. *La Guerre navale dans la Méditerranée*. Paris: Payot, 1929.

See also FRANCE, NAVY; *GOEBEN* AND *BRESLAU*; MEDITERRANEAN NAVAL OPERATIONS

Bourgeois, Léon Victor Auguste (1851–1925)

Leading French politician, diplomat, and proponent of the League of Nations. Born in Paris the son of a clockmaker on 29 May 1851, Bourgeois studied law before entering the French civil service in 1876, rising to prefect of police in 1887. In 1888 Bourgeois was elected to the Chamber of Deputies from the Department of the Marne, defeating General Georges Boulanger. As a Radical he held a number of cabinet posts and served as premier from 1895 to 1896. He distinguished himself as French plenipotentiary at the 1899 Hague Conference and four years later was nominated to the permanent Court of Arbitration. He was foreign minister during the 1906 Algeciras Conference and served as the French delegate to the Second Hague Conference in 1907. In June of 1914 Bourgeois briefly held the post of foreign minister and during the war was a minister without portfolio in the Aristide Briand cabinet.

Bourgeois is best known as the chief French proponent of a league of nations. He headed the government commission set up on 22 July 1917 to study the possibility of a league. Although an idealist, Bourgeois was a realist when it came to human nature. As the French representative on the committee at the Paris Peace Conference that drafted the league covenant, Bourgeois called for a stronger league than that favored by the United States and Great Britain. It had mandatory membership and a requirement that each member "be bound to use in common agreement with the others its economic, naval, and military power" to enforce league council decisions. Bourgeois proposed that a league military force be based on the French northeast frontier. The United States and Britain ignored his carefully prepared effort and pushed through their own Miller-Hurst draft, which had neither compulsory membership nor enforcement provisions.

See also ROMANIA

Bourgeois chaired the first meeting of the League of Nations and served as the principal French representative until 1924. In 1920 he was awarded the Nobel Prize for Peace. He died in Paris on 29 September 1925.

Spencer C. Tucker

References
Encyclopedia Britannica. Vol. 3, 1951.
Stevenson, D. *French War Aims Against Germany, 1914–1919*. Oxford: Clarendon, 1982.
The Times (London), 30 September 1925.

See also LEAGUE OF NATIONS; PARIS PEACE CONFERENCE

Brătianu, Ion (1864–1927)

Romanian premier. Born on 20 August 1864 in Florica, Romania, Brătianu was the main leader of the Liberal party of Romania in the early twentieth century and premier for most of World War I. While he declared Romanian neutrality at the outbreak of hostilities, he hoped for an eventual Austro-Hungarian defeat that would allow Romania to enter the war and seize Transylvania, where several million ethnic Romanians lived under Hungarian control.

For the first two years of the war, Brătianu assured the Central Powers that he was waiting only for a favorable moment to intervene on their side, while he bargained for the best deal over Transylvania that he could get from the Entente. At the same time, he worked to keep more impulsive anti-Austrian Romanian nationalists from stampeding the country into hostilities prematurely. Romania finally declared war against Austria-Hungary on 27 August 1916 in the wake of the Russian Brusilov Offensive. A German counteroffensive promptly overran much of the country. Brătianu triumphed in the end, however. At the 1919 peace conference, Romania secured both Transylvania from Austria-Hungary and Bessarabia from Russia. Brătianu died in Bucharest on 24 November 1927.

Gary W. Shanafelt

References
Glenn E. Torrey. "Rumania and the Belligerents, 1914–1916." In *1914: The Coming of the First World War*, edited by Walter Laqueur and George Mosse. New York: Harper, 1966.

Brest-Litovsk, Treaty of (3 March 1918)

The Bolsheviks, who had come to power under the slogan "Peace, bread and land," were hard pressed to fulfill these promises. By the end of 1917, however, there was no doubt that Russia had to quit the war, a position held even by British Ambassador George Buchanan. On 8 November, the day after the Bolshevik takeover, Lenin began to sound out his allies as to the possibility of a general peace conference. They categorically rejected such a proposal, especially since the Bolsheviks were publishing secret treaties to the embarrassment of France and Britain. The German position, however, was different. Because of the military stalemate in the west, the Hindenburg-Ludendorff clique, which now controlled the government, was thinking in terms of a major offensive in order to drive France and England to the conference table. For this to happen, Germany needed Russia out of the war and German eastern divisions transferred to the west.

On 28 November the Germans accepted a Russian armistice offer, and on 2 December the two delegations met at the Polish city of Brest-Litovsk, which was behind German lines. To demonstrate the proletarian character of the new government, the Russian delegation, led by the experienced diplomat Adolf Joffe, included a worker, a peasant, and a sailor. On 7 December they agreed to a ten-day truce (later extended) on the assumption that a peace treaty would soon be forthcoming.

In Petrograd, Commissar of Foreign Affairs Leon Trotsky took charge of the negotiations. Berlin was represented by the brilliant diplomat Richard von Kühlmann, from the foreign office, and General Max von Hoffmann, who spoke for the army. There was little doubt as to Bolshevik intentions. One had only to note the title of Trotsky's send-off speech: "Appeal to the Workers and Oppressed and Bled Peoples of Europe." The Bolshevik strategy was to stall by means of propaganda, hoping to incite the German people to rebellion against their own government, an event that would give the Russians more leverage at the peace table.

At the early sessions, which began on 22 December, the question of self-determination was raised by the Russians. In response to Trotsky's request for a German guarantee of independence for the former Russian provinces of Poland and the Baltic states, now occupied by the Germans, Hoffmann arrogantly replied that these areas had already voted for German rule. This German diplomatic miscalculation allowed the Russians to assume the high moral ground, which they exploited to the full. At this time, moreover, President Wilson announced his Fourteen Points, which called for the evacuation of Russian territory and an independent Poland. This seemed to strengthen the Russian position. From a practical standpoint, however, the Bolshevik position was tenuous. During the Christmas recess (22–28 December), Trotsky returned home and informed the Russian leaders of the German intention to annex the Russian territories previously cited. He then suggested a policy of "no war, no peace," which was summarily rejected by Lenin. To make matters worse, civil war had broken out in the Ukraine, where the White Army under General Aleksei Kaledin was in the process of occupying strategic cities.

In early January the peace talks resumed and deteriorated to a war of words. As Trotsky attacked the Kaiser and German militarism, and Hoffmann responded in kind, all pretense at courtesy disappeared. Only Kühlmann attempted to cool tempers, but to no avail. In the end, the Russians and Germans refused to eat together. Simultaneously, by radio from Petrograd and Brest-Litovsk, the Russians launched a propaganda barrage aimed at Austria and Germany, urging soldiers to rise against their officers and the masses against their governments. The main issue for the Russians, however, was the fate of Poland, Lithuania, Courland, and Estonia. The Germans openly stated that these lands were to remain with Germany.

Then, suddenly, the Ukraine declared its independence in accordance with a Bolshevik proclamation on the right of secession. Its new government, the Rada, was led by Simon Petlura. At the invitation of the Germans, the Rada sent a delegation to Brest-Litovsk on 9 January. This was to be a lever against the Russians; it became much more than that. During late January the Red army occupied the Ukrainian capital of Kiev, ousted the Rada, and installed a communist regime. To complicate matters even further, Count Ottokar Czernin, the Austrian delegate to Brest-Litovsk, informed Wilhelm II that Austria was starving to death, and in order to remain in the war she needed Ukrainian grain. Consequently, on 9 February Germany and Austria recognized the defunct Ukrainian Rada government, which in turn asked Germany for military assistance. The Germans quickly responded by sending troops into the Ukraine.

At the same time, Trotsky was back in Petrograd reporting to the Third Congress of Soviets on the situation at Brest-Litovsk. The news from the Ukraine only made the situation more critical. The whole question of German demands provoked an open debate among the Bolshevik leadership. There appeared to be only three options, all bad: outright acceptance of the German demands, favored by Lenin; a revolutionary war against Germany that no one endorsed, given the antiwar mood in Russia; and Trotsky's formula of no war, no peace, which was consistent with international revolutionary doctrine. Trotsky's plan would mean a German occupation with the hope that Bolsheviks could infect German troops with communism, which they would then carry back home. Lenin's contention, however, was that if the Russian state were lost it would also mean the end of the revolution. He, therefore, advised that Russia must survive even if in a truncated form. In a close vote in the Politburo, Lenin was defeated. Thus, Trotsky was sent back to the peace talks under instruction to continue to stall, in anticipation of a German revolution. And, given the mood in many of the German cities, that was not out of the question.

On 9 February, the same day that Germany recognized an independent Ukraine, General Hoffmann produced a map containing a yellow line delineating those territories that Russia had to recognize as German in order for Russia to quit the war. In addition to Poland and the Baltic states, these included the Moon, Dagö, and Oesel islands in the Baltic, which would put the Germans within striking distance of Petrograd. Trotsky was given a forty-eight hour ultimatum to agree to the territorial demands or face a German offensive. Trotsky responded: "We no longer wish to participate in this purely imperialist war. . . . We cannot place the signature of the Russian revolution under terms which carry with them oppression, sorrow, and misery for millions of lives."

On 12 February the Germans launched an offensive that crossed the Dvina River and captured the White Russian city of Pskov. In the south, Austrian troops entered the Ukraine. Under extreme pressure, Trotsky, for the last time, returned to Petrograd to face the Bolshevik leaders. After a bitter debate, Lenin's position carried by a 7–6 vote. The Germans were notified that the Russians were ready to sign. The Treaty of Brest-Litovsk was signed on 3 March 1918; Trotsky, who had been replaced as Commissar of Foreign Affairs by Georgi Chicherin, refused to attend the ceremony. By the treaty's provisions Russia officially left the war, but at a terrible price. She lost Poland, the Baltic states, part of White Russia, and the Baltic islands. Including the independent Ukraine, she gave up 1.3 million square miles and 63 million people. This included most of her industry and agriculture. This treaty was much harsher than the subsequent Treaty of Versailles. Moreover, in recognizing that the existence of Russia was essential to the revolution, Lenin poured international communism into a national mold. This contradiction reigned within the communist world until the very end.

John W. Bohon

References

Deutscher, Isaac. *Leon Trotsky: The Prophet Armed, 1879–1918.* New York: Oxford University Press, 1954.

Fischer, Louis. *The Soviets in World Affairs.* Princeton: Princeton University Press, 1951.

McCauley, Martin. *The Soviet Union Since 1917.* London: Longman, 1984.

See also HOFFMANN, MAX; KÜHLMANN, RICHARD VON; TROTSKY, LEON

Briand, Aristide (1862–1932)

French statesman. Born on 28 March 1862 in Nantes, Briand was the son of an innkeeper. A leftist, Briand served in the French Chamber of Deputies from 1902 to 1919. He was also a cabinet minister under Georges Clemenceau, Raymond Poincaré, and René Viviani from 1905 to 1915; and he was himself premier in 1913. Briand sought Franco-German understanding and colonial economic cooperation before 1914 but quickly joined the "Union Sacrée" government upon the outbreak of war.

Briand was an outspoken critic of the Allied fixation on a Western Front strategy. He favored an alternative approach focusing on southeastern Europe, which included an offensive in Salonika and the Dardanelles to threaten Austria, support Serbia, and force Greece and Romania into the war. Opposed by General

Joseph Joffre, the plan was implemented on Serbia's request in September of 1915.

In November of 1915 Briand became premier in a coalition government and sought to improve army efficiency and cooperation among the Entente powers. He made Joffre commander in chief in December of 1915 and advocated the defense of Verdun. Briand was frustrated by Joffre's lack of progress and replaced him with Robert Nivelle in December of 1916, but the continued stalemate brought the fall of Briand's government in March of 1917. Briand played a minor role in the abortive Lancken Affair in 1917.

Coming out of retirement in January of 1921 and again premier, Briand led the French delegation to the Washington Conference. During the interwar period he led eleven governments, served as foreign minister sixteen times, was a delegate to the League of Nations, and shared the 1926 Nobel Peace Prize with Germany's Gustav Stresemann. While he originally sought German containment, Briand later led moves toward German integration and reconciliation and became a proponent of a United States of Europe. He died in Paris on 7 March 1932.

Clayton D. Laurie

References

Suarez, Georges. *Briand.* 6 vols. Paris: Plon, 1941–52.

See also FRANCE, HOME FRONT; JOFFRE, JOSEPH

Brockdorff-Rantzau, Ulrich Count (1869–1928)

German diplomat and foreign minister. Born on 29 May 1869 on an ancestral estate in Holstein, Brockdorff-Rantzau studied law at Neuchâtel, Freiburg, Berlin, and Leipzig, where he passed his state examinations and earned a doctorate. After three years as a subaltern in the Prussian Guards, he entered the diplomatic service in 1894. Rising through a variety of foreign postings, Brockdorff-Rantzau eventually became German consul-general in Budapest and in 1912 was appointed German minister in Copenhagen, a location that assumed added significance as a listening post once the First World War began. During the war years, he promoted Danish trade with Germany (food for coal) and established a close relationship with

Alexander Parvus-Helphand, a colorful Russian socialist who played a major role in Berlin's efforts to undermine the czarist empire by seditious acts and propaganda.

After Germany's defeat and the collapse of the monarchical system, Brockdorff-Rantzau was approached by the new Social Democrat regime in Berlin, which on 20 December 1918 appointed him foreign minister. Although he was an aristocrat by breeding and lifestyle, his appointment reflected his flexible views on many matters. In an effort to obtain lenient peace terms from the Allies, he appealed to liberal sentiments abroad and at home and insisted that Wilson's Fourteen Points serve as the basis for a general settlement. His image as a "progressive" German statesman was badly undermined by his haughty demeanor and statements in Paris after the Allies had presented their peace terms to him on 7 May 1919. Eight weeks later, he resigned with the Scheidemann cabinet in protest against the harsh peace treaty Germany was expected to sign.

After over two years on the sidelines, in 1922 Brockdorff-Rantzau agreed to become the Weimar Republic's first ambassador to Soviet Russia. Once in Moscow, he worked hard to improve German-Soviet relations but consistently warned his superiors against any one-sided commitments to either the Soviet Union or the capitalist West. The count's work in Moscow was greatly facilitated by his good personal relationship with Soviet Commissar of Foreign Affairs G.V. Chicherin. Brockdorff-Rantzau died on 8 September 1928 while on sick leave in Berlin.

Ulrich Trumpener

References

Conze, Werner. "Brockdorff-Rantzau." *Neue Deutsche Biographie* 2. Berlin: Duncker and Humblot, 1953.

Fischer, Fritz. *Griff nach der Weltmacht: Die Kriegszielpolitik des kaiserlichen Deutschlands 1914/18.* Düsseldorf: Droste, 1961.

Haupt, Leo. *Ulrich Graf von Brockdorff-Rantzau: Diplomat und Minister in Kaiserreich und Republik.* Göttingen: Musterschmidt, 1984.

Luckau, Alma. *The German Delegation at the Paris Peace Conference.* New York: Columbia University Press, 1941.

Rosenbaum, Kurt. *Community of Fate: German-Soviet Diplomatic Relations 1922–1928.* Syracuse: Syracuse University Press, 1965.

See also VERSAILLES TREATY

Brooke, Rupert (1887–1915)

British poet. Born on 3 August 1887 at Rugby, where his father was a master, Brooke received his public-school education at Rugby before enrolling in 1906 at King's College, Cambridge, to read for the classical tripos. As an undergraduate he actively pursued his interest in drama and poetry, cultivated literary friends, enjoyed athletics, and served as president of the Fabian Society. He wrote, "There are only three things in the world—one is to read poetry, another is to write poetry, and the best of all is to live poetry."

Brooke's early circle of friends, who encouraged his writing, included many members of the Bloomsbury Group: Virginia Woolf, John Maynard Keynes, and Lytton Strachey. Brooke left Britain in May of 1913 for a journey that took him to the United States, Canada, and the South Pacific. He returned to Britain in June of 1914.

When the First World War began, Brooke accepted Winston Churchill's offer of a commission in the Royal Naval Division. He witnessed the campaign around Antwerp, which ended in a retreat by the British, and then spent the winter of 1914–15 preparing for the expedition to the Dardanelles. During this period he published his early war sonnets, most notably "Peace" with its familiar refrain expressing his generation's idealistic enthusiasm for the outbreak of military conflict:

> Now, God be thanked Who has matched us with His hour,
> And caught our youth, and wakened us from sleeping.

Brooke was on his way to Gallipoli when he became ill with blood poisoning and died on 23 April 1915; he was buried on the Greek island of Skyros. Three days later, in a tribute in *The Times,* Churchill wrote of Brooke's "simple force of genius" and "valiant spirit." Critics have long debated Brooke's literary merits, trying to separate their analysis of his poetry from the circumstances of his early death. In 1980, biographer John Lehmann stated this view: "Rupert Brooke was nevertheless a flawed poet of uneven quality, who might have grown considerably in stature if he had not died in the Aegean in 1915."

Thomas W. Davis

References

Hassall, Christopher. *Rupert Brooke, a Biography*. London: Faber and Faber, 1964.

Lehmann, John. *Rupert Brooke: His Life and His Legend*. New York: Holt, Rinehart, and Winston, 1980.

Marsh, Edward. *Rupert Brooke: A Memoir*. London: Sidgwick & Jackson, 1918.

See also LITERATURE: WRITERS OF THE FIRST WORLD WAR

Bruchmüller, Georg (1863–1948)

German colonel. Born in Berlin on 11 December 1863 to a family with no special military tradition, Bruchmüller was commissioned in the Foot Artillery in 1885. He spent the next twenty-eight years alternating between assignments with fortress guns and as an instructor in various military schools. In 1913 he was serving as an instructor at an artillery school when he fell off a horse and subsequently suffered a nervous breakdown. In October of that year he received a medical discharge and was placed on the retired list as a lieutenant colonel.

Upon the outbreak of World War I, Bruchmüller was recalled to temporary active duty on the Eastern Front. By the beginning of 1915 he had participated in numerous battles and won the Iron Cross Second Class and First Class in the process. His star really began to rise when he achieved stunning results during the Tenth Army's counterattack against the numerically superior Russians in the 1916 Battle of Lake Naroch. The German army continued to use him for increasingly larger attacks in the East. On 1 May 1917 Bruchmüller was awarded Prussia's coveted *Pour le Mérite*.

In August of 1917 General Max Hoffmann sent Bruchmüller to the Eighth Army to control the artillery for the Riga attack. After Riga fell, Bruchmüller was transferred to the Western Front. Although still only a retired lieutenant colonel on temporary active duty, Bruchmüller orchestrated the artillery for all five of Ludendorff's 1918 offensives. On 26 March 1918 Bruchmüller received the Oak Leaves to the *Pour le Mérite,* which were awarded only 122 times during the war. Later that month he was finally promoted to colonel and restored to the active list.

Bruchmüller was the first to employ many tactical techniques that were widely copied during and after the war. While massive artillery preparations on the Western Front had previously lasted seven and even fourteen days, his preparations lasted a matter of hours, with better effect. He pioneered a system of task-tailored artillery groupings for specific tactical missions and was the war's most successful user of artillery-delivered gas.

After the war Bruchmüller was again retired. He wrote several influential books about his tactical methods, which were translated into English, French, and Russian and widely studied in the 1920s and 1930s. Ironically, the postwar German army, obsessed with the tank-dive-bomber combination, abandoned most of Bruchmüller's World War I firepower principles and paid the price in World War II. The Soviets followed him very closely then and later. The fire-support tactics of most nations still bear his unmistakable imprint.

In August of 1939 the German army belatedly promoted the man who once commanded over six thousand artillery pieces to the rank of major general on the retired list. He died in Garmisch-Partenkirchen on 26 January 1948. During World War I German infantrymen in the trenches had a nickname for him that was a combination pun on his name and the German word for breakthrough, *Durchbruch.* They called him *Der Durchbruchmüller.*

David T. Zabecki

References

Zabecki, David T. *Steel Wind: Georg Bruchmueller and the Birth of Modern Artillery*. Westport, Conn.: Praeger, 1994.

See also ARTILLERY; LUDENDORFF OFFENSIVES; NAROCH, LAKE, BATTLE OF; RIGA, BATTLE OF

Brusilov, Aleksei Alekseevich (1853–1926)

Russian general and army commander. Born on 31 August 1853 in Tiflis, Georgia, Brusilov was the son of a Russian general of noble birth. Commissioned as a cavalry officer in 1872, he saw action in the Russo-Turkish War of 1877–78 and was decorated for heroism. Subsequently, he was posted to the Officer's Cavalry School. Upon graduating he became a teacher at the school, and from 1902 to 1906 he served as its commandant. He thus missed the Russo-Japanese War. In 1906 he was promoted general and given command of a division and then a corps. In 1912 he was deputy commander of the Warsaw Military District and shortly thereafter was posted to the Kiev Military District, where he became a member of a group of Russia's most innovative officers.

The outbreak of war in 1914 found Brusilov in command of the Eighth Army, positioned on the Galician frontier at the southern end of the southwestern front commanded by the mediocre General Nikolai Ivanov. With the Russian advance into Austrian Galicia in August of 1914, Brusilov's soldiers won two quick victories on the Lipa River. After the capture of the capital of Lemberg on 2 September, Brusilov started toward the main Galician fortress of Przemysl, but some of his units were diverted into the Carpathian Mountains to chase down fleeing Austrian units. This turned into a slugfest with heavy casualties on both sides, but the Russians seized the strategic passes. By the end of 1914 Brusilov's units controlled the Carpathians and were poised to debouch into the Hungarian plain, a major source of food for the Central Powers.

In May of 1915 German forces under General August von Mackensen opened a counterattack to drive the Russians out of Galicia. Brusilov's Eighth Army took the brunt of the attack, and entire divisions were wiped out. Brusilov contended that this was the end of the regular army. Russian general headquarters ordered evacuation, and Brusilov's 200-mile strategic retreat, based on vigorous small attacks often at night, won the admiration of Russians and Germans alike. He most likely saved the remnants of the Russian army in his sector.

During the winter of 1915–16 the battered Russian army was restored to combat readiness. Even so, it was assumed by her allies that Russia would not be able to conduct more than defensive operations in 1916. The French were soon calling for a Russian attack to relieve pressure at Verdun and to aid Italy, which had suffered a major defeat at the hands of the Austrians.

On 14 April Czar Nicholas II presided over a conference of senior officers to plan operations for 1916. Brusilov alone called for an offensive. Largely because of his reputation and experience, the general staff sanctioned an offensive operation for late May. The plan called for Brusilov to launch a diversionary attack; then General Aleksei Evert's divisions to Brusilov's north would start the main offensive. On 4 June Brusilov's units broke the Austrian lines in four places. When the overcautious Evert failed to attack, however, General Erich Ludendorff was able to move his units south to blunt Brusilov's offensive. By August it was all over for the Russians. Brusilov had lost 500,000 men. He later contended that if Evert had attacked as planned, Austria would have been driven from the war. Yet, as it turned out, the Brusilov offensive accomplished its objectives. German divisions were sent to the east, away from Verdun, and Austrian troops were transferred from Italy.

In May of 1917 Minister of War Aleksandr Kerensky appointed Brusilov commander of the army. The July 1917 offensive achieved initial success, but it was short-lived. Discipline in the army was nonexistent, and within three weeks of the start of the attack the Germans had launched deadly counterattacks. Totally exhausted, Brusilov was replaced by General Lavr Kornilov.

The aristocratic Brusilov remained in Russia after the Bolshevik Revolution. In 1920, during the war with Poland, he offered his services to the Bolsheviks. He retired in 1924 and died in Moscow on 17 March 1926.

John W. Bohon

References

Brusilov, General A.A. *A Soldier's Notebook*. New York: Macmillan, 1930.
Golovin, General N.N. *The Russian Army in the World War*. New Haven: Yale University Press, 1931.

See also BRUSILOV OFFENSIVE; EVERT, ALEKSEI; EAST GALICIA, 1914 CAMPAIGN; EASTERN FRONT; IVANOV, NIKOLAI; KERENSKY OFFENSIVE; MACKENSEN, AUGUST VON

Brusilov Offensive (4 June to 20 September 1916)

As a result of the Russian retreat from Galicia in 1915, a new Russian position was formed along a 500-mile line stretching from Riga on the Baltic through the Pinsk marshes to the Romanian frontier. At the time the most pressing need, if Russia were to continue in the war, was to restore the fighting capacity of her battered army. This was accomplished under the overall supervision of General Mikhail V. Alekseev, chief of staff to Czar Nicholas II and de facto commander of the army. Shortages of military equipment were largely made up and training programs were established for new recruits. By the beginning of 1916 the army had been largely restored. The 1915 military disaster had also had an adverse impact on Russian public opinion, which was reflected in urban demonstrations and large-scale criticism of the government and the high command. Consequently, Russia's allies recognized that she needed time to work out her problems and agreed not to press her during 1916. From October of 1915 to March of 1916 the Eastern Front was quiet.

This calm was short-lived, however. Once again, as in 1914, events in the west dictated the course of action in the east. France was severely strained by the German offensive at Verdun, and at an Allied conference at Chantilly in early 1916, Russia promised to resume the offensive by late June. At that time military dispositions in the east were as follows: In the north, German forces were commanded by Field Marshal Paul von Hindenburg, and, in the south, the Austrians were under Archduke Friedrich Josef. They faced three Russian armies. The northern front was commanded by General Aleksei N. Kuropatkin, whose record of timidity in the Russo-Japanese war was already established. The northwest front was under General Aleksei Evert, while General Nikolai Y. Ivanov presided over the southwestern front. The three Russian commanders ranged from mediocre to incompetent and had kept their positions largely because of Russia's archaic political system.

Under pressure from the French, in March of 1916 the Russians launched a preliminary strike against Colonel General Hermann von Eichhorn's Tenth Army in the Lake Naroch area, northeast of Vilna and adjacent sectors. The chief effort was to be made by General V.V. Smirnov's Second Army, which had been built up to a superiority of about five-to-one over the opposing German forces. Attacking in the spring mud, the Russians broke through the German lines. But the offensive was broken when the Germans brought up reinforcements and the Russians were subjected to withering German artillery fire. Russian losses numbered more than 100,000 men.

In the wake of this defeat, another external event called for Russia's attention. At the very time the battle of Verdun was reaching a climax, Italy suffered a major defeat at the hands of the Austrians in the mountains of the Trentino. Russia was called upon to relieve the pressure on the Italian front. On 14 April, at a general headquarters meeting presided over by the Czar, the question of a Russian offensive was raised. Generals Evert and Kuropatkin contended that Russian forces were too weak to sustain an attack and held out for remaining on the defensive. General Aleksei Brusilov, who had replaced Ivanov as commander of the southwestern front, thought otherwise. Brusilov, who had distinguished himself during the Carpathian retreat, was nevertheless a champion of the offensive. In answer to the objection that the Germans, with their superior railroads, could block any Russian attack, Brusilov suggested attacking in several areas at once in order to confuse the Germans as to the location of the main thrust. Based on this idea, a plan was devised wherein Brusilov would attack in the south, against the Austrians, toward the cities of Lutsk and Kovel. This was to be a feint. After the Germans moved their units south to block Brusilov's advance, Evert was to launch the main thrust toward Vilna through the gap vacated by the Germans. The plan was excellent in its overall conception. It was doomed, however, because of the inability of the Russians to coordinate such complex maneuvers and the timidity of Evert.

Brusilov commanded four armies over a 200-mile front. Facing these forces was an extremely strong Austrian position consisting of three belts of fortified trenches. Brusilov engaged in meticulous planning and preparations, such as had not been seen on the Eastern Front to that time. It even included the use of aerial photos to help in locating Austrian batteries. Front-line trenches were sapped forward, to as close as fifty yards of the Austrian lines. Tunnels were dug under the Austrian wire obstacles, huge dugouts were constructed to hold reserve troops, and the Russians made accurate models of the Austrian defenses and trained in them. Russian superiority in men was not that great: perhaps 600,000 Russian soldiers to 500,000 Austrians and Germans. The number of artillery still favored the enemy, but not as widely as in other operations. Brusilov had 1,770 light and 168 heavy guns, to 1,301 light and 545 medium and heavy for his opponents. The numerical disadvantage for the Russians was overcome by the fact that the

Russians knew the location of the Austrian guns and were cooperating with the infantry. The bulk of their guns were positioned no farther than two kilometers from the front, another innovation for the Russians. Brusilov was a tireless worker; he had constantly to deal with innumerable objections and lack of will in his subordinates, and doubts raised by General Alekseev. Despite objections, Brusilov set the attack for 4 June.

Brusilov was determined on surprise, and he achieved it to a considerable degree. On 4 June the Russians began a massive and accurate barrage, silencing many of the Austrian guns. The attack lasted the entire day, and on 5 June Brusilov's infantry moved forward. The Austrians had already sustained major casualties, as the majority of their troops were in the front-line positions hardest hit by the Russian artillery. Three of the four armies broke through, tearing wide gaps in the enemy lines. The Russians were aided by the defection of entire Czech units and by Austrian overconfidence. On 8 June Lutsk fell to the Russians. Austrian Archduke Friedrich Josef, enjoying a birthday luncheon in that city, barely escaped. On 12 June Brusilov's command reported it had captured from the four Austrian armies some 193,000 enemy officers and men and 216 guns. Although Austria-Hungary had almost collapsed, Brusilov could not immediately follow up his victory. His own losses had not been insignificant, and his forces had outrun their supply lines. He had only one cavalry division in reserve, commanded by General Carl Mannerheim.

Brusilov could do no more. It now rested on General Evert, with a million troops and two-thirds of the Russian army's artillery—a threefold superiority in men and guns—to attack in the north, against the Germans. His offensive was to have begun on 9 June. He had no stomach for the attack. He demanded vast quantities of shells and informed general headquarters that he could not possibly be ready to attack until 18 June. The result was inevitable.

Head of the German general staff, General Erich von Falkenhayn, refused to send forces from the west, and in Berlin on 8 June lectured his Austrian counterpart, Field Marshal Franz Conrad von Hötzendorff, insisting that he transfer troops from the Italian front. Four German divisions were to be sent, along with four and a half Austrian divisions. Some German troops arrived on 6 June and by the 20th

there were ten and a half new Austro-Hungarian and German divisions in place facing Brusilov. Under orders from Alekseev, Brusilov resumed the offensive on 28 July but was slowed by ammunition shortages. A third assault (7 August to 20 September) brought the Russians into the Carpathian foothills. During the next month the Russian offensive petered out. German General Alexander von Linsingen stabilized the front and eventually forced Brusilov to abandon Bukovina and Galicia.

Subsequently, Brusilov would contend that had Evert attacked on schedule, Austria would have been driven from the war. It seems probable that, without the German reinforcements, Austria-Hungary would probably have been defeated. The offensive probably finished Austria-Hungary as a major military power. More specifically, the Italian army was saved when Austrian units were transferred from the Trentino to the Russian front. The Brusilov Offensive also contributed to the weakening of the German attack at Verdun, helped lead to the fall of Falkenhayn, and encouraged Romania to declare war against Austria-Hungary. On the other hand, for Russia the cost of the Brusilov Offensive had been high and it was seen as another military failure. As such it contributed to revolution in that country in 1917.

John W. Bohon

References
Florinsky, Michael T. *Russia: A History and Interpretation.* 2 vols. New York: Macmillan, 1953.
Pushkarev, Sergei Germanovich. *The Emergence of Modern Russia, 1801–1917.* New York: Holt, Rinehart and Winston, 1963.
Stone, Norman. *The Eastern Front 1914–1917.* New York: Charles Scribner's Sons, 1975.
Taylor, A.J.P., ed. *A History of World War I.* London: Octopus, 1974.

See also ALEKSEEV, MIKHAIL; BRUSILOV, ALEKSEI; EAST GALICIA, 1914 CAMPAIGN; EVERT, ALEKSEI; NAROCH, LAKE, BATTLE OF

Bucharest, Treaty of (7 May 1918)
Treaty whereby Romania was forced to conclude peace with the Central Powers. Hopes of territorial aggrandizement and Russia's initial success in the 1916 Brusilov Offensive led Ro-

mania to declare war on Austria-Hungary on 27 August 1916. Romania proved ill prepared for war, however. By January of 1917 most of the country, including the capital of Bucharest, had fallen to the Central Powers. Since neither Russia nor its Western Allies were in a position to help, Romania had no choice but to sign an armistice on 9 December 1917. Had the Central Powers won the First World War, Romania would have paid dearly for entering the war on the Allied side.

In settling with its former ally, Germany sought to punish Romania severely. During a tour of the Romanian front in September of 1917, Kaiser Wilhelm II made it clear that he intended to draw Romania closer to Germany in order to secure its agricultural production, oil, and mineral resources. He was even prepared to grant Austria-Hungary hegemony over Poland in exchange for German control over Romania. When the German high command (OHL) objected to giving up Germany's position in Poland, German officials held a conference at Kreuznach on 7 October 1917 to resolve their differences. At the conference, State Secretary for Foreign Affairs Richard von Kühlmann succeeded in winning OHL's reluctant endorsement of the Kaiser's proposal. Chief of Staff Field Marshal Paul von Hindenburg and Quartermaster General Erich Ludendorff made their approval conditional, however, on forcing Austria to grant Germany special concessions in Poland, guaranteeing German economic and political control over Romania, and securing German control over the Dobrudja.

To secure Austrian support for the Kreuznach agreement, Kühlmann met with Austro-Hungarian Foreign Minister Count Ottokar von Czerzin on 22 October. Although they agreed that Poland was to be formally associated with Austria-Hungary, it was to be just a personal union through the Hapsburg Emperor, and Germany was to have close economic and military ties to Poland. While Austria-Hungary was to extend its Transylvanian borders by acquiring parts of Wallachia, Germany was to have virtually complete dominion over Romania. Finally, Austria-Hungary and Germany were also to sign a twenty-year military alliance.

The next problem for German diplomats was winning over Bulgaria. Although it had been promised the southern Dobrudja, which it had lost in the Second Balkan War, Bulgaria, now demanded the entire region. After long negotiations, Germany finally agreed to cede the entire Dobrudja to Bulgaria, but only after securing wide-ranging concessions. Germany was to control the naval base at Constanta, the railroad from Constanta to Cernavoda, and navigation on the Danube. In addition, Germany could build a canal from Constanta to Cernavoda to shorten the approach to the Black Sea. Finally, Bulgaria was to sign a permanent military alliance with Germany, fund its war debt through German banks, and transfer mines seized from Serbia and the railroad to Salonika to German ownership. Although OHL protested that giving up the Dobrudja violated the terms of the Kreuznach conference, German diplomats had in effect used it to tie Bulgaria closer to Germany.

Turkey proved the most difficult of the Central Powers. The Turks demanded that the Romanian settlement be linked to that with Russia. In this way the Turks hoped to secure compensation in the Caucasus, Georgia, Armenia, and Azerbaijan, as well as in western Thrace. Turkish demands, however, went far beyond what Germany had ever promised. In any event, Germany's success in establishing a puppet regime in the Ukraine and moving troops to the Caucasus ultimately gave the Turks no choice but to consent to the Treaty of Bucharest.

Once Germany had secured agreements with the other Central Powers, German military and diplomatic leaders held a series of conferences to work out the specific demands, which were finally presented to Romania in the form of an ultimatum on 27 February 1918. All agreements between Romania and the Allies were to be canceled. A German-controlled Central European Oil Company was to be given a ninety-year lease over Romanian oil deposits and mines. Romania was to have a 20 percent share in the company, while Germany was to control 56 percent and Austria-Hungary 24 percent. Since sales, production, and delivery were to be in German hands, this would ensure that German needs would be supplied first. OHL and the navy demanded that Constanta become a German naval base and that Romanian railroads be transferred to German ownership. Strict controls were also to be placed over Romanian agriculture. Until 1926 the entire agricultural surplus was to go directly to Germany and Austria-Hungary, and thereafter their needs would have to be met before Romania could export its grain to anyone else. Finally, Romania was to enter a military alliance against

Russia and join a Central European Customs Union.

Although Romanian leaders had expected a harsh peace, none were prepared for the terms presented on 27 February. In fact, pro-German conservatives Peter Carp and Alexander Marghiloman had hoped to secure better terms by offering to depose Ferdinand I and place Friedrich Karl of Hesse or the Kaiser's fifth son, Prince Oscar, on the throne. The Germans, however, refused to make concessions. Although the Romanian government was prepared to accept the economic and military conditions as terms for negotiations, and was willing to part with the southern Dobrudja and to adjust the frontier between Wallachia and Transylvania, it protested Bulgaria's demands for the entire Dobrudja. Faced with the further advances of German troops, however, on 2 March the Romanian government consented to the ultimatum of 27 February and on 5 March signed the preliminary peace of Buftea. Finally, on 21 March, a new government under Marghiloman took office to begin negotiations in Bucharest.

In the negotiations of the final treaty, signed on 7 May 1918 in Bucharest, Marghiloman succeeded in winning some minor concessions. Constanta was to become a free city instead of being annexed outright as a German naval base. Romania was also to retain control of its mines. On everything else, however, Romania was forced to accept the original German demands: a ninety-year lease on Romanian oil deposits; a German monopoly over Romanian trade through a Central European Customs Union; German and Austro-Hungarian control over Romania's agricultural surplus; German control of Romanian railways and the Danube; Bulgarian acquisition of the Dobrudja; and Austro-Hungarian gains in Wallachia. Although the Reichstag's Peace Resolution of July 1917 had called for "no annexations and indemnities," the same body quickly ratified the treaty. Ludendorff, however, denounced Kühlmann for failing to establish necessary "political controls," and he therefore left German troops in Romania to guarantee the flow of oil and grain to Germany. OHL's criticisms soon led to Kühlmann's dismissal.

Together with the Treaty of Brest-Litovsk, which ended the war between Germany and Russia, the Treaty of Bucharest marked the zenith of German expansionist policy in World War I. Ironically, in obtaining their excessive demands the Germans contributed to their own failure. The delay in negotiations and the need for occupation troops in the east meant that Ludendorff did not have as many troops as he might have had in the west for his great offensives in the spring of 1918. While the Ludendorff Offensives probably would have failed anyway, it is certain that the harsh terms imposed on Russia and Romania hardened the will of the Allies to resist, because they showed what could be expected from a *Pax Teutonica*. Fortunately for Romania, Germany's defeat in the west rescued it from the Treaty of Bucharest and in fact made Romania a principal beneficiary. In the Treaty of Trianon, the Allies forced Hungary to cede it Transylvania, Bukovina, and part of the Banat.

Justin D. Murphy

References

Fisher, Fritz. *Germany's Aims in the First World War*. New York: W.W. Norton, 1967.

Holborn, Hajo. *A History of Modern Germany. Vol. 3: 1840–1945*. Princeton: Princeton University Press, 1969.

Schmitt, Bernadotte E., and Harold C. Vedeler. *The World in the Crucible, 1914–1919*. New York: Harper and Row, 1984.

See also FERDINAND I; KÜHLMANN, RICHARD VON; ROMANIA; ROMANIAN CAMPAIGN, 1916; TRIANON, TREATY OF; WAR AIMS

Bulgaria

When the First World War erupted in August of 1914, the Bulgarian government avoided involvement. Bulgaria was still exhausted from the strenuous effort of the First Balkan War and the catastrophic defeat of the Second Balkan War. Much of the population demonstrated a traditional Russophile stance at the beginning of the war. The popular Balkan War hero Radko Dimitriev resigned his position as ambassador to St. Petersburg and became a general in the Russian army. Initially, Bulgaria proclaimed neutrality. Nevertheless, Bulgarian Czar Ferdinand, and the head of the Bulgarian government, Vasil Radoslavov, inclined toward the Central Powers. They sought to undo the consequences of the 1913 Treaty of Bucharest, which deprived Bulgaria of its long-sought goals in Macedonia as well as southern Dobrudja.

After the Ottoman Empire entered the war in October of 1914, both warring sides sought the assistance of Bulgaria because of its strategic location. The price of Bulgaria's participation on either side became Macedonia. Because Serbia held Macedonia, the Central Powers had a pronounced advantage in securing a Bulgarian alliance: They could promise the immediate occupation of all of Macedonia. The best the Entente could do in May of 1915 was to offer Bulgaria eastern Thrace, then in Ottoman hands, and a portion of Macedonia (the uncontested zone) at the end of the war if Serbia received compensation elsewhere. Also, the Entente promised to consider Bulgarian claims to southern Dobrudja and to Kavala (then under Greek control), and to render Bulgaria financial assistance. The reluctance of Serbia to surrender any of Macedonia naturally stymied the Entente in its negotiations with Bulgaria. The Bulgarians negotiated with both sides until the summer of 1915. Then Entente defeats in Galicia and Gallipoli persuaded Ferdinand and Radoslavov that the time was propitious to join the Central Powers. On 6 September 1915 Bulgaria signed an alliance with Germany and Austria-Hungary at German military headquarters at Pless, providing for a joint German-Austrian-Bulgarian invasion of Serbia and for the Bulgarian annexation of Macedonia. Concurrent negotiations with the Ottoman Empire obtained for Bulgaria the cession of the Maritsa Valley in Thrace.

On 14 October 1915 Bulgaria declared war on Serbia, and two days later Bulgarian troops crossed the Serbian frontier. The invasion quickly overwhelmed the Serbs, who had to retreat across the Albanian mountains to the Adriatic. Bulgarian forces repulsed an attempt launched from Salonika by the Entente to relieve the Serbs. Despite strong Bulgarian objections, the German high command would not permit the Bulgarian army to cross into Greece to pursue the defeated British and French troops; the Germans did not want to involve Greece in the war. The Central Powers' failure to destroy the Entente forces allowed them to regroup and maintain themselves in Salonika, where they posed a threat to the southeastern flank of the Central Powers for the rest of the war.

In 1916 the Germans withdrew their objections to a Bulgarian advance on the southeastern front. Some German troops arrived there to assist their Bulgarian allies. Without bloodshed, Greek forces handed over Fort Rupel on the Struma River northeast of Salonika to the Bulgarians in May of 1916. Later in the year Bulgarian forces occupied portions of northern Greece, including Drama, Kavala, and Seres. Bulgarian troops also assumed occupation duties in Serbia to free German soldiers for the planned Western Front offensive.

In August of 1916, after the Romanian declaration of war on Austria-Hungary, Bulgaria and the other Central Powers launched an attack on Romania. Bulgarian troops advanced into the Dobrudja against Romanian and Russian opposition, taking the port of Constanta in October. Bulgarian forces also crossed the Danube, together with German and Turkish troops, and overran Wallachia. These attacks effectively knocked Romania out of the war and restored to Bulgaria southern Dobrudja, which Romania had taken in the Second Balkan War. With the reoccupation of the southern Dobrudja, Bulgaria had accomplished its major war aims. Its policy now was largely defensive.

In the autumn of 1916 an Entente offensive from Salonika succeeded in taking a portion of southwestern Macedonia—including the city of Bitola (Monastir)—from the Bulgarians. Additional Entente attempts in 1917 to advance farther into Macedonia met strong Bulgarian resistance and failed to break through the Bulgarian positions.

By 1918 the Bulgarian situation had begun to deteriorate. Much of the food produced in Bulgaria left the country, legally and illegally going mainly to sustain the German war effort. Resentment against the Germans also developed because of German control of Bulgarian transportation and communication facilities. In addition, a dispute with Germany and Austria over the disposition of northern Dobrudja contributed to Bulgaria's disaffection with the war. The Treaty of Bucharest, signed in May of 1918 between the Central Powers and Romania, officially returned Dobrudja to Bulgaria but granted Germany considerable economic influence. This solution satisfied no one. Finally, the Bulgarian population suffered from a profound sense of war weariness. In May of 1918 Radoslavov resigned, ostensibly because of his failure to obtain northern Dobrudja. A government more conciliatory to the Entente and to a negotiated solution to the war replaced him.

An Entente offensive in September of 1918 in Macedonia quickly overwhelmed the Bulgarian forces at Dobropole and broke through the

Bulgarian lines into Macedonia. A rapid collapse of Bulgarian forces ensued. By 25 September British and French troops had crossed into Bulgaria proper. The same day the Bulgarian Czar and government decided to seek an armistice. On 29–30 September the Bulgarians signed the armistice at Salonika. According to its terms, the Bulgarians were required to demobilize their army and turn all their equipment over to the Entente forces. Furthermore, Bulgarian troops had to evacuate all Greek and Serbian territories, and Bulgarian territory and transportation systems were made available for Entente operations.

Meanwhile, many of the disaffected troops streaming back toward Sofia accepted the loose leadership of the Bulgarian Agrarian Union, which had opposed the war from its onset. These soldiers and Agrarians sought to inflict retribution on those responsible for Bulgaria's catastrophe. The disorganized rebels proclaimed a republic in Radomir, a small town southwest of the capital. Ragtag formations of these soldiers reached the outskirts of Sofia. On 30 September, however, a hastily collected force, including German troops and military cadets, defeated and dispersed them. With the signing of the armistice and the abdication of Czar Ferdinand on 4 October, the major objective of most of the soldiers, an end to the war, was accomplished, and the major culprit in their view, Ferdinand, had fled to Germany. Ferdinand's eldest son succeeded him as Czar Boris III.

The Bulgarians were the last to join the Central Powers and the first to leave. Within a month of the Bulgarian armistice the Ottoman and Hapsburg empires likewise gave up the fight. The Germans also understood that the war was lost. On 3 October General Paul von Hindenburg recognized that in view of the collapse of the Macedonian front "there was no longer a prospect of forcing peace on the enemy." Forty-eight hours later the Germans contacted President Wilson, seeking his mediation to end the war.

Richard C. Hall

References

Berov, Ljuben. "The Bulgarian Economy during World War I." In *East Central European Society in World War I,* edited by Bela K. Kiraly and Nandor F. Dreisziger. Boulder, Colo.: Social Science Monographs, 1985.

Crampton, R.J. *Bulgaria, 1878–1918.* New York: East European Monographs, 1983.

Vlahov, Tushe. *Otnosheniya mezhdu Bŭlgariya i Tsentralnite sili prez voinite 1912–1918.* Sofia: Bŭlgarskata komunisticheska partiya, 1957.

See also BALKAN FRONT, 1915, 1916, AND 1917; BULGARIA, ARMY; DIMITRIEV, RADKO; DOBROPOLE, BATTLE OF; FERDINAND, CZAR; RADOSLAVOV, VASIL; ROMANIAN CAMPAIGN, 1916

Bulgaria, Army

The Bulgarian army demonstrated impressive offensive capabilities in the First Balkan War against the Ottoman Empire in 1912–13. In the Second Balkan War in 1913, however, a combined Serbian-Greek-Romanian-Turkish attack overwhelmed the Bulgarian forces. When the First World War began in 1914, the Bulgarian army had not yet recovered from these campaigns. Losses in these wars had left Bulgaria with a shortage in matériel and men, especially in subalterns and noncommissioned officers.

Bulgarian soldiers came mostly from peasant backgrounds and were stolid and determined fighters. In 1915, when Bulgaria entered the First World War on the side of the Central Powers, the army mobilized 650,000 troops, about 12 percent of the total Bulgarian population.

According to the Bulgarian constitution, the military had few civilian constraints. The minister of war, who sat in every government cabinet, was always an army general who had no party affiliation. Czar Ferdinand was the nominal commander in chief of the Bulgarian army, but after the defeat of the Second Balkan War he declined to assume that position. Nevertheless, Ferdinand retained an important influence over appointments and army policy.

Bulgarian officers received their education in military academies throughout Europe, including Austria, Italy, and Russia. In preparation for war on the side of the Central Powers, Ferdinand selected those senior officers with decided Germanophile or Austrophile tendencies to lead the army. In 1915 Ferdinand chose the Italian-educated Major General Nikola Zhekov to command the Bulgarian army. Zhekov owed his position more to his association with the Czar than to his military abilities.

In the First World War, Bulgarian troops, together with the other Central Powers, participated in major campaigns under German command. In 1915 Bulgarian forces quickly overran southern Serbia and Macedonia. They also prevented the British and French from advancing from Salonika to aid the Serbs. Because of political and military considerations, however, the Germans refused Bulgarian demands to advance into Greece to eliminate the Entente positions around Salonika. In 1916 Bulgarian forces participated in the invasion of Romania and attacked Dobrudja, capturing the strongly held fortress of Tutrakan. That same year Bulgarian troops fought effectively in defensive battles around Salonika against the Entente armies and advanced into Greek territory, taking the important town of Kavala. An Entente counteroffensive, however, drove them from Bitola in Macedonia. This was the only important Bulgarian loss until the end of the war. From 1916 to 1918 the Bulgarians also carried out occupation responsibilities in Serbia.

Although Bulgarian forces had performed well, by the summer of 1918 the troops were tired of the war. Supply and command problems increased friction with Germany. Bulgarian troops collapsed in the face of an Entente offensive at Dobropole in September of 1918 and retreated in some disorder toward Bulgaria. Some participated in an attempt to overthrow the monarchy and replace it with a peasant republic.

Richard C. Hall

References

Aleksandŭr Ganchev. *Voinite prez tretoto bŭlgarsko czarstvo*. Sofia: Bŭkgarska akademiya na naukite i izkustvata, n.d.

Bŭlgarskata armiya, Shtab na voiskata voenno-istoricheski otdel. *Bŭlgarskata armiya v svetnata voina, 1915–1918*. Sofia: Dŭrzhavna pechatnitsa, 1943.

Noykov, Stilyan. "The Bulgarian Army in World War I, 1915–1918." In *East Central European Society in World War I*, edited by Bela K. Kiraly and Nandor F. Dreisziger, 403–15. Boulder, Colo.: Social Science Monographs, 1985.

See also BALKAN FRONT, 1915, 1916, AND 1917; BULGARIA; DOBROPOLE, BATTLE OF; FERDINAND, CZAR; ROMANIAN CAMPAIGN, 1916; ZHEKOV, NIKOLA

Bülow, Karl von (1846–1921)

German field marshal and army commander. Born in Berlin on 24 March 1846, Bülow participated in the Austro-Prussian War of 1866 and the Franco-German War of 1870–71 as a subaltern. Although he never attended the *Kriegsakademie*, he was posted to the Prussian general staff in 1876 and thereafter held a number of important staff and command positions. He was a corps commander in Berlin from 1903 to 1912 and was then appointed head of Third Army Inspection and promoted to colonel general. Upon mobilization Bülow took charge of the Second Army, initially composed of six corps, which was to sweep through Belgium into France on the German right wing.

It appears that neither Bülow, aged sixty-eight, nor his chief of staff, Lieutenant General Otto von Lauenstein, were in good health at that time. To make matters worse, the senior quartermaster of Bülow's army, Major General Erich Ludendorff, was called away to East Prussia just as the German offensive began. The advance of Bülow's troops, via Liège and Namur toward St. Quentin, was accompanied by repeated friction with the adjacent First Army of Colonel General Alexander von Kluck, and Moltke's decision to subordinate Kluck (and his recently ennobled chief of staff, Major General Hermann von Kuhl) to Bülow created further problems. By 6 September a thinly veiled gap of over twenty miles had developed between Bülow's and Kluck's armies, which were pushing across the Marne with scant regard for their exposed flanks. Bülow became increasingly concerned about the situation and on 8 September agreed with an emissary from OHL, Lieutenant Colonel Richard Hentsch, that a withdrawal of the entire German right wing might soon become necessary. The following afternoon Bülow ordered his own army to retreat, thus forcing Kluck to follow suit.

Bülow's Second Army eventually wound up in the St. Quentin region. He was promoted to field marshal in January of 1915, but his health deteriorated further, and he was placed on sick leave (and received the *Pour le Mérite* medal) on 4 April. Despite his subsequent attempts to return to active duty, Bülow was pensioned off in June of 1916. He died in Berlin on 31 August 1921.

Ulrich Trumpener

References

Bülow, Karl von. *Mein Bericht zur Marneschlacht*. Berlin: Scherl, 1919.

Gebsattel, Ludwig Freiherr von. *Generalfeldmarschall Karl von Bülow.* Munich: Lehmanns Verlag, 1929.

Jäschke, Gotthard. "Zum Problem der Marneschlacht von 1914." *Historische Zeitschrift* 190 (1960).

Müller-Loebnitz, Wilhelm. *Die Führung im Marne-Feldzug.* Berlin: Mittler & Sohn, 1939.

Reymann, Martin. "Bülow." *Deutsches Biographisches Jahrbuch* 3 (1927).

See also MARNE, FIRST BATTLE OF

Burian von Rajecz, Count Stephen (1851–1922)

Austro-Hungarian diplomat. Born near Pressburg on 16 January 1851, Burian was in the diplomatic service for much of his life, serving at the Moscow and Sofia embassies. From 1903 to 1913 Burian was Hungarian minister of finance and served as administrator of the provinces of Bosnia and Herzegovina. In June of 1913 Burian was appointed Hungarian minister to the Court of Vienna. In June of 1915, with Italy and Austria-Hungary moving toward war, the German foreign office pressured Austro-Hungarian Foreign Minister Count Leopold Berchtold to make territorial concessions to Italy to prevent a further expansion of the war. When Berchtold acquiesced to this German proposal, he was forced from office on 13 June by hardliners and replaced by Burian. Burian soon changed his policy from hardline to accommodating, but Italy joined the Allied Powers. Burian, however, won Bulgaria to the Austro-Hungarian side and arranged a political/military alliance with Turkey.

Burian insisted that Germany treat Austria-Hungary as an equal in all military, economic, and political activities. He opposed Germany's policy of unrestricted submarine warfare and insisted that Austria-Hungary be paramount in Poland. He further angered Germany by proposing a peace plan that called for the reestablishment of a free Belgium and the return of all captured French territory in exchange for Allied Powers' recognition of German and Austro-Hungarian rights to captured eastern lands. As a result of this peace proposal, he was forced to resign in December of 1916.

On 15 April 1918 Burian was reappointed foreign minister with instructions to end the war. On 14 September 1918 he issued a call for all nations to end the war by diplomatic negotiations. Burian's proposal fell on deaf ears, and he resigned from office. Thereafter, he took no active part in diplomacy or politics. Burian died at Vienna on 20 October 1922.

Charles H. Bogart

References
Kann, Robert. *A History of the Hapsburg Empire.* Berkeley: University of California Press, 1974.

Valiani, Leo. *The End of Austro-Hungary.* New York: Alfred A. Knopf, 1973.

See also AUSTRIA-HUNGARY, HOME FRONT

Byng, Julian Hedworth George (1862–1935)

British army general. Born at Wrotham on 11 September 1862, Byng was a career soldier who had entered the 10th Hussars in 1883 and saw action during the Boer War. He commanded the 3rd Cavalry Division at Ypres (1914) and took command of the Cavalry Corps for a period in 1915. He commanded IX Corps at Suvla Bay during the ill-fated Dardanelles Campaign, but in his defense he took command well after the landings had failed.

His rise to prominence began when he became commander of the Canadian Corps in 1916, succeeding the politically hamstrung Lieutenant General Sir E. Alderson. Byng directed the corps in its capture of the bastion of Vimy Ridge on 9 April 1917. He was promoted and moved to Third Army that spring. While in command of the Third Army, he led the most significant tank attack of the war at Cambrai. Using surprise and tanks en masse, Byng's forces penetrated deep into the German defense. Although German counterattacks eventually recaptured the ground won, the Battle of Cambrai proved the value of the tank in modern warfare.

Byng's units bore the brunt of the March (Ludendorff) Offensives of the German army in 1918, and he received considerable criticism for his decision not to pull V Corps out of the Flesquières salient on 21 March. Its pullout on 23 March would have been more easily accomplished two days earlier. He recovered from this setback to command his army with success during the counteroffensives from July to November. Byng proved a superior corps and a capable army commander, one of a number that the BEF produced during the war.

After the war, Byng was raised to the peerage as Baron Byng of Vimy. He served as Governor-General of Canada (1921–26) and was promoted to field marshal in 1932. He died at Essex on 6 June 1935.

Ian M. Brown

References

Travers, Tim. *The Killing Ground: The British Army, the Western Front, and the Emergence of Modern Warfare*. Boston: Allen & Unwin, 1987.

Williams, Jefferey. *Byng of Vimy*. London: Leo Cooper, 1983.

See also CAMBRAI, BATTLE OF; CANADA, ARMY; VIMY RIDGE

C

Cadorna, Luigi (1850–1928)

Italian general and chief of staff. Born in Pallanza on 4 September 1850, Cadorna was the son of Raffaele Cadorna, commander of the expedition that occupied the Vatican territories in September of 1870. Cadorna entered the army in 1866 and attained the rank of major general in 1898 and was promoted to divisional general in 1905. He took command of Genoa's army corps in 1910, but, having been passed over for command of Italian forces in Libya in 1911, he was ready to retire when he was named chief of the general staff of the Italian army on 20 July 1914.

Cadorna had no combat experience, he had been criticized for questionable conduct during the army's 1911 maneuvers, and his technical preparation was mediocre. While he had published three articles on infantry tactics, they were fairly simplistic exaltations of the superiority of shock over firepower during the Franco-Prussian war of 1870–71, an argument repeated in a small book, *Le forme di combattimento della fanteria* (1898).

Although not a theorist of the first rank, Cadorna saw strategic problems clearly and made up in self-confidence what he lacked in intellectual ability. Unfortunately, he had some difficulty cooperating with politicians and colleagues because he tended to be stubborn and touchy, and he had a reputation as a stern disciplinarian with no empathy for the rank and file. Many believed that his imposition of harsh discipline led to disaffection in the ranks and contributed indirectly to the disaster at Caporetto. By February of 1916 Cadorna's relations with minister of war General Vittorio Zupelli had become so strained that Cadorna's threat to resign, "*o via Zupelli o via io*" ("either

Zupelli goes, or I do"), led to Zupelli's resignation and replacement by General Morrone.

Cadorna had believed a war of movement possible in 1914, an illusion that he never quite relinquished. Although he has been criticized for being an unimaginative general, his conduct of the operations on the Isonzo was at worst competent, and he has had strong defenders, including Emilio Faldella and Angelo Gatti. Although made the primary scapegoat for the defeat at Caporetto, for which he was replaced and investigated, Cadorna repulsed the Austrians in 1916, broke into the Bainsizza in 1917, and held Austro-Hungarian and German forces on the Piave after Caporetto. He deserves a better reputation, therefore, than he has enjoyed. Cadorna died at Bordighera on 23 December 1928.

James J. Sadkovich

References

Cadorna, Luigi. *Altre pagine sulla grande guerra*. Milan: Mondadori, 1925.
———. *La guerra alla fronte italiana fino all'arresto sulla linea del Piave e del Grappa*. Milan: Treves, 1921.
———. *Pagine polemiche*. Milan: Garzanti, 1950.
Faldella, Emilio. *La grade guerra*. 2 vols. Milan: Longanesi, 1965.
Gatti, Angelo. *La parte dell'Italia, rivendicazioni*. Milan: Mondadori, 1926.

See also CAPORETTO; ITALY, ARMY

Caillaux, Joseph (1863–1944)

French finance minister and premier. Born in Le Mans on 30 March 1863, Caillaux was the son of a finance minister. He enjoyed a decade-long career as a bureaucrat before his election to parliament in 1898. The following year he became finance minister (a post he was to hold repeatedly over thirty-five years) in the Waldeck-Rousseau cabinet. Despite considerable wealth and generally moderate views, Caillaux made enemies on the right and center-right with his 1907 endorsement of an income tax. Premier in 1911, he insisted on a negotiated settlement of the Second Moroccan Crisis (compensating Germany with French territory in the Cameroons) and was denounced as a pacifist.

Caillaux became president of the Radical party in 1913 and a strong candidate for premier the next spring. When his wife confronted and killed one of his political enemies, the editor of *Le Figaro*, the scandal and trial forced Caillaux into political retirement just as the war began. Serving only a few months in the army, Caillaux positioned himself as a potential "peace" premier, willing to negotiate with the Germans. Although he declared that peace must bring the return of Alsace and Lorraine, his trips to Argentina (1914) and Italy (1917), as well as indiscretions at home, saw Caillaux associating with defeatists and German agents.

Premier Georges Clemenceau had Caillaux arrested in January of 1918, but his senate trial for treason was delayed until 1920. Protesting that he "sinned through frivolity," Caillaux was convicted on only a minor charge and amnestied in 1924. He returned to parliament and by 1925 was once again minister of finance. He died on 22 November 1944 at Mamers.

David L. Longfellow

References

Binion, Rudolph. *Defeated Leaders*. New York: Columbia University Press, 1960.

Caillaux, Joseph. *Devant l'histoire*. Paris: Editions de la Sirene, 1920.

Watt, Richard M. *Dare Call It Treason*. New York: Simon and Schuster, 1963.

See also FRANCE, HOME FRONT

Calais Conference (26 February 1917)

Called ostensibly to discuss railroad logistics for the Allies' spring offensive, the Calais Conference of 26 February 1917 was the first attempt to create a unified command for the Allied armies. British Prime Minister David Lloyd George attempted to force his commanders to accept subordination to the French commander in chief. This approach, however, furthered an atmosphere of mistrust and stubbornness that would blunt many future attempts to coordinate the Allied war effort.

Lloyd George had met General Robert Nivelle, France's new commander in chief, during the latter's visit to London in December of 1916. Lloyd George distrusted Field Marshal Sir Douglas Haig and thought his insistence on massive offensives in the west both incorrect and wasteful. In Nivelle he saw a chance to take control of the British army. After informing Chief of the Imperial General Staff Sir William Robertson, Haig's ally, that he did not need to be present, Lloyd George obtained the British war cabinet's approval for his plan to place Nivelle in supreme command.

When the conference convened at Calais, Lloyd George was ready. He spent a half hour closeted with French President Aristide Briand before the open conference. The railroad planners were summarily dismissed, as Lloyd George suggested they move on to the question of plans. Nivelle stepped forward, and after prompting by Lloyd George, chastised Haig for being unwilling to attack as requested. Stating that he was interested in responsibility, not tactics, Lloyd George asked Nivelle to prepare a proposal for a system of command, to be presented that evening.

Nivelle's proposal, which Lloyd George had presented to the war cabinet days earlier, gave the French commander in chief authority over all operational, supply, and administrative functions of the British Expeditionary Force after 1 March 1917. It further stipulated that the French commander be in direct contact with the war cabinet, leaving Haig responsible only for disciplining his troops and carrying out Nivelle's orders. When presented with this, Haig and Robertson were speechless; Robertson, in fact, showed every sign of having a fit.

Haig and Robertson met with Lloyd George the following morning. He agreed the demands were excessive but pointed out that the war cabinet had approved the plan and ordered a blueprint for implementation by the next day. Robertson then confronted Nivelle, who professed surprise that the British were unaware of a proposal their prime minister had suggested a fortnight earlier. Eventually, through negotiation and obstinacy, Robertson was able to win concessions from Nivelle and Lloyd George.

The final agreement left Nivelle in command of the BEF but only for the duration of the coming offensive. Haig and Robertson not only retained the right to appeal Nivelle's actions to the war cabinet but were also able to regain "operational control" over their forces. Even this Haig was willing to sign only "as a correct statement, but not as approving the arrangement."

The Calais agreement would be amended several times and never settled the issue of unity of command. It did, however, cause feelings of distrust on all sides.

Timothy C. Dowling

References

Robbins, Keith, ed. *The Blackwell Biographical Dictionary of British Political Life in the 20th Century*. Oxford: Basil Blackwell, 1990.

Terraine, John. *Douglas Haig, the Educated Soldier*. London: Hutchinson, 1963.

Warner, Phillip. *Field Marshal Earl Haig*. London: Bodley Head, 1991.

Young, Brigadier Peter, ed. *The Marshall Cavendish Illustrated Encyclopedia of World War I*. New York: Marshall Cavendish, 1984.

See also HAIG, SIR DOUGLAS; LLOYD GEORGE, DAVID; NIVELLE, ROBERT; ROBERTSON, SIR WILLIAM

Calthorpe, Sir Somerset Arthur Gough (1864–1937)

British admiral. Born in London on 23 December 1864, the second son of the seventh Baron Calthorpe, he entered the navy in 1878 and commanded the Second Cruiser Squadron, 1914–16, and was second sea lord in 1916. The mild-mannered Calthorpe was a somewhat surprising choice when the British decided to reinstate a Mediterranean commander in chief in the summer of 1917. Calthorpe had the difficult task of coordinating the scattered British naval commands, which ranged from Gibraltar to the Aegean. Although French Admiral Dominique Gauchet remained theoretical commander in chief of Allied forces in the Mediterranean, Calthorpe, who presided over the central direction for routing established at Malta, attempted to gain British control of the antisubmarine campaign. This, indeed, had been the primary British motive for

the establishment of his office. He was only partially successful.

It proved difficult to achieve unity among the Allies, particularly in regard to pooling escorts. An elaborate system of Mediterranean convoys was gradually introduced, although the lack of sufficient escorts remained a problem. Calthorpe remained somewhat skeptical about the value of convoys, especially those through the Mediterranean, since they did not provide complete immunity; he was tempted to divert resources to the Otranto barrage. Fortunately, the admiralty did not agree. On 30 October 1918 Calthorpe concluded an armistice with the Turks at Mudros—deliberately excluding the irate French—and on November 12 he had the satisfaction of leading the combined Allied fleet through the Dardanelles. Calthorpe was high commissioner at Constantinople, 1918–19, and he ended his active career as commander in chief, Portsmouth, 1920–23. He was also the first British naval representative on the armaments commission of the League of Nations. He died at Ryde, Isle of Wight, on 27 July 1937.

Paul G. Halpern

References

Beesly, Patrick. *Very Special Admiral: The Life of Admiral J.H. Godfrey, CB*. London: Hamish Hamilton, 1980.

Godfrey, J.H. *The Naval Memoirs of Admiral J.H. Godfrey*. 7 vols. Hailsham: Privately printed, 1964–66.

Halpern, Paul G. *The Naval War in the Mediterranean, 1914–1918*. Annapolis, Md.: Naval Institute Press, 1987.

———, ed. *The Royal Navy in the Mediterranean, 1915–1918*. Publications of the Navy Records Society, Vol. 126. Aldershot, England: Temple Smith for the Navy Records Society, 1987.

Marder, Arthur J. *From the Dreadnought to Scapa Flow*. Vol. 4, *1917: Year of Crisis*, and Vol. 5, *1918–1919: Victory and Aftermath*. London: Oxford University Press, 1969–70.

See also MEDITERRANEAN NAVAL OPERATIONS

Cambon, Paul (1843–1924)

French civil servant and diplomat. Born in Paris on 20 January 1843, Cambon, the wartime

French ambassador to Great Britain, began his career in 1870 as Jules Ferry's secretary and later served as resident-minister in Tunisia, 1882–86, ambassador to Spain, 1886–91, and Turkey, 1891–98. During the Fashoda Crisis in 1898, Cambon was sent as French ambassador to the Court of St. James, a post he held until 1920. Cambon sought to resolve Anglo-French differences and improve relations between the two countries. His efforts culminated in the creation of the Entente Cordiale in 1904, although he subsequently failed to get an unequivocal British military commitment to support France in case of a continental war against Germany. Cambon considered continuation of the Anglo-French alliance his primary mission, and he skillfully preserved the Entente through the 1904 Dogger Bank Incident and the 1905 Moroccan Crisis in spite of German efforts to destroy the relationship. Cambon supported the idea of Anglo-French military staff talks, as well as Britain's 1907 entente with Russia. During the crisis summer of 1914, Cambon pressed Foreign Secretary Edward Grey to stand by Britain's alliance with France. Cambon remained at his post as ambassador during the war and was an observer at the 1919 Paris Peace Conference. Dissatisfied with the Versailles Treaty, he retired from public life in 1920. Cambon died in Paris on 29 May 1924.

Clayton D. Laurie

References

Eubank, Keith. *Paul Cambon, Master Diplomatist.* Westport, Conn.: Greenwood, 1978.

See also ALLIANCES, PREWAR

Cambrai, Battle of (20 November–5 December 1917)

The battle of Cambrai, where tanks were used en masse for the first time, lasted from 20 November to 5 December 1917. On the British side it involved nineteen divisions and three tank brigades of General Julian Byng's Third Army; on the German side there were six divisions, later reinforced to twenty, of General Georg von der Marwitz's Second Army. Although the British had first used tanks at Flers in September of 1916, then and subsequently they had always deployed them in small packets. At Cambrai, however, more than 400 (including 376 of the latest Mark IV model) were employed under

their own commander, Brigadier General Hugh Elles, as the key element of the British plan.

The year 1917 had gone badly for the Allies—the Bolshevik Revolution had effectively put Russia out of the war, the Central Powers had routed the Italians at Caporetto, the U-boat campaign seemed on the brink of success, and the French and British armies had suffered appalling losses on the Western Front. The Allies wanted to keep as much pressure as possible on the Germans in the west before they could bring in large reinforcements from Russia. Toward that end, British commander in chief Field Marshal Douglas Haig chose for his next attack the sector near Cambrai, a town in northeastern France, 35 miles south of Lille. This area had three advantages: firm, dry ground; sufficient cover to assemble a large attacking force in secrecy; and a weakly held German line.

German defenses at Cambrai consisted of a series of outposts and three well-constructed lines: the main Hindenburg Line, supported by two others about one and four miles farther back. A thirteen-mile-long tunnel, thirty-five feet below the surface, allowed reserves to wait and rest in safety. The British plan had originally been conceived by Colonel J.F.C. Fuller as a large-scale tank raid in reaction against the expensive and ultimately futile tactics used in the Passchendaele Campaign. It was expanded by Byng into a full-blown offensive: His aim was to smash a six-mile-wide gap in the German defenses, capture Bourlon Ridge (a feature four miles west of Cambrai that overlooked this sector of the front) to secure their northern flank, and then launch five cavalry divisions through the gap to disrupt the German rear.

This plan was especially ambitious under World War I conditions. Its success depended on complete surprise and securing Bourlon Ridge before the Germans could deploy their plentiful reserves.

At 06:30 on the dry but foggy morning of 20 November, the well-planned British assault began. The initial attack was made by 374 tanks and five infantry divisions on a six-mile front. Their tactics were more akin to those of World War II, and the units had been well trained. Instead of a long and counterproductive preliminary bombardment, a thousand British guns put down a short but intense barrage on the enemy front line; they then shifted rearward to disrupt the movement of the German reserves and to blind enemy direct-fire artillery with smoke. The tanks, working in teams of three and each carrying a fascine (a large bundle of brushwood used to fill a trench for the passage of vehicles and men), led the advance, closely followed by the infantry—small groups in open order rather than the more usual extended-line assault formation.

Each tank in the team had a well-defined task. The first crushed a gap in the wire, then turned left to work its way down the near side of the front trench; the second used its fascine to cross the trench (often as much as thirteen feet wide) before turning left to work down the far side; the third then moved to the support trench, crossed it and also turned left. Mark IV tanks weighed twenty-eight tons, had a top speed of four MPH, a crew of eight men, and half-inch-thick armor. The "male version" was armed with two 6-pounders and four Lewis guns; the "females" with six Lewis guns. Since the German infantry had no weapon capable of knocking them out, demoralized defenders simply fled, an unusual event for the Germans in either world war. The role of the British infantry was to mop up survivors and to secure the captured trenches against counterattack, ready for the next move forward by the tanks.

On the first day events went largely according to plan. One participant, a British corporal in the Machine Gun Corps, described how he and his gun team plodded forward all day under their eighty-pound loads completely unmolested; they neither fired nor were fired at until after they had dug in that night.

The advance encountered only two setbacks. At Masnieres the Germans blew a canal bridge while a tank was crossing. This forced the infantry to fight without the support of tanks, impeding progress. At Flesquières the commander of the 51st (Highland) Division allowed his tanks to get too far ahead of the infantry. Allegedly, one German defender knocked out between five and sixteen of the tanks (depending on the account) with a field gun. Even on the first day of the age of armored warfare, one lesson was abundantly clear: Tanks, infantry, and artillery must cooperate and not act independently.

By the end of the first day's action the British had penetrated the German lines five miles deep on a front eight miles wide. Their gains included the villages of Graincourt, Flesquières, Ribecourt, Marcoing, Anneux, Cantaing, and Noyelles. In Britain church bells were rung in celebration, as they were to be after Alamein twenty-five years later. But on this occasion, the rejoicing was premature: The key Bourlon Ridge remained in German hands, many tanks had either been knocked out or had suffered mechanical failure, and German reserves were arriving to plug the gap. Mainly as a result of large losses in the Passchendaele Campaign, the British lacked the reserves needed to exploit their initial success. Of the great force of cavalry that Haig had amassed, only one Canadian squadron was actually used. It captured a field battery, dispersed an infantry company, and returned to the British lines on foot with their prisoners.

Fuller's words sum up the battle well: "By 4 P.M. on November 20 one of the most astonishing battles in all history had been won, and as far as the Tank Corps was concerned tactically finished, for, no reserves existing, it was not possible to do more than rally the now very weary and exhausted crews, select the fittest, and patch up composite companies to continue the attack on the morrow." He added: "November 21 saw, generally speaking, the end of any co-operative action between tanks and infantry." The battle now reverted to a typical World War I infantry slogging match.

Although they gained a foothold on Bourlon Ridge, the British never captured it and in the week following 20 November made virtually no more gains. With twenty divisions now available, most of them fresh, the Germans counterattacked on 29 November. Where the initial British attack had depended on the tank, the German counterattack made great use of low-flying aircraft—another foretaste of World War II. When the battle petered out on 5 December, the Germans had regained 75 percent of the territory lost on the first day, and in the extreme south of the battle front even made slight inroads into the original British line. Casualties amounted to 44,000 British and 53,000 Germans.

Whether they realized it at the time or not, on 20 November 1917 the British army initiated the age of armored warfare. Their tactics on that day are hard to fault. But, with insufficient reserves and many tank equipment failures, they were unable to exploit their tremendous success. Ironically, it was the Germans who, twenty-three years later, were to realize the tank's full potential with their *blitzkrieg;* on 18 May 1940 Cambrai was captured by Erwin Rommel's Seventh Panzer division in an afternoon.

Philip J. Green

References

Buchan, John. *A History of the First World War*. Moffat (Dumfries), Scotland: Lochar, 1991.

Chandler, David. *A Traveller's Guide to the Battlefields of Europe: From the Siege of Troy to the Second World War*. Wellingborough, Northhamptonshire, England: Patrick Stephen, 1989.

Livesey, Anthony. *Great Battles of World War I*. London: Michael Joseph, 1989.

See also BYNG, JULIAN; FULLER, J.F.C.; TANK WARFARE; TANKS

Camouflage

From the very beginning of human history, men have practiced the arts of deception and concealment when hunting or fighting their enemies. During the Great War this practice became known as camouflage and was used commonly by both the Central and Allied powers.

The word camouflage comes from the French word *camoufler* (to make up for the stage) and in its military definition relates to the art of concealment, deception, misdirection, and screening. The need for camouflage became increasingly important as binoculars, telescopic sights, and aerial photography came into military use, providing accurate means of target acquisition. The German use of aerial photography over the battlefields of Flanders has been said by some to have been the cause for the development of artificial camouflage. The French had used aerial photography since 1909, but the Germans were the first to fully appreciate its military significance. Also, the French generals had initially been reluctant to eliminate the army's traditional red trousers, but, after the bloody battles of August and September of 1914, even they recognized the need to make soldiers and equipment seemingly disappear into their surroundings.

In September of 1914 a French artist named Guirand de Scevola, who worked as a telephone operator for an artillery unit, came up with the idea of painting canvas sheets in earth colors and using them, instead of natural foliage, to cover artillery pieces when they were not in action. This so impressed the French general staff and President Raymond Poincaré that Guirand was transferred from the artillery, promoted to lieutenant, and became the head of the first *section de camouflage* not only in the French army but in military history. Appropriately, the chameleon became the symbol for the new unit.

Instead of the red kepi and trousers, French soldiers now wore a more neutral powder-blue uniform. Guirand recruited artists and designers to assist him in his new efforts at camouflage, and they did more than just hide big guns and other pieces of equipment under painted canvas. They created fake dead horses and cows to conceal observers. They constructed artificial trees that they then placed on the battlefield at night in place of real trees, which were cut down. An observer then climbed into this artificial tree, where a steel plate protected him. Such observers were frequently connected by telephone to a command post. The *camoufleurs* first built such an artificial tree near Lihors, France, in May of 1915 during the Battle of Artois.

Camouflage became increasingly popular in the French army, creating the need for the formation of new sections. Guirand received promotion to captain and became the overall adviser for camouflage operations on the general staff. By 1918 twelve hundred soldiers and eight thousand civilian women worked for the camouflage service.

The art movement of Cubism might very well have had an influence on the initial use and spread of camouflage. Upon seeing a camouflaged truck for the first time, Pablo Picasso cried out to his companion Gertrude Stein, "Yes, it is we who made it, that is cubism." Certainly the idea of concealment with camouflage does share a concept with Cubism, that the background and foreground should become one object. And Guirand knew of Picasso, saying: "In order to totally deform objects, I employed the means Cubists used to represent them—later this permitted me, without giving reason to hire in my [camouflage] section some painters, who, because of their very special vision, had an aptitude for denaturing any kind of form whatsoever." Picasso might have been right when he remarked, "That is cubism."

The British initially were not as taken with artificial camouflage as the French. In 1914 the artist Solomon J. Solomon proposed to the British army that muslin suspended by bamboo poles should be used to conceal trenches from aerial observation. The commander of the British Expeditionary Force in France, General Sir John French, rejected the idea, but his successor, General Sir Douglas Haig, was very much impressed with the French efforts at camouflage. In late 1915 he made Solomon technical adviser to the recently created British camouflage service. Solomon learned techniques from the French *camoufleurs,* such as the construction of an observation post that resembled a bomb-blasted willow. Made of steel, it weighed 784 pounds and was covered with willow bark from a decaying tree in Windsor Great Park. This observation post tree would eventually be taken to France, and it was used during the Battle of the Somme.

British camouflage operations grew rapidly. Solomon became a lieutenant colonel and recruited other artists and designers, including Walter Russell, an artist and later Keeper of the Royal Academy; L.D. Symington, a theatrical stage designer; Oliver Bernard, an artist-designer who was wounded in 1917; Harry Paget, an artist who became a specialist in tank camouflage; Ian Strang, an etcher of topographical subjects; Colin Gill, a war artist; and Leon Underwood, a sculptor and inventor. They were all put under the command of Lieutenant Colonel Francis Wyatt, an engineering officer. The section became known as the Special Works Park, and on 17 March 1916 they arrived in France and set up operations in an abandoned factory at Wimereux, near Boulogne.

They fulfilled a number of camouflage missions. The new tanks would be painted a pattern of different shades of brown and green, and smoke would be used, along with low-flying airplanes, to screen their movement and muffle their noise. Netting and scrim (a light, sheer, loosely woven cotton or linen cloth) replaced the heavier and more unwieldy canvas used earlier by the French to cover equipment and artillery. The British also used scrim to cover tracks made by vehicles, or to simulate such tracks to deceive the enemy. To confuse snipers, Symington created dummy soldiers that were raised above the trench line to draw fire. Rods were then run through the bullet holes, thus determining the direction of fire. He also created sniper suits of painted scrim material. These suits came in two types: a one-piece suit with detachable hood, and a loose coat with hood attached and separate leggings. The completed ensemble included gloves and a rifle cover. Symington also designed concealed machine-gun positions covered with gauze so that the gunner could see out while remaining invisible to the enemy. Camouflage came to play such a large part in the British army

that a camouflage school was set up in London to train officers in the art of camouflage for assignment to combat units, thus reducing the need for camouflage experts to be exposed to fire.

The Germans had used camouflage (*Tarnung*) in early 1916, employing expressionist painter Franz Marc to create nets and canvases to conceal German artillery at the Battle of Verdun, but they did not have a formal camouflage section until after the Battle of Cambrai in 1917. The Germans made several innovations in the area of structural camouflage. They disguised hangars and planes at an airfield near St. Pierre Capelle in Flanders in such a manner as to resemble a farmhouse, complete with garden and fields. The Germans also undertook large-scale camouflage operations in preparation for the big March 1918 Western Front offensive. Strategic roads to the front were laced with overhead netting and side curtains, and German *camoufleurs* constructed large camouflaged shelters to obscure troop activity from aerial and ground observation. These procedures gave the Germans an element of surprise in the offensive.

Camouflage was used at sea as well as on land during the First World War. The British admiralty used decoy vessels called Q-ships—tugs, fishing trawlers or tramp steamers armed with carefully concealed guns—to lure in unsuspecting German U-boats. Unrestricted submarine warfare lessened the effectiveness of Q-ships, so another act of concealment, dazzle painting, was employed by the British to cut losses to the U-boats. First suggested by Norman Wilkenson, a British naval commander, the dazzle concept of painting ships sought to harmonize light colors, white and blue, with the color of the sky, to distort the ship's shape by adding black and dark gray to a pattern of sloping lines, curves, and stripes. By 1917 the admiralty ordered most merchant ships to be painted in the dazzle pattern, with admittedly mixed results. The Germans did not use decoy ships or dazzle paint on their merchant vessels to any extent, largely because the Allies did not authorize attacks on merchant ships.

By the conclusion of World War I, camouflage became an integral part of strategic and tactical combat operations in the air, on land, and on sea. Even if only marginally effective, the value of concealment and deception became obvious to the military forces of both the Central and Allied powers.

Richard A. Voeltz

References

Addison, G.H. *The Work of the Royal Engineers in the European War, 1914–1918.* London, 1926.

Hartcup, Guy. *Camouflage: A History of Concealment and Deception in War.* New York: Charles Scribner's Sons, 1980.

Kern, Stephen. *The Culture of Time and Space, 1880–1918.* Cambridge: Harvard University Press, 1983.

Solomon, S.J. *Strategic Camouflage.* London, 1920.

Sumrall, Robert F. "Ship Camouflage (WWI): Deceptive Art," *U.S. Naval Institute Proceedings* (July 1971): 55–77.

See also Q-SHIPS

Canada, Army

When the news of war in Europe reached Canada on 5 August 1914, it was greeted with enthusiasm. Men flocked to the colors. A division was rapidly promised to Britain, and Sir Sam Hughes, the minister of militia and defense, instigated a bewildering system for the raising of troops. The first rush of men was accommodated at Valcartier Camp, Quebec, and prepared for their trip overseas. On 3 October 1914 the 1st Division, 31,200 strong, sailed for Britain. They endured a miserable winter on the Salisbury Plain before finally reaching France the next spring. Before they arrived in Britain, the Canadian government had made the offer of another division.

In April of 1915 the Canadian Division was holding a section of the line in the Ypres Salient when the Germans unveiled gas warfare, and the Canadians had their baptism of fire. A smattering of Canadian and British troops were thrown into the gap created by the gas, and they managed to hold up the Germans, who were unprepared for the scale of their success. A confusing battle ensued during which the Canadian Division held its ground at the cost of over six thousand casualties, in the process creating a reputation that Canadians would have to live up to for the duration of the war.

In September of 1915 2nd Division arrived in France (3rd Division arrived in early 1916 and 4th Division in August that year), and Lieutenant General Sir Edwin Alderson took command of the newly formed Canadian Corps, being replaced as 1st Division commander by a Victoria real estate man, Arthur Currie. The 2nd Division had its baptism attempting to hold the St. Eloi craters, a confusing and confused struggle that cost Alderson his command, but only because he, as corps commander, was ultimately responsible for the trouble. Alderson became a scapegoat.

Alderson's replacement in May of 1916 was Lieutenant General Sir Julian Byng, who had commanded IX Corps in the Dardanelles. Byng proved to be an extremely capable corps commander; he was determined to turn the four Canadian divisions into first-class troops deserving of their reputation. He first worked on discipline in the ranks, as he believed that acting like good soldiers was a prerequisite for becoming so. Byng was also a careful planner who did not believe in futile attacks that wasted the lives of his troops. Byng's program culminated in the capture of the bastion of Vimy Ridge on Easter Monday 1917. The Canadian Corps, attacking for the first and only time with all four divisions in the battle line, followed a dense creeping barrage and careful preparation and carried the ridge in a matter of hours. It gained them a reputation as formidable attacking troops, similar to the Australians. Byng was rewarded with an army command and replaced by Lieutenant General Sir Arthur Currie, a Canadian.

Under Currie the Canadians took Lens. Their capture of Hill 70 forced the Germans out of Lens. The battle for Hill 70, designed to divert German attention from Passchendaele by playing on the Canadian reputation, succeeded as an operation, although it failed as a diversion because the Germans simply felt that the Canadian Corps, no matter how formidable, was not as great a threat as two full armies attacking near Passchendaele. In the battle for Hill 70, the Canadians used the German propensity to counterattack against them. Their plan involved advancing to a limited depth, digging in, and repelling German counterattacks by artillery, machine gun, and rifle fire. It worked well, but that success led inevitably to Passchendaele.

Having exhausted the Australians in attempting to seize Passchendaele Ridge, Field Marshal Sir Douglas Haig turned to the Canadian Corps to finish the job. Currie did not want the corps to go and agreed only on the condition that he be given time to prepare the attack. Haig agreed and Currie had the luxury of time denied to the Australians. Once the logistic infrastructure in the salient was repaired, the corps launched four well-spaced attacks and took its objectives. It cost 16,000 casualties overall, almost exactly what Currie had predicted. Immediately afterward, the corps was moved to the Vimy-Arras region for the winter.

During the spring 1918 Ludendorff Offensives, the corps maintained its integrity because of Currie's political influence. The corps ended up holding nearly one-fifth of the British Expeditionary Force's frontage by April, but, unlike the Australians, saw no action. During this time, Currie opposed the expansion of the corps into an army on the grounds that it would promote inefficiency by doubling the staff component of the corps. Rather, he had the battalions of the corps strengthened, so that the corps, by the summer, had nearly the striking power of an army with the administrative overhead of a corps.

At Amiens on 8 August 1918 the Canadian Corps and Australian Corps spearheaded the attack that is generally acknowledged as the beginning of the end for the German army. They made an eight-mile advance, having been secretly inserted into the battle line beside the Australians when the Germans believed them to be in the north. Amiens began an unbroken, but costly, string of successes for the corps. Later in the summer, they cracked the Drocourt-Quèant Switch of the Hindenburg Line in eight hours and forced the Canal du Nord to a depth of some eight miles in one day. For the corps the war ended at Mons, which they recaptured some hours before the Armistice.

The Canadian "army" was embodied for most of the war in the Canadian Corps. Constituted in 1915, political pressure allowed it to fight together—unlike the Australians—for the duration of the war. The successes of the Canadian Corps in France helped to earn Canada's true independence from Britain, which was to be manifest in September of 1939 when the government declared war on Germany, independently of Britain.

Ian M. Brown

References

Duguid, A.F. *Official History of the Canadian Forces in the Great War, 1914–1919.* Ottawa: King's Printer, 1938.

Nicholson, G.W.L. *Canadian Expeditionary Force, 1914–1919.* Ottawa: Queen's Printer, 1964.

Swettenham, John. *Canada and the First World War.* Toronto: Ryerson, 1967.

See also ALLIED COUNTEROFFENSIVE; BYNG, JULIAN; CANADA, ROLE IN WAR; CURRIE, SIR ARTHUR; PASSCHENDAELE; VIMY RIDGE; YPRES, SECOND BATTLE OF

Canada, Navy

The Canadian navy of 1914 consisted of only 350 men of all ranks, with another 250 partially trained reservists working two old cruisers, two submarines, and a motley assortment of small craft. The prewar attitude in Ottawa and London had ignored the navy; the rationale was that the Royal Navy's protection meant that Canada did not need a navy. Early in the war that attitude was reinforced in England—London wanted troops for service in France, not a Canadian navy. Ottawa inquired informally in October of 1914 about increasing the navy's strength but was rebuffed by the admiralty, as ships took too long to build.

While such attitudes did not change appreciably, because of an understandable fixation on the Canadian Corps in France, there was a role for the navy in the war—primarily that of convoy protection. Indeed, the officers and men of the *Rainbow* had the distinction of being the first Canadians to risk their lives when they set out from Esquimalt to search for the German cruiser *Leipzig*. Luckily, they did not find her.

Convoy protection became particularly important in 1917 after the United States entered the war. Halifax, New Brunswick, and Sydney, Nova Scotia, were two major assembly ports for convoys in 1917. Halifax was to repeat its role in the Second World War, the legacy of a large, well-protected anchorage.

The largest incident involving the Royal Canadian Navy (RCN) was the explosion of the ammunition ship *Mont Blanc* in Halifax harbor on 6 December 1917. The *Mont Blanc* collided with another ship and caught fire. She blew up while an RCN scuttling party from *Niobe* was climbing her hull. The cargo of 2,700 tons of guncotton, pyric acid, and TNT below decks, with benzol on the decks, created the largest manmade explosion until Hiroshima. It leveled over one square mile of Halifax, killed 1,600 people, injured another 9,000, and left 50,000 homeless. In addition, it ruined Halifax as a convoy staging area at a time when the harbor and its facilities were badly needed.

By November of 1918, the RCN had grown to 9,600 men and officers and over one hundred small ships (destroyers, armed trawlers) plus an embryonic Naval Air Service. While this was a significant change, the RCN suffered throughout the war from a fixation on the Canadian Corps, the Western Front, and a lack of enthusiasm for an independent navy in London. The RCN would have to wait until the Second World War before becoming a significant factor in Canadian defense policy.

Ian M. Brown

References

Morton, Desmond. *Canada and War.* Toronto: Butterworth, 1981.
Stacey, C.P. *Canada and the Age of Conflict, Volume I: 1867–1921.* Toronto: University of Toronto Press, 1984.

See also CANADA, ROLE IN WAR

Canada, Role in War

When the First World War began, Canadians flocked to the colors and rallied behind Great Britain. That was no surprise, given the high proportion of Canadians who had emigrated from Britain or whose parents had emigrated from there. The scale of commitment during the ensuing four years was quite remarkable.

In 1914 Canada's population of eight million people was spread out on the second largest country on earth. An agrarian society blessed with vast areas for the production of food, Canada was able to send large amounts of grain and meat overseas to support Britain. The expansion of the industrial infrastructure was quite profound. By the end of the war the Imperial Munitions Board had supervised a wide variety of production not limited to munitions such as aircraft. The Canadian Vickers firm in Montreal had built submarines for Italy from parts provided by the Bethlehem Steel Corporation, after Congress decided that American neutrality would be violated if they were constructed in the United States. While Canada did not become an industrial nation, the foundation had been laid.

In 1914 Canada had a tiny army and a marginally trained militia. Nonetheless, Ottawa's offer of 25,000 men to Britain was immediate. The flood of volunteers in 1914 allowed for an overstrength division to be sent to Britain on 3 October 1914 for further training—three more would follow by 1916. Of more than 600,000 Canadians mobilized to fight in France, over 60,000 were killed and 173,000 wounded. It was a level of loss that could not be maintained by voluntary enlistment.

A manpower crisis in late 1916 led the government of Robert Borden (prime minister since 1911) to consider the conscription of men for overseas service. At the time it was perceived that Quebec was not pulling its weight in enlistments. While it was true that there were fewer Quebecois in the trenches, the cultural and social factors that made this so were overlooked. Borden was forced to call an election in December of 1917, and, while there were other considerations, the election was fought over conscription. Borden, a Conservative in 1911, was reelected as the Unionist (proconscription) prime minister in an election filled with dirty tricks. These included the selective enfranchisement of female relatives of servicemen; the use of overseas (serving soldiers') votes, usually where the issue was close; and the disenfranchisement of immigrants from belligerent countries, who tended to vote Liberal. On the whole, it was a crooked election, the result of which was not in doubt. Since most of Canada voted Unionist and Quebec came down Liberal, this led to Quebec's isolation and a crisis as grave as any Canada has ever faced.

The success of the Canadian Corps in battle in France led to an emergent nationalism in Canada. While most of the volunteers in the early phase of the war had been of English birth and thought of themselves as Englishmen, by 1917 many were thinking of themselves as Canadians. Recognizing the change in Canadian attitudes, Borden sought a greater voice in how Canadian troops were to be employed in France. Because Australia, South Africa, and New Zealand expressed similar nationalist sentiments, this ultimately led to the formation of David Lloyd George's Imperial War Cabinet.

Canada entered the war as a self-governing but dependent dominion of Great Britain. Canada's armed forces were negligible, her industrial infrastructure in its infancy, and she was dependent on London for the exercise of her diplomacy. Canada emerged from the war, having seen battlefield success in France, with a large army (rapidly demobilizing), and considerably more industrial capacity—a truly self-governing nation-state. The relationship with the United States changed dramatically in 1917, as the U.S. entry into the war led to a rapprochement and the end of decades of suspicion and mistrust. Canada had become a junior ally, rather than a dominion. This was to manifest itself in the 1931 Statute of Westminster, in which Canada became responsible for its own diplomacy, and, on 10 September 1939, in an independent declaration of war against Nazi Germany in support of Britain.

Ian M. Brown

References
Brown, R.C., and G.R. Cook. *Canada 1896–1921: A Nation Transformed.* Toronto: McClelland and Stewart, 1974.
Morton, Desmond. *Canada and War.* Toronto: Butterworth, 1981.
Stacey, C.P. *Canada and the Age of Conflict, Volume I: 1867–1921.* Toronto: University of Toronto Press, 1984.

See also BORDEN, SIR ROBERT; CANADA, ARMY; CANADA, NAVY

Capelle, Eduard von (1855–1931)

German admiral and state secretary of the naval office, 1916–1918. Born on 10 October 1855 in Celle, Capelle joined the German navy in 1872 and held primarily shipboard commands before becoming director of the Administrative Department of the Naval Office (1905–14). One of Admiral Alfred von Tirpitz's early associates, he showed expertise in preparing naval budgets, dealt skillfully with the Reichstag, and maintained a realistic view of the fleet's mission.

Having been raised into the Prussian nobility (1912) and made full admiral (1913), Capelle served as under secretary of the naval office early in the war. Appreciation for the primacy of political over military demands gradually alienated him from Tirpitz and hastened his retirement in late 1915. Upon Tirpitz's dismissal in March of 1916, Capelle was reactivated and succeeded his former mentor as state secretary. While promoting smoother relations with the Reichstag, Capelle increasingly felt that unrestricted submarine warfare might turn the tide of war after all. His lukewarm endorsement of additional battleship building programs, his uneasiness over how the naval mutinies were handled, and his ill-fated efforts to purge the Reichstag of leftist deputies soon estranged him from fellow officers and civilian leaders alike. Despite his growing unpopularity, Capelle managed to stay in office until Septem-

ber of 1918. He died at Wiesbaden on 23 February 1931.

Eric C. Rust

References
Görlitz, Walter, ed. *The Kaiser and His Court: The Diaries, Note Books and Letters of Admiral Georg Alexander von Müller, Chief of the Naval Cabinet, 1914–1918.* New York: Harcourt, Brace, World, 1964.
Herwig, Holger H. *The German Naval Officer Corps: A Social and Political History, 1890–1918.* Oxford: Oxford University Press, 1973.
Horn, Daniel. *The German Naval Mutinies of World War I.* New Brunswick: Rutgers University Press, 1969.
Hubatsch, Walther. *Der Admiralstab und die obersten Marinebehörden in Deutschland. 1848–1945.* Frankfurt: Bernard, Graefe, 1958.

See also TIRPITZ, ALFRED VON

Capello, Luigi Attilo (1859–1941)

Italian general. Born in Intra of humble origins on 14 April 1859, Capello was commissioned in the army as a lieutenant in 1878. He rose steadily and was made a major general in 1910; the following year he commanded a brigade against the Turks in Libya. Known for concern for his men, Capello's success in leading an infantry division at the Carso in June of 1915 led to his promotion to lieutenant general in September. Although his Sixth Corps won the first major triumph of Italian arms in the war at Gorizia in the summer of 1916, Capello nonetheless fell prey to politics when Cadorna exiled him in September to the quiet Trentino sector.

Capello returned to play a key role in the Eleventh Battle of Isonzo (19 August–12 September 1917) as commander of the Second Army, which was charged with attacking the Bainsizza Plateau. His success there caused the Austro-Hungarians to seek reinforcements from the Germans. In the resulting Austro-German breakthrough at Caporetto, the Second Army was broken. Capello must bear, along with Cadorna, responsibility for the debacle. Instead of following Cadorna's orders to withdraw artillery from the Bainsizza to the west bank of the Isonzo, he prepared for a counteroffensive to hit the attacker's flanks. He also placed his worst troops in the area of greatest danger.

Ill health forced Capello to leave his command before the Battle of Caporetto, but he returned by the time of the enemy attack on 24 October, when he suffered a complete physical collapse. Capello urged Cadorna to withdraw some thirty miles to the Tagliamento River; his sound advice was rejected, enabling the enemy to push well beyond the Tagliamento to the Piave Line.

Although Capello recovered his health, he did not again return to command. A subsequent parliamentary investigation into the Caporetto disaster blamed both Capello and Cadorna.

After the war, Capello was one of Mussolini's earliest supporters and joined him in the march on Rome. He assisted in negotiations with Germany in 1924 but parted company with Mussolini as the latter moved toward dictatorship. In November of 1925 he was arrested for complicity in a plot with socialist deputy Tito Zaniboni to assassinate Mussolini and was sentenced to thirty years imprisonment on Ponza Island. Health problems led to his release from confinement in 1936. Capello died in Rome on 25 June 1941.

Spencer C. Tucker

References

Capello, Luigi. *Caporetto, perché?* Turin: G. Einaudi, 1967.

Herwig, Holger, and Neil M. Heyman. *Biographical Dictionary of World War I.* Westport, Conn.: Greenwood, 1982.

Seth, Ronald. *Caporetto: The Scapegoat Battle.* New York: Macmillan, 1965.

Whittam, John. *The Politics of the Italian Army, 1861–1918.* Hamden, Conn.: Archon, 1977.

See also CADORNA, LUIGI; CAPORETTO, BATTLE OF; ISONZO, BATTLES OF, 5–9, 10 AND 11

Caporetto (Twelfth Battle of the Isonzo), 24 October to 25 December 1917

Caporetto is the only battle fought in Italy during the Great War that has survived in the popular memory. The overwhelming Italian defeat at Caporetto has preserved and reinforced the image of the Italian soldier who preferred desertion or surrender to fighting, as well as the legend that German troops and tactics were so superior to those of the Italians and Austro-Hungarians that the mere presence of seven German divisions almost drove Italy out of the war. Italian scholars Angelo Gatti and Mario Caracciolo recognized more than sixty years ago that the Italian defeat at Caporetto had been exceptional, and they pointed out that the Italian army recovered quickly to destroy the Austro-Hungarian forces at Vittorio Veneto a year later. Caracciolo thought that Italy's allies played up the rout of the Italian Second Army at Caporetto in order to cover their own lackluster performance during 1917, when the British Army was impotent, the Russian prostrate, and the French riddled with disaffection and mutiny.

The Italians themselves have kept the debate about Caporetto alive because the defeat was a rude shock after their earlier victories, and it triggered a search for scapegoats. Caporetto became a symbol for left-wing and papal defeatism as well as a synonym for political corruption and military incompetence, as generals without powerful friends were sacrificed to protect those with connections. But the Italian defeat at Caporetto was no more caused by socialists, the Pope, or an incompetent general staff than it was by congenitally inept Italian soldiers faced with superior German troops. The German presence and the use of a new tactic merely tilted the scales just enough to throw the Italians temporarily off balance, and the nature of the Italian front transformed a tactical victory into a strategic retreat, which ended with a solid Italian defensive performance on the Piave River.

Convinced that Italy's success on the Bainsizza Plateau in August of 1917 required Germany to aid Vienna to knock Italy out of the war, Berlin transferred seven divisions to the Isonzo, where they joined with Austro-Hungarian forces to form the Fourteenth Austrian Army under the command of German General Otto von Below. Overall command of the Central Powers along the Isonzo was under Austro-Hungarian Field Marshal Baron Svetozar Boroević von Bojna. To achieve local air superiority the Central Powers brought in air units from as far away as the Carpathians, giving them a squadron for every kilometer of front at Caporetto. In the three weeks leading up to the attack on 24 October nine days were too overcast for air reconnaissance, and conditions were so bad on the 24th that neither side could fly. It was therefore difficult for the Italians to ascertain the extent of the enemy buildup, and during the first day of the attack fog and rain hid the advance of German and Austrian units along the valley floors.

Even so, the Italians were aware that something was afoot between the Plezzo Gap and Tolmino, and on 21–22 October Czech and Romanian deserters warned that a major offensive was imminent. Ironically, the Italian command, which had doubted Austria-Hungary's intention to attack in the Trentino in 1916, now dismissed the possibility of a large-scale offensive on the northern Isonzo because they believed that the Austrians would attack in the Trentino, a suspicion that a diversionary attack there on 27 October seemed to confirm.

As Luigi Cadorna worried over the wrong sector, General Luigi Capello, commander of the Second Army, fretted about an attack on the northern stretch of the Isonzo. He reinforced his left wing and requested three additional divisions, but he received only seven battalions of alpine troops and a brigade of *bersaglieri*. Whether he might have done more had he not been incapacitated by an attack of nephritis, a painful kidney disorder, is not clear. But he had issued no specific orders regarding defensive dispositions prior to going to a clinic in Padua on 20 October, and he did not return to his command until the 24th, too late to affect events.

Cadorna had ordered Capello to deploy only covering forces in forward positions, to use his artillery to interdict the enemy's batteries, and to throw up a short, intense barrage prior to counterattacking, should the Second Army be attacked. These aggressive orders were apparently the result of Cadorna's conviction that the front line was always overrun and that the only maneuver possible in trench warfare was the use of reserves. But Cadorna checked defensive dispositions of the Second and Third armies only on 22 October, when his visit to Second Army's IV Corps upset him so much that, on the following day, he castigated Capello and General Pietro Badoglio, commander of XXVII Corps, for failing to look after their defenses. He complained, "My father took Rome, and it falls to me to lose it!"

Although the outburst was not prophetic, the IV Corps was extremely vulnerable, because the Second Army's reserves were too far to the south to help should it be hard pressed. Badoglio had also put three divisions on the left bank, leaving the 19th Division to cover thirty

kilometers of territory on the right; and he had deployed the Napoli Brigade so high that it could not quickly intervene on the floor of the Isonzo valley. Finally, Badoglio's headquarters were too far to the rear, and he hesitated to commit his reserves when the attack came, thereby facilitating the enemy's tactic of infiltrating Italian positions by advancing along the valley floors.

The new German/Austro-Hungarian Fourteenth Army under Below was to lead the assault, supported by the Austro-Hungarian Tenth Army on the right and the Fifth Army on the left. The Central Powers had deployed an additional 1,600 guns, bringing their total to 4,126, each with 1,000 rounds of shell. By slow, sporadic targeting of their artillery over several days, the Austrians had misled the Italians regarding the number of guns in the area, but, with a gun every 4.4 meters, the barrage on 24 October was intense. It was also deep, reaching four to five kilometers into the Italian lines; and short, opening at 02:00, lifting briefly at 04:15, then resuming as a massive mine blew off the top of Monte Rosso and overturned Italian positions on Monte Mrzli at 07:30. It peaked at 08:00, as the infantry went over the top. In the Plezzo Gap alone, one thousand gas shells landed in the first thirty seconds of the barrage, killing six hundred men.

With twenty-five divisions and two thousand guns on a twenty-five-kilometer front, Capello's Second Army was certainly capable of contesting the Austro-German advance, had it been able to coordinate its response. Although the Austro-German forces advanced six kilometers in the first twelve hours, resistance was fierce and the troops in the Plezzo Gap and on Monte Nero held through the evening. But heavy fog and the damage done to Italian telephone wires by the barrage disoriented the Italians. As gunners strained to see their targets, commanders hesitated to give orders to fire, and while some artillery units reacted, others did not. As a result, the first wave of attackers crossed into Italian lines with few casualties.

The collapse of the 46th Division near Sleme and Mrzli isolated the 43rd, which was still fighting, and allowed the 12th Silesian to reach the bridge at Caporetto at 15:00 on the 24th. Austrian and German units moved up thinly held valley floors against service units and reserve battalions hastily deployed in unprepared positions, even though front-line troops fought well. The IV Corps held, but it

C

lacked the reserves to do so for long. With the Napoli Brigade too high to intervene and communications links in the forward positions cut by the artillery barrage, its flank was turned on the 25th.

On the evening of the 24th the 19th Division remained viable, German units had failed to reach their objectives, and the 1st Austro-Hungarian Division had suffered heavy casualties. In the Italian army, however, services in forward areas had been battered by the barrage and had begun to melt away, even though there was little damage to Italian rear areas. Gunners also began to abandon their pieces, and at 18:00 the commander of the 50th Division decided to withdraw, opening a large gap in the Italian line. Still, the Italians held the Saga defile to Polounik in the north, the 43rd Division continued to resist, the VII Corps held the twenty-kilometer sector from Matajur to Kolovrat to Monte Xum, and Italian troops still occupied Globocak to the south.

The collapse of the 46th Division and retreat of the 50th opened crucial gaps in the Italian lines, raising concerns in the Italian high command that the flanks of the Third Army to the south and the Fourth and First to the north and west might be turned if the attackers reached the Tagliamento River, which also guarded the high command's headquarters at Udine. On the 26th, Cadorna therefore created a special army corps with the 20th and 33rd divisions under the command of General Di Giorgio to hold the bridges over the river. On the 26th, however, Badoglio's XXVII Corps retreated, the VII Corps collapsed, and General Villani of the 19th Division committed suicide as his division was finally overrun. With the key stronghold of Montemaggiore abandoned and his front disintegrating, Cadorna ordered a retreat to the Tagliamento, where he intended to resist until positions on the Piave River could be prepared. Caracciolo considered the decision "heroic," but it conceded the Austro-German forces a major tactical victory and forced a retreat in the north in order to close the gap that the collapse of the Second Army had opened between the Fourth and Third armies.

On 27 October the Italian command moved from Udine to Treviso. High waters of the Tagliamento funneled the Italian armies over a few permanent bridges, slowing the retreat and putting Third Army at risk as enemy forces advanced from the north almost as fast as d'Aosta's troops moved from the south. On the 28th the Italian command issued a bulletin blaming the failure to resist of a few units of Second Army for the rout and calling on everyone to fight as they had done since 1915 to stop the invader.

Although on 30 October the Second Army's retreating right wing could use only the bridge at Modrisio, by the evening of the 31st the Third Army was over the Tagliamento. The Italians repulsed Austrian efforts to cross it until the night of 2–3 November, when falling water allowed parts of the 55th Austro-Hungarian Division to ford the river at Cornino. At 10:00 on the 4th the high command ordered all bridges on the Tagliamento destroyed, and it withdrew behind the Piave. The bridges on the Piave were destroyed the morning of the 9th, the same day that Armando Diaz replaced Cadorna as supreme commander.

Forced to reorganize and bring up their artillery, the Central Powers could not press their attack. With only thirty-three divisions, 3,986 guns, and six airfields behind the Piave, the Italians faced fifty-five Austro-German divisions, worse odds than the Entente had encountered on the Marne in 1914. But Diaz now had two hundred fewer kilometers of front to defend, and his troops were entrenched behind a river line in the south and anchored on the Asiago Plateau and Monte Grappa to the north, a good strategic position for the first time in the war. They were facing troops flushed with victory but worn out after a seventy-kilometer pursuit. The last efforts by Boroević to pierce the Piave Line and flank it by overwhelming the Fourth Army on Monte Grappa failed between 11 and 18 December, and Boroević suspended the offensive on Christmas Day. The Italians had thus salvaged a situation that seemed lost, and by doing so they felt that they had reclaimed their honor and saved their war effort—especially since five British and six French divisions that arrived in early November refused to enter the line until the Italians had made it "safe" to do so.

Nonetheless, 3,152 guns had been lost; twenty-two airfields had been abandoned; 40,000 men had died; 280,000 had been taken prisoner; and 350,000 had lost touch with their units. Yet such losses were not unique: The French and the British would suffer similar losses during the German offensives in France in March and May of 1918, when German units advanced about seventy kilometers. As their allies would be in 1918, the Italians had been the victim of the new infiltration tactics first used by the Germans against the Russians at Riga in September of 1917.

Infiltration had certain constant characteristics and it tended to achieve similar results, which could not be exploited further because nonmotorized armies had limited pursuit capabilities. Intended to achieve breakthroughs and deep penetrations of enemy positions without armor, the German "Hutier" tactics amassed forces covertly by moving troops at night, keeping them hidden during the day, and targeting single artillery pieces over several days. Artillery barrages were short and intense, using high-explosive and gas shells in a single sector to disrupt enemy communications and disorient enemy artillery. Attackers bypassed, rather than reduced, strong points; they punched corridors deep into the enemy's rear, rather than trying to advance along a whole front. This isolated front-line units, disrupted communications, and reached the rear areas before significant enemy reserves could be brought into play.

If the Italian experience was repeated in France, there were factors specific to the Italian front that turned a tactical defeat into a strategic disaster. In Italy any breakthrough was a threat to the whole front, whereas in France and Russia a large salient could be gained with little threat to the rest of the front. With no reserves, and British and French troops unwilling to enter the line until it was "safe," the Italians could not count on their allies to help; the Austrians had the support of German troops. The movement of units and ordnance in mountainous terrain was more difficult than rushing reinforcements to the front in flat country. And, as in France, civilian morale in Italy was at a low ebb and the troops were worn out. Given a series of command errors and bad weather that masked the preparations and initial assault, the Italian defeat, if not inevitable, was explicable.

But it did not seem so at the time. Some blamed workers from Turin, who had been sent to the front as a punishment, for infecting the troops with their defeatist attitudes. Others castigated Cadorna and Capello for depressing morale with their harsh discipline and rigid personalities; Cadorna seemed to blame the troops in his communiqué of 28 October. The army resorted to summary execution and decimation to punish mutinous units and to make examples of those who had fled to the rear during the retreat; that reinforced the general impression of chaos and panic, with incompetent and bloodthirsty generals punishing their own troops rather than fighting the enemy.

Yet, by the summer of 1918, Diaz had 7,000 guns in line, including 1,100 Allied pieces, and the army had created 104 new infantry regiments; 47 infantry battalions; 812 machine-gun, 69 sapper, and 72 telegraph companies; and various other units from the 355,000 troops who had been "disbanded" during the retreat. By June of 1918 there were fifty Italian and four Allied divisions on the Piave to repulse Boroević's last major offensive. In October the Italians annihilated the Austro-Hungarian army at Vittorio Veneto, on the anniversary of their defeat at Caporetto.

James J. Sadkovich

References

Capello, Luigi. *Caporetto, perché?* Turin: Einaudi, 1967.

Caracciolo, Mario. *L'Italia nella guerra mondiale*. Rome: Edizioni Roma, 1935.

Fadini, Francesco, ed. *Caporetto dalla parte del vincitore: La biografia del generale Otto von Below e il suo diario inedito sulla campagna d'Italia del 1917.* Firenze: Vallecchi, 1974.

Gatti, Angelo. *La parte dell'Italia, rivendicazioni*. Milan: Mondadori, 1926.

Pieri, Piero. *L'Italia nella prima guerra mondiale (1915–1918)*. Turin: Einaudi, 1968.

Rochat, Giorgio. *L'Italia nella prima guerra mondiale. Problemi di interpretazione e prospettive di ricerca*. Milan: Feltrinelli, 1976.

Valori, Aldo. *La guerra italo-austriaca, 1915–1918*. Bologna: Nicola Zanichelli, 1920.

See also BADOGLIO, PIETRO; BELOW, OTTO VON; BOROEVIĆ VON BOJNA, SVETOZAR; CADORNA, LUIGI; CAPELLO, LUIGI; ITALY, ARMY; ITALY, HOME FRONT

Carden, Sir Sackville Hamilton (1857–1930)

British admiral. Born 3 May 1857 at Templemore, Tipperary, Carden first entered the navy in 1870; he was promoted to captain in 1887 and rear admiral in 1908. Carden was admiral superintendent at the Malta dockyard at the beginning of the war. He was replaced there in September of 1914 by Admiral Arthur Limpus, former head of the British naval mission in

Turkey. Churchill had originally wanted to give Limpus (with his presumed local knowledge) command of the naval forces blockading the Dardanelles, but the foreign office still hoped that Turkey would remain neutral and thought the choice of Limpus would offend the Turks. Carden, therefore, switched places with Limpus.

Carden was able to provide support for Churchill's plan to attack the Dardanelles. He did not believe that the Straits could be taken in a rush, but he did believe that the superiority of naval firepower over that of the Turkish forts would permit the Dardanelles to be forced after methodical operations. The first phase would be to reduce the forts at the entrance, then the inner forts, and finally the defenses of the narrows, which would permit clearing the minefields. Carden began his bombardment on 19 February. It proved relatively easy to dominate the outer Turkish defenses, but it was another story when ships had to operate in the restricted waters of the Straits to attack the inner defenses. Concealed guns and mobile howitzers made it impossible for the battleships to anchor for accurate fire, and spotting proved difficult to impossible. Turkish gunfire prevented the minesweepers from clearing the minefields, and that, in turn, prevented the battleships from closing. On 11 March the admiralty, believing Turkish ammunition to be low, ordered Carden to press for a decision, even at the cost of some loss. The British planned a daylight attack for the 18th, but on the 16th Carden was forced by ill health to relinquish his command to Rear Admiral John de Robeck. Carden thus became one of the great "might-have-beens" of history, although there is nothing to indicate that the results of 18 March would have been different under his leadership.

Admiral Carden retired from the navy as a full admiral in October of 1917. He died at Lymington on 6 May 1930.

Paul G. Halpern

References

Gilbert, Martin. *Winston S. Churchill*. Vol. 3, *The Challenge of War, 1914–1916*. Boston: Houghton Mifflin, 1971.

Halpern, Paul G., ed. *The Keyes Papers*. Vol. 1, *1914–1918*. Publications of the Navy Records Society, Vol. 117. London: Navy Records Society, 1972. Reprint. London: Allen & Unwin, 1979.

Keyes, Admiral of the Fleet Sir Roger. *The Naval Memoirs*. Vol. 1, *The Narrow Seas to the Dardanelles, 1910–1915*. London: Thornton Butterworth, 1934.

Marder, Arthur J. "The Dardanelles Revisited: Further Thoughts on the Naval Prelude." In *From the Dardanelles to Oran: Studies of the Royal Navy in War and Peace, 1915–1935*. London: Oxford University Press, 1974.

———. *From the Dreadnought to Scapa Flow: The Royal Navy in the Fisher Era, 1904–1919*. Vol. 2, *The War Years: To the Eve of Jutland*. London: Oxford University Press, 1965.

See also DARDANELLES CAMPAIGN; DE ROBECK, JOHN

Carrier Pigeons

Carrier pigeons were used throughout World War I as combat messengers. The German general staff early on perceived their potential and by 1887 had secured some 3,000 for the army. As the Germans advanced on Paris in 1914, they adopted a policy of destroying all pigeons captured in occupied Belgian and French territory. The British, who also feared enemy spies, reportedly ordered the relocation or destruction of pigeons found along the Channel coast. The British also used pigeons for communications assistance in minesweeping operations and in locating downed planes. Allied governments reported a 95 percent success rate for messages delivered by pigeons in combat, including one that read: "Take it away; I'm tired of carrying this damned bird."

Estimates of the number of pigeons used in the war range as high as 500,000. Some 20,000 were killed in action. A monument in Lille, France, commemorates their role in the war. Perhaps the most famous pigeon was Cher Ami. This British-bred carrier pigeon had compiled an impressive record at Verdun, and it was used by the AEF in the Argonne Forest on 22 October 1918 when the German army cut off its battalion. The battalion came under intense artillery fire from Allied lines and sought to inform headquarters of its position. Cher Ami, terrified, was finally coaxed to fly. Although badly wounded, with the loss of an eye, broken breast bone, and severed leg, he nonetheless delivered the message. In recognition of this service, which saved the "Lost

Battalion," Cher Ami was later stuffed and mounted at the Smithsonian Institution in Washington, D.C.

Jeffrey M. Pilcher

References

Levi, W.M. *The Pigeon.* Columbia, S.C.: R.C. Byran, 1940.

Lubow, Robert E. *The War Animals.* Garden City, N.Y.: Doubleday, 1977.

Casement, Roger (1864–1916)

British diplomat and Irish nationalist. One of six children, Roger Casement was born on 1 September 1864 to a Protestant father and Catholic mother in Ulster. Orphaned before he was ten, he left his Anglican school in Ireland at age fifteen. He arrived in 1883 in Africa, where he worked for twenty years as British consul in several regions. His reports in 1903 and 1904 from the Congo Free State described the abuse of native laborers and created a public outcry for reform. In Brazil from 1906 to 1911, he issued there his Putumayo Report, which was sharply critical of the exploitation of native workers in the rubber industry.

Casement received a knighthood in 1911 and soon retired to Ireland with a sympathetic interest in nationalism. He aided the formation of the Irish National Volunteers and traveled to the United States in 1914 to seek support and money for their cause. Opposed to Ireland's involvement in the war against Germany, Casement went to Berlin but failed to convince the German government to provide adequate soldiers and ammunition to assist an Irish revolt against England. Returning home in a U-boat in April of 1916 to caution against a rebellion, he was arrested on an Irish beach and transported to London, where he was tried and convicted of treason two months later. Selections from his personal diaries were deliberately and privately circulated during the trial and purported to reveal his homosexuality. Despite efforts to secure a reprieve, Sir Roger Casement was hanged on 3 August 1916.

Thomas W. Davis

References

Inglis, Brian. *Roger Casement.* London: Hodder and Stoughton, 1973.

Reid, Benjamin L. *The Lives of Roger Casement.* New Haven: Yale University Press, 1976.

Sawyer, Roger. *Casement: The Flawed Hero.* Boston: Routledge & Kegan Paul, 1984.

See also IRELAND

Castelnau, Noel Joseph Edouard de Curières de (1851–1944)

French general. Born in Saint-Affrique, Aveyron, Languedoc, on 24 December 1851, Castelnau left St. Cyr in 1870, served in the Franco-Prussian War, and later commanded various infantry units. From 1911 to 1914 he served as deputy chief of staff to the commander of the French army and helped formulate War Plan XVII. Castelnau then commanded Second Army in Lorraine. Deeply religious, Castelnau was accompanied by a personal chaplain and was a lay member of the Capuchin order, hence his nickname: *Le Capuchin Botte* (the Fighting Friar). A firm believer in the offensive, Castelnau's attacks in Lorraine were repulsed by the Germans; he then conducted defensive operations during which his forces halted the enemy, saved Nancy, and stabilized the front in Lorraine.

In 1915 Castelnau commanded Center Army Group and directed offensives in Champagne, after which he became chief of staff to French army commander General Joseph Joffre. During the Verdun crisis of 24–25 February 1916 he was given plenipotentiary powers and ordered to hold Verdun, while defending both the left and right banks of the Meuse River. He decided that General Henri Pétain would command the defense. These decisions had fateful implications, affecting not only the course of the Battle of Verdun and the war but subsequent French history as well.

When Joffre was replaced in December of 1916, Castelnau found himself unemployed; he was considered too Catholic and was discredited by his association with Joffre. In 1918, however, he returned to active service to command Eastern Army Group in Lorraine. After the war, Castelnau served in the Chamber of Deputies (1919–24). He died at Montastruc-la-Conseillère, near Toulouse, on 19 March 1944.

Donald F. Bittner

References

Horne, Alistair. *The Price of Glory: Verdun, 1916.* New York: Harper Colophon, 1962.

Le Grand Encyclopédie, Vol. 4. Paris: Librairie Larousse, 1974.

Le Grand Larousse Encyclopédique en dix volumes. Vol. 2. Paris: Librairie Larousse, 1962.

Porch, Douglas. *The March to the Marne: The French Army, 1871–1914.* Cambridge: Cambridge University Press, 1981.

See also CHAMPAGNE, BATTLES OF 1914 AND 1915; FRENCH WAR PLAN XVII; FRONTIERS, BATTLE OF, 1914; VERDUN, BATTLE OF

Casualties

When war broke out in Europe in August of 1914, all of the participants expected that it would be over by Christmas. Dreams of quick victory, however, turned into a four-year nightmare of trench warfare and massive slaughter. By the time German delegates signed the Armistice in the forest of Compiègne at 05:00 on 11 November 1918, more than half of all the mobilized forces had been killed or wounded: 65 million able-bodied men had been mobilized, and at least ten million of these had died (approximately 8 million from combat and the remainder from disease); approximately 21 million wounded. Some 7.8 million had been taken prisoner or declared missing. In addition, 6.6 million civilians perished.

While many military leaders had anticipated heavy losses, none were prepared for the massive slaughter that followed the outbreak of the war. Military tactics and strategy had failed to keep up with the changes that had occurred in military technology. The introduction of machine guns, long-distance rapid-firing artillery, and barbed wire shifted the advantage from the attacker to the defender. With armies numbering in the millions compressed in the limited space of the Western Front, the initial war of movement quickly turned into one of trench warfare. Wedded to the Napoleonic concept of attack, military commanders attempted to breach the lines at all costs. The result was a blood bath. Indeed, by 1916 military strategy had deteriorated to the point that attrition ("bleeding the enemy white") became the chief objective.

Compared with previous wars, World War I was unprecedented in its carnage, with twice as many casualties than in all the wars of the two preceding centuries combined. Ten percent of France's adult population was killed during the war; indeed, one out of every two French men between the ages of twenty and thirty-two in 1914 lost his life in battle. Nine percent of British men under age forty-five died as a result of combat. On 1 July 1916, the first day of the Somme Offensive, the British suffered almost 60,000 casualties, including 20,000 dead; in World War II it would take forty-five days after the Normandy landing in 1944 to match these figures. By the time the Battle of the Somme ground to a halt in mid-November of 1916, Allied and German casualties amounted to over 1.25 million, making it the bloodiest battle in history. During the course of 1916 the British advanced six miles on a thirty-mile front at a cost of one soldier dying or being wounded every forty-five seconds. The monumental Battle of Verdun created almost one million French and German casualties. Casualty rates for France and Russia reached an unprecedented 75 percent of the forces mobilized (see table).

In commenting on the American Civil War, Union General William Tecumseh Sherman had declared, "War is Hell." The same sentiment applies to the First World War. Through the fires of war, Europe was transformed. In addition to the dead and wounded, the war also destroyed the Ottoman and Austro-Hungarian empires; it overturned the Hohenzollern and Romanov dynasties, brought the Bolsheviks to power in Russia, disrupted the European economies, and brutalized the European soul. Both victors and vanquished were equally devastated. Indeed, even with the recovery of Alsace and Lorraine, France's postwar population was lower than its prewar. Finally, the peace that ended the war only intensified the hatreds that the war had aroused and eventually produced an even greater bloodletting in the Second World War.

Ingrid P. Westmoreland

References

Bogart, Ernest Ludlow. *Direct and Indirect Costs of the Great World War.* New York: Oxford University Press, 1919.

The Harper Encyclopedia of Military History. R. Ernest Dupuy and Trevor N. Dupuy, eds. 4th ed. New York: Harper Collins, 1993.

Hansen, Harry, ed. *The World Almanac and Book of Facts for 1957.* New York: New York World-Telegram, 1957.

Lyman, Robert Hunt, ed. *The World Almanac and Book of Facts for 1929.* New York: New York World, 1929.

Williams, M.J. *Thirty Percent: A Study in Casualty Statistics,* in the Royal United

CASUALTIES TABLE

Country	Total Force Mobilized	Military Battle Deaths	Military Wounded	Prisoners and Missing	Total	Percent	Civilian Deaths
Allies							
Belgium	267,000	13,715	44,686	34,659	93,060	35%	30,000
British Empire	8,904,467	908,371	2,090,212	191,652	3,190,235	36%	30,633
France and Empire	8,410,000	1,357,800	4,266,000	537,000	6,160,800	73%	40,000
Greece	230,000	5,000	21,000	1,000	27,000	12%	132,000
Italy	5,615,000	462,391	953,886	600,000	2,016,377	36%	n.a.
Japan	800,000	300	907	3	1,210	.15%	n.a.
Montenegro	50,000	3,000	10,000	7,000	20,000	40%	n.a.
Portugal	100,000	7,222	13,751	12,318	33,291	33%	n.a.
Romania	750,000	335,706	120,000	80,000	535,706	71%	275,000
Russia	12,000,000	1,700,000	4,950,000	2,500,000	9,150,000	76%	2,000,000
Serbia	707,343	45,000	133,148	152,958	331,106	47%	650,000
United States	4,355,000	50,585	205,690	4,500	260,775	6%	n.a.
	42,188,810	4,889,090	12,809,280	4,121,090	21,819,560		3,157,633
Central Powers							
Austria-Hungary	7,800,000	922,500	3,620,000	2,200,000	6,742,500	86%	300,000
Bulgaria	1,200,000	75,844	152,390	27,029	255,263	1%	275,000
Germany	11,000,000	1,808,546	4,247,143	1,152,800	7,208,489	66%	760,000
Turkey	2,850,000	325,000	400,000	250,000	975,000	34%	2,150,000
	22,850,000	3,131,890	8,419,533	3,629,829	15,181,252		3,485,000
Grand Total	65,038,810	8,020,980*	21,228,813	7,750,919	37,000,812	57%	6,642,633

* This does not include approximately two million additional deaths from disease, malnutrition, etc. Many of these figures (compiled from various sources) are approximations or estimates, since official figures are often misleading, missing, or contradictory.

Service Institution (R.U.S.I.) Journal (February 1964): 51–55.

Caucasus Front, 1914–18

Although the Allies considered Caucasia a secondary theater, Russia feared an invasion from that region, especially after the Crimean War and the Russo-Turkish War of 1877–78. The Turks wanted the fort at Kars and the port of Batum, both of which they had lost in 1878. The Young Turks believed that the Central Powers would grant territory in exchange for assistance. On 29 October 1914, Turkish naval vessels bombarded the Black Sea ports of Odessa, Sevastopol, and Theodosia. Consequently, Great Britain and France declared war on Turkey on 5 November 1914, in compliance with their treaty with Russia.

Even though Caucasia was 500 miles from the nearest Turkish railhead at Konia, Enver Pasha decided upon a campaign through Armenia to Caucasia. Following the declaration of war, the Third Turkish Army moved into Caucasia, hoping to surprise the Russians. Kars guarded the route from Erzerum, the Turkish advanced base, to the middle of Caucasia. A railroad crossed the province from the Black Sea to the Caspian Sea, with branch lines on both sides: One ran from Tiflis, one extended through Kars to Sarikamish, and a third ran southeast through Erivan and along the Persian border.

Despite the severe winter climate, Enver planned to seize Kars and isolate the Russian army in a series of rapid maneuvers. He hoped to envelop the Russian forces at Kars by a strategic concentration of the army at Erzerum and the corps at Trebizond. His strength was about 200,000 men. The XI Corps was to harass the Russian army at Kars, drawing it toward Erzerum, and the IX and X corps would move through Olta to envelop the Russian right. The I Corps from Trebizond would attack through Ardahan to cut the Russian line of communications.

On 20 November 1914 Russian forces under General Vorontsov advanced, occupied Keuprikoi, and engaged the Turkish XI Corps. While the Turkish XI Corps held the Russians, the IX and X corps advanced against Sarikamish and Kars, and the I Corps, landing at Trebizond, marched on Ardahan. When the Turkish X Corps threatened his flank, General Vorontsov defended against the XI Corps while

decisively defeating the X Corps on 1 December 1914. Nevertheless, the Turkish forces withstood the Russian assault and advanced until 25 December 1914, after which the Russians severely defeated the Turkish X Corps near Ardahan. Although the Turkish I Corps entered Ardahan on 1 January 1915, two days later Vorontsov decisively defeated it under Enver at Ardahan. Vorontsov then turned and defeated the IX Corps at Sarikamish on 17 January 1915.

The Russian winter victory over the Turks was not decisive. In 1915 the Russians had a capable commander, General Nikolai Yudenich, who believed that he faced only three or four divisions in the hills northwest of Lake Van. Actually, he faced eight Turkish divisions. On 10 July 1915, when General Organovski launched an attack to reduce those positions, he faced a potential disaster. By 16 July 1915, Turkish commander General Abdul Kerim was moving large reinforcements to the area west of Malazgirt, twenty-five miles north of Lake Van, and beginning counterattacks against the Russians. The fighting grew more severe, and, outnumbered three-to-one, Organovski did not comprehend the danger to which his forces were exposed. Belatedly the Russians withdrew to Malazgirt, where the highly motivated Turks quickly surrounded the town with a five-to-one superiority. On 22 July 1915 Yudenich sent an officer to Malazgirt to assess the situation, but the Russians had already lost the battle. By the end of the month Organovski's corps was retreating north. The victory was a morale booster for the Turks, and Enver ordered Abdul Kerim to pursue the Russians and drive them over the border. Although Abdul Kerim detached a large number of troops to secure his lines of communication, he had sufficient strength to defeat Organovski. Yet the threat of Russian reinforcements led Abdul Kerim to hesitate.

Yudenich gathered a force of 22,000 cavalry and infantry near Tashir to attack the Turks on their advance north from Malazgirt through Karakilise. When the Turks had advanced an appropriate distance, General Baratov was to move around the Turkish rear and cut their line of retreat. The straggling Turkish column stretched over twenty miles, and consequently the Russians did not envelop the entire force. The Russian cavalry captured many guns, large stocks of provisions in Karakilise, and 6,000 prisoners. The Turks lost 10,000 killed and wounded. Although he won a victory, Yudenich had insufficient forces for exploitation. On 2 September 1915, when Grand Duke Nicholas went to the Caucasus as viceroy, he retained Yudenich as the Russian military commander. Nicholas dispatched a force to northern Persia where it removed a pro-German government in Hamadan, completing Russian military operations for 1915.

Caucasia caused the Russians considerable trouble in 1916. The Allied evacuation of the Gallipoli peninsula permitted the redeployment of Turkish troops to Caucasia. Yudenich did not believe these troops could redeploy effectively prior to the end of March 1916. He intended, moreover, to attack the Turks before they could launch an offensive. Yudenich planned a feint, a secret concentration along the road from Kars to Erzurum, and a penetration of the Turkish defenses. Taking the Turks by surprise in mid-January 1916, he won a victory at Kopruky, but he did not envelop the enemy as planned. Consequently, Abdul Kerim withdrew rapidly to Erzurum, sustaining 25,000 casualties. With no siege artillery, the Russians attacked quickly between the forts and took Erzurum during the period 11–15 February 1916. On the 19th the Russians captured Mush; on 1 March, Kamak; and on 2 March, Bitlis. The Russians also seized a number of Turkish depots in the Erzurum area. Simultaneously, Yudenich initiated a secondary offensive along the Black Sea coast, where he employed naval gunfire from the Black Sea fleet and an amphibious landing in the Turkish rear. The naval bombardment was devastating, and the defense broke with numerous Turkish soldiers deserting. Consequently, on 18 April 1916, Yudenich's subordinate, General Lyakov, commanding two sea-lifted brigades, entered the port of Trebizond. This port, the best on the north Anatolian coast, became a valuable entrepot for Russian logistical support.

Enver sought to regain the initiative. Vehip's Third Army was to engage the Russians from the Black Sea to the Karasu River. Ahmet Izzet's Second Army, formed of Gallipoli campaign veterans, would move on Bitlis before the end of March 1916 to outflank the main Russian force and threaten its rear. Turkish communications were deplorable, and troops sent by rail to Ankara marched for one month to get within striking distance of the Russians.

Vehip attacked the Russians west of Erzurum on 29 May 1916. Initially successful, his attack soon faltered. Worried about Trebizond, through which the Russians were receiving reinforcements, Enver ordered Vehip to retake the port in June of 1916. Lacking sufficient means, Vehip followed orders and approached the Russians over the Pontic Alps. He achieved limited success but did not drive the Russians from Trebizond. Yudenich launched an offensive against the Turks on 2 July 1916, with the main attack at Bayburt, the apex of a triangle formed with Erzurum and Erzincan. His goal was to divide the Turkish forces. Although the Turks staged a determined resistance, once the Russians penetrated their positions they retreated. The Russians won the battle on 25 July 1916, when they captured the communications center of Erzincan. Cossacks wreaked havoc in pursuing the Turks some twenty miles. Yudenich thus rendered the Third Turkish Army ineffective for the rest of 1916.

The Turkish Second Army began a belated offensive on 2 August 1916, captured Mus and Bitlis, but lost what it won in the wilderness between the two branches of the Euphrates River. The Russians defeated the Second Army, and both belligerents retired early to winter quarters.

Although at the beginning of 1917 the Russian military situation on the Caucasus front was satisfactory, the March revolution undermined its position. By mid-March the officer corps had lost control of the army as discipline ceased to exist. Turkish troops were now free to support other fronts. In December of 1917, the Bolsheviks and the Germans met at Brest-Litovsk to discuss an armistice. The treaty signed there in March of 1918 withdrew Russia from the war. One of the terms of the Treaty of Brest-Litovsk was Turkish acquisition of the Caucasus. Russia evacuated Anatolia and ceded to Turkey the districts of Ardahan, Kars, and Batum. Furthermore, Russia was forbidden to interfere in the reorganization of these districts. A number of officers from the old Russian army who refused to accept this plan created the so-called Volunteer Army in the south, which participated in the Russian Civil War and set up contacts with the Don and Kuban Cossacks.

Montecue J. Lowry

References

Allen, George H. *The Great War*. Vol. 4. Philadelphia: George Barrie's Sons, 1919.

Cruttwell, C.R.M.F. *A History of the Great War: 1914–1918*. Oxford: Clarendon, 1934.

C

Halsey, Francis Whiting. *History of the World War*, Vols. 7 and 8. New York and London: Funk & Wagnalls, 1919.

Horne, Charles F., ed. *The Great Events of the Great War*. Vols. 2, 3, 4, and 5. London: National Alumni, 1920.

Howland, Colonel C.R. *A Military History of the World War*. Fort Leavenworth, Kans.: General Service School Press, 1923.

See also ENVER PASHA; OTTOMAN EMPIRE, ARMY; RUSSIA, ARMY, CIVIL WAR, NAVY; YUDENICH, NIKOLAI

Cavalry

Although a cavalry invasion of Belgium began World War I, infantry, artillery, and then mechanized forces overshadowed antiquated cavalry forces. Since the American Civil War, cavalry had declined as a vital military force. While there were 103 cavalry divisions with one million cavalry horses in World War I—the largest equine force for any war (in 1916 there were one million cavalrymen in Europe), mounted troops played a minimal role in the Great War. There were no major cavalry actions during the war on the Western Front; in the east, however, Russian Cossacks and German and Austro-Hungarian cavalry waged battles similar to those fought in wars centuries before.

In the initial stages of the war, cavalry did play some important roles. German cavalry assisted in the successful overrunning of Belgium, serving as advance guard and performing reconnaissance. French cavalry also performed reconnaissance. German and Allied cavalry patrols clashed in the early fighting in both Belgium and France before trench warfare proliferated. German cavalry used radios to intercept and decipher messages, but these maneuvers were rather dull compared with the thrilling cavalry charges of previous wars. Hussars, Lancers, and Dragoons found it unrealistic to charge on a battlefront pocked with shell holes and barbed wire entanglements.

It soon became apparent that cavalry was a romantic and outmoded means of war. Cavalry played an important role in covering the retreat from Mons in 1914, delaying German forces. There was also limited mounted action in the battles of Loos in 1916 and Cambrai in 1917, but the German infantry held the line, preventing the cavalry breakthrough for which

Allied generals longed. Canadian Cavalry mounted a famous charge at Moreuil Woods on 30 March 1918, in which three troops commanded by Lord Strathcona routed one hundred Germans with machine guns and prevented the enemy from moving forward. Four of 150 horses in the attack survived. Rarely were there other such opportunities on the Western Front, because of the changed nature of warfare.

The siege conditions of the Western Front forced the demise of mounted calvary because the enemy was entrenched and concentrated on the field. Trench warfare supported by machine guns and artillery forced cavalrymen into the role of mounted infantrymen who relied on their horse only to transport them from one location to the next. Dismounted, however, the force was reduced by 25 percent because one in four of the men acted as horse holder. Cavalrymen also had to learn about infantry weapons, with which they were unfamiliar.

Although British Prime Minister David Lloyd George criticized "the ridiculous cavalry obsession" of generals and their insistence on retaining so many cavalry mounts, both British commander General John French and his successor, General Sir Douglas Haig, refused to cut the size of their cavalry forces. They and other Allied military generals, mostly former cavalrymen, perpetuated the glamour of cavalry and yearned for the opportunity for a gallant charge and breach of enemy lines. They believed that as soon as the trenches were breached, cavalry would be necessary for exploitation. Such was shown only infrequently, however, as by Italian cavalry against the Austrians in the battle at Vittorio-Veneto.

Since cavalry could no longer be used as shock troops, cavalry proponents emphasized that cavalry could perform both distant and close reconnaissance, as well as guerrilla warfare and counterreconnaissance. Cavalry could provide security, and serve as both advance and rear guards and outposts. In addition to being attack forces, cavalry could counterattack, defend specific areas, cover withdrawals, fill gaps, and serve as a mobile reserve. Cavalry raids and rapid withdrawals were useful in surprising the enemy.

World War I cavalry was largely limited to these support roles, except in the Middle East, where the Desert Mounted Corps showed cavalry still could be decisive. As a result, some cavalry units were reorganized as infantry or cycle units. Cavalry horses were converted into draft animals for artillery. In addition to pulling guns and wagons, horses were used to deliver messages and for ceremonial funeral processions. In June of 1915 rumors abounded that the cavalry would be disbanded because cavalry horses required considerable maintenance, both grooming and feed, which made mechanized forces more attractive. Horses could carry 300 pounds of rider, weapons, and campaign kit, but tanks, which first appeared in 1916, could carry much more weight and were less vulnerable to enemy fire.

Despite their limited role in the war, after the Armistice, cavalry horses were showered with flowers, treats, and hugs by liberated villagers. Unfortunately, most were not rewarded by their war offices. Instead, many were destroyed or sold for labor or meat. Many led harsh lives in stone quarries, pulling wagons, or towing barges. Others were slaughtered as farms became mechanized in the 1920s. Still others eventually returned to somewhat placid lives, wearing their war medals on their bridles and participating in war-horse veteran events. In 1924 a Cavalry War Memorial was erected in Hyde Park, London, to commemorate the role of horse cavalry in the Great War. It also marked the end of an era.

Elizabeth D. Schafer

References

Brereton, John M. *The Horse in War*. New York: Arco Publishing, 1976.

Cavalry Combat. United States Army, the Cavalry School. Harrisburg, Pa.: Telegraph Press, 1937.

Home, Sir A. *Diary of a World War I Cavalry Officer*. Tunbridge Wells, Kent: Costello, 1985.

Rogers, Colonel H.C.B. *The Mounted Troops of the British Army 1066–1945*. London: Seeley Service, 1959.

Wakefield, J., and J.M. Weippert, eds. *Indian Cavalry Officer 1914–15: Captain Roly Grimshaw*. Tunbridge Wells, Kent: D.J. Costello, 1986.

Cavell, Edith (1865–1915)

English nurse in Belgium during World War I. Born in Swardesten, England, on 4 December 1865, Cavell was the daughter of a minister. After a short time as a governess in Belgium, she returned to England at the age of thirty to care for her ill father. She subsequently entered nursing school and was certified.

In 1907, Cavell returned to Brussels and started a nursing school that had modernized nursing in Belgium by the outbreak of World War I. When Brussels was occupied by the Germans in August of 1914, many Allied soldiers, separated from their units during the retreat from Mons and Charleroi, disguised themselves as civilians and were under threat of being executed as spies. Cavell was asked to hide a number of them in her nursing school. Motivated by humanitarian impulses, she allowed at least two hundred soldiers to take refuge there during the next year. But on 5 August 1915 the Germans arrested her. She was held in solitary confinement for nine weeks; although allowed a lawyer, she was not permitted to see him before her trial.

On 7 and 8 October 1915 the Germans tried Cavell, along with thirty-four other individuals similarly accused. Found guilty, Cavell was executed by firing squad before dawn on 12 October 1915. At the time, German and some British military authorities felt that Cavell's execution was justifiable under German military law; that, however, was not true. She was charged with violating the provision of the code stipulating the death penalty to anyone who "conducted soldiers to the enemy." Cavell had not done that; she had merely supplied Allied soldiers with medical attention, food, clothing, shelter, and a means by which to try to escape into Holland. There is no evidence that any of these men ever rejoined their units. On 12 October 1915, the Germans posted a decree in Brussels making individuals who knowingly aided, "in any manner whatsoever," an enemy of Germany subject to the death penalty.

Edith Cavell's execution was powerful propaganda for the Allies. Although many Allied soldiers vowed to avenge her death, it should be noted that French authorities had already executed a woman for the same actions, although French censorship kept it quiet. On 15 May 1919 Cavell's body was reinterred at Norwich Abbey, England.

Meredith L. Bragg

References

Beck, James Montgomery. *The Case of Edith Cavell: A Study of the Rights of Non-Combatants*. New York: G.P. Putnam's Sons, n.d.

Elkon, Juliette. *Edith Cavell: Heroic Nurse.*
New York: Julian Messner, 1956.
Herman, Gerald. *The Pivotal Conflict: A
Comprehensive Chronology of the First
World War, 1914–1919.* Westport,
Conn.: Greenwood, 1992.
Judson, Helen. *Edith Cavell.* New York:
Macmillan, 1941.

See also BELGIUM, OCCUPATION OF; PROPA-
GANDA, USE IN WAR

Censorship

Like much else, truth is a casualty of war. During the First World War all warring governments introduced censorship and disseminated
propaganda to their peoples. Belligerents
amended their constitutions with the justification that in times of war the survival of the state
takes precedence over freedom of the press. The
singular importance of national interest also
liberated governments from internal criticism of
repressive tactics that would not have been tol-
erated in peacetime.

Some censorship was self-imposed or private, such as when Lord Lansdowne sent a letter to *The Times* of London urging the necessity of peace through negotiation and the
editors refused to print it. But the vast majority of censorship was exacted by the state.

Censorship varied from belligerent to belligerent. It was most severe in Russia, which had
little tradition of a free press. In Germany the
severity of censorship depended on the local
military commander. In some states censorship
was quite strict; in others it was lax. In Germany censorship began with gentle prodding by
Kaiser Wilhelm II to put aside internal complaints in the face of an international crisis. But
as the war lengthened and grievances multiplied, the OHL (*Oberste Heeresleitung*) organized Section IIIb to address censorship and
propaganda. The government justified this action by the State of Siege Act, which provided
for the suspension of a number of key paragraphs in the constitution, such as those guaranteeing free speech, if the nation were endangered.

When Field Marshal Paul von Hindenburg
and General Erich Ludendorff took command
of the government, they attempted to impose a
more uniform and severe form of censorship,
but that was never entirely successful. The war
press office (*Krieaspressamt*) saw that nothing

positive was said about Germany's enemies,
little bad news about the war escaped to the
public, and criticism about the government was
circumscribed. Complaints were voiced to the
Reichstag about censorship, restrictions on freedom of association, and the reading of private
mail, but little was done. Hindenburg tried to
limit censorship to matters pertaining to military matters; yet, in wartime, all news can be
said to affect the military.

In practice, censorship was utilized not
only to control information the public received
but also to suppress liberal and radical factions
in Germany. To counter the 1917 Reichstag
Peace Resolution, the government circulated a
barrage of films, posters, newspapers, and
books, all of which predicted chaos from the left
if victory were not attained. The population was
urged to "think German, speak German, and
write German, and avoid anything foreign in
speech and print." Music in cafes and dance
halls had to be "suitable," and songs had to be
serious or patriotic (ragtime was banned). In the
end, censorship alienated the population from
its government, and Germans were grossly misinformed about events at the front. Defeat came
as a surprise to many Germans simply because
they were not accurately informed about the
realities of the war.

Conditions were similar in Great Britain.
The British relied on the Defense of the Realm
Act (DORA), passed on 8 August 1914, to justify severe censorship. Not only were leftist
journals suppressed, but *The Times* incurred
harassment as well. As in other nations, correspondents were first prohibited and then discouraged from front-line reporting. Instead, the
military conferred news to the press at regular
meetings. In the first week of the war, War
Minister Lord Horatio Kitchener and Lord of
the Admiralty Winston Churchill set up an office to supervise press censorship in order to
ensure "a steady stream of trustworthy information supplied both by the war office and the
Admiralty." Editors were liable to prosecution
for publishing anything that might be deemed
subsequently to have been a military or naval
secret. "It is not always easy to decide what
information may or may not be dangerous,"
said Lord Kitchener, "and whenever there is any
doubt, we do not hesitate to prevent publication." Not only did the government filter what
was printed, it also read private mail. In August
of 1914 there were only fourteen people assigned to screen mail, but by early 1917 some

3,700 censors in London and 1,500 more in Liverpool worked to ensure that front-line news was kept positive, and the enemy was always condemned and British soldiers exalted. As the war continued, the severity of British censorship increased. Laws and rules under the umbrella of the DORA infringed liberties in an unprecedented way. Civilians were prohibited from writing in invisible ink, buying binoculars, or flying kites.

Similar restrictions existed in France. On 5 August 1914 the French military issued orders prohibiting the publication of information of a military nature. The "State of Siege" allowed military authorities to ban all publications and meetings judged to be of a nature to excite or encourage disorder. As in other countries, the ministry of war organized a press bureau that checked all publications, and that office had the authority, under the Law Repressing Indiscretions of the Press in Time of War, to shut down any publications deemed in violation. The aim of French censorship, as one historian wrote, was not merely to prevent the propagation of news harmful to the army, nor was it to attack or support one specific group, but to persuade the press to propagate ideas and sentiments likely to contribute to final victory. As in most cases the most effective form of censorship was self-censorship. After the war the French journal *Evolution* and the magazine *Le Crapouillot* published some of the more bombastic remarks of the press throughout the political spectrum. In fact, exaggerated stories about German atrocities went too far even for the army, and the minister of war asked all prefects to instruct editors to avoid detailed descriptions of acts of cruelty because these were perceived as lowering morale.

As the war progressed, censorship in France was less concerned with divulgence of military secrets than with raising French morale. A few people, including Georges Clemenceau, protested the severe restrictions. Alfred Capus, editor of *Le Figaro,* joked that, provided journalists did not refer to the authorities, government, politics, the wounded, German atrocities, or the postal service, they were free to print everything—but under the inspection of two or three censors!

It did not seem to matter whether a nation was winning or losing; censorship was severe in all the belligerent states. When the war began, the Austrian government reached back to an 1869 law permitting "suspension of fundamental rights" during a state of emergency. This broadly worded law was used by authorities to detain and deport citizens, search private homes, restrict freedom of assembly, and censor the press. Under the newly passed War Service Law, the government also intruded on private businesses. In addition, many of the normal functions of civilian government were taken over by the army high command. This was especially true in non-German areas of the empire. The central government, worried that it was fighting a war not only against external enemies but internal ones as well, organized a War Surveillance Office to monitor all potentially "suspicious" activities.

In Austria suspicion of espionage was greater than in many of the other countries, because of the wide ethnic diversity within the empire. Many of the extraordinary laws decreed by the Hapsburg Empire seemed directed more at silencing internal nationalism and preventing sabotage than at protecting military secrets from the Entente. According to one author, the leaders of the Austro-Hungarian Empire believed "that a war could be carried through only by means of the permanent maintenance of emergency measures, that is . . . by the maintenance of a dictatorship in the full sense of the word." This tight control became ever more repressive as the war worsened, and it fell apart only when defeat was at hand.

In all countries dissent was tantamount to treason, and any information perceived as harmful to the cause was banned. In the United States, the Committee on Public Information circulated over 75 million pieces of patriotic literature. The government encouraged citizens to report anyone who "spreads pessimistic stories, divulges—or seeks—confidential military information, cries for peace, or belittles our efforts to win the war." Nothing less than 100 percent Americanism was required. Although the First Amendment clearly guaranteed freedom of speech, the Espionage Act of 1917 and the Sedition Act of 1918 were upheld by the Supreme Court. These prohibited German, socialist, and pacifist papers from the mails. In a famous case, Socialist leader Eugene Debs was given a twenty-year sentence for urging people to resist militarism wherever found. The Supreme Court rationalized these laws by stating that "when a nation is at war, many things that might be said in times of peace are such a hindrance to its effort that their utterance will not be endured so long as men fight."

Clearly, the national governments of the belligerents perceived free speech to be a possible deterrent to the primary goal of victory. In many instances, the government did not have to force the press to write patriotic stories, but when it was necessary all governments tried to keep morale high, no matter the cost. Each nation sanitized stories from the front, while rumors about atrocities committed by the enemy abounded. Michel Corday, a French writer, concluded that censorship and self-censorship inculcated an incessant hatred that "will remain one of the outstanding phenomena of our life during the war. The press will prove to have been one of its chief instigators."

Glenn R. Sharfman

References

Becker, Jean-Jacques. *The Great War and the French People*. Translated by Arnold Pomerons. New York: St. Martin's, 1986.

Breen, William. *Uncle Sam at Home: Civilian Mobilization, Wartime Federalism and the Council of National Defense, 1917–1919*. Westport, Conn.: Greenwood, 1984.

Kann, Robert, et al., eds. *The Habsburg Empire in World War I: Essays on the Intellectual, Military, Political, and Economic Aspects of the Habsburg War Effort*. New York: Columbia University Press, 1977.

Kitchen, Martin. *The Silent Dictatorship: The Politics of the German High Command under Hindenburg and Ludendorff*. New York: Homes and Meier, 1976.

Marwick, Arthur. *The Deluge: British Society and the First World War*. Boston: Little, Brown, 1965.

Redlich, Joseph. *Austrian War Government*. New Haven: Yale University Press, 1929.

Sanders, M.L., and Philip M. Taylor. *British Propaganda during the First World War*. London: Macmillan, 1982.

Williams, John. *The Home Fronts: Britain, France and Germany 1914–1918*. London: Constable, 1972.

See also FRANCE, HOME FRONT; GERMANY, HOME FRONT; GREAT BRITAIN, HOME FRONT

Champagne, First Battle of (December 1914–March 1915)

During November of 1914 the German high command, under General Erich von Falkenhayn, began to shift troops from the Western Front to Russia, gambling that the weakened but well-entrenched armies in France could hold while the Germans crippled the Russian army. Alerted to this by French military intelligence, General Joseph Joffre, long-time proponent of the importance of the offensive, believed that, with proper planning and adequate artillery preparation, his forces could rupture the weakened German lines. On 8 December 1914 Joffre issued General Instructions Number 8, which ordered simultaneous offensives by General Fernand de Langle de Cary's Fourth Army in Champagne and General Louis de Maud'huy's Tenth Army in Artois. The French sought to break through the German front, cut the vital Metz-to-Lille rail lines in the area of Mézières (Champagne) and Douai (Artois), and thereby force a German withdrawal from northern France. To divert German attention and resources, Joffre planned a series of French, Belgian, and British secondary attacks at various points from the North Sea coast to the Vosges. At the very least, Joffre calculated, this would provide the Russians much-needed relief.

Joffre wanted the Fourth and Tenth armies to attack simultaneously, but logistical problems posed by the rainy winter weather and the extremely poor roads in the undulating and thinly settled Champagne countryside delayed the Fourth Army's push. Undeterred, on 17 December 1914 Tenth Army's XXI, XXXIII, and X corps attacked units of Bavarian Crown Prince Rupprecht's Sixth Army on Vimy Ridge, a dominating geographic feature in Artois. General Henri Philippe Pétain's XXXIII Corps captured some of the German front line, but the assault faltered because of heavy rain, fog, and mud. To the north, Belgian, French, and British diversionary attacks around Ypres also met with very little success. By Christmas Day stiff German resistance and poor weather had convinced French commanders to restrict operations in Artois to besieging the stubbornly defended village of Carency. This effort continued unsuccessfully until early January, when Joffre allowed Maud'huy to suspend the Artois offensive until the Tenth Army could lay new plans, stockpile supplies, and replace its casualties.

Meanwhile, on 20 December, the Fourth Army launched its offensive in Champagne between the Suippe River, a small tributary of the Aisne, and the Argonne Forest. The initial assault began in the wooded hills between Souain and Massignes, where the XII, XVII, and Colonial corps (west to east) attacked the four weak divisions that made up the VIII Reserve Corps of German General Karl von Einem's Third Army. In support, Fourth Army's II Corps and the French Third Army made limited diversionary attacks in the Argonne. Initially, the XVII Corps gained some high ground near Perthes, while to the east the Colonials made some progress near Massignes. On 25 December, in hopes of expanding these slight gains, de Langle de Cary committed the fresh I Corps between the XVII and Colonial corps, but the three units quickly became intermingled, confused, and bogged down on such a narrow front. Hampered by fog and defective artillery shells, as well as German reinforcements and counterattacks, the Fourth Army's renewed attacks on 30 December also faltered. Further assaults enabled the French to take Perthes on 7–8 January, but, with their infantry exhausted, the offensive halted on 18 January.

Undaunted, Joffre and Langle de Cary decided to renew the Champagne offensive on a broader front in order to avoid a repetition of the confusion engendered by the commitment of the I Corps on Christmas Day. On 16 February the French reopened the Champagne offensive with some initial gains, but these could not be expanded because of poor weather, mud, and lack of surprise. Newly arrived German reserves launched fierce counterattacks, primarily at night, which enabled Einem's Third Army to hold its lines. Undaunted, Langle de Cary brought fresh troops into action on 25 February and again on 5, 7, and 12 March. Fighting was generally concentrated between Perthes and Massignes, with French gains confined to the center of this sector. By mid-March the Fourth Army was exhausted and the offensive spent. Although Joffre terminated the offensive on 17 March, he ordered Langle de Cary to maintain the image that a renewed assault was imminent for fear that suspension of the Champagne offensive would be interpreted as a tacit admission of failure and a blow to French morale.

Despite the minimal gains, Joffre claimed that the First Champagne Offensive succeeded, because it proved the superiority of French morale and forced the Germans to commit their reserves. Such claims cannot bear scrutiny. First, the offensive failed to achieve its strategic objective of breaking through the German front. Second, the minor tactical victories, such as those won in secondary attacks in the Vosges by the Chasseurs Alpins, paled in comparison with the 94,000 casualties taken by the French in

Champagne. Nonetheless, French commanders did learn some important tactical lessons from the First Champagne-Artois Offensive, such as the need for longer, heavier, and more accurate preparatory artillery barrages, the need to attack on a rather broad front to allow for the commitment of reserves, and the need to maximize each division's striking power by assigning each a relatively narrow assault front. The Germans, who lost 46,000 men, also learned important defensive lessons from the First Champagne-Artois Offensive. Most important, the Germans stepped up their efforts to deepen their defenses by building a second trench line in their rear all along the Western Front. Finally, the winter battles reinforced heightened German confidence that properly entrenched troops supported by machine guns, artillery, and reserves could defeat attacks by numerically superior troops. With these lessons in mind, both sides began to prepare for renewed battles in Artois and Champagne later in 1915.

David K. Yelton

References
Edmonds, James E., and G.C. Wynne. *Military Operations: France and Belgium, 1915. Vol. 1. In Great Britain, Historical Section of the Committee of Imperial Defence, History of the Great War Based on Official Documents*. London: Macmillan, 1927.

Falls, Cyril. *The Great War*. New York: Putnam, 1959.

Ministère de la Guerre. *Etat-Major de l'Armée Service Historique. Les Armées Française dans la Grande Guerre, Vol. II*. Paris: Imprimerie Nationale, 1931.

Reichsarchiv. *Der Weltkrieg 1914–1918*. Vol. 7. Berlin: E.S. Mittler und Sohn, 1931.

See also ARTOIS, SECOND BATTLE OF; EINEM, KARL VON; JOFFRE, JOSEPH; LANGLE DE CARY, FERNAND DE; MAUD'HUY, LOUIS ERNEST DE; RUPPRECHT, CROWN PRINCE OF BAVARIA

Champagne, Second Battle of (25 September–3 November 1915)

When the Second Battle of Artois ground to a halt in mid-June 1915, French General Joseph Joffre immediately began planning a massive fall offensive. As with the First Battle of Champagne and the Second Battle of Artois, Joffre, a dedicated believer in the myth of the French infantry's offensive superiority, wanted to exploit the favorable strategic situation created by the German decision in 1915 to concentrate their forces against Russia. Joffre believed that his previous offensives had miscarried because of a failure to attack simultaneously in Champagne and Artois and because of tactical errors, such as insufficient artillery preparation, poor infantry-artillery coordination, attacking on an overly narrow front, and inadequate planning. To ensure that such mistakes would not disrupt his fall offensive, Joffre and his commanders spent the entire summer laying the groundwork for the attack.

For his grand fall offensive, Joffre planned to return again to his General Instructions Number 8 of 8 December 1914. That called for numerous minor diversionary assaults along the length of the Western Front in support of simultaneous offensives in Champagne by General Henri Philippe Pétain's Second Army and General Fernand de Langle de Cary's Fourth Army, and in Artois by General d'Urbal's Tenth Army. Additionally, Joffre wanted supporting offensives by the BEF near Loos, just north of Artois, and by the newly allied Italians on the Isonzo front. In the relatively flat terrain of Champagne and Artois, a penetration could quickly sever the Germans' railborne logistical nexus, thereby forcing a general retreat from northern France, while concurrently relieving the pressure on the battered Russian armies. Originally, Joffre intended to concentrate his effort in Artois. He switched the main French emphasis to Champagne, despite its inadequate rail and road system, because it had fewer villages for the Germans to use as strongpoints with which to impede the offensive.

French confidence for the fall offensive ran high, because of their meticulous preparations. Joffre had created new formations by reducing the size of infantry companies, reorganizing territorial units, and calling up the class of 1915. General Noel de Castelnau, commander of the newly formed French Central Group of Armies, had carefully studied the lessons learned earlier in 1915, particularly by Pétain's XXXIII Corps at Second Artois. To minimize the first waves' exposure to fire, Castelnau had his troops dig communication trenches some 3,000 yards to the rear, construct protective bunkers in which to wait out the initial bombardment, and narrow the gap between the French and German trenches from 1,000 to less than 300 yards. To maximize the chances of maintaining communications, Castelnau's men laid double and triple phone lines. To ensure reliable logistical support, the Second and Fourth armies expanded Champagne's road and rail network. Finally, the French carefully sited some seven hundred heavy guns (many recently removed from unoccupied fortifications) and stockpiled 800,000 rounds for the artillery barrage designed to soften the German defenses. Clearly, the French believed that detailed planning and preparations were the key to a successful breakthrough in 1915.

On the German side of the Western Front, the summer lull was not wasted either. The outnumbered German troops had constructed a fallback position of interconnected defensive entrenchments some two to four miles behind the entire Western Front. Although weak in reserves in the west (only six infantry divisions, four infantry brigades, and a few cavalry and artillery units), General Erich von Falkenhayn was confident that the deepened German front would hold. After all, he reasoned, it had repulsed several major French offensives already in 1915, and the situation in Russia had improved to the point that he could safely divert some units from that theater should the need arise. Unfortunately for the Germans, Falkenhayn mistakenly believed that low French morale and British shortages would prevent them from launching any massive offensives in the fall of 1915. He therefore refused to send reserves to Champagne or Artois until early September.

With both sides anticipating success, on 21 September the French began a four-day artillery preparation. Of course, this sacrificed any hope for tactical surprise, but Joffre and his subordinates were convinced that planning, firepower, and élan would carry the day. On 25 September French infantrymen went over the top in both Champagne (at 09:15) and Artois (12:45). While the push in Artois faltered (see Third Battle of Artois), the offensive in Champagne opened promisingly with the French Second and Fourth armies' eighteen divisions (plus a further ten divisions and two cavalry corps in reserve) striking General Karl von Einem's German Third Army (eight divisions with one in reserve) and the right-wing corps of the German Fifth Army on a twenty-mile front. In the French center, a sector nine miles wide from west of Souain to Massignes, the Fourth and Second armies nearly shattered Einem's rather low-quality VIII Reserve

Corps. Lacking reserves, because Falkenhayn had insisted that the French would not attack, Einem faced a serious crisis.

On either side of the Bois de Perthes, in the center of the French assault, the XIV and II Colonial corps advanced nearly 2,500 yards in less than two hours. The assault, spearheaded by the 10th Colonial Division (under General Jean Marchand of Fashoda fame, who was killed in this attack), came to a grinding halt as it encountered the German second line of defense five hours ahead of schedule. French artillery, operating according to their meticulously prepared schedules, launched a fierce barrage on the German second line just as the 10th Colonials reached it; the infantry, unable to contact their own artillery, fell back in disarray. Thus a promising operation failed because infantry units in battle were unable to maintain contact with their artillery and commanders; as the 10th Colonials could attest, a carefully planned timetable was a poor substitute.

Meanwhile, troops of the Second Army's XIV and XI Corps had made serious penetrations to the east of the II Colonial Corps. This forced Einem to throw all available reserves, including dismounted cavalry and raw recruits, into the threatened VIII Reserve Corps sector in order to hang on to his second line of defense.

News of the near breakthrough had prompted the startled Falkenhayn to rush reserves—including two corps recently arrived in Belgium from Russia—to Champagne and Artois. On 26 and 27 September the French attacked with five fresh divisions at the Souain-Somme Py road, where the 10th Colonials had struck the previous day. So close did the French believe they were to a breakthrough that the Germans reported French cavalry moving forward; they even captured a number of cavalry officers on scouting missions. On the 28th the French briefly penetrated the German second line but were forced back by German counterattacks. By late that same day it was clear that the initial French assault had stalled, as substantial German reserves began to reach the beleaguered Third Army.

Castelnau ordered a pause in Champagne on 30 September to allow the Second and Fourth armies to rest and regroup. They renewed the offensive with nineteen divisions on 5–6 October, focusing again primarily on the center of the French line. The Germans held because of the arrival of reinforcements and a persistent fog, which hampered French artillery fire. Fighting was fiercest around Tahure, north of Perthes, where the French made minor gains; but the struggle there degenerated into a series of limited attacks and counterattacks by both sides, which lasted through October. With the offensive stalled, Joffre ordered the Second and Fourth armies to suspend the Second Champagne Offensive on 3 November.

The Champagne Offensive netted a gain of about fifteen square miles and a maximum penetration of two and a half miles—but at the cost of some 144,000 casualties. Given the degree of planning, the human and material resources committed, and the favorable strategic situation, the Champagne Offensive was a major French defeat. It damaged morale and forced many French commanders, including such ardent proponents of the offensive as Joffre and Foch, to modify, though not abandon, their faith in offensive operations. At the very least, they began to call for training and equipment, such as mortars, better suited to trench warfare. The failure of the Champagne-Artois offensives had political repercussions as well. It brought down the René Viviani government, which was replaced by Aristide Briand's cabinet. The massive casualty lists and minimal results also led the Chamber of Deputies to demand increased civilian control over the war effort, including the right to examine the performance of French generals. Not surprisingly, the French army looked to the British to carry the weight of offensive action in 1916 and confined their offensive focus to the Salonika Expedition in late 1915.

During 1915 the Germans learned a great deal about the power of a defense in depth. By early 1916 the entire German Western Front was four to six miles deep with dual interlocking defense lines and safe, comfortable bunkers for the troops, which eliminated the need to rotate front line units frequently. Despite the lessons learned in 1915 about the superiority of defense, both the Germans and the Allies would take the offensive in 1916 in the massive bloodlettings of Verdun and the Somme.

David K. Yelton

References

Falls, Cyril. *The Great War*. New York: Putnam, 1959.

Ministère de la Guerre. Etat-Major de l'Armée Service Historique. Les Armées Française dans la Grande Guerre, Vol. III. Paris: Imprimerie Nationale, 1923.

Reichsarchiv. *Der Weltkrieg 1914–1918*, Vol. 9. Berlin: E.S. Mittler und Sohn, 1933.

See also ARTOIS, THIRD BATTLE OF; JOFFRE, JOSEPH

Charles I, Emperor of Austria

See KARL I, EMPEROR OF AUSTRIA
(1887–1922)

Charteris, John (1877–1946)

British brigadier general. Born 8 January 1877 in Glasgow, Scotland, Charteris attended Woolwich and was commissioned in the Royal Engineers in 1896. He formed a lasting association with Douglas Haig before World War I. Charteris served with Haig as both intelligence officer and personal confidant at I Corps, First Army, and at General Headquarters. When Haig assumed command of the BEF in December of 1915, Charteris became his head of intelligence.

Charteris sought to sustain Haig's morale and self-confidence, and as a result his reports were overly optimistic concerning German weaknesses and the chances of victory. In 1917 Charteris's assessments also affected Haig's view of operations during the Passchendaele Offensive (Third Ypres) and the Battle of Cambrai. By then, Prime Minister David Lloyd George had lost confidence in Charteris (and Haig), and a cabinet inquiry into Cambrai targeted intelligence as a factor in the failure. Haig resisted pressure to remove Charteris but finally did so in January of 1918, making him deputy director of transportation at GHQ. Haig continued to consult Charteris on intelligence matters. Although at variance with views in London, Charteris predicted that the Germans would launch an offensive early in 1918.

Charteris retired in 1922 as a brigadier general; between 1924 and 1929 he served as a Conservative MP for Dumfriesshire. He wrote two highly laudatory biographies of Haig, *Field Marshal Earl Haig* (1929) and *Haig* (1933), and also published his own diary, *At G.H.Q.* (1931). Charteris praised Haig's prediction of a long war, preparation for field operations, belief that the war could be won only on the Western Front, calmness in crisis, and pressure for an Allied offensive in 1918 and not 1919. Charteris died on 4 February 1946 in Thorpe, Surrey.

Donald F. Bittner

References

Charteris, Brigadier General John. *Field Marshal Earl Haig*. London: Cassell and Company, 1929.

Duncan, G.S. *Douglas Haig as I Knew Him*. London: George Allen and Unwin, 1966.

Marshall-Cornwall, General Sir James. *Haig as Military Commander*. New York: Crane, Russak, 1973.

Terraine, John. *Douglas Haig, The Educated Soldier*. London: Hutchinson, 1963.

Warner, Philip. *Field Marshal Earl Haig*. London: Bodley Head, 1991.

See also CAMBRAI, BATTLE OF; HAIG, SIR DOUGLAS; INTELLIGENCE OPERATIONS

Chemical Warfare

On 22 April 1915, Germany carried out the first successful employment of poison gas in modern combat. At around 17:00 hours, French Algerian troops holding a section of line near Ypres, Belgium, noticed a greenish-yellow cloud advancing from the German front. The Germans had opened 6,000 cylinders, releasing 168 tons of chlorine; the resulting cloud covered a four-mile section of the French line. As it entered the Allied line, many panicked. Some ran wildly to the rear, blinded and terrorized; others were overwhelmed and died coughing and choking in the trenches. German infantry cautiously advanced behind the cloud, and by dark they had captured two thousand prisoners and fifty-one guns. Yet the effects of the attack surprised the Germans as well as the Allies. The Germans had failed to position reserves to exploit the breach in the French line, and French and Canadian troops later counterattacked and stabilized it.

Prior to World War I many had considered the possibilities of chemical warfare, and by the turn of the century concern had led to an attempt at The Hague International Peace Congresses to ban poison gas. The European powers were far too concerned with their own offensive doctrines to consider alternative weapons seriously. By the end of the war, however, both sides had violated the conventions and were guilty of deploying "poison or poisoned weapons" and arms that caused unnecessary suffering. Postwar arguments then surrounded the question of which side had deployed chemical weapons first.

The World War I trench stalemate led both sides to search for what Basil Liddell Hart called the "keys to the deadlock." While the French experimented with tear gas, the Germans, who had the most advanced chemical industry in the world, took the lead in development of chemical weapons. Fritz Haber, a German Jew at the Kaiser Wilhelm Institute, offered to develop chemical weapons for the German government, and it was Haber who unleashed the first deadly cloud of chlorine at Ypres.

After the attack, the Allies scrambled to organize their chemical defenses and to retaliate in kind. Both sides developed bureaucratic chemical empires that advocated continued gas warfare. While the French created the *Service Chimique de Guerre* to conduct chemical warfare, the British promoted Lieutenant Colonel Charles H. Foulkes to general and placed him in charge of a similar operation. What later became the British Special Brigade conducted projector, mortar, and gas-cylinder attacks, and also assumed the duties of smoke and flamethrower operations. When the Americans entered the war, they based their 1st Gas Regiment upon the British model. By the summer of 1918 the Allies had some nine thousand chemical warfare troops, while the Germans utilized five thousand. The Germans, the Allies, and the Americans all increased the scope of total industrialized warfare by utilizing academic scientists and chemical industries to fight the gas war.

On 25 September 1915, the British launched their first chlorine gas cloud along a twenty-five mile front in Loos, Belgium. When the wind changed direction, the British quickly discovered one of the main drawbacks to chemical warfare, its dependence on weather conditions. The British lost many of their own troops to gas in the assault, and the chemical specialists lost respect among their comrades as a result.

Chlorine clouds launched from trench lines had to be supported by winds blowing in the direction of the enemy lines, and any variation in wind conditions could end in disaster. All types of chemical warfare were reliant upon weather. Chemicals were most effective when deployed during temperature inversions, preferably in the early morning prior to sunrise. That let the gas clouds remain low to the ground and take a longer time to dissipate. A shower or wind shift could spoil an attack.

After Second Ypres the Allies scrambled to develop adequate chemical defense. At first,

British troops were advised to hold socks soaked in urine over their face to act as a breathing mask. The British and Germans also issued cloth masks soaked in triosulphate. Both sides soon realized the inadequacy of such measures and began developing other forms of protection. The British issued gas helmets with eyelenses, which were little more than fabric bags soaked in chemicals that the soldiers wore over their heads. The helmets tended to leak, stimulating the British to develop an effective gas mask. The result was the Small Box Respirator, or SBR. The SBR was worn over the head, and air was breathed through a tube leading to a box that contained a filter of soda lime and charcoal. Goggles protected the eyes, and the nose was held closed with a clip. Although the mask was awkward and uncomfortable, trained troops acquired confidence in it, and it worked well throughout the war.

The French were slow in developing an active response to gas attacks and suffered numerous casualties before they introduced a practical defense program. They settled upon the marginally effective M2 gas helmet. The Russians and the Italians were never properly trained or supplied, and paid a heavy cost for their negligence. The Americans, latecomers to the chemical war, suffered terrible casualties before they were willing to take proper defensive measures. They arrived in France with twenty thousand worthless gas masks and no defensive training. The Germans, on the other hand, used a reliable leather gas mask. In addition to their masks, troops also used powdered bleach to decontaminate areas and equipment. The chemical war degenerated into a technological race to develop a chemical that would "break" enemy masks and cause panic in the lines. When troops received proper defensive training, warning systems, and equipment, however, they rarely panicked under attack.

In December of 1915 the Germans introduced a new gas, the choking agent phosgene. Both sides had been experimenting with it, and the French retaliated in February of 1916 with phosgene-filled artillery shells. By using their highly efficient 75mm gun, the French were able to saturate their targets with gas.

Artillery improved the effectiveness of chemical warfare by giving the attacker more latitude in controlling elements such as wind and weather. The British contributed as well with their 1916 4-inch Stokes mortar. Mortar shells could carry more chemicals than artillery rounds, and their short range (1,000 meters) was ideal for trench conditions.

Captain William H. Livens aided British chemical operations in several ways. After working with his father to develop a flamethrower, he turned his attention to building a large mortar tube for shooting chemical projectiles. His Livens Projector consisted of a metal tube and breach plate buried at a 45-degree angle in the ground. When fired, it launched an 8"x 29" bomb containing thirty pounds of chemicals. It had a range of almost a mile and could be fired in volleys by twenty-five-tube batteries. The effect of concentrated Livens, Stokes, and artillery fire countered some of the drawbacks of cylinder attacks. Although once buried in the ground it could not be re-aimed, it was less dependent upon wind, and the massive volleys of gas gave defenders a very limited time in which to react and take protective measures.

In July of 1917 the Germans introduced dichloroethyl sulfide, better known as mustard gas, to their deadly arsenal. The men were already familiar with phosgene and chlorine, choking agents that attack the respiratory system and make it difficult to breathe. Mustard, classified as a blister agent, is far more hazardous. In its natural state mustard is a liquid, not a gas. When the shell burst, it vaporized and then condensed into a persistent liquid that could saturate its target and remain for long periods.

The effects of mustard gas were not immediate. Soldiers first noticed a strange smell that some described as being similar to horseradish or mustard. It would then take some time from the moment of contamination for the initial symptoms to appear. Several days passed before the full extent of the injury became evident. Mustard, a vesicant, would attack any part of the body with which it came in contact, leaving first- or second-degree chemical burns. The exposed areas of skin blistered and burst within four weeks. If not properly treated the blisters could become infected, compounding the injury. Good treatment for burns included keeping them clean and dry with absorbent dressings. The best treatment included cleaning and decontaminating the patient, issuing him a clean uniform, and evacuating him to the rear. By the end of the war, most of the belligerents had built chemical-treatment centers for their wounded.

In addition to burning exposed areas of skin, mustard attacked mucous membranes, the throat, bronchial tubes, and the lungs. Mustard gas also produced temporary blindness. Conjunctivitis became the most common form of mustard injury, but it was also the least dangerous; most patients fully recovered within ten days. While most victims recovered from their burns, about 1–3 percent died from respiratory problems. The fatally wounded would linger for a few days before drowning from the inflammation of their lungs. Some survivors suffered from respiratory illness the rest of their lives.

The Allies wanted to respond instantly with mustard gas of their own, but it took them over a year to do so. By the summer of 1918 they had reached near parity in the mustard-gas war, and by the end of the conflict the casualties caused by mustard were nearly equal on both sides.

The introduction of chemical warfare failed to break the trench stalemate. Like machine guns, tanks, and aircraft, the technology behind gas warfare outpaced tactics on the ground. In all, over twenty-eight chemicals were tested in combat, with mustard, chlorine, phosgene, and diphosgene becoming the most widely employed. Yet none of the agents could break the stalemate. Once troops were equipped and trained to defend themselves from gas, its offensive value became negligible. Without a tactical doctrine and commitment to its use followed by large-scale advances, the role of chemicals diminished. Eventually chemicals were relegated to psychological operations meant to harass the enemy.

In the attack, gas was used as antibattery fire and to make machine-gun and infantry emplacements untenable. Although the gas attacks no longer broke enemy lines, they did reduce the fighting ability of the defenders. By 1918 the Germans discovered that, while gas did not break the stalemate of the trenches, it could aid in defense. As the Germans retreated, they used mustard gas to contaminate areas and deny ground to the Allies.

The mythology surrounding the use of gas in World War I has continued. Although it was an unsuccessful weapon that had negligible effects, the public perceived it as a nightmare. The propaganda began during the war as casualty rates from both sides were distorted. After initiating the chemical war at Ypres, the Germans downplayed the effects of gas while the Allies, seeking moral support, tended to exaggerate it. While the exact numbers of casualties on both fronts will never be known, on the Western

Front, where records are the most accurate, about 500,000 men were casualties. Since most victims of gas recovered, the death rate was very low, especially when compared with the millions of men killed by conventional weapons.

By the end of the war most soldiers had had some exposure to gas, or at least chemical-defensive training. A handful of writers and artists survived, retaining deep emotional impressions of chemical warfare. Their views have colored historical perception ever since, and turned a relatively unimportant weapon into something that has been widely seen as being far more lethal than it ever was.

Thomas D. Mays

References

Haber, L.F. *The Poisonous Cloud: Chemical Warfare in the First World War.* Oxford: Clarendon, 1986.

Hartcup, Guy. *The War of Invention: Scientific Developments, 1914–18.* London: Brassey's Defence Publishers, 1988.

Moore, William. *Gas Attack! Chemical Warfare 1915–18 and Afterwards.* New York: Hippocrene, 1987.

Richter, Donald. *Chemical Soldiers: British Gas Warfare in World War I.* Lawrence: University Press of Kansas, 1992.

Spiers, Edward M. *Chemical Warfare.* Urbana and Chicago: Macmillan, 1986.

See also YPRES, SECOND BATTLE OF

China

Although the main focus of World War I lay in Europe, the war had important repercussions in China and throughout East Asia. After a century of Western military and economic penetration, China had been undergoing a period of traumatic change in the late nineteenth and early twentieth centuries. The last imperial dynasty, the Qing, or Manchu, was overthrown in 1912 and replaced by a tenuous military regime under the warlord Yüan Shu-kai (Yüan Shih-k'ai). His chief rival, Dr. Sun Yat Sen (Sun Yat-sen), had fled to Canton, where he presided over a coalition of nationalist groups known as the Nationalist party, or the Quomindong (Kuomintang).

To call China of the early twentieth century a unified nation would be a gross overstatement. Not only did independent warlords control their own fiefdoms, but the major coastal cities were virtually self-governing city-states. By 1900, moreover, the foreign powers had carved China into spheres of influence: France controlled the south and Indo-China; Britain, the central Yangtze valley; and Russia, Manchuria. Two imperial newcomers, Japan and Germany, had made more recent inroads. As a result of its victory in the Russo-Japanese War of 1904–5, Japan secured control of Korea as well as economic concessions in Manchuria and the Laodong (Liaotung) peninsula. In 1898 Kaiser Wilhelm II sent German troops into the Shandong (Shantung) peninsula, where they seized the port of Qingdao (Tsingtao), which became a German leasehold. Finally, it might be added that the United States had economic ties with China but no territorial claims.

As had been the case for most of the nineteenth century, China remained passive during World War I. With the European powers occupied in the West, Japan seized the opportunity to become the dominant power in China. In late August 1914, Japan entered the war on the side of Britain. Using that as an excuse, she sent troops into Shandong and occupied Qindao. Early in the following year the Japanese government pressured the Yüan Shih-k'ai regime in Beijing into accepting the so-called "Twenty-One Demands," which would have ceded Shandong to Japan and given Japan control of the Chinese government (Japan later dropped this last provision). In May of 1915, failing to receive help from abroad and faced with the threat of a major Japanese military presence, China accepted most of the Twenty-One Demands. Shortly thereafter, Yüan Shih-k'ai died, signaling the beginning of the total fragmentation of China as Beijing (Peking) fell under one unscrupulous general after another. Once again Japan took advantage of the political chaos. In return for lending Beijing large amounts of money (actually bribes), Japan received secret Chinese guarantees of Japanese hegemony in Shandong as well as other concessions in northern and central China.

In April of 1917, meanwhile, the United States entered the war. President Wilson's international idealism had already captured the imagination of many Chinese intellectuals. Wilson had hinted that the principle of self-determination would also apply to China. Consequently, it was assumed, at least by the Chinese intelligentsia, that the United States would openly press for the removal of the foreign military presence in China once the war ended. On that basis the Chinese leadership allowed themselves to be persuaded by President Wilson to enter the war in August of 1918, in order that China might secure a seat at the peace conference and present her case. Although no combat units were available, Chinese labor battalions were sent both to Europe and the Middle East.

In 1919 both Japan and China sent delegations to the Paris Peace Conference, the latter's headed by the distinguished Chinese diplomat Dr. Wellington Koo. The Japanese, armed with the secret treaties mentioned above, fully expected big-power acceptance of her dominant position in the Shandong peninsula. China, on the other hand, anticipated President Wilson's support for her own cause. The Americans were caught in the middle. While the great majority of the issues dealt with at Paris pertained to Europe, ironically, the Shandong dispute nearly wrecked the conference. Totally committed to the establishment of a League of Nations, Wilson had already endured an Italian walkout over a territorial dispute with the new state of Yugoslavia. The Japanese threatened the same if Wilson voted against them. After some tortured deliberation, Wilson, who feared a breakup of the conference, decided to support the Japanese, hoping to secure justice for China at some later date.

The news of the American "betrayal" had immediate repercussions in China. Student demonstrations and general riots broke out in nearly every major Chinese city. This tumult became known as the May 4th movement, after the date when the news from Paris was received in China. The date was subsequently installed as a major event in the modern Chinese revolutionary movement. Simultaneously, Chinese communism was born, aided to some degree by the shabby treatment China had received at Paris. Immediately after the Bolshevik coup in Russia in November of 1917, Lenin made a series of radio speeches collectively called "the Addresses to the Working Toilers of the East." In the address to China he announced the cancellation of all debts owed by China to Czarist Russia and the return of territories forcibly seized by Russia (Lenin later reneged on this). It goes without saying that this caused a sensation among Chinese intellectuals, who, with the backing of the Russian-led Comintern, would found the Chinese Communist party in July of 1921. While its original leadership consisted of eleven men representing a total membership of only fifty-seven, by 1925 its membership had risen to 100,000.

John W. Bohon

References

Fairbank, John, Edwin Reischauer, and Albert Craig. *East Asia in Modern Transformation.* Boston: Houghton Mifflin, 1965.

Falk, Edwin A. *From Perry to Pearl Harbor: A Struggle for Supremacy in the Pacific.* Garden City, N.Y.: Doubleday, Doran, 1943.

Feis, Herbert. *The China Triangle.* Princeton: Princeton University Press, 1953.

Li, Tien-yi. *Woodrow Wilson's China Policy, 1913–1917.* Kansas City, Mo.: University of Kansas Press, 1952.

See also JAPAN; PARIS PEACE CONFERENCE, 1919; QINGDAO (TSINGTAO), SIEGE OF

Chkeidze, Nikolai Semenovich (1864–1926)

Menshevik leader in Russia. Born in the western Georgian village of Puti in 1864 of a noble but poor family, Chkeidze was expected to become a civil servant. While studying at the University of Odessa in 1887 he became radicalized. Later, while continuing his studies at the Veterinary Institute in Kharkov, he was expelled for subversive political activities.

Nicknamed "Karlos" after Karl Marx, Chkeidze, like most Georgian Marxists, aligned with the Mensheviks. Although possessing no extraordinary political talents, Chkeidze consistently achieved influential positions, primarily through fortunate timing. Having served in the Third State Duma (1907–12), he was elected his faction's chairman for the Fourth State Duma (1912–17). He served as the Petrograd Soviet's first president and president of the Constituent Assembly of Georgia (1918).

A centrist during World War I, Chkeidze and the Social Democrats advocated more worker involvement in government. As the war continued, Chkeidze called for a revival of the Communist International in an effort to bring peace. After the February Revolution of 1917, Chkeidze's faction adopted a relatively moderate position. He was serving as a member of the Georgia Mission of the Paris Peace Conference when the Bolsheviks seized power in Georgia in 1921. Choosing not to return home, Chkeidze stayed on in Paris as a member of the Georgian government-in-exile. Depressed by the political situation at home and his inability to support his family, Chkeidze committed suicide in June of 1926.

Jeff Kinard

References

Jackson, George, ed. *Dictionary of the Russian Revolution.* Westport, Conn.: Greenwood, 1989.

Medvedev, Roy A. *The October Revolution.* New York: Columbia University Press, 1979.

Shukman, Harold. *Lenin and the Russian Revolution.* New York: Capricorn, 1966.

Christian X (1870–1947)

King of Denmark. Born at Charlottenlund on 26 September 1870, Christian ascended to the Danish throne on 14 May 1912, upon the death of his father, Frederick VIII. Christian was also king of Iceland from 1888 to 1944.

Christian enforced a policy of neutrality during World War I. He realized that Denmark was vulnerable in the Baltic and ordered the Danish navy to be on alert and reinforce sea forts. He also made Germany aware that he would not tolerate an invasion of his country. Early on, under some German pressure, Denmark mined the Skagerrak, in effect denying both sides in the war access to the Baltic from the North Sea.

Christian arranged for a continuation of Danish trade during the war, both import and export. In 1915 he signed a reformed constitution that included universal suffrage. Two years later Denmark sold the Danish West Indies (Virgin Islands) to the United States. In 1918 Christian recognized the complete independence of Iceland.

Although he succeeded in maintaining Danish neutrality during the First World War, Christian was not as fortunate in the Second World War. During the German occupation, however, he defied the Germans until he was incarcerated from 1943 to 1945. Christian X died in Copenhagen on 20 April 1947.

Elizabeth D. Schafer

References

Heckscher, Eli. *Sweden, Norway, Denmark and Iceland in the World War.* New Haven: Yale University Press, 1930.

Jones, W. Glyn. *Denmark: A Modern History.* London: Croom Helm, 1986.

Lauring, Palle. *A History of the Kingdom of Denmark.* Translated by David Hohnen. Copenhagen: Høst & Søn, 1973.

C

Churchill, Winston Spencer Leonard (1874–1965)

British Liberal party politician and cabinet member. Born at Blenheim Palace on 30 November 1874 to an American mother (Jennie Jerome) and an English father (Lord Randolph Churchill), he was sent to a boarding school near Ascot shortly before his eighth birthday. Less than a distinguished student, he attended Harrow for four years and later the Royal Military College, Sandhurst, where he was commissioned a lieutenant in the cavalry in 1895, the year of his father's death.

Between 1895 and 1900 Churchill had military assignments in Cuba, India, and the Sudan; he covered the war in South Africa as a journalist, became a prisoner of the Boers and escaped, and won a seat in the House of Commons as a Conservative one year after losing his first bid for parliamentary election.

Crossing over to the Liberal party in 1904, Churchill held a number of increasingly important posts under prime ministers Henry Campbell-Bannerman and Herbert Asquith: under-secretary of state for the colonies (1905–08), president of the Board of Trade (1908–10), and home secretary (1910–11). During the Second Moroccan Crisis in 1911, Churchill pressed his views on European defense issues and made no secret of his desire to succeed Reginald McKenna as first lord of the admiralty, a post he received on 24 October.

Churchill worked indefatigably in the next two years to ensure Britain's naval readiness in case of a major war. As late as July of 1914 he was still uncertain about the likelihood of war, but he was determined to put Vice Admiral Sir John Jellicoe in charge of the fleet in place of Sir George Callaghan. Just prior to the war's start, Churchill supported home rule for Ireland and moved naval forces to the Irish Sea in March of 1914, intending to restrain advocates of an Ulster rebellion. He grew closer to Horatio Herbert Lord Kitchener and fully supported his cabinet appointment as secretary of state for war in early August 1914.

Two months later, Churchill was deeply involved in the defense of Antwerp when that port city came under siege by the German forces sweeping through Belgium. He traveled to Antwerp and actively directed military operations, but the city eventually surrendered. His critics complained loudly, but defenders argued that his actions had slowed the Germans and provided time to save several important Channel ports, including Dunkirk.

The crucial war year for Churchill was 1915, when he became the chief advocate for the Dardanelles Campaign. It seemed a simple, straightforward idea: Secure the Straits, provide an easier means to aid Russia directly, and knock Turkey out of the war. Success might also enlist the support of several Balkan states against the Central Powers. The plan appealed to Churchill's feeling of a need for action, but it was poorly planned. Allied military operations in the eastern Mediterranean ended in disappointment and failure, in large part because Churchill had insisted (despite his disclaimers at the time and later) that the Dardanelles could be forced by ships alone and that naval gunfire could silence the Turkish shore batteries. When troops were brought in (the Gallipoli Campaign), they were too few and too late. In the storm of political debate that followed, Asquith brought in Conservatives and Labour M.P.s to a new coalition government and presided over a ministerial reshuffle. Churchill, though ardently defending his plan in the Dardanelles, ultimately resigned from the admiralty, thinking his political career finished. Asquith refused to accept David Lloyd George's suggestion that the outgoing minister be appointed to the colonial office. During this period of bitter personal disappointment, Churchill began a new endeavor—painting—which proved to be both a solace for the moment and a passionate pastime for the rest of his life.

By November of 1915 he had joined the army on the Western Front, spending time with the 2nd Battalion, Grenadier Guards, to get a firsthand look at trench warfare. In less than two months he received command of his own battalion, the 6th Royal Scots Fusiliers, 9th Division.

By May of 1916 Churchill was back in England, his wartime experience of troop command behind him. For over a year rumors of his return to the cabinet circulated in London, but Conservative party opposition and lingering public suspicions over the Dardanelles Campaign kept Churchill from office. He overcame those obstacles in July of 1917 when his friend and new prime minister, Lloyd George, named him minister of munitions. For the next fifteen months, until the war ended, Churchill concentrated on increasing the manufacture of ammunition in British factories and helped to create a shell surplus. He frequently visited the troops in France and met with such leaders as Field Marshal Sir Douglas Haig and Premier Georges Clemenceau.

Churchill's public career after the Great War was long and distinguished. He is best remembered for his service as prime minister during the Second World War (1940–45). He served again in the same post from 1951 to 1955. Churchill died in London on 24 January 1965 and is buried beside his parents and brother in the churchyard at Bladon, a short distance from Blenheim Palace. The years from 1914 to 1918 greatly influenced him; they were marked by both high achievement and disappointment. Perhaps the most perceptive remark came from J.L. Gavin, editor of the *Observer,* who made this observation in 1915 after Churchill resigned from the admiralty: "He is young. He has lion-hearted courage. No number of enemies can fight down his ability and force. His hour of triumph will come."

Thomas W. Davis

References

Brendon, Piers. *Winston Churchill: A Biography.* New York: Harper and Row, 1984.

Gilbert, Martin. *Churchill: A Life.* New York: Henry Holt, 1991.

Manchester, William. *The Last Lion: Winston Spencer Churchill, Visions of Glory: 1874–1932.* Boston: Little, Brown, 1983.

See also DARDANELLES CAMPAIGN; GALLIPOLI CAMPAIGN; GREAT BRITAIN, NAVY

Clemenceau, Georges (1841–1929)

French politician and premier. Born at Mouilleron-en Pareds in the Vendée, 28 September 1841, Clemenceau was the son of a doctor and atheist. He followed his father's religious views and leftist politics, although he was very much a political maverick. He first rose to national prominence as mayor of Montmartre during the Franco-Prussian War. Elected to the National Assembly, Clemenceau voted against peace terms that would give up

Alsace-Lorraine. A leader of the Radical party and newspaper publisher, he was a leading figure in the travails of the Third Republic. He found his role in championing Captain Alfred Dreyfus, the young Jewish captain wrongly accused of treason. His reputation as a skilled debater earned him the nickname "the Tiger." In the Chamber of Deputies Clemenceau opposed French imperial efforts, which he believed detracted from military preparedness against Germany.

Clemenceau first served as premier of France from 1906 to 1909. During that time he supported the use of troops to crush strikers, a move that earned him the enmity of the Left. In foreign affairs he kept French resolve at the Algeciras Conference over Morocco. Out of power, Clemenceau opposed French territorial concessions to Germany during the Second Moroccan Crisis in 1911 and also pushed extension of the term of military service from two to three years.

The outbreak of the First World War found Clemenceau an outsider and government critic. He attacked the government's handling of the war, while at the same time he pushed for an all-out effort to win. He criticized workers who put strikes for higher wages and improved benefits ahead of the war effort, governments that did not prosecute the war, and all defeatists. His moment came in the summer of 1917, when the failure of the Nivelle Offensive led to wide-scale French army mutinies. By the autumn of 1917 there was serious doubt about whether France could win the war, and Clemenceau attacked the government for pacifistic sentiments. The government fell in October and, the next month, Paul Painlevé's government collapsed. President Raymond Poincaré faced a dramatic choice: Either call on Joseph Caillaux, who would presumably try for negotiations with Germany, or call on Clemenceau to continue the fight. Poincaré's anger over Clemenceau's personal attacks on him was outweighed by his distaste for Caillaux's defeatism; he selected Clemenceau on 16 November 1917.

As premier, Clemenceau thoroughly dominated the government. Most of the members of his cabinet were Republicans, and none were of real prominence. The Right was not represented, and the Socialists went into opposition. For one of the few times during the Third Republic, parliamentary ascendancy went into eclipse. Clemenceau was called France's one-man Committee of Public Safety. He ordered

former minister of interior Louis Malvy arrested, as well as Caillaux. The Left never forgave him. In the crisis over the Bolshevik Revolution and Russia's withdrawal from the war, Clemenceau's oratory helped infuse the French with the will to fight through to final victory. He made it clear to the trade unions that he would support improvements in their working conditions but would crush any strikes; he also would not tolerate any defeatism or pacifism. He pressed both the British and Americans to increase the number of men drafted for the war effort. He also advanced the promotion of Ferdinand Foch as supreme allied commander and supported him in that post, even when the two quarreled. He frequently visited the front to show his concern for the welfare of the men. Clemenceau played a crucial role in stiffening French morale sufficiently to allow her to survive the final German drives of the spring and summer of 1918.

With victory secured, France faced daunting problems; not the least of these was reconstruction of the devastated areas. Clemenceau knew that winning the peace would be difficult. He was much criticized in Britain and the United States as a vengeful Shylock, determined to keep Germany in subjugation. His aim at the Paris Peace Conference, however, was quite simply the security of France. He had to try to balance the idealism of Wilson and Lloyd George's desire to revive German trade with the demands of the French Right (represented by Poincaré and Foch) to treat Germany harshly. Clemenceau realized that France would have lost the war but for the intervention of Britain and the United States and that it was essential to keep those two countries on the side of France in the event of a renewal of hostilities. Forced to compromise over the Rhineland issue (both on the separation of the territory from Germany and the length of the Allied occupation), Clemenceau endured bitter attacks by the French Right, including Foch. In the ratification debate Clemenceau pointed out that the Treaty of Versailles was not a perfect document and that its success rested not on its clauses but rather on enforcement and vigilance.

Clemenceau led a center-Right coalition into the elections of November 1919. This Bloc National won a sweeping triumph. In January of 1920, when Poincaré's term ended, Clemenceau allowed his name to be put forward as a candidate for the presidency. Most observers expected the "Father of Victory," now in his eighty-first year, to win election as a final reward for his services. But Clemenceau's many enemies, including Briand, Foch, Maginot, and Poincaré, felt free to attack him, and the National Assembly elected Paul Deschanel.

Clemenceau immediately resigned the premiership and went into embittered retirement. He spent his remaining years writing and trying to warn France about the need for vigilance and enforcement of the Treaty of Versailles. In this regard, his most important book was *Grandeur and Misery of Victory* (published posthumously in 1930). In it he cautioned his countrymen about putting too much faith in the League of Nations, and he attacked the Locarno Pacts as providing the illusion rather than the reality of security. Clemenceau died in Paris on 24 November 1929.

Spencer C. Tucker

References

Brunn, Geoffrey. *Clemenceau*. Cambridge: Harvard University Press, 1943.

Jackson, John Hampden. *Clemenceau and the Third Republic*. New York: Macmillan, 1948.

King, Jere C. *Foch Versus Clemenceau: France and German Dismemberment, 1918–1919*. Cambridge: Harvard University Press, 1960.

Watson, David R. *Georges Clemenceau: A Political Biography*. New York: David McKay, 1974.

See also FRANCE, HOME FRONT; PARIS PEACE CONFERENCE, 1919

Codebreaking

Wireless telegraphy (WT) offered governments and military leaders rapid, reliable, and seemingly secure mobile communications. With it, commanders could coordinate the actions of their forces across the breadth of Europe, even the world. Foreign ministries also realized its vast potential. WT was faster and apparently more secure than mail or diplomatic couriers. Others, however, saw wireless communications (even encoded communications), as a risk-free window into their opponents' plans and intentions. By 1908 all the European great powers were monitoring their neighbors' wireless communications. By war's end, the best military commanders were regularly exploiting codebreaking to shape their military plans.

Most prewar codebreaking operations were centered on their nations' respective "black chambers," offices that broke codes used by foreign embassies or dissident movements. Black chambers had been fixtures of all major European powers for centuries, with those of Russia and France being the most developed. France was the first to establish a similar organization to monitor wireless communications, and by 1905 each of her major ministries had cryptologic (codebreaking) bureaus. By 1914 the various French ministries had "broken" (that is, were reading) codes used by the Germans, British, and Italians. Meanwhile, the Russian Foreign Ministry had gained a similar level of success against the Swedes, Germans, Austro-Hungarians, and Romanians. Unfortunately for the Czar's army, its leadership saw no utility in reading its neighbors' wireless communications; it did not establish a cryptologic bureau of its own until mid-1915. More significantly, the Russian army placed little emphasis on encoding its own communications; this had disastrous consequences in the war's early battles, especially at Tannenberg.

Britain was slower in establishing a formal cryptologic bureau, waiting until 1909. Britain more than made up for lost time by coordinating the decoding efforts of competing agencies. By 1912, through the cooperation of the Royal Signal Corps, British military intelligence had established a series of stations to monitor wireless transmissions from the continent. Informal arrangements were made for decoded naval traffic to pass to naval intelligence, army signals to go to the War Office, and embassy communications to go to the Foreign Ministry. It was an effective and relatively efficient system that saw much improvement by war's end.

Although Italy established a cryptologic bureau in 1901, its work was primarily directed at protecting Italian codes, a job it performed with indifferent success. Italy was the only European power unable to read its neighbors' communications. In 1917, Great Britain sent a team of cryptologists to Italy to assist in the breaking of Austria-Hungary's military codes. By March of 1918 the combined Anglo/Italian cryptologists were regularly reading Austria-Hungary's diplomatic and naval wireless communications.

Although a latecomer in the war, the United States by 1917 was fairly proficient at breaking into minor military and diplomatic codes. The army's codebreakers enjoyed the greatest success, mainly because they were closer to the enemy and therefore able to intercept more signals.

Austria-Hungary, alone among the Central Powers, established a military codebreaking bureau before the war. Both its foreign and war ministries had such bureaus in operation by 1906. The military intelligence bureau in particular saw much expansion during the immediate prewar period because of its success in monitoring the Italo-Turkish and Balkan wars through codebreaking. By 1914 Austro-Hungarian military intelligence was reading Russian, Serbian, Italian, and Romanian military communications. In fact, Austro-Hungarian codebreakers gave their government thirty-six hours' notice of the Italian declaration of war in 1915 because they had read orders transmitted by the Italian naval ministry to its fleet. Unfortunately, the Austro-Hungarian Empire's moribund decision-making mechanism precluded all but its navy from exploiting this information.

Although Germany and Turkey had black chambers before the war, only the former had a cryptologic bureau established for wireless communications. The German Foreign Ministry monitored and attempted to break its neighbors' telegraphic codes. Its army and navy cryptologic bureaus monitored only *communications en clair* (not encoded), because it believed that codes could not be broken in time to affect the outcome of a battle. As in America, moreover, the military bureaus operated under the strict control of a jealous high command, which precluded cooperation and inhibited the effectiveness of the overall effort.

As the war progressed, all the cryptologic bureaus improved in their analytical techniques, but the Western Allies had by 1916 begun to demonstrate a marked superiority, especially in naval codebreaking. In October of 1914 the Russians provided the Royal Navy a German codebook taken from the *Magdeburg* before it sank. With it the British were able to read Germany's naval communications until well into 1918. That facilitated not only Allied operations against the German High Seas Fleet but also those directed against zeppelin and U-boat forces.

Nor were the British alone in their success. French codebreaking provided warning of Germany's final offensive along the Marne in 1918, while Italian codebreakers enabled their navy to thwart Austro-Hungarian naval operations in the Adriatic the same year. For the Central Powers, Austria-Hungary's codebreaking made a crucial contribution to successful Austro-German operations against Romania and Italy throughout the war. It also provided Austria-Hungary with advance warning of Bulgaria's intention to leave the war in 1918. Germany's codebreakers provided similar warning of Austria-Hungary's peace feelers in 1917–18. Moreover, few generals in the Great War were better served by their codebreakers than Germany's Paul von Hindenburg and Erich Ludendorff, who were given advance warning of virtually every Russian tactical maneuver and operation opposite their front from 1914 to 1917. That support was no doubt critical to their brilliant operations against a more numerous although less well equipped and ineptly led opposition.

Although World War I's codebreakers are not as well known as their more famous successors of World War II, their successes were every bit as important and contributed as much to their respective countries' operations. Moreover, the codebreakers of the First World War established the principles of codebreaking and signal traffic analysis used by intelligence agencies today.

Carl O. Schuster

References

Beesly, Patrick. *Room 40: British Naval Intelligence 1914–1918*. London: Hamish Hamilton, 1982.

Flicke, Wilhelm. *War Secrets in the Ether*. Vols. 1 and 2. Laguna Hills, Calif.: Aegean Park, 1977.

Gylden, Yves. *The Contribution of the Cryptographic Bureaus in the World War*. Laguna Hills, Calif.: Aeagean Park, 1978.

Kahn, David. *The Codebreakers*. London: Weidenfeld and Nicolson, 1967.

See also EAST PRUSSIA CAMPAIGN; MAGDEBURG; ROOM 40; ZIMMERMANN TELEGRAM

Congress of Oppressed Nationalities

The Congress of Oppressed Nationalities was an unprecedented, and allegedly spontaneous, meeting of approximately fifty prominent exiled Italian, Slovak, Czech, Polish, Romanian, and South Slavic nationalists whose ethnic homelands were ruled by Austria-Hungary.

Meeting in Rome between 1 and 8 April 1918 with the blessings of the Entente powers, the delegates proclaimed their common desire for individual national identities, the right of statehood, full economic and political independence, and an end to continued Hapsburg rule. In a heavily publicized resolution, the delegates denounced the Hapsburg Monarchy as an instrument of German domination and as an obstacle to national self-determination. They further vowed to work together to obtain complete liberation of their peoples.

The selection of Rome as the site for the congress was intended to demonstrate to ethnic groups within the Austrian Empire that the congress was not a tool of either Britain or France, or tied to Entente war aims. It also showed that Italy, which previously had claimed areas of the Austrian Empire as its own, was now willing to work with Balkan peoples to resolve mutual differences and territorial claims in the best interests of all.

While heralded by the Allies as an extemporaneous demonstration of ethnic self-determination, and unbeknownst to its participants, the Congress was actually planned, organized, and directed by Britain's chief of propaganda to enemy countries, Lord Northcliffe, and his assistants Wickham Steed and R.W. Seton-Watson. The congress was a landmark event in the anti-Austrian propaganda campaign that sought to weaken the Central Powers by fomenting ethnic unrest and rebellion within the Austrian Empire.

Clayton D. Laurie

References

Bruntz, George G. *Allied Propaganda and the Collapse of the German Empire in 1918.* Stanford: Hoover War Library, Stanford University Press, 1938. Reprint. New York: Arno, 1972.

Lasswell, Harold D. *Propaganda Technique in World War I.* London: Kegan Paul, Trench, Trubner, 1927. Reprint. Cambridge: MIT Press, 1972.

"Lord Robert Cecil and the Rome Congress." *New Europe,* 30 May 1918, 163–64.

Stuart, Campbell. *Secrets of Crewe House: The Story of a Famous Campaign.* London: Hodder and Stoughton, 1920.

Vencesi, Ernesto. "The Roman Congress of Oppressed Nationalities." *New Europe,* 2 May 1918, 54–63.

Conrad von Hötzendorf, Count Franz (1852–1925)

Austro-Hungarian field marshal and imperial army chief of staff. Born in a suburb of Vienna on 11 November 1852, Conrad proved to be a brilliant staff officer with a firm grasp of strategic concepts. A graduate of the prestigious Maria Theresa Akademie in Wiener Neustadt, he served only briefly with troops before being selected for general staff training in 1876. He distinguished himself as a staff planner two years later during the occupation of Bosnia-Herzegovina. He spent the next fourteen years serving in a variety of general staff positions, including four years as an instructor at the Imperial General Staff College (1888–92). He rose quickly in rank, acquiring the patronage of Archduke Franz Ferdinand, heir to the imperial throne. The archduke facilitated Conrad's rapid advancement, even lobbying for his appointment as chief of staff of the imperial army, a post Conrad achieved in 1906.

More a staff officer than a commander, Conrad was the forerunner of the modern military manager. He understood the advantages provided by the twentieth-century's new communications and transportation technologies. He did not, however, understand the negative impact other developments, such as nationalism and the machine gun, would have on the Austro-Hungarian army. Conrad was an intensely loyal and unrepentant supporter of the Hapsburg Monarchy and the conservative imperial policies that he believed were essential to the Austro-Hungarian Empire's survival. Among these policies was his ardent belief in preventive wars against the empire's enemies, such as Serbia and Italy (the latter technically still an ally). His views antagonized the empire's restive minorities and its liberal politicians, fueling the divisions that were tearing the empire apart. Nonetheless, Conrad was one of the most outstanding strategists of the war. Many of his contemporaries felt it a pity that such a brilliant planner led such a poor army.

Conrad was a hard-working and visionary chief of staff. Finding the army ill trained, poorly equipped, and totally unprepared for modern war, he embarked on an aggressive modernization program. His was the first army to establish a radio-interception and decryption service to monitor the communications of likely opponents. Conrad also established an aerial reconnaissance service and urged development of lighter, more mobile artillery. He often found his efforts frustrated by the empire's divided government structure, its inept and corrupt bureaucracy, and its grossly inadequate industrial base. Curiously, those problems did nothing to undermine his confidence in the army's ability to conduct any mission assigned to it.

Conrad worked his staff at a furious pace, presenting a new war plan annually to Emperor Franz Josef and continually updating previous plans to reflect the empire's changing internal and external situation. Despite his obviously good work, his active lobbying for wars his empire could ill afford placed him at odds with most of the empire's civilian officials. Conrad even urged the annexation of Serbia, seemingly oblivious to any potential Russian reaction. His outspoken views led to his resignation in 1911 over a dispute with the foreign ministry, but he was quickly reinstated when the Balkan Wars erupted in 1912.

Conrad was still chief of staff when Archduke Franz Ferdinand was assassinated in Sarajevo on 28 June 1914. Unable to decide whether to concentrate forces against Russia or Serbia, Conrad delayed the mobilization of Austria-Hungary's final echelon of troops. That effectively muddled an otherwise smooth mobilization and contributed to the army's dismal performance in its early battles. Neither the Russian nor the Serbian front received troops from that final echelon in time to affect the initial fighting. Conrad underestimated Serbia's ability to resist, and he overestimated the capabilities of his own army. The result was an almost constant string of defeats at the hands of both the Russians and the Serbs. Resentful of German assistance, Conrad cooperated only reluctantly with his ally, at the cost of their overall war effort. The defeats continued well into 1916 with only the Italian army, which entered the fray against the Central Powers in 1915, seemingly inferior to that of Austria-Hungary. Still, Conrad remained optimistic.

The same could not be said of most of the Austro-Hungarian government, particularly as Conrad's failings as a commander became more apparent. His fixation on the Trentino Offensive against Italy prevented the dispatch of troops to stop Brusilov's drive into Galicia in the summer of 1916. The resulting disaster ended any hopes for an Austro-Hungarian victory in the east. Archduke Karl, heir to the throne, blamed Conrad for the debacle. Although Conrad retained the confidence of Emperor Franz Josef, the emperor's death in December 1916 removed that last patron. Emperor Karl dismissed Conrad almost immediately upon assuming the throne.

Subsequently given command of the Austrian army in Tyrol in March of 1917, Conrad proved an adequate but undistinguished commanding general. He had only a small role in the successful Austro-German Caporetto Offensive that November and enjoyed little success in the failed Piave Offensive of June of 1918. He retired from service one month later.

Although he had been a brilliant staff officer, Conrad's failure to recognize his army's shortcomings led him into planning operations far beyond its capabilities. The resulting battlefield disasters, coupled with his advocacy of divisive domestic and foreign policies, did more to destroy the empire he loved than anything its enemies undertook. Conrad died in Bad Mergentheim on 25 August 1925.

Carl O. Schuster

References

Cruttwell, C.R.M.F. *A History of the Great War 1914–1918*. London: Paladin, 1986.

Dupuy, Trevor N., Colonel (U.S.A., Ret.). *The Harper Encyclopedia of Military Biography*. New York: Harper Collins, 1992.

Michel, Bernard. *La Chute de L'Empire Austro-Hongrois 1916–1918*. Paris: Editions Robert Laffont, 1991.

Rothenburg, Gunther. *The Army of Francis Joseph*. West Lafayette, Ind.: Purdue University Press, 1976.

Stone, Norman. *The Eastern Front 1914–1917*. London: Hoddard and Stoughton, 1975.

See also AUSTRIA-HUNGARY, ARMY; EAST GALICIA, 1914 CAMPAIGN; EASTERN FRONT, JANUARY TO APRIL 1915; OUTBREAK OF THE FIRST WORLD WAR

Constantine I (1868–1923)

King of Greece, 1913–22. Born in Athens on 12 July 1868, Constantine was the son of King George I. After study at Heidelberg University, Constantine graduated from the War Academy in Berlin and served for a time as an infantry officer in the Prussian army. In 1889 he married Sophia, sister of Kaiser Wilhelm II. All of this left him with decidedly pro-German sympathies.

Constantine led the Greek army to defeat in the 1897 war with Turkey, which nearly cost George I his throne. In 1909 he was forced into exile by disgruntled army officers but returned to Greece when Eleutherios Venizelos became premier. Constantine's military reputation was restored when he led the Greek army to victory over the Turks and seized Salonika in the First Balkan War. Upon the assassination of George I in March of 1913, Constantine became king.

Greece was plunged into crisis by the First World War. Constantine's pro-German sympathies were abetted by his belief that the Central Powers would win the war, but Allied naval power dictated neutrality. Premier Venizelos, however, favored bringing Greece into the war on the side of the Entente. The split between the two men produced muddled policies and finally Allied intervention in Greece.

In 1915, when the war shifted to the Mediterranean, Britain offered Greece major concessions if she would participate in the Dardanelles campaign. Venizelos wanted to send three Greek divisions, but Constantine refused, whereupon Venizelos resigned. Constantine's communications to Berlin made it clear that he favored the Central Powers.

Venizelos returned to office following victory in the June 1915 elections, and Constantine was forced (under a 1913 treaty between Greece and Serbia) to agree to mobilize the Greek army against a Bulgarian threat to Serbia. He was unable to prevent the Allies from landing at Salonika in October. Constantine then forced Venizelos from office and took real power himself, urging the Germans to invade Greece and attack the Allies at Salonika.

Following the Allied defeat in the Dardanelles campaign, Constantine openly supported the Central Powers. Greek surrender of Fort Rupel to Bulgaria in May of 1916 opened eastern Macedonia to attack and imperiled the Allies. In August the Bulgarians captured the port of Kavalla. Venizelos now established a rival Greek government in Crete and Salonika with assistance from the Allies, who, nevertheless, continued to recognize and negotiate with Constantine.

An attack by Greek royalist troops on a landing party of British and French sailors and marines at Athens on 1 December cost Constantine whatever credit he had with the Entente. He remained in power for a time because of monarchist sympathies among the Entente governments and the support of Premier Aristide Briand, a friend of the Greek royal family. By June of 1917, however, Briand was gone from office, and Constantine was forced into exile. He went to Switzerland, without formal abdication, along with his eldest son. Constantine left a younger son, Alexander, to rule in his absence. Venizelos returned to Athens as premier.

In exile, Constantine hoped that the Germans might yet win the war and restore him to his throne. In 1920, following the war, he returned to Greece after Venizelos was defeated in an election. Alexander had died from blood poisoning caused by the bite of a pet monkey, and Constantine took the throne. His decision to continue Greek imperial efforts in western Asia Minor proved his undoing. The resurgent Turks defeated the Greek army and the Greek people blamed Constantine. Following Greek losses in the spring of 1922 and the Turkish sack of Smyrna, Constantine in September abdicated for a second time, in favor of his eldest son, who became king as George II. He died four months later in Palermo, Sicily, on 11 January 1923.

Dennis J. Mitchell

References

Clogg, Richard. *A Short History of Modern Greece.* New York: Cambridge University Press, 1986.

Leontaritis, George B. *Greece and the First World War.* New York: Columbia University Press, 1940.

Young, Kenneth. *The Greek Passion.* London: Dent, 1969.

See also BALKAN FRONT, 1915, 1916, 1917; GREECE; SALONIKA CAMPAIGN; VENIZELOS, ELEUTHERIOS

Constantinople Agreements (Istanbul Agreements), 18 March 1915

A series of secret agreements regarding Turkey made by the Entente powers during the war. They were concluded by an exchange of notes among the foreign ministers of England, France, and Russia on 18 March 1915. Their main purpose was to decide who would control the city of Istanbul and the Turkish Straits.

After numerous disagreements among the powers, it was finally decided that Russia would be allowed control of Istanbul, the Bosphorus, and the Dardanelles. Istanbul, however, would be an open city for all the Entente powers; that would entitle them to free commercial navigation through the Straits. To be included among the Russian possessions were the islands in the Sea of Marmora and the islands of Imbros and Tenedos in the Aegean. These islands would give full control of navigation through the Straits, to the Russians, although they would not be allowed to build fortifications there. The Russians were also promised eastern Thrace to the Enos-Midia line, which was to be the boundary of Bulgaria. They would also get a stretch of Anatolia to the Sakarya River and the Gulf of Izmit. Britain would acquire the neutral zone in Persia, as established in 1907, and all of central Persia, including the Ispahan region. France would annex Syria and parts of Palestine and Cilicia.

After the Russian Revolution, when the Bolsheviks published the secret agreements and renounced the foreign policy of the Czarist regime, much in the Constantinople Agreements became obsolete.

Yücel Yanikdağ

References

Grey, Edward. *Twenty-Five Years*. 2 vols. New York: Frederick A. Stokes, 1925.

Howard, Harry N. *The Partition of Turkey: A Diplomatic History 1913–1923*. New York: Howard Fertig, 1966.

Shaw, Stanford J., and Ezel K. Shaw. *History of the Ottoman Empire and Modern Turkey*. 2 vols. Cambridge: Cambridge University Press, 1977.

Convoy System, Naval

The introduction of a general convoy system for merchant shipping in the late spring of 1917 is generally credited with turning the tide in the submarine campaign and causing the failure of Germany's unrestricted submarine warfare. Convoys were certainly not new; they were a common and generally successful method of protecting shipping in the age of sail. Moreover, they were used in the opening months of the war, but largely for troopships carrying men from Australia, New Zealand, Canada, South Africa, and India to European waters or other portions of the British Empire.

Apart from these so-called "Imperial Convoys," merchant shipping was allowed to proceed independently, following only general instructions from the admiralty about areas that were considered dangerous. Troopships were usually escorted, but, unless a ship was considered to be carrying exceptionally valuable cargo, escorts were not given to merchant shipping. The admiralty relied on dispersion for protection, that is, individual routes far removed from the usual shipping lanes. In March of 1916 the Allies adopted a system of patrolled routes in the Mediterranean. These measures were not successful—in fact, the safety of shipping depended more on the number of submarines the Germans were able to keep at sea and the rules under which they operated than any of the Allied countermeasures. Losses to submarines rose, and, after the Germans resumed unrestricted submarine warfare in February of 1917, losses vaulted to a shocking 860,334 tons in April. The Allies could not sustain losses of that magnitude and remain in the war.

The inevitable question is why there had been such an unconscionable delay in introducing methods that had worked so well in the past. The answer is that the weight of expert naval opinion—and not just in Great Britain—believed that the introduction of steam had altered the conditions of naval warfare. Convoys would now concentrate too many attractive targets in one vulnerable group and would be tied to the speed of the slowest ship. Merchant captains would not be experienced in maneuvering together with other ships under wartime conditions, particularly at night, when the number of navigational lights would be drastically reduced. The majority of merchant captains tended to agree with the admiralty.

There were also commercial objections. Ships would be forced to wait in port until convoys were formed. Furthermore, the arrival of a large number of ships at one time would overload port facilities, causing still further delay. It would be impossible to find the requisite number of escorts for convoys, given the volume of British and Allied shipping. Naval opinion also regarded convoys as merely "defensive." Naval officers instinctively preferred "offensive" actions like "hunting patrols," which searched for submarines wherever they were reported. Unfortunately, submarines rarely waited to be caught, and the patrols were a colossal waste of time and fuel.

The pressure of submarine losses did lead to the introduction of a few small convoys on an experimental basis before the crisis of April

1917. In July of 1916 the British began convoys to the Hook of Holland. That was as much in response to raids by German destroyers from the Flanders coast or Heligoland Bight as it was to the danger of submarines. Mounting losses or delays to shipping caused by submarines led the French in early 1917 to press for the protection of the coal traffic from the south of England; in February, French coal convoys began. Similar pressure from Norwegian shipowners for greater protection to traffic from Lerwick (Shetlands) to Bergen led to the gradual introduction of Scandinavian convoys; by the end of April the system was extended southward along the east coast of Great Britain.

These convoys accounted for only a relatively small proportion of trade. The decision to adopt a far-reaching system of oceanic convoys was not taken until the end of April. On the 25th the War Cabinet authorized the Prime Minister to investigate all means used in antisubmarine warfare. Lloyd George was by now thoroughly dissatisfied with the lack of progress in reducing losses and prepared for drastic measures.

By that time the admiralty had finally decided to introduce convoys. A pro-convoy officer, Commander R.G.H. Henderson of the Anti-Submarine Division, demonstrated that the admiralty had been using unreliable statistics, which greatly inflated the number of ships arriving at British ports, by not differentiating between long oceanic and coastal voyages; the result was to magnify the number of escorts that seemed necessary. It still would have been difficult to obtain the requisite number, but it was not impossible. The problem was to find the smaller escorts, the sloops and destroyers, to bring shipping through the danger zone around the British Isles. There was relatively little trouble finding a sufficient number of old battleships, cruisers, and armed merchant cruisers to protect convoys on the high seas. The entry of the United States into the war offered hope for a solution. Rear Admiral William Sims, future commander of United States naval forces in European waters, was horrified when he learned of the true situation upon visiting the admiralty in April of 1917. A proponent of the convoy system, he immediately recommended that the United States send as many destroyers as possible. The first group of six sailed shortly after the United States entered the war, and by the end of August 1917 there were thirty-five American destroyers working with the British under the command of Vice Admiral Sir Lewis Bayly at Queenstown.

On 27 April first sea lord admiral Sir John Jellicoe, approved the recommendation of Rear Admiral Alexander Duff, head of the Anti-Submarine Division, that all ships from the southern and northern Atlantic be convoyed. On 10 May the first trial convoy sailed from Gibraltar to the United Kingdom. It proved a success, and convoys were extended. It took time and enormous effort to establish the system, and losses, sometimes heavy, continued. Overall, the trend was down, something not always apparent to some who remained skeptical of the convoy system long after it had proved its usefulness.

The key to a successful convoy system was probably organization. A separate convoy section was formed at the admiralty under Fleet Paymaster H.W.E. Manisty to coordinate with both the Ministry of Shipping and the Intelligence Division. Cooperation of this sort had not always been the case in the past. Now, for example, intercepts of submarine wireless traffic obtained from "Room 40" were plotted on a large map showing the location of the convoys, which were then routed by wireless away from danger areas.

In June and July, an elaborate system of convoys developed. The most important were the HH convoys from Hampton Roads, the HS convoys from Sydney, Cape Breton Island (Halifax, Nova Scotia, in the winter), the HN convoys from New York, and the HG convoys from Gibraltar. The system was expanded to include South American convoys and, in October and November, outward (OE) and homeward (HE) convoys through the Mediterranean to Port Said. In the Mediterranean, the French and Italians also introduced their own convoy systems.

One of the reasons losses declined dramatically was that German submarine commanders found the seas empty. Formerly, they needed only wait along shipping routes for ships to appear. Convoys were now hard to find and harder to attack. The presence of escorts ruled out attack by gunfire on the surface, and, with the convoy zigzagging, it was much more difficult for a submerged submarine to maneuver into a favorable position for an attack. U-boat losses also rose, because convoys partially solved the problem of finding submarines. The submarines were now drawn to where the escorts had a chance to destroy them. Losses among outward-bound shipping, however, remained high. Consequently, in August the admiralty began a series of outward-bound convoys that eventually matched the homeward convoys. The admiralty attempted to solve the problem of obtaining enough escorts by having escorts that had taken an outward convoy through the submarine danger zone meet a homeward-bound convoy at a specified rendezvous. That called for precise scheduling and considerable coordination.

The Germans probed for weak spots, and in early October 1917 they increased attacks on shipping in coastal waters, that is, in the areas between the convoy assembly and dispersal points and the individual ports. The British then altered their convoy assembly points and, in 1918, began a series of local convoys to complement the ocean convoys. Coastal convoys also benefited from the increasing numbers of aircraft in service. The technology of the time rarely permitted aircraft to kill a submarine, but they could keep them down and restrict their ability to find a favorable firing position.

Convoys certainly did not provide immunity to submarine attack, but they did reduce losses to acceptable proportions. Submarines proved unable to impede the massive flow of American troops and supplies in the summer of 1918. That flow altered the balance on the Western Front.

Paul G. Halpern

References

Fayle, C. Ernest. *Seaborne Trade*. Vol. 3: *The Period of Unrestricted Submarine Warfare*. London: John Murray, 1924.

Hezlet, Vice-Admiral Sir Arthur. *The Submarine and Sea Power*. London: Peter Davies, 1967.

Marder, Arthur J. *From the Dreadnought to Scapa Flow: The Royal Navy in the Fisher Era, 1904–1919*. Vol. 4, *1917: Year of Crisis*, and Vol. 5, *Victory and Aftermath (January 1918–June 1919)*. London: Oxford University Press, 1969–70.

Newbolt, Henry. *Naval Operations*. Vols. 4 and 5. London: Longmans, Green, 1928–31.

MAJOR HOMEWARD AND OUTWARD CONVOY SYSTEMS, 1917–18

Convoy	Route	Net Number of Convoys
HH	Hampton Roads—east or west coast of England	75
HN	New York—east or west coast of England (later east coast only)	89
HX	Halifax (later New York)—west coast of England	55
HS	Sydney or Halifax—east or west coast of England	61
HC	Halifax—east or west coast of England	23
HB	New York—Bay of Biscay	19
HG	Gibraltar—east or west coast of England	119
HD	Dakar—east or west coast of England (slow)	56
HL	Sierra Leone—east or west coast of England (fast)	55
HJL	Rio de Janeiro—England (fast)	3
HJD	Rio de Janeiro—England (slow)	19
HE	through Mediterranean—England	22

Convoy	Port	Frequency	Net Number of Convoys
OB	Lamlash	every 8 days	87
OLB	Liverpool	every 8 days north (slow)	14
OLX	Liverpool	every 8 days north (fast—13 knots)	13
OL	Liverpool	every 8 days south (10–11.5 knots)	39
OE	Liverpool	every 16 days Mediterranean	24
OM	Milford	every 4 days	113
OF	Falmouth	every 8 days	57
OD	Devonport	approx. every 3 days	135
OC	Southend	every 16 days	10

Tables based on Admiralty, Technical History Section, *TH 14. The Atlantic Convoy System, 1917–1918* (October 1919), and *TH 15. Convoy Statistics and Diagrams* (February 1920).

Winton, John. *Convoy: The Defence of Sea Trade, 1890–1990*. London: Michael Joseph, 1983.

See also ASDIC; DEPTH CHARGES; ROOM 40; SUBMARINE WARFARE, CENTRAL POWERS

Corfu, Declaration of (20 July 1917)

On 15 June 1917, Serbian, Croatian, and Slovenian representatives met on the island of Corfu to begin discussions on the formation of a united and independent Balkan state. Serbian Prime Minister Nikola Pašić proposed a centralized state. Ante Trumbić, a Croat, favored federalization, but he was unable to convince his supporters that a federal solution would benefit them.

The discussions resulted in the Declaration of Corfu, signed 20 July 1917, in which the Yugoslav Committee, representing Croats and Slovenes, and the Serbian government agreed to cooperate on the establishment of a Yugoslav state. It was to consist of a constitutional monarchy under the Karađorđević (Serb) dynasty and a constituent assembly, elected on the basis of universal male suffrage. The representatives decided that the constituent assembly would draft the constitution, which would have to be accepted in its entirety by more than a simple majority. Final sanctioning would come from the king.

The declaration, representing a compromise between the Serbs and the Yugoslav Committee, recognized the Serbs, Croats, and Slovenes, their flags and religions, and the Cyrillic and Roman alphabets. It included Macedonians, Montenegrins, Albanians, and Bosnian Muslims under the heading of Serbs, Croats, and Slovenes. In this compromise the Serbs, with the larger population and under their own king, would have the advantage. This declaration bound the Serb government to a Yugoslav solution and contributed to the dissolution of the Hapsburg monarchy.

Susan N. Carter

References

Banac, Ivo. *The National Question in Yugoslavia: Origins, History, Politics*. Ithaca: Cornell University Press, 1984.

Grlica, George. "Trumbić's Policy and Croatian National Interests from 1914 to the Beginning of 1918." *Journal of Croatian Studies* 14–15 (1973–74): 74–112.

Jelavich, Barbara. *History of the Balkans*. Vol. 2, *Twentieth Century*. New York: Cambridge University Press, 1983. Reprint. New York: Cambridge University Press, 1989.

See also PAŠIĆ, NIKOLA; TRUMBIĆ, ANTE; YUGOSLAVIA, CREATION OF

Coronel, Battle of (1 November 1914)

Naval battle between Royal Navy and German East Asia Squadron. With the outbreak of war in 1914, German Admiral Maximilian Graf von Spee had moved his East Asia Squadron of two heavy cruisers (the *Scharnhorst* and *Gneisenau*) and three light cruisers (the *Nürnberg, Dresden* and *Leipzig*) out of their base at Tsingtao. By 14 October 1914 he had concentrated his forces at Easter Island. He had received word that British Vice Admiral Sir Christopher Cradock's flagship, *Good Hope,* another heavy cruiser (*Monmouth*) and the light cruiser *Glasgow* were in the near vicinity, and he hoped to engage and defeat them.

The Royal Navy, however, had learned of Spee's movement to Easter Island. In response, the admiralty prepared a force strong enough to overcome Spee's squadron. Cradock, however, feared that Spee's squadron would evade his own and have free reign to attack the Falkland Islands, English Bank, and the Abrothos coaling bases. He telegraphed London on 8 October, requesting that Royal Navy units be positioned on each coast of South America, with each force strong enough to bring the Germans into action.

The admiralty denied Cradock's request. Instead, Churchill ordered out the old battleship *Canopus,* with four 12-inch guns, despite Cradock's warnings that it would slow his squadron's speed to a mere twelve knots. It was unclear how Cradock, with a twelve-knot squadron, could engage and defeat Spee's squadron, which was capable of making twenty knots. Moreover, the *Canopus* had guns of an early type that could not outrange Spee's smaller guns, and her gun crews were reservists who had not had an opportunity to practice fire. The *Canopus* arrived at the Falklands on 22 October; there she underwent maintenance to improve her speed.

Cradock left *Canopus* at Port Stanley to go out in search of what he thought was a lone German ship, the *Leipzig*. At the same time, the Germans were hunting the *Glasgow*, which Cradock had detached to Coronel on 27 October under orders that it rendezvous with the rest of the squadron at noon on 1 November. This situation, in which both sides were searching for a single enemy ship, brought the two enemy squadrons together off the west coast of South America near Coronel.

At 16:40 on 1 November, Cradock, in his northward search for the *Leipzig*, sighted the German cruiser squadron. Although the two squadrons were approximately equal in total firepower, the Germans held a clear advantage. The *Good Hope* had only two 9.2-inch guns at bow and stern, and it was the only ship in the squadron with guns of that size. In broadsides, *Good Hope* had sixteen 6-inch guns. None of the other ships in Cradock's squadron had guns larger than 6-inch; without *Canopus*, Cradock was at a grave disadvantage.

The German force had more long-range guns. *Scharnhorst* and *Gneisenau* mounted a total of eight 8.2-inch guns with maximum range of 13,500 meters. These were the weapons that would decide the outcome of the battle. At 18:34 the Germans opened action at a range of 12,300 meters, barely within the 12,500-meter range of Cradock's largest guns. At 18:50 the *Monmouth* fell out of line, damaged and helpless; thirty-three minutes later, the Germans hit the *Good Hope,* which exploded. At 19:26 the German cruisers stopped firing. The *Good Hope* sank at about 20:00, with 895 of its total complement of 900 aboard, including Cradock.

The *Monmouth* drifted until about 21:00, when the *Nürnberg* located and sank her in the darkness. Her total complement of 675 men were lost. Just before his vessel was discovered, *Monmouth*'s captain ordered the *Glasgow* to escape, and both she and the armed auxiliary *Otranto,* which had kept at safe distance from the battle, were able to slip away in the night.

The Battle of Coronel was a demoralizing setback for the British admiralty and nation. The news shocked Britain, as the British public had not expected a defeat of this magnitude. There was some fear that Spee would steam around Cape Horn and attack all of the vulnerable British naval installations. Fortunately for the British, a month later Vice Admiral F.D. Sturdee caught and defeated Spee's squadron in the Battle of the Falkland Islands.

Mark A. Macina

References

Bennett, Geoffrey. *Coronel and the Falklands.* London: Pan, 1967.
Frothingham, Thomas. *The Naval History of the World War—Offensive Operations, 1914–1915.* New York: Books For Libraries, 1971.
Hough, Richard. *The Great War at Sea, 1914–1918.* Oxford: Oxford University Press, 1983.

See also CRADOCK, SIR CHRISTOPHER; SPEE, MAXIMILIAN GRAF VON

Cradock, Sir Christopher George Francis Maurice (1862–1914)

British rear admiral. Born at Hartforth on 2 July 1862, Cradock joined the Royal Navy in 1875. During the Boxer Rebellion in China, he directed the storming of the forts at Tientsin. Promoted to rear admiral in 1910, Cradock was given command of the North American and West Indies Station in February of 1913, with the task of protecting the North Atlantic trading routes.

When the war began, Cradock's squadron attempted to catch the German cruisers *Dresden* and *Karlsruhe* but failed. The admiralty then ordered Cradock south to the Falklands, where his squadron was to intercept German trade and attempt to destroy the German East Asiatic Squadron under Admiral Maximilian Graf von Spee. On 1 November 1914 off Coronel near the Chilean coast, Cradock's weak force of two elderly cruisers, one light cruiser, and one armed merchant cruiser faced Spee's larger, faster, and more heavily armed squadron. Cradock forced the engagement anyway, possibly hoping to inflict damage on the enemy far from its repair bases, even though it meant possibly sacrificing his own force. The battle lasted barely two hours. The Germans sank the *Good Hope* and the *Monmouth,* with the loss of all hands including Cradock (a total of 1,600 men). An inquiry exonerated Cradock of recklessness and blamed his defeat on late-arriving reinforcements and ambiguous admiralty orders.

Andrzej Suchcitz

References

Bennett, Geoffrey. *Coronel and the Falklands.* London: Pan, 1967.

Hough, Richard. *The Pursuit of Admiral von Spee.* London: George Allen and Unwin, 1969.

See also CORONEL, BATTLE OF; SPEE, MAXIMILIAN GRAF VON

Currie, Sir Arthur W. (1875–1933)

British Canadian lieutenant general. Arthur Currie was born near Strathroy, Ontario, on 5 December 1875. He moved to British Columbia after training as a teacher. There he served in the militia and made a living as a real-estate agent.

Currie commanded the 2nd Canadian Infantry Brigade at Ypres during the German gas attacks in 1915 and acquitted himself well. He made mistakes, but, as one associate put it, "Currie did not make the same mistake twice—a very great virtue in a soldier." Promoted in 1915, he took command of the 1st (Canadian) Division, which did well under his leadership at the Somme in 1916. He helped greatly with the planning and capture of Vimy Ridge by the Canadian Corps on 9 April 1917.

In June of 1917 Currie was promoted to lieutenant general and took command of the Canadian Corps. The corps achieved tremendous success throughout 1917–18, capturing Lens (1917) and Passchendaele (1917), attacking at Amiens (1918), breaking the Hindenburg Line (1918), crossing the Canal du Nord (1918), and finishing with the recapture of Mons on the last day of the war. After the Armistice, Currie commanded the Canadian portion of the occupation force in Germany.

Currie was one of a number of superb corps commanders produced by the BEF during the war. His maxim was "Thorough preparation leads to success, neglect nothing." His goal was minimal Canadian casualties through the maximum application of firepower and planning. Currie was chancellor of McGill University when he died in Montreal on 30 November 1933.

Ian M. Brown

References

Dancocks, Daniel. *Sir Arthur Currie: A Biography.* Toronto: Methuen, 1985.

Hyatt, A.M.J. *General Sir Arthur Currie.* Toronto: University of Toronto Press, 1987.

Urquhart, Hugh M. *Arthur Currie: The Biography of a Great Canadian.* Toronto: J.M. Dent, 1950.

See also CANADA, ARMY; VIMY RIDGE; YPRES, SECOND BATTLE OF

Czech Legion

From 1918 to 1920, the 45,000 men of the Czech Legion were the most effective fighting force in Russia. For much of that time, they controlled the Trans-Siberian railway and significantly influenced end-of-war diplomacy.

When World War I started, approximately one-tenth of the 100,000 Czech citizens of Czarist Russia joined the Druzina—a regiment of Czech nationals. In 1914 and 1915 thousands of additional Czechs, influenced by panslavism, surrendered without resistance and were interned in Russia. When Czar Nicholas II abdicated in 1917, the French encouraged the provisional government to combine the prisoners of war and the Druzina into a Czech army. Two divisions were created and based at Kiev.

The Czech divisions participated effectively in the Kerensky Offensive of July 1917 but, when Kerensky's government approached collapse that fall, Tomáš Masaryk began negotiations to send the Czech Legion to the Western Front, where they could continue to fight for the Allies. As part of the diplomatic maneuvering, France agreed to recognize the existence of a Czech state with the legion as its army.

Meanwhile, the Czech soldiers remained in Russia and came under immediate threat in January of 1918 when the Ukraine declared its independence and the German army began to converge on Kiev. On behalf of his new state, Masaryk declared war on the Central Powers. The legion moved north and defeated the Germans in March at Bakhmach. From there, the Czechs took the railway east to Moscow, destroying tracks behind them.

From Moscow, the Russian railway ran north to Petrograd and east in two lines—a northern one through Perm and Ekaterinburg and a southern through Samara and Chelyabinsk. The lines rejoined at Omsk and went on as a single track to Chita in eastern Siberia. At Chita the line branched again. The northern limb went through Kharbarovsk to Vladivostok, while the southern line crossed north China and Harbin on the way to the same city. This was to be the Czech route to freedom.

The British, the French, and the Bolsheviks had differing interests in the Czech Legion. Great Britain wanted them to guard supplies at the northern ports of Archangel and Murmansk. France wanted the soldiers to reinforce the Western Front. The Treaty of Brest-Litovsk obligated the Bolshevik government to expel foreign troops from Russian soil. Besides, the new government was uneasy about such a large fighting force operating inside Russian borders. Leon Trotsky was torn between a desire to have the Czechs out of his country and a wish to incorporate them into the Red Army.

The retreating Czech Legion scattered along the Trans-Siberian railway from Penza to Chelyabinsk and had been forced to trade much of its arms and ammunition for access to rolling stock. When an Austrian prisoner of war killed a Czech legionnaire on 14 March 1918, the first overt fighting between the Czechs and the Red Army began. The Czechs captured Chelyabinsk and began an organized campaign against the Bolsheviks; within six weeks they controlled the entire railway from the Volga to Vladivostok.

On 6 July 1918 President Wilson used the immense popularity of the Czech Legion to justify joining France, Great Britain, and Japan in the Siberian intervention. In fact, Wilson was more concerned with the possible return of German and Austrian prisoners of war to the Western Front and with the possibility of Germany and Japan dividing the Russian land mass than he was with the fate of the Czechs.

When an independent Siberian Republic was declared on 23 July 1918, the Czechs agreed to support it against the Red Army. By 3 August a combined force of Czechs, Cossacks, White Russians, British, Japanese, and Americans occupied Vladivostok. The Czechs who had reached that city were ordered to return to the Volga and to make contact with Allied forces that had landed at Archangel and Murmansk.

Trotsky personally took command of the Red Army contingent that defeated the Czechs as they moved west through Kazan on 5 September. Although the tired, demoralized Czech Legion wanted only to return home, Masaryk ordered them to stay in Siberia. He hoped that their cooperation with the Allies in Russia would favorably influence the coming peace negotiations.

When the Armistice was declared in November it applied only to the Western Front, leaving the Czechs stranded in Russia, facing the Siberian winter and the hostile Red Army. Their slow eastward retreat that winter brought them to Omsk by August of 1919. When the independent Siberian government collapsed and the Americans withdrew late in 1919, the Czechs' situation became desperate. Most of the legion was west of Lake Baikal, the Red Army was advancing from the east, and the counter-revolutionaries resisted a Czech retreat in hopes of forcing a fight that would weaken the Bolsheviks.

Over the next six months the legion was forced to defeat Ataman Semyonov's Cossacks to reach Vladivostok, where ships chartered by American Czechs and the Red Cross waited to take them to the United States. From San Francisco the Czech Legion crossed North America and the Atlantic and, eventually, returned home to form the nucleus of the new Czechoslovak army.

Jack McCallum

References

Hoyt, Edwin. *The Army without a Country.* New York: Macmillan, 1967.

Unterberger, Betty. *The United States, Revolutionary Russia, and the Rise of Czechoslovakia.* Chapel Hill: University of North Carolina Press, 1989.

See also CZECHS; MASARYK, TOMÁŠ; RUSSIA, ALLIED INTERVENTION IN; RUSSIA, CIVIL WAR IN

Czechs

World War I presented the Czechs of the Austrian Empire with the opportunity to regain national independence, which they had lost in the Thirty Years War (1618–48). As one of many nationalities within the Austro-Hungarian Empire, the Czechs struggled to gain a voice over their own affairs and underwent a great national revival during the nineteenth century. After universal male suffrage was instituted in the Austrian half of the empire in 1906, the Czech representatives in the *Reichsrat* in Vienna worked for a federated Austria in which the various nationalities would possess greater autonomy.

When World War I began, many Czech nationalists looked to the great Slavic empire of Russia as a possible liberator. Czech immigrants in Russia visited Czar Nicholas II in Moscow on

20 August 1914 to seek his support for Czech independence, but his response was minimal. In addition, in September Czech immigrants formed a volunteer army unit, Ceská druzina, which contained Czech deserters from the Austro-Hungarian army. Early Russian losses at Tannenberg and the Masurian Lakes shattered Czech expectations.

Other Czechs, led by Tomáš Masaryk, were not content to wait for Russia. Masaryk feared exchanging one imperial domination for another, because Russia would expect adequate compensation for her help. He also realized that the Central Powers could lose the war, and that a weak Russia would play a lesser role in the peace process than the Western nations. Masaryk therefore made several trips to neutral countries in 1914 to try to solicit Western help. While on one of those trips, he learned that the Austrian government had ordered his arrest; he therefore stayed abroad to continue his efforts. Masaryk left behind a group of loyal followers known as the Czech Mafia. In 1915 he was joined by two assistants, Edvard Beneš (his life-long collaborator) and the Slovak leader Milan Rastislav Stefánik.

Because the Western Allies still hoped to pull Austria-Hungary away from Germany, they were at first noncommittal on Czech autonomy, not wanting to side with any of Austria's nationalities. The Czechs persisted. On 14 November 1915 Czech exiles in Paris launched the Czech movement for independence when the Czech Foreign Committee, as they now styled themselves, issued a declaration demanding the establishment of an independent state. In 1916 the committee transformed itself into the National Council of the Czech Lands with its headquarters in Paris; Masaryk was chairman, with Josef Dürich and Stefánik as vice-chairmen and Beneš as secretary-general. Czech persistence began to pay off when, on 10 January 1917, the Allies issued a statement of war aims that included liberation of Czech lands.

In response, Austrian Foreign Minister Ottokar Count Czernin forced Czech *Reichsrat* members to repudiate Allied calls for liberation, and Emperor Karl put out peace feelers, intimating that Austria might make a separate peace if the Allies promised not to dismember the empire. Secret negotiations along those lines lasted from March of 1917 until April of 1918, making the Allies reluctant to commit to the Czechs.

Efforts with Russia, meanwhile, had grown complicated because of her internal problems. In 1916 Dürich had traveled to Moscow, where he joined the ultraconservative Panslavs, repudiated the Paris National Council, and, in January of 1917, formed a rival Czech council in Petrograd. That organization was short-lived, however, because of the revolution. By the time Masaryk arrived, in May of 1917, Alexander Kerensky was the new strongman. He was disinclined to help the Czechs because he feared the breakup of the Russian Empire along national lines. Kerensky shifted his stance after military victories on the Eastern Front in July in which the Czech unit distinguished itself. The Russian high command was authorized to organize an autonomous Czech army in Russia.

The November Bolshevik coup and Lenin's subsequent Peace Decree again changed Czech strategy. During the peace negotiations between Russia and the Central Powers, Czech leaders in Vienna demanded representation at Brest-Litovsk, but they were ignored. With the subsequent Russo-German armistice of 5 December 1917 and the United States declaration of war against Austria-Hungary on 7 December 1917, the Czechs turned their hopes to America. Before leaving for the United States, Masaryk arranged in March of 1918 for the Czech Legion to leave Russia and proceed to the Western Front via Siberia.

After negotiations with Austria-Hungary had failed, President Wilson openly encouraged Austro-Hungarian nationalities to revolt by announcing on 29 May 1918 that "nationalistic aspirations had U.S. sympathy." The French, British, and Italians concurred on 3 June 1918. The outbreak of conflict between the Czech army and the Soviet government in May of 1918 expanded the Russian Civil War, brought Allied intervention in Russia, and helped commit Wilson to supporting the Czechs. On preparing to intervene in Russia on 30 June, the French recognized the Czech National Council (CNC) as the official agency authorized to represent the Czech cause; the British followed suit on 9 August. The Americans went even further in September by recognizing the CNC as the de facto government of the Czechs.

By now Austria-Hungary was nearing its demise, and its leadership scrambled to preserve the empire. After two failed peace initiatives, Emperor Karl issued a manifesto on 16 October 1918 that federalized the Austrian half of the empire and authorized or sanctioned national committees. Masaryk (in the United States) issued a Czech declaration of independence. The empire began to disintegrate. The German-Austrian deputies withdrew from the *Reichsrat* on 21 October and constituted a provisional national assembly as an independent German-Austrian state, which they hoped to unite with Germany. Austria-Hungary sued for peace on 27 October.

The Prague National Committee, formed by Karel Kramář in July as preparation for such an event, issued its first law on 28 October, "the independent Czech state [having] come into being." Kramář and Beneš met at Geneva on 31 October to iron out the specifics for starting the new Czech state. It would be a democratic, parliamentary system with Masaryk as president, Kramář as premier, Beneš as foreign minister, and Štefánik as minister of war. On 13 November, two days after the emperor abdicated and one day after the declaration of the German-Austrian Republic, a provisional constitution was issued, creating a provisional national assembly. That body elected Masaryk president.

The dissolution of the Austro-Hungarian Empire was a *fait accompli* by the time of the Paris Peace Conference in 1919. Kramář and Beneš led the Czech delegation, which pushed for formal recognition of the new Czechoslovak state based on the historic boundaries of Bohemia, Moravia, Slovakia, Austrian Silesia, and Ruthenia. The Council of Ten at the conference created a Commission of Czech Affairs to advise them. The Treaty of St. Germain with Austria and the Treaty of Trianon with Hungary outlined the new Czech state. Czechoslovakia also had to sign a "minorities" treaty, which put her numerous ethnic minorities under League protection, as well as a treaty of financial settlement with the Allies. This financial treaty asserted that the new Czech state had to share in the financial obligations of the old empire; thus the new state had to pay reparations based on its ability to pay: For Czechoslovakia that came to 750 million gold francs.

A new independent Czech state had been created as a result of the breakup of the old Austro-Hungarian empire, a breakup speeded along by the Czechs themselves. Unfortunately, the new state faced many problems, particularly with her large German minority. Between the world wars Czechoslovakia remained the only democracy in Eastern Europe, but in 1938 she was sold out to her large German neighbor by her Western allies.

Laura Matysek Wood

References

Seton-Watson, Robert W. *History of the Czechs and the Slovaks*. London: Hutchinson, 1943.

Thomson, S. Harrison. *Czechoslovakia in European History*. Princeton: Princeton University Press, 1953.

Wallace, William V. Czechoslovakia. Boulder, Colo.: Westview Press, 1976.

See also BENEŠ, EDVARD; MASARYK, TOMÁŠ

C

Czernin, Count Ottokar (1872–1932)

Austro-Hungarian minister of foreign affairs. Born at Dymokury on 26 September 1872, Czernin entered the diplomatic corps upon graduating from the German university in Prague but resigned as a result of a lung infection. His close friendship with Archduke Franz Ferdinand led him to return to the diplomatic service. Upon the outbreak of World War I, Count Czernin was Austro-Hungarian minister to Bucharest. During the early months of fighting he strove successfully to keep Romania neutral, thanks in part to the support of the aged King Carol. Most Romanians did not share Carol's strongly pro-German sentiments, and Czernin could not persuade his own government to promise territorial concessions that might have prolonged Romanian neutrality. Romania entered the war on the side of the Allies in August of 1916.

With the accession of the new emperor, Karl I, Czernin was appointed minister of foreign affairs on 23 December 1916. He quickly discovered that Austria's increasing wartime dependence on Germany rendered a truly independent foreign policy impossible. His efforts in 1917 to persuade the German government of the need for a peace by compromise proved unsuccessful.

At the peace negotiations at Brest-Litovsk, 1917–18, Czernin agreed to cede Chelm to the newly created Ukrainian Republic. The "bread peace" of 9 February 1918 did not solve Austria's food-supply problem, but it did earn Czernin the hatred of Austrian Poles, who also claimed Chelm.

The Sixte Affair led to Czernin's fall from office. Emperor Karl, using Prince Sixte of

Bourbon-Parma as his intermediary, secretly assured French president Raymond Poincaré by letter (24 March 1917) that he would support France's claims to Alsace-Lorraine. Czernin was not kept fully informed of these negotiations. When Clemenceau published the letter a year later, Czernin, feeling himself betrayed by Karl, resigned on 15 April 1918. His diplomatic efforts to disengage his country from World War I failed to prevent the dissolution of the Hapsburg Monarchy. He died at Vienna on 4 April 1932.

William L. Mathes

References

Czernin, Ottokar. *In the World War*. New York and London: Harper Brothers, 1920.

Meckling, Ingeborg. *Die Aussenpolitik des Grafen Czernin*. Vienna: Geschichte und Politik, 1969.

Singer, Ladislaus. *Ottokar Graf Czernin; Staatsmann einer Zeitenwende*. Graz: Verlag Styria, 1965.

See also KARL I, EMPEROR OF AUSTRIA; SIXTE, PRINCE OF BOURBON-PARMA

D

Danilov, Yury Nikiforovich (1866–1937)

Russian army general. Born in the Ukraine on 13 August 1866, Danilov graduated from the Mikhailovsky Artillery School, served briefly as a line officer, and in 1892 graduated from the General Staff Academy. Although Danilov held some line posts, he made his reputation as a staff officer. He also taught at the General Staff Academy and wrote extensively on military subjects. Danilov rose rapidly in rank to the post of quartermaster general, which he held in 1914. Although the term quartermaster general implies supervising supplies and transportation, in the Russian army it was comparable in duties to an operations officer in Western armies. Danilov was therefore responsible for drafting military orders and supervising overall military planning.

Upon the outbreak of war in August of 1914, Danilov was chosen deputy chief of staff under General Nikolai Yanushkevich. Both were on the staff of commander-in-chief Grand Duke Nikolai Nikolaevich. After the war began Danilov and his colleagues moved to army field headquarters in the Polish town of Baranovichi, a rail center between Warsaw and Vilna. By most accounts, Danilov was one of the ablest members of the general staff. He was a hard worker, a strict disciplinarian, and "the brains" of the staff.

Danilov had a key role in planning Russia's East Prussian Campaign at the beginning of the war. Among the senior officers there were two schools of thought. One was headed by General M.V. Alekseev, who saw Austria as the weak link of the Central Powers and urged that Russia's offensive efforts be directed toward that target (as it turned out, this was a correct appraisal). Danilov, on the other hand, championed the anti-German faction, also correct in the long run, which held that victory was dependent on the defeat of Germany and that this should be the primary goal of the Russian army. Consequently, it was no surprise that shortly after the war began, in answer to French pleas for a Russian attack to relieve pressure in the West, Danilov wholeheartedly supported an offensive into East Prussia (although it is unclear whether it was his own idea). He pressed this issue on two grounds: that East Prussia was the shortest route to Berlin, and that it was a matter of honor that Russia help her ally. Since he was the most experienced officer on the general staff, his proposal was accepted by the grand duke. Consequently, much of the planning for this ad hoc campaign (the original Russian plan called for an invasion of Austrian Galicia) was left to Danilov. The result was the Russian disaster at Tannenberg.

In September of 1915, when Czar Nicholas II took personal command of the army, he chose General Alekseev as his own chief of staff. General Danilov then became chief of staff to General Nikolai Ruzsky, commander of the Northern Front. For a time he commanded Fifth Army. With the end of the monarchy he immigrated to France, where he wrote his memoirs. He died in Paris on 3 November 1937.

John W. Bohon

References

Danilov, Yury. *La Russie dans la guerre mondiale (1914–1917)*. Paris: Payot, 1927.

Gurko, General Basil. *Features and Figures of the Past*. Stanford, Calif.: Stanford University Press, 1939.

Showalter, Dennis E. *Tannenberg, Clash of Empires*. Hamden, Conn.: Archon, 1991.

See also EAST PRUSSIA CAMPAIGN

Dankl von Krasnik, Viktor (1854–1941)

Austro-Hungarian general. Born 18 September 1854 in Udine, Italy, Dankl brought forty-four years of experience as a cavalryman and staff officer to his first wartime command, the First Austro-Hungarian Army. A competent if unimaginative leader, in August of 1914 he attacked north into Poland. Blundering into a series of engagements, by mid-September Dankl found himself outflanked. Ordered to withdraw, Dankl was unable to prevent the retreat from degenerating into a rout. His army fell back upon Cracow and thereafter played a minor role in the seesaw fighting that raged across Galicia and Poland during the remainder of 1914.

In April of 1915 Dankl transferred to the Italian frontier, where he had one understrength corps with which to defend the Tyrolean passes against the Italians. The next summer Dankl spearheaded the Trentino Offensive. Commanding Eleventh Army, Dankl tried to force his way out of the Alps to the northern Italian plains, enveloping enemy positions along the Isonzo. Mountainous terrain, Italian heroics, and the meddling of headquarters thwarted Dankl's plans and led the entire offensive to grind to a halt short of its objectives. Archduke Eugen and Austrian Chief of Staff Franz Conrad von Hötzendorf ascribed the offensive's failure to Dankl's mismanagement. Infuriated, Dankl asked to be relieved of his command. The archduke complied in June of 1916, and Dankl never again commanded troops during the war. He died at Innsbruck on 8 January 1941.

Steven Eden

References

Rothenberg, Gunther. *The Army of Francis Joseph.* Princeton: Princeton University Press, 1976.

Stone, Norman. *The Eastern Front, 1914–1917.* New York: Charles Scribner's Sons, 1975.

Villari, Luigi. *The War on the Italian Front.* London: Cobden-Sanderson, 1932.

Young, Peter. *History of the First World War.* 8 vols. London: BPC Publishing, 1971.

See also POLAND: GERMAN OFFENSIVE OF SEPTEMBER–NOVEMBER 1914; TRENTINO OFFENSIVE

D'Annunzio, Gabriele (1863–1938)

Italian poet and war propagandist. Born at Pescara, Italy, on the Adriatic Sea on 12 March 1863, the son of a wealthy landowner, D'Annunzio was full of a vibrant, irrepressible energy that expressed itself in fast cars, fast airplanes, fast spending, and fast women. A poet, writer, and radical amateur politician who alternately passed from the extreme right to the extreme left, D'Annunzio nevertheless remained an ardent nationalist and irredentist who burned to reclaim Italian lands from Austria-Hungary. An unfulfilled, highly individualistic Romantic cast in the Nietzschean vein, D'Annunzio sought immortality through the compelling word and a heroically patriotic death.

In May of 1915 D'Annunzio facilitated Italian entry into World War I on behalf of the Allies during a whirlwind tour of speeches and oratorical harangues. From 1915 to 1918 he became an aficionado of propaganda, termed by some as an "arch-angel of battle." He was largely attached to the staff of General-in-Chief Luigi Cadorna as a freelancer dispensing "moral force." D'Annunzio entered the war as a lieutenant in the cavalry and ended as a colonel. He variously both led and participated in infantry attacks, actions with the Alpini, traveled in a submarine, raided the Austro-Hungarian fleet in a motorboat, and delivered speeches to the Italian navy. He is primarily known for his aerial exploits over enemy lines, which included the long-range bombing of Vienna with propaganda leaflets in August of 1918.

After the war D'Annunzio became the guiding light for nationalists disappointed with Italian gains at the Paris Peace Conference. In September of 1919 he and his followers resorted to aggression by attacking and capturing the Italian-speaking Adriatic port of Fiume, coveted both by Italy and the newly created Yugoslavia. Over the next year his attempts to force the Italian government to annex Fiume failed; he had gained a significant hearing, however, and nationalist elements spoke of him as leader, or *Duce*. Consequently, he has been viewed as a forerunner of Mussolini and fascism. D'Annunzio died at Lake Garda on 1 March 1938.

David L. Bullock

References

Antongini, Tom. *D'Annunzio.* London: William Heinemann, 1938.

Griffin, Gerald. *Gabriele D'Annunzio: The Warrior Bard*. Port Washington, N.Y.: Kennikat, 1970.

Jullian, Philippe. *D'Annunzio*. New York: Viking, 1973.

Mack Smith, Denis. *Italy: A Modern History*. Ann Arbor: University of Michigan Press, 1959.

Dardanelles Campaign

The Dardanelles Campaign in 1915 was the Allied attempt to open the Straits connecting the Black Sea with the Mediterranean. It was one of the great missed opportunities of the war.

German Rear Admiral Wilhelm Souchon's bombardment of Russian Black Sea bases had brought Turkey into the First World War on the side of the Central Powers, severing French and British access to the Black Sea and greatly increasing their difficulties in getting military supplies to Russia. It also denied Russia a means of exporting her goods to the West, thus exacerbating that country's financial difficulties.

Reopening the Dardanelles was at first not a high priority for Britain and France; their attention was fixed on the campaign in France. The stalemate there, however, led to increased interest in a flanking movement elsewhere. Early in the war, First Lord of the Admiralty Winston Churchill and secretary of state for war Field Marshal Earl Horatio Kitchener discussed a plan aimed at supporting a Greek landing on the Gallipoli peninsula to silence land batteries guarding the Straits, so that an Allied naval force could sail through them and threaten Constantinople. The Greeks initially turned down the project, and British and French generals said they could spare no manpower of their own.

At the end of December 1914 Lieutenant Colonel Maurice Hankey, secretary of the war council, submitted his own persuasive plan for a Dardanelles campaign. Hankey argued that, while the French armies held the deadlocked Western Front, Britain should use her sea power and newly raised land forces to strike a blow against Germany by attacking her weakest ally, Turkey. Hankey proposed the attack be made by three corps of Kitchener's New Army, preferably supported by both Greece and Bulgaria (both of which were then neutral).

A few French generals supported the plan; most, including French army commander Joseph Joffre, opposed it. They believed that a decision in the war could come only in its main theater and that all available forces should be massed on the Western Front. Churchill was the chief proponent of the plan; the Dardanelles offered an opportunity for action. First Sea Lord John Fisher went along, provided that the attack be "immediate" and supported by troops. Kitchener played the key role; originally skeptical, he was persuaded by a plea from Russian commander in chief Grand Duke Nikolai Nikolaevich.

By the beginning of 1915, the Russians, reeling from the effects of twin defeats at Tannenberg and the Masurian Lakes, appealed for a diversionary attack to relieve Turkish pressure in the Caucasus. Such a blow would free Russian troops to fight the German and Austro-Hungarian armies as well as reopen the Black Sea route for imports of arms and ammunition and the export of grain.

Kitchener opposed drawing troops from France and insisted on a purely naval operation. His newly raised land troops would go to France. After much debate, the war council decided on a naval action alone against the Dardanelles, with Constantinople as its objective. Churchill and other advocates of the plan believed that it would force Turkey out of the war and possibly bring some of the Balkan states into the war on the side of the Entente. It could also expose the Central Powers to a new line of attack from the southeast. Finally, it would diminish the possibility of an attack by the Central Powers on the Suez Canal, Cyprus, or Aden.

Churchill was probably correct in seeing the operation as a means of breaking the costly deadlock on the Western Front, but Fisher and the admirals of the War Staff Group saw what he did not, the need for a properly mounted combined-arms operation. Churchill did not appreciate the need for training and specialized equipment, the vulnerability of ships to shore fire, or the need for amphibious operations to silence them.

At the beginning of January Churchill sought the views of Vice Admiral Sackville Carden, commander of the blockading squadron off the Dardanelles. In response to Churchill's question as to whether he considered "the forcing of the Dardanelles by ships alone a practical operation," Carden replied: "I do not consider Dardanelles can be rushed. They might be forced by extended operations with large numbers of ships." This less-than-enthusiastic reply should have raised alarm bells in London.

On receipt of Carden's communication on 5 January Churchill consulted with his advisers (with the notable exception of Fisher) and asked Carden for a detailed plan, which arrived a week later. Carden requested a dozen battleships, three battlecruisers, four light cruisers, sixteen destroyers, six submarines, twelve minesweepers, some seaplanes, auxiliary vessels, and a considerable quantity of ammunition. He believed that, weather permitting, he could do the job in about a month.

Battleships were not a problem. Their slow speed would not be a factor in such an operation, and their heavy guns and armor would be needed against shore batteries. Battlecruisers were believed necessary to deal with *Goeben,* the powerful German battlecruiser that had escaped to Constantinople early in the war and was expected to contest the Allied naval presence. The admiralty went along with Carden's force projections, even adding the newest British dreadnought, the *Queen Elizabeth,* with eight 15-inch guns, which was scheduled to go to the Mediterranean for gunnery trials.

On 13 January the war council unanimously resolved "that the Admiralty should prepare for a naval expedition in February to bombard and take the Gallipoli peninsula with Constantinople as its objective." The war council assumed that once the fleet had reached Constantinople, the mere threat of naval bombardment would force Turkey out of the war. If the arrival of the *Goeben* had brought Turkey into the war, surely a fleet would force her out.

In the meantime, the solid front in London supporting the operation had broken. Fisher fell out with Churchill over the campaign. He believed it vital to contain the German High Seas Fleet and worried less about older battleships, which would be of little value in a decisive battle in the North Sea, than the possible loss of trained sailors. At length Churchill won Fisher over; he even added two additional predreadnought battleships to the operation. The French also sent a squadron of battleships and supporting vessels, commanded by Vice Admiral Emile Paul Guépratte.

Carden's force was the most powerful ever assembled in the Mediterranean. It consisted of the *Queen Elizabeth* (his flagship), the battlecruiser *Inflexible,* sixteen old battleships (four of them French), and twenty destroyers (six French). A flotilla of thirty-five minesweeping trawlers and a seaplane carrier were on their way. A number of cruisers and submarines were also available.

About a hundred land guns defended the Dardanelles. Seventy-two of these were in fixed emplacements in eleven different forts. Most of the guns were old, but the Germans had supplied two dozen 5.9-inch (15-centimeter) howitzers capable of quick redeployment, as well as a handful of other modern pieces. The heaviest guns, along with torpedo tubes, searchlights, and minefields, guarded the entrance of the Dardanelles. The defenders, however, lacked sufficient shells.

On 15 February Carden said that a naval bombardment by itself would not be sufficient and that land units were necessary, if only to secure the area after the fleet had passed through. He also stressed the need to wait for minesweepers and seaplanes. The critical political situation induced the war council in London to order him nevertheless to commence operations, but bad weather delayed bombardment of the outer Turkish forts until 19 February.

At 10:00 on the 19th the battleship *Cornwallis* fired the first shot of the campaign, against Fort Orkaniye. The outer Turkish forts, hit repeatedly, did not return fire. After about four hours, Carden closed the range to approximately 6,000 yards, whereupon some Turkish batteries returned fire. This encounter proved the need for ships to close to decisive range in order to knock out shore guns by direct fire. The British ships withdrew that afternoon. Bad weather then closed in, forcing a six-day interruption in the bombardment.

On 25 February the naval bombardment recommenced. The second in command, British Vice Admiral John de Robeck, led his flagship, the *Vengeance,* into much closer range. Naval shelling silenced all four outer Turkish forts, and minesweepers began clearing a path for the larger ships. They immediately encountered the swift current from the Black Sea into the Mediterranean.

The next day, largely unopposed, demolition parties, accompanied by marines, went ashore to complete destruction of the outer forts. The fleet then sailed into the Straits as far as they had been swept and began bombarding the inner forts. On 2 March Carden signaled London that unless bad weather intervened, he expected to be off Constantinople in two weeks' time.

Carden's optimism proved unfounded. Although the forts could be hit with the aid of spotter planes, damage was not great, and Turkish troops soon reoccupied abandoned forts. The Turkish howitzers, which could fire from behind the crests of the hills, were not easily accessible to flat-trajectory, high-velocity naval guns, and the mobile howitzers on both shores of the narrow Straits scored a growing number of hits on Allied vessels. Although this fire did not bother the battleships, it certainly affected minesweeping operations; each night the minesweepers were driven off by land fire. When weather allowed, the fleet kept up shelling during the day, while the minesweepers tried unsuccessfully to sweep the minefields at night. Until troops could be landed to destroy the mobile howitzers, fire from these guns prevented sweeping the minefields. And until the minefields were swept, the big ships could not be brought up close enough to destroy the modern Turkish earthworks, allowing passage to Constantinople.

On 3 March Admiral de Robeck reported that the operation would not succeed unless troops were landed to control one or both shores of the Straits. The repulse of a demolition party sent ashore on 4 March demonstrated this problem. London resisted the demand for troops, however. Kitchener contemplated "the employment of military force on any large scale [only] . . . in the event of the fleet failing to get through after every effort has been exhausted." Churchill had assured the war council that the navy would be able to force the Straits alone. He had refused not only to involve the army at the beginning but also to send out the entire Royal Naval Division, which was available.

Captain Roger Keyes, Carden's chief of staff, concluded that the fishermen and merchant seamen who made up the bulk of the crews on the mostly converted-trawler minesweepers were not up to the work. He offered them bonuses as well as additional naval personnel, and got permission from Carden for a night effort by six vessels on 10 March. Turkish searchlights illuminated the scene, and under intense fire one minesweeper struck a mine and sank. The flotilla promptly withdrew. The next night Keyes tried again, but as soon as the Turks opened fire, the minesweepers withdrew. On the night of the 13th Keyes used naval volunteers. Despite heavy fire that put out of action all but three minesweepers, many mines were swept. Minesweeping now went forward day and night.

Churchill kept up pressure on Carden. On 11 March he informed him that "the results to be gained are . . . great enough to justify loss of ships and men if success cannot be obtained without it." Three days later he told Carden to press on with the minesweeping operations regardless of reasonable casualties. He urged speed before the Germans sent submarines, and he passed along intelligence that the Turks were running out of shells.

Despite his near total lack of losses, Carden was terrified of taking responsibility for the destruction of any ships. On 16 March his health broke and de Robeck assumed command of the grand assault planned for 18 March.

The naval effort to force the narrows began on schedule at 11:30 on the 18th, when Allied battleships opened a heavy bombardment of land batteries in the narrows. Three ships (two British and one French) sustained damage, but most shore batteries were hit hard. Then disaster struck. The French battleship *Bouvet* took a hit in one of her magazines and blew up. She sank in less than two minutes with the loss of 640 men. Allied shelling of land batteries continued throughout the afternoon. De Robeck ordered his minesweepers forward, but they fled after coming under fire. Then the British battlecruiser *Inflexible* was crippled when she struck a mine. Her crew saved her, but she withdrew from action. A few minutes later, the battleship *Irresistible* also was disabled by a mine. Gunners ashore concentrated on her, and most of her men were taken off.

De Robeck ordered a withdrawal for the night but instructed Keyes to stay in the Straits with the destroyers and organize the *Irresistible* for towing with the help of two other battleships, the *Ocean* and *Swiftsure*. Instead of concentrating on the salvage operation, the *Ocean* shelled shore installations. She too was hit by an explosion, which disabled her steering. Keyes ordered the *Swiftsure* to retire with the crew of the *Ocean*. He then left to meet De Robeck on the *Queen Elizabeth* and secured permission to return that night to sink the *Irresistible* by torpedo and determine if the *Ocean* could be salvaged. As Keyes returned, there was a great explosion. No trace of the two battleships was found. Later, it was learned that all three battleships had run into a new and very small minefield, which had been laid along the Asian side of the Straits only ten days before the assault, and which Allied seaplane patrols had failed to detect.

De Robeck was depressed by the loss of his capital ships, but Keyes and other senior officers believed that one more determined push by the fleet would be decisive. In fact, the Turkish shore batteries had used up half of their supply of ammunition in that one day and were down to their last armor-piercing shells. The Turks were also virtually out of mines.

A great storm now blew up, damaging some British and French ships. Still, preparations for renewal of the offensive went forward. De Robeck replaced the minesweeper crews with British and French naval volunteers. On 19 March a message from the admiralty regretted the ship losses but ordered De Robeck to renew the assault. It promised five battleships (four British and one French); a squadron of land-based aircraft also arrived. On 20 March De Robeck had sixty-two vessels ready as minesweepers, and he said the offensive would be renewed in a few days. Two days later, however, after meeting with Army General Sir Ian Hamilton, he changed his mind. Keyes was outraged, as was Churchill. But, in an acrimonious session, the war council decided to let the views of commanders on the spot prevail. The naval offensive was not renewed.

The attempt to force the Dardanelles with warships alone cost the British and French 700 lives, three battleships sunk and two crippled, and damage to other ships. Turkish War Minister Enver Pasha quite correctly pictured the repulse as a great victory.

The focus of the campaign now shifted to land operations on the Gallipoli peninsula. The decision to continue the campaign brought Fisher's resignation as first sea lord; subsequent reshuffling of the British government also resulted in Churchill's removal as first lord of the admiralty. Naval activities from this point consisted chiefly of gunfire support and resupply.

Spencer C. Tucker

References

Churchill, Winston S. *The World Crisis*. Vol. 2. New York: Charles Scribner's Sons, 1923.

James, Robert Rhodes. *Gallipoli, The History of a Noble Blunder*. New York: Macmillan, 1965.

Moorehead, Alan. *Gallipoli*. New York: Harper and Row, 1956.

See also CARDEN, SACKVILLE; CHURCHILL, WINSTON; DE ROBECK, JOHN; GALLIPOLI, CAMPAIGN; GOEBEN AND BRESLAU; GUÉPRATTE, EMILE; HAMILTON, IAN; HANKEY, MAURICE; KEYES, ROGER; KITCHENER, EARL HORATIO

Dartige du Fournet, Louis René Charles (1856–1940)

French vice admiral and commander of the French Mediterranean Fleet in World War I. Born at Putanges (Orne) on 2 March 1856, Dartige du Fournet graduated at the head of his class from the Ecole Navale in 1874. He was senior naval officer in the international squadron at Constantinople during the Balkan Wars (1912–13); in 1915 he commanded the French squadron (3ème Escadre) off the Syrian coast, and in September the Dardanelles squadron. Dartige du Fournet succeeded Vice Admiral Augustin Boué de Lapeyrère as commander in chief of the French Mediterranean Fleet (1ère Armée navale) in October of 1915 and continued in that command until December 1916.

Dartige du Fournet was soon faced with the necessity of detaching destroyers to assist the Italians in the evacuation of the Serbian army from Albanian ports. His major challenge, however, proved to be the growing number of German submarines in the Mediterranean. Dartige du Fournet presided over an Allied conference at Malta in March of 1916 that decided to establish a series of patrolled routes for transport in the Mediterranean. This subsequently proved ineffective in reducing losses to submarines. In the second half of 1916 Dartige du Fournet found himself increasingly preoccupied with Greece, where the French favored the pro-Entente premier Eleutherios Venizelos over the neutralist King Constantine. The Allies applied periodic pressure against the Greeks, and on 1 December a predominantly French landing force was attacked in Athens. There were heavy losses, and Dartige du Fournet was accused of having been surprised and having placed excessive and naive reliance on the word of the king. Shortly afterwards he was relieved of his command. He died at Périgueux (Dordogne) on 17 February 1940.

Paul G. Halpern

References

Dartige du Fournet, Vice Admiral. *Souvenirs de guerre d'un amiral, 1914–1916*. Paris: Plon, 1920.

Halpern, Paul G. *The Naval War in the Mediterranean, 1914–1918*. London and Annapolis, Md.: Allen & Unwin and Naval Institute Press, 1987.

Laurens, Adolphe. *Le Commandement naval en Méditerranée, 1914–1918*. Paris: Payot, 1931.

Taillemite, Etienne. *Dictionnaire des Marins Français*. Paris: Editions Maritimes et d'Outre-Mer, 1982.

Thomazi, A. *La Guerre navale dans la Méditerranée*. Paris: Payot, 1929.

See also MEDITERRANEAN NAVAL OPERATIONS

Daszynski, Ignacy (1866–1936)

Polish socialist leader, born on 28 October 1866 at Zbaraż. He led Polish socialist deputies in the Viennese parliament. Until February of 1918 he advocated a Polish-Austrian solution to the question of Polish independence, meaning a triple monarchy of Austria, Hungary, and Poland. He actively supported Jósef Piłsudski's armed struggle against Russia, and within the Supreme National Committee he was Piłsudski's leading advocate. Following the Treaty of Brest-Litovsk, Daszynski turned his back on an Austro-Polish solution forever. With the collapse of the Hapsburg Empire he formed a Polish government in Lublin on 7 November 1918 composed of socialists and radical agrarians, as a counterweight to the Regency Council in Warsaw. He resigned on 14 November, following the appointment of Piłsudski as chief of state. After the war he was active in the politics of newly independent Poland and served as deputy premier of the national government (1920–21) and marshal (speaker) of the Sejm (lower house) from 1928 to 1930. Daszynski died on 31 October 1936 at Bystra.

Andrzej Suchcitz

References

Ciolkosz, Adam. *Ludzie P.P.S.* London: Centralny Komitet Polskiej Partii Socjalistycznej, 1981.

Feldman, Jozef. "Daszynski Ignacy," in *Polski Slownik Biograficzny*. Crakow: Sklad Glowny w Ksieg, Gebethnera; Wolffa, 1935.

See also PIŁSUDSKI, JÓSEF; POLAND

De Gaulle, Charles André Marie Joseph (1890–1970)

French army officer in World War I; later a prominent theorist of armored warfare, leader of the French government-in-exile in the Second World War, and then president of the Fifth Republic. Born in Lille, France, on 22 November 1890. De Gaulle's family was of staunch Catholic/conservative background, and his father was a professor in a Catholic high school in Paris. In 1909 Charles joined the 33rd Infantry Regiment, and the next year he entered St. Cyr. He graduated in 1912, thirteenth in a class of 211. He returned to his old regiment, now commanded by Colonel Henri Philippe Pétain, and won praise from Pétain and promotion to full lieutenant.

In August of 1914 de Gaulle received a severe leg wound during fighting at Dinant, Belgium. He took seven months to recover and rejoined his regiment as adjutant. Wounded again in March of 1915, he spent five months recovering. Promoted to captain in September of 1915, he returned to the 33rd, which was ordered to Verdun in February of 1916. Near Fort Douaumont, on 2 March, de Gaulle was again wounded and captured. He later received the Legion of Honor for this action. While a prisoner in Germany, de Gaulle made five attempts to escape, but his height (six feet, five inches) proved a detriment.

De Gaulle returned to France in November of 1918 with a suitcase full of writings and materials. Perhaps because he had spent so little time actually fighting, he retained a certain detachment and enthusiasm lost by those who had gone through the entire ordeal. His capture also perhaps enabled him to survive the war, saving him for the future greatness for which he believed he was destined. De Gaulle was the most prominent leader of the French Resistance to the Germans in World War II and headed the provisional government, 1944–45. He returned to power in 1958 and became president of the Fifth Republic (1958–69). De Gaulle died at Colombey-les-Deux Eglises on 9 November 1970.

Spencer C. Tucker

References

Cook, Don. *Charles De Gaulle, a Biography*. New York: G.P. Putnam's Sons, 1983.

Lacouture, Jean. *De Gaulle. The Rebel, 1890–1944*. Translated by Patrick O'Brian. New York: W.W. Norton, 1990.

Ledwidge, Bernard. *De Gaulle*. New York: St. Martin's, 1982.

Delcassé, Théophile (1852–1923)

French politician, born on 1 March 1852 at Pamiers. Delcassé entered the Chamber of Deputies in 1889 and was briefly minister of colonies. As minister of foreign affairs from 1898 to 1905, he was the architect of the Entente Cordiale with England but was forced to resign during the first Moroccan Crisis. As minister of the navy from March of 1911 until January of 1913, Delcassé wrote the naval law of 1912, which established a massive naval building program. He also strengthened ties with Britain in a 1912 naval agreement whereby, in the event of war, the French fleet would be concentrated in the Mediterranean while the British fleet would be concentrated in the North Sea, English Channel, and Atlantic Ocean. That agreement committed Britain to defend the French coastline in case of a Franco-German war. Together, these steps gave France the most powerful fleet in the Mediterranean. In 1913 Delcassé served as French ambassador to Russia. As a fervent supporter of the Franco-Russian alliance, Delcassé succeeded in persuading Russia to invest heavily in the building of railways serving the western frontier.

Delcassé served as minister of foreign affairs in the wartime government of René Viviani (1914–15). Delcassé's major accomplishment was the Treaty of London in April of 1915, whereby Italy agreed to join the Entente. In return, Italy was promised postwar territory on the Adriatic, the Tyrol, a portion of southwestern Turkey, and the Dodecanese Islands.

On the other hand, Delcassé's Balkan policy proved disastrous. To avoid a breach with the Russians, in March of 1915 Delcassé consented to their annexation of Constantinople and the Straits, an act that helped to drive neutralist Greece, Bulgaria, and Romania away from the Entente. Having earmarked Bulgaria as the main target of his diplomacy, Delcassé promised Serbian and Greek territory; the result was continued Greek neutrality. On 12 October 1915, Bulgaria, which had received better territorial promises from the Central Powers, declared war against Serbia. Delcassé immediately resigned, partly on account of the failure of his Bulgarian policy and partly as a protest against the decision of the René Viviani government to send troops to Salonika, Greece,

in an attempt to assist Serbia. Delcassé died 22 February 1923 at Nice.

Jan Karl Tanenbaum

References

Leon, George B. *Greece and the Great Powers, 1914–1917*. Thessaloniki: Institute for Balkan Studies, 1974.

Mitrakos, Alexander S. *France in Greece during World War I: A Study in the Politics of Power*. Boulder, Colo.: East European Quarterly, 1982.

Porter, Charles W. *The Career of Théophile Delcassé*. Philadelphia: University of Pennsylvania Press, 1936.

See also BULGARIA; LONDON, TREATY OF; ORIGINS OF THE FIRST WORLD WAR

Denikin, Anton Ivanovich (1872–1947)

Russian general and commander in chief of the Armed Forces of south Russia during the civil war. Born at Shpetal Dolnyi on 7 December 1872, this half-Russian, half-Polish only son of a poor former serf distinguished himself as an officer in the Imperial Russian Army. He attended the Kiev Junker School and Academy of the General Staff, and he served heroically in the Russo-Japanese War and during the Revolution of 1905. He was promoted to major general in June of 1914 and was serving as acting chief of staff of the Kiev district upon the outbreak of war.

Denikin then became deputy chief of staff to Aleksei Brusilov's Eighth Army, but he preferred combat to desk work. In September he secured command of the 4th Rifle "Iron" Brigade, a post in which he excelled over the following two years. Denikin fought successfully and gallantly in the Carpathians and in Galicia. In 1916 he was given command of VIII Corps and fought alongside the Romanians during Brusilov's Offensive. His next posting was chief of staff, Southwest Front.

Denikin welcomed the March 1917 Revolution that overthrew Czar Nicholas II. That summer he was selected chief of staff to the supreme commander in the Aleksandr Kerensky regime, a post in which he served, successively, Generals Mikhail Alekseev, Aleksei Brusilov, and Lavr Kornilov. In an effort to rejuvenate the tired and decimated Russian army, Kornilov attempted an abortive political coup in September. Denikin supported the coup and was sent to prison with Kornilov.

In December, following the Bolshevik Revolution, Denikin and Kornilov escaped to join Alekseev in Don Cossack territory in south Russia. There they formed the "White" Volunteer Army, a tiny force loyal to the Allies and dedicated to driving the Central Powers and the "Reds" from Russian soil.

After Kornilov was killed in the spring of 1918, Denikin assumed control of the field army. He led a series of brilliant campaigns in the Kuban, north Caucasus, and along the Don, emerging at the end of the year as commander in chief of the Armed Forces of South Russia. Having received limited Allied aid, Denikin, with his volunteers and Don, Terek, and Kuban Cossacks, launched a spectacular drive to capture Bolshevik Moscow in June of 1919. After reaching Orel his forces were defeated in October, and by March of 1920 they had been evacuated from Novorossiisk to the Crimea. Denikin resigned his post and passed the remainder of his life in exile. He died at Ann Arbor, Michigan, on 7 August 1947.

David L. Bullock

References

Denikin, Anton I. *The Career of a Tsarist Officer: Memoirs, 1872–1916.* Translated by Margaret Patoski. Minneapolis: University of Minnesota Press, 1975.

———. *The White Army.* London: Jonathan Cape, 1930.

Kenez, Peter. *Civil War in South Russia, 1918: The First Year of the Volunteer Army.* Berkeley: University of California Press, 1971.

———. *Civil War in South Russia, 1919–1920: Defeat of the Whites.* Berkeley: University of California Press, 1977.

Lehovich, Dimitry V. *White Against Red: The Life of General Anton Denikin.* New York: W.W. Norton, 1974.

See also KORNILOV, LAVR; RUSSIA, CIVIL WAR IN

Depth Charges

The depth charge came to be the most effective antisubmarine weapon used during World War I. Although the basic concept was proposed in 1911, it was not until 1916 that the British first successfully used the weapon.

Developed by the British, the first efficient depth charge was Type D, which contained three hundred pounds of TNT and was the most common type used during the war. When Type D was first introduced, it was set to explode at a fairly shallow depth, making it impractical for use by smaller patrol boats. Consequently, the British developed the Type D*, which contained only 120 pounds of TNT and was widely used by the smaller patrol and auxiliary boats.

The British suffered from a chronic shortage of depth charges. During 1916 and most of 1917 destroyers were issued only four depth charges apiece—two Type Ds and two Type D*s. Some patrol craft were equipped with only a single charge. Spurred on by the need to counter Germany's heightened submarine warfare, the British undertook a massive effort to increase stocks of depth charges. They were able to raise production of depth charges from 140 per week in July of 1917 to over 800 per week by December of the same year. By 1918 the British were able to equip their destroyers with between thirty and forty depth charges per ship.

The British were also able to improve the design of the Type D. In 1917 a new firing mechanism was developed, allowing the depth charge to be set to detonate at deeper depths. This gave smaller vessels the opportunity to distance themselves from the explosion. The improvement led to the discontinuation of the Type D*. For the remainder of the war, Type D was used exclusively by Allied forces.

The British also improved the delivery system of their depth charges. Originally, depth charges were simply rolled off the stern of a ship. In 1917 the British developed a thrower that could hurl a depth charge some forty yards. Destroyers were subsequently equipped with two launchers. These throwers allowed a ship to fire depth charges at a quicker rate as well as to broaden the scope of its depth-charge barrage.

The basic depth charge attack involved laying down a "ring" of explosions around the enemy submarine. Once the relative position of a submarine was ascertained, the attacking destroyer would launch as many depth charges as possible over the submarine. Since there was no way to find the depth of the submarine with any certainty once the attack began, depth charges were usually set to explode at varying depths. In order to actually destroy a submarine, a

D

depth charge would have to explode within fourteen feet of it. A depth charge could damage a submarine if it exploded within about forty feet of the vessel.

In 1918 depth charges accounted for the destruction of twenty-eight U-boats, more than any other source. By the end of the war, the depth charge had become the most effective antisubmarine weapon used by the Allies.

T.M. Lansford

References

Jellicoe, John. *The Crisis of the Navel War.* London, 1920. Reprint. New York: Books for Libraries Press, 1972.

Terraine, John. *The U-Boat Wars: 1916–1945.* New York: G.P. Putnam's Sons, 1989.

See also Submarine Warfare, Central Powers

De Robeck, Sir John Michael (1862–1928)

British admiral, born at Naas, County Kildare, on 10 June 1862. De Robeck was the second son of the fourth Baron de Robeck. He entered the Royal Navy in 1875 and served on two dozen warships before his promotion to commander in 1897. In 1911 he was promoted to rear admiral; he was admiral of patrols, 1912–14, and commanded the 9th Cruiser Squadron (Finisterre Station) in 1914.

In 1915 de Robeck suddenly emerged from relative obscurity as second-in-command of the Eastern Mediterranean Squadron when the commander, Vice Admiral Sackville Carden, was forced by ill health to relinquish his command on 16 March. It was de Robeck, therefore, who led the unsuccessful naval attack on the 18th. The attack failed when the battleships ran into an uncleared line of mines, resulting in the loss of one French and two British battleships and considerable damage to others. Buoyed by his fiery chief of staff, Commodore Roger Keyes, de Robeck was ready to renew the attack, but by the 22nd he recommended that the navy wait for the army to land and seize the heights that dominated the narrows. From then on de Robeck steadfastly resisted pressure—whether from a source as highly placed as First Lord of the Admiralty Winston Churchill or his own staff—for a renewed naval attack. He believed that even if the navy succeeded in passing the Dardanelles, the Turks would not capitulate without a successful advance by the army to seize and hold territory.

De Robeck's critics believed that he lost his chance for greatness and doomed the Dardanelles campaign to failure. His supporters, such as Admiral Sir Arthur Limpus, countered with the thought that it took a strong man to say no to probable disaster. De Robeck later commanded the 2nd Battle Squadron, Grand Fleet, 1916–19. He was commander in chief Mediterranean, 1919–22; high commissioner for Constantinople, 1919–20; and commander in chief Atlantic Fleet, 1922–24. He died at London on 20 January 1928.

Paul G. Halpern

References

Halpern, Paul G., ed. "De Robeck and the Dardanelles Campaign." In *The Naval Miscellany, Volume 5*, edited by N.A.M. Rodger, 439–98. Publications of the Navy Records Society, Vol. 125. London: Allen & Unwin for the Navy Records Society, 1984.

———. *The Keyes Papers.* Vol. 1, *1914–1918*. Publications of the Navy Records Society, Vol. 118. London: Navy Records Society, 1972. Reprint. London: Allen & Unwin, 1979.

Jellicoe, John. *The Crisis of the Naval War.* London, 1920. Reprint. New York: Books for Libraries, 1972.

Keyes, Admiral of the Fleet Sir Roger. *The Naval Memoirs.* Vol. 1, *The Narrow Seas to the Dardanelles, 1910–1915*. London: Thornton Butterworth, 1934.

Marder, Arthur J. "The Dardanelles Revisited: Further Thoughts on the Naval Prelude." In *From the Dardanelles to Oran: Studies of the Royal Navy in War and Peace, 1915–1935*. London: Oxford University Press, 1974.

———. *From the Dreadnought to Scapa Flow: The Royal Navy in the Fisher Era, 1904–1919.* Vol. 2, *The War Years: To the Eve of Jutland*. London: Oxford University Press, 1965.

Terraine, John. *The U-Boat Wars: 1916–1945.* New York: G.P. Putnam's Sons, 1989.

See also Carden, Sackville; Dardanelles Campaign

Diaz, Armando (1861–1928)

Italian general and chief of staff, 1917–18, born in Naples, on 5 December 1861. Diaz served in the Italo-Turkish War and led the Office of Operations when Italy entered the war in 1915. He was commanding the XXIII corps under d'Aosta's Third Army in November of 1917 when he was chosen to succeed General Luigi Cadorna as chief of staff. Diaz was ably assisted by Pietro Badoglio and Ugo Cavallero, who helped him plan the offensive that routed the Austro-Hungarian army in October of 1918, an action that earned Diaz the title Duke of Vittorio Veneto in 1920.

Enrico Caviglia portrayed Diaz as a gray man who was malleable as pasta but possessed that greatest of personal qualities, good luck. Compared with the stern Luigi Cadorna, Diaz was a general who cared for his men and did much to improve conditions for the average soldier after the debacle at Caporetto: Soldiers received better rations and regular periods of rest with government-sponsored entertainment, as well as insurance policies, a great share of medals, and the right to vote. Organizations were formed to care for veterans and for the families of the fallen, and peasant soldiers were promised a redistribution of land after the war, now presented as a popular struggle for the liberation of Italy.

When given command of Italian forces, Diaz had told the *camera*, "You have ordered me to fight with a broken sword; okay, we will fight all the same." But he was criticized for failing to act as Austria-Hungary began to unravel, and the war seemed poised to end in late 1918. By early October his inactivity had led to discussions of replacing him with Giardino, and even the collapse of Bulgaria on 25 September prompted Diaz to plan only to seize an extensive bridgehead in anticipation of a major offensive in the spring.

Although Diaz initially intended only to attack the Austrian Fifth and Sixth armies where they joined over the Piave River toward Ponte della Priula and Vittorio Veneto, his final plan aimed at a decisive breakthrough. Unfortunately, by placing Allied generals in command of the Eighth and Fourth armies, Diaz allowed the British and French to claim that they had won the battle, even though they were executing an Italian plan on an Italian front where fifty-two of fifty-seven Entente divisions and most of the guns and aircraft were Italian. Forced to act by Allied pressure, domestic criticism, and worries that Emperor Karl might sue for peace (following his concession of autonomy to the empire's Slavs and his appeal to the Pope to forestall an Italian offensive), Diaz still won a notable victory. It cost Italy 37,000 dead and wounded but annihilated the Austro-Hungarian armed forces and left the road to Vienna undefended.

In November of 1919 Diaz was replaced as chief of staff by Pietro Badoglio, and he told Malagodi that the military had done their job and now were merely "objects in a museum or display window." During the March on Rome in October of 1922 Diaz assured the king that the army, despite its sympathies for fascism, would do its duty, an ambiguous message that generated as much doubt as confidence in Victor Emmanuel III. Diaz subsequently served as minister of war under Mussolini (31 October 1922 to 30 April 1924) and reorganized the army to maximize Italy's one dependable resource, its manpower. He died in Rome on 29 February 1928.

James J. Sadkovich

References

Pieri, Piero. *L'Italia nella prima guerra mondiale (1915–1918)*. Turin: Einaudi, 1968.

Rochat, Giorgio. *L'esercito italiano da Vittorio Veneto a Mussolini*. Bari: Laterza, 1967.

———. *L'Italia nella prima guerra mondiale. Problemi di interpretazione e prospettive di ricerca*. Milan: Feltrinelli, 1976.

See also ITALY, ARMY; VITTORIO VENETO CAMPAIGN

Dimitrijević, Dragutin (1876–1917)

Serbian army colonel, leader of the Black Hand terrorist group that organized the assassination of Archduke Franz Ferdinand. Born on 17 August 1876 to an artisan family in Belgrade, Dimitrijević entered the Serbian Military Academy in 1892 and quickly gained recognition for his outstanding academic record. Assigned to the general staff in 1895 while only a lieutenant, Dimitrijević was a rabid Serbian nationalist. Also known by the name of Apis, he was so fanatical in his obsession with a greater Serbia that one contemporary called him a Garibaldi and Mazzini rolled into one. He was one of the leaders of a group of twenty-eight army officers who on 10 June 1903, murdered

King Alexander Obrenovich and restored the Karađordević family to the Serbian throne.

By the early twentieth century the Balkans were rent by illegal nationalist groups such as Mlada Bosnia (Young Bosnia) and the Serbian Narodna Odbrana (National Brotherhood). In 1911 Colonel Dimitrijević, on the general staff and also in charge of Serbian army intelligence, was the leader of a group of officers who formed the Black Hand, a conspiratorial terrorist group dedicated to speeding up the cause of a greater Serbia. In this they had the support of Pan-Slavic circles within the Russian government. The Black Hand became so powerful that it was virtually a state within a state. It was even feared by Serbian Premier Nikola Pašić.

In the spring of 1914 Vienna announced that the heir to the Austrian throne, Archduke Franz Ferdinand, would visit Sarajevo, the capital of Austria's newest possession of Bosnia. A number of young Bosnian radical nationalists, opposed to the Austrian occupation and sympathetic to Serbia, made plans to murder the archduke, who was to arrive in Sarajevo on 28 June. For help in this venture the two leaders, Gavrilo Princip and Nedeljko Charbrinovich, traveled to Belgrade to meet with Colonel Dimitrijević. While there are some questions about the part he played in the assassination, there is no doubt that, in his eyes, Archduke Franz Ferdinand was the enemy of Serbian nationalism because of his plans to grant autonomy to the Slavs within the Austrian half of the Hapsburg Monarchy. According to one view, the colonel took charge of the plan. From the Serbian army arsenal he issued to the conspirators four pistols, six bombs, 150 dinars, cyanide capsules, a map of Bosnia, and an official letter to get them across the frontier. Shortly after the assassination the name of Dimitrijević became linked to those of the terrorists. In December of 1916 he was arrested in Salonika, charged with having planned the assassination, and executed.

John W. Bohon

References

Stavrianos, Leften S. *The Balkans Since 1453.* New York: Holt, Rinehart and Winston, 1966.

Wolff, Robert L. *The Balkans in Our Time.* New York: W.W. Norton, 1974.

See also BLACK HAND; FRANZ FERDINAND; OUTBREAK OF THE FIRST WORLD WAR; PRINCIP, GAVRILO

Djemal Pasha (1872–1922)

Turkish army officer and leader of the Young Turks, born in Constantinople in 1872. Djemal graduated from the war college in 1895 and was assigned to Salonika, where he joined the Young Turk movement in 1906. In 1908 those rebels forced Sultan Abdul Hamid from the throne and reconstituted the government. After 1909, political power in Turkey became concentrated in the hands of Enver Pasha, Talât Pasha, and Djemal Pasha.

Djemal commanded a division in the Balkan Wars of 1912 and 1913. During that period the Turkish leadership unleashed a reign of terror aimed at crushing political opposition, and he played a prominent role. Djemal entered the cabinet in 1913 and became minister of the navy in 1914. During the July 1914 crisis that followed the assassination of Franz Ferdinand, a split arose among the Turk leaders. Minister of War Enver Pasha was pro-German and signed a secret agreement with Berlin promising that Turkey would join the Central Powers when they went to war with Russia. Djemal Pasha, on the other hand, was pro-Entente. British advisers were training the navy, and orders had been placed for powerful warships with British yards. Djemal attempted to arrange an alliance between Turkey and the Entente powers. The idea was rejected by Britain and France so as not to anger Russia, Turkey's traditional enemy. Djemal then supported friendly relations with the Central Powers, but he was a reluctant convert to joining the war on their side.

After Turkey entered the war on 4 November 1914, Djemal continued as navy minister. He also played a key role in the fighting in the Arab lands. In 1915 he became governor of Syria, where he treated the inhabitants with extreme ruthlessness, especially in Lebanon, helping to create revolts against Turkish rule. His inept raid on the Suez Canal in 1915 was easily defeated. Djemal then returned to Damascus. The British defeated Turkish forces in Syria and Palestine in 1917. After the fall of Jerusalem in December, Djemal left Syria for Constantinople. Djemal was forced from office, along with other Young Turks, in early October 1918, and the next month he fled the country. He was shot and killed by an Armenian assassin in Tbilisi on 21 July 1922.

John W. Bohon

References

Herwig, Holger H., and Neil M. Heyman. *Biographical Dictionary of World*

War I. Westport, Conn.: Greenwood, 1982.

Ramsaur, E.E. *The Young Turks*. Princeton: Princeton University Press, 1957.

Stavrianos, L.S. *The Balkans Since 1453*. New York: Holt, Rinehart and Winston, 1958.

See also OTTOMAN EMPIRE; PALESTINE AND SYRIA; SINAI CAMPAIGN

Dmitriev, Radko R. (1859–1918)

Bulgarian/Russian general, born on 24 September 1859 in Gradets, Bulgaria (then the Ottoman Empire). Dmitriev (also identified as Radko-Dmitriev), who became known as "the fiery Bulgarian," started his military career as a Bulgarian army officer. A strong russophile, on 20 August 1886 he and a group of other army officers forced Prince Alexander Battenberg to give up the Bulgarian throne in favor of a pro-Russian government. Dmitriev participated in the Serbo-Bulgarian War of 1885 and served as commander of the Bulgarian Third Army during the First Balkan War, and as the overall commander of Bulgarian forces in the Second Balkan War.

In August of 1914 Dmitriev resigned as Bulgarian ambassador to St. Petersburg in order to serve as a general in the Russian army. He obtained command of the Third Army, which was part of General Nikolai Ivanov's southwestern front. Along with General Alexei Brusilov's Eighth Army, Dmitriev's Third shared in the glory of the Galician campaign of the late summer of 1914. After Brusilov's units captured the Galician capital of Lemberg/Lvov, Dmitriev's army drove 100 miles to the west. The May 1915 German counteroffensive launched by General August von Mackensen was aimed at the flank of the Russian Third Army. Withering German artillery fire all but destroyed Third Army, which had failed to dig anything more than rudimentary trenches.

Dmitriev later commanded the Russian Twelfth Army without any great success. In the Russian Civil War that followed World War I, Red forces commanded by I.L. Sorokin shot Dmitriev at Rostov-on-Don on 18 October 1918.

John W. Bohon

References

Denikin, Anton J. *The Russian Turmoil*. London: Hutchinson, 1921.

Dmitriev, Radko. *Treta armiya v Baklanskata voina 1912 godina*. Sofia: Armeiski voenno-izdatelski fond, 1922.

Stone, Norman. *The Eastern Front 1914–1917*. New York: Charles Scribner's Sons, 1975.

Dmowski, Roman (1864–1939)

Polish statesman. Born in Kamionek on 9 August 1864, Dmowski was the son of a stonecutter. Educated at the University of Warsaw as a biologist, he became a leader of the National Democratic party from its foundation in 1893. Dmowski opposed revolutionary methods and favored Poland's autonomy within the Czarist Empire. He distinguished himself in the second and third Russian *Dumas* as the chief spokesman for Polish collaboration with Russia, France, and Britain against Germany.

At the beginning of World War I, Dmowski helped form a committee that sought to achieve Polish national aims through cooperation with Russia and its Western allies. In 1915 he went to Lausanne, Paris, and London, and worked for Poland's full national sovereignty. In August of 1917 he formed a Polish National Committee in Paris that later was recognized by the Allies as the official representative of Poland. In France he formed a Polish army of six divisions, headed by General Joseph Haller. After the war Dmowski represented the new Polish government at the Paris Peace Conference, and in June of 1919, together with Ignacy Jan Paderewski, he signed the Treaty of Versailles. Dmowski died on 2 January 1939 in Drozdowo.

M.K. Dziewanowski

References

Dillon, Emile J. *The Inside Story of the Peace Conference*. New York: Harper, 1920.

Dmowski, Roman. *Politvka Polska i Odbudowanie Panstwa*. Warsaw: PAX, 1988.

———. *Problems of Central and Eastern Europe*. London: Privately printed, 1917.

Komarnicki, Tytus. *Rebirth of the Polish Republic*. London: Heinemann, 1957.

Micewski, Andrzej. *Roman Dmowski*. Warsaw: Verbum, 1971.

See also POLAND

Dobropole, Battle of (September 1918)

Battle on the southeastern front in September of 1918 that caused the defeat of Bulgaria in World War I. For most of the war the Entente had experienced little success against Bulgarian troops along the southeastern (Macedonian) front. The Bulgarian army, with the assistance of some German formations, had strongly resisted Entente efforts to push into Macedonia. By 1918, however, the Entente was able to concentrate a large amount of men and matériel in Salonika for an attempt to break through the Bulgarian lines and push into Serbia and southern Austria-Hungary. Among the Entente forces were French, French colonial (Senegalese), Italian, Serbian, Greek, and British troops. By the beginning of September the Entente had achieved a manpower advantage of 3.4 to 1 and an artillery advantage of 8.3 to 1. At the same time an extreme case of war weariness affected the Bulgarian troops, who were also short of food and matériel. Bulgarian manpower reserves were exhausted, morale was poor, and a revolutionary mood infected many of the soldiers.

On 14 September 1918 Entente forces began an intense artillery barrage, which lasted most of the day, on the Bulgarian positions at Dobropole in southern Macedonia. The next day Entente soldiers launched their attack. For the first time on the southeastern front, Entente troops employed flamethrowers to overcome Bulgarian machine gunners. By the 16th, Entente forces had broken through the Bulgarian lines. The revolutionary disposition of many Bulgarian troops hampered attempts to counterattack. Bulgarian soldiers retreated in some disorder back toward Bulgaria. Discipline broke down, and there were mass desertions. Nevertheless, attempts by Entente forces to break through Bulgarian positions elsewhere along the front were unsuccessful. At Doiran, east of Dobropole, a British and Greek attack failed completely.

The collapse at Dobropole ended the Bulgarian war effort. The gap torn in the lines at Dobropole was too wide to fill, and Bulgaria lacked reserves to do so in any case. All along the lines Bulgarian and German troops received orders to retreat. British airplanes harassed the Bulgarian soldiers as they retreated, especially in the narrow Kresna Gorge. With Entente forces advancing on Bulgaria proper and with large segments of the army demonstrating revolutionary sensibilities, the government in Sofia decided that the war effort could not continue.

Bulgarian negotiators signed an armistice in Salonika on 29 September 1918.

Richard C. Hall

References

Cazeilles, Commandant de l'Infanterie coloniale. *La rupture du front bulgare.* Paris: Charles-Lavauzelle, 1929.

Dieterich, Alfred. *Weltkriegsende an der Mazedonischen Front.* Berlin: O.G. Stalling, 1925.

Palmer, Alan. *The Gardeners of Salonika.* London: Simon and Schuster, 1965.

See also BULGARIA, ARMY

Dogger Bank, Naval Battle of (24 January 1915)

Action between the British Battle Cruiser Force and the German First Scouting Group on 24 January 1915. Hoping to destroy some British light forces, German commander in chief Admiral Friedrich von Ingenohl directed Vice Admiral Franz von Hipper to patrol the Dogger Bank area. Hipper's flagship, SMS *Seydlitz,* led two other battle cruisers, *Derfflinger* and *Moltke,* plus the older and slower armored cruiser *Blücher.* Four light cruisers and nineteen destroyers rounded out the German force.

Hipper's orders were promptly intercepted and decoded at the admiralty, which sent Vice Admiral Sir David Beatty's command to intercept. Composed of five battle cruisers (flagship *Lion, Tiger, Princess Royal, New Zealand,* and *Indomitable*), seven light cruisers, and thirty-five destroyers, the British force sighted the German ships at 07:15. The day was clear, the seas calm, and visibility good.

Recognizing that the British force was superior, Hipper immediately reversed course and headed at best possible speed for his base. Slowed by the 25-knot top speed of the *Blücher,* Hipper's vessels came under fire at 20,000 yards at about 09:00. Beatty ordered his ships to engage their "opposite number," which led to uncertainty among the five British ships shooting at the four German. The resultant British fire distribution left *Moltke* unengaged for some time. The Germans, hoping to put Beatty's flagship out of action, concentrated their shooting on *Lion,* steaming in the British van.

Before the Germans succeeded, the British got in some punishing hits. *Blücher* suffered severely and, with her speed falling off, began to veer out of line. At about 09:30 the *Seydlitz* was struck by a 13.5-inch projectile from *Lion* that penetrated the rearmost barbette, setting off charges there. Flames engulfed the entire turret, spread to the adjacent rear turret, shot half as high as the mast, and burned 159 men to death. The ship was saved from total destruction by the heroism of a petty officer who doused the magazines by turning with his bare hands the red-hot wheels to the flooding valves.

Although the entire German force was now in dire peril, their gunfire began to tell on the *Lion*. Starting at about 10:00, that ship was hit several times by *Derfflinger*. As his flagship slowed to fifteen knots and in response to a false submarine sighting, Beatty ordered via flag hoist that the other ships in his squadron take a new course, press the enemy, and attack the German rear. Rear Admiral Archibald Moore, the next in command and well back in the line aboard the *New Zealand*, misunderstood Beatty to mean that the British ships should concentrate against the hapless *Blücher*, by now a flaming cripple.

Accordingly, Moore led the four sound British battle cruisers against that solitary ship, which fought to the bitter end, suffering hits from perhaps seven torpedoes and more than seventy shells. Of her complement of 1,026, 792 went down with her. Their sacrifice saved the other ships in Hipper's squadron. By the time Beatty shifted his flag to the *Princess Royal,* the German battle cruisers had escaped. Aside from the grievous injury to *Seydlitz,* *Derfflinger* sustained only slight damage from three shell hits.

For the British, the *Lion* had suffered seventeen shell hits, which surprisingly wounded only twelve of her crew. Material damage, however, was severe: The ship's port engine room was flooded, and her forward turret was disabled by a fire in its magazine. Repairs took four months. Two other British vessels were hit. Three German projectiles killed ten and wounded eleven on *Tiger*. The destroyer *Meteor* lost four dead and one wounded to a shell from *Blücher*.

Despite evidence that British protective measures were deficient, little was done to set them right. The Royal Navy did, however, take strong steps to amend and clarify their signaling procedures.

On the other side of the North Sea, the Germans improved their methods for handling ammunition (mainly by limiting the number of charges in opened cases at any one time), although *Derfflinger* neglected these procedures at Jutland and, like *Seydlitz* at Dogger Bank, suffered fires that put both of her after-turrets out of action. The Germans also dismissed Admiral Ingenohl, who came in for heavy criticism for making no arrangement to support Hipper's force with battleships. Kaiser Wilhelm II ordered Ingenohl's replacement, Admiral Hugo von Pohl, to take no risks with his heavy ships.

Dogger Bank was, unquestionably, a tactical victory for the Royal Navy. As is so often the case in military history, the losing side learned more from the battle than did the winners.

Malcolm Muir, Jr.

References

Conway's All the World's Fighting Ships 1906–1921. Annapolis, Md.: Naval Institute Press, 1985.

Marder, Arthur J. *From Dreadnought to Scapa Flow: The Royal Navy in the Fisher Era, 1904–1919*. 2nd ed. Oxford: Oxford University Press, 1978.

Parkes, Oscar. *British Battleships, "Warrior" 1860 to "Vanguard" 1950; a History of Design, Construction and Armament*. London: Seeley Service, 1957.

Sturton, Ian, ed. *Conway's All the World's Battleships: 1906 to the Present*. Annapolis, Md.: Naval Institute Press, 1987.

Young, Filson. *With the Battle Cruisers*. Annapolis, Md.: Naval Institute Press, 1921.

See also BEATTY, DAVID; HIPPER, FRANZ VON; INGENOHL, FRIEDRICH VON

Douhet, Giulio (1869–1930)

Italian general and leading air-power theorist. Born at Caserta on 30 May 1869. Douhet joined the Italian army as an artillery officer in 1882. Scientifically talented, by 1909 he commanded Italy's first military aviation unit. In 1913 Douhet wrote "Rules for the Use of Airplanes in War," publicizing the need for a separate air branch.

Outspoken about military aviation even when the Italian war ministry opposed his views, Douhet submitted plans for a tri-motored bomber to the war ministry, which rejected them. Despite this discouragement, Douhet built a successful prototype, and the

Caproni bomber was employed by Italy when it joined the Allied forces in 1915.

As chief of staff of the Division of Milan, Douhet suggested the use of bombers to attack Austrian cities in order to break the bloody stalemate between Italian and Austrian forces. When the ministry refused, he published his *War Diary,* criticizing the Italian high command's conduct of the war. In 1916 Douhet was court-martialed by a military tribunal for publicly denouncing Italy's military leaders in a memorandum to the cabinet. He was imprisoned for one year at Fenestrelle.

The irrepressible Douhet lobbied for air power from prison. The Italian defeat at Caporetto proved his claims, and the Italian government exonerated him and recalled him to service in December of 1917, as head of the Italian Army Aviation Service. In 1921 he was promoted to the rank of general and in 1922 became head of aviation under Mussolini.

Douhet is best known for his great work, *Command of the Air,* which he published in 1921. In this seminal work he stressed the need for air superiority to win total war: "To conquer the command of the air means victory; to be beaten in the air means defeat." Basing his ideas on his experiences in World War I, Douhet predicted that strategic bombing of major cities and industrial sites would shatter terrorized civilians' resistance. He viewed airplanes as solely offensive weapons and stressed that the air force must be independent, not an auxiliary to other branches. Douhet's works were translated and affected air doctrine worldwide. Even though his theories were incomplete and technologically outdated, they provided a valid framework for air doctrine and were proven in conflicts after World War I. Douhet died in Rome on 15 February 1930.

Elizabeth D. Schafer

References

Brodie, Bernard. "The Heritage of Douhet." *Air University Quarterly Review* 6 (1953): 64–69, 120–26.

Douhet, Giulio. *The Command of the Air.* Washington, D.C.: Office of Air Force History, 1983.

Sigaud, Louis A. *Air Power and Unification: Douhet's Principles of Warfare and Their Application to the United States.* Harrisburg, Pa.: Military Service, 1949.

———. *Douhet and Aeriel Warfare.* New York: G.P. Putnam's Sons, 1941.

Vauthier, Paul. *La doctrine de guerre du général Douhet.* Paris: Berger-Levrault, 1935.

Warner, Edward. "Douhet, Mitchell, Seversky: Theories of Air Warfare." In *Makers of Modern Strategy: Military Thought From Machiavelli to Hitler,* edited by Edward M. Earle. New York: Atheneum, 1966.

Doullens Conference (26 March 1918)

Called in the face of a German offensive that threatened to drive a wedge between the British and French armies near Amiens, the Doullens Conference on 26 March 1918 took the first step toward installing French General Ferdinand Foch as supreme commander of Allied forces on the Western Front.

Previous efforts to establish a unified command had been blunted by mistrust. The Supreme War Council was largely powerless, and the war effort in the West was managed through informal agreements between French commander in chief General Henri Philippe Pétain and British commander in chief Field Marshal Sir Douglas Haig. That arrangement broke down as the Germans drove toward Amiens in March of 1918 and threatened to rupture the Allied line. Pétain was convinced that the British were beaten, while Haig believed that the French commander would rather retreat to cover Paris than aid the British in holding the line. It soon became apparent that Haig was correct, and the British commander telegraphed Sir Henry Wilson in Paris asking for a meeting with the French leaders to name as supreme commander "Foch or some other determined general who will fight."

British secretary of war Lord Alfred Milner had already been sent to France by Prime Minister David Lloyd George and had met with the French leaders at Compiègne on 25 March. Without Haig no agreement could be made, however, and another meeting was set for the 26th at Doullens. On the way to Doullens Wilson convinced Milner of what he had earlier told Haig: Foch should be named commander in chief.

The conference itself was quite brief. French President Raymond Poincaré took the chair. Also representing the French were Minister of Munitions Louis Loucheur, Pétain, Foch, Premier Georges Clemenceau, and, by some accounts, General Weygand, Foch's chief of staff. The British representatives were Haig; Wilson; Milner; General Sir Herbert Lawrence, Haig's chief of general staff; and General Archibald Montgomery-Massingberd, British representative to the secretariat at Versailles. Haig spoke first, briefly describing the situation and again asking Pétain for assistance to hold the line at Amiens. In reply, Pétain cast a pallor over the meeting by opining that the British were beaten and by failing again to guarantee French aid.

After a brief silence, Milner and Clemenceau stepped aside for a private conference, in which Milner proposed installing Foch as supreme commander. Clemenceau quickly agreed, and the two approached their respective commanders in chief for approval, which was also rapidly forthcoming. Clemenceau then drafted a note charging Foch with the "coordination of the British and French armies in front of Amiens," which Haig amended to cover the entire Western Front and the Allied armies.

While this formula had a great effect on the morale of the Allied leaders and ended the dangerous selfishness and mistrust among commanders in chief, it left Foch virtually powerless. His position was strengthened on 3 April at Beauvais, but it was not until the end of April that Foch officially became general in chief of Allied armies.

Timothy C. Dowling

References

Stokesbury, James L. *A Short History of World War I.* New York: William Morrow, 1981.

Terraine, John. *Douglas Haig, the Educated Soldier.* London: Hutchinson, 1963.

Watson, David Robin. *Georges Clemenceau: A Political Biography.* Plymouth, England: Eyre Metheune, 1974.

Young, Peter, ed. *History of the First World War.* Vol. 6. London: Parnell, 1971.

See also FOCH, FERDINAND

Dowbor-Muśnicki, Józef (1867–1937)

Polish general, born at Garbów on 25 October 1867. Dowbor-Muśnicki joined the Russian army in 1884 and rose to command first an infantry division and, by 1917, XXXVIII Corps. In the summer of 1917 the Russian government chose Dowbor-Muśnicki to organize and command the I Polish Corps. Formed of Poles serving in the Russian army, its aim was to participate in operations against the Central Powers while remaining neutral in internal Russian politics.

During the winter of 1917–18, Dowbor-Muśnicki successfully carried out the concentration of the corps in the Bobrujsk area of White Russia (Byelorus). From January of 1918, in a series of skirmishes, Dowbor-Muśnicki successfully resisted Bolshevik attempts to disband the corps. German forces cut off and surrounded the I Polish Corps, however. Following the Treaty of Brest-Litovsk, Dowbor-Muśnicki signed an agreement with the Germans that led to the corps' disarmament in July of 1918.

Although Dowbor-Muśnicki was much criticized for not resisting the Germans, his decision did secure trained reserves of officers and NCOs for the new Polish army when Poland regained independence four months later. In 1919 Dowbor-Muśnicki commanded the successful Wielkopolska Rising against Germans attempting to hold on to the Posnanian province. He died at Batorowo on 26 October 1937.

Andrzej Suchcitz

References

Bauer, Piotr. *General Józef Dowbor-Muśnicki.* Poznan: Wydawnictwo Poznańskie, 1988.

See also POLAND

Dreadnought (HMS)

HMS *Dreadnought* represented such a major step forward in naval technology that her completion in 1906 rendered all existing battleships obsolescent. At the turn of the century, an average battleship displaced about 15,000 tons, was propelled with reciprocating machinery to a top speed of eighteen knots, and was armed with a mixed battery of four large guns (usually 12-inch) and a greater number of smaller pieces (typically twelve 6-inch guns). Given projected battle ranges of only a few miles, the lighter weapons were expected to be useful in shooting up an enemy's upper works. Over the next five years, designers increased the firepower of their battleships by adding guns of intermediate caliber. For example, the U.S.S. *Connecticut,* launched in 1904, carried four 12-inch, eight 8-inch, and twelve 7-inch guns, as well as a variety of small pieces.

Trials, however, showed that larger guns of varying calibers were difficult to control effectively. Their ballistic characteristics differed significantly, while splashes from their shells were of sufficiently similar size to make spotting very difficult. Innovative naval officers, such as William S. Sims, USN, and Sir John Fisher, RN, as well as naval architects such as W.H. Gard (Britain) and Vittorio Cuniberti (Italy), advocated doing away altogether with the medium guns, especially because improvements in fire control promised long-range hits with the largest projectiles.

Early results of the Russo-Japanese War validated such thinking. In March of 1905, the U.S. Congress authorized the construction of two battleships of the South Carolina class to be armed with two calibers only: eight 12-inch guns in four center-line turrets and small antitorpedo boat weapons. However advanced these two ships were in their armament details, they were still to be propelled by the cumbersome reciprocating machinery. Unfortunately, their construction was leisurely and the ships were not commissioned until 1910.

In the interim, Fisher, who became first sea lord in October of 1904, seized the initiative. His handpicked Committee on Designs settled in January of 1905 on the basic outline of what became HMS *Dreadnought*. Construction started in October of 1905 at Portsmouth Dockyard. Displacing 21,845 tons with 11-inch belt armor, the battleship carried a two-caliber armament: ten 12-inch guns and twenty-four 12-pounders for defense against torpedo craft. In a significant gamble, Fisher chose turbine machinery (which had, to that time, been fitted only in small vessels) to give increased reliability and a speed of twenty-one knots. Here was a ship that could outrun and outfight any other battleship.

Her construction time of little more than one year was remarkably rapid, in part speeded by diverting armament intended for other vessels on the stocks to *Dreadnought*. When her details became known, it was clear that all other battleships were rendered obsolescent at one stroke. A naval race ensued in which the dreadnought battleship seemed the only vessel that mattered.

HMS *Dreadnought* was herself quickly overshadowed by ever larger and more powerful battleships. During World War I she rammed *U-29* (commanded by the famous Otto Weddigen) on 18 March 1915, thus becoming the only battleship ever to sink a submarine. In May of 1916 she moved to Sheerness to serve as flagship of the second-line predreadnoughts and thus missed the Battle of Jutland. She was sold for scrap in 1922.

Malcolm Muir, Jr.

References

Burt, R.A. *British Battleships of World War One*. Annapolis, Md.: Naval Institute Press, 1986.

Conway's All the World's Fighting Ships 1906–1921. Annapolis, Md.: Naval Institute Press, 1985.

Friedman, Norman. *Battleship Design and Development: 1905–1945*. New York: Mayflower, 1978.

Parkes, Oscar. *British Battleships, "Warrior" 1860 to "Vanguard" 1950; A History of Design, Construction and Armament*. London: Seeley Service, 1957.

Sturton, Ian, ed. *Conway's All the World's Battleships: 1906 to the Present*. Annapolis, Md.: Naval Institute Press, 1987.

See also FISHER, JOHN; NAVAL ARMS RACE, ANGLO-GERMAN; WARSHIPS: BATTLESHIPS

Dubail, Auguste (1851–1934).

French general, born 11 April 1851 at Belfort. Dubail graduated from St. Cyr, served in the Franco-Prussian War, and graduated from the War College in 1878. In 1911 he became chief of staff of the French army. As a member of the Supreme War Council, Dubail negotiated with Britain regarding the size and disposition of British forces in a possible war with Germany.

When the First World War began, Dubail commanded the First Army. French War Plan XVII called for two offensive movements, the first into Lorraine, to be executed by Dubail and the Second Army, and a later offensive by the Third, Fourth, and Fifth armies into the Ardennes against what Joffre then supposed to be the main body of enemy forces. On 14 August Dubail's First Army and the Second Army advanced into Lorraine. Along the whole front, the Germans fell back and drew the French forward into a "sack" so that the First and Second armies could be engaged in battle while the decisive fighting occurred before Paris.

On 18 August Dubail's units entered Sarrebourg, which the enemy had voluntarily evacuated. The next day the Germans, who had prepared the region against the expected French attack with barbed wire, trenches, and gun emplacements, counterattacked; the French offensive ground to a halt. When the Second Army withdrew on his left, Dubail was forced to evacuate Sarrebourg. The Germans launched a frontal attack upon the French fortress line on the Moselle River between Toul and Epinal. From 25 August to 7 September the two German left-wing armies, the VI and VII, commanded by Crown Prince Rupprecht of Bavaria, fruitlessly dashed themselves against Dubail's army as French heavy artillery from Belfort and Epinal blazed away.

At the same time the French offensive further west, led by the Third, Fourth, and Fifth armies, failed in late August. Thereupon, the French armies retreated west and in early September won the Battle of the Marne. Neither the retreat nor the victory would have been possible had Dubail's First Army given way. Indeed, the First and Second armies had shut the eastern door of France.

In January of 1915 Dubail assumed command of the Eastern Group on the stalemated Western Front. His reputation suffered in the Verdun battle. Although in early 1915 Dubail had publicly stated that no German attack on the fortress was expected, by December he warned General Joseph Joffre of the possibility of an attack. Joffre, however, made him the principal scapegoat for the Verdun debacle and removed him from command. Dubail was subsequently appointed military governor of Paris, in which post he finished the war. He died in Paris on 7 January 1934.

Jan Karl Tanenbaum

References

Ministère de la Guerre, Etat-Major de l'Armée, Service Historique. *Les Armées françaises dans la grande guerre*, Tome 1, Vols. 1–3. Paris: Imprimerie Nationale, 1923–39.
Tuchman, Barbara. *The Guns of August*. New York: Dell, 1962.

See also FRONTIERS, BATTLE OF THE

Duchêne, Denis Auguste (1862–1950)

French general, born at Juzennecourt on 23 September 1862. Duchêne entered St. Cyr at age nineteen and joined the infantry upon graduation. From 1885 to 1887 Duchêne was a signaler in Tonkin; by 1912 he was a colonel in the 69th Infantry Regiment.

When war came, Duchêne was made general of a brigade and, in October of 1914, interim commander of the 42nd division. By March of 1915 he was general of a division and given command of XXXII Corps. As commander of Tenth Army, Duchêne led it in support of the Fifth and Sixth armies during the disastrous Nivelle Offensive of 16–20 April 1917, including the Second Battle of the Aisne, and the Third Battle of Champagne.

Duchêne became commander of Sixth Army in December of 1917 and was placed in charge of defenses along the Aisne River, where the Allies were informed of an impending spring attack. To retain the high ground of Chemin des Dames, Duchêne ignored Pétain's call for an elastic defense and placed the bulk of his twelve divisions forward in trenches along the twenty-five-mile front. As a result, large numbers of the men were casualties in the intense preliminary German artillery bombardment. Attacked by seventeen German divisions on 27 May 1918, Duchêne's troops collapsed, surrendering thirteen miles the first day. For this failure, Duchêne was sacked by Premier Georges Clemenceau on 9 June 1918.

Duchêne died at Bihorel-les-Rouen on 9 June 1950. He was buried at the church of St. Louis des Invalides.

Timothy C. Dowling

References

D'Amat, Roman, and R. Limorizin-Lamothe, dirs. *Dictionnaire de la Biographie Française*. Paris: Librairie Letouzey et Ane, 1967.
King, Jere Clemens. *Generals and Politicians. Conflict between France's High Command, Parliament and Government, 1914–1918.* Berkeley: University of California Press, 1951.

See also LUDENDORFF OFFENSIVES; NIVELLE OFFENSIVE

Dukhonin, Nikolai Nikolaevich (1876–1917)

Russian general, born 13 December 1876. The son of a nobleman of Smolensk Province, Dukhonin graduated in 1896 from the Aleksandr

Military Academy and in 1902 from the General Staff Academy.

Dukhonin rose rapidly in command in the course of the war. One key in his success was his straightforward approach to problem solving. If possible he preferred to see for himself rather than rely on reports by others. At the beginning of World War I Dukhonin was a regimental commander. In December of 1915 he became deputy quartermaster general of the southwestern front and in June of 1916 quartermaster general. From June to August of 1917 Dukhonin was chief of staff of the southwestern front and, from August to September of 1917, chief of staff of the Western Front.

In September of 1917 Dukhonin became chief of staff to Aleksandr Kerensky, supreme commander in chief. This meant that Dukhonin exercised effective command. After the Bolshevik Revolution, Dukhonin became acting supreme commander in chief. It had been an extraordinary rise from regimental commander just three years before. Dukhonin avoided direct challenge to the Bolsheviks, by ordering troops to halt their movement toward Petrograd. A staunch patriot, he refused to carry out a 20 November order from the Council of People's Commissars to open peace negotiations with the Central Powers. He stalled for a time but was relieved of his post on 22 November 1917 and then arrested. Before he was replaced, Dukhonin ordered the release of five prominent generals held since September at Bykhov, including Lavr Kornilov and Anton Denikin. On 3 December 1917, Dukhonin was in a railroad car at Mogilev. He was dragged from the train, beaten, and then shot to death by a crowd of soldiers enraged by news of the release of Kornilov.

Spencer C. Tucker

References

Bunyan, James, and H.H. Fisher. *The Bolshevik Revolution, 1917–18: Documents and Materials.* Stanford, Calif.: Stanford University Press, 1961.

Great Soviet Encyclopedia. Edited by A.M. Prokhorov. Vol. 8. New York: Macmillan, 1975.

Lincoln, W. Bruce. *Passage through Armageddon: The Russians in War and Revolution, 1914–1918.* New York: Simon and Schuster, 1986.

See also KERENSKY, ALEKSANDR

E

East Galicia, 1914 Campaign

Pre–World War I Russian military planning envisioned two options in response to German actions. A German main offensive against Russia would bring a Russian counterattack against Germany. If Germany's main blow should be against France, then Russia would strike against Austria. As it turned out, French pleas for help led the Russians to attempt both offensives at the same time, with the result that both failed.

The Austrians also had a number of plans. Vienna opted to dispatch two armies to finish off Serbia while employing her remaining four armies in an offensive against Russian Poland. This strategy seemed justified in that Poland formed a giant Russian salient pushing into Germany. Its westernmost tip was only three hundred miles from Berlin. Poland was also a potential springboard for a Russian strike into the industrial center of Silesia, but also a trap if the Austrians and Germans could attack the Russians from the south and north respectively, thereby pinching off the salient.

On 28 July, as one Austrian army invaded Serbia, the main Hapsburg force of three armies (First, Third, and Fourth) prepared to strike north into Poland. The Hapsburg chief of staff, Field Marshal Franz Conrad von Hötzendorf, was an able strategist, but his multinational forces suffered from numerous weaknesses.

On the Russian side, General N.I. Ivanov, who commanded the southwestern front, launched his own well-planned offensive. On 10 August the Southwestern Russian Army Group (Third, Fourth, Fifth, and Eighth armies) invaded Galicia (Austrian Poland), causing Conrad to halt his Polish offensive in order to stop the Russians. At the beginning of the Galician campaign neither army was where the other expected it to be. Consequently, two giant forces stumbled around aimlessly, finally joining battle in the vicinity of Lemberg, the capital of Galicia.

On 23–24 August, in the Battle of Kraśnik, the Austrian First Army drove back the Russian Fourth. In the Battle of Zamosc-Komarów (26 August–1 September), General Moritz von Auffenberg-Komarów and the Austrian Fourth Army won a great victory over General Paval Plehve's Russian Fifth Army.

Events went differently on the southern flank, where, on 26 August, Ivanov launched his own offensive and precipitated the Battle of Gnila Lipa (26–30 August). The Russian Third Army, commanded by General Radko Dmitriev and the Eighth Army under Aleksei Brusilov hit the Austrian Third Army. At the same time Plehve's Fifth Army was thrown into the Austrian gap north of Lemberg. The Austrians were defeated again, decisively, at Rava Ruska (3–11 September). The entire Austrian front now collapsed. Abandoning Lemberg, the Austrians were pushed back more than 100 miles to the Carpath-ian Mountains. Whole Austrian divisions of Slavic makeup surrendered and offered to fight with the Russians against the Hapsburg regime. Radko Dmitriev's units set off for the armed fortress of Przemysl, trapping another 100,000 Austrians there. In all, the Austrians suffered 250,000 killed and wounded and lost 100,000 prisoners, the bulk of her trained veterans. While Russian casualties were probably comparable, the extent of the Austrian defeat was staggering. Not only was her army broken, but the Russians held most of Galicia and were poised for further strikes into Silesia and Hungary.

The Austrian defeat in Galicia posed a major threat to Germany. Silesia was one of her main industrial centers. Moreover, the overall Russian commander, Grand Duke Nikolai Nikolaevich, had put Tannenberg behind him and amassed a huge force in Poland. It consisted of three armies on the Vistula River bend, with two armies on its northern flank and three more in the south.

General Paul von Hindenburg, German commander in the East, requested reinforcements, but chief of the general staff General Erich von Falkenhayn was mounting his own drive on the Channel ports and refused to release units. Hindenburg, therefore, stripped his forces in Prussia, taking four of his six corps to form a new Ninth Army, which was placed under the command of General August von Mackensen. It was located in the vicinity of the Polish city of Czestochova, where it linked up with the Austrian First Army in order to protect Silesia.

Within Russian military headquarters, meanwhile, there was a division of opinion as to the next objective. The grand duke favored another offensive into East Prussia, while General Ivanov and chief of staff General Mikhail Alekseev argued for a strike into Silesia, which held the possibility of forcing Austria out of the war. In the end, the grand duke compromised. He agreed to detach the Ninth Army from the northern force in order to launch a strike against Krakow, while retaining the Tenth Army under General Sievers and the First under General Pavel Rennenkampf for a northern offensive. By the end of September both sides were preparing for a new offensive.

Hindenburg held several advantages over his adversary. One was the excellent Prussian railway system, which allowed rapid troop movements. But the most important was that the Germans were intercepting Russian wireless messages, which were uncoded. Privy to all Russian plans, on 3 November Hindenburg made a historic decision. Within five days he moved the entire Ninth Army (some 250,000 men) from Czestochowa 250 miles to the north to Torun (Thorn) where it was situated to exploit a glaring gap between the Russian First and Second armies.

General Rennenkampf, veteran of the Masurian Lakes disaster, was supposed to protect the southern flank. But, as in the previous campaign, he was oblivious to the location of the Germans. On the other hand, Conrad, rec-ognizing the implication of Hindenburg's redeployment, pulled his Second Army out of the Carpathian Mountains to protect Silesia.

On 11 November the German Ninth Army launched its attack against the Russian First. On the 14th, before they were aware of what had occurred, the Russians began their own offensive against Silesia. Mackensen's troops caught the Russians by surprise as they were moving up to their staging areas. Rennenkampf's units were easily thrust aside (this time he was relieved of command and replaced by General Litvinov), and the Germans smashed into the flank of Sievers's Second Army.

In the ensuing bloody fighting of the Battles of Lódz and Lowicz (16–25 November) it was once again Russian bodies against German firepower. The Russian Second and Fifth army commanders decided not to continue with their invasion and instead swung back to the east, on their supply center, the large town of Lódz. Marching almost without stopping for two days, they beat the Germans to Lódz. When the Germans arrived there they found seven Russian corps on the town's perimeter. Their flank wrapped around the southeastern rim of the city, the Germans were actually surprised by Fifth Army's attack. For a very short time the Russians were in a position to envelop the Germans but were unable to exploit this rare opportunity. But neither were the Germans able to destroy the Russians as they had at Tannenberg.

Fighting continued until early December. Then, with winter coming on, the Russians evacuated Lódz (6 December) and retreated to the Bzura-Rawka River line. While the Battle of Lódz was not a clear-cut victory for either side, the Russians had called off their offensive. German losses in the Lódz campaign were some 35,000 killed and wounded; Russian casualties approached 100,000. The battle's real significance was in its psychological implications: The Russians were no match for the Germans. This perception became so fixed in Petrograd that by the end of the year there was some talk in Russian court circles of a separate peace.

John W. Bohon

References

Asprey, Robert B. *The German High Command at War. Hindenburg and Ludendorff Conduct World War I.* New York: William Morrow, 1991.

Florinsky, Michael. *Russia, A History and Interpretation*. 2 vols. New York: Macmillan, 1953.

Gurko, General Basil. *Russia 1914–1917*. New York: Macmillan, 1919.

Stone, Norman. *The Eastern Front, 1914–1917*. New York: Charles Scribner's Sons, 1975.

See also ALEKSEEV, MIKHAIL; AUFFENBERG-KOMARÓW, MORITZ VON; AUSTRIA-HUNGARY, ARMY; AUSTRO-HUNGARIAN WAR PLAN; BRUSILOV, ALEKSEI; CONRAD VON HÖTZENDORF, FRANZ; IVANOV, N.Y.; MACKENSEN, AUGUST VON; NIKOLAI NIKOLAEVICH; RENNENKAMPF, PAVEL; RUSSIA, ARMY

East Galicia, German Counteroffensive (18–28 July 1917)

On 1 July 1917, the Russians launched their Kerensky (Second Brusilov) Offensive, ranging from Riga in the north to the Carpathian Mountains in the south. The German high command in the east (*OberOst*) had anticipated such an offensive since April; indeed, the Germans knew its details several weeks before it was launched, and German Eastern Front commander General Max Hoffmann had already drawn up plans for a counteroffensive. Although the Russian offensive achieved gains of about thirty miles—many Austrian troops broke and fled—Brusilov had no reserves with which to force a breakthrough, and by mid-July the Russian offensive had ground to a halt.

Hoffmann then set in motion his counteroffensive. Mounted by both German and Austrian forces, it was made possible by six German divisions sent by General Erich Ludendorff from the Western Front. Hoffmann placed his newly acquired divisions in the area between Zoboroth and the Sereth River, with the intention of striking toward Tarnopol. The German assault, commanded by General von Eben and launched on a twelve-mile front on the right flank, began on 19 July. It was preceded by an intense bombardment planned by Georg Bruchmüller. Demoralized Russian armies disintegrated as they were pushed back, and the Central Powers' troops advanced nine miles the first day alone. Tarnopol fell on 25 July. Halicz and Stanislav were also taken within the week (24–26 July). Tarnopol's fall rendered the whole enemy position untenable. A Russian retreat there triggered similar withdrawals along the entire front to the Bukovina. Czernowitz fell on 3 August, and by early August the Russians had evacuated Galicia and the Bukovina. No Russian army existed south of the Pripet Marches.

The German offensive halted on the border of Galicia because there were insufficient resources to keep it moving forward. Additional gains were contingent on advances to the south, but neither Archduke Josef's Austro-Hungarian forces south of Czernowitz nor Field Marshal August von Mackensen's army group in Romania made significant progress.

Hoffmann was pleased with the results of the offensive, noting that he had won "in a style I could scarcely have dreamed of." Kaiser Wilhelm II rewarded him with the *Pour le Mérite*. Ludendorff was not as happy. Romania and Russia had yet to be knocked out of the war, a necessary precondition for a massive 1918 Western Front offensive.

Spencer C. Tucker

References
Asprey, Robert B. *The German High Command at War. Hindenburg and Ludendorff Conduct World War I*. New York: William Morrow, 1991.

Stone, Norman. *The Eastern Front 1914–1917*. New York: Charles Scribner's Sons, 1975.

See also BRUCHMÜLLER, GEORG; KERENSKY OFFENSIVE

East Prussia Campaign (August–September 1914)

Simultaneous with the German invasion of Belgium and France, fighting began in the east. The Eastern Front ran from the East Prussian marches in the north to the Carpathian mountains in the south. According to the original strategic plan hammered out by France and Russia before the war, France was to hold the Germans in the west for at least six weeks while Russia mobilized her millions of soldiers, who would roll over both Austria-Hungary and Germany. This plan was scrapped, however, at the onset of hostilities. By mid-August 1914, as the Germans put heavy pressure on France, Paris sent urgent pleas to St. Petersburg for an immediate offensive to relieve pressure in the west. The field commander of the Russian army, Grand Duke Nikolai Nikolaevich, vowed to do his utmost to save France. Consequently, a plan for a Russian offensive against East Prussia was patched together.

The Russian army in 1914 was woefully unprepared for modern war. For example, it suffered from incompetent military leadership. The field commander, Grand Duke Nikolai Nikolaevich, one of the Czar's uncles, had never actively commanded troops; his chief of staff, General N.N. Yanushkevich, had been a protocol officer at court and was promoted for political reasons. Even by his own admission he was totally ignorant of his responsibilities. The real work of military planning fell to the unimaginative deputy chief of staff, General Y.N. Danilov. Logistical planning, which was nearly nonexistent, was another glaring deficiency. At the beginning of the war, the Russian military had available only 418 motorized trucks; supplies were transported from the railheads by horse-drawn carts. Moreover, Russian and Prussian railroad gauges were of different sizes, so that the excellent German railroads would be of no use to the Russians. Throughout most of the war the Russian army suffered severe shortages. Troops were half starved, artillery units ran out of shells at critical moments, and headquarters could not communicate with units in the field because there was no wire.

In order to launch an offensive in two instead of six weeks, certain stages of the mobilization were omitted. Consequently, some Russian units were little more than groups of unarmed peasants. The overall commander of the Russian offensive was General Y. Zhilinsky. His command consisted of two large armies. First Army was led by General Pavel K. Rennenkampf, an undistinguished cavalry officer who had seen service against the Japanese in 1904. Second Army was commanded by General Aleksandr V. Samsonov, an aged officer who had found it difficult to lead even a single division in the Russo-Japanese War. Each of the two armies contained five corps totaling some 300,000 men. None had steel helmets. Many men did not have rifles, and others did not have boots.

The German strategic plan assumed a slow Russian mobilization; therefore only a skeleton force was assigned to defend East Prussia until the remainder of the German army defeated France. The German Eighth Army, stationed in the east, consisted largely of garrison troops and reserve units. Its commander, General Maximilian von Prittwitz und Gaffron, was obese to the point of near immobility (he was known to his soldiers by the unflattering appellation "the rotund soldier"). As with so many of his Russian counterparts, Prittwitz verged on incompetency. He was given his command because he was a favorite of the Kaiser. Fortunately, his deputy chief of staff, Colonel Max Hoffmann, was an officer of great ability. He formulated the plan for the resultant German victory but received little recognition for the achievement.

General Prittwitz was under orders, in the unlikely event of a Russian attack, to defend East Prussia; if that proved impossible, he was to retreat to the Vistula River, where a permanent defense line would be held until help arrived from the west. In other words, in this worst-case scenario the high command would temporarily cede to the enemy much of East Prussia.

August of 1914 was exceptionally hot, a factor that would lay a further burden on the ill-provisioned Russian soldiers. At dawn on 17 August the first units of Rennenkampf's army crossed the East Prussian frontier along a thirty-five-mile front. First Army's goal was the fortified city of Königsberg. Rennenkampf's force was to be the northern arm of a pincer. To the south, three days later, Samsonov's Second Army was to make its way around the heavily wooded Masurian Lakes and join up with Rennenkampf at Allenstein. Once the German defenders were destroyed in the Russian ring, the Russians would then drive into the heart of Germany, toward Berlin.

The first fighting occurred on the afternoon of the 17th only five miles inside the frontier, near the town of Stalluponen, when units of the German I Corps under the fiery General Hermann von François blocked the Russian advance. François informed Prittwitz that he intended to attack the Russians in force. The cautious Prittwitz, however, ordered François to retreat east to Gumbinnen, where a preliminary German line had been established. François partially ignored these orders. The Russians were subjected to their first artillery bombardment, and some 3,000 surrendered.

On the 19th Rennenkampf, whose troops were without food and water, halted his advance to restore order and also allow Samsonov, whose units had crossed the southern frontier late on 19 August, to catch up. At the same time, within the German staff there was a growing dissension between Prittwitz, who was showing signs of panic, and Colonel Hoffmann, who correctly recognized the weaknesses in the Russian situation and urged offensive action. Giving way to his more aggressive subordinates, Prittwitz sanctioned an attack in the Gumbinnen area. At 04:00 on the 20th, after a brief bombardment, units of General François's I Corps attacked the extreme right of Rennenkampf's line. The first two waves were mowed down by Russian artillery. But then the Russian guns ran out of shells and the Germans broke through. Under cavalry charges the Russian 28th Division sustained 65 percent casualties. The Russian center and left were ready for the Germans in strong defensive positions, however, and it was then the turn of the Germans to suffer heavy casualties. General August von Mackensen's 35th Division actually broke and ran under Russian artillery fire.

The Battle of Gumbinnen was perceived as a Russian victory, but, more important, it laid bare the weaknesses in the Russian leadership. Had Rennenkampf exploited his brief victory by pursuing the shaken Germans, he might have achieved a major breakout. But the Russian commander, assuming that the Germans were beaten, decided to stay put.

Prittwitz, sensing impending disaster, ordered a retreat to the Vistula River. Moreover, when he learned on the 20th that Samsonov's forces had entered East Prussia, his nerves gave way. He informed army headquarters at Coblenz that he might not be able to hold the Vistula line. This produced panic at the highest levels. Again, Hoffmann, after reading Russian uncoded radio intercepts, guessed the true situation—that Rennenkampf, whose army was in disarray, posed no threat and that it would be feasible to turn the entire German force against Samsonov in the south.

Virtually ignoring Prittwitz, Hoffmann issued orders to entrain the corps commanded by Generals François, Mackensen, and Otto von Below to move south. General von Scholtz's XX Corps was already there. The final act preliminary to the main battle was initiated at army headquarters when Prittwitz was sacked. A search for competent commanders for the East Prussian front began. Colonel Erich Ludendorff, "the hero of Liège," was appointed chief of staff. On 22 August he boarded a special train for Marienburg. On the way he joined the new Eighth Army commander, sixty-eight-year-old General Paul von Hindenburg, a Prussian Junker recalled from retirement. While still on the train, the two concocted a plan nearly identical to that already launched by Hoffmann. The resultant Battle of Tannenberg, fought between 26 and 31 August, was named after one of the towns in the area. It was also the name of a famous medieval battle involving the Teutonic Knights.

The Russian offensive had encountered serious problems. A pincer movement is one of the more complex military maneuvers even under ideal conditions—not the case with the Russians in East Prussia. The whole movement was coordinated by General Zhilinsky, whose headquarters was well behind the lines. His communications with Rennenkampf and Samsonov were tenuous, and his knowledge of the Germans' reactions was nonexistent. He did not sense that the Germans were making excellent use of their rail transportation to concentrate to the south in order to strike Samsonov's left flank. Zhilinsky also assumed that Rennenkampf and Samsonov were coordinating their movements when in actual fact the two armies had lost contact with each other. All during this time Zhilinsky sent messages via courier to Samsonov urging him to drive to the Vistula and close the pincers around the Germans. Samsonov replied that his troops had had no rations for three days and were near total exhaustion.

Samsonov assumed that his northern flank was protected by Rennenkampf's units. It was not. The final factor in the coming Russian disaster was German intelligence operations. Not only did the Germans have excellent aerial reconnaissance (the Russians had no aircraft), but all Russian radio messages were intercepted by the Germans. Each evening they were read by Ludendorff, who knew as much about the Russian plans as did the Russian generals themselves.

Early on 26 August, Mackensen's and Below's corps attacked Samsonov's exposed northern flank. It became immediately apparent that instead of enveloping the Germans, the Russians themselves were about to be enveloped. There were 5,000 casualties in the Russian VI Corps alone. Then, at 04:00 on the 27th, François's artillery opened up against the other flank. The Russian I Corps fled in panic. By the 28th the Germans had turned both Russian flanks, and Samsonov's Second Army was doomed. Rennenkampf, with his own army of 200,000 men to the north, was oblivious to the situation. Even Zhilinsky, upon reading Samsonov's dispatches, suspected something ominous, but his repeated urging to Rennenkampf to attack the Germans from the north was of no avail.

On the 28th Samsonov, in despair, quit his headquarters. Like the old cavalry officer that he was, he mounted a horse and, together with his staff, rode among the various units. On the following day he ordered his two central corps to retreat through the woods back to the Russian frontier. But it was too late. The Germans had closed their own pincers, and their artillery began to pound the exhausted Russian units. On the afternoon of 30 August General Samsonov committed suicide.

The battle of Tannenberg, the first of many Russian disasters, resulted in over 150,000 Russian casualties (92,000 prisoners). The Germans also captured some 500 guns. German losses were between 10,000 and 15,000 men. With the annihilation of the Russian Second Army, the German Eighth Army wheeled north to engage the First Army. From 9 to 14 September First Army took a tough beating in the Battle of the Masurian Lakes. François's I Corps played a leading role, forcing back the Russian left flank. Rennenkampf finally disengaged under cover of a two-division counterattack, thereby preventing a second German double envelopment. Russian losses in this First Battle of the Masurian Lakes were about 125,000 men and 150 guns. German losses were about 40,000 men.

Zhilinsky was sacked for incompetence, but Rennenkampf continued in command for the time being. The immediate impact of the disaster was masked by the Russian victory against the Austrians, but it eventually became apparent that the Russian military was unsuited for modern war. Allied confidence in Russia was shattered. On the German side, Tannenberg launched the Hindenburg myth. As the victorious commander, he began to project an aura of national hero and oracle.

John W. Bohon

References

Showalter, Dennis E. *Tannenberg, Clash of Empires.* New York: Archon, 1991.

Solzhenitsyn, Alexander. *August 1914.* New York: Farrar, Straus and Giroux, 1972.

Stone, Norman. *The Eastern Front 1914–1917.* New York: Charles Scribner's Sons, 1975.

See also BELOW, OTTO VON; DANILOV, YURI; FRANÇOIS, HERMANN VON; HINDENBURG, PAUL VON; HOFFMANN, MAX; LUDENDORFF, ERICH; MACKENSEN, AUGUST VON; NIKOLAI NIKOLAEVICH; PRITTWITZ UND GAFFRON, MAX; RENNENKAMPF, PAVEL; RUSSIA, ARMY; SAMSONOV, ALEKSANDR; YANUSHKEVICH, NIKOLAI; ZHILINSKY, YAKOV

Eastern Front, January to April 1915

On the Eastern Front in January of 1915, both sides were engaged in siege warfare along an extended line that ran in a southerly direction from Libau, to the west of Warsaw, to the east of Cracow, south of Przemysl, to the Romanian border.

During the winter of 1914–15 the Russians advanced for a second time into the Masurian Lakes region and continued their advance in the Carpathian Mountains, threatening East Prussia and Hungary. Russian planners believed that a spring 1915 advance on Budapest could precipitate the breakup of Austria-Hungary. The Germans realized the seriousness of the situation and agreed to assist Austria-Hungary in a major offensive to force Russia from the war.

In January of 1915 Field Marshal Paul von Hindenburg's forces consisted of two battle-experienced armies—the Eighth, commanded by General Otto von Below, and the Ninth, under General August von Mackensen. The Eighth Army held the line from Tilsit south to Ortelsberg. The Ninth Army was in the sector facing Warsaw. *Landwehr* and *Landsturm* troops occupied the gaps between the Eighth and Ninth armies and between the Ninth Army and the Austrians. Four additional corps arrived in late January of 1915. Hindenburg added one to the Eighth Army and used the remaining three to form the Tenth Army under General Hermann von Eichhorn. The Tenth Army secretly concentrated in the rear area west of Insterburg.

The major Russian defensive barrier in northern Poland lay along the Narev River, which flows into the Bug River about fifteen miles northeast of Novo Georgievsk. Fortified towns protected the primary crossings, one of which was Ostroleka, a convenient base of operations where three branches of the Warsaw-Petrograd railroad converged. Przasnysz, about fifty miles north of Warsaw, halfway between Ostroleka and Mlava between the Narev River and the Prussian frontier, was an important communications center from which eight major highways radiated. The Russian Twelfth Army, commanded by General Wenzel von Plehve, held the Narev River defensive line. A single Russian brigade covered Przasnysz. A Russian division occupied the high ground to the west of Przasnysz between the town and the Warsaw-Mlava railroad.

On 20 January 1915 two German corps, which for two days had concentrated between Mlava and Chorzele, began operations against the Russians. Capturing Przasnysz, they circled to the south and attacked the Russians on their flank and in their rear. Following a fierce defense against the vastly superior German-Austrian army, Russian forces launched a counterattack. From fortresses along the Narev River, strong Russian forces converged on the Germans, overpowered the Thirty-Sixth German Reserve Division at Orzec, reentered Przasnysz on the night of 26 January 1915, and secured the city the next day. The Russians were in complete control of Przasnysz by the 28th, and the Germans hastily retreated after suffering severe losses.

Not willing to accept defeat, the Germans made plans and preparations for a new offensive. Hindenburg's operations in East Prussia appear to have been the prelude to a decisive attack on Warsaw from the north. Prior to this operation, however, it was necessary to protect the German northern flank on the Niemen River and to reduce the Russian threat by cutting the Warsaw-Petrograd railroad east of the Russian Narev River line. Planners in the German High Command in the East arranged for the rapid, secret movement of forces to the frontier north of Warsaw in order to launch so rapid an attack that the enemy would not have sufficient time to maneuver to meet it.

Using the railroads to move troops from the Polish front, from Germany, and from the Western Front, Hindenburg concentrated the Tenth Army under the command of Eichhorn and reinforced the Eighth Army under the command of Below. The intent was to concentrate a strong force in East Prussia to destroy the Russian Tenth Army under the command of General Sievers. The Russian Tenth Army occupied more than 100 miles of front along the East Prussian frontier.

Austrian and German forces were to converge on the Russians. Hindenburg was to attack with a group of German armies from the north, drive the Russians from East Prussia, and cut the Russian lines of communication.

Austro-Hungarian chief of staff General Franz Conrad von Hötzendorf was to attack from the south with a group of Austrian armies, reinforced with German detachments and corps, to drive the Russians out of Hungary and relieve the siege of Przemysl.

The attack by the Central Powers began in a blinding snowstorm on 7 February 1915 with the right flank corps of the Eighth Army. The purpose of this attack was to create a diversion and cause the Russians to move troops away from the sector immediately in front of Eichhorn's Tenth Army. While the German center, opposing the Russian XX Corps, held the Russians in place, the left wing of Eichhorn's Tenth Army was to dislocate the Russian right flank near Tilsit and envelop it by advancing along the Tilsit-Mariampol-Grodno route. The Eighth Army was to penetrate the Russian line and envelop the left flank of the Russian Tenth Army by advancing in the direction of Johannisburg-Grodno.

The German Tenth Army attacked on the morning of 8 February 1915 and made significant gains. The Central Powers executed the double envelopment efficiently, under the most adverse weather conditions. By the 10th, the Central Powers had driven the right wing of the Russian Tenth Army back as far as Vilkoviski and Wirballen. There was fierce fighting in all sectors, and the Eighth Army pressed the left wing of the Russian Tenth Army at Lyck. The Germans continued to press forward, especially in the zone of the German Tenth Army, causing the Russians to execute a general withdrawal. Accordingly, from 11–14 February the Russian Tenth Army withdrew through the Augustow Forest, giving up Lyck on the 14th. Eichhorn sent his left flank corps around the Augustow Forest in an attempt to encircle the Russians. In three days of severe fighting the Russian XX Corps covered the withdrawal of the other three Russian corps of the Tenth Army, permitting them to escape. The XX Corps, however, was forced to surrender on 21 February. This battle is known as the Second Battle of Masurian Lakes; it cost the Russians a total of 200,000 casualties (90,000 prisoners).

To counter this defeat, Russian commander Grand Duke Nikolai Nikolaevich sent the Russian Twelfth Army under General Plehve north from Warsaw to assist the Tenth Army. The Twelfth Army attacked the southern flank of the German Eighth Army and, in a bloody battle on 26–27 February, defeated it.

In response the Germans brought forward fresh units and, in heavy fighting from 8–11 March, they pushed forward almost to Przasnysz; the general thaw beginning about 15 March, however, prevented further large-scale offensive military operations.

In the south Conrad commanded the southern converging force, the mission of which was to raise the siege of Przemysl and drive the Russians out of Hungary. Heavily reinforced with German troops, Conrad attacked simultaneously with Hindenburg's attack in the Masurian Lakes region to the north. He succeeded in recapturing Czernowitz and Kolomea and driving the Russians almost to the Dniester River; in the mountains and in the west, however, he lost many troops as prisoners and essentially made no progress.

Although the Second Battle of Masurian Lakes was a major tactical success for the Central Powers, the strategic importance was minimal. In the south, the Russians stopped Conrad's attack. The Austrians could not even retain the fortress of Przemysl, which the Russians recaptured on 22 March 1915. The Austrians lost 150,000 men and over 1,000 artillery pieces.

The recapture of Przemysl released 200,000 Russian soldiers for service elsewhere, made the Russians masters of the railroads in Galicia, and provided maneuver room for an advance across the Carpathian Mountains. Grand Duke Nikolai Nikolaevich perceived that the Russian victory, coupled with the spring thaw in Poland, would protect the Russian right flank from the Germans. Thus he decided to launch a major offensive against Hungary. The next maneuver, involving the most difficult of winter operations, yielded a victory over the Austrians at the end of April 1915 enabling the Russians to cross the passes and prepare to enter Hungary.

Montecue J. Lowry

References

Allen, George H. *The Great War*. Vol. 4. Philadelphia: George Barrie's Sons, 1919.

Howland, Colonel C.R. *A Military History of the World War*. Fort Leavenworth, Kans.: General Service Schools Press, 1923.

Stone, Norman. *The Eastern Front 1914–1917*. New York: Charles Scribner's Sons, 1975.

See also BELOW, OTTO VON; CONRAD VON HÖTZENDORF, FRANZ; EICHHORN, HERMANN VON; HINDENBURG, PAUL VON; LUDENDORFF, ERICH; MACKENSEN, AUGUST VON; NIKOLAI NIKOLAEVICH

Eastern Front, May to September 1915

The great German-Austrian spring-summer offensive of 1915 was a brilliantly planned, well-coordinated, and well-executed campaign. In the spring of 1915, chief of the general staff General Erich von Falkenhayn, acting under Kaiser Wilhelm II's orders, gave priority to the Eastern Front and assumed personal overall command. Russian successes against Austria had alarmed the Central Powers, and field marshal Count Franz Conrad von Hötzendorf had appealed for assistance. In return he agreed to allow the Germans to direct operations. Falkenhayn believed that, given her logistical problems, Russia would not be able to defend against an offensive supported by massive German artillery fire.

The attack was conceived as a converging maneuver to disgorge Russian forces from Galicia, but it also included an operation to push the Russians from Hungary. Field Marshal Paul von Hindenburg's army group was to apply pressure from the north on the Ossovietz-Warsaw line, but the main effort would be made south of Warsaw by the new Eleventh Army, commanded by General August von Mackensen. Additional forces on the right wing were to attack Russian positions at Przemysl and Lemberg. Other forces would provide flank protection.

The Eleventh Army was composed of forces from the Western Front. Falkenhayn took three battalions from each division, two guns from each artillery battalion, and cannibalized other units. As constituted, the Eleventh Army had four corps and eight divisions.

Hindenburg and his chief of staff, General Erich Ludendorff, favored a major envelopment of the Russian north flank, while Conrad wanted a penetration in the Gorlice-Tarnow area to force a Russian withdrawal from the Carpathian Mountains. After considering both courses, Falkenhayn accepted Conrad's plan, which entailed a penetration along a thirty-mile front between the Vistula River and the Carpathian Mountains. To ensure success, the Central Powers added the Austro-Hungarian Third and Fourth armies to the Eleventh Army. Although Conrad was the nominal commander, he could not give orders to Mackensen without Falkenhayn's approval.

To conceal preparations for the offensive, the Central Powers employed several diversions. At the end of April, Hindenburg attacked the Russians in the north, causing them to deploy troops there. In the west the Germans launched a gas attack at Ypres on 22 April. And in the Gorlice-Tarnow area, German officers and reconnaissance troops wore Austrian uniforms. Although the Russians had identified Germans in the area by 27 April, the concentration had been completed, and the Russians were ignorant of the size of the deployment. To maintain secrecy, up until the last minute German and Austrian troops were kept ignorant as to their destination and mission.

The secrecy was effective, and Russian commander Grand Duke Nicholas did not expect the attack. His forces were poorly equipped, short of supplies, and stretched thin. The Russian Third Army held a 100-mile front, and only two corps were in position opposite Mackensen's main attack positions.

Mackensen also enjoyed the greatest concentration of fire support thus far assembled. There was one light artillery piece for every forty-five yards of front and a heavy gun for every 130 yards. Each light gun battery was allotted 1,200 rounds and each heavy gun battery 600.

On 1 May 1915 the Germans registered their artillery and at dusk began harassing fire. Except for two hours, from 01:00 to 03:00, German artillery harassed the Russians throughout the night of 1–2 May. The pause permitted reconnaissance patrols to obtain the latest information on the enemy, and engineer troops to clear lanes through the barbed wire. Also during the night, infantry assault units quietly moved into forward positions. The Germans positioned reserve units and artillery closely behind the assault troops.

The Battle of Dunajec opened on 2 May 1915. The Germans began their bombardment of the Russian lines—the most massive artillery preparation to date—at 06:00 and continued it for four hours. At 10:00, following a rolling barrage, German troops began their assault. They met little resistance; Russian troops surrendered in droves or simply ran away.

Organized in depth and their attack closely coordinated, German troops moved rapidly and defeated hastily organized Russian counterattacks. The Germans advanced so rapidly that commanders allowed their troops to move beyond their phase lines, as long as they maintained contact between adjacent units. Although some Russian troops fought bravely, attacks from both flanks forced them to fall back from the Dunajec River to the San River between Warsaw and Przemysl.

The Central Powers completed the penetration on 4 May 1915. For all practical purposes they had eliminated the Russian Third Army. The Russian position in the Carpathian Mountains was now untenable, and the Russian Eighth and Eleventh armies rapidly withdrew. Although Mackensen's Eleventh Army did most of the fighting, the Austrian Third and Fourth armies, positioned on the German flanks, moved with the assault and assisted the victory. In the first two weeks the Germans and their allies advanced 100 miles. They then paused, enabling the Russians to establish defensive positions behind the San River. The Germans, however, soon resumed the offensive. For more than a month, four million men were engaged in fighting along the San River line. Finally, after being subjected to what seemed an endless bombardment by heavy artillery, the Russian troops evacuated Przemysl on 3 June 1915.

After Germans troops occupied Przemysl, leaders of the Central Powers met to decide on their next objective. Although the situation in other theaters indicated the advisability of moving troops from the Eastern Front, they decided to continue the attack. Part of the Austrian Third Army was sent to the Italian theater, and the remainder to other armies on the Eastern Front. Mackensen, however, received the Austrian Second Army and German reinforcements commanded by General Max von Gallwitz ("Army Detachment Gallwitz"). The latter, also known as the Bug Army, grew steadily in size and in August of 1915 was renamed the Twelfth Army.

With these reinforcements Mackensen resumed the offensive and captured Lemberg on 22 June. The Central Powers crossed the Dniester on 23–27 June. Following the loss of Lemberg, as well as most of Galicia, Russian positions formed a large salient around Warsaw. To reduce this salient, the German High Command ordered Mackensen to redirect his forces and attack north, with Brest-Litovsk as his final objective. At the same time Gallwitz's Twelfth Army was to attack southeast through the Mlava area, passing directly to the west of Warsaw.

On 13 July 1915 Gallwitz began his offensive with a rapid penetration of the Russian positions. Concurrently, by 15 July Falkenhayn had driven the Russians out of Hungary. He then began his converging maneuver. South of Gallwitz's force, the German Ninth Army and an Austrian army under General Remus von Woyrsch drove the Russians back toward the Vistula River. On 27 July Woyrsch crossed the Vistula River between Warsaw and Ivangorod. By the 29th Mackensen was moving rapidly toward Brest-Litovsk after breaking through the Lublin-Kholm line. The southern force turned north between Warsaw and the Bug River and on 30 July attacked Lublin and Kholm. In the north Hindenburg drove to Warsaw, captured Przasnysz, and forced the Russians across the Narev (Narew) River. Simultaneously, he exploited the success with his left wing by driving the Russians back along the Baltic coast. In the center, Prince Leopold of Bavaria's army group moved forward, guiding on Mackensen's army group, and on 30 July attacked Ivangorod.

The Russians continued their retreat to a line along the Vistula and Bug rivers, which they occupied on 30 July. To avoid encirclement, on 4 August Grand Duke Nikolai ordered the Russian evacuation of Warsaw and a day later began a general withdrawal to the interior of Russia. For the rest of August the Russians continued to retreat, and the Germans took Brest-Litovsk on the 25th and Grodno on 2 September.

In early September of 1915, Falkenhayn announced his intention to stabilize the line prior to going into winter quarters. During the next two weeks the Germans forced the Russians back another 100 to 150 miles. During that period, most fighting took place on the flanks. In the north, Hindenburg's forces captured Vilna on 19 September; in the south, the Austrians tried, but failed, to drive the Russians from eastern Galicia. By the end of September 1915, both sides, thoroughly exhausted by the fighting, went into defensive positions. Major Allied operations in other theaters of the war and a Turkish request for assistance prompted the Central Powers to cease operations against Russia and deploy some forces elsewhere. The 600-mile front extended from the Gulf of Riga to Czernowitz in Romania.

Russia's defeat in the Galician Campaign had profound consequences for the Russian war effort. Although Grand Duke Nikolai had at least managed to preserve the bulk of his forces and had withdrawn them in fairly good order,

Czar Nicholas II, urged on by Empress Alexandra, relieved the Grand Duke as commander in chief and assumed personal command of the Russian army. That decision would prove fatal to the Russian Empire.

Montecue J. Lowry

References

Allen, George H. *The Great War*. Vol. 4. Philadelphia: George Barrie's Sons, 1919.

Asprey, Robert B. *The German High Command at War*. New York: William Morrow, 1991.

Howland, Colonel C.R. *A Military History of the World War*. Fort Leavenworth, Kans.: General Service Schools Press, 1923.

Stamps, Colonel T. Dodson, and Colonel Vincent J. Esposito, eds. *A Short Military History of World War I*. West Point, N.Y.: United States Military Academy, 1950.

See also CONRAD VON HÖTZENDORF, FRANZ; FALKENHAYN, ERICH VON; GALLWITZ, MAX VON; HINDENBURG, PAUL VON; MACKENSEN, AUGUST VON; NIKOLAI NIKOLAEVICH

Eberhardt, Andrei Augustovich (1856–1919)

Russian admiral and naval commander. Born in November of 1856 on the Greek island of Patras, Eberhardt rose to become chief of the Russian Naval General Staff in 1908. Appointed commander in chief of the Black Sea Fleet in 1911, his new command was composed of old vessels. The first new replacements were not due until 1915. His efforts to obtain agreement for an active defense plan was met in St. Petersburg with stony silence. An able and vigorous commander, he organized mining operations in defense of Russia's Black Sea ports. He also carried out the bombardment of the Anatolian coast, concentrating on the mining areas and Bosphorus fortifications. His subsequent failure to counter the German submarine threat and to prevent the bombardment of the Russian coastline by enemy cruisers led to his replacement in July of 1916. He was then appointed a member of the State Council. Eberhardt died on 19 April 1919 in Petrograd.

Andrzej Suchcitz

References

Gozdawa-Golebiowski, Jan, and Tadeusz Wywerka Prekurat. *Pierwsza wojna swiatowa na morzu.* Gdansk: Wydawnictwo Morskie, 1973.

Herwig, Holger, and Neil Heyman. *Biographical Dictionary of World War I.* Westport, Conn.: Greenwood, 1982.

See also BLACK SEA, NAVAL WAR IN

Ebert, Friedrich (1871–1925)

Moderate German socialist, leader of the German Social Democratic party (SPD) through the First World War, and first president of the Weimar Republic. Born in Heidelberg on 4 February 1871 to modest working parents, Ebert apprenticed in the saddler's trade and traveled widely in Germany during his journeyman years. In Mannheim he encountered the moderate social democratic movement of Ferdinand Lasalle and became an active participant in the socialist trade-union movement. Union activities within the saddler's craft took him to numerous cities, and he began his climb in the social democratic movement. The position of presiding officer of the 1904 SPD Congress catapulted him into high visibility, and in 1905 he was elected secretary of the party's national leadership, which required relocation to Berlin. Skilled at creating harmony and consensus, Ebert was an adherent of the moderate reformist wing of the SPD and committed to cooperation with the German constitutional regime as outlined in the SPD's 1891 Erfurt platform. In 1912 Ebert was elected to the Reichstag and in September of 1913 to party chairman.

The crisis of July 1914 found Ebert out of the country and unable to exercise significant influence on the SPD's response. By early 1916 he had moved into leadership positions in the party's Reichstag delegation. Ebert opposed annexationist policies, although he insisted on the necessity of defending the Reich's territory, which in his view included Alsace and Lorraine. When in March of 1916 the minority caucus of the SPD challenged the party's adherence to the government's war aims in a full session of the Reichstag, Ebert initiated the decision to rescind party recognition of the minority caucus. The result was the splintering of the SPD, which drove Ebert and the SPD majority closer to middle-class Catholic and Progressive parties.

As a German victory became increasingly problematic, Ebert helped press for crucial constitutional changes in Prussia and the Reich. This included revision of the electoral franchise in Prussia, which had suffered under a property-based three-class voting system since the constitution of 1850. Ebert also helped draft the 1917 Reichstag Peace Resolution and in October of 1917 called for the dismissal of Chancellor Georg Michaelis.

Ebert was swept along against his will by the events that brought the war to an end and toppled the monarchy. Many of the SPD's demands for a genuine parliamentary constitution in the Reich were fulfilled by the October 1918 reforms, but Ebert worried about the possibility of revolution. He had pinned his hopes on a constitutional monarchy to forestall this alternative and disagreed with Philip Scheidemann's peremptory 9 November 1918 declaration of a republic. Nonetheless, he accepted Prince Max von Baden's offer of the chancellorship the same day. To secure authority in the Reich and provide an element of practical support for the new regime, Ebert concluded a controversial telephone pact with General Wilhelm Groener of the army to defend order and stability in Germany.

On 10 November Ebert called into being a provisional executive drawn from mainstream Social Democrats and Independent Socialists, further to the left. The Independents, however, broke fully with Ebert and the moderate Socialists over the repression of Spartacist and other leftist uprisings in 1919 and 1920 and because they felt Ebert was relying too heavily on the army.

To create a new regime, Ebert had pressed almost immediately for a national constitutional assembly, for which elections were held in January of 1919. On 11 February this body elected him Provisional Reich president. In October of 1922 the now legitimated Reichstag extended his tenure until June of 1925. Throughout these early years of the Weimar Republic, Ebert sought to steer a constitutionally grounded middle course between the forces of the left and right. His efforts were especially crucial in 1923 when the French and Belgians occupied the Ruhr because of nonpayment of war reparations. This event led to the worst phase of the postwar hyperinflation.

On 23 December 1924, in a highly publicized and political affair, a Magdeburg court convicted Ebert of technical complicity in a

January 1918 strike by workers at a munitions plant. Although in ill health, Ebert insisted upon appearing in court. The verdict upset him deeply, and he died in Berlin on 12 February 1925.

J. Ronald Shearer

References

Ebert, Friedrich. *Schriften, Aufzeichnungen, Reden*. 2 vols. Dresden: C. Relssner, 1926.

Eyck, Erich. *A History of the Weimar Republic*. Vol. 1. Translated by Harlan P. Hanson and Robert G.L. Waite. Cambridge: Harvard University Press, 1967.

Freund, Michael. "Friedrich Ebert." *Die grossen Deutschen*. Vol. 4. Berlin: Propylaen-Verlag, 1957.

Kotowski, Georg. *Friedrich Ebert: Eine politische Biographie*. Vol. 1. Wiesbaden: F. Steiner, 1963.

Peters, Max. *Friedrich Ebert*. 2nd ed. Berlin: Arani, 1954.

Schorske, Carl. *German Social Democracy, 1905–1917*. Cambridge: Harvard University Press, 1955.

See also GERMANY, REVOLUTION OF 1918

Egypt in World War I

Egypt was in a politically and religiously contradictory situation when the war began. Although occupied by the British since 1882, Egypt was an Ottoman province, and the Turkish sultan was also the caliph, or leader of Egypt's Moslems. When war began, British High Commissioner Sir Herbert Kitchener was vacationing in London, and the Egyptian Khedive Abbas Himli II was in Constantinople. British junior officials in Cairo assumed control of the government and, on 5 August 1914, coerced the Egyptian Council of Ministers to sign a document effectively placing them at war with their Ottoman suzerains. Martial law was declared in Egypt on 2 November, and on 18 December British King George V declared the ties between Cairo and Constantinople dissolved. The British established a protectorate, deposed Abbas, and placed Hussein Kamil in the new office of Sultan of Egypt.

Professionals in the British army of occupation were called to France and replaced by an assortment of territorial brigades and units from Australia and New Zealand charged with maintaining order in a restive population of thirteen million people, while protecting the Suez Canal, the western deserts, and the southern reaches of the Nile. During the war Egypt served as a staging area for Gallipoli and the desert campaigns and as a source of cotton, camels, and labor for Allied armies in Europe and the Middle East.

After the Turks were driven from the Sinai peninsula in 1917, Egyptian interest in the war—never particularly acute—waned perceptibly. The continuing draft of Egyptian peasants for the Auxiliary Labor Corps, the commandeering of one-fifth of Egypt's camels, and British control of price and distribution of Egyptian cotton became sources of deep resentment. Egyptian unrest was fed by hopes of Wilsonian self-determination, and in 1918 and 1919 there were riots led by Saad Zaghlul and his Nationalist party. Ultimately, General Sir Edmund Allenby was posted as high commissioner to restore civil order.

Jack McCallum

References

Elgood, P.G. *The Army in Egypt*. London: Oxford University Press, 1924.

Fromkin, David. *A Peace to End All Peace: The Fall of the Ottoman Empire and the Creation of the Modern Middle East*. New York: Avon, 1989.

See also ALLENBY, EDMUND; SINAI CAMPAIGN

Eichhorn, Hermann von (1848–1918)

German field marshal and army group commander and the only German of his rank to suffer a violent death during the war. Born on 13 February 1848 in Breslau into a bourgeois family of civil servants and savants, Eichhorn received a patent of nobility (through his father) in 1856 and joined the Prussian Foot Guards in 1866. After attending the Kriegsakademie, he rose rapidly through various staff and command positions and was a corps commander by age fifty-six. In 1912 he was appointed head of the Seventh Army Inspection at Saarbrücken, and soon thereafter he was promoted to colonel-general.

As a result of injuries suffered in a riding accident, Eichhorn did not get a posting at the beginning of the war. Indeed, he had to wait until January of 1915 before being entrusted with the command of a newly formed force in

East Prussia, the Tenth Army. With this army and, later, with an enlarged army group under his simultaneous command, Eichhorn operated against the Russians in the northern sectors of the Eastern Front until March of 1918. His solid performance during these years was rewarded by the *Pour le Mérite* medal in 1915 and promotion to field marshal at the end of 1917.

Following the signing of the Peace Treaty of Brest-Litovsk, the elderly field marshal was sent to Kiev as commander of a new army group in the southern regions of the defunct Czarist empire. Although he was assisted by a very capable chief of staff, Lieutenant General Wilhelm Groener, Eichhorn had only limited success in stabilizing the political situation in the Ukraine and in harnessing its resources for the war effort of the Central Powers. On 30 July 1918 he was assassinated in Kiev by a young Left Social Revolutionary.

Ulrich Trumpener

References

Baumgart, Winfried. *Deutsche Ostpolitik 1918: Von Brest-Litowsk bis zum Ende des Ersten Weltkrieges*. Vienna and Munich: Oldenbourg, 1966.

Fedyshyn, Oleh S. *Germany's Drive to the East and the Ukrainian Revolution, 1917–1918*. New Brunswick: Rutgers University Press, 1971.

Reichsarchiv. *Der Weltkrieg 1914 bis 1918: Die militärischen Operationen zu Lande*. Vols. 7–13. Berlin: E.S. Mittler und Sohn, 1931–42.

Strutz, Georg. "Hermann von Eichhorn." *Deutsches Biographisches Jahrbuch*, 2. Stuttgart: Deutsche Verlagsanstalt, 1928.

See also EASTERN FRONT, 1915; GROENER, WILHELM; UKRAINE

Einem, Karl von (1853–1934)

German colonel general, born at Herzberg on 1 January 1853. Einem's father was a cavalry captain in the Royal Hanoverian Army who was killed in action against Prussian troops during the War of 1866. That did not deter his son from entering Prussian service. Commissioned in the cavalry during the Franco-Prussian War, Einem was eventually admitted to the general staff corps without prior training at the Kriegsakademie. In August of 1903 the Kaiser appointed him to the Prussian cabinet as minister of war, a position he exchanged for a corps command (at Münster) six years later.

After leading his corps into France as part of General Karl von Bülow's Second Army, Einem was chosen on 12 September 1914 to replace the ailing commander of the adjacent Third Army, Colonel General Max Baron von Hausen. Promoted to colonel general in January of 1915, Einem remained in charge of the Third Army until the end of the war. Assisted by a number of capable staff officers, he successfully held his sector of the Western Front (the Champagne) against a succession of Allied attacks.

Immediately after the Armistice and the fall of the Hohenzollern dynasty, Einem was given command of the army group previously led by the German crown prince, and he presided over its return to Germany. He officially retired in January of 1919 and thereafter wrote his memoirs. He died on 7 April 1934 at Mülheim.

Ulrich Trumpener

References

Einem, Karl von. *Ein Armeeführer erlebt den Weltkrieg: Persönliche Aufzeichnungen*. Edited by Junius Alter. Leipzig: v. Hase & Koehler, 1938.

———. Personal Papers (*Nachlass*). N 324. Bundesarchiv-Militärarchiv, Freiburg i. Br.

———. *Erinnerungen eines Soldaten, 1853–1933*. Leipzig: Koehler, 1933.

Möller, Hanns. *Geschichte der Ritter des Ordens 'pour le mérite' im Weltkrieg*. Berlin: Bernard & Graefe, 1935.

See also CHAMPAGNE, FIRST AND SECOND BATTLES OF; NIVELLE OFFENSIVE

Emden (SMS)

The German light cruiser *Emden*, commanded by Captain Karl von Müller, began the war assigned to Vice Admiral Maximilian von Spee's East Asia Squadron. A powerful ship in her class, she was armed with ten 10.5cm rapid-fire guns and two torpedo tubes. She had a top speed of more than twenty-four knots and a cruising range of 6,000 miles.

After a brief sortie during the first week of the war in which she captured a Russian freighter, the *Emden* joined her squadron at Pagan Island in the Mariana Archipelago on 12

August 1914. The next day Spee granted Müller's request that his vessel be detached to conduct an independent cruiser campaign in the Indian Ocean.

On 9 September, southeast of the Indian coast, the *Emden* captured a Greek steamer carrying British coal. Over the next two months she captured twenty additional ships totaling more than 89,000 tons. Most of them were stripped of useful supplies and then sunk, but some carrying coal were kept to provide fuel for the *Emden*. When the number of captured crew members and passengers grew too large, Captain Müller released a ship to carry them to India and safety.

The *Emden* also carried out attacks against two military targets in the Indian Ocean. The first operation was particularly dangerous— against the fortified city of Madras, India. Fort St. George's 5.9-inch guns could easily wreck the *Emden,* and British warships would probably be in the harbor. On the night of 22 September the *Emden* approached Madras aided by the city lights. The crew planned carefully, so that the *Emden*'s fire would hit only the Burma Oil Company's storage tanks or the city's shore batteries. The *Emden* stopped engines at about two miles from the harbor entrance, turned on her searchlights, and commenced fire. Her shells quickly set fire to the large oil storage tanks and scored some hits on the shore batteries. Answering shells failed to find the *Emden*, and she escaped unscathed.

On 28 October the *Emden* conducted a second raid, on Penang harbor. Captain Müller planned an early-morning attack on the ships at anchor. The *Emden* approached from the north, aided by the port's lights and navigational aides. She entered the harbor at dawn and sank the Russian cruiser *Zhemtchug* and a French destroyer, *D'Iberville*. The *Emden* suffered no casualties and evaded her pursuers. No fewer than fourteen major Allied warships were now searching for the *Emden*.

The German warship's final mission was to destroy the powerful radio transmitter on Direction Island in the Cocos (Keeling) group. As the *Emden* approached her target early on 9 November, the island's radio operator challenged her and, after not receiving an answer, sent an S.O.S. The *Emden*'s landing party of fifty men, commanded by first officer Lieutenant Helmuth von Mücke, was ashore for about three hours when they saw the *Emden* weigh anchor and steam off at full speed. *H.M.A.S.*

Sydney, an Australian cruiser escorting the nearby Anzac convoy, had arrived to answer the S.O.S.

Although the *Emden* was a formidable ship in her own class, the *Sydney* was faster (26 knots), larger, and had more powerful armament (eight 6-inch and four 3-pounder guns, plus two 21-inch torpedo tubes). In the ensuing engagement the *Sydney* maintained a distance of 7,000 yards, out of *Emden*'s range but well within her own. With the *Emden*'s fire-direction system knocked out and her guns no longer operable, Müller chose to beach. Of the ship's company, 141 were dead and 65 were wounded; only 117 were unhurt. Müller was the last to leave his ship.

In her three-month cruise the *Emden* had sunk or captured twenty-three merchant ships, an enemy cruiser, and a destroyer, and had inflicted considerable damage ashore. Her exploits were legendary in Germany, and the British had great respect for her captain's bravery, chivalry, and humanity. At one time or another the *Emden* tied down nearly eighty enemy warships.

Meanwhile, the *Emden*'s landing party under Lieutenant Mücke appropriated a dilapidated yacht, provisioned her, and put to sea flying the German naval ensign. More than seventeen hundred miles later they encountered a German freighter off the coast of Sumatra, whereupon they scuttled the yacht. On 9 January 1915 they disembarked on the southern tip of Arabia and over the next four months made their way up the peninsula. On 23 May 1915 Lieutenant Mücke and his men reached Constantinople and reported for duty to Admiral Souchon.

Randall J. Metscher

References

Hoyt, Edwin P. *Kreuzerkrieg*. Cleveland, Ohio: World Publishing, 1968.

———. *The Last Cruise of the Emden*. New York: Macmillan, 1966.

Lochner, R.K. *The Last Gentleman of War: The Raider Exploits of the Cruiser Emden*, Translated by Thea and Harry Lindauer. Annapolis, Md.: Naval Institute Press, 1988.

Van der Vat, Dan. *Gentleman of War: The Amazing Story of Captain Karl von Müller and the S.M.S. Emden*. New York: William Morrow, 1984.

See also GERMANY, NAVY

Enver Pasha (1881–1922)

Turkish general and one of the Young Turks. Son of an advisor to Sultan Abdul Hamid II, Enver was born in Constantinople on 22 November 1881. He graduated from the military academy there and entered the Ottoman army. While a major serving at Third Army headquarters in Salonika, Enver joined the Young Turks and was one of the organizers of the Young Turk Revolution of 1908. Enver chose to continue with his military career and secured posting to Berlin as military attaché (1909–11). He served with distinction during the 1911–12 war with Italy, and during the First Balkan War he led the coup that gave the Young Turks full power (23 January 1912). Enver gained national renown leading forces that recaptured Adrianapole in 1913.

Promoted to brigadier general, in February of 1914 Enver became minister of war while still in his early thirties. He was the most pro-German among the Young Turk leaders, although he always put Turkey's interests first. Certainly, he played a key role in bringing Turkey into the war on the side of the Central Powers. It was his order that allowed the *Goeben* and *Breslau* to enter Turkish territorial waters. Enver was also chief architect of wartime military policy, which was marked by efforts to expand Turkish power into the Caucasus region and Russian Central Asia.

When in October of 1914 Turkey entered World War I, Enver assumed personal command of the Third Army opposite Russia. His plans there showed his tendency toward grandiose and unrealistic schemes. The offensive began in winter and resulted in disaster at Sarakamish (29 December 1914). That was followed by other major defeats at the hands of the capable Russian commander General Nikolai Yudenich. Enver's continued concentration on the Caucasus area of operation almost led to a rupture with Germany.

Enver's interest in the Caucasus intensified with the March 1917 Russian Revolution, depriving the Germans of Turkish forces with which to meet Allenby's Palestine offensive. Enver's reputation was further damaged by Turkish massacres of civilians in Armenia.

When the Young Turks fell from power, in October of 1918, Enver was forced to flee the country. He was killed by the Red Army near Baljuvan, Uzbekistan, on 4 August 1922, while leading anti-Soviet Turkic rebels.

Spencer C. Tucker

References

Ahmad, Feroz. *The Young Turks: The Committee of Union and Progress in Turkish Politics, 1908–1914.* Oxford: Clarendon, 1969.

Allen, William Edward David, and Paul Muratoff. *Caucasian Battlefields: A History of the Wars on the Turco-Caucasian Border, 1828–1921.* Cambridge: Cambridge University Press, 1969.

Shaw, Stanford J., and Ezel Kural Shaw. *History of the Ottoman Empire and Modern Turkey.* Vol. 2. Cambridge: Cambridge University Press, 1977.

Trumpener, Ulrich. *Germany and the Ottoman Empire, 1914–1918.* Princeton: Princeton University Press, 1968.

See also CAUCASUS FRONT; OTTOMAN EMPIRE, ARMY

Erzberger, Matthias (1875–1921)

German politician and leader of the Center party. Born in the southern German state of Württemburg on 29 September 1875, Erzberger trained as a schoolteacher but pursued that profession for only a few years before turning to political newspaper editing for the Center party in Stuttgart in 1896. After helping establish the Catholic trade union movement in the city of Mainz in 1899, he was elected a Center party representative to the Reichstag in 1903. An advocate of parliamentary reform, Erzberger was one of the new politicians of this era: energetic, ambitious, and familiar with the viewpoints of ordinary people. In the Reichstag he focused his energies on Germany's colonial policies, which he opposed, and on financial reform. An ardent Catholic, he steadfastly rejected a coalition with the Social Democrats (SPD) before the war.

The war opened numerous political and diplomatic opportunities for Erzberger. He organized favorable German propaganda for foreign Catholic circles and, along with Prince Bernhard von Bülow, participated in the futile effort to prevent Italy from entering the war. He was an early advocate of annexationist policies, supporting in September of 1914 the German absorption of Belgium, though he later vigorously opposed implementation of unlimited German U-boat warfare in 1917. As an outgrowth of his disagreement with naval policy, Erzberger supported the Reichstag's peace resolution of 1917 and sought to convince the right wing of his party of its necessity. Erzberger was also suspected by the radical German Right in the leaking of a highly pessimistic assessment of the war effort by the Austrian Foreign Office in 1917; the assessment fell into Allied hands.

Although Erzberger helped engineer the downfall of Chancellor Theobald von Bethmann Hollweg in 1917, he enjoyed little influence in the regime that followed. With the war effort collapsing and with the advent of the new regime of Prince Max von Baden in October of 1918, Erzberger found himself appointed state secretary without portfolio with special responsibility for propaganda. In the turbulent events after the Kaiser's abdication and the end of hostilities, he advocated immediate elections to the national assembly and suppression of the Spartacist uprising.

Erzberger served in the Weimar Republic's first cabinet under Philip Scheidemann as a minister without portfolio with responsibility for all issues of the Armistice. He was finance minister in the succeeding Bauer cabinet. Opposition coalesced against him for his policies in both positions. In a legal action against him in Berlin-Moabit in early 1920, he was not fully cleared of mixing public and private concerns in his political activities. Forced to resign as finance minister, he was reelected to the Reichstag in June of 1920. Associated politically in the minds of the radical Right with the alleged abuses of the fledgling Weimar regime in finance, tax, and Armistice policies, he was murdered on 26 August 1921 by two former naval officers recruited by the nationalistic Germanic Order.

J. Ronald Shearer

References
Epstein, Klaus. *Erzberger and the Dilemma of German Democracy.* Princeton: Princeton University Press, 1959.
Erzberger, Matthias. *Erlebnisse im Weltkrieg.* Stuttgart: Deutsche Verlagsanstalt, 1920.

See also BETHMANN HOLLWEG, THEOBALD VON; GERMANY, HOME FRONT; GERMANY, REVOLUTION OF 1918

Essen, Nikolai von (1860–1915)

Russian vice admiral, born on 24 December 1860 in St. Petersburg. Essen graduated from the Naval College in 1880 and the Nikolaevsky Naval Academy in 1886. He served in the Pacific and the Mediterranean. During the Russo-Japanese War he commanded a battleship and was taken prisoner in 1905 during his defense of the Tiger Peninsula. In 1908 Essen was promoted to rear admiral. The next year he became commander in chief of the Russian Baltic Fleet. His principal task was to secure the defense of Petrograd against a preemptive attack by blockading the Gulf of Finland. On his own initiative he ordered a protective minefield laid across the entrance of the gulf. Essen also hoped to prepare his forces for offensive actions, which were prevented by his superiors. Regardless, he ordered his units to spend as much time as possible training at sea. In 1913 Essen was promoted to admiral.

Essen was under authority of the army general commanding Petrograd. In the autumn of 1914 Essen managed to secure a free hand for his light forces to begin limited offensive operations. These included an extensive mining operation of the south and west Baltic Sea aimed at disrupting German trade and communications. There were also a number of minor naval skirmishes with the Germans, but the overall defensive policy of his superiors meant that an opportunity to catch a large part of the German Baltic Fleet's light forces at Libau in early May of 1915 was not exploited. Essen's untimely death on 20 May 1915 deprived the Russian Baltic Fleet of an energetic, decisive, and able leader.

Andrzej Suchcitz

References
Kosiarz, Edmund. *Pierwsza wojnaświatowa na Bałtyku.* Gdansk: Wydawnictwo Morskie, 1979.
Mitchell, Donald W. *History of Russian and Soviet Sea Power.* New York: André Deutsch, 1974).

See also BALTIC NAVAL OPERATIONS; RUSSIA, NAVY

Eugen, Archduke (1863–1954)

Austro-Hungarian field marshal and commander of the Italian front, 1915–18. He was born on 21 May 1863 in Gross-Seelowitz, Moravia.

Eugen's early military career reflected his imperial connections. The only archduke to undergo formal general-staff training, Eugen became a general of cavalry at thirty-seven and commanded XIV Corps before the war. Handsome and popular, Eugen replaced General Oskar Potiorek as commander of the Serbian front following the disastrous winter offensive of 1914. In May of 1915 he assumed command along the Italian frontier, overseeing every major action on that front until the end of the war. Throughout the period he was hampered by constant interference by Austrian chief of staff Field Marshal Franz Conrad von Hötzendorf and frustrated by the unwillingness of the Germans to subordinate themselves to Austrian command.

His own faults compounded these handicaps. Although devoted to his troops, Eugen overestimated their abilities and advocated offensive action in a theater that should have been strictly defensive. At the same time his unwillingness to take risks resulted in dispersion of the Austrian effort, a factor that doomed several offensives from the start. Finally, the aristocratic Eugen often allowed dynastic politics to interfere with his military judgment, a fault that contributed to the failure of the Trentino Offensive, in which the archduke fiddled with the plans in order to ensure a leading role for the future Emperor Karl, one of his corps commanders.

After the war, Eugen fled to Switzerland, returning to Austria in 1934. Much honored by his countrymen, he died at Merano on 30 December 1954.

Steven Eden

References
Rothenberg, Gunther. *The Army of Francis Joseph*. West Lafayette, Ind.: Purdue University Press, 1976.
Villari, Luigi. *The War on the Italian Front*. Cobden-Sanderson, 1932.
Young, Peter. *History of the First World War*. 8 vols. London: BPC, 1971.

See also AUSTRIA-HUNGARY, ARMY; ISONZO, BATTLES OF, NOS. I–II

Evan-Thomas, Sir Hugh (1862–1928)

British admiral, born on 27 October 1862 in Glamorganshire, Wales. Evan-Thomas entered the Royal Navy in 1876. He rose steadily in responsibility and served as naval secretary to first sea lord admiral Sir John Fisher. In 1915 Evan-Thomas was made commander of the 5th Battle Squadron, a concentration of the newest, fastest, and most powerful battleships. The squadron was assigned to Admiral Sir David Beatty's battle cruiser force, the advance guard of the Grand Fleet.

At the Battle of Jutland, a crucial, controversial incident occurred at the moment that Beatty learned of the presence of the German High Seas Fleet (14:32, 31 May 1916). Beatty signaled to turn toward the enemy and increase speed. The signal was not received in the *Barham*, Evan-Thomas's flagship, until 14:37; meanwhile, Beatty's battle cruisers were eight miles away. Beatty opened fire at 15:49, Evan-Thomas at 16:00. In his multivolume work *The World Crisis*, Winston Churchill singled out Evan-Thomas for criticism for the confused delay at Jutland. Others, however, cited Evan-Thomas as the most effective tactical leader on the British side. Both Beatty and Admiral John Jellicoe consistently praised him in despatches and summary reports. Sir Leslie Shane's epic poem *Jutland* was an apology for Evan-Thomas.

Evan-Thomas was promoted, awarded several prominent honors, and remained commander of the squadron until the end of the war. His last service was as commander of the Nore squadron in 1921. He retired in 1924 and died on 13 August 1928 in Charlton near Shaftesbury.

Eugene L. Rasor

References
Baddeley, V.W. "Sir Hugh Evan-Thomas," *DNB, 1922–1930 Supplement*. London: Oxford University Press, 1937, 291–92.
Churchill, Winston. *The World Crisis*. Vol. 3. New York: Charles Scribner's Sons, 1923–31.
Evan-Thomas Papers, British Library, London.
Jones, Geoffrey P. *Battleship Barham*. London: Kimber, 1979.
Shane, Leslie. *Jutland: A Fragment of Epic*. London: Ernest Benn, 1930.

See also JUTLAND, BATTLE OF

Evert, Aleksei Ermolaveich (1857–1918?)

Russian general, born on 20 February 1857. Evert was a graduate of both the Aleksandrovsky Military College (1876) and the General Staff Academy (1882). His experience in both the Russo-Turkish War and the Russo-

Japanese War led to his assignment in 1912 as commander of the Irkutsk Military District in eastern Siberia.

In August of 1914 Evert commanded the Fourth Army in central and southwestern Poland during Grand Duke Nikolai Nikolaevich's general offensive into Silesia. The resultant stalemate was broken in the spring of 1915 as Austro-German armies split Evert's Fourth Army from the rest of the Russian troops. Forced to fight while retreating, Evert led his embattled troops for three months over 300 miles to the Pripet Marshes. In September of 1915 Evert was given command of the expansive Russian western front, a command that included a majority of both Russian field artillery and infantry divisions.

A commander of limited abilities and disdain for the offensive, Evert reluctantly commanded two offensives in 1916. A battle near Lake Naroch on 18 March resulted in over 70,000 Russian casualties and a collapse of morale. Fighting alongside General Aleksei Brusilov's army group in June and September, Evert's troops failed to keep pace with Brusilov's rapid advance. Instead, Evert held back, building up stockpiles of ammunition and guns. Evert's inability to capitalize on Brusilov's successes meant that the Russians lost their chance to secure the vital rail link at Kovel on 27 July.

In March of 1917 Evert refused to back Czar Nicholas II in his domestic crises. He was subsequently dismissed and disappeared. He is believed to have died the next year.

Tom Zucconi

References

Glovine, N.N. *The Russian Army in the World War*. New Haven: Yale University Press, 1931.

Herwig, Holger, and Neil M. Heyman. *Biographical Dictionary of World War I*. Westport, Conn.: Greenwood, 1982.

Stone, Norman. *The Eastern Front 1914–1917*. New York: Charles Scribner's Sons, 1975.

See also BRUSILOV, ALEKSEI; NAROCH, LAKE, BATTLE OF; NIKOLAI NIKOLAEVICH

F

Faisal, Prince (1885–1933)

Arab leader. Born in Mecca on 20 May 1885, Prince Faisal was the son of the Sharif of Mecca. He was an advocate of the Arab home rule party and served in the Turkish parliament.

In World War I Faisal was assigned a Syrian military post, but in June of 1916 he fled to Hejaz to assist his father in leading an Arab revolt against Turkish rule. He led the Northern Hijazi Army with Colonel T.E. Lawrence as his liaison and staged guerrilla attacks on Turkish towns and railways.

Faisal's forces captured Aqaba in 1917 and moved north to Syria with Lawrence to protect the British right flank under General Edmund Allenby. His troops performed admirably in the Transjordan and routed the Turks at the Battle of Megiddo in September of 1918.

Faisal's troops liberated Damascus from Turkish rule on 3 October 1918. Because British leaders had promised him a united Arab state, he was dismayed to discover that Britain had agreed to give France a mandate over Syria. At the Paris Peace Conference he emphasized, "We desire, passionately, one thing—independence."

The Syrian National Congress proclaimed him king in March of 1920, but the French expelled him. Faisal was named King of Iraq under British mandate in August of 1921. He died on 8 September 1933 at Bern.

Elizabeth D. Schafer

References

Erskine, Beatrice. *King Faisal of Iraq*. London: Hutchinson, 1933.
Kedourie, Elie. *England and the Middle East: The Destruction of the Ottoman Empire, 1914–1921*. London: Bowes & Bowes, 1956.
Lawrence, T.E. *Seven Pillars of Wisdom*. New York: Doubleday, 1936.
Rihani, Amin F. *Faysal al-Awwal*. Beirut: Matbaat Sadir, 1934.
Russell, Malcolm B. *The First Modern Arab State: Syria Under Faysal, 1918–1920*. Minneapolis, Minn.: Bibliotheca Islamica, 1985.

Falkenhayn, Erich Georg Anton Sebastian von (1861–1922)

German general and chief of the general staff, 1914–16. Born at Burg Bechau on 11 November 1861, Falkenhayn came from an old Prussian military family and attended cadet school before joining the infantry. From 1899 to 1903 he served as a military instructor in China, and he served on the staff of the relief expedition to Beijing during the Boxer Rebellion (June 1900 to May 1901). Kaiser Wilhelm II was impressed by Falkenhayn's reports from China and took a personal interest in advancing his military career. In 1902 Falkenhayn returned to Germany to command a battalion of infantry, and in 1906 he was appointed chief of staff of the Sixteenth Army Corps. In June of 1913 he was named Prussian minister of war. Falkenhayn's prewar career was truly meteoric, but his rapid rise caused some jealous feelings among some of the older officers on the general staff.

After General Helmuth von Moltke suffered a nervous breakdown after the Battle of the Marne (6–14 September 1914), Wilhelm II chose Falkenhayn as the new chief of the general staff. Falkenhayn directed the movements of the German army during the so-called "race to the sea" that established the Western Front. Once the armies in France and Belgium had settled down to the stalemate of trench warfare, Falkenhayn sent troops to the East at the urging of Field Marshal Paul von Hindenburg and General Erich Ludendorff. Falkenhayn would not gamble on weakening his armies on one front to achieve superiority on another, but preferred marginal strength on all fronts. His cautious nature may have lost Germany her only chance to win the war after the failure of the Schlieffen Plan.

As a "Westerner," Falkenhayn maintained that peace could be achieved only by a victory on the Western Front. Believing Britain to be Germany's most deadly foe, he chose instead to attack France as an indirect method of hitting Britain. Carrying this convoluted thinking further, Falkenhayn decided to attack the strongest point on the French line, a fortress that France would never surrender: Verdun. The city itself was important to France for historical reasons as well as for reasons of national prestige. Knowing this, Falkenhayn planned a battle of attrition in order to "bleed the French white." The resulting battle, lasting from 21 February to 18 December 1916, bled the German army as well as the French; total casualties reached nearly one million. The battle also cost Falkenhayn his command, when Hindenburg, assisted by Ludendorff, was named to replace him on 29 August 1916.

Falkenhayn was given command of the Ninth Army, which was assigned the task of driving back the Romanians, who had entered the war on 29 August. He led a brilliant campaign that threw the Romanians back and drove them across the Carpathian Mountains. His army entered the Romanian capital of Bucharest on 6 December 1916.

Following his victory over the Romanians, Falkenhayn was sent to command Turkish forces in Palestine in 1917. On 31 October his forces were defeated at Gaza by British General Edmund Allenby. The primary cause of that defeat was the lack of adequate supplies furnished to the Turkish army. In February of 1918 Falkenhayn was relieved of command by General Otto Liman von Sanders. For the remainder of the war, Falkenhayn commanded the remote Tenth Army in Lithuania. He retired to his home in Lindstadt, where he died on 8 April 1922.

Steven D. Fisher

References

Falkenhayn, Erich von. *The German General Staff and Its Decisions, 1914–1916.* New York: Dodd, Mead, 1920.

Horne, Alistair. *The Price of Glory: Verdun 1916.* New York: St. Martin's, 1963.

See also PALESTINE AND SYRIA; RACE TO THE SEA, 1914; ROMANIAN CAMPAIGN, 1916; VERDUN, BATTLE OF

Falklands, Battle of (8 December 1914)

Following the Battle of Coronel on 1 November 1914, Vice-Admiral Graf Maximilian von Spee, commanding the German East Asia Squadron, decided to leave the southeast Pacific Ocean. His force, consisting of the heavy cruisers *Scharnhorst* and *Gneisenau* and the light cruisers *Dresden, Leipzig,* and *Nürnberg,* had been at sea since before the war started and consequently were low on ammunition. Spee planned to move into the southwest Atlantic Ocean to meet a resupply ship.

The German squadron arrived without incident in the Strait of Magellan on 3 December and remained at anchor in shallow inlets until the 6th. While anchored, Spee received a message, purportedly from German nationals living in Argentina, that there were no British warships in the Falkland Islands. Based on that information Spee decided to attack the Falklands, burn coal stored there, and destroy the wireless station.

Spee's information was, however, erroneous. In response to the loss at Coronel, the British Admiralty decided to put together an overwhelmingly superior force based at Port Stanley, Falkland Islands. The old battleship *Canopus* was scuttled on a mud flat near the harbor's entrance to serve as a fortress. Vice Admiral Sir Frederick Doveton Sturdee's force arrived at Port Stanley on 7 December 1914. Under his command were two modern battle cruisers, the *Invincible* and the *Inflexible* from the Home Fleet, along with the cruisers *Carnarvon, Bristol, Kent, Glasgow,* and *Cornwall,* and the auxiliary cruiser *Macedonia.*

As the German ships approached the Falkland Islands early on 8 December, Spee detached the *Gneisenau* and *Nürnberg* to conduct the raid while the remaining ships stood out to sea to search for British warships. At about 08:30 Sturdee received word that the Germans were approaching.

At Port Stanley the British squadron frantically tried to get ready for the coming engagement. All of the cruisers were in need of maintenance, coaling, or both. Three British cruisers were coaling, two had their engines open for repairs, one had not yet coaled, and two had put out their boiler fires. As the German raiding force neared the harbor mouth, the smoke produced by the British ships trying to raise steam caught the attention of the captain of the *Gneisenau*. As the German ships turned away, two salvoes from the *Canopus* splashed near them. Sturdee set out in pursuit at 09:45, leaving the *Kent* and the *Macedonia* behind.

The battle cruisers *Invincible* and *Inflexible* were faster than the *Scharnhorst* and *Gneisenau* and began to overtake them. In the ensuing battle Sturdee chose to use the size and quality advantages of his ships to fight a long-range battle that the Germans could not win. The battle cruisers carried eight 12-inch guns, which gave them a greater range and striking power than the 8.2-inch guns on the *Scharnhorst* and *Gneisenau*. The British cruisers also enjoyed an advantage. Excluding the *Scharnhorst* and *Gneisenau*, the smallest cruiser in Sturdee's squadron displaced a thousand tons more than the largest cruiser in Spee's squadron.

Sturdee opened fire on the trailing German cruisers just before 13:00. Spee ordered the slow light cruisers to disperse and attempt to escape. Sturdee sent his cruisers in pursuit, while his heavy ships continued to chase the *Scharnhorst* and *Gneisenau*.

Admiral Sturdee kept his battle cruisers at or just beyond maximum range of the German guns for most of the day. He initially targeted Spee's flagship, the *Scharnhorst*, which endured the overwhelming barrage until 16:17. The British ships, joined by the *Carnarvon*, then concentrated their fire on the *Gneisenau*. The *Gneisenau* was running short of ammunition and had a bad list to starboard when her captain ordered her scuttled. She sank just before 18:00.

The German light cruisers fought a running battle with the heavier British cruisers. The captain of the *Leipzig*, slowest of the German cruisers, fought a delaying action against the *Cornwall* and *Glasgow* before succumbing at 21:21. The *Kent*, the fastest of the British cruisers, sank the *Nürnberg* at 19:27 after a short, intense action. The remaining German cruiser, *Dresden*, escaped and remained at large for over three months; she finally was scuttled off the Chilean coast on 14 March 1915.

The death of the German East Asia Squadron ended the one major surface threat to the Royal Navy outside the North Sea. Sturdee's force suffered only six killed and fifteen wounded. The German survivors were few: 157 from the *Gneisenau*, eighteen from the *Leipzig*, and only eight from the *Nürnberg*; no survivors were rescued from the *Scharnhorst*. In all, the Germans lost some 2,000 men.

Randall J. Metscher

References

Bennett, Geoffrey. *Coronel and the Falklands*. New York: Macmillan, 1962.

Bingham, Commander The Hon. H. *Falklands, Jutland and the Bight*. London: J. Murray, 1919.

Hoyt, Edwin P. *Kreuzerkrieg*. Cleveland: World, 1968.

Spencer-Cooper, Henry Edmund Harvey. *The Battle of the Falkland Islands*. London: Cassell, 1919.

See also CORONEL, BATTLE OF; SPEE, MAXIMILIAN GRAF VON; STURDEE, SIR FREDERICK

Fayolle, Marie-Emile (1852–1928)

French marshal, born on 14 May 1852 at Puy. Fayolle was educated at the Ecole Polytechnique and commissioned in the artillery in 1877. In 1889 he entered the Ecole de Guerre, where he later served as professor of artillery (1897–1907). While there he stressed the need for concentration of artillery fire against an attacking enemy. Fayolle became a general in 1910.

In 1914 Fayolle was given command of the 70th Infantry Division, composed largely of reservists. As part of General Ferdinand Foch's XX Corps, his division took part in the advance toward Morhange and then the retreat and defensive battle east of Nancy in late August and early September of 1914. General Henri Philippe Pétain then became the corps commander, and much of Fayolle's subsequent wartime service was as a subordinate to Pétain. Both generals agreed on the futility of massive infantry assaults unsupported by adequate artillery fire.

In June of 1915 Fayolle was promoted and succeeded Pétain in command of XXXIII Corps during the costly Artois Offensive. In February of 1916 he was named commander of the Sixth Army and ordered to support the British in the impending Somme offensive. He developed a valuable friendship with British General Sir Henry Rawlinson. In the first days of the Somme Offensive, Fayolle's Sixth Army advanced beyond their objectives and took over 4,000 German prisoners. Fayolle's troops captured far more ground than did the British, whom he criticized for "infantile tactics."

In May of 1917, when Pétain became commander in chief, Fayolle succeeded him as head of the Central Army Group holding the Champagne and Verdun fronts. After a brief period in Italy in command of Tenth Army, helping to hold the northern flank of the Piave line, Fayolle returned to the Western Front in February of 1918. By 31 March he commanded the Reserve Army Group (GAR) of forty divisions on the front line south of the Somme, the critical hinge where the French and British armies met. At the peak of action during the last phase of the war Fayolle commanded fifty-two French divisions. Torn by conflicting directives from Pétain stressing the defensive and Foch ordering attack, Fayolle came to accept as virtue Foch's aggressive approach. His troops first mopped up German salients and then drove steadily forward until the Armistice.

After the Armistice Fayolle served as commander of French forces in occupation of the Rhineland until October of 1919. After his retirement the following year, public demands that his service be recognized (technically he was retired a brigadier general) led to his promotion to marshal of France on 21 February 1921. Fayolle undertook missions to Canada and Italy and technically remained on active duty as a member of the Supreme War Council until his death in Paris on 27 August 1928.

Meredith Kulp

References

Barnett, Correlli. *The Sword Bearers: Supreme Command of the First World War.* New York: William Morrow, 1964.

Herwig, Holger H., and Neil M. Heyman. *Biographical Dictionary of World War I.* Westport, Conn.: Greenwood, 1982.

See also FRONTIERS, BATTLE OF THE; SOMME, BATTLE OF

Ferdinand (1861–1948)

Bulgarian Czar. Born on 26 February 1861 in Vienna, fifth and youngest son of Prince Augustus of Saxe-Coburg and Gotha and Princess Clementine de Orléans, daughter of Louis Philippe. Ferdinand became prince of Bulgaria in 1887 after the Russians had arranged the deposition of the previous prince, Alexander of Battenberg. Thereafter, Ferdinand maintained a deep personal suspicion of Russia.

Ferdinand pursued an ambitious foreign policy that vacillated between the two European alliance systems. In 1908 he proclaimed Bulgaria's full independence from the Ottoman Empire and assumed the title of czar. In 1912 his country earned significant victories in the First Balkan War, but in the Second Balkan War in 1913 Bulgaria suffered catastrophic defeats and by the Treaty of Bucharest lost much of the territory gained the previous year. After the outbreak of the First World War, Ferdinand again wavered between the two warring sides in an effort to obtain concessions to reverse the verdict of the Treaty of Bucharest. In 1915 Ferdinand and Prime Minister Vasil Radoslavov led Bulgaria into an alliance with the Central Powers. Bulgaria's defeat in 1918 forced Ferdinand from his throne. On 4 October 1918 he abdicated in favor of his eldest son, Boris of Turnovo, and fled to Germany, where he lived in Coburg until his death on 10 September 1948.

Richard C. Hall

References

Constant, Stephen. *Foxy Ferdinand Tsar of Bulgaria.* New York: Watts, 1980.

Iovkov, Ivan, *Koburgйt.* Sofia: Partizdat, 1980.

Madol, Hans Roger. *Ferdinand von Bulgarien, der Traum von Byzanz.* Berlin: Universitas, 1931.

See also BALKAN WARS; BULGARIA; RADOSLAVOV, VASIL

Ferdinand I (1865–1927)

Romanian king, born in Sigmaringen, Germany, on 24 August 1865. The son of Prince Leopold of Hohenzollern-Sigmaringen, Ferdinand was the nephew of King Carol I of Romania. Carol I had no direct heirs and in 1889 adopted Ferdinand and declared him his successor. In 1893 Ferdinand married Princess Marie of Great Britain, the granddaughter of Queen Victoria of Britain and Alexander II of Russia. When Carol I died on 27 September 1914, Ferdinand I succeeded to the throne.

Ferdinand I continued Carol's policy of neutrality in spite of offers of territory by both the Allied and Central powers throughout the first years of the war. Ferdinand's two brothers, both of whom were serving with the German army, as well as his cousin Wilhelm II, pressured him to join the Central Powers. Allied offers of more territory, Premier Ion Brătianu's advice, and the persuasion of Ferdinand's wife drew Romania into the war on the Allied side. Throughout the war Brătianu was a major influence on Ferdinand. In May of 1918, however, Romania was overrun by the Central Powers and forced to make a separate peace. Ferdinand avoided signing the Treaty of Bucharest, an action that he felt allowed the Romanians to reenter the war on the Allied side on 10 November 1918. Ultimately, Romania received Transylvania, Bessarabia, Bukovina, and part of the Banat. In October of 1922, Ferdinand I was crowned King of Greater Romania. He died on 20 July 1927 at Sinaia.

Meredith L. Bragg

References

Castellan, Georges. *A History of the Romanians.* New York: Columbia University Press, 1989.

Georges, Vald. *The Romanians: A History.* Columbus: Ohio State University Press, 1984.

Herwig, Holger, and Neil M. Haymen. *Biographical Dictionary of World War I.* Westport, Conn.: Greenwood, 1982.

See also BRĂTIANU, ION; BUCHAREST, TREATY OF; ROMANIA

Film and Television and World War I

Films and television programs about the First World War were made during the conflict and continue to be produced to this day. World War I has been the subject of news reels, documentaries, musicals, dramas, TV miniseries, and even a British comedy series. The Great War, as it was originally called, was the first major conflict to be captured on film, and those images conveyed both the pageantry of war and its horrors. Seventy-five years later the photos taken of the First World War still have meaning; the images of few wars can convey the horror of modern conflict more effectively.

The United States Army Signal Corps recorded much of the war on film. Those, plus the archives of the other warring powers, have been the basis for many documentary movies and television programs. One of the best documentary series, *World War I* (1964), was produced by CBS News and featured Robert Ryan as narrator. The twenty-four-episode series focuses on America's role although the series presents a balanced picture. More recently, the Arts and Entertainment Network's series *Our Century,* with Edward Herman as host, featured several World War I episodes produced in Europe that contain footage not often seen in the United States. One of the more famous documentaries was the 1969 production *The Guns of August,* based loosely on Barbara Tuchman's book of the same name. That film examines how the interlocking alliance systems of Europe led to the outbreak of war in August of 1914.

Patriotism and duty to one's country are important themes depicted in many World War I movies. Probably the most popular American hero of the war was Sergeant Alvin York, who single-handedly captured 132 German soldiers in 1918. In 1941 Gary Cooper played the title character in *Sergeant York,* a film detailing York's life in the Tennessee hills and his decision to enter the army despite his being a conscientious objector. In the movie, York's act of bravery is intended ultimately to save more lives than it takes. Patriotism and duty to one's country, regardless of personal convictions, is a major theme.

The Fighting 69th (1940), starring James Cagney, has a patriotic theme and depicts the famous U.S. Army regiment from New York City. Cagney plays a character who is a coward but who later finds courage and dies in battle. Courage and cowardice are also the theme of Stanley Kubrick's classic antiwar film *The Paths of Glory* (1957). In this film Kirk Douglas plays a French lawyer turned officer who must defend three of his men, being tried for the cowardice of the entire unit. The story focuses on men made scapegoats by a high-ranking officer because of their failure to capture a strongly held German redoubt called the "ant hill" (probably Vimy Ridge). The officer had hoped that a successful attack would result in his own promotion; when the attack failed, he turned his wrath on Douglas's men, who had fought but failed to take the objective. Ultimately, after a kangaroo court trial, the men are executed by firing squad.

A similar theme of courage and cowardice is depicted in the British-made film *For King* and *Country* (1964), in which Dirk Bogart portrays a British officer who tries to defend a soldier on trial for desertion. This black-and-white film is one of the most depressing of antiwar movies. The accused soldier is a simpleton suffering from shell shock, and the high command has already found him guilty even before his trial begins. The night before his execution his drunken friends give the unfortunate soldier a mock execution. Incessant rain and mud in the film contribute to its somber nature.

Another French film, Jean Renoir's *La Grand Illusion* (1937), is the story of a group of French prisoners of war held in a German POW camp. They attempt to dig tunnels out of the camp and outwit their German captors. Many elements from this film can be found again in later POW camp movies.

By far the best and most important antiwar film about World War I is *All Quiet on the Western Front* (1930), based on the book by Erich Maria Remarque. Directed by Lewis Milestone and starring the young Lew Ayres as Paul Baumer, the film tells the story of a group of young, idealistic, German youths who volunteer for war service. The film chronicles the years of war and how the men and boys come together in the bonds of comradeship. The characters are played by American actors and represent all youths destroyed by the war. One by one Baumer's friends are killed and wounded, until finally he himself is killed at the end of the war by a sniper's bullet. When the film was released in Germany, Nazis demonstrated in front of theaters showing the movie. In 1979 the film was remade, starring Richard Thomas and Ernst Borgnine.

Also released in 1930 was director G.W. Papst's *Westfront 1918,* starring Gustav Diessl. As with *All Quiet on the Western Front,* this antiwar film depicts a war without heroes. Made in Germany, the film lacks the technical sophistication of *All Quiet* but uses silent-film techniques combined with sound to produce a film strong in social critique and powerful in its antiwar message. The film tells the story of Karl, a typical German soldier, during the last months of the war. When Karl goes home on leave he discovers his wife in bed with the butcher—the only means she has to obtain more food. Upon returning to the front Karl discovers that his friend, the "student," has been killed in a French raid. Finally, the French make a major attack. Using tanks, they overrun the out-gunned Germans; Karl is wounded. The film ends with Karl lying in a hospital thinking of the wife he refuses to forgive.

Another German film, without an antiwar theme, is *Douaumont; Die Hölle von Verdun.* Made in the 1930s, it is a docudrama about the capture and occupation of this important Verdun fort. The movie depicts important moments during the fort's occupation by the Germans, including its capture, an explosion that kills 679 German soldiers, and its final abandonment.

In 1936 the film *Standschütze Bruggler* was released. It tells the story of Toni Bruggler, a young man living in the Tyrolian Alps. The film is noteworthy because of its photography of alpine warfare. The Standschütze was a militia to which all Austrians living in the Alps were required to belong, serving as a border guard against the Italians.

Russia's role in the war has been depicted in many movies, among them *Nicholas and Alexandra* (1971), which tells the story of the last czar and his ill-fated family. *Dr. Zhivago* (1965) also tells the story of the Russian Revolution and the civil war that followed through the eyes of a Russian doctor, played by Omar Sharif. The perspective of the former Soviet Union is portrayed in Sergei Eisenstein's *October/Ten Days That Shook The World* (1928), an important film of the Stalinist period.

Perhaps one of the best-known movies about the war's lesser front was *Lawrence of Arabia* (1962), starring Peter O'Toole and Omar Sharif. The film traces Lawrence's adventures in Arabia, where he was sent to get Arab support for the British against the Turks. Lawrence organizes rebellion against Turkish rule and plants the seeds of Arab nationalism. Lawrence is shown to be egotistical and corrupted by his new-found power, making him indifferent to those around him. His grandiose plans for an Arab state fall apart after the capture of Damascus. Without the Turkish enemy to unite them, the Arabs return to fighting among themselves.

Australia has recently produced movies about her soldiers in the Great War. Among these is *Gallipoli* (1981) starring Mel Gibson. This antiwar film tells the story of two friends who join the army in order to get into the elite Light Horse Regiment. The men share a common interest in cross-country running and, as athletes, both are desirable to the army. After training in Egypt they lose their horses and are sent along with the expedition to Gallipoli, where they experience war for the first time. The two friends are employed as runners to carry important messages. The character played by Gibson is chosen as a runner during a major attack on the Turkish trenches. The attack is canceled, but Gibson fails to reach his unit and friend in time to prevent them from going over the top against Turkish machine guns.

The 1987 release *The Light Horseman* tells the story of the Australian Light Horse during the 1917 attack on Beersheba in Palestine. The story focuses on the camaraderie of a group of Australian cavalrymen. The last great successful cavalry charge in modern history is the highlight of the story. Eight hundred Australian cavalrymen charge the Turkish fortifications at Beersheba and capture the town, which had repelled all previous attacks by infantry and tanks. The main character, who doubts his ability to take another human life, redeems his presumed cowardice by saving one of his comrades during the battle.

1915 is the title of an Australian television miniseries about a group of young Australians during the war. The men go to war, where they find themselves struggling to survive in the trenches at Gallipoli. The series is at its best when depicting the conditions and hazards at Gallipoli.

Another Australian miniseries is *ANZACs: The War Down Under* (1982), starring Paul Hogan. It traces the adventures of a group of friends who join up to fight for Australia and the empire. A major theme of the series is the growth of Australian nationalism. The story traces the history of the Anzacs (Australian and New Zealand Army Corps) from Gallipoli through Passchendaele to the end of the war. As in many Australian movies about the Great War, the British general staff are shown as bunglers and incompetent butchers.

A British Broadcasting Corporation series for television is based on the book *The Monocled Mutineer*. The series, by the same name, tells the true story of the British mutiny at Etaples, allegedly led by Percy Toplis, a young con artist. The story relates Toplis's adventures leading up to his wounding and return to service at the training camp at Etaples known as the "bull ring," which derived its name from the severe training given to returning men recuperating from wounds. Toplis, a stretcher bearer, becomes the leader of the mutiny after it has already begun. To escape the authorities, he assumes the identity of a British officer with a monocle. He proves quite skillful in taking on the manners and speech patterns of the British officer class. Finally, after the war is over, he is tracked down and killed by the police.

BBC production in quite a different light is *Blackadder Goes Forth* (1989), the fourth comedy series about the descendants of the original Blackadder, a bungler who killed "Good" King Richard III while looking for his horse. The series finds Captain Edmund Blackadder (Rowan Atkinson) and his faithful batman Baldrick (Tony Robbins) on the Western Front in 1917. Despite the comedic content of this series, the final episode ends with Blackadder going over the top and vanishing in a burst of German machine-gun fire.

One of the most recent appearances of World War I themes has been in the TV series *The Young Indiana Jones Chronicles* (1991). Although fictitious, the stories are based on real incidents: Indy meets a broad spectrum of true participants in the war, such as Paul von Lettow-Vorbeck, Siegfried Sassoon, and Colonel Charles DeGaulle. Indy gives us yet another side of the war when he joins the Belgian rather than the British army.

The history of the war is told in biting satire in the musical *Oh, What a Lovely War*. The war is depicted in brief narrated episodes connected by musical numbers made up of period soldiers' songs. The soldiers' parodies contrast with the jingoism of the civilians' songs, providing most of the irony of the film. Tunes include "The Bells of Hell," "Bombed Last Night," "I Don't Want to Be a Soldier," "Belgium Put the Kiabosh on the Kaiser," and "I Want to Go Home."

The First World War was a war of new technology, and nowhere was the new technology more evident than in the birth of modern airpower. The aces were the first and most remembered heroes of the war in the air, and many newsreels and films were made about them. The first successful film about the air war was *Wings* (1927), starring Clara Bow, Charles Rodgers, and Richard Arlen. The film centers around two friends who join the air service together and later become rivals for the attention of Clara Bow. The flying footage is the most memorable aspect of this silent film, equaled only by Howard Hughes's *Hell's Angels* (1930), which gathered an immense number of planes to refight World War I in the skies over California.

F

The Dawn Patrol (1930), later remade as Flight Commander in 1938, did much to popularize the air war on film. In the 1938 version, David Niven and Errol Flynn portray Royal Flying Corps pilots who suffer from the strain of war as they see their fellow pilots killed one by one. The two friends come into conflict when Flynn becomes the flight commander and sends up Niven's younger brother, who is shot down. A similar theme is portrayed in The Eagle and the Hawk (1933), starring Cary Grant and Frederic March. March flies an observation plane and is awarded decorations for bringing down many German aircraft, but the strain of war and the thought of having to kill other young men proves too much for him, and he commits suicide. The Blue Max was the nickname for Germany's highest military award, the order Pour le Mérite. In The Blue Max (1966) George Peppard stars as a young German ace seeking the medal to compensate for his low social origins.

This is but a brief overview of movies and television programs about the First World War. The antiwar theme runs strongly through most of them. World War I, with its heavy artillery, poison gas, rotting bodies, machine guns, and death in the air, seems particularly suited to this message.

Steven D. Fisher

References

Farmer, James H. Celluloid Wings: The Impact of Movies on Aviation. Blue Ridge Summit, Pa.: Tab, 1984.

Woodward, David R., and Robert F. Maddox. America and World War One: A Selected Annotated Bibliography of English Language Sources. New York: Garland, 1985.

See also ART DURING THE WAR; LITERATURE: AUTHORS OF DISILLUSIONMENT, AND WRITERS OF THE FIRST WORLD WAR

Finland, Role in War

The position of the Grand Duchy of Finland within the Russian Empire during the years 1809–17 was marked by a good deal of uncertainty resulting from persistent Finnish claims to autonomy and inconsistent czarist responses to those claims. The last thirty-five years of the empire's existence saw frequent attempts to bring Finnish institutions under closer Russian

control. Nevertheless, until the outbreak of World War I the Finns were not involved in systematic efforts to achieve independence.

When the war began, the Finns had no enthusiasm for the Russian cause, and publication in Helsinki on 17 November 1914 of a czarist plan for the total Russification of the duchy created deep public resentment. The Finns refused to form an army to fight on the Russian side and stuck to their traditional policy of passive resistance. Of course the duchy did not escape the impact of the commercial blockade, food rationing, inflation, and restrictions on civil liberties characteristic of total war. Some Finnish youths did volunteer for the Russian army, but many more left for Germany via Sweden for military training as future "Jägers." By May of 1916 the Lockstedt detachment of Finnish volunteers in Holstein had grown into a battalion of 2,000 men. The 27th Prussian Light Infantry Battalion, composed of these Finns, later served as the core of a Finnish army of liberation.

The abdication of Czar Nicholas II in March of 1917 produced a crisis of authority. The new Russian Provisional Government hoped to win over the Finnish people to the war effort. On 20 March the provisional government issued a manifesto that repealed the Russification laws, granted political amnesty, and convened the Finnish diet. The manifesto did not, however, concede to Finland the degree of internal independence then being demanded by socialists and nationalists alike. The provisional government also held to the theory that the powers of the former czar-duke had to be passed on intact to a future constituent assembly, in whose name it was acting as temporary trustee. Meanwhile, a Finnish coalition "senate" began to function as the actual government of the duchy.

By mid-1917 all political groups in Finland desired independence, but they were not in agreement on the timing and methods to be used. In an effort to break the constitutional deadlock between the coalition senate and the Russian provisional government, the Finnish diet on 18 July adopted the so-called "power law." It would have transferred the legal authority of the former czar-duke to the diet, though the Russian government would have retained control of foreign policy and defense. Despite its own precarious position, the Russian Provisional Government vetoed the bill as unconstitutional, dissolved the diet, and called for new elections. In fact, the Aleksandr Kerensky government had neither the time nor the will to settle this problem by negotiations.

The Bolshevik coup in November of 1917 presented the Finns with a unique opportunity to separate from Russia, for Lenin had only six months before publicly promised to liberate Finland. Pehr Evind Svinhufvud, leader of the Young Finns, quickly organized a coalition government from the nonsocialist parties. At the suggestion of his senate, on 6 December 1917 the diet formally declared Finland to be a sovereign republic. The Russian Council of People's Commissars (Sovnarkom) somewhat grudgingly recognized the independence of the new "bourgeois" state on New Year's Eve.

Peaceful separation from Russia did not spare Finland civil war and foreign intervention. On one side, left-wing forces gained control of the Social Democratic party, set up a Finnish Red Guard, and early in 1918 seized Helsinki and the industrial centers of southern Finland. Forty thousand Russian troops still in the country provided the insurgents with arms and some military support. On the other side, the legal government, which had fled to west-central Finland, was supported by a defense corps and the German-trained Finnish Jägers. Carl Gustav Mannerheim was picked as commander in chief by the Svinhufvud government. Finland found herself involved in a war of liberation and a civil war at the same time.

Because Russian troops were not withdrawn from Finland as agreed upon by the Treaty of Brest-Litovsk, Svinhufvud called on Germany to dispatch an expeditionary force. Mannerheim, who reasoned that German assistance would taint the liberation movement and further aggravate class antagonisms, at first opposed this move and threatened to resign. A compromise was worked out in which German forces under General Rüdiger von der Goltz would be subordinated to Mannerheim's orders.

In order to gain a decisive Finnish victory before the Germans arrived in force, Mannerheim accelerated attacks against the Reds. On 6 April Tampere was taken after stubborn resistance. A German Baltic division had disembarked at Hangö on 3 April, but it played no role in Mannerheim's Tampere victory. The German troops pressed on to Helsinki, and by May the rebellion had been suppressed. About 20,000 captured rebels either were executed or died in prison camps. A few Finnish revolutionaries escaped to Russia, where they established the Finnish Communist party in Moscow.

After the victory of the Whites, the Finns had difficulty ridding themselves of their German allies. The rump Finnish diet, from which all Social Democrats had been ejected, was persuaded in October of 1918 to offer a Finnish crown to the Kaiser's brother-in-law, Prince Friedrich Karl of Hessen. When the German Empire collapsed a month later, he had the good sense to withdraw his candidacy. Mannerheim, named regent in December of 1918, resigned in 1919 when a republican constitution was adopted.

William L. Mathes

References

Hannula, Joose Olavi. *Finland's War of Independence*. London: Faber and Faber, 1939.

Kirby, David G., ed. *Finland and Russia, 1808–1920: From Autonomy to Independence. A Selection of Documents.* New York: Barnes and Noble, 1976.

Smith, Clarence Jay. *Finland and the Russian Revolution, 1917–1922.* Athens: University of Georgia Press, 1958.

Upton, Anthony F. *The Finnish Revolution, 1917–1918.* Minneapolis: University of Minnesota Press, 1980.

See also GOLTZ, RÜDIGER VON DER; MANNERHEIM, CARL GUSTAV; RUSSIA, HOME FRONT AND REVOLUTIONS OF 1917

Fisher, John Arbuthnot, Lord Fisher of Kilverstone (1841–1920)

British admiral of the fleet, born in Ceylon, 25 January 1841. The son of an army captain, Fisher became a naval cadet in 1854 and experienced battle under fire in China in 1859. He served several times at the admiralty and was commander of the prestigious Mediterranean fleet at the turn of the century. In an injudicious appointment, he represented Great Britain at the second Hague Arms Limitation Conference of 1907.

Fisher was an exciting, dynamic, colorful, and highly controversial personality. His extensive correspondence, which is published, is filled with outlandish phrases, overly dramatic characterizations, and biblical quotations.

During the height of his career he was Admiral Sir John Fisher, first sea lord of the admiralty, the highest professional position in the Royal Navy; ultimately, he became First Baron Fisher of Kilverstone, admiral of the fleet. At that very time the Royal Navy and Great Britain itself were at their highest point of global power and prestige. To the most renowned of the historians of the Royal Navy, Fisher best represented the period. Arthur J. Marder entitled his standard history of the British navy before and during World War I *From Dreadnought to Scapa Flow: The Royal Navy in the Fisher Era, 1904–1919* (5 vols., 1961–1970).

Fisher became first sea lord on the ninety-ninth anniversary of the battle of Trafalgar, 21 October 1904, and ostentatiously launched a series of wide-ranging reforms in a Royal Navy that he depicted as technologically backward, lethargic, and inefficient. His regime was to be a "new broom." There was increasing concern about the rising naval competition from Germany. Fisher stressed three themes: efficiency, economy, and the German threat.

The *Dreadnought* and the battle cruiser, two major contributions in naval warship design, were actually touted as factors for economy. The *Dreadnought* has been seen as the most far-reaching innovation. It effectively made all predreadnought battleships obsolete: It was an all-big-gun, high-speed, turbine-powered battleship whose concept would dominate capital ship construction until the development of the aircraft carrier. Fisher's personal preference was the battle cruiser, which he saw as a powerful but cheap capital ship. It had little armor protection but was very fast (about 21 knots), and Fisher rationalized that its advantage in speed precluded the need for extensive armor. The battle cruiser did not fare as well as Fisher planned. Three blew up in the battle of Jutland, and the *Hood,* a derivation, was sunk in a battle with the German battleship *Bismarck* early in World War II.

Other Fisher reforms were responsive to the German threat: a redistribution of fleets, bringing home capital ships from foreign stations so that they could be concentrated in the North Sea, and a ruthless scrapping of obsolete ships. Admiral Sir Percy Scott initiated a gunnery renaissance, stressing centralized fire control and accuracy. Fisher's support of Scott and other dynamic young naval officers led to accusations of favoritism: Fisher's "Fish Pond." Fisher deserves credit as well for significant "lower deck" improvements. On the negative side, the Royal Navy during his reign was seriously deficient in naval staff structure, effective war planning, and intraservice cooperation.

Inevitable opposition in the tradition-bound Royal Navy soon developed. Leading opponents included Admiral Lord Charles Beresford and others, dubbed "the Syndicate of Discontent" or, by Fisher, "Adullamites." Fisher had always exploited his close contacts with prominent journalists of the day, and he accelerated those machinations as first sea lord. He also cultivated powerful members of the opposition Conservative-Unionists party, notably former prime Minister Arthur James Balfour.

The Royal Navy was seriously disrupted by these inner conflicts, the "Fish Pond" versus the "Syndicate." Fisher resigned as first sea lord in January of 1910. Shortly after World War I began First Lord of the Admiralty Winston Churchill recalled Fisher, but their relationship deteriorated rapidly. Fisher served until the Dardanelles imbroglio in May of 1915, at which time his resignation precipitated a shake-up in the government, Churchill being one of the casualties. For a time he served as chairman of the Board of Invention and Research.

Conflict, controversy, and schism characterized the Fisher era within the Royal Navy. Historians have similarly disagreed over assessments of Fisher and his regime at the Royal Navy before and during World War I. Marder and Richard Hough praised Fisher and his reforms unequivocally. Others, such as Peter Kemp, have presented more balanced perspectives, arguing that the personnel reforms were effective and that the "early" Fisher was a model of dynamic and innovative change, while criticizing him for later developments. Churchill as historian was understandably critical of Fisher. At the anti-Fisher extreme is Jon Sumida. Whereas Marder presented Fisher as virtually flawless, Sumida has written a series of scholarly articles and an intensively researched book in which he blames Fisher and the prewar Liberal government for later catastrophes. He notes that there was a financial crisis in 1904 when Fisher came to the admiralty. A government welfare program was being implemented and pressure was exerted to reduce naval expenditures. Fisher insisted upon cheap, simple warships. To get that, corners were cut, such as use of less armor and adoption of an inferior, flawed central-fire-control system. All along, the Pollen fire-control system had been available; it was superior, being effective and accurate for high-speed problems. The consequences of these short-sighted decisions were seen during the Battle of Jutland.

Fisher died on 10 July 1920. He was buried at Kilverstone.

Eugene L. Rasor

References

Fisher, Sir John. *Memoirs and Records.* 2 vols. London: Doran, 1919, 1920.

Hough, Richard. *First Sea Lord: An Authorized Biography of Admiral Lord Fisher.* London: Unwin, 1969. Reprint, 1977.

Mackay, Ruddock F. *Fisher of Kilverstone.* New York: Oxford University Press, 1973.

Marder, Arthur J. *Fear God and Dread Nought: The Correspondence of Admiral of the Fleet Lord Fisher of Kilverstone.* 3 vols. London: Cape, 1952–59.

———. *From Dreadnought to Scapa Flow: The Royal Navy in the Fisher Era, 1904–1919.* 5 vols. London: Oxford University Press, 1961–70, 1978.

Roberts, John. *The Battleship Dreadnought.* London: Conway, 1992.

Sumida, Jon T. *In Defence of Naval Supremacy: Finance, Technology, and British Naval Policy, 1889–1914.* Boston: Unwin, 1989.

See also CHURCHILL, WINSTON; DARDANELLES CAMPAIGN; *DREADNOUGHT;* GREAT BRITAIN, NAVY; JUTLAND, BATTLE OF; NAVAL ARMS RACE, ANGLO-GERMAN; WARSHIPS, BATTLE CRUISERS

Flamethrowers

Flamethrowers, as a means of projecting flame at an enemy, date back to the eighth century A.D. In ancient wars they were used primarily at sea. A bellows apparatus could be mounted on the bow of a ship to propel flames at an enemy vessel. Because ships were made of wood the weapons were effective—but they were as dangerous to the user as his enemy.

World War I saw the first widespread use of automated flamethrowers. Like their human-powered predecessors, these were also dangerous to operate. Use of compressed oxygen as a propellant for the burning fuel led to many explosions and accidental deaths. It was discovered later in the war that deoxygenated air could serve as an inert propellant.

The weapon design was relatively simple. Steel tubes were connected to tanks containing the fuel and propellant. Separate trigger mechanisms were located on the steel tubing to control output and ignition.

Two types of flamethrowers were used in World War I. The fixed-mount design involved a trench or underground gallery, which contained the fuel tanks. Only a portion of the steel tubing and the nozzle were above ground, and they could be lowered when not in use. The advantages to this design were concealment prior to use and larger tanks than those on portable types.

Portable flamethrowers were more dangerous to the operator than their stationary counterparts. Infantrymen had to carry the fuel tanks on their backs. The tanks were cumbersome, and accidental explosions resulted in certain death for the carrier. Furthermore, the flames created enormous clouds of black smoke that gave away the position of the flamethrower and left its carrier vulnerable to machine-gun fire. For those reasons the flamethrower was not very effective for purely military purposes, and it came to be used mainly as a weapon of terror.

There is some evidence that the French may have used flamethrowers as early as 1914, but it is generally accepted that the Germans were the first to employ them in any numbers. The first German use came at the Bois de Malancourt, northeast of Verdun, in February of 1915. The Germans continued to use them against both the French and British in the summer of that same year, but it was not until 1916 that flamethrowers were used on a grand scale.

Throughout the Battle of Verdun, the Germans utilized portable flamethrowers as assault weapons. Wherever the flames made an appearance, panic struck the French lines. In one case, an officer and thirty-six men surrendered to a single German flamethrower detachment. But flamethrower units alone were never sufficient to break through the French lines, for their twenty- to thirty-yard range made the carriers easy targets for French machine gunners. And, of course, many of them died in compressed-oxygen explosions.

Although the Allies characterized the flamethrower as an "inhuman projection of the German scientific mind," they not only used the weapon themselves but they also improved on it. F.H. Livens, a young British army officer, produced a fixed-mount flamethrower with a

F

range of approximately seventy yards. He also did away with oxygen as a propellant and used deoxygenated compressed air. The inert properties of the air cut down on the number of accidental explosions. Livens applied the compressed air principle to portable flame packs but could still get only twenty to thirty yards' range from them. This breakthrough in flamethrower technology did much for user safety but little to improve the weapon's effectiveness.

Livens's flamethrower, while exploding less often, still created huge clouds of black smoke. The British used it throughout the war without much success. The French and Germans were not very successful with their flame packs either. The flamethrower is simply not effective for assault purposes on an open battlefield; it tends to handicap the user as much as the enemy facing it.

While the flamethrower was merely a terror weapon during the First World War, it was an important invention. American marines used the weapon successfully in the Pacific theater during the Second World War. With Japanese concealed in underground passages and caves, flame packs were effective at burning them or drawing them out in the open. In those battles, short flame range did not matter. Also, the smoke would often fill the cave and aid in drawing out the Japanese. Thus the flamethrower's minimal success in the trenches of France did not preclude its success on other fields of battle.

Mark A. Macina

References

Hartcup, Guy. *The War of Invention, Scientific Developments 1914–1918.* New York: Brassey's Defense Publishers, 1988.

Horne, Alistair. *The Price of Glory—Verdun, 1916.* New York: St. Martin's, 1963.

Macksey, Kenneth. *Technology in War—The Impact of Science on Weapon Development and Modern Battle.* New York: Prentice Hall, 1986.

Terraine, John. *White Heat. The New Warfare 1914–1918.* London: Leo Cooper, 1992.

Foch, Ferdinand (1851–1929)

Marshal of France and generalissimo of the Allied armies in 1918. Born in Tarbes, southwestern France, on 2 October 1851, Foch was the son of a civil servant. He interrupted his education during the Franco-Prussian War to enlist in the army but did not see action and entered the Ecole Polytechnique in 1871. Three years later he was commissioned a lieutenant in the artillery. His peacetime advance was rapid. During 1885–87 he attended the war college and graduated near the top of his class, which won him assignment in 1890 to the general staff headquarters in Paris. In 1895 he was recalled to the war college to teach military history, strategy, and applied tactics. During his five years at the college, Foch gained the reputation as a gifted military thinker. His book *The Principles of War* (published in 1903) stressed his belief in the importance of the commander's will and the necessity of offensive operations.

In 1900 Foch left the war college for a minor field command, the result of his undisguised Catholicism in the wake of the Dreyfus Affair. The popularity of his doctrines and writings overcame this drawback, and in 1907, after his appointment as chief of staff to V Corps, Foch was promoted to brigadier general. In 1908 Premier Georges Clemenceau selected him to head the war college. After his 1912 promotion to major general, Foch received command of a division. The following year he took charge first of the VIII, then the elite XX Corps, the part of Fifth Army charged with guarding the Lorraine sector against Germany.

In the Battle of the Frontiers in August of 1914, XX Corps attacked toward Morhange but was quickly forced to withdraw to its jumping-off point of Nancy after fierce German counterassaults. Foch, nonetheless, gained notice for his skill in the initial drive on Morhange and the fighting retreat that followed.

Foch's reputation as a military leader was now established, and on 28 August French army commander in chief General Joseph Jacques Césaire Joffre appointed him to take command of the new Ninth Army, forming to fill a gap on the Marne front. Before leaving for his new command, Foch was joined by Lieutenant Colonel Maxime Weygand, who served as his chief of staff for the next four years.

From 4 to 9 September, during the Battle of the Marne, Ninth Army held a crucial sector of the front in the face of repeated German attacks. Foch demonstrated that counterattacks are important even to defensive operations. He was always known for his optimism and determination under pressure. During the Marne battle Foch reported: "I am hard pressed on my right; my center is giving way; situation excellent; I am attacking."

On 4 October 1914, in recognition of his prominent role in the Battle of the Marne, Foch was appointed Joffre's deputy commander in chief and given the task of coordinating operations in the northern wing of armies during the "Race to the Sea." This involved extensive contact with British and Belgian military leaders.

In January of 1915 Foch received formal command of the Northern Army Group, a post he held until December of 1916. In that capacity, he directed offensives in Artois in May and September of 1915. By the close of that year, Foch had come to the conclusion that the key to Allied victory lay not in the hope of decisive breakthrough but in coordinated attacks on various sectors, designed to wear down the enemy.

Joffre's plan for a vast Anglo-French Somme offensive in 1916 was dashed by the German attack at Verdun in February. Enormous Allied losses there and during the Battle of the Somme in the summer and fall of 1916 hurt Foch's career because of his close association with Joffre, even though Foch had questioned the value of the offensive. When Joffre was dismissed in favor of General Robert Nivelle in December of 1916, Foch was transferred to an unimportant advisory post. It was not until May of 1917, when Henri Philippe Pétain became commander in chief of the French army, that Foch returned to prominence as chief of the general staff, although command authority rested with Pétain. In this post Foch advised the Italian government after the disaster at Caporetto (October 1917) and helped secure British and French divisions for Italy. In November of 1917 Georges Clemenceau became French premier and appointed Foch, who now had the reputation as a high-level coordinator, to the military committee of the new instrument of permanent inter-Allied military coordination, the Supreme Allied War Council at Versailles.

Foch's great opportunity came in the spring of 1918 when the Allies were close to defeat during the Ludendorff Offensive. Heretofore, British and French forces had operated largely independently; now coordinated Allied operations were crucial. Pétain, the pessimist, developed a plan for his generals to withdraw, if necessary, southward to defend Paris, and this alarmed the British. British army commander

Field Marshal Douglas Haig believed that survival of his forces rested on maintaining a continuous front with the French. He advocated to London the idea of a supreme commander, "one who would fight." It was a foregone conclusion that this post would go to a Frenchman, and the choice was largely Clemenceau's to make. He was put off by Pétain's defeatist tendencies and selected Foch, largely for his fighting spirit. Originally, Foch had power only to "coordinate" Allied operations, but he soon gained control over "strategic direction"; and on April 14, he was named commander in chief of the Allied armies, first on the Western Front and then over all other operations. When Foch took risks to shore up the British sector of the front, it produced clashes with Pétain. Soon Pétain lost the right, as commander of the French army, to appeal Foch's orders to Clemenceau. Foch and Clemenceau also disagreed on occasion, but to Clemenceau's credit he backed Foch through the remainder of the war.

As generalissimo of the Allied armies, Foch directed the defeat of the German offensive. Even as the offensive raged, Foch had husbanded a small reserve; in July, when the German drive had spent itself, he launched his own attack, a succession of offensives over the whole of the Western Front to give the Germans no time to regroup. This continued for the next three months until victory. In gratitude for that achievement, on 6 August Clemenceau awarded Foch the rank of marshal of France.

Foch headed up the Allied side in armistice negotiations with the Germans at Compiègne in November of 1918, insisting on terms that would make it impossible for Germany to renew the war. During the Paris Peace Conference of 1919, he consistently advocated a tough stance toward Germany, including the demand that the Rhine become France's eastern frontier. Whatever Clemenceau's attitude, this was not possible in the teeth of British and American opposition. Foch's meddling in diplomacy led to an irreparable break with Clemenceau. Foch later denounced the Treaty of Versailles, prophetically predicting that the Germans would invade France again within a generation.

The postwar period brought numerous honors to Foch. He was elected to the Académie française and was the only French general named a British field marshal. He also was made a field marshal of Poland. Foch died in Paris on 20 March 1929.

Spencer C. Tucker

F

References

Foch, Ferdinand. *The Memoirs of Marshal Foch*. London, 1931.

Hunter, T.M. *Marshal Foch: A Study in Leadership*. Ottawa, 1961.

King, Jere Clemens. *Foch Versus Clemenceau: France and German Dismemberment, 1918–1919*. Cambridge: Harvard University Press, 1960.

———. *Generals and Politicians: Conflict between France's High Command, Parliament, and Government, 1914–1918*. Berkeley, California, 1951.

Marshall-Cornwall, Sir James. *Foch as Military Commander*. London: Batsford, 1972.

See also ALLIED COUNTEROFFENSIVE, 1918; ARMISTICE; ARTOIS, SECOND BATTLE OF; ARTOIS, THIRD BATTLE OF; FRANCE, ARMY; MARNE, FIRST BATTLE OF, 1914; PARIS PEACE CONFERENCE; PÉTAIN, HENRI-PHILIPPE; RACE TO THE SEA, 1914; SUPREME WAR COUNCIL; WEYGAND, MAXIME

Fokker, Anthony Herman Gerard (1890–1939)

Aircraft designer and manufacturer. Born in Java on 6 April 1890 to a wealthy Dutch plantation owner, Fokker, whose family returned to the Netherlands while he was still a boy, built his first airplane in 1910 and taught himself to fly. His genius was not understood at first, for he disliked being taught, wanting instead to find things out for himself. Although his schoolwork suffered, Fokker showed a flair for woodworking tools and metals. In 1912 he opened a small aircraft factory at Johannisthal near Berlin. During World War I Fokker introduced the world's first true synchronization gear, which made it possible to fire a machine gun through the propeller arc of a plane without hitting the blades; the propeller itself, by means of levers and gears, operated the gun at properly timed intervals. Although he had offered his airplane designs to both sides at the beginning of the war, the Allies had declined. Fokker became a leading builder in Germany and was forced to become a German citizen. Many German aces, including Oswald Boelcke, Max Immelmann, and Manfred von Richthofen, flew Fokker airplanes, including the D VII, one of the greatest fighters of the war.

As the war ended, Fokker managed to take most of his equipment and plans out of Germany and back to the Netherlands, where he opened a new aircraft factory. Fokker seemed able to sense a sound airplane design when he saw it, and his aircraft developed a reputation for safety flying worldwide for the Dutch airline, KLM. By the early 1920s, he sold an increasing number of aircraft to the American military, and, in 1922, he established the Atlantic Aircraft Corporation in New Jersey. The first nonstop flight across the U.S. was accomplished in a Fokker T-2, and Richard Byrd flew over the North Pole in a Fokker trimotor in 1926. By the 1930s Fokker concentrated on commercial aircraft, many of which were used in the fledgling U.S. commercial aviation industry. Fokker, who died in New York on 23 December 1939 from an infection following surgery, displayed outstanding energy, a zest for work, and unflagging perseverance throughout his short life.

Laura Matysek Wood

References

Fokker, Anthony H.G. *Flying Dutchmen: The Life of Anthony Fokker*. New York: Arco, 1972.

Hegener, Henri. *Fokker: The Man and the Aircraft*. Letchworth, Herts, Great Britain: Harleyford, 1961.

See also AIR WARFARE: FIGHTER TACTICS; AIRCRAFT, FIGHTERS; AIRCRAFT, PRODUCTION DURING THE WAR; RICHTHOFEN, MANFRED VON

France, Army, 1914–18

World War I officially began for the French army at 17:00 on 1 August 1914, when mobilization orders were posted in cities and villages throughout the nation. The next day all the railroads of France came under military control. Mobilization plans called for 4,278 trains to transport troops to their points of assembly. More were needed, and in the next sixteen days 7,136 trains, at times traveling only eight minutes apart, carried 3,781,000 men to the front lines. Only nineteen trains arrived late.

On 18 August the assembled French army consisted of 823,000 three-year conscripts (including 46,000 colonials) and 2,887,000 reservists called to active duty. In the next ten months, government orders brought an additional 2.7 million men into the army. Between

July of 1915 and the end of the war, another 1,907,000 troops were mobilized. Between 1914 and 1918 some 1,100,000 volunteered for active service. In all, a total of 8,417,000 men, of whom 475,000 were colonials, served in the French army in World War I. That was 20 percent of the total population of metropolitan France.

Providing a troop strength sufficient to match that of Germany on the Western Front required a tremendous national effort. The nation's birth rate had declined after 1875, and by 1914 the total population stood at 39,600,000, less than 60 percent that of Germany. After the Franco-Prussian War, both nations passed laws requiring men to serve in the active army, followed by assignment to reserve forces for a set number of years. The 1905 Two-Year Law made all able-bodied Frenchmen aged twenty to forty-five eligible for military duty. Since no exemptions were granted except for physical unfitness, the law placed a significant burden on the French people. The burden increased when French military intelligence discovered that significant additions to the German army in 1912 meant that the French army of 567,000 would face an enemy force of 870,000 in the event of war. To counter the imbalance, the 1913 army bill required all fit men to serve three years on active duty followed by twenty-five years in the regular and territorial reserves. That added another 100,000 soldiers to the active army and gave France a total of four million trained men available in August of 1914.

Prewar planning divided the army into twenty corps, nineteen headquartered in metropolitan France and one in Algiers. Those headquarters were to serve as assembly depots during a general mobilization. Initially, each corps consisted of two infantry divisions (sometimes three), a cavalry regiment, four groups of field artillery, and support services including eight field hospitals. In 1912 France created an additional corps to match the increase of German forces in Alsace-Lorraine and to act as a covering force for the Vosges.

France began the war with five field armies. Between 1914 and 1918 sixteen additional armies, including forces overseas, were organized and sent into combat. Three army groups were created in 1915 (Center, East, North) to improve planning and provide better administrative control. Two reserve army groups, established in 1917 and 1918, included

Allied forces as well as divisions held in reserve for assignment to combat as needed.

When war came, the army organized sixty-two infantry divisions on the Western Front: forty-three active, four colonial, and fifteen reserve. Each division numbered about fifteen thousand men organized into two brigades of infantry, a field artillery regiment, a cavalry squadron, and support troops including an engineer company. The infantry of the active army was divided into 173 line regiments. Divisions initially contained four line regiments, but the total was reduced to three after July of 1915 to increase the ratio of guns to infantry. Thirty-nine new divisions were added to the army between 1914 and 1918, although the total number of infantry on active duty declined steadily after May of 1915 from a high of 1.5 million to less than 850,000 at the end of the war.

French infantrymen entered combat in 1914 with an inferior rifle. The 8mm Lebel, introduced in 1886, required individual loading of each cartridge and had a rate of fire significantly lower than that of German and British clip-loading weapons. In 1916 the Berthier rifle, with a five-round clip, replaced the Lebel; by the end of the year it had been issued to every infantryman serving on the front lines.

The high number of casualties in 1914 caused the general staff to recognize the need for increased numbers of machine guns to support infantry operations. Several models were used by the army, the most effective being the Model 1915 CSRG light machine gun, with a rate of fire of 240 rounds per minute. More than 250,000 were produced between 1915 and 1918, many of them used to equip Allied forces. By 1918 a front-line infantry company contained between twelve and sixteen machine-gun teams. Compared with a total of 2,156 in September of 1914, by March of 1918 there were 19,300 heavy and 47,800 light machine guns in front-line service.

The French army entered the war with ninety-one cavalry regiments on active duty. Those not assigned to service with infantry were organized into ten divisions, each containing three brigades of cavalry, a horse artillery brigade (two 4-gun batteries), a machine-gun company, a cyclist company, and support services including three mobile blacksmith shops. The total strength of each division was about 4,500 men. The Model 1890 carbine, with a three-round Mannlicher clip-fed magazine, became the standard rifle for cavalry units. Most cavalrymen thought the weapon useless, as it could not be fired effectively during a mounted charge. Swords were discarded after October of 1914, but cavalry lances continued in use throughout the war. In 1914 there were 106,700 mounted cavalrymen. By early 1918 seventy-three regiments were dismounted and assigned to infantry duty, leaving 33,500 cavalrymen in active service.

French artillerists began the war convinced that the 75mm Puteaux field gun would give them battlefield dominance. The weapon's mobility, rapid rate of fire (fifteen rounds per minute), and range of nine thousand yards made it a superb weapon for certain types of offensive operations. It could also inflict heavy casualties on troops advancing across an open field. But the gun was incapable of high-angle fire, making it ineffective in hilly or enclosed country, and its shells were too light to be useful against entrenchments. Despite these deficiencies the army organized its artillery units around the 75mm gun; 4,098 of them were in service in 1914, as compared with 389 heavy guns. By November of 1918 there were 4,398 heavy guns in front-line service. The sixty-two field artillery regiments on active duty in 1914 contained 296,000 men. The number of regiments doubled by 1918, and 608,000 men were serving in the artillery at the end of the war.

The army's lack of heavy artillery in 1914 reflected a commitment by the general staff to a false doctrine of war—the *offensive à outrance*. Colonel Ferdinand Foch became the leading proponent of this doctrine. Analysis of the Franco-Prussian War led Foch and his supporters to conclude that the army's defeat in 1870 and 1871 had come because of a defensive posture that allowed the Prussian commanders to dictate the course of battle. Only by seizing the offensive could the army hope to win a war with Germany. Foch argued that the effects of decisive infantry attacks would decide the outcome of modern battles. Victory would be achieved by the élan of the French infantryman, whose superior will to win was more important than firepower, terrain, or even maneuver. During six years as an instructor at the Ecole de Guerre (1895–1900), Foch used his gifts as a charismatic teacher to convince more than four hundred senior officers of the value of the doctrine of the offensive. His ideas were eagerly accepted by those officers, most of whom commanded divisions or brigades or occupied senior staff positions in 1914.

Foch's concepts became official policy when his star pupil, Colonel Louis de Grandmaison, became head of the general staff's Operations Bureau in 1908. Under his aegis the bureau developed War Plan XVII, which committed the French army to the offensive on all fronts. Grandmaison envisioned the direct attack of the French infantry carrying all before it. Soldiers would rush forward, engage the enemy, and let the cold steel of their bayonets decide the issue. If the German army seized the offensive every foot of French soil must be defended to the death and, if lost, regained by an immediate counterattack, no matter what the cost.

The offensive spirit of Plan XVII dominated the strategy and tactics of the entire army. The deficiencies of the infantry rifle and the cavalry carbine were recognized but thought to be unimportant by Army Operations Bureau planners. The rapidity of the infantry charge gave no time for deployment into the open firing-line formations that would give maximum effect to long-range rifle fire. The ferocity of the cavalry charge made it unnecessary to develop dismounted tactics. A general staff officer speaking to a parliamentary commission about the army's lack of heavy guns said, "Thank God we have none. The strength of the French Army is in the lightness of its guns."

The few high-ranking officers who questioned the offensive doctrine were forced to leave the general staff. In 1911 General Victor Michel, commander in chief designate in the event of war, attempted to convince the minister of war and his council of senior generals to include a defensive strategy in the army's war plans. Michel predicted that the main German offensive, using both active and reserve corps, would come through central Belgium. He wanted to counter the German plan by standing on the defensive along the Alsace-Lorraine border and placing the majority of his forces, including reserves, along the Belgian frontier. His ideas were rejected, and Michel resigned. His replacement, General Joseph Joffre, did not choose to argue with the strategists of the Operations Bureau.

Army training sought to imbue French soldiers with the spirit of the offensive. Men entering active service after 1911 were expected to memorize portions of a training manual that stated: "From the moment of action every soldier must ardently desire the assault by bayonet as the supreme means of imposing his will on the enemy and gaining victory." Divisions and brigades were trained in offensive maneuver; defensive tactics received no attention. Noncommissioned officers told their men to avoid the use of cover while advancing on the enemy. The army refused to provide training in entrenchment techniques or the preparation of stationary defenses. Thus, the infantry entered combat poorly trained and led for the war they were to fight. When war came, Joffre's headquarters staff, the Grand Quartier Général, remained comfortably isolated from the realities of front line combat and refused to change their ideas concerning infantry tactics. French soldiers were forced to learn on the field of battle and paid a heavy price for the army's commitment to the *offensive à outrance.*

The high intrinsic quality of the 1914 French army was clearly demonstrated by the ability of the infantryman to survive and rise above the lethal results of the implementation of Plan XVII. Between 18 August and 1 September, army casualties totaled 306,515 men killed, wounded, and missing, a rate of loss never again equaled during the war. Ten percent (4,478) of the officers serving in front-line units were killed in the first twelve days of battle. During that same period 26,582 noncommissioned officers died, a loss of 49 percent of the NCOs in front-line service. The ability of the infantry to endure these losses and keep on fighting was the key ingredient enabling Joffre to achieve victory at the Marne.

The Battle of Verdun broke the offensive spirit of the French army. The German attacks, begun in February of 1916, were designed to "bleed France to death" by annihilating her best troops. The battle lasted for 298 days, and before it ended 75 percent of the army had been drawn through it. During the ten months of fighting the army lost 78 percent of its infantry officers below the rank of lieutenant colonel. Those casualties, and the loss of 39,217 noncommissioned officers, ended the army's commitment to the doctrine of the offensive.

Army morale broke down after the failure of the Nivelle Offensive. From 16 April to 9 May 1917, French troops, most of whom were serving under newly appointed officers, flung themselves against barbed wire, entrenched machine guns, and presighted artillery. The fighting produced 130,000 casualties, and the hopes raised by Nivelle's promise of an easy victory collapsed in a bloody shambles. In early May a front-line battalion, scheduled for re-

placement, was ordered instead to attack. They mutinied. Word of the rebellion traveled along the trenches. Soldiers driven to despair by bad food, inadequate medical services, and the refusal to grant them even a few days of leave suddenly realized they had power. Whole regiments refused to go into the line, and by the end of June of 1917 only two reliable divisions stood between the front line and Paris.

General Henri Philippe Pétain replaced Nivelle as commander of the army. He quickly restored morale and regained the soldiers' confidence with reforms in the policies on pay and leave, and a promise that no attacks would be made without some real hope of success. Unlike most general officers, Pétain recognized the futility of the *offensive à outrance* and the need to develop new tactics in order to avoid senseless casualties.

The army responded to Pétain's leadership. When the Germans launched a tentative offensive in July of 1917, to test the will of the French to continue fighting, the attack ran up against one of Pétain's reconditioned divisions. The Germans broke off their attack after incurring 4,752 casualties in two hours of heavy fighting. An attack by French troops at Verdun on 20 August 1917 resulted in the capture of over 10,000 German prisoners, and showed that the army's ability to fight an offensive battle had been restored.

The fighting quality and, more especially, the recuperative powers of French soldiers allowed the army to overcome adversities throughout the war. Casualties (killed, wounded, and missing) totaled 6,160,800 by November of 1918. One quarter of those losses came after the mutinies of 1917. The spirit of the headlong offensive decimated the officer corps. But the Operations Bureau, living and working in the isolation of the Grand Quartier Général, clung to the doctrine to the very end. The general officers of the army failed to learn from their early mistakes, and even though 41 percent of them were relieved in 1914, most of those who remained never grasped the realities of modern war. They continued to send their troops forward in disastrous frontal attacks. Service in the trenches imposed unimaginable burdens on front-line units, but the infantry demonstrated an amazing ability to endure. In four years of war the overall desertion rate never rose above 6.3 percent. The sacrifices of the French army became a cornerstone of the Allied victory. Yet the moment of final triumph was bittersweet at best. The seeds of future defeat were sown in the soil of peace and came to fruition twenty years later.

Thomas G. Oakes

References

Fyfe, Albert J. *Understanding the First World War: Illusions and Realities.* New York: Peter Lang, 1988.

Gorce, Paul De La. *The French Army: A Military-Political History.* New York: Braziller, 1963.

Haythornthwaite, Philip J. *The World War One Source Book.* London: Arms and Armour, 1992.

Ministere de la Guerre. *Les Armées Francais dan la Grande Guerre.* 34 vols. Paris: Etat-Major de L'Armée, Service Historique, 1922–38.

Palat, General Barthelemy. *La Grande Guerre sur le Front Occidental.* 14 vols. Paris: Chapalet, 1918–29.

Percin, General Andre. *Le Massacre de notre Infanterie.* Paris: Geoffrey Bles, 1931.

Porch, Douglas. *The March to the Marne: The French Army 1871–1914.* New York: Cambridge University Press, 1981.

Terraine, John. *White Heat: The New Warfare 1914–1918.* London: Leo Cooper, 1992.

See also FOCH, FERDINAND; FRENCH 75MM FIELD GUN; FRENCH ARMY MUTINY, 1917; FRENCH WAR PLAN XVII; GRANDMAISON, LOUIS DE; JOFFRE, JOSEPH; MICHEL, VICTOR; NIVELLE OFFENSIVE; NIVELLE, ROBERT; PÉTAIN, HENRI-PHILIPPE; VERDUN, BATTLE OF

France, Colonial Troops

At the outbreak of the war, French colonial forces were scattered around the empire with few stationed in France. The government had ignored pleas from experienced colonial commanders who urged recruitment of colonial troops to enlarge the French army. Those limited numbers of Algerian, Moroccan, and Senegalese soldiers available, however, fought bravely against the initial German thrust into France. The Senegalese suffered such severe casualties in the Battle of the Marne that afterward their units were disbanded because too few men had survived. Moroccan and Algerian units played key roles ln the defense of Paris,

and the Moroccans went on to become the most decorated unit in the French army.

France had only recently acquired Morocco, and it was not fully pacified, so only limited numbers of troops could be raised there. French settlers in Algeria opposed the enlistment of Algerians. That left West and Equatorial Africa as the promising areas for recruitment. The French hesitated to utilize fully those resources because of the general European fear of arming black Africans. After the initial deployment of Senegalese at the Marne, black units were shifted to the Dardanelles and later to Thrace. By 1915 no black combat units remained in France, and the Chamber of Deputies balked at enlarging colonial recruitment. During the Dardanelles Campaign the British commander criticized the Senegalese in racist terms, and the Turks used an airplane to drop leaflets on French African troops urging them to desert the "white" men. The Germans also condemned the use of colonials as "uncivilized."

Despite reservations, the French led other Europeans in accepting colonial soldiers. Individual Senegalese from the "quatre communes," which were recognized as part of France, continued to join the army and to serve alongside other Frenchmen. Only the French accepted such integration. Colonial strength grew steadily through enlistment. Colonial troops garrisoned the empire, fought the Germans in Togo and Cameroon, and by 1916 reappeared in France. Every colony contributed men, but black Africa and Algeria contributed the most. To utilize black troops the French organized "regiments mixtes," comprising two black battalions and one white. To protect blacks from cold weather, the army agreed that they would be withdrawn to the south during the winter.

France did not take full advantage of its colonial manpower resources until Georges Clemenceau came to power in 1917. The previous government had wavered to the end on the question. Colonial forces suffered severe losses in the disastrous Nivelle Offensive of 1917, causing some to doubt their effectiveness. Rumors of Anamese (Vietnamese) troop riots contributed to the French army mutinies. The Banta rebellion in Algeria toward the end of 1916 generated arguments against drafting colonials, but the army never wavered in its commitment to colonial troops. Clemenceau, by his own account, was the "least colonialistic of all the French," but he needed men desperately. He listened to advocates of the "force noire" such as Charles Mangin, who advised him to draft men from the colonies.

To produce the numbers required from black Africa, the government turned to Blaise Diange, the Senegalese deputy from the "quatre communes," who functioned as spokesman for colonial soldiers throughout the war. In the 1918 draft, Diange delivered 72,000 soldiers from black Africa and 50,000 from Algeria. The colonial draft created resistance everywhere, but no major rebellions.

By 1917 the French had earned the reputation of being able to extract the best from colonials. When the United States failed to integrate American forces, a black American combat battalion was transferred to French army control. Both they and French colonial troops reported a warm reception from the French people.

Few problems developed over the inevitable sexual encounters between the soldiers and French women, but the occupation of the Rhineland after the war brought racial tensions to the surface. The Germans created an international incident by accusing the African colonial soldiers of atrocities. Despite the lack of any evidence to support the charges, political pressures led to their withdrawal. Other colonials replaced them.

The French were not devoid of racism, but they were less racist than their enemies or allies—and more desperate, leading them to mobilize colonial forces. Their success frightened other powers, which attempted to restrict France's use of colonial troops. At Versailles the French insisted on retaining their right to arm colonials and considered the possibility of maintaining a large colonial force. Grappling with the politics of peace, however, France soon dropped those plans and forgot its promises to extend French citizenship to colonial veterans.

Dennis J. Mitchell

References

Balesi, Charles John. *From Adversaries to Comrades in Arms: West Africans and the French Military, 1885–1918.* Waltham, Mass.: Crossroads, 1979.

Davis, Shelby Cullom Davis. *The French War Machine.* London: Allen and Unwin, 1937.

———. *Reservoirs of Men.* Chambrey, France: Imprimeries Réuniés, 1934.

Michel, Marc. *L'Appel à l'Afrique. Contributions et Reactions à l'Effort de Guerre en A.O.F. (1914–1919).* Paris: Publications de la Sorbonne, 1982.

Porch, Douglas. *The March to the Marne: The French Army, 1871–1914.* New York: Cambridge University Press, 1981.

See also FRANCE, ARMY; MANGIN, CHARLES

France, Home Front

Although sharp political and ideological divisions had plagued the Third Republic since its inception in 1870, when the guns of August erupted in 1914, Frenchmen rallied behind President Raymond Poincaré's call for unity within France. Premier René Viviani established a government of national unity that drew support from across the political spectrum, including Jules Guesede, the first Socialist member to serve in a Third Republic cabinet. The Ministry of Interior even shelved its Carnet B, the list of three thousand individuals earmarked for arrest in time of emergency. The laws against religious orders were also suspended. Unfortunately for France, this *union sacrée* finally foundered in the glut of French blood, which by 1917 had intensified antiwar and revolutionary agitation, producing work stoppages, street demonstrations, and, eventually, sabotage in munitions factories and power plants. When Georges Clemenceau became premier in November of 1917, he was determined, no matter the cost, to pursue the war to a victorious conclusion and forcefully silenced all doubters.

France's economic planning for wartime had assumed a short war fought with existing supplies. On 4 August 1914 normal economic activity was interrupted. The *Bourse* temporarily shut down, banking was disrupted, a short-term moratorium on rents and debts was decreed, and railroads were commandeered. The mobilization of workers denuded both industry and agriculture and forced over half of French factories to close temporarily. A number of contracts for ammunition were not renewed because it was assumed that the war would be over before the matériel could be produced.

As the illusion of a quick victory disappeared, efforts, though often chaotically lacking in central direction, were taken to restore and expand the production of food and clothing, as well as war matériel. Some 500,000 skilled workers were demobilized, and other soldiers were temporarily assigned to war work. Those temporarily assigned were housed in barracks and received the normal military pay, twenty-five centimes a day, while other workers received as much as fifteen francs. For many women the war was a liberating experience, as they left low-paying domestic service for higher paying factory jobs that were previously the preserve of men. Although some special provisions, such as nurseries, were made for women workers, they worked longer hours than men at a lower hourly rate. Refugees were put to work, and France imported workers, many from her colonies. Armament factories were enlarged, and other factories were converted to war production. The need to replace factories located in the heavily industrialized areas captured by the Germans in 1914 forced the introduction of twenty-four-hour shifts.

German-controlled French territory had accounted for 66 percent of French textile production, 60 percent of its coal production, 55 percent of its metal industry, and 14 percent of its industrial population. Despite the frantic construction of new factories, France's industrial production sank to 60 percent of its prewar level. The nature and locale of France's industry were transformed. Metallurgy replaced textiles, and Paris became a center of heavy industry. The working class was altered as well. With the expansion of nonskilled factory jobs, the work force became more radical and more unionized. Trade unions gained a million new members during the war.

The war placed considerable hardship on the families of soldiers, whose miserable pay did not replace lost wages or salaries. Workers on the home front suffered as well, because wages were controlled with much more vigor than prices. By 1916 the cost of living had risen by 40 percent over its prewar level, and by August of 1917 by 80 percent. Only the price of bread was controlled at first. Piecemeal rationing was introduced in 1917, and maximum prices were established in 1918. In 1917 interior lighting in residences was limited to one bulb per room, upon penalty of losing electricity for three weeks. Long hours of work, inadequate nutrition, and shortages of fuel and clothing undermined the health of the urban working classes. Tuberculosis increased, and French medical services, already inadequate, were further strained by the war. Fortunes increased, however, as money from war production (some of the goods were criminally shoddy) flowed into the pock-

ets of the well-connected families of the upper bourgeoisie. Those with enough money could get whatever they wanted.

Almost every French family was directly touched by the war. During the duration of the conflict 7,948,000 men between the ages of eighteen and fifty-one were mobilized. Of these 16 percent, or 1,315,000, died. Half of the men who in 1914 were between the ages of eighteen and thirty did not live to see 1919. The peasantry and intelligentsia, neither of which received the exemptions given skilled workers, were hit hardest. Even though food shortages forced the government to send 300,000 peasant soldiers back to the fields between April of 1917 and January of 1918, peasants still made up half of France's casualties. Those who stayed on the land enjoyed a unique if temporary period of prosperity. Many peasant soldiers who survived were seduced by their contact with city life and did not return to the countryside. Others returned, but without their proverbial prewar passivity.

The decision to finance the war through borrowing and inflation rather than taxation transformed the franc from one of the world's more stable currencies into a very unstable one, as the postwar years would soon demonstrate. Although parliament introduced an income tax in 1916, its rates were so low that little revenue was generated. Tax revenue during the war barely exceeded the prewar level. Although the franc depreciated by only 15 percent during the war, within a year of the war's conclusion the franc had depreciated by over 50 percent.

Victory was unable to compensate for the deep physical and psychological wounds the war inflicted upon France. The nation lacked the physical and moral strength to face another 1914. Even having regained Alsace and Lorraine with their 1.8 million inhabitants, France had fewer people in 1919 than it had had without Alsace and Lorraine in 1914. Seven million acres in northern France had been ravaged. Some 250,000 buildings had been totally destroyed, and 350,000 others partially wrecked. All this had an impact on the French position at the Paris Peace Conference and future French demands for security.

Bernard A. Cook

References

Becker, Jean-Jacques. *The Great War and the French People*. New York: St. Martin's, 1986.

Fridenson, Patrick, ed. *The French Home Front 1914–1918.* Providence and Oxford: Berg, 1992.

Williams, John. *The Other Battleground, The Home Fronts: Britain, France and Germany 1914–1918.* Chicago: Henry Regnery, 1972.

See also CLEMENCEAU, GEORGES; POINCARÉ, RAYMOND; VIVIANI, RENÉ

France, Navy, 1914–18

In the 1880s the French navy underwent a period of tactical and strategic disputes. These disagreements centered on the theories of the so-called *Jeune Ecole,* which advocated torpedo boats and cruiser warfare against commerce, as opposed to traditional battle fleets. This strategic dispute, coupled with a lax building policy, resulted in a heterogeneous "fleet of samples." Partly as a result of that fact, in 1905 the German navy overtook the French as the world's second most powerful. To add to the French navy's problems, two battleships were lost in 1907 and 1911 to explosions caused by unstable powder.

It was only in 1912, two years prior to World War I, that the French navy began a gradual improvement. Two capable ministers of marine, Admiral Augustin Boué de Lapeyrère and Théophile Delcassé, secured passage of a new naval law. It provided for a regular program of shipbuilding with the aim of gaining supremacy in the Mediterranean Sea. The plan called for a French fleet by 1920 to consist of twenty-eight first-class battleships, ten light cruisers, fifty-two destroyers, ten ships for overseas stations, and ninety-four submarines.

The French built three dreadnoughts in 1913 (the *Bretagne, Lorraine,* and *Provence*). Bretagne-class dreadnoughts could cruise at twenty knots; their belt armor was 10.75 inches and their deck armor 1.75 inches thick. Main batteries consisted of ten 13.4-inch guns. That was an improvement over the Courbet class of 1910 (*Courbet, Jean Bart, Paris,* and *France*), which also could cruise at twenty knots. Main batteries in this class were only twelve 12-inch guns. Their armor was thicker than that of the Bretagne class, however: 11.75 inches on the belts and 2.75 inches on the main deck.

French battleships built in 1907 were the latest to participate in World War I. Known as the Danton class, they included the *Danton,* *Mirabeau, Diderot, Condorcet, Vergniaud,* and *Voltaire.* The major improvement in these battleships over those of the 1891, 1894, 1899, and 1901–3 types was speed. The newer ships could steam at 19 knots, whereas the earlier ships could get only 15.5 to 19 knots. Their four 12-inch-gun main battery was the same as that of the 1899 and 1901–3 series. Belt armor was thinner than all the earlier series; it was 10 inches on *Danton* and *Mirabeau,* and 10.5 inches on the remaining four ships. Deck armor was 3 inches throughout the Danton class. That was relatively thin compared with the 19.5 inches on the belts and 5 inches on the decks of certain of the 1894 series battleships.

The latest cruiser series in the French navy during the First World War dated back to 1907–8. These vessels could make 23 knots, an improvement over the 1901–4 series, which could get only 21–22 knots. Their main armament was 7.6-inch guns, the number of which differed among classes. The Waldeck Rousseau class (*Waldeck Rousseau* and *Edgar Quinet*) was the latest. It mounted a main battery of fourteen 7.6-inch guns. The 1906 ship *Ernest Renan* contained a main battery of only four 7.6-inch guns; a battery equal to that of the most advanced ship in the 1901–4 series. The *Edgar Quinet, Waldeck Rousseau,* and *Ernest Renan* had 6.75-inch-thick belt armor and 2.5-inch decks, no improvement over the 1901–4 series.

The most advanced destroyers in the French navy were the Tribal class of 1917 (*Algerien, Annamite, Arabe, Bambara, Hova, Kabyle, Marocain, Sakalave, Sénégalais, Somali, Tonkinois,* and *Touareg*). They were built in Japanese yards and were virtually replicas of the Japanese Kaba class destroyers. Their maximum speed was 29 knots, 3 knots slower than the 1914 Enseigne Gabolde class. Main armament on these ships consisted of four 18-inch torpedo tubes in two twin-deck mountings, only half the number of tubes on the Enseigne Gabolde class. Exact armor thickness aboard these ships is unknown.

The French built submarines for war service as late as 1917, some of which were not completed until after the war. The Joessel class (*Joessel* and *Fulton*) were oceangoing vessels capable of 16.5 knots on the surface and 11 knots submerged. The 1913 Gustave Zédé class could get 19 surface knots, but only 10 knots under water. Main armament of the Joessel submarines consisted of eight to ten torpedo tubes carried in external cradles. Exact skin thickness for these vessels is unknown. The *Fulton* was finished in 1919, after the war.

By the outbreak of World War I, the French fleet numbered some twelve dreadnoughts, twenty-one battleships, nineteen armored cruisers, nine protected cruisers, ten small warships, eighty-four destroyers of several classes, seventeen torpedo boats, seventy-six submersibles, ten auxiliary ships, and seven miscellaneous ships. These figures include ships still being built at the beginning of the year. Regardless, the improved French fleet would have been large enough to play only a supportive role in the blockade of Germany. It had to take a dominant position elsewhere.

During World War I French naval strength was concentrated in the Mediterranean Sea. A convention signed in London on 6 August 1914 gave France control of Mediterranean naval operations. The agreement provided for the British to cooperate with the French fleet until the escaped German cruisers *Goeben* and *Breslau* were destroyed. When that occurred, and provided Italy did not break its neutrality on the side of the Central Powers, most of the British force would be freed for service elsewhere. What remained of British Mediterranean naval strength would be placed under French command. Also, Malta and Gibraltar would become French naval bases.

Protection of British and French commerce throughout the Mediterranean was a paramount concern. If war were to be declared between Austria and France, the French fleet would act against the Austrians and conduct strict surveillance of the entrance to the Adriatic Sea. The French were also to keep watch on the Suez Canal and Straits of Gibraltar.

In acting against the Austrian fleet in the Adriatic, the French ran into problems. Blockades require fuel and maintenance facilities, and there was no available port near the entrance to the Adriatic. Furthermore, Admiral de Lapeyrère detailed several larger ships for escort duties, leaving mostly destroyers and torpedo boats for blockade duty. Those vessels were a poor selection; they were not as durable as larger ships and suffered from frequent boiler-room fires.

De Lapeyrère planned a naval sweep into the Adriatic in the hope of drawing the Austro-Hungarian navy into a decisive battle. On 16 August 1914 the French encountered two Austrian warships: the cruiser *Zenta* and the de-stroyer *Ulan*. French gunfire sank the *Zenta* but the *Ulan* escaped northward. The Austrian fleet did not accept the French challenge, never coming out in force. De Lapeyrère still lacked a nearby base and was forced to institute a rotation system whereby some of his ships could return to Malta while others remained on blockade duty.

The French fleet also played a role in the failed effort in 1915 to force the Dardanelles, committing four old battleships (the *Suffren, Bouvet, Charlemagne,* and *Gaulois*) to the operation. In the subsequent effort to force the straits the *Bouvet* took a hit in one of her magazines and blew up, sinking in less than two minutes with the loss of 640 men. The French naval commitment at the Dardanelles won renewed British recognition of French command in the Mediterranean. The French did not make a great naval effort at the Dardanelles, however, fearing that, if the operation failed, their extensive interests in the Near East would be threatened. Also, the Dardanelles action was in addition to their other Mediterranean operations, and the French felt they could ill afford to divert any ships from their Adriatic blockade.

Despite the failure to destroy the *Goeben* and *Breslau* early on and war with Austria-Hungary, the French fleet maintained supremacy in the Mediterranean. That allowed transport of colonial forces from North Africa to France, the maintenance of Mediterranean trade routes, and the evacuation of thousands of Serbian troops from Albania. It also helped to force Greece into the war on the Allied side.

French naval losses throughout the war were light in comparison to those of Britain and Germany, because the bulk of actual naval warfare took place elsewhere. French warship losses amounted to 109,000 tons (plus 56,000 tons of merchant shipping requisitioned for navy use). An additional 925,000 tons of French merchant shipping was sunk during the war.

Mark A. Macina

References

Coletta, Paolo E. *Sea Power in the Atlantic and Mediterranean in World War I.* Lanham, Md.: University Press of America, 1989.

Halpern, Paul G. *The Naval War in the Mediterranean, 1914–1918.* Annapolis, Md.: Naval Institute Press, 1987.

Moore, John, ed. *Jane's Fighting Ships of World War I*. London: Jane's, 1919.

Valluy, General J.E., ed. *La Première Guerre Mondiale*. Vol. 2. Paris: Larousse, 1968.

See also Boué de Lapeyrère, Augustin; Delcassé, Théophile; Mediterranean Naval Operations; Submarines; Warships: Battleships, Cruisers, Destroyers

Franchet d'Esperey, Louis Felix François (1856–1942)

Marshal of France, born in Mostaganem, Algeria, on 25 May 1856, Franchet d'Esperey graduated from St. Cyr in 1876 and entered the French army. He served in France's North African and Asian colonies and also traveled extensively in southeastern Europe.

When the war began, Franchet d'Esperey's I Corps, Fifth Army, won a significant victory at Guise on 29 August that won him command of Fifth Army on 3 September. He helped negotiate the participation of the BEF in the Marne Offensive and remained a popular French general with the English. In late 1914 Franchet d'Esperey urged President Poincaré to make a major military effort in southeastern Europe, but the plan was vetoed by Joffre. In 1916 he was promoted to head Army Group East and in 1917 Army Group North.

The failure of General Maurice Sarrail's 1917 Balkan offensive, low morale in the Allied army there, and Franchet d'Esperey's familiarity with the region finally led to his appointment as commander in Salonika in June of 1918. His energy and diplomatic skills set the stage for a 15 September offensive that soon forced Bulgaria to request an armistice. Belgrade fell on 1 November and by the end of the war Franchet d'Esperey's armies stood on the Danube.

Named Marshal of France in 1922, Franchet d'Esperey remained on active service well into his seventies. Admitted to the French Academy in 1934, he died at Albi on 8 July 1942.

David L. Longfellow

References
Azan, Paul. *Franchet D'Esperey*. Paris: Flammarion, 1949.

Larcher, Maurice. *La Grande guerre dans les Balkans*. Paris: Payot, 1929.

See also Dobropole, Battle of

François, Hermann von (1856–1933)

Prussian army corps commander. The descendant of seventeenth-century Huguenot immigrants, François was born on 31 January 1856 at Luxembourg, where his father, a Prussian army officer, was stationed. Fourteen years later, his father, by then a major general, was killed during the invasion of France. Hermann von François began his military career in the Foot Guards and, after graduating from the Kriegsakademie in 1887, served in a variety of staff and command positions. Although not yet a three-star general he was entrusted with the East Prussian I Corps on 1 October 1913, and it was in that position that he would become widely known in August of 1914.

Headstrong and believing in the value of the offensive, François played a major role in the first encounters with the Russians, especially at Gumbinnen. His penchant for ignoring orders, however, caused much difficulty to both his superiors and his chief of staff. Promoted to general of infantry, François was briefly employed as acting commander of the Eighth Army (October-November of 1914), but thereafter he had to be satisfied with yet another corps command. As leader of the newly formed XXXXI Reserve Corps, he served initially on the Western Front but was sent back to the east in April of 1915. Two months later he was appointed commander of the Westphalian VII Corps, a position he would retain until the summer of 1918. In addition, from July of 1916 on François was responsible for "Meuse Group West," coordinating German operations in the left-bank section of the Verdun region.

Decorated with both the *Pour le Mérite* and its oak leaf cluster, François gave up his command on 6 July 1918. He stayed on the standby list until October and was then pensioned off. He died at Berlin on 15 May 1933.

Ulrich Trumpener

References
Elze, Walter. *Tannenberg: Das deutsche Heer von 1914, seine Grundzüge und deren Auswirkung im Sieg and der Ostfront*. Breslau: F. Hirt, 1928.

François, Hermann von. "Der Grenzschutz im Osten im August 1914 und seine Reibungen." *Wissen und Wehr*, X (1929).

F

———. *Marneschlacht und Tannenberg: Betrachtungen zur deutschen Kriegsführung der ersten sechs Kriegswochen.* Berlin: A. Scherl, 1920.

———. Personal papers (*Nachlass*), N 274. Bundesarchiv-Militärarchiv, Freiburg i. Br.

Showalter, Dennis E. *Tannenberg: Clash of Empires.* Hamden, Conn.: Archon, 1991.

See also EAST PRUSSIA CAMPAIGN

Franz Ferdinand (1863–1914)

Archduke and heir to the throne of Austria-Hungary. His assassination by Bosnian terrorists in Sarajevo on 28 June 1914 was the immediate cause of the outbreak of the First World War. As heir to the throne, Franz Ferdinand intended to overhaul the constitutional structure of the Austro-Hungarian monarchy, through force if necessary. Because his life was abruptly cut short, his plans for reform and his ability to carry them out have remained subjects of controversy to this day.

Franz Ferdinand was born on 18 December 1863 in Graz, Austria. A series of tragedies made him the heir to the Hapsburg throne. Rudolf, the only son of Emperor Franz Josef, committed suicide at Mayerling in 1889, and Franz Ferdinand's father, one of the emperor's younger brothers, died in 1896 during a pilgrimage to the Holy Land. Franz Ferdinand was not originally trained to be a ruler. Rather, like other Hapsburg archdukes, he was given a primarily military upbringing, and he eventually became inspector general of the Austro-Hungarian army.

In his lifetime, Franz Ferdinand was not a popular figure. Intelligent and forceful, he was also quick to anger and a man of strong prejudices, which he made little effort to hide. When he was diagnosed with tuberculosis in 1895 and forced to spend several years in semiretirement, he reacted furiously to reports that people were anticipating his demise. He reacted even more forcibly to the opposition aroused by his decision to marry Countess Sophie Chotek. Chotek was not of sufficiently noble blood to be eligible for marriage to a Hapsburg, and Franz Ferdinand overcame his uncle Franz Josef's opposition to the match only by agreeing to a morganatic marriage. The ceremony took place in 1900. Thereafter, at all official functions, to the Archduke's continued outrage, his wife was placed not at his side but at the bottom of the royal protocol list. By all accounts, however, he was a devoted husband and father, a side of his complex personality largely hidden from the general public.

Franz Ferdinand believed fervently that the established constitutional structure of Austria-Hungary would lead to the demise both of the Hapsburg dynasty and of the state itself. Austria-Hungary was a "Dual Monarchy" by virtue of the *Ausgleich* of 1867. While the monarchy comprised nine major nationalities, the 1867 settlement split it into two parts, Hungary in the east and Austria in the west and north. Each half had its own separate parliament and administration, centered on Budapest in the east and Vienna in the west. What united them was a common army, foreign ministry, and monarch. In practice, it vastly complicated the process of governing, for common policies became almost impossible to implement with two administrative structures instead of one. Moreover, the Dual Monarchy's nationality conflicts were only exacerbated by the arrangement: the nonprivileged groups demanded the same status as the Germans and Magyars, who fiercely resisted their demands, causing the virtual paralysis of much of public life in the years before 1914. Franz Ferdinand's support for change clashed repeatedly with Emperor Franz Josef's inertia, chilling relations between them even without the added complication of the archduke's marriage.

Although without formal power, Franz Ferdinand began attracting supporters with an eye on the future, advisers who became known as his "Belvedere Circle" (from the name of his palace in Vienna). They included Count Ottokar Czernin, later Austro-Hungarian foreign minister; the Transylvanian politician Alexandru Vajda-Voevod; Friedrich Funder, editor of the Christian Social newspaper the *Reichspost* and an associate of Vienna mayor Karl Lueger; and a host of others on greater or lesser terms of intimacy. This circle was reinforced by the creation of Franz Ferdinand's Military Chancery, headed by Alexander Brosch von Aarenau from 1906 and Karl Bardolff after 1911. It gave Franz Ferdinand a vehicle with which to collect information about the current situation in the monarchy, to influence major figures in the government, and finally to lay plans for the day when he would ascend the throne.

There is no doubt that major upheavals would have taken place if Franz Ferdinand had ever become emperor. Less clear is whether they would have saved the Hapsburg monarchy or merely accelerated its collapse. He intended to end the *Ausgleich* as quickly as possible, and with it what he considered the Magyars' dangerous position of power in the realm. He hoped to win the support of the discontented non-Magyar nationalities in Hungary and, through the enactment of universal suffrage, to use their votes to swamp the Magyar gentry in the Budapest parliament. Magyar resistance would be met by the imposition of martial law throughout Hungary. Franz Ferdinand toyed with a number of alternative institutional arrangements to the 1867 system. One was trialism, or making the dual monarchy a triune monarchy through creation of a third autonomous area in the south for the monarchy's Croats, Slovenes, and Serbs. If two administrations caused major institutional problems, though, three would have been even more cumbersome. More likely is that the archduke would have liked to create or re-create the Greater Austria (*Großösterreich*) of the 1850s, with a single, centralized administration in Vienna responsible directly to the emperor. He was a dynast rather than a democrat; he has sometimes been compared to Counter-Reformation Hapsburg rulers like Ferdinand II, autocratic and staunchly Catholic. How well a program like that was suited to the needs of the twentieth century is an open question. But Franz Ferdinand was also a pragmatist and might have modified his ideas in the process of actually trying to carry them out.

It is not hard to see why the archduke was chosen for assassination by the Serbian Black Hand terrorist organization. It hoped that the growing discontent of the Serbs and Croats with the 1867 system in Austria-Hungary would make them ripe for future annexation by the neighboring state of Serbia. If Franz Ferdinand really initiated trialism in the monarchy, however, they might become loyal Hapsburg subjects and lose all interest in being annexed. On the other hand, if he created a centralized but effective bureaucracy, they might remain discontented but be deprived of any power to agitate further against the Hapsburg government. In either case, Serbian nationalism would be stymied. Franz Ferdinand's negative public image made him an easy target of hatred in any case.

The Black Hand's opportunity came with the archduke's trip to Bosnia-Herzegovina in June of 1914 to attend army maneuvers, followed by a well-publicized visit with his wife to the Bosnian capital, Sarajevo. Although the parade route through Sarajevo was printed in the local papers, Oskar Potiorek, the military governor of the province, did little to provide security, beyond stationing a few policemen along the streets. A number of Bosnian youth, armed with guns or bombs supplied by the Black Hand, positioned themselves amid the crowds on the morning of 28 June. One, Nedjelko Čabrinović, threw a bomb at the car containing Franz Ferdinand and his wife as it passed him. It bounced off the archduke's vehicle and exploded behind it. The party reached the city hall unscathed. When they left, however, there was some confusion about the correct route to take; the car's chauffeur stopped to turn the car around directly in front of another conspirator, Gavrilo Princip. Princip's two bullets killed both Franz Ferdinand and his wife.

The Sarajevo assassination was the occasion for the Austro-Hungarian ultimatum to Serbia that led to World War I, even though many leading figures in the monarchy were probably relieved that Franz Ferdinand had been killed. Ironically, while the archduke had constantly advocated strengthening the monarchy's military forces, he had generally counseled against using them in risky foreign adventures. He wanted a strong military to back up his future reform program and sensibly hoped to keep foreign affairs on ice until his internal changes had been carried out. His death thus led to the very war that, while alive, he had so much desired to avoid.

Gary W. Shanafelt

References

Cassels, Lavender. *The Archduke and the Assassin: Sarajevo, June 28th, 1914.* London: Frederick Muller, 1984.

Dedijer, Vladimir. *The Road to Sarajevo.* New York: Simon and Schuster, 1966.

Kann, Robert A. *Erzherzog Franz Ferdinand Studien.* Vienna: Verlag für Geschichte und Politik, 1976.

Kiszling, Rudolf. *Erzherzog Franz Ferdinand von Österreich-Este: Leben, Pläne, und Wirken am Schicksalsweg der Donaumonarchie.* Graz-Cologne: Böhlaus Nachfolger, 1953.

F

See also BLACK HAND; CZERNIN, OTTOKAR; DIMITRIJEVIĆ, DRAGUTIN; OUTBREAK OF THE FIRST WORLD WAR; POTIOREK, OSKAR; PRINCIP, GAVRILO

Franz Josef I (1830–1916)

Emperor of Austria. Franz Josef reigned for sixty-eight years (1848–1916) and presided over the creation of the Dual Monarchy in 1867, which made him King of Hungary (1867–1916). As emperor, Franz Josef always maintained an air of royal dignity, and his devotion to duty was legendary. As head of the Hapsburg royal family, he sought to extend and enhance the dynasty, and he brooked no dissension or deviance from the royal line. The empire over which he ruled, however, declined in prestige as the various ethnic groups demanded more power and his family suffered a series of tragedies.

Born on 18 August 1830 in the Schönnbrunn Palace near Vienna, Franz Josef was the oldest son of Archduke Franz Karl and Archduchess Sophia. When the Revolutions of 1848 broke out, conservatives saw Franz Josef as the best hope for preserving the Hapsburg monarchy. On 2 December 1848, therefore, Chancellor Prince Felix zu Schwarzenberg persuaded Emperor Ferdinand, who was epileptic, mentally deficient, and childless, to abdicate the throne because he had been compromised by promising to meet all the demands of the Viennese revolutionaries. Ferdinand's brother, Franz Karl, agreed to forgo his rights of succession in favor of his son, and Franz Josef became emperor at age eighteen.

Franz Josef personally campaigned with his armies to put down the revolution in Hungary, and he viewed the army as the major support of his rule. With the help of Russian military intervention, Franz Josef defeated the Hungarian revolutionary army of Louis Kossuth. By 1850 he ruled as an absolute monarch, and the next ten years were known as the era of neo-absolutism. In reaction, János Libényi attempted to assassinate the emperor in February of 1853.

In foreign affairs, Franz Josef's policies soon proved disastrous for Austria. During the Crimean War of 1854, Franz Josef angered both the Russians and the allied powers by not entering the war. In June of 1859 the Sardinians and their French allies goaded Franz Josef into war and decisively defeated him at Solferino. In the subsequent Armistice of Villafranca, he surrendered Lombardy. In 1864 Franz Josef was drawn into a war with Denmark, and in 1866 Prussian Minister-President Otto von Bismarck maneuvered him into a disastrous war with Prussia in which the Austrians were routed at Königgrätz (Sadowa). In the peace treaty that followed, Austria lost Venetia and was excluded from the new North German Confederation.

In 1867 Franz Josef faced more problems as Hungary used Austria's defeat to press again for independence. He appointed Count Julius Andrássy as minister-president of the independent Hungarian government, and on 8 June Franz Josef was crowned king of Hungary. The creation of the Dual Monarchy, in which the Austrian and Hungarian halves coexisted in equal partnership, gave the Hungarians considerable power and influence in the empire.

After the Prussian victory over France in 1871, Austria began a close relationship with the new Germany, which was sealed by the Dual Alliance in 1879. That relationship remained the centerpiece of both German and Austrian diplomacy through World War I.

After having lost Austrian possessions in Italy and Germany, having angered his giant neighbor Russia with the illegal annexation of Bosnia-Herzegovina in 1908, and with internal pressures mounting, Franz Josef in 1914 committed his empire to a war that would destroy it. Hungary's prejudicial policies toward its Slavic brethren in the eastern half of the empire had created anger and resentment among the Slavs, which neighboring Serbia sought to exploit. After Bosnian terrorists assassinated Franz Joseph's nephew and heir to the throne, Archduke Franz Ferdinand, in Sarajevo on 28 June 1914, imperial leaders such as Chief of the General Staff Franz Conrad von Hötzendorf and Foreign Minister Leopold von Berchtold pressed for action against Serbia, which they believed to have been behind the murder plot. Upon urging from his ministers and with German backing, the aging Franz Josef issued an intransigent ultimatum to Serbia on 23 July. Although Serbia complied with most of the demands, Austria-Hungary declared war on 28 July 1914. Serbia's ally, Russia, responded, and soon all of Europe was at war. Franz Josef had failed to foresee or grasp the possible European reaction, particularly on the part of Russia. During the war his age and failing health left him mainly a figurehead, while his ministers carried out the day-to-day affairs of state.

In his family life, Franz Josef fared little better. He was dominated by his mother, Sophia, and spoke rarely to his father. In 1854 Franz Josef married the beautiful Elizabeth, his first cousin. They had four children, the first of whom (Sophie) died in childhood. The empress, whom he had fallen for at first sight, differed greatly from the austere, regal Franz Josef, and in 1860, seeking to escape her rigid husband and overbearing mother-in-law, she began a series of foreign excursions that kept her away from the emperor for most of the rest of her life. She was immensely popular in Hungary. While vacationing in Geneva in 1898 she was assassinated by Luigi Lucheni. The imperial couple's only son, Rudolf, clashed with his father on almost every idea; outgoing, charming, intelligent, liberal, and witty, Rudolf was isolated from his father. Finally, in 1889 at Mayerling, he apparently committed suicide with his mistress. Franz Josef's brother, Maximilian, was executed by firing squad in Mexico in 1867. In addition, the emperor's heir and nephew, Franz Ferdinand, married beneath his royal status; Franz Josef responded with his usual grace, denying the Countess Sophie the title of archduchess and all of its perquisites by forcing a morganatic marriage. Sophie died with her husband at Sarajevo.

In all family matters, Franz Josef sought to keep up appearances of royal dignity. He believed himself to be above not only his subjects but all other European monarchs as well; he ruled his family with an iron hand. His rigidity and punctiliousness prevented most friendships. He was a man of very narrow views who resisted change. He never rode in an elevator and only near the end of his life did he consent to ride in an automobile. An archconservative, Franz Josef sought to quell all liberalism within his empire; he also failed to understand the internal problems that had begun to destroy his empire even before his death. He had tried to pursue a policy of peace through personal contacts among sovereigns, while blind to the realities of European diplomacy. After having led his country into World War I, he died on 21 November 1916 at Schönnbrunn Palace. He was succeeded by his grandnephew Karl, the last emperor of Austria-Hungary.

Laura Matysek Wood

References

Marek, George Richard. *The Eagles Die: Franz Josef, Elizabeth, and Their Austria*. New York: Harper and Row, 1974.

Murad, Anatol. *Franz Josef I of Austria and His Empire*. New York: Twayne, 1968.

Redlich, Josef. *Emperor Francis Joseph of Austria: A Biography*. Hamden, Conn.: Archon, 1965.

Tschuppik, Karl. *Francis Joseph I: The Downfall of an Empire*. Translated by C.J.S. Sprigge. New York: Harcourt, Brace, 1930.

See also AUSTRIA-HUNGARY, HOME FRONT; KARL I, EMPEROR

French, John Denton Pinkstone, Earl of Ypres (1852–1925)

British field marshal and first commander of the British Expeditionary Force (BEF). Born on 28 September 1852, the son of a Royal Navy officer, French was educated at Eastman Naval Academy and posted to naval service as a midshipman in 1866. Preferring a career in the army, however, he joined the militia in 1870 and then transferred to the regular army. French saw periods of colonial service in Egypt and India and established his military reputation by his performance as a cavalryman in the Boer War. After the war, French was selected for command at Aldershot and went on to serve as inspector general of the army. In 1912 he was named chief of the Imperial General Staff and promoted the next year to the rank of field marshal. Although he resigned in April of 1914 in the aftermath of the Curragh Mutiny of March 1914, the outbreak of war in August made him the logical choice to command the BEF, because he had prepared the British forces for service in France.

French's performance proved disappointing. His mercurial temperament, quick mood swings, and lack of understanding of modern war made him a far from ideal military leader. French's actions in the earliest engagements of the war called into question his judgment and resolution. Only the actions of General Sir Horace Smith-Dorrien saved the British army from defeat at the battle of Mons and in the 200-mile retreat that followed. As the decisive moment drew near in the first great campaign of the war, French urged that the BEF withdraw from the line in order to refit. It required the personal intervention of Secretary of War Sir Horatio Herbert Kitchener to stop French from pulling out of the line on the eve of the critical battle of the Marne.

After the Marne the BEF was shifted to Flanders to shorten the line of communications to Britain. French, confident that he could breach the German lines, launched attacks in March and May of 1915 on Neuve Chapelle and Auber Ridge; the attacks proved costly failures. French quickly moved to place the blame on the shortage of shells and on Kitchener at the war office. He found an ally in the Northcliffe press, but the "Shell Scandal" failed to dislodge Kitchener and served to raise further questions about French's judgment. The field marshal's habit of blaming others for his failures and the unsuccessful battle of Loos fought in September of 1915 proved his undoing.

French and General Sir Douglas Haig disagreed over the conduct of the battle. The dispute centered on the use of the general reserve. In a desperate attempt to save his career, French changed military orders to make it appear that he had made the reserves available, which in fact he had not. Growing criticism in the press and in the House of Lords ushered in French's removal from command. King George V, increasingly concerned over French's handling of the BEF, urged that Prime Minister Herbert Asquith relieve French. Asquith gave French the option of resignation or sacking. French resigned and took the post of commander in chief of the Home Forces (1916–18). That was followed by appointment as Lord-Lieutenant of Ireland (1918–21). French was made an earl in 1921 and died of cancer at Deal Castle on May 22, 1925.

Van Michael Leslie

References

Bourne, J.M. *Britain and the Great War 1914–1918*. London: Edward Arnold, 1989.

Cassar, George H. *The Tragedy of Sir John French*. Newark: University of Delaware Press, 1985.

Cruttwell, C.R.M.F. *A History of the Great War 1914–1918*. Oxford: Clarendon, 1940.

Wilson, Trevor. *The Myriad Faces of War: Britain and the Great War 1914–1918*. Cambridge: Polity, 1986.

Woodward, Sir Llewellyn. *Great Britain and the War of 1914–1918*. London: Methuen, 1967.

See also ARTOIS, SECOND AND THIRD BATTLES OF, 1915; FRONTIERS, BATTLE OF THE, 1914; GREAT BRITAIN, ARMY; NEUVE CHAPELLE, BATTLE OF 1915; RACE TO THE SEA, 1914; YPRES, FIRST BATTLE OF, 1914

French 75mm Field Gun

The French 75mm (2.95-inch) field gun, model 1897, was one of the most important developments in field artillery history. Known by the French as the *Canon de 75* or *soixante quinze,* it was the mainstay in both the French and American armies of the First World War and influenced the design of all twentieth-century artillery.

The 75 was designed by Captains Sainte Claire Deville and Remailo and manufactured at Pautreaux Arsenal. Its revolutionary feature was its smooth, soft, hydro-pneumatic recoil system that allowed the gun to maintain its position while firing. This meant that the gun did not have to be re-aimed and its sights reset after every round, thus enabling rapid fire with accuracy.

The recoil system consisted of two hydraulic cylinders, a floating piston, a connected piston, a head of gas, and a reservoir of oil. The recoil of the connected piston pushed the oil against the floating piston below the head of gas; this gently but increasingly broke the recoil, at the end of which the pressure of the gas returned the tube to "in-battery" position. The whole cycle took less than one second.

The length of the gun tube was 36 calibers (106 inches). The 75 used shell and shrapnel ammunition, and its normal rate of fire was twenty rounds per minute (thirty in an emergency). Range for shrapnel of 11.66 pounds was 6,800 meters (7,440 yards), or 8,500 meters (9,350 yards) for a shell of 15.84 pounds. Other valuable features of the 75 were wheel brakes, a trail spade, and a shield to protect the crew against small-arms fire. Quite light, at 1,544 kg (3,400 pounds), the 75mm gun could be transported with its ammunition by four horses or even by two.

The French army had more than 4,000 75s in service by August of 1914; by the end of the war more than 17,000 had been produced. Initially, the French failed to take advantage of the weapon's advantages. French tactical doctrine was geared to direct fire only and had no provision for artillery fire beyond 4,000 meters. On the other hand, the capabilities of the 75mm gun convinced the French army that the gun could handle all battlefield tasks, when it was not as effective as heavier pieces in trench warfare. Thus, France entered World War I with fewer than 300 medium and heavy artillery pieces, as opposed to more than 2,500 for Germany. Some 75s were employed as antiaircraft guns, coast-defense guns, and tank weapons. The French referred to it as "The Father, Son, and Holy Ghost of Warfare."

The 75 continued in service until the early 1970s in some Third World armies. It is also remembered in a lethal drink consisting of a jigger of gin or brandy in champagne.

Spencer C. Tucker

References

"The French 75, a New Gun for a New Century." Fort Sill, Okla.: U.S. Army Field Artillery Museum, 1987.

See also ARTILLERY

French Army Mutiny, 1917

In the spring and early summer of 1917 a crisis of major proportions threatened the capacity of the French army to continue the war. Low morale led to mutinous eruptions in numerous military units. Almost three years of unavailing yet costly warfare, horrible conditions for front-line troops, evidence of political corruption, the proliferation of defeatist pamphlets and pacifist newspapers, and the incompetence of military commanders had combined to cause the troops to question their role in the conflict. Most immediately, the failure of the Nivelle Offensive demoralized the soldiers to the point of rebellion.

Beginning on 16 April 1917 with the launching of the assault on the Hindenburg Line, especially on the southern extremity at the Chemin-des-Dames, there were isolated instances of dereliction and desertion. The first mutiny was registered on 29 April when the 2nd Battalion of the 18th Infantry Regiment, already decimated and exhausted after the 16 April offensive, rebelled against orders to return to the front lines. The men drank their wine rations along with additional bottles that had been hoarded and in drunken defiance refused to march, shouting "Down with the War!" By midnight, however, the alcohol had worn off, and the unit was dispatched to the front by 02:00. About a dozen men were pulled from the line, charged with mutiny, and tried. Five were sentenced to execution and the others to terms in a penal colony.

The next uprising occurred on 3 May in the 2nd Division of the Colonial Infantry, which was billeted outside Soissons. In years of fruitless attacks this unit had lost its most reliable and best officers and men, and it had incurred heavy losses during the early days of the Nivelle Offensive. When called to the front lines again, the soldiers sullenly fell in but without their weapons. Incited by pacifist pamphlets, they refused to resume the attack against the Chemin-des-Dames. Only after being persuaded by their officers of their duty to relieve their fellow soldiers in the trenches could the men be motivated to move. While they occupied the front positions, they refused to attack. Punishment was forgone because the mutineers were too numerous. Other mutinies followed.

Although the Nivelle Offensive ended on 9 May 1917, mutinies spread along the front. The fever of mutiny most severely affected the Soissons-Aubérive sector. The May mutinies followed a similar pattern: Rebelliousness generally arose in infantry regiments that had suffered severe losses during the Nivelle Offensive and had been out of the lines only a short time before being ordered back to the front. The Sixth Army was the most mutinous, followed in order by the Fourth, the Tenth, the Fifth, and the Second.

In June another round of mutinies occurred because of miserable conditions in the "rest camps," lack of leave, exaggerated but widely believed casualty figures, and loss of confidence in the military leadership. The largest of these incidents began on 2 June outside Coeuvres, where the 310th Infantry Regiment had been in a rest camp. The troops had become rebellious a few days earlier when another defiant regiment had passed through the town. The 310th refused to return to the front, marched down the main road for a short distance, established a camp, and remained there for four days until food supplies were exhausted. They then surrendered to the cavalry. After a short period at the front, the unit was withdrawn and a court of inquiry convened. Sixteen soldiers received death sentences; lesser sentences were imposed on a number of others.

The publication of left-wing internationalist sentiments and the dissentient influence of two Russian brigades contributed to rebelliousness that continued throughout June. Left-wing sentiment helped inspire the mutiny of the 298th Infantry Regiment, which captured the

F

town of Missy-aux-Bois and held it three days before surrendering to the 1st Cavalry Division. Six mutineers were executed.

The failure of the Nivelle Offensive and the disorder within the army caused Nivelle's dismissal on 15 May 1917. General Henri-Philippe Pétain replaced him. Pétain's "directives" gradually brought the situation under control. He personally visited disaffected units and talked to the men, assuring them that he would not spend their lives needlessly on costly offensives. He told them that he was "waiting for the Americans and the tanks." Pétain ordered limited offenses with maximum artillery by loyal units, and he rotated unaffected units into position. Pétain also worked to improve the men's conditions, including mail and medical services. He gave precise orders for establishing leaves, and he created *conseils de guerre* to render justice speedily. Additionally, officers received considerable latitude in dealing with recalcitrants. Most important, Pétain and the French were able to conceal the mutinies from the Germans until it was too late for them to capitalize on the situation. The British heeded Pétain's calls for a diversion by launching the ill-fated Passchendaele Campaign.

In the initial stages of the crisis, from 29 April to 10 June, ninety cases of serious mutinies were reported—an average of more than two per day; from 11 June to 1 July, the number dropped to twenty—an average of less than one per day; for the month of July the average dropped to one every four days. Overall, "indiscretions" arose in fifty-four divisions—half the French army. Officially, the crisis ended by 14 July 1917. Twenty-three mutineers were executed. Mutinies continued to occur, however; although few in number (and the true punishment figure was much higher), for decades thereafter the French Army Mutiny was shrouded in secrecy and the details deliberately obscured.

Edward L. Byrd, Jr.
Ingrid P. Westmoreland

References
Pedroncini, Guy. *Les Mutineries de 1917.* Paris: Presses Universitaires de France, 1967.
Watt, Richard M. *Dare Call It Treason.* New York: Simon and Schuster, 1963.

See also FRANCE, ARMY; NIVELLE OFFENSIVE, 1917; PÉTAIN, HENRI-PHILIPPE

French War Plan XVII
The seventeenth revision of France's plan for war since the end of the Franco-Prussian War, Plan XVII became notorious as a costly failure. The faith of its framers in an all-out offensive resulted in the massacre of French infantry in the war's opening campaign, but Plan XVII was actually a plan for mobilization and concentration and left the French commander maximum flexibility to determine the best axis of attack.

Plan XVII was born out of the political and ideological controversies that perpetually swirled around the French High Command. Previous French war plans, most notably Plan XVI, had attempted to concentrate the French army so that it could fight an initially defensive battle, changing to a counteroffensive once the direction and weight of the German attack were gauged.

Yet inside the French army there was important opposition to that strategy. A new "offensive school," *offensive à outrance,* increasingly dominated French tactical thought. French military theorists such as General Ferdinand Foch and Lieutenant Colonel Louis Loyzeau de Grandmaison reasoned that only offensive operations won wars, and that moral not material factors were the most important determinant of victory in battle.

This school of thought has been rightly derided for failing to appreciate the important material changes in warfare, most notably the tremendous increases in firepower. For all its faults, however, the "offensive school" at least married the French army to a doctrine that placed scant reliance on heavy artillery and fire preparation, sophisticated tactics, and intense training—all effectively denied to the army by a suspicious and penurious government. Thus it can be argued that in opting for an all-out offensive doctrine the army made a reasonable choice, given the political constraints of the period and the almost universal belief that the coming war would be short.

In 1911 General Joseph Césaire Joffre became French chief of staff. Historians debate how committed he was to the new offensive doctrine. He was, however, dissatisfied with Plan XVI, since it did not adequately provide for an anticipated German thrust through Belgium. It must be emphasized, however, that the French completely underestimated the size and strength of the German advance through that neutral country. Joffre believed that the plan contemplated by his predecessor, General Victor Michel, was completely defensive and too passive. As early as 1912, Joffre and his subordinates began revising Plan XVI.

Joffre himself seems to have preferred an offensive into Belgium to meet the advancing Germans, but Britain made it clear that she regarded Belgium as inviolable. In 1913 Plan XVII was unveiled. Unable to attack through Belgium, Joffre proposed to meet (what French intelligence expected to be) the bulk of the German forces head on, with an offensive in the general direction of the Franco-German frontier. The new war plan married French doctrine and strategy: Joffre's stated intention was that "whatever the circumstances, it is the commander in chief's intentions to advance with all forces united to attack the German armies." The exact axis of attack was left up to the commander's discretion.

Plan XVII deployed French forces in five armies: First Army with headquarters at Epinal, 256,000 troops; Second Army, HQ at Neufchâteau, 200,000; Third Army, HQ at Verdun, 168,000; Fourth Army, HQ at St. Dizier, 193,000; Fifth Army, HQ at Rethel, 254,000 men. In addition, the plan assigned left and right flank guards of three divisions, as well as a cavalry corps of three mounted divisions. This deployment brought no additional protection to the French left flank to guard against a German thrust through Belgium. It did create in Fourth Army, however, a formation concentrated behind the other four French armies that could serve as a strategic reserve.

The French executed Plan XVII in August of 1914 and very nearly lost the war as a result. French intelligence had persistently failed in evaluating German intentions; thus Joffre committed his forces to the attack (20–23 August) even as the massive German right wing marched against his virtually denuded left, protected by his flank guard (three divisions) and the British Expeditionary Force. The so-called "red-trouser" battles that Joffre's plan produced—the French infantry in their greatcoats and red pants moving with assumedly irresistible ardor to the attack—ended in complete defeat: At least forty thousand French soldiers were killed in abortive attacks against German positions in Lorraine and in the Ardennes. Only the French lateral railway lines and Joffre's supreme *sang froid* saved France from utter defeat.

Plan XVII has come to symbolize the myopia and ignorance of European militaries in the years before 1914. Modern commentators, while not diminishing the consequences of this deployment plan and French offensive doctrine, have stressed the importance of seeing Plan XVII in the context of the politics of the Third Republic and its army, as well as the prevailing pan-European views of war and society.

Gary P. Cox

References

House, Jonathan M. "The Decisive Attack: A New Look at French Infantry Tactics on the Eve of World War I." *Military Affairs* 40 (December 1976): 164–68.

Porch, Douglas. *The March to the Marne: The French Army 1871–1914.* Cambridge: Cambridge University Press, 1981.

———. "The Marne and After: A Reappraisal of French Strategy in the First World War." *Journal of Military History* 53 (October 1989): 363–85.

Williamson, Samuel R., Jr. *The Politics of Grand Strategy: Britain and France Prepare for War, 1904–1914.* Cambridge: Harvard University Press, 1969.

See also FOCH, FERDINAND; FRONTIERS, BATTLE OF THE, 1914; GRANDMAISON, LOUIS; JOFFRE, JOSEPH; MICHEL, VICTOR

Friedensturm: Peace Offensive, 15–16 July 1918

The last of the German offensives in 1918 was christened Friedensturm, or peace offensive, by the attack's planner, General Erich Ludendorff. Its dismal failure, coupled with the high expectations of the troops, proved extremely damaging for German morale. The Allies called the attack and the Allied counterattack the Second Battle of the Marne. Ludendorff directed the attack toward either side of Reims in the south and to Lys in the north. Ludendorff committed two major mistakes, by launching the offensive almost a month after the previous offensive had ended on 11 June and by failing to take enough precautions to keep his objectives secret. As a result, the Allies had time to prepare an expertly constructed defense in depth.

When Friedensturm began on 15 July with the usual bombardment of high explosives and gas shells, the French, who knew of the attack ahead of time, launched a bombardment on the forward German trenches ten minutes before the German attack was set to go forward. This killed many of the attacking

F

troops before they left their trenches. When German storm troops attacked, beginning at 01:10, most of the enemy lines were empty except for scattered machine-gun positions. Once they reached the limit of their own barrage, the Germans found the enemy's main line of resistance untouched and heavily manned. In the ensuing battle assault troops had no chance of breaking through the undamaged Allied defenses.

Although Ludendorff canceled the offensive after two days, the Allies counterattacked against the base of the salient created by the German attack and sent the Germans reeling in retreat. The Allied counterattack ended any further German efforts at offensive operations. After the failure of Friedensturm, the German army was increasingly on the defensive, and the troops lost their belief in a successful conclusion to the war.

Steven D. Fisher

References;
Pitt, Barrie. *1918 the Last Act*. London: Cassell, 1962.

See also ALLIED COUNTEROFFENSIVE, 1918; LUDENDORFF, ERICH; LUDENDORFF OFFENSIVES

Friedrich, Archduke (1856–1936)

Commander in chief of the Austro-Hungarian armed forces from 1914 to 1916. A member of the Hapsburg royal family and cousin of the last Austro-Hungarian emperor, Friedrich was born at Gross-Seelowitz, Moravia, on 4 June 1856. He emerged from semiretirement to serve as titular head of the Imperial Armed Forces during the first two years of the war. Often characterized as elderly and ineffectual, he was no older than many who served under him, while his assessment of Austria's prospects was grimly realistic.

Nominal chief of the Army High Command (*Armee Oberkommando*) and commander of Austro-Hungarian forces on the Eastern Front, Friedrich actually served as a mere figurehead in both roles for his chief of staff, General Franz Conrad von Hötzendorf. Nevertheless, he maintained his position as a trusted advisor of the failing Emperor Franz Josef, who rewarded him with promotion to field marshal in the summer of 1915.

Tough minded and reactionary, Friedrich feared that war would destroy the regime he had served all his life. He consistently advised against dissipation of the empire's limited re-

sources. He believed that the entry of Italy and Romania doomed the Austro-Hungarian war effort to failure. After ascending to the throne, Emperor Karl found Friedrich's gloomy outlook disquieting and removed him as commander in chief in December of 1916. He was kept on briefly as the emperor's assistant before being forced into retirement in February of 1917. After the war Friedrich settled in Hungary, where his son had some pretensions to the throne. He died on 30 December 1936 at his estate in Magyarovar.

Steven Eden

References
Rothenberg, Gunther. *The Army of Francis Joseph*. West Lafayette, Ind.: Purdue University Press, 1976.
Stone, Norman. *The Eastern Front, 1914–1917*. New York: Charles Scribner's Sons, 1975.
Villari, Luigi. *The War on the Italian Front*. London: Cobden-Sanderson, 1932.
Young, Peter. *History of the First World War*. 8 vols. London: BPC Publishing, 1971.

Frontiers, Battle of the (August 1914)

As the respective campaigns of the adversaries developed along the Franco-German and Franco-Belgian borders, the resulting haphazard series of engagements, known collectively as the Battle of the Frontiers, established the two sides' fronts for the duration of the war.

The Schlieffen Plan, as modified by chief of the German General Staff General Helmuth von Moltke, had prescribed envelopment of the entire French strength by way of Belgium. After just over two weeks, the powerful German right wing had approached the French borders, as ancillary blocking forces farther south had braced to check the anticipated French drive to regain the borderlands lost to Germany in 1870.

The French at once activated their Plan XVII. That consisted of a rapid thrust into Lorraine toward the Saar River by First and Second armies. On the left, Third and Fifth armies faced Metz and the Ardennes, respectively, poised to launch either an offensive between Metz and Thionville or to strike at the flank of a possible German drive through the Ardennes or Belgium. The Schlieffen Plan had proposed merely an active defense on the German left to limit these principal French axes of advance.

The Battle of the Frontiers actually encompasses four separate engagements. Proceeding from right to left in a generally northwesterly direction, they were: 1) the Lorraine offensives, 2) the Ardennes battles, 3) the Battle of Charleroi (or the Sambre), and 4) the British clashes at Mons and Le Cateau.

Lorraine

As noted, the Schlieffen Plan had anticipated the French thrust into Lorraine. A planned, phased German retrograde movement would absorb the anticipated French assault sufficiently to keep the committed forces from reinforcing units protecting the northern flank. That quarter was where the main effort, the vital enveloping German right wing, would ultimately threaten the French from the rear.

A French army corps prematurely thrust into Alsace on 7 August 1914, while the Plan XVII mobilization and deployment process were still underway. It captured Mulhouse by the 8th. This was an impetuous, politically motivated move risked in order to reassure the French-speaking people of Alsace that their countrymen would liberate them. The makeshift assault was rolled back to its starting line on 9 August by the German Sixth and Seventh armies, nominally led by Crown Prince Rupprecht of Bavaria but in fact directed by his chief of staff, General Konrad Krafft von Dellmensingen.

Based on his assessment of communications problems at Mulhouse, French army commander General Joseph Joffre reorganized the command in that sector to form three corps into the Army of Alsace. He instructed that army to cover the right flank of the advancing French First Army as part of a combined northeastward drive by First Army (led by General Edouard de Castelnau) and Second Army (led by General Auguste Dubail), starting just below Metz and moving toward Strasbourg.

The French jumped off on 14 August. The Germans conducted a methodical fighting withdrawal and mounted a series of punishing blows, in accordance with the Schlieffen Plan, as they fell back to the general line of Morhange-Sarrebourg-Vosges Mountains. On 20 August, from prepared positions near the lakes of Diuze and in the thickly wooded hills of Morhanges, the German Sixth and Seventh armies re-formed and counterattacked along converging axes to drive the French back into the fortified heights of Nancy, where they barely contained the German assault. The French Second Army had managed a rather orderly withdrawal, but First Army was prevented from disintegration only by the determined stand of the French XX Corps (known thereafter as the Iron Corps) under General Ferdinand Foch.

Moltke was overly optimistic about the further prospects for the Sixth and Seventh armies. On that basis he modified the Schlieffen Plan's right hook to accommodate a double envelopment. That was to be done by exploiting the supposed forward momentum of the left anchor, formerly allocated a mere containment role.

Originally, the German forces in Alsace were to have been detached to reinforce the all-important right wing once the French drive had been blunted. Instead, those two armies were tied down for two weeks in an increasingly futile push against the solid French defensive belt running from Metz south to Luneville.

Ardennes

On 21 August the French Third Army (under General Pierre Ruffey) and Fourth Army (under General Ferdinand de Langle de Cary) were ordered to thrust abruptly into Luxembourg, which contained the high wooded hills of the Ardennes forest and where intersecting valleys afforded cover. Joffre hoped to catch the supposedly inactive German defenders unawares; he expected to get his forces through this rough country and into the open before contact with the Germans. That was the decisive element of Plan XVII, designed to smash the German center and thereby outflank the turning movement through Belgium. Originally, Fifth Army under General Charles Lanrezac was to have joined the offensive, but after French intelligence convinced Joffre that the Germans were mounting a strong attack through Belgium, as Lanrezac had been insisting all along, his army was detached to meet the threat on the north.

As it happened, the forward elements of the German Fourth and Fifth armies were already on the move as the hinge of Moltke's decisive right wing and were thus quite well situated to strike at the French. The French initiative had been launched with inadequate reconnaissance into low-lying fog, each corps blindly negotiating its assigned slice of ground until stumbling upon the advancing Germans in an encounter battle.

A combination of rugged terrain, deficient intelligence, and poor spotter-gunner coordination dissipated the firepower advantage of the French rapid-firing but flat-trajectory 75mm field artillery. German high-angle artillery and their agile tactical handling of machine guns were the determining factors. The unsuspecting French columns, without proper artillery support, were mauled by well-concealed German automatic fire and methodical howitzer and mortar barrages.

After two days of fierce resistance, both French armies pulled back, the Third to anchor its right flank on Verdun, just about where it had started, and the Fourth to Stenay and Sedan on the west side of the Meuse. Crown Prince Friedrich Wilhelm's German Fifth Army left a contingent of siege troops to take the fortress at Longwy as it pressed on into France.

By 28 August, Fourth Army had checked the German Fourth on the Meuse, but the two-day battle opened a gap between it and the French Fifth Army, now fifty miles to the west. Joffre filled the breach with a three-corps group under Foch. The latter formed the new Ninth Army two weeks later.

The German General Staff was convinced that it had won a great victory, having smashed a major component of the French front. But even though they had taken heavy losses, Third and Fourth armies had not been eliminated and were still capable of mounting offensive operations. Joffre was in fact doing some much-needed reorganization and weeding out of timid commanders, all while preparing to spring a trap on the vaguely comprehended German advance.

The Sambre (Charleroi)

The French Fifth Army, under Lanrezac, was ordered to move up into the angle of the Meuse and Sambre rivers on 15 August in order to check German forces of unknown size that had just taken Dinant (Belgium) on the Meuse. Joffre still was uncertain about any German flank threat to his contemplated Ardennes operation. This difference of perception created a communications breakdown between French GHQ and Lanrezac, compounding the latter's tactical indecision. Unknown to Joffre or Lanrezac, the Fifth French Army was blocking the primary line of advance of the German Second Army (under General Karl von Bülow) and Third Army (under General Max von Hausen), while the British Expeditionary Force on the seaboard flank was in the path of the First German Army. Joffre still believed he could salvage at least part of the Plan XVII offensives; thus, he waited until 21 August

to order Lanrezac to push his Fifth Army directly to the north. By that time, the Battle of the Sambre was already underway.

At noon on 20 August, after a grueling five-day, ninety-mile march in August heat, advanced units of the Fifth Army reached the Sambre River. Lanrezac now contemplated his options: crossing the Sambre and occupying the southern heights of the river, or taking up position on the high ground some distance south. During a two-day period no orders were issued and no positions prepared. Finally, late in the afternoon of the 21st, Lanrezac ordered the army to occupy the heights south of the Sambre. To his credit, Lanrezac was among the first to discern the true bearing and implications of the main German advance to his north.

By the time Joffre had concurred, advance guards of the Second German Army had reached the Sambre River line. The German Third Army pushed up the Meuse after taking Dinant, threatening Lanrezac's right flank. At the same time, General Bülow, after detaching troops from his Second Army to besiege Namur, forced two crossings of the Sambre between Namur and Charleroi, about twenty-one miles to the southwest. The Germans won the resulting fight for the bridges. Bülow had originally expected to push over the Sambre upon arrival at the river; his orders, however, called for a combined attack of the Second and Third armies. Inasmuch as Hausen's command could not reach the Meuse until late on the 21st, Bülow decided not to cross the Sambre until he was assured that the German Third Army would be in position.

Bülow's directive for the 22nd prescribed a consolidation of the position south of the Sambre, but he delayed his advance until he could ascertain the intentions of the French Fifth Army, regrouping to his front. On the morning of the 22nd the French counterattacked but met failure. The next morning Bülow launched a general attack and requested that Hausen attack across the Meuse in a westerly direction. Hausen had already issued orders for an advance southwest on Givet in order to arrive behind the Fifth French Army and obliterate it. He conformed his movements to Bülow's instructions, thereby forfeiting his original prospect of blocking the retreat of the Fifth French Army.

Bülow encountered little resistance as Lanrezac withdrew. Had Bülow allowed the German Third Army to continue its original movement and get behind Lanrezac, the French Fifth Army might have been destroyed or captured, achieving the decisive results contemplated by the Schlieffen Plan. Instead, the Fifth Army continued its withdrawal and, along with the other largely intact French forces, was available for reorganization and redeployment.

Mons—Le Cateau

The French High Command did not at first comprehend the scope of the German incursion in Belgium. Before the war it assumed that the small British Expeditionary Force would serve as an adjunct to the French armies. The BEF was thus expected to be employed as Joffre required to help deal with any threat to Flanders from the north, although that was considered unlikely.

On 20 August as Lanrezac's Fifth French Army was taking up positions on the Sambre, General Sir John French's BEF, embracing four infantry divisions and one cavalry division, had nearly completed their concentration in the Le Cateau area. Moltke's headquarters mistakenly informed Bülow, who commanded the key right-wing army group comprising General Alexander von Kluck's First Army and his own Second, that British troops had not yet appeared in France in meaningful numbers but would eventually assemble in the vicinity of Lille.

So as to ensure that his Second Army would have adequate flank support in the imminent showdown with Lanrezac's forces, Bülow ordered Kluck to pivot his line of advance from southwest to south, thereby driving directly into the front of the undetected BEF rather than advantageously circuiting its left flank, as would have otherwise been the case. London had instructed French that, although he was not attached to Joffre's armies, he was expected to conform his strategy to the latter's plans and dispositions. After consulting with Joffre's headquarters, the 70,000 or more men of the BEF took up position at Mons, thirty-five miles west of Charleroi, preparatory to advancing to seek out any German forces nearby. The two-mile gap between the BEF's right and Lanrezac's left flank was defended by a British cavalry brigade and the weary French Cavalry Corps. During the night of 22 August, the hard-pressed Lanrezac requested French to rotate his forces to the right to hit the German Second Army in the flank; British air reconnaissance had discovered heavy columns of German troops approaching

Mons, however, and French declined to detach any of his units.

On the night of the 22nd the German cavalry screen skirmished with British cavalry at Castreau, north of Mons. The next morning news arrived of Lanrezac's defeat and withdrawal from Charleroi. The British II Corps under General Sir Horace Smith-Dorrien hastily entrenched just behind the Mons Canal from Condé to Mons, while General Douglas Haig's I Corps hooked around to face southeast in order to protect the now-uncovered French flank.

In broken terrain some thirty thousand men of Britain's regular army faced over ninety thousand Germans. The Germans attacked in textbook fashion, advancing doggedly and repeatedly in massed formation in the face of startlingly accurate British rifle fire. The British reloaded and fired their rifles so quickly that the Germans mistook it for machine-gun fire. The sheer weight of the German attacks, supported by devastating artillery fire, however, forced the British to fall back to the southwest, although they did so skillfully and inflicted additional heavy casualties on their pursuers. Neither a British victory nor a defeat, Mons was a fruitful delaying action. For a price of 1,650 casualties the British had bought precious time for the French to redeploy.

Kluck erroneously assumed that the BEF was based on the Channel ports of Boulogne and Calais. He thus continued to attempt to envelop the British west flank so as to cut them off from those bases. That produced greater pressure on Smith-Dorrien's II Corps than on Haig's I Corps, which had not been as heavily engaged at Mons. Smith-Dorrien had intended to pause temporarily to reorganize his three divisions at Le Cateau with Haig on the east flank, whereupon the BEF would then withdraw and form a new defense line. The Germans, however, were in close pursuit, and II Corps was fatigued by three days of combat and marching. Deciding that his corps could not resume its march, Smith-Dorrien resolved to resist at Le Cateau on 26 August and retreat the following night. Haig, meanwhile, continued to pull his men back, uncovering II Corps' right flank and separating his forces from it by the Oise River.

Having to mask its eastern approach as well as counter the head-on German assault, II Corps dug in. Kluck, who assumed he was still stalking a fleeing enemy, virtually stumbled over Smith-Dorrien's troops. II Corps' center held well, but the right flank was driven back under heavy artillery fire. When his left flank was turned, Smith-Dorrien had to extricate his forces to avoid disaster. Fortunately, the French Cavalry Corps arrived from the southwest in time to distract the Germans and allow II Corps to make an orderly retreat. British casualties at Le Cateau ran 20 percent of effectives, some eight thousand men and thirty-six guns. As at Mons, the BEF delayed the deadly German right hook and bought essential time for the Allies to regroup at the Marne.

James J. Bloom

References

Asprey, Robert. *The Battle of the Marne.* Philadelphia: Lippincott, 1962.

Edmonds, Sir James E., comp. *Military Operations: France and Belgium, 1914,* Vol. I. London: Macmillan, 1933. (British Official History.)

Kluck, A. von. *The March on Paris and the Battle of the Marne, 1914.* London: Edward Arnold, 1920.

Spears, Edward L. *Liaison, 1914: A Narration of the Great Retreat.* Rev. ed. New York: Stein and Day, 1968.

Tyng, Sewell. *Campaign of the Marne, 1914.* New York: Longmans, Green, 1935.

See also BÜLOW, KARL VON; CASTELNAU, NOEL JOSEPH EDOUARD DE; DUBAIL, AUGUSTE; FOCH, FERDINAND; FRENCH, JOHN; FRENCH WAR PLAN XVII; HAIG, SIR DOUGLAS; JOFFRE, JOSEPH; KLUCK, ALEXANDER VON; KRAFFT VON DELLMENSINGEN, KONRAD; LANGLE DE CARY, FERNAND DE; LANREZAC, CHARLES; MOLTKE, HELMUTH VON; RUPPRECHT, CROWN PRINCE; SCHLIEFFEN PLAN; SMITH-DORRIEN, HORACE

Fuller, John Frederick Charles (1878–1966)

British army officer. Born on 1 September 1878 in Chichester, England, the son of an Anglican clergyman, Fuller was educated at Sandhurst. Commissioned in 1898, he served in the Boer War and afterward studied military history and wrote professionally. He was promoted to captain in 1911 and appointed to the Staff College at Camberley in 1913. There he studied the army's *Field Service Regulations,* found them lacking, and suggested modifications, for which he was reprimanded. In response, in 1914 Fuller published his first book, *Training Soldiers for War,* which described training based on psychological and educational principles and emphasized the military's need to accept new technological developments.

A general staff officer at the onset of World War I, Fuller soon realized the offensive capabilities of the tank to overcome trench warfare. In December of 1916 he became chief of staff for the new Heavy Branch of the Machine Gun Corps (actually the new Tank Corps). Seeing the tank as an offensive weapon, Fuller planned the November 1917 attack at Cambrai, which used them in mass for the first time. The attack proved less than a success because of mechanical breakdowns.

After 1917 Fuller continually pressed for an expansion of the Tank Corps, but with little success. His subsequent "Plan 1919" called for a coordinated attack of tanks and airplanes to win the war by attacking enemy command centers. The war ended before his plan could be put into effect, but Fuller continued to urge reform in the British army. He called for a general staff coordinated under a single commander in chief to lead a totally mechanized army that was coordinated with aircraft. His ideas were ignored in Britain.

In late 1926 Fuller was chosen to command the new Experimental Force (or Tank) brigade—the pinnacle of his military career. His condescending attitude and sharp tongue, his advocacy of reform and tanks, and his intolerance created many enemies and brought an end to his military career. In December of 1933 the British army retired him. Fuller began a new career as a journalist and historian and embraced fascism.

As an early developer of tank tactics, Fuller ranks as one of the premier military theorists, and his effect on Sir Basil Liddell Hart and others helped revolutionize warfare in the late 1930s and the Second World War. Fuller died on 10 February 1966 at Tehidy Hospital in Cornwall.

Laura Matysek Wood

References

Fuller, John Frederick Charles. "The Development of Sea Warfare on Land and Its Influence on Future Naval Operations." *RUSI Journal* 65 (May 1920): 281–98.

———. *Memoirs of an Unconventional Soldier.* London: Ivor Nicholson and Watson, 1936.

———. *Military History of the Western World.* New York: Funk and Wagnalls, 1954–56.

Trythall, Anthony John. *Boney Fuller*. New
  Brunswick, N.J.: Rutgers University
  Press, 1977.

See also CAMBRAI, BATTLE OF; LIDDELL
HART, SIR BASIL; TANKS

F

G

Galicia

See EAST GALICIA

Gallieni, Joseph Simon (1849–1916)

Marshal of France. Born on 24 April 1849 at St. Beat, Haute Garonne, Gallieni attended St. Cyr. He was commissioned in the French Naval Infantry (Marines) in 1870 and fought with distinction in the Franco-Prussian War. He later served in the French colonies, most notably Niger, Senegal, Tonkin, and Madagascar. He then returned to France and commanded XIII and XIV corps. In 1908 he joined the general staff, serving there until retiring for reasons of age in 1914.

On 28 August 1914 Gallieni became military governor of Paris and designated successor to French Commander in Chief General Joseph Joffre, if the latter were killed or otherwise incapacitated. Gallieni vowed to defend Paris and quickly spurred his commander to action. As Alan Palmer noted, "Gallieni believed it his duty to save Paris and thus France, Joffre to save France and thus Paris." By early September the French government had left Paris for Bordeaux, and 500,000 citizens had departed the city.

Although General Michel Maunoury's Sixth Army was temporarily under Gallieni's command, Paris's defenses were in poor condition. On 31 August a major change occurred when German General Alexander von Kluck decided to turn his First Army southeast of Paris while still north and east of the French capital, rather than moving west of it and then turning south and east. Gallieni knew of this through aerial reconnaissance, verified by French cavalry patrols and documents found on the body of a dead German officer. Kluck's army, advancing down the River Ourcq and the corridor between Meaux and Chateau-Thierry on the Marne, was vulnerable to a counterattack by the French Sixth Army and the Paris garrison, and Gallieni took advantage of this moment.

Gallieni pressed upon Joffre the need for an immediate counterattack, while at the same time on 3 September he ordered Sixth Army to prepare to attack. On the afternoon of 5 September units of Sixth Army clashed with those of Kluck's First Army on the Ourcq River. Although operations occurred elsewhere, this sector became the vital one. While Kluck maneuvered his forces on 7 September to counter the French threat, a gap developed between his army and General Karl von Bülow's Second Army, into which the British Expeditionary Force moved. The same day Gallieni sent desperately needed reinforcements to Sixth Army: the "taxi army" that moved from Paris in six hundred vehicles commandeered to carry six thousand troops. Although the actual effect of these troops did not match the post-event mythology, the dramatic event symbolized the linkage of Paris with the battle raging thirty miles away. By 9 September the Germans had fallen back all along the front. Paris was saved, and a stabilized front in the west ensued.

There is controversy over whether a greater victory might have been won. It focuses on Gallieni's desire to attack Kluck's flank rather than his front, as Joffre had ordered. Regardless, the Battle of the Marne wrecked the German plan and changed the course of history. If Joffre had ultimate command responsibility for what occurred, Gallieni, in the words of Basil Liddell Hart, "dictated both the site and the promptness of the thrust."

Between October of 1915 and March of 1916, Gallieni served as minister of war in the Aristide Briand government. Poor health forced his retirement from that post, and he died at Versailles on 27 May 1916. In May of 1921 he was created Marshal of France, and in 1925 a statue of him was erected at the Invalides in Paris. Between 1885 and 1905 Gallieni published five books dealing with his colonial experiences. His children later published two others, one of which concerned his role in the defense of Paris in 1914: *Les Mémoires du Maréchal Gallieni, Défense de Paris* (1926).

Donald F. Bittner

References

Le Grand Encyclopédie, Vol. 9. Paris: Librairie Larousse, 1974.
Le Grand Larousse Encyclopédique en dix volumes. Vol. 5. Paris: Librairie Larousse, 1962.
Liddell Hart, B.H. *The Real War, 1914–1918.* Boston: Little, Brown, 1930.
Palmer, Alan. "The Marne." In *Decisive Battles of the 20th Century: Land-Sea-Air,* edited by Noble Frankland and Christopher Dowling. New York: David McKay, 1976.
Porch, Douglas. *The March to the Marne: The French Army, 1871–1914.* Cambridge: Cambridge University Press, 1981.

See also MARNE, FIRST BATTLE OF

Gallipoli Campaign

The Gallipoli campaign was the 1915–16 unsuccessful Allied ground effort to help secure the Dardanelles and force Turkey from the war. The naval effort to force the Dardanelles failed, but for political reasons the campaign had to be continued. This meant the belated injection of land troops.

London had in fact already taken the decision before the naval bombardment of 18 March 1915 to send out land forces. As First Lord of the Admiralty Winston Churchill sought to exhort Vice Admiral Sackville Carden, commander of the blockading squadron off the Dardanelles, to greater action, First Sea Lord John Fisher and secretary of state for war Field Marshal the Earl Horatio Kitchener came to the conclusion that troops would have to be landed on the Gallipoli peninsula at the northern entrance to the Dardanelles. On 1 March Prime Minister Eleutherios Venizelos of Greece had offered three divisions, but the Russian government vetoed the plan; Greek success might leave them in control of the Straits and deny Russia one of her principal war aims.

On 19 February Kitchener released the crack 29th British Division, but opposition from British and French generals caused him to substitute the untrained Australian and New Zealand Corps (ANZAC) of two divisions, then in Egypt. On 10 March Kitchener decided to send the 29th and Royal Navy divisions. The French also agreed to send a division.

General Sir Ian Hamilton commanded this army of 75,000 men. He arrived at the Dardanelles in time to watch the naval bombardment of 18 March; no plans had been developed for the deployment of ground forces, however. Although Admiral John de Robeck originally believed that the navy could do the job alone, after meeting with Hamilton on 22 March on the *Queen Elizabeth* at Lemnos, he felt that it could not be accomplished without army support. Captain Roger Keyes, de Robeck's chief of staff, was outraged at this decision. Churchill agreed, but after an acrimonious meeting, the war council decided that the views of the commanders on the spot should prevail.

There was little preliminary army planning, maps were few and inaccurate, and intelligence information about the Turkish forces was virtually nonexistent. Hamilton also lost valuable time when he chose to concentrate his forces in Egypt.

Tipped off by the naval bombardment, the Turks used the interval to prepare for the Allied landings. German General Otto Liman von Sanders, head of the German military mission and now inspector general of the Turkish army, was given charge of preparations to resist the Allied invasion. Liman von Sanders had available the Fifth Army, consisting of six widely dispersed divisions. Hilly and rocky, the Gallipoli peninsula was ideal defensive terrain, and Liman von Sanders organized strong positions in the hills immediately behind likely invasion beaches. He was ably assisted by Turkish Colonel Mustapha Kemal, later the father of modern Turkey.

A vast armada of two hundred Allied ships gathered off Mudros on Lemons for the landings, which were to be supported at close range by a naval force of eighteen battleships, twelve cruisers, twenty-nine destroyers, eight submarines, and a host of small craft. On Sunday morning, 25 April 1915, Allied troops landed at five beaches around Cape Helles (the extremity of the peninsula) and on the southwest side of the peninsula to the north near Gaba Tepe, at a beach that is still called Anzac. Turkish opposition was fierce and Allied casualties heavy, but by nightfall the invasion forces were well established ashore.

At the same time, French troops landed on the Asiatic side of the Straits at Kum Kale, where they met a larger Turkish force. An advance there was impossible, and the French were lifted off and transferred to Helles on the 27th. From that point on, the naval aspect of the campaign consisted of gunfire support and resupply activities. A number of ships were hit by land fire.

Meanwhile, Allied troops on shore were in two lodgements about fifteen miles apart, controlling only small pieces of territory. The fighting was virtually trench warfare, similar to that of the Western Front; opposing lines were often only a few yards apart. The Turks were well dug in and could easily detect in advance any Allied moves to drive them from their almost impregnable positions. Their artillery was also ideally situated to shell the beaches.

Early in May the Allies sent out two additional divisions—one each from Britain and France—and a brigade from India. Some ground was gained on 6 May, but stalemate soon followed. The British then sent out five additional divisions, monitors for shore bombardment, more naval aircraft, and armored landing barges, but Turkish strength increased apace to sixteen (smaller) divisions.

A new naval attack was abandoned in mid-May after the Turks sank the British battleship *Goliath*. Only submarines could make the passage through the narrows to interfere with Turkish shipping. Of twelve boats sent (nine British and three French), seven were lost. One, *E-14*, got into the Sea of Marmara and sank a troopship with 6,000 men aboard, all of whom died. *E-11* blew up an ammunition ship. German submarines were also active. One, *U-21*, torpedoed and sank two old British battleships, the *Triumph* and *Majestic*.

The Allies decided to employ two of their new divisions at Suvla Bay to the north of Anzac, successfully landing on the night of 6–7 August. Mustapha Kemal, now a corps commander, helped contain the Allied landing to little more than a toehold. At the same time, reinforced Allied units at Anzac planned to break out and seize the high ground to the east of Suvla that dominated the landing areas. Although Liman von Sanders shifted his resources north to meet the new threat at Suvla Bay, inept Allied ground commanders wasted the opportunity to exploit conditions presented by the Turkish dispersal.

At the end of August the French offered to send out a whole army, and the British found two additional divisions for yet another invasion, planned for November. It had to be postponed, however, when Bulgaria, emboldened by the Allied failures at the Dardanelles and Gallipoli, entered the war on the Central Powers' side. This move immediately threatened Serbia and impacted on the situation at Gallipoli, as Hamilton was obliged to shift two of his divisions to Salonika in northern Greece. Bulgaria's entry into the war also provided a direct rail link for sending Central Powers' munitions to Turkey.

By the middle of September the French government concluded that there was no hope for the Gallipoli campaign. The British government persisted, unwilling to sacrifice a venture into which so much had been invested. When Hamilton was asked for his views, he replied that he was strongly opposed to evacuation. Meanwhile, a drumfire of criticism appeared in the Australian and British press, based on reports by war correspondents about the incompetence of British land commanders at Gallipoli. In October of 1915 Lieutenant General Sir Charles Monro replaced Hamilton. He pointed out that Allied positions ashore were not satisfactory, that there was little prospect for improving those positions without substantial reinforcements, and that the army ran serious risks in trying to cling to its positions in the impending winter without a major supply base.

At the end of October, Monro pressed London for evacuation. Keyes went there to press the case for a renewal of the naval assault. Kitchener, initially sympathetic to Keyes, went to Gallipoli to see for himself. A blizzard at the end of November, the worst in recent memory, resulted in Allied casualties of 10 percent on the Gallipoli peninsula. Kitchener argued for evacuation as the only justifiable course. With both the French and Russians arguing for the Salonika front, the British cabinet decided on 7 December 1915 in favor of evacuating Gallipoli, despite Monro's prediction of up to 40 percent losses. Kitchener predicted there would be no losses. Orders went out on 8 December for Monro to withdraw forces from Suvla and Anzac, while retaining the lodgement at Helles. Night after night the Allies withdrew vast stocks of supplies, and on the night of 18–19 December the troops were taken off from Suvla Bay and Anzac. Amazingly, the Turks were unaware of what was going on, although at points the opposing lines were only a few yards apart. Turkish defenders awoke to find the enemy gone.

Liman von Sanders decided to concentrate on the last redoubt, at Cape Helles. Here the Allies had four divisions totaling 35,000 men. On 17 December the British cabinet decided to evacuate them as well. The French withdrew unscathed on 1 January 1916. Because of the obvious gap in the lines, the British 29th Division moved round the coast by ship and made another landing to fill the hole. On successive nights, men and equipment were gradually withdrawn. The weather was not good, and Turkish shells caused a number of casualties on the beaches. On 7 January the Turks launched a determined attack, but the defensive fire was such that not one attacker reached the British lines. The Turks then mistakenly concluded that the final evacuation was not imminent. The difficult evacuation of the Helles Beaches was carried out on the night of 8–9 January 1916, again without loss. Bad weather prevented some ordnance and ammunition from being evacuated. Its demolition by the British informed the Turks that the evacuation at Helles was over.

The evacuation of the Gallipoli Peninsula was the largest operation of its kind prior to the extraction of the British Expeditionary Force from Dunkirk in 1940. Much to the astonishment of the Allied command, it was carried out without loss.

Accurate casualty totals for the entire 259-day campaign are not available. Turkish records are incomplete, and their official figures of 86,692 killed and 164,617 ill and wounded are undoubtedly underestimated. The Turks lost a great many men from sickness and disease. One source gives their casualties at 470,000 men, but a more reasonable figure might be 300,000. Total Allied casualties were about 265,000, of whom some 46,000 died. While these were not as large a percentage as Western Front losses, they were nonetheless substantial.

The failure at the Dardanelles meant that the Straits remained closed, Turkey continued in the war, and Russia was cut off from aid. The effect of this failure in bringing about the military collapse of Russia and the Bolshevik Revolution can only be guessed.

At the time and for years afterward, Churchill received most of the criticism for the failure. In August of 1916 the British appointed a commission to investigate the campaign; at the end of 1917 it concluded that the campaign had been a mistake. As its chief instigator, Churchill reaped most of the contemporary abuse. Although this criticism may have been excessive, Churchill did make serious errors in judgment, none of which he admitted in his own historical defense of his actions.

Although it failed, the Gallipoli landing was much studied in the years following the war. The operation utilized considerable experimentation in naval aviation and landing/resupply techniques, which proved quite influential in the development of U.S. Marine amphibious doctrine in the Second World War.

If the Allies had been prepared to commit, at the beginning of the campaign, the resources they ultimately deployed, they would have been successful. The campaign failed because of faulty planning, poor leadership, and indecision.

Spencer C. Tucker

References

Churchill, Winston S. *The World Crisis*. Vol. 2. New York: Charles Scribner's Sons, 1923.

Great Britain, Dardanelles Commission. *The Final Report of the Dardanelles Commission*. London: HMSO, 1919.

Hamilton, General Sir Ian. *Gallipoli Diary*. New York: George H. Doran, 1920.

James, Robert Rhodes. *Gallipoli, The History of a Noble Blunder*. New York: Macmillan, 1965.

Moorehead, Alan. *Gallipoli*. New York: Harper and Row, 1956.

See also ANZAC; CARDEN, SACKVILLE; CHURCHILL, WINSTON; DARDANELLES CAMPAIGN; DE ROBECK, SIR JOHN; FISHER, JOHN; HAMILTON, IAN; KEMAL, MUSTAFA; KEYES, ROGER; KITCHENER, HORATIO; LIMAN VON SANDERS, OTTO; MONRO, SIR CHARLES

Gallwitz, Max von (1852–1937)

German general and army group commander. Although he was of lower middle-class origin and a devout Roman Catholic, Gallwitz became a major figure in Imperial Germany. Born at Breslau on 2 May 1852, Gallwitz joined the Prussian army during the Franco-German War and was commissioned in the field artillery two years later. After attending the Kriegsakademie, he held positions both in the general staff and the Prussian War Ministry, commanded a division (at Cologne), and in 1911 became inspector of field artillery.

Raised to noble status in 1913, Gallwitz took command of the Guards Reserve Corps at the outbreak of hostilities. After participating in the invasion of Belgium, the corps was sent to East Prussia in late August to help throw the Russians out of that province. In November of 1914 the Garde-Reservekorps was split up, and Gallwitz assumed command of a mixed German/Austro-Hungarian corps in Poland. Three months later he was entrusted with the defense of East and West Prussia as head of Army Detachment Gallwitz. Growing steadily in size, that force eventually, in August of 1915, was renamed the Twelfth Army.

Seven weeks later, Gallwitz participated in the conquest of Serbia as commander of the Eleventh Army. In March of 1916 he was given a major role in the Battle of Verdun as commander of Meuse Group West. When the Battle of the Somme intensified, however, he was dispatched to that region to take charge of the Second Army and temporarily to supervise the operations of the First Army as well. Toward the end of 1916 Gallwitz was sent back to the Verdun sector as commander of the Fifth Army. Later, his authority was broadened by placing both his own army and the adjacent Army Detachment C under his headquarters, thus elevating him to the position of army group commander. In 1918 Gallwitz's divisions generally gave a good account of themselves in the defensive battles in the Meuse-Moselle region.

According to reliable sources, Gallwitz was repeatedly guided by his religious convictions into opposing harsh measures ordered by his superiors. He was also considered by many to be a suitable candidate for the German chancellorship. After his retirement from the army he entered politics and from 1920 to 1924 held a seat in the Reichstag. He died at Naples, Italy, on 18 April 1937. His only son, Werner, became a general in Hitler's army and was killed near Sevastopol in 1944.

Ulrich Trumpener

References

Gallwitz, Max von. *Erleben im Westen, 1916–1918.* Berlin: E.S. Mittler und Sohn, 1932.

———. *Meine Fuhrertätigkeit im Weltkriege, 1914/1916: Belgien, Osten, Balkan.* Berlin: E.S. Mittler und Sohn, 1929.

Möller, Hanns. "Max von Gallwitz." *Neue Deutsche Biographie.* Vol. 6. Berlin: Duncker & Humbolt, 1964.

Reichsarchiv. *Der Weltkrieg 1914 bis 1918: Militärische Operationen zu Lande.* 14 vols. Berlin: E.S. Mittler und Sohn, 1925–44.

Trumpener, Ulrich. "*Junkers* and Others: The Rise of Commoners in the Prussian Army, 1871–1914." *Canadian Journal of History* 14 (1979).

See also ALLIED COUNTEROFFENSIVE; EAST GALICIA, 1914 CAMPAIGN; SOMME, BATTLE OF; VERDUN, BATTLE OF

Gauchet, Dominique Marie (1857–1931)

French vice-admiral and commander in chief of the fleet in the Mediterranean from 1916 to 1919. Born in Vains, Manche, on 14 August 1857, Gauchet entered the Ecole Navale in 1874 and at the beginning of the war was commander of the navy's department of administration and supply. In October of 1915 Gauchet was given command of the French squadron at the Dardanelles and became closely involved with the French landing at Salonika and the frustrations and complexities of dealing with the Greeks at the beginning of the Macedonian expedition.

Appointed commander of the Second Squadron of the French Mediterranean Fleet in March of 1916, Gauchet earned such a reputation for vociferously upholding French rights at Salonika that there was some trepidation among the Allies when he succeeded Admiral Louis Dartige du Fournet as commander in chief of the French fleet in the Mediterranean (1ère Armée navale) in December of 1916. Once in office, with his status clearly recognized, Gauchet proved more mellow and became increasingly preoccupied with maintaining French battle squadrons at Corfu in a state of readiness to meet any sortie on the part of the Austrian fleet. This was a contingency that never arose, although the inability of the French and Italians to agree on who would command a combined fleet made the great Allied superiority on paper far less effective than it might have been.

The dispute need not have threatened the balance at sea, but in 1918 Gauchet faced the threat that the Germans might seize control of the Russian Black Sea fleet, and he was forced to send substantial reinforcements to the Aegean. In 1917–18 the British increasingly assumed control of the antisubmarine campaign in the Mediterranean, while Gauchet, although theoretically Allied commander in chief, seemed preoccupied with preparing for a classical naval battle that would never occur. He remained commander in chief in the Mediterranean until the Armistice. Gauchet retired from active duty in May of 1919. He died at Vains on 4 February 1931.

Paul G. Halpern

References

Docteur, Admiral. *Carnet de bord, 1914– 1919*. Paris: La Nouvelle Société d'Edition, 1932.

Halpern, Paul G. *The Naval War in the Mediterranean, 1914–1918*. London and Annapolis, Md.: Allen & Unwin and Naval Institute Press, 1987.

Laurens, Adolphe. *Le Commandement naval en Méditerranée, 1914–1918*. Paris: Payot, 1931.

Taillemite, Etienne. *Dictionnaire des Marins Français*. Paris: Editions Maritimes et d'Outre-Mer, 1982.

Thomazi, A. *La Guerre navale dans la Méditerranée*. Paris: Payot, 1929.

See also FRANCE, NAVY; MEDITERRANEAN NAVAL OPERATIONS; SALONIKA CAMPAIGN

Geddes, Sir Eric Campbell (1875–1937)

British businessman and administrator. Born on 26 September 1875 in India and educated in Scotland and at the Oxford Military College, Geddes spent his early life working in the United States and India. While in India he gained invaluable experience in railway management. On his return to Britain in 1906 Geddes went to work for the North Eastern Railway, and by 1914 he had become general manager. The outbreak of war saw him involved in the mobilization of railway employees for military service.

In 1915 Geddes was named deputy director-general of munitions supply. His work caught the attention of David Lloyd George,

and he was subsequently put in charge of transportation for the British Expeditionary Force in France. Geddes went on to hold the post of inspector-general of transportation for all British theaters of operations, receiving the honorary rank of major general. In May of 1917 he was transferred to the admiralty as controller with the honorary rank of vice admiral in charge of marshaling British shipbuilding resources. Within a few months, however, Geddes was appointed first lord of the admiralty and elected to the House of Commons. While at the admiralty, Geddes pushed for an administrative reorganization.

Geddes made an important contribution to the British war effort. His administrative talent and energy greatly facilitated the efficient operation of Britain's wartime transportation network, especially in France. He retired from politics after the fall of Lloyd George's coalition in 1922 and went on to become chairman of Dunlop Rubber and Imperial Airways. Geddes died on 22 June 1937.

Van Michael Leslie

References

Bourne, J.M. *Britain and the Great War 1914–1918*. London: Edward Arnold, 1989.

Grieves, Keith. *Sir Eric Geddes: Business and Government in War and Peace*. New York: St. Martin's, 1990.

Woodward, Sir Llewellyn. *Great Britain and the War of 1914–1918*. London: Methuen, 1967.

George V (1865–1936)

British king and emperor, born on 3 June 1865 in London, George Frederick Ernest Albert ruled as King George V of Great Britain and emperor of India from 1910 to 1936. As the second son of King Edward VII, George had been groomed for a military career before he became heir to the throne in 1892 upon the death of his elder brother, Prince Albert Victor. In the same year he became Duke of York and subsequently, in 1901, upon his father's accession to the throne, the Duke of Cornwall and Prince of Wales. He married his elder brother's fiancee, Princess Mary of Teck, in 1893. George ascended to the throne on 8 May 1910 and was crowned on 22 June 1911.

Sensible, straightforward, conscientious, and orderly, George differed greatly from his continental, romantic father, Edward VII. George and his family came to represent what was uniquely British. During World War I, in response to domestic criticism, he changed the family name from the German Saxe-Coburg-Gotha to the singularly British Windsor (for the beloved Windsor Castle). George V and Queen Mary buoyed the spirits of Englishmen by visiting military bases, reviewing troops, conferring decorations, visiting hospitals, and touring factories. Few previous British monarchs had so closely interacted with their subjects. George went to France five times to survey the battlefields, and on one such visit the king suffered a broken pelvis when his horse reared and threw him. Two royal sons served in the military during the war: the Prince of Wales in the army, and Prince Albert in the navy. Throughout the war the royal family remained a bastion of British courage and steadfastness, and the British crown was one of the few in Europe to survive the war in a strong position.

Later in his reign, George handled well the first Labour government and the creation of the British Commonwealth. His four surviving sons (one died as a child) served as able representatives of the crown on many trips. Unfortunately, the Prince of Wales developed an affection for the American divorcee Wallis Warfield Simpson and, as King Edward VIII, would abdicate the throne, thus allowing George V's second son, Albert, to become king as George VI. George V died on 20 January 1936 at Sandringham.

Laura Matysek Wood

References

Arthur, George Compton Archibald, Sir. *George V.* New York: J. Cape and H. Smith, 1930.

Nicolson, Harold George, Sir. *King George the Fifth: His Life and Reign.* Garden City, N.Y.: Doubleday, 1953.

Rose, Kenneth. *King George V.* New York: Knopf, 1984.

German Armed Merchant Raiders

Even before the outbreak of World War I, merchant ships were included as auxiliary vessels in the naval lists of all major sea powers. As with other naval powers, the German Imperial Navy listed passenger ships capable of speeds above eighteen knots as auxiliary cruisers.

Operations involving large German auxiliary cruisers began immediately after the commencement of hostilities. The first of these ships, *Kaiser Wilhelm der Grosse* (14,349 tons), commanded by Commander Max Reymann, left Bremerhaven on 4 August 1914. Once in the Atlantic she sank three merchant ships totaling 10,685 tons but was destroyed on 26 August 1914 off the coast of the Spanish colony of Rio de Oro by the British cruiser *Highflier.*

The steamer *Cap Trafalgar* (18,805 tons), at anchor at Buenos Aires when the war began, was outfitted as an auxiliary cruiser using components from the old gunboat *Eber;* she was soon sunk by the superior British auxiliary cruiser *Carmania* (19,524 tons) on 14 August 1914. Her commanding officer, Lieutenant Commander Julius Wirth, and fourteen others of the crew perished. The *Carmania* was hit seventy-nine times and suffered nine dead.

The passenger ship *Kronprinz Wilhelm* (14,908 tons), while returning from New York, was fitted with two 8.8cm guns from the cruiser *Karlsruhe,* then operating in the Atlantic. This auxiliary cruiser, commanded by Lieutenant Paul Wolfgang Thierfelder, operated for half a year in the South Atlantic, sank fourteen Allied merchant ships totaling 55,939 tons, and covered 37,666 nautical miles in 250 days. On 27 April 1915 a shortage of coal and the poor condition of her engine led to her internment at Newport News, Virginia.

The same reasons forced Lieutenant Commander Max Thierichens to have his auxiliary cruiser, *Prinz Eitel Friedrich* (8,797 tons), interned at Newport News on 9 April 1915, but only after he had sunk eleven ships (totaling 33,153 tons) in the Atlantic.

During the night of 22–23 October 1914 the auxiliary cruiser *Berlin* (17,324 tons), commanded by Captain Hans Pfundheller, laid 200 mines north of Tory Island. These sank the British battleship *Audacious* (23,000 tons) and auxiliary cruiser *Viknor* (5,386 tons), among other ships. But during the night of 17–18 November 1914 the poor condition of her boilers and a shortage of coal forced the *Berlin* into Drontheim, where she was interned.

The high coal consumption of auxiliary cruisers was a strong limiting factor in their deployment. Very little could be done, moreover, to change their characteristic appearance. Consequently, the admiralty decided to deploy a second wave of less conspicuous but heavily armed freighters, which would, it was thought, have a much better chance of breaking through the blockade. These ships were also equipped with means for greatly altering their appearance.

The most successful auxiliary cruisers of this new wave were the *Mowe* (4,788 tons), commanded by Lieutenant Commander Nikolaus Graf zu Dohna-Schlodien, and the *Wolf* (5,809 tons), under Commander Karl August Nerger. The *Mowe* put to sea for the first time on 29 December 1915. She laid mines off Cape Wrath on 2 January and before the mouths of the Gironde and Loire rivers on 9 January 1916. Before her return to port on 4 March 1916, the *Mowe* had sunk fifteen ships totaling 57,835 tons. Her mines sank the British battleship *King Edward VII* (16,350 tons). On her second mission, from 22 November 1916 to 22 March 1917, the *Mowe* sank twenty-three merchant vessels totaling 108,821 tons and captured the *Yarrowdale* (4,652 tons).

The *Wolf* made the longest voyage of all, from 30 November 1916 to 21 February 1918, a total of 444 days. In addition to her guns and 465 mines, the *Wolf* carried a reconnaissance aircraft. She laid mines off Capetown, Cape Agulhas, Colombo, Bombay, New Zealand, and Singapore, and converted the *Turitella*—a steamer of 5,528 tons captured in the Indian Ocean—into an auxiliary cruiser that was given the name *Iltis* and placed under the command of Captain Iwan Brandes.

The *Wolf* captured fourteen ships and sank approximately 280,000 tons of shipping, including nineteen freighters destroyed by the mines she laid. The *Iltis* captured two sailing vessels totaling 1,442 tons and laid twenty-five mines off the coast of Aden, but her crew blew up the ship on 5 March 1917 when she was approached by the British sloop *Odin*.

The smallest German auxiliary cruiser was the *Meteor* (1,912 tons). Commanded by Lieutenant Commander Wolfram von Knorr, she laid 285 mines in the White Sea in June of 1915 and 374 in the Firth of Morey in August. On her return voyage the *Meteor* sank the British auxiliary ship *Ramsey* (1,443 tons), saving forty-two of her ninety-eight crewmembers. On the following day, however, approached by British cruisers, her crew scuttled her near Horns Riff. Several steamers and the destroyer *Lynx* (935 tons) sank on the barricades.

The auxiliary cruiser *Greif* (4,962 tons) was not able to break through the blockade. Attacked on 29 February 1916 northwest of Bergen by the British auxiliary cruisers *Alcantara* (15,300 tons) and *Andes*, she sank the *Alcantara* by torpedo but suffered such heavy damage herself that her crew was forced to surrender. In all, ninety-seven men died, among them the commanding officer, Commander Rudolf Tietze. There were 209 survivors.

The only sailing vessel among the German auxiliary cruisers was the *Seeadler* (1,543 tons), previously the *Pass of Bahama,* captured by U-36. Beginning on 21 December 1916 she was commanded by Captain Felix Graf Luckner in the Atlantic and Pacific, sinking fourteen ships totaling 28,140 tons. The first time she put to sea, the *Seeadler* successfully survived an inspection by a British prize crew. On 2 August 1917 the *Seeadler* ran aground on the island of Mopelia.

The captured merchant ship *Yarrowdale* became the auxiliary cruiser *Leopard*. Last of the German auxiliary cruisers, she put to sea in March of 1917 under Commander Hans von Laffert. On 16 March 1917, while attempting to break through the blockade between Norway and Iceland, the *Leopard* engaged the British armored cruiser *Achilleus* and auxiliary cruiser *Dundee* and was lost with her entire crew of 319 men.

After the December 1914 Battle of the Falklands, German military options on the high seas were severely limited. Armed merchant raiders were the only viable surface threat the High Seas Fleet could offer. They performed admirably, sinking Allied merchantmen and tying down large numbers of the enemy's smaller combat ships around the globe, denying them the opportunity to concentrate against U-boats.

Gerhard Hümmelchen

References

German Admiralty Office. "Der Krieg zur See." Division 6: *Der Kreuzerkrieg in den auslandischen Gewassern.* Vol. 3. Eberhard von Mantey. *Die deutschen Hilfskreuzer.* Berlin: E.S. Mittler und Sohn, 1937.

Langsdorff, Werner von. *Kaperkrieg im Atlantik.* Gutrersloh: Verlag C. Bertelsmann, 1933.

Schoen, Walter von. *Auf Kaperkurs. Heldentaten deutscher Hilfskeuzer.* Berlin: Ullstein, 1934.

Thomas, Lowell. *Count Luckner, The Sea Devil.* Garden City, N.Y.: Garden City Publishing, 1927.

German Channel Destroyer Raids (1917)

From February to April of 1917 the German navy conducted a series of raids on Allied ports in and around the English Channel. The raids were part of an attempt by German naval forces to regain the offensive after the Battle of Jutland.

There were twenty-two German destroyers stationed at Zeebrugge and Ostend. These ports were within seventy miles of the English port of Dover. A typical German raid involved the use of eleven or so destroyers, supported by torpedo boats and submarines. The ships would steam out during the day and conduct their attack under the cover of darkness. By daybreak, the Germans could be back in port. During this three-month period, the Germans attacked the English towns around Dover and the French ports of Calais, Boulogne, and Dunkirk. In addition, the Germans attacked Allied convoys in the Channel. Often the raids involved little more than the shelling of enemy towns or ports. Fear of British patrols meant that the Germans did not want to remain in one area for any length of time. Many of the raids lasted only a few minutes. As a result, their ability to inflict damage was somewhat limited.

The arduous task of defending against the raiders fell to the Dover Patrol. Based in the port of Dover, this force consisted of one light cruiser, eighteen modern destroyers, and eleven older destroyers. The German destroyers were superior to the British ships in armor, speed, and armament. In fact, the eleven older British destroyers were not even considered fit to engage the German ships. When the Germans began their raids, the British force was wholly unable to defend the English coast against the attacks. The Dover Patrol had to provide escorts for the sundry Allied convoys as well as patrol several hundred miles of coastline. Thus, while the Germans could concentrate their resources against a specific target, the British were usually too spread out to provide an adequate defense. At first, there were only four to six British destroyers ready to respond to a German attack.

The raids did little military damage, but they were damaging to British morale and prestige. Consequently, the admiralty took several steps that ultimately ended the raids. Spotlights and shore batteries were installed along the English coast. Heavily armed monitors were moored near the more frequent targets. More important, eleven new destroyers were attached to the Dover Patrol. These actions produced the desired effects. The monitors and shore batteries were able to drive off the German raiders. The last German raid occurred on the night of 20 April. A force of six German destroyers was intercepted by two British destroyers. The British sank two of the German ships and damaged the others.

The suppression of the raids by the British marked the real end of naval surface warfare during the war. After April of 1917 the Germans relied almost exclusively on their submarine forces to fight the British on the high seas.

T.M. Lansford

References

Frothingham, Thomas. *Naval History of the World War, 1915–1916*. Cambridge: Massachusetts Historical Society, 1924–26.

Hough, Richard. *The Great War at Sea, 1914–1918*. New York: Oxford University Press, 1983.

See also GERMANY, NAVY; GREAT BRITAIN, NAVY; WARSHIPS: DESTROYERS

German Cruiser Raids, 1914

Despite the massive German naval building program, on 1 August 1914 the British Grand Fleet enjoyed an advantage over the German High Seas Fleet of 20:13 in battleships and 4:3 in battle cruisers. During the next six months the British could expect the addition of up to ten other capital ships, while the Germans had only five new ships coming into service in the same time period. As a result, Grand Admiral Alfred von Tirpitz developed a multiple strategy of reducing the British numerical advantage through U-boat attacks, mine fields, and limited engagements with inferior British forces. Only then would he risk a decisive fleet battle. That was the background to the German battle cruiser raids against the British coastal cities of Great Yarmouth on 3–4 November 1914 and Hartlepool, Whitby, and Scarborough on 15–16 December 1914.

These German plans were undermined by a naval action with the Russians. On 26 August 1914 the German light cruiser *Magdeburg,* engaged in a mine-operation against the Russians in the Finnish Gulf, was stranded off the island of Odensholm and had to be scuttled. The Russians searched the wreck and sent in divers, who salvaged the signal book used to encode radio signals of fleet units before they were super-enciphered with a simple transposition table. The Russians passed this book on to the British. Thanks to the work of Room 40, by early December 1914 the admiralty could read German naval signals.

In late November 1914, after an unsuccessful raid by the Grand Fleet into the German Bight, commander in chief of the German High Seas Fleet Admiral Friedrich von Ingenohl planned again to send his battle cruisers, under Vice Admiral Franz von Hipper, to bombard the British coast and lay mines along the coastal shipping route. On 14 December, after some delays because of bad weather, the German battle cruisers and their accompanying cruisers and destroyers, lying at anchor at Schilling Reede of the Jade, received a radio message to begin their operation.

This signal was intercepted and decrypted by the British. Without exact information about the German target, the admiralty assumed a probable attack against the central East Coast. As a result, Whitehall sent south from Cromarty and Scapa Flow the First Battle Cruiser Squadron under Vice Admiral David Beatty with the *Lion, Tiger, Queen Mary,* and *New Zealand,* accompanied by the First Light Cruiser Squadron with four cruisers and the Third Cruiser Squadron with four armored cruisers and seven destroyers. Also sent was the Second Battle Squadron under Vice Admiral Sir George Warrender, with dreadnoughts *King George V, Orion, Ajax, Conqueror, Centurion,* and *Monarch.* The Grand Fleet was to follow the night of 16 December from Scapa Flow, and the Third Battle Squadron, with its eight predreadnought battleships, would sail from the Firth of Forth.

The British did not know that the entire German High Seas Fleet, composed of fourteen modern and eight older battleships, two armored cruisers, seven light cruisers, and fifty-three destroyers, was approaching as a covering force. This force had received its orders before departing the harbor of Wilhelmshaven and remained undetected because it observed strict radio silence. At about 01:00 on 16 December the five German battle cruisers had just crossed the course of the approaching ten British capital ships at a distance of less than six to ten miles, but bad weather limited visibility to only four miles. At about 06:15 the seven British destroyers on the eastern flank of the British formation clashed with German destroyers and

the cruiser *Hamburg.* This led Ingenohl to order a turn to avoid torpedo attacks. As a result, the British destroyers did not learn of the presence of the German battleships.

At 09:15 the German battle cruisers *Derfflinger* and *Von der Tann* began the bombardment of Scarborough, followed a few minutes later by the *Seydlitz, Moltke,* and *Blücher* against Hartlepool. At 10:06 the first group opened fired against Whitby. When first reports of the bombardments arrived at the admiralty, Churchill and the operations officers were pleased, because they knew that the British capital ships were between the Germans and their home bases. They sat down for breakfast to await news of the coming great battle.

Meanwhile, the heavy British ships had turned northeast in the direction of reports of the enemy received from the destroyers. They were closing on the German High Seas Fleet until the news of the coastal bombardments caused them to turn westward to intercept the German ships when they came out of the gap in the mine barrages. Because of increasingly bad weather, Hipper had earlier detached his light forces. At 12:30 the cruisers *Stralsund* and *Straßburg,* with their destroyers, suddenly encountered the British battle cruisers coming out of the mist, but because of signaling mishaps on the part of the British, the German ships escaped to the south at high speed. Turning east again, the Germans also evaded the Second British Battle Squadron, but missed an opportunity to lure the six British battleships against the High Seas Fleet battle line.

Hipper learned about the British attempt to intercept him from the signals of his light cruisers and by listening to British radio traffic. As he left the minefields, Hipper turned north, while Beatty, only about ten miles distant, turned again to the east, thus opening the distance and allowing Hipper to go around the British forces in the north. By 16:00 the German ships were beyond reach of the British.

In the admiralty, Churchill and his officers waited in vain for the great battle they had anticipated. On the next day Churchill had to endure tough questions in Parliament. He was unable to reveal how the efforts of Room 40 had almost trapped the Germans. He did not then know how close the ten British capital ships had come to an encounter with eighteen German capital ships (not counting the weaker *Blücher* and the predreadnought battleships) and a greatly superior number of German destroyers. Never in the following years did the Germans come as close to the *Kräfteausgleich* desired by Tirpitz.

Churchill and the admiralty could hardly have learned in more dramatic fashion the possibilities and limits of radio intelligence. Unknown to each other, the opposing forces had passed each other three times just out of view. Six weeks later, the Royal Navy was more fortunate in the Battle of the Dogger Bank. This experience with radio intelligence was the reason for Churchill's intense interest in that aspect of modern warfare. It would bear fruits in the Second World War.

Jürgen Rohwer

References

Beesly, Patrick, and Jürgen Rohwer. "Room 40 and the German Bombardment of Hartlepool, Scarborough and Whitby on 15/16 December 1914." Unpublished papers presented at the 4th Naval History Symposium of the U.S. Naval Academy, Annapolis, Md., 1979.

Corbett, Julian Stafford, and Henry Newboldt. *Naval Operations*. Vols. 1–5. London: Longmans Green, 1920–31.

Groos, Otto. *Der Krieg in der Nordsee: Zweiter Band: Von Anfang September bis November 1914; Dritter Band: Von Ende November 1914 bis Anfang Februar 1915. Der Krieg zur See 1914–1918.* Herausgegeben vom Marine-Archiv. Berlin: Verlag E.S. Mittler und Sohn, 1922 and 1923.

See also BALTIC NAVAL OPERATIONS; BEATTY, DAVID; GERMANY, NAVY; HIPPER, FRANZ VON; INGENOHL, FRIEDRICH VON; ROOM 40; TIRPITZ, ALFRED VON

German Cruiser Raids, 1916

Raids by the cruiser forces of the High Seas Fleet were the main element of German naval strategy in 1916. These raids were directed against the English coast and were designed to draw the British Grand Fleet out of its home ports. In the end the strategy worked very well—the one great fleet engagement of the war, the battle of Jutland, was the result of an attempted raid by the High Seas Fleet.

The appointment of Reinhard Scheer as commander of the High Seas Fleet in 1916 led to the adoption of a more offensive strategy by the German navy. Instead of avoiding contact with the British, Scheer actively sought confrontation. One of the first signs of this was a raid against the English coast. On 24 April 1916 the High Seas Fleet set out for the English coast. The German plan was for the cruisers and battle cruisers of the fleet to bombard the English towns of Lowestoft and Yarmouth. Lowestoft was a port for British minelayers and Yarmouth was a British submarine base. The cruiser bombardment was to be supported by airship raids on surrounding towns. Since the British fleet was actually based at two different ports, Rosyth and Scapa Flow, Scheer hoped that the British would arrive in two different groups. Thus Scheer could concentrate the combined firepower of the High Seas Fleet on one section of the British fleet.

The Germans began their bombardment at 05:00 on 25 April. The cruisers met little resistance during the bombardment. After shelling the towns for an hour or so, the fleet retired. During the whole course of the raid, the German fleet encountered only a light force of British cruisers. While the raid did little military damage, it destroyed a number of houses and caused some civilian casualties.

The most important aspect of the raid was that it created a public outcry in Great Britain. It appeared that German naval units were able to attack the English coast with impunity. Twice before, once in 1914 and once in 1915, the German navy had attacked the coast of England and the British navy had failed to intercept the raiders. The April raid forced the first lord of the admiralty, Arthur Balfour, to announce publicly that if the Germans attempted to raid the coast again they would definitely be met by the Grand Fleet. Consequently, as Scheer planned the next German raid, he was confident that the raid would result in contact with the main British fleet.

Early in May of 1916 Scheer drew up plans for a raid on the English town of Sunderland. Scheer planned for the raid to follow the same pattern as the Lowestoft raid. He hoped to be able to draw the British cruiser squadron into battle but retire before the British heavy ships arrived on the scene. Unfortunately for the Germans, in 1914 British intelligence had gained access to German cipher codes. The British had set up a secret department known as Room 40, which was able to decipher German wireless messages and plot naval movements. Thus forewarned, on 30 May the British Grand

Fleet sailed a full two hours before the Germans. On the afternoon of 31 May the two fleets engaged each other in the battle of Jutland. Although the battle was really inconclusive, it did force the Germans to retire before they had carried out their raid. The action also introduced a measure of caution into the commanders of both fleets.

After Jutland there was a period of relative inactivity on the part of the High Seas Fleet, but, by August, Scheer was ready to undertake another raid. On the 19th he attempted to carry out the failed raid on Sunderland. Again forewarned of the German fleet's movements, the British fleet set out to engage the enemy. Both fleets turned back, however, before they were even close to each other. The Germans withdrew after an airship spotted elements of the approaching British fleet. After a light cruiser was torpedoed, the British retreated for fear of further U-boat attacks. This foray was the last instance in which the Germans attempted to use capital ships to raid the English coast. By the end of 1916 the Germans switched to utilizing destroyers to conduct raids against the British.

Throughout the war, the German cruiser raids inflicted very little military damage on the British. The most important result of the raids was the adoption of a more aggressive naval strategy by the British. In turn, the more aggressive strategy led to the battle of Jutland.

T.M. Lansford

References

Hough, Richard. *The Great War at Sea, 1914–1918*. New York: Oxford University Press, 1983.

Scheer, Reinhard. *Germany's High Sea Fleet in the World War*. London: Cassell, 1920.

See also BALFOUR, ARTHUR; GERMANY, NAVY; JUTLAND, BATTLE OF; ROOM 40; SCHEER, REINHARD

Germany, Army

In 1914, Germany as a single entity did not exist. As a compromise during unification, the King of Prussia became Kaiser, while allowing the monarchs and princes of the other German states to retain their titles and privileges. The German Empire was composed of twenty-six states: four kingdoms, five grand duchies and principalities, three free cities, and the imperial territory of Alsace-Lorraine. Three states maintained some measure of independence and had their own armies, war ministries, general staffs, and inspectorates; these were Bavaria (11 percent of the army), Saxony (7 percent), and Württemberg (4 percent). All of the rest of the army (78 percent) was controlled by Prussia, the dominant state. In time of war, all the armies were united under the command of the Kaiser, who was the all-highest warlord. Actual operations were directed by the German General Staff.

The German army was composed of twenty-five army corps. Each had its own district from which it recruited its contingent of soldiers. Prior to the war, the peacetime strength of the army was 34,870 officers and 663,578 NCOs and men. Recruitment was based on the concept of universal military service (*Wehrpflicht*), which required every male to serve over a twenty-seven-year period from his seventeenth birthday until his forty-fifth. Upon reaching age seventeen the man was enlisted in the first level (*Ban*) of the territorial reserve (*Landsturm*). At twenty he began his period of active service (*Dienstpflicht*), consisting of two years in the regular army (three years for the cavalry), followed by five in the active reserve (four years for cavalry). After leaving the reserves at age twenty-seven, the man joined the first *Ban* of the inactive reserve (*Landwehr*) and transferred into the second *Ban* upon reaching age thirty-two. At thirty-nine he transferred into the second *Ban* of the *Landsturm*, until his discharge at age forty-five. The system was intended to provide a regular army and a large reservoir of trained reserves who attended training sessions periodically during each year. Another category of recruit was that of one-year volunteers (*Einjahrige Freiwilligen*); these were young men of good birth and education who served one year at their own expense. At the end of that year they were allowed to transfer to the reserve as a reserve officer aspirant. During the war another category was created, the war volunteers (*Kriegsfreiwilligen*), young men who volunteered to serve before their call-up.

Although in theory all German males were obligated to perform military service, large numbers never served at all. This was in part because of the large expenditures involved and the fact that the Reichstag would need to approve raising additional troops. Another reason was the lack of officers of the required social class and the army's reluctance to enlist urban workers, for fear they would spread socialist ideas to rural recruits. Despite not serving, those exempted were carried on the muster rolls of the first or second *Ban* of the *Landsturm*, or if they were between the ages of twenty and thirty-two, they were placed in the Replacement Reserve (*Ersatz*). When fully mobilized, the German army consisted of active regiments, active reserve regiments, supporting *Landwehr* regiments, and the *Landsturm* (which operated only within Germany itself).

Reserve regiments were intended to form duplicate regiments of the regular army; for example, the regular army Regiment 111 had as its counterpart Reserve Regiment 111. The *Ersatz* Reserve was intended to form a pool from which replacements could be drawn for the reserve and regular army regiments. In 1914 there were 218 active regiments, 113 reserve regiments, 96 *Landwehr* regiments; by 1918 that had increased to 698 active, 114 reserve, and 106 *Landwehr*.

The German army was socially conservative. Its officer corps was drawn primarily from the landed *Junker* class, although in the years just prior to the war, increasing numbers of non-*Junkers* were permitted to become officers. That was because of the increasing German population and the *Junkers'* low birthrate, which made them an ever smaller percentage of the population. The officer corps was bound by oath and class to the Kaiser and the nobility of the various German states. Although the officer corps was founded on birth, it also placed great importance on ability; thus a commoner, Erich Ludendorff, was to reach the high rank of quartermaster general.

The men who made up the German army came primarily from rural backgrounds and were deeply patriotic. Urban recruits were a problem for the army because of the socialist leanings often found in an industrial society. Service in the German military was looked upon as an honor, and the military had a high level of prestige. The military was also used to imbue soldiers with the conservative beliefs of the ruling class.

Command of the army rested with the all-highest warlord, Kaiser Wilhelm II, but actual administrative command was exercised by the German General Staff. Later in the war, the Kaiser became practically a figurehead; decisions were made by Field Marshal Paul von Hindenburg and his chief of staff, Quartermaster General Erich Ludendorff. German armies in the field operated with two heads, the army group commander assisted by his chief of staff. This allowed many of Germany's high nobility to lead armies with the aid of a thoroughly professional soldier.

The German army was organized around the twenty-six army corps; these were in turn divided into two divisions incorporating infantry and cavalry, a rifles (*Jäger*) battalion, a train battalion, a pioneer (engineer) battalion, and a foot artillery regiment. This organization was not always uniform for each corps; some had more support battalions, some fewer. The number of divisions in each corps often increased during the war, and by 1918 it was not unusual to find army corps with up to six divisions. Another factor in the increased size of the army corps was the new support units required because of changing technology. Battalions of gas pioneers, storm companies, flamethrower units, flak units, trench mortar units, and aviation units were added.

When the war began, there were fifty infantry divisions in the army, two of elite guard units, and six in the Bavarian army. Divisions consisted of four brigades: two infantry, one cavalry, and one artillery. Auxiliary troops consisted of three squadrons of cavalry used for escort and reconnaissance, one or two pioneer companies who performed engineering operations, one or two companies of medical personnel (stretcher bearers), and a bridging train. This basic organization changed during the war into a "triangular" division, which consisted of a brigade of three infantry regiments and one regiment of field artillery in three battalions. Additional changes occurred by 1917; support troops consisted of two pioneer companies, a trench mortar company (*Minenwerfer*), and searchlight sections. Medical support was also increased.

The years 1917 and 1918 saw the faltering German war machine calling up troops early and scrambling to relieve manpower shortages. Many new divisions were created using men who were too young or too old, as well as recovered wounded and called-up factory workers. Divisions were classed as first to fourth class, depending on their suitability for offensive operations (1st) or for holding operations in quiet sectors (4th).

Brigades consisted of two regiments of either infantry, cavalry, or field artillery. The regiment was the primary organization to which the soldier owed allegiance; it was the regiment's number or cipher that adorned his shoulder boards and the cover of his spiked helmet. The regiment was composed of battalions numbered I, II, and III. Each battalion was in turn divided into four companies. The companies were numbered from one to twelve; the thirteenth company was the heavy machine-gun company and was unattached to the three battalions. Companies were further broken down into three platoons (*Zug*), each with four sections (*Korporalschaften*) composed of two groups (*Gruppen*) of eight men. In all, each company had five officers, 259 enlisted men, ten horses, and four wagons.

The German army was organized around its regular army of 217 infantry regiments composed of currently serving conscripts and regular officers. In time of war, reservists were called to the colors and filled out the regular regiments. A duplicate organization of reserve regiments (numbering 113) and divisions was also created during wartime. The reserve units mirrored their regular regimental namesakes and allowed the German army to nearly double its size. Reserve units did not take on the honorary titles of the regular regiments, however. Regiment 111 had the honorary title "Markgraf Ludwig Wilhelm" and carried an "LW" monogram on its shoulder boards. Reserve Regiment 111 had no title and wore the number 111 on its shoulder boards.

Regular German army regiments often carried honorary titles relating to earlier elite unit status, such as Grenadier and Fusilier. Actual elite formations were designated as Guards, Grenadier Guards, or the Bavarian *Leib* Guards (Body Guards). In addition, there were formations designated as *Jäger,* elite units composed of men trained in marksmanship and woodland skills and intended to give close support to cavalry. The eighteen *Jäger* units were originally organized as battalions but were later grouped to form *Jäger* divisions: the *Deutsche Jäger* Division, the *Alpenkorps,* and the 200th Infantry Division.

Pioneer battalions were attached to each army corps before the war and were responsible for bridging operations and other engineering projects. During the war their role expanded, and they were called upon to train the infantry in their special skills. These included handling grenades, destroying barbed wire, the use of mortars (*Minenwerfer*), and other technical skills. In addition, many of the new weapons, such as flamethrowers (*Flammenwerfers*) and

early operations using poison gas, were entrusted to the pioneers. With their diverse skills, the pioneers became the nucleus of the elite storm troops.

Storm troops and the tactics they employed became the hallmark of the German army in World War I. Originally raised as special battalions, their special skills were passed on, and many unofficial storm battalions were created for special attacks and raids. Storm battalions were composed of young, aggressive soldiers, hand-picked for their talents. They employed a large number of specialized weapons including grenades, light machine guns, flamethrowers, infantry cannons, and trench mortars. They were shifted around the front and used for special assaults or raids. They were skillful at penetrating enemy trenches and capturing prisoners. Storm troopers were often treated like star athletes and given better food and billets than the average soldier. In special schools they taught the infantry their tactics of infiltration, surprise attack, and coordination of various weapons.

Unquestionably the premier infantry weapon was the machine gun. German machine guns were initially organized into special machine-gun companies armed with six heavy, sled-mounted Maxim MG-08 guns. The German army appreciated the usefulness of machine guns prior to the war; even they, however, were unprepared for the vast numbers of these weapons the war would demand. In addition to the regular regimental machine-gun companies, special independent machine-gun companies were established. In late 1915 a lighter version of the MG-08 appeared, designated the MG-08/15. This gun was mounted on a bipod. The 08/15 was distributed within the various companies of each regiment. In 1916 special elite machine-gun companies were formed, designated machine-gun sharpshooter troops (*Maschinengewehr-Scharfschützen-Truppen*). These troops were armed with the heavy MG-08 and were given special training.

On a battlefield dominated by the machine gun and artillery, there was little place for the cavalry, although the German army (like all the others) contained many cavalry units. The 110 regiments of cavalry were made up of many different types, all equally archaic. Dragoons were intended to fight dismounted, Uhlans (lancers) were armed with a rifle and steel lance; Hussars, light cavalry, were used for scouting; Curassiers, equipped with steel helmets and breastplates, were heavy cavalry intended to charge into the enemy, and *Jäger zu Pferd* were mounted sharpshooters. Upon mobilization, thirty-six additional cavalry units were created. The German High Command soon realized that this large number of men (over 100,000) was being wasted serving in the cavalry, and that the horses could be better used elsewhere. Many cavalry units were dismounted and served as infantry. Cavalry was still needed for scouting on the vast Eastern Front, but many officers looking for excitement sought other commands. The famous Baron Manfred von Richthofen (the Red Baron) was originally an Uhlan officer before joining the air service.

Artillery finally came into its own during the First World War. German artillery was divided into two branches, the field artillery, which consisted of light guns, and the foot artillery, which was made up of heavy guns of the corps and army artillery. In a war that used massive artillery bombardments lasting many days, artillery took on a new importance.

The prewar field artillery was organized into 101 regiments and the artillery school at Jüterborg. Regiments were divided into two *Abteilung,* each with three batteries usually of six guns each. The normal armament of the field artillery consisted of the 7.7cm field gun. Some regiments were equipped with the 10.5cm light field howitzer instead of the normal complement of 7.7cm guns. The prewar strength in guns was 5,580 pieces; during the war the number of field artillery units expanded and by 1918 had risen to 11,280 pieces. Expansion was achieved by production as well as by pressing captured weapons into service.

Although organized into twenty-four regiments, the foot artillery (heavy artillery) was allocated to different commands in batteries and groups of batteries. The foot artillery's principal weapons included 15cm heavy field howitzers, 10cm field guns, and 21cm Mörsers. During the war, the types of guns available increased as captured guns were pressed into service and new, larger pieces were developed. By the end of the war, the number of guns was eleven times that at mobilization.

Aiding the guns in their task was the German Air Service, which supported both the army and navy. The Air Service was divided into three arms, the airship troops (*Luftschiff-Truppen*), balloon troops (*Feldluftschiffer-Abteilungen*), and the flying troops (*Flieger-Abteilungen*). Airship troops manned and operated airships such as the zeppelins, which made long-range bombing raids and scouted the North Sea for the fleet. Balloon troops manned observation balloons suspended over the front and spotted for the artillery. Flying troops operated reconnaissance machines, which aided the artillery and took photographs. Fighter squadrons defended the reconnaissance machines and balloons, while attacking enemy observation aircraft and balloons. Later in the war, huge bombers were built for long-distance bombing raids.

In addition to the main combat services, the army had vast numbers of support units serving such functions as transportation, signals, communications, medical transport, hospitals, veterinary services, supply depots, military police, and *Etappen* (which administered the occupied areas and controlled the local population). These services were important in sustaining the war effort and allowed the fighting troops to concentrate on fighting the war.

Despite the efforts of the support and supply services, German troops often were hungry; as the blockade of Germany tightened, food grew scarce. The high command tried to ensure that the troops received priority in food allocation, but it was often not enough. Shortages in materials resulted in the use of many substitute materials, called *Ersatz*. Shortages in rubber resulted in aircraft landing wheels being made from wood, and rubberized gas masks were replaced with ones made from oiled leather. By the end of the war, cannon barrels were so worn that they frequently fired short and killed their own men. The German soldier continued on and fought well in a war that increasingly engulfed and overwhelmed him. The Germans called the later stages of the war the "war of material" (*Materialschlacht*).

In the end what mattered most was material resources; bravery, courage, and honor were irrelevant in this impersonal war that brutalized the soldier. For over four years the soldiers of all armies were forced to live in mud, with lice, rats, and filth. The battlefield during World War I resembled an open graveyard, full of unburied corpses. The proud German army of 1914 died in this hellish world, and a new, hard, brutalized army emerged in 1918 to return home to more privation and revolution.

Steven D. Fisher

References

Nash, D.B. *Imperial German Army Handbook, 1914–1918*. London: Ian Allan, 1980.

See also ARTILLERY; CAVALRY; HINDENBURG, PAUL VON; LUDENDORFF, ERICH; MACHINE GUNS; STORMTROOPERS; WILHELM II

Germany, Home Front

When Germans marched to war in 1914, they, like the other participants, expected that the war would be over by Christmas. Each side was confident that its army could crush the other quickly, and none would admit the possibility of a long, drawn-out war.

Germany was not prepared for a protracted war; even in peacetime she needed to import 20 percent of her food and many of the raw materials for her factories. German military planners knew that their country could survive a British blockade for only up to eighteen months before the food situation would become critical; they hoped to win the war before supplies ran out. Meanwhile, industrialist Walther Rathenau began organizing War Industries Companies to convert Germany's immense industrial capacity to production of war materials in an attempt to get the government and private sector into a cooperative effort.

The Reichstag, however, was not entirely in favor of the war. The Social Democrats (SPD) agreed to call a truce (*Burgfrieden*) and support the war effort if the government would assure them that the war was necessary for Germany's defense. By mid-1915 the SPD realized that it had been misled and issued a manifesto calling for peace. Throughout 1915 and into 1916 some members of the SPD voiced increasing opposition to the war, which culminated in a split in the party after seventeen of its members voted against the emergency budget in March of 1916. This dissenting faction formed the Social Democratic Labor Fellowship, which attracted some trade union leaders and other left-wing sympathizers and led to government countermeasures against revolutionary activities. But, at least for the first two years of the war, the antiwar liberals did not enjoy the support of the masses.

During the initial mobilization, the German public was united in support of the war effort. Bands played patriotic songs, crowds cheered the soldiers as they marched off to war, and well-meaning women met troop trains and handed out food, drink, and cigarettes to the men on their way to the front. People subscribed to government-sponsored war loans and gave up their gold jewelry. Shopkeepers did a steady trade in patriotic souvenirs and postcards of the Kaiser and his generals.

The government quickly stepped in to regulate public morale and behavior. It encouraged a hate campaign directed at Britain, which it considered the only serious threat to Germany's war aims, as a move to unify civilians and make them feel part of the war effort. English could not be spoken in public or on the telephone. People automatically greeted each other with the phrase, "God punish England." Newspapers came under military control and could print only stories cleared by a central press office, resulting in little real war news but plenty of rumor. Officials banned dancing, theatrical comedy, and ragtime music, requiring that public performances present patriotic and serious themes.

But the worst threat to civilian morale was the food shortage caused by the British blockade and inefficient distribution practices. By early spring of 1915, food was becoming scarce and expensive. The harvest fell almost 40 percent short of the expected yield. A severe drought in June and July withered much of the grain and indicated a bad harvest to come. Food prices had increased 65 percent over July 1914 prices, so the government fixed maximum prices for many foods and instituted ration cards for milk and bread. One could no longer buy pork, because the butchers were losing 30 pfennig per pound by selling at the government's fixed price. By the summer of 1916, food was rationed even more: four pounds of bread and one-half pound of meat per week, one pound of potatoes per day, and one pound of sugar for the month. Women stood in line for hours before the food shops opened only to find that there was no milk, bread, eggs, meat, or butter to buy. In September of 1916 the women in one Silesian city rioted outside the town hall, demanding butter and pasting their ration stamps to the door, forcing the mayor to call out Home Defense troops to end the disturbance.

Fruit and vegetables rarely made it as far as the market; farmers sold them at inflated prices or officials requisitioned them. People with money could usually buy food on the black market or from local farmers; in fact, the black market supplied up to one-third of all food. Unfortunately, poorer people could not afford the black market. Part of the drastic rise in the wartime crime rate, particularly juvenile delinquency, resulted from food theft.

Wartime rationing was not limited to food. Clothing and shoes grew scarce because raw materials were needed for military equipment. Resourceful manufacturers wove a substitute fabric from twisted paper. An exhibition in Breslau featured articles made of this paper cloth: stockings, dresses, underwear, and drive belts for machinery. The government published lists of rationed clothing; if a person owned more than his allotment, he was supposed to surrender the surplus to the government so that it could recycle the fibers. If one wished to replace a garment, the old one had to be given up before purchasing the new one. Women could keep only one Sunday dress, two workday dresses, and two pair of shoes or boots. Even yard goods were rationed according to the garment one planned to make; for a blouse, one could buy only 1.6 meters of fabric; for a dress, 4.25 meters.

Labor and material shortages limited production of badly needed munitions and equipment for the army. In desperation the government passed the Auxiliary Service Law (known as the Hindenburg program) in December of 1916. It demanded that all men between seventeen and sixty who were ineligible for military service must work in a war-related industry such as manufacturing, agriculture, or the government. Women were not required to serve under this law, but a central organization provided employment for women who wished to do so. The Hindenburg program resulted in a significant increase in production but devoured Germany's already depleted raw materials and exhausted her labor force.

By 1917 German patriotism had all but dissolved. A poorly clothed, poorly fed civilian population had no desire to prolong the war and no strength to continue the rate of industrial production demanded by the government. In April of 1917 a cut in the bread ration sparked massive workers' strikes in Berlin and Leipzig, followed by other demonstrations throughout the summer and a significant munitions workers' strike in January of 1918. The ideals of the Russian Revolution attracted some workers, and the unrest soon spread to the navy. The public and many politicians clamored for peace. The Reichstag voted 212 to 126 for a Peace Resolution on 19 July 1917, but the other warring nations took little notice of it. As the industrial, social, and political framework began to disintegrate, the government was forced to seek peace, although the British blockade continued. After the Armistice, German officials exaggerated the extent of the food shortages in order to make Germany appear threatened by Bolshevism and so gain aid from the Allies.

Suzanne Hayes Fisher

References

Gerard, James W. *My Four Years in Germany*. New York: George H. Doran, 1917.

Offer, Avner. *The First World War: An Agrarian Interpretation*. New York: Oxford University Press, 1989.

Williams, John. *The Other Battleground: The Home Fronts: Britain, France, and Germany, 1914–1918*. Chicago: Henry Regnery, 1972.

See also BLOCKADE, NAVAL, OF GERMANY; PROPAGANDA, USE IN WAR; RATHENAU, WALTHER

Germany, Navy

Prussian military tradition was so rooted in land warfare that the navy was less than an afterthought prior to the ascendancy of Wilhelm II. Prussia obtained its first armor-clad, steam-powered ship (the *Arminius*) in 1864, and the *König Wilhelm*, built in 1868, remained the largest German warship until 1891. The German navy of the 1870s and 1880s was solely a coastal defense force and, until 1888, was commanded by army generals. General Georg Leo von Caprivi took command of the navy in 1882, and, unaware of Bismarck's Reinsurance Treaty, was convinced that Germany's military resources had to be preserved for a two-front land war with France and Russia. He bought only inexpensive eighty- to ninety-ton torpedo boats for his navy.

When Wilhelm II became kaiser, he demanded a more impressive sea-going force and replaced Caprivi with Alexander von Monts (an admiral) in 1888. Monts designed and ordered four 10,000-ton battleships to begin the German blue-water navy.

Alfred Thayer Mahan's *Influence of Sea Power upon History* (1890) and the kaiser's personal interests in sea power and competition with Great Britain changed the course of German naval development. Wilhelm moved from the *Jeune Ecole* school, which emphasized coastal defense with small boats and commerce raiding with fast cruisers, to Mahan's projection of power with large fleets led by large ships. Alfred von Tirpitz was appointed state secretary of the navy 18 June 1897 and immediately launched the German naval propaganda campaign to garner public support for a larger navy. The campaign culminated in overwhelming passage (212–139) of the first Navy Bill on 26 March 1898. The bill authorized construction of seven battleships without mention of cost and without possibility of review by the Reichstag. The building program was enhanced by the second Navy Bill of 1900 and the Novelles (Supplementary Navy Laws) of 1906, 1908, and 1912. The cumulative result called for eventual construction of forty-one battleships. Between 1898 and 1911, the naval budget increased from 20 percent of that of the army to 54.8 percent. It did shrink to 32.7 percent by 1913, but defense consumed 90.1 percent of the German national budget that year. Because indirect consumer taxes were the only funding for this immense expense, the naval buildup added 1,040,700,000 GM to the national debt between 1897 and 1914. With that the Germans bought the world's second largest navy.

German battleships were built in four series. The 1907 series comprised four ships (*Westfallen, Nassau, Posen,* and *Rheinland*) which carried twelve 11-inch guns mounted six forward and six aft. Their maximum speed was 19.9 knots and they were said to be cramped but steady gun platforms. The 1908 series (*Thuringen, Helgoland, Ostfiesland,* and *Oldenburg*) were completed in 1910. They carried twelve 12-inch guns and their speed was 20.5 knots. The Kaiser series of 1909–10 (*Kaiser, Friedrich Der Grosse, Kaiserin, Prinz Regent Luitpold,* and *Konig Albert*) carried only ten 12-inch guns and had a maximum speed of 20 knots, but they incorporated several structural improvements devised by Professor Alfred Dietrich. They were the first European capital ships to employ watertight compartments, coal bunkers along the ships' sides as protection below the waterline, and steel plates around the propulsion plants. The 1911 series (*Kron Prinz Grosser Kurfürst König* and *Markgraf*) were all completed in 1913. They carried ten 12-inch guns mounted four forward and six aft and could steam at 21.5 knots. The last two German super dreadnoughts (*Bayern* and *Baden*) were laid down in 1914 and completed in 1915. Two additional ships of this class (*Sachsen* and *Württemberg*) were not complete by war's end.

Each carried eight 15-inch guns mounted four forward and four aft and were capable of 21 knots. For comparison, the British 1913–14 dreadnoughts carried eight 15-inch guns and steamed at 23 knots, though they were less well protected, carrying only 13-inch belt and 2-inch deck armor (see table). Ten of the dreadnoughts were scuttled at Scapa Flow and one was sunk at Jutland.

The German battle cruisers played a more prominent combat role than their larger cousins. They were built in four series beginning with the 1907 *Von der Tann,* which carried eight 11-inch guns and could achieve 25 knots. The 1909 series (*Goeben* and *Moltke*) carried two additional 11-inch guns and could steam at 27 knots. The *Seydlitz* of 1911 also mounted ten 11-inch guns, had a maximum speed of 26.5 knots, but was said by Jane's to be of "immensely strong construction." The 1912 series (*Derflinger, Lützow,* and *Hindenburg*) were completed between 1914 and 1916. They mounted eight 12-inch guns and could achieve 26–27 knots. The British 1915 series of battle cruisers carried six 15-inch guns and were capable of 28–30 knots. Six battle cruisers were scuttled at Scapa Flow and the *Lützow* was lost at Jutland.

The Imperial Navy also listed twenty-eight predreadnought battleships constructed between 1887 and 1904. Most carried four 11-inch guns, though some of the older models had only three or four 9.4-inch guns. Their best speed was between 17 and 18 knots. Fifteen armored cruisers built between 1895 and 1904 carried between four and twelve 8.2-inch guns and were capable of 19–24.5 knots. The three newest of these were all lost in action—the *Blücher* at Dogger Bank and the *Scharnhörst* and *Gneisenau* in the Battle of the Falklands. Another was sunk by a mine and a fifth by a torpedo.

The Germans had ten light cruisers built after 1905 and five older models. The newer ships carried six to eight 5.9-inch guns and sailed at 26–28 knots. The *Magdeburg* ran aground in the Baltic in 1914, the *Ebling* was lost at Jutland, and the *Dresden, Köln, Karlsruhe, Bremse, Brunner,* and *Frankfurt* were scuttled at Scapa Flow.

The Imperial Navy had 178 destroyers of which 90 were modern and 88 older. Of the modern ships, only forty-five were complete at war's end and twelve to fifteen of the older ships were obsolete or so damaged as to be useless. Fifty-nine were sunk during the war and thirty-eight were scuttled at Scapa Flow. They carried 3.1–4.1-inch guns and had speeds ranging from 35–thirty-eight knots in the newer ships to as little as 26 knots in the older ones.

Germany had 134 torpedo boats of which 74 could be considered modern. Of these, twenty-six were sunk during the war and sixteen reverted to the Belgian navy after being abandoned in the German withdrawal. They were of two general types, one capable of about 29 knots with a range of up to 600 and an older model with a range of 470 miles and a maximum speed of only 18 knots. Both carried two 3–4-pound guns. The navy also possessed 138 minesweepers and minelayers, of which 28 were lost in battle and 12 were never completed. In addition, the Imperial Navy had 17 gunboats, about 100 trawlers, and an assortment of tenders, training ships, and yachts.

Germany was the last of the major powers to adopt the submarine; Tirpitz did not order the first German submarine until 1904. It had a range of only 50 miles and a top speed submerged of 8.7 knots. When the First World War began Germany possessed only twenty-eight submarines, a third the number France possessed and half that of Britain. By the end of the war Germany had produced four types of submarines. They included 143 coastal submarines deployed from the Mediterranean to the Irish Sea. These were capable of 9–13.5 knots on the surface and 5.5–8 knots submerged and were detailed primarily as commerce raiders. Germany also deployed seven large submarines as cargo carriers, designed to go beneath the British blockade. One of these, the *Deutschland,* successfully completed two cargo-carrying missions to the United States. Patrol submarines, of which there were 109, served scout and attack duty in the North Sea. They were capable of 15.5–17.7 knots on the surface and 8–10.7 knots submerged. In ad-dition, there were 123 U-boats designated as mine layers, one of which deployed the mine that sank the *HMS Hampshire* off Marwick Head and cost Lord Horatio Kitchener his life. A total of 203 submarines were lost in battle, the majority being "sunk in the North Sea."

German mine warfare was especially effective during the war. The 50,000 German mines laid sank a total of 8 battleships, 3 armored cruisers, 2 light cruisers, 44 destroyers, 207 auxiliary ships, and 1.1 million tons of merchant shipping.

At the war's outset, units of the German navy were scattered over the world. In August of 1914 Admiral Graf Maximilian von Spee's cruiser squadron left the German port of Quingdao (Tsingtao). Spee dispatched the *Emden* into the Indian Ocean and called the light cruisers *Leipzig* and *Nürnberg* from the Americas and the *Dresden* from the Caribbean to join him.

The *Emden* sank the Russian light cruiser *Zhemtchug,* the French destroyer *Mousquet,* and 68,000 tons of merchant shipping before being sunk at Keeling Island by the Australian cruiser *Sydney.*

Spee met three British light cruisers under Rear Admiral Sir Christopher Cradock at Coronel off the west coast of Chile. He sank the cruisers *Good Hope* and *Monmouth* in an engagement that cost Cradock his life.

Karlsrühe stayed in the South Atlantic and enjoyed a successful period of commerce raiding. The *Königsberg* sank the British cruiser *Pegasus* off Zanzibar and stayed in east Africa to help Paul von Lettow-Vorbeck defend Germany's colony there. For a brief period, it seemed that Spee had control of the Indian Ocean, the South Pacific, and the South Atlantic. Moreover, on 29 September the submarine U-9 sank three British cruisers in rapid order; on 27 October the British battleship *Audacious* was sunk by a German mine off northern Ireland; on 30 October Russia declared war on the Ottoman Empire after the *Goeben* and the *Breslau* shelled Odessa; and Admiral Franz von Hipper bombed Yarmouth on 3 November. German naval fortunes were at a zenith.

Spee decided to press his advantage by attacking the British naval station in the Falkland Islands. He rounded Cape Horn and approached Stanley in December. The British, embarrassed by Coronel, had dispatched Vice Admiral Sir David Sturdee with four armored and two light cruisers and the battle cruisers *Inflexible* and *Invincible* to the south Atlantic. The two forces met by chance on 8 December. Spee lost all of his ships except the *Dresden* and two older cruisers, as well as his own life and those of two of his sons.

Karlsrühe was destroyed when her magazine exploded as she prepared to attack Barbados. *Königsberg* was blockaded in East Africa and would eventually be sunk there. *Dresden* was sunk off the coast of Chile in March of 1915, and the two other cruisers were interned in Norfolk for the balance of the war. Things were not going well in the North Sea either. A squadron of British cruisers and destroyers had made a sweep through Heligoland Bight on 28 August 1914. In a confused battle, Germany lost three cruisers and a torpedo boat, while the British suffered only reparable damage to the cruiser *Arethusa* and the destroyer *Laertes*. Sagging German naval confidence received a mild boost when Hipper managed to take four heavy and four light cruisers to the British coast and lob a few ineffective shells into the town of Yarmouth.

Three intelligence disasters befell the Germans in the latter half of 1914. On 11 August the Royal Australian Navy took a German steamer in Port Phillip Bay and captured the codes used to communicate with the merchant marine, zeppelins, small ships, and U-boats. That same month, the Russians captured the major unit codes from the *Magdeburg* after she ran aground on Odensholm Island. The czar's navy obligingly delivered the codes to the British admiralty. Finally, the *Verkehrsbuch,* which contained codes Berlin used to communicate with its embassies and consulates, was dredged up in a chest full of cipher materials by a British fishing vessel. The admiralty had the entire set of German naval codes. Inexplicably, Germany continued to use these codes unaltered through the balance of the war.

In December of 1914 Hipper took three of his heavy cruisers and again bombarded the British coast, this time damaging the towns of Scarborough, Whitby, and Hartlepool. Only a heavy mist, British ineptitude, and luck allowed him to get back to Germany without having his escape cut off from behind. Hipper's luck ran out the following month when he was sent on a scouting mission over Dogger Bank. The admiralty intercepted and decoded radio signals ordering the mission and were waiting for him. The first engagement between dreadnoughts (albeit battle cruisers) resulted in a decisive British victory. The *Blücher* was sunk, *Seydlitz* suffered severe damage, and *Derflinger* and *Kölberg* suffered lesser damage. On the British side, only *Lion* and the destroyer *Meteor* were significantly damaged. Dogger Bank impressed the German navy with their disadvantage in comparison with the heavier and longer-range British guns. Even though the Imperial Navy's guns had a higher muzzle velocity and could fire reliably for twice as many rounds, they were no match for the greater range of the larger British weapons. The Kaiser, unwilling to further risk his fleet, replaced Admiral Friedrich von Ingenohl with the more passive Hugo von Pohl and declared all waters around the British Isles a war area—in effect initiating a policy of unrestricted submarine warfare.

In January of 1916 the ailing Pohl was replaced by the more aggressive Vice Admiral Reinhard Scheer. For the first time the kaiser authorized a commander of the High Seas Fleet to undertake offensive operations without his personal approval. Increased mining and the continuation of unrestricted submarine warfare were integral parts of Scheer's battle plan, but he also envisioned a more active role for the surface fleet. In April of 1916 Scheer led a group of cruisers on a successful shelling raid of the British coastal towns of Yarmouth and Lowestoft.

By mid-1916, Jellicoe was coming under increasing pressure to establish control of the Baltic, a goal he had always reckoned impossible without destroying the High Seas Fleet. Taking the Baltic would allow direct contact with Russia, would sever the trade routes between Germany and Scandinavia, and would force the Germans to commit much-needed reserves to protecting their own coastline. These pressures and a more willing competitor resulted in the Battle of Jutland in May of 1916. After the inconclusive engagement, the German surface navy, with the exception of occasional light cruiser or destroyer forays, remained in port and the offensive naval effort devolved upon the U-boat fleet.

Underemployed and poorly supplied, the sailors fell victim to poor morale, culminating in mutinies that began on the battleship *Prinzregent Luitpold* on 2 August 1917 and helped spark the November Revolution that overthrew the Kaiser in 1918.

The navy's final humiliation came on 21 November 1918 (*Der Tag*) when the High Seas Fleet surrendered, to be interned at Scapa Flow. The Treaty of Versailles allowed the German navy only 15,000 men with no more than 1,500 officers and a fleet composed of six small battleships, six light cruisers, twelve destroyers, twelve torpedo boats, no submarines, and no aircraft. The Kaiser's proud experiment had reached an ignominious end.

Jack McCallum

References
Frost, Holloway. *The Battle of Jutland.* New York: Arno, 1980.

Herwig, Holger. *"Luxury" Fleet: The Imperial German Navy 1888–1918*. Atlantic Highlands, N.J.: Ashfield, 1987.

Massie, Robert. *Dreadnought: Britain, Germany, and the Coming of the Great War*. New York: Random House, 1991.

Moore, John, ed. *Jane's Fighting Ships of World War I*. London: Jane's, 1919.

See also CORONEL, BATTLE OF; DOGGER BANK, NAVAL BATTLE OF; FALKLANDS, BATTLE OF; HELIGOLAND BIGHT, BATTLE OF; INGENOHL, FRIEDRICH VON; JUTLAND, BATTLE OF; POHL, HUGO VON; SCAPA FLOW, SCUTTLING OF GERMAN FLEET; SPEE, MAXIMILIAN VON; SUBMARINES; TIRPITZ, ALFRED VON

Germany, Revolution of 1918

From November of 1918 through January of 1919 Germany endured revolutionary upheaval that gave birth to the Weimar Republic. The German Revolution was the product of military defeat, the disintegration of the imperial government, and a desperate effort to stave off a seizure of power.

By the end of August 1918, Field Marshal Paul von Hindenburg and General Erich Ludendorff had concluded that Germany could not achieve military victory. By the end of September their pessimism had turned to desperation. On 29 September they demanded the formation of a new government capable of winning the backing of a majority in the Reichstag and, hence, better able to obtain an acceptable armistice and peace from the Allies. Prince Max of Baden became chancellor and formed a government with the support of the majority wing of the Social Democrats, the Center party, and the Progressives.

Allied insistence upon terms that amounted to capitulation, the unwillingness of the kaiser to abdicate in favor of a grandson, and the spread of chaos in Germany, all rendered Max's position untenable. The German request for an armistice sapped the willingness of many Germans to continue a futile struggle. At the end of October, sailors at Keil mutinied rather than obey orders to set to sea. Revolutionary councils, modeled after the Russian soviets, were established, and early in November mutinies broke out at other ports and spread inland. On 7 November, following the capitulation of Austria, revolutionaries in Bavaria under the leadership of the Independent Socialist Kurt Eisner overthrew the monarchy and proclaimed the Bavarian People's Republic.

Friedrich Ebert, leader of the majority Social Democrats, feared that without an abdication or an armistice a continuation of the impasse would play into the hands of the radical left-wing Spartacists led by Karl Liebknecht and Rosa Luxemburg. A reformist, Ebert did not desire revolution but favored maintaining the monarchy until a constituent assembly decided its fate. To forestall a Bolshevik-style revolution, he insisted that Max secure the Kaiser's abdication by 9 November. On that day Max announced the abdication of the still-resisting Kaiser, who was then forced to seek exile in the Netherlands. Max then handed his office over to Ebert.

Although Ebert expressed his desire to establish a "people's government," he deferred any decision on the establishment of a republic. Ebert's colleague, Philip Scheidemann, however, having been informed that Liebknecht was at that moment leading a massive demonstration at the Hohenzollern Palace, moved to seize the initiative from the Spartacists. From a Reichstag balcony at 14:00 on 9 November he proclaimed to the crowd the establishment of a German republic.

Ebert's paramount concern was not to socialize Germany but to obtain peace and to secure the order necessary for Germany and Germans to survive. To achieve this, he believed, required unity, and he did not want to alienate the bourgeoisie. He hoped that a constituent assembly could be elected as soon as possible by all Germans so that the assembly could draw up a democratic constitution. Pressed by the Left within his own party as well as by the Independent Socialist party, he agreed to a temporary Council of People's Commissars composed of three majority Socialists and three Independents. Under pressure from the Left, he also agreed to call a National Congress of Workers' and Soldiers' Councils, which the Spartacists hoped would serve as the basis for a revolutionary socialist government.

Ebert moved immediately to consolidate support for the new provisional government by launching a number of reforms. On 12 November he declared an end to martial law and the restoration of civil liberties, and he established equal, direct, universal suffrage (male and female). Three days later he negotiated agreements with industrialists that won the recognition of the independent trade unions and secured the right of collective bargaining.

When the National Congress met on 16 December, Ebert and the moderate leadership of the Majority Social Democrats were able to forestall most radical measures and win support for an elected national assembly. Another step by Ebert greatly aided his victory over the Spartacists, but had its own negative impact upon the development of German democracy. A very uncertain and beleaguered Ebert received a telephone call on the night of 9 November from the Supreme Army Command over a private line in the chancellery. An agreement was made between Ebert and General Wilhelm Groener, Ludendorff's successor: In return for Groener's promise to support him against the Left, Ebert agreed not to tamper with the authority of the officer corps. Although the support of the army proved crucial to his regime, Ebert was unable to purge it of undemocratic elements.

On 24 December Ebert called upon the army to drive the radical People's Naval Division from the Hohenzollern Palace. The Spartacists came to the aid of the revolutionary sailors, and the army temporarily withdrew. The clash led to the resignation of the Independent Socialists from the Council of People's Commissars on 29 December and emboldened Liebknecht and the Spartacists, who, in preparation for a direct challenge to Ebert, formed the Communist party of Germany.

The challenge came in January of 1919 when Liebknecht, to the dismay of Luxemburg, whom he ignored, decided on a precipitate uprising. Liebknecht, whose call was initially answered by a massive outpouring of support, provided inadequate leadership and inspiration. Ebert's support, however, was well-organized and proved decisive. Gustav Noske, an opportunistic and ambitious Social Democrat, joined the provisional government when the Independents left it. He expressed his willingness to be a "bloodhound" and supported the establishment by the army of volunteer *Freikorps* units composed of demobilized soldiers willing to fight the Spartacists. On 9 January Noske was ready to counterattack, and by 15 January the Spartacists had been crushed. Both Liebknecht and Luxemburg were taken prisoner and murdered by their captors. In all, over one thousand people lost their lives in the fighting in Berlin.

Elections for the National Assembly were held on 19 January 1919. The Social Democrats emerged as the largest party but were far from commanding a majority. Ebert surrendered his power to the new body, which then elected him president. When the Independents refused to cooperate with the "killers of Marxists," the Social Democrats, led by Scheidemann, formed a coalition with the Center and the Democrats.

Ebert had succeeded in steering Germany toward a pluralistic parliamentary democracy. The constitution drafted and proclaimed at Weimar on 14 August gave the regime its name. Unfortunately, the Weimar Republic bore the onus of Germany's defeat in the First World War, lengthening the odds against its survival.

Bernard A. Cook

References

Morgan, David W. *The Socialist Left and the German Revolution: A History of the German Independent Social Democratic Party, 1917–1922.* Ithaca: Cornell University Press, 1975.

Ryder, A.J. *The German Revolution of 1918.* Cambridge: Harvard University Press, 1968.

Waldmann, Erich. *The Spartacist Uprising and the Crisis of the German Socialist Movement.* Milwaukee, Wis.: Marquette, 1958.

Watt, Richard M. *The Kings Depart: The Tragedy of Germany at Versailles and the German Revolution.* New York: Clarion, 1968.

See also EBERT, FRIEDRICH; GROENER, WILHELM; HINDENBURG, PAUL VON; LIEBKNECHT, KARL; LUDENDORFF, ERICH; LUXEMBURG, ROSA; MAX OF BADEN, PRINCE; NOSKE, GUSTAV; SCHEIDEMANN, PHILIP; STAB-IN-THE-BACK MYTH; WILHELM II

Giolitti, Giovanni (1842–1928)

Italian politician and premier, born at Mondovi (Piedmont) on 27 October 1842. Giolitti was a master of the politics of *trasformismo* and gave his name to the prewar liberal era of Italian history, even though radicals like Gaetano Salvemini condemned him for presiding over a *ministero della mala vita* (criminal ministry). He began his career in the Italian civil service (1862–82), then served as a deputy (1882–1928), minister of the treasury (1889–90), and premier (1892–3, 1903–5, 1906–9, 1911–14, and 1920–21). Despite seizing Libya from Turkey in 1911, Giolitti opposed intervention in 1914 because Italy could avoid the costs of war and obtain *parecchio* ("something") simply by remaining neutral. Interventionists, who contended that the defeat of the Central Powers would benefit both Italy and Western civilization, saw his position as cynical, mean, and pro-Austrian. Giolitti believed, however, that Rome could benefit by remaining neutral, because he was convinced that Vienna would make major concessions to keep Italy out of the war.

Giolitti's December 1914 meeting in Rome with Bernhard von Bülow gave rise to rumors that he was selling Italy out to Germany. But like Antonio Salandra and Giorgio Sonnino, Giolitti blamed Vienna for failing to concede Rome its demands for compensation for Austro-Hungarian gains in the Balkans. Yet efforts to win the Piedmontese politician over to intervention failed, and although 300 deputies and senators deposited calling cards with him in early May as a sign of their support for his position, Salandra was able to win a vote of confidence. Soundly defeated, Giolitti left for his estates at Cavour in Piedmont, where he remained until Vittorio Orlando replaced Salandra in 1916. He then participated indirectly in government.

After the war Giolitti defended his neutralist stance, denounced war profiteers, and criticized Luigi Cadorna's vilification of his troops. But he thought that the "great misfortune" of Caporetto had unified and instilled a spirit of discipline in the country, and he supported the terms of the 1915 Treaty of London and Italian claims to Fiume. He also praised the Orlando government's conduct of the war after 1916 but implied that its performance at the peace conference was less than sterling. Although Giolitti was the shrewdest practitioner of *trasformismo*, his efforts to resurrect the prewar practice in the postwar era only facilitated the triumph of Mussolini and Fascism. He died at Cavour on 17 July 1928.

James J. Sadkovich

References

Carocci, Giampiero. *Giolitti e l'età giolittiana. La politica italiana dall'inizio del secolo alla prima guerra mondiale.* Turin: Einaudi, 1961.

Coppa, Frank J. *Planning, Protectionism and Politics in Liberal Italy.* Washington, D.C.: Catholic University of America Press, 1971.

Giolitti, Giovanni. *Memoirs of My Life.* New York: Howard Fertig, 1923. Reprint, 1973.

Salomone, Arcangelo William. *Italy in the Giolittian Era: Italian Democracy in the Making, 1900–1914.* Philadelphia: University of Pennsylvania Press, 1960.

Salvemini, Gaetano. *Il ministro della mala vita.* Milan: Feltrinelli, 1962.

See also ITALY, HOME FRONT; SALANDRA, ANTONIO

Goeben and Breslau

Two German warships, the *Goeben* and *Breslau,* changed the course of the First World War by bringing Turkey into the conflict on the side of the Central Powers.

The *Goeben* was laid down in 1909 and commissioned in 1912. One of two *Moltke*-class battle cruisers in the German navy, she displaced 22,640 tons and mounted ten 11-inch guns in five turrets. Her secondary armament consisted of twelve 5.9-inch and twelve 3.4-inch, 22-pounder guns. She also had four 19.7-inch submerged torpedo tubes. Unlike her British counterparts, she was heavily armored. *Goeben* was extremely fast, up to twenty-seven knots. The light cruiser *Breslau*, completed in 1911, displaced 4,550 tons; she was armed with ten 4.1-inch guns and was very lightly armored. She had a normal top speed of twenty-eight knots.

On the outbreak of the First World War these two ships, commanded by Rear Admiral Wilhelm Souchon, constituted the Mediterranean Division of the Imperial German Navy. The *Goeben,* however, was the most formidable warship in the entire Mediterranean. Although British and French naval units heavily outnumbered his own force, Souchon was determined to get his ships to the Dardanelles. Souchon capitalized on ineffective Allied leadership, poor coordination, overestimation of the *Goeben*'s abilities, and failure to anticipate that the Germans would steam east instead of toward the Atlantic. Despite her formidable armament and great speed, the *Goeben* had serious handicaps, including defective boilers.

The escape of the *Goeben* from her Allied pursuers remains one of the black marks in the history of the Royal Navy. The French navy, however, could have brought the two ships into action early on, but Vice Admiral Augustin

Boué de Lapeyrère disobeyed orders and insisted that his warships continue escorting convoys carrying the army of Africa to France. The British, who had responsibility for the eastern Mediterranean, absorbed the blame. Rear Admiral Sir Ernest Troubridge was made the scapegoat (his superior, Admiral Sir A. Berkeley Milne, was let off because his own shortcomings were also those of the admiralty). Troubridge was later court-martialed for failing to close with his light cruiser squadron. He judged such an action suicidal against the longer-range guns and greater speed of the *Goeben*. The court agreed and acquitted him.

The arrival of the *Goeben* and *Breslau* at Constantinople helped those Turks wishing to take their country into the war on the German side. Turkey had a secret alliance with Germany, but the cabinet had delayed putting it into effect. The Turkish leadership was in fact sharply divided, and a majority favored continued neutrality.

Without Berlin's concurrence Souchon arranged to "sell" both warships to Turkey as replacements for two Turkish dreadnoughts sequestered by Britain (*Goeben* was known in Turkish service as the *Sultan Yavuz Selim*, the *Breslau* as *Midilli*). Although the Turkish government renewed its declaration of armed neutrality, the two warships retained their German crews, and on 15 August Souchon became commander in chief of the Turkish navy, while at the same time retaining his position in the German navy.

With the secret support of Turkish Minister of War Enver Pasha (the leading supporter of the German alliance), Souchon used his warships to bring about war between Russia and Turkey. On 29 October 1914 he carried out a bombardment of Russian bases, under the guise of training exercises in the Black Sea. The Turkish cabinet was not informed in advance, and Souchon even reported that the Russians had attacked him first, an outright lie.

The result was a new theater of war in the Middle East. Russia declared war on Turkey on 2 November 1914. The next day, British ships off the Dardanelles shelled Turkish forts; when this failed to bring about a change in Turkish policy, Britain and France declared war on Turkey on 5 November. Having Turkey as an active military opponent forced Russia to divert resources from the fight against Germany and Austria-Hungary. Her southern (and most accessible) supply route for Western war materi-

als was cut off, as was the export of Russian grain to the West. These burdens added to Russia's internal difficulties and helped bring about the Bolshevik revolution three years later.

During the rest of the war the *Goeben* and *Breslau* made numerous forays into the Black Sea. On 17 November 1914, accompanied by a Turkish cruiser and some destroyers, both warships were involved in an inconclusive battle with five Russian battleships. The *Goeben* took a 12-inch shell in her third casemate, which blew one of her 5.9-inch guns into the sea. Quick action in flooding a magazine probably saved the ship. On 21 December 1914 she was badly holed when she struck two Russian mines at the approach to the Bosphorus. She was still undergoing repairs and unable to intervene in the British/French attack on the Dardanelles in February of 1915, although some of her smaller guns were removed for land service to resist the Allied landings at Gallipoli. On 9 May 1915 the Russians laid a trap for the *Goeben*, and she came up against seventeen Russian ships, including five battleships. She took two direct hits from 12-inch shells but damaged three of the five Russian battleships, as well as a submarine. Her great speed enabled her to escape. In July of 1915 the *Breslau* was holed by a mine while returning from patrol. In 1916 both warships had close brushes with two new Russian dreadnoughts, *Imperatriza Maria* and *Ekaterina II*.

The *Goeben* and *Breslau* made a final sally into the Mediterranean on 20 January 1918, when they fought the Battle of Imbros off the entrance to the Dardanelles. The *Goeben* struck a mine and sustained minor damage, but the *Breslau* sank two British monitors, *Raglan* and *M28*. Subsequently engaged with two British destroyers, *Breslau* struck two mines and sank. Although she hit another mine trying to come to the rescue of the *Breslau*, the *Goeben* survived; she soon grounded, however, and was in desperate straits. Sufficient British naval assets were available to destroy the *Goeben*, but poor command decisions prevented their utilization. British aircraft carried out 250 sorties against the German battle cruiser, but most of their bombs missed and, in any case, were too light. The Germans and Turks finally towed the *Goeben* free on the 26th. She arrived at Constantinople the next day and never again fired a shot in anger.

The major role played by these two German ships in World War I was to keep in check Russian naval units in the Black Sea. That was especially true during the 1915 Allied attack on the Dardanelles, when the Russian navy might otherwise have moved from the East to support their Western Allies.

At the end of the war the Turkish government refused to hand over the battle cruiser, and she was allowed to rust until being rebuilt in 1927–30. Renamed the *Yavuz*, the *Goeben* reemerged as flagship of the Turkish navy and was not retired until 1950. She became a museum and was finally scrapped in 1976.

Spencer C. Tucker

References

McLaughlin, Redmond. *The Escape of the Goeben*. London: Seeley Service, 1974.

Milne, Admiral Sir A. Berekely. *Flight of the Goeben and Breslau*. London: Eveleigh Nash, 1921.

Van Der Vat, Dan. *The Ship that Changed the World. The Escape of the Goeben to the Dardanelles in 1914*. New York: Adler and Adler, 1986.

See also BLACK SEA, NAVAL WAR IN; BOUÉ DE LAPEYRÈRE, AUGUSTIN; MILNE, A. BERKELEY; SOUCHON, WILHELM; TROUBRIDGE, ERNEST

Goltz, Colmar Freiherr von der (1843–1916)

Prussian and Ottoman field marshal. Born on 12 August 1843 at Labiau, East Prussia, Goltz belonged to an impoverished branch of an old Brandenburg family. He joined the Prussian army in 1861 and participated in the Wars of German Unification. A man of high intelligence, Goltz spent much of his subsequent career in staff or teaching posts and became a military advisor in the Ottoman Empire in 1883. Upon his return to Germany in 1895, he rapidly rose into the top echelons of the Prussian army, becoming a corps commander (at Königsberg) in 1902 and an army inspector general in 1908.

Widely known for his close ties with the Ottoman army and as the author of several major works on military matters, Goltz was promoted to field marshal in 1911. Two years later, on the eve of his seventieth birthday, he was placed on the standby list.

When the Great War began, Goltz was eager to get a major field command, but he eventually had to be satisfied with becoming the governor-general of occupied Belgium (23 August 1914). Dissatisfied with his job (and criticized by some as "too soft"), the elderly field marshal welcomed his transfer to Constantinople in December as a senior advisor to the Ottoman High Command. Frequent friction with the head of the German military mission in Turkey and with General Otto Liman von Sanders, as well as other problems, marred his stay in the Ottoman capital. In the fall of 1915 he eagerly accepted his transfer to the Persian-Mesopotamian theater of war. As commander of the Ottoman Sixth Army, Goltz succeeded in halting the British advance toward Baghdad. He died of spotted fever on 19 April 1916, ten days before the Turks received the surrender of General Charles Townshend's Anglo-Indian division at Kut-el-Amara. The field marshal's remains were buried in Constantinople.

Ulrich Trumpener

References

Goltz, Generalfeldmarschall Colmar Freiherr von der. *Denkwürdigkeiten*. Edited by Friedrich Freiherr von der Goltz and Wolfgang Foerster. Berlin: E.S. Mittler und Sohn, 1929.

Teske, Hermann. *Colmar Freiherr von der Goltz: Ein Kämpfer für den militärischen Fortschritt*. Gottingen: Musterschmidt, 1957.

Trumpener, Ulrich. *Germany and the Ottoman Empire, 1914–1918*. Princeton: Princeton University Press, 1968.

Wallach, Jehuda L. *Anatomie einer Militärhilfe: Die preussisch-deutschen Militärmissionen in der Türkei 1835–1919*. Dusseldorf: Droste, 1976.

Wende, Frank. *Die belgische Frage in der deutschen Politik des Ersten Weltkrieges*. Hamburg: Bohme, 1969.

See also BELGIUM, OCCUPATION OF; LIMAN VON SANDERS, OTTO; MESOPOTAMIA

Goltz, Rüdiger Count von der (1865–1946)

Prussian general, born on 8 December 1865 at Züllichau in Brandenburg. Goltz joined the Prussian army in 1885. He attended the

Kriegsakademie in the 1890s and eventually rose to command an infantry regiment (March of 1914).

Wounded during the battle of the Marne, Goltz was made a brigade commander in November of 1914, serving thereafter both on the Russian and Western fronts. Promoted to major general in August of 1916, he was, the following summer, entrusted with the 37th Infantry Division, which was deployed in the Chemin des Dames sector. On 28 February 1918 he became commander of the 12th Landwehr Division (the "Baltic Division").

In response to requests by Finnish nationalists, the German High Command decided to send German assistance to Finland and dispatched Goltz's division to Finland. Landing at Hangö early in April of 1918, the division advanced toward Helsinki against Russian and Finnish Bolshevik resistance. After seizing control of the city (13 April), the German troops moved north, and, in cooperation with General Baron Carl Gustav Mannerheim's White Guards, eventually surrounded the bulk of the Red Army, which surrendered on 2 May.

Goltz and some of his troops remained in Finland until December of 1918. Two months later, he was appointed commander of the German VI Reserve Corps and Governor of Libau (Lipaja) in Courland. Originally acting with tacit Allied approval, the general organized a force of German volunteers and some local groups to expel the Bolsheviks from the Baltic region, but during the ensuing seven months the political situation in that region became increasingly complex and Goltz was eventually ordered home by the German government.

Discharged from the army, Goltz became deeply involved in right-wing politics and from 1924 on served as president of the United Patriotic Associations of the Reich. He died at Kinsegg in Bavaria on 4 November 1946.

Ulrich Trumpener

References
Goltz, Rüdiger Graf von der. *Meine Sendung in Finnland und im Baltikum.* Leipzig: Koehler, 1920.
Maller, Hanns. *Geschichte der Ritter des Ordens "pour le mérite" im Weltkrieg.* 2 vols. Berlin: Bernard & Graefe, 1935.
Smith, C. Jay. *Finland and the Russian Revolution, 1917–1922.* Athens: University of Georgia Press, 1958.

Vogelsand, Thilo. "Rüdiger Graf von der Goltz." *Neue Deutsche Biographie 6* (1964).
Volkmann, Erich Otto. *Revolution über Deutschland.* Oldenburg: Stalling, 1930.

See also FINLAND, ROLE IN WAR; MANNERHEIM, CARL

Goremykin, Ivan (1839–1917)

Russian politician and prime minister. Born on 27 October 1839 in Novgorod province into a noble family, Goremykin held a string of important government positions. A complacent and unenlightened bureaucrat, Goremykin was typical of the advisers with whom the czar surrounded himself in the last years of the Russian Empire. Appointed prime minister at age seventy-four in January of 1914, Goremykin came to symbolize the incapacity of the czarist regime to deal with the political complexities caused by the outbreak of the First World War.

As prime minister, the aged monarchist failed to utilize the national enthusiasm that followed the declaration of war. Instead of rallying Russians into the war effort, he chose instead to rely on exclusively bureaucratic means to mobilize the resources of the nation. He ignored the public and the Duma. The disastrous military defeats of 1915 revealed the bankruptcy of his policy. The public held Goremykin and his inefficient, corrupt government responsible for both the supply crisis and the shocking conditions under which Russia's troops were compelled to fight. In that crisis the Duma called for Goremykin's dismissal and the creation of a government of public confidence.

In August of 1915 Czar Nicholas II responded to the crisis by assuming personal command of Russia's forces, a disastrous decision that Goremykin alone of all the czar's ministers supported. Thereafter, Russia's government remained in Goremykin's hands—with the full support of the Empress Alexandra and Rasputin—until January of 1916 when, with considerable personal regret, the czar replaced the now clearly senile Goremykin. He died shortly thereafter, on 11 December 1917, in the Caucasus.

Sylvia Russell

References
Lincoln, Bruce. *Passage Through Armageddon. The Russians in War and Revolu-*

tion 1914–1918. New York: Simon and Schuster, 1987.

Pares, Bernard. *Russia between Revolution and Reform.* New York: Schocken, 1962.

Pipes, Richard. *The Russian Revolution.* New York: Knopf, 1990.

See also RUSSIA, HOME FRONT AND REVOLUTIONS OF 1917

Göring, Hermann Wilhelm (1893–1946)

German army officer, born 12 January 1893 in Rosenheim, Bavaria. Göring, the son of a judge, gained fame in World War I as an air ace and last commander of the Richthofen Fighter Squadron. Having attended the military academy at Gross Lichterfelde, Göring joined the army in 1912 as an infantry lieutenant. In 1915 he requested and received a transfer to the air force as a combat pilot. Shot down and severely wounded, he returned to combat in 1916. He notched twenty-two kills and received the Iron Cross (First Class), as well as the *Pour le Mérite* (2 June 1918). In July of 1918 Göring became commander of the Richthofen Squadron and led it until the end of the war.

After the war Göring moved to Scandinavia, where he became a show flier and married a Swedish baroness. Upon returning to Germany in 1922 he became a prize recruit for the Nazi party, which seized upon his background as a hero and aristocrat and made him commander of the SA Brownshirts. Seriously wounded during the Beer Hall Putsch of 1923, Göring fled Germany for four years, during which period he became addicted to morphine. He returned in 1927, rejoined the Nazis, and was one of the party's first representatives elected to the Reichstag in 1928. Göring's contacts throughout German society were his biggest contributions to the rise of Nazism, and he led the 1932 electoral triumph that bought him the presidency of the Reichstag. Once Hitler was made chancellor, Göring garnered numerous titles and positions, including those of *Reichsminister* for Air and *Reichsmarschall.* He amassed a fortune through the giant industrial conglomerate named for him. Popular with the German people in the early years because of his accessibility, he grew satiated and lethargic and his popularity plummeted. He was stripped of his posts when he sought to take control of Germany before Hitler's death. Captured by the Americans in May of 1945 and tried at Nuremburg, Göring committed suicide on 15 October 1946, two hours before his scheduled execution.

Laura Matysek Wood

References
Frischauer, Willi. *Goering.* London: Oldhams, 1951.
Manvell, Roger. *Herman Goering.* London: Heinemann, 1962.
Mosley, Leonard. *The Reich Marshal: A Biography of Herman Goering.* Garden City, N.Y.: Doubleday, 1974.

Gough, Sir Hubert (1870–1963)

British general, born on 12 August 1870 of a prominent Irish military family. An ancestor, Field Marshal Hugh Gough (1779–1869), had conquered the Punjab; his father, uncle, brother, and a cousin were all VCs. Gough was educated at Eton and Sandhurst and commissioned into the 16th Lancers in 1889. Gough's first taste of action came in the Tirah campaign of 1897–98. In the Boer War he proved a successful commander of mounted troops in antiguerrilla operations before being severely wounded and returned to Britain. After the war he served as professor at the Staff College, Camberley, and as commander of the 16th Lancers.

In 1914 Gough played a prominent part in the "Curragh Incident" as commander of the 3rd Cavalry Brigade in Dublin. He and fifty-seven of his officers threatened to resign if ordered to use force to impose Irish home rule on the Protestants of Ulster, effectively forcing the government to back down. Later that year, in the First World War, he commanded the same brigade in the retreat to Mons and the Marne. Although Gough's aggressive nature was not well suited to trench warfare, rapid promotion followed. He commanded successively 2nd Cavalry Division at First Ypres and Messines Ridge, 7th Infantry Division at Festubert, and I Corps at Loos. In the Battle of the Somme in 1916 he commanded the new Fifth Army, for which he was knighted.

In July of 1917 Gough led the opening phase of the ill-fated Passchendaele Campaign but, because of high casualties, command was shifted to General Herbert Plumer. After this campaign, Haig sent Gough to take over forty miles of front from the French army. The defenses were in a poor state, divisions were too thin on the ground, and there were virtually no reserves. Gough warned Haig of the dangers, but at that stage of the war few reinforcements could be found. On 21 March 1918 the Germans fell on Gough's weak army and achieved a breakthrough, despite a series of valiant British rearguard actions. Some French help arrived, but slowly and often without artillery. Gough was held responsible for the disaster and after a week was removed from command. Some figures will help to put his performance into perspective. Gough's fourteen divisions were attacked by about forty German divisions, and each of his divisions held an average of 6,750 yards of front; the comparable figure for Byng's adjacent Third Army was 4,700.

Gough's last job before his retirement with the rank of general in 1922 was as chief of the military mission to the Baltic. He was recalled on the grounds that his views were too radical for this politically sensitive post. He and many others felt that he had been made a scapegoat in 1918 for the failings of his superiors. His book, *Fifth Army,* published in 1931, put his case before the public and defended the reputation of his men. The award of Knight Grand Cross, Order of the Bath (GCB) in 1937 was widely seen as belated recompense for his treatment.

He was a director of Siemens Brothers between the wars. Despite his age, Gough served until 1942 as a colonel in the Home Guard in the Second World War. Gough died in London on 18 March 1963.

Philip J. Green

References

Gough, Sir Hubert. *Fifth Army.* London: Cassell, 1931.
Terraine, John. *The Western Front.* London: Hutchinson, 1964.

See also LUDENDORFF OFFENSIVES; PASSCHENDAELE CAMPAIGN; SOMME, BATTLE OF

Gouraud, Henri Joseph Eugène (1867–1946)

French general, born in Paris on 17 November 1867, known as the "Lion of Champagne" for his role in stopping the Germans in the Second Battle of the Marne. Gouraud entered St. Cyr in 1888 and was commissioned in the infantry two years later. Prior to World War I he spent virtually his entire service overseas and won military distinction in Morocco. He was promoted to brigadier general just before the war and major general in 1915. In May of 1915 he replaced the lackluster General d'Amade as commander of French forces at Gallipoli, where he performed credibly and lost an arm to a shell.

In December of 1915 Gouraud returned to active duty as commander of the Fourth French Army in Champagne, but, when Marshal Lyautey became minister of war in December of 1916, Gouraud took his place in Morocco as resident general. In July of 1917 he was back in France to command Fourth Army.

Gouraud's army held about fifty miles of the front line in Champagne. Gouraud was convinced that the Germans would attack in his sector, because once they had conquered the hills they would have rolling terrain that offered little opportunity to the defenders. The Germans could then press on to Chalons, split the French lines, and win the war. Under these circumstances Gouraud issued his famous "stand or die" order to French and American troops in his command. Gouraud also implemented Pétain's new plan of defense in depth, although it apparently took some time to persuade him to do so. To Gouraud, any retreat was a personal stain on his honor.

On the night of 14 July a trench raid netted German prisoners who revealed the timing of the German attack—an artillery barrage beginning at 22:00 on the next night with the infantry assault at 04:00 on the 16th. Gouraud ordered counterbattery fire fifteen minutes before the German guns opened, and this fire badly smashed German artillery and decimated assembly areas.

Perhaps the most critical battle of the Ludendorff Offensives was the attack on Reims, directed at the French Fourth and Fifth armies on either side of the city. As a result of only light garrisoning of the front trenches, the German artillery barrage fell on nearly empty space; their infantry attack was defeated on the second positions. Gouraud's successful defensive operation here allowed some of his resources to be shifted to Fifth Army, which had been forced back. These reserves and American troops halted the German drive on the other side of Reims.

On 26 September 1918, Fourth Army went on the offensive in cooperation with the U.S. First Army. Two American divisions were a part of Gouraud's forces. While the first days of the offensive gained only limited ground, it did help to destroy German morale. On 1 November Fourth Army and the U.S. First Army returned to the offensive, and by 11 November they had pushed the Germans back to the Meuse River. On the eve of the Armistice Gouraud's forces had the honor of retaking Sedan, scene of the catastrophic French defeat of 1870.

After the Armistice, Gouraud remained at Strasbourg as military governor. In October of 1919 he became high commissioner of Syria and commander in chief in the Levant from 1919 to 1923. He later served as governor of Paris and member of the Supreme Allied War Council (1923–37). Gouraud was one of the best known French military figures in the United States, because so many American troops had served under his command. He died in Paris on 16 September 1946.

Spencer C. Tucker

References

Cruttwell, C.R.M.F. *A History of the Great War, 1914–1918*. Chicago: Academy Publishers, 1934. Reprint, 1991.

Moorehead, Alan. *Gallipoli*. New York: Harper and Row, 1956.

Pitt, Barrie. *1918—The Last Act*. London: Cassell, 1962.

Porch, Douglas. *The Conquest of Morocco*. New York: Alfred A. Knopf, 1983.

Ryan, Stephen. *Pétain the Soldier*. New York: A.S. Barnes, 1969.

See also ALLIED COUNTEROFFENSIVE, 1918; GALLIPOLI CAMPAIGN; LUDENDORFF OFFENSIVES

Grandmaison, Louis Loyzeau de (1861–1915)

French general and military theorist, born at Le Mans, Sarthe (Poitou) on 21 January 1861. Grandmaison joined the army in 1881 and was commissioned two years later. He saw extensive service both in France and her new colonial empire, but is best known for his association with the French school of offensive warfare. While serving on the French army general staff as director of military operations (1908–14), Grandmaison articulated the doctrine of the resolute offensive; this rested on the foundation of "élan," culminating in an emotional, determined response to any invader. That would ensure retention of the initiative in a future war against Germany. The concept of the "*offensive à outrance*" was incorporated into French War Plan XVII, approved in May of 1913, and in the Regulations for the Conduct of Major Formations of October of 1913.

Grandmaison thought that it was more important to develop a conquering state of mind than to argue over tactical details. He stressed aggressiveness on the battlefield by continual advancement toward the enemy, thus throwing him off balance and disrupting his plans. In the revised infantry regulations of 1913, Grandmaison wrote that the French army, "returning to its traditions, recognizes no law save that of the offensive." Referring to advancing under fire, Grandmaison wrote, "We have to train ourselves to do it and train others, cultivating with passion everything that bears the stamp of offensive spirit. We must take it to excess, perhaps even that will not go far enough." Such ideas won wide acceptance in France before World War I.

Grandmaison's ideas are contained in two published works: *Dressage de l'infanterie en vue de l'offensive* (1906) and *Deux conférences faites aux officiers de l'état-major de l'armée* (1911). Grandmaison was promoted to major general in January of 1915 and died of wounds received in combat at Soissons on 19 February 1915 while commanding the Fifth Army Group of reserve divisions.

Donald F. Bittner

References

Carver, Field Marshal Lord (Michael). *Twentieth Century Warriors: The Development of the Armed Forces of the Major Military Nations of the Twentieth Century*. New York: Weidenfeld & Nicolson, 1987.

France. Extract, Official Service Record, Général de Division Loyzeau de Grandmaison (François Jules Louis).

Griffith, Paddy. *Forward into Battle: Fighting Tactics from Waterloo to the Near Future*. Novato, Calif.: Presidio, 1991.

Howard, Sir Michael. "Men against Fire: The Doctrine of the Offensive in 1914." In *Makers of Modern Strategy from Machiavelli to the Nuclear Age*, edited by Peter Paret. Princeton: Princeton University Press, 1986.

Porch, Douglas "Bugeaud, Gallieni, Lyautey: The Development of French Colonial Warfare." In *Makers of Modern Strategy from Machiavelli to the Nuclear Age*,

G

edited by Peter Paret. Princeton: Princeton University Press, 1986.

———. *The March to the Marne: The French Army, 1871–1914.* Cambridge: Cambridge University Press, 1981.

See also FRENCH WAR PLAN XVII

Great Britain, Army

Great Britain fought World War I with two very different armies—her small Regular Army, which bore the brunt in the early months of the war, and the enormous citizen army she placed in the field from 1915 onwards. The former was 250,000 strong, the latter almost four million at its peak early in 1918 (from a population of forty-eight million).

In 1914 Great Britain was the center of the greatest maritime empire the world had ever seen. Her traditional defense policy rested on maintaining the largest navy in the world, with a small Regular Army designed mainly for imperial expeditions and a part-time militia (rechristened the Territorial Army in 1907 as part of the Haldane reforms) for home defense.

The key feature of the Regular Army was its regimental system, particularly in the infantry and cavalry. In the cavalry a regiment denoted a lieutenant colonel's command. In the infantry a battalion was the equivalent, and the word "regiment" denoted a recruiting and training organization without any tactical significance. These infantry regiments were based in a particular region (usually a county) with a permanent regimental depot near the main town of the area. They manned two regular and one or more territorial (that is, part-time) battalions. Of the two regular battalions, one would be full-strength and stationed overseas; the other would be under-strength, composed mainly of men below twenty years of age, and stationed at home. To provide a professional element, regulars held some key officer and senior NCO appointments in territorial battalions.

Most soldiers enlisted for nine years of regular duty, with an additional three in the reserves. Soldiering did not stand high in public esteem (in 1914 the army was 6 percent below established strength), and John Bull thought that his army was best kept out of the public eye looking after the empire. Officers tended to come from landed, professional, or church families—very few from commercial

backgrounds—and were noted more for their courage and integrity than their intellect.

This army had fought no fewer than sixty-four colonial campaigns during Queen Victoria's reign, but only in the Crimean and Boer wars had it faced a sophisticated enemy. It was essentially designed for defense of the overseas empire. Although a European war was becoming ever more likely, the Committee of Imperial Defense had decided, as recently as 1906, that this was only one of four contingencies to be prepared for—the others being a Russian attack on India, another Boer rebellion, and an American invasion of Canada. As a result of lessons learned at the hands of the Boers, great reforms in training, tactics, organization, and improvements in equipment were made in the decade before 1914. At the regimental and individual level this was among the most professional armies in the world; its particular strengths were skill-at-arms, endurance, discipline, esprit de corps, and the leadership of its junior officers.

In August of 1914, 12 of its 31 cavalry regiments and 74 of its 157 infantry battalions were overseas. Nonetheless, by 22 August a British Expeditionary Force (BEF) of 100,000 men, including many reservists recalled to the colors, was in France. The BEF was organized into one cavalry and four infantry divisions and was joined on 29 August by two more infantry divisions. In the opinion of many historians, it was the finest military force ever sent abroad by Great Britain. Small in relation to the armies of the French and Germans (each with more than 1.5 million men), this professional force played a part out of all proportion to its size on the northern flank of the Allied line, first in its fighting retreat from Mons, then on the Marne, and finally at First Ypres, where it established positions never to be lost for the rest of the War.

Interestingly, twenty-seven of the regiments that fought so well at First Ypres bore the battle honor "Inkerman" for their heroism under similar circumstances against the Russians sixty years earlier almost to the day—a testament to the value of regimental tradition in a tight corner. It is alleged that Kaiser Wilhelm II ordered Chief of the General Staff Helmuth von Moltke "to sweep this contemptible little army out of his path." Whether he said that or not, it has passed into British history as a fact, and to their dying day the regular soldiers who had fought with the BEF were proud to call themselves Old

Contemptibles, to distinguish themselves from other veterans.

By the end of 1914 this splendid army had virtually ceased to exist—90 percent were casualties, and those who survived were needed to train the mass citizen army being raised. Clearly, the war was not going to be over by Christmas as the optimists had believed, and Britain was now involved in a large-scale continental conflict. After some deliberation, the government decided on an army of seventy divisions; it is not clear whether that target was based on an estimate of available manpower or an analysis of the need. Two methods of achieving this expansion were not open in 1914. The Territorial Army had no legal obligation to serve overseas, and that would apply equally to new recruits or units. Conscription, the standard method of raising armies in Europe, was regarded as unconstitutional in Great Britain. Although the National Service League had been stressing the need for compulsory service since 1902, it was not needed until 1916.

The number of men who volunteered is an outstanding feature of the British army in World War I. Of the total of 5.7 million who served in the army, no fewer than 2.5 million did so voluntarily. The number that had volunteered by the end of 1915 was greater than that conscripted in 1916 and 1917. In the first month alone, a staggering 463,000 came forward "to take the King's shilling." Neither the government nor the army had any contingency plans for such an expansion, and initially much of the recruiting effort fell to committees of civilians at the local level—even to the extent of clothing, housing, and feeding the new units and selecting officers. The 142 battalions formed in this way usually adopted local titles and are known generically as "Pals Battalions." When they were taken over by the war office in 1915, the committees had their expenditures refunded.

Despite the seeming lack of organization, by 1917 the army had achieved its target of seventy divisions: By mid-1915 its strength had reached 2 million (1,400 battalions); by mid-1916, 3 million (1,500 battalions); and by early 1918, about 4 million. A subsequent slight decline occurred mainly because of the transfer of the Royal Flying Corps (RFC) to form the new Royal Air Force. At the end of the war the British army was seven and a half times its 1914 size (regular and TA combined), but because of the nature of the fighting, not every part of the service had increased at the same rate. Of the main fighting arms, cavalry, infantry, artillery, and engineers had grown by ratios of 1.6, 5.5, 6.1, and 14.9 to 1, respectively (the infantry to a massive 1,648,000 men). The increases of 22.5 to 1 (Service Corps) and 54 to 1 (Veterinary Corps) reflect the importance of transport and logistical support, as does the formation of a new Labour Corps of 390,000. The impact of new technology is seen in the size of three new corps: RFC (formed just before war), 144,000; Machine Gun Corps (formed 1915), 130,000; and Tank Corps (formed 1916), 28,000. Surprisingly, in view of the enormous casualties, the Medical Corps grew by only 7.8 to 1. For the first time women served in the British army other than as nurses—by November of 1918 the Women's Auxiliary Army Corps numbered 41,000, 10,000 of them overseas.

Field Marshal Earl Horatio Kitchener presided over this enormous and unprecedented expansion. A professional soldier who was appointed secretary of state for war in August of 1914, Kitchener remained in that position until he was lost in 1916 when the warship taking him on a mission to Russia struck a mine and sank. Although he probably knew more about Egypt and India than his own country, Kitchener was a hero to the British people, and his appointment was extremely popular. The psychological impact of having this great imperial hero at the helm (he had been commander in chief in Egypt, South Africa, and India) undoubtedly provided a great boost to voluntary recruitment, and the great citizen army he created is often referred to as Kitchener's Army.

With the realization that Britain was up against a dedicated and efficient enemy, the old prewar concept of the soldier as a ne'er do well was quickly replaced. Soldiers were now seen as heroes, and there was thus no longer any reason why men of any social class should not consider enlisting. In 1914 British society possessed a sturdy self-confidence, and the vast majority of its citizens were motivated by duty and patriotism. As one infantry officer wrote in his war memoirs: "If any soldier had delivered a speech on love of country, or the justice of our cause, consternation would have reigned among his comrades. These were matters that were taken for granted." He added that most men found soldiering a disagreeable job, but one that had to be done and that they took seriously. The combination of this national mood and the

G

appeal of a great imperial hero encouraged many men to volunteer.

Napoleon once opined that there were no good or bad regiments, only good or bad officers, and that was as true in 1914 as a hundred years before. One of the greatest problems Kitchener faced was how to select and train the officers and NCOs who would lead this great mass of willing but unmilitary citizens. Approximately 30,000 new officers were needed, in addition to replacements for battle casualties. Kitchener had recognized the problem early on and had taken prompt steps as early as August of 1914. He ordered all battalions leaving for France with the BEF to leave behind three officers and some NCOs. Finding that there were 500 officers of the Indian army on home leave, he kept them in Britain.

Even as new officers were trained there was a constant dilemma, particularly acute in the early part of the war: should they be sent to France to replace casualties, or kept at home to train the new units? There was no easy answer, for they were needed in both places at once. Rapid expansion brought a problem at higher levels of command, too. The pre-1914 British army was a collection of superb regiments but had very few officers trained in command and staff work at brigade and higher levels. Yet, as the army increased from eight to seventy divisions in three years, officers for these posts had to be found. The only solution was to pick the best available and weed out those who failed. If the standards of British generalship in 1914–18 are sometimes criticized, that factor should be borne in mind.

Local committees that raised the Pals battalions chose their officers from prominent local families or from men with military experience, subject to formal endorsement by the war office. This system generally worked well. Finding officers for other new units, especially battalion and company commanders, proved more difficult. Recourse was usually to retired officers (known colloquially as "dugouts"). Some were excellent and despite their age performed admirably. Inevitably, some were unfit and out of date in training and tactics.

Obtaining new subalterns was relatively easy, given the patriotic zeal of middle- and upper-class men of that generation. Most had received rudimentary military training in the officer training corps at private schools and universities, and by March of 1915 that source had produced 21,000 new officers, which helped maintain the traditional class composition of the officer corps.

For the first year of the war, these new officers had to learn on the job in order to keep one step ahead of the men they were training and were to lead into battle. In mid-1915, Young Officer companies were established to provide training, and in February of 1916 this system was regularized by the formation of Officer Cadet battalions; henceforth, commissions were granted only to those who successfully completed a four-month course.

NCOs for new units were eventually promoted from their own ranks, but this was obviously not possible in the early days. "Dugout" regular NCOs were used with mixed success. NCOs who had served with the old Regular Army, whose recruits were usually of low education, often found it hard to adjust to the intelligence of the citizen soldiers of Kitchener's Army.

Britain's World War I army was eventually the largest military force she ever fielded. Of its seventy divisions, sixty served in France grouped into five armies under the command of Field Marshal Sir Douglas Haig. The army also fought in Italy, Salonika, Gallipoli, Palestine, East and South West Africa, and Mesopotamia (now Iraq), and continued to garrison the empire. The contribution of dominion and Indian troops must be acknowledged. Australian, Canadian, Indian, New Zealand, and South African divisions served in France and other campaigns with courage and distinction, although their contribution is often hidden by the all-embracing use of "British" when "British Empire" is meant.

The infantry, relying heavily on the artillery and engineers for support, bore the brunt of the fighting. Outside the Middle East, the cavalry played only a small role, and by the end of the war was being replaced by tanks. A standard British division consisted of three brigades, each of four battalions (reduced to three in January of 1918). A battalion comprised 33 officers and 883 men, with each of its four companies having 6 officers and 191 men, split further into four platoons of an officer and 44 men. When a battalion went into battle, it left a cadre of 108 senior NCOs and specialists behind, around which the unit could reform if casualties were high. The weapons of a battalion were simple by today's standards: the Lewis Gun (a LMG), Lee Enfield rifle and bayonet, Mills Bombs, and a primitive mortar.

In 1915, all machine guns were concentrated into a Machine Gun Corps. By 1918 this corps had fifty-seven battalions in France, each of four companies of sixteen weapons. In the artillery, each division had three "brigades" (regiments or battalions in other armies' terminology) of sixteen 18-pounders and one of sixteen 4.5-inch howitzers. In addition to these divisional weapons the Royal Artillery deployed a mass of medium and heavy pieces, ranging in caliber from 6- to 15-inch. A feature of the artillery was the development of massed fires from many batteries; though technically feasible, these great barrages were to prove tactically cumbersome and inflexible until the introduction of reliable radios in the Second World War.

The British army, composed almost entirely of men with little or no military experience and even less wish to be soldiers, fought the highly professional German army from the first to the last day of the war (only the British fought the Germans from the beginning to end of both world wars). After enduring appalling casualties at such battles as the Somme (and Passchendaele), its breakout and advance in August of 1918 represents one of the greatest feats of British arms. The endurance, courage, sense of duty, and ability to learn the soldiers' trade is a remarkable testament to the character of that generation of the British nation. In its ranks served men who were to be famous as political or military men in a later conflict—Churchill, Attlee, Macmillan, Eden, Alexander, Slim, Montgomery, to name but a few. In addition, hundreds of thousands of ordinary Britons, whose names are remembered only on parish war memorials, served; half of them were volunteers.

Philip J. Green

References

Chandler, David G. *Great Battles of the British Army*. London: Arms & Armour, 1991.

MacDonald, Lyn. *1914—1918, Voices and Images of the Great War*. London: Penguin, 1988.

Myatt, Frederick. *The British Infantry 1660–1945, The Evolution of a Fighting Force*. London: Blandford, 1983.

Perry, Frederick W. *The Commonwealth Armies: Manpower and Organization in Two World Wars*. Manchester: Manchester University Press, 1988.

Simkins, Peter. *Kitchener's Army: The Raising of the New Armies, 1914–16*. New York: St. Martin's, 1988.

See also GREAT BRITAIN, HOME FRONT; KITCHENER, HORATIO

Great Britain, Home Front

In terms of significant domestic developments, the Great War in Britain was a true twentieth-century watershed. The war began with great enthusiasm and a "business as usual" approach; it later reached stages characterized by bitter disillusionment, despair, and a degree of state intervention and control unimaginable in the prewar era. In a war of unprecedented battlefield casualties, the home front was shaken by conditions and events that blurred class distinctions, challenged sacred economic principles, and thrust women into roles previously reserved for men. With the passage of time, the scene at home indeed resembled a topsy-turvy world.

Britain's problems on the home front were common to any wartime situation: producing enough soldiers and military supplies while maintaining high morale and adequate living conditions. In the words of A.J.P. Taylor, life after August 1914 initially "rolled on almost unaffected. There was plenty of food, and, indeed, of everything else. Statesmen still appeared in top hats. Businessmen rarely lapsed into bowlers." Men flocked to enlistment centers to fill "Kitchener's armies" in such large numbers that the war office worried about its capacity to clothe and train them. Patriotism ran at such a fever pitch that able-bodied men walking the streets of English towns ran the risk of having the infamous white feather thrust upon them, a symbol of cowardice for not having joined up. Factory men working to produce the materials for war were given special badges to wear to justify their being at home, but the gesture met with limited success in the jingoistic atmosphere; pacifists and internationalists were even more at risk of public condemnation. Conscription finally arrived in the spring of 1916, but only after heated debate within Asquith's coalition government. Forcing men into the army proved a grim necessity to fight a war of attrition that dragged on at the Western Front and eventually brought six million British soldiers to arms.

For a country wedded to the principles of laissez-faire, the shift to a controlled economy was difficult. The term that best symbolized this shift was D.O.R.A. (Defense of the Realm Act), an August 1914 statute whose provisions were periodically amended and expanded as the government's need to manage the economy grew. In time came price controls, the regulation of imports and exports, subsidies for agricultural production, food rationing, and the directing of the labor supply to specific wartime industries. So too came an accelerated and directed effort for progress in science and technology. The shortage of shells in 1915 did more than anything to further state intervention in the economy; it also led to David Lloyd George's taking over a new government department, the ministry of munitions.

For the most part the spirit of cooperation prevailed in labor-management relations, although trade union leaders looked with wary suspicion on wartime profiteering. Labor unrest was spotty throughout the country, with noted worker discontent existing around Glasgow and "Red Clydeside." Union leaders also expressed concern about the dilution of labor caused by the rapid introduction of women into the workforce to replace men departed for military service and to fill the need for administrative assistance in the expanding bureaucracy. For most Englishmen, seeing women working as secretaries was fairly easy to accept; recognizing them in engineering works and as tram operators was far more disturbing. These new roles for women led directly to a decline in the number of domestic servants, as well as to the success in 1918 of the suffragette campaign—votes for women finally came to those age thirty and over.

The effort to sustain high morale at home had many manifestations. Zeppelin raids and airplane bombings were shockingly new. Although limited in effect, these incidents, as well as the sinking of the *Lusitania,* increased anxiety and caused a number of anti-German actions. German-sounding names had to be changed and sauerkraut disappeared from menus. The royal family even changed its dynastic name from the German Saxe-Coburg-Gotha to Windsor. Wartime atrocity stories, real and imagined, fed the fuel of anti-German hysteria and increased Britain's determination to destroy the dreaded Huns. Lord Northcliffe's *Daily Mail* contributed to this atmosphere, as did speechmakers at Speakers Corner in Hyde Park and on the floor of the House of Commons. Information was officially controlled and

managed, too, with propaganda ultimately organized by Lord Beaverbrook at the newly established ministry of information. In retrospect, the low points in morale are easy to pinpoint: the Easter rebellion, the loss of Kitchener, the aftermath of the Somme Offensive, the government crisis that resulted in Asquith's resignation in 1916; the unrestricted submarine warfare that led to food shortages, the Passchendaele Campaign (Third Ypres) in 1917, and the renewed German offensive in 1918. Not surprisingly, there was an uncontrolled three-day outburst of celebration once Armistice Day arrived.

The war brought totally unintended developments to the home front, ranging from a new casualness in relationships between the sexes to British Summer Time (daylight savings). Brassieres and zippers were in, camisoles and buttons were out; long skirts and long hair disappeared in favor of rising hemlines and "the bob." While sentiment was favored in the novels of Victoria Cross and nostalgia reigned in such popular songs as "Tipperary," cultural standards in classical music and opera rose and audiences were increased by the efforts of the energetic and popular Sir Thomas Beecham. Liquor consumption declined, aided by more restrictive pub hours, as did church attendance. Throughout the war years the overall standard of living for working-class families rose in terms of real wages and access to material comforts. Arthur Marwick summarized that the Great War destroyed the old world but helped create the new: "Out went gold sovereigns, chaperons, muffin men, and the divine right of private enterprise; in came State control, summer time, a new prosperity and a new self-confidence for families long submerged below the poverty line, and, in the aftermath, a biting skepticism and challenge to established authorities."

Thomas W. Davis

References

Fussell, Paul. *The Great War and Modern Memory*. New York: Oxford University Press, 1975.

Marwick, Arthur. *The Deluge: British Society and the First World War*. Boston: Little, Brown, 1965.

Taylor, A.J.P. *English History, 1914–1945*. New York: Oxford University Press, 1965.

Winter, J.M. *The Great War and the British People*. Cambridge: Harvard University Press, 1986.

See also GREAT BRITAIN, ARMY

Great Britain, Navy

For three centuries after the defeat of the Spanish Armada, Great Britain had assumed the role of naval as opposed to continental military power. The English had used seapower to create an economy and empire without precedent. By the eighteenth century, the Royal Navy was the foundation upon which the edifices of the *Pax Britannica* and the Victorian British Empire were built.

Having defeated their only legitimate naval rival at Trafalgar in 1805, Great Britain passed into a century almost devoid of major conflict. Save for a few coastal forays and isolated battles with pirates and slavers, British sailors were forced to join land actions to acquire combat experience.

Although the nineteenth century was bereft of significant naval conflict, it saw the most significant technological advances in all of maritime history. The French laid down the first ironclad capital ship in 1858, and the British responded with the *Warrior,* the first truly modern warship, in 1860. The weight of armor demanded a new source of propulsion, and the age of sail passed through steam-sail hybrids to fully steam-powered vessels in the next three decades. By the late 1880s the admiralty had realized that the work of operating a sail-powered vessel detracted from its efficiency as a gun platform. The result was the Naval Defense Act of 1889, which authorized construction of eight steel battleships (the *Royal Sovereign* class) designed to displace 14,000 tons and to steam at 16 knots.

Coincident with that act, the British government explicitly stated their commitment to maintain a fleet of a strength equal to the next two strongest in Europe combined. Earlier in the nineteenth century, with France defeated, the Dutch and Spanish in decline, and the Russians, Germans, and Americans dedicated land powers, that was an attainable goal. By the latter part of the century, however, the French were resurgent and the continental powers each had naval aspirations. Besides, the new technology had made maintenance of a dominant navy prohibitively expensive.

Admiral Sir John Arbuthnot (Jacky) Fisher became first sea lord in 1904 and set out to apply as much of the new technology as possible to the tradition-laden Royal Navy. He was the first naval administrator to recognize publicly that Britain's next likely opponent would be Germany rather than France—even predicting that a naval "Battle of Armageddon" between the two would take place on 21 October 1914. He thought the best ship to fight that battle would be large, heavily armored, and fast, and that it would carry only heavy guns of a single large caliber. The "dreadnought" design reflected Fisher's belief that the short-range battles characteristic of the wooden-walled navy would, in the age of steam and steel, be supplanted by accurate gunnery delivered from long range.

Britain's principal advocate of improved gunnery was Admiral Sir Percy Scott. Scott helped develop rudimentary computers to replace manual aiming by gunlayers and ultimately devised a central fire-control system to synchronize firing from the guns of Fisher's new dreadnoughts.

In addition to the dreadnoughts, Fisher pushed a wide range of innovative naval weapons into the Royal Navy. He augmented the battleships with fast, heavily armed but lightly armored battle cruisers. These ships were meant to mirror the function of Nelson's frigates— scouting, raiding, and protection of merchant commerce. Unfortunately, their heavy guns led to confusion about their role and to their being employed against battleships, a use for which they were disastrously inadequate. Fisher feared the effect of faster, more powerful torpedoes on his capital ships and developed a class of turbine-driven, agile ships to counter torpedo boats—the destroyers. He also recognized the potential of submarines, and forced them on those in the admiralty who thought underwater warfare devious and un-English.

Fisher's innovations were expensive. Alfred von Tirpitz and the German navy began a concomitant naval building program, and their success led to the British Naval Scare of 1909. The British were convinced that their nation's naval supremacy was at risk when finances forced the government to retreat from the Two Power Standard to a policy of being 60 percent stronger than the Germans alone. Between 1907 and 1913 Great Britain spent £229 million on its navy, an amount estimated to be twice as much as needed to solve most of its social problems—and sufficient to precipitate a constitutional crisis.

When the war began (or shortly thereafter), the Royal Navy had several advantages.

G

The most obvious was its numerical superiority. Fisher had reorganized the fleets by bringing most of the ships home and retiring those that were too old to be of effective service. In August of 1914 Great Britain had twenty first-line battleships and four battle cruisers in the North Sea, while the Germans had only thirteen first-line battleships and four battle cruisers. In addition to the Grand Fleet at Scapa Flow, commanded by Admiral Sir John Jellicoe with twenty-four battleships and battle cruisers, Admiral Sir Cecil Burney's Channel Fleet at Portsmouth had eight second-line battleships. The battle cruisers were subsequently separated under Admiral Sir David Beatty and based at Rosyth. The British Mediterranean Fleet at Malta had three battle cruisers, four armored cruisers, four light cruisers, and their attached destroyers.

The Royal Navy also benefited from geography. When Germany failed to capture France's Atlantic ports, its only effective North Sea egress was the gap between Norway and Scotland. The excellent harbors at Scapa Flow, Cromarty Firth, and Rosyth gave the British a base from which they could effectively blockade German shipping without leaving their home waters. Close blockade of the estuaries of the Ems, Jade, Weser, and Elbe, or an attack on the High Seas Fleet at its home ports, was not necessary. Germany, on the other hand, was forced to operate beyond the British blockade and well away from its home bases to attack shipping approaching Great Britain from the Atlantic.

Early in the war, the admiralty came into three astounding bits of luck. On 11 August 1914 the codes used to communicate with merchant shipping, U-boats, zeppelins, and small ships were captured from a German steamer in Australia. The same month, the German ship *Magdeburg* ran aground on Odensholm Island and the Russians captured and gave to the British Germany's major unit codes. The third and final set of German codes came to the British when a chest of cipher materials was dredged up by a fishing vessel. The codes allowed the Royal Navy to repeatedly anticipate the movements of the High Seas Fleet.

The British had disadvantages as well. Their guns, though larger, were not as effective as those of the Germans. The German 30.5cm (12-inch) guns had the same penetrating ability as the British 13.5-inch and were effective for an average of two hundred rounds, whereas the British guns would fire only an average of one hundred rounds. Although British seamen enlisted for twelve years and the Germans only for three, German gunnery was consistently more accurate. In part this was because British ships were narrower of beam and thus less stable gun platforms than those of their opponents. Perhaps the most significant difference was in ship protection. After the Battle of Dogger Bank, the Germans recognized the importance of isolating gun turrets from powder magazines, a lesson the British failed to learn and one that cost them three battle cruisers at Jutland.

Except for two battle cruisers, all of the Royal Navy's capital ships were built before the war. The *Dreadnought* (1906), the three ships of the *Bellerophon* class (1907), the three *St. Vincent*s (1908), the *Neptune* (1909), and the two *Collossus*es (1909) were propelled by coal-fired turbines, carried 8–11-inch armor belts, mounted ten 12-inch guns, and could steam at 19–21.5 knots. The four *Orion*s (1909) and the four *King George V*s (1911) were also coal-fired, but they carried 9–12-inch armor, mounted ten 13.5-inch guns, and were capable of up to 23 knots. The *Agincourt* (1911) was begun as the Turkish *Sultan Osman I* but was commandeered at the war's onset. She was coal-fired, had only 3.6–9-inch armor, and carried fourteen 12-inch guns at a maximum speed of 22.5 knots. The *Erin* (1911) had also been laid down for the Turks and carried ten 13.5-inch guns and 8–12-inch belt armor. The *Canada,* begun for Chile, carried ten 14-inch guns and a 7–9-inch belt. The four *Iron Duke*s (1912) were the last coal-fired battleships, carried 9–12-inch armor and ten 13.5-inch guns and were capable of 21.5 knots. The five *Queen Elizabeth*s (1912–13) and the five *Royal Sovereign*s (1913–14) were oil-fired, carried 6–13-inch armor and eight 15-inch guns and were capable of 21.5 knots.

The eleven battle cruisers were built in three prewar and one wartime series. The three *Invincible*s (1906) carried 4–6-inch belt armor and mounted eight 12-inch guns, were coal-fired, and steamed at 28.5 knots. The two *Lion*s (1909) had 4–9-inch belts, mounted eight 13.5-inch guns, were coal-fired, and were capable of 28 knots. The two *Indefatigable*s (1910) were similar in armor and armament to the *Invincible*s and included the *New Zealand,* which had been given to the Royal Navy by the dominion for which it was named. The *Queen Mary* and the *Tiger* (1911) had only a 2–9-inch belt but mounted eight 13.5-inch guns and reached 29 knots. In 1915 the navy acquired the two *Renown* class dreadnoughts with 1.3–9-inch belts, six 15-inch guns, oil-fired turbines, and speeds of 32.5 knots. The battle cruisers were nearly as well-gunned as the battleships, and they were much faster. The cost for the extra speed was armor too thin to stop battleship shells.

The Royal Navy inventory included forty predreadnought battleships commissioned between 1894 and 1904. They carried an assortment of guns, the largest of which were 12-inch, and their belt protection varied from 4–6 inches. Their speeds varied from 16 to 18.5 knots because their coal-fired engines were piston rather than turbine designs.

The British had forty-eight old cruisers (including the *Minotaur, Warrior, Duke of Edinburgh,* and *Cressy* classes) carrying 6–9.2-inch guns and capable of only 20–24 knots. The two newer *Courageous*-class cruisers were oil-fired, carried four 15-inch guns, and could steam at 31.5 knots.

The light cruiser fleet comprised eighty-eight coal-fired ships built from 1890 to 1914 and mounting four 6-inch guns. Twenty-nine more light cruisers were built during the war. These were designated alphabetically—*Birmingham*s, *Cambrian*s, *Centaur*s, *Caledon*s, *Ceres*es, *Carlisle*s, and the D class. They carried five or six 6-inch guns, except for the *Birmingham*s, which had seven 7.5-inch guns. They were oil-fired, turbine-driven, and were capable of 28–29 knots.

Much wartime construction was devoted to destroyers. The navy listed 178 prewar ships, the oldest of which was built in 1895, but 301 more were built during the war. The older ships carried 12-pound guns, most wartime series had three 4-inch guns, and the final wartime ships (the *Admiralty V* series) had 4.7-inch guns. The destroyers were designated alphabetically from A to I, K to M, R, S, V, and Yarrow classes. After 1906 (midway through the E series) they were propelled by oil-fired turbines and were trial platforms for that engine. The Royal Navy also had about 220 assorted patrol boats, gun boats, and torpedo boats. This group's nineteen PC boats were the original antisubmarine Q-ships and carried a single, deck-mounted 4-inch gun hidden behind artificial cargo.

Although traditionalists felt submarine warfare devious, the Royal Navy had built an undersea force beginning with the A series of 1904. The submarine fleet was divided into oceangoing (the first of which were in the wartime G series), seagoing, coastal, and minelaying boats. The thirty-three seagoing E series boats saw extensive duty in the Baltic, and twenty-seven of them were sunk during the war. The single boat of the M class mounted a 12-inch gun retrieved from a retired battleship. After loading the gun on the surface, the submarine submerged enough to leave only the barrel exposed, and aimed with a bead sight visible through the periscope. Of the 200-boat submarine fleet, 73 were prewar and 127 were built during the emergency wartime program.

In 1916 a cruiser initially designed for the *Courageous* class was converted into an aircraft carrier with an afterdeck for landing and a shorter foredeck for launching aircraft. The ship was built at a cost of £6 million and carried four Short seaplanes and six Sopwith pups. The *Argus,* begun as an Italian passenger liner, was converted into an aircraft carrier in 1917. It was the Royal Navy's first true "flat top" with a bow to stern flight deck, and carried Sopwith Cuckoo torpedo planes. The light cruiser *Cavendish* was converted to the carrier *Vindictive* in 1918. Like the *Furious,* it had fore and aft flight decks and carried six aircraft. The Royal Navy also had four ships designed to deploy seaplanes.

At the beginning of the war, the Royal Navy moved to sweep German ships from the seas. The German navy had cruisers deployed in both the Atlantic and the Pacific. Admiral Maximilian Graf von Spee divided his Far Eastern Fleet, sending the *Emden* into the Indian Ocean and the *Scharnhorst* and *Gneisnau* east across the Pacific. The *Emden* was sunk by the Australian cruiser *Sydney,* and the *Scharnhorst* and *Gneisnau,* after sinking the cruisers *Good Hope* and *Monmouth* off Coronel, were destroyed by Sir David Sturdee's battle cruisers in the Battle of the Falklands. The German commerce-raider *Karlsruhe* sank off Barbados when her magazine exploded, and the *Konigsberg* was blockaded and later sunk after she destroyed the British cruiser *Pegasus* off Zanzibar. By March of 1915 the remaining German commerce raiders were either sunk or interned, justifying Winston Churchill's claim that, after the Battle of the Falklands, Britain controlled all the world's oceans except the landlocked Black Sea, the Baltic Sea, and Heligoland Bight.

The British achieved a much-needed naval victory in the 28 August 1914 raid on Heligoland Bight. In September three of the Royal Navy's

G

older cruisers were sunk in a single day by U-29, and on 27 October the predreadnought battleship *Audacious* was sunk by a German mine. German Admiral Franz von Hipper's raids on England's east coast were facilitated by the Grand Fleet's having moved north to blockade Germany's Atlantic access. The Battle of Dogger Bank (23 January 1915) was significant for several reasons. It was the first engagement fought between dreadnoughts—albeit battle cruisers rather than battleships. Damage done to the *Seydlitz* led the Germans to install flash protection between their turrets and magazines, a lesson the British failed to learn and one that would cost them dearly at Jutland. Finally, the damage suffered by the High Seas Fleet led directly to decisions to keep the surface ships close to port and to pursue unrestricted submarine warfare in British waters.

Except for its participation in the Dardanelles Campaign, short forays into the North Sea, and Scheer's raid on the coastal towns of Lowestoft and Yarmouth, the Royal Navy was unchallenged until mid-1916. In May, Scheer decided to confront the Grand Fleet, and Jellicoe, under pressure to restore British access to the Baltic Sea, was willing to accept, although Churchill pointed out that it made the Royal Navy able to lose the war in a single afternoon. Although the British lost more ships than the Germans at Jutland and the admiralty and the public were disappointed at the decidedly un-Nelsonian outcome, the German surface navy ceased to be a factor after that battle.

During the war, Britain lost two dreadnoughts, eleven predreadnoughts, three battle cruisers, thirteen cruisers, twelve light cruisers, sixty-seven destroyers, and fifty-four submarines. For that cost, the Royal Navy gained control of the world's oceans, confined their major competitor to port, and effected a blockade that strangled the German economy.

Jack McCallum

References

Frost, Holloway. *The Battle of Jutland.* New York: Arno, 1980.

Goldrick, James. *The King's Ships Were at Sea: The War in the North Sea. August 1914–February 1915.* Annapolis, Md.: Naval Institute Press, 1984.

Keegan, John. *The Price of Admiralty: The Evolution of Naval Warfare.* New York: Viking, 1988.

Massie, Robert. *Dreadnought: Britain, Germany, and the Coming of the Great War.* New York: Random House, 1991.

Moore, John, ed. *Jane's Fighting Ships of World War I.* London: Jane's, 1919.

Wegener, Wolfgang. *The Naval Strategy of the World War.* Annapolis, Md.: Naval Institute Press, 1989.

See also CORONEL, BATTLE OF; DOGGER BANK, NAVAL BATTLE OF; FALKLANDS, BATTLE OF; HELIGOLAND BIGHT, BATTLE OF; JUTLAND, BATTLE OF

Greece

By August of 1914 Greece was exhausted from the Balkan Wars of 1912 and 1913 and by growing political divisions. In March of 1913 King George was assassinated, and his son, Constantine, brother-in-law to the Kaiser, became king. With the outbreak of World War I, Greece tried to preserve its neutrality, but its intense opposition to Turkey and Bulgaria plus continued Allied pressure made that course almost impossible. Gradually, the Greek government dissolved into two camps: The first, centered on the king, feared the Allies more than the Central Powers; the second, centered on Premier Eleutherios Venizelos, feared that if the Central Powers won, Bulgaria and Turkey would claim Greek territory.

In 1915, when the Serbian army was driven out of Serbia, the Allies requested permission of the Greek government to evacuate the army to Salonika. On 24 September 1915, Constantine privately consented to this arrangement. His public reversal caused the fall of the government headed by Eleutherios Venizelos. On 8 November the new government declared Greece a Benevolent Neutral favoring the Allies.

Political division, meanwhile, intensified in Greece. The Allies increased pressure on Greece to join the war, while the Central Powers made no serious moves to bring Greece to their side. The Germans felt confident that with the Central Powers positioned along Greece's northern frontier, they could easily contain any move north. The Central Powers were able, with second-line troops, to hold the Allies at Salonika until October of 1918.

By mid-1916 King Constantine stood for neutrality, while Venizelos, who had fled to Crete and set up a provisional government, supported the Allied cause. Since the Allies occupied some Greek territory, Constantine allowed the Central Powers also to occupy defensive positions on Greek soil. When the Allies tried to expand their bases in Greece, they met Greek resistance. On 8 December 1916 the Allies declared Greece under blockade and on 19 December recognized Venizelos's provisional government. The Greek people rallied to the king. The Central Powers took no action; they were pleased to see the Allies tied down in a minor theater. After six months of blockade, Constantine abdicated in favor of his second son, Alexander, on 12 June 1917. The new king appointed Venizelos to head a new government, which declared war on the Central Powers on 27 June 1917.

Having joined the Allies, Greece found herself without an army, since it had been disbanded for remaining loyal to Constantine. The nucleus of the new Greek army was formed from units organized under British control. By early 1918 a Greek army of some 20,000 men had been equipped and trained. These troops went into battle in May of 1918 against the Bulgarians at the Skra di Legan salient. In a surprise attack, the Greeks destroyed a Bulgarian regiment and captured its position. This successful action led to an influx of volunteers. In September and October of 1918 the Greek army took part in General Marie Guillaumat's Balkan offensive that helped end the war.

After the war, Greece expected to be awarded predominantly Greek territories in the Balkans and Asia Minor. Unfortunately for Greece, those claims ran afoul of Turkish nationalism. In May of 1919 fighting broke out between Greece and Turkey. Greece was successful in the early battles and occupied Turkish territory. The Treaty of Sèvres, 10 August 1920, awarded Greece Bulgarian and Turkish territory, but Turkey refused to ratify the treaty. The Greeks responded by sending an army to Smryna, on the coast of Anatolia, but they were ultimately defeated by the Turks led by Mustafa Kemal (Atatürk).

In 1920 King Alexander died and his father Constantine returned to the throne. Although Constantine reorganized the army and government, poor management lost Greece all the territory she had won. This disaster led to a revolt in Greece, and Constantine was forced into exile. On 13 October 1922, with both Greece and Turkey militarily exhausted, they signed the Treaty of Lausanne—a victory for Turkey.

Charles H. Bogart

References

Andrew, Prince of Greece. *Towards Disaster: The Greek Army in Asia Minor.* London: B.J. Murry, 1930.

Dakin, Douglas. *The Unification of Greece 1770–1923.* New York: St. Martin's, 1972.

Palmer, Alan. *The Gardeners of Salonika: The Macedonian Campaign 1915–1918.* New York: Simon and Schuster, 1965.

See also BALKAN FRONT, 1915, 1916, 1917; CONSTANTINE, KING; SALONIKA CAMPAIGN; VENIZELOS, ELEUTHERIOS

G

Grenades, Hand

One of the most important weapons in trench warfare was the grenade. Grenades were explosive devices that utilized a percussion or timed fuse and were either thrown (hand grenades) or fired from rifles (rifle grenades). They caused damage from shrapnel and by the bursting charge itself. Grenades were ideal for use in trench warfare because of the need for a weapon that could be thrown or lobbed over no-man's-land or around the traverse of a trench.

Grenades came in two types, those relying on shrapnel and those relying on explosive effect. Shrapnel, which consisted of the case fragments or metal pieces inside the case, was used in situations in which the thrower was protected from the fragments—for example, down in a trench. High-explosive grenades, because of their limited fragmentation effect, were more suitable for offensive warfare in which the attacker was moving toward his opponent in an open area. Both types were very effective within the confined spaces of a trench.

In 1914 most armies did not have a ready supply of grenades, because their use in previous wars had been limited and their development crude. The German army had some supplies of grenades, but they were considered a specialist's weapon and only combat-engineer (*Pionier*) units were supplied with them. Trench warfare required a weapon that could be thrown from one trench system to another, and soon troops in all the armies resorted to making their own crude grenades, which were often as dangerous to the thrower as to the intended victim.

The two most common types of early grenades were the "jam pot" and "racquet." The jam pot grenade was widely used by the British until their production grenades became available in 1916. As its name implies, the jam pot was made of empty jam tins filled with explosive and nails, and occasionally parts of clocks. These were thrown and used a simple fuse to ignite the charge. The racquet, sometimes called a hair brush grenade, was favored by the French. It consisted of a piece of pipe wired onto the end of a stick and filled with explosive. The ends of the pipe were blocked up and a simple fuse ignited the charge. Both the racquet and jam pot were very dangerous to make and to use. Soldiers using them were often forced to work in isolated traverses of the trench in case of accidents.

Early German grenades were the "baseball," a heavy sphere of iron ignited when thrown by means of a friction primer attached to the bomber's arm. When thrown, the primer was pulled as the grenade left the bomber's hand. Another type was the "tortoise," which was saucer-shaped with four percussion plungers around the outer edge. The grenade had to land on one of the plungers in order to go off. Neither of these types was ideal, so others were developed.

In 1916 the British developed the Mills bomb, which, with minor improvements, would see service throughout the war. It was a shrapnel grenade that used a spring-loaded time fuse released by pulling a pin. In 1918 the Americans produced their pineapple grenade along the same idea.

The French developed grenades similar to the Mills bomb but in several shapes. They all used a time fuse activated by a spring-loaded igniter released by a pin. They used thin-skinned percussion grenades as well as thick-skinned shrapnel grenades with shapes including the oval, pear, and sphere.

German grenades after 1915 were produced in two types, the egg grenade and the stick grenade. The egg grenade, so named because of its shape, was a shrapnel grenade that operated by means of a friction primer in a tube on top of the grenade. The stick grenade, which went through several models, was a charge in a thin-skinned tin can mounted on a stick. A friction fuse attached to a pull cord ran through the hollow stick. Before throwing, the bomber unscrewed a metal cap on the end of the stick and pulled on a porcelain ball attached to the pull cord. Later in the war (1918), German troops used stick grenades wired in a bundle

around a central grenade as an antitank weapon. The bundle was thrown under the tank to destroy its tracks. Some airmen also dropped these bundled grenades from airplanes.

Both the French and British (and later, the Americans) produced several styles of multi-pocketed vests to aid their bombers in carrying the heavy grenades. The Germans strung old sand bags around their necks like water wings. Grenade sacks were perhaps one major distinction of the kit worn by elite German stormtroops. One disadvantage to the German system was the immense bulk of stick grenades, making large numbers difficult to carry.

Both sides produced rifle grenades, but they were not as effective as the hand-thrown variety. Their primary drawback was the lack of accuracy, which eliminated any advantage of longer range. Rifle grenades were launched by means of a rod that fit into the barrel of the weapon, or from a special cup that fit on the end of the rifle, the discharge being provided by a blank round. One French type used a live round passing through the grenade to both launch and ignite the grenade. With all rifle grenade launchers, the rifle was fired with its butt on the ground to absorb the recoil.

Grenades were also thrown by mechanical means. Early in the war, catapults and slingshots were tried as means of throwing grenades farther. Bombers also experimented with devices that fired grenades from a crossbow mechanism. Later, special throwing devices were produced; the grenades fired from these were equipped with fins and served as light mortar rounds. As with rifle grenades, accuracy was the greatest disadvantage of these devices, although they did serve as a means of harassing the enemy.

Grenades used by countries such as Italy, Austria-Hungary, and Russia generally followed the designs of their more technically advanced allies. The Russians used a type of stick grenade, and Turkey used a spherical bomb. British troops at Gallipoli used a similar type, known as a Malta Grenade after its place of manufacture.

As the use of grenades became more common, special tactics were developed for their use. Grenade attacks were usually conducted by squads of about eight men. Two men were designated throwers; the others were either riflemen or grenade carriers. The system for clearing a trench was to have one thrower in front who would throw his bombs over traverses into a trench. Once the grenades detonated, the riflemen would rush around the traverse and kill any surviving enemy soldiers before they could recover from the shock. The process was repeated trench by trench. Dugouts and machine-gun posts were also special targets of bombers.

Steven D. Fisher

References

Delhomme, Patrice. *Les Grenades Françaises de la Grande Guerre*. Paris: Hegide, 1984.

Messenger, Charles. *Trench Fighting 1914–1918*. New York: Ballantine, 1972.

Nash, David. *German Infantry 1914–1918*. London: Almark, 1971.

See also INFANTRY TACTICS; STORMTROOPERS; TRENCH WARFARE

Grey, Edward (1862–1933)

British politician and foreign secretary. Born on 25 April 1862 in London, Grey was a descendant of the second Earl Grey. He was educated at Winchester and at Balliol College, Oxford (where he was sent down for idleness by the famed Benjamin Jowett), and succeeded to his grandfather's country estate at Falloden in Northumberland and to his baronetcy in 1882. Three years later he won election to the House of Commons as a Liberal and retained his seat until he retired from government in 1916.

He quickly established lasting friendships with other junior M.P.s, notably Herbert Asquith and R.B. Haldane. Grey worked as parliamentary undersecretary at the Foreign Office in the 1890s, where he became increasingly alarmed at threats to European peace. During the Boer War he supported the Liberal Imperialists, arguing that, once started, a war effort must be vigorously pursued and successfully concluded.

Grey became foreign secretary following the 1905 Liberal landslide. During the tense years of diplomatic negotiations that followed to 1914, Grey sought to preserve peace, cultivate England's recent entente with France, establish friendly relations with Russia and Japan, maintain good communications with the United States, and remain cordial with Germany. During the Moroccan Crises of 1906 and 1911 he cautiously supported France's position against Germany, causing some critics to say that he created diplomatic confusion by sending mixed signals and that he made other European powers uncertain about England's intentions. G.M. Trevelyan stated that Grey believed that his diplomatic approach was the best means to avert war and a lesser evil than encouraging France and Russia to be more bellicose.

In July of 1914 Grey worked tirelessly to prevent the outbreak of war following the assassination of Archduke Franz Ferdinand in Sarajevo. He urged Germany to restrain Austria-Hungary, and he cautioned France and Russia against hostilities. Once Germany invaded neutral Belgium, however, Grey reluctantly recognized the inevitability of a Europeanwide conflict he had tried so hard to prevent. As he put it, "The lamps are going out all over Europe; we shall not see them lit again in our lifetime."

During the first two years at war, Grey's attention went to isolating and blockading Germany, luring Italy to join the Allies, dealing with the Balkans, and fostering good relations with the United States. A chance for retirement came when David Lloyd George replaced Asquith as prime minister in December of 1916. During the next seventeen years, Grey accepted a peerage as Viscount Grey of Falloden, promoted the League of Nations, wrote his memoirs, and pursued his love of birds. He died on 7 September 1933.

Thomas W. Davis

References

Hinsley, Francis H., ed. *British Foreign Policy Under Sir Edward Grey*. New York: Cambridge University Press, 1977.

Robbins, Keith. *Sir Edward Grey: A Biography of Lord Grey of Falloden*. London: Cassell, 1971.

Trevelyan, George M. *Grey of Falloden*. London: Longmans, 1940.

See also ALLIANCES, PREWAR; ORIGINS OF THE FIRST WORLD WAR; OUTBREAK OF THE FIRST WORLD WAR

Grigorovich, Ivan Konstantinovich (1853–1930)

Russian admiral and minister of the navy, born on 7 February 1853. Grigorovich was a graduate of the Naval College in 1874 and served in the Russo-Turkish War of 1877–78. He then held numerous commands in the Baltic and Far East, as well as serving as naval attaché to Great

Britain from 1896 to 1898. He was decorated for heroism in the Russo-Japanese War.

In 1905 Grigorovich was appointed chief of staff for the Black Sea Fleet; in 1906 he took command of the Baltic port of Libau, and in 1908 he commanded Kronstadt, Russia's most important naval base. As assistant to the minister of the navy, Grigorovich was promoted to admiral and was himself minister of the navy in 1911, a post he held until the March Revolution of 1917.

An able administrator and skilled in bureaucratic politics, Grigorovich had good relations with both the Duma and Czar Nicholas II. He was instrumental in securing Duma approval of the navy's massive nineteen-year naval building program, designed to provide Russia with seven new battleships and a number of cruisers and destroyers.

Grigorovich's naval doctrine called for concentrating Russian naval forces in the Baltic and modernizing their bases. Fear of a German offensive strike into the Gulf of Finland, however, prompted him to establish a defensive strategy based on massive mine fields. In 1912 Grigorovich personally quelled mutinies in the Black Sea Fleet. Upon the outbreak of World War I, the navy came under the supervision of Grand Duke Nikolai Nikolaevich, who placed the Baltic Fleet under command of the Sixth Army in the Gulf of Finland. Grigorovich, in spite of the land-oriented military command arrangement and a lack of aggressive admirals, continued to give subtle but important support to the navy.

Grigorovich avoided ministerial infighting and even refused to run for premier in the summer of 1915, when his allies in the Duma suggested him as a replacement for Ivan Goremykin. In September of 1915 he refused to sign the protest against Czar Nicholas II's decision to take direct command of the Russian armies, but in 1916 he warned the czar of growing unrest in the Russian fleet. Through March and November of 1917 Grigorovich tried unsuccessfully to control unrest in the navy. In 1923 he was granted permission to emigrate, and he died in France on 3 March 1930.

Tom Zucconi

References

Herwig, Holger, and Neil M. Heyman. *Biographical Dictionary of World War I*. Westport, Conn.: Greenwood, 1982.

Pavlovich, N.B., ed. *The Fleet in the First World War*. New Delhi: Published for the Smithsonian Institution and the National Science Foundation, Washington, D.C., by Amerind Publishing, 1979.

Saul, Norman E. *Sailors in Revolt: The Russian Baltic Fleet in 1917*. Lawrence, Kans.: Regents Press of Kansas, 1978.

Wieczynski, Joseph L., ed. *Modern Encyclopedia of Russian and Soviet History*. Vol. 13. Gulf Breeze, Fla.: Academic International, 1979.

See also RUSSIA, NAVY

Groener, Wilhelm (1867–1939)

Württemberg general and quartermaster-general of the OHL at the end of the First World War. Born at Ludwigsburg, near Stuttgart, on 22 November 1867, Groener was the son of a regimental paymaster in the Royal Württemberg Army and his middle-class wife. After attending grammar school, he entered a local infantry regiment on his seventeenth birthday and received a commission two years later. Upon graduation from the Kriegsakademie in 1896, Groener progressed through a variety of staff and command positions and in October of 1912 became head of the Railroad Branch of the general staff in Berlin. In that capacity, he played a key role in the rapid mobilization and deployment of the German army in August of 1914.

Rapidly promoted to colonel (September 1914) and major general (June 1915), Groener continued in charge of German railway operations until October of 1916 and simultaneously dispensed advice to the successive heads of the Army High Command (OHL) on a broad range of issues. After participating in the allocation of Germany's limited food resources, Groener was promoted to the rank of lieutenant general and appointed head of a new war office on 1 November of the same year. That office, in the Prussian ministry of war, was responsible for directing the Hindenburg Program, mobilizing Germany's manpower for war production and a huge increase in the output of arms and ammunition.

From his previous work, Groener fully understood the importance of motivating the working masses by flexible social policies, although he drew the line against work stoppages and denounced strikers in the spring of 1917 as "scoundrels." Watched with increasing concern by some of Germany's conservative industrialists and their friends at OHL, notably Lieutenant Colonel Max Bauer, Groener was eventually removed from the war office and sent to the Western Front as a divisional commander (16 August 1917). Four months later he was elevated to a corps command, leading first XXV Reserve Corps in the Aillette sector and then I Corps in the Ukraine.

When Field Marshal Hermann von Eichhorn was made Germany's senior commander in the Ukraine late in March of 1918, Groener was assigned to his headquarters in Kiev as chief of staff. For the next seven months he labored diligently under Eichhorn and, after the latter's assassination on 30 July, under Colonel General Günter Count von Kirckbach to stabilize the political situation in the Ukraine and to exploit its resources for the benefit of the Central Powers.

After General Erich Ludendorff resigned from his position as the first quartermaster-general at the OHL (26 October 1918), Field Marshal Paul von Hindenburg invited Groener to take Ludendorff's place. With Germany's military situation declining rapidly, Groener realized that he would become the whipping boy for many frustrated Germans, but he nevertheless decided to accept Hindenburg's offer. Aside from supervising the orderly withdrawal of Germany's western armies to the Antwerp-Meuse line, he made it clear to the government on 6 November that, in view of the revolutionary turmoil in several regions of the *Reich,* armistice talks should be initiated immediately. Three days later, Groener informed the kaiser that the army "no longer stood behind" him, thereby squashing the monarch's efforts to stay on the throne. The following day, 10 November, Groener assured the head of the new socialist government in Berlin, Friedrich Ebert, that the army was prepared to work with the new regime as long as it kept radical elements in check.

Remaining at Hindenburg's side throughout the following months of turmoil, Groener repeatedly took personal responsibility for various "unpopular" decisions and measures. After counseling acceptance of the Versailles Treaty in June of 1919, Groener retired from active service three months later. In June of 1920, he joined the *Reich* government as minister of transport and effectively served in that portfolio until August of 1923. During the next four and a half years he wrote extensively on Germany's military preparations for war and the opening campaign in the west, emphasizing the genius of the Schlieffen Plan and deploring its partial abandonment by General von Moltke.

In January of 1928 Groener was persuaded for the second time to assume political office, this time as minister of defense. From October of 1931 onward, he also took on the position of minister of the interior in the Brüning Cabinet. In both positions he soon incurred the enmity of the Nazis as well as of some *Reichswehr* generals. After much harassment from his various opponents, in May of 1932 Groener resigned from the cabinet and went into well-deserved retirement with his second wife. He died at Bornstedt, near Potsdam, on 3 May 1939.

Ulrich Trumpener

References

Groener, Wilhelm. *Der Feldherr wider Willen: Operative Studien über den Weltkrieg.* Berlin: E.S. Mittler und Sohn, 1930.

———. *Lebenserinnerungen: Jugend, Generalstab, Weltkrieg.* Edited by Friedrich Freiherr Hiller von Gaertringen. Göttingen: Vandenhoeck & Ruprecht, 1957.

———. Personal papers (*Nachlass*), N 46, Bundesarchiv: Militärarchiv Freiburg i.Br.

———. *Das Testament des Grafen Schlieffen: Operative Studien über den Weltkrieg.* Berlin: E.S. Mittler und Sohn, 1927.

Hürter, Johannes. *Wilhelm Groener: Reichswehrminister am Ende der Weimarer Republik 1928–1932.* Munich: Oldenbourg, 1993.

See also ALLIED COUNTEROFFENSIVE; ARMISTICE, AT COMPIÈGNE; GERMANY, REVOLUTION OF 1918

Guchkov, Aleksandr Ivanovich (1862–1936)

Russian politician and minister of war, born in Moscow on 14 October 1862. Guchkov was an oddity in pre-1917 Russia—a self-made man who stood for the principles of nineteenth-century bourgeois classical liberalism. His grandfather had been a serf and his father built a major merchant business that Guchkov took over and expanded. In the Boer War he traveled to South Africa and served as a volunteer in the Boer army. During the Russo-Japanese War he organized the Russian Red Cross, which ran the medical service. It is no exaggeration to say that

Guchkov was an individualist in a nation with no real individualist tradition.

Politically, Guchkov wanted to see Russia transformed into a liberal constitutional monarchy. To that end, in October of 1905, during the political turmoil of that year, he founded the Octobrist party (the Party of the Union of 17 October), which for its time was considered conservative. In 1906 he formed a political alliance with Prime Minister P.A. Stolypin, who shared the same ideals. Together they attempted to modernize Russia. As president of the Third Duma (1907–12) Guchkov took the lead in getting Stolypin's agrarian reforms enacted into law. Guchkov also chaired the Duma National Defense Committee, which publicly exposed Russian military backwardness and the need for both military and political reform. That, of course, put him on a collision course with reactionary court circles. In 1909, in a confrontation with the monarchy, Guchkov resigned from the Duma. After being defeated in the election to the Fourth Duma, he was elected to the State Council (the upper house of the Russian legislature). During the war he chaired the War Industries Committee, which coordinated efforts to spur war production.

In March of 1917 Guchkov was one of two delegates sent to Pskov to accept the czar's abdication. And in the first coalition of the provisional government Guchkov served as minister of war, only to be replaced by Aleksandr Kerensky in April. Guchkov left Russia following the Bolshevik Revolution to live in western Europe. He settled in Paris, where he died on 14 February 1936.

John W. Bohon

References

Gurko, Vladimir Iosifovich. *Features and Figures of the Past. Government and Opinion in the Reign of Nicholas II.* Stanford: Stanford University Press, 1939.

Pushkarev, Sergei G. *The Emergence of Modern Russia 1801–1917.* New York: Holt, Rinehart and Winston, 1963.

See also RUSSIA, HOME FRONT AND REVOLUTIONS OF 1917

Guépratte, Emile Paul Amable (1856–1939)

French admiral, born at Granville (Manche) on 30 August 1856. Guépratte entered the Ecole Navale in 1871 and at the beginning of World War I commanded the *Division de complément.* That division of old battleships escorted convoys between North Africa and France. Guépratte was later ordered to the Dardanelles and joined the British in the bombardment of 3 November 1914, and those of February and March 1915. He advocated a naval offensive despite the extreme vulnerability of his obsolete ships, and he has been described as a latter-day knight, full of concern for honor and glory. Guépratte won the respect and affection of his British allies but was not universally loved in his own navy. Some French leaders even considered him "unbalanced." Minister of Marine Victor Augagneur curbed his independence by sending a vice admiral to command an expanded French squadron at the Dardanelles, and in October Guépratte was sent ashore to be *Préfet Maritime* at Bizerte, with promotion to vice admiral as compensation. He retired from active service in August of 1918 and subsequently served in the Chamber as a deputy from Finistère, 1919–24. He died at Brest on 21 November 1939.

Paul G. Halpern

References

Cassar, George H. *The French and the Dardanelles.* London: Allen & Unwin, 1971.

Guépratte, Vice-Admiral P.-E. *L'Expédition des Dardanelles, 1914–1915.* Paris: Payot, 1935.

Taillemite, Etienne. *Dictionnaire des Marins Français.* Paris: Editions Maritimes et d'Outre-Mer, 1982.

Thomazi, A. *La Guerre navale aux Dardanelles.* Paris: Payot, 1926.

See also DARDANELLES CAMPAIGN; FRANCE, NAVY; MEDITERRANEAN NAVAL OPERATIONS

Guillaumat, Marie Louis Adolphe (1863–1940)

French general, born in Bourgneuf on 4 January 1863. Guillaumat was one of France's most experienced generals at the beginning of World War I, having taken part in twelve colonial campaigns. Guillaumat graduated from St. Cyr in 1884 and served three years as an officer in the Foreign Legion. In 1900 he was wounded at Tientsin, China, while serving in the Boxer Rebellion. In 1903 he returned to St. Cyr as professor of military history and lecturer in infantry tactics. In 1911 he became director of infantry and in 1914 aide to the minister of war.

With the outbreak of World War I, Guillaumat rose to command French forces in many important battles. His first assignment was command of an infantry division in the battles of the Marne in 1914 and the Argonne in 1915. Promoted to commander of I Corps, he took part in the battle of Verdun and the Somme. From December of 1916 to December of 1917 he commanded Second Army in the epic battles to recapture areas around Verdun. In December of 1917 he replaced General Maurice Sarrail as commanding officer of the Armies of the East at Salonika. His principal tasks were to restore the morale of the Allied troops and train the Greek army. The only major offensive action centered on the seizure of Srka Di Legen Ridge by Greek troops. In July of 1918 Guillaumat was recalled to France to command troops defending Paris. In October of 1918 he was given command of the Fifth Army.

Guillaumat's exploits in the war ensured him a prominent role in the postwar French army. He helped reorganize the Greek army, commanded the French Army of Occupation in the Rhineland from 1924 to 1926, and served briefly as minister of war in July of 1926. Guillaumat died in June of 1940.

Charles H. Bogart

References

Beaufre, General André. *La France de la Grande Guerre, 1914/1919*. Paris: Culture, Art, 1971.

King, Jere Clemens. *Generals and Politicians. Conflict between France's High Command, Parliament and Government, 1914–1918*. Berkeley, Calif.: University of California Press, 1951.

Palmer, Alan. *The Gardeners of Salonika: The Macedonian Campaign 1915–1918*. New York: Simon and Schuster, 1965.

See also SOMME, BATTLE OF; VERDUN, BATTLE OF

G

H

Haber, Fritz (1868–1934)

German chemist, born on 9 December 1868 in Breslau, Silesia. Haber was the son of a well-to-do chemical merchant and pursued the study of chemistry and chemical technology at several universities and at the Technische Hochschule in Karlsruhe, where he also obtained his first academic position. A concern that the growing demand for nitrogen fertilizer could not be met by Chilean nitrate led him to concentrate on the problem of nitrogen fixation. By 1909 he had developed a method of synthesizing ammonia from hydrogen and nitrogen, which made large-scale commercial production of ammonia feasible. Imbued with German patriotism, Haber was also aware of the significance of nitrogen fixation for the production of explosives during wartime.

As director of the prestigious Kaiser Wilhelm Institute for Physical Chemistry in Berlin after 1912, he placed himself and his laboratory at the service of the German government when the war began in 1914. He played a major role in the development of poison gas as a weapon and personally directed its use at Ypres, Belgium, in April of 1915. Before long he was put in charge of the chemical warfare service in Germany. At war's end he was charged with war crimes, but this accusation was silenced by the award of the Nobel Prize in chemistry in 1919 for his method of ammonia synthesization. As a Jew, he left Germany in 1933 because of Hitler's anti-Semitic policies. He died of a heart attack in Basel, Switzerland, on 29 January 1934.

George P. Blum

References

"Fritz Haber." *Dictionary of Scientific Biography*. Vol. 5. New York: Charles Scribner's Sons, 1972.

Goran, Morris Herbert. *The Story of Fritz Haber*. Norman: University of Oklahoma Press, 1967.

See also CHEMICAL WARFARE; YPRES, SECOND BATTLE OF

Hadik, Count János (1863–1933)

Hungarian politician and premier. Born in Pálóc on 23 November 1863, Hadik was the grandson of General András Hadik, who fought for Empress Maria Theresa. On 25 October 1918 Mihály Károlyi formed the Hungarian National Council in Budapest, which demanded Hungarian autonomy. Oszkár Jászi worked out a twelve-point reform program. Meanwhile, a number of politicians and organizations, including the Budapest police force, rallied to the National Council. It was assumed that King Charles (Emperor Karl) would appoint Károlyi minister-president to replace Sándor Wekerle. Increasing public demonstrations demanded his appointment and implementation of the reform program. On 28 October there was a public march from the inner city to Buda Castle, and police fired on demonstrators on Chain Bridge. Urged by the ruling elite, Charles appointed not Károlyi but János Hadik minister-president. This was a stopgap arrangement to prevent a Károlyi government in Hungary. During the night of 30–31 October, soldiers and civilians espousing the ideas of the Hungarian National Council seized public buildings in Budapest, captured the military governor, and released political prisoners. Early on the morning of the 31st, Hadik resigned. He then fled the country, and Count Károlyi came to power. Hadik died in Budapest on 10 December 1933.

Spencer C. Tucker

References

Hanák, Péter, ed. *The Corvina History of Hungary. From Earliest Times until the Present Day.* Translated by Zsuzsa Béres. Budapest: Corvina, 1991.

Hoensch, Jörg K. *A History of Modern Hungary, 1867–1986.* New York: Longman, 1988.

Jászi, Oskár. *Revolution and Counter Revolution in Hungary.* London, 1924.

Károlyi, Mihályi. *Memoirs. Faith without Illusion.* London: Jonathan Cape, 1956.

See also KÁROLYI, MIHÁLY

Haig, Sir Douglas (1861–1928)

British field marshal and commander in chief of the British Expeditionary Force from December of 1915 to Armistice Day in 1918. For many critics, Haig's name is synonymous with the horrendous number of casualties on the Western Front. He is most noted for his role in directing two campaigns that resulted in a record number of dead and wounded British soldiers: the Battle of the Somme in 1916 and the Passchendaele Campaign (Third Ypres) in 1917.

Born in Edinburgh on 19 June 1861, Haig was the ninth child in a Scottish family. His father was founder of a prosperous whisky firm that still bears the family name. A graduate of Brasenose College, Oxford, and the Royal Military College, Sandhurst, Haig was an accomplished polo player who was commissioned in the cavalry. In 1885 he joined his regiment, the 7th Hussars, in India. In 1896 he attended the Army Staff College at Camberley and two years later participated in cavalry charges at the Battle of Omdurman. During the Boer War he served as chief of staff to General John French; there his concerns grew about the military training of British soldiers. Following marriage and further service in India, Haig went to the war office in 1906 to work for Secretary of State for War R.B. Haldane of the Liberal party, who referred to Haig as "the most highly equipped thinker in the British Army." For the next three years he worked diligently to prepare a British Expeditionary Force for possible deployment in a European war. He concentrated on forming a general staff and a Territorial Army, plus im-

proving military training. Haig was knighted in 1909 and promoted to lieutenant general the following year.

When the Great War began, Haig envisioned lengthy hostilities involving large numbers of soldiers. He initially commanded I Corps, which included such famous regiments as the Grenadier Guards, the Black Watch, and the Coldstream Guards. Before 1914 ended, he was promoted to full general with command of First Army. A year later (December of 1915) Haig was a popular successor to Sir John French as commander of British forces in France.

Haig's name is forever linked with the Battle of the Somme, which began on 1 July 1916. The battle was preceded by a full week of the heaviest artillery bombardment in history. When British soldiers went over the top and advanced in a tightly packed line along an eighteen-mile front, they expected nothing but a mopping-up operation. In contrast to the expectations, the British suffered a record 60,000 casualties on that first day, as wave after wave of infantry were mowed down by German machine gunners. The offensive Haig had championed lasted until mid-November, the front line advanced six miles, and British casualties approached 500,000 men. Defenders of Haig underscored his determination to fight against all odds; critics said his battle plan at the Somme exceeded his army's capacity to succeed, that he foolishly refused to employ tanks in support of the infantry, and that his rigidity rendered him blind to the campaign's futility and the senseless loss of thousands of soldiers to gain a few miles of insignificant terrain. It was the Somme that above all led to Haig's subsequent reputation, perhaps best summarized in Paul Fussell's evaluation: "He was stubborn, self-righteous, inflexible, intolerant—especially of the French—and quite humorless."

The Battle of Passchendaele (Third Ypres) was to 1917 what the Somme had been to 1916: a battle commanded by Haig (now promoted to field marshal) and fought by British soldiers, with a similar result of high casualties (approximately 350,000) suffered for a small advance (four miles) along the front lines in Flanders. It is difficult to sort out responsibility for this battle, which began on 31 July with terrible conditions of torrential rain that continued for weeks. Some blame David Lloyd George and the cabinet for getting too involved in military campaign planning and causing delays because of the prime minister's dislike of Haig. Others point to France's hesitancy while waiting for the Americans to arrive in greater numbers and the previously disastrous Nivelle Offensive, which had failed to weaken the German positions before Haig's troops attacked. Passchendaele provoked more bitterness at home than did the Somme, as war-weary Britons were repulsed by battlefield accounts such as that of Cyril Cruttwell: "All the combatants on either side regarded it as the culmination of horror. The rain was pitiless, the ubiquitous mud speedily engulfed man and beast if a step was taken astray from . . . the macabre grotesqueness of this blasted and mangled land."

In 1918 Haig's military fortunes improved, in part because he worked well with Ferdinand Foch, overall commander of the Allied forces since April. Haig helped repulse German offensives early in the year, and he planned the final successful counterattack in August, most notably the action around Amiens.

When the war ended, Haig remained in France until April of 1919, working in part on his war records and his meticulous diary. He then returned to Scotland where he lived in a castle on a hill high above the River Tweed. Created Earl Haig, Viscount Dawick and Baron Haig in 1919, he spent much of his time seeking support for Britain's soldiers, the British Legion, composed of military veterans, and Poppy Day. He also devoted himself to promoting the welfare of wartime veterans, while controversy surrounding his responsibility for the battlefield losses in the war of attrition continued to grow. He also defended his war record to the end of his days, yielding no point to his critics. Although Haig was associated with incompetence in high command during the Great War, his defenders argue that his leadership helped the Allies win the war, that determination and bulldog tenacity are much admired as cultural traits, and that Lloyd George never replaced him as commander in chief despite numerous opportunities. He died in London on 29 January 1928.

Thomas W. Davis

References

Sixsmith, Eric K. *Douglas Haig*. London: Weidenfeld and Nicolson, 1976.

Terraine, John. *Douglas Haig, the Educated Soldier*. London: Hutchinson, 1963.

Winter, Denis. *Haig's Command: A Reassessment*. New York: Viking, 1991.

See also ALLIED COUNTEROFFENSIVE; PASSCHENDAELE CAMPAIGN; SOMME, BATTLE OF

Haldane, Richard Burdon, Viscount (1856–1928)

British reformer and statesman, born on 30 July 1856 at Edinburgh, Scotland. Haldane served as a Liberal member of Parliament between 1885 and 1911 and as secretary of state for war under Liberal prime ministers Henry Campbell-Bannerman and Herbert Asquith between 1905 and 1912.

Acting on recommendations from the 1903–4 Esher Committee Report and 1906 Anglo-French staff talks, Haldane secured legislation modernizing the British army along European lines by creating the Imperial General Staff, the British Expeditionary Force, the Territorial Army, and the Officer Training Corps. Although fiscally minded Liberals were indifferent to them, Haldane's reforms were welcomed by the war office and made possible the rapid deployment of the BEF to France in 1914.

In 1912 Haldane undertook an unsuccessful mission to Germany to persuade Kaiser Wilhelm II to slow warship construction and was later accused of pro-German sympathies. Following 1912 Haldane served as lord chancellor, but he was dropped as a liability when Asquith formed his coalition government in 1915. He again served as lord chancellor in 1924, joined the Labour party, and headed the opposition in the House of Lords, 1925–28. Haldane died at Cloan, Perthshire, Scotland, on 19 August 1928.

Clayton D. Laurie

References

Haldane, Richard B. *Autobiography*. London: Hodder and Stoughton, 1929.

Koss, Stephen E. *Lord Haldane: Scapegoat for Liberalism*. New York: Columbia University Press, 1969.

Sommer, D. *Haldane of Cloan*. London: Allen and Unwin, 1960.

Spiers, Edward M. *Haldane: An Army Reformer*. New York: Columbia University Press, 1980.

See also NAVAL ARMS RACE, ANGLO-GERMAN; ORIGINS OF THE FIRST WORLD WAR

Hall, William Reginald (1870–1943)

Prominent British naval intelligence officer and vice admiral, born at Britford, Wiltshire, on 28 June 1870. Hall joined the navy in 1884. Known in the Royal Navy for his deep interest in the welfare of sailors, Hall was a reform-minded and imaginative officer who won promotion to commander in 1901 and to captain in 1905. In 1913 he was appointed captain of the new battle cruiser *Queen Mary* but for reasons of health was reassigned to naval intelligence duties in London in November of 1914. Hall was then appointed director of naval intelligence (DNI) and became instrumental in the establishment of the War Trade Intelligence Department for censorship operations.

Hall was an enormously successful DNI throughout the war. In particular, he emphasized and expanded the admiralty's cryptologic operations, called Room 40, that controlled British code-breaking activities against the Germans. Hall organized a "flying squad" to be ready at a moment's notice to search fallen zeppelins for secret information, especially signal books. Similarly, he arranged with the salvage service to raise, or at least search, any sunken U-boats. "Blinker" Hall, fondly named because he blinked incessantly, would say to one of his assistants upon learning of a German wreck, "Willoughby, go and fetch the rum!"

Under Hall's direction Room 40 achieved significant breakthroughs into German codes, especially at the time of the 1916 Battle of Jutland and the Zimmermann telegram in 1917. Promoted to rear admiral in April of 1917, Hall was that same year given a knighthood for his brilliant handling of the Zimmermann telegram affair.

At the end of the war Hall stepped down as DNI. In 1919 Room 40 was combined with the army's MI1–b to form the Government Code and Cypher School in London, which soon was placed under the jurisdiction of the foreign office.

Admiral Hall was a member of Parliament in the 1920s and a distinguished internationalist in the 1930s; but, as naval historian Arthur Marder put it, he was the greatest of all DNIs. Hall died in London on 22 October 1943.

Carl Boyd

References

Hoy, Hugh Cleland. *40 O.B. or How the War was Won.* London: Hutchinson, 1932.

James, William. *The Eyes of the Navy: A Biographical Study of Admiral Sir Reginald Hall, K.C.M.G., C.B., LL.D., D.C.I.* London: Methuen, 1955.

Marder, Arthur J. *From the Dreadnought to Scapa Flow.* 5 vols. London: Oxford University Press, 1961–70.

Von Rintelen (Franz Rintelen von Kleist). *The Dark Invader: Wartime Reminiscences of a German Naval Intelligence Officer.* London: Peter Davies, 1933.

See also INTELLIGENCE OPERATIONS; ROOM 40; ZIMMERMANN TELEGRAM

Haller, Józef (1873–1960)

Prominent Polish general, born at Jurczyce on 13 August 1873, Haller became a professional soldier in the Austro-Hungarian army, retiring in 1911 as a captain. Active in the Polish independence movement, Haller organized the Field Sokól Troops (based on the patriotic sports organization) in 1912. From 1914 to 1918 he served with the Austrian-backed Polish Legions and commanded the 3rd Infantry Regiment and the 2nd Legionary Brigade. To protest the signing of the Treaty of Brest-Litovsk by the Central Powers and Russia, Haller switched sides. At Rarańcza he defeated the Austrian 53rd Infantry Regiment. Haller joined his forces to the Polish II Corps in the Ukraine and became its commander. Although superior German forces attacked and defeated the Polish II Corps at Kaniów on 11 May 1918, Haller escaped capture and eventually ended up in France in July of 1918, where the Paris-based Polish National Committee appointed him commander in chief of Polish forces in France.

In the summer of 1920, during the Russo-Polish War, Haller commanded the entire Polish northern front during the crucial Battle of Warsaw. From 1940 to 1943 he was a minister in General Władysław Sikorski's wartime government. Haller died in London on 4 June 1960.

Andrzej Suchcitz

References

Aksamitek, Stefan. *General Józef Haller. Zarys biografii polityczenj.* Katowice: Wydawnictwo "Ślask," 1989.

Haller, Józef. *Pamietniki: Z Wyborem Dokumenton I Zdjec.* London: Veritas, 1964.

Wrzosek, Mieczyslaw. *Polski czyn zbrojny podczas pierwszej wojny śiatowej 1914–1918.* Warsaw: Wiedza Powszechna, 1990.

See also POLAND

Hamilton, Ian (1853–1947)

British general who commanded Allied forces in the Gallipoli Campaign. He was born at Corfu on 16 January 1853. Hamilton joined the army in 1872, and as a protegé of Field Marshals Frederick Roberts and Horatio Kitchener, he served with distinction during the Boer War. He held a variety of posts before World War I, including those of commander in chief of Mediterranean forces and inspector general of overseas forces.

At the outset of the war, Hamilton was given command of Britain's home defense forces. In March of 1915, after naval operations failed to open the Dardanelles, Kitchener picked Hamilton to command an amphibious assault on the Gallipoli Peninsula. An intelligent, brave, and popular officer, Hamilton proved inadequate in this command. He was given a mixed force of 490,000 British, Commonwealth, and French troops. Unfortunately, he was not given the proper intelligence information or logistical support to conduct the invasion.

Hamilton's conduct during the invasion compounded these deficiencies. He spent forty days assembling the invasion force on the islands off the coast of Gallipoli; this delay negated the original naval bombardment. It provided the commander of the Turkish forces, German General Otto Liman von Sanders, the opportunity to repair and strengthen the defenses. Hamilton's invasion plan failed to provide for the possibility of heavy resistance. On 25 April the Allied forces made twin landings at Cape Hellus and farther north at "Anzac Cove." Although Hamilton's troops established bridgeheads, the reinforced Turkish defenses stalled the attack. A war of attrition followed. By 8 May Hamilton had lost a third of his original invasion force.

Throughout the battle, Hamilton remained isolated both physically and intellectually. He established his headquarters on an island off the coast and relied on falsely optimistic reports from his field commanders. Hamilton also failed to control the actions of his front-line commanders. He often issued "suggestions" to his subordinates rather than direct orders. As a result, generals who should have been replaced were allowed to continue to squander the lives of their men. As casualties mounted, Hamilton remained overly optimistic and resisted calls for evacuation.

On 7 August Hamilton attempted to force a breakthrough by ordering a second landing, north of Anzac Cove, at Suvla Bay. This landing coincided with attacks from the two established beachheads. The main goal of the landing was to cut the north-south supply line of the Turks. Unfortunately, errors by subordinates prevented the landings from achieving a breakthrough or disrupting the Turkish supply lines. After the landings at Suvla Bay, a stalemate similar to that on the Western Front ensued. By October, London had lost confidence in Hamilton and he was relieved on 15 October.

Because of his mismanagement of the Gallipoli campaign, Hamilton never again held active command. He died in London on 12 October 1947.

T.M. Lansford

References

Hamilton, Ian. *Gallipoli Diary.* 2 vols. London: Edward Arnold, 1920.

Moorehead, Alan. *Gallipoli.* New York: Harper, 1956.

See also GALLIPOLI CAMPAIGN

Hankey, Sir Maurice (1877–1963)

British civil servant, born at Biarritz, France, on 1 April 1877. Hankey was educated at Rugby. He served in the Royal Navy (1895–1907) before becoming assistant secretary of the Committee of Imperial Defense in 1908. Between 1912 and 1938 Hankey served as secretary of the CID and during World War I as chief of the Imperial War Cabinet Secretariat. While in those posts he formalized procedure, prepared the agenda, recorded proceedings, and took responsibility for implementing cabinet decisions, all new innovations.

After the war Hankey combined the posts of secretary of the war cabinet and CID with that of the clerk of the Privy Council, holding the new post until retiring in 1938. It is in this position that he is generally credited with developing the modern cabinet form of British government. During this same period Hankey served as secretary of the British delegation at the Paris Peace Conference and of the Council of Four, at imperial conferences, and at conferences in Washington, Genoa, London, Lausanne, and The Hague. Granted a peerage in 1939, Hankey served in Neville Chamberlain's war cabinet and acted as paymaster-general in Churchill's government until dismissed in 1942. He died at Redhill, Surrey, England, on 25 January 1963.

Clayton D. Laurie

References

Hankey, Maurice. *The Supreme Command, 1914–1918.* 2 vols. London: Allen and Unwin, 1961.

———. *The Supreme Control at the Paris Peace Conference, 1919: A Commentary.* London: Allen and Unwin, 1963.

Naylor, John F. *A Man and an Institution: Sir Maurice Hankey, the Cabinet Secretariat and the Custody of Cabinet Secrecy.* Cambridge: Cambridge University Press, 1984.

Roskill, Stephen W. *Hankey: Man of Secrets.* 2 vols. Annapolis, Md.: Naval Institute Press, 1979.

Harmsworth, Alfred, Lord Northcliffe (1865–1922)

British newspaper editor and proprietor, born in Ireland on 15 July 1865. Alfred Harmsworth (created Baron Northcliffe in 1905 and Viscount in 1917) was one of the most influential "press lords" of the war. His publishing empire included the *Daily Mail* (1896) and *The Times* (1908). Prior to 1914 Northcliffe warned of the growing danger posed by Germany. The outbreak of hostilities saw him use his position to push for vigorous conduct of the war. That was translated into a number of press campaigns that included the demand for a Ministry of Munitions, the adoption of compulsory military service, and criticism of the Dardanelles Campaign. In 1917 Northcliffe headed the British War Mission to the United States. The following year he was appointed as director of propaganda for enemy countries. With the end of the war, his influence declined as his health failed and the excesses of wartime journalism were exposed. He died on 14 August 1922.

Van Michael Leslie

References

Bourne, J.M. *Britain and the Great War 1914–1918.* London: Edward Arnold, 1989.

Pound, Reginald, and Harmsworth, Geoffrey. *Northcliffe.* London: Cassell, 1959.

See also GREAT BRITAIN, HOME FRONT

Haus, Anton (1851–1917)

Naval commander and chief of the navy section at the ministry of war of the Austro-Hungarian navy, 1913–17. Born at Tolmein (Küstenland), on 13 June 1851, Haus was a brilliant and multitalented individual. He entered the navy in 1869 and after a successful career was named fleet inspector in 1912. He became naval commander (*Marinekommandant*) in February of 1913 at a time when the first Austrian dreadnoughts were entering service, transforming the Austro-Hungarian navy into a blue-water navy from a merely coastal-defense force. In 1913 Haus was also designated commander of the combined Triple Alliance fleets in the Mediterranean in the event of war, destined to lead a major naval encounter against the French and British. That possibility ended when Italy remained neutral, and Haus and his fleet, hopelessly outnumbered, were condemned to a strictly defensive role in the Adriatic.

In the beginning of the war Haus rejected German demands that he proceed to the assistance of the *Goeben* at Messina. His fleet was not yet fully mobilized, and he did not know the location of the far superior French forces. The most he would do was steam southward to escort the *Goeben* when she reached Austrian territorial waters. The operation was aborted when the Germans elected to dash for the Dardanelles. Haus was equally firm in rejecting the German and Austrian high commands' proposals that he deploy the fleet to Constantinople for operations against the Russians in the Black Sea. He regarded that as impracticable and insisted that the big ships be preserved as a fleet-in-being to watch his former ally, the Italians. After Italy entered the war on the Allied side, he still did not risk his capital ships in a major action but made full use of his light forces as well as submarines and aircraft. Haus subsequently became an ardent supporter of the German submarine campaign in the Mediterranean and the concept of unrestricted submarine warfare. While returning from a meeting on the subject with the German High

Command at Schloss Pless, he contracted pneumonia. He died aboard his flagship at Pola on 8 February 1917.

Paul G. Halpern

References

Bayer von Bayersburg, Heinrich. *Unter der k.u.k. Kriegsflagge, 1914–1918.* Vienna: Bergland Verlag, 1959.

Halpern, Paul G. *The Naval War in the Mediterranean, 1914–1918.* London and Annapolis, Md.: Allen & Unwin and Naval Institute Press, 1987.

Sokol, Hans Hugo. *Österreich-Ungarns Seekrieg.* 2 vols. Vienna: Amalthea Verlag, 1933. Reprint. Graz: Akademische Druck und Verlagsanstalt, 1967.

Wagner, Walter. *Die Obersten Behörden der K. und K. Kriegsmarine, 1856–1918.* Vienna: Ferdinand Berger, 1961.

See also AUSTRIA-HUNGARY, NAVY; MEDITERRANEAN NAVAL OPERATIONS

Helfferich, Karl (1872–1924)

German economist and politician. Born on 22 July 1872 in Neustadt in the Palatinate, Helfferich was the son of a textile-factory owner. He studied law and economics before joining the German Colonial Office in 1901. Known as an expert on finance and currency, he became director of the Baghdad Railroad in Constantinople in 1906 and later director of the Deutsche Bank in Berlin.

During the First World War Helfferich embarked on the second phase of his ambitious career when he was appointed state secretary of the treasury early in 1915 and, one year later, state secretary of the interior and deputy chancellor. He advocated a problematic policy of financing the war through loans rather than taxation, thereby exacerbating inflation. Conservative politically, somewhat arrogant and rigid in temperament—a contemporary called him a "Jesuit in frockcoat"—he opposed wartime efforts at political reform. Although he warned against unrestricted submarine warfare, fearing that it would bring the United States into the war, he defended it once it was implemented. Even when he resigned his ministerial appointments in 1917 he sympathized more with the army leaders than the politicians, who advocated a moderate course.

Although close to the National Liberals before 1914, Helfferich became a leader of the German National People's party after the war and a bitter enemy of the Weimar Republic and the policy of fulfillment. His death in a train wreck in Bellinza, Switzerland, on 23 April 1924 was met with relief by many contemporaries.

George P. Blum

Reference

Williamson, John G. *Karl Helfferich, 1872–1924: Economist, Financier, Politician.* Princeton: Princeton University Press, 1971.

See also GERMANY, HOME FRONT

Heligoland Bight, Battle of (28 August 1914)

Heligoland Island, located in the North Sea to the west of the Schleswig-Holstein Peninsula, guarded the strategically important anchorages of the German High Seas Fleet in the bight, south of the island. Heligoland also protected the western entrance to the newly widened Kiel Canal across the Schleswig-Holstein Peninsula, which allowed the High Seas Fleet to move undisturbed between the North and Baltic seas. Heavily fortified, Heligoland Island served as the cornerstone of the German fleet's security around the bight. Destroyers, U-boats, minesweepers, and light cruisers patrolled the bight, with the destroyers positioned farther out; the destroyers and U-boats were withdrawn at night and returned to duty in the morning.

The original British plan called for two squadrons of destroyers and some submarines to approach the bight early in the morning, get behind the newly arriving destroyers, inflict as much damage as possible, and then leave before heavy German ships could arrive. On 28 August 1914 the Royal Navy implemented the plan to cover the movement of 3,000 Royal Marines to Ostend, Belgium.

The British set out with thirty-one destroyers and two light cruisers, the *Arethusa* and *Fearless,* all commanded by Commodore Sir Reginald Tyrwhitt. These warships were supported by six light cruisers under the command of Commodore W.E. Goodenough and three submarines. As the surface ships arrived at their rendezvous, they were joined by Admiral Sir David Beatty's five battle cruisers. The admiralty had sent Beatty to support the operation but did not inform the other commanders because of the need to maintain radio silence. Communications problems were to be the hallmark of this operation. There was so much radio traffic between the British ships that the Germans knew that some kind of operation was in progress.

Shortly before 07:00 Tyrwhitt's force sighted two squadrons of German destroyers, which turned for port with the British in pursuit. Tyrwhitt's flagship, the *Arethusa*, was then engaged by the German light cruiser *Stettin*, which was soon joined by another light cruiser, the *Frauenlob*. By the time the German cruisers retired into a patch of mist, the *Arethusa* had only one functional gun, no radio communication, and one engine room flooded. After the engagement, *Fearless* came alongside *Arethusa;* using semaphore and radio on the *Fearless*, Tyrwhitt reassembled his scattered destroyers and began moving west at about 09:00.

The next engagement resulted in the sinking of the German destroyer *V-187,* which had run into a force of British destroyers, turned away only to find two British light cruisers, and turned again directly into the line of fire of four British destroyers. During this initial move to the west, the British ships spent much of their time chasing other British ships in and out of patches of mist that made target identification difficult. Twice a submarine reported German cruisers, really Goodenough's light cruisers. In one instance a British cruiser attempted to ram a British submarine, but the submarine survived by diving. Shortly after 10:00 Tyrwhitt had regained control of his force and again moved west.

The first German ships sent in response began to arrive on the scene an hour later. When the first of these, light cruiser *Strassburg*, was sighted, the fog gave her the appearance of a much larger ship, and Tyrwhitt signaled Beatty for help. The first reinforcements to arrive, however, were four of Goodenough's cruisers. The *Strassburg* quickly retired, but another German light cruiser, the *Mainz*, arrived moments later. She succeeded in fending off attacks by the destroyers, but when Goodenough's light cruisers joined the attack, their firepower quickly wrecked her. Even after Beatty's battle cruisers joined the fracas and despite enormous damage, the *Mainz*'s captain managed to alert other German units to the presence of heavy British warships in the bight. At about 13:10 Beatty's squadron destroyed two more cruisers, the *Köln* and *Ariadne*.

By 13:30 Admiral Beatty withdrew rather than risk an engagement with the German battle cruisers that he believed had already been dispatched. That ended the Battle of Heligoland Bight. While the British suffered one light cruiser and two destroyers badly damaged, they had sunk three German light cruisers and one destroyer. The British lost thirty-five men killed, while the Germans lost over one thousand. More important, the battle caused the Germans to pursue a more cautious strategy with their capital ships.

Randall J. Metscher

References

Bingham, Commander The Hon. H. *Falklands, Jutland, and the Bight*. London: J. Murray, 1919.

Frothingham, Thomas G. *The History of the World War*. 3 vols. New York: Books for Libraries Press, 1924–26. Reprint, 1971.

Hough, Richard. *The Great War at Sea 1914–1918*. Oxford: Oxford University Press, 1983.

Knight, E.F. *The Harwich Naval Forces*. London: Hodder and Stoughton, 1919.

Henry, Prince of Prussia (1862–1929)

German admiral and naval commander in the Baltic Sea, 1914–18. Born at Potsdam on 14 August 1862, Henry was the younger brother of Kaiser Wilhelm II. Widely traveled, he commanded the cruiser squadron based at Kiaochow and led German naval units during the Chinese Boxer Rebellion in 1900. Promoted Grand Admiral, Henry was named commander of German naval forces in the Baltic Sea in 1914. Henry understood the importance of controlling the Baltic in order to maintain the iron ore shipments from Sweden and prevent Allied shipments of war matériel to Russia. He mounted aggressive operations and persistently argued for greater forces in his theater. He exercised only nominal command, however, when major High Seas Fleet units operated in the Baltic, such as against the Gulf of Riga in 1915 and in the amphibious assault on the Baltic Islands in 1917. He died of cancer of the throat at Hemmelsmark on 20 April 1929.

A. Harding Ganz

References

Gemzell, Carl-Axel. *Organization, Conflict, and Innovation*. Lund, Sweden: Berlingska Boktryckeriet, 1973.

Herwig, Holger H., and Neil M. Heyman. *Biographical Dictionary of World War I.* Westport, Conn.: Greenwood, 1982.

See also Baltic Naval Operations

Hentsch, Richard (1869–1918)

Saxon staff officer and key figure in the Battle of the Marne. Born at Cologne on 18 December 1869 into a lower-middle-class family, Hentsch joined the Royal Saxon Army in 1888. After graduating from the Kriegsakademie, he served intermittently in various staff positions and, by the summer of 1914, had become the head of the Prussian General Staff's Third Branch (which tracked military developments in France and certain other Western countries). Upon mobilization, Hentsch took charge of the *Nachrichten-Abteilung* (the intelligence evaluation branch) of the high command (OHL); in that capacity he became a member of General Helmuth von Moltke's inner circle.

Once the German armies on the right wing had swept through Belgium into northeastern France, friction arose between them, and eventually a wide gap developed between General Alexander von Kluck's First and General Karl von Bülow's Second Army. While the Battle of the Marne was raging, Moltke, at German headquarters in Luxembourg, sent Lieutenant Colonel Hentsch to the front with sweeping powers to make whatever adjustments seemed appropriate. On 9 September, after having reviewed the situation with a deeply pessimistic Bülow and some other army commanders on the previous day, Hentsch ordered First Army to withdraw from its exposed positions. The order was reluctantly obeyed once it became clear that Bülow's troops had already begun their retreat toward the Aisne.

Following Moltke's replacement by General Erich von Falkenhayn, Major Leopold von Rauch took over the *Nachrichten-Abteilung* at the OHL, while Hentsch was sent off to Crown Prince Rupprecht of Bavaria as a "liaison officer." Later, Hentsch distinguished himself as a staff officer at the Eastern Front and was promoted to colonel in January of 1916. Fourteen months later he was made chief of staff to the military administrator of occupied Romania. While serving in that post, he not only received an official confirmation from the OHL that he had acted properly in 1914, but also a *Pour le Mérite* medal in recognition of his services since

that time. Hentsch died in Bucharest on 13 February 1918 after undergoing a gallbladder operation. His role in the Battle of the Marne became the subject of lively controversy during the 1920s and 1930s and even today there is no consensus on how much his actions on 8 and 9 September 1914 changed the course of the war.

Ulrich Trumpener

References

Barnett, Correlli. *The Swordbearers: Supreme Command in the First World War.* New York: William Morrow, 1964.

Jäschke, Gotthard. "Zum Problem der Marneschlacht von 1914." *Historische Zeitschrift* 190 (1960).

Möller, Hanns. *Geschichte der Ritter des Ordens "pour le mérite" im Weltkrieg.* 2 vols. Berlin: Bernard & Graefe, 1935.

Müller-Loebnitz, Wilhelm. *Die Führung im Marne-Feldzug 1914.* Berlin: E.S. Mittler und Sohn, 1939.

Reichsarchiv. *Der Weltkrieg 1914 bis 1918: Die militärischen Operationen zu Lande.* Vol. 4. Berlin: E.S. Mittler und Sohn, 1926.

See also Marne, First Battle of; Moltke, Helmuth von

Hertling, George Graf von (1843–1919)

Philosophy professor and politician. Born in Darmstadt on 31 August 1843 into a noble Catholic family, Hertling accepted a post teaching philosophy at the University of Bonn but was denied promotion because of his defense of the Catholic Church during Otto von Bismarck's *Kulturkampf.* In 1882 he became a professor of philosophy at Munich University but was increasingly active in politics. During 1877–90 and 1896–1912, Hertling represented the Catholic Center party in the Reichstag and became leader of its conservative wing; between 1912 and 1917 he served as Bavarian prime minister.

When Chancellor Bethmann Hollweg resigned in July of 1917, he recommended Hertling to succeed him, but Hertling declined because of advanced age. After Chancellor Georg Michaelis failed to mediate between the supreme command and Reichstag members who wanted peace, Hertling accepted the office on 1 November 1917 and served concurrently as Prussian minister-president.

Hertling attempted to placate the Reichstag by advocating minor reforms, such as reducing the degree of press censorship, but he refused to reform the three-tier system of Prussian voting. Not wanting to upset the high command of Field Marshal Paul von Hindenburg and General Erich Ludendorff, and hoping to secure Germany's eastern annexations, Hertling criticized Wilson's peace proposal before the Reichstag in January of 1918.

Like his predecessors, Hertling avoided promising restoration of Belgian sovereignty and refused to discuss Alsace and Lorraine. His effectiveness was greatly weakened by the totality of the high command's power. As a Catholic and a Bavarian, Hertling never earned the trust of Prussian conservatives or Kaiser Wilhelm II. He also lacked the desire and experience to govern Prussia effectively.

Hertling resigned on 2 October 1918, a month before Germany's defeat. He was replaced by Prince Max von Baden. Although retaining a better reputation than the obsequious Michaelis, Hertling has been regarded as a weak chancellor caught between a high command bent on victory and a Reichstag pushing for peace and domestic reform. Hertling died in Ruhpolding, Upper Bavaria, on 4 January 1919.

Glenn R. Sharfman

References

Holborn, Hajo. *A History of Modern Germany, 1840–1945*. New York: Alfred A. Knopf, 1969.

Jarausch, Konrad H. *The Enigmatic Chancellor: Bethmann Hollweg and the Hubris of Imperial Germany*. New Haven: Yale University Press, 1973.

Kitchen, Martin. *The Silent Dictatorship: The Politics of the German High Command under Hindenburg and Ludendorff, 1916–1918*. New York: Holmes and Meier, 1976.

See also GERMANY, HOME FRONT

Hindenburg, Paul von (1847–1934)

Field marshal and chief of the German General Staff, 1916–18. Born at Posen (Poznan) on 2 October 1847, he was the son of a junior army officer of ancient noble lineage and a bourgeois mother. He entered the Prussian cadet corps at age twelve and received a commission in the Foot Guards in 1866. After participating in the Seven Weeks' War and the Franco-Prussian War, Hindenburg attended the Kriegsakademie and thereafter held a variety of staff and command positions. From 1900 to 1903 he commanded the 28th (Badenese) Division in Karlsruhe and then spent eight years in Magdeburg as commanding general of IV Corps, becoming well-known for his calm and steadfastness. Made a three-star general in 1905, Hindenburg was placed on the inactive list in January of 1911 at the age of sixty-three.

When the opening weeks of the Great War led to a command crisis in East Prussia, the Army High Command (OHL) called Hindenburg out of retirement and sent him east as the new commander of the Eighth Army (22 August 1914). At the same time, it chose the versatile and energetic Major General Erich Ludendorff to serve as Hindenburg's chief of staff. This began a special relationship between the two men that would last until October of 1918.

Aided by the preparatory work already done by Eighth Army's brilliant GSO 1, Lieutenant Colonel Max Hoffmann, the new team decisively defeated Russian General A.V. Samsonov's Second Army in the Battle of Tannenberg (26–31 August 1914) and subsequently chased General Pavel Rennenkampf's First Army out of East Prussia after the First Battle of Masurian Lakes (9–14 September 1914). Promoted to colonel general, in mid-September Hindenburg assumed command of a new German force, the Ninth Army, which was supposed to relieve Russian pressure on Austria-Hungary by offensive action in Russian Poland. After weeks of campaigning against numerically superior Russian forces, the Ninth Army had to withdraw toward the German border. On 2 November Hindenburg was placed in overall charge of all German forces on the Eastern Front, assuming the title of *Oberbefehlshaber Ost* (Oberost). Promoted to field marshal a few weeks later, Hindenburg, with Ludendorff and Hoffmann at his side, henceforth presided over the operations of the German Eighth and Ninth armies, to which a Tenth Army (under Hermann von Eichhorn) was added in January of 1915.

After several grim battles in Russian Poland and in East Prussia during the winter, Oberost badgered the German High Command for additional troops with which to deliver a knockout blow against Russia, but General

Erich von Falkenhayn felt unable to accommodate those wishes. Although they achieved a breakthrough in Galicia in May of 1915 and had cleared the Russians out of Poland (and Courland), Hindenburg and Ludendorff were frustrated by Falkenhayn's refusal to allot to them all the divisions they wanted. They therefore became increasingly involved in efforts to get rid of the chief of the general staff; but Falkenhayn effectively countered their efforts (and those of others) and retained the kaiser's support until August of 1916. It was then that the kaiser, faced with Romania's intervention on the Allied side and under growing pressure from the eastern duumvirate as well as his imperial chancellor, finally agreed to replace Falkenhayn with Hindenburg at the OHL. Simultaneously, the kaiser authorized General Ludendorff to assume co-responsibility for military operations as first quartermaster-general.

During their first nine months at OHL, Hindenburg and Ludendorff presided over a successful campaign against Romania and a general stabilization of the Eastern Front. They also ruined French offensive plans by implementing Operation Alberich, a phased withdrawal of several German armies in the west to a shorter line (the Siegfried, or Hindenburg, Line) in March of 1917. But these successes were counter balanced by OHL's decision to back the proponents of unrestricted submarine warfare (which brought the United States into the war) and by its radical program of economic and manpower mobilization that led to technical and political problems.

The OHL's increasing interference in the internal affairs of the country was highlighted in July of 1917 by the dismissal of Chancellor Theobald von Bethmann Hollweg and a series of other personnel changes. Moreover, despite growing evidence of instability and exhaustion among Germany's allies, Hindenburg continued to support imperialistic war aims and the repression of any attempts to liberalize Germany's political system. In a big gamble, he also agreed with Ludendorff that Germany should launch major offensives on the Western Front in the spring of 1918, a strategy that led to some spectacular gains but eventually also exposed the German armies to devastating counterstrokes by the Allies.

As German setbacks multiplied and after Bulgaria dropped out of the war, Ludendorff demanded that the government sue for peace, but eventually he changed his mind and called for continuation of the war. When stymied in his plans, Ludendorff resigned from his post on 26 October but Hindenburg refused to follow his example—a decision that led to a permanent alienation between the two generals. With General Wilhelm Groener as his new right-hand man, the elderly field marshal reluctantly agreed to the conclusion of an armistice with the victorious Allies and thereafter presided over the withdrawal and demobilization of the German army. He resigned from his position on 25 June 1919, three days before representatives of the German government signed the Treaty of Versailles. After the war, Hindenburg contributed his prestige to the "Stab-in-the-Back" Myth.

Widely admired by many Germans ever since the Battle of Tannenberg, Hindenburg enjoyed his well-earned second retirement until 1925. When the president of the Weimar Republic, Friedrich Ebert, died in February of that year, conservative German circles persuaded Hindenburg to run for the presidency. Elected by a plurality of the popular vote, Hindenburg served as head of state for the next seven years, all the while thinking of himself as a man who might facilitate the eventual restoration of the monarchical system in Germany.

In 1932, by then approaching his eighty-fifth birthday, Hindenburg reluctantly agreed to stand for reelection. Running against both Adolf Hitler and Communist party leader Ernst Thälmann, Hindenburg emerged the winner in the runoff elections. Faced with serious economic and political instability in the country, Hindenburg in January of 1933 was persuaded by some of his friends and advisers to appoint Hitler, leader of the largest single party in Germany, chancellor in a coalition government. Though Hindenburg continued in office as Reich president, he proved unable (and, occasionally, unwilling) to keep Hitler and his Nazi henchmen from building up their power through trickery and violence. More and more withdrawn from public life, Hindenburg died at his Neudeck estate in East Prussia on 2 August 1934. He was buried with his wife at Tannenberg.

Ulrich Trumpener

References

Dorpalen, Andreas. *Hindenburg and the Weimar Republic.* Princeton: Princeton University Press, 1964.
Hindenburg, Paul von. *Aus meinem Leben.* Leipzig: Hirzel, 1920. Kitchen, Martin.

The Silent Dictatorship: The Politics of the German High Command under Hindenburg and Ludendorff, 1916–1918. London: Croom Helm, 1976.

Reichsarchiv et al. *Der Weltkrieg 1914 bis 1918: Militärische Operationen zu Lande.* Vols. 2, 5–14. Berlin: E.S. Mittler und Sohn, 1925, 1929–44.

Showalter, Dennis E. *Tannenberg: Clash of Empires.* Hamden, Conn.: Archon, 1991.

See also ALBERICH, OPERATION OF; EAST GALICIA, 1914 CAMPAIGN; EAST PRUSSIA CAMPAIGN; EASTERN FRONT, 1915; HITLER, ADOLF; HOFFMANN, MAX; LUDENDORFF, ERICH; LUDENDORFF OFFENSIVES; STAB-IN-THE-BACK MYTH

Hintze, Paul von (1864–1941)

German naval officer and diplomat. Like most senior officers in the kaiser's navy, Hintze (ennobled in 1908) came from a provincial middle-class family, his father being a tobacco processor at Schwedt on the Oder River. Born there on 13 February 1864, Hintze joined the navy in 1882. Thanks to his intelligence and versatility, he eventually became a staff officer and spent over seven years at St. Petersburg, first as a naval attaché (1903–08) and then as the kaiser's military plenipotentiary at the czar's court.

In 1911 Hintze retired from the navy as a rear admiral and joined the diplomatic service. After serving three years as the German minister to Mexico, he made his way to China to serve as minister there. After his return to Europe in 1917, he was appointed German minister to Norway. In July of 1918, after Richard von Kühlmann had run afoul of General Erich Ludendorff and other right-wingers, the kaiser chose Hintze to take over the German foreign office. Much to the amazement of the high command (OHL), the former admiral during the next twelve weeks tried hard (and often effectively) to continue the moderate policies of his predecessor, particularly by pushing for the abandonment of unrealistic war aims and for the establishment of better relations with Lenin's Bolshevik government.

When Prince Max of Baden formed a new government on 3 October Hintze relinquished his portfolio to Wilhelm Solf and joined the kaiser's entourage as liaison between the monarch and the chancellor. In that position he pushed the kaiser into a further liberalization of the German government system. Moreover, in the days preceding the Berlin November Revolution, Hintze was one of the leading figures at the German general headquarters who felt that, for the sake of the country, the kaiser should abdicate.

After the war, Hintze remained politically active and eventually became head of the VDA (Association of Germans Abroad). He died on 19 August 1941 at Merano, South Tyrol.

Ulrich Trumpener

References

Baumgart, Winfried. *Deutsche Ostpolitik 1918.* Vienna and Munich: Oldenbourg, 1966.

Hentig, Hans Wolfram von. "Hintze." *Neue Deutsche Biographie* 9 (1972).

Hull, Isabel V. *The Entourage of Kaiser Wilhelm II, 1888–1918.* Cambridge: Cambridge University Press, 1982.

Ritter, Gerhard. *The Sword and the Scepter: The Problem of Militarism in Germany.* Vol. 4. Coral Gables, Fla.: University of Miami Press, 1973.

Trumpener, Ulrich. "The Service Attachés and Military Plenipotentiaries of Imperial Germany, 1871–1918." *International History Review* 9 (1987).

Hipper, Admiral Franz Ritter von (1863–1932)

German admiral and chief of the high seas fleet in 1918, born on 13 September 1863 in Weilheim. Hipper was one of the few Catholics, Bavarians, and unmarried officers among Germany's naval leaders. Hipper, who served between 1881 and 1918, first saw service overseas before returning to home waters after 1890. While endorsing Tirpitz's battle-fleet concept, he spent most of his career on smaller vessels, commanding torpedo boats and cruisers. Recognized for his nautical skills and tactical expertise and liked for his joviality, Hipper rose to flag rank by 1912 and took over the scouting forces of the High Seas Fleet. He held that command until 1918 with Erich Raeder, the future grand admiral, as his chief of staff.

Coastal operations against England in 1914 and the Dogger Bank engagement in 1915 marked Hipper as a fearless and imaginative tactician. He shared, however, the dilemma common among Germany's naval leaders: desiring to avoid a decisive showdown with the superior Grand Fleet while fearing a decline in morale and reduced parliamentary appropriations if the fleet remained inactive.

Hipper's most conspicuous performance came in the Battle of Jutland. On 31 May 1916 his scouting force of six battle cruisers led Admiral Reinhard Scheer's main body of sixteen battleships on northerly courses along Denmark's Jutland Peninsula. At the same time the British Grand Fleet under Admiral John Jellicoe and its cruiser force under Vice Admiral David Beatty approached from the west. By afternoon Hipper had engaged Beatty's units in relatively poor visibility. The German battle cruisers, though outnumbered, proved superior to their British counterparts and sank two of them without losses of their own. Encouraged by these developments, Hipper moved to draw the enemy in the direction of Scheer's dreadnoughts, while Beatty sought to bring Hipper within range of Jellicoe's battleships, closing in from the northwest. Soon the battle broadened into a furious artillery duel involving both capital ships and lighter units, until darkness engulfed the combatants. Jellicoe twice succeeded in "crossing the T," thus forcing Scheer to respond by turning maneuvers that exposed his ships to heavy fire. Hipper eventually transferred to the *Moltke* when his flagship, *Seydlitz,* went down. During the night the Germans gradually disengaged and, badly mauled, managed to slip away to their bases. Only later did they learn that the British had suffered greater losses in ships, tonnage, and personnel.

Analysts have credited Hipper with sound judgment in the battle's early phase and praised his leadership under difficult and confusing conditions. In recognition for his efforts he received the order *Pour le Mérite* and a knightship from the King of Bavaria. In the shake-up of Germany's naval command structure in August of 1918, Hipper was promoted to full admiral and succeeded Scheer as chief of the High Seas Fleet. He planned the abortive last-minute sortie of the battle fleet against England on 30 October that caused crippling mutinies on his ships and presaged the end of hostilities.

Hipper retired from active duty in December of 1918. The *Kriegsmarine* later named a heavy cruiser after him. He died on 25 May 1932 in Altona.

Eric C. Rust

References

Bennett, Geoffrey M. *The Battle of Jutland.* Philadelphia: Dufour, 1964.

Macintyre, Donald. *Jutland.* New York: Norton, 1958.

Marineministerium (Berlin). *Der Krieg zur See, 1914–1918.* 24 vols. Berlin, 1922–66.

Scheer, Reinhard. *Germany's High Seas Fleet in the World War.* London: Cassell, 1920.

Waldeyer-Hartz, Hugo von. *Admiral von Hipper: Das Lebensbild eines deutschen Flottenführers.* Leipzig: R. Kittler, 1933.

See also DOGGER BANK, NAVAL BATTLE OF; GERMAN CRUISER RAIDS, 1914; GERMANY, NAVY; JUTLAND, BATTLE OF

H

Historiography of the Outbreak of the War

No sooner had Europe gone to war than controversy over its outbreak began. All the various governments published a series of "color books" that presented selected diplomatic documents to try to prove that they had been forced into the war. The Allies' victory in 1918, however, placed them in the position to impose not only peace terms but also blame. Article 231 of the Versailles Treaty forced Germany to accept responsibility for causing the war. That, of course, provided justification for reparations. The controversy over the "War Guilt" clause has fueled the debate over the outbreak of the war ever since.

For obvious reasons, German historians were the first to attempt to revise the guilty verdict handed down by the Paris Peace Conference. The War Guilt Section of Weimar Germany's foreign ministry appointed a team of historians (Albrecht Mendelssohn-Bartholdy, Johannes Lepsius, and Friedrich Thimme) to edit and publish German diplomatic documents of the prewar era in an effort to show that Germany had not premeditated the war. The result was the multivolume collection *Die große Politik der europäischen Kabinette.* British and French papers did not come out until the 1930s, and thus historians examining the origins of the war relied extensively on the German documents, encouraging the revisionist school.

The War Guilt Section also began publishing the journal *Die Kriegsschuldfrage* (War Guilt Question), which, under editor Alfred von

Wegerer, a former military officer working in the foreign office, launched the revisionist assault against the Versailles Treaty. Employing a self-righteous tone, Wegerer asserted that the Central Powers had been fully justified in their actions toward Serbia because it had plotted the assassination of Archduke Franz Ferdinand and was bent on the destruction of Austria-Hungary. Whereas Germany and Austria-Hungary were trying to protect their vital interests, Russia and France had intervened for selfish motives: Russia to gain the Straits and establish dominance in the Balkans, and France to recover Alsace and Lorraine. Thus it was the Entente powers that turned what would have been a localized conflict into a European war.

While Wegerer's position received strong support in his own country, his influence outside of Germany was minimal because he had made no effort at objectivity. Count Max Montgelas, however, helped spread the German revisionist message. In 1923 Montgelas published *Leitfuden zur Kriegsschuldfrage* (translated into English as *The Case for the Central Powers*), which was certainly sympathetic to the German side but more objective. Montgelas concluded, for example, that the Black Hand's involvement in the assassination of Franz Ferdinand did not necessarily indict the Serbian government. More important, he pointed out three critical mistakes made by German policy makers during the July Crisis: (1) The German government believed that European monarchies, including Russia, would rally behind Austria-Hungary in the wake of the assassination; (2) Germany failed to recognize the resolve of France and Russia to prevent Austria-Hungary from crushing Serbia; and (3) Germany had a misplaced faith in British neutrality. What gave Montgelas's interpretation greater appeal outside of Germany was his assertion that neither the Entente nor the Central Powers were bent on war, but that a series of miscalculations in diplomacy led to the conflict. As a result, he could clear Germany of war guilt without passing it to the Entente.

German revisionists were soon joined in the protest against the "War Guilt" clause by American historian Harry Elmer Barnes, professor of historical sociology at Smith College. In a series of articles published in such journals as *Current History*, Barnes played upon the postwar disillusionment sweeping the United States by challenging the notion that the Germans had forced war on the Entente. In his most important work, *The Genesis of the World War* (1925), Barnes exonerates the Central Powers from any guilt in causing war. For Barnes, Austria-Hungary had no choice but to punish Serbia; it was a matter of survival. More important, he cites "informed Serbs" in asserting that Premier Nikola Pašić and Crown Prince Alexander were fully aware of the assassination plot against Franz Ferdinand. While he admits that Wilhelm II's blank check was poor judgment, he maintains that it was not a premeditated step to war but a necessary attempt to prop up a tottering ally. France, on the other hand, had given Russia an "open-ended commitment" to support its "expansionist" Balkan policies. With Russian mobilization the die was cast and war became unavoidable.

More successful than Barnes in undermining the Versailles Treaty was American historian Sidney Bradshaw Fay. A colleague of Barnes's at Smith College, Fay's objectivity made his two-volume *Origins of the World War* (1928) the most influential book of the revisionist school. Indeed, it won him a position at Harvard University. The key to Fay's interpretation is his conclusion that all the powers, rather than Germany and her allies alone, shared a degree of blame. After dismissing Barnes's claim that the Serbian government was involved in the assassination of Franz Ferdinand, Fay points out the stupidity of Wilhelm II in giving the Austrians a free hand in the Balkans. More important, he asserts that German Chancellor Theobald von Bethmann Hollweg believed that the best way of preventing Russia from intervening in an Austro-Serbian conflict was to give the appearance of full support for Austria-Hungary. Only too late did Bethmann Hollweg realize the folly of his policy, and, while his belated efforts to mediate were sincere, they came too late; Russian mobilization left Germany no choice but to go to war. He also faults British Foreign Minister Sir Edward Grey for not clearly stating British policy. Fay was so influential in making his arguments that not until Fritz Fischer would any historian attempt to lay sole blame for the war upon the Central Powers; instead, the debate shifted to the degree that each power was responsible for the war.

Although the revisionist school had found support within the United States, it was not well received within other Allied countries, such as France. Indeed, after the initial salvos were fired by Wegerer and Montgelas, French historian

Pierre Renouvin quickly responded. In *Les Origines immédiates de la guerre* (1925) Renouvin clears the Entente of premeditating the war. While he speculates that the Serbian government may have inspired the assassination attempts, he points out that there was no direct evidence that they did so. Although Renouvin admits that Russian mobilization played a role in producing the war, he maintains that the Russians were merely responding to actions carried out by the Germans and Austrians. Noting the divisions within the British cabinet, Renouvin also excuses Grey for not clearly stating British policy earlier in the crisis. Although Renouvin does not charge Germany and Austria-Hungary with desiring a general war, he asserts that, in pursuing a localized war to neutralize Serbia, the Central Powers were well aware that they risked a European war.

Although Fay had won a large audience in the United States, American historian Bernadotte Everly Schmitt emerged as the leading American antirevisionist during the 1930s. His two-volume work, *The Coming of the War, 1914* (1930), challenges almost every element of Fay's interpretation. Where Fay excused Wilhelm II's "blank check" as stupidity, Schmitt asserts that Wilhelm was fully aware of Austria-Hungary's intentions and in fact urged them to take an even more vigorous stance. He also points out that there is no evidence that French President Raymond Poincaré and Premier René Viviani plotted war during their visit to St. Petersburg. German efforts to rein in Austria-Hungary were halfhearted at best and cynical at worst. According to Schmitt, the Central Powers were bent on altering the balance of power in the Balkans. Their mistake was in believing that Russia would back down as it had in the Bosnian Annexation Crisis of 1908 and the First Balkan War. Certainly they knew they risked war, but, as Schmitt reminds his readers, war was unfortunately considered an acceptable option by all powers in any diplomatic dispute.

The most significant antirevisionist work was written by the Italian journalist Luigi Albertini. His expertise in European languages allowed him to become the first historian to examine all the major diplomatic collections of the powers involved in the July Crisis. The result was the massive three-volume work *Le origini della guerra del 1914*. While Albertini faults Serbian Premier Pašić for not taking adequate steps to warn the Austrians after he became aware of the plot to assassinate Franz Ferdinand, he concludes

that it was Germany that played the key role in the July Crisis. In urging Austria-Hungary to take a hard line against Serbia, German leaders were gambling that the Entente would stay out of a Balkan war. Thus Germany was not only aware of the Austrian ultimatum before it was issued but applauded it. As for the Entente powers, Albertini asserts that while the French did not plot a war, they clearly attempted to capitalize on German and Austrian blunders. While condemning Russian mobilization as a fatal blunder, he asserts that Russia was merely reacting to the policies being pursued in Berlin and Vienna. Although Albertini believed that the Germans should have realized that the British could not remain neutral in a Franco-German war, he nevertheless faults Grey for not giving a warning earlier. Despite the divisions in the British cabinet, Grey could have at the very least warned the Germans that their actions risked British intervention.

For almost two decades, Albertini had the last word on the outbreak of the First World War. Because the Second World War overshadowed the earlier conflict, it also dominated historical commentary in the late 1940s and 1950s. Gradually, however, some historians began to see a continuity between German policy in both wars. Ironically, it was a German, Fritz Fischer, a historian at the University of Hamburg and a former Nazi, who renewed the debate over the origins of the First World War.

Although Fischer had been trained in Reformation history, the Second World War broadened his horizons. After traveling abroad and studying in the United States he became acquainted with the antirevisionist school, which had been muted in Germany. After returning to Germany in 1955 he began an intensive study of German archival records, including those in East Germany. He discovered that many of Germany's prewar diplomatic papers had never been published, and for obvious reasons: they revealed a much more aggressive role than German leaders had wanted to become known.

After publishing some of his findings in articles in the *Historische Zeitschrift,* in 1961 Fischer published his landmark work, *Griff nach der Weltmacht* ("Grasping for World Power"), which was later published in English under the title *Germany's Aims in the First World War*. While the bulk of the book concentrated on German objectives during the war and was widely accepted, the most controversial part was the first two chapters in which Fischer

H

examined Germany's imperialistic aims for world power and its role in the July Crisis. From the beginning there is no doubt about German responsibility for the war. Fischer makes it clear that under Wilhelm II Germany made a determined effort to become the leading world power. When that led to the formation of the Triple Entente, Fischer asserts that German military leaders began looking to a preventive war, and the assassination of Franz Ferdinand provided them the opportunity. Fischer continues this theme in *War of Illusions* (1969) by tying the objectives of military leaders together with those of politicians and industrialists who sought additional territory and economic supremacy in Europe. He even asserts that in December of 1912 the German war council decided to precipitate a war.

It is not surprising that Fischer's interpretation created a storm of controversy, especially within Germany, which was struggling to paint the Third Reich as an aberration in German history. If Fischer were correct, however, the Nazis were a natural progression in German history. For that reason many West German historians denounced Fischer as a traitor. In articles in the *Historische Zeitschrift* and his four-volume work *Staatskunst und Kriegshand Werk* (published in English as *The Sword and the Scepter*), Gerhard Ritter rejected any hint at a continuity in German diplomacy. Where Fischer had interpreted such German actions as the blank check and rejection of arbitration as a sign of a premeditation, Ritter saw them as tragic blunders. Thus for Ritter, Bethmann Hollweg finally realized the errors in judgment and sincerely tried to reign the Austrians in, but it was too late. Ritter also discounts Fischer's reliance upon the bellicose statements of generals and political figures. More important, Ritter rejects Fischer's thesis that the German people were bent upon an offensive war. Finally, Ritter and other historians point out that Fischer often confused the aims that developed during the war with Germany's prewar policy.

While Ritter attacked Fischer, Imanuel Geiss rose to his defense. In a collection of over 700 documents, published in two volumes as *Julikrise und Kriegsausbruck, 1914,* Geiss provided the public with a glance at the papers that had influenced Fischer's work. In light of these revelations even Fischer's critics had to agree that German policy played the leading role in causing the outbreak of the war, though they continued to discredit his assertion that Ger-

many plotted war. Wolfgang Mommsen, for example, argues in *Das Zeitalter des Imperialismus* (1969) that while Bethmann Hollweg had consistently rejected the idea of a preventive war, he sought to use the crisis resulting from the assassination of Franz Ferdinand to split the Entente. He miscalculated that France and Britain would not support Russia over Serbia. Likewise, Egmont Zechlin in a series of articles recognizes Germany's principal role, but argues that German policy was defensive, rising out of fear of encirclement.

Although historians continue to debate the outbreak of the First World War today, many of the central issues that were first raised in the aftermath of the war have been settled, following the controversy over Fritz Fischer's work. No one can seriously conclude that Germany or any other power bears sole responsibility for the war or that the war was premeditated. Historians are generally agreed that all the powers played a role in producing the conflict, though they differ on which powers and which actions played the critical role. In many ways these issues are pointless. What is important is that war remained an option for all the powers during the July Crisis. Had they known the destruction that would follow the outbreak of a European war, they might have acted differently. Unfortunately, a historian's hindsight was not available to the diplomats of July 1914.

Justin D. Murphy

References

Geiss, Imanuel. *July 1914: The Outbreak of the First World War*. New York: Norton, 1974.

Fischer, Fritz. *Germany's Aims in the First World War*. New York: W.W. Norton, 1967.

Herwig, Holger H. *The Outbreak of World War I*. 5th ed. Problems in European Civilization series. Lexington, Mass.: D.C. Heath, 1991.

Langdon, John W. *July 1914: The Long Debate, 1918–1990*. Oxford: Berg, 1991.

See also ALLIANCES, PREWAR; ORIGINS OF THE FIRST WORLD WAR; OUTBREAK OF THE FIRST WORLD WAR

Hitler, Adolf (1889–1945)

German corporal and future dictator of Nazi Germany. Adolf Hitler was born on 20 April

1889 in Braunau, Austria, to an imperial customs officer, Alois, and his third wife, Klara Pölzl. Although Hitler later claimed to have grown up in poverty and privation, his father retired with a pension in 1895. Hitler aspired to a career in art but twice was denied admission to the Vienna Academy of Fine Arts. From 1908 he lived in Vienna in virtual obscurity, often staying in a charity hotel. In 1913 he left Austria, probably to avoid the draft that he had evaded since 1910, and settled in Munich.

With the outbreak of World War I, Hitler petitioned and was allowed to join 1st Company of the 16th Bavarian Reserve Infantry Regiment. He saw action in the First Battle of Ypres in 1914 and subsequently participated in the battles of Nueve Chapelle in 1915 and the Somme in 1916. After being wounded in the leg on 7 October 1916 near Bapaume, he was sent back to Germany for the first time in nearly two years. Upon recuperation, Hitler returned to the front in March of 1917 and was promoted to lance corporal, taking part in the battles of Arras and Passchendaele. Having participated in the 1918 spring offensives, Hitler was gassed in an attack by the British on 13–14 October 1918. Temporarily blinded, he ended the war in a hospital.

Throughout the conflict, Hitler served as a *Meldegänger,* or runner, carrying messages between the company and regimental headquarters. He thus spent nearly four years at or near the front. In December of 1914 Hitler had been awarded the Iron Cross Second Class. On 4 August 1918 he received the Iron Cross First Class, a quite uncommon award for someone of his rank. It is unclear for which action he received this award, since the official regimental history says nothing about it.

World War I made a major impression on Hitler and probably was one of the happiest times of his life. After its end, he worked in Munich for the army by reporting on developing political parties. He soon embraced politics full time and joined the German Workers' party. Soon he was the driving force in the party, which changed its name to the National Socialist German Workers' party.

Under Hitler's leadership, the Nazis embraced his ideas of terror and intimidation. The party rose to prominence in Germany by the early 1930s, and Hitler became chancellor in January of 1933. For the next twelve years he would rule Germany with absolute authority—plunging the world into war in 1939 and systematically murdering millions in concentration camps. He died by his own hand in his bunker in Berlin on 30 April 1945.

Laura Matysek Wood

References

Bullock, Alan. *Hitler: A Study in Tyranny.* Rev. ed. New York: Harper and Row, 1962.

Flood, Charles Bracelan. *Hitler: The Path to Power.* Boston: Houghton-Mifflin, 1989.

Ho Chi Minh (1890–1969)

Indo-Chinese nationalist and one of the outspoken advocates of freedom for colonial peoples during the Paris Peace Conference. Born on 19 May 1890 in northern Annam, son of a Mandarin official whose career had been halted as a result of anti-French activity, Ho Chi Minh's real name was Nguyen Tat Thanh; later he changed it to Nguyen ai Quoc ("Nguyen the Patriot") and finally to Ho Chi Minh ("He who brings enlightenment"). Ho attended Vietnam's best high school at Hué, but in 1911 at age nineteen he left Vietnam on a French merchant ship. He lived in London for several years working as an assistant chef in the kitchens of the Hotel Carlton. He also claimed to have visited the United States and lived in Harlem. Ho came to Paris during the war and worked as a pastry chef, retoucher of photographs, and designer of "Asian antiquities" produced in France. There were many Vietnamese living in France at the time (during the war some 100,000 went there to work as laborers), and Ho became one of their leaders.

In 1919 Ho and two of his compatriots drew up an eight-point memorandum to the Great Powers at the Paris Peace Conference, in which they demanded that Wilsonian principles of self-determination of peoples be applied to Indo-China. This call went unheeded, and Ho's activities earned him a police dossier. The French socialist newspaper *Le Populaire* did publish the memorandum and a number of Ho's later articles. Ho joined the Socialist party, and in 1920 he was one of the founders of the French Communist party when it split off from the socialists.

He became active in the Comintern and in 1930 was one of the founders of the Indochinese Communist party. Ho Chi Minh led the struggle of Vietnamese nationalists to free their country, first against the Japanese, then the

French, and finally the Americans. Ho died on
3 September 1969.

Spencer C. Tucker

References

Karnow, Stanley. *Vietnam, A History*. New
York: Viking, 1973.

Lacouture, Jean. *Ho Chi Minh, A Political
Biography*. New York: Random House,
1968.

Sainteny, Jean. *Ho Chi Minh and His Vietnam*. Translated by Herma Briffault.
Chicago: Cowles, 1972.

Hoffmann, Carl Adolf Maximilian (Max) (1869–1927)

German general. Born in Homberg near Kessel
on 25 January 1869, Hoffmann was the son of
a judge. Despite his lack of family military tradition, Hoffmann attended the Kriegsschule.
After serving a term as adjutant in an infantry
regiment he was selected to attend the
Kriegsakademie at Torgau, where he was conspicuous for his brilliant, albeit indolent, mind
and intuitive grasp of practical solutions to map
problems. His superiors esteemed his military
aptitude despite his marked indifference to soldierly deportment, drill, and sports.

Hoffmann served a six-month tour in Russia in 1898–99, where he gained insight into its
military system. Upon his return to Germany, he
was assigned to the Russian section of the general staff. His special gifts soon attracted the
attention of General Schlieffen, who appointed
him as a German military observer with Japanese forces in the Russo-Japanese War. That
experience increased Hoffmann's knowledge of
Russian military methods and command style
and helped him gain the post of operations chief
of the Eighth Army under General Max von
Prittwitz, charged with defending East Prussia.

Hoffmann urged his commanders to take
risks when dealing with the Russians, and he
reassured them that intercepted Russian *en clair*
radio messages were authentic. Hoffmann
anticipated that Russian General Pavel Rennenkampf's column would not hasten to the assistance of General Aleksandr Samsonov's force.
He attributed this to attrition and supply and
transportation problems, rather than malicious
indifference, as popularly imputed. Hoffmann's
Tannenberg battle plan precisely foretold the
one prepared by Ludendorff and Hindenburg,
who were en route to take charge in the East.

Hoffmann received the Iron Cross, First Class,
for the German victory at Tannenberg and for
planning and staff work for the February 1915
Masurian Lakes campaign. He claimed that the
medal was won sitting at the telephone. The trio
of Hindenburg, Ludendorff, and Hoffmann
were a smoothly operating machine on the Eastern Front. Hindenburg provided social prominence and steadfastness, Ludendorff the driving
energy and organizing ability, and Hoffmann
the fertility of ideas and caustic sense of reality.

Throughout the last half of 1916, Hoffmann worked to brace the German position in
Poland against heavy Russian attacks. When
Hindenburg and Ludendorff were posted to
command the Third Army in the West in August
of 1916, Hoffmann was promoted to colonel
and appointed chief of staff to the new overall
commander in the East, Field Marshal Prince
Leopold of Bavaria. Hoffmann was the hidden
hand behind Leopold's successes in the East:
halting the July 1916 Brusilov Offensive, mounting an offensive against the Russians in Galicia
that defeated them near Zloczov, orchestrating
the attack on Riga, and planning Baltic amphibious operations in the fall of 1917. In recognition
of his key role in these operations, Hoffmann
was promoted to major general.

In December of 1917 Hoffmann concluded
an armistice with the Bolsheviks, representing
the Hindenburg-Ludendorff team at peace talks
in Brest-Litovsk. Hoffmann insisted on considerable Russian territorial concessions, although
less than those demanded by Ludendorff. In
January of 1918, when Hoffmann suggested
that the kaiser might modify his demands for
Polish territory, he was rebuked by Ludendorff's
right-wing supporters as succumbing to
"Semitic" influences. In any event, in February
of 1918, when Trotsky tried stonewalling,
Hoffmann sent fifty-two divisions against the
disorderly, demobilizing Russian army. The
Germans captured, in rapid succession, Duna-
berg, Pskov, and Kiev, after which Lenin ordered Trotsky to sign a peace on German terms.

After his retirement from the army in
1920, Hoffmann plotted with agents from the
victorious Allies (some say including Sidney
Reilly) to topple the Bolsheviks from power in
Russia. His postwar publications, including an
analysis of Germany's fatal command decisions,
his war diaries, and an anti-Bolshevik alarmist
tract, were all critical of Hindenburg and
Ludendorff. Hoffmann died at Bad Reichenhall
on 8 July 1927.

It is quite probable that had Hoffmann curbed his acid wit and been posted to the vital Western Front, instead of working in the shadow of notables or royalty in a secondary theater, he would be ranked among the most brilliant and successful German commanders of the war.

James J. Bloom

References

Asprey, Robert B. *The German High Command at War: Hindenburg and Ludendorff Conduct World War I*. New York: William Morrow, 1991.

Churchill, Winston S. *The Unknown War*. New York: Charles Scribner's Sons, 1932.

DeWeerd, H.A. "Hoffmann" in *Great Soldiers of the Two World Wars*. New York: W. Norton, 1941.

Hoffmann, Max. *War Diaries and Other Papers*. 2 vols. Edited by Karl Novak. Translated by Eric Sutton. London: Martin Secker, 1929.

Stone, Norman. *The Eastern Front 1914–1917*. New York: Charles Scribner's Sons, 1975.

See also BREST-LITOVSK, TREATY OF; EAST PRUSSIA CAMPAIGN; EASTERN FRONT, 1915; HINDENBURG, PAUL VON; RIGA, BATTLE OF

Holtzendorff, Henning von (1853–1919)

German grand admiral and chief of the admiralty staff, 1915–18. Born on 9 January 1853 in Prentzlau into an old Prussian noble family, Holtzendorff joined the navy in 1869, fought in the Franco-Prussian War, and subsequently served both overseas and in home waters. With expertise in capital ships, he commanded a battleship during the Boxer Rebellion and by 1906, with flag rank, Germany's First Battle Squadron. In 1909 he became chief of the high seas fleet and was promoted to full admiral a year later. Conservative and subscribing to "old school" doctrine, Holtzendorff soon disagreed with Tirpitz over the pace of naval expansion, training methods, and contingency planning. He reluctantly retired in April of 1913.

In September of 1915 Holtzendorff was reactivated as chief of the admiralty staff. Known to be critical of Tirpitz, he cultivated close relations to the kaiser, Chancellor Theobald Bethmann Hollweg, and chief of the naval cabinet Admiral Georg von Müller. While supporting Scheer's fleet operations in 1916, Holtzendorff convinced himself that ultimately only all-out submarine warfare ensured a German victory over England. He was primarily responsible for persuading the kaiser to resume unrestricted U-boat activities in February of 1917, promising monthly sinkings of 500,000 tons and England's collapse before the end of the summer. Even though disappointed in his expectations, Holtzendorff retained imperial favor until August of 1918 when he retired for good as part of Scheer's reorganization of the navy's command structure. Already close to death, in 1918 Holtzendorff received the honor of promotion to grand admiral and the *Pour le Mérite*. He died on 7 June 1919 in Jagow.

Eric C. Rust

References

Görlitz, Walter, ed. *The Kaiser and His Court: The Diaries, Note Books and Letters of Admiral Georg Alexander von Müller, Chief of the Naval Cabinet, 1914–1918*. New York: Harcourt, Brace, World, 1964.

Herwig, Holger H. *The German Naval Officer Corps: A Social and Political History, 1890–1918*. Oxford: Oxford University Press, 1973.

———. *"Luxury" Fleet*. London: Allen, Unwin, 1980.

Hubatsch, Walther. *Der Admiralstab und die obersten Marinebehörden in Deutschland. 1848–1945*. Frankfurt: Bernard, Graefe, 1958.

Tirpitz, Alfred von. *My Memoirs*. 2 vols. New York: Dodd, Mead, 1919.

See also GERMANY, NAVY; SUBMARINE WARFARE, CENTRAL POWERS

Horne, Baron Henry Sinclair (1861–1929)

British general, born at Stirkoke, County Caitness, on 19 February 1861. Horne was commissioned in the artillery from the Royal Military Academy, Woolwich, in 1880. He saw service in the Boer War and began the First World War as a brigadier general, commanding the artillery of I Corps. In 1915 Horne commanded the 2nd Division. He served briefly on Lord Horatio Kitchener's staff during the latter's visit to the Dardanelles that same year. In 1916 he commanded XV Corps on the

Somme before being promoted again to command First Army later the same year.

Horne was a competent and steady leader who worked well with subordinate corps commanders. That was important, because the Canadian Corps (by 1917 acting as a national army) was often attached to First Army. In 1917, for example, Horne had to deal with Lieutenant General Sir Arthur Currie, who refused to fight at Passchendaele if it meant serving under General Sir Hubert Gough. First Army's successes included Vimy Ridge (1917) and the battles on the left flank of the BEF during the summer advance of 1918, in particular the breaching of the Hindenburg Line and the Canal du Nord.

Horne was a capable army commander on par with Herbert Plumer and Henry Rawlinson. Created baron after the war, Horne died at Stirkoke on 14 August 1929.

Ian M. Brown

References

Dancocks, Daniel G. *Spearhead to Victory.* Edmonton: Hurtig, 1987.

Travers, Tim. *The Killing Ground: The British Army, the Western Front and the Emergence of Modern Warfare.* London: Allen & Unwin, 1987.

See also ALLIED COUNTEROFFENSIVE; VIMY RIDGE

Horthy de Nagybána, Miklós (1868–1957)

Austro-Hungarian admiral and navy commander from February to October of 1918. Born at Kenderes on 18 June 1868, Horthy, a Hungarian, entered the Naval Academy at Fiume in 1882 and subsequently became a naval aide-de-camp to Kaiser Franz Josef from 1911 to 1914. At the outbreak of the war he commanded the battleship *Hapsburg.* Horthy earned a reputation for boldness in 1915 while in command of the new light cruiser *Novara.* He planned the 15 May 1917 raid on the drifter line maintaining the Otranto barrage, which led to the largest naval action of the war in the Adriatic. The Austrians emerged from their encounter with superior Entente forces relatively unscathed, although Horthy himself was wounded. After the Cattaro mutiny in February of 1918, widespread demand for a rejuvenation of the naval command led young Kaiser Karl to select Horthy over many more senior officers to lead the Austrian fleet.

Horthy lived up to his reputation by planning another raid on the Otranto Straits in June. The raid would be supported by the battleships, a distinct departure from the cautious policy of his predecessors, which had been to preserve the fleet-in-being. Unfortunately, while the heavy ships were steaming south during the night, a division ran into a pair of Italian Mas boats off Premuda. The dreadnought *Szent István* was torpedoed and sunk, and Horthy was obliged to abort the operation. Horthy managed to keep the fleet intact until the end of the war, maintaining the essential sea communications with the Austrian army in Albania and supporting the German submarine campaign in the Mediterranean.

Horthy has the melancholy distinction of being the last commander of the Austro-Hungarian fleet. He is better known for leading the counterrevolution that overthrew the Communist regime of Belá Kun and established himself as Regent of Hungary, 1919–44. Horthy nevertheless clung to the title of admiral and frequently wore naval uniform. During the Second World War Horthy brought Hungary into the war on the side of the Germans, only to be overthrown by the latter and the rabidly pro-Fascist Arrow Cross party when he tried to bring his country out of the war. He spent the last years of his life in exile in Portugal. He died at Estoril on 9 February 1957.

Paul G. Halpern

References

Bayer von Bayersburg, Heinrich. *Unter der k.u.k. Kriegsflagge, 1914–1918.* Vienna: Bergland Verlag, 1959.

Halpern, Paul G. *The Naval War in the Mediterranean, 1914–1918.* London and Annapolis, Md.: Allen & Unwin and Naval Institute Press, 1987.

Horthy, Admiral Nicholas. *Memoirs.* London: Hutchinson, 1956.

Sokol, Hans Hugo. *Österreich-Ungarns Seekrieg.* 2 vols. Vienna: Amalthea Verlag, 1933. Reprint. Graz: Akademische Druck und Verlagsanstalt, 1967.

See also AUSTRIA-HUNGARY, NAVY; HUNGARY, REVOLUTION IN; MEDITERRANEAN NAVAL OPERATIONS

Hungary, Revolution in (1918–19)

With the military collapse of Russia, Germany, and Austria-Hungary in 1918, a series of revolutions swept through Central and Eastern Europe. In Hungary there would be two revolutions, as Hungarians attempted to shape a new existence.

In the first revolution a coalition of Social Democrats, Radical Bourgeois party members, and supporters of Count Mihály Károlyi declared an end to the Hapsburg Monarchy on 31 October 1918, thereby severing Hungary's last tie to Austria. With Károlyi installed as president, the new provisional government immediately faced serious problems. It had to negotiate a favorable peace treaty with the representatives meeting at Versailles, organize a new government capable of governing, solve the nationality problem, divide land among the peasants, raise the standard of living, and integrate former prisoners of war into the country's economic and political life.

The efforts of the Károlyi government failed on most counts. The victorious Allies meeting at Paris imposed an unfavorable territorial settlement that meant repeated boundary changes, all at Hungary's expense, especially the loss of Transylvania to Romania. Elections were delayed, and the nationality question remained unresolved as the non-Magyar groups did not gain autonomy. Land reform was not initiated, and Károlyi and his coalition partners failed to agree on a number of crucial issues.

Powerful groups within Hungary desired to see the Károlyi government fall. Aristocratic landholders did not like its plans to distribute land. The military, disbanded at the end of the war, felt betrayed. The Social Democrats, the largest political party, hoped to come to power through an expanded electorate; its leadership, however, remained divided on issues and tactics. The Hungarian Communist party also grew in importance, particularly as a result of propaganda efforts among Hungarian prisoners of war in Russia. In fact, during the revolution of late October 1918, Hungarian communists called upon the former prisoners of war to return home and spread revolution. Only several hundred strong in November of 1918, the Hungarian Communist party quickly established contact with other groups opposing the Károlyi government and gained support among the masses and workers.

Events in the spring of 1919 led to the second revolution. A communist-led demonstration in Budapest on 20 February turned violent, and the coalition government responded strongly. As many communists as could be found were arrested, including the party's leader, Béla Kun. While the public was initially sympathetic to the government (several policemen had been killed in the demonstration), the beating of Kun quickly turned sentiment against the government. The Károlyi government also failed to enforce its ban on communists. More important, conditions within Hungary continued to worsen as the democratic government weakened in the face of a military threat, rising unemployment, and widespread hunger. On 20 March an Allied ultimatum demanded Hungary surrender large tracts of territory. That action toppled the Károlyi government.

On 21 March 1919 the Hungarian Soviet Republic, a coalition of Social Democrats and Communists, took power under the leadership of Béla Kun. The establishment of a Soviet regime in central Europe shocked and alarmed Western leaders in Paris. A delegation went to Budapest but failed to reach an agreement, and military action against the Soviet Republic came from Romania and Czechoslovakia, as each country tried to grab more territory. Hungarian armed forces were hastily mobilized and halted the Romanian and Czechoslovak advances. Many Allied leaders, while not sympathetic with these land grabs, recognized the need to aid them in order to combat the spread of communism. France supplied both advisors and equipment, and on 7 June the Allied Powers issued an ultimatum demanding cessation of hostilities. On 13 June another ultimatum demanded the withdrawal of Hungarian troops to newly drawn boundaries. The Béla Kun government had no choice but to accede, because the Hungarian armed forces were simply too weak.

Dissatisfaction with the Soviet Republic grew, particularly among Hungarian nationalists, who saw the country being partitioned. On 24 June 1919, a military coup was attempted in Budapest. Afterwards, Béla Kun launched an offensive against Romania, perhaps hoping to regain nationalist support. When this offensive failed and a Romanian counterattack carried all the way to the gates of Budapest, Béla Kun and his government were forced from power on 1 August 1919 and fled. His 133 days of revolutionary rule were over, but they left a deep mark. The ensuing political reaction installed Admiral Miklós Horthy as regent. Meanwhile, a White Terror targeted Jews in the name of combating Bolshevism. In 1920 and 1921 King Charles IV made two attempts to regain his throne but was prevented by the Allied Powers. Revisionism was strong in Hungary following the peace settlement (some 3 million ethnic Hungarians were included in other states and much territory had been lost), and that ultimately led the government to side with Nazi Germany in the Second World War.

Robert G. Waite

References

Carsten, F.L. *Revolution in Central Europe, 1918–1919.* Berkeley: University of California Press, 1972.

Pastor, Peter, ed. *Revolutions and Interventions in Hungary and Its Neighbor States, 1918–1919.* Highland Lakes, N.J.: Atlantic Research and Publications, 1988.

Siklós, András. *Revolution in Hungary and the Dissolution of the Multinational State, 1918.* Budapest: Akademiai Kiado, 1988.

Völgyes, Iván, ed. *Hungary in Revolution, 1918–19.* Lincoln: University of Nebraska Press, 1971.

See also AUSTRIA-HUNGARY, HOME FRONT; HORTHY, MIKLÓS; KARL I, EMPEROR OF AUSTRIA; KÁROLYI, MIHÁLY; KUN, BÉLA; TRIANON, TREATY OF

Hunter-Weston, Sir Aylmer Gould (1864– 1940)

British general. Born on 23 September 1864 at Hunterston, West Kilbride, Ayrshire, Hunter-Weston attended Woolwich and was commissioned in the Royal Engineers in 1884. He then saw considerable field service and received three brevet promotions and the DSO.

In 1914, as a brigadier general, Hunter-Weston took the 11th Infantry Brigade to France. He was then promoted to major general and assumed command of the 29th Division, which landed at Cape Helles in the Gallipoli Campaign. His role there was controversial. General Ian Hamilton left tactical dispositions to Hunter-Weston, who focused attention on the contested "W" and "V" beaches, preventing exploitation of unopposed landings at "S," "X," and "Y" beaches. Also, Hunter-Weston issued no orders to the forces there. His division suffered heavy losses, the Turks had time to respond and reor-

ganize, and the opportunity was lost. The British gained only two small footholds and the fighting lapsed into stalemate and trench warfare similar to that on the Western Front.

Despite this failure, Hunter-Weston was promoted to lieutenant general and given command of VIII Corps. Sunstroke forced his medical evacuation from the Dardanelles, but he retained command of VIII Corps until the end of the war and led it to France.

Hunter-Weston retired from the army in 1920. Elected to the House of Commons in 1916, he served there until 1935. Hunter-Weston died on 18 March 1940 at the home where he was born.

Donald F. Bittner

References

Lee, John. "Sir Ian Hamilton and the Dardanelles, 1915." In *Fallen Stars: Eleven Studies of Twentieth Century Military Disasters,* edited by Brian Bond. London: Brassey's, 1991.

Liddell Hart, B.H. *The Real War, 1914–1918.* Boston: Little, Brown, 1930.

Owen, C.V. "Weston, Sir Aylmer Gould Hunter-Weston," *Dictionary of National Biography, 1931–1940,* edited by L.G. Wickham Legg. London: Oxford University Press, 1949, 900–901.

The Times (London), 19 March 1940.

See also GALLIPOLI CAMPAIGN

Hussein Ibn-Ali (1852–1931)

Sharif, emir of Mecca, and king of the Hejaz. Hussein was born at Constantinople in 1852 into the family of Hashem, traditionally held as descendants of Mohammed and, therefore, holders of the title sharif. Sultan Abdul Hamid II brought him to Istanbul in 1892 and, though placing him on the Council of State, held him in virtual captivity until 1903, when Hussein was appointed emir of Mecca. Although he maintained a lifetime loyalty to the sultan, Hussein resented the Hejaz railroad as an encroachment on Arab autonomy and feared the Young Turks, who effectively controlled the Ottoman government.

In 1915 Hussein discovered written proof that the Young Turks planned to depose him after the war. Through his son Abdullah, he had initiated talks with the British government in Cairo in 1913 and again in 1914. The threat from Istanbul caused him to pursue that relationship, and he initiated the Arab Revolt in 1916. Hussein wanted personal power, autonomy within the existing empire, and the hereditary right to the title of emir of Mecca. Lord Horatio Kitchener wanted military support from an Arab guerilla force, the support of a descendant of the Prophet for its propaganda value, and the transfer of the caliphate from Istanbul to Mecca as the cornerstone of a British Arab Empire similar to that in India. The military value of the Arab forces has been subject to debate, but, at best, it diverted 20 to 30,000 Turkish troops. The propaganda and political value of the caliphate were never as great as Kitchener believed.

After the war Cairo reluctantly continued to support Hussein over the wishes of the Foreign Office and the India Office, which favored his son Feisal and his enemies, the Sauds. Feisal was given Syria but was deposed and became king of Iraq under British protection. Abdullah became king of the newly created Transjordan. Hussein declared himself king of the Hejaz, but, lacking committed British support, was deposed by his Saudi enemies in 1924. He spent most of the rest of his life in Cyprus and died in Transjordan on 4 June 1931.

Jack McCallum

References

Fromkin, David. *A Peace to End All Peace: The Fall of the Ottoman Empire and the Creation of the Modern Middle East.* New York: Avon, 1989.

Glubb, Sir John. *A Short History of the Arab Peoples.* New York: Dorset, 1969.

Hourani, Albert. *A History of the Arab Peoples.* Cambridge: Harvard University Press, 1991.

See also ABDULLAH, EMIR; ARAB REVOLT; FAISAL, PRINCE; IBN SA'UD, ABD-AL-AZIZ

Hussein, Kamil (1853–1917)

Sultan of Egypt, 1914–17. Born in 1853, Kamil Hussein was a member of the ruling Mehemet Ali dynasty. His prewar interests were centered in agricultural development. World War I catapulted him into national prominence.

Prior to 1914 Britain exercised a "veiled protectorate" over Egypt. The declaration of war allowed a "lifting" of this veil and brought full protectorate status. Nationalist Khedive

Abbas II Hilmi (1874–1944) was at Constantinople, but the real power in Egypt was Britain's high commissioner, Sir Henry McMahon. He deposed Abbas while the latter was on a visit to Constantinople and replaced him with his uncle, Hussein. On 19 December 1914, to demonstrate severance of ties with Turkey, the British declared Hussein Sultan of Egypt.

This was a personal triumph that saved dynastic power but was purchased at a heavy price. The majority of Egyptians saw Hussein for what he was, a representative of British interests. Over the next two years he was the subject of repeated assassination attempts. Despite these attempts, it was tuberculosis that took his life, on 9 October 1917.

John P. Dunn

References

Beaman, Ardern George Hulme. *The Dethronement of the Khedive.* London: Allen & Unwin, 1929.

Cromer, Earl of (Evelyn Baring). *Abbas II.* London: Macmillan, 1915.

al-Kaylani, Muhammad Sayyid. *Al-Sultan Husayn Kamil.* Al-Qahirah: Dar al-Qawmiyah al-Arabiyah lil-Tibach, 1963.

Lloyd, George Ambrose. *Egypt Since Cromer.* 2 vols. New York: AMS, 1970.

See also EGYPT IN WORLD WAR I

Hutier, Oskar von (1857–1934)

German general, born in Erfurt on 27 August 1857. Hutier was commissioned into the army in 1874. In 1885 he entered the Kriegsakademie, earning appointment as a general staff officer in 1890. In the years before the war he served in alternating command and general staff assignments. In 1911 he was chief quartermaster on the Great General Staff, and the following year he assumed command of the prestigious 1st Guards Division in Berlin.

During the first year of the war Hutier commanded the 1st Guards Division on the Western Front at Namur, the Marne, and Arras. In 1915 he assumed command of XXI Corps on the Eastern Front and participated in the battles at Wilno, Kowno, and Lake Naroch. In 1917 he was promoted to general of infantry (*general der infantrie*) and given command of the Eighth Army. On 1–3 September 1917 Eighth Army captured the Baltic port of Riga, which effectively knocked Russia out of the war. In December of 1917 Hutier was transferred back to the Western Front to assume command of the Eighteenth Army, which he led in the Ludendorff Offensives at St. Quentin and Noyon.

Hutier is best remembered for Riga and St. Quentin. Riga saw the first large-scale introduction of the new infantry tactics that were to revolutionize twentieth-century ground combat. At St. Quentin, Hutier's Eighteenth Army achieved the amazing tactical success of penetrating sixty-seven kilometers in only fifteen days—the single deepest and fastest penetration of the war, with the exception of Chemin de Dames two months later. For both the Riga and St. Quentin attacks, Hutier's armies also employed radically new artillery tactics developed by Colonel Georg Bruchmüller.

Riga and St. Quentin stunned the Western Allies, who struggled to come to grips with new German tactical methods. The French in particular were anxious to identify one specific "military genius" as the source of their troubles. Thus, for many years German stormtroop tactics were also known as "Hutier Tactics." That was a misnomer, however, since the new tactics were not the product of any single theorist but rather of the careful and methodical staff work that characterized the German army. Hutier was simply the commander of the first large-scale operation in which the new doctrine was applied. Still, Hutier must be given substantial credit for being the first commander to achieve a major success with the tactics and to combine them with the new artillery tactics developed on the Eastern Front.

Hutier retired from the army in January of 1919. From 1919 to 1934 he was president of the German Officers' Association. He died in Berlin on 5 December 1934.

David T. Zabecki

References
Alfoldi, Laszlo M. "The Hutier Legend." *Parameters* 5 (February 1976): 69–74.
Pitt, Barrie. *1918: The Last Act*. New York: W.W. Norton, 1963.

See also BRUCHMÜLLER, GEORG; INFANTRY TACTICS; LUDENDORFF OFFENSIVES; RIGA, BATTLE OF; STORMTROOPERS

Hymans, Paul (1865–1941)

Belgian statesman, diplomat, teacher, and author, born in Ixelles, Belgium, on 23 March 1865. Hymans passed his barrister examination in 1885. From 1898 to 1914 he was professor of parliamentary history at the Free University of Brussels. Hymans was also active in Belgian politics, and in 1894 he was elected to the parliament, where he led the Liberal party. In 1914 Hymans followed the Belgian government into exile, and later that year he traveled to the United States to plead his country's case. He returned to Great Britain and served as Belgian ambassador to the United Kingdom from 1915 to 1917.

In 1917 Hymans became minister of economic affairs and from 1918 to 1920 was minister of foreign affairs. He represented Belgium at the Paris Peace Conference, where he became the spokesman for the minor powers. In 1920 he was Belgium's delegate to the League of Nations and was elected that organization's first president. During 1921 he was a leader in forming the Belgium and Luxembourg Custom Union. Hymans helped to win acceptance of the 1924 Dawes Plan. He held various government positions and was Belgian foreign minister almost without break from 1924 to 1935.

Hymans wrote numerous historical and political works. He fled Belgium after the German invasion of 1940 and died in Nice, France, on 6 March 1941.

Charles H. Bogart

References
Goldberg, George. *The Peace to End Peace*. New York: Harcourt, Brace, and World, 1969.
Methuen, Eyre. *Portrait of a Decision*. Birkenhead: William Brothers, 1972.

See also PARIS PEACE CONFERENCE, 1919

I

Ibn Sa'ud, Abd-al-Aziz, of the House of Sa'ud (1880–1953)

King of Nejd and Saudi Arabia and founder of the Kingdom of Saudi Arabia. Born in Riyadh about 1880, Sa'ud was the son of Abd al-Rahman and descended from the founder of the Wahhabi sect. Forced to flee from the invading Rashidis in 1891, he lived a short time in exile in Kuwait. In 1902 Sa'ud captured the town of Riyadh to reestablish rule by his family in the Nejd. By 1915 the British recognized him as ruler of the Nejd and Hassa. During World War I, he maintained a position of benevolent neutrality and received a subsidy of £5,000 monthly from Britain. He also continued to harass the Rashidis, allies of the Turks.

In 1920–21 he defeated his enemy, the Rashidis, and became the Sultan of the Nejd. In 1924 he dispelled Sharif Hussein of Mecca, who had assumed the title of kalif. He continued to expand his rule and became the "King of the Hijaz and the Nejd." Sa'ud extended his holdings by having his sons marry into families of tribal rulers. In 1932 he proclaimed himself King of Saudi Arabia and soon granted oil concessions that made his country immensely wealthy. A remarkable ruler, Sa'ud worked to create a spirit of nationalism within his Arab state. As David Bongard stated, "He was a charismatic leader, a talented tactician, and a gifted strategist." He died in Mecca on 9 November 1953.

Raymond L. Proctor

References

Allen, Richard. *Imperialism and Nationalism in the Fertile Crescent*. London: Oxford, 1974.

Fisher, Sydney Nettleton. *The Middle East*. 3rd ed. New York: Knopf, 1979.

Lebkicher, Roy. *The Arabia of Ibn Saud*. New York: Russell F. Moore, 1952.

Shimoni, Yaacov. *Political Dictionary of the Arab World*. New York: Macmillan, 1987.

See also Arab Revolt; Hussein, Ibn-Ali

India, Role in the War

As the certainty of a war in Europe became apparent, India's British government rushed to pledge its support to the empire's war effort. Upon mobilization, Indian Expeditionary Force A (IEF A), composed of the Lahore and Meerut divisions, sailed from India in early September of 1914 en route to France. After stopping at Suez to post a detachment for temporary guard duty of the canal, the bulk of IEF A continued on to join the British Expeditionary Force in France.

As the war escalated, so did India's commitment. IEF A was soon followed by IEF B, posted to East Africa, and IEF C, which sailed for Mesopotamia. Finally, IEF D joined IEF C as reinforcements.

Led by British officers, Indian troops acquitted themselves well on the Western Front. Going into the line near Bassée in November of 1914, the Indian Corps served with distinction in the First Battle of Ypres. During the Neuve Chapelle Offensive of May of 1915, IEF A suffered heavy casualties at the Battle of Aubers Ridge. They were also engaged in the Battle of Frezenberg Ridge. While IEF A was fighting in Europe, the British government assigned the task of taking German East Africa to their counterparts in Delhi. The Indian government organized and dispatched IEF B for that purpose.

After the Royal Navy refused to land the troops at the port of Tanga for fear of mines, IEF B was forced to make an amphibious landing on 30 October 1914. Their choice for a landing zone was unfortunate. The peninsula they chose consisted mainly of swampland and was some distance south of Tanga. After a three-day contest with German-led native troops, heat, snakes, and mosquitoes, the landing forces retreated to their ships. Their unsuccessful efforts had resulted in 817 Indian casualties and a considerable boost to German morale. Despite this setback, IEF B participated in other operations in German East Africa until early 1917.

Indian troops also fought in the Mideast. In February of 1915 the Tenth and Eleventh Indian divisions successfully defended the Suez Canal from attack by 20,000 German-led Turkish troops. In 1918 Indian forces, including two divisions sent from Mesopotamia and a unit of cavalry sent from France, fought with General Sir Edmund Allenby's forces in the Battle of Megiddo in Palestine.

India's mission to Mesopotamia proved to be one of the most disorganized sideshows of the war. On 19 October 1914, in a campaign directed by Indian authorities in Delhi, IEF C landed at Bahrain on the Persian Gulf. Its primary objective was to protect the 140-mile oil pipeline from southern Persia to the Anglo-Persian refineries at Abadan. Although not immediately threatened by the nearby Turks, these oil facilities were vital for the Royal Navy. The colonial force's presence was also intended to confirm the allegiance of the local sheiks.

In November, Indian forces pushed north into Turkish territory. After an inspection tour by Lord Harding, viceroy of India, two more brigades, designated IEF D, were authorized and dispatched from India as reinforcements. Encouraged by his rapid successes and under pressure from Delhi, General Sir John Nixon, commander of Indian troops in Mesopotamia, devised a hasty plan for seizing complete control over lower Mesopotamia. In one of the more colorful incidents of the war, Major General Charles Townshend, commander of the Sixth Indian Division, assembled a polyglot fleet for the expedition known as "Townshend's Regatta." After some early initial success, Townshend's forces were checked by the Turks at Ctesiphon and retreated downriver to the town of Kut-el-Amara, where they were surrounded and besieged from November of 1915 to late April of 1916. Devastated by starvation

and disease, the Indians were forced to surrender on 29 April 1916.

The demoralizing defeat at Kut graphically illustrated the Indian government's lack of expertise in planning military operations beyond its immediate borders. The whole affair, which cost the empire 40,000 casualties, moved Britain to restructure its command in Mesopotamia. Indian authorities who had failed to provide adequate logistic support to their forces were relieved of command. Their British replacements quickly remedied the situation, and the Mesopotamian theater soon settled into uneventful obscurity.

The effects of the war on India were profound. Responding enthusiastically to the war effort, India had contributed £80 million in military supplies, millions in other types of material, as well as a gift of £100 million in cash. India had also contributed approximately one million troops, of whom some 100,000 became battle casualties.

Britain's gratitude at the close of hostilities was hardly magnanimous. Indian veterans, who had left a repressive, colonially ruled homeland to fight bravely for Britain, found little changed upon their return home. Although some Indian troops had at last won British officer commissions and promises of more independence, they found these gains and promises to have little real value. Indians' rights were still rigidly controlled. In addition, unemployment soared as India suffered a severe postwar depression and staggering loss of life from the 1918 influenza pandemic.

The Indian nationalist movement, which had remained relatively dormant during the war, gained new momentum after the Armistice. In the spring of 1919, as a response to continuing British repression, terrorist groups began a new wave of violence against their colonial rulers.

In contrast to the militant nationalists, Mohandas K. (Mahatma) Gandhi instituted his policy of noncooperation against the colonial regime. As leader of the 1920 Indian National Congress, Gandhi, who had once recruited troops for the British war effort, emerged as the primary leader of the Indian independence movement that culminated in India's independence in 1947.

Jeff Kinard

References

Dodwell, H.H., ed. *The Cambridge History of India*, Vol. 6, 1858–1918. Delhi: S. Chand, 1932.

Edmonds, Brigadier-General Sir James E. *A Short History of World War One*. New York: Greenwood, 1968.

Golant, William. *The Long Afternoon, British India 1601–1947*. New York: St. Martin's, 1975.

MacDonald, Lyn. *1914*. New York: Athenium, 1988.

Naidis, Mark. *India, A Short Introductory History*, New York: Macmillan, 1966.

Sydenham of Combe, Lord. *India and the War*. London: Hodder and Stoughton, 1915.

Wilson, Trevor. *The Myriad Faces of War, Britain and the Great War, 1914–1918*. Cambridge: Polity, 1986.

See also AFRICA, 1914–18; MESOPOTAMIA, 1914–18; TOWNSHEND, CHARLES

Infantry Tactics

Between the end of the Franco-Prussian War in 1871 and the outbreak of the First World War in 1914, there were no major wars in Europe. During that period, however, a technological revolution produced entirely new types of weapons—smokeless gunpowder, recoiling and quick-firing artillery, magazine-fed repeating rifles, and the machine gun—that would dramatically alter warfare. All these weapons represented large-scale improvements in range, accuracy, volume of fire, and lethality that placed the soldier in the open at a distinct disadvantage to the soldier fighting from a protected position.

Inasmuch as tactics are largely a function of technology, these new weapons should have radically altered the tactics of the day. But most of the European armies of 1914 had had little recent combat experience against which to evaluate their old tactics. While the Boer War and the Russo-Japanese War should have shown the nature of future warfare, the experiences of both conflicts were largely dismissed because combatants were not considered proper European armies. As World War I approached, the Balkan fighting also provided hints for the future, but it came too close to 1914 to be analyzed and understood completely.

Thus, most of the major armies entered World War I doctrinally committed to the rigid tactics in use since Napoleon's day. About the only difference was that linear attack formations were more widely spread out, a response to the greater volume of firepower encountered in the Franco-Prussian War. Typical skirmish lines moved forward with one to three meters between soldiers. Many military professionals continued to believe that an aggressive spirit on the part of the attacker would overcome greater firepower. For the most part prevailing doctrines did not envision frontal attacks anyway, preferring instead to attack open flanks with envelopments and turning movements. The credo of the German army, for example, was Moltke's "*Umfassen, Einschliessen, Vernichten*" (Fix, Encircle, Destroy). The fatal flaw in this logic was that by 1914 the density of forces was so great along the German, French, and Belgian borders that open flanks were rare.

The early battles of August and September of 1914 were characterized by considerable maneuver. But as both sides jockeyed for the ever-illusive open flank, firepower took its grim toll. The interval between individual soldiers in skirmish lines progressively widened until it reached five meters, although France retained the one-meter interval as late as 1916. Regardless, the soldiers themselves soon realized the near impossibility of survival on the surface and began digging. By the end of 1914 the Western Front had evolved into two roughly parallel lines of foxholes and hasty trenches, running from the Swiss border to the North Sea. As time dragged on these defenses became more sophisticated and semipermanent. Thus, firepower technology had gained the upper hand over maneuver tactics, and the result was trench warfare. Although the Eastern Front never quite bogged down into the static and rigid network of trenches and fortifications that characterized the Western Front, the flat terrain and wide-open spaces in the East, combined with the increased firepower yet limited mobility of the World War I armies, produced its own special brand of stagnation.

Most commanders on all sides came to regard the static lines of fixed fortifications as an unnatural and temporary situation. They therefore spent most of the war looking for a way to break through their enemy's defenses and restore the natural condition of maneuver warfare. The key flaw in this approach was that military tacticians of the period failed to comprehend that the central paradigm of war itself had shifted. Rather than a contest between two opposing forces of blood, muscle, and bayonets, war had become a contest between two machine armies, where man's most important roles involved the operation and direction of those machines. Muscle power had been replaced by mechanical power. Yet most of World War I was taken up with an effort to prevail with manpower in history's first truly mechanized war.

More important, the new technologies made coordination among the various arms more critical than ever. Gone were the days when large infantry units could win battles on their own. By the end of World War I the foundations of combined-arms warfare had emerged, with infantry, artillery, and even armored fighting vehicles and airplanes complementing each other's strengths. For the most part, the Germans were ahead of the Allies in evolving their tactical doctrine—especially in artillery. After the failures of 1914 the Germans went over to the strategic defensive on the Western Front and concentrated on driving their Eastern Front opponents out of the war. Thus until the end of 1917 the Allies focused on the problem of achieving that ever-illusive decisive breakthrough, while the Germans concentrated on preventing it.

The rapidly evolving role of artillery created serious problems for coordination with infantry on the battlefield. Indirect fire techniques and the increased range of the guns themselves, combined with the still primitive communications systems, made close support of infantry increasingly difficult the farther it moved from the attack line of departure. Corrections and requests for fire had to be conveyed by messenger, which sometimes took hours. The solution to the problem was to move the artillery fire forward on a precise schedule, controlled by phase lines on a map. That eventually evolved into the creeping or rolling barrage, with advancing infantry trained to follow closely behind the moving wall of their own fire. Shrapnel, the shell used in these barrages, burst in the air and sent most of the blast effect forward along the line of the shells' trajectories. Infantry could, therefore, follow very closely behind it, often as close as fifty meters. Infantry commanders were encouraged to keep their troops as close to the barrage as possible, even though they might take some casualties from friendly fire. The belief was that such an approach resulted in fewer overall casualties.

The main problem with the creeping barrage and phase line was that they wholly subordinated the infantry advance to the artillery schedule. This in turn reinforced the use of rigid linear tactics. In addition, tactical decisions became centralized at higher and higher levels, which meant slower response times, because primitive communications could not support the greater centralization of control. Thus, front-line infantry commanders ignored terrain in their planning, came to have less and less control of the tactical situations around them, and soon even forgot how to maneuver their forces on the battlefield.

With the Germans on the strategic defensive on the Western Front, the Allies continued to try to achieve decisive penetrations. As the war progressed that became increasingly difficult, because fixed defenses became more dense and elaborate. By 1916 a typical defensive line consisted of at least three parallel lines of trenches reinforced with bunkers. The leading edges of these positions were protected with massive barbed-wire entanglements extending out into no-man's-land. Behind these trench lines both sides massed huge supply depots and stationed reinforcing units that could be moved up to wherever a breach was threatened.

By 1916 attack planning had been almost reduced to fixed sets of mathematical formulae: so many heavy guns per yard of front in the primary attack sector, so many machine guns, so many riflemen, so many rounds in the artillery prep, and so forth. Enemy first positions could always be taken and usually his second positions—if the attacking commander was willing to pay the price in casualties and ammunition. The real problem came when attempting to move more deeply into enemy territory. By that stage of the attack the initial infantry force was totally depleted and supporting artillery most usually was at its maximum range. To advance, therefore, fresh infantry units had to be brought up and artillery had to displace forward. That took time, especially because those forces had to move over shattered terrain, blocked with the refuse of war. Such movements were always by foot, with scattered horse transport. The defender, meanwhile, could reinforce the threatened area much more quickly by taking advantage of roads and even rail networks in his own rear area. Motor vehicles could operate there without problem, but not in the cratered and muddy morass of no-man's-land. The essence of the problem, then, was that the defender's strategic mobility worked against the attacker's lack of tactical mobility.

Attack formations varied greatly during the war, but the principle was essentially the same. In some armies the regiments attacked in echelon, with two battalions in the first echelon, and one or two in the second. In other armies whole regiments were committed to the first echelon, while additional regiments made up the second echelon. Most armies, however, attacked using some variation of the wave system.

The formation used by many British battalions in the Somme attack was typical: a battalion, consisting of four rifle companies of four platoons each, attacked in ten waves, with 100 meters between each. Company A, for example, would make up the first two waves, with two platoons (a total of eighty men) in the first wave and two in the second. The company commander and the small company headquarters section moved between the two waves. Company B made up the third and fourth waves. The battalion's fighting platoons were in these first four waves. Company C made up the fifth (mop-up platoons) and the sixth wave (support platoons). The seventh wave consisted of the battalion headquarters and signal sections. Company D made up the eighth and ninth waves, the carrying platoons. Stretcher bearers came in the tenth wave. Soldiers in the preceding waves were not to stop to help wounded comrades, leaving them for the stretcher bearers. The entire formation moved forward at the rate of 100 meters every two minutes.

Attacking soldiers moved across the torn-up terrain, through barbed wire, and against enemy fire while carrying heavy loads. Each man in the first five waves typically carried his rifle, bayonet, gas mask, ammunition, wire cutters, a spade, two empty sandbags, flares, and two grenades. The grenades were not to be thrown by the soldier, but passed to specially trained troops called "bombers." A soldier's individual kit weighed up to seventy pounds. Troops in the carrying platoons were essentially human pack-animals. In addition to their individual kits, they also carried heavy loads of ammunition, barbed wire, duck board, and construction material to help fortify the objective, once it was captured.

During the early years of the war defensive tactics focused on rigid defenses with the bulk of combat power concentrated in the forward trenches—a concept known as forward defense. As the human cost of taking ground increased, it seemed almost sacrilegious to yield even a few inches of it. Thus the defensive credo became one of holding "at all costs," regardless of the actual tactical situation. Allied commanders in particular felt that allowing units to withdraw

under pressure (even when that made the most sense tactically) would be bad for morale and an inducement to mass cowardice. The fatal flaw of the forward defense was that it was suicidal. It placed the bulk of the defender's combat power in densely packed areas well within the range of the attacker's artillery. Standing on the defensive in the West, the Germans were the first to recognize the problem, particularly as a result of their heavy losses on the Somme.

By the end of 1916 the Germans had begun to develop their concept of the "elastic," or flexible, defense-in-depth. They organized positions into three zones: the outpost zone, 500 to 1,000 meters in depth and manned with sparsely located early-warning positions; the battle zone, up to 2,000 meters deep; and the rearward zone, where reserves and counterattack units were held, often in deep, reinforced bunkers. The leading edge of the battle zone was the main line of resistance, with three or more successive trench lines. Between the battle zone and the rearward zone came another line of multiple trenches that served as the protective line for the artillery. The Germans also decreased the strength of the forward positions. While the French were putting two-thirds of their combat strength into the first two lines, the Germans put only 20 percent into those positions. The Germans even came to regard their forward-most trenches as useful only in quiet periods. During an artillery bombardment prior to an Allied attack, the forces in the rear would move into deep, protected bunkers to ride out the storm. Troops in the thinly held outpost line would slip out of their trenches and take cover in nearby shell holes—while the Allied artillery pounded the empty trenches.

The Germans formalized their defensive concepts in a set of tactical instructions, *The Principles of Command in the Defensive Battle in Position Warfare,* issued by headquarters on 1 December 1916. The German doctrine rested on the three key principles of flexibility, decentralized control, and counterattack. While the command and control of the Allied attacks became centralized at ever higher levels, German commanders in the defense had an impressive amount of autonomy at the lower levels. A front-line battalion commander had the authority to withdraw from forward positions under pressure as he saw fit. More important, he had authority to order remaining battalions of his regiment (positioned to his rear) to counterattack when he judged the timing right. The Germans used immediate and violent counter-attacks to hit the attacker before he could consolidate his gains and when he was at his most vulnerable.

At higher echelons the Germans began distinguishing between two types of divisions, each with different tactical functions. Defensive positions in the line were manned by *Stellungsdivision* (trench divisions). Farther back in the operational rear the Germans positioned their *Eingriefdivision* (attack divisions) to conduct larger-scale counterattacks. When the Germans went over to the offensive in 1918, this distinction played a key role.

When the Germans withdrew to the Siegfried, or Hindenburg, Line in early 1917, they added a new twist to the flexible defense-in-depth. The Germans planned this withdrawal very carefully, and made extensive preparations of their new positions before occupying them. In as many places along the line as possible, the trenches of the main line of resistance were sited on high ground on the reverse slope, facing away from the Allies. The concept of reverse-slope defense ran counter to the conventional wisdom of the time because it did not utilize the maximum range of the machine gun. Actually, it gave the defender significant advantages. It placed his positions out of the line of sight of the attacker's base position, thereby complicating the attacker's communications and the coordination of his artillery. At the same time, these positions remained within the line of sight of the defender's rear positions and artillery, giving the defending commanders the advantage of knowing where and when to move reserves and counterattack.

By mid-1917 many Allied commanders had realized that decisive penetration was not to be. General Henri-Philippe Pétain, among others, began advocating limited objective attacks, designed to eat away at an enemy's position in small chunks. Other tactical thinkers, however, were thinking along bolder lines. In May of 1915 French Captain André Laffargue wrote a pamphlet suggesting that main attacks be preceded by specially trained teams of skirmishers. Armed with light machine guns and grenades, these teams would infiltrate the German lines ahead of the main attack, locate and neutralize machine guns, and even penetrate deeply enough to attack artillery positions. The British and French largely ignored Laffargue's pamphlet; but the Germans captured a copy during the summer of 1916, translated it, and issued copies to their front-line units.

On the German side of the line, Captain Willy Rohr was one of the earliest leaders in the development of the new offensive tactics. In August of 1915 Rohr took command of the recently formed *Sturmabteilung* (Assault Detachment) on the Western Front. Under Rohr's guidance the Assault Detachment conducted numerous successful counterattacks, using infiltration tactics drawn from the traditional tactics of the German *Jäger* (hunter) units. Armed with grenades, automatic weapons, trench mortars, and flame throwers, their operations were very similar to those suggested by Laffargue. Rohr's detachment eventually grew into a *Sturmbattalion* and was used to train other such units. The Germans created special schools to train these troops, and other units (usually Pioneer and Jäger) were converted into assault units. They became known as *Stosstruppen* (Stormtroops). It is important to note here that these highly effective units bore no connection whatever to Adolf Hitler's brown-shirted thugs, who several years after the war usurped and forever sullied what had been the perfectly honorable title of Stormtrooper.

By 1917 Rohr's infiltration tactics became the official German counterattack doctrine on the Western Front. In September of 1917 the Germans made their first attempt to apply the tactics to a large-scale offensive operation—on the Eastern Front at Riga. Instead of the typical attack formations of rigid lines, the German Eighth Army of General Oskar von Hutier attacked in fluid leaps and bounds, with one element moving forward while another element provided fire cover. Then the two elements would reverse roles and leap-frog each other. The forward-most units completely bypassed the defender's strong points, isolating them and leaving them for heavier follow-on forces to eliminate. Reserves were used only to reinforce success, rather than being thrown in where the attack was faltering. These were radical tactics by the standards of World War I.

Riga was also the first time the new infantry tactics were combined with the new artillery tactics developed on the Eastern Front by Colonel Georg Bruchmüller. The Germans also used similar tactics during their successful attack at Caporetto in Italy. The new tactics, or more precisely their results, shocked the Western Allies. The French, in particular, looked for a single tactical mastermind as the source of the new tactics and settled on Hutier. Thus, they somewhat erroneously dubbed the new German tactics, "Hutier Tactics." In fact, the German advances in both offensive and defensive tactical doctrine throughout the war were more a product of corporate effort and sound methodical staff work.

The British, meanwhile, achieved a tactical revolution of their own during their attack at Cambrai in November of 1917. For the first time in the war the tank was used in massed formations with mutual infantry support (one platoon for each tank in the main body). Up to that point in the war the tank had been committed only in "penny packets," with little result. As initially planned by the Royal Tank Corps' brilliant Chief of Staff, Colonel J.F.C. Fuller, the attack was to be a rapid but limited-objective thrust into the Hindenburg Line. By the time British commander Field Marshal Sir Douglas Haig's staff finished reworking the plan, it was a much more ambitious offensive—far more ambitious than available British resources could support. Initially the attack was a stunning success, with nine battalions of tanks and supporting infantry crashing deep into the German defenses. But once there, the British had insufficient reserves to exploit their success or even to hold what they had gained. Ten days later the Germans counterattacked and retook all the lost ground.

The Cambrai counterattack marked the first large-scale appearance on the Western Front of the new German offensive tactics. With the final defeat of Russia the Germans transferred as many units as possible from East to West for a rapid shift to the offensive. Many of the key leaders from the East, including Hutier and Bruchmüller, were also transferred to the West. The Germans started a massive program to train their Western Front units in the new tactics in preparation for what would become Ludendorff's 1918 Offensives. On 1 January 1918 Ludendorff's headquarters issued the new tactical instructions, *The Attack in Position Warfare,* with Captain Hermann Geyer as the principal compiler.

On 21 March 1918, the Germans launched the first of what would be five great offensives on the Western Front. Early results were stunning, with the Germans taking more ground in a few days than the Allies had managed to take in the last four years. In the end, however, the German attack ran out of steam, mainly because Germany was completely spent after four years of a two-front war. The Germans did manage to inflict massive casualties on the Allies, but those losses were more than made up for by newly arriving American units. The Germans experienced similar results in their four following offensives. By the third offensive (Chemin des Dames), the Allies finally realized the fatal error of the forward defense and quickly copied the German defense-in-depth.

The last great offensive by the Germans (Champaign-Marne) started on 15 July 1918. Compared with the previous four it was a failure. Three days later the Allies counterattacked and Germany remained on the defensive for the rest of the war. Here too the Allies copied the German tactics, abandoning the old linear formations and adopting both the infiltration techniques and artillery tactics learned at such great cost at the hands of the Germans.

Neither side in World War I ever broke the pattern, but Germany came within a hair's breadth between March and May of 1918. In the end Germany finally succumbed to four years of a two-front war of attrition. But the tactical principles that had begun to solidify in late 1917 and 1918 changed the face of land warfare forever and formed the origins of modern tactics. With the exception of nuclear weapons, every element of the modern combat equation can be seen in World War I. The major blind spot in the German tactics was the tank—a mistake they would correct by World War II.

David T. Zabecki

References

Balck, Wilhelm. *Entwickelung der Taktik im Weltkriege*. Berlin: R. Eisenschmidt, 1920.

Bidwell, Shelford, and Dominick Graham. *Firepower: British Army Weapons and Theories of War, 1904–1945*. London: Allen and Unwin, 1982.

Gudmundsson, Bruce I. *Stormtroop Tactics: Innovation in the German Army, 1914–1918*. New York: Praeger, 1989.

Lucas, Pascal Marie Henri. *L'Evolution des Idées tactiques en France et en Allemagne pendant la guerre de 1914–1918*. 4th ed. Paris: Berger-Levrault, 1932.

Paschall, Rod. *The Defeat of Imperial Germany, 1917–1918*. Chapel Hill, N.C.: Algonquin, 1989.

Travers, Timothy. *The Killing Ground: The British Army on the Western Front and* the *Emergence of Modern Warfare, 1900–1918*. London: Allen and Unwin, 1987.

Wynne, Graeme C. *If Germany Attacks; the Battle in Depth in the West*. London: Faber and Faber, 1940.

See also ALBERICH, OPERATION OF; ARTILLERY; CAMBRAI, BATTLE OF; FULLER, J.F.C.; GRANDMAISON, LOUIS DE; HUTIER, OSKAR VON; LUDENDORFF, ERICH; PASSCHENDAELE CAMPAIGN; RIGA, BATTLE OF; SOMME, BATTLE OF; STORMTROOPERS; TANKS; TRENCH WARFARE

Influenza Pandemic

As the First World War ended, an epidemic of unparalleled severity swept around the world. Between 1918 and 1920, influenza affected one-fifth of the world's population and killed twenty to forty million people, a greater mortality than any other twentieth-century catastrophe save the two great wars.

Although it probably originated in a United States Army training facility at Fort Funston, Kansas, it was known around the world as the Spanish flu. The pandemic spread in three or four waves, beginning in the spring of 1918. In the first wave, the influenza virus caused chills, fever, and upper respiratory symptoms, but lacked the virulence it would later display. This wave spread from North America to Europe, then from west to east across Asia and the Pacific. It reentered the United States, having caused more inconvenience than mortality.

In the fall of 1918, the virus underwent a lethal mutation. It reemerged almost simultaneously at troop staging points in Boston, Brest, and Freetown, Sierra Leone. The second wave of Spanish flu started much as the first but was followed by a particularly deadly pneumonia. The illness showed a predilection for young adults, was extremely contagious, and was associated with significant mortality.

Because wartime censors deliberately underreported its incidence and the public health establishment in much of the world was incapable of accurate statistics, it is impossible to be sure exactly how many people died of the Spanish flu in 1918 and 1919. Officially, the United States and France reported only 10,000 deaths each, and Great Britain only 3,500. In fact, over 4,000 a week died in the ninety-six great towns of Britain alone during the pandemic's zenith. About 668,000 Americans died of the flu during 1918 and 1919 (compared with a total of 425,000 who lost their lives during World War I, World War II, and the Korean Conflict), and that number may be undercounted by as much as 25 percent.

Both the cause and the treatment of the flu were a mystery to the contemporary medical establishment. It was hypothesized that gases released from rotting human and animal corpses were made toxic by the effects of explosives on European battlefields. The resulting poisons were thought to cause flu. Since no effective treatment existed, medical measures were limited to attempts at quarantine. Military camps were isolated by armed guards, and in Washington, D.C., it was made illegal to communicate the disease—in effect making it against the law to contract the illness.

Although concealed by censors, the flu's effect on the armies of the warring powers was devastating. In 1918 alone 40 percent of the U.S. Navy contracted the illness. The U.S. army registered 621,000 ill, over nine million man-days lost, and about 38,000 dead from influenza. In that year, 60 percent of the army's deaths were from Spanish flu.

At the Western Front, 69,000 Americans contracted flu in the fall of 1918, and the disease brought the Meuse-Argonne Offensive to a halt. Ludendorff initially thought that influenza in the Allied armies might save his wavering forces, but the virus moved east and proved as lethal for Germans as for their opponents. Ludendorff later blamed Spanish flu for the failure of his 1918 offensive.

On the day of the Armistice, the flu-related mortality rate declined in Britain for the first time since the epidemic began. An additional wave of what was probably the same illness in a less virulent form circled the world in 1920 before the infection vanished permanently. It is likely that the virus took refuge in pigs and may have made a less dramatic appearance as the swine flu of the 1970s. A significant number of flu survivors later suffered from Parkinson's disease. Otherwise, the virus disappeared without a trace.

Jack McCallum

References

Beveridge, William. *Influenza, the Last Great Plague: An Unfinished Story of Discovery*. New York: Prodist, 1978.

Crosby, Alfred. "The Influenza Pandemic of 1918." In *Influenza in America: 1918–*

1976, edited by June Osborn. New York: Prodist, 1977.

Hoehling, A.A. *The Great Epidemic*. Boston: Little, Brown, 1961.

See also CASUALTIES; MEDICINE, MILITARY

Ingenohl, Friedrich von (1857–1933)

German admiral and chief of the High Seas Fleet from 1913 to 1915, born on 26 June 1857. Ingenohl was an early supporter of Admiral Alfred von Tirpitz and a subscriber to "old school" naval doctrine. He distinguished himself in various shipboard and shore commands before the war. By 1908, while commanding the Second Battle Squadron, he attained flag rank and was raised into the Prussian nobility a year later. Competence as a squadron leader and loyalty to Tirpitz earned him promotion as chief of the High Seas Fleet in April of 1913 and the rank of full admiral.

Ingenohl became the first of several German fleet commanders to agonize over the dilemma of not being allowed to commit his ships fully against a possibly superior enemy while being simultaneously accused of inefficiency and inaction. Generally credited for keeping the fleet well trained and at high levels of combat readiness, Ingenohl reluctantly respected imperial orders that limited offensive operations to surprise raids, mining operations by lighter units, and U-boat warfare. Ingenohl's battleships rarely participated in Hipper's limited offensive actions against British shipping in the North Sea or coastal installations, or arrived on the scene too late. Setbacks such as the Falklands disaster and the loss of the battle cruiser *Yorck* to friendly mines hurt Ingenohl's standing with the kaiser and led to his replacement by Pohl on 2 February 1915, just one week after the unfortunate Dogger Bank engagement. Dogger Bank seemed to underscore Ingenohl's shortfalls as a decision-maker.

Ingenohl subsequently commanded the Baltic Naval Station until his retirement in August of 1915. He died in Berlin on 19 December 1933.

Eric C. Rust

References

Görlitz, Walter, ed. *The Kaiser and His Court: The Diaries, Note Books and Letters of Admiral Georg Alexander von Müller, Chief of the Naval Cabinet,* *1914–1918*. New York: Harcourt, Brace, World, 1964.

Herwig, Holger H. *The German Naval Officer Corps: A Social and Political History, 1890–1918*. Oxford: Oxford University Press, 1973.

Marineministerium. *Der Krieg zur See, 1914–1918*. 24 vols. Berlin: 1922–66.

See also DOGGER BANK, NAVAL BATTLE OF; GERMAN CRUISER RAIDS, 1914; GERMANY, NAVY

Intelligence Operations

The difference between military information and military intelligence is the same as the difference between a large pile of vegetables recently harvested from a garden and a wonderful soup prepared from those same vegetables. Military intelligence is processed information, that is, information sifted and organized with specific objectives in mind.

Depending on the level of detail and scope, intelligence operations may be categorized as strategic, operational, or tactical. Strategic intelligence deals with policy and planning matters at national or international levels. Operational and tactical intelligence pertain to combat operations within a theater of war. Military intelligence may be a component of all three categories of intelligence operations.

At the outbreak of World War I most European powers had well-organized military-intelligence agencies, with the French and Germans in the front rank. By 1914 military and naval attachés were recognized by all countries as accredited intelligence officers. Although violation of a host nation's laws would result in recall of a foreign attaché, it was presumed by all intelligence agencies that foreign attachés in their country were actively gathering information of military value. This was known as "positive" intelligence.

In addition to gathering information about foreign armed forces, intelligence officers and the agents they controlled also engaged in counterintelligence operations to deceive their enemies, prevent sabotage, and protect their military forces. This was known as "negative" intelligence. The problems associated with organizing intelligence forces, collecting information, transmitting it safely, processing it into useful military intelligence, and disseminating it in a timely and protected way were immense.

Counterintelligence forces always counted on foreign intelligence operations being less than perfect, so that "enemy" vulnerabilities could be exploited. The controlling organization of a major intelligence agency always had to worry about its agents being "turned" against the parent agency, usually for money, sex, or revenge.

At the conclusion of their war with Japan in 1905, the Russians made Germany their principal intelligence target, believing that they were cooperating with French intelligence to the detriment of Germany. Of course, both France and Russia were targeted by German intelligence in the decade before 1914. So was Britain, principally to monitor naval construction and technology matters and to assess British interest in the German and Danish coastal areas. Germany also kept an eye on its potential allies, Austria-Hungary and Italy; and the interest was reciprocal, perhaps preventing effective collaboration among the nations composing the Central Powers during the war.

The British General Staff did little to prepare in this area until 1912. As the result of thoughtful, energetic work by Colonel George M.W. Macdonogh, a royal engineer who identified potential intelligence officers beginning in 1912, and Colonel (later Lieutenant General) David Henderson, who had lobbied aggressively after the Boer War for an intelligence service for the soon-to-be-organized British Expeditionary Force (BEF), the BEF had fifty competent, if marginally trained, intelligence officers in August of 1914.

British strategic intelligence efforts, prior to the outbreak of war and during its early months in France, improved quickly. John Charteris, who rose to the rank of brigadier general, was Field Marshal Sir Douglas Haig's intelligence officer at corps, army, then British Expeditionary Force level. From 1916 to the end of the war, the Western Allies had good information about the German army from prisoner-of-war interrogations and analyses of captured documents. In the first two years of the war the British and French armies could dedicate their radios to intercept operations, because the French used their own wire-cable network for tactical communications. But the Germans were very skilled at concealing information about their field forces. For example, the existence of the heavy siege artillery used to batter Verdun's outer fortifications was successfully concealed, and the use of reserve di-

visions in front-line corps likewise came as a surprise to the Allies.

General Charteris continued to enjoy the confidence of his commander in chief, despite his erroneous estimates of the supposed strategic disintegration in Germany. His manipulation of the enemy strength picture prior to the attack at Cambrai in November of 1917 and his growing unpopularity with the British cabinet finally led a reluctant Haig to sack him. Charteris knew his commander's tendency to be resolute in his decision once it was made, so he tailored his advice on intelligence matters accordingly. Within the British army, moreover, it was customary in World War I to assign officers with little training or inclination to intelligence duties.

Professionalism had hardly penetrated the practice of combat intelligence operations at the outset of the war in most European armies. But by the end of the war, intelligence operations had made substantial gains. New technologies, such as radio interception, direction finding, and aerial photography, were refined. But the obvious utility of coordinating strategic and operational/tactical intelligence operations did not occur to those who should have known better.

During World War I, the field armies of the belligerent nations had staff sections dedicated to field, or tactical, intelligence. As Colonel Nicolai's spy-based intelligence network began to dry up, General Helmuth von Moltke appointed Lieutenant Colonel Richard Hentsch as chief of the Foreign Armies Section of the general staff in the field. Hentsch later became Moltke's messenger in the affair that changed the Schlieffen Plan's grand encirclement of Paris into a withdrawal from the Marne. It has been suggested that general staff conservatism, which reinforced the army chief's own conservatism, and the natural tendency to overrate the capabilities of the enemy deprived the German field armies of their best opportunity to win the war. The separation of strategic from operational intelligence matters indicated that the intelligence priorities had shifted to combat support after hostilities began.

In most cases, the military staff "G-2s" would receive information from local agencies as well as from the national, or central, intelligence organization at home. Likewise, battlefield intelligence was bundled up and transmitted to the national intelligence center for analysis. The staff intelligence section had as its principal focus the provision of timely information about enemy dispositions and capabilities, upon which the commander would base his own plans. This appreciation of the enemy situation was a critical step in the commander's estimate and would influence the course of action he adopted.

The colorful exploits of some spies notwithstanding, most productive intelligence activities were accomplished quietly by faceless bureaucrats and staff officers working behind the scenes. American Major Herbert O. Yardley's "Black Chamber" operation (M.I. 8, Cable and Telegraph Section) was in reality a cryptographic agency during World War I. Despite its early establishment in June of 1917, Yardley's unit was not actively decoding intercepted foreign messages until August of 1918. Yardley's group did react quickly to the possibility that the Germans were decoding American messages sent over transoceanic cables, and they developed safer codes and ciphers. Some of the most important cryptographic work during the war was that performed by the Royal Navy's Room 40.

Communications security varied widely. Colonel Walther Nicolai, chief of the German Secret Service of the Imperial General Staff since 1913, who was an unusually well qualified diplomat and linguist, commented after the war that the Allies quickly learned how to protect their wireless message traffic, but the Russians "were the most harmless and clumsy in their code system."

As the war moved to a conclusion at the end of 1918 and during the peace negotiations in 1919, counterintelligence operations dominated the work of most intelligence services, particularly the American agencies. Intelligence operations occurred at the highest levels of government of each of the belligerent powers, as well as at battalion and regimental levels on the battlefield. In most instances, intelligence organizations were vertical "stovepipe" affairs running from the lieutenant in the infantry battalion to the top analyst in the national intelligence organization. Information went up this stovepipe and processed intelligence went down.

John F. Votaw

References

Bidwell, Colonel Bruce W., U.S. Army (Ret). *History of the Military Intelligence Division, Department of the Army General Staff: 1775–1941.* Frederick, Md.: University Publications of America, 1986.

Dorwart, Jeffrey M. *The Office of Naval Intelligence: The Birth of America's First Intelligence Agency, 1865–1918.* Annapolis, Md.: Naval Institute Press, 1979.

Drake, Lieutenant-Colonel Reginald John, D.S.O. "Intelligence, Military." In *Encyclopaedia Britannica*, 12th ed. Vol. 32, 504–12. New York: Encyclopaedia Britannica, 1922.

Ferguson, Thomas G. *British Military Intelligence, 1870–1914: The Development of a Modern Intelligence Organization.* Frederick, Md.: University Publications of America, 1984.

May, Ernest R., ed. *Knowing One's Enemies: Intelligence Assessment before the Two World Wars.* Princeton: Princeton University Press, 1984.

Millett, Allan R., and Williamson Murray, eds. *Military Effectiveness. Volume 1: The First World War.* Boston: Unwin Hyman, 1988.

Strong, Major-General Sir Kenneth, K.B.E., C.B. *Men of Intelligence: A Study of the Roles and Decisions of Chiefs of Intelligence from World War I to the Present Day.* London: Cassell, 1970.

Sweeney, Lt. Colonel Walter C., U.S. Army. *Military Intelligence: A New Weapon in War.* New York: Frederick A. Stokes, 1924.

Yardley, Herbert O. *The American Black Chamber.* Indianapolis, Ind.: Bobbs-Merrill, 1931.

See also CHARTERIS, JOHN; HALL, REGINALD; HENTSCH, RICHARD; ROOM 40

Ireland

During World War I Ireland proved to be a huge, annoying, and bloody distraction for Great Britain. The war came at a bad time for both Ireland and Britain, as the British Parliament was on the verge of granting Irish home rule. Although many individual Irishmen volunteered to fight against Germany, Irish nationalists in league with the German government rose in rebellion on 24 April 1916; the "Easter Rebellion" ended in disaster. Afterwards, the disaffected population refused to enlist in British service and in 1918 violently resisted conscription. Eventually, the "Irish Question" caused hundreds of casualties on both sides and diverted British resources badly needed elsewhere.

Anglo-Irish relations have historically been unsettled. Since the English conquest of Ireland in the sixteenth century, latent Irish nationalism has occasionally erupted into open rebellion, often with the aid of a foreign power as coconspirator. Without exception, these risings met with bitter results. In the early twentieth century, a fresh breed of Irish nationalist (taking the name Sinn Fein) introduced a new tactic into the long struggle. These idealists sought political solutions and semi-autonomous "home rule" as a preliminary step toward eventual independence. The method gained momentum, eventually eclipsing the more radical nationalists, and by the spring of 1914 a home rule bill was before parliament.

Pro-British Irish Protestants in Ulster bitterly fought home rule. Arguing that they would be targets for Catholic reprisals, they promised armed opposition to the impending legislation and formed the Ulster Volunteers, a paramilitary army. In the Curragh Mutiny of April of 1914, British troops stationed in Ireland declared that they would not use force against the Ulster Protestants. At the urging of King George V of England, Parliament refused to act on the issue of home rule until further investigation. This conundrum stymied and discredited the efforts of Sinn Fein, as radicals on both sides of the issue began arming themselves.

The eruption of war in Europe in August of 1914 temporarily averted civil war in Ireland. Sinn Feiners, hoping to gain political influence in Britain, urged Irishmen to enlist in the British ranks for service against Germany. Although thousands did, a large number joined the more radical volunteer forces arming in Ireland. Hoping to stave off any violence in Ireland, Parliament passed home rule early in 1916, but only through the expediency of permanently partitioning Ireland into a Protestant north (Ulster) and Catholic south.

For radical Irish nationalists, the war seemed to be the providential moment to strike for independence against a distracted Britain. With the aid of former British diplomat Sir Roger Casement, nationalists in the United States and in Ireland opened communications with Germany to obtain support in the form of weapons and money. The Germans agreed to assist the Irish nationalists and plans for rebellion accelerated. Despite intricate planning the rebellion was doomed to disaster.

German enthusiasm for the venture cooled, but the promised weapons left Kiel, Germany, on schedule on 9 April aboard the *Aud,* a tramp freighter flying Norwegian colors. The *Aud* was to rendezvous in mid ocean with German U-boats but missed the meeting point and proceeded to Ireland unescorted. On 21 April off Tralee Bay two patrolling British trawlers investigated the suspicious ship, which quickly made steam and slipped back to the open sea. Two other Royal Navy vessels, the corvettes HMS *Bluebell* and HMS *Zinnia,* gave chase and ordered the *Aud* to follow them to Queens-town, Ireland. The next day, as the vessels entered the harbor, Lieutenant Karl Spindler of the *Kreigsmarine,* skipper of the *Aud,* ordered his vessel scuttled at the harbor entrance in a gesture of defiance.

Meanwhile, Casement and a two-man escort traveled to Ireland aboard *U-19* to alert their countrymen as to German intentions. Coming ashore by dinghy at remote Tralee Bay on 21 April, they traveled by foot toward Dublin. Local children, however, discovered their abandoned boat and alerted police. Two rural patrolmen reacted to the report and arrested the party just hours after they had landed on Irish soil.

Even with the element of surprise lost, and desperately short of modern weapons, the nationalists decided to proceed with their rebellion. The Sinn Fein leadership opposed them, however. Confused by the mixed signals they were receiving from their leaders, many outlying units of the Irish Citizen Army disbanded.

In Dublin, rebels armed themselves with old rifles, homemade bombs, and even pikes. At noon on 24 April approximately 200 insurgents attacked Dublin Castle but then withdrew to seize key locations in downtown Dublin. From his headquarters at the General Post Office, self-proclaimed president Patrick Pearse declared Ireland an independent republic.

The British response was swift and violent. Troops from nearby units, including detachments from a variety of empire battalions, hurried to Dublin. Meanwhile, in England, anxious officials wondered if the Irish rising served as a cover for a German invasion. They sent some reservists to the coast to begin digging trenches.

The bulk of the British forces sent to Ireland came from the 178th North Midland Division, including the four battalions of the 7th

Sherwood Foresters and the 2/6th South Staffordshire. These men arrived after a hurried crossing, fully believing they were in France and quite surprised to find themselves in Dublin. On 25 April they began a block-by-block reduction of the rebel positions. HMS *Helga,* stationed in the River Liffy, added gunfire support, which set many parts of the city on fire. By 29 April the rebellion had been crushed, and Pearse ordered his followers to surrender.

The British rounded up their prisoners and transported the majority of them to camps in Wales. Leaders of the rebellion met with swift execution by firing squad at the Kilmainham jail. Casement languished for months in the Tower of London and tried to commit suicide on three occasions. After a trial, he was hanged at Pentoville Prison, London, on 3 August 1916.

The Easter Rebellion cost three thousand casualties, including fifty-six rebel and 130 British dead. Nearly two hundred buildings in central Dublin lay in ruin. Some 100,000 Irish civilians were homeless or in need of public relief after the battle.

Many considered the subsequent treatment of Easter Rebellion prisoners cruel, and Irish propagandists turned the disaster to their favor. In the months following the event, scattered rebel groups initiated guerrilla warfare that proved to be a constant distraction for Great Britain during the rest of World War I and forced tens of thousands of British troops to serve as a permanent garrison in Ireland. The presence of a common enemy on Irish soil also served to fuse the various nationalist factions together under the leadership of Sinn Fein. In 1918 efforts to conscript Irishmen into the British army met with violent opposition, requiring even more empire soldiers in garrison duties on the island.

By war's end Irish nationalists had a host of new patriot martyrs, and support for home rule and eventual independence had gathered momentum. Although the war on the European continent had ended, violence and guerrilla warfare in Ireland increased. In 1919 Sinn Fein declared Irish independence. By 1921, Great Britain had found it necessary to commit some 100,000 troops and constabulary forces to the island. That year, Parliament granted Ireland dominion status within the empire in exchange for peace. A year later the country again declared itself independent, this time successfully.

Donald Frazier

References

Bell, J. Bowyer. *The Secret Army: The I.R.A., 1916–1970.* New York: John Day, 1971.

Caulfield, Max. *The Easter Rebellion.* New York: Holt, Rinehart, and Winston, 1963.

Figgis, Darrell. *Recollections of the Irish War.* New York: Doubleday, Doran, n.d.

Jones, Francis P. *History of the Sinn Fein Movement and the Irish Rebellion of 1916.* New York: Kennedy and Sons, 1917.

Macardle, Dorothy. *The Irish Republic: A Documented Chronicle of the Anglo-Irish Conflict and the Partitioning of Ireland with a Detailed Account of the Period 1916–1923.* New York: Farrar, Straus, and Giroux, 1937.

McHugh, Roger, ed. *Dublin 1916.* New York: Hawthorn, 1966.

O'Broin, Leon. *Dublin Castle and the 1916 Rising.* New York: New York University Press, 1971.

See also CASEMENT, ROGER

Isonzo, Battles of, Nos. 1–4 (1915)

The Italian front was over four hundred miles long, but most of the fighting occurred on sixty miles of jagged karst uplands, rugged mountain ridges, and precipitous river valleys along the Isonzo River from Tolmino to the Adriatic Sea. The forbidding nature of the terrain elsewhere on the front, the need to deny Austria the plains of the Veneto, and the closeness of such military objectives as Trieste made this the logical place for Italy to attempt to mount its major offensive operations. Consequently, as early as May of 1915, Italian commander General Luigi Cadorna deployed fourteen of his thirty-five divisions along the sixty-mile Isonzo front and another fourteen on the mountains that stretched for 350 miles from Carnia to Mount Stelvio.

The first four Italian offensives along the Isonzo occurred between 23 June and 2 December 1915. The Italians gained some ground but suffered 40,000 casualties in the first two offensives and 117,000 in the last two. By the end of 1915 they had suffered 235,000 casualties along the Isonzo, including 54,000 dead, 160,000 wounded, and 21,000 prisoners.

Italy's entry into the war on 24 May 1915 was predicated on promises that both Russia and

Serbia would attack, thereby distracting Austria-Hungary and giving the Italian army an opportunity to drive deeply into Austrian territory. Because mobilization did not begin until early May, however, it could not be completed until mid-June. That forced Cadorna to choose between attacking quickly and perhaps catching Austro-Hungarian commander Field Marshal Franz Conrad von Hötzendorf off guard, or waiting a month and running the risk that his opponent would reinforce the frontier, where Austro-Hungarian forces already controlled the heights. He chose to attack quickly, but his 195 battalions had neither helmets nor battle experience. His decision has been severely criticized, but Cadorna could not have attacked earlier and waiting longer would have given Conrad more time to prepare and man defensive positions. As it was, Conrad was able to move a division from the Balkans and two battered divisions from Russia. He was, therefore, able to increase the number of battalions on the Italian front from 36 on 27 April to 127 by late May, giving him a force of 114,000 men supported by 230 guns with which to contest Cadorna's advance.

Although Cadorna had 400,000 men in the Veneto in May, he had little artillery and few alpine troops. Consequently, he ordered a brief "offensive push" *(balzo offensive)* by Second and Third armies, which were to advance and cross the Isonzo River where possible in order to improve their positions for a later attack. Meanwhile, First and Fourth armies were to consolidate their defensive positions in the Trentino and Carnia. Second Army captured Caporetto, Kolovrat, and Korada, and the Third occupied the area from Gradisca to Monfalcone. The Austrians, however, were strongly emplaced on the right bank of the Isonzo at Gorizia and Tolmino, had fortified the valley of the Vipacco River, and held the high ground from the Triestine karst to the coast.

Italian forces on the Isonzo had few aircraft and no bridging equipment. Hand grenades had not yet been distributed, and some units even lacked wirecutters. In the Trentino, First Army had six divisions, and in Carnia the Fourth had five divisions supported by 36 mountain guns, 220 field guns, and 16 heavy howitzers. Cadorna could concentrate neither his artillery nor his infantry. For his "offensive jump" of 7 to 13 June, he used twenty-two of his thirty-five divisions, keeping seven in reserve at Lake Garda. They had no artillery support until after the 10th.

While the Austrians had few permanent fortifications, Conrad had 220 battalions—the equivalent of eighteen Italian divisions—and the thirteen battalions of the German Alpenkorps. Even so, the initial Italian attack succeeded in approaching Monte Sabotino and Podgora east of Gorizia, crossing the Isonzo at Monfalcone in the south and Plava in the center, isolating the Austrian bridgeheads at Gorizia and Tolmino, taking Monte Nero on 16 June and briefly holding Monte Mrzli, just north of Tolmino. Each side suffered around 11,000 casualties, as the Austrians maintained their bridgeheads at Gorizia and Tolmino and kept the heights at Sabotino and San Michele. Having already moved eight divisions and a brigade to the Italian front in May, Conrad transferred six divisions and a brigade by September and added two divisions and two brigades by Christmas, for a total of twenty-two divisions along the Isonzo by the end of 1915.

The First Battle of the Isonzo began on 23 June, ten days after the suspension of the initial advance, and ended on 7 July. Cadorna hoped to break into the Vipacco valley and extend the Italian bridgehead at Plava, thereby flanking Gorizia and the hills east of the city as his troops overcame Austro-Hungarian resistance on Monte Sabotino and Peuma with frontal attacks. Although he hoped to break through to the karst, doing so would be difficult because Italian infantry would have to attack uphill with little artillery support over broken terrain against strong positions. By pushing on the Austro-Hungarian left and applying pressure in a series of frontal attacks, there was a chance that Cadorna might turn his enemy's flank.

Fighting was heavy, with the Italians suffering 14,950 casualties, the Austrians 10,400. While Third Army reached the karst and took Sagrado, Second Army was checked to the north. Still, the Italians had extended their bridgehead at Plava and established themselves on the right bank of the Isonzo. That they did no better was to be expected, since Conrad had concentrated 113 battalions and 132 batteries from Monte Nero to the sea, and during the battle he threw three more divisions into line.

The Second Battle on the Isonzo resulted from an agreement on 7 July by an inter-Allied conference at Chantilly to support Russia. Once again Serbia stood by passively from 18 July to 3 August as Italy carried out its offensive. The immediate objectives were the strongpoints of

San Martino and San Michele, two of the defensive pillars supporting Gorizia and guarding the Vipacco valley and the karst plateau. Third Army, with thirty-four battalions and eight squadrons of aircraft on a ten-mile front, bore the brunt of the attack. Seven Italian divisions against five and a half Austro-Hungarian divisions were too few to prevail, and while the Italians took San Michele, an Austrian counterattack quickly recaptured it. The Italians retook the position, but poor use of reserves and artillery allowed the Austrians again to reoccupy San Michele, where 6,000 Italians and Austrians died fighting. Total casualties reached 10,700 Italians and 5,400 Austro-Hungarians. Second Army had also attacked Monte Rosso, and in August and September the Italians mounted a series of local actions, including one against the Plezzo Gap north of Caporetto. If disappointing, the second offensive nonetheless forced Conrad to withdraw his last mobile units from the Balkans and transfer four divisions from Russia.

The entry of Bulgaria into the war on 21 September, the Serbian collapse in early October, and French pressure to support their offensive in Champagne on 25 September pushed Cadorna to act. Because he insisted on waiting until his units had replenished their ammunition stocks, the third battle on the Isonzo did not begin until 18 October, when the Serbs and Montenegrins were already in full retreat. Cadorna once more hoped to break into the Vipacco valley by attacking on the wings against the karst in the south and Plava and Tolmino to the north, while mounting attacks in the center against Gorizia, San Michele, Monte Sabotino, and Podgora. He was still desperately short of artillery, however, and after a series of small gains, he suspended the attack from 4 to 10 November to reorganize and resupply.

The final Italian offensive on the Isonzo front in 1915 occurred in miserable conditions between 10 November and 2 December. Fighting was especially fierce around Podgora, which saw forty separate attacks. Although the Italians failed to take either San Michele or Gorizia, they pushed the Austrians back, penetrated the Gorizia salient, and further expanded their bridgehead at Plava. They did so at great cost, as some of the units on the karst lost up to 50 percent of their effectives. During the third and fourth offensives, which had been fought with twenty-five Italian divisions along a fifty-mile front, the Italians suffered 116,000 casualties (67,000 in the third and 49,000 in the fourth offensive), the Austrians about 67,000 (42,000 and 25,000).

During the course of these battles Italian aircraft gained in importance, being used when weather permitted for artillery spotting and reconnaissance. Also, by the end of 1915 Italian aviators were flying an Italian aircraft, Gianni Caproni's heavy bomber.

Cadorna has been criticized for staging a series of unimaginative offensives that did little more than kill large numbers of Italian troops and slightly lesser numbers of Austro-Hungarian soldiers. His defenders, however, believe that heavy losses were the result of difficult terrain, too few experienced units, and poor training, rather than poor command decisions. They point out that the Italian casualties of 116,000 in the fall of 1915 were fewer than the British and French losses of 247,699, and they note that if the Italians had taken 246,400 casualties in six months, the French and British had suffered 622,699 in twelve. Still, there is no question that Cadorna had mounted the first four battles with too little artillery and an unfavorable position. At best, his decision can be defended as having forced Austria-Hungary to divert eight divisions from the Serbian front and six from the Russian front and tied up the six brigades of the German Alpenkorps. Italian troops inflicted 200,000 casualties on Austria-Hungary in 1915, and their successes raised morale even if they improved their tactical position only slightly. Cadorna praised the fourth offensive as "the harshest and most glorious" period in the war, and authors like Caracciolo have argued that Italy "replaced" Russia and Serbia in 1915, as the one faltered and the other collapsed.

James J. Sadkovich

References

Caracciolo, Mario. *L'Italia nella guerra mondiale*. Rome: Edizioni Roma, 1935.

Faldella, Emilio. *La grande guerra*. 2 vols. Milan: Longanesi, 1965.

Molfese, Manlio. *L'aviazione da ricognizione italiana durante la guerra europea (maggio 1915–novembre 1918)*. Rome: Provveditorato Generale dello Stato, Libreria, 1925.

Pieri, Piero. *L'Italia nella prima guerra mondiale (1915–1918)*. Turin: Einaudi, 1968.

Porro, Felice. *La guerra nell'aria, 1915–1918.* Milan: Corbaccio, 1935. Reprint. Milan: Mate, 1965.

Valori, Aldo. *La guerra italo-austriaca, 1915–1918.* Bologna: Nicola Zanichelli, 1920.

See also CADORNA, LUIGI; ITALY, ARMY

Isonzo, Battles of, Nos. 5–9 (1916)

Although Caproni bombers raided Ljubljana in February of 1916 and Rome dispatched two divisions to Albania, the offensives of 1915 had exhausted Italy. On the Isonzo the Second Army had only 85,000 of its complement of 148,000 riflemen, and if Italian commander General Luigi Cadorna maintained odds of two to one on the Isonzo, with 200 battalions to 116 enemy battalions, and 330 batteries with 1,300 guns against 135 Austro-Hungarian batteries with 650 guns, he was in the process of rebuilding his forces. He therefore launched the fifth Italian offensive on the Isonzo on 6 March 1916 only after France urged him to relieve pressure on Verdun and to support a projected Russian offensive that got underway only in early June.

With no definite objective, the Italian attack on the Isonzo, like the short-lived offensive in the Trentino's Valsugana, degenerated into a series of local actions that proved futile and costly. Fought in mud and deep snow, the battle dragged on through late April, costing the Italians 50,000 casualties and the Austrians 40,000. If the offensive achieved little, Rome's accommodation of its allies convinced Conrad that the Italians posed no threat on the Isonzo and that he could go ahead with his plans for an offensive in the Trentino. Yet by doing so, he opened the way to successful Italian offensives later in the year. While the sixth Italian offensive was extremely bloody, the next three battles on the Isonzo were very brief and less costly, the Italians suffering 75,000 casualties and the Austrians 63,000 as Cadorna's forces gained significant advantages along the Isonzo.

The idea for the sixth battle originated in late June when the Duke d'Aosta, who commanded the Third Army, suggested that a large-scale offensive might overwhelm Austro-Hungarian positions from Monte Sabotino to the Adriatic Sea. Cadorna agreed, but the Italians needed until 27 July to recover from Conrad's spring offensive in the Trentino, which they had managed to stem only by committing their reserves of twenty-seven divisions. As a result, only seven divisions were available for an offensive on the Isonzo. That limited the Italian attack to an assault on Monte Sabotino, which, with San Michele, defended the Austrian bridgehead at Gorizia on the right (Italian) side of the river. Moreover, while Cadorna and D'Aosta had discussed the first phase of the attack, they had not elaborated on a second, so that there were no plans beyond securing the right bank of the river and taking Monte Sabotino.

Nonetheless, the Italian attack was formidable. The Third Army had sixteen divisions (203 battalions) with 1,094 guns on a twenty-four-kilometer front from Monte Sabotino, just north of Gorizia, to the sea. Each army corps also had a squadron of aircraft with which to reconnoitre the battlefield prior to, then spot for artillery during, the attack. For the nine-hour barrage that opened the battle, the Italians deployed thirty-nine guns per kilometer, their largest effort to date on the Isonzo. By moving fifty-eight battalions and twenty-two batteries to the Isonzo from 27 July to 3 August Cadorna had achieved surprise, which he then squandered, according to Pieri, by mounting two more-or-less equal actions against the anchors of the Austrian position at Gorizia, thereby losing his chance for a major breakthrough.

The initial attack opened on 4 August with a diversion at Monfalcone to draw off the reserves of Field Marshal Svetozar Boroević von Bojna. The attack on San Michele, San Martino, Monte Sabotino, Podgora, and Gorizia got underway two days later with a massive barrage from 07:00 to 16:00. The VI Corps, with six divisions and two-thirds of the Third Army's 750 medium and heavy guns, was to attack the sector between Monte Sabotino and Podgora, and the XI Corps, with three divisions, was to take San Michele. But d'Aosta and Cadorna sent three reserve divisions to the karst and only one to the VI Corps, wasting a third of Third Army's strength on a three-kilometer front against San Michele. The infantry took both Sabotino and San Michele. Because the Italians failed to occupy the flanks of these positions, however, especially Peuma and Podgora, the Austrians were able to attack and stage a fairly orderly if hurried retreat over the river on the night of 7–8 August, losing 18,000 of 23,000 troops on the right bank of the river. On the following day, the Italians occupied Gorizia, and Luigi Capello, commander of the VI Corps, believed that he had routed the Austrians. He therefore requested permission, which Cadorna granted, to create a "fast" army corps of two battalions of cyclists and eighteen squadrons of cavalry.

But Boroević had only been falling back to more defensible positions, and he had been steadily reinforced, getting three battalions on the 7th, two brigades on the 10th, and a division after the 13th. Consequently, although Cadorna sent a cavalry and two infantry divisions from the Trentino—so that by 9 August Capello had six divisions and a *celere* group on the left bank of the Isonzo—the Italian pursuit bogged down as they ran into strong positions during the afternoon of 9 August. They reached their culminating point the following day, when they were checked at Monte Santo and elsewhere.

It seemed that the Italians had let a big victory slip away by not concentrating their forces on a single point, and a debate followed over whether Capello had been right to pursue, or whether he should have allowed d'Aosta to press the second phase of the attack. But, as Mario Caracciolo noted, at the time the capture of Sabotino and Gorizia were viewed as major victories, because both had become symbols of Austrian resistance and Italian frustration. The price of 51,221 Italian casualties had been high, but the Austrians had suffered 37,458, and Cadorna had obliterated the Austro-Hungarian bridgehead at Gorizia, dramatically improved his own position, forced Vienna to transfer four more divisions from Russia to the karst, and won the first Italian victory against a foreign army in a major battle since the days of Rome. In effect, the capture of Gorizia had redeemed the reputation of the Italian military and given a considerable boost to morale in Italy. Moreover, if they did not manage to secure as dramatic a victory in the next three offensives, the Italians did maintain their advantage through the end of 1916 by launching a series of short, intense "pushes" against the Austro-Hungarian line along the Isonzo River.

The idea of shifting from protracted offensives over large areas to short, powerful "pushes" (*spallate*) against the enemy line evolved from Cadorna's appreciation that the war had become one of attrition, one in which reserves could always check breakthroughs. Experience had shown that while the impetus of the initial attack might allow an advance of several kilometers, a culminating point was quickly reached. Drawing out the attack only increased casualties. By September of 1916, Cadorna had become convinced that breakthroughs were impossible and that it was therefore best to suspend the attack once it was clear that a "dead" point had been reached, in order to avoid exhausting his units and discouraging his troops. It was a tactic that author Mario Caracciolo considered "really useful" and "a great advance over previous methods of attack."

If successful, his new tactic would allow Cadorna to keep the initiative, because he would be able to renew the offensive quickly by rotating fresh forces to the front lines. In fact, while he used forty-five brigades in his *spallate* of late 1916, only seven were in all three battles, nineteen in two, and nineteen in one only. Given that most Italian objectives were only twenty to thirty kilometers away, that even brief attacks would relieve Austrian pressure on Romania, that the fall of a coastal city like Trieste would have significant political ramifications in Austria-Hungary, and that the Dual Monarchy had been decimated by the Russian summer offensive, it seemed reasonable to adopt a strategy of wearing down Austria-Hungary by mounting a series of limited offensives calculated to reach Italian strategic objectives by what amounted to offensive leaps and bounds.

Unfortunately, divisional, corps, and army commands were reluctant to stop fighting once they were engaged, especially if they fell under the illusion, as Capello had at Gorizia, that a bit more effort might pay huge rewards. In addition, the Italians had too few guns and too little ammunition to support such a strategy, especially inasmuch as Italian infantry were typical in their psychological dependence on artillery to overcome static defenses.

The Third Army, with ten divisions and 960 guns, opened the seventh battle of the Isonzo on 14 September. Intended to advance against Trieste over the karst by taking the Monte Faiti, Monte Trstelj, and the Vipacco valley, the offensive began with a massive artillery barrage that lasted from dawn to 15:00. D'Aosta's troops quickly advanced two kilometers, taking 4,100 POWs and suffering 18,000 casualties. They then bogged down, and a disappointed Cadorna suspended the attack after three days.

The next *spallata,* the eighth battle of the Isonzo, was designed to strike east of Gorizia and break into the Vipacco valley. But the Second Army's offensive was delayed by the weather and its attack on 10 October frustrated by Austro-Hungarian counterattacks. Cadorna suspended the action on the 12th, but by then Italy had suffered 23,000 casualties for paltry gains. Still, the action impressed Boroević, who had lost 8,200 POWs and concluded that his Italian opponents had learned a great deal about the waging of war since 1915.

The last *spallata* in 1916, the ninth battle of the Isonzo, was also delayed by weather and got underway only on 1 November. Once more, Cadorna aimed at the Vipacco valley, and once more gains were small and casualties high; about 29,000 in three days. While the Third Army advanced five kilometers, the Second Army stalled, and the offensive was suspended on 4 November. Nonetheless, the action forced Vienna to deploy two more divisions on the Isonzo, and it seemed that the Italians were wearing down Austria-Hungary. Cadorna's armies had inflicted 74,000 casualties on the Dual Monarchy, but they had suffered 77,000 themselves. Even so, from August to November of 1916 the Italians had taken 40,000 POWs, killed or wounded 90,000 enemy troops, and pinned down thirty-eight divisions. If the *spallate* had disappointed expectations raised by the capture of Gorizia in August, the Italians had at least ended 1916 in a better tactical position than they had started it, and they seemed to be evolving their own brand of trench warfare, which had enjoyed some success at Gorizia.

James J. Sadkovich

References

Caracciolo, Mario. *L'Italia nella guerra mondiale*. Rome: Edizioni Roma, 1935.
Faldella, Emilio. *La grande guerra*. 2 vols. Milan: Longanesi, 1965.
Király, Béla, and Nándor F. Dreisziger, eds. *War and Society in East Central Europe*. Vol. 19. New York: Columbia University Press, 1985.
Pieri, Piero. *L'Italia nella prima guerra mondiale (1915–1918)*. Turin: Einaudi, 1968.
Valori, Aldo. *La guerra italo-austriaca, 1915–1918*. Bologna: Nicola Zanichelli, 1920.

See also BOROEVIĆ VON BOJNA, SVETOZAR; CADORNA, LUIGI; CAPELLO, LUIGI; TRENTINO OFFENSIVE

Isonzo, Battles of, Nos. 10 and 11 (1917)

The tenth battle of the Isonzo was fought between 12 and 18 May 1917. Italian commander General Luigi Cadorna had been concerned over another attack in the Trentino and wanted to coordinate his offensive on the Isonzo with Allied attacks elsewhere, in order to force Austria-Hungary to disperse its forces as widely as possible. With snow four meters deep in the mountains and its army exhausted from the campaigns of 1916, the Italian command planned only a limited offensive. The objectives were to enlarge the Plava bridgehead, reach Hermada on the Karst, and secure a foothold on the edge of the Bainsizza Plateau by taking Monte Kuk, Monte Santo, and San Gabriele.

Luigi Capello's Second Army (twelve divisions supported by 140 light and 528 medium guns) was to open the attack with a diversionary action against Tolmino, then turn to the area around Gorizia as it ceded some of its guns to the Third Army. By "maneuvering" his artillery in this way, Cadorna hoped that, in a third phase of the battle, d'Aosta's Third Army (sixteen divisions with 190 light and 530 medium guns) would be able to make significant advances on the Karst.

Second Army's attack was preceded by a barrage between 12 and 14 May. For the first time the Italians had enough artillery to do real damage to the Austrian lines. During the seventeen days of the battle, their 2,238 guns fired three million shells, opening large gaps for the Italian infantry. Italian pilots controlled the air and staged large-scale attacks, using up to thirty-four Caproni bombers against Austrian positions. Because it surprised the Austrian Fifth Army, led by Field Marshal Svetozar Boroević von Bojna, the Italian Second Army quickly occupied the flanks of Monte Kuk, Vodice, and Monte Santo. Unfortunately, as in 1916, Capello again thought that he had routed the Austrians and so kept his medium artillery, rather than ceding it to d'Aosta. That delayed Third Army's attack by two days. Bad weather postponed it further, so that by the time d'Aosta's troops moved, on 23 May, Bojna had gained five days to reorganize his defenses, bring up two divisions from the East, and deploy two of his four reserve divisions at Gorizia.

Capello's troops succeeded in taking the summit of Monte Kuk, but they failed to secure Monte Santo. His optimism had undermined d'Aosta's attack. Austro-Hungarian resistance was fierce, with violent counterattacks from 14 to 31 May, and Boroević's counterattack near Hermada in early June cost the Italians over 20,000 casualties. Although they had again improved their tactical position, inflicted 75,700 casualties on the Austrians, and forced Boroević to transfer two more divisions from the Eastern Front, the Italians had suffered 111,873 casualties.

Cadorna's persistent offensives were clearly wearing down his enemy, who had also suffered heavily in the East. While Italian forces also had taken heavy casualties, they had not been bled on a second front. By the summer of 1917 Cadorna had fifty-one divisions and 3,600 guns on the Isonzo. Capello's Second Army had increased to a cavalry and 26.5 infantry divisions supported by 2,366 guns. D'Aosta's Third Army had eighteen infantry divisions with 1,200 guns. With reserves of 6.5 infantry and 1.5 cavalry divisions, the Italians were poised for a major effort on the Isonzo, but Cadorna was not satisfied. During a conference in Paris on 24–26 July he asked Generals Ferdinand Foch and Sir William Robertson for ten divisions and four hundred guns to enable him to mount a "decisive" attack from Tolmino to the sea, shatter Austria-Hungary's forces on the Isonzo, and force Vienna to sue for peace.

Italy's allies continued to see France as the decisive front, and Russia's collapse in July led them to worry that large numbers of German divisions would shortly be arriving in France. Hence they rejected Cadorna's requests. Cadorna himself was worried that Austro-Hungarian units might soon arrive from Russia, so he rushed the attack on the Isonzo. Moreover, he diluted his forces by launching a three-pronged offensive against Tolmino to the north, the Bainsizza plateau to the east, and San Gabriele to the south.

The eleventh battle of the Isonzo was intended to occupy the Bainsizza Plateau, with the Second Army to take Monte Mrzli, Tolmino, and Ternova, while the Third occupied Comen. But the Second had to attack over the Isonzo against strong positions, and Boroević's Fifth Army had been reinforced by three divisions from Russia. That brought his strength to twenty-three divisions by mid-August. Against them, Cadorna could throw forty-three divisions (593 battalions) supported by 3,743 guns and 1,882 bombards. How the Isonzo had come to dominate the Italian war effort can be appreciated by noting that while only 11 of 85 alpine battalions were used in the offensive, 88 of 116 infantry brigades and 36 of 72 *bersaglieri* battalions fought in the eleventh battle, from 17 to 29 August.

The artillery preparation was staggered. Second Army's guns opened up on 17 August, and Third Army's the next day, with an attack by the Italian infantry on the 19th. Because bridging proved difficult, and only six of fourteen were usable, the attack on Tolmino faltered and had failed by the 20th. Enrico Caviglia's XXIV corps occupied Monte Santo and Kuk by 24 August, however, forcing Boroević to withdraw to Chiapovaro the night of 23–24 August. Third Army also made progress on the right wing, but its attack was suspended on the 23rd because Capello again thought that he had routed the enemy. Instead, his pursuit met heavy resistance from Austro-Hungarian rear guards. His forces had no heavy artillery and could do little on 25 August when they ran up against prepared positions manned by fifty-two Austro-Hungarian battalions supported by Fifth Army's artillery. The Italian command therefore suspended the offensive on 29 August, although fighting on San Gabriele raged until 10 September and isolated actions occurred until the 15th.

Although the Italians had been frustrated, before their attack stalled they had advanced ten kilometers. That was the farthest advance by any army in Western Europe. They had inflicted 110,000 casualties on the Austrians, captured 145 guns, and established control of the air. The army's air force had kept 230 aircraft serviceable daily: Italian pilots had flown 2,474 missions, including 70 by Caproni bombers, which dropped 750 bombs (125,629 kg) on auto parks and depots in the Vallone di Chiapovaro. But if the Italians now had large numbers of guns and were honing combined arms operations, their success in wearing down Austria-Hungary contained the germ of their own defeat. Once again they paid a high price for their successes, suffering 8,867 casualties in the fighting for San Gabriele and 143,074 during the offensive. Without the help of their allies, they could not defeat Austria-Hungary, but the British and French continued to focus their attention in France. The Germans, alarmed by the setbacks suffered by their ally, began to consider ways in which they might help Vienna knock Italy out of the war. The incomplete Italian victory on the Bainsizza during the Eleventh Battle of the Isonzo would lead to an incomplete German-Austro-Hungarian victory at Caporetto later in 1917.

James J. Sadkovich

References

Caracciolo, Mario. *L'Italia nella guerra mondiale*. Rome: Edizioni Roma, 1935.

Faldella, Emilio. *La grande guerra*. 2 vols. Milan: Longanesi, 1965.

Pieri, Piero. *L'Italia nella prima guerra mondiale (1915–1918)*. Turin: Einaudi, 1968.

Valori, Aldo. *La guerra italo-austriaca, 1915–1918*. Bologna: Nicola Zanichelli, 1920.

See also BOROEVIĆ VON BOJNA, SVETOZAR; CADORNA, LUIGI; CAPELLO, LUIGI

Isonzo, Battles of, No. 12 (24 October to 25 December 1917)

See CAPORETTO

Italy, Army

Although Italy's military budget rose after 1907 to allow the army to modernize, and two-year service enlistments increased the annual number of conscripts by 30,000 (bringing the number of front-line troops to 600,000), the Italian army was ill-prepared for war in 1914. Indeed, the army received only 148 of the 551 million lire in extraordinary funds requested and was not prepared to join the fighting.

While the army placed its first order for 500 motortrucks in 1907 and opened a school of aviation in 1910, by 1914 it had only 595 vehicles and only eight squadrons of aircraft. All of Italy had only 20,000 vehicles in 1914, and the army depended on 200,000 horses and other draft animals. Despite arsenals at Turin and Naples, arms factories at Brescia, Terni, Turin, and Torre Annunziata, and ordnance plants at Genova, Bologna, Capua, Fossano, and Fontana Liri, Italian industry could not satisfy the army's needs. A monthly production of 2,500 rifles forced the use of older models, and even in early 1916 there were only 112,000 rifles with which to train 228,000 conscripts. With only 618 machine guns in 309 sections, the Italians had only two to six weapons per regiment, while the Austrians had two per battalion.

The army had only fourteen batteries of 149mm howitzers, built by the German firm Krupp, and was just replacing the older, rigid 75mm guns when the war began. With a monthly production of only 100 rounds per gun and 40 per rifle, and stocks of only 1,200 shells per gun and 700 rounds per rifle, the army could not mount either a prolonged offensive or a massive artillery barrage. As late as May of 1915 Italy produced only 23,000 artillery shells per month, about 27,000 fewer than needed. Not until 26 June 1915, after Italy had entered the war, did minister of war General Vittorio Zupelli order industrial mobilization. Consequently, the army lacked good artillery support until later in 1916. Of 40.9 million artillery rounds fired during the war, only 3.3 million were fired in 1915 and 8 million in 1916, compared with 29.6 million rounds in 1917 and 1918.

To compound the army's matériel problems, there was a change of leadership on the eve of hostilities. General Alberto Pollio, chief of staff since 1908, died unexpectedly of a heart attack on 1 July 1914 and was succeeded by Luigi Cadorna. Cadorna's strained relations with the Ministry of War hampered efforts to obtain money. Also, his revision of prewar plans to mobilize and assemble simultaneously from the Piave to Tagliamento rivers, in favor of mobilizing in peacetime assembly areas and then moving to the Po Valley to assemble, proved cumbersome. In addition, he had to call back as many of the 62,000 troops in Libya as possible, cover a shortage of 7,500 officers, and find 350,000 uniforms for reservists.

Uncertain prior to the outbreak of war whether Italy would fight with the Entente or the Central Powers, the Italian command had to provide for a 600-kilometer front split into three distinct areas: the Trentino salient; the "wall" formed by the Dolomites and Julian alps; and the Isonzo River, which included the Karst region. Cadorna's desire for an all-out war of movement clashed with Antonio Salandra's policy of waging a "small war" to obtain Italy's "terra irredenta." Because he was not privy to the negotiations for Italy's entry into the war, it was not until a few weeks before the Treaty of London was publicly announced that Cadorna learned that his government had pledged to attack Austria-Hungary. The army had a nominal strength of 1,058,000 men in 35 infantry, 4 cavalry, and one *bersaglieri* division, and 4 groups of alpine troops, but on 24 May 44,000 troops remained in Libya. Although there were 400,000 troops in the Veneto area, no more than two of seventeen army corps were complete, and only 15,858 of its 45,099 officers were career men, who accounted for about 22,000 of Italy's 186,000 officers in 1918.

Unprepared for a European war, the army did not even issue steel helmets until 1916, and regiments did not have eighteen machine guns until 1917. The army slowly grew to forty-eight infantry and four cavalry divisions in twenty corps by late 1916, then to seventy divisions in late 1917, when some 2.9 million men were at the front. By then the army also had increased its stocks of artillery shells tenfold to 34 million and it had 3,828 small-calibre, 2,933 medium, and 157 heavy-caliber guns at the front, supported by 2,402 bombards. At the same time, air support available to the infantry grew from 244 aircraft in fourteen squadrons in September of 1915 to 553 aircraft in seventy squadrons by October of 1918. During the battle of Vittorio Veneto, Italian pilots flew everything from mass bombing missions to artillery spotting and photo reconnaissance, the latter needing only thirty-seven minutes to deliver a photo to the local command.

The Italian army reached its nadir in the battle of Caporetto (24 October–12 November 1917), when a combined German and Austro-Hungarian army, using "Hutier Tactics" thrust the Italians back from the Isonzo and advanced some 100 kilometers to the Piave. Italian losses were devastating: approximately 40,000 killed and wounded, 275,000 prisoners, 2,500 guns, and large amounts of supplies and munitions. Some estimates of casualties and prisoners have reached as high as 600,000 men. In any case, the Italian army was reduced to thirty-three divisions supported by 3,782 guns. Faced with these losses and Allied pressure, Cadorna resigned on 7 November 1917 and was replaced by General Armando Diaz.

Although the arrival of eleven British and French divisions under Sir Herbert Plumer helped stabilize the Italian front after Caporetto, much credit should be given to the Italians for their recovery in 1918. By June of 1918 the army had increased from thirty-three to fifty divisions and from 3,782 guns to over 7,000. When the Italians launched the battle of Vittorio-Veneto in October of 1918, they fired some three million shells in just nine days (the equivalent of their entire stock in May of 1918) and advanced seventy kilometers. This was a remarkable achievement for an army that had seemed close to total collapse just one year earlier.

Despite its success in 1918, the Italian army's debacle at Caporetto has left a lasting picture of an army with little *esprit de corps* and a low fighting efficiency. Indeed, by 1917 even the Italian High Command believed that the Italian soldier had little faith in his officers and even less in his country. During the war 128,527 deserted, and military tribunals handed down 1,006 death sentences, of which 729 were carried out (some sources estimate that as many as 834 soldiers were executed). Despite these figures, it is important to note that more French soldiers were executed in 1917 than Italian (528 versus 359). In addition, in 1916 the army had established elite *arditi* formations, which fought well throughout the war and went on to form the core of Benito Mussolini's Fascist party in 1919.

In the aftermath of Caporetto, the army launched a massive propaganda campaign. One of the themes struck by the propaganda office of the Eighth Army was that the war was "to free our people from their dreary role of the eternal day laborer" and to make "every Italian" equal to "every other European." The effectiveness of such propaganda is unclear, but it certainly raised expectations and fueled resentment after the war. Emilio Lussu's memoirs suggest that a large number of troops despised the general command and considered turning their rifles on the "real enemy," their own government. Luigi Gasparotto depicted southern peasants as rude stoics, for whom conditions at the front were not much worse than those in the sulfur mines or on the latifundia of Sicily. Frontline troops had their own rough classification of patriots, in which they were idiots (*fessi*) because they were in the trenches dying for Italy. Those who had it made (*fissi*) were in the rear areas with divisional, corps, and army commands. The Italians (*Italiani*) were farther yet to the rear, and the "100 percent Italians" (*italianissimi*) were in Italy proper. Poor peasant conscripts, who were used to seeing the gentlemen (*signorotti*) enjoying the good life while they languished in poverty, deeply resented the spectacle of workers earning ten lire a day and living in relative comfort and safety while they suffered and died at the front for half a lire a day. Still, if both officers and common soldiers were often bitter, cynical, and occasionally overwhelmed by nostalgia for their home and family, many saw the war as just and even noble. Their letters, many of which Adolfo Omodeo later published, were idealistic as well as resigned.

The Italian army was deployed on a number of fronts. About 100,000 men were stationed in Albania by 1918, where they held the port of Valona and established an Italian presence. Two divisions of infantry and 80,000 laborers were sent to France, where they found their German POWs more congenial company than their allies, and 50,000 fought in Macedonia. In theory, the Italian infantryman spent five days in the trenches, five in front-line reserves, ten in rear-area reserves, and twenty in rest areas. In reality, shortages of troops, constant offensives, and a high command that had little regard for the rank-and-file prevented such a rotation.

The Italians took their share of casualties, suffering an average of 1,220 dead and wounded daily in 1915, 1,670 in 1916, 2,155 in 1917, and 614 in 1918. Total casualties amounted to 1,275,800, of which the infantry accounted for 1,210,000. Of these, 231,860 were suffered in 1915, 357,400 in 1916, 461,240 in 1917, and 119,720 in 1918. Even so, the number of forces operating at the front climbed from 984,000 in 1915 to 1,539,000 in 1916, to 2,197,000 in 1917, and to 2,194,000 in 1918. The infantry suffered incredible losses, as 314,000, or 1 in 10, died and 896,000, or 3 in 10, were wounded. The next highest losses were suffered by engineers, artillery men, and cavalry, who lost about 1 in 100 (3,900, 9,200, and 1,000, respectively) and who suffered 3 in 100 wounded (14,600, 28,000, and 3,400, respectively). Service personnel had low rates of only 1 in 1,000 killed (1,600) and 3 in 1,000 wounded (4,100).

If not generally considered one of the best armies in the war, the Italian army slowly pushed back Austro-Hungarian forces during the first eleven battles of the Isonzo, held Conrad's Trentino Offensive in 1916, survived the Austro-German attack at Caporetto in late 1917, turned back an Austro-Hungarian offensive in June of 1918, and annihilated the Austro-Hungarian army in October of that year. The Austrians signed an armistice at Villa Giusti on 4 November. If, as many Italians complained, the army had been ready to "undergo" a war only in 1915, by 1918 it had clearly learned how to "wage" one.

James J. Sadkovich

References

Caracciolo, Mario. *L'Italia nella guerra mondiale*. Rome: Edizioni Roma, 1935.
Ceva, Lucio. *Storia delle forze armate italiane*. Turin: Intergest, 1981.
Edmonds, James E., and H.R. Davies. *Military Operations in Italy, 1915–1919*. London: His Majesty's Stationery Office, 1949.
Faldella, Emilio. *La grande guerra*. 2 vols. Milan: Longanesi, 1965.
Italy, Ministero della Guerra, Commando del Corpo di Stato Maggiore, Ufficio Storico. *L'Esercito italiano nella grande guerra (1915–1918). I. Le forze belligeranti*. Rome, 1927.
Melograni, Piero. *Storia politica della grande guerra*. Bari: Laterza, 1971.
Monticone, Alberto, and Enzo Forcella. *Plotone di esecuzione. I processi della Prima guerra mondiale*. Bari: Laterza, 1968.
Pieri, Piero. *L'Italia nella prima guerra mondiale (1915–1918)*. Turin: Einaudi, 1968.
Rochat, Giorgio. *L'esercito italiano da Vittorio Veneto a Mussolini*. Bari: Laterza, 1967.
———. *L'Italia nella prima guerra mondiale. Problemi di interpretazione e prospettive di ricerca*. Milan: Feltrinelli, 1976.
Valori, Aldo. *La guerra italo-austriaca, 1915–1918*. Bologna: Nicola Zanichelli, 1920.
Villari, Luigi. *The Macedonian Campaign*. London: T. Fisher Unwin, 1922.

See also CADORNA, LUIGI; CAPORETTO; DIAZ, ARMANDO; SALANDRA, ANTONIO; VITTORIO VENETO CAMPAIGN

Italy, Home Front

The First World War shattered the liberal Italian state, undermined the Italian Socialist party, and gave birth to new political forces, from Gabriele D'Annunzio's legionnaires to Benito Mussolini's Fascists. In 1914 the Italian socialists obtained 22.9 percent of the votes (1,146,948) in the national elections, and their newspaper, *Avanti!*, boasted a circulation of 60,000. The question of intervention in 1915, however, split the Italian Left. The socialists became identified as defeatist because of their policy of neither supporting nor undermining the war in 1915 (*né aderire né sabotare*), their resistance to the war in 1916 and 1917, and their ambiguous policy in 1919 when they would neither attempt a revolution nor support the reconstruction of a liberal social and political order.

Many on the Left, including revolutionary syndicalists like Alceste De Ambris and Filippo Corridoni, revolutionary socialists like Benito Mussolini, and radicals like Gaetano Salvemini, supported the war effort. They were joined by the ultra-nationalists led by Enrico Corradini and the ANI (Associazione Nazionalista Italiana) in urging that Italy enter the war on the Entente's side. For some, intervention was a moral imperative; for others it was a shrewd diplomatic ploy. And for a few students, like Paolo Caccia Dominioni, it was an opportunity to continue his family's *Risorgimento* tradition by liberating Trentino and Trieste—a romantic way to avoid examinations. During the "radiant May days," the decadent poet Gabriele D'Annunzio whipped up popular enthusiasm for the war, while the old master of *trasformismo*, Giovanni Giolitti, saw his efforts to keep Italy out of the war by settling for "something" *(parecchio)* crumble.

The debate between advocates of neutrality and proponents of intervention was often settled in the streets rather than in the parliament, and Italy's entry into the war on 24 May 1915 left the country deeply divided. As the Italian war effort reached its nadir in late 1917, following the collapse of the Second Army at Caporetto and the long retreat to the Piave River, 150 deputies and 90 senators formed the *Fascio parlamentare di difesa nazionale* to press for a united war effort. But while the Italians pulled together to win the war, deep rifts among classes and political factions surfaced as soon as the firing stopped. Symbolic of these divisions were the middle-class landowners, whose return to the Veneto to reclaim their property meant the eviction of those peasants to whom the Austrians had given the abandoned farms.

The hostility that developed between town and countryside was particularly acute. It was reflected in the stereotypes of the peasant-infantryman *(fante-contadino)* and the worker-shirker *(operaio-imboscato)*. There were also hard feelings among the officers. Those officers with degrees in the humanities, the infantryman-lawyer *(fante-avvocato)*, who tended to come from the south, were usually assigned to front-line units where the ratio of officers to soldiers was 1 to 26. Those officers with technical degrees, the engineer-shirker *(ingegniere-imboscato)*, who were predominantly northerners, were usually posted to the artillery and technical services inside the country. There, the ratio of officers to soldiers was 1 to 7. And

while 441,000 industrial workers were excused from military service, only 163,000 agricultural laborers were exempted.

The war took a heavy economic toll on peasant families. Because only one in ten rural Italian families owned land, most depended on the wages earned by both male and female members of the household. The loss to the war effort of about half the males in rural areas effort depleted the countryside of laborers—especially in the south, where three-quarters of the rural workforce was male. Women and children had to shoulder much of the burden on the farms. During the war the standard of living declined in the countryside, because the government took not only men but also livestock, fodder, and timber, paying only half the market value for requisitioned goods. Higher prices for manufactured products and price controls on agricultural products led to decreased consumption in the countryside, while in urban areas higher wages spurred consumption, especially in the tertiary sector for such things as entertainment. Since the predominantly peasant infantry had taken the highest casualties of any branch of the army, after the war relatively fewer men returned to the countryside than to the city. Rural areas had relatively more consumers and fewer producers in 1919 than in 1914.

In industry Italy was no more ready for war than it was politically, and while decrees mobilizing industry were quickly issued, not until 1917 was Italian industry able to supply its armed forces with adequate quantities of machine guns, artillery, aircraft, and ammunition. The government paid generous prices for war matériel—and raised the wages of industrial workers—while it contained the price of agriculture products. This policy of "spending freely," and the tendency of 167,000 officers assigned to oversee war plants to act as advocates for their firms, stimulated Italy's war industries by keeping prices high. By 1918 Italy had added 1,288,342 new industrial workers, including 200,000 in metallurgy and 50,000 in aviation. About 196,000 members of the industrial work force (22 percent) were women, a shift that had dramatic ramifications for Italian social and economic life.

Large concerns, especially those in the metallurgical, chemical, and electrical fields, were the main beneficiaries of government spending, while small firms were hard pressed to survive the war. By 1917–18, 40 percent of war expenditures were on arms and 49 percent on necessities for the soldiers. Among the firms that expanded during the war was Ilva, a steel consortium backed by the Banca Commerciale, which increased its capital holdings to 500 million lire and its workforce to 50,000.

Ansaldo, another metallurgical giant, saw its capital worth expand from 30 million lire in 1915 to 500 million in 1918; its workforce grew from 6,000 to 111,000 employees. During the war it manufactured 10,900 guns, 3,800 aircraft, 95 ships, and 10 million artillery shells. But it was broken up after the war, shrinking to a tenth of its size. Breda suffered a similar fate, but Fiat maintained its wartime gains, which saw the automaker increase its capital worth from 25 to 125 million; its workforce from 4,000 to 40,000: It manufactured everything from trucks to aircraft. The rapid growth of Italy's war industries and the enormous resources committed to the war led to shortages in civilian consumer goods that became severe by 1917, triggering social unrest throughout the country.

In June of 1915 General Dallolio took over the newly created Undersecretary (later Ministry) of Arms and Munitions, which was to control government spending, settle wage disputes, allocate resources, and oversee working conditions. Industries defined as "auxiliary" were favored, and their number consequently grew from 221 in 1915 to 1,976 by the end of the war. By 1918 almost two-thirds of all Italian industrial workers were employed in war production; their wages, which had been slightly above agricultural wages in 1914, were double those in rural areas by the end of the war. Daily earnings for factory workers rose from 3.9 lire in 1913 to 10.0 lire in 1917 to 20 lire or more by 1919, while peasant wages languished at 4 to 5 lire and infantrymen earned a mere half lira a day.

The cost of living doubled from 1914 to 1916, then doubled again by 1919, as notes in circulation went from 2.26 billion lire in 1914 to 19.2 billion in 1921. While public spending increased fivefold, private consumption grew by only 6 percent. The real wages of some workers, therefore, kept pace with inflation, but the wages of rural workers plummeted, as did the salaries of white-collar workers and middle-class professionals. As a result, the war was seen as benefiting only industrialists, factory workers, and those soldiers lucky enough to be assigned to rear areas. Of 571,000 employees in war industries, 404,000, or 70 percent, were in

the Milan-Turin-Genoa industrial triangle in northern Italy.

Smallholders in the north, rural laborers in the south, some landowners, and the semirural middle class were all hard hit by higher taxes, inflation, and rent control. All classes suffered as the Spanish flu claimed 600,000 victims in 1919. The middle class saw its savings disappear, and those in urban areas who did not benefit by the expansion of war industries saw both workers and the rural classes as profiteers. Even those who did benefit very often did so at the cost of putting the whole family to work: Not only were 200,000 of the 900,000 new industrial workers women, 60,000 were children.

While the war benefited some large industries, it hurt small concerns and disrupted prewar social and economic relationships. By cutting off emigration, it closed a safety valve that had allowed the poor and unemployed to find remunerative work abroad. It also ended reimbursements to relatives by emigrants, funds that had fed Italy's hard-currency accounts and stimulated its economy. Unable to emigrate in 1919, peasants "occupied" large estates and workers took over industrial plants.

The war had deprived the poor of escape from economic misery and social inequality; it had also taught millions of lower-class infantrymen the habits of mass action and the efficacy of violence. It was therefore not just the *arditi,* members of elite units whose black shirts became the symbol for the Fascist *squadristi,* who were aggressive after the war. Veterans in Catholic unions "occupied" large estates in the Cremona district, and socialists and syndicalists occupied the latifundia in the south and the factories in the north. The interventionist debate of 1914–15 had polarized and militarized politics, as groups took to the streets and piazzas of Italy to argue their case. These tactics were resurrected in 1919 by new political formations composed largely of veterans who had little patience with parliamentary procedures and polite debate. The number of workers in unions jumped precipitately, as the socialist Cgl *(Confederazione generale del lavoro)* reached 1,150,062, doubling its size, and the Cil *(Catholic confederazione italiana dei lavoratori)* enrolled 500,000 members in 1919, five times its prewar membership.

If the war had created a new consciousness of being Italian, it also made many Italians bitter toward allies who seemed to have robbed them of their gains at the peace table.

It alienated others from the liberal state that failed to live up to promises of a more equitable postwar social order based on land and economic reform. The defeat at Caporetto and the victory at Vittorio Veneto a year later took the Italian national psyche on an emotional roller-coaster ride and created some real physical hardships. From October of 1917 to the end of the war, Austria occupied 12,500 square kilometers of Italian territory with a population of 1.2 million. Some 250,000 refugees had fled before the advancing Austrian forces in 1917 and had to be accommodated at the same time that the Italians were reconstructing their armies, trying to assess blame for the disaster, and reestablishing their national resolve. The drain of manpower from the rural areas resulted in the reversion of 500,000 hectares of land to pasturage and fallow—ideal breeding ground for the mosquitoes that caused 120,000 cases of malaria during the war. The conflict left 280,096 children orphaned, most (179,326) in rural areas. When the veterans returned home to "settle accounts" *(fare i conti)*, they found unemployment in the cities, and homesteads devastated by neglect and requisitioning in the countryside. Some also encountered hostility from those who had opposed the war, and many veterans believed that the Left had betrayed the country and was now, with the liberal government, betraying them.

Although there was a good deal of exaggeration to such feelings, there had been opposition to the war, particularly in early 1917 as hopes for victory receded, rationing increased, and the standard of living declined. From early December 1916 to the middle of April 1917 the police reported five hundred demonstrations against the war, most by women from small towns and rural areas. In May of 1917 women from the countryside around Milan roamed the city, stoning war plants and demanding that the government return their husbands; in Turin women demanded higher rations and an end to the war. That Pope Benedict XV issued an appeal for peace and condemned the "useless slaughter" in August, just after an Italian victory on the Bainsizza Plateau and just before the disaster at Caporetto, seemed to show that the Vatican favored Vienna. Many, therefore, later blamed the Papacy and the Left for the protests against the war, for sowing the seeds of defeatism and, by extension, for the defeat at Caporetto. The Italians emerged from the conflict as deeply divided politically and socially as they had been in 1914, but with four years of scores to settle.

James J. Sadkovich

References

De Felice, Renzo, et al. *Il trauma dell'intervento, 1914–1919*. Florence: Vallecchi, 1968.

Dominioni, Paolo Caccia. *1915–1919*. Milan: Longanesi, 1965.

Einaudi, Luigi. *La condotta economica e gli effetti sociali della guerra italiana*. Bari: Laterza, 1933.

Melograni, Piero. *Storia politica della grande guerra*. Bari: Laterza, 1971.

Monticone, Alberto. *Gli italiani in uniforme, 1915–1918*. Bari: Laterza, 1972.

Omodeo, Adolfo. *Momenti della vita di guerra, dai diari e dalle lettere dei caduti (1915–1918)*. Turin: Einaudi, 1935. Reprint, 1968.

Serpieri, Arrigo. *La guerra e le classi rurali italiane*. Bari: Laterza, 1930.

Speranza, Gino. *The Diary of Gino Speranza: Italy, 1915–1919*. New York: Columbia University Press, 1941.

Thayer, John A. *Italy and the Great War*. Madison: University of Wisconsin Press, 1964.

Trevelyan, G.M. *Scenes from Italy's War*. Boston: Houghton Mifflin, 1919.

See also BENEDICT XV; CAPORETTO, D'ANNUNZIO, GABRIELE; GIOLITTI, GIOVANNI; MUSSOLINI, BENITO; PARIS PEACE CONFERENCE, 1919; VITTORIO VENETO CAMPAIGN

Italy, Navy

The Italian navy played a relatively minor, but important, role in World War I by bottling up the Austro-Hungarian fleet in the Adriatic Sea. Throughout the conflict, Austrian warships enjoyed secure anchorages at Boka Kotorska, Šibenik, Zara, and Pula, while the Italians had no good ports between Venice and Taranto. They therefore improved Taranto, expanded their naval base at Venice to accommodate the whole fleet, developed the port of Valona in Albania, and built up Brindisi in southern Italy. Of 4.8 billion lire spent by the navy during the war, 90 million went to port improvements, including 21.6 million on Venice, 13.0 on Brindisi, and 14.7 on Taranto.

The war opened for Italy with a series of raids by light Austrian vessels on Italian ports in July and early August of 1915, leading Italy to employ armored trains to defend their vulnerable coast. Some 2,600 tons of shipping were also converted to floating batteries, which mounted 381mm guns able to support land operations on the Isonzo front from the Gulf of Trieste. The navy increased the number of its radio telegraphic stations from 35 to 107, and set up 22 radio locators, 150 new telegraph offices, 1,250 new telephone installations, and 10 radiotelephones. During the war it consumed about 700,000 tons of coal and fuel oil annually, using an average of 90 ships totaling 300,000 tons and 250 tugs and tankers to service the fleet.

In 1915 Italy had two dreadnoughts, the *Duilio* and *Doria,* ready to enter service, but four super-dreadnoughts, which had just been laid down, were canceled in favor of building light vessels and submarines because Italian shipyards suffered a lack of everything from raw materials and weaponry to skilled labor.

Although the navy grew from 2,000 to 6,000 officers, and from 40,000 to 139,000 enlisted men from July of 1915 to November of 1918, it suffered from a shortage of manpower because it had to man 948 guns and 523 radio-telegraph stations on merchant ships, as well as provide crews for 214 small vessels engaged in antisubmarine activity. Some 13,800 naval personnel were even pressed into service on land during and after the battle of Caporetto.

During hostilities the navy laid 15,760 mines in the Adriatic, as well as twenty-three kilometers of antitorpedo and thirty-nine kilometers of antisubmarine netting. The most ambitious project was undertaken when, in less than five months beginning in April of 1918, five Italian and two French ships laid sixty-six kilometers of antisubmarine netting and 1,200 mines. Supported by 429 buoys and 180 kilometers of steel cable, each of the 720 nets deployed was 91.5 by 50 meters. The barrier claimed its first victim, the German submarine *UB.53,* on 3 August 1918, but its effect on the outcome of the war was practically nil.

Italian naval aviation antedated the war, with men such as Alessandro Guidoni pioneering the use of torpedoes as early as 1913, but a concerted effort to provide aircraft and airships did not get under way until the war had begun. As a result, the navy had only two dirigibles and fourteen aircraft in August of 1914 and twenty-five aircraft in May of 1915. By the end of the war, however, it deployed 675 aircraft and 17 dirigibles at forty bases. Naval aviation grew from 30 pilots in 1915 to over 500 by 1918, supported by 5,000 personnel, as the number of missions rose from 314 in 1915 to 17,284 during 1918.

During the war naval aircraft conducted 2,362 bombing raids against Austrian ports, including 1,382 in 1918, when Austria-Hungary attacked Italian ports only 145 times. The navy claimed to have shot down 130 enemy aircraft, and it produced one ace, Lieutenant Orazio Pierozzi. It lost only thirty-eight aircraft and two dirigibles, although 119 Italian naval airmen were killed. The navy used fifteen Curtiss aircraft to train fifty student pilots at Taranto's flight school in 1915, and the first naval fighter, the Macchi L.2, was a copy of the Austrian Lohner, two of which had been captured in May of 1915 during a raid on Venice. Naval aviation could do little in 1915, but by the spring of 1916 seaplanes were attacking rear areas, and by late 1916 naval aviation had its own inspectorate, having previously shared one with the submarine arm. In August Italian naval aircraft staged a daylight raid on Trieste, and in 1917 seaplanes spotted for floating artillery off the Isonzo front and attacked enemy shipping. In 1918 naval aircraft raided coastal targets from Istria to Albania, and seaplanes flew 549 missions on the Piave in 1918, as naval aircraft began to support operations inland.

The Italian navy concentrated its ASW in the Adriatic, where Austria lost ten submarines to Italian ships and mines and four to the British and French. ASW activity was intense, especially after the creation of the Inspectorate for the Defense of Maritime Traffic under Rear Admiral G. Mortola in February of 1917; the navy began to use aircraft to hunt subs in 1917. It lost two destroyers, three torpedo boats, and thirteen escorts protecting merchantmen, but the merchant marine lost 800 men, 242 steamers (769,450 tons) and 395 sailing vessels (102,891 tons). In all, 46 percent of Italian shipping extant in June of 1915 was lost, mostly to submarines, which accounted for 410,000 of the 769,450 tons sunk.

From December of 1915 to April of 1916 the Italian navy took part in the evacuation of the Serbian army from Albania and its relocation to Corfu. During that period the Italian, French, and British navies supplied 28,299 tons of matériel to Serbian forces and transported 260,895 men, 10,153 draft animals, and 68 guns. Italy supplied the majority of naval and merchant ships used, including 45 (93,000 tons) of the 81 (130,000 tons) merchantmen. The navy then transported and supplied Italian forces in Albania and Macedonia, which had grown to 146,000 men by late 1918.

In 1914 the navy had nine hospitals on land with 1,916 beds; by 1918 it was administering 7,000 hospitals with 44,000 patients, as hotels and other buildings were converted to wartime use. Four hospital ships with 2,300 beds cared for a total of 126,727 wounded during the conflict. Four "armed" hospital ships transported 12,500 British troops, and four others cared for 2,500 men. Naval medical personnel fought diseases ranging from malaria to cholera in Albania.

One of the boats most associated with the Italian navy during the war was the MAS (*Motoscafi Siluranti* or *Motoscafi Antisommergibili*), of which about three hundred were built. The prototype for MTBs (motor torpedo boats), these small craft displaced sixty tons and generally carried a variety of weapons, including machine guns, a 20mm gun, torpedoes, depth charges, and mines. Some also carried radiotelephones and hydrophones. They were used for coastal defense and raids, including one of the more famous of the war by the poet Gabriele D'Annunzio, who penetrated the naval base at Buccari with Costanzo Ciano in February 1918. Prior to that, Italian MAS had forced Durazzo five times and Pula twice, and in June of 1918 two MAS boats sank the warship *Szent Istvan*.

From 1915 to 1918 the Italian navy sank fourteen warships displacing 51,496 tons and twenty-three merchantmen totaling 41,583 tons. The Italian fleet spotted and chased the Austrian fleet five times but managed only to damage the cruiser *Helgoland* on 29 December 1915. Although some of the Italian fleet was deployed outside the Adriatic, its major opponent was Austria-Hungary. Italy could deploy twenty-one battleships to Austria's eighteen; fifteen scouts and cruisers to six; fifty-two destroyers to thirty; 102 torpedo boats to 89; and seventy-five submarines to Austria-Hungary's twenty-seven. The Italian navy thus enjoyed an overall numerical advantage of eighty-five ships. By 1916 the Italians had twenty-one battleships in the Adriatic area compared with only four Austrian; thirty-nine

scouts and destroyers to Austria-Hungary's thirteen; sixty-four torpedo boats to none; and twenty-four submarines to twenty-one: a total of 211 Italian naval vessels to Austria's 38. This advantage increased, and by the end of the war the Italians had deployed 377 naval vessels in the Adriatic.

During the war the Italian navy carried out approximately 86,000 missions, and its ships logged an average of 25,000 km at sea daily. But the Italian fleet was never able to close with the Austrians, and the naval war resolved itself into raids, skirmishes, and patrols. Italian submarines had few targets, since Austrian traffic was light and well-protected by the rugged Dalmatian coastline. As MAS forced more harbors the Austrians adopted defensive measures, just as the Italians had done earlier to thwart raids by small naval forces and aircraft on their ports. It was thus appropriate that the Italian actions most remembered were the forcing of harbors by MAS boats, the sinking of the *Szent Istvan* by MAS 15 and 21 in June of 1918, and the sinking of the *Viribus Unitis* in Pola by a special assault team at dawn on 1 November 1918. Rather than a naval war on the Mahanian model, the Italo-Austrian war was a guerrilla war, in which light vessels, submarines, and aircraft were crucial. The lessons to be learned were far from clear-cut.

James J. Sadkovich

References

Chiggiato, Artù. "Il Cantiere S.V.A.N. di Venezia: Ricordi di un cantiere scomparso." *Rivista marittima* (1979).

Fioravanzo, Giuseppe. "L'attività area della Marina durante la guerra, 1915–1918." *Rivista marittima* (1965).

Halpern, Paul. *The Mediterranean Naval Situation, 1908–1914.* Cambridge: Harvard University Press, 1972.

Hurd, Archibald. *Italian Sea-Power and the Great War.* London: Constable, 1918.

Italy, Ministero della Marina. *The Italian Navy in the World War, 1915–1918.* Rome: Stabilimento Poligrafico per l'Ammiragliato dello Stato, 1927.

Manfroni, Camillo. *Storia della marina italiana durante la guerra mondiale, 1914–1918.* Bologna: Zanichelli, 1925.

See also MEDITERRANEAN NAVAL OPERATIONS

Ivanov, General Nikolai Yudovich (1851–1919)

Russian general, born 3 August 1851. In 1869, Ivanov graduated from Mikhailovsky Artillery College. Many believed he came from a peasant background, which contributed to his common touch and popularity with the rank and file of the army. He fought in the 1877–78 war with Turkey, and by the end of the Russo-Japanese War he had advanced to corps command. In 1906, as governor general of Kronstadt, he put down a military mutiny on a base near St. Petersburg and earned the gratitude of Czar Nicholas II. Promoted general of artillery in 1908, Ivanov commanded the Kiev Miliary District prior to the war.

When World War I began Ivanov took command of the southwestern front, consisting of four armies facing Austria-Hungary. Although he was admired by his staff and troops, Ivanov proved to be a poor field commander. He could best be described as an anachronism, belonging to an older military tradition; he seemed unable to comprehend the events around him. On the battlefield Ivanov suffered from an inability to react to changing conditions, often with disastrous results.

Although many expected much from Ivanov, during the Galician Campaign (August to September of 1914) he demonstrated a McClellan-like inability to understand and react to quickly moving battlefield conditions. In August, after the Austrian First Army defeated the Russians at Krasnik, Ivanov panicked and ordered a retreat to Brest-Litovsk. He then directed General Pavel Pleve's Fifth Army to make an unsupported advance into the Austrian right flank. Pleve saved his force from being cut off and destroyed only after usurping Ivanov's orders and retreating from his advanced and exposed position. In September, even though his forces vastly outnumbered the Austrians, Ivanov advanced at a snail's pace, stopping and resting his troops several times even after the Austrian retreat had become a rout. Ivanov let a great opportunity escape.

In March of 1915 the Russian High Command (*Stavka*) ordered Ivanov to assault though the Carpathians and threaten the Hungarian plain in order to support the Allied invasion of the Dardanelles. This time the Austrians requested German assistance. In early May, the Germans smashed Ivanov's line at Gorlice and moved into the Russian rear. The Russians attempted to make a stand on the Sand River before retreating. In August, after four months of continuous retreat, the Russians finally solidified their lines near Luck while the Germans captured Poland.

In November of 1915 Stavka ordered Ivanov to advance in eastern Galicia in hopes of reinvigorating the defeated Serbs. Ivanov failed to properly support his advancing infantry with artillery, thus ensuring his replacement. In March of 1916 Ivanov was appointed to the Council of Empire as a military advisor to the czar. Although such an appointment usually meant forced retirement, Ivanov's close relationship with the czar kept him involved in events.

Ivanov remained loyal to the czar during the March Revolution. On 12 March 1917 he was given command of eight hundred veterans with orders to march on Petrograd and put down the rebellion. The procession became a farce as the nation fell apart and as promised reinforcements failed to arrive. As troops arrived from the front, they quickly deserted and joined the revolution. Ivanov's mission failed.

In October of 1918 Ivanov took command of the White Southern Army on the Don. This force soon diminished, and Ivanov's military career came to an end. On 27 January 1919 Ivanov died in south Russia from typhus.

Thomas D. Mays

References

Herwig, Holger H., and Neil M. Heyman. *Biographical Dictionary of World War I.* Westport, Conn.: Greenwood, 1982.

Knox, Alfred. *With the Russian Army 1914–1917.* New York: Arno Press & *The New York Times,* 1971.

Stone, Norman. *The Eastern Front 1914–1917.* New York: Charles Scribner's Sons, 1975.

See also Brusilov, Aleksei Alekseevich; East Galicia, 1914 Campaign

Izzet Pasha, Ahmed (1864–1937)

Turkish general and politician, born in Albania in 1864. Izzet's military experience included study in Germany and active service in Greece and Yemen. Despite his best efforts, he was unable to avoid the turbulent Ottoman political scene. As a result, Izzet's career was one of ups and downs. During the first two years of the war, he was in semiretirement.

In April of 1916 Izzet took command of the Second Army in Anatolia. As part of Enver Pasha's overly ambitious plan to recapture Erzurum, Izzet attacked late and failed to concentrate his forces. Despite local successes, Izzet's forces were driven back by the Russians under General Nikolai Yudenich. Within five months, Izzet was back to his starting position and done as a combat leader.

Izzet continued to serve the empire in a variety of diplomatic and administrative roles that culminated with his elevation to Grand Vizier in October of 1918. That ended on 11 November, and despite several ministerial positions in Sultan Mehmed VI's shadow government (1918–22), Izzet soon retired. He died in Istanbul on 1 April 1937.

John P. Dunn

References

Allen, W.E.D., and Paul Muratoff. *Caucasian Battlefields: A History of the Wars on the Turco-Caucasian Border, 1828–1921*. Cambridge University Press, 1953.

Izzat Pasha, Ahmad. *Denkürdigkeiten des Marschalls Izzet Pascha* Translated and edited by Karl Klinghardt. Leipzig: K.F. Koehler, 1927.

Pomiankowski, Joseph. *Der Zusammenbruch des Ottomanischen Reiches* Zurich: Amalthea-Verlag, 1928.

See also CAUCASUS FRONT; ENVER PASHA; MEHMED VI

I

J

Jackson, Sir Henry Bradwardine (1855–1929)

British admiral and first sea lord from May of 1915 to November of 1916. Born at Barnsley on 21 January 1855. Jackson joined the Royal Navy in 1868 and fought in the Zulu War. He was naval attaché in Paris in 1897. As a captain he met Marconi, and this association led to the introduction of radio (W/T) into the Royal Navy in 1900. As third sea lord and comptroller of the Navy (1905–8) Jackson supported development of the *Dreadnought* and battle cruiser *Invincible*. After subsequent service in the Mediterranean, Jackson headed the new Naval War College at Portsmouth and trained the first war staff officers. In 1913 he became chief of the war staff of the admiralty.

At the outbreak of the war Jackson was president of the Oversea Attack Committee and charged with coordinating attacks on Germany's colonial possessions. When Admiral John Fisher was forced to resign as first sea lord, Jackson replaced him. Jackson, however, lacked the drive and imagination of his predecessor. A bureaucrat by nature, Jackson found it difficult to delegate responsibility. His forte lay rather in scientific innovation. He ordered extensive mine-laying operations in the North Sea. During the Dardanelles campaign Jackson believed that a naval operation made sense only if it were supported by a land occupation of the Gallipoli Peninsula. He was one of those who opposed Winston Churchill's demands that Admiral John de Robeck force the Straits with the fleet alone.

The disappointment of the Battle of Jutland, increasing losses of merchant shipping, and German Channel raids, led to Jackson's replacement as first sea lord by Admiral John Jellicoe at the end of November of 1916. Jackson ended the war as president of the Royal Naval College at Greenwich and aide-de-camp to King George V. Promoted to admiral of the fleet in 1919, Jackson retired from the navy in 1924 and died at Salterns House, Hayling Island, on 14 December 1929.

Andrzej Suchcitz

References

Hough, Richard. *The Great War at Sea, 1914–1918*. New York: Oxford University Press, 1983.
Roskill, Stephen. *Admiral of the Fleet Earl Beatty*. London: Collins, 1980.

See also FISHER, JOHN; GALLIPOLI CAMPAIGN; JELLICOE, JOHN

Jagow, Gottlieb von (1863–1935)

Prussian statesman and diplomat. Born in Berlin into an old Brandenburg family on 22 June 1863, Jagow studied law before entering the diplomatic corps in 1895. He served in Luxembourg (1907–9) and Italy (1909–13), aided in the renewal of the Triple Alliance in 1912, and was state secretary of the Foreign Office between 1913 and 1916.

Jagow was convinced of the inevitability of war with Russia but did not believe that the summer of 1914 was the most opportune time for Germany. In the prewar years he encouraged Austrian ambitions, while seeking to strengthen Anglo-German ties by avoiding tensions over colonial and naval issues. He disagreed with Admiral Alfred von Tirpitz's naval ambitions and disapproved of the Schlieffen Plan because of its inherent violation of Belgian neutrality.

In 1914 Jagow was absent from Berlin during the critical days following the assassination of Franz Ferdinand; he returned only after Germany had offered the "blank check" to Austria. Even though he doubted Britain would remain neutral, Jagow supported Chancellor Theobald von Bethmann Hollweg and continued to cling to the hope that Russia would accept Austrian hegemony in the Balkans to avoid a general European war. When war appeared inevitable, he yielded to German military leaders.

After victory eluded Germany at the Battle of the Marne, Jagow foresaw his nation's ultimate defeat and urged a moderate peace, supporting Bethmann Hollweg's concept of a German-dominated, but not occupied, Mitteleuropa. Jagow's staunch opposition to the 1916 resumption of unrestricted submarine warfare, which he predicted would bring American intervention, prompted his dismissal and retirement from public life. He died at Potsdam on 11 January 1935.

Clayton D. Laurie

References
Zeman, Z.A.B. *A Diplomatic History of the First World War*. London: Weidenfield and Nicolson, 1971.

See also BETHMANN HOLLWEG, THEOBALD VON

Japan, Role in the War

Japan's declaration of war on Germany on 23 August 1914 was the product of almost complete unanimity within Emperor Taisho's government. There was some hesitancy within the ranks of high officers in the imperial army, who recalled with gratitude Germany's military mentorship of past decades. Japan's Diet, encouraged by Prime Minister Okuma Shigenobu, stood firmly behind joining the Allied Powers. Prior diplomatic agreements, such as the 1902 Anglo-Japanese Alliance, proved inconsequential in determining Japan's direction in 1914. The lure of Germany's Asian possessions and the opportunity to extend the Japanese Empire in the East during a European war served Japan's imperial ambitions perfectly.

Ultimately, the war, which proved so disastrous for much of the Western world, brought easy gains for Japan. In large part this was because Japanese military operations could be confined to the eastern Pacific, Siberia, and the Shandong Peninsula, all areas in which Japanese power could easily be projected. The European Allied nations were loath to request Japanese intervention on the continent in 1914, and when such requests were posed later, the Japanese government unashamedly demurred. Although Japanese naval vessels did serve as far away as the Mediterranean Sea, most of Japan's naval and military forces remained positioned to serve the empire's objectives exclusively.

From the war's earliest days Japan pursued clearly defined and self-serving objectives, often with Allied approval. Beginning in September of 1914, the imperial army moved against German-leased territory on the Shandong peninsula, capturing Qingdao in November. German prisoners received unusually good treatment. Naval operations against Germany's Pacific-island possessions commenced in October and brought rapid conquests of the Mariana, Caroline, and Marshall islands. In less than three months, Japanese arms had won control of all of Imperial Germany's Far-Eastern holdings.

With major military operations over by early 1915, Japan was free to pursue national interests through other means. Enjoying an enviable position in a war-torn world, Japanese industry now found significant profit in the sale of arms and materials to the Allies, and Japan's merchant fleet provided convenient and profitable logistical support. A diplomatic offensive was aimed at securing one of Japan's most ambitious imperial goals—a strengthened Japanese foothold on the Chinese mainland. With the Allies distracted, Japan seized the opportunity to demand extensive territorial, political, economic, and military concessions from a disorganized China. The Twenty-one Demands, presented to Yuan Shih-K'ai's ineffectual government in January of 1915, were imposed under threat of war in late May.

There were several consequences of Japan's imperial ambitions. Its egregious bullying provoked a broad wave of volatile Chinese nationalism, resulting in boycotts, strikes, demonstrations, and violent protests. Relations between the two Asian nations deteriorated rapidly in subsequent years. The Twenty-one Demands, together with Japan's evident unwillingness to contribute to Allied efforts to end the stalemated struggle in Europe, brought about a Western reevaluation of its Asian ally. By 1919, as the victors met in Paris, Japan was viewed with growing suspicion by her former allies.

Even before Japan's diplomats could make known their nation's desires at Paris, circumstances conspired to present the rising Pacific power with another chance to expand its influence on the Asian mainland. The Bolshevik Revolution of October of 1917 not only signaled the end of political stability in Russia, but also a probable weakening of the territorial integrity of the border regions of the former czarist empire. Only a month after the Bolshevik coup, the imperial army's general staff was considering how Japan might take advantage of the situation. Although both military and civilian officials opposed forceful intervention against Moscow, it was agreed that Japan might well move to improve her position in eastern Siberia and northern Manchuria. An additional inducement to act was the lure of large stocks of Allied war materials at Vladivostock.

Ironically, the opportunity for significant Japanese intervention was unwittingly provided by the United States. The Wilson administration, in hopes of facilitating the evacuation of the Czech Legion from Russia, suggested that both the United States and Japan dispatch troops to Vladivostock. Japan's general staff objected to a proposed troop ceiling of 7,000 men and restrictions on deployment. Eventually a compromise granted the Japanese army a limit of 12,000 troops and the authority to move inland if necessary.

As the Siberian expedition was launched in August of 1918, the army leaders proceeded with plans that went far beyond what the Western Allies had intended and what Japan's civilian cabinet had sanctioned. Determined to shape the political and economic future of the region, the generals deployed 70,000 troops, more than the combined strength of all other Allied forces in Russia. They dominated the Chinese Eastern Railway zone and the Amur valley, giving Japan *de facto* control of an immense area.

Permanent political and economic gains proved illusory, however. Anti-Bolshevik forces organized by the Japanese were ephemeral at best. Economic penetration, most manifest through the opening of *zaibatsu* branch offices on the Asian mainland, remained contingent upon the presence of military forces. The destiny of some 50,000 new Japanese settlers was likewise dependent on the army's protection. Following the withdrawal of the Western expeditionary forces by 1920, Japan faced growing pressure to follow suit. Doggedly remaining until 1922, the imperial army finally withdrew, abandoning the settlers to the vengeful Bolsheviks.

At the Paris Peace Conference, Japanese delegates strove for international recognition of their nation's wartime gains. Success came with little opposition. Japan was awarded Germany's prior rights in Shantung and also the Pacific-island possessions seized from Germany early in the war. The latter were to be administered as Class C mandates and remain unfortified. Japan's diplomats saw additional opportunities in the new League of Nations, hoping that it could secure international recognition of the principle of racial equality. The Japanese were sorely disappointed. The Western powers, most notably the United States, found the suggestion troublesome and rejected it as superfluous.

Altogether, belligerency served Japan well, greatly strengthening the nation's position on the Asian mainland and in the Pacific. Japan's international stature, it was felt, was enhanced at the cost of comparatively light casualties. Negative consequences, while initially obscured, were nonetheless soon evident. Ironically, the relatively undemanding nature of Japan's military campaigns had left the imperial army behind the West in strategic, tactical, and technological innovations. Having avoided the demands of war on the Western Front, the imperial army remained unaware of its lessons. Few Japanese, for that matter, had been intrigued by the European war. The postwar domestic climate fostered antimilitarism, driven by rumors of army atrocities in China and then Korea. As political dissent grew, draft evasion became respectable.

More ominously, Japan's wartime actions brought distrust in the West. The perception of a Japanese threat in the Pacific fueled a naval building-frenzy in the United States. Former allies more readily viewed Japan as shamelessly opportunistic, having expanded and profited from a murderous conflict in the West. Even as the West grew more suspicious of Japanese expansion, Japan's military leaders grew more confident that the path to regeneration and national greatness lay in further conquests.

Blaine T. Browne

References

Beasley, W. *Japanese Imperialism, 1894–1945.* Oxford: Oxford University Press, 1987.

Burdick, C. *The Japanese Siege of Tsingtao.* Hamden, Conn.: Archon, 1976.

Harries, Meirion and Susie. *Soldiers of the Sun: The Rise and Fall of the Imperial Japanese Army*. New York: Random House, 1991.

Morley, James W. *The Japanese Thrust into Siberia*. New York: Columbia University Press, 1957.

See also CHINA; PARIS PEACE CONFERENCE, 1919; QINGDAO, SIEGE OF; RUSSIA, ALLIED INTERVENTION IN

Jaurès, Auguste Marie Joseph Jean (1859–1914)

French trade unionist and Socialist party leader, born on 3 September 1859 in Castres, France. Jaurès taught philosophy at the University of Toulouse. Elected to the Chamber of Deputies in 1885, by 1905 Jaurès was one the leaders of the unified French Socialist party (S.F.I.O.). With his socialist views and belief in political reconciliation, Jaurès was a staunch opponent of militarism prior to World War I. He was, however, a moderate on the volatile issue of military conscription. On the one hand, he condemned military professionals who indoctrinated working-class conscripts to support the political and economic status quo. On the other hand, he did not believe that socialists should work to undermine the French military as an institution. Although Jaurès agreed that a national army was necessary, he also clamored for a new force patterned on the "inherently defensive" militia armies of 1792–95. With all eligible Frenchmen serving short periods in *L'Armée Nouvelle*, the French military would recapture the democratic spirit of 1792, promote social cohesion, and preserve class consciousness in an institution once dedicated to its eradication.

Ultimately, Jaurès's program to democratize the military proved unpopular, as did his call for a political reconciliation between Germany and France and his commitment to arbitration as the best method to resolve disputes. His beliefs inspired the French chauvinist Raoul Villain—who thought Jaurès's seeming pacifism a national liability—to assassinate him in Paris on 31 July 1914.

Peter R. Faber

References

Goldberg, Harvey. *The Life of Jean Jaurès*. Madison: University of Wisconsin Press, 1962.

Jaurès, Jean. *L'Armée Nouvelle*. Paris: Les Editions Rieder, 1932.

Weinstein, Harold R. *Jean Jaurès: A Study of Patriotism in the French Socialist Movement*. New York: Columbia University Press, 1936.

Jellicoe, John Rushworth, First Earl (1859–1935)

British admiral of the fleet and commander of the Grand Fleet, born 5 December 1859 in Southampton. Jellicoe entered the Royal Navy in 1872. He served abroad in Egypt and the Far East, where he was seriously wounded during the Boxer Rebellion of 1900 in China.

During Sir John Fisher's first term as first sea lord, Jellicoe served in the key position of director of naval ordnance. Even then Fisher was preparing him to be "admiralissimo when Armageddon comes." When war began in August of 1914, Jellicoe immediately became commander of the Grand Fleet.

Fleet mobilization and organization for war operations went smoothly. During the first two years there were several minor confrontations both in the North Sea and abroad: that is, at Heligoland Bight and at the Falkland Islands, where a German squadron was annihilated. Meanwhile, Jellicoe made it clear to all that he would act in the most careful, considered fashion when and if the German and British battle fleets met. He was later faulted, by Winston Churchill and David Beatty among others, for being overcautious and lacking aggressive initiative.

"Armageddon" finally occurred between 31 May and 1 June 1916 off the western coast of Denmark, in the Battle of Jutland. Jellicoe and the entire Grand Fleet were out, with Beatty and the advanced battle cruiser force to the south, and Jellicoe with the entire battle fleet ready to the north. Contact was made in mid-afternoon and the battle continued in phases through the night and into the early morning. The results were indecisive, and the British were bitterly disappointed.

Several problems during the two-day conflict plagued Jellicoe: communications, military intelligence, navigation, and the lack of training in the fleet, especially in night fighting. Collectively, these meant a significantly diminished capacity to respond effectively to the unparalleled opportunity. On two occasions Jellicoe turned the entire battle fleet away from the Germans on reports of torpedo attacks. Despite all of the serious limitations and the confusion of battle, it was Jellicoe alone who was credited with a brilliant deployment of the fleet at precisely the correct time, in the proper direction, and with the appropriate formation during the time of the major fleet confrontation. Twice the Grand Fleet "crossed the T" of the High Seas Fleet, the ultimate battle situation when a fleet is fighting in line ahead formation. It was at that time that extensive damage was inflicted upon the German fleet.

In December of 1916, several months after Jutland, Jellicoe was made first sea lord, but within a year he was abruptly dismissed by Prime Minister David Lloyd George. Jellicoe became a victim of the crisis of the German U-boat campaign. Lloyd George apparently believed that Jellicoe was incapable of resolving the threat.

After the war, Jellicoe was recalled to service, this time in the capacity of diplomat and imperial elder statesman. During 1919–20 he led a Commonwealth Tour, going to all of the prominent empire capitals and conducting investigations on Commonwealth defense matters and strategic considerations. He concluded an impressive career with imperial service. During the early 1920s he served with distinction as governor general of New Zealand. Jellicoe wrote two books summarizing his experiences as fleet commander and first sea lord. He was anxious to justify his actions at Jutland and to review and highlight the seriousness of the U-boat threat during the war. Jellicoe died on 20 November 1935 in Kensington. He was buried in St. Paul's Cathedral near Lord Nelson.

Eugene L. Rasor

References

Bacon, Sir Reginald. *Life of John Rushworth, Earl Jellicoe.* London: Cassell, 1936.

Jellicoe, John Rushworth. *The Crisis of the Naval War.* London: Cassell, 1920.

———. *The Grand Fleet, 1914–1916: Its Creation, Development, and Work.* New York: Doran, 1919.

Marder, Arthur J. *From Dreadnought to Scapa Flow: The Royal Navy in the Fisher Era, 1904–1919.* 5 vols. New York: Oxford University Press, 1961–70, 1978.

Patterson, A. Temple. *Jellicoe: A Biography.* London: Macmillan, 1969.

See also FISHER, JOHN; GREAT BRITAIN, NAVY; HELIGOLAND BIGHT, BATTLE OF; JUTLAND, BATTLE OF

Jewish Legion

The Jewish Legion, which fought for the Allies in the First World War, was a factional potpourri of Zionist Jewish volunteers. Participants sought a prominent role in the liberation of Palestine from the Turks in order to gain approval for a Jewish homeland in any postwar division of the liberated territory.

In 1914 Russian émigré Zionist leaders Vladimir Jabotinsky and Joseph Trumpeldor raised volunteers from Palestinian Zionists who had fled to Alexandria, Egypt, in the wake of the Turkish expulsion. Judging a Palestinian campaign premature, British military authorities redirected the five-hundred-man Jewish group to be utilized as a mule transport unit in Gallipoli. Designated the Zion Mule Corps, it saw service in the Gallipoli campaign of 1915–16 and performed well under fire in a noncombatant role.

After the Gallipoli evacuation, Jabotinsky continued worldwide efforts to recruit Jews. Much of the Zionist leadership was opposed, fearful of reprisals against Jewish populations in enemy territory. The British War Office also opposed Jabotinsky's efforts, although this evaporated with the late 1917 decision to allow Russian Jews living in Britain to enlist in the British army. Shortly thereafter, an all-Jewish battalion, organized as the 38th Royal Fusiliers and commanded by Colonel J.H. Patterson, was raised in England. It shipped out to Egypt where it was joined by a Canadian/American unit, the 39th Battalion. A third battalion, the 40th, drawn from Jews from liberated areas of Palestine, was ready only after the conclusion of the decisive campaign for Damascus and did not take part in any fighting.

The 38th Battalion was initially posted along the heights opposite a Turkish camp twenty miles north of Jerusalem. Its aggressive patrolling confined Turkish movements. Over the next several months, however, the battalion's fighting strength was severely depleted by malaria.

In September of 1918 the 38th battalion, reinforced by two companies from the 39th, took the fords of the Jordan River at Umm Shart and marched eastward to take the town of Es Salt in Jordan. Although the official Australian history claims that the Jews had to be prodded to advance into machine-gun fire, Colonel Patterson disputes this.

In 1919 the three battalions of the Jewish Legion, with more than five thousand men, were disbanded, and the British reneged on their promise to allow the men to settle in Palestine. A few remnants of the legion vainly attempted to protect Jewish life and property during the Arab riots of 1920–21.

James J. Bloom

References

Jabotinsky, Vladimir. *The Story of the Jewish Legion.* New York: Beachhurst, 1945.
Patterson, Lt. Col. John Henry. *With the Judeans in the Palestine Campaign.* London: Hutchinson, 1922.
———. *With the Zionists in Gallipoli.* London: Hutchinson, 1922.

See also PALESTINE AND SYRIA

Joffre, Joseph Jacques Césaire (1852–1931)

French general and commander in chief of the army. Born on 12 January 1852 at Rivesaltes, France, Joffre interrupted his studies at the Ecole Polytechnique to serve in the Franco-Prussian War. After the war he reentered the Ecole Polytechnique, and after graduation he served as an officer of the Engineer Corps in Formosa and Indo-China, led an expedition to Timbuktu in 1893, and served as a fortifications specialist in Madagascar from 1900 to 1905. In 1910 he was appointed to France's Supreme War Council, and in 1911 he was named chief of the general staff and, if war were to occur, commander in chief of the French armies.

When war broke out in August of 1914, Joffre was ignorant of Germany's strategic intentions. His plan of attack, known as Plan XVII, failed to anticipate where the enemy would deploy its forces. The French High Command did not anticipate the basic elements of Germany's Schlieffen Plan: the massing of troops on the German extreme right wing, the violation of neutral Belgium, and the crossing of the Meuse River. Joffre was convinced that the Germans would not use their reserves on the front lines. Without reservists, the Germans would lack sufficient manpower to extend from Mulhouse to Brussels. Consequently, Joffre

expected the main German attack to originate from Lorraine.

As the Germans prepared to make their major strike from the north, Joffre's Plan XVII deployed five French armies facing east and northeast for an attack between Belfort and Mézières. As soon as the French concentration was completed Joffre ordered a general offensive with the two armies of his right wing, to be followed a day later by his center, which was to launch the principal attack in the Ardennes and Luxembourg. On 20 August the two armies on the right were defeated at Sarrebourgh and Morhange. Three days later the Third and Fourth armies, forming the center, were beaten and forced to retreat. In the next two days the Fifth Army and the British contingent on the left were defeated. The French armies were in retreat everywhere as the German right-wing tentacle, led by Generals Alexander von Kluck and Karl von Bülow, moved through Belgium and headed in the direction of Paris.

As the French and British fell back toward the Marne, Joffre proved unflappable, which was vital in preventing panic in this difficult situation. Transferring forces from the east to the west to give the allies the advantage of numbers, Joffre organized a new army (the Sixth) just to the north of Paris under the command of General Michel Maunoury. On 31 August Maunoury informed Joffre that Kluck's army was veering to the southeast of Paris; that meant that Kluck's exposed right flank was vulnerable to a French attack. Joffre wanted Maunoury to move to the south bank of the Marne before he ordered a counterattack. General Joseph Gallieni, military governor of Paris, preferred the north bank of the Marne, for if the attack were to spring from the south bank the German flank would not have been turned; rather, it would have been a frontal collision.

Gallieni persuaded Joffre to strike north of the Marne. Joffre gave the order for the Battle of the Marne to begin on 6 September. In the ensuing days, as Kluck's army came to a grinding halt in the face of Sixth Army's attack, French troops began to penetrate between Kluck's and Bülow's armies. The Germans were forced to withdraw. Joffre, as the general in chief, naturally won much of the fame for the "Miracle of the Marne."

The Battle of the Marne was the high point of Joffre's career. All of the major offensives of 1915 and 1916, including Champagne, Somme, and Artois, were failures, but Joffre believed, as did the Germans, that a breakthrough was possible. Joffre justified these bloody offensives by maintaining that they convinced Italy to join the Entente in 1915, that they took pressure off Russia on the Eastern Front, and that they eased German pressure on Verdun in 1916.

By the end of 1916 Joffre came under severe criticism. The offensives were failures, and the casualties were horrendous. The situation was a hopeless deadlock, and Joffre's critics argued that France would have done better to confine herself to a strictly defensive strategy. In addition, the German attack against Verdun in 1916 had caught Joffre by surprise. He had neglected the Verdun defenses and the lines of communications into Verdun, in spite of warnings from colleagues. Joffre was also blamed for the Romanian disaster in late 1916.

In December of 1916 the French government removed Joffre as commander of French forces on the Western Front. He was named marshal and appointed technical advisor to the government. In the spring of 1917, just as the United States entered the war, Joffre made a goodwill tour of the United States. He died in Paris on 3 January 1931.

Jan Karl Tanenbaum

References

Porch, Douglas. *The March to the Marne. The French Army, 1871–1914*. Cambridge: Cambridge University Press, 1981.
Varillon, Pierre. *Joffre*. Paris: Arthème Fayard, 1956.
Williamson, Samuel R., Jr. *The Politics of Grand Strategy; Britain and France Prepare for War, 1904–1914*. Cambridge: Harvard University Press, 1969.

See also FRANCE, ARMY; FRENCH WAR PLAN XVII; MARNE, FIRST BATTLE OF; VERDUN, BATTLE OF

Josef Augustin, Archduke (1872–1962)

Austro-Hungarian archduke and general, born into the House of Hapsburg near Budapest on 9 August 1872. Archduke Josef devoted his life to the Austro-Hungarian army, commanding IV Corps, based in Hungary, prior to the outbreak of World War I. During the war he was a corps, army, and army group commander on the Russian, Romanian, and Italian fronts, 1914–18. Handsome and popular, favoring the dashing uniform of a Hungarian hussar, Josef rose to command the Tyrolean Army Group by the end of the war. An energetic leader who demonstrated personal bravery on several occasions, Josef displayed considerable talent at the corps level but was less effective commanding larger formations.

As the war entered its final year, Josef began to shift his loyalties from the empire to his native Hungary. At a royal council in January of 1918, Josef was the only commander present to vote for the creation of a separate Hungarian army. He hoped thereby to reinvigorate the flagging enthusiasm of Magyar troops. Growing increasingly pessimistic after the failure of the Piave Offensive, by October Josef openly advocated an immediate armistice.

Josef became deeply involved in Hungarian postwar politics. Appointed the emperor's personal representative in Hungary at the end of the war, he witnessed the revolution that brought first the liberal Count Mihály Károlyi and then the communist Béla Kun to power. In April of 1919 Josef joined a provisional government, supported by Romanian and French troops, dedicated to overthrowing Kun's communist dictatorship. In August he briefly took control of Hungary as regent but resigned the next month in the face of Allied protests over a Hapsburg's serving as head of state. He retired to his estates near Budapest, abjuring politics and producing a massive three-volume history of the war in Magyar. Josef died at Regensburg, Germany, on 7 July 1962.

Steven Eden

References

Rothenberg, Gunther. *The Army of Francis Joseph*. West Lafayette, Ind.: Purdue University Press, 1976.
Stone, Norman. *The Eastern Front, 1914–1917*. New York: Charles Scribner's Sons, 1975.
Villari, Luigi. *The War on the Italian Front*. London: Cobden-Sanderson, 1932.
Young, Peter. *History of the First World War*. 8 vols. London: BPC Publishing, 1971.

See also HUNGARY, REVOLUTION IN

Josef Ferdinand, Archduke of Austria (1872–1942)

Austro-Hungarian archduke and general, born in Salzburg, Austria, on 24 May 1872. Josef

Ferdinand was one of the less competent commanders of the Austro-Hungarian army during World War I. After the outbreak of hostilities, he was put in charge of a number of military units on the Eastern Front, culminating with his appointment as commander of the Austrian Fourth Army in Galicia. Believing his defenses impregnable, he organized hunting parties with his aristocratic friends while the Russians sapped their trenches forward to his lines. On 4 June 1916 Fourth Army received the initial assault of the Russian Brusilov Offensive, at Luck (Lutsk). The Fourth Army was destroyed as an effective fighting force in a matter of hours, and only massive German reinforcements saved the whole Austro-Hungarian army from disintegration. Josef Ferdinand was relieved of his command three days after the start of the attack. He died in Vienna on 25 August 1942.

Gary W. Shanafelt

References

Rothenberg, Gunther. *The Army of Francis Joseph*. West Lafayette, Ind.: Purdue University Press, 1976.

Stone, Norman. *The Eastern Front, 1914–1917.* New York: Charles Scribner's Sons, 1975.

See also BRUSILOV OFFENSIVE

Jutland, Battle of

The Grand Fleet of Great Britain and the High Seas Fleet of Germany met on the afternoon of 31 May 1916 off the western coast of Denmark (the Danish peninsula is called Jutland). The battle was near the outer entrance to the straits into the Baltic Sea, the Skagerrak, as the battle is known in Germany. The battle began during the afternoon of the 31st and concluded in the early hours of 1 June.

Ever since the decisive British naval victory at Trafalgar in 1805, there had been anticipation of another major fleet confrontation. The spectacular Anglo-German naval arms race of the two decades before 1914 was preparation for it: the British for another Trafalgar and the Germans for "*Der Tag*," The Day. All were certain that there would be some final Armageddon, and the victor would win the war. Jutland was the only occasion during the four years of World War I where such decisive naval results were possible.

Personalities were important in the battle. Winston Churchill, first lord of the admiralty when the war began, noted that the commander of the Grand Fleet, Admiral Sir John Jellicoe, was the only person who could lose the war in an afternoon. Jellicoe has been criticized for being overly cautious at Jutland. His opposite number in May of 1916 was Admiral Reinhard Scheer. Seconds in command (or commander of the advanced or scouting force for each fleet) were, respectively, Admiral Sir David Beatty and Admiral Franz von Hipper. Mention must also be made of the two naval professionals who oversaw the making of these "blue water" fleets of battleships: Admirals Sir John Fisher and Alfred von Tirpitz.

On 31 May 1916, both battle fleets were out in full force. The British had by far the most powerful fleet ever sent to sea to that point under the command of one man: twenty-eight battleships, nine battle cruisers, thirty-four cruisers, and eighty destroyers. The Germans had sixteen battleships, six predreadnoughts, five battle cruisers, eleven cruisers, and sixty-three destroyers.

Admiral Scheer, more aggressive than his predecessor, sought the battle. His hope was to sail with the entire High Seas Fleet and engage and destroy a portion of the British Grand Fleet. That would even the odds at sea considerably. Scheer put to sea on 30 May. The British had intercepted radio signals and broken a German naval code, and so were warned of the German plans. Whitehall ordered out the Grand Fleet before the Germans sailed. Scheer sent an advanced force of some forty fast warships, built around a nucleus of five battle cruisers and under command of Hipper, out in front. Well behind them was the main fleet, with the sixteen battleships and six predreadnoughts. Scheer's plan was to decoy the British ships back into the concentration of High Seas Fleet battleships.

Rushing to meet the Germans across the North Sea, independent of the rest of the Grand Fleet, was Beatty's scouting force of some fifty-two ships, including his six battle cruisers and Admiral Hugh Evan-Thomas's 5th Battle Squadron of four new, fast battleships. Both were steaming in line ahead. At about 14:30 on 31 May 1916, some 100 miles off Jutland, cruisers of the two fleets first made contact. Hipper, having sighted the British ships, had already turned south toward Scheer. A British light cruiser made the signal that both sides had anticipated for two years: enemy battlefleet in sight.

Most accounts of the Battle of Jutland treat the complex series of movements and actions in four discrete phases. At the time that the scouting cruisers of the opposing fleets first made contact, Hipper and his advanced force of battle cruisers were out ahead of Scheer and the body of the High Seas Fleet, headed generally north. Beatty's force was to the west, and Jellicoe and the Grand Fleet were about sixty miles to the north.

In Phase I, or the Run to the South, Hipper seemingly fled south. Beatty, as Hipper had hoped, turned on a parallel course south and signaled Evan-Thomas to follow him in turning toward Hipper. At about 15:45 both sides opened fire at a range of about nine miles. Evan Thomas's battleships missed the signal, however, and were slow to close. The result was a disaster for the British battle cruisers. Beatty's flagship, the *Lion,* took a hit on one of her midships' turrets. A fire started, and the ship was saved only by quickly flooding the midships' magazines. The *Indefatigable* blew up and immediately sank. Only two of her crew were saved. Within thirty minutes another battle cruiser, the *Queen Mary,* had suffered the same fate. Beatty did not slacken; his response was to order his remaining ships to engage more closely.

Phase II, the Run to the North, followed Beatty's discovery of the High Seas Fleet at 16:42. He at once reversed course to join Jellicoe and try to lure Scheer in turn into the Grand Fleet. The chase to the north continued for over an hour. Both fleets, nearly 250 warships, were now rushing toward one another at an aggregate speed of about forty knots.

Phase III was the Main Battle Fleet Confrontation, which some divide into two episodes because Jellicoe was able to "cross the T" of the Germans twice. This phase occurred between 18:00 and 21:00. Shortly after 18:00 a third British battle cruiser, the *Invincible,* was struck by a shell and split in two. The three British battle cruisers that blew up suffered almost 100 percent losses, about 1,000 men per ship. Observing the loss of the *Invincible,* Beatty made his much quoted assessment: "Chatfield (commanding officer of HMS *Lion*), there seems to be something wrong with our bloody ships today."

Shortly after 18:00 Beatty sighted Jellicoe's warships approaching from the northwest. The British fleet was still over the horizon from the Germans. Shortly before 18:30, as the High Seas Fleet proceeded north, Scheer sighted Admiral Sir Horace Hood's battle squadron out in front; about the same time British battleship shells began to fall around the German battle line. Within a matter of minutes all ships were within range. Three of Scheer's leading ships were soon hit. At 18:35 Scheer ordered a 180-degree turn, masterfully executed by his captains under cover of smoke screen and destroyer attacks. The German warships disappeared back into the mist. Jellicoe, instead of pursuing, continued southward in an effort to cut the Germans off from their base. At 18:55 Scheer executed another 180-degree turn, in hopes of finding a better position, but they were spotted by British cruisers. Once again Jellicoe was able to "cross the T" of the German line. This time it appeared the Germans would not escape, but Scheer again reversed course. Scheer's destroyers launched torpedoes at the British ships and laid a smokescreen.

There were two ways a commander might deal with a torpedo attack. The first was to present a small silhouette by meeting the attack bow on. The second was to reverse course and run out of range. Jellicoe chose the latter course, and in the process he lost sight of the enemy and never regained it.

With darkness there was mass confusion. Numerous individual encounters occurred throughout the night of 31 May–1 June during Phase IV, Night Action. The British fleet was between Scheer and his home ports. Scheer knew his fleet could not withstand a renewed general battle. After dark he turned toward the southeast, managing to cross Jellicoe's track of light cruisers astern. Scheer's warships were attacked by British destroyers. The Germans were able to slip away by early morning and escape through their main minefield to their base, thus ending the battle of Jutland.

In the battle the British lost fourteen ships: three battle cruisers, three cruisers, and eight destroyers. The Germans lost eleven warships: one battleship, one predreadnought, four cruisers, and five destroyers. The British lost 6,094 killed (6,945 total casualties), the Germans 2,551 killed (3,058 total casualties). Total tonnage losses were 111,980 to 62,233 tons, respectively. The day after the battle, twenty-eight capital ships of the Grand Fleet were fully ready for battle, whereas only ten capital ships of the High Seas Fleet were ready. The latter would not be operational for several months.

To a large extent the debate over the battle still rages, both within the naval organizations of each power and at the international level among historians. For at least a decade serious and acrimonious conflict raged within the Royal Navy between those who backed Jellicoe and his cautious strategy and those who favored Beatty and his more aggressive approach.

In the overall assessment, several problems were readily apparent. For the Grand Fleet, they were warship design, military intelligence, communications, and navigation. Communications failure during the first and crucial phase of the Run to the South resulted in fatal delays involving the 5th Battle Squadron under Admiral Sir Hugh Evan-Thomas. The four most powerful battleships in the world failed to engage the enemy expeditiously because of confusion over signals between Beatty and Evan-Thomas.

Jellicoe was the direct victim of two of the problems. Intelligence information that could have proved decisive was available in London at the admiralty and among the various outlying Royal Naval forces both on 31 May and 1 June, but it never was transmitted to the commander where it could be used. For example, British destroyers and cruisers during the Night Action engaged the High Seas Fleet directly, and, in addition, the admiralty knew the exact track Scheer was following to escape to Germany. But Jellicoe was not informed in either case.

Navigation in the Grand Fleet was horrendous. From later reconstruction it was determined that navigational errors were as great as eleven miles in some cases. That proved to be most crucial at the moment when the two battle fleets met, Jellicoe's being consistently misinformed of the locations of the various forces. It was important that he deploy the Grand Fleet in a single line ahead at the exact time and place to be most effective. Despite all the errors, Jellicoe at least accomplished the deployment brilliantly.

The Germans had their problems as well, particularly their cumbersome command structure and the less effective leadership of Scheer. Indeed, the organizational structure of the German navy was hopelessly complicated and ultimately fatal.

Affecting both sides was the poor weather: A heavy haze forced German reconnaissance zeppelins to turn back, and there was poor visibility for all. A British seaplane "carrier" launched one forty-minute flight that sighted three enemy cruisers, but this information never reached the proper commanders.

N.J.M. Campbell, a metallurgist, has conducted a detailed investigation of gunnery during the battle: the firing from all calibers of guns on both sides, specific hits, description of damage, and damage control. A sample of his statistical conclusions includes the following: Number of British shells fired, 4,500; German, 3,574. Hits on German ships, 102; on British ships, 85. During crucial phases: In the Run to the South, hits on British ships, 62; on German ships, 36. At the main fleet confrontation, hits on British ships, 23; on German ships, 68. The overall percentage of hits for each side was about equal, 3 percent.

British losses were certainly more spectacular. The three battle cruisers lost each blew up. Theories about the reasons abound: insufficient armor protection, especially the horizontal armor plating, poorly designed flash protection for the magazines, the volatility of propellent charges, sacrificing armor weight in order to gain speed, an inferior and faulty fire control system, and Beatty's inadequate staff work. The German ships appeared to be better designed. Yet, the German damage was clearly extensive and caused long delays until repairs could be completed.

Among recent historical accounts much is made of the Pollen Fire Control System, a superior gun fire-control mechanism available to the Royal Navy during the decade before the war but rejected for a system incapable of solving complex problems of high-speed naval battles. Its inventor, Arthur Pollen, was compensated £25,000 by the Admiralty in a postwar settlement.

Who won and who lost? The Germans gained a psychological advantage by an early announcement of what they claimed to be a decisive victory. The British failed to dispute that; their official announcement was delayed and pessimistic. Nothing, however, changed as a result of the battle. Jutland meant that the British continued to enjoy absolute domination of the surface of the seas all over the world. The much touted second Trafalgar or *Der Tag* was not to be.

Eugene L. Rasor

References

Campbell, N. John M. *Jutland: An Analysis of the Fighting.* Annapolis, Md.: Naval Institute, 1986.

Corbett, Sir Julian, and Sir Henry Newbolt. *Naval Operations: Official History of the Great War.* 5 vols. London: Longmans, 1920–1931, 1938, 1940.

Frost, Holloway H. *The Battle of Jutland.* Annapolis, Md.: Naval Institute, 1936.

Groos, Otto. *Der Krieg sur See, 1914–1918.* 6 vols. Berlin: E.S. Mittler und Sohn, 1920–1937.

Marder, Arthur J. *From Dreadnought to Scapa Flow: The Royal Navy in the Fisher Era, 1904–1919.* Vol. III: *Jutland and After.* London: Oxford University Press, 1966, 1978.

Rasor, Eugene L. *The Battle of Jutland: A Bibliography.* Westport, Conn.: Greenwood, 1992.

See also BEATTY, DAVID, FIRST EARL; EVAN-THOMAS, SIR HUGH; FISHER, JOHN ARBUTHNOT, LORD FISHER OF KILVERSTONE; HIPPER, ADMIRAL FRANZ RITTER VON; JELLICOE, JOHN RUSHWORTH, FIRST EARL; NAVAL ARMS RACE, ANGLO-GERMAN; SCHEER, REINHARD; TIRPITZ, ALFRED VON

J

K

Kamio, Mitsuomi (1856–1927)

Japanese general, born into a samurai family in 1856. Kamio served as a sergeant in the Satsuma Uprising of 1877 and was promoted to officer rank in 1879. His next thirty-five years mixed an excellent record of training plus active service. This combination made Kamio a divisional commander by 1912.

Two years later, in World War I, he was directed to lead a unit in an assault on Germany's powerful naval base at Qingdao (Tsingtao), China. Kamio demonstrated considerable skill in the course of the siege. He avoided grinding infantry tactics and used every opportunity to deploy his vastly superior artillery assets. On 7 November 1914 Kamio overcame the last German lines with a night assault and forced the city's surrender.

His rewards included governorship of the captured territory and, a year later, command of the Tokyo garrison. These in turn were followed by his advancement to full general in 1916. Kamio continued his military career until 1925. He died in Tokyo in 1927.

John P. Dunn

References

Burdick, Charles B. *The Japanese Siege of Tsingtau: World War I in Asia*. Hamden, Conn.: Archon, 1976.

Canning, Craig Noel. "The Japanese Occupation of Shantung during World War I." Ph.D. dissertation, Stanford University, 1975.

Gipps, G. "Siege of Tsingtao Manuscript." NMM MSS JOD/117. Greenwich, England: National Maritime Museum.

Hoyt, Edwin Palma. *The Fall of Tsingtao*. London: A. Barker, 1975.

Presseisen, Ernst. *Before Aggression: Europeans Prepare the Japanese Army*. Tucson, Ariz.: Published for the Association for Asian Studies by the University of Arizona Press, 1965.

See also JAPAN; QINGDAO, SIEGE OF

Karl I, Emperor of Austria (1887–1922)

Last Austrian emperor and Hungarian king (Charles IV), November 1916 to November 1918. Born Karl Franz Josef on 17 August 1887 at Persenbeug Castle in Austria, he was the grandnephew of Emperor Franz Josef. Educated at the Scottish High School in Vienna, Karl later attended lectures at Prague University. He married Princess Zita of Bourbon-Parma in 1911. Karl served as a cavalry officer until the assassination of his uncle Franz Ferdinand on 28 June 1914, at which time the young Karl became heir presumptive to the Austro-Hungarian throne because of the morganatic marriage of Franz Ferdinand.

In August of 1914, with the rank of colonel, Karl was attached to the Austro-Hungarian army in Galicia as imperial liaison. In the summer of 1915 he was promoted to major general and recalled to Schönbrunn for routine court functions. During the Austrian offensive against the Italians in May of 1916, Karl commanded the XX (Edelweiss) Corps, but after the defeat at Luck he was quickly sent to Eastern Galicia as commander of a new army corps, with German General Hans von Seeckt as his chief of staff.

When Franz Josef died on 21 November 1916, Karl succeeded to the throne as emperor of Austria, and on 30 December he was crowned king of Hungary. Karl began to put his imprint on the empire. His refusal to swear allegiance to the Austrian constitution caused the resignation of Minister-President Ernst von Körber, who was replaced by Heinrich von Clam-Martinic. After Foreign Minister Burian von Rajecz's 12 December 1916 peace offer went unanswered, Karl replaced him with Count Ottokar Czernin. Karl then forced Field Marshal Franz Conrad von Hötzendorf to resign and appointed the pliable General Athur Arz von Straussenburg as chief of staff. Finally, the new Emperor moved the army's headquarters from Teschen to Baden, near Vienna.

Genuinely concerned about the welfare of his subjects, young Emperor Karl lacked the experience, confidence, and willpower to make decisions and stick with them. He yearned to command the armed forces personally, which greatly concerned his military leaders. They also worried about his seeming desire to make peace at almost any price and to permit his wife a powerful voice in the affairs of state. He undermined morale and discipline in the army with a series of reforms in 1917 that abolished dueling, ended physical punishments for civilians and soldiers, halted air bombings, ended the use of gas without imperial approval, and granted amnesty for political crimes. In foreign affairs, Karl resented his dependence on the Germans, objected to the previously agreed-upon command structure, and protested Germany's decision to resume unrestricted submarine warfare. Karl even attempted to negotiate a separate peace with the Allies.

On 24 March 1918 Empress Zita's brothers, Sixte and Xavier, who were members of the Belgian army, met with Karl to plot his strategy. Unfortunately, the French were merely using the two young men to try to divide Germany and Austria. In April of 1918 the French government published parts of the correspondence between Karl and Sixte. Karl was accused of duplicity and treachery by the Germans and actually became more dependent on them, as seen in the minor role accorded the empire in the Treaty of Brest-Litovsk.

As the war turned increasingly sour for the Central Powers, the different nationalities of the empire pressed for autonomy or independence. After two more attempts at peace failed, Karl issued a manifesto on 16 October 1918 that transformed the western part of the empire, Austria, into a federated state with self-government for the various nationalities. At the same time, he assured the Magyars of the integrity of the Kingdom of Hungary. On 31 October he permitted officers to accept service in the national armies being formed. Karl had effectively disemboweled the old Empire. With the signing of an armistice on 4 November 1918, Karl stepped down on 11 November as head of the Austrian government. Ambiguous to the end, he refused to abdicate his throne but in March of 1919 was driven into exile in Switzerland, where he renounced his decision of 11 November.

Karl resisted his fate, however. On Easter Sunday in 1921 he attempted to regain his Hungarian throne but was foiled by the passive resistance of Admiral Miklós Horthy and by Allied opposition. On 21 October 1921, Karl and Zita flew to Hungary to try again to claim his crown. Horthy forcibly opposed the attempted coup, and Karl failed. After a brief incarceration, the royal couple was transported by British warship to exile in Madeira. Karl died at Quinta do Monte on Portuguese Madeira on 1 April 1922.

Laura Matysek Wood

References

Brook-Shepherd, Gordon. *The Last Habsburg.* New York: Weybright and Talley, 1968.
Rothenberg, Gunther. *The Army of Francis Joseph.* West Lafayette, Ind.: Purdue University Press, 1976.

See also AUSTRIA-HUNGARY, HOME FRONT; FRANZ JOSEF; HUNGARY, REVOLUTION IN; SIXTE, PRINCE

Károlyi, Count Mihály (1875–1955)

Prime minister of Hungary and president of the Hungarian Republic, 1918–19. Károlyi played a major and controversial role in Hungarian politics during World War I. Born in Fóth on 4 March 1875 into a wealthy and politically influential family, Károlyi began his political career as a Liberal but in 1913 became chairman of the Independence party. Before the war he advocated ending Austria-Hungary's alliance with Germany and joining the Entente powers, a stance that received little support from the other members of the party.

In the summer of 1916 Károlyi left the Independence party to organize a new opposition party, the United Party of Independence and of

1848, otherwise known as the Károlyi party. Its political stance included peace without annexations; loosening Hungary's bonds with Austria; general suffrage; land reforms to include breaking up the great estates; and social welfare legislation. In 1917, following the resignation of the Austro-Hungarian prime minister Count István Tisza, the Károlyi party, the Social Democrats, and other democratic parties formed a liberal revolutionary bloc. Recognizing the eminent defeat of the Central Powers, the Károlyi party pushed for a settlement on the basis of peace without annexations and self-determination for national minorities, in return for complete Hungarian autonomy.

On 31 October 1918, Emperor Karl (King Charles IV of Hungary) appointed Károlyi prime minister of Hungary in the hope that that would forestall a nationalist revolt. In fact it merely accelerated it. On 1 November Károlyi asked Karl to absolve him of his oath of allegiance, and the emperor agreed. Károlyi was then responsible only to the Hungarian nation; on 16 November he proclaimed the Hungarian Republic. From January to March of 1919 he was Hungary's president. He hoped that his pro-Western views would secure for Hungary lenient treatment at the peace conference, while his liberal nationality stance would appease non-Magyar groups in Hungary. Both notions proved illusory. As the nationalities declared their independence and the peacemakers ordered one Hungarian territorial concession after another, Károlyi's support dwindled. He resigned his office on 20 March 1919, to be succeeded by the Communist regime of Béla Kun.

Károlyi spent most of his remaining years in exile. He returned to Hungary in 1946, after the reactionary Horthy regime had been overthrown by the Red Army. He served as Hungarian minister to France, 1947–49, but resigned in protest against the Communist show trials. Károlyi died in Vence, France, on 19 March 1955.

Judith Podlipnik

References

Hoensch, Jörg K. *A History of Modern Hungary, 1867–1986*. New York: Longman, 1988.

Károlyi, Catherine. *A Life Together: The Memoirs of Catherine Károlyi*. London: Allen and Unwin, 1966.

Károlyi, M. *Memoirs. Faith without Illusion*. London: Jonathan Cape, 1956.

Volgyes, I. *Hungary in Revolution, 1918–19*. Lincoln: University of Nebraska Press, 1971.

See also HUNGARY, REVOLUTION IN; KARL I, EMPEROR OF AUSTRIA

Kemal, Mustafa (Atatürk) (1881–1938)

Turkish general and first president of the Republic of Turkey. Born in Salonika in 1881, Mustafa Kemal lost his father in early childhood and was raised by his mother, Zübeyde Hanim. Against his mother's wishes, he entered the military *Rüşdiye* school in Salonika in 1893. In 1895 he went on to the military high school *(Askeri Idadi)* in Monastir. He later entered the War College *(Harbiye)* in Istanbul as an infantry cadet. Finally, after attending the staff college, he graduated with the rank of staff captain in 1905. He served with distinction in the Italian and Balkan wars. In 1913 he was posted to Sofia as military attaché, and in March of 1914 he was promoted to lieutenant colonel.

After Turkey entered the Great War on 29 October 1914, Mustafa Kemal requested combat duty. On 2 February 1915 he was assigned the command of the Nineteenth Division, which was forming in Tekirdağ. This unit was a part of the Fifth Army, defending the Dardanelles under the command of German General Otto Liman von Sanders; it was delegated the pivotal role of a floating unit.

The first Allied attacks came on 18 March. The Allies suffered heavy casualties and decided not to press the attack. The next Allied attack came on 25 April against four points on the Gallipoli peninsula and one on the Asiatic shore. Kemal was convinced that the key to holding the southern half of Gallipoli was Conkbayiri and the Kocaçimen Plateau. Without waiting for orders from headquarters, he moved his troops against the British, who were advancing toward the hill of Conkbayiri. The battle raged on through the night of 25 April, and the British were finally pushed back to the last ridges overlooking the sea. As a result of this unauthorized but brilliant attack, he was promoted to full colonel on 1 June.

On the night of 6–7 August 1915, the Allies landed 20,000 troops in order to take the key town of Anafartalar. The attack was directed at the sector held by Kemal's division. He informed Liman von Sanders that the only remedy to the situation was to put all the forces in the area under his command. On 8 August he was appointed commander of the Anafartalar Group and immediately ordered an attack on the Allies, which in the end pushed back the superior Allied forces.

He informed his superiors that he believed the enemy was getting ready to withdraw. His suggestion for a general offensive was denied, as there were no troops to spare. Kemal announced his resignation, but Liman von Sanders convinced him to take leave instead. On 19 December 1915 the Allies, having lost all hope of success, withdrew.

On 14 January 1916, Kemal was assigned the command of the Sixteenth Army Corps in Edirne. Only a month later, the corps was transferred to Diyarbakir in southeastern Turkey to fight the Russians on the Caucasus front. By the time he reached his new post, Kemal was promoted to brigadier general (Pasha).

He was appointed deputy commander of the Second Army on 5 March. During the next two days he recaptured the cities of Muş and Bitlis from the Russians. In recognition of his victories, Kemal was awarded the distinguished order of *Imtiyaz* (Golden Sword).

After the March Revolution, the Russians withdrew to Tiflis. Kemal, now freed on the Caucasus front, was sent to Damascus. There the British were mounting strong pressure against the hold of the Ottomans in the Hejaz. He recommended to the acting commander in chief, Enver Pasha, that the whole Arabian peninsula be abandoned in order to reinforce the Syrian front. Enver Pasha dismissed his recommendation.

On 5 July 1917 Kemal Pasha was appointed to the command of the new Seventh Army, which was attached to the *Yildirim* (Lightning) Armies Group forming in Aleppo under the command of German General Erich von Falkenhayn. He submitted a detailed report on 20 September 1917 to Enver Pasha and the war ministry on the army's weaknesses and defects. He went on to state his objection to the sacrifice of Turkish soldiers by German commanders in pursuit of glory. When the high command disagreed with his views, Kemal relieved himself of his command. The Turkish government convinced him to take sick leave instead.

While Kemal was on leave, British forces under General Edmund Allenby captured Jerusalem. His next assignment was to the en-tourage of the Ottoman Crown Prince Vahdeddin (later Mehmed VI) for the latter's state visit to Germany.

On 7 August 1918 Kemal was for the second time appointed to the command of the remnants of the Seventh Army in Syria. Liman von Sanders, who had replaced Falkenhayn as the head of the *Yildirim* Army Group, gave him the command of the Fourth, Seventh, and Eighth Ottoman armies as he left Syria.

Although Kemal now had three armies under his command, he was still outnumbered two to one by the British. A tour of the Turkish positions was enough to convince him that any battle against the British was already lost. Hoping to save as many Turkish lives as possible, he abandoned most of the Arabic provinces of the Ottoman Empire to the British. His plan was to defend Anatolia, the Turkish heartland. On 26 October 1918 his forces halted the advance of the British a few miles north of Aleppo.

On 30 October Kemal received orders to cease fire, as the Turkish government had signed the Armistice of Mudros. After four years of fighting, he was the only undefeated Ottoman field commander.

Once the war was over, Kemal was appointed to the post of inspector-general of the Ninth Army in Anatolia. He used that position to organize a national resistance movement against the invading Allies, specifically, the Greeks. On 8 July 1919 he resigned from the army. The nationalist government he established in Ankara later became the actual government of Turkey. Kemal was chosen the first president of the Republic of Turkey and given the surname Atatürk, "Father Turk." He remained president until his death of cirrhosis of the liver on 10 November 1938.

Yücel Yanikdağ

References

Atay, F.R. *Atatürk'ün Hatiralari 1914–1919*. Ankara: Turkiye Is Bankasi Kultur Yayinlari, 1965.

Kinross, Patrick Balfour. *Atatürk: A Biography of Mustafa Kemal, Father of Modern Turkey*. New York: Quill, 1992.

Lewis, Bernard. *The Emergence of Modern Turkey*. London: Oxford University Press, 1969.

Volkan, Namik, and Norman Itzkowitz. *The Immortal Atatürk*. Chicago: University of Chicago Press, 1984.

See also Caucasus Front; Gallipoli; Ottoman Empire; Palestine and Syria

Kerensky, Aleksandr Fedorovich (1881–1970)

Russian politician and leader of the provisional government, born on 4 May 1881 in Simbirsk in the central Volga region. His father, Feodor Kerensky, was the principal of the high school attended by both his son and Vladimir Ulianov (Lenin). In fact, it was Feodor Kerensky's letter of recommendation that secured admission for young Ulianov to the University of Kazan. After high school, Aleksandr Kerensky studied law at the University of St. Petersburg. Subsequently, as a young lawyer in that city he specialized in political cases. Indeed, politics was his main interest. As a person who stood politically just to the left of center, he became the leader of the small, moderate-socialist Labor (Trudovy) party. In 1912 Kerensky was elected as a delegate to the Fourth Duma.

On 26 July 1914, on the eve of the war, the czar invited the Duma leaders to the Winter Palace in order to obtain their support. Kerensky, along with the others, pledged to support the government in a defensive war and shortly thereafter voted for war credits, a symbolic gesture of unity within the government during a national emergency. During the war Kerensky flirted with the Socialist Revolutionaries, but there is no evidence that he supported their radical land-reform program. In the State Duma he was a member of the Progressive Bloc, a group of centrist legislators who banded together to goad the government into reorganizing itself so as to successfully manage the war effort. It goes without saying that this group was not popular with the imperial family and the numerous incompetent ministers who held posts early in the war. Kerensky's colleagues described him as an excellent orator but prone to nervousness and fits of anxiety and given to heavy cigarette smoking. From late 1915 to mid-1916 Kerensky was out of the political arena because of serious illness.

When Kerensky returned from recuperation in Finland he found Russia at the breaking point, as heavy war casualties, severe food shortages in the cities, economic dislocation, and the incompetence of the central government—now in the hands of the Empress Alexandra and Rasputin—brought open talk in every level of society of the need to get rid of Czar Nicholas II. In February of 1917 Kerensky called for an end to Russia's "medieval regime."

On 8 March 1917 riots broke out in the industrial section of Petrograd and soon spread throughout the entire city. On the 11th the Duma refused to obey an imperial decree of dissolution and instead formed a Provisional Committee, which included Kerensky. The avowed aim of this group was to restore order to the city. At the same time the more radical Duma members constituted themselves into the Petrograd Soviet of Workers Deputies in order to transform the riots into a revolution. These two bodies found themselves in competition for political power. On the 15th the czar abdicated, and on the following day, realizing that this political stalemate could not continue, the provisional committee and the Soviet came to an agreement. The Soviet would recognize the legitimacy of a provisional government but would retain a veto power over it. It was also agreed that the army would remain at the front, but only for defensive purposes.

The provisional government lurched from crisis to crisis. In April, Foreign Minister Paval Miliukov pledged to Russia's allies that Russia would fulfill her war obligations. This caused demonstrations in Petrograd and led to the fall of the first government coalition. In the new government, the "eloquent lawyer" Kerensky, who had been minister of justice, was elevated to the post of minister of war; in that capacity he was known as "the persuader in chief." On several trips to the front he explained to the soldiers the political situation back home and the possible need for an offensive action in order to achieve more favorable terms at the peace conference.

In July there occurred two simultaneous events that propelled Kerensky to the head of the provisional government. First, a Russian offensive against the Austrians in Galicia failed, and when the Austrians and Germans counterattacked, the whole southwest front collapsed. The Russian Eleventh Army disintegrated. At the same time, in Petrograd the Bolsheviks launched a demonstration that got out of hand; once more, riots threatened to engulf the city. In the midst of these "July Days" Kerensky replaced Prince Lvov as the head of the government. He immediately blamed the Bolsheviks for the current turmoil and sent the police to arrest their leaders. Trotsky and several others were jailed for a short time, but Lenin went underground into Finland.

In August and September, Kerensky, at the head of the government of a nation in total disintegration, faced an untenable situation. He was almost forced into an alliance with right-wing General Lavr Kornilov in order to restore discipline in the army. Kornilov, who headed the antirevolutionist faction within the general staff, was appointed commander in chief of the army on 31 July. It was not long before all of the revolutionary leaders, including Kerensky, saw Kornilov as a potential demagogue intent on overthrowing the revolution and imposing a dictatorship. But events interceded. In early September the Germans captured Riga, leaving Petrograd exposed. That, and the threat of more Bolshevik demonstrations, led Minister of War B. Savinkov to request a cavalry corps from General Kornilov to defend the capital. The troops, under General Krimov, immediately began to entrain for the city, resulting in panic within both the Soviet and the government at the thought of a counterrevolution. The military trains were halted by sympathetic workers short of the capital, however, and Bolshevik agitators persuaded the hungry and demoralized troops to go home. The danger from the right had ended.

In the wake of the Kornilov affair the second government coalition fell. It was not until 8 October that Kerensky was able to form a new government, which included a socialist majority. To forestall another collapse, Kerensky declared Russia a republic and announced plans for a constitutional convention. But the political situation was too far gone. On 7 November the Bolsheviks seized the government. Kerensky fled the city in an auto flying an American diplomatic flag. He attempted to gather military support to oust the Bolsheviks but was unsuccessful. Consequently, he fled Russia and after a short stay in Paris went to the United States, where he lived in New York City until his death on 11 June 1970.

John W. Bohon

References

Kerensky, Alexander. *Russia and History's Turning Point*. New York: Duell, Sloan and Pearce, 1965.

Kochan, Lionel. *Russia in Revolution 1890–1918*. London: Granada, 1981.

Sukhanov, Nikolai N. *The Russian Revolution 1917*. 2 vols. New York: Harper, 1962.

See also KORNILOV, LAVR; RUSSIA, HOME FRONT AND REVOLUTIONS OF 1917

Kerensky (Second Brusilov) Offensive (1 July 1917)

Despite the overthrow of Czar Nicholas II in the March 1917 Revolution, Russia's provisional government remained committed to the war effort—even though the Russian people were war-weary, the army was disintegrating, and the economy was in a shambles. If for no other reason, the government sought to use the war to focus attention on external affairs and away from more pressing problems at home; they wished as well to maximize whatever aid might come from the United States. The decision to continue the conflict not only proved futile, but did more than anything else to bring the Bolsheviks to power.

The Eastern Front for the first half of 1917 was static. The Central Powers and the Russians (and their allies) maintained positions on a line running from Riga in the north, west of Minsk, down the eastern slope of the Carpathian Mountains to the Black Sea, halfway between Constanta and Odessa. There were approximately eighty Central-Power divisions on the western side of the line and about forty-five Russian divisions to the east.

The Russian forces included the Eleventh Army, under the command of Erdelli, poised for a strike at Ztoczów and anchoring the right side of the line. Next to them, in the middle, Belkovitch's Seventh Army was aimed at Brzezany; Kronilov's Eighth Army, south of the Dniester River, prepared to make a flank movement and attack Kalusz.

Several of the Central Powers' divisions, mostly Austrian, were aligned opposite the war-weary Russians. The Austrian Second Army was located north of Lemberg. Opposite Brzezany and south of Lemberg was the "Sudarmee," consisting of one Turkish, three Austrian, and four German divisions. Just north of the Dniester River was the Austrian Third Army, and, finally, the Austrian Seventh Army was located just south of Kalusz. The tacit commander of German forces on the Eastern Front was Major General Max Hoffmann. General Count Felix von Bothmer commanded the Sudarmee, and General Tersztuanky commanded the Third Austrian Army.

The Germans felt no particular urgency to initiate an attack. They were fully aware of the turmoil inside Russia, especially after the abdication of the czar, and were willing to wait out the Russians. Not only were they unwilling to take any military action that might solidify the country, the Germans became politically involved in Russia's internal affairs when they assisted Lenin in his triumphant return to Moscow. Although they were to regret that decision twenty years later, that was with the benefit of hindsight. Most would agree that any action leading to the internal political instability of an enemy was an action worth pursuing, as it would inevitably prove of military benefit at the front.

On the Russian home front, with the abdication of the czar, politics and the military were inextricably entwined. Aleksandr Kerensky had become the Russian war minister, as well as the nominal leader of the Russian government. He knew that his position was precarious. The Bolsheviks were urging strikes and actions against authority both at home and in military units at the front. Further, Lenin was gaining strength among the populace. In addition to the internal problems and politics, Kerensky was also under pressure from the Allies to attack the Central Powers' forces, thus opening two fronts.

Succumbing to political pressures from home and abroad, Kerensky ordered General Aleksei Brusilov, now commander of the Russian forces on the Eastern Front, to launch an attack against the enemy. The immediate objectives were the oil fields near Drohobycz, with the ultimate objective being Lemberg, in Galicia.

The attack began on 1 July. For the first few days, the offensive went well. The tired, ill-equipped Russian forces made significant headway against the superior armies of the Central Powers. To the south, General Lavr Kornilov's armies pushed forward past Stanslau and reached Kalusz. On the far right flank, Erdelli's Eleventh Army reached Ztoczów. The Seventh Army, under the command of General Belkovitch, successfully drove against the Sudarmee, pushing them back nearly 30 kilometers.

The Russians had launched a total of forty-five divisions along a forty-mile front in this last-gasp effort to salvage something from their years of war. (Russia's divisions consisted of about 3,000 men in World War I, unlike the 12,000- to 15,000-man divisions of modern armies.) The Bolsheviks opposed this effort, preferring instead to sue for peace with the Germans and turn their attention to internal problems.

The Bolsheviks' opposition, however, did not blunt the initial efforts of the armies, and the Russian forces reached positions over thirty miles behind enemy lines before giving out. Even at the end, had the soldiers obeyed their commanders, it might have been possible to win the battle and reach the objective.

Although Bolshevik activity was widespread, both at home and in the various military units at the front, that activity alone did not lead to defeat. In many units there were significant weapons shortages, and many soldiers did not have weapons of any kind. Further, poor military planning and execution resulted in needless deaths. For instance, one division attacked an entrenched artillery position, although it was outnumbered twelve to one. As a result, fewer than 500 men out of more than 3,000 survived.

Ironically, although this battle was the end of Russia's participation in World War I, future leaders of the Soviet Union were being shaped in the effort. Several future generals, marshals, and political leaders of the Soviet Union were serving, most as enlisted soldiers, in the decaying forces of Russia. Michael Frunze, who would become the academician of the military, was a Bolshevik fomenter in his unit. Georgii Zhukov, destined to become the Soviet Union's most renowned military leader, was also a Bolshevik in his front-line cavalry unit. Stalin and Khrushchev were both visible political figures at the front in these waning days of World War I. Others included Ivan Koniev, promoted to corporal for his bravery during this final push; in the Second World War he led Soviet forces in their final dash across Germany to the Oder River. Konstantin Rokossovsky would become one of the four officers most trusted by Zhukov. Finally, future Marshal A.I. Eremenko had been drafted into the czar's army, but joined the Soviet forces after the overthrow of the Bolsheviks.

Russia played out this final hand, serving the goals of the Allies by keeping thousands of the Central Powers' soldiers tied up in a largely meaningless battle on the Eastern Front. Her withdrawal from the war probably had little impact on the final outcome, but it was a prelude to the next act to follow, twenty years later.

The defeat signaled the end of Kerensky's government. Brusilov, commander in chief in the field, was relieved and replaced by Kornilov. Kornilov had gained near-hero status by his actions against the czar but would prove inept in the final defense against the counterattacking Central Powers. Kornilov was replaced by Dukhonin, who would have the distinction of being the last of the czar's officers to serve as commander in chief. On 3 December 1917 he was dragged from his railroad car and killed by rioting Bolshevik sailors. Thus ended the Russian, and the czar's, army.

Tom Cagley

References

Brusilov, General A.A. *A Soldier's Note Book 1914–1918*. London: Macmillan, 1930.

Golovine, Lieut.-Gen. Nicholas N. *The Russian Army in the World War*. New Haven: Yale University Press, 1931.

Stone, Norman. *The Eastern Front 1914–1917*. New York: Charles Scribner's Sons, 1975.

Wildman, A. *The End of the Russian Imperial Army*. 2 vols. Princeton: Princeton University Press, 1980.

See also BRUSILOV, ALEKSEI; EAST GALICIA, GERMAN COUNTEROFFENSIVE; KERENSKY, ALEKSANDR; RUSSIA, HOME FRONT AND REVOLUTIONS OF 1917

Keyes, Sir Roger John Brownlow (1872–1945)

British admiral, born on 4 October 1872 at Tundiani, North West Frontier of India. Keyes first entered the navy in 1885. He had an adventurous career, which included capturing a Chinese destroyer with a boarding party while in command of a destroyer during the Boxer Rebellion. On the outbreak of the First World War he was Commodore (S)—the head of the submarine service. An aggressive and natural leader, Keyes was the instigator of the sweep on German light forces in the Bight that resulted in the Heligoland action of 28 August 1914. He ran afoul of first sea lord Admiral Lord Fisher and left in February 1915 to become chief of staff to Admirals Sackville Carden and John de Robeck at the Dardanelles.

Keyes was undismayed by the failure of the naval assault of 18 March and, having reorganized the minesweeping service, tried to persuade de Robeck to make another attempt. De Robeck, however, decided to wait for the army. After the landings at Gallipoli failed to progress beyond the beachheads, disagreement between de Robeck and Keyes intensified. It grew sharper when the new landings at Suvla in August also failed to break through. De Robeck permitted Keyes to return to London in October to argue his plan for a new attack. Keyes, still relatively junior in rank, was unable to prevail, and London decided to evacuate. Keyes remained convinced for the remainder of his life that a great opportunity had been squandered and that the reorganized fleet with new ships, such as specially bulged cruisers, would have been able to break through, appear off Constantinople, and force Turkey out of the war.

Keyes returned to the Grand Fleet in 1916 and in September of 1917 went to the admiralty as director of plans. He clashed with Admiral Reginald Bacon, commander of the Dover Patrol, over how to bar the Dover Straits to German submarines and superseded Bacon as commander of the Dover patrol on 1 January 1918. Keyes implemented his plan for a deep minefield in the Straits, illuminated by trawlers burning flares in order to force submarines to dive into the mines. He also executed Operation Z.O., the attempt to block the entrances to the canals at Zeebrugge and Ostend leading to the submarine base at Bruges. The raid on the night of 23 April was one of the most gallant events of the war, but the blocking attempt was only partially successful at Zeebrugge and failed at Ostend, as did a second raid. In the long run, however, the raids contributed to making the Belgian ports insecure for the German Flanders flotillas, and Keyes's less dramatic Dover barrage eventually stopped German submarine traffic through the Straits.

After the war Keyes was created a baronet in 1919, commanded the battle cruiser squadron, 1919–21, was deputy chief of naval staff, 1921–25, commander in chief Mediterranean, 1925–28, and ended his naval career as commander in chief Portsmouth, 1929–31. Keyes became MP for Portsmouth North in 1934 and during the Second World War was director of combined operations, July 1940–October 1941. His name was always linked with the raid on Zeebrugge, and when he was raised to the peerage in 1943 he took the title Baron Keyes of Zeebrugge and of Dover. He died at Tingewick, Buckinghamshire, on 26 December 1945.

Paul G. Halpern

References

Aspinall-Oglander, Cecil. *Roger Keyes*. London: Hogarth, 1951.

Halpern, Paul G., ed. *The Keyes Papers*. Vol. 1: *1914–1918* "Publications of the Navy Records Society, Vol. 117." Reprint. London: George Allen and Unwin, 1979.

Keyes, Admiral of the Fleet Sir Roger. *The Naval Memoirs*. 2 vols. London: Thornton Butterworth, 1934–5.

See also DARDANELLES CAMPAIGN; OSTEND AND ZEEBRUGGE, RAIDS OF, 1918

Keynes, John Maynard (1883–1946)

Prominent economist and critic of the Versailles settlement, born in Cambridge on 5 June 1883. Keynes joined the civil service and went to Paris in 1919 as the British treasury representative. Vehemently opposing the reparations demanded of Germany, in June of 1919 he resigned in disgust. He then published *The Economic Consequences of the Peace* (1919), predicting that what he felt was French insistence on a Carthaginian peace with Germany would provoke future German aggression. The book attained such fame that one scholar even blamed Keynes for the Versailles Treaty's failure; in fact, rejection of the treaty by the United States was certain even before the book went to press. Keynes's most important work was his *General Theory of Employment, Interest and Money* (1936), which overturned the foundations of classical economic theory by demonstrating that economies do not tend automatically toward full equilibrium. At the Bretton Woods conference of 1944, Keynes played a leading role in establishing the International Monetary Fund and the World Bank. The system of fixed exchange rates he helped to construct governed international finance until the 1970s. He was raised to the peerage in 1942 as Baron Keynes of Tilton. Lord Keynes died at Tilton on Easter Sunday, 21 April 1946.

Jeffrey M. Pilcher

References

Harrod, Roy Forbes. *The Life of John Maynard Keynes*. New York: Harcourt, Brace, 1951.

Moggridge, Donald E. *Keynes*. 3rd ed. Toronto: University of Toronto Press, 1993.

Sharp, Alan. *The Versailles Settlement: Peacemaking in Paris, 1919*. New York: St. Martin's, 1991.

Skidelsky, Robert J.A. *John Maynard Keynes: A Biography*. 2 vols. New York: Viking Penguin, 1994.

See also PARIS PEACE CONFERENCE, 1919; VERSAILLES TREATY

Kiel Canal

Known to German contemporaries as the Kaiser Wilhelm Kanal, this sixty-two-mile-long artificial waterway connecting the North Sea with the Baltic across the Prussian province of Schleswig-Holstein took eight years to build. It first opened in June of 1895. The canal represented the culmination of efforts, some going back to the Vikings, to find a shortcut between the two bodies of water without having to round Denmark's Jutland Peninsula. Named in honor of the founder of Germany's Second Reich, Wilhelm I, the canal has terminals at Brunsbüttel on the Elbe River and at Holtenau, a suburb of Kiel, Germany's major naval base on the Baltic. A pair of locks at each terminal allow for smooth, two-way traffic. They also keep the water level of the canal steady while adjusting shipping to tidal variations.

The launching of HMS *Dreadnought* in 1905 prompted the German government to deepen and widen the canal and build a new set of locks, so that Germany's own dreadnoughts could transfer freely between the Baltic and the North Sea. This modernization was completed on 24 June 1914, just prior to the war. The canal became a major asset during the conflict, since no German ships had to face the perilous detour around Jutland. The new locks measured 330 by 45 by 11 meters and accommodated even the largest German battle cruisers. They also placed limits on the size of future capital ships. The time of passage, at ten knots, averages about eight hours.

Eric C. Rust

References

Herwig, Holger H. *"Luxury Fleet": The Imperial German Navy, 1888–1918*. London: Allen and Unwin, 1980.

Jane's Fighting Ships of World War I. New York: Military Press, 1990. Reprint of 1919 edition.

K

Kiggell, Sir Launcelot Edward (1862–1954)

British general, born on 2 October 1862 in Ballingarry, Limerick, Ireland. Kiggell attended Sandhurst and in 1882 entered the Royal Warwickshire Regiment. From 1897 he made his career in staff assignments. He served at Sandhurst and Camberley and was commandant of the staff college between 1913 and 1914.

During World War I Kiggell initially served in the war office, but with General Sir Douglas Haig's appointment in December of 1915 he became his chief of staff. Kiggell had limited field experience in modern war, and that affected his performance. He recommended the tactics of successive waves for the Somme offensive in 1916, postponement of the use of tanks at Cambrai from August to September so as not to divide the British effort while the Passchendaele Offensive was in progress, and, in October, continuation of that offensive despite heavy British casualties, exhaustion, and bad weather. Kiggell was promoted to lieutenant general in 1917. Although Haig continued to support him, in January of 1918 Kiggell gave up his post for medical reasons.

Kiggell then served as general officer commanding and lieutenant governor, Guernsey. He retired in 1920. After the war, he worked on the official history of the war, but poor health forced him to abandon his participation. Kiggell died on 23 February 1954 at Felixstowe, Suffolk.

Donald F. Bittner

References

Barnett, Correlli. "Kiggell, Sir Launcelot Edward," *Dictionary of National Biography, 1951–1960.*
Duncan, G.S. *Douglas Haig as I Knew Him.* London: George Allen and Unwin, 1966.
Marshall-Cornwall, General Sir James. *Haig as Military Commander.* New York: Crane, Russak, 1973.
Terraine, John. *Douglas Haig, the Educated Soldier.* London: Hutchinson, 1963.
The Times (London), 25 February 1954.

See also SOMME, BATTLE OF

Kitchener, Earl Horatio Herbert (1850–1916)

British field marshal and secretary of state for war from 5 August 1914 until his death on 5 June 1916. Kitchener was born on 24 June 1850 to English parents living near Listowel in County Kerry, Ireland. He studied engineering at the Royal Military Academy, Woolwich, obtaining his commission in 1871 and starting his military career with extensive survey work in Palestine, Cyprus, and Anatolia. In 1883 he was part of the relief expedition that failed to save General Gordon at Khartoum in the Sudan, an experience he remembered vividly fifteen years later when he commanded the British and Egyptian forces at the Battle of Omdurman (1898), which resulted in the recapture of Khartoum and his elevation to the peerage. In the Boer War he was initially chief of staff to Field Marshal Roberts, then his successor as commander in chief. From 1902 to 1909 he served as commander in chief in India. In 1911 Kitchener returned to Egypt where he served as consul general until 1914.

From the moment of his appointment to Herbert Asquith's cabinet as minister of war on 3 August 1914, Lord Kitchener envisioned a long and costly war, one that would require the training of thousands of new soldiers. His stern and resolute image, complete with his characteristic full moustache, appeared on the Great War's most famous poster, with the clear words "Your Country Needs YOU" standing out boldly beneath his index finger, pointing to all observers. He was England's most famous soldier when the war began, having established his reputation with distinguished service in Egypt, South Africa, and India. Besides his title of Earl Kitchener of Khartoum and of Broome, his honors included the Order of the Bath, Order of the Garter, and Order of Merit. In assessing his fame with the British public, one commentator reduced Kitchener's success to two attributes: "an unparalleled thoroughness, and an unparalleled drive."

Kitchener's record as a cabinet member for twenty-two months during the Great War is mixed. Admirers point to his early vision of a long and extended war, an unpopular view with his civilian colleagues who were certain of a quick and decisive engagement that would end by Christmas in 1914. Furthermore, some civilian leaders distrusted the idea of a career military officer's serving as minister of war, while others complained about his insistence that the war could not be won at sea and about his lack of enthusiasm for the Territorial Army.

Kitchener presided over the mobilization and training of an unprecedented British military force that expanded in a few months from seven to seventy divisions. Known as "Kitchener's armies," these units, amounting to nearly 3 million men, were formed by patriotic enlistments rather than conscription, and they suffered enormous casualties in the war of attrition on the Western Front in 1915 and 1916. Critics later blamed Kitchener for the lack of leadership up and down the ranks in the later stages of the war, England's best and the brightest having been killed in earlier months.

Kitchener and Churchill often supported the same war strategies, although the latter took the primary blame for the failed Gallipoli campaign. Kitchener offered to resign from the cabinet too but was asked to stay for the sake of his country; the unkind story circulated that the minister for war was not a great man but was a great poster. In addition to the Gallipoli failure in the spring and summer of 1915, Kitchener also became a target of criticism after the Battle of Loos in September. But he continued to work—some say autocratically and with aloofness—in recruiting troops, planning strategy, and reorganizing industrial production for increased munitions. Cooperating with civilian colleagues in the cabinet was never his strong point, nor was delegating responsibility to others.

By early 1916 his influence on war policy had clearly diminished, in proportion to David Lloyd George's rise. Yet he stayed in office, grudgingly acknowledging the government's need for his name. He was never a great admirer of French general Joseph Joffre, and he supported the replacement of Sir John French by General Sir Douglas Haig as commander of the British Expeditionary Force in December of 1915. In the same month Field Marshal Sir William Robertson became chief of the general staff and assumed greater control of strategic planning. Kitchener's influence in the cabinet was minimal by early 1916, but the public still admired him greatly, and he worked in harmony with Haig and Robertson in planning the western offensive in 1916. He also showed an increased interest in deploying tanks.

Kitchener agreed to visit Russia at Nicholas II's invitation, in order to advise the czar on methods to improve the fighting ability of the Russian army. On 5 June 1916 Kitchener was aboard the *Hampshire* steaming toward Archangel when the cruiser struck a German mine west of the Orkney Islands and sank in rough seas within fifteen minutes. There were few survivors, and Kitchener's body was never recovered; a shocked nation received the news a day later. Two memorial statues stand in London today in tribute to this great and enigmatic soldier, one at St. Paul's Cathedral, the other at the Horse Guards.

Thomas W. Davis

References

Farwell, Byron. *Eminent Victorian Soldiers*. New York: W.W. Norton, 1985.
Magnus, Philip. *Kitchener: Portrait of an Imperialist*. New York: E.P. Dutton, 1959.
Warner, Philip. *Kitchener: The Man behind the Legend*. New York: Atheneum, 1986.

See also GREAT BRITAIN, ARMY

Kluck, Alexander von (1846–1934)

Prussian general and army commander, born at Münster in Westphalia on 20 May 1846. His father was a construction engineer, his mother the daughter of a merchant. In 1865 Kluck joined a Westphalian infantry regiment as an officer aspirant and was commissioned ten months later. After participating in the wars against Austria (1866) and France (1870–71), Kluck rose slowly through the ranks, serving for long periods either as an adjutant or as a specialist in the training of NCOs. Without war academy training or any experience on the general staff, Kluck nevertheless received a divisional command in East Prussia (1902) and a corps command at Posen (Poznan) four and a half years later. In 1907 he was transferred to Königsberg in East Prussia to assume command of I Corps. Fourteen months later he was elevated to noble status.

Perhaps because of his successes in one of the annual maneuvers, Kluck was made head of the Eighth Army Inspection (at Berlin) in October of 1913 and promoted to colonel general shortly thereafter. Upon mobilization he assumed command of the First Army, a force of six corps assigned to the far right wing of the German armies deploying for the invasion of France (and Belgium). Assisted by the most cerebral of all senior staff officers, Major General Hermann von Kuhl (a recently ennobled Rhenish Catholic with a doctorate in philology), Kluck led his troops into Belgium, took Brussels on 20 August, left behind one reserve corps to cover Antwerp, and encountered the BEF at Mons on the 23rd and again at Le Cateau three days later.

For a variety of reasons, some of which were entirely beyond his control, Kluck's army gradually deviated from the intended route through northeastern France and eventually arrived at the Marne, to the east of Paris, rather than enveloping the city from the west. Headstrong and given to taking the offensive, Kluck and Kuhl permitted some of their corps to push across the river in hot pursuit of the Allies—and paid only limited attention to their growing exposure to French counterstrikes from the west. To the annoyance of General Karl von Bülow, commander of the adjacent Second Army, Kluck and Kuhl did not do much about a broad gap that was opening between the two armies. Indeed, when the growing danger on their right flank finally became clear to them, Kluck and Kuhl hastily moved more and more divisions from their southern front to the threatened right wing of the First Army, thereby widening the gap further. In the end, the high command (OHL), through its special emissary, Lieutenant Colonel Richard Hentsch, induced Kluck and Kuhl to stage a withdrawal to the Aisne River (9 September).

In the ensuing months Kluck's First Army wound up in the Oise-Aisne region, where it became involved in several major battles—near Noyon (September 1914), Roye (October 1914), and Soissons (January 1915). On 28 March Kluck was seriously wounded by shrapnel while inspecting his lines near Vailly. His position as commander of the First Army was filled by General Max von Fabeck, and, even after Kluck had recuperated, he received no further appointments. Decorated with the *Pour le Mérite* as of the day he was wounded, he was placed on the inactive list in October of 1916.

After the war, both Kluck and his erstwhile chief of staff, Kuhl, wrote about their experiences during the 1914 western campaign and the German failure at the Marne. Historical assessments of their role in the debacle still range from highly positive to mildly negative. In 1928 the Bavarian University of Erlanger conferred an honorary doctorate on the retired general. Kluck died in Berlin, aged 88, on 19 October 1934.

Ulrich Trumpener

References

Groener, Wilhelm. *Der Feldherr wider Willen: Operative Studien über den Weltkrieg*. Berlin: E.S. Mittler und Sohn, 1931.

Jäschke, Gotthard. "Zum Problem der Marne-Schlacht von 1914." *Historische Zeitschrift* 190 (1960).

Kluck, Alexander von. *The March on Paris and the Battle of the Marne, 1914*. London: E. Arnold, 1920.

———. *Wanterjahre, Kriege, Gestalten*. Berlin: R. Eisenschmidt, 1929.

Kuhl, Hermann von. *Der Weltkrieg 1914–1918 : Dem deutschen Volke dargestellt*. 2 vols. Berlin: Vaterländischer Verlag Weller, 1930.

See also FRONTIERS, BATTLE OF THE; MARNE, FIRST BATTLE OF

Kolchak, Aleksandr Vasilevich (1874–1920)

Russian admiral, born on 16 November 1874 at St. Petersburg. Kolchak commanded a destroyer in the Russo-Japanese War and took part in two polar expeditions. On the outbreak of war in 1914 he was chief of operations of the Baltic Fleet. Ambitious and aggressive, he proved to be one of Russia's ablest naval commanders. During his Baltic years, apart from staff appointments, he also commanded a destroyer flotilla in the Windau operation of November 1915, resulting in the withdrawal of German picket lines further south, away from Russian bases. Promoted to rear admiral on 27 April 1916, he was given command of the Baltic Fleet's Destroyer Division. In June of 1916 he took part in the action in the Gulf of Norrkoping against a German convoy bound from Sweden. Although Kolchak's destroyers sank an auxiliary cruiser and a number of ships, his poor tactics and refusal to comply with his superiors' plan to cut off the enemy's retreat into Swedish territorial waters meant that a large-scale victory was denied Russia. Nevertheless, he was promoted to vice admiral and, on 17 July 1916, to commander of the Black Sea Fleet.

Kolchak's aggressive tactics soon bore fruit, and by the end of the year he had established Russia's dominance of the Black Sea through large-scale mining operations, continual operations against Turkish coastal shipping, and the bombardment of coastal installations. Following the March Revolution, Kolchak intensified operations to quell revolutionary ardor among the sailors; he was forced by them to resign, however, on 19 June 1917. Sent by the provisional government to Washington to discuss naval cooperation, his return coincided with the Bolshevik Revolution.

Kolchak was determined to keep Russia in the war against Germany and took nominal command of White forces in Siberia. His spring 1919 advance westward soon collapsed. In early 1920 Kolchak fell into Bolshevik hands at Irkutsk and was shot outside the city on 7 February 1920.

Andrzej Suchcitz

References

Lincoln, W. Bruce. *Passage through Armageddon: The Russians in War and Revolution*. New York: Simon and Schuster, 1986.

———. *Red Victory: A History of the Russian Civil War*. New York: Simon and Schuster, 1989.

See also RUSSIA, CIVIL WAR IN; RUSSIA, HOME FRONT AND REVOLUTIONS OF 1917

Königsberg (SMS)

SMS *Königsberg*, completed in 1907, was a German light cruiser of 3,814 tons, protected by a thin armored deck and armed with ten 4.1-inch guns and two underwater torpedo tubes. Her small size and shallow draft of seventeen feet made her ideal for employment on colonial station, where her modest top speed of twenty-three knots represented no great handicap.

In August of 1914 *Königsberg* was the station ship at Dar-es-Salaam in German East Africa. Under Commander Max Loof, she enjoyed modest success as a commerce raider in the Indian Ocean. On 6 August she captured *The City of Winchester,* the first British merchant ship taken in the war, and on 20 September she sank the small British cruiser *Pegasus* and the picket ship *Helmut* at Zanzibar. Because the *Königsberg* had machinery problems, in October Loof took her to the remote Rufiji River delta, but she was discovered and blockaded in that wilderness by the cruiser HMS *Chatham,* soon joined by additional warships. The larger British vessels with their deeper drafts were unable to get upriver and within range of the *Königsberg*. The stalemate lasted until the next spring, at which time the British brought up reinforcements while Loof shifted position and camouflaged his ship by lashing tree trunks to her masts.

The British Admiralty finally dispatched to the theater two shallow-draft monitors purchased at the outbreak of the war from Brazil, HMS *Mersey* and *Severn*. Each armed with two 6-inch guns, the craft were diverted from the Gallipoli campaign. They left Malta in April and reached Mafia Island on 3 June. Over the next month, the British made extensive preparations, including building an airfield ashore for spotter planes. On 6 July the two monitors pushed up the Rufiji. With three aircraft correcting their shooting by wireless, *Mersey* and *Severn* damaged the German cruiser, although both were hit in return. Forced to withdraw, the monitors renewed the action five days later. Loof, with inadequate means of directing his gunfire, scuttled his ship after fighting for five hours. The crews of the monitors and of the airplanes split £1,920 in naval prize money, the first distributed since the Crimean War.

From the wreckage of the *Königsberg* the enterprising Germans salvaged her ten 4.1-inch artillery pieces. Fitted with wheels and mountings at Dar-es-Salaam and served in part by the ship's sailors, these guns proved of great value to forces commanded by General Paul von Lettow-Vorbeck in German East Africa. Four of the pieces were still in the field as late as the fall of 1917. Before she had been scuttled, the *Königsberg* had tied down, by one estimate, twenty-seven British ships. In recognition of the fact that the *Königsberg* had caused the Allies trouble out of all proportion to her actual military prowess, Loof was promoted to captain and decorated with the Iron Cross, First Class. Lesser medals were liberally bestowed on his crew.

Malcolm Muir, Jr.

References

Conway's All the World's Fighting Ships 1906–1921. Annapolis, Md.: Naval Institute Press, 1985.

Farwell, Byron. *The Great War In Africa (1914–1918)*. New York: Norton, 1986.

Hoyt, Edwin P. *The Germans Who Never Lost: The Story of the Königsberg*. New York: Funk and Wagnalls, 1968.

Miller, Charles. *Battle for the Bundu: The First World War in East Africa*. London: Purnell, 1974.

Korfanty, Wojciech (1873–1939)

Polish nationalist politician, born at Sadzawka near Katowice on 20 April 1873. Korfanty was elected to the German Reichstag in 1903. He initially supported the notion that Poles should side with Germany as the best way to secure Poland's independence, but by the end of 1914 Korfanty had become disenchanted with that approach. A member of the executive committee of the League for Independence, he was a member of the Polish Circle (Polish parliamentary grouping) in the German Reichstag from 1916. In October of 1918 Korfanty made a powerful speech in the Reichstag demanding the unification of all Polish lands, including those annexed by Prussia: Pomerania, Danzig, Wielkopolska (Greater Poland), and Silesia. After the war Korfanty played a key role in the Greater Poland and Silesian Risings against German rule. He was later a deputy in the Polish Parliament, where he joined the Christian Democratic party. He died at Warsaw on 17 August 1939.

Andrzej Suchcitz

References

Krzywobłocka, Bozena. *Chadecja, 1918–1937*. Warsaw: Ksiazka i Wiedza, 1974.
Orzechowski, Marian. "Wojciech Korfanty." In *Polski Słownik Biograficzny*. Vol. 60. Warsaw: Polska Akademia Nauk, 1968.

Kornilov, Lavr Georgievich (1870–1918)

Russian general. Born 30 August 1870 at Ust Kamenogorsk in eastern Siberia of Mongol ancestry, he was the son of a retired Cossack junior officer. After graduating from the General Staff Academy, Kornilov gained a reputation for personal courage and, at times, reckless bravery, the stuff from which heroic legends are molded. During service on the Afghan frontier he led a daring reconnaissance mission through enemy lines. During the Russo-Japanese War he again demonstrated his bravery by leading the rear-guard action as the Russian army retreated from the Mukden front. Between 1907 and 1911 he was a Russian military attaché in China.

The outbreak of the war in 1914 saw General Kornilov in command of 48th Division in General Radko Dmitriev's Third Army. During the Carpathian Offensive against the Austrians in the autumn of 1914, Kornilov's units were the only ones to actually descend into the Hungarian plain. Before the German counterattack of the following spring, while directing the rear-guard action, Kornilov was taken prisoner and spent nearly a year in an Austrian prison camp. In early 1916, disguised in an Austrian uniform, he made a daring escape to Romania. News of the event made Kornilov a national hero. Upon his arrival back at Russian lines he was given command of XXV Corps, stationed on the Transylvanian (Romanian) border. While in that post, he worked vigorously to restore the fighting capacity and spirit of his own units, which, along with the remainder of the Russian army, had become demoralized after the military defeats of the preceding year. Shortly thereafter, Kornilov participated with distinction in the Brusilov Offensive in the summer of 1916.

In early 1917, in the wake of the riots in Petrograd, the new provisional government saw the need to restore order in the streets. For this task they called General Kornilov from the front and appointed him commander of the Petrograd Military District. He was chosen because of his popularity and his reputation as a strict disciplinarian. On 15 March the czar abdicated. On the 21st, leading a group of rabble from a local soviet, Kornilov arrived at the Palace at Tsarskoe Selo, where he placed the empress and her children under arrest "for their own protection." On the following day the czar arrived from headquarters at Mogilev, under armed escort, to join his family. They would not see liberty again. In April General Kornilov resigned his post in disgust because he had no authority over his troops, who now insisted that every order be countersigned by a member of the Petrograd Soviet.

General Kornilov was a major participant in the vicissitudes of the provisional government. In July, after a half-hearted offensive against the Austrians, the entire Russian southwest front collapsed. Premier Aleksandr Kerensky succumbed to the advice of Minister of War B.V. Savankov and appointed Kornilov commander of that sector. On 18 July he was made commander in chief of the Russian army, in order to restore discipline. True to his word, Kornilov immediately presented a plan to the provisional government aimed at bringing order to the army. Its centerpiece was the reimposition of the death penalty. After a heated debate, the plan was accepted. By August, however, there was a split within the Petrograd leadership. Kerensky and most of the members of the Soviet began to perceive Kornilov as a threat to the revolution from the right. Surrounded by his fierce-looking Caucasian Horse Guard and making provocative speeches, it is little wonder that the general was seen as a potential

Bonaparte. He was definitely the champion of the antirevolutionary generals on the staff *(stavka)*. In reality, Kornilov was nothing more than a simple soldier with no understanding of politics.

In September of 1917 another crisis occurred when the Germans took Riga, leaving Petrograd exposed. On the 6th, amid rumors of Bolshevik demonstrations, Savinkov asked Kornilov to dispatch a cavalry corps to defend the capital. Troops under the command of General Krimov began to entrain. Among the Petrograd revolutionary leadership there was something akin to panic at the thought of a Kornilov dictatorship. The Bolshevik leader Leon Trotsky was charged with the defense of the city and was authorized to arm the Red Guard. The Kornilov danger, however, was exaggerated. Workers and Bolshevik propagandists were sent to stop the military trains well before they reached the capital. After lengthy, and at times heated, debates, the hungry and demoralized troops melted away. General Krimov was arrested and shot himself. Kornilov, who had remained at headquarters at Mogilev, surrendered to the authorities and was jailed at Bykov. The threat of a counterrevolution was past. The end of the provisional government was near, and Russia was in a process of disintegration.

Immediately after the Bolshevik takeover but before they could extend their power, many incarcerated czarist officers were set free. The liberated Kornilov made his way to the Don River area, where he took part in the organization of an anti-Bolshevik volunteer army. He hoped to see the Bolsheviks overthrown and Russia reenter the war. On 13 April 1918, in a skirmish at Ekaterinodor, northeast of the Black Sea, he was killed by an artillery shell.

John W. Bohon

References

Florinsky, Michael. *Russia, A History and Interpretation.* New York: Macmillan, 1958.

Gurko, General Basil. *Features and Figures of the Past.* Stanford, 1939.

———. *Russia 1914–1917, Memories and Impressions of War and Revolution.* New York: Macmillan, 1919.

Kerensky, Aleksandr F. *The Prelude to Bolshevism, The Kornilov Rebellion.* London: T. Fisher, 1919.

See also KERENSKY, ALEKSANDR; RUSSIA, CIVIL WAR IN; RUSSIA, HOME FRONT AND REVOLUTIONS OF 1917

K

Kövess von Kövessháza, Baron Hermann (1854–1924)

Austro-Hungarian field marshal, born in Temesvár (Timişoara), now in Romania, on 30 March 1854. Kövess had an undistinguished early career in the Austro-Hungarian army and was actually slated for retirement in 1914 when World War I began. He commanded the Austro-Hungarian Third Army in the Central Powers' 1915 offensive against Serbia and captured Belgrade on 9 October. His forces went on to occupy Montenegro and northern Albania. In May of 1916 he was involved in the Asiago offensive on the Italian Trentino front. The attack achieved only limited success and was eventually canceled because of the Brusilov breakthrough in Galicia, where Kövess spent the next two years.

With the collapse of Bulgaria in 1918 Kövess was made commander of all Austro-Hungarian troops in the Balkans, but he was unable to stop the advance of the Allies. In the final days of the war he became the last commander in chief of the dissolving Austro-Hungarian army. Kövess was an unassuming personality, and his successes came more from unflappable persistence than brilliant leadership. A quiet retirement ended with his death in Vienna on 22 September 1924.

Charles H. Bogart

References

Rothenburg, Gunther. *The Army of Francis Joseph.* West Lafayette, Ind.: Purdue University Press, 1976.

Steinitz, Eduard. "Hermann Baron Kövess von Kövessháza." In *Neue Österreichische Biographie 1815–1918.* Vol. 2, 138–46. Vienna: Almathea-Verlag, 1925.

See also BALKAN FRONT, 1915; TRENTINO OFFENSIVE

Krafft von Dellmensingen, Konrad (1862–1953)

Bavarian general, born at Laufen, Upper Bavaria, on 24 November 1862. His father, a public notary, was of noble stock; both his mother and future wife came from bourgeois families. His career was enhanced by a high level of intelligence and energy. Krafft joined a Bavarian artillery regiment in 1881 and later attended the Munich War Academy.

Having served for many years in various important staff positions and as a major general since 1912, in August of 1914 Krafft was appointed chief of staff to Crown Prince Rupprecht of Bavaria, the commander of the Sixth Army. Initially deployed in Lorraine, that army was subsequently moved to northern France, where it participated in the futile German fall offensive. In May of 1915 Krafft was promoted to lieutenant general and sent to the Tyrol as the commander of the newly formed German division of mountain troops, the *Alpenkorps*. Intended initially as a standby reserve in case of an invasion of Tyrol, the unit was moved to the Balkans in October to participate in the invasion of Serbia. The following spring the *Alpenkorps* was sent to the Western Front; later in September it participated in the campaign against Romania.

Decorated with both the Prussian *Pour le Mérite* medal and its oak leaf cluster for his accomplishments, in March of 1917 Krafft was reassigned to the Western Front as chief of staff of "Army Group Duke Albrecht." Six months later, he accompanied General Otto von Below to the Isonzo region for a major strike at the Italians at Caporetto. When Below was called back to the Western Front (in January of 1918) to assume command of the new Seventeenth Army, Krafft once again served as his chief of staff and thus played a major role in the great German spring offensive.

Promoted to corps commander, Krafft spent the last six months of the war in the northern sections of the Western Front. He retired in December of 1918 and devoted himself to historical work. He died on 22 February 1953 at Seeshaupt, Upper Bavaria.

Ulrich Trumpener

References

Krafft von Dellmensingen, Konrad. *Der Durchbruch am Isonozo*. 2 vols. Oldenburg & Berlin: Stalling, 1926.
———. *Der Durchbruch: Studie an Hand der Vorgange des Weltkrieges 1914–1918*. Hamburg: Hanseatische Verlagsanstalt, 1937.
———. *Kritischer Streifzug durch die Studien des Generalleutnants a.D. Wilhelm Groener: Das Oberkommando in den Reichs landen im Sommer 1914*. Munich: Max Schick, 1931.
———. *Personal Papers (Nachlass)*. W-10, Nrs. 50642–51. Bundesarchiv-Militarzwischenarchiv Potsdam.
Moller, Hanns. *Geschichte der Ritter des Ordens "pour le merite" im Weltkrieg*. 2 vols. Berlin: Bernard & Graefe, 1935.

Kreuznach Conference, 23 April 1917

A high-level German conference held 23 April 1917 at temporary imperial headquarters in Bad Kreuznach. It was held in response to repeated demands by the high command (OHL) that, in view of recent political developments in Russia, Germany's war aims be defined more clearly. Presided over by the kaiser, the meeting was attended by Imperial Chancellor Theobald von Bethmann Hollweg, head of the foreign office Arthur Zimmermann, and chief political adviser to the German governor-general in Belgium, Oskar Baron von der Lancken. Representing the military were chief of the general staff Field Marshal Paul von Hindenburg, first quartermaster general General Erich Ludendorff, and chief of naval staff Admiral Henning von Holtzendorff.

While Bethmann Hollweg had always had serious misgivings about the territorial gains sought by Ludendorff and other right-wing elements of German society, he did not openly challenge the military and their annexationist demands during the meeting. He eventually signed the protocol recording the decisions made at the conference (henceforth known as the Kreuznach Program). At the same time, though, the chancellor declared and filed notes to the effect that the war-aims program adopted at Kreuznach could be implemented only if Germany won the war decisively, and that he had no intention of prolonging the war for the sake of getting those demands accepted by Germany's enemies.

The Kreuznach Program stipulated that Germany should acquire Lithuania and Courland as well as certain parts of Russian Poland. To make these losses more palatable to the Russians, the Hapsburg Monarchy should cede eastern Galicia to Russia and receive compensation for that sacrifice in various parts of southeastern Europe. As for the rump of Russian Poland, it was to form a satellite state closely linked to Germany. In the west, Belgium, likewise, was to come under close German control; in addition, it was to cede its coastal region with Brugge and the Liége area outright to Germany. France was expected to surrender the ore-rich Longwy-Briey region as well as certain other border districts. A number of other changes—in the Balkans, Asia Minor, Africa, and elsewhere overseas—were desirable as well, but specific decisions in these areas were to be postponed until all relevant government agencies had been consulted.

Reflecting demands that had been articulated by various German individuals or pressure groups in previous years, the Kreuznach Program is seen by some historians as the typical manifestation of a broadly based German imperialism. Other historians insist that it was primarily a reflection of what the German military wanted; that Germany's political leaders, from Bethmann Hollweg on down, were far more moderate in their outlook—and more realistic as well. Suffice it to add that the chancellor, under growing pressure from both the military and certain other groups, resigned less than three months after the Kreuznach Conference.

Ulrich Trumpener

References

Fischer, Fritz. *Griff nach der Weltmacht: Die Kriegszielpolitik des kaiserlichen Deutschland 1914/18.* Düsseldorf: Droste, 1961.
———. *Welmacht oder Niedergang: Deutschland im ersten Weltkrieg.* 2nd rev. ed. Frankfurt: Europäische Verlagsanstalt, 1966.
Gatzke, Hans W. *Germany's Drive to the West (Drang nach Westen): A Study of Germany's Western War Aims during the First World War.* Baltimore: Johns Hopkins Press, 1950.
Kitchen, Martin. *The Silent Dictatorship: The Politics of the German High Command under Hindenburg and Ludendorff, 1916–1918.* London: Croom Helm, 1976.
Ritter, Gerhard. *Staatskunst und Kriegshandwerk: Das Problem des "Militarismus" in Deutschland.* Vol. 3. Munich: Oldenbourg, 1964.

See also BETHMANN HOLLWEG, THEOBALD VON; LUDENDORFF, ERICH

Krobatin, Alexander Freiherr von (1849–1933)

Austro-Hungarian general and minister of war, born on 12 September 1849 in Olmütz (Olomouc) in what is now the Czech Republic. Krobatin was a specialist in the construction and use of artillery. He became Austro-Hungarian minister of war in December of 1912. Before the war he urged increases in military spending and generally supported Franz Conrad von Hötzendorf's urgings for war against Serbia and Italy at the first favorable moment.

After the outbreak of hostilities, his job became that of supplying the field army as best the economy would allow, particularly in attempting to increase its stocks of artillery. He remained minister of war until 1917, when Emperor Karl transferred him to active duty as commander of the Tenth Army on the Italian front. His troops forced the Italian Fourth Army to retreat in the Battle of Caporetto in the fall, but a year later they were routed at Vittorio Veneto. He lived on in relative obscurity until his death in Vienna on 27 December 1933.

Charles H. Bogart

References

Dedijer, Vladimir. *The Road to Sarajevo.* New York: Simon and Schuster, 1966.
Kiszling, Rudolf. "Alexander Freiherr von Krobatin (1849–1933)." *Neue Österreichische Biographie ab 1815.* Vol. 17, 202–6. Vienna: Almathea-Verlag, 1968.

See also CAPORETTO; VITTORIO VENETO CAMPAIGN

Kucharzewski, Jan (1876–1952)

Polish historian and politician, born at Wysoko Mazowieckie on 27 May 1876. Kucharzewski was active in the Polish National Democratic Movement. During the first part of the war, he worked in Switzerland for Poland's independence by publishing articles, pamphlets, and books, mainly in French. The 1916 establishment by the Central Powers of a Polish state (albeit limited in size and restricted in sovereignty) led Kucharzewski to return to Poland.

From December of 1917 to February of 1918 Kucharzewski was premier of the Kingdom of Poland. He attempted to create a Polish army on the Eastern Front and to secure

Polish representation at negotiations between the Germans and the Russians at Brest-Litovsk. He failed on both counts. The Brest-Litovsk Treaty was injurious to Polish interests, and Kucharzewski resigned with the whole of his government. After the war he left politics to return to academic interests. In 1925, he was named to the International Court of Arbitration at The Hague. Kucharzewski died in New York City on 4 July 1952.

Andrzej Suchcitz

References

Kucharzewski, Jan. *The Origins of Modern Russia*. New York: Polish Institute of Arts and Sciences in America, 1948.
Maternicki, Jerzy. "Jan Kucharzewski." In *Polski Sownik Biograficzny*. Vol. 68. Warsaw: Polska Akademia Nauk, 1971.

See also BREST-LITOVSK, TREATY OF

Kühlmann, Richard von (1873–1948)

German state secretary for foreign affairs, born on 3 May 1873 in Constantinople. Kühlmann was a career diplomat who served in a number of diplomatic posts until called back to Berlin to be German state secretary for foreign affairs from the summer of 1917 to July of 1918. Kühlmann believed a total German victory in World War I was unattainable, and that the war should, therefore, be ended through flexible diplomacy before it was too late. He hoped that Germany's strong battlefield position would allow it to retain some of its gains at the close of hostilities, particularly in Central and Eastern Europe.

Kühlmann headed the German delegations to both the Brest-Litovsk and Bucharest peace conferences and worked closely with his Austro-Hungarian counterpart, Ottokar Czernin, for peace conditions that at least to the general public would appear moderate. The rigid annexationism of the German military led by Erich Ludendorff undermined what little bargaining room he had with the Entente. Ludendorff forced him from office in July of 1918. He died on 6 February 1948 in Ohlstadt bei Murnau, Germany.

Gary W. Shanafelt

References

Fischer, Fritz. *Germany's Aims in the First World War*. New York: Norton, 1967.
Kühlmann, Richard von. *Erinnerungen*. Heidelberg: L. Schneider, 1948.

See also BUCHAREST, TREATY OF; CZERNIN, OTTOKAR

Kun, Béla (1886–1939)

Hungarian revolutionary, founder of the Hungarian Communist party, and leader of the Hungarian Soviet Republic of 1919. Born into a Jewish family in the mixed ethnic area of Transylvania in February of 1886, Béla Kun was brought up in an essentially secular and Magyar fashion. His first political beliefs appear to have focused on the tradition of Hungarian nationalism. Kun dropped out of law school and became a journalist and then a trade-union official.

With the outbreak of the First World War, Kun joined the Austro-Hungarian army and fought for fifteen months on the Eastern Front. Captured by the Russians during the 1916 Brusilov Offensive, he became a prisoner of war at Tomsk. Rudolf T. Tökés argues that it was at this point that Kun began his final transformation into a full-fledged Bolshevik revolutionary, and it does seem that Kun's study of Marxism while he was a prisoner of war, along with the impact of the Russian revolutions, made him into a convinced revolutionary.

Kun understood that four years of war had transformed the social and economic conditions of most European countries. The collapse of the Hapsburg Monarchy once again gave bourgeois nationalists in Hungary the chance to create their own national government, and on 16 November 1918 a left-of-center coalition under Count Mihály Károlyi declared a Peoples' Republic. But the loss of Hungarian lands resulting from the 13 November armistice, rising inflation and unemployment, the nationalities question, starvation in the cities, and the threat from the Romanian army, all meant that Károlyi's government was short-lived. The Vyx ultimatum from the Romanians finally broke the back of the Károlyi regime. Unlike Károlyi, Kun and the new Communist party of Hungary (formed in November of 1918) were willing to fight the Romanians, and, as a result, Kun took over the government at the head of a socialist-communist coalition in March of 1919.

Kun sought to combine elements of both nationalism and Bolshevism to create a two-part transformation of Hungary, and thus he was very much a product of his time. He failed, however, to grasp the subtleties of Lenin's seizure and consolidation of power in Russia; instead, Kun tried to force a too-rapid transformation of Hungary's already weakened economy. Of necessity, such action meant that Kun had to use the techniques of the Red Terror. Worse still for the Hungarian communists, their newly formed Red Army proved to be no match for the invading Romanians. June of 1919 also saw the arrival in Hungary of French interventionist forces, which aided Admiral Miklós Horthy's White Army. Further Romanian victories gave Kun no option, and on 1 August 1919 he resigned the presidency and fled the country, leaving many of his erstwhile comrades to fall victim to the White Terror.

Kun later became active during the Russian Civil War, where he was personally responsible for ordering the murder of twenty thousand White prisoners of war in the Crimea, along with thousands of Nestor Makhno's anarchists. These murders did nothing to reconstruct Kun's reputation after the failures of his Hungarian Red Army. Yet Kun was a survivor, and by attaching himself to powerful figures in the Soviet hierarchy he was able to continue his revolutionary career. But practical success eluded him again, when he bungled a revolutionary attempt in Prussian Saxony in March of 1921. Once again, Kun escaped to carve a new career for himself, this time as a party bureaucrat in the Soviet Union. In June of 1937 he was arrested by the Russian secret police (NKVD), tortured over a span of six months, and finally executed on 10 November 1939.

Stephen M. Cullen

References

Szilassy, Sándor. *Revolutionary Hungary, 1918–1921.* Astor Park, Fla.: Danubian, 1971.

Tökés, Rudolf T. *Béla Kun and the Hungarian Soviet Republic.* New York: Praeger, 1967.

Völgyes, Iván, ed. *Hungary in Revolution, 1918–19.* Lincoln: University of Nebraska Press, 1971.

See also HUNGARY, REVOLUTION IN; KÁROLYI, MIHÁLY

Kuropatkin, Aleksei (1848–1925)

Russian general and commander of the Northern Army Group, born on 29 March 1848 at Pskov. The son of a retired army officer, Kuropatkin graduated from the Pavlovsky Military School in 1866 and earned a favorable military reputation in campaigns during the conquest of Turkestan (1866–83). He served in staff positions during the Russo-Turkish War (1877–78), was promoted to major general in 1882 at the age of thirty-four, and was Russia's minister of war from 1898 to 1903. At the outbreak of the Russo-Japanese War, Kuropatkin was appointed commander of the Manchurian army, and by mid-October 1904 he was placed in charge of all Russian forces in the Far East. Military abilities, which had served him well in Central Asia, were insufficient to deal with the far more complicated problems in the Far East. Kuropatkin suffered repeated defeats, and in March of 1905 he was relieved of his post after his defeat in the Battle of Mukden.

The First World War gave Kuropatkin another chance to prove himself. In late 1915 he was given command of the Grenadiers Corps, even though the czar himself expressed reservations about the appointment. In one misadventure Kuropatkin initiated a nighttime attack with the aid of searchlights, intended to dazzle and confuse the Germans. Instead, the lights silhouetted his own men, eight thousand of whom were killed. Despite such mistakes in military judgment, Kuropatkin was picked in February of 1916 to head up Russia's Northern Army Group.

Pessimistic and indecisive, Kuropatkin failed to come to the aid of General A.E. Evert in the Lake Naroch (Narocz) Offensive, the purpose of which was to relieve pressure on the French at Verdun. This mismanaged campaign, begun as the spring thaw converted the battlefield into a quagmire, was a complete fiasco. Russian casualties exceeded 100,000. Kuropatkin also failed to support the Brusilov Offensive, resigned in July of 1916, and was again posted to Turkestan. In April of 1917 he was arrested but later released by the provisional government. Refusing to emigrate, Kuropatkin lived the remainder of his life as a schoolteacher. He died on 16 January 1925.

William L. Mathes

References

Kuropatkin, Aleksei Nikolaevich. *Dnevnik A.N. Kurupatkina.* Nizhnii Novgored: Nizhpoligraf, 1923.

———. *The Russian Army and the Japanese War.* 2 vols. London: J. Murray, 1909.

Stone, Norman. *The Eastern Front, 1914–1917*. New York: Charles Scribner's Sons, 1975.

See also <small>NAROCH, LAKE, BATTLE OF</small>

L

Lacaze, Marie Jean Lucien (1860–1955)

French vice admiral and minister of marine, October 1915 to August 1917. Born at Pierrefonds (Oise) on 22 June 1860, Lacaze entered the Ecole Navale in 1877 and served as chef du cabinet to Minister of Marine Théophile Delcassé from 1911 to 1913. He assumed the same office himself near the end of the Dardanelles campaign and apparently would have been prepared to support a new naval attempt to force the Straits.

The Salonika campaign added greatly to his responsibilities, and he was forced to devote increasing attention to the submarine war. The French made desperate efforts to increase the number of small craft, ordering a dozen destroyers from Japanese yards and purchasing large numbers of trawlers from Allied and neutral countries. They also reorganized the system of patrols. The painful losses from submarines continued, however, and Lacaze faced mounting criticism in parliament, where the Chamber of Deputies forced the creation of a special directorate for antisubmarine warfare (*Direction générale de la guerre sous-marine*).

Lacaze eventually resigned after Premier Alexandre Ribot accepted the demand for a commission with inquisitorial powers, which Lacaze regarded as prejudicial to discipline. He was subsequently préfet maritime of Toulon, commanded the French patrols of the Western Mediterranean, and represented the French navy in the League of Nations. Lacaze retired from active service in June of 1922. He died in Paris on 23 March 1955.

Paul G. Halpern

References

Halpern, Paul G. *The Naval War in the Mediterranean, 1914–1918* Annapolis, Md.: Naval Institute Press, 1987.

Jolly, Jean, ed. *Dictionnaire des parlementaires français*. Vol. 6. Paris: Presses Universitaires de France, 1970.

Salaun, Vice-Amiral. *La Marine française*. Paris: Les Editions de France, 1934.

Taillemite, Etienne. *Dictionnaire des marins français*. Paris: Editions Maritimes et d'Outre-Mer, 1982.

See also FRANCE, NAVY; SALONIKA CAMPAIGN

Lake, Sir Percival (1855–1940)

British general and commander in Mesopotamia from 1916 to 1917, Lake was born in Tenby, Wales, on 29 June 1855. He entered the army in 1873 and served his first active duty in the Second Afghan War (1878–79). He graduated with honors from the staff college and served in the Intelligence Department of the war office, with the British forces in India, and with the Canadian militia. From 1908 to 1910 he was chief military advisor to the Canadian government.

In 1915 Lake was sent to Mesopotamia to guard British interests in the oil fields. On 24 January 1916 he replaced General Sir John Nixon as commander in chief in Mesopotamia and was directed to make a second attempt to relieve General Charles Townshend and 13,000 British troops besieged in the fortress of Kut.

Although Lake had 63,000 troops, only 14,000 men and forty-six guns could be prepared. An additional 11,000 men and 28 guns were available as reinforcements. Opposing Turkish forces were well dug in and had roughly equivalent manpower (10,000 troops plus reserves). This and two successive attempts to relieve Kut failed, and Townshend was forced to surrender on 29 April 1916. In all, the relief operations claimed 23,000 British casualties, in addition to the 13,000 lost in Kut. Turkish casualties were approximately 10,000.

Lake returned to England to testify before the Mesopotamia Commission and was subsequently posted to the Ministry of Munitions in May of 1917. He retired in November of 1919 and moved to Victoria, British Columbia, where he died on 17 November 1940.

Meredith Kulp

References

Barker, A.J. *The Bastard War. The Mesopotamian Campaign of 1914–1918.* New York: Dial, 1967.

Wickham-Legg, L.G., ed. *The Dictionary of National Biography: 1931–1940.* London: Oxford University Press, 1985.

Lake Naroch, Battle of, March 1916

See NAROCH, LAKE, BATTLE OF

Langle de Cary, Fernand de (1849–1927)

French general and army commander, born on 4 July 1849 at Lorient. Langle de Cary served with distinction in the Franco-Prussian War (1870–71). Thereafter, he served at several garrisons in France while advancing through the military bureaucracy. In 1912 he was appointed to the Supreme War Council and retired from the army in July of 1914.

In August of 1914 Langle de Cary was recalled to active duty to command the Fourth Army. Under Plan XVII the Fourth Army was to undertake the principal French offensive action. On 22 August the Fourth Army, supported by the Third Army, attacked into the forests of the Luxembourg Ardennes; Langle de Cary's mission was to take Neufchâteau.

French commander in chief General Joseph Joffre expected these two armies to lop off the arm of the German right wing as it made its swing through Belgium. Joffre's confidence was predicated upon a profound misconception that Langle de Cary's army greatly outnumbered the German Fourth Army in the Ardennes. Such was not the case, as the next three days demonstrated. German artillery, superior manpower, and well-entrenched guns stopped Langle de Cary's advance. In particular, the Colonial Corps, hope-lessly outnumbered and completely surrounded, was badly mauled at Rossignol, south of Neufchâteau. On 24 August Langle de Cary ordered the retreat of his army behind the protection of the Meuse River.

For the next two weeks the Fourth Army, together with the Fifth and Third armies, retreated while fighting a savage holding action against the German advance. On the morning of 5 September Langle de Cary received orders to stop the retreat, stand his ground, and prepare to resume the offensive. French forces, stretched from the outskirts of Paris to Verdun, were now in position to fight the Battle of the Marne.

In the Marne fighting Langle de Cary's Fourth Army took the full brunt of Duke Albrecht of Württemberg's Fourth Army attack. On neither flank was Langle de Cary's army in close contact with its neighbor. On its left the twelve-mile Gap of Mailly separated Langle de Cary from General Ferdinand Foch's Ninth Army; on its right the Gap of Revigny lay between it and General Sarrail's Third Army. Langle de Cary's principal concern was to prevent German exploitation of either gap. For three days Langle de Cary's army held off the Germans on his left flank. The decisive event was the arrival of the 21st Corps from Lorraine, which put an end to the possibility that the Gap of Mailly would be breached.

On the morning of 11 September the German armies began to retreat along the front. Langle de Cary had accomplished his mission of holding the Germans at bay, while farther to the west the French Fifth and Sixth armies, as well as the British Expeditionary Force, inflicted the decisive blows to the German armies.

Langle de Cary continued to command the Fourth Army on the stalemated Western Front until December of 1915. He was then appointed commander of France's Center Army Group. Unfortunately, the German attack against Verdun in early 1916 revealed that the French fortresses were inadequately prepared. Langle de Cary was removed from the Western Front in March of 1916 and sent on an insignificant inspection tour of North Africa. He was removed from the army entirely in 1917 and died at Pont-Scorff on 19 February 1927.

Jan Karl Tanenbaum

References

Ministère de la Guerre, Etat-Major de l'Armée, Service Historique. *Les Armées françaises dans la grande guerre*. Tome 1, Vols. 1–3. Paris: Imprimerie Nationale, 1923–39.

Tuchman, Barbara. *The Guns of August*. New York: Dell, 1962.

Tyng, Sewell. *The Campaign of the Marne, 1914*. London: Oxford University Press, 1935.

See also FRONTIERS, BATTLE OF THE; MARNE, FIRST BATTLE OF; VERDUN, BATTLE OF

Lanrezac, Charles Louis Marie (1852–1925)

French general, born on 31 July 1852 at Pointe-à-Pitre, Guadeloupe. Lanrezac left St. Cyr in 1870 to fight in the Franco-Prussian War. Promoted to colonel in 1902, he was made professor at the French War College and became a brigadier general in 1906. In the spring of 1914, Lanrezac, a protegé of General Joseph Joffre, was appointed commander of the French Fifth Army. The Fifth Army's purpose, as designated by the high command's Plan XVII, was to face northeast and prepare to support the Third and Fourth armies' offensive into the Ardennes. Lanrezac warned on several occasions that Plan XVII had a major shortcoming: It left much of the French-Belgian border uncovered. If the Germans made a wide move west of the Meuse and then struck southward across the open border while French armies were moving into the Ardennes and Lorraine, the French army could be enveloped.

On 18 August, two weeks after the start of the war, the French High Command realized that German troops were indeed crossing the Meuse. It therefore ordered Lanrezac to move a portion of his army northwest to the Sambre River to hold the Germans, while the remainder of his troops would support the main French offensive to the northeast through the Ardennes. Unfortunately, that was not adequate. When Joffre ordered the French offensive to begin on 20 August, Lanrezac discovered that there were thirty German divisions opposite his fifteen French. French forces were overwhelmed at Charleroi on 23 August, and the Third and Fourth armies fared no better in the Ardennes. Joffre ordered a retreat on 24 August.

In order to relieve pressure on the BEF, Joffre ordered Lanrezac to counterattack northwest against von Kluck's First Army; he reluc-

tantly obeyed. The French counterattack at Guise had strategic repercussions; it caused the Germans to abandon their plan for a wide sweep west of Paris. After taking heavy losses and threatened by envelopment, Lanrezac again retreated in order to disengage the Fifth Army and bring it into line with the other retreating French armies. In early September the Fifth Army successfully crossed the Marne out of reach of the German enveloping move. Lanrezac never participated in the Battle of the Marne; on 5 September Joffre replaced him as army commander with the more aggressive General Louis Franchet d'Esperey, victor at Guise. Joffre claimed that Lanrezac was exhausted, but more important he was displeased with Lanrezac's reluctance to counterattack and work effectively with the British. He also considered him a defeatist and resented Lanrezac's frequent warnings that Plan XVII had been flawed.

In 1917 the Painlevé government offered Lanrezac another military post, but he refused. In 1920 Lanrezac published a very critical account of Joffre's conduct as commanding general. In 1924 Pétain decorated Lanrezac for his wartime service, seeming to vindicate him. Lanrezac died in Paris on 18 January 1925.

Jan Karl Tanenbaum

References
Lanrezac, Charles L.M. *Le Plan de Campaigne française et le premier mois de la guerre*. Paris, 1920.

Ministère de la Guerre, Etat-Major de l'Armée, Service Historique. *Les Armées françaises dans la grande guerre*. Tome 1, Vols. 1–2. Paris: Imprimerie Nationale, 1923–39.

Tuchman, Barbara. *The Guns of August*. New York: Dell, 1962.

See also FRENCH WAR PLAN XVII; FRONTIERS, BATTLE OF THE

Latin America, Role in the War

World War I had a dramatic impact on Latin America. Brazil, British Guiana, Costa Rica, Cuba, French Guiana, Guatemala, Honduras, Nicaragua, and Panama declared war and, while their combat troops played no significant role in Europe, raw materials from the region were critical to the Allied war effort. In turn, the war's economic dislocations profoundly influenced Latin American development, most significantly by replacing European influence with United States hegemony. Anglo-American economic coercion also fueled the growth of Latin American nationalism.

Capitalist development had accelerated rapidly in Latin America since the 1880s. The process, which derived from agrarian foundations, resulted in urban industrialization. Railroads were built to carry goods such as Argentine wheat, Brazilian coffee, Chilean copper, and Mexican silver from farms and mines in the interior to coastal cities for export. The demand for workers led to massive immigration, especially to Argentina, where the population rose from slightly more than one million in 1860 to almost eight million by 1914. In addition, cities, such as Buenos Aires and Rio de Janeiro, grew rapidly. Finally, native industrialists began to develop textile mills and food-processing plants to profit from the new urban markets.

Latin America's dependence on foreign credit and shipping became dramatically apparent with the outbreak of World War I. On 31 July 1914, four days before the German invasion of Belgium, when the London Stock Exchange closed its doors, lines began forming outside banks in Buenos Aires and São Paulo. The governments of Argentina, Brazil, and Peru declared bank holidays and banned the export of gold. Nevertheless, European banking houses began calling in loans, forcing mines to close in Chile and workers to go without pay in Peru. Allied requisition of ships likewise contributed to the collapse of commerce. Brazil alone had an adequate merchant fleet to carry on independent overseas trade. Argentina attempted to remedy this shortage during the war, but its shipyards failed to meet the challenge.

Wartime dislocations caused an immediate slump throughout the world. By 1915 the global economy had begun to adjust to the situation, and for the rest of the decade the prosperity of each Latin American nation depended on the strategic value of its export commodities. Great Britain, and after 1917 the United States, were ruthless in exerting economic coercion over the region. To supply their own economies and to strangle the German war effort, they resorted to merchant blacklists, market manipulations, and military threats. Latin American nations depended on these two powers not simply for credit and shipping but also for manufactured goods, fuel, and in some cases even food.

Countries with valuable export goods found themselves subjected to ever greater coercion. Argentina, one of the world's great agricultural producers, had directed much of its prewar grain trade with Germany. In 1915 it rather suspiciously redirected its exports to European neutrals. The Allies finally halted this circuitous German trade in 1916 by imposing blacklists on merchants. In 1917 Great Britain coerced Argentina into exporting wheat during a grain shortage by threatening to withhold loans, coal, and shipping. Latin American sugar production also became vital after the loss of Austro-Hungarian suppliers. Price control efforts through the Royal Sugar Commission were only partially effective, and Cuban and Peruvian planters gained windfall profits. Higher sugar production in Cuba and Peru also led to rural hunger, as export crops supplanted staple grains.

The war proved disastrous for countries exporting nonessential agricultural goods. Coffee growers in Brazil, Colombia, and Central America suffered from falling demand and the lack of shipping, although Brazil possessed some merchant ships. The large German market was lost completely through the tight Allied blockade and blacklists, and other Europeans sharply limited their purchases. When U-boat wolfpacks began indiscriminate attacks in 1917, Britain prohibited the importation of coffee and cocoa.

Producers of raw materials also lived and died with the vagaries of Allied supply officers. Petroleum was essential for the war effort, and Mexican drilling boomed during the war. Oil wells along the coast increased production despite the ravages of the Mexican Revolution of 1910. Petroleum was also discovered in Peru, but Standard Oil and its subsidiaries gained the majority of profits from drilling throughout Latin America. Chile and Peru benefited temporarily from the rising price of nitrates, which were needed for the production of gunpowder. In the long run, however, the war proved disastrous for the market because Germany, cut off from South American sources, developed industrial substitutes. By the 1930s these synthetics were permanently displacing natural sources. Latin American rubber production also suffered from the competition of industrial substitutes and plantations in the Far East.

The most contentious question for historians is the effect of World War I on Latin American industrialization. Scholars ask in particular if the loss of imports from Europe and the United States led to the growth of domestic manufacturing. Advocates of dependency theory, who believe that Third World development is impossible under the influence of First World capital, look for signs of economic growth during the war. If Latin American industry prospered in wartime isolation, then European domination of international trade subverts development in the periphery. And, in fact, Brazilian industrial production doubled during the war, primarily in light industries. Critics of the dependency theory believe that the war did not result in the growth of import substitution. They observe that since raw materials earned such high prices during the war, Latin American capitalists concentrated more than ever on export markets.

Latin American political reactions to the war were shaped largely by domestic concerns. Former British and French colonies in the Caribbean declared war in support of the Allies. A large neutral block developed in pro-German countries such as Argentina, Chile, Colombia, and Venezuela. Mexico maintained neutrality to counterbalance the overwhelming presence of the United States. Peru, on the other hand, severed relations with Germany in part to gain U. S. support against pro-German Chile. Brazil likewise favored the Allies because Argentina supported Germany.

German war efforts in the hemisphere had mixed success. Espionage efforts generally failed, including plans to sabotage the Panama Canal and to destroy Mexican oil fields. The goal of establishing a permanent U-boat base in the hemisphere failed. Propaganda campaigns made greater headway. German agents constructed a radio transmitter in Mexico City to spread news from the front, and printing presses churned out anti-American pamphlets. Balanced against this propaganda campaign was the destruction caused by U-boats. In October of 1917, after a number of ships were torpedoed, Brazil declared war on Germany. The Brazilian navy henceforth assisted the British in South Atlantic antisubmarine patrols.

World War I also had a significant impact on Latin American society. Working class militancy became particularly marked toward the end of the war. After years of falling real wages, and buoyed by the success of Russian workers in the October Revolution, Latin American labor took to the streets. A 1917 general strike brought the city of São Paulo to a standstill.

Government troops were sent to crush the strike, but they refused to fire on the workers. Peruvian labor activism culminated in January of 1919 with a three-day general strike. Protests also spread through Argentina, Chile, and other regions. Elites assumed that strikes resulted from foreign agitators. Anti-immigrant leagues were formed and passed laws to deport alien labor organizers. Many union activists were expelled from Brazil and Argentina, but in Chile the government could find no foreigners to deport. Strikes between 1917 and 1920 succeeded in raising wages but did not significantly improve living conditions.

The middle classes also pressed for a larger voice in the government. In Córdoba, Argentine militant students went on strike in 1918 demanding university reforms. Within a year student strikes had spread throughout Argentina, Peru, and Chile. The war coincided with the growth of popular politics throughout much of Latin America. The Mexican Revolution broke the closed ranks of the government of Porfirio Díaz, and the rise of the Radical party brought increasing middle-class political participation in Argentina. Peruvian President Augusto Leguía forged a coalition of labor and capital to counter the landed elite. This trend was far less advanced in Brazil, but even there the middle class eroded the old oligarchy, culminating with the Lieutenant's Revolt of 1922. The war did not actually cause these movements, but it did hasten their development.

World War I wreaked havoc with the international economy and with British hegemony. The United States gained influence in Latin America, so that while Britain dominated declining industries such as railroads, North American investors opened new markets for radio, telegraphs, and motion pictures. At the same time, Latin Americans asserted a new cultural nationalism, rejecting European models repudiated by the war. Racist doctrines of Social Darwinism gave way to new emphasis on native American civilizations, especially in the Mexican murals of Diego Rivera and in the Peruvian populism of Victor Raúl Haya de la Torre. Foreign capitalists continued to dominate world markets, but Latin America was carving its own destiny.

Jeffrey M. Pilcher

References

Albert, Bill. *South America and the First World War: The Impact of the War on*

Brazil, Argentina, Peru and Chile. Cambridge: Cambridge University Press, 1988.

Katz, Friedrich. *The Secret War in Mexico: Europe, the United States and the Mexican Revolution.* Chicago: University of Chicago Press, 1981.

Keen, Benjamin, and Mark Wasserman..*A Short History of Latin America.* Boston: Houghton Mifflin, 1980.

Smith, Robert Freeman. "Latin America, the United States and the European Powers, 1830–1930." In *The Cambridge History of Latin America*, Vol. 4, c. 1870–1930, edited by Leslie Bethell. Cambridge: Cambridge University Press, 1986.

See also MEXICO

Lausanne, Treaty of (24 July 1923)

Signed on 24 July 1923, the Treaty of Lausanne was one of a series of documents produced by the Conference of Lausanne, one of the last conferences associated with World War I (22 November 1922 to 23 July 1923). The treaty provided a sweeping settlement of Turkish affairs after the Great War.

Reaching a settlement between Turkey and the Allied Powers proved difficult. Representatives of the splintered Ottoman Empire did sign a peace treaty at Sèvres, France, on 10 August 1920, but it was a stillborn affair. The treaty went unratified because a group of ardent nationalists, headed by Mustafa Kemal, were the true center of Turkish power. These "Young Turks" repudiated the nominal authority of Sultan Mehmet VI, established an alternate government at Ankara, and championed their own blueprint for Turkey's future, the National Pact of 28 January 1920.

When the Ankara faction managed to defeat invading Greek forces in Anatolia, an invasion which had been triggered by Turkish unwillingness to recognize the Greek mandate over Smyrna, the legitimacy of the Sultan and his government disappeared. As a result, on 23 September 1922 the major Allied Powers invited the Ankara government to a Turco-Greek peace conference. The Turkish nationalists accepted but demanded an armistice conference first. The latter occurred at Mudania on the Sea of Marmara and led to the signing of an armistice convention on 11 October. With its diplomatic legitimacy now recognized, the Ankara

government next sent a delegation to Lausanne, Switzerland, at the invitation of Great Britain, France, and Italy.

The first part of the Lausanne Conference lasted from 20 November 1922 to 4 February 1923. It included representatives from the principal Allied Powers (Great Britain, France, Italy, and Japan) and from Greece, Romania, Bulgaria, and Yugoslavia. The United States sent an observer who did not sign any documents or assume any commitments. Initially, the conferees failed to arrive at a formal agreement. One impediment to success was the organization of the conference itself: The delegates, rather than stage plenary sessions, negotiated through a series of commissions and subcommissions. Also, the Turkish delegation, led by General Ismet Inönü, was extremely sensitive about Turkey's national sovereignty and its treatment by other nations. Despite fragmented discussions conducted with oversensitive Turkish negotiators, the conference members did present a draft treaty on 31 January 1923, one day after a separate Turco-Greek convention that arranged for the compulsory exchange of national minorities, with the exception of Turks living in western Thrace and Greeks living in Istanbul.

Because of Lord Curzon's influence and his sympathy for Turkish nationalism, the terms of the draft treaty favored Turkey. The treaty set the Turco-Greek border at the Maritsa River in Thrace, although it did guarantee Turkey a terminal railroad station on the Greek side of the river. It put the fate of Mosul, an established Turkish province in Iraq, in the hands of the League of Nations. It also abolished the "special régimes" enjoyed by foreign powers in Turkey and opened the Dardanelles Strait to all commercial ships and a limited number of warships.

Despite the liberal terms of the British-inspired treaty, Ismet Pasha asked for an eight-day delay to review them. The Turkish National Assembly, for reasons that remain obscure, subsequently rejected the draft treaty. Russian demands for unfettered naval access through the Dardanelles may have been a factor. Nevertheless, the National Assembly did authorize further negotiations and sent a conciliatory 115-page note asking that the economic sections of the treaty be negotiated separately. Lord Curzon reacted to this suggestion by meeting with French and Italian representatives in London, 21–28 March 1923. The Allied Powers refused to separate the economic sections from the rest of the treaty, and it was under these circumstances that the Lausanne Conference resumed on 24 April.

The second part of the conference lasted from 24 April to 24 July 1923. The Turkish and Allied delegations expected to resolve their differences, but two major issues stood in their way. First, there was the lingering dispute over the economic sections of the draft treaty. The Allies claimed initially that further financial concessions were impossible, but they had no other choice. As a result, they agreed to minor economic adjustments that cumulatively benefited Turkey. Secondly, there was the problem of granting Turkey a railway point on the Greek side of the Maritsa border. The Turks wanted Karagach, which served the city of Adrianople and was located on the line to Dedeagach and Constantinople. The Greeks first resisted Turkish demands, but after considerable Allied pressure, they grudgingly agreed to let the Turks have Karagach.

With the above problems resolved, delegates to the conference signed the Treaty of Lausanne on 24 July 1923, along with sixteen other diplomatic instruments. The treaty was basically the same one rejected by the Turkish National Assembly the previous February, and it gave Turkish nationalists virtually everything they had demanded in the National Pact of 1920.

The Treaty of Lausanne formalized Turkey's borders. In contrast to the boundaries specified by the Treaty of Neuilly (1919), the Treaty of Lausanne adopted the existing Turco-Bulgarian border from the Rezvaya River on the Black Sea to the Greek frontier on the Maritsa River, northwest of Adrianople. The Turco-Greek border then continued southward along the Maritsa to the Aegean Sea, with the exception of Karagach. The Turco-Syrian border, established by Turkey and France in the Angora Agreement of 20 October 1921, remained intact, while Turkey and Great Britain (the mandatory power in Iraq) agreed to establish a border between Turkey and Iraq within nine months. Lastly, Turkey denied Kurdish demands for autonomy and did not relinquish disputed territory to Armenia.

The Treaty of Lausanne also divided various territories among its signatories. Turkey recognized Great Britain's annexation of Cyprus and Italian suzerainty over the Dodecanese Islands in the Aegean Sea. Turkey also renounced any rights to Egypt and the Sudan,

retroactive to 5 November 1914. Turkey did, however, acquire the islands of Imbros and Tenedos south of the Dardanelles Strait; the Rabbit Islands, which controlled the entrance to the Dardanelles; and the islands in the Sea of Marmara. Greece received the islands of Samothrace, Lemnos, Lesbos, Chios, Samos, and Ikaria. Lastly, the status of Mosul remained a problem for the League of Nations to resolve at a future date. Ultimately, Turkey lost the former Arab provinces of the Ottoman Empire, but it recovered the majority of its 1914 frontiers (one step in the recovery process was the abolition of Italian and French spheres of influence in western Anatolia).

In addition to establishing borders and apportioning territories, the Treaty of Lausanne also resolved an assortment of other problems. It prohibited future meddling in Turkey's financial or military affairs, divided the Ottoman public debt between Turkey and those states that had benefited from the division of Ottoman territory since the Balkan Wars of 1912–13, and established irrevocable laws protecting the religious and political rights of non-Moslem minorities living in Turkey.

Finally, conference participants signed various conventions that supplemented the basic Treaty of Lausanne. For example, the Regime of the Straits agreement demilitarized the length of the Bosphorus and both sides of the Dardanelles for seventy-five miles. (In the first case, the depth of the demilitarized zone was 9.5 miles, while in the second case it fluctuated from three to fifteen miles.) The agreement also established the freedom to navigate the Dardanelles Strait, the Sea of Marmara, and the Bosphorus. Under most circumstances, merchant vessels and aircraft could transit the area without interference or taxation, while a maximum force of three warships, each weighing less than ten thousand tons, could pass into the Black Sea. Neutral merchant ships would remain unmolested if Turkey were at war, provided they did not carry contraband. In the latter case, Turkey had the right to search suspicious vessels. It also had the right to bar the passage of enemy naval vessels in wartime. A commission formed under the auspices of the League of Nations, made up of ten states, would ensure that the signatories of the Regime of the Straits Convention honored its provisions.

Other agreements included the Thracian Convention, which demilitarized approximately 18.5 miles of the land frontier between Turkey and Bulgaria and Turkey and Greece; the Commercial Convention, which set the tariff for Turkish imports and exports at the level freely adopted by Turkey on 1 September 1916; the Convention on Conditions of Residence, Business, and Jurisdiction, which ensured that Turkish courts would protect the legal and property rights of foreign nationals living in Turkey; and the convention dealing with the Exchange of Greek and Turkish Populations, which represented a capitulation to Turkey's desire to resettle Greeks outside its territories.

The above conventions, coupled with the basic Treaty of Lausanne, ultimately yielded Turkey four major benefits: (1) It freed her from foreign spheres of influence; (2) It markedly reduced her national debt; (3) It demilitarized her borders and thus decreased the immediate chances for war; and (4) It solidified her political and economic ties to the West. For these reasons, the Treaty of Lausanne was a pact that clearly redounded to Turkey's advantage.

Peter R. Faber

References

Final Act of the Lausanne Conference, July 9, 1932. Cmd. 4126. London: H.M.S.O., 1932.

Further Documents Relating to the Settlement Reached at the Lausanne Conference, June 16–July 9, 1932. Cmd. 4129. London: H.M.S.O., 1932.

Lausanne Conference on Near Eastern Affairs, 1922–23: Proceedings and Draft Terms of Peace. Cmd. 1814. London: H.M.S.O., 1923.

See also BULGARIA; GREECE; OTTOMAN EMPIRE; SÈVRES, TREATY OF

Lawrence, Colonel Thomas Edward (1888–1935)

Archaeologist and a prominent figure in the Arab Revolt during World War I. Born in Tremadoc, North Wales, on 15 August 1888, he was the second of five illegitimate sons of Sir Thomas Chapman. He was about ten years old when he learned of this, and many believe that it had a lasting effect on his personality. Lawrence was of high intellect and a prolific reader. Educated at Jesus College, Oxford, in 1909 he made his first trip to the Middle East, where he worked and lived with the Arabs.

In August of 1914 Lawrence, who failed to meet the height requirement of five feet five inches to join the army, was assigned to the Geographical Section of the war office. When Turkey joined the war, Lawrence was posted as an intelligence officer to British headquarters in Cairo. His Arab dress and generally abrasive conduct shocked the professional regular officers.

With the Arab revolt against Turkey, Lawrence was posted as liaison officer to Emir Faisal's army. He quickly learned that tribal warriors should not be used as a European-style assault force against well-trained and -equipped troops. They would be most effective as a rapid moving guerrilla force utilizing speed and surprise. Against orders, he convinced Emir Faisal they should cut Turkish rail communications and capture the vital port of Aquaba. Again against GHQ orders, he led a small camel force in an amazing ride of some five hundred miles across the desert to capture Aquaba in August of 1917 from the rear.

Major Lawrence convinced the new British commander in Egypt, General Edmund Allenby, as to how the Arabs should be used. Lawrence recommended that they form the right flank of the British advance through Palestine to Damascus, which Lawrence (unknown to GHQ) was determined to capture before the British arrived. He felt that Damascus should be the capital of an independent, free Arabia. Shortly, the Turks posted rewards of 20,000 pounds for Lawrence alive, or 10,000 pounds dead.

Lawrence had learned earlier about the Sykes/Picot Agreement and felt that this knowledge was making him live a personal lie, as he had encouraged the Arabs in their war for independence. He correctly felt that Emir Faisal and his Arabs would be discarded once they had fulfilled their task of aiding the British and French in their destruction of the Ottoman Empire.

The Arabs continued north, disrupting Turkish communications on the British east flank. As Faisal's forces regrouped, Lawrence visited Allenby's headquarters, now in Jerusalem, and obtained from him 2,000 camels from the Imperial Camel Brigade. This added to the mobility and speed of his Arab forces. The Arabs now made a strong attack on Deraa to draw Turkish attention from Allenby's main objectives in the east, and north, through Palestine. But Lawrence was ordered not to close on Damascus. This was to be a British victory. Once again he violated orders.

Shortly, the Turkish forces in most all sectors were in retreat. The Turks withdrew from Damascus on 30 September 1918, and the following morning Lawrence (in his Arab robes), Faisal, and their men entered the city three hours ahead of Allenby's forces. Lawrence's force of 3,000 Arabs had tied down some 15,000 Turkish troops stationed south of Damascus.

Lawrence, now a colonel, resigned at the moment of triumph. He returned to Britain on 11 November 1918. There and in France, Lawrence attempted, at the highest levels, to save the independence for which he, Faisal, and the Arabs had fought. A master of guerrilla tactics, Lawrence of Arabia was also one of the most colorful, legendary, and at the same time controversial figures of the Great War.

The peace settlement was a bitter disappointment for Lawrence. He wrote his memoirs and was briefly at All Souls College and the colonial office. He then enlisted, at the lowest rank, in the RAF under the name John Hume Ross. His identity was learned, and he was cashiered. He then joined the Tank Corps under the name of T.E. Shaw in 1923 but was permitted back into the RAF in 1925, where he served until 1935. He died at Bovington Camp Hospital on 19 May 1935 following a motorcycle accident.

Raymond L. Proctor

References

Aldington, Richard. *Lawrence of Arabia*. London: Collins, 1955.

Lawrence, T.E. *Seven Pillars of Wisdom*. New York: Garden City Co., 1938.

Liddell Hart, B.H. *T.E. Lawrence in Arabia and After*. London: Jonathan Cape, 1934.

Mousa, Suleiman. *T.E. Lawrence, an Arab View*. London: Oxford, 1966.

Nutting, Anthony. *Lawrence of Arabia: The Man and Motive*. New York: Potter, 1961.

See also ALLENBY, EDMUND; ARAB REVOLT; FAISAL, PRINCE; PALESTINE AND SYRIA

League of Nations, Covenant of

Conceived of as the basis for permanent world peace, the Covenant of the League of Nations served as the constitution, philosophical heart, and source of the organization's existence. It established the various League offices, dictated their size and composition, defined their areas of expertise, and guided their operations. The covenant served as the supreme authority on all matters with which the League dealt, but it failed to foresee or provide the means for dealing with many of the crises faced by the institution during the interwar period.

The League of Nations idea originated from several diverse quarters: (1) from plans made by a British group of lawyers, diplomats, and historians known as the Phillimore Committee; (2) from a similar French group bearing the name of its chairman, Léon Bourgeois; (3) from a pamphlet by South African Jan Christiaan Smuts entitled *The League of Nations: A Practical Suggestion*, which distilled years of European thinking on the subject; and (4) from President Woodrow Wilson, who referred to such a body in his Fourteen Points.

Of the various writings on the League concept, the most important was Smuts's work. In his pamphlet Smuts argued that the League should be more than just another organization superimposed on preexisting national and international structures. The new League, he maintained, should be a revolutionary organ that would transform the whole system of international relations. He envisioned an institution that would regulate the vast political and social changes and upheavals that had occurred during the war and manage those sure to come in the postwar world. The League would have three basic functions: preserving the peace, organizing and regulating international commerce and business, and serving as the international center where every nation could go for help and counsel. In addition to providing the philosophical foundation for this "ever visible, living, working organ of the polity of civilization," Smuts outlined an organizational structure consisting of a general assembly, a nine-member governing council, and courts of conciliation and arbitration.

In the United States President Wilson, a relative latecomer to the League idea, shared Smuts's vision. In the Fourteen Points he called for the creation of "a general assembly of nations . . . under specific covenants" to afford mutual guarantees of political independence and territorial integrity to all nations. On arriving in Paris in December of 1918, Wilson urged the immediate drafting of a covenant for a

League of Nations before the actual Peace Conference began. He feared that if action were delayed until a peace treaty was signed, the League idea would fall victim to the tiring process of peacemaking and to post-settlement indifference. He further visualized the League as the proper vehicle by which to adjust the inevitable imperfections of the peace treaty and to ensure proper enforcement of the settlement.

Acting in conjunction with many like-minded individuals, Wilson and Smuts introduced a resolution calling for the establishment of a League of Nations as an integral part of the general peace settlement. The resolution was adopted by a plenary session of thirty-two states and dominions assembled at the Peace Conference on 25 January 1919. A provisional covenant was drafted by Colonel Edward House and Lord Robert Cecil, assisted by David Hunter Miller and Sir Cecil Hurst. It drew heavily from the plans of the Phillimore and Bourgeois committees, the Smuts pamphlet, Wilson's Fourteen Points, and the ideas of House and Cecil.

On 3 February 1919 the Covenant Committee met for the first time, with Wilson as its chairman. Cecil and Smuts represented the British Empire and Commonwealth; Léon Bourgeois and Ferdinand Larnaude, France; Vittorio Orlando and Vittorio Scialoja, Italy; and Baron Makino and Viscount Chinda, Japan. Belgium, Brazil, China, Portugal, and Serbia were also asked to participate. Following their protests that the major powers were overrepresented on the committee, additional members were included from Greece, the Polish National Council, Romania, and Czechoslovakia.

The committee worked quickly and efficiently, preparing a draft covenant for presentation to a plenary session of the Peace Conference in just eleven days. Following delegate suggestions and criticisms, the Covenant Committee returned to refine the February draft during five additional meetings lasting until 11 April. On 28 April 1919 Wilson presented the final text of the covenant before a plenary session, where it was unanimously approved. The covenant (and the League of Nations) formally and officially began functioning after the last nation signed the Versailles Peace Treaty on 10 January 1920.

The covenant consisted of twenty-six articles contained within the Treaty of Versailles. The first seven articles dealt with League membership, admission, and withdrawal; the character and power of the assembly and council; the means for appointing a secretary-general and his staff; and the establishment and funding of the League headquarters in Geneva, Switzerland.

Articles 8 and 9 dealt with disarmament and the desire of League members to reduce arms to the lowest possible levels. The articles also obligated members to engage in a full and frank exchange of information on armaments.

In Article 10 all League members pledged to respect the territorial integrity and political independence of fellow members and to aid in their protection. Article 11 addressed the rights of member nations to bring disputes between League members, and between League members and nonmember nations, to the attention of the council.

Articles 12–15 described the settlement of disputes through arbitration, or by reference to the court, council, or assembly. These articles also contained the members' pledge not to resort to force until the dispute was heard by the appropriate League body, and then only in certain circumstances and after the passage of three months.

Article 16 required each member to take action against any other member that went to war in violation of the covenant, through either economic and financial sanctions or armed force. This article also dealt with member expulsions from the League. Article 17 guaranteed each member the same protection from attack by nonmember states.

Articles 18–21 defined the effect of the covenant on other treaties, and required that all agreements entered into by League members had to be first submitted to the secretary-general for posting; it gave the assembly power to amend treaties; and affirmed that the covenant did not affect the validity of the Monroe Doctrine. Furthermore, the articles declared that any treaty that was inconsistent with the covenant was immediately abrogated.

Article 22 instituted the mandate system and gave the League the responsibility for exercising good government in the mandates through the members chosen to administer the territories as trustees.

Article 23 required member proclamations of their intention to use League offices for dealing with a whole host of international issues such as finance, trade, commerce, land, sea and air transportation, disease prevention, drug trafficking, and other matters that transcended national boundaries. Article 24 transferred to League of Nations control all international bodies that had been independent prior to the war. In Article 25 League members promised to support the activities of the various national Red Cross organizations, while Article 26 described the procedure for amending the covenant.

Although the League as established generally entailed most of what the Covenant Committee had suggested and while it did function for the most part along the lines envisioned, it never became the all-encompassing organization that Wilson and Smuts had hoped to create. Critics present at the Peace Conference and in later years found the covenant flawed in many respects. It was charged that the authors had excluded several major nations from draft discussions, including the Soviet Union and the countries of the former Central Powers, as well as many neutrals. The covenant gave too much influence to the major powers and failed to provide for compulsory arbitration of all justifiable disputes. Others charged that the covenant created a weak, unrepresentative League of Nations consisting primarily of European or European-settled or -dominated nations.

A major criticism centered on the idea that the League, as configured, could not prevent international disputes, nor could it have halted the outbreak of World War I had it existed in 1914. This was because the covenant did not outline any plan to enforce compliance with League decisions. The organization did not have its own military force and, despite French proposals, lacked the authority for raising or controlling any sort of multinational military organization. According to the Japanese the covenant failed to endorse the principle of equality of nations, while a clause regarding freedom of religion, suggested by Wilson, was stricken from the final draft.

Ironically, the most outspoken critics of the League of Nations Covenant were in the United States. The Republican-controlled Senate, angered by Wilson's refusal to consult them during the settlement and suspicious of the entire League idea as well as covenant provisions that seemed to imply entangling alliances, a surrender of national sovereignty, and a denial of congressional prerogatives, rejected both the covenant and, because it was part of the larger peace settlement, the Treaty of Versailles itself.

Repeated attempts were made during the interwar years to amend the covenant to improve League of Nations effectiveness. Special efforts were focused on Articles 10–17, which dealt with the prevention of war. By and large these efforts failed, although a total of sixty-three countries agreed to adhere to the provisions as members of the League of Nations.

Clayton D. Laurie

References

Mee, Charles L., Jr. *The End of Order: Versailles, 1919*. New York: E.P. Dutton, 1980.

Miller, D.H. *The Drafting of the Covenant*. New York: Putnam, 1928.

Walters, Francis P. *A History of the League of Nations*. London: Oxford University Press, 1952. Reprint. Westport, Conn.: Greenwood, 1986.

See also BOURGEOIS, LÉON; PARIS PEACE CONFERENCE, 1919; SMUTS, JAN; VERSAILLES TREATY

Leman, Gérard (1851–1920)

Belgian general and the defender of Liège, born at Liège on 8 January 1851. Leman was commissioned from the Ecole Militaire at Brussels and was later head of the school before being appointed commander of the ring-fortress of Liège in January of 1914. The twelve forts and the Meuse were athwart the Maastricht-Ardennes gap, through which the Germans would funnel two armies. But the Brialmont-type forts were obsolete, proof against 21cm (8.2-inch) shells only. Although fieldworks slowed the German advance, a special task force under Lieutenant General Otto von Emmich began to reduce the forts, and Major General Erich Ludendorff, deputy chief of staff to Second Army, brazenly led a brigade into the city itself and bluffed the garrison into surrendering. Superheavy Skoda 30.5cm (12-inch) and Krupp 42cm (16.5-inch) howitzers cracked the forts like eggshells. Leman himself was captured, wounded and unconscious, in the ruins of Fort Loncin on 15 August. After the Armistice he returned to Belgium a hero. He died in Brussels on 27 October 1920.

A. Harding Ganz

References

Atkinson, Major Charles F. "Gérard Leman." *Encyclopaedia Britannica*. 12th edition, 1922. Vol. 31, 745.

———. "Liège." *Encyclopaedia Britannica.* 12th edition, 1922. Vol. 31, 162–64.

See also BELGIUM, INVASION OF

Lenin, Vladimir Ilyich (1870–1924)

Leader of the Russian Bolshevik party. Born on 23 April 1870 (10 April 1870, Old Style) in the provincial town of Simbirsk, Vladimir Ilyich Ulianov (Lenin) was the third child of Ilia Nikolaevich Ulianov, a titled senior-school official, and Maria Alexandrovna Ulianov, daughter of an army doctor. He enjoyed a privileged childhood.

In the spring of 1887 Lenin's older brother, Aleksandr, a student at the University of St. Petersburg, and his eldest sister, Anna, were arrested for an abortive assassination attempt on Czar Alexander III. Anna was sentenced to exile on their grandfather's Kokushkino estate. Refusing clemency, Aleksandr was hanged on 8 May 1887.

Sitting for gymnasium final examinations the week of Aleksandr's execution, the seventeen-year-old Lenin was graduated with a gold medal and enrolled as a law student at Kazan University. Deeply affected by his brother's death, Lenin soon involved himself in radical student activities. Within three months, he was arrested and expelled from the university for participating in a student demonstration. Sentenced to join his sister in internal exile, Lenin continued his law studies independently but devoted much of his three-year exile to the study of Marx and Plekhanov. Upon his release he was a committed Marxist dedicated to revolution.

Graduated first in his class in 1891 as an external candidate of St. Petersburg University, Lenin passed the bar the following year and practiced as a provincial lawyer until his departure for St. Petersburg in 1893. Associating with S.I. Radshenko's Marxist group, the twenty-three-year-old lawyer proved himself a skilled debater and propagandist. While in St. Petersburg Lenin met his future wife, Nadezhda Krupskaya, a member of Radshenko's group.

Extending his revolutionary activities, Lenin traveled to Switzerland in 1895 to contact expatriate Marxist Georgii Plekhanov and the Liberation of Labor Group. He returned to St. Petersburg later that year and joined with Yuli Martov to establish the Social Democrat faction, "Union of Struggle for the Emancipation of the Working Class." These efforts were soon curtailed when Lenin and the majority of the Marxist leadership were arrested in a December police crackdown.

Jailed for fifteen months and subsequently exiled internally for three years, Lenin continued his revolutionary work, completing *The Development of Capitalism in Russia.* Joined by the recently exiled Nadezhda Krupskaya, the two were married in July of 1898.

Leaving Nadezhda to complete her sentence, the newly freed Lenin left for Stuttgart in February of 1900. Collaborating with Plekhanov and Yuli Martov, he began publication of the Marxist journal *Iskra* (the Spark). Constantly moving to elude Russian agents, Lenin completed *What Is to Be Done?* in March of 1902. Outlining a new direction of Marxist strategy, it called for a core of professional revolutionaries to lead the revolution, thus reducing internal dissension and the threat of infiltration.

With its first congress (1898) ineffective because of the exile of its top leadership, the Marxist Russian Social Democrat Labor Party (RSDLP) held its Second Party Conference in July of 1903. The congress evidenced profound organizational and ideological differences among the party's leadership. The RSDLP ultimately split into two factions: the Mensheviks (minority party) led by Martov, and the Bolsheviks (majority) under Lenin. Lenin's strategy of a rapidly realized proletariat- and peasant-backed dictatorship clashed irreconcilably with Martov's concept of a gradual, bourgeoisie-based evolution of government from monarchy to socialism.

Having lost control of *Iskra* in the congress, Lenin began publishing the journals *Vpered* (Forward) in 1905 and *Proletarii* in 1906. Issues raised in the short-lived 1905 Russian Revolution continued to divide the RSDLP. Internal dissension escalated until Lenin and the Bolsheviks separated from the party at the Prague Conference of the Bolshevik party in 1912, at which time he began publication of *Pravda.*

Isolated in Cracow at the outbreak of World War I, Lenin was stunned by the socialists' unexpected nationalism. Rather than revolt against what he viewed as a capitalist, imperialist conflict, world socialists supported their countries' war efforts. Briefly detained in Austria for suspicion of spying, Lenin returned with his wife to Zurich, where in 1917 he published *Imperialism: The Highest Stage of Capitalism.* In this analysis of the causes of the war, he attacked the foundations of capitalism and espoused world revolution.

On 15 March 1917, with rapidly deteriorating conditions on both the military and domestic fronts, Czar Nicholas II abdicated. Announcing its intention to keep Russia in the war, the provisional government under Aleksandr Kerensky alarmed both Lenin and the Germans. The German Foreign Ministry then made one of the profound decisions of the war: Providing a sealed train, it allowed Lenin and thirty-two other Russian revolutionaries safe passage to Petrograd (formerly St. Petersburg) via neutral Sweden. Lenin's arrival, on 16 April 1917, was marked by his immediate denunciation of Kerensky's moderate provisional government and his call for its overthrow.

Returning from an inspection of the front, Kerensky fanned anti-Bolshevik sentiments by blaming military reversals on defeatist Bolshevik agitators. Lenin, accused as a German spy, was forced into hiding, where he completed *The State and Revolution*. Kerensky, meanwhile, attempted to avert anarchy by forming the short-lived Third Coalition. As Kerensky's new government rapidly collapsed, Lenin returned in secret to Petrograd. Recognizing the need for immediate action, Lenin called for the Bolsheviks to seize power and secured party leadership for such action. The October Revolution was realized as Petrograd Soviet Chairman Leon Trotsky's Red Guards seized the Winter Palace, overthrowing the provisional government. On 8 November 1917 Lenin assumed power as chairman of the Council of People's Commissars.

Consolidating his government, Lenin quickly moved for a separate peace with the Central Powers. Overcoming strong leftist-communist pressure to continue a "revolutionary war," Lenin pressed for an immediate end to Russian involvement in the conflict. On 3 March 1918 Trotsky reluctantly signed the Treaty of Brest-Litovsk, removing Russia from the war. Threatened by the Bolshevik's pacifism and refusal to repay war loans, and fearful of war matériel's falling into German hands, the Allies supported the anti-Bolshevik Russian White Army. The resulting civil war pitted the Bolshevik Red Army against the Whites. Aided by peasant support, the Reds defeated the Whites by the end of 1920. The following March, Lenin acknowledged the need to deal with economic collapse and meet peasant needs by introducing the New Economic Policy.

Lenin's health rapidly deteriorated after the Bolshevik Revolution. A series of strokes, aggravated by wounds from a 1918 assassination attempt, left him partially paralyzed and unable to speak. He died on 21 January 1924, and his body was subsequently embalmed and placed on display in a mausoleum in Red Square.

Jeff Kinard

References
Clark, Ronald W. *Lenin*. New York: Harper and Row, 1988.

Mailloux, Kenneth F. and Heloise P. *Lenin, The Exile Returns*. Princeton: Auerbach, 1971.

Medvedev, Roy A. *The October Revolution*. New York: Columbia University Press, 1979.

Pearson, Michael. *The Sealed Train*. New York: G.P. Putnam's Sons, 1975.

Pipes, Richard. *The Russian Revolution*. New York: Alfred A. Knopf, 1990.

Possony, Stefan T. *Lenin: The Compulsive Revolutionary*. Chicago: Henry Regnery Company, 1964.

Shukman, Harold. *Lenin and the Russian Revolution*. New York: Capricorn, 1966.

Shukman, Harold, ed. *The Blackwell Encyclopedia of the Russian Revolution*. Oxford: Basil Blackwell, 1988.

Ulam, Adam B. *Lenin and the Bolsheviks*. London: Secker and Warburg, 1965.

See also Brest-Litovsk, Treaty of; Russia, Home Front and Revolutions of 1917

Lettow-Vorbeck, Paul Emil von (1870–1964)

Commander of the German armed forces in German East Africa. Son of a German general, he was born at Saurlovis on 20 March 1870 and was commissioned an artillery officer upon graduating from the Kriegsakademie in 1899. He served in China during the Boxer Rebellion (1900–1901), saw action in Southwest Africa during the Hottentot and Herero rebellions (1904–8), and was promoted to major in 1913. In 1914 he was appointed commander of the German *Schutztruppen* in German East Africa and promoted to lieutenant colonel.

Lettow-Vorbeck believed in the inevitability of conflict with other colonial powers, especially Great Britain. He worked diligently to prepare his German troops and their twelve companies of native Askaris for the war he foresaw. Lettow-Vorbeck was a proponent of offensive warfare, so when war came, in August of

1914, he immediately launched raids against the British in Kenya. His goal was to tie up as many British and Allied troops as possible and prevent their use in decisive European battles.

Cut off from supplies from Germany, Lettow-Vorbeck's small army used great skill in improvising weapons, fuel, medicine, and clothing. Realizing the usefulness of a friendly native population, Lettow-Vorbeck made sure that the Africans were treated with justice. His own native Askaris showed great loyalty and, despite their lack of supplies, fought bravely against British Empire troops who had discounted the fighting abilities of native soldiers.

Lettow-Vorbeck's command, which never numbered more than 3,000 German troops and 11,000 Askaris, diverted over 130,000 Allied troops from use on the Western Front. Driven from East Africa, Lettow-Vorbeck's troops continued the fight. He invaded Portuguese Mozambique and then moved into Rhodesia, where he repeatedly proved himself a master of guerrilla warfare. Upon learning of the armistice in Europe, he negotiated the surrender of his undefeated army on 25 November 1918.

Upon his return to Germany, Lettow-Vorbeck was promoted to major general and paraded triumphantly down *Unter den Linden*. After the war he involved himself in the conservative *Freikorps* movement against the left-wing Spartacists. Later, he served briefly in the Reichstag (1928–30), where he opposed Nazi politics. He retired from public life in 1930 and died on 9 March 1964 in Hamburg.

Steven D. Fisher

References

Farwell, Byron. *The Great War in Africa.* New York: Norton, 1986.
Hoyt, Edwin P. *Guerrilla: Colonel von Lettow-Vorbeck and Germany's East African Empire.* New York: Macmillan, 1981.
Lettow-Vorbeck, Paul von. *My Reminiscences of East Africa.* London: Hurst and Blackett, 1920.

See also AFRICA

Levetzow, Magnus von (1871–1939)

German naval commander and staff officer, born in Flensburg on 8 January 1871. Levetzow received his navy commission and was an admiralty staff officer during the European blockade of Venezuelan ports in 1903. Promoted to cap-

tain in 1913, he commanded the battle cruiser *Moltke* in the Yarmouth and Hartlepool raids of November and December of 1914 and at the Dogger Bank clash in January of 1915. At Jutland in 1916 he was chief of the Operations Division under Captain Adolf von Trotha, chief of staff to Vice Admiral Reinhard Scheer, commander of the High Seas Fleet. In 1917 Levetzow helped plan Operation Albion, the amphibious invasion of the Baltic Islands off the Gulf of Riga.

In August of 1918 now-Commodore Levetzow became chief of staff of Admiral Scheer's new Naval Supreme Command, which unified the three previous naval departments. He planned the last fleet sortie, but mutiny paralyzed the fleet. An ardent nationalist, Levetzow later joined Hitler's Nazi party. He died in Berlin on 13 March 1939.

A. Harding Ganz

References

Gemzell, Carl-Axel. *Organization, Conflict, and Innovation.* Lund, Sweden: Berlingska Boktryckeriet, 1973.
Herwig, Holger H., and Neil M. Heyman. *Biographical Dictionary of World War I.* Westport, Conn.: Greenwood, 1982.

See also DOGGER BANK, NAVAL BATTLE OF; GERMAN CRUISER RAIDS, 1914; SCHEER, REINHARD

Lichnowsky, Count Karl Max (1860–1928)

German diplomat, born on 8 March 1860 in Kreuzenort, Kreis Ratibor, in Oberschlesien. Lichnowsky began his career in London in 1883 with the German Foreign Service. He gained additional diplomatic experience in posts in Stockholm, Constantinople, Bucharest, and Vienna. After he was several times passed over for promotion, Lichnowsky resigned in July of 1904.

Thereafter, Lichnowsky wrote political articles for the German press, and in 1912 he warned of the possibility of a "German-English Misunderstanding." This led Kaiser Wilhelm II to send him as envoy to London, so that in the event of a conflict between Germany, Russia, and France, Lichnowsky would ensure that Britain remained neutral.

Lichnowsky soon realized that Britain was determined to uphold the balance of power on the Continent and that she would be on the side opposing Germany. He reported this to Berlin.

Nevertheless, one of Lichnowsky's diplomatic dispatches was interpreted to mean that Britain would remain neutral in the event Germany were to attack only Russia. For this, he was soon branded a scapegoat for Germany's unfavorable military position.

Lichnowsky did not play a role in Weimar Republic politics after the war. Evaluation of his 1927 *Auf Dem Weg zum Abgrund* establishes Lichnowsky as one of the very few German statesmen who clearly foresaw the First World War and tried to prevent it. Lichnowsky died on 27 February 1928 in Kuchelna in Oberschlesien.

Ekkehart P. Guth

References

Bach, August. *Deutsche Gesandtschaftsberichte zum Kriegsausbruch 1914*. Berlin: Quader-Verlag, 1937.

Mann, Golo. *Geschichte und Geschichten*. Frankfurt: Fischer-Verlag, 1962.

Neue Deutsche Biographie. Berlin: Duncker-Verlag, 1985.

See also ORIGINS OF THE FIRST WORLD WAR

Liddell Hart, Sir Basil (1895–1970)

British military historian and strategist who helped lead the fight for a mechanized army in Britain in the years before the Second World War. Born Basil Hart in Paris on 31 October 1895 to an upper-middle-class family, he changed his last name to Liddell Hart in 1921 (his mother's family name was Liddell). The outbreak of World War I cut short his schooling at Cambridge, and he joined the army as a lieutenant in the infantry in December of 1914. He served on the front lines in France throughout 1915. He was gassed during the Somme Offensive of 1916 and he spent the rest of the war in England training infantrymen.

After the war, Liddell Hart began a long and distinguished writing career. In 1920 he wrote the army's official *Infantry Training* manual, which included his "expanding torrent" strategy that had evolved out of World War I German infiltration tactics. Liddell Hart was heavily influenced by the writings of J.F.C. Fuller on mechanized warfare and the use of air power. He himself soon became a leading advocate for military reform through his "indirect approach," which aimed at dislocating the enemy and reducing his means of resistance. He remained in the army until 1924 when he was invalided out because of a heart problem; he retired as a captain in 1927. In 1925 Liddell Hart became a military correspondent for the *Daily Telegraph* and moved to *The Times* (London) in 1935 as a military advisor. Throughout the 1920s and 1930s Liddell Hart published extensively on strategy and tactics and soon developed a great reputation as a military expert.

Liddell Hart's reputation brought him access to government officials. He strongly advocated a defensive strategy for Britain and spoke against raising a large army to fight in France. In 1937 Liddell Hart became personal adviser to Leslie Hore-Belisha, secretary of state for war in Neville Chamberlain's government, and helped shape British strategic decisions. His ideas to mechanize the army with tanks and antiaircraft forces were strongly resisted, however. During the war his reputation suffered from his repeated calls for a negotiated settlement with Hitler, and when his predictions failed to materialize. A correspondent for the *Daily Mail,* he spent the war on the sidelines.

Liddell Hart's reputation rebounded in the 1950s, and by the 1960s he was regarded as a brilliant military strategist. He wrote extensively on military affairs and criticized the concept of massive retaliation. His post–World War II writings often contradicted what he had said and done before the war and seemed to show him as the lone figure warning against the German danger. Liddell Hart's influence also spread through many young historians who studied and worked with him. He was knighted by Queen Elizabeth in 1966 and died on 29 January 1970 at Buckinghamshire, England.

Laura Matysek Wood

References

Bond, Brian. *Liddell Hart: A Study of His Military Thought*. London: Cassell, 1977.

Liddell Hart, Sir Basil. *Memoirs*. London: Cassell, 1965.

———. *The Remaking of Modern Armies*. London: J. Murray, 1927.

———. *The Tanks*. 2 vols. London: Cassell, 1959.

Mearsheimer, John J. *Liddell Hart and the Weight of History*. Ithaca, N.Y.: Cornell University Press, 1988.

See also J.F.C. FULLER

Liebknecht, Karl (1871–1919)

German political leader and co-founder of the Spartacists. Born in Leipzig on 13 August 1871, he was the son of Wilhelm Liebknecht, one of the co-founders of what became the German Social Democratic party. Liebknecht studied law and political economy at Leipzig and Berlin and sought to follow his father in expanding the influence of socialism in Germany.

During World War I Liebknecht was a delegate to both the Reichstag and the Prussian *Landtag*. He became an early and energetic opponent of Germany's goals in the war, seeing them as imperialist rather than merely defensive, as the kaiser's government claimed. He was the first member of the Reichstag to vote against war credits. In early 1916, as the mainstream German Social Democratic party (SPD) began to crumble over the issue of support for the war, Liebknecht was expelled for opposing party policy.

Along with Rosa Luxemburg, another prominent radical Social Democrat, Liebknecht founded the subversive and revolutionary Spartacus League. Jailed for revolutionary activity during a 1 May workers' celebration in 1916, Liebknecht was released in October of 1918, shortly before the collapse of the kaiser's regime on 9 November 1918. In the social and political confusion that followed, the Spartacus League undertook a revolutionary uprising in Berlin in January of 1919. On 15 January, counterrevolutionary right-wing troops detained both Liebknecht and Luxemburg on questionable legal grounds as leaders of the uprising. They were both shot to death the same evening.

J. Ronald Shearer

References

Meyer, Karl W. *Karl Liebknecht: Man without a Country.* Washington: Public Affairs Press, 1957.

Schorske, Carl E. *German Social Democracy, 1905–1917. The Development of the Great Schism.* Cambridge: Harvard University Press, 1955.

See also GERMANY, REVOLUTION OF 1918; LUXEMBURG, ROSA

Liman von Sanders, Otto (1855–1929)

German general and commander of Turkish forces at Gallipoli and in Palestine, born at Stolp on the Pomorze in Prussia, 18 February 1855. Liman's military career began when he entered the Hessian Life Guards in 1874 with assignment to the 115th Infantry Regiment. In 1879 he transferred to the cavalry. After becoming a general staff officer in 1887, he held a number of assignments on the general staff. In 1906 he commanded the 15th Cavalry Brigade; five years later he was appointed lieutenant general commanding the 22nd Infantry Division at Kassel. In 1913 Wilhelm II ennobled him, at which time he added the name of his deceased Scottish wife, Sanders, to his own. Liman von Sanders developed the reputation as a man of energy, ability, and strong character.

In late 1913 Wilhelm II sent Liman von Sanders on a special military mission to the Ottoman Empire. The mission originated with the Young Turks' desire to westernize and modernize the administration of the empire. Accordingly, they invited several distinguished foreigners to assist them, including French, British, and German subjects. Liman von Sanders was not the first German officer assigned to assist the Turkish army. His predecessor, General Colmar von der Goltz, had lacked the authority to transform the old Turkish officers and soldiers into disciplined troops in accordance with the Prussian methods. Prolonged negotiations between the Young Turks and German officials led to Liman von Sanders's subsequent mission. Initially, he was to command a Turkish army corps at Constantinople.

Liman von Sanders's 1913 appointment exacerbated the tense situation in the Middle East and Eastern Europe. On 2 November 1913, the Russian ambassador at Constantinople, M.N. Giers, sent a telegram to St. Petersburg informing his government of a rumor about the forthcoming German military mission to Turkey. On 5 November 1913, when Russian Foreign Minister Sergei Sazonov heard that Liman von Sanders was to command Turkish troops, he became indignant and reacted with such impropriety that he misrepresented the situation to the other nations of the Triple Entente. Although the major European powers had been informed of the mission, Sazonov felt insulted and slighted at the lack of information sent to Russia. Accordingly, Sazonov demanded "compensation" and suggested that the other major powers do likewise. The British and French initially accepted this misrepresentation, and had diplomats of these two nations not quickly determined the facts, World War I might have begun in November of 1913.

Heightened diplomatic tension followed Giers's telegram of 2 November 1913. Diplomatic intervention by France and England resulted in a compromise on 15 January 1914. As a consequence of the "Liman von Sanders Affair" and the compromise that had followed it, Liman von Sanders lost command of the First Turkish Army and instead became inspector general of Turkish troops, with the rank of a Turkish Field Marshal. Up to the outbreak of World War I, he did much to improve the Turkish army, which was in deplorable condition following the Balkan Wars.

At the outbreak of the First World War, Liman von Sanders worked diligently to bring Turkey into the conflict on the side of the Central Powers. Thwarted in his efforts, he asked the kaiser to recall him. Later in August, however, he was appointed commander of the Turkish First Army in the Bosphorus. In March of 1915 Enver Pasha sent him to command the Fifth Turkish Army at Gallipoli. Although his forces were outnumbered, he succeeded in containing the Allies on the beachhead and ultimately forced them to evacuate the peninsula. In November of 1916 Liman von Sanders tried to halt the deportation of Armenians to Smyryna. He also opposed an October 1917 convention, to take effect after the war, that gave Turkey control over all German officers in that country.

On 27 February 1918 Liman von Sanders received command of Army Group F, consisting of the Fourth, Seventh, and Eighth Turkish armies, in Syria and Palestine. For a time he held up the British advance north, but under pressure from Allied forces commanded by General Edmund Allenby, Liman von Sanders withdrew most of his force to Aleppo.

After the armistice of Mudros, Liman von Sanders returned to Constantinople to organize the repatriation of German soldiers. When he attempted to return to Germany in February of 1919, the British detained him at Malta for six months as a suspected war criminal. Liman von Sanders retired from the German army in October of 1919 and died in Munich on 22 August 1929.

Montecue J. Lowry

References

Die Grosse Politik der Europäischen Kabinette, 1871–1914, Vol. 38. Berlin: German Foreign Ministry, 1927.

Fay, Sidney B. *The Origins of the World War.* Vols. 1 and 2. New York: Free Press, 1966.

Gooch, G.P., and Harold Temperley, eds. *British Documents on the Origins of the War.* Vol. 10. London: His Majesty's Stationery Office, 1936.

Grey, Sir Edward. *Twenty-Five Years.* New York: Frederick A. Stokes, 1925.

Liman von Sanders, Otto. *Five Years in Turkey.* Annapolis, Md.: The United States Naval Institute, 1927.

See also GALLIPOLI CAMPAIGN; OTTOMAN EMPIRE, ARMY; PALESTINE AND SYRIA

Linsingen, Alexander von (1850–1935)

Prussian colonel general and army group commander. Son of a Hanoverian civil servant, Linsingen was born at Hildesheim on 10 February 1850. He joined the Prussian army in 1868, held a number of adjutant's positions, and thereafter slowly rose through the ranks. Although he had never served on the general staff, Linsingen became a divisional commander in 1905 and a corps commander four years later.

During the opening campaigns in the West, Linsingen's II Corps formed part of General Alexander von Kluck's First Army, but it was eventually transferred to the Russian front (in November of 1914). Two months later Linsingen was appointed commander of the so-called *Südarmee,* a mixed force of German and Hapsburg troops that would henceforth hold a crucial sector in the Austro-Hungarian front. After General August von Mackensen's successful advance into central Poland, Linsingen was moved to that region as head of a newly formed *Bugarmee* (6 July 1915). Ten weeks later his authority was broadened through the creation of "Army Group Linsingen," which initially consisted of his own *Bugarmee* and the German Eleventh Army. Later, the Austro-Hungarian Fourth Army was assigned to him as well.

Holding the south-central portions of the Eastern Front, Linsingen's army group was hit hard by superior Russian forces, particularly during the Brusilov Offensive in 1916; on each occasion, Linsingen was able to restabilize the situation. After the Treaty of Brest-Litovsk Linsingen's army group was dissolved, and he was promoted to the rank of colonel general. Aged sixty-eight, he was then placed in charge of the German capital and its environs, assuming the title of *Oberbefehlshaber in den Marken und Gouverneur von Berlin.* In that capacity he tried to stop the revolutionary tide flowing toward Berlin from Germany's naval bases and elsewhere, but, hampered by bureaucratic infighting, he eventually gave up (8–9 November) and tendered his resignation.

After the Nazis came to power in Germany, Linsingen experienced some discrimination at their hands for his less-than-perfect "Aryan background." He died on 5 June 1935 at Hanover.

Ulrich Trumpener

References

Glaise-Horstenau, Edmund, et al., eds. *Osterreich-Ungarns letzter Krieg 1914–1918*. Vols. 2–6. Vienna: Verlag der Militärwissenschaftlichen Mitteilungen, 1931–36.

Reichsarchiv et al. *Der Weltkrieg 1914 bis 1918. Militärische Operationen zu Lande*. Vols. 1, 3–13. Berlin: E.S. Mittler und Sohn, 1925–42.

Schmidt, Ernst-Heinrich. *Heimatheer und Revolution 1918*. Stuttgart: Deutsche Verlags-Anstalt, 1981.

Stone, Norman. *The Eastern Front 1914–1917*. New York: Charles Scribner's Sons, 1975.

See also BRUSILOV OFFENSIVE

Literature: Authors of Disillusionment

Even before the guns had fallen silent, the Great War had produced a new strain of war literature characterized by its stark contrasts to traditional, romanticized depictions of war. Shocked by the yawning chasm separating the heroic legends of war and the realities of the trenches, and disillusioned by the abject failure of any country to achieve its lofty objectives, poets, novelists, and memoirists from among all the major European combatants contributed to this new literary realism. Especially prominent were the contributions of the French, Germans, and British. The major themes of this literature included the sense of victimization suffered by all combatants on both sides of the lines, the cant and hypocrisy of political and social leaders who pushed their young men into the slaughter of the front, and the myth of the "Lost Generation"—the feeling that an entire generation of young men, the best and brightest of their society, had been utterly destroyed by the war. To convey their stories, these authors relied upon realism, irony, and the inversion of conventional literary symbolism.

Although the movement had no definite beginning, Henri Barbusse (1873–1935) published in 1916 one of the earliest examples of this literature with his novel *Le Feu* (translated as *Under Fire* in 1917). The novel was read by soldiers of all the warring countries, who found in Barbusse's treatment of the human experience of trench warfare a horribly accurate drama that transcended any national boundaries. A forty-two-year-old reservist, winner of the Croix de Guerre in 1915, invalided from the service in 1917, Barbusse wrote of the miseries of trench life, of the boredom and terror of frontline duty, and of the camaraderie among those who endured it. He emphasized through classical allusions the primitive power of war with continual references to the four elements (fire, water, wind, and earth) as encountered by Neanderthal soldiers in the trenches. In many ways Barbusse gave voice to the spirit of the French army at the time of the mutiny and encouraged writers in other countries to express similar views.

Probably the most famous book to depict the miseries of the war is Erich Maria Remarque's *All Quiet on the Western Front*, first published in 1927. Translated into more than a dozen languages with several cinematic versions, this novel about Paul Bäumer and his comrades in many ways epitomizes the genre. Drafted into the army in 1916 where he served as a sapper until wounded, Remarque (1898–1970) describes in vivid detail the petty authoritarianism of the army, the insensitivity toward human suffering, and the loss of innocence experienced by young men pulled straight from the classroom to the battlefield. The irony conveyed in the title—Paul is killed on a quiet day when nothing militarily significant happened at the front—crops up elsewhere in the book and is a characteristic of the genre. Sweeping aside traditional heroic romanticism, the authors of disillusionment use irony to emphasize incongruities between expectations and actualities. Remarque uses ironic situations frequently to explore the shared humanity of German, French, and Russian soldiers and the physical and psychological isolation of the front soldiers from their former civilian lives. Although not lauded for its purely literary merits, *All Quiet on the Western Front* remains prominent in the genre for its emotive, realistic story of wartime experience.

Several other German authors wrote of their disillusionment in the war. In his novel *Seven before Verdun* (1930) Josef Magnus Wehner (1891–1973) wrote an account of the battles around Verdun, where he was badly wounded, as an allegory for the tragedy of the German nation. The seven men he chronicles are officers and enlisted men representing a cross-section of the German people. Five of the seven are killed in the savage fighting on different parts of the battlefield, their youthful vitality—and that of the country—wasted under the direction of senile and decrepit leaders.

The first two volumes of Arnold Zweig's tetralogy, *The Strange Case of Sergeant Grischa* (1927) and *Education before Verdun* (1935), represent his best work. Zweig (1887–1968) explores issues of personal responsibility and accountability through the central figures in the two novels. Both General von Lychow and Lieutenant Eberhard Kroysing, representing old aristocratic values and modern situational morality, respectively, are ultimately defeated by the brutally impersonal, mechanistic forces mobilized by the state in a war fought for greed and without moral justification.

Ludwig Renn (1889–1979), the pseudonym of A.F. Vieth von Golssenau, a high-ranking, aristocratic staff officer, utilized his wartime diary in writing *War* (1928). The war he describes is so horrible and monstrous that the individual can do nothing but surrender to its elemental force, over which he has no control. The inability of men to control their own destiny is another characteristic of the genre that places it in sharp contrast to the heroic tradition.

Edwin Erich Dwinger (1898–1981), the son of a German father and Russian mother, went into the army at age seventeen and fell, severely wounded, in 1915. In *Army behind Barbed Wire* (1929) he recounts the experiences of a soldier held prisoner in Siberia and swept up in the subsequent war between the Reds and Whites. German literature was generally more politicized than is the case in France or Britain, especially for Zweig and Dwinger, who dealt with the Eastern Front. Because they often clashed with conservative, nationalistic authors who found redemption in defeat and the subsequent rise of the National Socialists, many of the authors of disillusionment in Germany became expatriates during the interwar period.

In some respects the British offer the most refined literature of disillusionment to come out of the war. The poets, novelists, and memoirists who chronicled their wartime experience came primarily from upper-middle-class backgrounds with classical educations in the public schools, often continued at Oxford or Cambridge. All served in the army, most as frontline officers, and virtually all of those who survived the war carried deep physical and psychological scars long thereafter. The myth of the lost generation was strongest among these survivors, and many labored under a sense of their own unfitness and guilt that all the best men had died in the trenches.

Siegfried Sassoon (1886–1967) was typical of the eager, well-bred gentlemen who rushed to the colors in August of 1914 and provided most of the reserve officers of the British Expeditionary Forces. Leaving behind a quiet, well-to-do rural life of fox hunting and writing (several volumes of dreamy, romantic verse), Sassoon early on switched from the cavalry to the Royal Welch Fusiliers. He proved a brave and capable officer, even after his initial enthusiasm faltered with the trench deadlock and the long series of futile, bloody British offensives. A 1917 collection of antiwar—or, more accurately, anti–home front—poems in *The Old Huntsman* announced Sassoon's rejection of the war.

After recovering from wounds, physical and psychological, Sassoon returned to the war and the men he felt he was selfishly abandoning. In June of 1918 he brought out his most famous collection of war poetry in *Counter-Attack and Other Poems*; the next month he was wounded in the head and invalided home. Not until 1926 had he recovered from his experiences sufficiently to resume writing. The three-volume *Memoirs of George Sherston* represented what became his lifelong obsession—stretching into six autobiographical volumes—with his wartime experiences and the sharp dichotomy between his prewar innocence (*Memoirs of a Fox-Hunting Man* [1928]) and his transformation (*Memoirs of an Infantry Officer* [1930]) to the man who emerged from the war in 1918 (*Sherston's Progress* [1936]).

A friend of Sassoon's and a fellow officer in the Royal Welch Fusiliers, Robert Graves (1895–1985) wrote his autobiographical *Goodbye to All That* as a means of breaking free from his former associations in England, including his recollections of the war, before moving to Majorca and continuing his prolific literary career, which produced more than fifty volumes of verse and many fictional works, including his well-known historical novel *I, Claudius*. Like Sassoon, a bitter, injured soldier with mixed feelings of devotion to his men and anger at those behind the lines, Graves expressed his feelings in two collections of poems during the war, *Over the Brazier* (1916) and *Fairies and Fusiliers* (1917). Written almost as a theatrical performance a dozen years later, *Good-bye to All That* (1929) shunned melodrama in favor of farce. Graves felt comedy more appropriate for his generation's experience because tragedy presupposed elements of guilt and responsibility for events that he did not accept.

Edmund Blunden (1896–1974) is often considered the third member of the literary triumvirate of the English authors of disillusionment. Eventually becoming professor of poetry at Oxford in 1966, Blunden left Queens College in 1915 to join the Royal Sussex Regiment. A shy officer nicknamed Rabbit and later Bunny, Blunden won the Military Cross before being gassed and invalided home in March of 1918. His best-known work on the war is his memoir, what one author has labeled "an extended pastoral elegy in prose," *Undertones of War* (1928). A master at utilizing classical English literature to present an ironic, understated picture of the war, Blunden does not express the bitter obsession of Sassoon or the mocking humor of Graves, and yet quietly conveys many of the same general concerns.

There were several other notable British authors who contributed to the rich literature of the war. Richard Aldington (1892–1962) was a member of the prewar literati, an "imagist" poet of great promise. Enlisting in 1916, Aldington emerged from the war with a captain's commission and a severe case of shell shock. Aside from his poetry, including *Images of War* (1919), he is best known for the autobiographical novel *Death of a Hero* (1929). The central character, Winterbourne, a participant in what Aldington labeled Europe's suicide, is less troubled by the physical horrors of war than by the mental degradation of military service. His experience cuts him off from his prewar intellectual roots and alienates him from his wife. All that is beautiful to a sensitive, poetic young man—and ultimately his life—is destroyed in the war.

Three additional poets also stand out. Wilfred Owen (1893–1918), a friend of Sassoon's and Graves's, returned to the front from convalescence in 1918, where he was killed shortly before the Armistice. His poems, most of which were published posthumously, are among the most vivid and evocative of the sights and sounds of the trenches. Isaac Rosenberg (1890–1918) was another of the poet-officers killed late in the war. He tapped his Jewish heritage to find connections with the human suffering he witnessed in the war. There is little bitterness in his work; he had not enlisted in late 1915 with any illusions about war's grandeur. Nevertheless, the deep irony he uses conveys effectively the plight of humanity caught in the barbed wire of the trenches. Charles Sorley (1895–1915) was an earlier casualty of the war, whose work was not as well developed. Nevertheless, he was a bridge between the romantic visions of Rupert Brooke and the poets who emerged in 1917–18.

It is also worth noting one important exception to the British officers' perspectives represented here. David Jones (1895–1974) was an artistic genius—carver, painter, sculptor, writer—who enlisted in the Royal Welch Fusiliers in late 1915, serving in the ranks until March of 1918. *In Parenthesis* (1937) is a remarkably sophisticated epic poem-memoir that encompasses elements of Welsh and English folklore, Roman Catholic liturgy (Jones converted in 1921), Old Testament history, and especially Arthurian legend. It does not give vent to the bitterness of Sassoon or Owen but conveys well the obsessive force of recollection and myth-making that was at the core of the others' disillusionment.

Although the soldier-writers are those most closely associated with the authors of disillusionment, women also made important contributions to this literature. Sassoon, Graves, and Owen attacked women for their unthinking acceptance of the war and their active role in pushing young men into the maelstrom. German authors most often ignored women or relegated to them traditional tropes as care-giving mothers and nurses. But authors like Vera Brittain (1893–1970) gave voice to women's experiences, offering an important corrective to those of the men just mentioned. Traumatized by the deaths of her fiancé and brother, Brittain became a VAD nurse serving on Malta and later in France. That experience helped strip her of any romanticized illusions she had entertained earlier, and, like Sassoon, this wartime transformation became a lifelong obsession. *Testament of Youth* (1933), *Testament of Friendship* (1940), and *Testament of Experience* (1957) offered Brittain's efforts to assess the war's impact on her personal and public life, and gave some recognition to the women of her generation who she felt had sacrificed as much as the men without the recognition.

The authors of disillusionment taken as a whole represent an important literary bridge between Victorian romanticism and postwar realism and modernism. Most of the authors were politically liberal; several, like Barbusse, Renn, and Zweig, were active socialist ideologues. Most had received classical educations that were reflected in their works. All the British poets, for example, borrowed heavily from the imagery of the Romanticists and others in order to establish the ironies of contemporary experience. Ultimately, the liberal experience of war merged with more conservative accounts, which emphasized cause and camaraderie, to create a retrospective synthesis. The First World War permanently changed the language and imagery of war. Efforts to combine the elements of realism and irony after the Second World War generally failed, and gave way to absurdism. Thus, the wartime accounts that emerged from the Great War are unique and provide essential insights into the conflict not available anywhere else.

Craig Cameron

References

Fussell, Paul. *The Great War and Modern Memory*. New York: Oxford University Press, 1975.
Leed, Eric J. *No Man's Land: Combat and Identity in the First World War*. New York: Cambridge University Press, 1979.
Silkin, Jon. *Out of Battle: The Poetry of the Great War*. New York: Oxford University Press, 1972.

See also LITERATURE: WRITERS OF THE FIRST WORLD WAR

Literature: Writers of the First World War

In August of 1914 a cultural fever swept Europe. As successive European powers entered the war, so their populations swarmed onto the streets to celebrate. Outside the Imperial Palace in Berlin, on the Nevsky Prospekt, in Trafalgar Square, ecstatic crowds greeted the news of the first general European war in a century. Many intellectuals also celebrated, capturing the nationalist enthusiasm of the moment in verse and prose. Later, as the initial excitement of 1914 disappeared in the bloodletting of Verdun, the Somme, and the Brusilov Offensive, writers turned their attentions to the horrors of war.

It appeared then that there was a clear division between those writers of 1914 who, like Rupert Brooke, had welcomed the war, and those who fought in the terrible battles of attrition and wrote, like Wilfred Owen, of the "pity of war." Yet, although there were those in 1914 who greeted the war with unbounded enthusiasm, there were others, such as Edward Thomas, August Stramm, and Lucien Rolmer, who sensed what was coming and took refuge in a stoicism built upon duty and honor. Still others, such as Gerrit Engelke, expressed a clear sense of unease in their writing. Finally, there were writers, such as Hermann Hesse, who condemned the war outright. Whether the writers of 1914 responded with ecstasy or condemnation, none of them were unaware of the historic moment they were living through and in which many of them were to die.

Rupert Brooke (1887–1915) has come to symbolize a naive patriotism that characterized much of the response to the declaration of war. His five sonnets, collectively entitled *1914*, celebrated the comfortable middle-class English life that Brooke had led. They seemed to weigh the pleasant, idealized, English life in the balance, and argue that its preservation, and more important, its revitalization depended on the sacrifice of England's youth. Sonnets I, "Peace," and V, "The Soldier," became particularly famous, with the first line of "Peace"—"Now, God be thanked Who has matched us with His hour"—becoming familiar throughout England. That, and the opening lines of Sonnet V, have entered into the English national consciousness:

If I should die, think only this of me:
That there's some corner of a foreign
   field
That is for ever England.

Brooke himself died on the way to Gallipoli, and thereafter his fame spread, with 300,000 copies of *1914 and Other Poems* and his *Collected Poems* being sold within ten years.

Brooke wasn't alone in his ecstatic response to the war (although there are few reasons to think that his view would have remained the same had he lived beyond April of 1915). William Noel Hodgson (1893–1916) also caught the mood of 1914 in "Happy Is England Now," with its assertions that:

Happy is England now, as never yet! . . .
Happy is England in the brave that die
For wrongs not hers and wrongs so
    sternly hers;
. . . happiest is England now
In those that fight, and watch with pride
    and tears.

That poem and others, such as "The Call,"
and "England to Her Sons," became universally
popular in 1914 and remained so, even after the
Battle of the Somme, on the first day of which
Hodgson was killed.

In France the belief that the war was a
great and necessary adventure was, if anything, more pronounced than in any of the
combatant nations. French concern at being
left far behind in the industrial and demo-
graphic race that Germany led, along with the
general desire to avenge the national humiliation of the loss of Alsace and Lorraine in the
Franco-Prussian War, added extra impetus to
the common belief that France had a civilizing
role to play in the world. The writer and professional soldier Ernest Psichari (1883–1914)
represented one strand of this belief in the
importance and necessity of war. Psichari had
been brought up in the Republican tradition
but had found fulfillment as a soldier in
France's African colonies, and later, as a convert to Catholicism. To him, as for many others on the right, the army and the church were
the true repositories of France's greatness, they
represented eternal France. Psichari's books
about life in the colonial army and his novel,
The Call to Arms, celebrated the virtues of
soldiers. So it is not surprising that he could
write, on 20 August 1914, two days before he
was killed at the front:

We hear only vague news about the war,
but what we hear fills us with joy and
confidence. We are certainly heading for
great victories, and I feel less inclined
than ever to repent at having desired a
war, which was necessary for the honor
and greatness of France. It has come at
the time and in the manner that we required. Let Providence remain with us in
this great and magnificent adventure.

The sort of views held by Psichari were
not confined to those on the right of French
politics. Others, such as Charles Péguy (1873–
1914) and Lucien Rolmer (1880–1916), also
saw the war as a mission to reinvigorate and
save France and civilization. Rolmer wrote: "I
want to live, but above all I want France to live
and impose her Republican will on these feu-
dal Germans—and I'm suffering willingly for
our France and willingly for future freedom."
Rolmer was shot through the head after capture during the Battle of Verdun—the battle
that bled France white.

Not all writers expressed outright enthusiasm for the war in 1914. Many, like the great
working-class poet Isaac Rosenberg (1890–
1918), believed that the war would reinvigorate
civilization but at the same time recognized the
horrors that awaited Europe. In his "On Receiving News of the War" he wrote:

O! ancient crimson curse!
Corrode, consume.
Give back this universe
Its pristine bloom.

Rosenberg was himself poor material for a
soldier, being a very small man and in poor
health, but he joined up in 1915. He was determined that his poetry should not be undermined
by the war, and in fact, before his death in action on 1 April 1918, he had written some of the
finest and most poignant poetry of the war in
poems such as "The Dying Soldier," "Break of
Day in the Trenches," and "Dead Man's
Dump."

In Germany, poet and artist Gerrit Engelke
(1890–1918) was also skeptical from the start
about the value of the war. Engelke was in neutral Denmark when the war began and was
unsure as to whether he should return to Germany to enlist or remain there to work on a
novel, in order that he could "do my people the
major service of increasing the intellectual
worth of the German Empire." He did return
to Germany and had a distinguished career
fighting in the terrible battles of Langemarck,
St. Mihiel, the Somme, Champagne, Dünaberg.
and Verdun. All the while he remained skeptical and convinced that the war was essentially
antispiritual, as when he wrote:

Our war is lacking a soul—just consider
the thread which binds here with over
there as the three threads of capitalism,
party politics and diplomacy. As a concept, this war will surely only ever be
portrayed in the arts as a time-dictated
great and insanely bloody event.

Engelke was mortally wounded during a British attack on 11 October 1918 and died the following day.

If there were writers whose ambivalence toward the war was clear from the outset, there were those who condemned it completely, either openly or in their private diaries and letters. The great German writer Hermann Hesse (1877–1962) was in Switzerland when the conflict began. He refused to serve in the war, condemning it in a series of articles that were later collected as *If the War Goes On. . . .* In September of 1914 Hesse wrote his article "O Freunde, nicht diese Töne!" In the article he attacked the insane chauvinism that had overtaken many of those he termed "the neutrals"—the "scientists, teachers, artists, and men of letters [who] are engaged in the labours of peace and of humanity." Hesse took the fatalistic line that "since shooting is the order of the day, let there be shooting," but he called upon all of "the neutrals" to preserve the universal values of humanity and peace, even in the midst of war.

Gustav Sack (1885–1916) was another German living in Switzerland when the war broke out, and he was reluctant to return to his homeland. Sack was a complex individual who had enjoyed his earlier period of national service, while hating the military. He had no illusions about the causes of the war, nor its real nature. He wrote the following, after he had returned to Germany to fight:

We, the "good soldiers," fight because we are soldiers and are here to save our skins and want to survive at all costs. We are not fighting for an aim, nor for the Fatherland, nor for a united Germany— that is all stuff and nonsense.

Sack's death during the German advance on Bucharest in 1916 was particularly ironic, for he had only just begun to make a literary name for himself. His novels were successfully published after his death.

There were many other writers of 1914 who saw through the jingoistic hysteria of the moment and condemned the idiocy of the war. Amongst them were the Alsatian poet and Rhodes scholar Ernst Stadler (1883–1914), who was killed by a British grenade at First Ypres, and the poet and drug addict Georg Trakl (1887–1914), whose precarious mental balance was disturbed by the horrors of the war on the Eastern Front and who died from an overdose in November of 1914. In France the poet Marc de Larreguy de Civrieux (1895–1916), author of *La Muse de Sang*, wrote poetry against the wartime mentality, but he fought from 1915 until his death at Verdun in November of 1916—another artist victim of Europe's collective insanity.

Although it has become commonplace to ascribe prowar attitudes to the writers of 1914, it can be seen that something new was happening, and that the tired years of "La Belle Epoque" were behind them. Yet others writers sensed or realized what terrors were about to overcome Europe, including, for many, their deaths.

Stephen M. Cullen

References

Bridgwater, Patrick. *The German Poets of the First World War*. London: Croom Helm, 1985.

Cross, Tim, ed. *The Lost Voices of World War I*. London: Blomsbury, 1988.

Field, Frank. *Three French Writers & the Great War*. Cambridge: Cambridge University Press, 1975.

Hamburger, Michael. *A Proliferation of Prophets*. Manchester: Carcanet, 1983.

Wohl, Robert. *The Generation of 1914*. Cambridge: Harvard University Press, 1979.

Lloyd George, David (1863–1945)

Prominent British politician and prime minister from 1916 to 1922. Born 17 January 1863 in Manchester of Welsh parents, Lloyd George was reared by his mother and an uncle in Wales; his father, a schoolmaster, died in 1864. From an early age Lloyd George was exposed to Welsh nationalism, nonconformity in religion, and Liberal politics. In the 1880s he became a successful solicitor. He was elected as a Liberal candidate for an 1890 by-election and held the seat of Carnarvon Boroughs for the next fifty-five years.

In his first fifteen years as an MP, he established his reputation as a spirited debater and a man of charm. He bitterly opposed the Boer War. Following the Liberal party's victory in 1905, he served as president of the Board of Trade for three years and in 1908 became Herbert Asquith's chancellor of the exchequer. His controversial 1909 "People's Budget" was his attempt to provide increased tax revenue for both the naval armaments race and domestic programs. He was a great champion of old-age pensions, plus health and unemployment insurance.

Lloyd George's attitude toward Germany in the immediate prewar years was a mixture of caution and occasional belligerence. He hoped that England could remain uninvolved in any European-wide conflict but abandoned this view once Germany invaded Belgium. By the end of 1914 he favored a vigorous prosecution of the war and supported Churchill's proposed Dardanelles Campaign. He also envisioned a protracted struggle in Europe that would require Britain's total involvement.

In the early months of 1915 Lloyd George was critical of Lord Kitchener and the war office for the shortage of shells on the Western Front. His chance to address that issue directly came in May of 1915, when Asquith appointed him to the new cabinet post of minister of munitions. His determination and zeal to eliminate red tape and to increase shell production became legendary. In reaction to Kitchener's suggestion that each battalion be granted no more than four machine guns, he stated: "Take Kitchener's maximum . . . square it; multiply that result by two; and when you are in sight of that, double it again for good luck." That equation produced sixty-four machine guns per battalion. With energy and vigor he reorganized munitions factories within Britain and placed overseas orders with many countries, including the United States. He also visited workers on site to inspire their efforts to manufacture more ammunition. He was an early proponent of conscription, believing that manpower needs would easily keep pace with the need for more munitions.

Early in 1916 Lloyd George distanced himself somewhat from Asquith with speeches in the Commons that called for more decisive action in the war. Both men were still Liberals and cabinet colleagues, but their personal relationship became more correct than cordial. Following the Easter Rebellion in Dublin, the prime minister asked Lloyd George to pursue an Irish settlement, a new mission that by chance prevented him from accompanying Kitchener on his trip to Russia in June of 1916. When Kitchener died at sea, the question of his successor as secretary of war dominated political discussions. Lloyd George got the office, not Andrew Bonar Law, and he went to the war office just as the Somme Offensive began. During the next six months, he increasingly questioned both Asquith's ability to lead wartime Britain at home and the competence of Douglas Haig and William Robertson as military commanders.

The circumstances surrounding Asquith's resignation and Lloyd George's promotion to prime minister on 7 December 1916 have elicited extensive comments. Various suggestions circulated in London prior to the event, one calling for Asquith to remain in office but with Lloyd George as chairman of a smaller, more powerful war committee. Others proposed the Conservative leader Bonar Law as a suitable replacement for Asquith. In the end, Lloyd George emerged as the only acceptable alternative, perhaps because men of influence recognized the salient characteristic of his personality, as noted by his friend and subsequent biographer, Thomas Jones: "Lloyd George had a passion to win the war."

Lloyd George served as prime minster for the last two years of the Great War. His decisions reflected his earlier work as munitions minister. He reorganized government offices with active new leaders, and he established the five-member war cabinet to make major decisions. He worked with tireless determination and confidence, and he placed a high priority on lifting the nation's morale. Good news and bad came in the difficult year of 1917. While welcoming America's declaration of war, he knew that several months would pass before that decision would have a direct military impact. Russia's exit from the war allowed Germany to concentrate on the Western Front, and U-boat activity had a devastating impact on supply routes. Finally, the prime minister's confidence in Britain's two leading generals, Haig and Robertson, continued to wane. By 1918, however, conditions had improved noticeably: American men and supplies arrived in significant numbers; Robertson was dismissed in favor of another general, Sir Henry Wilson; Haig's campaigns were more successful and less costly; and France's Marshal Ferdinand Foch became the supreme allied commander. Also, the naval convoy system, supported by the Americans and Lloyd George, proved its worth against the U-boats.

Lloyd George led the British delegation at the Versailles Peace Conference, where he tried to maintain the pragmatic middle ground between Wilson's idealism and Clemenceau's penchant for imposing a harsh and punitive settlement on the Germans. On most key issues he sided with the Americans. Lloyd George continued as the head of a coalition government until 1922, but his dependence on Bonar Law and the Conservatives became increasingly clear. His one notable success in this period was the Government of Ireland Act, in 1920, which established Northern Ireland while setting the southern counties on the road to independence. Although he resigned from the government in October of 1922, Lloyd George remained an important person in the Liberal party for another twenty years. Churchill asked him to join the war cabinet in 1940, but Lloyd George politely declined. He was created 1st Earl Lloyd-George of Dwyfor by the New Year's honors list in 1945, a few short months before his death on 26 March. He was buried in Wales, beside the Dwyfor River.

Thomas W. Davis

References

Constantine, Stephen. *Lloyd George*. New York: Routledge, 1992.

Grigg, John. *Lloyd George, from Peace to War*. Los Angeles: University of California Press, 1985.

Jones, Thomas. *Lloyd George*. Cambridge: Harvard University Press, 1951.

Morgan, Kenneth O. *The Age of Lloyd George*. New York: Barnes and Noble, 1971.

Mowat, Charles L. *Lloyd George*. London: Oxford University Press, 1964.

See also ASQUITH, HERBERT; GREAT BRITAIN, HOME FRONT

London, Treaty of (26 April 1915)

The secret Treaty of London ended Italy's neutrality in World War I and formalized its temporary hegemony over its neighbors.

Although formally allied to Germany and Austria-Hungary in the Triple Alliance when the First World War began, Italy sought refuge in neutrality in order to protect its fragile nation-state, created only in the second half of the nineteenth century. Italians worried that any conflict with Great Britain would ruin trade, that their armed forces were unprepared for combat, and that the fractious Chamber of Deputies would reject any effort to join the Allied cause.

Several developments, however, began to tilt the government of Antonio Salandra (1914–16) toward intervention on the side of the Allies. These included the failed German offensive culminating in the Battle of the Marne, the possibility of Allied success in the Dardanelles, and the expectation of a Russian victory against Austria-Hungary in Galicia. If the Allies were to succeed on each of these fronts, Salandra and his advisors feared an exodus of Balkan nations to the Allied cause, thus robbing Italy of the continued political benefits of neutrality. The Salandra government believed that it had to act if it were going to complete its irredentist aims and legitimize Italy's claim to great-power status. The government had to either sell its support to the highest bidder or watch its political options disappear. As a result, on 4 March 1915, the Italian government presented its price for intervention to the Allies.

The Italian government had two major preconditions for entering the war on the Allied side. First, it wanted to annex southern Tyrol up to the Brenner Pass and thus eliminate an Austrian salient on its northern front. Secondly, it wanted to establish political hegemony over the Adriatic. Since the Italians did not have a suitable naval base between Venice and Brindisi, a distance of five hundred miles, they did not want to trade an old vulnerability to the Austro-Hungarian Empire for a new vulnerability to an aggressive Yugoslav confederation. The Italians sought control over both coasts of the Adriatic and the denial of naval ports to Serbia and Montenegro. The Italians also feared that Serbian seaports might provide access to the Russian navy.

Regardless of her demands, both Great Britain and Germany wanted Italy as an ally. The British hoped to tap Italian military capabilities, which they overestimated, and they expected nearby Balkan states to follow Italy's example and join the Allied cause. The British were sufficiently eager for Italy's support that they neither complained about her demands nor threatened to strangle Italian maritime trade, which was an obvious bargaining option. At the same time, the British secured Russian compliance by threatening them with reduced aid. As a result, the Russians muted their support for a Serbian-dominated greater Yugoslavia.

The German General Staff was well aware of what might be the effect of Italian intervention on the Allied side. It was worried that a hostile Italy would inspire military interventions by Romania, Bulgaria, and Greece, and thus force a major diversion of German troops to the Balkans. The Germans subsequently pressured Austria-Hungary to satisfy Italy's demands, but Vienna steadfastly refused.

On 26 April 1915 Italy abandoned its "sacred egoism" and signed the Treaty of London. A formal denunciation of the Triple Alliance followed on 3 May, as did a declaration of war against the Central Powers on 23 May. The treaty offered a great deal to the Italians and required little in return. It stipulated that the British and French fleets would protect Italian interests, and that Russia would prevent Austria-Hungary from concentrating its troops against its neighbor. Additionally, the treaty promised Italy the following territories: the Trentino, the Tyrol (south of the Brenner Pass), the counties of Gorizia and Gradisca, Trieste, the Istrian peninsula and adjoining islands, North Dalmatia and the islands off it, the Port of Vlonë (Valona) in Albania and a zone around it, and the province of Antalya/Adalia (in the event the Allies divided up Turkey). It also promised gains for Italy in Eritrea, Somaliland, and Tripolitania if Britain and France were to gain territory in Africa at the expense of Germany. Lastly, the treaty guaranteed Italy's sovereignty over the Dodecanese Islands, a share of future war indemnities, and a British loan of at least £50 million. The demands placed on Italy, in contrast, were relatively modest—it would not oppose the division of Adriatic territories, including Albania, between Croatia, Montenegro, Serbia, and Greece.

From an Italian perspective, the terms of the Treaty of London seemed beneficial, but they ultimately yielded mixed results. First, the Italians had based their negotiations on the expectation of rapid military success, but by late May neither Galicia nor the Dardanelles were in Allied hands. As a result, Italy's entry into the war did not break the stalemate. What it did do was destroy domestic social and political cohesion, especially since the number of Italians lost in combat almost equaled the number gained through annexation and occupation. Secondly, Russia divulged the general provisions of the treaty to Serbia, thus undermining any attempt to keep the treaty secret from disaffected Slavs. The Serbians subsequently worked to revise the accord, especially any provisions that yielded Dalmatia to Italy. Indeed, Serbian opposition lasted until the Treaty of Rapallo in 1920, which saw Italy modify its claims to Dalmatia,

but only after ensuring that Fiume would become a free state.

Lastly, Italian irredentism collided with President Wilson's vision of a postwar peace as expressed in his Fourteen Points. Italy argued that the Treaty of London remained binding and demanded that the Allies honor its provisions at the Versailles Conference. The resulting differences of opinion over the treaty remained largely unresolved until the bilateral Italo-Yugoslav accord signed at Rapallo.

Peter R. Faber

References

Gottlieb, Wolfram. *Studies in Secret Diplomacy During the First World War.* London: Allen and Unwin, 1957.

Stevenson, David. *The First World War and International Politics.* New York: Oxford University Press, 1988.

Zeman, Z.A.B. *The Gentlemen Negotiators.* New York: Macmillan, 1971.

See also ITALY, HOME FRONT; PARIS PEACE CONFERENCE, 1919; SALANDRA, ANTONIO; VERSAILLES TREATY

Loßberg, Friedrich von (1868–1942)

Prussian staff officer. Born on 30 April 1868 at Homburg von der Höhe to a family that had a long tradition of military service, Friedrich "Fritz" von Loßberg was commissioned an officer in the prestigious Guards Regiment in 1888. By 1911 he had become principal of the Kriegsakademie and in 1913 was promoted to chief of staff of the XIII Württemburg Army Corps.

In 1915 Loßberg was promoted to colonel and became the chief of operations for General Erich von Falkenhayn. He directed and organized the German defense during the Champagne battles of 1915 and the Somme battles of 1916. He believed in allowing his subordinate commanders freedom to make important decisions regarding the timing of their counterattacks, which was effective in stopping the Allied offensives. Loßberg began to distill defensive knowledge into a formula, which became the idea of the defense in depth, or "elastic" defense.

After taking command of the German armies, Field Marshal Paul von Hindenburg and General Erich Ludendorff embraced Loßberg's new ideas of defense. In the fall of

1916 Loßberg was placed in charge of Operation Alberich, the planning of the *Siegfriedstellung,* or Hindenburg Line. Loßberg directed its construction and saw to it that the most up-to-date ideas on defense were incorporated into its design. In a war characterized by mediocrity, Loßberg was one of the few masters of his craft.

From the summer of 1918 until the end of the war, Loßberg was chief of the general staff for General Max von Boehn's army group. After the war ended, Loßberg was placed on Hans von Seeckt's staff and was charged with supervising the securing of Germany's eastern border.

After the war, Loßberg held high positions in the *Reichswehr,* including general chief of staff in Kassel from 1920 to 1921 and commander of the Sixth Division in Münster. He retired in 1927 as general of the infantry and died on 14 May 1942 in Lübeck.

Steven D. Fisher

References

Wynne, G.C. *If Germany Attacks: The Battle in Depth in the West.* London: Faber and Faber, 1940.

See also ALBERICH, OPERATION OF; CHAMPAGNE, FIRST AND SECOND BATTLES OF; SOMME, BATTLE OF

Ludendorff, Erich (1865–1937)

German quartermaster general. One of the central figures in World War I, Ludendorff was also one of the most peculiar characters in military history. Born on 9 April 1865 near Posen (Poznan), Ludendorff was the son of a rural estate agent. He was educated in the Cadet Corps and entered the army, gaining his commission as an infantry officer in 1883.

Ludendorff's whole focus was the military, and, as a result, he lacked a wider vision. His stern character and fierce intellect earned him admission to the Kriegsakademie at the relatively young age of twenty-eight. In 1895, as a captain, he joined the general staff. Starting in 1904, he spent almost nine straight years in the mobilization planning section of the general staff and became chief of the mobilization section in 1908.

Ludendorff's 1913 call for sharp increases in the military irritated his superiors and led to his transfer to regimental command. Later that same year he assumed command of a brigade in Strasbourg. When the war began, Ludendorff became chief quartermaster of General Karl von Bülow's Second Army.

In August of 1914 Ludendorff rescued his military career when the commander of the 14th Infantry Brigade was killed before Liège. Ludendorff took command and won the *Pour le Mérite* for his daring capture of the fortress.

He was then posted as chief of staff of General Paul von Hindenburg's Eighth Army on the Eastern Front. It was the start of the team that the Allies came to refer to as "H&L." The two men were an odd but apparently complementary couple. Ludendorff was dynamic and very excitable in crisis, while Hindenburg was known for his stoic facade and iron nerves.

Although planning for the Battle of Tannenberg was the work of Colonel Max Hoffmann, Ludendorff planned most of the key eastern battles for the next two years, such as at the Masurian Lakes, Lodz, and Gorlice-Tarnów.

In August of 1916, after the failure of the Verdun offensive, the kaiser relieved General Erich von Falkenhayn and brought H&L to the West to assume supreme military control. Hindenburg became chief of the general staff, while Ludendorff assumed the post of first quartermaster general. Despite his title, his job had nothing to do with supplies and logistics. Nominally the number-two man in the German army, Ludendorff in a very short time became de facto generalissimo, although he never held a rank higher than *general der infantrie* (equivalent to lieutenant general).

Before the end of the First World War, Ludendorff also became the virtual military dictator of Germany. In 1917 he endorsed the navy's plan for unrestricted submarine warfare, which eventually brought the United States into the war. He also brought about the dismissal of German Chancellor Theobald von Bethmann Hollweg. In 1917 he approved the plan to transport Lenin from Switzerland with the idea that the Bolsheviks might cause enough internal chaos to take Russia out of the war.

After H&L took command, the German army went on the strategic defensive in the West and concentrated on eliminating Russia from the war. Once that was accomplished, the army again looked westward. By that time, however, the United States had entered the war on the Allied side. Ludendorff knew he had to act before American troops arrived in sufficient number to tip the balance against Germany. He

L

planned a great offensive to take Britain out of the war, reasoning that France would then collapse.

Between 21 March and 17 July 1918, the Germans mounted five great offensives. The first three of these were great tactical successes, with the first and third each capturing more ground than the Allies had managed to take in the previous three and a half years combined. Strategically, however, none of the offensives achieved their objectives. The final outcome was in part the result of strategic errors on Ludendorff's part.

From 18 July until the end of the war, Germany never again gained the initiative. During the final months of the war Ludendorff first called for an armistice, then reversed himself when he learned of Allied terms. Ludendorff then offered his resignation to the kaiser, who accepted it on 26 October. Rather than face the chaos in Germany, Ludendorff went into exile in Sweden and wrote his war memoirs.

Ludendorff returned to Germany in the spring of 1919. The remaining years of his life can only be described as a bizarre binge of extreme-right-wing politics mixed with fanatical Nordic religion. He participated in the 1920 Kapp Putsch and in Hitler's 1923 Beer Hall Putsch. Acquitted in subsequent trials, Ludendorff in 1925 ran for president against Hindenburg, whom he had come to despise since the end of the war.

At first Ludendorff was an ardent supporter of the Nazis and served as a National Socialist member of the Reichstag from 1924 to 1929. By the early 1930s, however, Ludendorff had effectively withdrawn from public life. He spent a great deal of his time writing on his theories of "total war," in which he reversed the concept advanced by Carl von Clausewitz. For Ludendorff, politics was nothing but an extension of war.

In 1925 Ludendorff divorced his first wife and married Mathilde von Kemnitz, a neurologist and popular philosopher who was every bit as eccentric as he. Together they concocted theories of the "divine destiny" of the German people and of the conspiracies to thwart that destiny by the "supernational powers" of Christianity, Jewry, and Freemasonry.

During World War I Ludendorff was ennobled by the kaiser, thus allowing him to call himself von Ludendorff. He had, however, refused to let the kaiser make him a count. By the mid-1930s Ludendorff had turned completely against the Nazis, and he refused promotion to field marshal from Hitler. By the time of his death at Munich on 20 December 1937, Ludendorff was warning about Hitler's tyranny.

David T. Zabecki

References

Aspry, Robert B. *The German High Command at War. Hindenburg and Ludendorff Conduct World War I*. New York: William Morrow, 1991.

Goerlitz, Walter. *History of the German General Staff—its History and Structure 1657–1945*. Translated by B. Battershaw. Westport, Conn.: Praeger, 1953.

Goodspeed, D.J. *Ludendorff. Genius of World War I*. Boston: Houghton Mifflin, 1966.

Ludendorff, Erich. *My War Memories*. 2 vols. London: Hutchinson, 1919.

See also BELGIUM, INVASION OF; EAST PRUSSIA CAMPAIGN; EASTERN FRONT, 1915; GERMANY, HOME FRONT; HINDENBURG, PAUL VON; LUDENDORFF OFFENSIVES, 1918

Ludendorff Offensives, 1918

Following the failure to take Verdun in 1916, Germany's overall strategy had been to remain on the strategic defensive against the Allies in the West and concentrate on defeating Russia in the East. With the German victory at Riga in September of 1917 effectively taking Russia out of the war, General Erich Ludendorff was freed to turn his attention back to the West. In the fall of 1917 the German army transferred thirty-five divisions with their organic artillery and over one thousand heavy guns. That put some 194 of Germany's 251 divisions on the Western Front and gave them a superiority of roughly eighteen divisions over the Allies at the start of 1918.

Ludendorff knew he had to move quickly to end the war because of the United States' entry into the war. While there were not sufficient American troops to play a significant factor at the end of 1917, by the middle of 1918 they could be expected to tip the balance of power in the Allies' favor. In the spring of 1918, however, Ludendorff believed that he still had the resources and the numerical superiority for one decisive blow.

Ludendorff considered the British, located on the northern flank, the more dangerous of his two principal opponents. Britain, he felt, would continue to fight without France. But if the British could be defeated decisively on the battlefield, Ludendorff was sure that France would collapse. On 11 November 1917, exactly one year before the end of the war, Ludendorff called a meeting of all his key staff section heads and chiefs of staff of the subordinate commands. They met at Spa, Belgium, to consider various courses of action. Opinions were widely divided, so Ludendorff deferred the final decision and ordered the OHL (*Oberste Heeresleitung*, German General Headquarters on the Western Front) to draw up detailed plans for the most promising options.

Rather than the one great assault envisioned by Ludendorff, the Germans actually mounted five large offensives during the spring and early summer of 1918. They also planned and were preparing for a sixth assault, which they never launched. This group of offensives is significant in the history of military tactics because they saw the first major applications on the Western Front of what became known as "Stormtrooper Tactics." The artillery tactics were new too, with fire planning for all five handled by Colonel Georg Bruchmüller, brought from the Eastern Front for that purpose.

The St. Quentin Offensive

On 21 January 1918 Ludendorff selected the operations plan code named Michael. The attack was designed to strike at the boundary between the British and French armies in Flanders. Once the British were cut off from French reinforcements and pinned against the sea, they could be rolled up from the flank and defeated in detail. Then the Germans could turn their attention to the French.

Michael called for an attack by sixty-seven German divisions along a seventy-kilometer front running from La Fère to Arras. Three field armies would control the action: General Fritz von Below's Seventeenth Army in the north, General Georg von der Marwitz's Second Army in the center, and General Oskar von Hutier's Eighteenth Army in the south. The Second Army was to launch the main attack, while the Eighteenth Army was to prevent the French from closing the gap and reinforcing the British, and the Seventeenth Army was to prevent the British from moving reinforcements down from the north.

Facing the attacking force were thirty-three British divisions in the Third Army of General Sir Julian Byng and the Fifth Army of General Sir Hubert Gough. Fifth Army, on the British southern flank, was in the most precarious position. Having suffered heavy casualties in the Passchendaele Offensive of 1917, it had only recently moved into its present sector of the line. When the British took over their new positions from the French, they found the trenches and defensive works in poor condition, and, in some places, nonexistent.

In preparation for the attack, the Germans moved in huge quantities of artillery. When the attack started, the three German field armies had a total of 6,608 guns, approximately 2,598 of which were heavy or superheavy. Facing them the two British armies had a total of 2,686, only 976 of which were heavier than light field guns. This gave the Germans a superiority of 2.5:1.

The German artillery opened fire at 04:40 on 21 March 1918. The preparations lasted only five hours. The St. Quentin preparation was the greatest artillery bombardment in history to that time. The sound of the firing could be heard as far away as London. The Germans fired 3.2 million rounds on the first day. At 09:40 hours the creeping barrage started to move forward followed closely by the German infantry. Heavy fog until late that morning favored the attackers and tended to prolong the effects of the German gas. Initial results were spectacular, with the German infantry pushing farther and faster than anyone in early 1918 could have believed possible.

Gough's Fifth Army took the blow especially hard. By the end of the first day eight frontline battalions of its XVIII Corps could count a total of only fifty combat effectives still in the line.

The Allies' initial response only contributed to the German success. British commander in chief Field Marshal Sir Douglas Haig knew his center of gravity was the Channel ports. He had put all his reserves behind his north wing and was counting on the French to cover him in the south. But French army commander General Henri-Philippe Pétain believed the attack was only a feint. Fearing the German main attack would come near Reims and drive straight for Paris, he refused to commit his reserves in support of the British. In desperation Haig called for a meeting of the Supreme Allied War Council, which met on 26 March at Doullens. Their response to the crisis was to appoint French General Ferdinand Foch as Allied commander in chief on the Western Front. For the first time in the war all the Western Allies recognized a unified command structure. Foch responded in turn by ordering French reinforcements to move in support of the British.

Despite its early success, the German drive soon started to slow down. By the end of the second day only the Eighteenth Army was still advancing rapidly. But it was not supposed to be the main effort. On 28 March Ludendorff tried to restore momentum in the north by launching the Seventeenth Army against Arras. This second wave was actually the Mars operation, which came out of the 11 November conference. When Mars failed, Ludendorff decided to shift the main attack to the Eighteenth Army, and he ordered Hutier to push toward Amiens. That change in plans caused a wrenching shift in the logistical support network behind the German lines, as supplies and follow-on forces were poured in behind the Eighteenth Army. Shortly, however, Hutier started running up against the French reinforcements sent by Foch. Hutier's drive also soon ran out of steam, and the Eighteenth Army never reached Amiens.

When Ludendorff called off the great St. Quentin Offensive on 5 April, the German army had taken more ground than the Allies had during four years of fighting. German forces captured 1,200 square miles of territory—compared with the 125 square miles the British had to show for three months of fighting on the Somme in 1916. Besides the lost ground, the attack cost the Allies 160,000 casualties, 90,000 prisoners, and 1,100 pieces of artillery. Despite their astounding tactical success, the Germans suffered casualties almost as high, most of them in the specially trained shock divisions.

The St. Quentin Offensive almost worked, and the reasons for its failure are varied and complex. For one thing, Ludendorff violated the principle of unity of command at the operational level. Originally all three attacking armies had been under the Army Group of Bavarian Crown Prince Rupprecht. Less than two months prior to the attack, however, the Eighteenth Army was transferred to the Army Group of German Crown Prince Wilhelm.

One of the most striking features of the operation was the uneven advance of the three armies. Eighteenth Army in the south penetrated almost sixty-seven kilometers. In the end it advanced too far, too fast, and finally halted when it outran its logistical chain. Seventeenth Army in the north made the least progress, advancing barely twenty-five kilometers. Second Army in the center did only slightly better. Seventeenth Army did have the toughest mission and faced the better prepared opponent. But, curiously, the Germans failed to weight the main attack with artillery. While Second Army was designated to make the main effort, it attacked with significantly fewer mortars, guns, and even fewer heavy guns than either Seventeenth or Eighteenth armies.

The Lys Offensive

St. Quentin was a brilliant tactical success, but it was a strategic failure. When the fighting stopped, the Allies were shaken to their very core. They had suffered massive casualties and equipment losses and had lost huge tracts of territory. Physically and politically, however, the coalition was still intact. The Germans had created a huge salient in Allied territory, which really meant an additional eighty-five kilometers of front line to man and defend. The worn and strained German logistics system was stretched to the point of breaking.

Meanwhile, fresh American divisions continued to pour into Europe. In retrospect, Germany had already lost the war at that point. But, as Ludendorff saw it, his offensive came so close to succeeding that one more hard drive would shove the Allies over the edge. He therefore ordered immediate preparations for another large attack against the British.

Ludendorff wanted to execute Plan George against the main British positions in the north. But the Germans had expended so much in trying to exploit the tactical success at St. Quentin that they did not have the resources for the George attack. OHL analyzed the British situation and concluded it would not be necessary to penetrate all the way to the Channel. If the Germans could capture the strategic rail center at Hazebrouck, twenty-six kilometers east of Armentières, it would put an arrow straight through the heart of the British logistics network. After some quick revisions of the George operation plan, a scaled-down version emerged—Georgette.

On 28 March, right after the Mars attack died, Ludendorff ordered Georgette in eight to ten days' time. This second great German offensive pitted the German Fourth and Sixth armies on the extreme north of the German line against the British Second and First armies and the small Belgian army. The Germans massed a total of sixty-one divisions against thirty-four Allied.

Plan Georgette called for the Sixth Army under General Ferdinand von Quast to make the main attack south of Armentières and drive straight toward Hazebrouck. On the following day the Fourth Army would mount a secondary attack north of Armentières to contain any British reinforcements. This time the main attack got the preponderance of artillery. Fourth Army had 522 guns and Sixth Army 1,686 guns, to face the 511 guns of the British First Army. This gave Sixth Army a superiority of 3.3:1. With Sixth Army attacking on a seventeen-kilometer-wide front, it had an artillery density of one hundred guns per kilometer—the highest density the Germans achieved in the war.

Sixth Army's artillery opened up at 04:15 on 9 April, with the preparation lasting four and a half hours. At 08:45 the infantry moved out behind the creeping barrage. The Sixth Army fired a total of 1.4 million rounds of ammunition that first day.

Like St. Quentin the month before, the initial results were an overwhelming success. Sixth Army advanced five kilometers in the first few hours of the assault. Two weak Portuguese divisions assigned to the British First Army virtually disintegrated. On 10 April the German Fourth Army on the extreme north flank started the supporting attack. By 12 April the situation looked desperate for the British, and Field Marshal Haig issued his famous "Backs to the Wall" message to his troops. Two days later the attack of the Sixth Army started to falter. The fighting finally stopped on 29 April, with the Germans halted eight kilometers short of their objective at Hazebrouck.

Judged by the standards of World War I battles, the Lys Offensive was another tactical success—although not on quite the same scale as St. Quentin. But it too was a strategic failure. It failed primarily through a lack of reserves to exploit the initial success—reserves Ludendorff had squandered when he tried to shift the weight of the St. Quentin attack. Since 21 March the Germans had achieved two tactical victories, but with heavy and irreplaceable losses. Two-thirds of the German army on the Western Front had been committed to the two offensives, and Germany had run out of manpower resources. Although the Allies had also suffered heavy losses—fifty-three out of a total of sixty British divisions had fought in one or both battles—the Allies still had the advantage of the fresh American units that continued to pour into the theater.

The Chemin des Dames Offensive

Ludendorff fell victim to the lure of his spectacular but purely tactical successes. Rather than husbanding his forces and going on the defensive, he continued to believe the Allies were on the verge of collapse and that just one more hard push would end the war. He still saw the British as the center of gravity; but by this time the Allies understood that too, and Foch had moved considerable numbers of French reserves into Flanders. Ludendorff was realistic enough to know that the German army did not have enough strength left for an attack in the north, where the French and newly arrived Americans would be sure to counter. He therefore conceived another one-two punch on a massive scale.

On 18 April 1918, OHL issued the warning order for Operation Blücher to Crown Prince Wilhelm's Army Group. Ludendorff intended this attack as a diversionary drive toward Paris, designed to scare the French into pulling all their reserves and the new American units into a tight defensive perimeter around the French capital. The plan called for the attack to halt after advancing about twenty kilometers. The German army would then follow up with Operation Hagen, a rapid shift north and another thrust against the British.

The Blücher attack was planned for the area just south of St. Quentin, along the Chemin des Dames ridge. The German Seventh Army would make the main effort, supported by First Army. OHL massed forty-one divisions along the fifty-five-kilometer attack front. Facing that force, the weak French Sixth Army had about nine divisions (including some British units) on the front line.

Again the Germans weighted the attack heavily with artillery. Facing 1,422 French and British guns, the Germans massed 5,263 guns. The resulting 3.7:1 ratio was the highest artillery superiority the Germans achieved during any of the battles on the Western Front between 1914 and 1918. At 02:00 on 27 May 1918, German guns opened fire and caught the Allies almost completely by surprise. This preparation was Bruchmüller's masterpiece. All firing was done by using calculations of the new "Pulkowski Method." There was no adjustment of rounds, and therefore no need to observe; thus all the firing was done during darkness. The

L

preparation lasted just two hours and forty-five minutes. The effect was accurate and devastating. The German gunners hardly missed a single forward position, communications trench, command post, or Allied battery. The carnage was even worse than it should have been because General Denis Duchêne, commander of the Sixth Army, had ignored Pétain's instructions on the use of elastic defense and defense in-depth techniques. Refusing to yield an inch of sacred French soil, he packed all of his troops into the front lines, where they were sitting ducks for Bruchmüller's guns. The German artillery fired three million rounds on the first day of the battle. Fifty percent of that total was gas.

The German infantry assaulted at 04:40, twenty minutes before first light. Following behind a double creeping barrage, they managed to take the eastern end of the ridge by 06:30. By 10:00 the first German units were across the Aisne, about five kilometers beyond the Chemin des Dames ridge line. The Germans moved so fast that the French could not withdraw their artillery in battery on the north side of the river, allowing the Germans to capture some 650 guns as they swept along.

By the end of the first day of the attack the German infantry had advanced twenty-two kilometers, exceeding the objective for the entire offensive. That was the largest single-day advance of any attack in World War I. On the evening of the second day the German penetration was twenty-five kilometers deep and seventy wide. Ludendorff had accomplished his goals far more quickly than he could have thought possible. But rather than following through with his overall strategic plan, his own tactical success pulled him in once again. Ludendorff ordered the Seventh Army to drive on Paris, and he threw in the reserves he had been building up for Hagen.

For the next few days the German juggernaut rolled along, with all French resistance crumbling in its path. General Pétain committed his sixteen reserve divisions with little effect. Then, doing exactly what Ludendorff originally had wanted him to do, he requested the immediate shifting of the Allied theater reserves from Flanders to his sector. General Foch was convinced the attack was a feint. Ironically, Foch seemed to possess a better appreciation of the strategic situation than Ludendorff. At first Foch did not send Pétain any additional help, but he finally started to trickle reinforcements into the sector, including the U.S. 2nd and 3rd

infantry divisions. The U.S. 3rd Infantry Division was rushed by motor and rail to Château-Thierry on the Marne. In three days of savage fighting starting 1 June they beat back all German attempts to cross, earning the nickname they still carry—"The Rock of the Marne." The United States Army had finally arrived.

On 6 June, Crown Prince Wilhelm's Army Group called a halt to the attack and ordered Seventh and First armies to consolidate their gains. The Germans were less than seventy kilometers from Paris. At first glance it looked like the low point of the war for the Allies, but the Germans were in no position to exploit their advantage. Ludendorff had squandered the resources he needed for Hagen, and all he had to show for it was another large salient to defend and a longer front line to hold with fewer resources.

The Noyon Offensive

Operation Gneisenau had been planned originally as the second phase of the Chemin des Dames Offensive. Both attacks were designed to pull the Allied theater reserves down from Flanders; but that was before Ludendorff abandoned the limited objectives of the Chemin des Dames attack. Now Operation Gneisenau was imperative for an entirely different reason. After St. Quentin and Chemin des Dames the Germans were left holding two large salients into Allied territory—something like a huge but sloppy-looking letter M. The Gneisenau attack, centered around Noyon, was intended to straighten out the inward bulge in the German line and connect the extreme points in the two outward bulges. That would shorten the overall line the Germans had to man and free up resources for another chance at the Hagen attack. Even before the Chemin des Dames fighting came to an end, Hutier's Eighteenth Army had received a warning order to prepare to attack on 7 June with fifteen divisions against the nine of the French Third Army.

Preparations for the Noyon Offensive were hasty at best. Many of the external assets, including the heavy artillery, were still tied up at Chemin des Dames. As a result, the attack had to be delayed forty-eight hours so that all the guns could get into place. The rapid and somewhat slipshod preparations were difficult to conceal. German activities in fact were so obvious, compared with those of the first three attacks, that French intelligence at first thought it was all part of a crude and rather obvious deception plan.

The German artillery preparation lasted three hours and forty-five minutes. Eighteenth Army fired 1.4 million rounds the first day. Despite the lack of surprise, the initial results were good. The French apparently had not learned the lessons of Chemin des Dames and still had more than 50 percent of their troops within 2,000 meters of the front line. By the end of the first day Eighteenth Army had advanced ten kilometers, taken eight thousand prisoners, and virtually destroyed three French divisions. On 20 June Hutier reached his objectives and halted to consolidate his gains.

The Champagne-Marne Offensive

By the middle of June, Germany no longer had a significant chance of winning a decisive victory. Twenty American divisions were now in France, each twice as large as a European division, and they could field three times the actual trench strength of the understrength German divisions. But Ludendorff refused to yield the initiative. He still believed that he could defeat the British if he could pull the Allied reserves away from the north. Thus Ludendorff issued a warning order for another large offensive in the south. This one was called *Friedensturm* (Peace Offensive). It was an unfortunate code name, because it gave the *Landser* in the trenches the impression that it would be the last big attack, which would end the war. Ludendorff actually planned *Friedensturm* as yet another feint, preparatory to the long-delayed Hagen.

Crown Prince Wilhelm's Army Group got the *Friedensturm* mission. The ambitious plan called for a double envelopment of the Reims salient, making it the farthest south of all the great 1918 attacks. It also was in a location where the overall frontline trace ran east and west, so the Germans would be attacking from north to south. West of Reims a large section of the line ran along the Marne River. The German Seventh Army would have to start its attack with a deliberate river crossing. East of Reims, in Champagne, the Marne was anywhere from twenty to thirty kilometers south of the line of departure. First and Third armies would have to attack over relatively open ground and then conduct a hasty crossing of the Marne. The western wing of First Army also had the mission of conducting a holding attack against the front of Reims itself.

The French Fourth Army held the ground east of Reims. Fifth Army was on the west side, extending almost to the tip of the Château-Thierry salient. The overall correlation of forces gave the attackers an advantage, with forty-five German divisions facing thirty-three French.

As in Noyon, the Germans failed to achieve the same level of surprise they had for the attacks in March, April, and May. They had enough time to prepare, but conditions did not favor secrecy. The short, bright nights aided Allied observation, and prevailing northeasterly winds carried sounds from the German lines.

The French anticipated the German attack as early as 1 July. On the night of 14 July a trench raid bagged twenty-seven German prisoners, who divulged that the attack was scheduled to commence the following morning with artillery preparation starting at 01:10. At 01:20 hours, ten minutes after the German opening time, the French artillery started a full-scale counterpreparation. The fire was far more intense than anything the Germans could have thought possible. At 04:50 on 15 July the German infantry moved out behind a double creeping barrage. Although the wind direction favored the attackers, it was too strong and quickly dissipated the German gas.

West of Reims the French counterpreparation disrupted the Seventh Army's river-crossing operation. Right from the start the French fire separated the German infantry from their creeping barrage. The infantry stalled, but the barrage kept moving along. French fire also played havoc with the bridging operation. As the bridges finally started going up, far behind schedule and under heavy fire, small groups of infantry got across the Marne in boats. For the most part they landed in the wrong locations and had little support because they could not get their artillery across.

After the third try, the Germans got some bridges across the river. By nightfall on 15 July they had some six divisions on the south bank but hardly any artillery. The bridgehead was about twenty kilometers wide and five deep. At that point French artillery, working in conjunction with the air force, started concentrating on the bridges, to cut off the German force on the south bank.

East of Reims, meanwhile, First and Third armies encountered far heavier French artillery fire than anticipated but almost no resistance on the ground. Despite taking stiff casualties the German infantry advanced rapidly—at first. About 07:30 their creeping barrage reached its maximum range and lifted. The attackers found themselves facing a fully manned zone defense that had been hardly touched by the preparation or the barrage. The French had sucked them into a trap. Knowing the exact time of the attack, Fourth Army had abandoned its front-line positions except for a very light security force. It reestablished the main line of defense along its intermediate position, between their first and second sets of trench lines. The massive German artillery prep, for the most part, had struck empty ground.

By nightfall on 15 July it was obvious to everyone that the German attack was going nowhere. Fighting dragged on through the next day. Ludendorff realized that he was not going to accomplish another spectacular break-through, but, ever the optimist, he still believed he could scare the Allies into shifting their the-ater reserves if the Germans took Reims. He ordered the Seventh Army on the west flank to consolidate its gains. Early on the 17th, OHL started shifting much of the reinforcing artillery away from Seventh Army to support the con-tinued attacks on Reims.

Foch launched a surprise counterattack early on 18 July. Two French armies, heavily augmented with American divisions, hit either side of the Château-Thierry salient on Seventh Army's extreme western flank. This was exactly the area where OHL had withdrawn most of its reinforcing artillery just the day before. This time the French had a 2.3:1 gun superiority. They also committed almost 750 tanks. The French counterattack spelled the end of the German's Champagne-Marne Offensive— Ludendorff's fifth great drive. It also aborted Operation Hagen. After 18 July 1918 the Ger-mans never again regained the initiative in the Great War.

Aftermath

Within days of Foch's counterattack Luden-dorff realized that the war was lost. On 20 July he wired Prince Rupprecht that Operation Hagen probably never would be launched. The German army remained on the defensive for the rest of the war. Ludendorff's five great offensives cost the Allies almost 948,000 casu-alties in just four brief months. They also lost 225,000 POWs and some 2,500 guns. But the Germans fared no better, taking 963,000 casualties. During that same period the Amer-icans put more than one million troops in-to Europe, almost making up the Allied losses. After 18 July the Allies were clearly win-ning the war, but they too failed to achieve a decisive breakthrough. In the end the Allies won the Great War by sheer weight of num-bers.

David T. Zabecki

References

Essame, Hubert. *The Battle for Europe, 1918*. New York: Charles Scribner's Sons, 1972.

Middlebrook, Martin. *The Kaiser's Battle*. London: Penguin, 1978.

Paschall, Rod. *The Defeat of Imperial Ger-many, 1917–1918*. Chapel Hill, N.C.: Algonquin, 1989.

Pitt, Barrie. *1918: The Last Act*. New York: Norton, 1963.

Zabecki, David T. *Steel Wind: Colonel Georg Bruchmueller and the Birth of Modern Artillery*. Westport, Conn.: Praeger, 1994.

See also BRUCHMÜLLER, GEORG; LUDENDORFF, ERICH

Ludwig III (1845–1921)

King of Bavaria. The son of Prince Luitpold, Ludwig was born at Munich on 7 January 1845. He replaced his father as regent of his first cousin, the insane King Otto, in December of 1912, and was crowned king as Ludwig III in November of 1913.

He hoped to acquire territory during World War I; his son, Crown Prince Rupprecht, commanded German forces. At first Bavarians were patriotic, but as economic devastation worsened, sentiments shifted. Bavarians criti-cized Ludwig for not defending their interests to the Berlin government; many distrusted him because he focused on preserving his regime and did not share their sacrifices.

Popular unrest simmered as rumors circu-lated of Allied invasion from the south. Ludwig altered his goals toward peace without territo-rial gains. On 2 November 1918 he approved constitutional reforms, such as a revision of the electoral system. Despite Ludwig's concessions, insurgents led by Kurt Eisner wrested control of the Bavarian government on the 7th. Ludwig fled across the Austrian border by car, and Eisner declared Bavaria a republic.

At his castle refuge in Anif, Ludwig re-leased his subjects from fealty oaths but never formally abdicated, hoping one day to return to the throne. He died on 18 October 1921 at the Wittelsbachs' Sarvar estate in Hungary.

Elizabeth D. Schafer

References

Beckenbauer, Alfons. *Ludwig III. von Bayern. 1845–1921. Ein König auf der Suche nach seinem Volk.* Regensburg: Friedrich Pustet, 1987.

Bosl, Karl, ed. *Die bayerischen Herrscher von Ludwig I. bis Ludwig III. im Urteil der Presse nach ihrem Tode.* Berlin: Duncker & Humblot, 1974.

Garnett, Robert S., Jr. *Lion, Eagle, and Swastika: Bavarian Monarchism in Weimar Germany, 1918–1933.* New York: Garland, 1991.

Hümmert, Ludwig. *Bayern: Vom Königreich zur Diktatur 1900–1933.* Munich: Verlag W. Ludwig, 1979.

Mitchell, Allan. *Revolution in Bavaria 1918–1919: The Eisner Regime and the Soviet Republic.* Princeton: Princeton University Press, 1965.

See also GERMANY, REVOLUTION OF 1918; RUPPRECHT, CROWN PRINCE OF BAVARIA

Lusitania, Sinking of

The *Lusitania*, built at a cost of £1,250,000 and launched on 7 June 1906, was (with her sister ship the *Mauritania*) the fastest, largest, and most luxurious transatlantic liner. Although built by Cunard Lines, both her construction and operating expenses were subsidized by the admiralty. In return for financial support, Cunard equipped the liner with gun mounts concealed below the wooden decks, a power plant below the water line, and magazines in the forward "coal bunkers." In 1914 Jane's listed the *Lusitania* as an "auxiliary cruiser," recognizing that she was designed for ready conversion from passenger ship to warship.

After the Battle of Dogger Bank, Germany declared the waters around the British Isles a war zone in which enemy and neutral ships would be sunk on sight, but U-boat captains usually followed "cruiser rules" and gave warning and time for evacuation prior to sinking their prey. The British, however, resorted to the use of "mystery (Q) ships," armed vessels disguised as merchantmen, to sink U-boats when they surfaced prior to attack. That practice caused the Germans to institute occasional attacks without warning.

The *Lusitania* began her 201st crossing from New York bound for Liverpool on 1 May 1915. The admiralty, taking advantage of de-coded German radio traffic, knew that there were three U-boats operating south of Ireland, but the *Lusitania*'s captain was given no warning and was not told that her escort, the cruiser *Juno*, had been withdrawn. On 7 May, U-20, commanded by Kapitän-Leutnant Walter Schweiger, placed one torpedo just forward of *Lusitania*'s bridge as she passed about ten miles off the Old Head of Kinsale in southwest Ireland. A second explosion, almost certainly from a cargo of contraband munitions, caused the ship to sink rapidly by the bow, drowning 1,201 of the 1,965 passengers, over 100 of whom were Americans. Bodies washed up on the Irish beaches for weeks, and Cunard offered £1 for each Englishman retrieved, £2 for Americans, and £1,000 for the body of Albert Vanderbilt.

Although the United States delivered a harsh protest to Germany, the sinking of the *Lusitania* did not result in America's prompt entry into the war on the Allied side. In the investigations following the sinking, care was taken to protect the financial and political interests of Cunard, Great Britain, and the United States. The British went to great lengths to conceal the fact that the ship carried contraband and was, in effect, armed. Some of the documents relative to the sinking remain classified.

Jack McCallum

References

Bailey, Thomas A., and Paul B. Ryan. *The Lusitania Disaster.* New York: The Free Press, 1975.

Simpson, Colin. *The Lusitania.* Boston: Little, Brown, 1972.

See also SUBMARINE WARFARE, CENTRAL POWERS

Luxembourg

Although the great powers, including Germany, had long guaranteed the neutrality of the Grand Duchy of Luxembourg, when Germany faced the prospect of a two-front war it did not hesitate to invade France through Luxembourg and Belgium. On 1 August 1914, therefore, German soldiers occupied Troisvièrges, a northern Luxembourg village a few miles south and east of Belgium, and broke up 150 meters of railroad line. The next day the German army invested the whole of the Grand Duchy, although Germany had not yet declared war against France. From 30 August to 28 September Kaiser

Wilhelm II and the general staff were in the capital city, and for the next four years Germany controlled every aspect of Luxembourg's social, economic, and political life.

Although Germany had violated its guarantees of Luxembourg's neutrality (Treaty of London of 1867 and Fifth Convention of The Hague in 1907), the Luxembourg government decided that its best hope lay in maintaining neutrality toward Germany and friendly powers alike. A government statement of 3 November 1914 proclaimed: "Scrupulous respect for our treaties has been our strength in the past. More than ever it will be our line of conduct in the present and our safeguard for the future." Nevertheless, during the long German occupation and the peace that followed, Luxembourg was plagued by economic and political troubles deriving from that policy.

In 1914 Luxembourg was enjoying a prosperity that had grown steadily in the seventy years since its independence. At the outbreak of war its per capita national wealth was estimated at more than twice that of Germany and France. Its national budget had increased tenfold in seventy-five years; its savings deposits had increased by fifty times. The iron-steel industry grew prodigiously. Over the forty years prior to 1914, iron production had increased 1,000 percent. Indeed, by 1900 Luxembourg accounted for one-seventh of the total production of the Zollverein, twenty-seven times the cast-iron production of Belgium and thirty times that of France. It had railroads and roads connecting it with all of Europe. While Luxembourg was reaching these heights of success, as Christian Calmes noted, "The east and west winds send clouds charged with hatred and sulphur scudding across the sky of an idyllic Luxembourg."

The German occupation of Luxembourg in 1914 brought four years of decline in productivity, growing unemployment, and labor unrest. Thousands of Luxembourg men who had been out of the country when the invasion occurred joined French forces fighting the Germans. In 1915 Germany declared Luxembourg a theater of war and claimed the right, according to military code, to kill spies and traitors.

The war saw a steady movement toward crises in 1918 and 1919 that threatened the very existence of Luxembourg. These had to do with the sovereign, the authority of government, sufficiency of food, employment, suffrage, and the brutality and dictatorship of the German military.

Grand Duchess Marie Adelaide ruled Luxembourg in 1914. Barely twenty years old at the time of the German invasion, she was the first native-born sovereign, a fervent Catholic in a fervently Catholic country, beautiful, appealing, and immensely popular. Of Germanic birth, educated by Germans and intimately related to Germans, she made errors in dealing with the German oppression until forced to abdicate, an action that threatened Luxembourg independence.

After the experienced minister of state (since 1888), Paul Eyschen, died in 1915, Marie Adelaide met opposition in the Chamber of Deputies. It came from both the people at large and from the Allies, a state of affairs that continued through changes of government. In the midst of this political dissension unemployment grew, pay lagged behind the cost of living, unions clashed with one another, farmers opposed townspeople, hunger spread, strikes occurred, and markets disappeared. In short, during the war Luxembourgers suffered severely.

The troubles of the war years came to a head following the Armistice of 11 November 1918. On 9 January 1919, Marie Adelaide announced her abdication. She was succeeded by her sister, Charlotte. Uncertainties over sovereignty, independence, and economic relations continued, and the Chamber of Deputies ordered a plebiscite for 28 September. Socialists and republicans had grown strong enough to make a bid for power, but the monarchy won the election with 80 percent of the vote. Defeated were those citizens worn down by the war years who favored surrendering independence to France or Belgium. The government of Luxembourg persuaded the Allies to reaffirm the grand duchy's independence. It also made suffrage universal and gave women the power to vote.

Germany was forced in the Treaty of Versailles to relinquish its interests in Luxembourg. Formal economic ties with Germany were supplanted by an economic union with Belgium. The article in the Treaty of Versailles pertaining to the Grand Duchy stated: "Germany recognizes that the Grand Duchy of Luxembourg ceased being a part of the German Zollverein dating from January 1, 1919, renounces all rights over the management of the railroads, supports the abrogation of the position on neutrality on the part of the Grand Duchy, and accepts in advance all international arrangements agreed on by the allied powers and associated powers relative to the Grand Duchy."

After World War I Luxembourg defined itself more clearly. It shaped a future for itself as an independent participant in European and world political life, and it began the economic development that would place it among the most prosperous of nations.

James Newcomer

References

Calmes, Christian. *The Making of a Nation: From 1815 to the Present Day.* Luxembourg: Imprimerie St. Paul, 1989.

Majerus, Pierre. *Le Luxembourg Indépendant.* Luxembourg: Imprimerie Beffort, 1945.

Melchers, Emile-Théodore. *Kriegsschauplatz Luxemburg, August 1914–Mai 1940.* Luxembourg: Sankt-Paulus Druckerei, 1977.

Newcomer, James. *The Grand Duchy of Luxembourg: The Evolution of Nationhood.* Lanham, Md.: University Press of America, 1984.

Trausch, Gilbert. *Le Luxembourg, Emergence d'un Etat et d'une Nation.* Anvers: Fonds Mercator, 1989.

Weber, Paul. *Histoire de l'Economie Luxembourgeoise.* Luxembourg: Chambre de Commerce, 1950.

See also SCHLIEFFEN PLAN

Luxemburg, Rosa (1871–1919)

German revolutionary socialist, born 5 March 1871 in Zamosc, Poland (then part of the Russian Empire). A member of the German Social Democratic party, Rosa Luxemburg (Raya Dunayevskaya) emerged as one of the most important theorists of a revitalized revolutionary socialism in the decades before 1914. Her unshakable belief in the direct revolutionary potential of the masses brought her into conflict with the reformist mainstream of Germany's Social Democratic party (SPD), which had come to rely on trade union organizing and political accommodation. Luxemburg also clashed sharply with Lenin over his assertion of the necessity for an intellectual elite to guide the proletarian revolution.

Along with Karl Liebknecht, Luxemburg formed the Spartacus League (later to become the German Communist party) out of the radical left wing of Germany's splintering Social Democrats in early 1916. Luxemburg and the Left Social Democrats increasingly opposed Germany's war effort as more imperialist than defensive, especially following the overthrow of Czar Nicholas II in March of 1917. The Spartacists attempted a revolutionary uprising in Berlin in January of 1919 in the chaos that followed the end of the war and the assumption of power by the majority Social Democrats. Detained on questionable legal grounds as ringleaders of the uprising on 15 January 1919, both Luxemburg and Liebknecht were beaten and shot to death by nationalist right-wing army troops that evening.

J. Ronald Shearer

References

Abraham, Richard. *Rosa Luxemburg: A Life for the International.* New York: St. Martin's, 1989.

Luxemburg, Rosa. *Rosa Luxemburg. Selected Political Writings.* Edited by Robert Looker. London: Jonathan Cape, 1972.

Schorske, Carl E. *German Social Democracy, 1905–1917. The Development of the Great Schism.* Cambridge: Harvard University Press, 1955.

See also GERMANY, REVOLUTION OF 1918; LIEBKNECHT, KARL

Lvov, Prince Georgi (1861–1925)

Russian zemstvo leader and first premier of the Russian Provisional Government, March–July 1917. Born on 2 November 1861, Lvov was the owner of large estates in Tula province, where he became active in zemstvo affairs upon graduation in 1885 from Moscow University. He combined an essentially populist approach to peasant problems with a wariness of Russia's emerging party politics. The czarist government's mismanagement of wartime relief work, however, drew Lvov first into public service and then into politics. During the Russo-Japanese War he was active in organizing an all-Russian zemstvo effort to aid the sick and wounded. He also became a lukewarm member of the Constitutional Democratic *(Kadet)* party and, as such, was elected to the first and second Dumas in 1906 and 1907.

At the outbreak of World War I, Lvov resumed his leading roles in zemstvo relief work. Under the patriotic spell of the "sacred union," the czar in August of 1914 approved the creation of an All-Russian Zemstvo Union for Aid to Sick and Wounded Soldiers, with Lvov as its chairman. The Zemstvo Union was far superior to the Medical Division of general headquarters in providing relief services and medical supplies. The government, despite its suspicions of any voluntary organizations, was obliged to advance huge ruble credits to support this essential work of the zemstvos. Prince Lvov was also a leader in the Union of Towns and the Central War Industry Committee. The three voluntary relief organizations collaborated closely, and in 1917 the Zemstvo Union and the Union of Towns were in fact united in the so-called *Zemgor.*

Despite Lvov's initial efforts to remain politically neutral, antagonism between the zemstvos and the czarist government grew more pronounced as the Zemstvo Union took on the additional tasks of provisioning troops and manufacturing munitions. Lvov won the respect of army commanders and the attention of Russia's political liberals. The prince's public criticism of governmental bungling of the war effort was taken by the Progressive Bloc within the Duma as a sign that he fully shared the bloc's political goals. In behind-the-scenes maneuvering to secure the appointment of a responsible government, Pavel Miliukov worked assiduously to bypass Duma President M.V. Rodzianko in favor of Lvov, even though he later admitted that he did not know Lvov well. Thus the abdication of Nicholas II was accompanied by a decree naming Lvov as premier and minister of interior of the provisional government (15 March 1917).

In the face of the intractable realities of war weariness, an agrarian revolution, and workers' demonstrations, the provisional government lasted approximately eight months. Lvov lasted four. His repeated appeals to the peasants to await the decision of the Constituent Assembly on land redistribution fell on deaf ears. His public commitment to a defensive war and to a peace "without annexations and indemnities" saved him during the May crisis, which drove Miliukov from office, but he had to reorganize the cabinet to include Aleksandr Kerensky and four other socialists. Under pressure from the Allies, the government attempted to continue the war effort, but the Russian military offensive failed. After a major left-wing demonstration (the July Days) threatened to topple the provisional government, Lvov resigned on 21 July 1917 and was succeeded by Kerensky. Lvov was arrested by the Bolsheviks early in 1918, but he escaped and eventually settled in Paris, where he died on 6 March 1925.

William L. Mathes

References

Miliukov, Paul N. *Political Memoirs, 1905–1917.* Ann Arbor: University of Michigan Press, 1967.

Polner, Tikhon I. *Russian Local Government during the War and the Union of Zemstvos . . . with an Introduction by Prince George E. Lvov.* New Haven: Yale University Press, 1930.

———. *Zhiznennyi put' Kniazia Georgiia Evgenievicha L'vova* Paris: Sovremennyia zapiski, 1932.

See also KERENSKY, ALEKSANDR; RUSSIA, HOME FRONT AND REVOLUTIONS OF 1917

Lyautey, Louis Hubert Gonzalve (1854–1934)

French minister of war and marshal of France, born on 17 November 1854 in Nancy. Lyautey earned fame as a colonial administrator and specialist in military pacification in Indo-China, Madagascar, and Algeria between 1894 and 1910. In 1912 he became high commissioner (and de facto governor) of the French protectorate in Morocco, a post he held until 1925.

Lyautey remained in Morocco until he was named minister of war in Prime Minister Aristide Briand's December 1916 reorganization of the cabinet. He arrived to find that a new commander in chief, Robert Nivelle, had been appointed without his consultation. Unsupported in his questioning of Nivelle's plans for a new offensive, Lyautey soon resigned (14 March). By the end of May he was back in Morocco.

Made a marshal in 1921, Lyautey died in Thorey, Lorraine, on 27 July 1934.

David L. Longfellow

References

King, Jere Clemens. *Generals and Politicians.* Berkeley: University of California Press, 1951.

Maurois, André. *Lyautey.* New York: D. Appleton, 1931.

M

Machine Guns

In 1884 Hiram Maxim invented the first modern machine gun. Unlike such predecessors as the Gatling gun, which were hand-cranked, Maxim's gun began firing when a trigger was pressed and ceased when it was released. The Maxim gun used the force of its own recoil to eject a spent cartridge, chamber another, and fire it; the true revolution, however, was that the Maxim gun had only one barrel. Its predecessors had all been multibarreled. The Maxim gun was the first truly automatic weapon, and its impact on warfare was to be profound because it greatly increased the infantry's fire power. Over time others came up with their own versions of the Maxim, and they became collectively known as machine guns.

In 1914 the three major manufacturers were Maxim, Hotchkiss, and Vickers. All of the major European powers used one or more of these types of machine guns. Germany and Austria-Hungary generally used the Maxim design as their primary machine gun, though the unsatisfactory Bergmann automatic rifle appeared in 1916 and the excellent MG-08/15 light machine gun (a light Maxim) in 1917. Some 37,000 of the MG-08/15 had been produced by January of 1918. By 1918 the German army was utilizing 2,500 twelve-gun machine-gun companies. The French army used the Hotchkiss as its primary machine gun during the war. The British choice was the Vickers, which was to become a common sight on battlefields in the next war as well. Vickers produced over 71,000 weapons between 1915 and 1918. The British also used Birmingham Small Arms Company's Lewis gun, an automatic rifle. The Lewis gun was a successful design widely and aggressively used by the BEF. Captured Lewis guns were also a popular choice of the German stormtrooper units until early 1918. When the United States joined the war, it found itself with a number of outdated and useless weapons and ended up using a wide variety—Vickers, Hotchkiss, the Lewis gun, the obsolete Benet-Mercié, the nearly useless Chauchat, and the excellent Browning.

Until 1914 the advantages of the machine gun were not well understood by those who used it. Machine guns had been employed in many colonial and frontier campaigns, but their main battlefield use came in the Russo-Japanese War of 1904–5. There they were used in defense by both sides, but the lesson that they had changed the face of defense was missed by most of the men who later studied reports from the battlefront. Instead, European military analysts chose to focus on the martial spirit of the Japanese and maintained a belief in the power of the bayonet in attack. This resulted in strategic schemes favoring the offensive in Europe. They neglected the fact that the Japanese were able to absorb tremendous numbers of casualties without their units becoming combat ineffective, and that their near-suicidal martial spirit was not in evidence in European armies.

Chief of the German General Staff Count Alfred von Schlieffen's great wheel through Belgium was based on the German need for swift victory in the West, as it anticipated a two-front war. French Plan XVII was based on the spirit of the offensive, *élan,* and the assumption that the power of the offensive was greater than that of the defensive. Even the small British Expeditionary Force (BEF) followed an offensive plan of action early on in the war. Belief in the power of the bayonet was unchallenged. The lesson that the defense had been made much more powerful by new weapons like the machine gun was not learned until late in the war.

The power of a machine gun is based on the type of fire it produces and on its small size. It can be used as an indirect fire weapon and creates a beaten zone roughly elliptical in shape in which unprotected men are vulnerable to a fall of bullets at a rate of 400–500 per minute. It was therefore possible to create a machine-gun barrage, akin to an artillery barrage, by forming machine guns into batteries and designing fire plans wherein a series of overlapping beaten zones swept areas of the battlefield. Alternatively, machine guns could be used directly to sweep the battlefield in front of their positions. Both methods of firing made the machine gun a useful defensive tool, though the common perception and image of the machine gun is in its direct-fire mode.

The inherent weight of the machine gun (they generally had barrels wrapped in a water jacket to prevent the warping of the barrel during prolonged automatic fire) made it much more difficult to use in attack. The small size of a machine gun (it could be concealed in an area as small as a few square feet), its nerveless nature (no wobbling in aim, because of its fixed platform), and the large volume of fire it produced all made it an excellent defensive weapon. Finally, it was very hard to destroy, again because of its small size.

When the great powers of Europe clashed in 1914, the machine gun was one of the main factors contributing to the advent of trench warfare. Others were the increased firepower of artillery and rifles. Confronted with a sleet of metal in the air, infantrymen quite naturally tried to dig under it. By December of 1914 a network of trenches stretched from Switzerland to the North Sea, and the difficulty both sides had in coming to terms with modern warfare meant that the trenches stayed in largely the same places until 1918.

Machine guns had a profound impact on the battlefield in the early years of the war. Situated defensively, with interlocking zones of fire, they proved a dominant weapon and the backbone of the defense.

The power of machine guns in defense is perhaps best shown by the action of 1 July 1916, the first day of the Somme Offensive. Disregarding the strategic arguments underpinning the offensive, its lack of success was blamed on an artillery failure. The British plan for the Somme was largely based on the idea of destroying the Germans by artillery fire, leaving a shattered defense over which the assaulting infantry would have an easy stroll. Unfortunately for the assaulting troops, artillery did not yet have the highly coordinated fire plans that emerged later, and the lack of the 106 fuse (an instantaneous contact fuse that later allowed for far more effective destruction of wire by high-explosive shells) meant that wire was ineffectively cut. The artillery concentrated on German trenches and defensive positions. The Germans, however, had just implemented a new defensive policy of pulling their machine guns out of the trenches, siting them inconspicuously in areas between the trench lines, and providing deep dugouts in which they could shelter from a barrage. In essence, they were missed by the bombardment and barrage, or they were well protected in their dugouts and came into action as soon after the barrage had passed as possible. As a result they took a heavy toll of the assault troops, who were held up by uncut wire. The cost to the British was very high, though it must be stressed that German artillery also took a heavy toll of the attackers. In that single day 19,000 British troops were killed, the greatest single one-day loss in the history of the British army.

After the Somme, the use of artillery began to change. The development of the 106 fuse allowed for far more efficient cutting of wire, and the concept of the creeping barrage emerged. The creeping barrage, by lifting in much smaller and more rigidly controlled intervals, effectively swept the ground between trench lines. Where assaulting infantry kept right up with the barrage, the German machine guns could not come into play effectively; rather, they made only a piecemeal contribution to the defense. In essence, the concept of suppressing defensive positions, rather than their outright destruction, had emerged. An example of this is the Vimy Ridge attack by the Canadian Corps on 9 April 1917.

Lieutenant General Sir Julian Byng's Canadian Corps was tasked with the capture of Vimy Ridge as its part in the larger Arras Offensive. Byng took a great deal of time to lay the groundwork for the assault. The troops were carefully trained, the logistic infrastructure for the attack was painstakingly created, and the artillery had a long period of preparation. The artillery fire plan was designed to disrupt the defense by destroying strongpoints, by aggressive counterbattery fire designed to destroy German artillery, and by disruption of the German logistic infrastructure. Canadian machine gunners put down nuisance barrages in rear areas that were designed to coincide with meal times and the movement of supplies. When the attack went in, the creeping barrage was supported and thickened by a machine-gun barrage, and the attack succeeded. The cost was still high, but the ridge was captured after two years of previously costly failures. The key to the success was the suppression of the defense by artillery. Vimy marks a period in which the power of the machine gun began to wane because of an increase in the sophistication of the use of artillery. The machine gun's power was not to wane into uselessness; rather, it was to be balanced by the evolution of new operational systems.

The BEF in general found that machine gunners should be specialists. A machine gunner's perception of ground was quite different from that of an infantryman. At the time, the relative immobility of the machine gun meant that it was caught in a doctrinal no-man's-land. It was not an artillery piece, though it shared the ability for indirect fire. Nor was it a true infantry weapon, since it was far too heavy to be easily moved about the battlefields of the First World War. The British eventually adopted a policy of treating machine gunners as a separate branch of the service, much like artillery or engineers.

The impetus for this came from the Canadian Corps, which after Vimy grouped its machine guns into batteries and used them in a coordinated fashion. Most of the available guns were situated forward in the trenches and given the role of direct support for the infantry. That was because, despite their relatively cumbersome nature, they had far more tactical flexibility than the artillery. Remaining batteries were used in the rear and had the more artillery-like role of barrage fire; they were used to supplement and support the artillery. Indeed, they were used as if they were light artillery pieces, and their role was to interdict the battlefield and to harass the Germans. Additionally, the Canadian Corps experimented with the mounting of machine guns in motor vehicles—the Canadian Motor Machine Gun Corps. On occasion (for example, after the breaking of the Drocourt-Quèant Switch of the Hindenburg Line in 1918), partially successful attempts were made to use armored cars with the Motor Machine Gun Corps.

On 21 March 1918 the Germans launched their spring offensives, their last massive effort to win the war. New German methods employed infiltration to slip through weak points in the defensive system, get into rear areas, and disrupt communications. Troops were armed with weaponry designed to give them great firepower from small numbers (trench mortars, flamethrowers, grenades, and light machine guns or automatic rifles). Follow-on troops were tasked with neutralizing the defenders once they were cut off from communications, while the spearhead continued to advance. It proved to be a method that was effective at isolating large areas of the defense and in disrupting the coordination of the defensive schemes in place.

It was costly, however. Those defenders who stayed and fought, despite being cut off, took a heavy toll of the follow-on troops, who had not received the sophisticated training of the assault troops. British machine gunners found tremendous opportunities to fire at densely packed German units and often fired until their ammunition was exhausted. They survived to find these targets because the German artillery bombardment, though short and tremendously heavy, was comparatively primitive—it lifted from trench line to trench line—and because the British (like the Germans in 1916) did not keep their machine guns in the trenches. The German attack, though successful on a scale not seen in the West before 1918, suffered greatly for not having learned the lessons of previous years, primarily the concept of suppressing defensive systems. The assault troops, therefore, had to come up with human solutions to the British machine gunners. The British had learned their lessons, and when the German offensives finally lost momentum, they had their chance to counterattack.

On 8 August 1918 the Allies counterattacked at Amiens. By deception and tremendous secrecy, the BEF had managed to place the Canadian Corps in the line beside the Australian Corps, while convincing the Germans that the Canadians were in Belgium and the Australians were not in a position to attack. The operational surprise that resulted combined with good tactics and operational planning to snuff out any chance of the German army's mounting further attacks. The BEF's artillery fire came down suddenly and was designed to destroy hard points and to suppress the defense in general. The whole of the Tank Corps was committed to the two Dominion Corps, and, where the assaulting infantry came upon unsuppressed machine guns, tanks aided greatly in their destruction. Although the Germans had machine guns in their positions, they were not able to influence the battle decisively, because they had been destroyed by the barrage, or suppressed by the barrage and captured by the infantry before they could come into action, or they came into action and were destroyed by combined infantry-tank tactics.

Later in the summer, the Hindenburg Line was taken, and the line of the Canal du Nord. After early October, the Germans were forced to adopt a defense composed largely of machine guns and artillery disposed in great depth and designed to slow, rather than stop, the Allied advance. Although this period was costly, and the German Maxims took their toll of Allied infantry, they were no longer the dominant weapon they had been in 1914–17. The machine gun had become a part of an army's arsenal, along with the rifle, the automatic rifle or light machine gun, artillery, and the new technologies of aircraft and the tank.

Hiram Maxim's invention came of age during the First World War. In the early battles it proved a decisive weapon, and all powers had difficulty coming to terms with defenses in which machine guns were used. Although by 1918 new tactics such as the creeping barrage and new weapons like the tank lessened the superiority that machine guns had previously enjoyed, the machine gun remained an important element of all defensive systems. If not dealt with effectively, it had the ability to exert a decisive effect on a battle. While the machine gun was not the dominant weapon that artillery was during the war, it was of significant importance.

Ian M. Brown

References

Bidwell, Shelford, and Dominick Graham. *Fire-Power: British Army Weapons and Theories of War 1904–1945*. Boston: Allen and Unwin, 1982.

Ellis, John. *The Social History of the Machine Gun*. London: Croom Helm, 1975.

Gudmundsson, Bruce. *Stormtroop Tactics*. New York: Praeger, 1989.

Hutchison, G.S. *Machine Guns: Their History and Tactical Employment*. London: Macmillan, 1938.

Millet, Allan R., and Murray Williamson, eds. *Military Effectiveness, Vol. 1: The First World War*. Boston: Unwin Hyman, 1988.

See also INFANTRY TACTICS; SOMME, BATTLE OF; TRENCH WARFARE; VIMY RIDGE

Mackensen, August von (1849–1945)

German field marshal, born on 6 December 1849 into a bourgeois family in Schmiedeberg, Saxony (on an estate managed by his father). Mackensen served as a reserve officer in the Franco-German War (1870–71), then studied agronomy at Halle University. In 1873 he reentered the Prussian army as a cavalry subaltern and in 1880 was posted to the general staff. Although he had not been trained at the Kriegsakademie, his career flourished. From 1891 to 1893 he served as the senior aide-de-camp to Count Alfred von Schlieffen. After commanding a famous hussars regiment at Danzig, he was posted to the kaiser's personal entourage (1898) and ennobled (1899).

After extended service as a brigade and divisional commander, in 1908 Mackensen was promoted to lieutenant general and assumed command of XVII Corps at Danzig. During the opening campaign in East Prussia, his corps was badly mauled at Gumbinnen but did better in the ensuing battles of Tannenberg and the Masurian Lakes. The XVII corps was subsequently assigned to Hindenburg's newly formed Ninth Army and participated in its war of movement in Russian Poland. When Hindenburg was made commander in chief on the Eastern Front (2 November 1914), Mackensen succeeded him as head of the Ninth Army. After bitter fighting in Poland during the winter, Mackensen (by now a colonel general) was reassigned to western Galicia, where he took charge of an army group composed of the German Eleventh and the Austro-Hungarian Fourth Army. Assisted by his chief of staff Colonel Hans von Seeckt, Mackensen presided over the famous breakthrough at Gorlice-Tarnow in May of 1915, which unhinged the Russian front in the Carpathians and eventually led to the expulsion of the czar's armies from most of Galicia and all of Russian Poland.

Promoted to field marshal on 22 June, Mackensen was entrusted with a new mission in September. Once again combining German and Austro-Hungarian troops under his command, he directed the invasion of Serbia (October of 1915) from the north and from the east with the Bulgarian First Army. After defeating the Serbs and driving the remnants of their armies into the mountains, Mackensen's army group took up defensive positions in Macedonia. During the first half of 1916, the OHL withdrew many of Mackensen's German units from the Balkans, so that he eventually presided over a force mainly Bulgarian in composition.

When Romania entered the war on 27 August 1916, Mackensen was given a mixed force of German, Bulgarian, and Austro-Hungarian units (and later some Turkish troops) and instructed to invade Romania from the south. Entering the Dobrudja in early September, Mackensen's troops gradually fought their way north and took the important port of Costanza by 19 October. Four weeks later they crossed the Danube and advanced upon Bucharest, which they entered on 6 December along with troops of General Erich von Falkenhayn's Ninth Army (the latter having become part of Mackensen's command one week earlier).

After pushing the remnants of the Romanian army and their Russian allies out of Wallachia, Mackensen established himself in Bucharest as head of the army of occupation. In November of 1918 he presided over the repatriation of his troops via Hungary. In mid-December he himself was taken into custody in Budapest, on French orders, and not released until the end of the following year.

Admired by many Germans, the elderly field marshal remained in the public eye throughout the 1920s and 1930s. Two of his sons rose to high positions in the Third Reich—one became state secretary of the foreign office and the other an army commander—but the field marshal himself maintained a healthy skepticism toward the Nazis. He died at Burghorn, near Celle, on November 8, 1945.

Ulrich Trumpener

References

Mackensen, August von. *Brief und Aufzeichnunoen des Generalfeldmarschalls aus Krieg und Frieden.* Edited by Wolfgang Foerster. Leipzig: Bibliographisches Institut, 1938.
———. Personal Papers *(Nachlass).* N 39. Bundesarchiv-Militärarchiv, Freiburg i.Br.

Niemeyer, Joachim. "Mackensen." *Neue Deutsche Biographie.* Vol. 15. 1987.
Showalter, Dennis E. *Tannenberg: Clash of Empires.* Hamden, Conn.: Archon, 1991.
Stone, Norman. *The Eastern Front 1914–1917.* New York: Charles Scribner's Sons, 1975.

See also BALKAN FRONT, 1915, 1916, 1917; EAST PRUSSIA CAMPAIGN; EASTERN FRONT

Madden, Sir Charles Edward (1862–1935)

British admiral, born on 5 September 1862 at Brompton, Gillingham, Kent. Madden entered the Royal Navy as a cadet in 1875. A specialist in torpedoes, with limited sea service before achieving flag rank, by 1904 Madden was identified by Admiral Sir John Fisher as one of the "brains" of the navy. He served on the design committee that produced the *Dreadnought* and *Invincible* classes of battleship and battle cruiser. He later commanded the *Dreadnought,* was promoted to flag rank in 1911, and, between 1912 and 1914, commanded three squadrons of the Home Fleet.

When Admiral John Jellicoe took command of the Grand Fleet, he requested Madden as his chief of staff. Madden held that important post until David Beatty assumed command of the fleet in 1916. Jellicoe had recommended that Madden succeed him, but the appointment went to Beatty and Madden received command of the 1st Battle Squadron and was second in command of the Grand Fleet.

Promoted to admiral in 1916, Madden served at sea throughout World War I and into the postwar years. After the war he assumed command of the Atlantic Fleet, the main element of the reorganized Royal Navy. Between 1927 and 1930, Madden served as first sea lord and chief of staff of the Royal Navy. In 1919 Madden was created a baronet and in July of 1924 promoted to admiral of the fleet. He died in London on 5 June 1935.

Donald F. Bittner

References

Baddeley, Vincent W. "Madden, Sir Charles Edward." *Dictionary of National Biography, 1931–1940.* London: Oxford University Press, 1985.

Kemp, Peter. "Madden, Sir Charles Edward." *The Oxford Companion to Ships and the Sea*. Oxford: Oxford University Press, 1988.

Marder, Arthur J. *From the Dreadnought to Scapa Flow*. Vols. 1–5. Oxford: Oxford University Press, 1969.

See also BEATTY, DAVID; JELLICOE, JOHN

Magdeburg (SMS)

One of the greatest counterintelligence coups of the war occurred after the German light cruiser *Magdeburg* ran aground on the island of Odensholm off the Estonian coast in August of 1914. SMS *Magdeburg* had been on a reconnaissance of the entrance to the Gulf of Finland when the accident occurred. Shortly thereafter, Russian warships arrived and prevented German attempts to destroy her. As a result, the Russians salvaged three copies of the German naval code book (SKM, or *Signalbuch der Kaiserlichen Marine*) along with the current key. The Russians gave a copy to the British. Possession of the *Magdeburg* code book, along with others captured by the British, allowed British cryptographers (Room 40) to decipher wireless intercepts, including the famous Zimmermann Telegram.

Paul G. Halpern

References

Beesly, Patrick. *Room 40: British Naval Intelligence, 1914–1918*. London: Hamish Hamilton, 1982.

Grant, Robert M. *U-Boat Intelligence, 1914–1918*. London: Putnam, 1969.

James, Admiral Sir William. *The Eyes of the Navy: A Biographical Study of Admiral Sir Reginald Hall*. London: Methuen, 1955.

Kahn, David. *The Code Breakers: The Story of Secret Writing*. New York: Macmillan, 1967.

Mäkelä, Matti E. *Das Geheimnis der "Magdeburg."* Coblenz: Bernard & Graefe Verlag, 1984.

See also ROOM 40; ZIMMERMANN TELEGRAM

Maistre, Paul (1858–1922)

French general, born in Joinville on 20 June 1858. Maistre was commissioned in the French army from St. Cyr and later taught tactics at the war college. In 1914 he was chief of staff of the Fourth Army and was rewarded after the Marne with command of the XXI Corps, which fought at Vimy, Verdun, and the Somme. On 1 May 1917 Maistre took over Sixth Army, butchered under General Charles Mangin at the Chemin des Dames, and nursed it back to fighting effectiveness. His carefully prepared attack at Malmaison in October, employing tanks and concentrating 1,800 guns on a 12-kilometer front, characterized Marshal Henri-Philippe Pétain's policy of selective, limited attacks to restore French army morale.

Maistre briefly commanded French forces dispatched to stabilize the Italians after the Caporetto disaster. He returned to the Western Front to command the Tenth Army, slowing the German advance between the Aisne and the Ourcq in the spring of 1918. He then succeeded to command the four armies of the Center Army Group in the Allied counteroffensive, reaching Charleville by the Armistice. He died in Paris on 24 July 1922.

A. Harding Ganz

References

Atkinson, Captain C.T., Major General Sir John Humphrey Davidson, and Captain Hoffman Nickerson. "Battles in Artois." *Encyclopaedia Britannica*. 12th ed., 1922. Vol. 30, 264–81.

Conger, Colonel Arthur L., Major General Hans von Haeften, and General Charles M.E. Mangin. "Battles in Champagne." *Encyclopaedia Britannica*, 12th ed. 1922. Vol. 30, 604–20.

Herwig, Holger H., and Neil M. Heyman. *Biographical Dictionary of World War I*. Westport, Conn.: Greenwood, 1982.

See also ALLIED COUNTEROFFENSIVE

Mangin, Charles Marie Emmanuel (1866–1925)

French general, born on 6 July 1866 in Sarrebourg, in Lorraine, which was lost to Germany during the Franco-Prussian War (1870–71). He graduated from St. Cyr in 1888. His early career was spent primarily in the French colonies fighting rebellious natives. Aggressive and brave, Mangin was wounded three times during his colonial service. In 1898 he led the advance guard of Colonel Jean Baptiste

Marchand's expedition across Africa to the Nile at Fashoda. In 1914 Mangin returned to France to take command of a brigade. His service in Africa led him to admire greatly the soldierly qualities of African troops, whom he used whenever possible as his attacking force. Service in Africa also contributed to some of Mangin's eccentric behavior: Whenever possible, he chose to sleep in a desert tent.

Mangin was one of France's most skilled soldiers. He combined an aggressive style with excellent technical ability; his attacks were always carefully coordinated and launched on time. His recklessness with the lives of his troops was legendary, and his beloved Africans always suffered heavy losses. Mangin was often called "the butcher" or "eater of men." His confidence in his men was superseded only by their confidence in him. He was utterly fearless and was often seen inspecting his troops at the front, where he was wounded several times.

In August of 1914 he distinguished himself at a battle near Charleroi and was promoted to general of division in early 1915, later taking over the 5th Division of General Robert Nivelle's III Corps. In 1916 his division was responsible for the recapture of forts Douaumont and Vaux at Verdun. During this period he became General Nivelle's favorite commander. Mangin later commanded the Sixth Army under Nivelle during the ill-fated Nivelle Offensive on the Aisne (1917), but his troops failed to capture their objective, the German-held Chemin des Dames. Nivelle, attempting to shift the blame for the failed offensive, relieved Mangin of command in May. Later, Mangin was absolved and brought back to command the Tenth Army, where he was successful in halting the last of the German attacks, on 18 July 1918. Foch appointed Mangin to launch the first of the counterattacks against the exhausted Germans.

After the war, Mangin was placed in command of French occupation troops in the Rhineland. He became involved with the Rhineland separatists but died on 12 May 1925 in Paris before their scheme could come to fruition.

Steven D. Fisher

References

Horne, Alistair. *The Price of Glory: Verdun 1916*. New York: St. Martin's, 1962.

King, Jere Clemens. *Foch versus Clemenceau: France and German Dismemberment, 1918–1919*. Cambridge: Harvard University Press, 1960.

———. *Generals and Politicians: Conflict between France's High Command, Parliament, and Government, 1914–1918*. Berkeley: University of California, 1951.

See also ALLIED COUNTEROFFENSIVE; FRANCE, COLONIAL TROOPS; NIVELLE OFFENSIVE; NIVELLE, ROBERT; VERDUN, BATTLE OF

Mannerheim, Carl Gustav (1867–1951)

Finnish statesman and field marshal, born in Villnäs (near Turku) on 4 June 1867. While Finland was part of the Russian Empire, Mannerheim was educated as a cavalry officer. He began his military service in the elite Chevalier Guards in St. Petersburg. Mannerheim saw action in the Russo-Japanese War (1904–5), after which he commanded cavalry units in Poland for seven years.

During World War I Mannerheim served on the Eastern Front against the Austrians. He commanded the 12th Cavalry Division in the Galician Campaign of 1915 and participated in the Brusilov Offensive of 1916. After Romania joined the Entente, Mannerheim was transferred late in 1916 to the newly formed front in the Transylvanian Alps. In June of 1917 he was promoted to lieutenant general and given the command of the 6th Cavalry Corps.

After the Bolshevik coup of 7 November 1917 Mannerheim returned to Finland, where, during the three-month War of Independence in 1918, he led the Finnish Defense Corps to victory against the Red Guards and Russian troops still left in the country. He was named regent of Finland in December of 1918 but resigned in 1919 when a republican constitution was adopted. He was made field marshal in 1933 and marshal of Finland in 1942.

Mannerheim led Finland's forces in the Winter War of 1939–40 and in the Continuation War of 1941–44. He was president of Finland from 1944 to 1946, when he retired because of ill health. He died in Lausanne, Switzerland, on 27 January 1951.

William L. Mathes

References

Mannerheim, Carl Gustav. *The Memoirs of Marshal Mannerheim*. New York: E.P. Dutton, 1954.

Screen, John E. *Mannerheim: The Years of Preparation*. London: Hurst, 1970.

See also Brusilov Offensive; Finland, Role in War

Marne, First Battle of (5–10 September 1914)

The series of engagements fought 5–10 September 1914 across the Western Front from Paris to Verdun. By stopping the great German offensive short of the French capital, it ended the Schlieffen Plan's attempt to knock France out of the war quickly and thus led directly to the tactical stalemate of the next four years. The battle takes its name from a river of east-central France that joins the Ourcq River northeast of Paris; together, the two rivers flow into the Seine just southeast of the capital.

After the German First Army, on the extreme right wing of the offensive, bypassed Paris to the north and east, French forces guarding the city struck the German right flank. In a confused series of engagements they forced the Germans to stop their offensive and redeploy forces to contain the French counterattack. It is one of the curious features of this battle that while the Germans were almost everywhere successful in halting the Allied counteroffensive, and thus could be termed the victors in a tactical sense, the Marne has been rightly seen as a brilliant Allied operational and strategic success that played a decisive role in shaping the next four years of warfare.

The First Battle of the Marne was the culminating engagement of the campaign that developed during the first three weeks of confused fighting. It was the result of both sides' attempting to carry out their prewar plans. French Plan XVII had called for an all-out offensive by five French armies against the center and left of the expected German line, including offensive thrusts into the lost provinces of Alsace and Lorraine. French chief of staff General Joseph Jacques Césaire Joffre expected to rupture the German line, recapture lost French territory, and divide the German right from the left wing. Persistent reports before the war indicated that Germany was preparing a massive attack against the French left flank by invading Belgium in great strength. The reports were either dismissed or accepted as ready proof that, by so strengthening their right wing, the Germans would lack sufficient reserves to man the rest of their line—thus allowing the French attack to cut the German forces in half.

The German campaign plan, the famous Schlieffen Plan, was developed by General Count Alfred von Schlieffen during his tenure as chief of the general staff (1891–1906) to meet the strategic dilemma of fighting a two-front war against France and Russia. Schlieffen planned to violate the neutrality of Belgium and the Netherlands, attack and turn the French left, penetrate below Paris, then turn east to encircle and destroy the French army in a giant battle of annihilation. In order to obtain success, Schlieffen had deployed fifty-nine divisions on the right wing north of Metz and only nine to the south. Schlieffen even planned to allow the German left and center to withdraw before the anticipated French offensive.

In order to maximize his strike force against the French, Schlieffen had virtually denuded the Eastern Front facing the Russian "steamroller." Precise calculations allowed only six weeks in which to defeat the French before German units would be desperately needed in the East to check the slow-deploying but ultimately massive forces of czarist Russia. Although Schlieffen's successor, General Helmuth von Moltke "the Younger," nephew of the victor of the Franco-Prussian War, modified the Schlieffen Plan, the basic strategy remained the same. Moltke canceled Schlieffen's projected violation of Dutch territory and allocated new divisions both to the Eastern Front and, in the West, to the German center and left wing. In 1914 the German right would comprise fifty-five divisions, the center and left, twenty-two. Altogether, seven German armies would move westward: Three of these armies would compose the critical right wing.

Trial by combat proved that both sides had developed unrealistic plans that were beyond their powers to carry out. The French were the first to have their shortcomings brutally revealed. After three weeks of mobilization and rapidly escalating fighting, Joffre launched his great assaults on 20 August. Over the next four days, French forces attacked along the Sambre River and into the Ardennes, the so-called Battle of the Frontiers. In their red trousers and dark blue greatcoats, the French infantry launched often uncoordinated but furious bayonet attacks against the German center and left. The result was disaster. Not only were these attacks everywhere repulsed, but French losses were horrific. French historian Henry Contamine estimates that between 20 and 23 August about 40,000 French soldiers were killed or mortally wounded. The 22nd of August, with 27,000 French dead, was, in Contamine's words, "the bloodiest day of [French] history." When the number of wounded are factored in—unknown, but scarcely less than two to three times the number killed—the extent of the disaster is apparent. Some authorities put total French losses in these frontier battles as high as 300,000 men.

Even as the French infantry raced forward in gallant if fruitless attacks, the true nature of the German plan was at last discerned by the French army. Because the Germans had placed reserve formations in the front line of combat—something the French had long considered harmful to the morale and combat spirit of regular troops and thus an unlikely German expedient—they were everywhere stronger than the French had expected. At the same time, the threat to the French left from Schlieffen's massive right wing became apparent.

In these increasingly desperate circumstances, with Plan XVII in shambles, Joffre's true greatness emerged. As early as 25 August, in his General Instruction No. 2, Joffre began reorganizing French forces to blunt the German offensive. While ordering the retreat of his three westernmost armies (Third, Fourth, and Fifth), Joffre began withdrawing forces from the east to form a new army, the Sixth, in order to cover Paris and extend the Allied left flank. Utilizing the excellent French lateral railway system, reinforcements streamed toward Paris. It was ironic that the Germans, who pioneered the use of railways in European war, developed an operational plan that did not seek to cut these crucial rail links. It was clear that, even at this early date, Joffre was contemplating a French counteroffensive.

Over the next twelve days, the Allied left wing, which included the British Expeditionary Force (BEF), steadily retreated, often marching twenty to twenty-five miles a day. As the Allies pulled back, Joffre relieved scores of incompetent officers: By 6 September, two army commanders, seven corps commanders, and twenty division commanders had been "limogés," relieved from command and sent to Limoges to await reassignment.

Although fighting continued, by 4 September the French and British armies stretched on an east-west line from Paris to Verdun. Virtually all accounts stress the fatigue and lowered morale that infected both French and British troops after a fortnight of retreat.

German commanders, meanwhile, believed themselves close to victory. Not only had the French offensive been repulsed with devastating French losses, but on the critical right wing good progress had been made. On 23 August and again on the 27th, the German First Army under General Alexander von Kluck had encountered and pushed back individual British corps at Mons and Le Cateau. While the British had fought well—at Le Cateau the BEF's II Corps had fought virtually the entire German First Army in avoiding a double envelopment—British casualties had been relatively heavy and the BEF was in full retreat. Its commander, Sir John French, believed that nothing but rest and reinforcement could revive his exhausted troops. So certain was German supreme headquarters of victory in the West that it dispatched two army corps from the German right wing to reinforce the Eastern Front, where early Russian advances seemed to make German defeat likely. At this critical juncture, however, the German campaign began to unravel.

The pace of the advance had exhausted the German infantry, and German logistical support was unable to keep up with the offensive. Then came yet another French attack, this time by Joffre's left wing (Fifth Army, under General Charles Lanrezac), in order to gain some respite for the weary BEF. Like previous French offensives, this attack (the Battle of Guise, 29 August 1914) also failed, but it led General Karl von Bülow, commander of the German Second Army on the right wing, to request that Kluck's First Army slide east in support to close a growing gap between the two German armies. Poor communications led to the isolation of Moltke and abetted his general unwillingness to exercise strong command during the entire campaign. Moltke's reticence left the decision squarely up to German First Army commander Kluck. Apparently unaware of the new French concentration, Joffre's Sixth Army forming north of Paris, Kluck complied with Bülow's request.

On 30 August Kluck left one corps facing Paris as a flank guard and turned his columns southeast, a course that would take them north and east of Paris, not west and south of the city, as in the original German operations plan. Allied aviators quickly picked up this change in direction, and its intent was confirmed from maps taken from a slain German staff officer.

The German turn southeast prompted the French staff, as early as 1 September, to urge

Joffre to go over to the attack. But the French commander wanted a double envelopment, based on an eastward thrust by Sixth Army to meet a westward attack from forces near Verdun, a plan that called for a coordinated attack along 100 miles of front. In addition to committing French forces, Joffre needed British participation, but he obtained only grudging support through political intervention; an appeal from the French government to Whitehall resulted in the arrival in France of British war minister General Horatio Kitchener, to ensure that British forces would participate in the offensive. To allow his forces additional time to regroup and to permit the Germans to move even farther southeast, Joffre ordered the great counterattack to begin on 6 September.

In fact the battle began on 5 September, when French forces around Paris, attempting to position themselves for the next day's assault, struck Kluck's flank guard on the Ourcq River. Kluck, by now south of the Marne, apparently believed that this was only a spoiling attack; he therefore detached one additional corps to return northwest and continued his advance. Only after the Battle of the Ourcq raged for two additional days (5–7 September) did Kluck realize French intentions. With the same driving energy that had marked each stage of his advance, he then swung his army back to the northwest and launched a savage counterattack that the French barely contained.

By this time the Allies were engaged all along the front from Paris to Verdun. Their attacks were met by German counterattacks, and the battle hung in the balance. Two events swung the battle in Joffre's favor. Kluck's precipitate turn to the northwest to oppose the attack from Paris had reopened a gap between the German First and Second armies. Into that gap, covered only by a German cavalry screen, the BEF now timidly advanced, threatening Kluck's left flank and rear, as well as the right wing of the German Second Army.

This threat from the BEF coincided with perhaps the most controversial event of the campaign. In a belated attempt to regain control over the battle, Moltke dispatched a general staff officer, Lieutenant Colonel Richard Hentsch, to survey the army commanders. Moltke apparently empowered Hentsch to coordinate the actions of the armies, though Hentsch's mission is still shrouded in controversy. Hentsch arrived at Second Army headquarters just as a French counterattack and the

BEF's advance seemed to threaten its right wing (9 September), convincing the always cautious Bülow that he must retreat. Hentsch attempted to coordinate this retreat with Kluck, ordering him in Moltke's name to conform with the retreat of the Second Army. Kluck reluctantly complied, and Moltke himself then ordered all his armies to retire. Since the French and British forces were exhausted, this retreat was completed with little Allied interference. By 14 September the Battle of the Marne was over.

The Marne, at best a tactical draw, was one of the decisive battles of world history. It made the prospect of a long war a virtual certainty and thus ensured that the war would become total, a development that obviously favored the richer, more numerous Allies over the Central Powers. The war could not be waged with a "business as usual" approach; it would be fought with economic as well as purely military means, and an increasingly interdependent economic system would spread the war to the major players of the world economy. Such a war would place extreme stress on all participants. The Marne thus helped bring about the entry of the United States into the war, the Russian Revolution, the collapse of Central Europe, and a major realignment of the great powers' colonial holdings, with all the momentous consequences those events brought to world history. Joffre had saved France, but at a cost—including 1.4 million French dead and a revolution in world affairs—that for many called into question the victory and produced much of the controversy that has dogged Joffre and the war itself over the past seventy-five years.

Gary P. Cox

References

Asprey, Robert B. *The First Battle of the Marne.* Philadelphia: J.B. Lippincott, 1962.

Barnett, Correlli. "The Tragic Delusion: Colonel-General Helmuth von Moltke." In *The Swordbearers: Supreme Command in the First World War.* Bloomington: Indiana University Press, 1963.

Isselin, Henri. *The Battle of the Marne.* Translated by Charles Connell. Garden City, N.Y.: Doubleday, 1966.

Porch, Douglas. *The March to the Marne: The French Army 1871–1914.* Cambridge: Cambridge University Press, 1981.

Tuchman, Barbara. *The Guns of August.* New York: Macmillan, 1962.

See also Bülow, Karl von; French War
Plan XVII; Frontiers, Battle of the;
Hentsch, Richard; Joffre, Joseph;
Kluck, Alexander von; Moltke,
Helmuth von; Schlieffen Plan

Marshall, Sir William Raine (1865–1939)

British army general, born on 29 October
1865 at Stranton, near Hartlepool, County
Durham, Marshall attended Sandhurst and in
1885 was commissioned in the Sherwood Foresters. Before World War I he served in Ireland
and Malta and with distinction in wars in India and South Africa, receiving two brevet
promotions.

In 1914–15 Marshall served in France as
a battalion commander. He then led a brigade
of the 29th Division at Gallipoli. In June of
1915 he was promoted to major general and
commanded the 42nd, 29th, and 53rd divisions. After Gallipoli, he commanded the 27th
Division at Salonika and then the III (Indian)
Corps in Mesopotamia, which he led in the
campaign that resulted in the defeat of the
Turkish army at Kut-el-Amara (24 February
1917) and the capture of Baghdad (11 March).
After the death of General Frederick Maude,
Marshall commanded the Mesopotamia Expeditionary Force, and in October of 1918 he
received the surrender of the Turkish army on
the Upper Tigris.

After the war, Marshall was appointed
commander in chief, Southern Command, India. He remained there until 1923 and retired
a year later. He wrote *Memories of Four Fronts*
(1929). Marshall died on 29 May 1939 at
Bagnoles de l'Orne, France.

Donald F. Bittner

References

Maurice, F. "Marshall, Sir William Raine."
*Dictionary of National Biography,
1931–1940*. London: Oxford University
Press, 1985.

See also Gallipoli Campaign;
Mesopotamia; Salonika Campaign

Marwitz, Georg von der (1856–1929)

Prussian army commander. Scion of an old, established, noble clan, Marwitz was born on his
father's Pomeranian estate (near Stolp) on 3 July
1856. Commissioned in the Guards Cavalry in
1875, he later graduated from the Kriegsakademie and held a number of staff and command
positions. Made inspector-general of the cavalry
in 1912, Marwitz assumed command of a
group of cavalry divisions at the beginning of
the war and soon thereafter was promoted to
lieutenant general.

After participating in the invasion of Belgium and France and the subsequent campaigns
in Artois and Flanders, Marwitz's cavalry group
was dissolved in late December of 1914; he was
posted to the Eastern Front as a commander of
the newly formed XXXVIII Reserve Corps. For
his contributions in the grim February 1915
Battle of the Masurian Lakes, Marwitz received
the *Pour le Mérite.* Shortly thereafter, he was
sent to the Carpathians as commander of the
Beskiden-Korps: there he once again distinguished himself and was rewarded with the oak
leaf cluster in May.

Following a long illness, in November of
1915 Marwitz was posted to the Western
Front as commander of VI Corps in the
Péronne area. Hastily moved to the East in the
summer of 1916, Marwitz and his troops successfully dealt with the problems caused by the
Brusilov Offensive. At the end of the year, he
returned to France as commander of the Second Army. First deployed in the St. Quentin
area and later in the Siegfried Line, the Second
Army was hit hard by the tank-supported British attack at Cambrai (November of 1917),
but Marwitz eventually regained most of the
lost ground. The following March, Marwitz's
divisions participated in the Michael Offensive, but they failed to take Amiens. After
months of bloody fighting, Marwitz's army
suffered a major setback on 8 August when
several of its divisions were smashed. Although
Ludendorff called it "the black day of the German army," Marwitz retained his command,
and it was only six weeks later that he was
reassigned (to the Fifth Army, in the Verdun
sector). Marwitz retired in December of 1918.
He died of heart failure at his Pomeranian estate on 27 October 1929.

Ulrich Trumpener

References

Bose, Thilo von. *Die Katastrophe des 8. Au-
gust 1918.* Berlin and Oldenburg: Stall-
ing, 1930.
Marwitz, General von der. *Weltkriegsbriefe.*
Edited by Erich von Tschischwitz. Berlin:
Reimar Hobbing, 1940.

Möller, Hanns. *Geschichte der Ritter des Ordens "pour le mérite" im Weltkrieg.* 2 vols. Berlin: Bernard & Graefe, 1935.

Reichsarchiv et al. *Der Weltkrieg 1914 bis 1918: Militärische Operationen zu Lande.* 14 vols. Berlin: E.S. Mittler und Sohn, 1925–44.

Stone, Norman. *The Eastern Front 1914–1917.* New York: Charles Scribner's Sons, 1975.

See also BRUSILOV OFFENSIVE; CAMBRAI, BATTLE OF; EAST PRUSSIA CAMPAIGN; LUDENDORFF OFFENSIVES

Masaryk, Tomáš Garrigue (1850–1937)

Czech nationalist leader, born on 7 March 1850 at Hodonín, Moravia. His Slovak father was a coachman, his Czech mother a servant. Masaryk showed great intellectual promise and attended the University of Vienna, where in 1876 he obtained a doctorate in philosophy. Masaryk pursued postdoctoral studies at Leipzig, where he met his future wife, an American student. In 1882 he secured a post as lecturer at the newly created Czech section of the University of Prague. He wrote extensively on a variety of subjects, including history, religion, and philosophy.

In Prague Masaryk joined the Young Czech (Liberal) party and from 1891 to 1893 was its deputy in the Austrian *Reichsrat* and the Bohemian *Landtag*. In 1907 he was again a *Reichsrat* deputy, this time for the moderately leftist Realist party, which he helped to found. As the party's sole deputy in the *Reichsrat*, Masaryk was branded a traitor by both radical young Czechs and the imperial authorities. Travels to Slavic regions of the empire and Russia aroused suspicion, which was enhanced by his criticism of the ruling classes in Vienna. As a deputy, Masaryk opposed both the alliance with Germany and the 1908 annexation of Bosnia-Herzegovina.

When World War I began, Masaryk favored the Allied cause. In Prague he and his adherents formed an underground network, known as the Mafia, operating in behalf of Czech independence. In December of 1914 he fled abroad, where, as president of the Czechoslovakian National Congress, he was the chief spokesman for Czech interests. He visited Switzerland, Britain, Italy, Russia, France, and the United States. In Britain he won the friendship and support of influential historian Hugh Seton-Watson. As a spokesman, Masaryk was ably assisted by the secretary of the council and his former student, Edvard Beneš. Another former student, Milan Stefánik, worked to further the cause in Paris.

Masaryk went to Russia to negotiate with the Bolsheviks over the Czech Legion, composed largely of deserters from the Austro-Hungarian army. This fighting force later won much Western sympathy for the Czech cause. In March of 1918 he traveled to the United States, reaching Chicago two months later. There he worked among the 1.5 million Czechs and Slovaks living in the United States to raise substantial sums for the cause. He also met and became friends with President Wilson. In May of 1918 Secretary of State Robert Lansing issued a declaration favoring Czech and Yugoslav independence, subsequently approved by the Allied governments on 3 June. On 30 June, in the so-called Pittsburgh Declaration, Masaryk got Czech and Slovak leaders to agree to a declaration calling for a common state.

On 14 November 1918 Masaryk was elected president of the new state of Czechoslovakia by a provisional parliament in Prague. He was three times reelected president of the Czechoslovakian republic. Upon his retirement in 1935, Masaryk entrusted the government to Beneš. Fortunately, he did not live to see his beloved country dismembered by the Germans. Masaryk died in Castle Lana, near Prague, on 14 September 1937.

Spencer C. Tucker

References

Beneš, Edvard. *Masaryk's Path and Legacy: Funeral Oration at the Burial of the President-Liberator, 21 Sept. 1937.* Prague: Orbis, 1937.

Herben, Jan. *T.G. Masaryk.* 3 vols. Prague: Manes, 1926–27.

Lowrie, Donald A. *Masaryk of Czechoslovakia, A Life of Tomáš G. Masaryk, First President of the Czechoslovak Republic.* New York: Oxford University Press, 1937.

Ludwig, Emil. *Defender of Democracy, Masaryk of Czechoslovakia.* New York: Robert M. McBride, 1936.

Selver, Paul. *Masaryk.* London: Michael Joseph, 1940.

Street, C.J.C. *President Masaryk.* London: Geoffrey Bles, 1930.

See also BENEŠ, EDVARD; CZECHS; SLOVAKS

Wagenaar, Sam. *Mata Hari: A Biography.*
New York: Appleton, 1966.

Mata Hari (1876–1917)

Probably the best known spy in the world; but the truth is that she was never a spy at all, at least not in any professional sense. Born Margaretta Gertrude Zelle in Holland on 7 August 1876 in Leeuwarden, Netherlands, Mata Hari was her stage name. When she took Paris by storm in 1905 as the top exotic dancer of her day, Mata Hari claimed to have been born in the Dutch East Indies and raised as a sacred dancer in a Hindu temple. In reality she married at age eighteen to a Dutch colonial official twenty years her senior and moved with him to the Indies. The marriage ended badly, and they separated. With no other means of livelihood, she went to Paris, became a dancer and courtesan and invented the strip-tease. Never a good dancer, she was however an extraordinary courtesan; her biographer says she slept with lovers "on an almost industrial scale." Her conquests included both French diplomat Jules Cambon and the Crown Prince of Germany.

Mata Hari had the misfortune to be linked romantically to a German police official at the outbreak of the First World War, and by the time she made her way back to Paris she was under suspicion as a German agent. Confronted by the chief of French counterintelligence, she agreed to work for French intelligence for money so that she might marry her lover, a young Russian officer she had met in France. The British knew nothing about her dealings with French officials and turned her back when she tried to get to Germany by sea. Mata Hari ended up in Spain, where she endeavored to win over a German diplomat. He easily saw through this guise and fed her some meaningless and incorrect informa-tion. When she returned to France, Mata Hari was arrested, tried, and found guilty of being a German agent. Incompetence and duplicity on the part of French and British counter-intelligence officers, as well as the circumstances of 1917 France (it was the low point in the war for the Entente), were the chief factors in her conviction. Mata Hari protested her innocence and died bravely before a firing squad at Vincennes on 15 October 1917.

Spencer C. Tucker

References

Howe, Russell Warren. *Mata Hari. The True Story.* New York: Dodd, Mead, 1986.

Maude, Sir Frederick Stanley (1864–1917)

British army corps commander, born at Gibraltar on 24 June 1864. Maude served with the Guards Brigade during the advance on Pretoria in the Boer War. He then served as military secretary to the governor general of Canada. In August of 1914 Maude was posted to III Corps staff. In August of 1915 he went to Gallipoli to command 13th Division, and he took the division to Egypt after the evacuation. In 1916 13th Division was sent to Mesopotamia to take part in the aborted relief expedition to Kut-Al-Amara, and it then remained on the Tigris confronting the Turks.

In September of 1916 Maude became army commander in Mesopotamia and spent the remainder of 1916 reequipping and training his troops. In December of 1916 he went on the offensive and drove the Turks back, recapturing Kut-Al-Amara. He continued the advance, taking Baghdad on 11 March 1917. He then paused to consolidate for the next offensive but was stricken with cholera and died in Baghdad on 18 November 1917.

Charles H. Bogart

References

Moberly, F.J. *Operations in Persia 1914–18.* London: Imperial War Museum, 1987.
Moorehead, Alan. *Gallipoli.* New York: Harper and Row, 1956.

See also GALLIPOLI CAMPAIGN; MESOPOTAMIA

Maud'huy, Louis Ernest de (1857–1921)

French general, born in Metz on 17 February 1857. Maud'huy entered the service in 1879 and became a professor of the general staff and general by 1912.

In late September of 1914 Maud'huy was given command of four divisions of I Cavalry Corps for operations north of Arras. His forces soon came under heavy pressure from three German corps and were ready to retreat. Told by Foch to "hang on like lice," Maud'huy's newly christened Tenth Army managed to repulse the attack and even take the offensive. The French attacks halted on 17 December 1914 at

Artois, where Maud'huy's forces suffered over 7,000 casualties and were victims of heavy fog and poor preparation.

Maud'huy was soon replaced as commander of Tenth Army and in April of 1915 was transferred to the Vosges Army. There he oversaw a series of indecisive attacks and retreats along a limited front throughout the summer of 1915.

By 1916 Maud'huy had been given command of XV Army Corps; he led them in a tour of duty at Verdun. Transferred to XI Army Corps in 1917, he served as commander of that unit in the battles of Chemin des Dames along the Aisnes River in May of 1918. While faring no worse than most other French commanders in the face of a German offensive that advanced thirteen miles on its first day, Maud'huy was sacked in June of 1918 by Clemenceau for his shortcomings.

Maud'huy's military career closed in his hometown of Metz, where he was appointed military governor of the city by Foch only seventeen days after the war. He died there on 16 July 1921.

Timothy C. Dowling

References
Gray, Ronald, with Christopher Argyle. *Chronicle of the First World War.* 2 vols. New York: Facts on File, 1990.
Hammerton, Sir J.A., ed. *Concise Universal Biography.* Vols. 3 and 4. London: Educational Book Co., 1975.

See also LUDENDORFF OFFENSIVES, 1918; RACE TO SEA, 1914; VERDUN, BATTLE OF

Maunoury, Michel Joseph (1847–1923)

French army commander and field marshal, born at Maintenon on 17 December 1847. Maunoury was an artillerist. He won a battlefield promotion to captain and was wounded in the Franco-Prussian War. Named general of division in 1906, Maunoury was serving as military governor of Paris and a member of the Supreme War Council when he retired (at sixty-five) in 1912.

Hurriedly recalled in August of 1914, Maunoury was given command of the new Army of Lorraine (composed of seven reserve divisions) on 19 August. Moved by rail to Paris on the 26th and designated Sixth Army, Maunoury's forces fought north of the capital but were forced back into the city's defenses. Maunoury was put under the command of General Joseph Gallieni, the military governor, who in turn urged an attack on Alexander von Kluck's right flank as his First Army passed east of Paris, a plan that General Joseph Joffre accepted on 5 September.

Later that same day, Maunoury struck the German flank-guard (IV Corps, First Army) along the Ourcq River in the opening action of the Battle of the Marne. Although the attack forced a German withdrawal, Kluck shifted three corps and drove Maunoury back three days later. When the Germans began their retreat to the Aisne on 9 September, Maunoury's battered units joined in the pursuit.

Maunoury's battlefield career ended abruptly the following March when he was wounded while touring his front lines. Partially blinded, he served as military governor of Paris until he left the service in 1916. He died on 28 March 1923 and was posthumously named a marshal.

David L. Longfellow

References
Asprey, Robert B. *The First Battle of the Marne.* Philadelphia: J.B. Lippincott, 1962.
Tuchman, Barbara. *The Guns of August.* New York: Macmillan, 1962.

See also GALLIENI, JOSEPH; KLUCK, ALEXANDER VON; MARNE, FIRST BATTLE OF

Max of Baden, Prince (1867–1929)

Imperial Germany's last chancellor. Born 10 July 1867 at Baden-Baden, nephew of Grand Duke Frederick I, Max was heir to the Badenese throne and president of the Upper House at Karlsruhe.

Educated as a lawyer, he resigned his military post as brigade commander in 1911. When World War I began in 1914, he believed that Russian mobilization had forced war on Germany. During the war Max mitigated conditions for prisoners of war. By 1915 he was aware that a conciliatory peace would be necessary. He protested against the 1917 resumption of unrestricted submarine warfare, fearing that the United States would enter the war.

On 3 October, upon the resignation of Count Georg von Hertling, Max became chancellor. Max cabled Woodrow Wilson, requesting that the president arrange an immediate armistice. He communicated Germany's acceptance of the Fourteen Points and declared that he spoke for the majority in the Reichstag and the German people. Wilson informed Max that Allied military leaders would outline the armistice.

Max appealed to Wilson on the 20th, asking him to oppose demands "irreconcilable with the honor of the German people and with paving the way to a peace of justice." Max realized that surrender, not peace negotiations, was being forced on Germany. He suggested the dismissal of General Erich Ludendorff, warning the kaiser to look for a new chancellor if his request were not honored.

Max suffered from influenza the last week of October, which hindered his activity. He realized that liberal reforms had to be enacted to save Germany from revolution. He also understood that to aid negotiations, the Allies would have to be convinced that Germany was trying to become a liberal democracy.

On 28 October Max, a prince of the blood, agreed to democratic constitutional changes that limited the kaiser's powers and initiated Germany's first parliamentary regime. The kaiser fled Berlin to army headquarters at Spa, Belgium, to avoid implementing these constitutional reforms. On 1 November Max broke down physically and mentally for thirty-six hours after a bitter telephone conversation in which he warned Wilhelm that if he did not abdicate, revolution would erupt.

On 5 November, Wilson agreed to an armistice, and on the next day Social Democrat Friedrich Ebert demanded the kaiser abdicate by the 9th. Max suggested that the kaiser's grandson might retain the German throne under a regent, but Wilhelm refused. Hindenburg and the German army supported abdication, and Wilhelm was forced into exile.

On 9 November Max publicly announced that both Wilhelm and the crown prince had abdicated. By that afternoon Philipp Scheidemann declared a German Republic. Max relinquished power to Ebert, who was named chancellor and began to establish order while Max returned to Baden.

Max was denounced by fellow monarchists for being the messenger of the abdication. He defended his actions, stating that he did so reluctantly but realistically, having knowledge of a mutinous German fleet and that several German princes had abdicated from fear of revolution. Max retired, penned his memoirs, and died at his Salem castle at Constance on 6 November 1929.

Elizabeth D. Schafer

References

Baden, Max von. *The Memoirs of Prince Max of Baden.* 2 vols. Translated by William M. Calder and C.W.H. Sutton. London: Constable, 1928.

Berghahn, Volker R., and Martin Kitchen, eds. *Germany in the Age of Total War.* Totowa, N.J.: Barnes & Noble, 1981.

Matthias, Erich, and Rudolf Morsey. *Die Regierung des Prinzen Max von Baden.* Dusseldorf: Droste, 1962.

Miller, Susanne, and Gerhard A. Ritter. *Die deutsche Revolution 1918–1919.* Frankfurt/Main: Fischer, 1968.

Orlow, Dietrich. *A History of Modern Germany 1871 to Present.* Englewood Cliffs, N.J.: Prentice-Hall, 1987.

Westarp, Kuno Friedrich Vikton, Graf von. *Die Regierung des Prinzen Max von Baden und die Konservative Partei.* Berlin: Deutsche Verlagsgesellschaft für Politik und Geschichte, 1928.

See also EBERT, FRIEDRICH; GERMANY, HOME FRONT AND REVOLUTION OF 1918; SCHEIDEMANN, PHILIPP; WILHELM II, GERMAN KAISER

Maxse, Sir Frederick Ivor (1862–1958)

British general, born on 22 December 1862. The son of an admiral, Maxse was an infantryman and guardsman. He saw service as a staff officer in South Africa during the Boer War and worked his way up through the Coldstream Guards to command of the 1st Guards Brigade in 1914.

Maxse was promoted to major general in 1915 and took command of 18th Division. Maxse insisted on preparation and thorough training, and his division had considerable success in the 1916 Battle of the Somme. Maxse then went to XVIII Corps. During the shake-up of the general staff at GHQ in early 1918, he became inspector-general (training) for British forces in France and preached the new gospel of infiltration and maneuver. These techniques contributed in no small measure to the economical British victories that autumn.

Maxse was noted for his determination to beat the Germans without losing large numbers of men, something he was able to do as both a division and corps commander. He was promoted to full general in 1923 and retired three years later. He died at Midhurst, Sussex, on 28 January 1958. Maxse was known as probably the most dynamic trainer of troops of the World War I British army and a superb corps commander.

Ian M. Brown

References

Bidwell, Shelford, and Dominick Graham. *Fire-Power: British Army Weapons and Theories of War 1904–1945*. Boston: Allen and Unwin, 1982.
Travers, Tim. *The Killing Ground: The British Army, the Western Front and the Emergence of Modern Warfare*. London: Allen and Unwin, 1987.

See also SOMME, BATTLE OF

Maxwell, Sir John Grenfell (1859–1929)

British general and commander in Egypt, 1915–16, born at Aigburth, Liverpool, on 11 July 1859. Maxwell was commissioned in the British army from Sandhurst in 1879. He served in Egypt in 1882, 1884–85, and 1892–1900. From 1900 to 1902 he was military governor of Pretoria. Promoted to major general in 1906, he took command of British troops in Egypt in 1908. He remained there until 1912, shortly after his promotion to lieutenant general. He then went on half pay.

On the outbreak of World War I Maxwell was sent to French headquarters as head of the British military mission, where he remained until the Battle of the Marne. He then resumed command of British forces in Egypt, which soon proved a demanding assignment.

When Turkey declared war, Maxwell had to defend the Suez Canal, the Sinai, and the western deserts. The British repulsed a Turkish attack in February of 1915, but Maxwell was unable to pursue because of inadequate transportation and Kitchener's instructions to avoid any reverse that might endanger British prestige among the Muslims. Maxwell's command responsibilities were made more difficult by the fact that Egypt was the staging ground for the Gallipoli Campaign and, after the evacuation for refitting, for the Salonika Campaign. In 1915 there were 400,000 British troops in Egypt.

In December of 1915, when General Murray arrived in Egypt, Maxwell retained command west of the Suez Canal. In January of 1916 he repelled an attack by the Senussi in the western desert. In March of 1916 he was called home on his own request. Shortly afterward, the Irish Easter Rebellion began, and Maxwell was appointed commander in chief in Ireland with extensive powers to reestablish order, which he did in a few days. In November of 1916 he was appointed commander in chief, Northern Command, in which post he remained until 1919. He later was a member of Lord Milner's mission to Egypt. He was promoted to general in June of 1919 and retired in 1922. Maxwell died at Cape Town on 20 February 1929.

Montecue J. Lowry

References

Falls, Cyril. *The Great War, 1914–1918*. New York: Capricorn, 1959.
Halsey, Francis Whiting. *History of the World War*. Vol. 8. New York and London: Funk & Wagnalls, 1919.
Liddell Hart, B.H. *The Real War, 1914–1918*. Boston: Little, Brown, 1930.
Martin, F.X., ed. *Leaders and Men of the Easter Rising: Dublin 1916*. London: Methuen, 1967.

See also EGYPT; IRELAND; SENUSSI AND SULTAN OF DARFUR REBELLIONS; SINAI CAMPAIGN

Medals and Decorations

While the award of military medals dates back to antiquity, both the variety and numbers issued during World War I were probably greater than the total of all previous conflicts. The vast scale of fighting between 1914 and 1918 was an obvious cause for such an increase. Other factors were the realization of the greater need for high morale at the front and the propaganda value of "heroes" back home. The end result was tens of millions of badges, medals, and decorations given to both military and civilian participants of the Great War.

The German Empire, with its many grand duchies, principalities, and free cities, granted more awards than any other nation. Each of these regions was allowed a separate collection of civil and military decorations. It is interesting to note, however, that at the national level, only four types of award were available. Of those, the most prestigious was the *Pour le Mérite,* known as the "Blue Max." It was given for outstanding displays of bravery or military achievement. Struck at first in gold, the *Pour le Mérite* was reduced to a silver gilt due to the wartime economy measures of 1916.

Much more common was the *Ehrenkruz des Weltkrieges* (Honor Cross of the Great War). Often called the Hindenburg Cross, it was authorized for display by veterans in 1934. Widows and orphans of such could also obtain a copy. Another often-seen award is the Wound Badge. With a different design for the army and navy, these came in three grades, depending on the severity of the wound.

Finally, there was the *Eiserne Kreuz* (Iron Cross), one of the best-known military decorations of all times. Although strictly speaking a Prussian award, it was granted for acts of bravery to all Germans beginning in 1914 and to those allied with Germany after 1915. Large numbers were issued in a "second" or "first" class; in addition, five Grand Crosses and one Star of the Grand Cross were awarded.

Franz Jozef's Dual Monarchy produced the next largest group of Central Powers decorations. The Maria Theresa Order came in three grades and was awarded for outstanding military achievement. There was also a War Cross for Civil Merit issued to industrialists whose efforts fueled the Austro-Hungarian military machine. The *Tapferkeits* (Bravery medal) was the Hapsburg equivalent of the Iron Cross. Among the easier awards to acquire were an Iron Cross for Merit, created in 1916, "for soldiers without rank" and the Karl Troop Cross, given to any man with twelve months of service and veterans of major battles.

Bulgaria's ill-fated decision to enter the Great War was acknowledged by a medal issued in 1933. It was awarded to all soldiers of the Central Powers who served with Bulgarian forces, or their widows or orphans. Bulgaria also issued a Military Order for Bravery and a premature medal to commemorate the 1916 victory over Serbia.

The Ottoman Empire granted its *Nichan-i-Imtiaz* (Order of Merit) to high-ranking officers. Lesser ranks could win the *Imtiaz* medal, which featured crossed swords bearing the Moslem date 1332 (1914/15). An Iron Cross equivalent, known as the "Iron Crescent," was also awarded for bravery.

Certain decorations from Finland, the Ukraine, Poland, and Georgia tie in with those of the Central Powers. These were issued by military detachments fighting for the independence of such proto-nations. The Order of Queen Tamara is among the more interesting, being granted to all members of the Georgian Legion and those German soldiers who agreed to fight in that nation after 4 November 1918.

Allied awards were just as diverse. They ranged from the familiar French *Croix de Guerre* to exotic decorations such as Thailand's Order of the White Elephant or Denmark's *Slesvig* medal, granted to French and British soldiers supervising the plebiscite there in 1920. Possibly the most interesting was the Inter-Allied Victory Medal. Proposed by Marshal Ferdinand Foch at the Paris Peace Conference, it was approved on 24 January 1919. The basic idea was for each country to utilize a common rainbow-colored ribbon, from which would hang a bronze medal with that individual nation's concept of victory. Those from American and European powers are similar in design, all depicting a classically styled winged victory. Japan and Siam show a Samurai warrior and a many-limbed goddess respectively. China went even further away from the common theme with a silver medal issued only to selected officers and Allied legation guards stationed in Peking and Tientsin.

France produced more decorations than any other Allied power. These included the five-leveled Legion of Honor, the *Medaille Militaire,* a *Medaille des Evades* for escaped POWs, and the famous *Croix de Guerre.* Over two million of the latter were awarded, to fighting men, military units, civilians, towns, and even the carrier pigeon Cher Ami.

British decorations reflected that nation's more conservative and class-conscious society. England gave medals to enlisted men and crosses to officers. Some, such as the Medal for Distinguished Conduct on the Field, came with a significant annual gratuity. While only officers could obtain a *Kaiser-i-Hind,* Order of the Garter, or Distinguished Flying Cross, all men were entitled to the Victoria Cross. Only 576 of these most coveted decorations were issued during the Great War. Nearly 10 percent of them went to the "Old Contemptibles" during the months of August to December of 1914. Possibly the best-known winner of the Victoria Cross was sixteen-year-old Jack Cornwell, whose posthumous award came for his gallant action at the Battle of Jutland in 1916.

M

Czarist Russia was even more rigid in regard to class distinctions and the award of military decorations. It issued a wide array of orders, crosses, and medals. The most important was the Order of St. George. It came in four classes for officers, one of which was an actual sword with a gold handle and orange and black knot—the colors of its ribbon. The St. George Cross was given to enlisted personnel and came with an annual cash annuity plus the proviso that its owner could not be reduced in rank save by court martial.

The earliest Italian decoration of the Great War was the Balkan Cross. It went to all troops serving in this theater, including those who occupied Albania before Italy declared war on the Central Powers. The old Sardinian Military Valor Medal was the highest award for bravery. Only twenty-six living men could claim its gold version in 1918.

United States awards reflected the republican traditions of the nineteenth century. Before 1917 only a Certificate of Merit, for enlisted men, or a Medal of Honor, for all ranks, could be given for acts of bravery. In January of 1918 President Wilson by executive order established the Distinguished Service Cross and Medal. Other awards included the fixing of silver or bronze stars to the Victory Medal, which indicated courageous actions of a degree less than those gaining a Distinguished Service Cross. Service Clasps were also placed on this medal to indicate duty in a particular battle or theater of operations.

John P. Dunn

References

Bowen, V.E. *The Prussian and German Iron Cross*. n.p.: Iron Cross Research Publications, 1986.

Laslo, Alexander J. *The Interallied Victory Medal of World War I*. Albuquerque, N.M.: Dorado, 1992.

Werlich, Robert. *Orders and Decorations of All Nations*. Washington, D.C.: Quaker, 1974.

Wyllie, Col. Robert. *Orders, Decorations and Insignia. Military and Civil*. New York: G.P. Putnam's Sons, 1921.

Medicine, Military

World War I came at a pivotal time in medicine's development. The battle for status between physicians and surgeons had been put to rest, Lister's antiseptic technique was generally accepted, and diagnostic methods such as roentgenography and bacteriology were available to field hospitals. On the negative side, modern surgery was in its infancy, and there was no effective treatment for most infectious diseases.

The American Civil War and the Crimean War had witnessed the beginnings of military nursing, effective triage and transport, and anesthesia. A system of field hospitals close to the front extending to fixed base hospitals well behind the lines had been tried by the Prussians in 1870. After the Boer War, in which twenty times as many men were hospitalized for disease as for wounds, the British Royal Army Medical Corps reorganized on the German model. The Queen Alexandra's Imperial Military Nursing Service was organized in 1902 and the Royal Army Medical Corps got its own journal and medical school by 1903. A school of sanitation was formed in 1906, and the first "field ambulance" (after the French *hopital ambulante*) was organized the same year.

The kaiser's Army Medical Corps was well prepared for war by 1914. German physicians had adopted Listerian techniques of asepsis, and a cadre of academic physicians and surgeons considered the best in the world were available for service. The British were relatively well prepared in spite of having only 18,000 hospital beds in the entire empire—a number that would rise to 637,000 by 1919.

The French and Russians were abysmally unprepared. The French still kept their medical corps under command of line officers and had no route of medical supply except through the quartermaster corps. French physicians refused to accept sterile techniques for wound treatment and made no provision for ordinary sanitation. The Russians were even worse. They had a severe shortage of physicians and little respect for those they did have. Russian physicians were dismally short of supplies and had no organized triage or hospital system.

The various medical corps would be asked to care for 63 million men. More than 21 million of them were wounded in the war; another 8 million died. In each army, former civilians assumed most nursing responsibilities. The Red Cross supplied Voluntary Aid Detachments (VADs)—women trained to work as orderlies and to do the simplest, most demanding, and most demeaning jobs. As the war progressed, the responsibility taken on by the VADs steadily increased in spite of protests by professional nurses. Volunteers, soldiers, and prisoners of war absorbed the physically taxing and incredibly dangerous jobs of retrieving wounded from the battlefields. Ambulances were usually driven by volunteers—often from noncombatant countries such as the United States. Physicians were in chronically short supply: When the war began the entire medical corps of both the Territorial and Regular British armies totaled only twenty thousand men. This corps cared for 316,000 casualties during the Somme Offensive alone. From early 1915 volunteer American physicians augmented meager British and French forces, when the United States entered the war, twelve hundred American doctors were formally seconded to the Royal Army Medical Corps.

The war brought a series of unique medical and surgical problems. Trench warfare posed almost insoluble sanitary problems, making diseases of fecal contamination such as dysentery, typhoid, and cholera common. Infectious diseases such as measles, mumps, and meningitis were inevitable when large populations of men were thrown together. Tropical theaters such as Mesopotamia and Africa brought their own diseases, especially malaria. Trench foot and trench fever, previously unknown diseases, were serious problems, and poor hygiene bred lice and the resultant scabies. Venereal diseases were common in the West, while in the East each Russian division had to reserve one hundred beds for scurvy caused by inadequate diets. Typhoid could be prevented by a newly available serum, and some diarrheal illnesses were rendered less common by improved sanitation. Still, for most infectious diseases there was no effective therapy. A final, bitter blow came in 1918, when the influenza pandemic swept across Europe on its way around the world and for one summer killed more men than died in battle.

The war posed difficult problems in wound treatment. The fields of northern France and Flanders were heavily contaminated with manure, and the organisms that caused tetanus and gas gangrene were endemic. Mortality from tetanus was appalling in the first months of the war but rapidly declined with the arrival of an effective antiserum. The incidence of gas gangrene decreased when surgeons adopted wide debridement of wounds and irrigation with an antiseptic solution of sodium hypochlorite (Carrel-Dakins fluid). Wound mortality in 1915 was 28 percent, but these measures resulted in a drop to a more respectable eight percent by 1917.

New technology brought special problems. Rather than clean, high-velocity wounds typical of the Boer War, most injuries in the trenches were caused by large, slow-moving shrapnel fragments that destroyed large amounts of tissue and carried contaminated material into the depths of the wound. Early in the war Germany began using soft-jacketed "dum-dum" bullets that slowed and expanded as they entered the body and had the same damaging effect as shrapnel. Irritant and asphyxiant gases generated frightful skin and respiratory problems. Zeppelins capable of flying at twenty thousand feet necessitated measures to combat and treat hypothermia and hypoxia—thus the beginning of aviation medicine.

Treatment of these problems was a mixture of success and frustration. Adopting and improving on wartime experiences of the last half of the nineteenth century, transport and triage reached a new level on the Western Front. Wounded who had previously been left on the battlefield for days were evacuated (often at great risk and difficulty) within hours. Stretcher bearers were equipped with rudimentary dressing kits and morphine. Field dressing stations in the trenches stopped active bleeding, dressed wounds, splinted fractures, and prepared the seriously injured for transport. Early in the war, wounded were evacuated in supply wagons returning from the front; these were later replaced by motorized ambulances that carried men to casualty clearing stations placed seven miles behind the front. These stations, just outside the range of enemy artillery, typically had two hundred beds and could be expanded to as many as one thousand. Twenty to twenty-five miles behind the front, and usually located on a rail line, were base hospitals where the more difficult surgery was performed and the sickest were treated. By 1918 each base hospital operating table could account for twenty-five operations in twenty-four hours. Behind the base hospitals were thousand-bed evacuation hospitals on the coast, where wounded were accumulated for transport back to Britain. The system's underlying principle was to keep every patient moving, either back to the front or to the rear and, eventually, to England or the south of France.

M

Military surgery saw significant advances during the war. Anesthesia had been used since the American Civil War, but it became routinely available to forward hospitals during World War I. X-ray machines moved from the laboratories of large hospitals to tents at the front. Intravenous fluids became commonplace, and the Americans taught Europeans to anticoagulate donor blood so transfusion could be routine. Before the war orthopedics had dealt primarily with congenital deformities, leaving fractures to the generalist. The vast number of bone injuries forced training of four hundred new orthopedists, the establishment of dedicated orthopedic hospitals, and development of hospitals dedicated to rehabilitation. In 1915 a bone injury carried a 40 percent likelihood of amputation; that number had dropped to 10 percent by 1917.

Facial and head wounds were an inevitable result of trench warfare. Early in the war the British commissioned artists to build plaster masks to hide the more grotesque facial injuries. By war's end the artists gave way to a cadre of reconstructive plastic surgeons trained to deal with these injuries. Mortality from penetrating brain injuries dropped from 60 percent to 25 percent as the war progressed. Hemostats, reusable syringes, adequate surgical lights, and even magnets to retrieve shell fragments lodged in the brain entered the medical armamentarium. As in other aspects of combat, dedication and inventiveness ameliorated but did not eliminate the worst effects of the technology of war.

Jack McCallum

References

Ashburn, P.M. *A History of the Medical Department of the United States Army*. Boston: Houghton Mifflin, 1929.

Gabriel, Richard, and Karen Metz. *A History of Military Medicine from the Renaissance through Modern Times*. New York: Greenwood, 1992.

Lovegrove, Peter. *Not Least in the Crusade: A Short History of the Royal Army Medical Corps*. Aldershot: Gale & Polden, 1952.

Mediterranean Naval Operations, 1914–18

In November of 1912 the German navy, according to an agreement with the Italians and Austro-Hungarians—Germany's two partners in the Triple Alliance—sent to the Mediterranean the battle cruiser *Goeben* and light cruiser *Breslau*. These two warships were immediately employed by their commander, Rear Admiral Wilhelm Souchon, at the outbreak of the war. On 4 August 1914 they bombarded the barracks of Bône and the port of Philippeville in Algeria.

British intervention at midnight the same day and the decision of Italy to remain neutral convinced the *Kaiserliche Marine* to withdraw its two warships from the Mediterranean sea. Consequently, Berlin ordered Souchon to reach Constantinople, where German diplomacy had been trying to gain Turkish entry into the war on the side of the Central Powers. Souchon easily accomplished this, leading his two ships into the Dardanelles on the evening of 10 August.

The arrival of *Goeben* and *Breslau* at Constantinople disclosed deficiencies in Anglo-French naval cooperation. More important, it strongly influenced the Turkish decision to enter the war on 29 October 1914. Shortly after their transfer to the Turkish navy, the two warships were renamed *Yavuz Sultan Selim* and *Midilli*, respectively.

These circumstances helped prompt London's traditional "peripheral strategy," using naval units to attack distant "soft bellies" of enemy coalitions. The subsequent effort to force the Dardanelles and bring Constantinople under the guns of the Royal Navy was designed to open a supply route to Russia, remove pressure on that nation by Turkey, and perhaps drive Turkey from the war.

The Dardanelles Campaign and Gallipoli Campaign, discussed in detail elsewhere, may be briefly summed up here. An Anglo-French fleet began bombardments of the outer Dardanelles forts on 19 February 1915 and of the inner forts in early March. This last task, considered essential before the combined fleet could force the narrows, was made difficult by the restricted waters of the Straits, mobile Turkish batteries, and mines laid by the defenders.

On 18 March the principal naval attack began. Six British and four French battleships moved forward, but an undetected row of twenty mines, previously laid by a Turkish steamer, proved deadly effective in those narrow and shallow waters. The British predreadnoughts *Irresistible* and *Ocean*, and the French predreadnought *Bouvet* were sunk, while the British battle cruiser *Inflexible* was badly damaged. Moreover, the French predreadnoughts *Gaulois* and *Suffren* were damaged by gunfire, and the former had to be beached to prevent its sinking.

Faced with these events, further naval attacks were deferred until troops were available and a joint operation mounted. Finally, on 15 April 1915, Allied troops landed on the Gallipoli Peninsula. The Turks, who had had sufficient time to prepare defenses, held the high ground, and the campaign soon turned into a stalemate and a major military failure.

Naval setbacks in the Dardanelles continued. On 13 May a Turkish destroyer sank the British predreadnought *Goliath*, and on 25 and 27 May German submarine *U-21* sent to the bottom British predreadnoughts *Triumph* and *Majestic*. Troop reinforcements, landed at Suvla Bay on 6–7 August, failed to penetrate inland. Evacuation of Allied troops from the Gallipoli Peninsula became inevitable, and a highly successful withdrawal took place between 23 November 1915 and 9 January 1916.

During the Dardanelles Campaign a British submarine, *E-11*, commanded by Lieutenant Nasmith, made three trips into the Sea of Marmara and sank the Turkish predreadnought *Kheireddin Barbarossa* and a large transport at Constantinople.

Meanwhile, French naval units in the Mediterranean were employed defending seaborne traffic and conducting operations in the Adriatic against the Austrian navy. The major naval engagements in this theater were the sinking of the French cruiser *Zenta* on 16 August 1914 and the French naval bombardment of Cattaretao on 1 September. On 20 December the Austrians captured the French submarine *Curie* when it entered Pola harbor. Another Allied setback was the 27 April 1915 torpedoing of the French cruiser *Léon Gambetta* by an Austrian submarine.

On 10 May an Anglo-French-Italian Naval Convention was signed as a result of Italian demands for major Allied support. A First Allied Fleet was constituted, to include four British battleships, four British light cruisers, twelve French destroyers, and numerous French torpedo boats, submarines, minesweepers and aircraft. It was headquartered at the Italian ports of Taranto and Brindisi under command of the Italian Fleet Vice Admiral Luigi Amedeo di Savoia, Duke of the Abruzzi. If this First Allied Fleet were deployed to the northern Adriatic, a second Allied fleet would be formed, under the commander of the French fleet. It would include those French battleships, cruisers and destroyers, and Italian and British warships, not already assigned to the Italian fleet commander.

The Italian fleet was itself much larger than the Austrian fleet. Italian appeals for Allied naval support were based chiefly on the geographical configuration of the Adriatic, which favored the Austrians (and had conditioned Italian policy since the 1866 Austrian naval defeat of Italy off Lissa).

Italy opened hostilities against Austria on 24 May 1915. War against Germany was declared on 28 August 1916. Chief of the Italian Naval Staff was Vice Admiral Paolo Thaon di Revel. He considered the narrow Adriatic waters unsuitable for the main battle fleets and advocated exclusive use of light craft and submarines. This policy kept the Italian battle fleet inactive at Taranto throughout the war. It also led to bitterness among Allied naval liaison officers (British Captain Herbert Richmond and French Captain Ren Daveluy) regarding Italian naval competence.

The Italian navy suffered a number of reversals. The Austrian fleet bombarded many cities along the Italian coast from Rimini to Barletta on the very first day of the war and sank the destroyer *Turbine*. On 18–19 June 1915 the Austrians attacked cities at the mouths of the Tagliamento, Pesaro, and Monopoli rivers. The Italian navy also lost two armored cruisers, *Amalfi* and *Garibaldi,* to enemy submarines in July, as well as other vessels (two torpedo boats and two submarines). On 27 September the predreadnought *Bene-detto Brin* blew up inside the port of Brindisi with the loss of 456 men. The explosion was later attributed to sabotage. Admiral Thaon di Revel then resigned and was replaced as chief of naval staff by the minister of the navy, Vice Admiral Camillo Corsi, who combined the two offices.

A favorable opportunity to avenge the Italian defeats seemed to be at hand on 29 December 1915, when an Austrian flotilla of one light cruiser (*Helgoland*) and five destroyers attacked Durazzo, one of the southern Adriatic ports used by the Allies for the evacuation of the defeated Serbian army. The Austrians sank three cargo ships and a French submarine but lost two destroyers in a minefield. They were pursued by four British and Italian cruisers and nine French and Italian destroyers. The Austrians managed to avoid destruction, however, and escaped with only slight damage. This was one of only two remarkable surface engagements of the whole war in the Mediterranean; the other was on 15 May 1917.

The Mediterranean submarine threat, meanwhile, had become cause for Allied concern. German U-boats had arrived in April of 1915 by sea or were sent overland in sections by rail to Pola, where they were assembled. The German navy had employed U-boats against the French and British in the Dardanelles since May.

American protests following the sinking of the liners *Lusitania* and *Arabic* offered the Germans further reason to shift their attentions to the Mediterranean, where American interests were less pronounced.

The German navy ordered five large U-boats and two smaller UC-boats (minelayers) into the Mediterranean in October and employed them in the Aegean and along the North African coast. These submarines achieved remarkable success, sinking seventy-nine merchant ships totaling 290,471 gross tons in the last three months of 1915. Nonetheless, prompt Allied countermeasures, in the form of patrols and extensive intelligence activities, reduced German successes in the first six months of 1916, when only twenty-four Allied cargo ships were sunk by U-boats in the Mediterranean.

Austrian submarines also registered successes, despite their small number, poor endurance, and scanty experience. Many of the victories initially ascribed to Austrian U-boats must be assigned to German submarines that hoisted the Austrian flag while surface cruising, above all in the Adriatic, to avoid diplomatic protests from Italy, which was not yet at war with Germany.

The submarine threat in the Mediterranean led to an Allied conference at Taranto on 30 October 1916. The Allies decided to strengthen defenses in the Straits of Otranto, through which the German U-boats based at Pola were obliged to pass, and to install there a barrage formed of British trawlers with tow nets. These little fishing boats should have been protected by warships as well as larger vessels at the nearby port of Brindisi, but things went differently.

Light Austrian warships carried out raids against the barrage, the most important of which occurred on 15 May 1917, giving rise to the second, and largest, noteworthy Adriatic naval battle of the war. Three Austrian light cruisers and two destroyers, commanded by Captain Admiral Horthy (with his flag in the *Novara*), supported by thirteen aircraft and three U-boats, moved against the barrage. En route the Austrians encountered a small convoy and sank the Italian destroyer *Borea* and a munitions ship. The Austrians broke through the barrage early on the morning of the 15th and sank fourteen trawlers. They also damaged another four, three badly. The Austrians picked up seventy-two prisoners. Once the alarm was raised, sizable Allied forces were set in motion, including two British light cruisers, an Italian cruiser and three flotilla leaders, seven Italian destroyers, and three French destroyers. Most were slow to close, however, and all Austrian ships succeeded in escaping and returning to base (*Novara* was taken in tow but became operational a week later). The Italian flotilla leaders *Aquila* and *Mirabello* were hit by gunfire, and the British cruiser *Dartmouth* was torpedoed and damaged by the German submarine *UC-25* while returning to Brindisi, but it eventually reached Malta.

Further misfortunes, meanwhile, struck the Italian navy. On 2 August 1916 the modern dreadnought *Leonardo da Vinci* shared the fate of the *Benedetto Brin* by falling victim to sabotage; it sank inside Taranto harbor. On 11 December the predreadnought *Regina Margherita* struck two mines and sank, with the loss of 674 lives.

Despite these losses, it was the German submarine threat that remained the main concern for the Allies, despite their introduction of a convoy system in October of 1917. The Italians even requested Japanese naval assistance, which was supported by the British government. The Japanese finally agreed, sending the light cruiser *Akashi* and eight destroyers into the Mediterranean in April of 1917.

The German submarines were tamed at last, but not before they sank a total of 3,355,262 gross tons of enemy shipping in the Mediterranean. Among the sixty submarines sent by Germany into that sea during the war was *U-35*, commanded by Lieutenant-Commander Lothar von Arnauld de la Perière. It sank the highest tonnage in history: 446,708 gross tons.

Despite its failures, the Italian navy achieved remarkable results with small craft, especially the MAS boats, basically fast motor torpedo boats. MAS boats obtained their first success on 26 June 1916, sinking two enemy freighters in Durazzo harbor. They increased their activity after the return of Vice Admiral Thaon di Revel to the post of chief of the naval staff on 9 February 1917.

Three MAS boats boldly but ineffectively attacked two Austrian battleships off Cortellazzo on 16 November 1917. In a daring raid on 10 December, *MAS.9* and *MAS.13,* commanded by Lieutenant Luigi Rizzo, sank the predreadnought *Wien* inside Trieste harbor. On 10 June 1918, *MAS.15* and *MAS.21,* again commanded by Luigi Rizzo, sank the dreadnought *Szent Istvan* off Premuda, despite seven escorting torpedo boats. The Austrian force (three remaining battleships) thereupon abandoned its planned attack against the Otranto barrage.

The Italian navy also developed a new underwater weapon called the mignatta, similar to the two-man torpedo employed by the Italians in the Second World War. On the night of 31 October–1 November 1918, one mignatta, manned by two Italian officers, Raffaele Paolucci and Raffaele Rossetti, entered the Austrian navy base at Pola and sank the dreadnought *Viribus Unitis.* The latter, three days before, had been transferred to the newly formed Yugoslav navy.

This was the last naval episode of the Mediterranean war. Turkey surrendered on 30 October, Austria on 4 November, and Germany on 11 November 1918.

Alberto Santoni

References

Halpern, Paul G. *The Naval War in the Mediterranean, 1914–1918.* Annapolis, Md.: Naval Institute Press, 1987.

Laurens, Adolphe. *Le Commandement naval en Méditerrané, 1914–1918.* Paris: Payot, 1931.

Marder, Arthur J. *From the Dreadnought to Scapa Flow. The Royal Navy in the Fisher Era, 1904–1919.* 5 vols. London: Oxford University Press, 1961–70.

Sokol, Hans H. *La guerra marittima dell'Austria-Ungheria, 1914–1918.* 4 vols. Rome: Ufficio Storico della Marina Militare, 1932.

Ufficio Storico della Marina Militare, La Marina italiana nella grande guerra. 8 vols. Florence: Vallecchi, 1935–42.

See also ABRUZZI, AMEDEO; AUSTRIA-HUNGARY, NAVY; DARDANELLES CAMPAIGN; *GOEBEN* AND *BRESLAU*; FRANCE, NAVY; ITALY, NAVY; SUBMARINE WARFARE; THAON DE REVEL, PAOLO

Mehmed V, Sultan (Mehmed Reşad) (1844–1918)

Sultan of the Ottoman (Turkish) Empire and the caliph (religious leader) of Moslems. Born in Istanbul on 2 November 1844, Mehmed V was brought to the throne by the revolutionary Young Turk government in 1909. His constitutional status as supreme commander was a mere formality; throughout his reign Mehmed V was a puppet of the Young Turks. It is doubtful that he had any prior knowledge of the Turco-German Treaty of Alliance of 2 August 1914 that brought Turkey into the Great War. On 14 November 1914 he declared Jihad, Holy War of Islam, on the Entente nations, although his hopes of a general revolt in Islamic regions against the Entente did not materialize. Mehmed V's main role during the war was to represent the country at state visits and to sign laws and military orders brought to him by the government.

Mehmed V died in office on 3 July 1918 of natural causes. He was replaced by Mehmed VI.

Yücel Yanikdağ

References

Lewis, Bernard. *The Emergence of Modern Turkey.* London: Oxford University Press, 1969.

Shaw, Stanford J., and Ezel K. Shaw. *History of the Ottoman Empire and Modern Turkey.* 2 vols. Cambridge: Cambridge University Press, 1977.

See also OTTOMAN EMPIRE

Mehmed VI, Sultan (Vahdeddin) (1861–1926)

Last sultan of Turkey, born on 2 February 1861 in Istanbul. Mehmed VI became sultan on 3 July 1918 after the death of his brother, Mehmed V. Mehmed VI's role in Turkish politics was only ceremonial. When it became obvious that the war was lost, Young Turk government leaders fled the country. Four months after his accession, Mehmed VI appointed a commission led by Minister of Marine Rauf Bey to sign the armistice of Mudros, 30 October 1918, which called for the unconditional surrender of the Turkish forces. Mehmed VI collaborated with Allied occupation forces in the suppression of the nationalist forces headed by Mustafa Kemal. On 10 August 1920 his government signed the Treaty of Sèvres that partitioned the Turkish Empire. The nationalist government accused him of treason for signing the treaty, and Mehmed VI fled the country on 17 November 1922. He lived in several places until his death in San Remo on 15 March 1926.

Yücel Yanikdağ

References

Kinross, Lord. *Atatürk: The Rebirth of a Nation*. Nicosia, Northern Cyprus: K. Rustem and Brother, 1981.

Sertoglu, Midhat. *Resimli-Haritali Mufassal Osmanli Tarihi*. Vol. 6. Istanbul: Guven, 1963.

See also KEMAL, MUSTAFA; OTTOMAN EMPIRE

Mesopotamia, 1914–18

From the beginning of the First World War Great Britain assumed the initiative in Mesopotamia (Iraq) and generally held it throughout the war, though with varying degrees of success. Their lack of success was especially evident at Kut al-Amara, where, after a prolonged siege, in April of 1916, the Turks captured an entire British division. Their defeat was actually a turning point for the British, who responded by organizing their forces and undertaking a series of offensives that resulted in the takeover of the entire region. Britain's presence in Iraq continued long after the war was over, despite the stirrings of nationalism among the Kurdish, Sunni, and Shiite tribes who inhabited the area.

Even prior to Turkey's entry into the war in late October of 1914, the British had dispatched a reinforced brigade to the mouth of the Shatt-al-Arab to protect the Anglo-Persian oil installations on the Persian Gulf. After Britain declared war on the Turks and increased its strength to a division, Major General Sir Arthur A. Barrett's Indian Expeditionary Force D moved upriver to Basra and took the city by 22 November. Several weeks later Barrett's troops occupied Qurna, five miles above Basra, at the confluence of the Tigris and Euphrates rivers, thereby securing the area.

Commentators have long questioned whether Britain should have remained at Basra rather than advancing farther into this outlying Ottoman region, with its forbidding climate and often hostile tribes. By the end of 1914 Baghdad had become an exceedingly desirable political objective in the minds of officials in India and London. In April of 1915 the India Office directed the British forces, now under Lieutenant General Sir John Nixon, who had replaced the ailing Barrett, to fan out across Lower Mesopotamia. Major General Sir George Gorringe had by now led his 12th Indian Division to Ahvaz in Persia and had driven the Turks out, thereby ensuring the flow of oil to the Abadan refinery. Major General Sir Charles Townshend then took his 6th Indian Division and a cavalry brigade and, with the assistance of a small naval flotilla, defeated the Turks at Amara on the Tigris on 3 June. Gorringe, after contending for over a month with heat and marshland as well as the Turkish enemy, occupied Nasiriya on the Euphrates on 25 July.

Next, Nixon ordered Townshend to head for Kut, 150 miles farther up the Tigris. At that point, differences between London and Indian authorities came to a head. Officials in India, as well as Nixon, viewed the proposed advance as a preliminary offensive with the eventual objective of taking Baghdad; the war office in London, because of the difficulties on other fronts, urged caution and restraint. By 29 August, British leaders allowed Townshend to push forward to Kut. By 11 September he had assembled about 11,000 soldiers, and, again assisted by a "regatta" of gunboats, steamers, barges, and tugs, the offensive began. On the 26th it reached Kut, captured the city, and pursued the Turks to Aziziya, halfway between Kut and Baghdad.

Although Nixon had ordered Townshend to stop, the lure of Baghdad and the desire to compensate for the disaster at Gallipoli led the British to continue. Townshend's superiors even promised him two additional Indian divisions from France, though they set no date for their arrival. As it turned out, however, it was General Nur al-Din's Turkish Sixth Army that received reinforcements, not Townshend. Although the latter's 14,000 troops moved forward and fought the Turks to a standstill at Ctesiphon, twenty-three miles south of Baghdad, his 4,600 casualties meant that he could not continue. The Turks had suffered 9,500 casualties, but they now held the initiative. They forced Townshend to retreat back to Kut, which he reached on 3 December. By the

7th they had surrounded his force of about 10,000 soldiers. On Christmas Eve the Turks attempted to storm Townshend's positions, but, after having been repulsed, they settled down to starve the British and Indian troops into submission.

During the next three months the British undertook three relief expeditions to try to extricate the 6th Division from Kut. Major General Sir Fenton J. Alymer made the first two attempts in January and March with his Tigris Corps of two divisions (actually those shipped from Europe) plus cavalry; General Gorringe commanded the third try in April; and even the Russians undertook a halfhearted operation from northwestern Iran. None succeeded, and on 29 April 1916 Townshend and 2,750 British and 6,500 Indian troops capitulated. His incarceration was less than onerous—the Turks gave him permission to go hunting, and he lived in a villa on an island near Constantinople—but his troops were treated horribly and many died in captivity. The only other mar on Turkey's victory was the death of one of Germany's most effective advisers, Field Marshal Colmar von der Goltz, who was helping direct the siege. Turkish forces, now under Khalil Pasha, were in control of central Iraq.

The British defeat at Kut forced their military leaders and officials to reassess their generally lackluster performance to date. They concluded that they could not take Mesopotamia "on the cheap," and that changes were in order. London now took over sole direction of operations in the theater. Lieutenant General Sir Percy Lake, who had succeeded the ailing General Nixon, had already started to develop the communications and transport necessary to sustain offensives in the interior. Lieutenant General Sir Frederick S. Maude began his meteoric rise, which eventually led to his promotion as commander of all British forces in the area.

The pace of the buildup quickened during the summer and fall of 1916. The British continued to increase the port capacity at Basra. In April they started construction of a major railway north of Basra and reached Amara by November. They augmented their river fleet and expanded the Royal Flying Corps, which had first flown at the front in 1915 and now gained air superiority over the enemy (primarily made up of German pilots). By December, Maude, who had replaced the aging Lake in late summer, had at his disposal two corps—I Corps under Lieutenant General A.S. Cobbe and III

Corps under Lieutenant General Sir William R. Marshall—with two divisions each, another division in the rear, and two cavalry brigades. Of a total of 340,000 troops in Iraq, the fighting force numbered about 166,000, of which two-thirds were Indians. Opposing them was Khalil Pasha's Sixth Army of 42,000.

On the 13th Maude began his slow but determined advance toward Baghdad. His joint army, navy, and air force recaptured Kut early in February and took Turkish defensive positions at Sanaiyat later in the month. Following several days of fighting along the Diyala River south of Baghdad the British gained the upper hand, forcing the Turks to begin pulling out on the evening of 10 March. Although Arab looters got to the city before the British, the next day the Black Watch regiment had the honor of first entering the town center. The Union Jack finally flew over Baghdad.

Throughout the rest of 1917 fighting became less intense. After the fall of Baghdad the British captured Samarra, a railhead ninety miles to the north, but there was little combat during the grueling summer months. The possibility of complications between Britain and Russia in northern Iraq dissipated as a result of the Russian revolutions. A possible threat from a combined Turco-German force being organized by General Erich von Falkenhayn did not materialize because it was diverted to the Palestine front. In the fall, British troops scattered over a wide area, engaging the Turks from the Euphrates in the west to the Diyala in the east. The British were usually successful, while Turkey's mounting defeats indicated its waning strength.

On 19 November Maude died of cholera and was replaced by his corps commander, General Marshall. By this time London considered Iraq a sideshow, and Marshall's Mesopotamian Expeditionary Force underwent considerable changes. By the summer of 1918 Marshall had been forced to send two divisions to Palestine, a battalion from each of his remaining brigades to the Balkans, and a company from each of the Indian battalions to form cadres for new units being raised in India. Such reinforcements as he received were not of the caliber or experience of the force Maude had commanded.

Nevertheless, combat in Mesopotamia had not ended. By October of 1918 the Turks were in dire straits on several fronts, and by mid month they sought an armistice. London thereupon directed Marshall to take as much of northern Iraq as possible, and on the 23rd his army began to advance. Tactically, they used frontal assaults combined with flanking attacks when forces were available. They made particularly effective use of armored-car companies, known as Lewis-gun detachments because of the Lewis light machine guns they had at their disposal. Air formations carried out bombing attacks and reconnaissance missions. On 29 October the force commanded by Turkish general Ismail Hakki surrendered. Although the Turks signed an armistice at Mudros the next day, it was not until 14 November, after a good deal of wrangling between Marshall and the local Turkish commander, Ali Ihsan Pasha, that the British occupied Mosul, Iraq's major northern city. The campaign in Mesopotamia was over.

British casualties in the Mesopotamian fighting totaled 92,501, of which 15,814 were deaths in battle and 12,807 from disease. British actions included victories near Basra and at Amara; the offensive that led to the taking of Baghdad had helped restore Britain's prestige. But Britain had also suffered defeats, most notably at Kut. The campaign also revealed Britain's administrative shortcomings and the difficulty of conducting operations in inhospitable terrain. The British also experienced problems in using second-rate troops and equipment, since the best went to the Western Front. Despite her military problems, Britain achieved her political goals by maintaining control of the area for decades to come. The British exercised control either directly through a mandate, or later, even after Iraqi independence, through favorably disposed governments. In the meantime, ethnic and religious hatreds among Iraq's peoples—and the exploitation of oil—made the "Land of the Two Rivers" a volatile place.

Alan F. Wilt

References
Barker, A.J. *The Neglected War: Mesopotamia, 1914–1918*. London: Faber & Faber, 1967.
Falls, Cyril. *The Great War*. New York: Capricorn, 1959. Longrigg, Stephen H. *Iraq, 1900 to 1950: A Political, Social, and Economic History*. London: Oxford University Press, 1953.
Moberly, Sir F.J. *Official History of the Great War: The Campaign in Mesopotamia 1914–1918*. 4 vols. London: HMSO, 1923–30.

Wilson, Sir Arnold T. Loyalties. *Mesopotamia, 1914–1917; A Personal and Historical Record*. New York: Greenwood, 1969.

See also GOLTZ, COLMAR VON DER; LAKE, PERCIVAL; MARSHALL, WILLIAM; MAUDE, FREDERICK; NIXON, JOHN; MAUDE, FREDERICK; OTTOMAN EMPIRE, ARMY; TOWNSHEND, CHARLES

Messines, Battle of (7–14 June 1917)

Messines was one of the finest set piece battles of the war. Field Marshal Sir Douglas Haig planned a great offensive in 1917 to gain the Belgium coast by attacking the Germans in Flanders. Before this attack could begin, the French launched their disastrous Nivelle Offensive that resulted in the mutiny of units of the French army. The need to distract enemy attention away from now-threatened sectors of the Allied line and the belief that the German army was approaching exhaustion pushed forward the British plan for a great offensive in Flanders.

As a preliminary to this attack, the British targeted the high ground of Messines Ridge, measuring six by eight miles, which dominated the Ypres salient. The main effort to gain the coast was to follow several weeks later. Planning for the Messines operation was given to the methodical commander of the British Second Army, General Sir Herbert Plumer, known as "Daddy" to his troops, and his highly capable chief of staff, General Sir Charles Harington.

As far back as 1915, the British had begun digging shallow tunnels under Messines Ridge, with plans to place small charges under the German lines. The following year the plan was expanded into nineteen deep tunnels, a hundred feet underground, to be packed with high explosives. By early 1916 five miles of tunnels were underway, some over half a mile long, dug at the rate of ten to fifteen feet a day. They were filled with over a million pounds of high-explosive ammonal.

On 21 May 1917 the British began an intensive artillery bombardment with 2,500 guns firing three and a half million shells. Meanwhile, the Royal Flying Corps achieved air superiority over the salient. Plumer massed his artillery at the rate of one piece for every twenty yards of ground along an 8.5-mile front. Then, shortly before dawn on 7 June and after the long preliminary bombardment, the great mines beneath Messines Ridge were exploded simultaneously without a single failure. The sound of the blasts could be heard as far away as London. The explosions created mine craters, some seventy feet in depth and three hundred feet across, and blasted away frontline German companies. This was followed by a massive artillery barrage and assault by nine Allied divisions, including Australian and New Zealand troops, accompanied by seventy-two Mark IV tanks. To add to the attack, oil and gasoline were projected into the German lines.

The German front trenches were easily overrun by the attackers. Entire enemy companies were nearly wiped out. More than ten thousand German troops were killed on the day of the assault, and many of those who survived the explosions and bombardment surrendered. The British advance was so rapid that the tanks were unable to keep up with the infantry. By late afternoon, the British forces were moving down the eastern side of the ridge. Plumer committed his three reserve divisions to press forward the attack. As the shock of the initial assault subsided, German resistance began to stiffen, but their counterattacks failed to stop the advancing troops.

The battle, which ended on 17 June, was entirely successful in straightening the Ypres salient and was a great boost to British morale. The Allies achieved success at Messines because of methodical planning and preparation by Plummer and Harington, the effective use of artillery, and the pursuit of a limited, obtainable objective. British casualties in the Battle of Messines were 17,000 men; German losses were 25,000, of whom 7,500 were prisoners.

After securing the southern flank of the Ypres salient at Messines, Haig was free to launch his long-awaited offensive, but the Passchendaele Campaign (Third Battle of Ypres) that followed proved a grim failure, with high casualties and little gain.

Van Michael Leslie

References

Bourne, J.M. *Britain and the Great War 1914–1918*. London: Edward Arnold, 1989.

Cruttwell, C.R.M.F. *A History of the Great War 1914–1918*. Oxford: Clarendon, 1940.

Falls, Cyril. *The Great War 1914–1918*. New York: Capricorn, 1959.

Wolff, Leon. *In Flanders Fields: The 1917 Campaign*. New York: Ballantine, 1958.

Woodward, Sir Llewellyn. *Great Britain and the War of 1914–1918*. London: Methuen, 1967.

See also HAIG, DOUGLAS; NIVELLE OFFENSIVE; PLUMER, HERBERT; TUNNELING AND MINE WARFARE

Metaxas, John (1871–1941)

Greek military leader, born on 12 April 1871 in Ithaca, Greece. Metaxas graduated from the Greek Military Academy and continued his studies at the Military Academy of Berlin. He gained distinction through his participation in the Greco-Turkish War (1897) and received an appointment to the Greek General Staff during the Balkan Wars of 1912–13. As chief of staff he remained a colonel during World War I until his promotion to general in 1916.

At the beginning of World War I, Metaxas favored a Greco-Turkish alliance and believed that Greek interests coincided more closely with those of the Central Powers than the Allies. He harbored strong Germanophile feelings, but division within the country and Greek vulnerability to Entente attack convinced Metaxas to support King Constantine's policy of Greek neutrality. In 1917 Metaxas left Greece following the forced abdication of Constantine, returning with the king in 1920. In 1936 he became dictator of Greece and remained so until his death in Athens on 29 January 1941.

Susan N. Carter

References

Alastos, Doros. *Venizelos: Patriot, Statesman, Revolutionary*. London: Lund Humphries, 1942.

Jelavich, Barbara. *History of the Balkans Vol. 2: Twentieth Century*. New York: Cambridge University Press, 1983. Reprint, 1989.

Leon, George B. *Greece and the Great Powers 1914–1917*. Thessaloniki: Institute for Balkan Studies, 1974.

See also CONSTANTINE I; GREECE

Mexico, Role in the War

With its almost 2,000-mile border with the United States, Mexico became an important theater of covert activity in World War I. While spies from Europe, Japan, and America fought for imperial advantage, Mexicans were engaged in the first great social revolution of the century. Just as the world powers played off revolutionary factions, Mexican leaders used imperial rivalries to realize their nationalist ambitions.

During the dictatorship of Porfirio Díaz (1876–1911), Mexico was fertile territory for imperialist ventures. United States capitalists gained control of mines and haciendas; the British built railroads and exploited Mexican oil reserves; and French and German investors dominated much of the country's industry.

Foreign ownership of the national wealth and the peasants' loss of their village lands set the stage for the decade-long Mexican Revolution. Francisco Madero led a popular army that overthrew Díaz in 1911, but he was assassinated two years later. When General Victoriano Huerta attempted to establish a new dictatorship, the rebel armies of Francisco "Pancho" Villa, Venustiano Carranza, Alvaro Obregón, and Emiliano Zapata deposed him in July of 1914. The victorious revolutionaries then began fighting among themselves for control of the country. The outbreak of World War I in August sent ammunition prices skyrocketing, which made it difficult for the Mexicans to obtain arms. The Villistas and Zapatistas subsequently lost a series of climactic battles in the spring of 1915. Carranza became president with the help of munitions supplied directly by the United States Army.

Villa, infuriated by the complicity of American President Woodrow Wilson, determined to exact revenge. On the morning of 9 March 1916 he sent 500 men to attack Columbus, New Mexico. The rebels burned the town and slaughtered eighteen people before U.S. troops drove them back across the border. Wilson responded by ordering a punitive expedition into Mexico to capture Villa and disperse his followers. A week later General John J. Pershing led his column into Mexico. Some scholars have speculated that German secret agent Felix Sommerfeld, a former Villista purchasing agent, provoked the attack on Columbus in order to embroil the United States in a Mexican war and forestall its involvement in Europe.

In any event, U.S. troops soon ran into conflict with Mexican authorities. President Carranza demanded that Pershing withdraw, and after an initial drive deep into Mexican territory, the Americans reluctantly complied, though only gradually. Frustrated by his inability to capture Villa, Pershing employed two Japanese secret agents in an attempt to poison the revolutionary. Villa actually drank the poison but somehow survived. In June the two nations came to the brink of war when American cavalry troops engaged a Mexican garrison at Carrizal. After tense negotiations the crisis eased, and in February of 1917 the expedition finally withdrew. If German agents were in fact responsible for the Columbus raid, their efforts proved counterproductive: The United States government used the punitive expedition to prepare for war in Europe by mobilizing the national guard and gaining organizational experience.

A United States/Mexican war remained the goal of German Foreign Minister Arthur Zimmermann. In January of 1917 he sent a telegram to President Carranza proposing a military alliance in which Germany would supply war materials for Mexico with which to reconquer Texas, New Mexico, and California. British intelligence (Room 40) obtained and deciphered Zimmermann's fateful telegram, then passed it along to the American president. At the time, Wilson was seeking congressional approval for measures against U-boat attacks. The note's publication on 1 March and the subsequent confirmation by Zimmermann himself two days later helped Wilson obtain a declaration of war. Car-ranza declined the German proposal.

After the Zimmermann fiasco Germany attempted to use Mexico as a base for espionage activities against the United States. Agents built a radio station in Ixtapalapa, a suburb of Mexico City, and disseminated anti-American propaganda to Mexican audiences. Carranza allowed German spies to operate freely in Mexico but denied the Germans permission to build a U-boat base. Allied secret services meanwhile sought to neutralize the German threat. Felix Sommerfeld was interned for the duration of the war, and two other leading spies, Anton Dilger and Kurt Jahnke, were kept under surveillance. Counterintelligence officials made their greatest coup by capturing Lothar Witzke during his attempt to enter the United States on an espionage mission.

European and American agents sought to manipulate rival Mexican revolutionary factions for their own imperial ends during World War I. But at the same time, Carranza manipulated imperial rivalries in his attempt to forge a nationalist revolutionary government.

Jeffrey M. Pilcher

References

Hall, Linda B., and Don M. Coerver. *Revolution on the Border: The United States and Mexico, 1910–1920*. Albuquerque: University of New Mexico Press, 1988.

Harris, Charles H., and Louis R. Sadler. *The Border and the Revolution*. Las Cruces, N.M.: Center for Latin American Studies/Joint Border Research Institute, New Mexico State University, 1988.

Hart, John M. *Revolutionary Mexico: The Coming and Process of the Mexican Revolution*. Berkeley: University of California Press, 1987.

Katz, Friedrich. *The Secret War in Mexico: Europe, the United States and the Mexican Revolution*. Chicago: University of Chicago Press, 1981.

See also ZIMMERMANN, ARTHUR; ZIMMERMANN TELEGRAM

Michael, Grand Duke (1878–1918)

Russian noble and younger brother of Czar Nicholas II. Born on 22 November 1878, the fourth of five children, Michael was the one most indulged by his father, Alexander III. He developed a penchant for automobiles and high living. When his brother Nicholas II denied him permission to marry a twice-divorced commoner, Nathalie Cheremetevskaya, Michael left Russia with his lover and lived abroad. In 1910 they had a son and two years later were married in Austria. He was allowed to return to Russia only after the outbreak of the war, and, even then, neither Nicholas nor Alexandra ever spoke to Nathalie.

During World War I Michael served in the Caucasus as commander of the Savage Division and the II Caucasian Corps. He was said to be a gentle and modest man, uninterested in power. On 15 March 1917 Czar Nicholas II abdicated in favor of Michael, who renounced the throne unless it were offered by a popularly elected constituent assembly. Many conservatives complained that it was illegal for Nicholas to bypass his own son, Aleksei, and bestow the title on Michael, who was married to a commoner and divorcée. Some members of the moderately conservative Octoberist party urged Michael to accept, but the grand duke believed that the public would not tolerate another Romanov. He therefore threw his support behind the provisional committee. In his manifesto renouncing the crown Michael wrote:

> Inspired by the same thought that permeates the nation, that the well being of our Fatherland is the supreme good, I have taken the firm decision to accept sovereign authority only in the event that such will be the desire of our great nation . . . through its representatives in the Constituent Assembly, to determine the form of government and the new constitution of the Russian state.

Michael retired to his estate near Petrograd. Lenin had him exiled in March of 1918 and brought under surveillance by the Cheka. Naively, Michael made no attempt to flee; he was killed in June of 1918, most likely by the secret police, although the Communists blamed the White Army. His wife escaped to England.

Glenn R. Sharfman

References

Lincoln, Bruce. *Passages through Armageddon: The Russians in War and Revolution, 1914–1918*. New York: Simon and Schuster, 1986.

———. *The Romanovs: Autocrats of All the Russians*. New York: Dial, 1981.

Massie, Robert K. *Nicholas and Alexandra*. New York: Macmillan, 1967.

Pipes, Richard. *The Russian Revolution*. New York: Alfred Knopf, 1990.

See also NICHOLAS II; RUSSIA, HOME FRONT AND REVOLUTIONS OF 1917

Michaelis, Georg (1857–1936)

German imperial chancellor. Born on 9 August 1857 in Haynau, Silesia, Michaelis was descended from an old Prussian civil service family. He studied law and theology and then entered the Prussian civil service in 1879. After teaching at the German Law School in Tokyo from 1885 to 1889 he reentered the Prussian civil service, serving in administration and the ministry of culture. Following rapid promotion, he became undersecretary of state in the Prussian Ministry of Finance in 1909.

After the outbreak of the First World War, Michaelis was appointed chairman of a newly formed war grain trade society and later director of the imperial grain-supply department. In 1917 he was named Prussian state commissioner for the national food supply. Colorless but energetic and hard working, Michaelis had achieved a notable record as a ministerial bureaucrat. In July of 1917, on General Erich Ludendorff's suggestion and to the surprise of many, he was appointed to succeed Theobald von Bethmann Hollweg as imperial chancellor and Prussian minister-president.

Endowed with at best modest political talents and lacking experience in foreign affairs, Michaelis faltered when he had to rely on the backing of the army against a Reichstag majority that had opposed his appointment. He was forced to accept the Reichstag Peace Resolution of 19 July 1917, which demanded an end to the war without annexations. He qualified it by adding his famous "as I understand it." When Pope Benedict XV initiated peace proposals, he was unable to make any concessions on Germany's expansionist policy toward Belgium. The majority parties in the Reichstag were angered by his foot-dragging on suffrage reform in Prussia and his blaming of the Independent Social Democratic party for instigating a naval mutiny. Without parliamentary support and with diminished backing from the army, he was forced to resign his short-lived chancellorship in October of 1917. After a short term as governor of Pomerania, Michaelis left government service and worked on behalf of the Protestant church and student welfare. He died on 24 July 1936 at Bad Saarow, Germany.

George P. Blum

References

Fischer, Fritz. *Germany's Aims in the First World War.* New York: W.W. Norton, 1967.

Ritter, Gerhard. *The Sword and the Scepter: The Problem of Militarism in Germany.* Vol. 4: *The Reign of German Militarism and the Disaster of 1918.* Coral Gables, Fla.: University of Miami Press, 1973.

See also Bethmann Hollweg, Theobald von; Germany, Home Front

Michel, Victor (1850–1937)

French general and commander in chief of the French army before World War I. Born on 30 January 1850 at Auteuil, Michel held several field positions before his appointment in 1907 to the supreme war council. In January of 1911 he was selected as vice president of the supreme war council and commander in chief designate. When Michel assumed his position, the French High Command believed that, if war broke out with Germany, the enemy would unleash an offensive from Lorraine and perhaps through eastern Belgium. Accordingly, French troops were to concentrate along Alsace, Lorraine, and the eastern portion of the Franco-Belgian border.

Michel rejected the high command's assumptions. Michel understood the core of German military strategy, the Schlieffen Plan. The Germans, making full use of the reserves on the front lines, intended to make a wide swing through western Belgium and then strike south across the unguarded Franco-Belgian border. If they were successful, the French army would be encircled.

Michel proposed a radical plan as a means to stop the German march through western Belgium. While reducing the traditional concentration of forces along the Alsace-Lorraine frontier, Michel wanted approximately 700,000 troops to be placed along the entire Franco-Belgian border. To obtain the manpower needed to defend the French border from Switzerland to the English Channel, Michel's plan, very much like the Schlieffen Plan, called for use of the reserves on the front lines. The French army would be in a position to stop the German swing maneuver and then launch a counteroffensive once the German attack had been identified.

Michel's proposals were rejected by much of the high command, and in December of 1911 he was forced to resign as vice-president of the supreme war council. The high command rejected Michel's belief that the reserves could fulfill a fighting function. It was widely thought that only the active army was physically and psychologically prepared to engage in frontline fighting. Distaste for a prominent role for the reserves also was shaped by political factors. The political Left, suspicious of the professional office corps' loyalty to the French Republic, sought to minimize the role of the active army, arguing that a few months' training would be adequate to produce the citizen-soldier. The conservative officer corps, on the other hand, believed that to emphasize the role of the reserves was to take a first step toward the socialist ideal of a militia. Lastly, the high command did not appreciate Michel's defensive counterattack strategy, since they believed that only an all-out offensive *(offensive à outrance)* as soon as war broke out would allow the French to break through the German lines and produce a victorious end to the short war universally anticipated.

Michel served the next two years as military governor of Paris. Unfortunately, when war began in 1914, Michel had failed to prepare Paris adequately for the anticipated German onslaught. Fortifications, construction of gun emplacements, and the laying of barbed wire were at best only half finished by the end of August. Michel was relieved of his command and placed on the inactive reserve list. He died on 7 November 1937 at Meulan.

Jan Karl Tanenbaum

References

Tanenbaum, Jan Karl. "French Estimates of Germany's Operational War Plans." In *Knowing One's Enemies,* edited by Ernest R. May. Princeton: Princeton University Press, 1984.

Williamson, Samuel R., Jr. *The Politics of Grand Strategy: Britain and France Prepare for War, 1904–1914.* Cambridge: Harvard University Press, 1969.

See also FRANCE, ARMY; FRENCH WAR PLAN XVII; SCHLIEFFEN PLAN

Micheler, Joseph Alfred (1861–1931)

French general, born in Phalsbourg, France, in 1861. Micheler commanded the French Tenth Army in the 1916 Battle of the Somme. His performance there earned him promotion to command the Reserve Army Group. In 1917 during the planning stages for General Robert Nivelle's Champagne offensive, Micheler and other French generals began to have serious doubts about its potential for success. Unwilling to confront Nivelle directly and thwarted in his efforts to change the plans by Sixth Army commander General Charles Mangin, Micheler contacted political leaders such as Minister of War Paul Painlevé. At an April meeting of political and military leaders Nivelle threatened to quit if his plans were changed and the subject was dropped.

When the Reserve Army Group was dissolved in May, Micheler took command of Fifth Army. By Autumn of 1917 Micheler was critical of Pétain's "inertia" and his orders for defense-in-depth, which Micheler believed extreme. When Micheler's Fifth Army and

General Duchêne's Sixth Army were attacked along the Chemin des Dames by the German First and Seventh armies on 27 March 1918, however, their forces were quickly overrun because they had placed the bulk of their troops forward in shallow trenches, spread out over a twenty-five-mile front. Micheler and Duchêne were among those French generals relieved of their commands.

Micheler died in Nice, France, 18 March 1931.

Tom Zucconi

References

Herwig, Holger, and Neil M. Heyman. *Biographical Dictionary of World War I.* Westport, Conn.: Greenwood, 1982.

King, Jere Clemens. *Generals and Politicians: Conflict between France's High Command, Parliament, and Government, 1914–1918.* Berkeley: University of California, 1951.

Ryan, Stephen. *Pétain the Soldier.* New York: A.S. Barnes, 1969.

See also LUDENDORFF OFFENSIVES; NIVELLE OFFENSIVE; NIVELLE, ROBERT; SOMME, BATTLE OF

Miliukov, Pavel Nikolaevich (1859–1943)

Russian minister of foreign affairs, born in Moscow on 27 January 1859, the son of a prominent architect. Miliukov was a member of the group of oftentimes utopian intellectuals who occupied a unique position in pre-Soviet Russian society. By education and training he was a historian. His major book, *The Russian State under Peter the Great,* is still considered an important work. Politically, Miliukov was on the left wing of the liberal movement, a faction that worked for a legal end to the Russian monarchy and the creation of a republic. During the political turmoil of 1905 he was one of the founders of the Constitutional Democratic (Kadet) party, which became the bastion of constitutionalism in Russia.

Because of his well-publicized statement "We have no enemies on the Left," Miliukov was considered dangerous by the czarist regime and therefore was disqualified from running for the First State Duma in 1906 on a legal technicality. After the dissolution of that body, however, he orchestrated a protest of Duma members against the government, the Viborg Manifesto, which called for the Russian people to stop paying taxes until the government moderated its position against the legislature. Miliukov was elected to the Third and Fourth dumas. In the latter body after 1914 he became one of the most strident critics of the czarist regime's inept prosecution of the war. Finally, in October of 1916, from the floor of the Duma, Miliukov accused Empress Alexandra of being either a traitor or a fool.

With the March 1917 Revolution, Miliukov was appointed foreign minister in the new provisional government. It was in that post that he displayed the naivete typical of many Russian intellectuals. He viewed the March Revolution as nothing more than a popular protest against an unpopular czar, as such having nothing to do with Russia's foreign policy. Consequently, in March and April of 1917 Miliukov made a number of public and private statements promising that Russia would continue to support her allies and strive for victory. At a 23 March press conference, Miliukov reiterated Russia's war aims: liberation of the Slavs in Austria-Hungary, annexation of the Austrian Ukraine (Galicia), and annexation of Constantinople and the Straits. This statement was completely at odds with the official provisional government position of "peace without annexations." Miliukov's foreign-policy pronouncements may have been welcome in Paris and London, but they created an uproar in Petrograd, where there were demonstrations verging on riots. On 2 May Miliukov resigned, and the provisional government was reorganized.

Shortly after the Bolshevik seizure of power Miliukov and several other political leaders traveled to the Rostov region, where an anti-Bolshevik army was being organized. With the creation of the Aleksandr Kolchak government, he went to Paris as its official representative. After the Civil War, Miliukov, like so many other Russian exiles, became a gadfly, showing up at various international gatherings such as the Washington Disarmament Conference of 1921 as a representative of the defunct Kadet party. His last years were spent in Paris and London; he died in France on 21 March 1943.

John W. Bohon

References

Gurko, General Basil. *Features and Figures of the Past*. Stanford: Stanford University Press, 1939.

Miliukov, Pavel N. *Russia and Its Crisis*. Chicago: University of Chicago Press, 1905.

Pares, Sir Bernard. *The Fall of the Russian Monarchy*. New York: Vintage, 1939.

See also RUSSIA, HOME FRONT AND REVOLUTIONS OF 1917

Millerand, Alexandre (1859–1943)

French politician, born in Paris on 10 February 1859. Millerand studied law and was elected a member of the Chamber of Deputies at the young age of twenty-six. He became a socialist and accepted the post of minister of commerce in 1899, prompting a crisis that disrupted the Second International. Premier Raymond Poincaré appointed Millerand minister of war in January of 1912, and he served in that post until January of 1913, and from August of 1914 to October of 1915.

In his first term as minister of war, Millerand believed that only a formidable army and powerful fleet would enable France to preserve its independence. He fostered a "nationalist revival" by strengthening military discipline and morale, by supporting an increase in the size of the navy and army, and by instilling a martial spirit in the public at large.

As minister of war (1914–15) in the René Viviani government during World War I, Millerand played a significant role in mobilizing the economy for war production: Existing factories were enlarged, new ones created, production goals were established, and 500,000 workers were recalled from the front and returned to armament factories.

Although the war minister served as an intermediary between the military and political leaders, Millerand shielded French army Commander in Chief Joseph Joffre from civilian political interference and control. Parliamentary determination to reassert civilian control surfaced dramatically when Joffre dismissed General Maurice Sarrail as commander of the Third Army in mid-1915. Sarrail was a republican general who had strong support from the political Left. To the Left, Sarrail's dismissal demonstrated Millerand's subservience to Joffre. Left-wing politicians not prepared to accept Sarrail's dismissal intervened; the Viviani government overrode Joffre's decision for the first time during the war and appointed Sarrail commander of the newly created French army in the Balkans. Millerand, who had defended Joffre's prerogatives, resigned in October of 1915. Millerand's departure illustrated the gradual shift in the balance of power away from the high command and toward the civilian politicians.

Millerand had an illustrious postwar career, most notably as premier and president of the republic, 1920–24. He died 6 April 1943 at Versailles.

Jan Karl Tanenbaum

References

Farrar, Marjorie Milbank. *Principled Pragmatist. The Political Career of Alexandre Millerand*. New York: Berg, 1991.

King, Jere Clemens. *Generals and Politicians: Conflict between France's High Command, Parliament and Government, 1914–1918*. Berkeley: University of California Press, 1951.

Weber, Eugen. *The Nationalist Revival in France, 1905–1914*. Berkeley: University of California Press, 1959.

See also JOFFRE, JOSEPH; SARRAIL, MAURICE

Milne, Sir Archibald Berkeley (1855–1938)

Royal Navy admiral, born at the admiralty on 2 June 1855, Milne was the only surviving son of Admiral of the Fleet Sir Alexander Milne. He attended Wellington College briefly and entered the navy in 1869. Milne was an inferior officer who lacked imagination and determination. An intimate at court and friend of Queen Alexandra, he owed his promotions primarily to connections. Milne was promoted to rear admiral in 1904, vice admiral in 1908, and admiral in 1911. He was appointed commander in chief in the Mediterranean in November of 1912.

In August of 1914 Milne was ordered to watch the mouth of the Adriatic for two German warships commanded by Admiral Wilhelm Souchon: the battle cruiser *Goeben* and light cruiser *Breslau*. Assuming they would head west, Milne sent his own battle cruisers *Indomitable* and *Indefatigable* to locate them. They were spotted at 10:30 on 4 August, but neither side was technically at war until the expiration of the British ultimatum to the German government at midnight, and so the ships passed one another on opposite courses and without the customary signals. Never suspecting that the Germans might make for the Dardanelles, Milne sent only one ship, the light cruiser *Gloucester* (Captain Howard Kelly), to block that route. Although the *Gloucester* located and tailed the two ships while reporting their position and even engaged the *Breslau* at long range, Milne failed to take decisive action. He was convinced that the German warships would eventually reverse course for the western Mediterranean and Atlantic. Ultimately, the *Goeben* and *Breslau* escaped to the Dardanelles. Their arrival at Constantinople was an important factor in bringing Turkey into the war on the side of the Central Powers.

On 30 August 1914 the admiralty issued a paper exonerating Milne of any blame in the escape of the *Goeben* and *Breslau*; this was in part a recognition of its own failures in the dismal affair. Nevertheless, press criticism of Milne was severe, and he was never employed again by the admiralty. He retired at the end of the war and in 1921 published a book in defense of his actions. He died in London on 5 July 1938.

Spencer C. Tucker

References

Corbett, Julian S., and Henry Newbolt. *History of the Great War: Naval Operations*. Vol. 1. London: Longmans, 1920.

Dictionary of National Biography, 1931–1940. London: Oxford University Press, 1985.

Marder, Arthur J. *From the Dreadnought to Scapa Flow: The Royal Navy in the Fisher Era, 1904–1909*. Vol. 2. London: Oxford University Press, 1961.

McLaughlin, Redmond. *The Escape of the Goeben*. London: Seeley Service, 1974.

Milne, Admiral Sir A. Berkeley. *Flight of the Goeben and Breslau*. London: Eveleigh Nash, 1921.

Van Der Vat, Dan. *The Ship that Changed the World. The Escape of the Goeben to the Dardanelles in 1914*. New York: Adler and Adler, 1986.

See also GOEBEN AND BRESLAU; MEDITERRANEAN NAVAL OPERATIONS

Milne, Baron George Francis (1866–1948)

British army commander in the Balkans, born in Aberdeen, Scotland, on 5 November 1866.

Milne was a graduate of the Royal Military Academy at Woolwich (1885) and Staff College at Camberley (1897). He directed artillery at the Battle of Omdurman (1898) and was a brevet lieutenant colonel on Kitchener's intelligence staff during the Boer War.

In 1914, as commander of the 4th Division artillery, Milne participated in the battles of Le Cateau, the Marne, and the Aisne. Promoted to brigadier general in October of 1914, he became a major general in 1915 and was assigned to the staff of the Second Army. Milne was appointed commander of the 27th Division in Salonika under overall Allied commander General Maurice Sarrail and in 1916 commanded all British forces under Sarrail and later General Franchet d'Esperey.

As Milne had only a small force that had been decimated by sickness, Chief of the Imperial General Staff Sir William Robertson would not allow him to undertake offensive action until April of 1917. Milne's troops suffered heavy losses in fighting near Lake Dorian, however, and did not advance again until after the collapse of the Bulgarian government in 1918. After the fall of the Ottoman Empire, his troops occupied Constantinople.

Milne remained in Turkey until 1920, when he was promoted to general. In 1922 he was named to head the eastern command and four years later was appointed chief of the Imperial General Staff. In 1928 he was promoted to field marshal. He retired in 1933 as Baron Milne of Salonika and Rubislaw, county of Aberdeen. Milne was active in the Home Guard during the Second World War. He died in London on 23 March 1948.

Tom Zucconi

References
Dictionary of National Biography, 1941–1950. London: Oxford University Press, 1985.
Falls, Cyril. *The Great War: 1914–1918.* New York: Capricorn, 1959.
Guinn, Paul. *British Strategy and Politics, 1914–1918.* Oxford: Oxford University Press, 1965.
Herwig, Holger, and Neil M. Heyman. *Biographical Dictionary of World War I.* Westport, Conn.: Greenwood, 1982.

See also MARNE, FIRST BATTLE OF; SALONIKA CAMPAIGN

Milner, Alfred, Viscount (1854–1925)

British colonial administrator and statesman, born 23 March 1854 in Germany. Educated at King's College and Oxford University, Milner served as under secretary of finances in Egypt and later as high commissioner of South Africa. With the outbreak of war he took on the role of troubleshooter, dealing with problems of food and coal production. When David Lloyd George became prime minister, Milner joined the war cabinet, where he dealt with issues ranging from shipping to the production of spirits.

Second only to Lloyd George in influence, Milner undertook several important diplomatic missions to France and Russia. He was instrumental in the inclusion of the dominion prime ministers in the war cabinet and in the appointment of Foch as commander of Allied forces. He attended the peace conference and signed the Versailles Treaty. Milner died on 13 March 1925 at Sturry Court in England.

Van Michael Leslie

References
Bourne, J.M. *Britain and the Great War 1914–1918.* London: Edward Arnold, 1989.
Gollin, A.M. *Proconsul in Politics: A Study of Lord Milner in Opposition and in Power.* New York: Macmillan, 1964.

See also GREAT BRITAIN, HOME FRONT; LLOYD GEORGE, DAVID

Mine Warfare, Sea

Despite the use of primitive mines in the American War of Independence, the Napoleonic Wars, the Crimean War, the American Civil War, and the Russo-Turkish War of 1877, the first mining campaigns of real consequence took place in the Russo-Japanese War of 1904–5. In early April of 1904 the Japanese sent the *Koryo Maru*, a merchant ship rebuilt as a minelayer, together with some destroyers to block the entrance to Port Arthur with moored mines. On 13 April the Russian battleship *Petropavlovsk*, flagship of the Russian squadron, with commander in chief Admiral S. Makarov aboard, struck the mines and blew up. The Japanese mines also damaged the Russian battleship *Pobeda*. The Russians replied in kind. Noting the tracks of the Japanese blocking ships, the captain of the *Amur*, the first purpose built minelayer, laid a barrage. In May of 1904 two Japanese battleships, the

Hatsuse and *Yashima,* ran into this minefield and sank. These and other successes led many navies to intensify development of mines, construct special minelaying vessels, and rebuild old gunboats or torpedo boats as minesweepers.

In 1914 most navies had stocks of different types of mines. There were controlled moored or ground mines to be fired from shore observation stations for the defense of harbors and anchorages. More important were the independent mines, most of which were moored types with a hydrostatic depth-taking device. They exploded when a ship touched and broke one of the horns, or set off the pendulum exploder.

Most minesweeping was conducted by small surface craft, usually fishing-type vessels. Two or more of them would trail long cables between them or individually towed long cables. The minesweepers were equipped with means to cut the mooring lines of the mines so that they would float to the surface and could be neutralized, usually by gunfire.

While the Royal Navy had only seven old and relatively slow rebuilt light cruisers of the *Apollo* class, the German navy had two special, fast, minelaying ships, and all modern light cruisers and destroyers were equipped to lay 100 to 120 or 18 to 40 mines, respectively. In addition there were some small fast passenger vessels that had been used to transport guests to seaside resorts; these were reequipped as camouflaged minelayers for up to 200 mines each. During the night of 4–5 August 1914 one of them, the *Königin Luise,* laid a minefield forty miles off Lowestoft on which the British light cruiser *Amphion* sank the next day, after she had intercepted and sunk the German minelayer.

During the night of 25–26 August 1914 the minelayers *Albatros* and *Nautilus,* covered by the light cruisers *Strassburg* and *Mainz* and destroyers, each laid two hundred mines off the Tyne and Humber. When the mines were discovered over the next days, minesweeping operations were started, during which the minesweeping gunboat *Speedy* and some trawlers were sunk.

Both sides also used defensive mine barrages to cover their own sea lanes against submarines or surface attacks. After the British raid into Heligoland Bight on 28 August 1914, the Germans used their minelayers to lay mine barrages to cover their passages in and out of Heligoland Bight. The British and French started in September to lay mine barrages to cover routes in the Channel by which the British Expeditionary Forces were transported to France, in order to protect them against German U-boats. For this purpose they used the converted old cruisers *Intrepid, Iphigenia, Andromache,* and *Apollo.*

While some other German offensive mining operations had to be canceled owing to fears of being detected, the armed merchant cruiser *Berlin* was sent in October of 1914 to the north of Ireland and laid barrages off Tory Island. On 27 October the dreadnought *Audacious* went down from one of these mines, the largest ship lost to a mine in World War I.

During the German battle cruiser raids against Yarmouth on 3 November 1914 and against Hartlepool, Whitby, and Scarborough on 16 December 1914, the light cruisers *Stralsund* and *Kolberg* laid mine barrages off the British coast. During their minesweeping operations the British lost minesweepers, merchant ships, and fishing vessels. In August of 1915 the German armed merchant raider *Meteor,* disguised as a neutral merchant ship, laid a minefield in the Moray Firth and sank by gunfire the armed boarding steamer *Ramsey,* but the *Meteor* had to be scuttled off Horns Reef when the British Harwich Force intercepted her. On 2 January 1916 the armed merchant raider *Möwe* laid 252 mines west of the Pentland Firth, and four days later the battleship *King Edward VII* capsized after hitting one of them.

After a January 1915 operation with four of the old slow minelayer-cruisers in Heligoland Bay, the British Admiralty ordered the replacement of these ships by some rebuilt fast merchant ships. In the latter half of 1915 the Royal Navy laid additional minefields defensively off the east coast of Britain and offensively in Heligoland Bay. In April of 1916, during German fleet operations, first the light cruiser *Graudenz* and then the battle cruiser *Seydlitz* were damaged by such mine barrages.

The most successful British minelayer was the rebuilt fast destroyer *Abdiel,* which had laid 68 minefields and 6,293 mines by the end of the war. Its most successful operation was laying a minefield off Horns Reef during the night of 31 May–1 June 1916 in which the German dreadnought *Ostfriesland,* returning from the Jutland battle, was heavily damaged.

Baltic

In August of 1914 the Germans had available only a few light cruisers, some torpedo boats and U-boats, and four merchant ships equipped as minelayers. On 3 August the cruisers *Augsburg* and *Magdeburg* laid mines off Libau, and on 17 August the auxiliary minelayer *Deutschland,* covered by the two cruisers, laid two hundred mines off the Finnish Gulf, on which three Russian minesweepers were lost. In addition, U-boats laid some mine barrages.

The Russian Baltic Fleet possessed five minelayers of high capacity, two of them built after the Russo-Japanese War, and three rebuilt old armored cruisers. They were used first to lay 3,280 mines in the entrance to the Finnish Gulf. In addition, the armored cruisers *Rjurik, Admiral Makarov,* and *Rossija,* the protected cruisers *Oleg* and *Bogatyr,* as well as more modern destroyers, especially the big new *Novik,* were equipped to lay mines. From October of 1914 to February of 1915, in eight operations together with the minelayers *Amur* and *Yenisei* they laid 1,598 mines in German shipping routes. These led to the loss of the armored cruiser *Friedrich Carl,* thirteen steamers, and three minesweepers, as well as damage to the light cruisers *Augsburg* and *Gazelle.*

In the spring and summer of 1915 the Russians used their minelayers mainly to block the entrances to the Gulf of Riga and German operational routes. The Germans continued to lay mines in the area west of the Irben Strait, off Gotland, and off the Finnish Gulf. During such operations the Russian minelayer *Yenisei* was sunk by the German U-boat *U-26,* and the German minelayer *Albatross* had to be beached on the approach of superior Russian forces. In October of 1915 German minelayers tried to block the approaches to Courland with 1,210 mines.

From October to December of 1915 Russian cruisers and destroyers again laid five mine barrages in the central Baltic east of Gotland and off Windau, on which the German cruiser *Bremen* and three smaller vessels sank and the cruisers *Danzig* and *Lübeck* were damaged. After the ice melted in 1916, Russian minelayers, cruisers, and destroyers laid new mine barrages in the Finnish Gulf, with 6,264 mines, and in the Botten Sea, with 1,000 mines. The Russians also laid 6,320 mines in the Gulf of Riga to block the Irben Strait. These had some effect on German landings on the Baltic Islands in October of 1917. Notwithstanding intensive efforts at minesweeping, the German dreadnoughts *Grosser Kurfürst Markgraf,* and *Bayern* were damaged by the mines, which also resulted in the loss of smaller vessels.

Black Sea and Mediterranean

Mine warfare was also conducted in the Black Sea and the Mediterranean. When the Turkish-German navies started the war against Russia on 29 October 1914, the Turkish auxiliary minelayer *Nilufer* laid a barrage off Sevastopol, as did the German cruiser *Breslau* off the Kerch Strait. The Russians countered with an operation by their Black Sea Fleet against the entrance to the Bosphorus, where four modern destroyers laid 240 mines. This was repeated in November when two minelayers laid 400 mines off Trabzon, and in December when four minelayers and four destroyers laid 607 mines again off the Bosphorus. On 26 December the German battle cruiser *Goeben* and on 2 January the Turkish gunboat *Berk* were heavily damaged by these mines. The Turkish cruiser *Medjidiye* was lost to a mine during a raid off Odessa on 1 April 1915 but was raised by the Russians.

During the Allied efforts to force the Dardanelles in the spring of 1915, the Turkish-German defenders tried with a small stock of mines of different designs to block the narrows. The Allies employed fishing trawlers to sweep the mines to open the way for their heavy ships. During the night of 7–8 March the new small Turkish minelayer *Nusrat* was able to lay twenty-six new mines in the entrance of the Dardanelles. This was the most successful mine barrage in history: When the Allied battleships entered the Dardanelles on 18 March, in their effort to break through to the Sea of Marmara, the French *Bouvet* took a hit in her magazine from shore gunfire and blew up; the minefield claimed the British ships *Irresistible* and *Ocean,* and damaged the battle cruiser *Inflexible.* This barrage was certainly the principal factor causing the Allies to cancel the operation to force the Dardanelles by ship alone.

From the spring of 1915 to the spring of 1917 the Russian Black Sea Fleet mounted a large number of mine operations against the Bosphorus, Turkish coal harbors, and the Bulgarian harbor of Varna. For these operations they used mostly destroyers but also their only minelaying submarine, *Krab,* and some specially built shallow-draft minelayers. These mines greatly hampered Turkish traffic along the Anatolian coast and led to heavy losses in transport shipping. On the German side the cruiser *Breslau,* repaired after mine damage off the Bosphorus in mid-1915, and the mine U-boat *UC-15* laid some mine fields in 1916 and 1917.

In the Mediterranean Allied minelayers in 1915 laid some barrages off Smyrna and other places off the Turkish coasts. These operations were followed in 1916–17 by the laying of additional fields off the Austrian Adriatic coast by the British minelayer submarine *E 46* and a strengthening of fields off the Dardanelles by French and British auxiliary minelayers. When on 20 January 1918 the German *Goeben* and *Breslau* left the Dardanelles to attack Allied guard vessels off Imbros and Mudros, the *Breslau* was lost and the *Goeben* heavily damaged by Allied defensive minefields. An Allied plan to close the Otranto Strait by an anti–U-boat mine barrage of 60,000 mines was not realized before the end of the war.

Submarine Minelayers

The first specially built minelaying submarine was the Russian *Krab*. She was designed in 1908 but completed only in 1915. So the first German minelaying U-boats of the *UC-I* type, ordered in November of 1914, became operational before the *Krab*. The *Krab* displaced 512 tons and could carry sixty mines in two horizontal tubes within the hull casing aft, transported by an electrically powered chain conveyor. The *UC-I* series of fifteen boats displaced only 168 tons and had six vertical mine tubes for twelve mines. They were followed by sixty-four of the bigger *UC-II* type of 400 to 434 tons with six mine tubes for eighteen mines. The *UC-II*s became operational between June of 1916 and May of 1917. In addition, sixteen units of an improved *UC-III* type were ready in the last weeks of 1918, with many more boats unfinished or canceled. There were also two types of bigger oceangoing U-boats: the *U-71* to *80* of 755 tons, each with two horizontal stern tubes holding a total of thirty-eight mines, which became operational in 1916, and the *U-117* to *126*, of 1,164 tons, which carried forty-two mines in two horizontal stern tubes, plus thirty mines in deck stowage. These boats were ready only in the summer of 1918.

The British rebuilt six of their E-class submarines of 667 tons to take twenty mines in two horizontal stern tubes. They were ready in late 1915 and 1916. Later, they also equipped five submarines of the *L*-class for minelaying from vertical chutes in the saddle tanks. They were ready only in the last weeks of the war. The few new Russian, French, and Italian minelaying submarines were not operational before the end of the war.

Most of the German minelaying U-boats were used from bases in Flanders to operate off the east and southeast coasts of England, and off the Channel ports. The first barrage with twelve mines was laid by *UC-11* on 21 May 1915 near the Goodwin Light Vessel. The next day the British destroyer *Mohawk* was damaged on this barrage. Up to September of 1915 forty additional minelaying operations were completed, followed by several hundred during the next three years. The British tried to block the German U-boat bases in Flanders by laying large mine barrages and mined nets off the coast and in the Dover-Calais narrows. These were laid mainly by former merchant ships rebuilt as minelayers. At least fifteen German U-boats were lost to mines in this area. Mine losses were high on both sides.

Some of the German minelaying U-boats were also transferred to the Mediterranean and laid mines off the French and Italian coasts, as well as in the eastern Mediterranean, resulting in many losses. Mines laid by German U-boats led to the loss of at least 752 Allied and neutral merchant ships of 1,121,000 gross tons. But besides many minesweepers, destroyers, and auxiliaries, some large warships were lost to U-boat mines. The British armored cruiser *Hampshire* was lost to a mine on 5 June 1916 off the Orkneys, with Field Marshal Lord Kitchener on board. In the North Sea the British cruiser *Arethusa* sank on 11 February 1916 from a mine laid by *U-73*. In the Mediterranean on 27 April 1916 the battleship *Russell* sank from a mine laid by *U-73*. On 11 December 1916 the Italian battleship *Regina Margherita* was sunk on a mine laid by *UC-14*. On 4 January 1917 the Russian battleship *Peresviet* sank from a mine laid by *U-73* off Port Said, and on 27 June 1917 the French armored cruiser *Kléber* was sunk by a mine laid by *UC-61*. Off the eastern coast of the U.S., on 19 July 1918 the U.S. navy armored cruiser *San Diego* sank from a mine laid by *U-156*, and the battleship *Minnesota* was damaged on 29 September 1918 by a mine from *U-117*.

The Russian submarine *Krab* laid two mine barrages in the entrance of the Bosphorus, on 10 July 1915 and 31 July 1916, and one more off Varna on 15 September 1916. The British E-class minelayers carried out many additional operations, especially into inner Heligoland Bay. The first of these was on 7 March 1916. They resulted in losses of German minesweepers and some U-boats.

Minesweepers and New Mines

While most navies used fishing vessels equipped with trailed cables or similarly equipped old gunboats or torpedo boats, the Russian navy in 1910 ordered the first purpose-built minesweepers, *Fugas* in the Baltic and *Albatross* in the Black Sea. These were followed by similar vessels of 150 to 445 tons' displacement, construction of which continued during the war.

In 1914 first the German and then the British navies started to build seagoing minesweepers in greater numbers. By the end of the war the Germans had ordered 176 minesweepers of the M-class, of 456–576 tons. From July of 1915 to November of 1918, sixty-six of them were completed, while twenty-eight were lost during minesweeping operations. The British began with "Fleet Sweeping Sloops" of the *Flower* class, of 1,200 tons. These were multipurpose vessels also used for U-boat hunting. Seventy-two were completed during the war. In 1916 this type was replaced by the more specially equipped Hunt-class minesweepers, displacing 750 tons, of which fifty-two were commissioned during 1917 and 1918.

To sweep mines in shallow waters and estuaries, in 1916 the Germans started to build smaller river minesweepers of the *FM*-type, of 193–205 tons. Fifteen were completed before the Armistice. The British built thirty-two "paddle" minesweepers of 810 tons. In 1916 the Italian navy began construction of fifty-seven small minesweepers of the *RD*-class, of 196–205 tons. The French navy used fishing vessels for minesweeping. In 1916 the U.S. navy ordered fifty-four ocean minesweepers of the *Bird* class. These displaced 950 tons, but they were ready only after the end of the war. Because there were never enough minesweepers to clear the ways for warships, several navies equipped their screening destroyers and also bigger ships with bow paravanes, which would push mines away from the ship and cut their moorings. The German navy also used some merchant ships as *Sperrbrechers,* by loading their holds with empty wooden barrels to give the ships additional buoyancy when exploding mines.

In the second half of the war several new types of mines appeared. To counter U-boats, special antenna-mines and deep-laid mines were used. Against surface ships, magnetic and acoustic firing devices were developed. To protect mine barrages against sweeping, special devices to destroy sweeping gear came into use.

From the end of 1916 on, the sea war in the North Sea and the Channel increasingly became a war of mines. The British used mine barrages to try to block the exits of German ships and especially U-boats from Heligoland Bay and the Flanders ports. The innermost minefields were laid by the few minelaying submarines. The bigger fields were laid by newly commissioned light cruisers and destroyers. The outer fields were laid mostly by the rebuilt merchant ships like the *Princess Margaret,* which laid the most mines of any vessel during the war: 25,242.

German minelaying was done mostly by U-boats. The two newly built special mine cruisers, *Bremse* and *Brummer,* of 4,385 tons' displacement and a capacity of 400 mines each, were seldom used in their intended role. The German High Sea Fleet was increasingly used as a screen for the minesweepers against possible attacks of British heavy ships, and the main task of the minesweepers was to keep exits open for German U-boats.

After the American entry into the war a new effort was started to close routes out of the North Sea to German U-boats. But it was 2 March 1918 before the biggest mining operation of history could start. This was the Northern Barrage, between the Orkneys and the Norwegian coast off Bergen. British minelayers first laid field B east of the Orkneys. That was followed, beginning on 8 June 1918, by fields A and C, up to the Norwegian coast. In the five months prior to 26 October 1918, ten American minelayers, most of them rebuilt merchant ships, laid no fewer than 56,033 mines. Four British minelayers, including the rebuilt battleship *London,* laid 15,093 mines. But even that effort did not stop U-boats from going out into the Atlantic. There were actually only a few U-boat losses to these mines. From November of 1917 to August of 1918 more than 10,000 additional mines were laid in a new anti–U-boat barrage between Folkestone and Cape Griz Nez in the Channel.

In all, during the war the Allies laid 256,200 mines. The Central Powers laid 51,900, the neutrals 1,600. Even if it is not possible to establish all losses from mines, especially regarding submarines or U-boats, the Allies lost at least eight battleships, three armored cruisers, two light cruisers, more than forty destroyers, thirty-four purpose-built minesweepers, and thirty submarines, as well as more than 294 auxiliaries and 900 merchant and fishing vessels. The Germans and their allies lost two armored cruisers, two light cruisers, fifty-one destroyers and torpedo boats, twenty-eight minesweepers, and at least fifty-nine U-boats, as well as about 120 auxiliaries and many merchant ships.

When the war was over the German navy had to sweep most of the remaining minefields, an operation finished only after 1922. At least 111 more ships were lost to mines after the end of the war.

Jürgen Rohwer

References

Conway's All the World's Fighting Ships 1906–1921. London: Conway, 1985.

Corbett, Julian S., and Henry Newbolt. *Naval Operations.* 5 vols. London: Longmans, Green, 1920–31.

Cowie, J.S. *Mines, Minelayers and Minelaying.* Oxford: Oxford University Press, 1949.

Greger, René. *The Russian Fleet 1914–1917.* London: Ian Allan, 1972.

Der Krieg zur See. 23 vols. Edited by the Marine-Archiv (up to 1944) and the Bundesarchiv-Militararchiv (since 1956). Berlin and Frankfurt/Main: Mittler, 1920–66.

Ledebur, Gerhard Freiherr von. *Die Seemine.* München: Lehmanns, 1977.

Ruge, Friedrich. *Torpedo- und Minenkrieg.* München: Lehmanns, 1940.

See also Dardanelles Campaign; Mines, Sea

Mines, Sea

During World War I sea mines were one of the most important naval weapons used by either side. More naval vessels were lost to mines than to combat. Minelaying and minesweeping became some of the more significant duties of the opposing naval forces.

During the war three basic types of mines were used. The most common was the contact mine. These mines were covered with detonator pins that protruded in all directions from the main body of the mine. It was moored to the ocean floor and detonated by contact with a ship's hull. Large fields of these mines were commonly deployed in shipping lanes or around harbors. The second type of mine commonly used was the controlled mine, which was utilized mainly to protect harbors or shore installations; it required an operator to detonate it from shore. The final type was the magnetic mine, which was detonated by magnetic fields generated by passing ships; developed in 1917, magnetic mines saw only limited use, during the last year of the war.

At the outset of the war the Germans possessed a considerable lead over the British in mine technology. The 1907 Hague Conventions outlawed laying mines outside a nation's territorial waters. Consequently, the British Admiralty did not foresee the potential of mines; the Germans were less scrupulous about the conventions and spent the decade before the war developing both mine and torpedo technology. Admiral Alfred von Tirpitz realized that mine warfare presented a possible way to negate the numerical superiority of the Royal Navy. As the Germans devoted substantial resources to mine technology, the British were concentrating their research on gunnery and ship design, neglecting mine research. As a result, British mines were notoriously inefficient at the outset of the war. It was not until 1917 that the British were able to develop an effective mine.

A major innovation in mine warfare was the development of the time-delay mine. Devised by the Germans, these mines had a time delay mechanism that allowed them to remain on the sea bed for a period of time before they were deployed. Thus minesweepers could clear an area only to have mines reappear on the surface. The British experimented with a chain-sweep that was carried along the ocean floor, but rocky bottoms or debris easily fouled the sweep. The British never developed an effective defense against time-delay mines.

The Germans and their allies were able to use mines quite successfully. By laying a deep field of mines around Germany's coastline, the German navy was able to prevent the sort of tight blockade that the British Admiralty had hoped to achieve. Germany also used mines aggressively as offensive weapons.

The British were less successful in their use of mines. While the Germans laid over 43,000 mines, the British deployed only some 33,000 (most of which were laid in 1917 and 1918). The British attempted to use mines as a weapon against German submarines, but the unreliability of their mines and the ability of submarines to evade them largely negated the British efforts. Ironically, as the British increased their efforts to use mines as an antisubmarine weapon, the Germans increased their use of submarines to deploy mines. By the end of the war, submarines were the primary minelaying craft of the German navy.

By the war's end, the British had destroyed some 24,000 mines. Clearly, there remained a considerable number unaccounted for. Rogue mines would be a problem for shipping for years to come.

T.M. Lansford

References

Haythornwaite, Philip. *The World War One Source Book*. London: Arms and Armour, 1992.

Hough, Richard. *The Great War at Sea, 1914–1918*. New York: Oxford, 1983.

Jellicoe, John. *The Crisis of the Naval War*. London: Cassell, 1920. Reprint. New York: Books for Libraries Press, 1972.

See also MINE WARFARE, SEA

Mišić, Živojin (1855–1921)

Serbian statesman and field marshal, born near Valievo on 7 July 1855. Mišić fought in the Serbian-Turkish War of 1877, the Serbian-Bulgarian War of 1885, and the First and Second Balkan Wars of 1912 and 1913. He was on General Radomir Putnick's staff during the Bosnian annexation crisis of 1908–9. In November of 1914 he commanded First Army on the right flank of Belgrade, defending against Austro-Hungary, and he won a decisive victory at Rudnik in December of 1914. That victory forced the withdrawal of all enemy troops from Serbia by January of 1915.

In the winter of 1915 Mišić led his troops to the Adriatic coast during the retreat of the Serbian army. At Corfu he performed staff and political duties. In August of 1917 he took command of the First Army at Salonika until June of 1918, when he became chief of staff. Mišić, the ablest soldier of the Balkan countries, actively promoted Yugoslavian nationalism. He died at Belgrade on 20 January 1921.

Charles H. Bogart

References

Falls, Cyril. *History of the Great War. Military Operations: Macedonia*. 2 vols.

London: H.M. Stationery Office, 1928–30.

Palmer, Alan. *The Gardeners of Salonika: The Macedonian Campaign 1915–1918*. New York: Simon and Schuster, 1965.

See also BALKAN FRONT, 1914, 1915, 1916, 1917; SERBIA

Mitteleuropa

Mitteleuropa (German for "Central Europe") was a term implying a general extension of German power throughout Central Europe in the event of German victory in World War I. The term was popularized by the 1915 bestseller of that name by the German politician Friedrich Naumann. The core of the idea was the permanent integration of the German and Austro-Hungarian economies in a single German-dominated customs union, reinforced by tighter political and military ties. Some advocates hoped also to include Belgium, Poland, Romania, and Scandinavia.

Gary W. Shanafelt

References

Meyer, Henry Cord. *Mitteleuropa in German Thought and Action, 1815–1945*. The Hague: Nijhoff, 1955.

See also BUCHAREST, TREATY OF; WAR AIMS

Moltke, Graf Helmuth Johannes Ludwig von (1848–1916)

German general and chief of the German General Staff from 1906 to 1914 and deputy chief of staff from 1914 to 1916. He is remembered chiefly as the man who modified the Schlieffen Plan of 1905, resulting in the failed German offensive of August of 1914.

Born into a Junker family in Gersdorf, Mecklenburg, on 23 May 1848, Moltke joined the army in 1869. He was a nephew of Helmuth von Moltke ("the Elder"), who commanded Prussian armies to victory in the Austro-Prussian War of 1866 and the Franco-Prussian War of 1870–71. Although similar greatness was expected for the younger Moltke, he unfortunately possessed little of his uncle's innovative military genius.

Contrary to the traditional career progression followed by Prussian officers, Moltke received little formal military schooling. He gained line experience while commanding a number of guards regiments, however, and was trained in staff operations while adjutant to the elder Moltke. Later he served the kaiser in the same capacity. He was promoted to colonel in 1895 and major general four years later. In 1900 he was a lieutenant general commanding the First Guards Division; four years later he was appointed quartermaster general. Kaiser Wil-helm II found Moltke's military appearance and bearing a welcome alternative to that of the aloof and aging Alfred von Schlieffen; he named him chief of the general staff in 1906, soon after Schlieffen's retirement in 1905. Moltke accepted the post with severe reservations, because he did not believe that he could make quick decisions in wartime. As chief of staff, Moltke believed that war with the Entente was inevitable and felt that it was better that it come sooner than later.

Moltke's major contribution to the Great War was his ill-conceived revision of the Schlieffen Plan, which called for a rapid offensive against France. A weaker German left wing was to go on the offensive in order to bring the bulk of the French forces to battle in the vicinity of Metz, while the stronger right marched through the Netherlands and Belgium, swung north around Paris, and then headed east to catch enemy forces from the rear and push them against the Rhine. In the Moltke modification of this plan, unveiled in 1911, the Germans would not march through the Netherlands but would violate only Belgian neutrality. This would constrict over 600,000 soldiers of the German First and Second armies between the Dutch border and the Meuse as they marched to invest the formidable fortress network at Liège.

Fear of a possible French offensive through Alsace and Lorraine led Moltke to create a serious imbalance between the left and right wings of his armies. Adding newly created corps, he deployed fifty-five divisions to the north of Metz, where Schlieffen had called for fifty-nine. To the south he deployed twenty-three divisions, to Schlieffen's nine. Thus, by August of 1914 Moltke had weakened his right sufficiently that it was unable to reach Paris and encircle the enemy.

On 25 August Moltke exacerbated matters when he pulled two corps and a division from the right and sent them against the Russian offensive at Tannenberg. That action was curious, inasmuch as General Erich Ludendorff, chief of staff to General Paul von Hindenburg, commander of the German Eighth Army, had already informed him that the troops would arrive too late for the battle then being fought.

At his headquarters in Luxembourg, meanwhile, Moltke attempted to remedy the failed envelopment of the French forces. Abandoning his usual noninterference leadership style, he instructed his commanders to push the enemy away from Paris to the southwest. This order resulted in the abortive Battle of the Marne (5–10 September 1914). The exhausted Germans fell back on a line between Noyon and Verdun and lost their final opportunity to knock France out of the war before Russia could bring sizable forces to bear in the east. Depressed during the battle, Moltke issued no orders whatsoever to his army commanders during its critical period.

On 14 September Moltke was relieved of his post, and General Erich von Falkenhayn became chief of the general staff. Demoted to deputy chief of staff, Moltke died suddenly from a heart attack in Berlin on 18 June 1916.

Paul B. Hatley

References

Craig, Gordon A. *The Politics of the Prussian Army, 1640–1945*. London: Oxford University Press, 1964.

Görlitz, Walter. *History of the German General Staff, 1657–1945*. New York: Frederick A. Praeger, 1953.

Kennedy, Paul M., ed. *The War Plans of the Great Powers, 1880–1914*. London: Allen and Unwin, 1979.

Paret, Peter, ed. *Makers of Modern Strategy from Machiavelli to the Nuclear Age*. Princeton: Princeton University Press, 1986.

Rosinski, Herbert. *The German Army*. New York: Frederick A. Praeger, 1966.

See also FRONTIERS, BATTLE OF THE; MARNE, FIRST BATTLE OF; SCHLIEFFEN PLAN

Monash, Sir John (1865–1931)

Australian general and engineer, born of Jewish descent in Melbourne on 27 June 1865. Monash obtained his engineering degree from Melbourne University in 1891. As an engineer, Monash pioneered construction of reinforced concrete bridges in Tasmania and Melbourne. Monash also served as a part-time officer in the militia, eventually reaching the rank of colonel. When the war began in 1914, he joined the Australian Imperial Force (AIF).

Monash served as commander of the 4th Infantry Brigade at Gallipoli and later commanded the 3rd Australian Division in France. In March of 1918 he replaced General Sir William Birdwood as commander of the Australian Army Corps. As a military tactician, Monash earned high marks for careful planning, organization, and leadership, especially in the last battles of the war, when the British based their final offensive on plans devised by him. Monash once wrote, "A perfected battle plan is like nothing so much as a score for musical composition." Monash recorded his war experiences in *The Australian Victories in France in 1918 (1920)* and *War Letters* (1933).

Lieutenant General Monash was called "the most outstanding Australian general of World War I" and "the greatest Jewish soldier of modern times." After the war he became a fervent advocate of the Jewish Lads' Brigade, a youth organization established before the war to turn Russian and Polish immigrant Jewish boys into Anglo-Jewish sportsmen and gentlemen who were integrated into British society. In 1921 he became head of the State Electricity Commission of Victoria, and in 1928 he assumed the presidency of the Zionist Federation in Australia. Monash died on 8 October 1931 in the city of Melbourne, where Monash University is named after him.

Richard A. Voeltz

References
Edwards, C. *John Monash*. Melbourne: State Electricity Commission of VIC, 1970.
Hetherington, J. *John Monash*. Oxford and Melbourne: Oxford University Press, 1962.
Monash, John. *The Australian Victories in France in 1918*. Sydney: Angus & Robertson, 1936. Reprint.
Serle, Geoffry. *John Monash, a Biography*. Melbourne: Melbourne University Press, 1982.

Monro, Sir Charles Carmichael (1860–1929)

British general, born at sea on 15 June 1860. Monro joined the army in 1879 and saw ser-

vice in various colonial actions. A major during the Boer War of 1899–1902, Monro served on the army staff. Returning to Britain at war's end, he became commandant of the Hythe School of Musketry, where he was promoted to colonel. A major general by the time Britain entered World War I, Monro went to France in command of the 2nd Division of I Corps and took part in the retreat from Mons and the Battle of First Ypres. In December he was promoted to lieutenant general and given command of I Corps. He served with distinction in the battles of Aubers Ridge, Festubert, and Givenchy, and in July of 1915 he assumed command of the newly formed Third Army.

In October of 1915 he was sent east to take command of the Mediterranean Expeditionary Force. Upon arrival Monro immediately recommended the evacuation of Allied forces from Gallipoli. Churchill concluded, "He came, he saw, he capitulated." Although he was initially opposed to evacuation, Kitchener concurred after an inspection tour. Monro's evacuation plan was among the most brilliantly executed of the war. After the close of the Dardanelles Campaign Monro returned to the Western Front as head of First Army. In October of 1916 he was appointed commander in chief in India and used his position to support General Maude in his advance up the Tigris River. From 1923 to 1928 Monro was governor and commander in chief of Gibraltar. Created a baronet in 1921, Monro died in London on 7 December 1929.

Charles H. Bogart

References
Moberly, Brig.-Gen. F.J. *Military Operations in Persia 1914–1919*. London: Imperial War Museum, 1987.
Moorehead, Alan. *Gallipoli*. New York: Harper and Row, 1956.

See also GALLIPOLI CAMPAIGN

Montenegro

By 1914 the Kingdom of Montenegro, chronically impoverished and exhausted from its effort in the Balkan Wars, seriously contemplated some form of union with the Kingdom of Serbia. When Austria-Hungary declared war on Serbia, Montenegro naturally aligned itself with the Serbs and on 6 August declared war on Austria-Hungary. King Nikola (prince from 1860 to 1910; king from 1910 to 1918), as supreme commander of the Montenegrin army, adopted a cooperative policy with Serbia. Montenegro fielded 35,000 poorly equipped and poorly trained troops, amounting to about one-seventh of the total population. Nikola's troops assumed defensive positions in both the rugged heights above the Bay of Kotor and with the Serbian Uzice Army Group along the northwestern frontier of Montenegro.

Offensively, Montenegrin forces advanced short distances into Albania and Herzegovina. In June of 1915 Montenegrin troops entered Skodar (Scutari), which the Great Powers had denied Montenegro during the First Balkan War. Nikola demanded the annexation of Skodar, northern Albania, Herzegovina, and parts of Dalmatia and Bosnia.

Montenegrin forces covered the retreat of the Serbian army across the Albanian Alps in November and December of 1915. An Austro-Hungarian invasion in January of 1916 quickly overwhelmed the Montenegrin army. By 13 January the invaders had captured the Montenegrin capital, Cetinje. Austro-Hungarian forces occupied Montenegro until the end of the war. The civilian population, although suffering greatly from lack of food and fuel and from disease, carried out guerrilla warfare on the occupation forces.

King Nikola, after having failed to reach an accommodation with the invaders, fled with his family across the Adriatic to his son-in-law, King Victor Emmanuel III of Italy. Nikola later moved on to Paris, where he worked for his restoration as part of a peace settlement. In Geneva, a Montenegrin Committee advocated the inclusion of Montenegro in a Yugoslav state at the end of the war. Nikola's second son, Prince Mirko, however, remained behind in Montenegro and later went to Vienna in an unsuccessful attempt to achieve an arrangement with Austria-Hungary.

After the war Nikola's desire to return to his kingdom was undermined by his hasty departure in 1916 and by the dealings of Prince Mirko with Austria-Hungary. A National Assembly at Podgorica on 26 November 1918 voted to join the new Kingdom of Serbs, Croats, and Slovenes and deposed Nikola and the Petrovich-Njegosh dynasty. King Nikola never accepted this decision and bitterly contested it during the Paris Peace Conference,

without success. He died in the Antibes on 1 March 1921.

Richard C. Hall

References

Djilas, Milovan. *Montenegro*. New York: Harcourt, Brace and World, 1962. (Historical novel)

Rakochevich, N. *Crna Gora u prvom svjetskom ratu 1914–1918*. Cetinje: Istorijski institut, 1969.

Zhivkovich, Dragan. "Serbia and Montenegro: The Home Front, 1914–18." In *East Central European Society in World War I*, edited by Bela K. Kiraly and Nandor F. Dreisziger, 239–59. Boulder: Social Science Monographs, 1985.

SEE ALSO BALKAN FRONT, 1914, 1915; NIKOLA

Mountbatten, Louis (von Battenberg) (1854–1921)

British admiral and first sea lord, 1912–14. Born into the Hessian nobility on 24 May 1854 at Graz, Austria, Mountbatten was a career officer in Britain's Royal Navy. He compiled a distinguished record and commanded several warships. He also invented the Battenberg Compass, which was later used in naval gunnery.

In 1899 Battenberg was appointed assistant director of naval intelligence, in which service he improved the overall staff efficiency. Three years later he became director of naval intelligence. Known as a naval reformer, Battenberg published several "white papers" espousing better living conditions and pay for seamen. He also advocated a modern staff system for the navy. His marriage to Queen Victoria's granddaughter, Victoria of Hesse, gave him intimate access to the royal houses of Europe. This allowed him to gather intelligence on the German naval buildup and its consequences for Britain, as Kaiser Wilhelm II freely discussed the German navy at social functions they jointly attended.

Battenberg was appointed first sea lord on 9 December 1912. His major achievement during the next two years was to improve naval operations and serve as a buffer between the fleet and First Lord of the Admiralty Winston Churchill. Churchill had no naval experience, and many of his policies, such as allowing seamen to contradict their officers publicly, would have destroyed discipline in the fleet. Battenberg was able to talk Churchill out of ideas that were contrary to the efficiency of the navy. Battenberg also supported an air arm for the Royal Navy. Both he and Churchill saw the airplane as the preeminent future naval weapon.

By July of 1914 a general European war seemed imminent, and Battenberg prepared the fleet for hostilities. Churchill directed the fleet be kept at full strength following the annual summer maneuvers, and on 28 July 1914 he ordered it to battle positions off Scotland. On 4 August 1914 the fleet received orders to commence hostilities against Germany. While Battenberg was first sea lord, the army was transported across the channel without loss, a blockade of Germany was implemented, and three German cruisers were sunk.

Battenberg was undermined by British setbacks at sea: two German ships, the *Goeben* and the *Breslau,* reached Turkish harbors despite attempts to intercept and sink them; U-boats sank three British cruisers in one day; and Germany scored a clear victory off the Coronel Islands. For the first time since Napoleon Britain suffered invasion hysteria, and the admiralty was openly questioned by the British public and press. The final blow to Battenberg's prestige occurred on 27 October 1914, when the first-line dreadnought *Audacious* went down to a German mine.

On 28 October 1914, with reversals piling up, Prime Minister Herbert Asquith asked for Battenberg's resignation, which he tendered. He spent the remainder of the war as a member of the King's Privy Council. Battenberg took the name of Mountbatten, Marquess of Milford Haven, in 1917, to protect his children from the anti-German bias he suffered throughout his naval career. He retired from the navy in 1919 and died of natural causes on 11 September 1921 in London.

Julius A. Menzoff

References

Hough, Richard. *The Mountbattens.* New York: E.P. Dutton, 1975.
Massie, Robert K. *Dreadnought, Britain, Germany, and the Coming of the Great War.* New York: Ballantine, 1991.

See also GREAT BRITAIN, NAVY

Müller, Georg Alexander von (1854–1940)

German admiral and chief of the naval cabinet from 1906 to 1918, born in Chemnitz on 24 March 1854. Müller joined the navy in 1871. Before becoming the kaiser's principal advisor in naval matters as chief of the naval cabinet in 1906, Müller held numerous shore and shipboard commands, several of them overseas. Originally a protégé of Tirpitz and raised into the Prussian nobility in 1900 while still a captain, Müller soon adopted views considerably more elastic and reform-oriented than those of his erstwhile mentor.

During the war Müller, by then a full admiral, shared the kaiser's desire not to risk the fleet rashly against superior British forces, appreciated political and diplomatic objections to unrestricted submarine warfare, and sought to liberalize the "feudalized" naval officer corps. While retaining the kaiser's trust, Müller gradually lost the support of frontline officers and finally retired in November of 1918. His candid diaries offer a fascinating glimpse of life at the imperial court. Müller died on 18 April 1940 in Berlin.

Eric C. Rust

References

Görlitz, Walter, ed. *The Kaiser and His Court: The Diaries, Note Books and Letters of Admiral Georg Alexander von Müller, Chief of the Naval Cabinet, 1914–1918.* New York: Harcourt, Brace, World, 1964.
Herwig, Holger H. *The German Naval Officer Corps: A Social and Political History, 1890–1918.* Oxford: Oxford University Press, 1973.
———. *"Luxury" Fleet.* London: Allen and Unwin, 1980.
Hubatsch, Walther. *Der Admiralstab und die obersten Marinebehörden in Deutschland. 1848–1945.* Frankfurt: Bernard, Graefe, 1958.
Tirpitz, Alfred von. *My Memoirs.* 2 vols. New York: Dodd, Mead, 1919.

See also GERMANY, NAVY; TIRPITZ, ALFRED VON

Murray, Sir Archibald James (1860–1945)

British commander in Egypt, 1915–17. Born in Woodhouse, Hampshire, on 21 April 1860, Murray attended Sandhurst and in 1879 reported to the 27th Regiment. He served in Hong Kong, Singapore, and the Cape Colony, and attended the staff college (1897–99). He served in the Boer War (1899–1901), India (1901), and South Africa (1902). He held a series of positions after the war, including director of military training at the war office (1907–12), inspector of infantry (1912–14), and commander of the 2nd Division, BEF (1914). At the beginning of World War I, Murray served as chief of staff to Sir John French and participated in the battles of Mons, Le Cateau, the Marne, Aisne, and First Ypres, before being returned to England in 1915 suffering from illness and exhaustion.

In February of 1915 Lord Kitchener appointed General Murray deputy chief of the Imperial General Staff and, in September of 1915, chief. After General Douglas Haig replaced French, Murray became commander of the Egyptian Expeditionary Force in December of 1915. Murray's capabilities were reduced early in 1916 by the transfer of ten of his fourteen divisions to other theaters. He prepared defenses along the prized Suez Canal and defeated the Turks at Români in August. Although his attack at Gaza on 26–29 March 1917 ended in defeat, Murray attacked and failed again on 17–19 April 1917. With the arrival of General Edmund Allenby on 29 June 1917, Murray returned to the command at Aldershot (1917–19). Promoted to general in August of 1919, he retired in 1922 and died on 23 January 1945 at Makepiece, Reigate.

Montecue J. Lowry

References

Falls, Cyril. *The Great War, 1914–1918.* New York: Capricorn, 1959.

Halsey, Francis Whiting. *History of the World War.* Vol. 8. New York and London: Funk and Wagnalls, 1919.

Herweg, Holger H., and Neil M. Heyman. *Biographical Dictionary of World War I.* Westport, Conn.: Greenwood, 1982.

Howland, Colonel C.R. *A Military History of the World War.* Fort Leavenworth, Kans.: General Service Schools Press, 1923.

Liddell Hart, B.H. *The Real War, 1914–1918.* Boston: Little, Brown, 1930.

See also EGYPT IN WORLD WAR I

Music in the War

The music of World War I helped create a sense of unity and common experience among soldiers and civilians alike, but the popular music of the home front bore little resemblance to the songs sung in the trenches. The fighting man's songs were often unprintable but sprang from his own experience. The civilian's songs were written by professional songwriters and served as a form of propaganda to foster patriotism and support for the war effort. These popular songs continue to function as propaganda even today in coloring our perceptions of the war. When we listen to "Over There" or "Tipperary" we might envision American troops being welcomed by flag-waving French girls, or soldiers marching proudly down Fifth Avenue. Seldom do we associate these songs with the reality of war: the horrible conditions in the trenches, the death and suffering. The popular, commercial music of World War I reflects the war as civilians wanted to see it, but the soldiers' songs more often reflect the war as it actually was.

The outbreak of war saw a proliferation of patriotic songs, both new and old. The British and French popularized many of these songs in the music hall, and sheet music and gramophone records helped spread wartime music to the masses. Britain produced some songs designed to recruit young men by appealing to their (or their sweethearts') patriotism, such as: "I'll Make a Man of You" or "Your King and Country Want You" (immediately parodied by the soldiers).

Early World War I French songs were extremely militaristic, with lyrics calling for revenge on the Germans for the Franco-Prussian War and commanding the French people to die for liberty. One nationalist French songwriter composed a bloodthirsty song, "Rosalie," about a bayonet, and later wrote another about a soldier's true love—his machine gun. The most popular French song of the entire war, "Madelon," told of a girl who worked in an estaminet and was a platonic friend to all of the soldiers. "Madelon" commemorated the idealized male-female relationship during wartime and later came to symbolize the experience of the *poilu* in the postwar period. On a more serious note, the "Chanson de Craonne" was written during the French army mutinies in the summer of 1917. An unusually fatalistic song, it begins, "Farewell to life, farewell to love. . . ."

The Americans held fast to their noncombatant status with "I Didn't Raise My Boy to Be a Soldier," but after the United States entered the war, American composers quickly turned out songs like "Over There" and "Goodbye Broadway, Hello France," which epitomized the brash self-confidence of the Americans. "Oui Oui Marie" and "When Yankee Doodle Learns to Parlez-Vous Français" depicted the innocent American farmboy turned loose in Paris. Some songs boasted of beating the Germans (personified by Kaiser Wilhelm), such as "Bring Back the Kaiser to Me," "Bing Bang Bing 'Em on the Rhine," and "Just like Washington Crossed the Delaware, General Pershing Will Cross the Rhine."

Singing was an integral part of a soldier's life; it helped keep up morale and kept the men from getting bored. A German artilleryman remarked, "The hearing of one's own voice gives courage and a feeling of security." Wartime journalists of both sides reported men charging into battle while singing patriotic songs, but the soldier accounts reveal that singing was confined to the march or off-duty hours. At first soldiers sang current popular tunes as they marched off to war in 1914 ("Tipperary," for instance, was a music hall hit of 1913, and the Canadian soldiers used "Alouette" as one of their first marching songs), but soon they created songs reflecting their own concerns. Most of these songs were humorous, satirical, and often vulgar; somewhat sanitized versions survive in recordings or wartime songbooks.

Unlike the commercialized civilian music that appeared on gramophone records, the music hall, and in sheet music, soldiers's songs spread mostly by word of mouth and occasionally in various frontline publications. Few were standardized, and men created new verses or parodies of popular and religious tunes in response to persons and events that directly touched their lives. In their book *The Long Trail: Soldiers' Songs and Slang 1914–1918,* John Brophy and Eric Partridge classified British soldier songs into the following categories: satire on war ("Gassed Last Night" and "Oh! What a Lovely War"), satire on the military system ("We Are Fred Karno's Army"), satire on superior officers ("If You Want to Find the Sergeant"), civilian bliss ("Take Me Back to Dear Old Blighty"), celebrations of drink and other comforts ("Mademoiselle from Armentières" and "Who Stole the Rum Last Night"), and nonsense and burlesque ("The Bells of Hell Go Ting-a-Ling-a-Ling").

The Germans took their singing somewhat more seriously than did the British or Americans. In 1916 the German Folk Song Archive (DVA) began a systematic study of soldiers' songs, "to preserve these songs for future generations and to show what a high importance they have in the life of the soldier." The Austro-Hungarian War Ministry circulated a similar questionnaire in which it also asked for popular words to regimental bugle calls. In addition to its request for lyrics, the DVA asked fifteen questions regarding types of songs, where they came from, who was most likely to sing, and under what circumstances. Lyrics taken from songbooks were not permitted, as the DVA wanted to study the oral tradition and the spread of songs among the men at the front.

The DVA's collection of nearly four hundred songs shows that the German soldier sang more patriotic and religious songs than his British counterpart but lacked the black humor and satire found in so many British lyrics. Many German soldier songs were folk tunes or regimental songs dating back to the Franco-Prussian or Napoleonic wars and were familiar to the men from the time of their compulsory army service. Because of this military tradition, a larger number of soldier songs were known to the general public in Germany than in Britain. Each of the German states had its own folk songs, often describing the beauties of a particular region or garrison town; local pride frequently competed with nationalism in the songs of Bavarians, Saxons, Württembergers, or Badeners.

Although the music of German, British, American, and French soldiers shared characteristics of humor, patriotism, and vulgarity, these songs often reflected stereotypical cultural values. In general, British songs frequently understated or satirized hardships; American songs were optimistic and brash; French songs could be both erotic and patriotic; German songs glorified the military life (but usually former rather than current battles). Soldiers of all nations sang about drinking and women. Civilian songs were usually more serious and nationalistic than those of the soldiers; the civilians had less realistic views of the war and were often more bloodthirsty than the soldiers, who frequently developed a laissez-faire attitude toward the enemy. The World War I songs that have survived in today's popular culture tend to be the civilian ones that were recorded or printed as sheet music; the true songs of the soldiers were not acceptable to the public, partly because of their coarse lyrics, but also because the sentiments expressed in them did not reinforce official and public attitudes toward the war.

Suzanne Hayes Fisher

References

Olt, Reinhard. *Krieg und Sprache: Untersuchungen zu Deutschen Soldatenliedern des Ersten Weltkriegs.* Vol. 4: *Beiträge zur deutschen Philologie.* Giessen: Wilhelm Schmitz Verlag, 1981.

Palmer, Roy. *"What A Lovely War:" British Soldiers' Songs from the Boer War to the Present Day.* London: Michael Joseph, 1990.

Mussolini, Benito Amilcare Andrea (1883–1945)

Italian socialist and subsequent dictator. Born into a socialist family at Dovia di Predappio, in the "red" province of Romagna on 11 January 1883, Mussolini as a youth was a militant socialist who imbibed the voluntarist beliefs associated with Sorel and embraced the syndicalist ideas of such union leaders as Filippo Corridoni. His nationalist sentiments were stimulated during his stay in the Austrian Trentino in 1909. He opposed Italy's conquest of Libya in 1911 and supported a major strike by syndicalist autoworkers in 1912. Two years later he helped to provoke "Red Week" (7–11 June 1914), a massive strike by Italian unions that was ended by the more moderate elements within the socialist CGL (*Confederazione generale del lavoro*). As editor of the socialist newspaper *Avanti!* after 1912, he doubled its circulation to sixty thousand and emerged as the uncontested leader of the Socialist party's revolutionary wing.

During the fall of 1914 Mussolini became increasingly convinced that Italy should enter the war on the side of the Entente. On 18 October 1914 he wrote "*Dalla neutralità assoluta alla neutralità attiva ed operante,*" in which he argued that formulas must be adapted to events, implying that intervention might be in the interest of the workers. He resigned the editorship of *Avanti!* to begin publication of his own newspaper, *Popolo d'Italia*, which favored intervention and attacked the neutralist stance of the PSI (*Partito socialista italiano*). The paper had a large circulation in northern Italy. Rumors abounded that he had been bought by the French, but Mussolini appears to have followed his own nationalist line of development, which owed a good deal to syndicalism and was evident by 1909.

After Italy joined the war on the Allied side, Mussolini volunteered for service and fought in the trenches until wounded in 1917 and honorably discharged, having risen to the rank of corporal. As with other veterans of the war, he believed that the military high commanders were little better than butchers. After the defeat at Caporetto, Mussolini combined principles of revolutionary syndicalism with those of class collaboration and looked to the veterans of World War I, the *trincerocrazia* (aristocracy of the trenches), to save Italy from both Marxism and the old corrupt political forces of the prewar liberal era. In March of 1919 he founded the *Fasci di combattimento,* whose original members included a large number of veterans, especially those from the elite *arditi* units, and many revolutionary syndicalists. The war, therefore, influenced Mussolini's evolution toward a national syndicalist interpretation of socialism, a novel approach that developed into Fascism after 1918.

Mussolini took power in Italy in 1922 and sought to increase Italy's standing by playing a complex and subtle diplomatic game, which became impossible after Hitler came to power in Germany. Convinced that Italy could not remain neutral he reluctantly joined the Second World War on Germany's side in June of 1940, only to be overthrown by his own party leadership in July of 1943. On 28 April 1945, while trying to escape to Germany, Mussolini was caught by partisans at Dongo and executed. He was then strung upside down next to his mistress in Piazzale Loretto in Milan.

James J. Sadkovich

References

Cordova, Franco. *Arditi e legionari dannunziani.* Padua: Marsilio, 1969.

De Begnac, Ivon. *L'arcangelo sindacalista (Filippo Corridoni).* Verona: Mondadori, 1943.

De Felice, Renzo. *Mussolini il rivoluzionario, 1883–1920.* Turin: Einaudi, 1965.

Gregor, A. James. *Young Mussolini and the Intellectual Origins of Fascism.* Berkeley: University of California Press, 1979.

Lyttleton, Adrian. *The Seizure of Power: Fascism in Italy, 1919–1929*. New York: Charles Scribner's Sons, 1973.

See also ITALY, HOME FRONT

N

Naroch, Lake, Battle of (March 1916)

Approximately sixty miles east of Vilnius in generally marshy terrain, Lake Naroch and several other lakes of smaller size had become part of the Eastern Front since the fall of 1915. Faced with French appeals for help following the onset of the German offensive at Verdun, the Russian High Command decided to unleash a major attack against parts of Colonel General Hermann von Eichhorn's Tenth Army in the Naroch region and adjacent sectors. The chief effort was to be made by General V.V. Smirnov's Second Army, which was built up to a superiority of about five-to-one over the opposing German forces.

Planned while most of the lakes and swamps in the region were solidly frozen, the Russian offensive began on 18 March 1916—several days after warm winds had weakened the ice in many places and produced enormous mud flats in others. While Russian artillery fire on the German positions was unprecedented in its volume and intensity, the shelling was not well directed. Mass attacks by Russian infantry north and south of Lake Naroch were stopped by the Germans in most places, and it was only on 21 March that one of the German units, the 75th Reserve Division, began to crumble under the Russian onslaught. Hastily brought-up German reserves eventually stopped the further advance of the Russians south of Lake Naroch. Farther north in the area near Postawy the 42nd German Infantry Division lost some of its trenches, and its situation remained precarious until it received support from the 107th Infantry Division. On 27 March further German reserves were thrown into the battle and eventually regained much of the ground previously lost. Five weeks later, in late April, the Germans recaptured the remainder of their original positions.

Although it put considerable strain on the German Tenth Army and led to the loss of about 20,000 men (including several thousand captured by the Russians), the Battle of Lake Naroch was definitely a major Russian setback. The attempt to break through the German lines had ended in complete failure, and total casualties on the Russian side exceeded 100,000 men. Poor leadership at the top, poor coordination between artillery and infantry, and a host of other problems had once again bedeviled the operations of the Czarist Army. Lake Naroch, according to Norman Stone, represented the "last real effort by the old Russian army—as distinct from the new, which emerged in summer 1916 on General Aleksei Brusilov's front," and it was "an affair that summed up all that was most wrong with the army."

Ulrich Trumpener

References

Immanuel, Friedrich. "Der Krieg auf der deutschen Ostfront 1916." In *Der Weltkampf um Ehre und Recht*. Vol. 2, edited by Max Schwarte. Leipzig, Barth/ Berlin: de Gruyter, n.d.

Stone, Norman. *The Eastern Front 1914– 1917*. New York: Charles Scribner's Sons, 1975.

Der Weltkrieg 1914 bis 1918: Die militärischen Operationen zu Lande. Vol. 10. Berlin: E.S. Mittler und Sohn, 1936. Reichsarchiv.

See also Eichhorn, Hermann von; Russia, Army

Naval Arms Race, Anglo-German

One of the principal causes of the First World War was the Anglo-German naval arms race. As late as the 1880s and even the 1890s, the British and Germans were friendly and collaborators. During the late 1890s relationships became more strained and by about 1905 serious antagonisms were obvious. Although many factors contributed to the rivalry—trade and economic competition, colonialism and imperialism, ultrapatriotic nationalism, domestic pressures, navalism and militarism, "Yellow" journalism, antagonistic public opinion, and dynastic jealousies—historians of all sides and persuasions have come to agree that one of the primary factors contributing to the rising Anglo-German antagonism was the naval arms race between the two powers.

During the nineteenth century the British enjoyed imperial, maritime, and naval hegemony throughout the world. In fact, the British saw themselves as enjoying a God-given right to dominate the seas. By the Naval Defence Act of 1889 Britain committed itself to having a fleet larger than the next two naval forces combined. The British initiated rapid and sustained naval warship expansion, which continued for three decades.

Although Prussia/Germany had not been known as a naval power, when Kaiser Wilhelm II succeeded to the throne in 1888, he was determined to secure Germany's "place in the sun." Germany already had the largest, most powerful army in the world, which had demonstrated its superiority in the Wars of Unification. To secure his imperial and world-power ambitions, however, Wilhelm aspired to a large navy. Beginning in the late 1890s, a series of German naval laws were passed providing for a large German battle fleet. The German naval leader responsible for building the German battle fleet was Admiral Alfred von Tirpitz, whose advocacy of a "Risk Fleet Theory" committed Germany to having a navy large enough that no other power (that is, Great Britain) would risk battle. When the naval laws of the early 1900s accelerated the expansion of the German High Seas Fleet, Great Britain was convinced that the Germans were bent on achieving naval supremacy. A full-fledged naval arms race soon ensued. This had important ramifications in foreign policy; as Otto von Bismarck had predicted, construction of a powerful German battle fleet drove Britain into the arms of France.

HMS Dreadnought added a new dimension to the competition. During the early 1900s the British Admiralty grew increasingly alarmed at the emerging German naval threat and began to bring home all capital ships from foreign stations. That meant Tirpitz's dream of concentration against a lesser force in the North Sea was now meaningless. Introduction of the *Dreadnought* in 1905, however, meant that the Germans could compete on a more equal basis, in a technological naval race. It was the *Dreadnought* that "raised the naval question to a position of central importance." Indeed, British fears culminated in the Naval Panic of 1909, when some British authorities and journalists accused the Germans of secretly accelerating their building rates. There were wild predictions that Germany might have twenty-one dreadnoughts by 1912. In fact, there were only nine. Nevertheless, Parliament approved construction of eight British capital ships.

The German perspective is best presented by Volker Berghahn, who contended that it was the Tirpitz naval program that provoked the naval arms race and, additionally, poisoned domestic relations within Germany. The international climate was upset, and the containment of Germany was the consequence. By 1911 the government precipitated a foreign policy crisis, the Agadir incident, to distract from serious domestic and financial problems.

Great Britain was definitely not innocent in all of this, but efforts were made to stop the arms race: the Haldane Mission of 1912, and the Churchill "Naval Holiday" proposal of 1913. Tirpitz and others in Germany were able to obstruct potential limitation agreements.

The naval arms race was also influenced by powerful single-interest pressure groups within Great Britain and Germany. In Britain, these groups included the Navy League, the National Service League, the Tariff Reform League, the Union Defence League, and the Imperial Maritime League; in Germany, the Pan-German League, the Navy League, and the Colonial League. The agenda of most of these groups had to do with agitation for better preparation against the potential threat from the increasingly dangerous opponent, Germany or Great Britain. They exerted expansive propaganda value.

In this particular conflict, several forms of writing influenced developments: "Yellow" journalism, the spy novel, and fictional invasion scares. It was an era of rapidly rising sensationalist newspapers and uncontrolled journalist license in both countries. Pauline Anderson documented these public opinion factors from the German perspective. The phenomenon of the invasion scare was actually launched in 1871 in *Blackwood's Magazine* in "The Battle of Dorking" by Sir George Chesney. The story depicted a fictional futuristic war between Britain and Germany. Fredrich von Bernhardi's *Germany and the Next War* (in German, 1911) and Arthur Conan Doyle's reply, *Great Britain and the Next War* (1913), generated emotional reactions in both countries. These were overly patriotic cautionary tales that stressed failure to prepare for war. Their propaganda influence was enormous.

Public opinion, journalism, pressure groups, unlimited nationalism, naval panics, dreadnought and battle cruiser building-races, provocative naval leaders, and super-patriotic authorities—all contributed to the rise of Anglo-German antagonism. These particular factors were all variations of the naval arms race. The Anglo-German naval race drove Britain and France together in the Entente Cordiale of 1904 and led to the 1912 naval convention between those two states. Certainly, it had decisive influence on World War I.

Eugene L. Rasor

References

Anderson, Pauline R. *The Background of Anti-English Feeling in Germany, 1890–1902.* New York: Octagon, 1969.

Art, Robert J. *The Influence of Foreign Policy on Seapower.* London: Sage, 1973, 1978.

Berghahn, Volker. *Germany and the Approach of War in 1914.* "Making of the Twentieth Century" series. New York: St. Martin, 1973.

Childers, Erskine. *The Riddle of the Sands.* London: Nelson, 1903, 1913.

Herwig, Holger H. *"Luxury Fleet": The Imperial German Navy, 1888–1918.* London: Allen, 1980, 1987.

Kennedy, Paul M. *The Rise of the Anglo-German Antagonism, 1860–1914.* Boston: Unwin, 1980, 1982, 1987.

Massie, Robert K. *Dreadnought: Britain, Germany, and the Coming of the Great War.* New York: Random House, 1991.

Padfield, Peter. *The Great Naval Race: Anglo-German Naval Rivalry, 1900–1914.* New York: McKay, 1974.

See also ALLIANCES, PREWAR; FISHER, JOHN; GERMANY, ARMY; GREAT BRITAIN, NAVY; ORIGINS OF THE FIRST WORLD WAR; TIRPITZ, ALFRED VON

Netherlands

The Kingdom of the Netherlands is strategically positioned both militarily and economically. The Netherlands was long an important trading nation, and the cities of Rotterdam and Amsterdam were important entrepôts between central Europe and overseas.

The Netherlands found itself in a precarious position on the outbreak of the First World War. The government immediately declared the kingdom's neutrality and mobilized its army. The Dutch feared that Germany might demand passage through Limburg or invade to establish submarine bases along the Dutch coast. They also feared that Britain might occupy the mouth of the Scheldt (closed by the Dutch to Britain when the war began) to protect supply lines to Antwerp. In October of 1914, after the fall of Antwerp to the Germans, some 30,000 Belgian troops crossed into the Netherlands and were interned.

The Dutch military remained mobilized for the duration of the war. Although costly, the Dutch thought it a necessary sacrifice. Luckily, the military was not tested. Its artillery was obsolete, fortifications and small arms were inadequate, and there were enough shells for only ten days' fighting.

Economically, the Netherlands was hard hit by the war because of its position as a trading nation. Much of Dutch trade ran afoul of the British Trading with the Enemy Act. The British withheld raw materials for fear that goods manufactured from them might reach Germany. The only advantage that accrued from this was that during the war the Dutch enhanced their industrial capability.

The war also affected agriculture, as the Dutch changed from wheat production to vegetables. In 1916 the Dutch arranged to ship vegetables to Britain provided she allowed fertilizers to come into the country from Germany under a similar reciprocal agreement. Nonetheless, food stocks dwindled during the war (food from the Dutch East Indies was cut off because the Dutch navy was unable to provide shipping protection), and the government imposed bread rationing after 1917.

A Royal Relief Committee, under Queen Wilhemina's personal guidance, was established in 1914 and did much useful work. Nonetheless, economic suffering brought agitation for constitutional change, which in turn provoked widespread support for the House of Orange. In November of 1917 a constitutional change did introduce proportional representation and universal suffrage at age twenty-five.

Dutch public opinion generally favored the Allies, especially given the severe losses of the Dutch merchant marine to German unrestricted submarine warfare. Nonetheless, the Netherlands remained neutral. This negated any claim to territory that might have come after even a short participation on the Allied side. It also helped fan postwar controversies with Belgium, which was strengthened territorially from the war.

Two controversial issues at the end of the conflict were war-related. The first was the Dutch decision to allow part of the German army to return to Germany through Limburg. The second was the decision to grant Kaiser Wilhelm II refuge in the Netherlands and to refuse Allied demands for his surrender and possible trial. Wilhelm lived in retirement at Amerongen, then Doorn, where he died in 1941.

Spencer C. Tucker

References

Landheer, Bartholomew, ed. *The Netherlands*. Berkeley: University of California Press, 1943.

Newton, Gerald. *The Netherlands: An Historical and Cultural Survey 1795–1977*. Boulder, Colo.: Westview, 1978.

Vlekke, Bernard H.M. *Evolution of the Dutch Nation*. New York: Roy, 1945.

Voorhoeve, Joris J.C. *Peace, Profits and Principles: A Study of Dutch Foreign Policy*. The Hague: Martinus Nijhoff, 1979.

Neuilly, Treaty of (27 November 1919)

Peace treaty between Bulgaria and the Allied Powers, signed in the Parisian suburb of Neuilly-sur-Seine on 27 November 1919. The Allies intended to punish Bulgaria for participating in the First World War on the side of the Central Powers. As a result of the treaty, Bulgaria lost significant territories. It had to relinquish all territories occupied during the war, including Macedonia and southern Dobrudja.

In the west, Bulgaria lost the four territorial salients of Strumitsa, Tsaribrod, Bosiligrad, and Timok to the new Kingdom of the Serbs, Croats, and Slovenes (Yugoslavia). Although these territories contained an overwhelmingly Bulgarian population, they were awarded to Serbia in order to eliminate any potential Bulgarian threat to the Salonika-Belgrade railroad. In the south, Bulgaria lost western Thrace to Greece, depriving it of its only outlet on the Aegean Sea. The victorious powers promised to afford Bulgaria economic access to the Aegean, but because of continuing rancor between Bulgaria and Greece that never occurred. The territory lost in Thrace had a mixed population with a significant Bulgarian component. Overall, Bulgaria lost 90,000 people and 5,500 square miles of territory. The Allies ignored Bulgarian requests for plebiscites in these territories. In addition, the great national objective of Macedonia, for which Bulgaria had fought the Balkan Wars as well as the First World War, again was denied.

The Treaty of Neuilly limited the Bulgarian armed forces to 20,000 volunteers, prohibited conscription, and forbade an air force. The treaty obligated Bulgaria to pay a reparation of 2,250,000 gold francs to the Entente powers within thirty-seven years. Bulgaria had to deliver specified quantities of livestock and railroad equipment to Serbia, Romania, and Greece. Any materials proven to have been taken from Serbia, Greece, and Romania during Bulgarian occupation had to be returned. Finally, Bulgaria had to deliver 50,000 tons of coal annually for five years to Yugoslavia.

The strenuous terms of the Treaty of Neuilly profoundly shocked and disappointed the Bulgarians. They had hoped for a more moderate treaty because they had strong ethnic claims to most of the territories they had occupied during the war, including Macedonia, and because they had never declared war on the United States. Woodrow Wilson's rhetoric of national self-determination provided some basis for Bulgarian expectations. The Bulgarians also had hoped that their delegation leader, Alexander Stamboliski, might also gain them sympathy at the conference. Stamboliski had resolutely opposed Bulgaria's participation in the war and had suffered imprisonment because of his opposition. In both of these expectations the Bulgarians were disappointed. The Yugoslavs, Greeks, and Romanians, with French support, rejected all attempts by the Bulgarians to justify their national claims to the territories on an ethnic or moral basis.

The terms of the treaty imposed a heavy economic burden on Bulgaria. The amount of reparations was reduced in 1923 and finally eliminated in 1932. Nevertheless, a significant portion of Bulgaria's produced wealth went out of the country without any kind of compensation. In addition, a new wave of refugees from the lands taken by Yugoslavia, Greece, and Romania flooded into the country and added to Bulgaria's financial problems.

The treaty increased the sense of national wrong and frustration in Bulgaria that had begun with the Treaty of Berlin in 1878 and the Treaty of Bucharest in 1913. Thus, the Treaty of Neuilly helped to destabilize Bulgarian politics. Nationalist elements assassinated Prime Minister Alexander Stamboliski when he sought a rapprochement with Yugoslavia in 1923. Like the Treaty of Bucharest in 1913, the Treaty of Neuilly left Bulgaria an international outcast in the Balkans. At first Bulgaria found friends in revisionist Hungary and Fascist Italy. By the 1930s Bulgaria increasingly followed the economic and political lead of Nazi Germany. Finally, in 1941 Bulgaria became a German ally and participated in the Second World War in yet another vain attempt to obtain Macedonia.

Richard C. Hall

References

Bulgaria, Ministry for Foreign Affairs. *Observations of the Bulgarian Delegation on the Conditions of Peace with Bulgaria.* Paris: H. Elias, 1919.

Genov, Georgi P. *Bulgaria and the Treaty of Neuilly.* Sofia, Bulgaria: H.G. Danov & Co., 1935.

Ivanoff, J. *Les Bulgares devant le Congrès de la Paix.* Berne: P. Haupt, 1919.

See also BULGARIA

Neuve Chapelle, Battle of (March 1915)

Battle launched by British forces in an attempt to expand the French-held Ypres salient and remove the German threat to Paris. The battle provided the army with a model for offensive trench warfare, the lessons of which remained valid for the war's duration.

By late winter 1915 the British Expeditionary Force, under the command of Sir John French, was organized into two armies: the First, on the right, commanded by Sir Douglas Haig, who worked out the detailed plans and carried out the attack at Neuve-Chapelle; the Second Army, under General Sir Horace Smith-Dorrien. The seam between the two pivoted on Armentières.

Initially, the offensive was planned as a joint operation with the French. The British objective was to capture Aubers Ridge in order to threaten the German railroad supply hub at Lille, while the French seized Vimy Ridge, dominating the Douai plain. The Allied pincers would then converge and choke communications feeding the German spearhead directed toward Paris at Noyon. The French, however, became bogged down in the costly Champagne Campaign and were unable to take part in the offensive. Moreover, French Commander in Chief General Joseph Joffre requested a British diversion in the Ypres sector to relieve his overextended troops from the burden of holding that perimeter.

British headquarters was anxious to restore self-confidence after the bloody fiasco at the German trenches fronting Messines Ridge in December of 1914. Thus, British Commander in Chief French shouldered the Neuve Chapelle project independently of French support. The objective remained Aubers Ridge, from which German spotters had been menacing the British lines. From that base, two reserve cavalry corps would exploit the breakthrough by raiding Lille.

Fourteen battalions of British infantry backed by sixty-four artillery batteries were to attack a mere three German battalions manning twelve known machine-gun positions concentrated along a 2,000-meter front. This concentration of force was unprecedented in the war. Also unique was the planned curtain-raiser: a secretly prepared, highly focused, surprise "hurricane" barrage in lieu of the usual prolonged, unsystematic shelling. The fire plan was attuned more to the recently divulged shell shortage than to calculated tactical analysis. Regardless of the incentive, the operation marks a watershed in the evolution of trench warfare.

The meticulous planning was innovative this early in the war. Aerial photos facilitated the production of large-scale trench maps on which were penciled blue and red phase lines designating sequential infantry objectives. Each battalion commander received a copy covering his sector. Each artillery unit was assigned designated targets, to be shifted forward on a timetable conforming with the expected arrival of the consecutive infantry waves at their assigned phase lines. Multicolored flares would signal the batteries to reposition fires and commence the next stage of the walking barrage. Realistic rehearsals were held behind British lines on a specially constructed model of enemy-held terrain and emplacements.

At 07:30 on 10 March, after thirty-five minutes of hurricane bombardment, the first wave (12,000) of the 40,000-man British infantry moved up to the primary phase line without significant resistance. They were delayed there after the opening surprise. Although the 18-pounders had sufficed to take out the wire obstacles, they failed to destroy dug-in bunkers; nor had the fire plan contemplated machine gun positions in houses and thickets behind the German lines.

Owing to demolished lateral communications, local commanders were slow to regroup and direct their units forward. Contact with the rear was hindered by the inevitable destruction of telephone lines. Because guns could not be quickly switched to obstacles delaying the preceding group, overlapping infantry waves became entangled. Lack of timely information also meant that reinforcements could not be redirected at will to new objectives.

As had been accurately forecast by British intelligence officers, enemy reserves swiftly adjusted to the shock of the opening assault; they moved up to fill gaps in their lines during the hiatus. German artillery was well-registered on the familiar abandoned positions, and a stalemate developed.

All gains had been confined to the first three hours of the attack, during which First Army lost about 13,000 men in advancing 1,000 yards. They were held there by the 16,000 reserves that General Erich von Falkenhayn rushed forward over the next twenty-four hours.

This first British set-piece attack was also the last to maintain the element of surprise through secrecy of preparation until the tank breakthrough at Cambrai two years later. In assessing their failure at Neuve Chapelle, Allied generals overlooked the role of surprise in achieving the initial success. Instead, they focused on the reasons for their defeat, which they saw as inadequacy of artillery support caused by a shortage of shells. That brought demands for greater production of shells and longer, more intense, preparatory bombardments.

James J. Bloom

References

Baynes, John. "Neuve Chapelle." In *Purnell History of the First World War*. Vol. 2, no. 11, 733–43. London: Pan, 1974.

Cruttwell, C.R.M.F. *History of the Great War, 1914–1918*. 2nd ed. Oxford: Clarendon, 1936.

Edmonds, Sir James E., and Captain G.C. Wynne, comp. *Military Operations: France and Belgium, 1915*. Vol. 2. London: Macmillan, 1928.

Falls, Cyril B. *The Great War*. New York: Putnam's, 1959.

McEntee, Girard Lindsley. *Military History of the World War*. New York: Charles Scribner's Sons, 1937.

Stamps, Col. T. Dodson, and Col. Vincent J. Esposito. *A Short Military History of World War I*. West Point, N.Y.: U.S. Military Academy, 1954.

See also FRENCH, JOHN; HAIG, DOUGLAS

New Zealand

With the outbreak of war in Europe in 1914, the British dominion of New Zealand loyally followed the United Kingdom into the conflict. For many New Zealanders who joined the military, the war was an opportunity to leave the isolation of the southwest Pacific and see the world. A total of 128,449 of New Zealand's population of 1,090,000 volunteered to join the New Zealand Expeditionary Forces.

In 1914 elements of the NZEF captured the German Pacific possession of Western Samoa. But it was at Gallipoli in 1915 that New Zealand's forces were immortalized in the annals of military history. When Turkey entered the war against the Allies in November of 1914 the NZEF was diverted to Egypt, where British Field Marshal Lord Horatio Kitchener combined it with forces from Australia into the Australian New Zealand Army Corps, or Anzac, for the Gallipoli Campaign.

After eight months of bitter fighting, the New Zealanders and the other Allied divisions were forced to retreat from the peninsula. Nevertheless, the NZEF had quitted itself well and would continue its gallantry in Europe, including the Western Front, until the end of the war.

The Royal New Zealand Navy, which consisted of five ships, was attached to the Royal Navy during the war. Units were present at

Jutland and participated in other engagements in the European theater.

New Zealand also made other important contributions to the war. Although a small country, it was the largest exporting nation in the world in proportion to population. During the war New Zealand shipped large amounts of foodstuffs to Great Britain.

New Zealand paid a terrible price in World War I. Some 100,000 New Zealanders left their country to fight in the Great War. That force sustained 58,000 casualties, including 17,000 dead, a casualty rate of 58.6 percent (compared with 47.1 percent for Great Britain). In sum, New Zealand made a tremendous sacrifice for the British Empire.

Stephan C. Palmer

References

Pugsley, Christopher. *Gallipoli: The New Zealand Story*. Auckland: Hodder and Stoughton, 1984.

Robertson, John. *The Tragedy and Glory of Gallipoli: ANZAC and Empire*. Darlinghurst, Australia: Mead and Beckett, 1990.

See also Anzac; Gallipoli Campaign

Nicholas II (1868–1918)

Czar of Russia, 1894–1917. At the center of the tumultuous events in Russia between 1914 and 1918 stood Czar Nicholas II. Born in 1868 the eldest son of Czar Alexander III, he was a delicate youth who later became imbued with a religious fatalism. He seemed to be the very opposite of his physically powerful and domineering father. The latter attempted to mold his son by the harsh discipline reminiscent of that of an army drill sergeant, a policy that clearly failed. Much has been written about the character flaws of Nicholas II, how he detested controversy and strong advisors, his tendency toward indecision, and his inability to understand complex issues. Beneath the surface, however, was the will of an autocrat determined to preserve the monarchy in an era in which it was becoming increasingly out of date if not harmful to the functioning of a modern nation. That determination was infused in the future czar by his tutor, the brilliant and reactionary K.K. Pobedonotsev, who considered political terrorism a mere police matter but who counseled his charge that the one unforgivable sin on the part

of a monarch was to give up even an iota of his power under a constitution. Nicholas II was clearly out of touch with his time.

The year 1894 saw two events that changed his life. First was his marriage to Princess Alice of Hesse (the Empress Alexandra Feodorovna), who was even more reactionary than he and came to be the dominant influence in the czar's life. The second was the death of his father, Alexander III, shortly after the marriage, which catapulted Nicholas into the czardom, a position for which he was almost totally unprepared.

Nicholas and Alexandra truly loved each other and were able to escape the affairs of state by arranging picnics and other excursions. After giving birth to four daughters the empress produced a son, the Czarevich Alexei, who was born with severe hemophilia. This tragic disease was to color the whole reign of Nicholas II, if for no other reason than it brought the debauched holy man and peasant Rasputin into the bosom of the imperial family, because he alone was able to stop the bleeding of the czarevich after the boy's several accidents.

During the early reign of Nicholas Russia experienced the political and social turmoil typical of a nation in transition from a medieval kingdom to a modern industrial nation. It was an attempt to divert Russian attention from its domestic problems that led Nicholas to plunge Russia into war with Japan in 1904. His minister of interior, N. Pleve, had insisted that the war would produce an easy victory that would unite the Russian people around the czar. Instead, the Russo-Japanese War was a military disaster, which exposed the numerous weaknesses within the army and navy. More important, the war produced a political explosion at home that nearly toppled the monarchy. To save it, Nicholas had to agree to share his power with an elected legislature, the Duma, under the so-called constitution of 1905.

In foreign policy Nicholas II attempted to play a leading role in the Balkans by supporting Slavic national movements. At the center was an independent Serbia, which championed the Yugoslav (South Slav) nationalist movement that, in turn, threatened the very existence of Austria-Hungary. At issue for Russia was the fate of the Ottoman Empire's Balkan Orthodox subjects, over whom Russia had posed as "protector" since the eighteenth century, as well as the age-old Russian dream of seizing Constantinople. The road to Constantinople ran through the Balkans, especially Bulgaria and Serbia, both of which Russia sought to dominate. Pan-Slav zealots in the Russian Foreign Ministry and the army who had the czar's ear stirred up ethnic and religious hatreds throughout the Balkans.

In the diplomatic crisis that followed the assassination of Archduke Franz Ferdinand, heir to the Austrian throne, on 28 June 1914, Nicholas felt compelled to support Serbia against Austrian reprisal. Since Russia had been unable to resist Austrian annexation of Bosnia-Herzegovina in 1908 and the creation of Albania after the Balkan Wars, both of which upset Serbian territorial ambitions, Nicholas and his advisors feared that, if Russia did not support Serbia now, it would lose the support of Slavs in Eastern Europe. After the Austrian ultimatum to Serbia, therefore, chief of staff General Nikolai Ianushkevich placed a mobilization order in front of the czar. With little difficulty Nicholas signed it. Russia had, after all, guaranteed the existence of Serbia. This brought an immediate response from Berlin. Simultaneously, German mobilization was ordered. By 4 August 1914, Europe was at war.

Although he committed Russia to war, Nicholas II had done little to prepare Russia to fight. Prior to 1914 the czar himself had taken no part in the operation of the government. That was left to his ministers, most of whom were products of the Russian bureaucracy. A few were competent but most, such as aged Prime Minister Ivan Gorymkin and Minister of War Vladimir Sukhomlinov, were ill suited for government service. The early military disasters clearly revealed the failings of the czarist regime. Although many Russians tried to help organize the war effort through the local zemstvos and other organizations, Nicholas failed to incorporate the popular forces into his government. More important, after the collapse of Russian armies in Galicia in September of 1915, Nicholas made the fatal mistake of dismissing his uncle, the popular Grand Duke Nikolai Nikolaevich, as commander in chief and assuming personal command of the army. It appears that the empress was the motivating force behind this decision. Jealous of the grand duke's popularity and under the naive medieval notion that kings were supposed to lead their armies into battle, she urged her husband to be more autocratic. Ever glad to be away from the problems of the government, he left for Baranovichi. Although Nicholas never participated in formulating strategy, his presence at the front meant that he was held responsible for Russia's mounting defeats.

In heading for the front, Nicholas committed another fatal blunder by leaving Alexandra and her confidant and personal advisor, Rasputin, in charge of the government. Ten of the twelve ministers in the cabinet signed a letter urging the czar to reconsider his decision to be commander of the army. The empress took this as a personal insult and challenge to the czar's authority. Consequently, she set out to replace these ministers, many of whom were among the most competent men in the Russian government. The new prime minister, Boris Sturmer, was held in universal contempt. The minister of interior, Aleksandr Protopopov, was close to insanity. Through this process of "ministerial leapfrog" the empress and Rasputin dismantled the government. In the summer of 1916 both were openly attacked on the floor of the Duma, and there was talk on the streets of replacing the czar. Although Rasputin was murdered in December of 1916 by conservative politicians who saw him as a symbol of Russia's ills, it was too late to save the dynasty.

By 1917 it was apparent that Nicholas II should abdicate in favor of someone else. Others were not so charitable and called for outright revolution. On 6 March, with the Duma in session, the czar left for the front at Mogilev. On the following day riots broke out in Petrograd. By 9 March the Duma had formed a provisional committee, and the czar's ministers were placed under arrest. On the 11th the Duma president Mikhail Rodzianko wired the czar urging him to grant immediate political reform. At this Nicholas ordered his train back to Petrograd, but it was stopped at the city of Pskov by revolutionary workers. There he was visited by General Nikolai Ruzsky, commander of the northern front, and his chief of staff, General Mikhail Alekseev. Both urged him to abdicate. A few days later the provisional committee sent its own delegation of A.I. Guchkov and V.V. Shulgin carrying an abdication decree. On the afternoon of 15 March, Nicholas greeted them with a calm fatalism, so typical of him in trying circumstances. He signed the paper on condition that his sick son would not assume the throne. When his uncle, the Grand Duke Michael, refused it, the imperial era of Russian history was over.

With the abdication of the czar events moved rapidly. The former imperial family was placed under house arrest at Tsarskoe Selo. Although their safety was guaranteed by the new provisional government, after the Bolshevik takeover in November and the beginning of the civil war, the czar became an important political symbol. After several moves Nicholas and his family were taken to Ekaterinburg in western Siberia, which was under the control of a radical soviet. In July of 1918 their security was placed under Jacob Yarovsky, a CHEKA officer who commanded a detachment of Lettish and Hungarian Chekists. In mid-July the local soviet voted to execute the former czar and his family. When Moscow was informed of this decision, it gave its approval. On 16 July, at midnight, the czar and his wife, their four daughters and son, along with various servants, were taken into the basement of the Ipatiev house and shot to death.

John W. Bohon

References

Florinsky, Michael. *Russia, A History and Interpretation.* New York: Macmillan, 1958.

Massie, Robert. *Nicholas and Alexandra.* New York: Antheneum, 1967.

Pares, Sir Bernard. *The Fall of the Russian Monarchy.* New York: Vintage, 1939.

See also ALEXANDRA FEODOROVNA; RASPUTIN; RUSSIA, HOME FRONT AND REVOLUTIONS OF 1917

Nikola (1841–1921)

Prince and king of Montenegro, 1860–1918. Born at Njegšo on 7 October 1841, Nikola succeeded his assassinated uncle, Danilo, as Prince of Montenegro in 1860. In 1910 he took the title of king. During his reign Nikola modernized his country and doubled its territory. A manipulative diplomat, he took advantage of both foes' and allies' weaknesses and often provoked conflict between them.

Austria-Hungary proffered territorial incentives in exchange for Montenegro's neutrality in World War I. Nikola, enticed by such offers, visited Montenegrin troops, who had mobilized in late July, and demanded they hold fire. He personally intervened at anti-Austrian demonstrations. Ultimately, hoping to preserve his throne, he sided with the Allied powers against Austro-Hungary. Nikola telegrammed his grandson Alexander, prince regent of Serbia, agreeing to defend Serbia's independence. Instead, Nikola sought personal goals of strengthening Montenegro and his leadership of a pan-Serbian territory.

He arranged a northern offensive into Bosnia-Herzegovina in October of 1914 that failed. Next, Montenegro troops attacked the port of Scutari in Turkish-controlled Albania, but Serbians distrusted his motives. A political chameleon who abruptly changed policies, Nikola initiated communications with Austro-Hungary as early as 1915.

After Serbia fell in late 1915, Austria-Hungary occupied Montenegro in 1916 and Nikola's cabinet resigned, protesting rumors that Nikola was seeking a separate peace with Austria. He fled to exile in Italy while Montenegro was still at war.

A political assembly accused Nikola of accommodating with the Central Powers and deposed him in November of 1918. After his supporters were defeated in a postwar election, Montenegro was named a province of the new Kingdom of Serbs, Croats, and Slovenes (Yugoslavia) in 1921. Nikola, Montenegro's last king, died at Antibes on 1 March 1921.

Elizabeth D. Schafer

References

Baerlein, Henry. "The First and Last King of Montenegro." *Contemporary Review* 187 (August 1955): 170–74.

Durham, Mary Edith. "King Nikola of Montenegro." *Contemporary Review* 119 (April 1921): 471–77.

Nikola I Petrović Njegoš. *Cjelokupna djela Nikole I Petrovića Njegoša.* Cetinje: Obod, 1969.

Treadway, John D. *The Falcon and the Eagle: Montenegro and Austria-Hungary, 1908–1914.* West Lafayette, Ind.: Purdue University Press, 1983.

von Hubka, Gustav. "König Nikolaus von Montenegro." *Deutsche Revue* 46 (April/June 1921): 23–32, 174–84.

See also BALKAN FRONT, 1914, 1915, 1916; MONTENEGRO

Nikolai Nikolaevich (1856–1929)

Russian army commander in chief, July 1914 to August 1915; born 6 November 1856. Grand Duke Nikolai Nikolaevich was a professional soldier who, prior to the war, had held a variety of high posts in the Russian army, including adjutant general, general of cavalry, commander of the guards detachments and the St. Petersburg military district, and chairman of the Council of State Defense. On 20 July 1914, on the eve of Russian mobilization for war, he was appointed commander in chief of Russia's armed forces by his nephew, Czar Nikolai II. His appointment came as a surprise to military circles; it proved unfortunate because of the grand duke's lack of wartime experience as well as the administrative and tactical skills necessary for so demanding a position.

As commander in chief, Nikolai Nikolaevich assumed sweeping powers both in the military and in civilian spheres in areas adjoining the front. In practice, however, the decentralized conduct of military operations, with the combat zone divided into several fronts each with its own commander and strategic plan, meant that he did not assume day-to-day control of operations.

Under his overall command, Russian forces in 1914 were defeated in East Prussia but were able to repulse a German thrust toward Warsaw and achieve significant success in the Galician offensive against Austria-Hungary. The campaigns of 1915, however, produced major defeats that culminated in the general retreat of Russia's armies, staggering casualties, and three million civilian refugees. The grand duke paid for that disaster with his command. On 23 August 1915, against all advice except that of his wife, the Empress Alexandra, and her advisor Rasputin, the czar dismissed the popular Nikolai and assumed personal command of Russia's armed forces.

Nikolai was then appointed local administrator of the Caucasus region and commander of the Caucasian front, established after Turkey had entered the war in October of 1914. Russian forces there were able to reverse the earlier successes of a Turkish offensive launched by Enver Pasha in December of 1914. Under Nikolai's direct command the subsequent course of the war on the Caucasian front was largely favorable to Russia and led to the invasion of Armenia and the capture of Erzerum in February and Trebizond in April of 1916.

During the March 1917 revolution the grand duke was instrumental in persuading Nikolai II to resign on 15 March 1917, in order to save the country and, it was hoped, the dynasty. Once again appointed commander in chief, Nikolai Nikolaevich was immediately forced to renounce his command because of the pressure placed on him by the Petrograd Soviet and the provisional government. In March of 1919 he emigrated aboard a British warship and traveled to Italy and later to France. During his years in exile he was considered the supreme chief of all Russian military organizations but played no part in political life. He died in France on 5 January 1929.

Sylvia Russell

References

Lincoln, Bruce. *Passage through Armageddon. The Russians in War and Revolution 1914–1918*. New York: Simon and Schuster, 1987.

Stone, Norman. *The Eastern Front, 1914–1917*. New York: Charles Scribner's Sons, 1975.

Wieczynski, Joseph L., ed. *The Modern Encyclopedia of Russian and Soviet History*. Gulf Breeze, Fla.: Academic International, 1976.

Wildman, Allan K. *The End of the Russian Imperial Army*. Princeton: Princeton University Press, 1987.

See also EAST PRUSSIA CAMPAIGN; EASTERN FRONT; RUSSIA, HOME FRONT AND REVOLUTIONS OF 1917

Nivelle (Chemin des Dames) Offensive (April–May 1917)

The Nivelle, or Chemin des Dames, Offensive (also known as the Second Battle of the Aisne) marked the last attempt of the French army to achieve a decisive military breakthrough on the Western Front. Its failure led to major changes in French military leadership and strategy.

General Joseph Joffre's offensive operations in 1915—the First (February–March) and Second (September–November) battles of Champagne and the Second Battle of Artois (May–June)—had produced desperate fighting and appalling casualty lists but left the basic strategic picture on the Western Front unchanged. French operations in 1916 were dominated by the colossal Battle of Verdun, which added another 375,000 French dead and wounded, but left the prospect of a decisive breakthrough as illusive as ever. One inevitable consequence of these successive bloodbaths was a steady loss of confidence in the French commander in chief. In December of 1916 Premier

Aristide Briand provided Joffre with an ostensible promotion and the title of Marshal of France but effectively removed him from direct command of the armies.

The search for Joffre's successor culminated in the unexpected choice of General Robert Nivelle, who had risen from colonel to army commander in two and a half years but had little or no experience of strategic operations. Other, arguably more qualified, generals were ruled out for political and religious reasons (Sarrail, de Castelnau, and Franchet d'Esperey) or recent military failures (Foch). In many ways, Henri-Philippe Pétain, the "hero of Verdun," seemed Joffre's logical successor, but he had become skeptical of the chances of France's winning a decisive victory and was urging the adoption of a more cautious, defensive strategy. Most French politicians did not yet share Pétain's convictions, and few found his open contempt for the government's management of the war appealing.

Thus, it was Pétain's deputy, Nivelle, who had carried out a series of successful local attacks at Verdun in late 1916 and remained optimistic about the prospect of military victory, who was promoted over his higher-ranking colleagues in December. An artilleryman, Nivelle owed his success at Verdun to skillful use of his guns to silence enemy artillery and provide cover for specially trained assault units with "creeping" barrages. Nivelle was convinced that these tactics, effective on a small scale, could be used as the basis for a general offensive.

Joffre and British generals had worked out preliminary plans for coordinated February offensives in 1917, but these were little more than revivals of the attacks on the Somme that had petered out the preceding autumn. In January Nivelle proposed a new plan, focusing on the seventy-mile-long westward bulge in the German lines between Arras and Craonne. Nivelle proposed that the British and French armies attack the "shoulders" of the bulge, east of Arras and north of the Aisne, with the British delivering a preliminary blow in the north to draw off German reserves before the French carried out the principal assault farther to the south. Using the "Verdun method" of heavy preliminary bombardment, creeping barrages, and troops trained to move rapidly around enemy strongpoints to achieve maximum penetration, Nivelle promised that his attacking troops could "rupture" the German defenses, overrun their lines, and achieve a breakthrough within

forty-eight hours. Reserves would be pushed forward relentlessly to exploit initial successes, and, as the German salient collapsed, a huge gap would open in the enemy lines through which the Allies might pour, ending the war in a single decisive battle.

Nivelle sold his plan to the British and French governments in January, winning operational authority over all Allied troops. He also reorganized French armies for the offensive. A Reserve Army Group (composed of the Fifth, Sixth, and Tenth armies) of more than fifty divisions was to make the breakthrough northward from the Aisne River, supported by the Third Army (Army Group North) on its left, and the Fourth Army (Army Group Center) on its right. Command of the new army group was given to General Joseph Micheler, who seemed enthusiastic about Nivelle's plans. Fifth, Sixth, and Tenth armies were commanded by Generals Mazel, Charles Mangin, and Denis Duchène, respectively. Mangin, who had enjoyed considerable success with French colonial troops and planned to use them as the spearhead of the coming offensive, had been Nivelle's protégé at Verdun. As a result, he usually dealt directly with the commander in chief, ignoring his putative superior General Joseph Micheler and disrupting the chain of command.

French units were withdrawn from the line for training in the "Verdun method," while Nivelle built up morale with impassioned promises of victory and harangued his commanders about the need for a vigorous offensive mentality: "I insist that the stamp of *violence,* of *brutality* and of *rapidity* must characterize your offensive; and, in particular, that the first step, which is the *rupture,* must in one blow capture the enemy positions and all the zone occupied by his artillery."

As supplies were accumulated, roads built, and batteries sited, the date for beginning operations was repeatedly postponed but finally fixed at mid-April. By late February, however, problems with the French plans were apparent. The first lay in the area selected for the French attack. After serious fighting in September of 1914, the Aisne River valley had remained a relatively quiet part of the front. In the area selected for the attack, the river ran generally eastward from Soissons to Berry-au-Bac, then southeastward to Reims, a distance of approximately thirty miles. In the east, French lines lay north of the river (and the Aisne-Marne canal, which ran beside it), but for two thirds of the front the fifty-yard-wide river lay just in front of the German lines, or behind them, and thus posed a significant obstacle to attacking troops. North of the Aisne, lying across the French line of advance and rising nearly five hundred feet above the valley floor, was a large, flat, limestone plateau. Its southern slope was a broken series of narrow gorges, bluffs, and escarpments, many of them too steep for vehicles or artillery to ascend.

Along the top of the plateau, from Malmaison to Craonne, lay the Chemin des Dames, an eighteenth-century road originally laid out for the convenience of the daughters of Louis XV. The reverse slopes of the plateau led down into the marshy valley of the Ailette River, which was bordered on its north by another limestone ridge, beyond which lay the town and plain of Laon. Nivelle was proposing that the Reserve Army Group attack across two river valleys and two ridgelines, all likely to be fortified by the Germans, and surmount all of these obstacles in a matter of hours.

A second problem lay in German knowledge of the plans for, and even the date of, the French operation. Aerial reconnaissance provided early indications of the French buildup, and intercepted Italian diplomatic traffic confirmed that the French and British were planning an April offensive. German spies added more information, and on 4 April German trench-raiders captured a sergeant major who had in his possession the assault plans for two entire corps. To cap these breaches of security, the French and English military attachés in The Hague revealed at a diplomatic dinner party on 15 April that the French offensive would begin the next day.

Even before the final details reached the German High Command, steps to blunt the impact of the Allied offensive were being taken. Briefly considering a spoiling attack, Quartermaster General Erich Ludendorff decided that the major German offensives in 1917 would still be launched in Italy and Russia. In France Ludendorff decided to evacuate the bulge that was Nivelle's target. Beginning on 9 February engineers in the salient began Operation Alberich, the systematic demolition of roads, bridges, towns, and even natural features that might be of use to the Allies. Between 15 and 19 March, German units along the front withdrew across this artificial wasteland to a new defensive position, the Siegfried Line (called the Hindenburg Line by the Allies), which had been prepared for them in the rear.

Along the Siegfried Line and those parts of the front not evacuated (including the Aisne valley), Ludendorff restructured the German defenses. Instead of concentrating manpower in the front trenches, the Germans created an "elastic" defense, constructing hundreds of concrete machine-gun emplacements in checkerboard patterns on the forward slopes of their positions. Behind these lay two or three separate trench lines, further apart than was customary, with numerous underground bunkers built into the reverse slopes of hills to shelter reserve troops from shellfire. Machine guns and coils of concertina barbed wire (eight feet high in places) would channel assaulting troops into killing zones, where they could be ground down and then crushed in counterattacks by reserve units.

Above the Aisne, the limestone quarries, caves, and narrow southern gorges of the Chemin de Dames plateau were ideally suited to Ludendorff's plans, and General von Boehn's Seventh Army worked throughout February and March to strengthen its defenses. Although Nivelle believed that his preliminary artillery bombardment would destroy the German fortifications, precise information about them, as well as accurate spotting for French batteries, was severely restricted by the Germans' success in maintaining air superiority over the battlefield. Shortening their line by abandoning the salient had added fourteen divisions to the German reserve, and the hoped-for French superiority in numbers on the Aisne was correspondingly reduced.

The German evacuation, combined with fragmentary reports on the strength of the new German defenses, convinced a growing number of French generals and politicians that Nivelle's plan was no longer practicable. While the commander in chief insisted that the April breakthrough was still possible, Paul Painlevé, who became minister of war in March, shared the doubts of his predecessor, General Louis Herbert Lyautey. Painlevé soon learned that the commanders of the Northern and Center army groups, Pétain and Franchet d'Esperey, had little enthusiasm for the offensive, and that even General Micheler was hinting that he had lost confidence in the plan.

Although Painlevé held a series of conferences to discuss these criticisms, it proved difficult to take action. Nivelle's subordinates were reluctant to state their objections in his presence, and the commander in chief energetically defended his plans. He argued that American entry into the war, Allied defeats in Italy, and the March revolution in Russia all necessitated a show of strength from France. When Nivelle threatened to resign on 6 April, the prospect of a collapse in the army's morale was more than the politicians could contemplate, and Painlevé and President Raymond Poincaré gave their reluctant approval to the attack.

By the time Nivelle offered his resignation, the preliminary bombardment had already begun. Although French guns pounded the German positions for two weeks, the bombardment left many of the defenses intact. On 9 April, after a shorter bombardment, the British attack (the Battle of Arras), led by General Edmund Allenby's Third and General Henry Horne's First armies, pushed eastward. The local German commander, General Falkenhausen, had not adopted the new German defensive system along all of his front and he had kept his reserve divisions farther to the rear than Ludendorff recommended. That enabled Horne's Canadian troops to capture Vimy Ridge. Although British troops penetrated nearly four miles into the German lines, no breakthrough occurred and no German reserves were drawn away from the Aisne front.

There, the night of 15–16 April brought rain and sleet, which soaked the ground and left many of Mangin's African units chilly and demoralized. Sixth Army (seventeen divisions) was to strike at the left end of the sector, Fifth Army (sixteen divisions, including two Russian brigades and 128 tanks) on the right. When they penetrated the defenses, Duchène's Tenth Army (which included an entire corps of cavalry) would move up to exploit the breakthrough. Mangin's first-day objective was the second ridgeline, beyond the Ailette. The opening assault waves, which moved forward at 06:00, ran into tenacious resistance from the start. Decimated by German machine guns and soon outpaced by rolling barrages predicated on the assumption that the attack was moving rapidly, French troops struggled forward through mud and unbroken barbed wire toward the concealed German defenses. Nivelle's plans called for reserves to be fed steadily into the battle, but lack of progress by advanced units meant reserve divisions were jammed into forward trenches under heavy enemy artillery fire. Troops trained to look for gaps in the defenses were drawn instead into the German killing zones, and Boehn, who had seventeen divisions in reserve, launched immediate counterattacks wherever the French threatened to gain footholds.

Absorbing terrible losses, Mangin's 42nd and 69th divisions were able to advance two and a half miles up the Chemin de Dames plateau. Everywhere else his troops made minimal advances or were repulsed; Mazel's divisions made little or no progress on their sector of the front, losing all their tanks to German artillery fire. Fifth Army took approximately 7,000 German prisoners and the Sixth 3,500, but in turn the French suffered nearly 90,000 casualties, overwhelming their medical services and further demoralizing reserve units waiting to be committed to the battle. On the 17th, after another night of freezing rain, Nivelle directed Mangin and Mazel to exploit what gains they had made, but further attacks gained only little additional ground. A diversionary attack by Fourth Army (Center Army Group) on 17 April also stalled, and bringing Tenth Army up to the front line (on the 19th) merely added more men to what had already degenerated into a grinding battle of attrition—the very sort of battle Nivelle's plans were designed to avoid.

By 25 April the French had captured about 20,000 German prisoners, 147 guns, and 300 machine guns, but their most advanced position on the Chemin des Dames plateau lay only four miles beyond their starting point on 16 April. For these modest gains they had lost nearly 100,000 dead and wounded, and 4,000 men taken prisoner, taking 80 percent of these losses on the first day of fighting. The French artillery faced a serious shortage of shells, and morale collapsed in some units. Nivelle and Micheler engaged in a public shouting match as each tried to fix blame for the offensive's failure on the other. When President Poincaré questioned the value of further attacks on 23 April, Nivelle indignantly protested that he was the victim of scurrilous "rumors . . . without foundation" about the situation at the front. But he had already lost the government's confidence, and on 29 April Pétain was named chief of the general staff with the understanding that he would restrict Nivelle's efforts to continue the attacks.

On 2 May Mangin was relieved of duty, and on the 6th the Reserve Army Group was dissolved, with Micheler reduced to command of a single army. On 15 May Nivelle finally stepped down and was replaced as commander in chief by Pétain. The offensive officially ended on 9 May, by which time the French had suffered 30,000 dead and 100,000 wounded. These figures were not released for some time, and in the interim rumors that casualties had been even higher circulated among the troops, who already had to reconcile the optimistic rhetoric that had preceded the fighting with their own experiences. While the Germans had hardly escaped unscathed—83,000 casualties in addition to their losses in prisoners—they could regard the largely successful defense of their positions with some pride.

Isolated incidents of "collective indiscipline" were reported in French units as early as 17 April. On 21 April the 1st Colonial Infantry Division (Sixth Army) engaged in openly mutinous behavior, disobeying their officers and shouting "Long live peace!" On the 29th the second battalion of the 18th Regiment (Sixth Army), which had suffered two-thirds casualties on 16 April, refused to return to the trenches, drunkenly defying its officers and crying "Down with the war!" By late May more than half of the frontline divisions were mutinous to some degree, but the phenomenon appeared first in units of the Reserve Army Group, which had undergone the bitter ordeal of the Chemin des Dames. The mutinies confronted France's military and civilian leadership with the greatest crisis of the war between the original German invasion in 1914 and Ludendorff's 1918 offensive.

Pétain forswore further large-scale assaults, promising to wait for "tanks and the Americans" to swing the military balance decisively against the Germans. In the meantime, he worked to rebuild the morale and the fighting qualities of the French army.

David L. Longfellow

References

King, Jere Clemens. *Generals and Politicians.* Berkeley: University of California Press, 1951.

Paschall, Rod. *The Defeat of Imperial Germany 1917–1918.* Chapel Hill, N.C.: Algonquin, 1989.

Watt, Richard M. *Dare Call It Treason.* New York: Simon and Schuster, 1963.

Young, Peter, ed. *The Marshall Cavendish Illustrated Encyclopedia of World War I.* New York: Marshall Cavendish, 1984.

See also ALBERICH, OPERATION OF; ALLENBY, EDMUND; FRENCH ARMY MUTINY; MANGIN, CHARLES; MICHELER, JOSEPH; NIVELLE, ROBERT; PÉTAIN, HENRI-PHILIPPE

Nivelle, Robert (1856–1924)

French general and commander in chief of the French army (December 1916–May 1917). Born at Tulle on 15 October 1856, Nivelle was the son of a Protestant officer and an English mother. Graduating from the Ecole Polytechnique in 1878, he entered the artillery. Between 1900 and 1908 he rose to the rank of lieutenant colonel and saw service in China, Korea, and Algeria. In 1911, he was promoted to colonel of the Fourth Artillery Regiment at Besançon.

After fighting around Mulhouse in August of 1914, his regiment joined Maunoury's new Sixth Army near Paris. In action along the Ourcq (Battle of the Marne) on 6 September, Nivelle pushed batteries ahead of his infantry and broke up a German attack with a rapid-fire barrage, a tactic he used again on the Aisne on 16 September. Imaginative handling of his guns won Nivelle promotion to general in October. By February of 1915 he was commanding a division and by early 1916 he was commander of Third Corps at Verdun. It was at Verdun that Nivelle and General Charles Mangin (his Fifth Division commander) developed the tactics that would bring him to prominence.

When General Henri-Philippe Pétain provided him with sufficient heavy artillery, Nivelle withdrew selected units from the front and trained them to assault specific objectives in small groups. Attacks were to be preceded by a "deception" bombardment (shelling halted to encourage the Germans to reveal their artillery positions, then renewed). With enemy guns silenced, assault units would advance to their objectives behind a creeping barrage. In April of 1916 General Joseph Joffre gave Nivelle command of the Verdun front (Second Army). Proclaiming "We have the formula!" Nivelle launched a series of local attacks on 1 May that led, after initial setbacks, to the recapture of Fort Vaux on 7 June and Fort Douaumont on 24 October. Because of his success at Verdun, Nivelle was named commander in chief on 13 December, replacing Joffre.

Although only four years younger than his predecessor, Nivelle projected a deliberate air of energy and optimism—"good looking, smart, plausible, and cool," in the words of British General Spears. Anticlerical deputies preferred his Protestantism to the aristocratic Catholicism of generals like Noel de Castelnau and Louis Franchet d'Esperey. His fluent English helped win Nivelle operational command of the British armies, and his assurance that his tactical innovations at Verdun could be applied on a wider scale made more experienced generals like Pétain and Ferdinand Foch seem overly cautious.

Nivelle overhauled existing plans for simultaneous February offensives by the French and the British and shifted the French effort to the Aisne. In January of 1917 he presented a plan "to break the enemy's front in such a manner that the rupture can be immediately exploited; to overcome all the reserves with which our adversary can oppose us; to exploit with all our resources the result of this decisive battle." The key to success was to be the Verdun "formula" or "method," despite the difficulties encountered in applying small-unit tactics to entire armies and in achieving artillery superiority on a front several dozen miles in length.

While preparations delayed the offensive into early April, the Germans (who were well aware of the French plan) shortened their front and withdrew to the heavily fortified Hindenburg Line. Politicians and generals raised doubts about the wisdom of the offensive, and on 6 April a conference at Compiègne in the presence of President Raymond Poincaré, Premier Alexandre Ribot, and Minister of War Paul Painlevé revealed that even General Alfred Micheler, whose army group was to make the assault, was pessimistic. Nivelle's threat to resign halted such criticism, however, and, following a diversionary British attack on 9 April, the initial French push by thirty-three divisions began on the 16th.

The "Nivelle Offensive" from 16 April to 9 May produced minimal gains but 130,000 French casualties; it sparked mutinies in the French army. When Nivelle persisted in ordering further attacks, Poincaré named Pétain chief of the general staff with instructions to end them. On 15 May Pétain replaced Nivelle as commander in chief and began to deal with the mutinies that were spreading through the army.

Nivelle declined command of an army group and in October of 1917 submitted to review by a military commission of inquiry, which whitewashed him. He commanded French troops in Algeria in 1918 and served on the supreme war council after the war, dying in Paris on 23 March 1924.

David L. Longfellow

References

King, Jere Clemens. *Generals and Politicians.* Berkeley: University of California Press, 1951.

Paschall, Rod. *The Defeat of Imperial Germany 1917–1918.* Chapel Hill, N.C.: Algonquin, 1989.

Watt, Richard M. *Dare Call It Treason.* New York: Simon and Schuster, 1963.

Young, Peter, ed. *The Marshall Cavendish Illustrated Encyclopedia of World War I.* New York: Marshall Cavendish, 1984.

See also MARNE, FIRST BATTLE OF; NIVELLE OFFENSIVE; VERDUN, BATTLE OF

Nixon, Sir John (1857–1921)

British general. Born at Brentford on 16 August 1857, Nixon was educated at Wellington College and Sandhurst. He fought in the Afghan War of 1879–80 and the Boer War and then served in India. In 1904 he was promoted to major general and in 1909 to lieutenant general. In 1912 Nixon received command of the Indian Southern Army; two years later he was promoted to full general and in 1915 received command of the Indian Northern Army.

In April of 1915 Nixon assumed command of British forces in Mesopotamia. His appointment marked a turning point in the theater. London favored a defensive strategy to protect the oil fields, but before Nixon left India, Sir Beauchamp-Duff, India's commander in chief, instructed him to advance on Baghdad. That was not known to London until later.

Nixon set about preparing for the offensive. He received additional reinforcements, although not a requested cavalry brigade. At first the British were successful. In June of 1915 British forces commanded by General Charles Townshend took Amara, followed by Kut el Amara in September. London then authorized Nixon to march on Baghdad, promising two Indian divisions from France. This strategy suited Nixon well; he was a man who was prepared to gamble to achieve success. He also depreciated the ability of Turkish troops and overestimated the ability of his own. Townshend indicated to Nixon his opposition to an advance on Baghdad without reinforcements. Having registered his objections, in late November Townshend followed Nixon's orders and began a march on Baghdad. Blocked by the Turks at Ctesiphon Townshend fell back on Amara, where he was besieged by the Turks in December and forced to surrender in April of 1916.

In January of 1916 Nixon gave up his command, ostensibly for reasons of health. He was called to London to testify before the Mesopotamia Commission, which, between August of 1916 and April of 1917, investigated the military failures of the region. Although the commission found Nixon had to make do with "wholly insufficient means," he was among those blamed: "The weightiest share of responsibility lies with Sir John Nixon, whose confident optimism was the main cause of the decision to advance." Plans to bring Nixon before a special court of inquiry were overtaken by the end of the war, but his career had been ruined. Nixon died at St. Raphael, France, on 15 December 1921.

Spencer C. Tucker

References

Barker, A.J. *The Bastard War—The Mesopotamian Campaign of 1914–1918.* New York: Dial, 1976.

Dictionary of National Biography, 1912–1921. Third Supplement. London: Oxford University Press, 1966.

See also MESOPOTAMIA; TOWNSHEND, CHARLES

Njegovan, Maximilian (1858–1930)

Admiral and commander of the Austro-Hungarian navy. Born at Agram on 31 October 1858 to Croatian parents, Njegovan graduated from the Naval Academy at Fiume in 1877. At the beginning of the war he assumed command of the I Geschwader and the First Division in the Geschwader. This command represented the most powerful warships, the dreadnoughts and predreadnoughts. While serving as *Marinekommandant* of the Austro-Hungarian navy (February 1917–February 1918) and *Chef des Marinesektion* at the ministry of war (April 1917–February 1918), he continued his predecessor Anton von Haus's essentially defensive policy of preserving the capital ships of the Austrian navy as a fleet-in-being.

During his command the Austrians lost their early edge, and the Italians became bolder and deployed new weapons such as the Mas boats, fast torpedo boats. Mas boats sank the coastal defense ship *Wien* in Trieste harbor in December of 1917. Njegovan was also criticized for not using the navy aggressively enough to exploit the success of the Caporetto Offensive. He had the misfortune to be in power at a moment when war weariness had spread through the Dual Monarchy and there were disturbances in the fleet—the most serious of which was the mutiny at Cattaro in February of 1918. Shortly after the mutiny was quelled, and with a widespread demand for "rejuvenation" of the naval high command, Njegovan retired at his own request. He died at Agram on 1 July 1930.

Paul G. Halpern

References

Bayer von Bayersburg, Heinrich. *Unter der k.u.k. Kriegsflagge, 1914–1918.* Vienna: Bergland Verlag, 1959.

Halpern, Paul G. *The Naval War in the Mediterranean, 1914–1918.* London and Annapolis, Md.: Allen and Unwin and Naval Institute Press, 1987.

Sokol, Hans Hugo. *Österreich-Ungarns Seekrieg.* 2 vols. Vienna: Amalthea Verlag, 1933. Reprint. Graz: Akademische Druck und Verlagsanstalt, 1967.

Wagner, Walter. *Die Obersten Behörden der K. und K. Kriegsmarine, 1856–1918.* Vienna: Ferdinand Berger, 1961.

See also AUSTRIA-HUNGARY, NAVY; MEDITERRANEAN NAVAL OPERATIONS

Noske, Gustav (1868–1946)

German Social Democratic leader. Born into an artisan family on 9 July 1868 in Brandenburg, Prussia, Noske trained as a basket-maker before joining the Social Democratic party in 1886 and later serving as an editor on several party newspapers. Elected to the Reichstag in 1906, he specialized in military and colonial affairs; in the following year he attracted national attention with a parliamentary speech asserting that workers had a duty to defend their fatherland if it were attacked.

At the outbreak of World War I, Noske became a socialist war correspondent. He supported the Reichstag peace resolution of 1917 and called for reform of the Prussian suffrage. Under the last imperial government he was commissioned to subdue the sailors' mutiny at Kiel in early November of 1918, which he accomplished successfully by his rhetorical skill. The new government under his fellow socialist Friedrich Ebert entrusted Noske with the task of rebuilding the German army after the war ended. Noske was dedicated to maintaining order and fearful of a Bolshevik-type revolution. Appointed to the provisional government, Noske used the *Freikorps* to suppress the Spartacist insurrection of January 1919. He reluctantly accepted the task, saying, "Someone has to be the bloodhound. I shall not shirk the responsibility." Made minister of defense in February, Noske used troops to suppress a worker uprising in the capital the next month. Unable to deal with the Kapp Putsch, Noske was forced to resign on 18 March 1920.

Noske ended his political career, as governor of Hanover from 1920 to 1933, when the Nazi government ousted him from office. Implicated in the 20 July 1944 plot against Hitler, he escaped trial and execution by feigning illness while imprisoned. He died in Hanover on 30 November 1946.

George P. Blum

References

Noske, Gustav. *Erlebtes aus Aufstieg und Niedergang einer Demokratie.* Offenbach-Main: Bollwerk Verlag, 1947.

Ryder, A.J. *The German Revolution of 1918.* Cambridge: Cambridge University Press, 1967.

Wette, Wolfram. *Gustav Noske: Eine politische Biographie.* Dusseldorf: Droste, 1987.

See also GERMANY, HOME FRONT; GERMANY, REVOLUTION OF 1918

Origins of the First World War

Inasmuch as the First World War was an event of unparalleled tragedy in European history, much effort has been made to try to discover what caused it. While some historians have attempted to reduce the origins of the war to one single cause, such as Bernadotte E. Schmitt's blaming of the alliance system, they have greatly oversimplified the complexity of European affairs in the prewar era. They have, moreover, made the war appear inevitable, when, in fact, it was not. Unlike 1939, when Hitler actively pursued war, no power in 1914 set out to plot a general European war. There were, however, a number of factors that provided a setting conducive to war. An examination of these will help to explain why the assassination of the Archduke Franz Ferdinand on 28 June 1914, provided the spark necessary to set Europe ablaze.

Of the long-term causes of the First World War, perhaps none was more powerful than the spread of nationalism. First arising in France during the French Revolution, modern nationalism forever changed the nature of European war. In place of wars between rulers, nationalism released the combined energies and hatreds of entire peoples, producing "total" wars of one nation against another. Nationalism also altered European diplomacy by forcing all governments, even the most autocratic, to take the passions of the masses into consideration. The presentation of the Austrian ultimatum to Serbia, for example, provoked such popular outrage in Russia that Russian Foreign Minister Sergei Sazonov was convinced that a revolution would break out if Russia did not support Serbia.

Just as religious identity had disrupted European relations during the Reformation and Counter Reformation of the sixteenth and early seventeen centuries, nationalism became a divisive force in the nineteenth century. That was especially the case in Eastern Europe, where there were a plethora of nationalities and ethnic groups desiring nations of their own. While the decline of the Ottoman Empire resulted in the establishment of an independent Greece, Serbia, Montenegro, Romania, and Bulgaria, each of these states looked to expand by incorporating members of their nationality in other countries: Romania coveted Transylvania and Bessarabia, with their large Romanian populations; Serbia hoped to establish a greater Serbia by uniting with Montenegro and the South Slavs (Serbs, Croats, Slovenes, and Muslim Bosnians) living within the Austro-Hungarian Empire; and both Greece and Bulgaria looked to expansion in Macedonia and Thrace. While Austria-Hungary and the Ottoman Empire were directly threatened by these movements, Pan-Slavs in Russia saw the opportunity to gain control of Eastern Europe by sponsoring their fellow Slavs. Likewise, the Pan-German League founded by Karl Peters in 1890 hoped to unite people of Germanic descent (Austrian Germans, Danes, Swedes); while its efforts did not necessarily reflect German policy, its propaganda aroused fears in other countries.

What made nationalism an even more disruptive force was the lack of an effective international organization to check nationalist aspirations. Although the Hague Conventions had established a world court for arbitration and prescribed rules of warfare, each nation followed its own interests, with no concern for Europe as a whole. Even if two nations did decide to submit to arbitration in the world court, it had no authority to impose its decision. Thus, after the assassination of Franz Ferdinand, each nation followed its own interests. While Britain and Germany belatedly called for arbitration between Austria-Hungary and Serbia, they could not force them without resorting to war. At the 1919 Paris Peace Conference the creation of an international organization, the League of Nations, to try to maintain peace in the future showed that the diplomats realized that unhindered nationalism had played a major role in causing the First World War.

Without international guarantees of peace prior to the war, each nation had sought to protect its interests through military alliances. As a result, by 1914 Europe had become divided into two hostile camps: the Triple Alliance of Germany, Austria-Hungary, and Italy, versus the Triple Entente of France, Russia, and Great Britain. By prescribing each country's actions and reactions in advance of a crisis, these alliances virtually destroyed any room for diplomatic maneuvering. With the great powers aligned against each other, any action, even one caused by a minor power, could provoke a European crisis of epic proportion. As Joachim Remak has put it: "The tail could wag a whole pack of dogs." The security of the alliances also contributed to the brinkmanship that European diplomats followed in July of 1914. Had Austria-Hungary not been ensured of German support in the event Russia intervened to protect Serbia from Austrian reprisals, it might have reacted to the assassination of Archduke Franz Ferdinand with greater restraint. Likewise, if Russia had not been confident of French support, it would not have risked antagonizing Germany. Finally, the alliance systems were not designed as much to prevent war as they were to prepare each state for war should it become necessary. Had the many secret military clauses been public, European diplomats might have acted with more caution. Indeed, President Wilson's call in the Fourteen Points for "open covenants arrived at openly" was a direct response to the secret diplomacy of the prewar era.

As if nationalism had not unleashed enough tensions within Europe, imperialism resulted in conflicting interests in areas far removed from Europe. Beginning in the 1870s the great powers, with the exception of Austria-Hungary, began scrambling to carve out colonies and spheres of influence in Africa and Asia. The British entered the imperial race with a huge lead and by 1914 ruled over 20 percent of the world's territory and 25 percent of its population. Germany, France, Italy, and even tiny Belgium had entered the race for overseas territories and by 1900 had been joined by the United States and Japan as imperial powers.

Of all the overseas empires, only the British Empire made sense economically; the others produced greater expenses than economic benefits. If colonies were not economically productive, why then did European countries allow their imperial pursuits to strain diplomatic relations? The answer goes back to nationalism. Imperialism was a sign of national greatness. For the French an overseas empire symbolized France's "civilizing mission," provided a much-needed psychological boost after the 1870 debacle at Sedan, and helped offset Germany's population advantage. For Kaiser Wilhelm II an overseas empire represented "Germany's place under the sun."

While much has been made of Germany's supposed desire to dominate the world, the fact is that the British not only aspired to world dominance but had already achieved it. More important, Englishmen acted as though they had some God-given right to it. As Raymond Sontag has put it: "Englishmen forgot their history and assumed that their supremacy resulted from the operation of a beneficent moral law. To challenge British supremacy was to challenge moral law." Certainly, if any power attempted to establish a colony virtually anywhere in the world, it was bound to conflict with British imperial interests. In the Fashoda Crisis of 1898, for example, French efforts to establish control over the Sudan almost resulted in war with Britain.

Nowhere can the impact of imperialism upon diplomatic relations be better illustrated than in the Anglo-German rivalry. Although relations between Germany and Great Britain had been cordial in the 1870s and 1880s, by the time of the accession of Wilhelm II in 1888 the relationship was showing signs of strain. German unification in 1871 had unleashed an economic expansion that by 1914 propelled Germany past Britain in most industrial categories. Wilhelm II's pursuit of *Weltpolitik*, through such actions as the "Berlin-to-Baghdad Railroad," were seen in London as an encroachment. Germany's support of the Boers in South Africa also antagonized the British. It was Wilhelm's naval buildup, however, that soured relations beyond repair and eventually drove the British into the arms of France and Russia.

If nationalism and imperialism created sparks, it was the press that fanned the flames. Members of influential groups such as the German Naval League and the British Naval League gave speeches and published books, pamphlets, and letters that played upon public fears. Just as important, however, was the role of the mass-circulation press in poisoning relations between nations, especially in the case of Britain and Germany. Since sensationalism increased the profit margin, publishers often appealed to the very worst in their readers. In 1909 the *London Daily Mail* helped fuel the Naval Panic by publishing a series of articles in which it concluded that "Germany is deliberately preparing to destroy the British Empire" and that only a larger navy could prevent "Germany's realization of world-power and domination." A few years earlier, the *Saturday Review* had been even more blunt, declaring, "Were every German to be wiped out tomorrow, there is no English trade, no English pursuit that would not immediately expand."

The danger of inflaming popular passion was even more inherent in an age in which war remained the ultimate and permissible resort in settling disputes. War had, after all, solved the questions of Italian and German unification. Social Darwinism had won a wide following among military leaders who came to see war as a product of "survival of the fittest." Had Europeans realized that the revolution in military technology was going to produce a mass slaughter of epic proportion, they might have feared it enough to try to avoid it. Instead, they prepared for it in one of the greatest arms races the world has ever seen. More important, in drafting war plans, military considerations often surpassed political and diplomatic considerations. Under the Schlieffen Plan, for example, the German General Staff insisted on the need for violating Belgian neutrality in order to defeat France, even though this would clearly risk war with Great Britain. War plans drove diplomacy.

As Europe entered the twentieth century, all of these factors (nationalism, imperialism, yellow journalism, the arms race) had combined to make European relations extremely volatile. In fact, the great powers had narrowly avoided war on several occasions in the decade preceding the First World War. In 1905 Wilhelm II provoked the First Moroccan Crisis by traveling to Tangiers and offering Morocco support against French plans to annex it. If France had not still been reeling from the Dreyfus Affair and her Russian ally had not been engaged in a war with Japan and embroiled in a revolution at home, war might easily have erupted. Instead, the differences were smoothed over through a conference of great powers, held at Algeciras, Spain. Three years later, in 1908, Austria-Hungary outraged Serbia and Russia by annexing Bosnia-Herzegovina. Serbia lost its access to the sea, while Russia felt betrayed because Austria-Hungary had failed to support Russia's acquisition of the Straits. In 1911 the Second Moroccan Crisis brought Europe to the brink of war again after a German gunboat, *Panther,* arrived at the Moroccan port of Agadir to protest French military intervention in Morocco and to demand compensation elsewhere. Finally, the Balkan Wars of 1912 and 1913 threatened to draw the great powers into the conflict because Austria-Hungary forced the creation of an independent Albania, which again thwarted Serbian access to the sea.

Although war was by no means inevitable in 1914, European diplomacy clearly needed a breathing spell if the threat of war were to diminish. The assassination of Archduke Franz Ferdinand, however, provoked a crisis of the first magnitude. Unfortunately, the great powers pursued the same brinkmanship policies that they had used in the previous crises to achieve their goals, and this time their actions plunged Europe into a war that would be more devastating than anything the world had seen before.

Justin D. Murphy

References

Fay, Sidney Bradshaw. *The Origins of the World War*. 2nd ed., revised. New York: Macmillan, 1949.

Hale, Oron J. *The Great Illusion, 1900–1914*. New York: Harper and Row, 1971.

Hayes, Carlton J.H. *A Generation of Materialism, 1871–1900*. New York: Harper and Row, 1941.

Remak, Joachim. *The Origins of World War I, 1871–1914*. New York: Holt, Rinehart and Winston, 1967.

Schmitt, Bernadotte E. *Triple Alliance and Triple Entente*. New York: Henry Holt, 1934.

Schmitt, Bernadotte E., and Harold C. Vedeler. *The World in the Crucible, 1914–1919*. New York: Harper and Row, 1984.

O

Turner, L.C.F. *Origins of the First World War*. New York: W.W. Norton, 1970.

See also ALLIANCES, PREWAR; BALKAN WARS; BLACK HAND; FRANZ FERDINAND; NAVAL ARMS RACE, ANGLO-GERMAN

Orlando, Vittorio E. (1860–1952)

Italian premier, 1917–19. Born in Palermo on 19 May 1860, Orlando was the scion of a wealthy Sicilian family. He taught law at the University of Palermo and became an eminent jurist and parliamentarian. He entered the Chamber of Deputies in 1897 and rose quickly through the ranks. He served as minister of public instruction (1903–5) and minister of justice (1907–9) in the Giolitti cabinet. He became minister of the interior in June of 1916 and ascended to the premiership in 1917, a critical time for Italy. After the military debacle at Caporetto, he successfully rallied popular support behind the government. Orlando organized the *Unione Sacra,* a patriotic national front, and with help from the other Entente powers presided over Italy's defeat of Austria-Hungary at Vittorio Veneto.

Orlando is most famous, however, for representing Italy in the Council of Four at the Paris Peace Conference in 1919. Along with Woodrow Wilson, Georges Clemenceau, and David Lloyd George, he hoped to write a treaty that would secure a lasting peace. Unfortunately, Orlando was handicapped by the conflict between the secret Treaty of London of 1915 (by which Great Britain and France promised to compensate Italy with territory along the Adriatic Coast—Dalmatia—in return for joining the Entente) and Wilson's ideal of self-determination. He proved inflexible to compromise, especially when it came to the Italian-speaking port of Fiume, which was not included in territory promised to Italy in the Treaty of London. Orlando had to pacify domestic turmoil caused by the high number of Italian military casualties (500,000 dead) and a large war debt.

Orlando's fiercest rival at the conference was Wilson, who abhorred the Treaty of London because it smacked of prewar secret diplomacy and ran counter to many of his Fourteen Points. Orlando was at a disadvantage at the conference because, while he spoke French, he did not understand English.

Orlando and his foreign minister, Sidney Sonnino, tried to work a deal whereby they would support Wilson's dream, the League of Nations, if Wilson would agree to give Italy Fiume. More than the other leaders, Orlando was influenced by his foreign advisor, who wanted to use the peace conference to maximize Italian gains. Wilson refused to deal, and Orlando retorted: "Mr. Wilson, there are at least 30,000 Italians in that most Italian of cities. We cannot abandon them to the by no means tender mercies of the Yugoslavs—treaty or no treaty." In fact, the city of Fiume was largely Italian, but its surrounding areas were heavily Slavic, and the Yugoslavs wanted the port equally as much as the Italians. Orlando opposed making Fiume a free port city in the same mold as Danzig.

Orlando wept as he realized that his ministry depended on receiving the port city. In his heart, he believed Italy was due. Both Lloyd George and Clemenceau favored giving Italy Fiume in return for other territorial considerations, but Wilson remained steadfast. The American president was not bound by the London Treaty and not likely to countenance annexationist claims. Remembering the warm welcome he had received in Italy before the conference, Wilson tried to appeal directly to the Italians. He published a manifesto addressed to all Italians urging them to reject what he thought were exaggerated and unjust demands. Orlando was so shaken by Wilson's betrayal that he left the conference confidently remarking that he would let the Italians choose between them.

Orlando attempted to employ Wilson's argument of self-determination by declaring that the whole Dalmatian coast had been a "boulevard of Italy throughout the centuries, which Roman genius and Venetian activity have made noble and great, and whose Italianity . . . today shares with the Italian nation the same feelings of patriotism." Orlando also warned of political upheaval if Italy were denied Fiume. He had little success with either argument, however. Other Allied leaders criticized Orlando for demanding implementation of the Treaty of London while claiming Fiume, contrary to the treaty's provisions. Clemenceau pointed out the irony of Italy demanding Fiume in the name of self-determination while denying Dalmatia the same right. Even Lloyd George thought Orlando's demands excessive.

The Italian people seemed to support Orlando, who remained in Italy from late April to early May waiting for an apology from Wilson that never came. Orlando's gain was ephemeral. The Italian delegation finally returned to Paris, "Fiuming" it is said, just in time to sign the final treaty. Orlando feared that more harm than good would come from not signing the Versailles agreement. He was disappointed, especially since France and Britain seemed to him to come away fulfilled, and the Italian press castigated him for selling Italy out. He was defeated in parliament in June of 1919 (262 to 78) and replaced by Francesco Nitti. From the beginning, Orlando's domestic position had been more tenuous than had been that of the other leaders at Paris.

In general, most Italian political parties were not satisfied with the addition of only Trent, Trieste, Istria, and the Brenner; they demanded more. The Yugoslav question was not settled until 1920, when Italian forces under Gabriele d'Annunizio marched into Fiume to the delight of the Italian people. The issue was resolved in November of 1920, when Italy gained Fiume and the surrounding areas.

Orlando retired from politics in 1925, after the assassination of Matteotti, when it became clear that democracy was no more than a sham. After World War II Orlando reentered politics, serving as president of the postwar constituent assembly. He died in Rome on 1 December 1952.

Glenn R. Sharfman

References

Elcock, Howard. *Portrait of a Decision: The Council of Four and the Treaty of Versailles*. London: Eyre Methuen, 1972.

Goldberg, George. *The Peace to End Peace: The Paris Peace Conference of 1919*. New York: Harcourt, Brace, and World, 1969.

Lowe, C.J., and F. Marzari. *Italian Foreign Policy 1870–1940*. London: Routledge and Paul, 1975.

Mayer, Arno. *Politics and Diplomacy of Peacemaking: Containment and Counterrevolution at Versailles 1913–1919*. New York: Knopf, 1967.

Mee, Charles. *The End of Order: Versailles 1919*. New York: Dutton, 1980.

See also ITALY, HOME FRONT; PARIS PEACE CONFERENCE, 1919; VERSAILLES TREATY

Ostend and Zeebrugge, Raids of (1918)

In April of 1918 the British navy launched raids against the Belgian ports of Ostend and Zeebrugge. Connected by canals to the inland port of Bruges, where the Germans had constructed concrete submarine pens, Zeebrugge and Ostend were valuable bases for submarines and torpedo craft of the German Flanders Flotillas because of their proximity to the strategic Dover Straits.

The final scheme and execution of Operation Z.O was the responsibility of Vice Admiral Roger Keyes, who assumed command of the Dover Patrol on 1 January 1918. Three obsolete cruisers were prepared as blockships to be sunk in the entrance to the Zeebrugge-Bruges canal. Simultaneously, another pair of blockships would be sunk at the entrance to Ostend harbor. The blockships at Zeebrugge would have a particularly difficult task, for they had to steam more than 3,400 feet through the harbor to reach the entrance to the Bruges canal. The harbor was formed by a massive stone mole, connected to the coast by a 300-yard viaduct. The curved mole was 1,840 yards long and 80 yards wide and had batteries at its northern tip, which was at the entrance to the harbor. The British planned to neutralize those batteries by temporarily occupying the northern portion of the mole with approximately 700 Royal Marines and 200 armed sailors. This force would be carried to the seaward side of the mole in the old cruiser *Vindictive* and Mersey ferries *Daffodil* and *Iris II*. *Vindictive* was extensively modified, including ramps and specially hinged brows to be lowered onto the mole for landing the troops.

The attack on the mole was coordinated with an attack on the viaduct by two obsolete submarines, which were to be blown up in order to sever links with the shore. There would be widespread use of smoke screens, and air raids and long-range bombardments of the coastal batteries by monitors would serve as diversions. The crews of the blockships would scuttle them and be picked up from their lifeboats and rafts by motor launches and CMBs (motor torpedo boats). Keyes commanded the operation from the destroyer *Warwick;* he had 82 officers, 1,698 Royal Marines and seamen, and no fewer than 165 vessels.

The operation could take place only under certain conditions of moon and tide and was canceled four times. The first postponement was caused by the unavailability of the requisite amount of smoke-making chemical and the late arrival of ships delayed in conversion. On 11 April the operation was aborted when the force was only some sixteen miles from the objective, because the wind shifted and would have prevented the smoke screen from being effective. On the 13th the force again raised steam, but the wind rose and the sea became too rough.

Operation Z.O was finally carried out on the night of 23 April but it did not go as planned. The wind shifted a few minutes before the *Vindictive* was scheduled to reach the mole; the Germans opened fire and destroyed many of the smoke floats, and the smoke screen lost much of its effectiveness. The *Vindictive* was illuminated by starshells and searchlights, and her upper works were swept by gunfire in the final stages of her approach. There were heavy casualties, and her commander, Captain Alfred Carpenter, increased speed. That, however, caused the *Vindictive* to stop 340 yards farther along the mole than planned and meant that her landing parties could not reach their objective, the batteries on the northern tip of the mole. To make matters worse, the *Vindictive*'s guns could not bear on the troops defending the batteries, and the special grapples failed to grip the mole. The *Daffodil* had to push the cruiser against the mole before the special brows for landing troops could be lowered. By then not all were serviceable, and the ferry had to keep up her efforts the entire time the raiding party was on the mole. The raiders were also fewer than planned, for the *Iris* could not anchor to the mole and eventually had to go alongside the *Vindictive* to discharge her troops. By that time approximately fifty-five minutes had elapsed, and Carpenter sounded the recall after the blockships were observed entering the harbor. The raiders on the mole acted with great valor, but it proved impossible to reach the batteries. It was a wonder any survived, or that the three ships could escape without being sunk.

The British were successful in severing the mole from the shore. The submarine *C.3* was blown up and cut the viaduct. The three blockships were also at least partially successful. Smoke and the heavy fighting on the mole permitted them to escape detection until they were virtually on top of the batteries at the northern tip. They were then subjected to virtually point-blank fire, and the *Thetis* grounded and sank before reaching the canal entrance. Nevertheless, the crews of the *Intrepid* and *Iphigenia* succeeded in scuttling them in the canal.

Crews of the *Brilliant* and *Sirius,* the blockships at Ostend, were less fortunate. The wind suddenly shifted, negating the smoke screen and permitting German gunners to sink the calcium light buoys the British had laid to mark the entrance to the harbor. The Germans had also shifted the light buoy marking the entrance to the harbor a mile to the east, and the blockships were scuttled in the wrong place.

Keyes tried again at Ostend on the night of 10–11 May, but the battered *Vindictive* was sunk in a position blocking only about one-third of the fairway. Keyes was ready to make a third attempt in June, but the admiralty canceled the operation.

The Zeebrugge raid gave a tremendous psychological boost to the British at a moment when it was badly needed because of the substantial success of the Ludendorff Offensive. At last the navy had taken the offensive instead of merely reacting to German initiatives. Losses had been high: 170 killed, 400 wounded, and 45 missing; a destroyer and two motor launches were sunk. But it appeared as if the canal at Zeebrugge was blocked. In reality—and apparently the British Naval Intelligence Division knew soon after the raid—the Germans were able to deepen and widen the channel between the stern of the blockships and the western side of the canal fairly quickly. Furthermore, the Germans claimed with some justification that the raid, in order to have been successful, had to block *both* Zeebrugge and Ostend, for submarines were able to proceed by canal from Bruges to either place. Nevertheless, the psychological factor was of great importance, and Zeebrugge will remain one of the most daring and courageous exploits in the history of the Royal Navy and Royal Marines.

Paul G. Halpern

References

Gladisch, Walter. *Der Krieg in der Nordsee.* Vol. 7: *Vom Sommer 1917 bis zum Kriegsende 1918.* Frankfurt/M: E.S. Mittler und Sohn, 1965.

Halpern, Paul G., ed. *The Keyes Papers.* Vol. 1: *1914–1918.* Publications of the Navy Records Society, 117. Reprint. London: Allen and Unwin, 1979.

Keyes, Admiral of the Fleet Sir Roger. *The Naval Memoirs.* 2 vols. London: Thornton Butterworth, 1933–34.

Newbolt, Henry. *Naval Operations.* Vol. 5. London: Longmans, Green, 1931.

Pitt, Barrie. *Zeebrugge: St. George's Day, 1918.* London: Cassell, 1958.

See also KEYES, SIR ROGER

Ottoman Empire

The defeats sustained by the Ottoman Empire in the First Balkan War discredited Sultan Mehmed V's government. In February of 1913 three members of the Committee on Union and Progress, a political organization formed by the Young Turks in 1909, took control in Constantinople: Enver Pasha became war minister, Talât Pasha served as minister of the interior, and Jemal Pasha took control of the navy as minister of marine. Enver Pasha invited Germany to assist in reorganizing the army, and a military mission led by General Otto Liman von Sanders arrived in December of 1913. The influence of this mission moved far beyond reforming the military. As a result, the leaders of the Ottoman Empire signed a secret alliance with Germany on 2 August in which both parties promised joint action if Russia intervened militarily in the conflict between Austria-Hungary and Serbia. The Ottoman Empire declared its neutrality on 3 August, but it also began mobilization the same day.

Enver Pasha, seeking to gain advantage for the empire, offered to maintain neutrality if Great Britain, France, and Russia agreed to make a large loan and modify the financial capitulations that had given European powers special economic concessions and virtual control of the empire's foreign trade. The Entente refused to negotiate and demanded the dismissal of the German military mission. At the same time the British government took possession of two Turkish dreadnoughts under construction in English shipyards. The empire had paid for the ships with money raised by public subscription, and British seizure of the ships turned public opinion against the Entente. When Enver Pasha accepted Germany's offer to give the warships *Goeben* and *Breslau* to the Turkish navy, further attempts to maintain neutrality by negotiation ended.

The Ottoman Empire abolished all financial capitulations on 8 September. When British naval units refused to allow a Turkish destroyer to enter the Dardanelles on 26 September, German officers closed the Straits. On 28 October the *Goeben* and *Breslau,* still under German command, attacked Russian ships and ports in the Black Sea. Russia declared war on 4 November. Britain and France took the same action the following day. On 14 November Mehmed V proclaimed a holy war against the Entente.

The entry of the Ottoman Empire into World War I on the side of the Central Powers produced far-reaching consequences. The empire controlled land and sea routes to three continents and thereby held a dominant position in the Near East. The closure of the Dardanelles isolated Russia economically and strategically and severely weakened its ability to wage war. Great Britain recognized the empire's ability to threaten land and sea routes to India and committed major resources to the protection of the Suez Canal. The Ottoman Empire thus found itself involved in military campaigns on the Egyptian, Mesopotamian, and Caucasian frontiers, as well as at the Dardanelles. The Turkish army successfully defended the Straits, but it lost Trebizond, Erzurum, Erzinjan, and Sivas to Russia. An attack on the Suez Canal failed and British forces took control of Palestine and Mesopotamia.

During the battles on the Caucasian front, Armenian partisans attacked supply depots behind the Turkish lines. Their actions threatened the ability of the Turkish army to maintain its lines of communication, and the Ottoman government responded to the attacks by ordering Talât Pasha to begin a general deportation of the Armenian population to other areas of the empire. When the Armenians resisted, Turkish troops committed atrocities on a large scale in several forced evacuations. Up to 800,000 Armenians died. After the defeat of the Turkish field armies on the Caucasian frontier, Armenian troops serving in the Russian army entered Anatolia and committed similar atrocities, though on a far smaller scale.

The Ottoman Empire committed all of its economic resources to sustain its ability to wage war. As a result, between 1914 and 1918 the civilian population in all regions suffered hardships of starvation and disease. In 1916 civil unrest forced the Ottoman government to declare martial law for the remainder of the war.

The collapse of Russia and the military victory of Germany on the Eastern Front resulted in the Treaty of Brest-Litovsk, by which the empire regained its Trans-Caucasian territories as well as areas ceded to Russia in 1878.

The government committed military forces to reoccupy and pacify these areas.

When Arab nationalists declared independence at Mecca in June of 1916 the government had no available reserves to send to Palestine. Arab forces occupied Jeddah, laid siege to Medina, and cut the Hejaz railway. In December of 1916 Great Britain formally recognized Arab control of the Hejaz.

On 30 October 1918 an armistice was signed at Mudros ending the war between the Ottoman Empire and the Entente. The government at Constantinople collapsed and its leaders fled. The Ottoman Empire ceased to exist on 15 November when Sultan Mehmed VI (who had succeeded to the throne the previous month on the death of Mehmed V) established a new government under the control of Greek and British troops. At the Versailles peace conference the Entente distributed Ottoman territories among themselves and their allies. These actions led to the Turkish Revolution and four more years of local warfare.

Thomas G. Oakes

References

Ahmed, Amin. *Turkey in the World War.* New Haven: Yale University Press, 1930.

Blaisdell, Donald. *European Financial Control of the Ottoman Empire.* New York: Columbia University Press, 1929.

Kent, Marian, ed. *The Great Powers and the End of the Ottoman Empire.* London: Allen and Unwin, 1984.

Lewis, Geoffrey. *Turkey.* New York: Praeger, 1960.

SEE ALSO CAUCASUS FRONT; EGYPT; KEMAL, MUSTAFA; MEHMED V, AND VI; OTTOMAN EMPIRE, ARMY, NAVY, AND TURKISH REVOLUTION; SÈVRES, TREATY OF

Ottoman Empire, Army

Military defeats in the Balkan Wars immediately preceding World War I led Turkey to seek the assistance of Germany in modernizing and reforming its military forces. A German military mission, led by General Otto Liman von Sanders, arrived at Constantinople in December of 1913. The influence of this military mission involved much more than the reorganization of the Turkish army. Supported by War Minister Enver Pasha, German officers assumed advisory roles at all levels of the Turkish military establishment and, on 2 August 1914, Turkey and Germany signed a secret military alliance. The agreement affirmed Turkish neutrality in the conflict between Austria-Hungary and Serbia, and also provided for mutual action if Russia intervened militarily. This alliance was one of the principal factors bringing Turkey into World War I on the side of the Central Powers at the end of October.

Turkey's entry into the war proved highly significant. The closing of the Dardanelles prevented Russia from receiving vital military supplies and ended the shipment of Russian wheat to Allied military forces on the Western Front. Turkish moves against the Suez Canal threatened British access to India and the Near East. Thus, the Ottoman Empire, whether in the region of the Straits, in Palestine and Syria, or in Mesopotamia, became one of the major areas of conflict. Between 1914 and 1918 Great Britain, France, and Russia committed more than 2.5 million troops as well as naval and air forces to the task of defeating the Ottoman Empire.

The Turkish Army entered World War I unprepared for modern war. The German military mission instituted several reforms in early 1914. Army officers participated in intensive training programs, and units at all levels conducted military exercises, critiqued by German advisors, in order to improve their ability to function effectively. In May of 1914 the government passed an Army Act, making all men liable for military service at eighteen years of age. Two years were to be served in the regular army and twenty-three in the reserves. Exemptions from further service could be purchased after five months of active duty, thus limiting long-term military service to the lower classes; the Arab regions and Anatolia provided most of the men conscripted into military service after the outbreak of war. The law required Christians and Jews to serve in labor battalions rather than regular military units.

Despite their best efforts, the attempts of the German military mission to reform the Turkish army proved ineffective. Turkey's entry into the war in October of 1914 left little time for the reforms to have a positive effect. War Minister Enver Pasha controlled military strategy but proved unequal to the task. Except for the successful defense of the Dardanelles and the capture of British forces at Kul-el-Amara, Turkish military operations consistently ended in defeat.

Enver's attempts to create a new Ottoman Empire diverted military units from vital combat zones and contributed to defeats in Palestine and Mesopotamia. The collapse of Russia and the high quality of its individual soldiers were the key elements in the ability of the Turkish army to sustain operations through 1918. Turkish soldiers fought well throughout the war, despite the hardships imposed by a lack of proper supplies and by inadequate medical services and inept military leadership.

Turkey began the war with four field armies of varying size and composition. The First Army, headquartered at Constantinople, consisted of five infantry corps and one cavalry brigade. The Second Army, based on the opposite side of the Straits in Constantinople, contained one infantry corps and a cavalry brigade. Third Army, with headquarters in Erzurum, deployed two infantry corps near the Russian border. Fourth Army, headquartered at Damascus, consisted of three infantry corps. Between 1914 and 1916 five additional armies were created and sent into combat. These nine armies remained active until the end of the war.

Each Turkish infantry corps consisted of one active and one or two reserve divisions. The army contained thirty-six divisions in October of 1914. By 1918 the army deployed seventy divisions. Each division consisted of three regiments of three battalions, a cavalry squadron, and an artillery regiment of twenty-four to thirty-six field guns. Each battalion contained up to twenty-four officers and 900 men organized in three infantry companies and one machine-gun company. Theoretically, each division totaled 19,000 effectives of all arms, but most never reached that level.

In 1914 the army contained 115 regular cavalry squadrons. Another 135 reserve squadrons were mobilized by the end of 1915. Poor equipment and a lack of good horses made the cavalry ineffective throughout the war.

Turkish artillery units were organized into 211 field batteries and 124 fortress batteries in October of 1914. Field artillery operated at the divisional level. Fortress batteries normally received orders from a field army headquarters or from naval commanders.

Throughout the war, the army failed to supply its troops with high-quality equipment. Infantry units utilized an 1892-design 7.65mm Mauser rifle. Some reserve divisions entered combat with single-shot Martini-Henry rifles. Cavalry units carried Mauser carbines, swords, and revolvers. One third of the artillery units utilized the 75mm Krupp field gun. Other batteries used older 87mm German field guns as well as several smooth-bored howitzers. A lack of modern field guns remained a problem to the end of the war in field-combat situations. Fortress batteries achieved greater success, especially when utilized against naval targets. Machine-gun companies were equipped with Maxim and Hotchkiss guns.

The Turkish army suffered from a lack of adequate support services. The German military mission provided technicians in an unsuccessful attempt to improve production in the Turkish armaments industry. Shortages of weapons and ammunition remained a principal factor in Turkish military defeats throughout the war. The medical corps, lacking proper supplies and facilities, proved unable to cope with the high number of casualties sustained by Turkish troops. Desertion rates increased as soldiers sought medical care in civilian facilities. Lack of medical care also caused many to avoid conscription into military service.

Approximately two million soldiers served in the Turkish army during the war. Up to 750,000 deserted, and casualties probably totaled 500,000 in killed, wounded, and missing. A lack of accurate record-keeping prevented the development of precise figures, and military commanders above the battalion level never knew the exact number of men serving in their commands. Declines in the strength of military formations continued throughout the war. By November of 1918 the largest field army contained fewer than 15,000 effectives, and no infantry corps contained more than one division.

The collapse of the Ottoman Empire in 1918 brought with it the dissolution of the Turkish army. But the excellent qualities of its individual soldiers allowed Mustafa Kemal to quickly rebuild the army as an effective fighting force. The military victories achieved by the army between 1920 and 1923 contributed significantly to the ability of the government to establish an independent republic.

Ekkehart P. Guth
Thomas G. Oakes

References

Ahmed, Amin. *Turkey in the World War.* New Haven: Yale University Press, 1930.

Haythornthwaite, Philip J. *The World War One Source Book.* London: Arms and Armour, 1992.

Larcher, Maurice. *The Turkish War in the World War*. Washington: Army War College, 1931.

Pomianski, Josef. *Der Zusammenbruch des Ottomanischen Reiches*. Leipzig: Karl Ludwig, 1928.

Trumpener, Ulrich. *Germany and the Ottoman Empire 1914–1918*. Princeton: Princeton University Press, 1968.

See also GALLIPOLI CAMPAIGN; KEMAL, MUSTAFA; OTTOMAN EMPIRE

Ottoman Empire, Navy

The Turkish navy had been on the verge of taking delivery of two super dreadnoughts being built in England when the war began, but the ships were seized by the British. Taking advantage of the situation, the German government "sold" (to avoid the obligations of international law concerning neutrality) the battlecruiser *Goeben* and light cruiser *Breslau* to the Turks. The two ships flew the Turkish ensign and were renamed *Sultan Yavuz Selim* and *Midilli,* respectively. They were the newest and most effective ships of the Ottoman navy.

The overwhelming sea power of the British and French in the Mediterranean forced the Ottoman navy, with rare and fleeting exceptions, to confine its operations to the Black Sea. The remainder of the Turkish fleet consisted of a pair of old battleships purchased from Germany in 1910, an ancient coast defense ship of scant value, two protected cruisers, eight relatively modern destroyers, and a handful of older and smaller torpedo boats and gunboats. The material condition of the fleet and state of training left much to be desired, although that could be partially explained by the relative inactivity imposed by the Tripolitan War (1911–12) and Balkan Wars (1912–13).

Rear-Admiral Wilhelm Souchon, commander of German Mediterranean forces, was named commander of the Turkish navy, and German naval officers monopolized the most important positions. That situation was enhanced by the fact that Ottoman Minister of Marine Djemal Pasha was also commander of the Fourth Turkish Army, military governor of Syria, and usually absent from Constantinople. Ottoman Minister of War Enver Pasha and the high command made the final decisions, but in practice the Germans had a good deal of leeway. German officers and men were seconded to Turkish ships, and it would be more accurate to speak of "Turkish-German" rather than "Ottoman" forces. The battleships and even the protected cruisers were too slow to work effectively with the *Goeben* at sea, and the destroyer flotilla therefore had the more important role. A German officer served as commodore of the flotilla, and other German officers commanded its divisions. In the larger ships there were two commanders: a German to command in battle and a Turkish officer to command in port and handle internal administration.

Souchon, with the connivance of Enver Pasha and a pro-war clique of Turkish officials, was able to precipitate Turkey's entrance into the war with an attack on the Russian Black Sea coast on 29 October. The Russians suffered little loss, and in 1915 their new dreadnoughts, their fast, large destroyers, and their submarines forced the Ottoman fleet into a strictly defensive role. The navy could do little to oppose the Allied naval forces during the Dardanelles Campaign, although the minelayer *Nousret* is credited with laying a row of mines that subsequently sank three Allied battleships on 18 March. It was not the Ottoman navy, however, that doomed the Anglo-French attack, but the failure to silence the shore batteries protecting the minefields. The destroyer *Muvanet* later sank the old British battleship *Goliath,* but the Turks lost a battleship and coast defense ship to British submarines in the Sea of Marmara. After the Dardanelles Campaign, the Ottoman navy proved unable to counter the large Russian destroyers that threatened to cut the important traffic in coal from Zonguldak and Eregli to Constantinople, nor could it hinder Russian amphibious operations on the coast of Lazistan in 1916. The Russian navy controlled the Black Sea until Russia's collapse at the end of 1917. Turkish naval forces in Mesopotamia were also eventually overwhelmed.

Paul G. Halpern

References

Conway's All the World's Fighting Ships, 1906–1921. London: Conway Maritime Press, 1985.

Halpern, Paul G. *The Naval War in the Mediterranean, 1914–1918*. London and Annapolis, Md.: Allen and Unwin and Naval Institute Press, 1987.

Köppen, Paul. *Die Überwasserstreitkräfte und ihr Technik*. Berlin: E.S. Mittler und Sohn, 1930.

Lorey, Hermann. *Der Krieg in den türkischen Gewässern*. 2 vols. Berlin: E.S. Mittler und Sohn, 1928–38.

Mäkelä, Matti E. *Auf den Spuren der Goeben*. Munich: Bernard & Graefe, 1979.

See also BLACK SEA, NAVAL WAR IN; DARDANELLES CAMPAIGN; DJEMAL PASHA; GOEBEN AND BRESLAU; RUSSIA, NAVY; SOUCHON, WILHELM

Ottoman Empire: The Turkish Revolution

The Ottoman Empire signed an armistice agreement with the Entente powers at Mudros on 30 October 1918. The terms of the armistice opened the Dardanelles, guaranteed access to the Black Sea and gave Entente troops the right to occupy all strategic areas and installations. Also, the Dardanelles were to be open to all nations. The Turkish army was to be demobilized, except where military units were needed to preserve order. The armistice also required Turkey to withdraw its troops from Persia, Syria, Mesopotamia, Palestine, and the Trans-Caucasian frontier. Finally, German, Austrian, and Hungarian military personnel were to leave Turkey within thirty days.

The Entente's occupation and partition of Turkey angered many Turkish leaders. When Greek troops landed at Izmir in May of 1919 and advanced into the Anatolian interior, General Mustafa Kemal protested and demanded that the government resist, even if it meant using Turkish military forces. The Greek landings enraged the Turkish population and inspired a resurgence of national patriotism. Thus, when the government assigned Kemal to the position of inspector general of the Third Army in Eastern Anatolia, he used the opportunity to call for an end to foreign occupation and for the reassertion of Turkish sovereignty. Resistance groups in the area formed the Eastern Anatolian Society for the Defense of National Rights, and they elected Kemal as their chairman. The government at Constantinople ordered Kemal's arrest, but local authorities refused to comply. At the Congress of Erzerum in July of 1919, Kemal and his supporters adopted a resolution calling for the restoration of national frontiers and the convocation of a national assembly. The Congress of Sivas in September of 1919 called for a free and independent Turkey. A representative committee was chosen, with Kemal as president.

Elections in February of 1920 established a nationalist majority in the parliament at Constantinople. The British occupied the capital in March of 1920, arrested several nationalists, and exiled others to Anatolia, where they enlarged the number of Kemal supporters. On 23 April 1920, a Grand Assembly met at Ankara and proclaimed the Turkish Revolution and established an independent republic. The assembly declared that Sultan Mehmed VI's government no longer represented the Turkish people.

Kemal and his supporters refused to accept the Treaty of Sèvres, dictated by the Entente in August of 1920. The Kemal government signed an agreement with the Soviet Union on 16 March 1921 and obtained military supplies that allowed the Turkish army to rearm. The army, which had been rebuilt by Kemal, launched an offensive and, after several months of campaigning, on 22 August 1922 decisively defeated the Greeks at the Battle of Sakriya. By 9 September the Greeks had been driven from Anatolia and the Entente negotiated a new armistice agreement with Kemal that provided for the withdrawal of all foreign troops from Anatolia and Eastern Thrace.

A new peace agreement, the Treaty of Lausanne, was signed on 23 July 1923. On 23 October 1923, the National Assembly proclaimed Turkey a republic and elected Mustafa Kemal as the first president of the new nation. By the end of the year Great Britain, France, Germany, and the Soviet Union had all formally recognized the Kemal government and established diplomatic relations. On 3 March 1924, the government abolished the caliphate, thus completing the Turkish Revolution.

Ekkehart P. Guth
Thomas G. Oakes

References

Ahmed, Amin. *Turkey in the World War*. New Haven: Yale University Press, 1930.

Kedourie, Elie. *The Destruction of the Old Ottoman Empire, 1914–1921*. Manchester: Hassocks, 1978.

Kent, Marian, ed. *The Great Powers and the End of the Ottoman Empire*. London: Allen and Unwin, 1984.

Lewis, Geoffrey. *Turkey*. New York: Praeger, 1960.

See also KEMAL, MUSTAFA; LAUSANNE, TREATY OF; OTTOMAN EMPIRE; SÈVRES, TREATY OF

Outbreak of the First World War

The gunshots that killed Austrian Archduke Franz Ferdinand and his wife Sophie in Sarajevo on 28 June 1914 reverberated across Europe. As German Chancellor Otto von Bismarck had predicted, "some damned fool thing in the Balkans" provoked a general European war. Coming on the heels of a series of crises—Morocco in 1905, Bosnia-Herzegovina in 1908, Morocco again in 1911, and the Balkan Wars in 1912–13—the assassination raised the specter of immediate European war.

Obviously, Austria-Hungary was the great power most directly affected. Although Franz Ferdinand had not been popular, the news that the heir to the throne had been assassinated outraged Austrians, who immediately and correctly suspected Serbian involvement. Those members of the imperial government who had been clamoring for a punitive war against Serbia now had their excuse. In February Austro-Hungarian chief of the general staff General Franz Conrad von Hötzendorf had written to his German counterpart, Helmuth von Moltke, "What are we waiting for?" He now remarked, "The hour has struck with shrill clangor." Foreign Minister Count Leopold von Berchtold joined in the hard-line approach. Even Emperor Franz Josef, who in 1913 had warned his ministers that a confrontation with Serbia must be avoided because it would result in a general war, had come to the position that conflict with Serbia was unavoidable. Hungarian Premier Count István Tisza was the only major official to urge caution.

It was largely to overcome Tisza's opposition that the imperial government decided to take two preliminary steps before taking action against Serbia. The first was to seek assurances of German support in case an Austro-Serbian war resulted in Russian intervention. The second was the appointment of senior diplomat Friedrich von Wiesner to lead the investigation of the assassination and seek proof of Serbian involvement. Historian Joachim Remak has argued, however, that Austria-Hungary might have been better served had it retaliated imme- diately while world opinion was still on its side. That might have localized the conflict. By de- laying, Remak asserts, Austria-Hungary made itself appear to be using the assassination as an excuse to crush Serbia, thereby increasing the likelihood of foreign intervention.

While Wiesner began his investigation, Berchtold sent a special envoy, Alexander Hoyos, to Berlin with a personal letter from Franz Josef to Kaiser Wilhelm II. On Sunday, 5 July, Austrian ambassador Count Laszlo Szögyeny presented the letter, in which Franz Josef warned that Austria-Hungary could not survive the "Pan-Slav flood" unless "Serbia's role as a power factor in the Balkans is ended." It concluded by asking for German support in that effort. Over lunch, the ever-bombastic kai- ser, who had been a personal friend of Franz Ferdinand's and had visited him just two weeks before his assassination, told Szögyeny to in- form Franz Josef that he could count on "Germany's full support" even if it meant "se- rious European complications." More specifi- cally, he promised aid should Russia intervene and even encouraged Austria-Hungary to at- tack quickly before Russia had time to prepare. After Chancellor Theobald von Bethmann Hollweg confirmed Wilhelm's promises later that afternoon, Szögyeny wired Berchtold in- forming him of Germany's "blank check."

Armed with the "blank check," Austrian authorities awaited Wiesner's report on the in- vestigation. Although Austrian authorities had succeeded in apprehending the conspirators, they were unable to substantiate any direct link to the Serbian government or to the secret ter- rorist organization *Narodna Odbrana*, "Black Hand," which had in fact orchestrated the as- sassination. After poring over the evidence, on 13 July Wiesner issued his report. While he had been able to determine that the bombs used were of Serbian manufacture, that the guns used had been issued from Serbian army stocks, and that minor Serbian officials had helped the as- sassins cross the border into Bosnia, Wiesner concluded: "There is nothing to indicate, or even to give rise to suspicion that the Serbian government knew about the plot, its prepara- tion, or the procurement of arms. On the con- trary, there are indications that this is impos- sible."

Despite Wiesner's report, Vienna was de- termined to teach Serbia a lesson whether its role in the assassination could be proved or not. The attitude of the Serbian government in the aftermath of the assassination certainly encouraged hard-liners within the Austro-Hungarian government and undermined Tisza's efforts to urge caution. Serbian officials, including Premier Nikola Pašić, who had known about the plot beforehand, made no effort to launch an investigation of their own or arrest Serbian officials known to be involved. Indeed, the government warned Milan Ciganović, a Serbian railroad employee whom the Austrians knew had aided the assassins, to go into hiding. In addition, the Serbian government took no steps to muzzle the Serbian press, which not only launched a series of tirades against Austria-Hungary but also glorified the assassination as a patriotic act. In response, the Austrian press naturally demanded retaliation. On 19 July, therefore, the joint council of the Dual Monarchy approved the text of an ultimatum that was to be presented to Serbia on 23 July.

Although the Austrians had hoped to keep the ultimatum secret until it could be sprung on Serbia on 23 July, rumors of its contents were already in circulation. Indeed, on 18 July, one day before the text was formally approved, Russian Foreign Minister Sergei Sazonov informed the Austrian ambassador: "Russia would not be indifferent to any effort to humiliate Serbia. Russia would not permit Austria to use menacing language or military measures against Serbia." Although this should have given Austrian officials pause, for any Austro-Serbian conflict clearly threatened Russian intervention, it did not. Even when French President Raymond Poincaré—who had arrived in St. Petersburg on 20 July on a state visit—warned the Austrian ambassador that Austria should act cautiously because "Russia has an ally, France," the Austro-Hungarian government went forward with its plans. At 18:00 on 23 July, the ultimatum was presented to the Serbian government in Belgrade.

The ultimatum began by citing the 1909 promise that Serbia had made in the aftermath of the Bosnian Annexation Crisis to "desist from the attitude of protest and opposition . . . and to live on the footing of friendly and neighborly relations with [Austria-Hungary] . . . in the future." It then detailed Serbia's failure to comply: its toleration of anti-Austrian statements in the press; the participation of Serbian officers and officials in subversive intrigues; the activities of the *Narodna Odbrana* in planning the assassination. As a result of these actions,

the Austro-Hungarian government declared that it could no longer "maintain the attitude of patient tolerance which it has observed for years toward these agitations which center in Belgrade and are spread thence into the territories of the Monarchy." Instead, Austria-Hungary felt that it was under the "obligation to put an end to those intrigues, which constitute a standing menace to the peace of the Monarchy."

The terms of the ultimatum were deliberately direct and brutal in their demands on the Serbian government and were designed not to be accepted. The Serbian government was to condemn all propaganda directed against Austria-Hungary and publicly apologize for the assassination. Any anti-Austrian publications and organizations, such as *Narodna Odbrana,* were to be shut down immediately, and steps were to be taken to prevent anti-Austrian propaganda in the public schools and army. The Serbian government was "to institute a judicial inquiry against every participant in the conspiracy of the twenty-eighth of June who may be found in Serbian territory" and allow Austrian officials to participate in the proceedings. It was to arrest Major Voja Tankosić and Ciganović, Serbian officials who had aided the assassins, and it was to dismiss and punish its border guards. Serbia was given exactly forty-eight hours, until 18:00 on Saturday, 25 July, to respond.

When the Serbian reply came on 25 July at 17:58—two minutes before the deadline—it was evasive on the key points. Serbia promised to enact strict penalties against anti-Austrian propaganda in the press, to dissolve the *Narodna Odbrana,* and "severely punish" the border guards responsible for helping the assassins cross into Bosnia. While Tankosić had been arrested, the Serbs would not turn him over to the Austrians. Since Ciganović held an Austrian passport and could not easily escape extradition, the government declared him "missing," when in fact it had ordered him to go into hiding. On the most critical issue, Serbia refused to allow Austrian officials to participate in any investigation on Serbian soil. While Serbia cited the need to protect its sovereignty, the real reason was to keep the Austrians from discovering that the plot to assassinate Franz Ferdinand led straight to the Serbian chief of military intelligence, Colonel Dragutin Dimitrijević, and that high-ranking officials, including Pašić, had known about the plot in advance.

As had been intended all along, the Austrian envoy informed Pašić that the reply was unacceptable and that diplomatic relations were thereby severed. By 20:00 Conrad ordered the mobilization of Austro-Hungarian forces against Serbia. Serbia had certainly anticipated the Austrian response, for it had issued orders for mobilization even before making its reply. What really mattered, however, was how the great powers would react, for that would determine whether an Austro-Serbian conflict remained localized or became a general European war.

The key response to Austria-Hungary's rejection of the Serbian reply came from Russia. When the terms of the ultimatum had become public on 24 July, Pan-Slavic opinion in Russia was outraged and demanded action. Having failed to support Serbia in the Bosnian Annexation Crisis of 1908 and the Balkan Wars of 1912–13, Russian officials feared that, if they allowed Austria to humiliate Serbia a third time, not only would Russia lose its influence in the Balkans but the czarist regime would face a popular revolution at home as well. The Russian council of ministers, therefore, approved Sazonov's proposal to mobilize several army corps along Austria-Hungary's borders to show support for Serbia. On 25 July, after Sazonov had received French Ambassador Maurice Paléologue's assurances of French support, Czar Nicholas II ordered "partial mobilization."

While it is unclear how the Russian response affected the Serbian reply, it had a dramatic impact upon Germany. Although German government officials acted surprised by the severity of the terms, they clearly knew what was coming. On 18 July, in fact, Foreign Minister Gottlieb von Jagow had wired German ambassador to England Prince Karl Max von Lichnowsky that Austria-Hungary intended "to force a showdown with Serbia" and that, while Germany hoped to keep the conflict localized, if Russia intervened it would mean war. Bethmann Hollweg echoed those sentiments in his instructions of 23 July to German ambassadors in Paris, London, and St. Petersburg, who were to demand nonintervention.

If German diplomats had hoped to keep the Austro-Serbian conflict localized, Russian mobilization finally caused them to realize that their "blank check" was about to be cashed. The German general staff was particularly alarmed for fear that its military plans would be compromised. Facing the prospects of a two-front war against France and Russia, it had developed the Schlieffen Plan, which committed the German army to a "quick" victory against France before Russia could complete its mobilization. With each passing minute that Russian mobilization went unanswered, the German timetable for victory was increasingly compromised.

The British and French were slow to realize that a general European war was looming on the horizon. Although British Foreign Minister Sir Edward Grey proposed a conference of Great Britain, France, Germany, and Italy—the four powers not directly affected—in an effort to arbitrate the dispute, he never clearly stated the British position. Indeed, although many in Britain considered the Austrian note harsh, they thought it was justified. Poincaré and Premier René Viviani, who also served as foreign minister, were at the time at sea returning to France from their visit to St. Petersburg, and thus the French response devolved upon Paléologue. He urged the Russians to take a firm stance and assured them of France's fullest support. More important, Paléologue deliberately misinformed officials in Paris about Russian plans and exaggerated France's support for Russia's hard line against Austria-Hungary. By the time Poincaré and Viviani arrived in Paris, events were beyond their control.

Ironically, it was Wilhelm II who finally recognized the possibility of war and began belated efforts to halt it. Although he rejected Grey's proposals for a four-power conference, on 27 July he urged the Austrian government to accept the Serbian reply as a basis for negotiation. Indeed, after reading the Serbian reply on 28 July, Wilhelm expressed great relief by declaring: "A great moral success for Vienna, but with it, all reason for war is gone." On that same day, however, Austria-Hungary declared war on Serbia without consulting Berlin.

Despite the Austrian declaration of war, Wilhelm II tried to stave off a general European war by ordering the foreign office to propose a "pledge plan" to Vienna whereby Austria would occupy Belgrade as a Serbian pledge of fulfillment. The great powers would then have time for talks to resolve the crisis. Bethmann Hollweg delayed transmitting the kaiser's proposal for several hours, however, and instructed the German ambassador in Vienna to "avoid giving rise to the impression that we wish to hold Austria back." The proposal was, he explained:

simply a matter of finding a way to realize Austria's desired aim, that of cutting the vital cord of the Greater Serbia propaganda, without at the same time precipitating a world war, and, if the latter cannot be avoided in the end, of improving, in so far as possible, the conditions under which we shall have to wage it.

Although Bethmann Hollweg sent a stronger demand the following day (29 July), German Chief of Staff Helmuth von Moltke wired Conrad and urged him not to negotiate and "to mobilize immediately against Russia." It is thus hardly surprising that Vienna did not take the kaiser's plan seriously and rejected a similar British proposal offered by Grey later on 29 July.

The little room that remained for diplomatic maneuvering quickly disappeared on 29 July when Austro-Hungarian forces began the bombardment of Belgrade. Mass demonstrations broke out in Russian cities as Nicholas II yielded to pressure from his ministers and ordered a general mobilization of Russian forces. After receiving a personal appeal from Wilhelm II to work together to resolve the crisis, however, the czar canceled his earlier order for general mobilization in favor of partial mobilization against Austria alone. Sazonov and the Russian general staff, however, berated Nicholas for taking partial measures. Indeed, chief of staff General Nikolai Yanushkevich declared that partial mobilization was impossible; it had to be all or nothing. In any event, they argued that Russia needed as much preparation as possible should a general war occur. Unable to withstand their pressure, on 30 July Nicholas again reversed course and ordered general mobilization. This time Sazonov instructed Yanushkevich to "smash your telephone" so the czar could not again change the orders.

Russian mobilization was the key factor in turning the Austro-Serbian conflict into a general war. On 31 July, after repeated demands from Moltke, Bethmann Hollweg finally proclaimed a "threatening danger of war" and gave Russia twelve hours to cease its mobilization. At the same time Germany sent an ultimatum to France, giving the French eighteen hours to promise to remain neutral in the event of war between Germany and Russia. More important, as a sign of "good faith," the French would allow Germany to occupy the fortresses of Toul and Verdun. Grey, meanwhile, demanded that Germany and France give Britain assurances that

they would respect the neutrality of Belgium. While the French quickly affirmed they would, the Germans remained silent. Finally, Austria-Hungary, having previously mobilized only against Serbia, declared general mobilization.

By 1 August military necessity had taken priority over diplomacy. While France had avoided provoking Germany, it had made no efforts to reign in the Russians. On 1 August, moreover, Paris replied to the German ultimatum by announcing that it would follow "its own interests." At 15:55 France ordered mobilization, which was followed at 16:00 by German mobilization. Having received no reply from Russia, at 19:10 Germany declared war on Russia.

With the German declaration of war, the die was cast. Since the Schlieffen Plan required that France be defeated before Russia's mobilization was complete, on 2 August Germany invaded Luxembourg and demanded that the Belgium government give it right of passage through Belgium. The British cabinet, meanwhile, voted to assure France that Britain would honor its agreement under the 1912 Anglo-French Naval Convention to protect the French coast. It was Germany's violation of Belgian neutrality that hastened Britain's entry into the war. As German troops entered Belgium on 3 August, Germany declared war on France on the excuse of "frontier violations." When Germany rejected a British ultimatum to stop its invasion of Belgium, Britain declared war at midnight on 4 August.

Although none of the European powers actually wanted a general European conflict, the crisis precipitated by the Archduke Franz Ferdinand's assassination quickly escalated into war. European diplomats were slow to realize the implications of their actions. Having narrowly avoided war in earlier crises, they failed to learn how to prevent potential conflict from arising. In issuing its "blank check," for example, German diplomats failed to realize the domino effect of a "localized" Balkan war. Russia, likewise, pursued a brinkmanship policy against Austria-Hungary that forced Germany's hand. Like the Germans, the French failed to reign in their allies. The British, alone of the great powers, might have been able to serve as an "honest broker," but the cabinet was divided and by the time Grey offered arbitration it was too late. Before anyone knew it, the July crisis gave way to the guns of August. Perhaps Grey summed it up best: "The lamps are going out all over Europe; we shall not see them lit again in our lifetime."

Justin D. Murphy

References

Hale, Oron J. *The Great Illusion, 1900–1914.* "The Rise of Modern Europe" series. New York: Harper and Row, 1971.

Langdon, John W. *July 1914: Long Debate, 1918–1990.* New York: Berg, 1991.

Remak, Joachim. *The Origins of World War I, 1871–1914.* New York: Holt, Rinehart, and Winston, 1967.

Schmitt, Bernadotte E., and Harold C. Vedeler. *The World in the Crucible, 1914–1919.* "The Rise of Modern Europe" series. New York: Harper and Row, 1984.

See also BETHMANN HOLLWEG, THEOBALD VON; CONRAD VON HÖTZENDORF, FRANZ; FRANZ FERDINAND; FRANZ JOSEF; GREY, EDWARD; HISTORIOGRAPHY OF THE OUTBREAK OF THE WAR; LICHNOWSKY, COUNT KARL MAX VON; NICHOLAS II; ORIGINS OF THE FIRST WORLD WAR; PALÉOLOGUE, GEORGES MAURICE; PAŠIĆ, NIKOLA; SAZONOV, SERGEI; WILHELM II

P

Paderewski, Ignacy Jan (1860–1941)

Polish virtuoso pianist, composer, and politician. Born on 18 November 1860 at Kurylówka, Paderewski studied at Warsaw and then Vienna, where he made his professional debut. He quickly made his reputation as an interpreter of Schumann, Chopin, and Liszt. At the outbreak of the war, Paderewski was co-organizer of a "general committee of assistance for the victims of the War in Poland," established in Switzerland. In 1915 he went to the United States as its representative. Through concerts and speeches, Paderewski raised funds and lobbied for the cause of an independent Polish state. In 1917 he became the representative in Washington of the Paris-based Polish National Committee, and he played a crucial role in winning President Wilson's support for the re-creation of an independent Poland.

After the war Paderewski returned to Poland, where he formed a coalition ministry. From January to December of 1919 he was Poland's premier and foreign minister and represented her at the Paris Peace Conference. During the Second World War Paderewski was again involved in the cause of an independent Poland as chairman of the National Council (the mini parliament-in-exile in London). Paderewski died in New York on 29 June 1941.

Andrzej Suchcitz

References

Drozdowski, Marian. *Ignacy Jan Paderewski. Zarys biofrafii politycznei.* Warsaw: Wydawnictwo Interpress, 1979.
Zamoyski, Adam. *Paderewski.* London: Collins, 1982.

See also POLAND

Painlevé, Paul (1863–1933)

French premier (September-November 1917), born in Paris on 5 December 1863. Painlevé's prodigious gifts in mathematics earned him numerous awards and a prestigious academic career with successive appointments to the universities of Lille and Paris, and chairs at the Ecole Normale Supérieure and the Ecole Polytechnique. He entered parliament in 1910 as an independent socialist.

A prewar interest in aviation and military technology made Painlevé an active member of the parliamentary committees on air and naval affairs when the war began. He used his first cabinet post, that of minister of education and military inventions under Aristide Briand, to familiarize himself with France's generals and military policy. An early and persistent critic of Joffre, Painlevé supported General Maurice Sarrail's Balkan strategy. In March of 1917 he became minister of war in the new Alexandre Ribot government.

Increasingly influenced by General Henri-Philippe Pétain's arguments for a defensive strategy and deeply skeptical of the prospects of General Robert Nivelle's offensive, Painlevé was still unable to prevent that April debacle. Afterward, however, he engineered Nivelle's replacement by Pétain in May and worked vigorously to bring to an end the army mutinies that followed the failed offensive. Reviewing individual death sentences personally, Painlevé later claimed to have limited executions of mutineers to twenty-three.

As premier from September to November of 1917, Painlevé continued to support Pétain, visited Italy with David Lloyd George after the Battle of Caporetto, and worked to develop a unified Allied war strategy. He was replaced as premier by Georges Clemenceau. Painlevé served as minister of war in several postwar governments and again as premier in 1925. He died in Paris on 29 October 1933.

David L. Longfellow

References

King, Jere Clemens. *Generals and Politicians.* Berkeley: University of California Press, 1951.

Painlevé, Paul. *Comment j'ai nommé Foch et Pétain.* Paris: F. Alcan, 1924.

Watt, Richard M. *Dare Call It Treason.* New York: Simon and Schuster, 1963.

See also FRANCE, HOME FRONT; NIVELLE OF-FENSIVE; PÉTAIN, HENRI-PHILIPPE

Palestine and Syria, 1914–18

The escape of the *Goeben* and *Breslau* into Turkish waters was a flashpan that did not immediately explode. Enver Pasha, dynamic leader of the Young Turks, and his German allies needed more time in which to steer a wavering Ottoman Empire into war. Conversely, the already overburdened Entente clung to the desperate illusion of Turkish neutrality weeks after it was obvious that full mobilization was taking place. Nevertheless, on 27 October elements of the Turkish navy bombarded Russian Black Sea ports and within days the Middle East was at war.

From November of 1914 to the summer of 1916 the Entente was on the defensive in the southwestern front of the Middle East. Britain had been in Egypt since the 1882 intervention, ostensibly to protect the Suez Canal. Aggressive Young Turks and the German Military Mission in Constantinople, therefore, had a double reason to take the offensive against Egypt—to block critical Allied shipping in the Suez Canal and to reclaim a lost province.

From November of 1914 to January of 1915 Djemal Pasha assembled some 25,000 men in Palestine. That January the expeditionary force crossed the Sinai Desert to assault the canal; Djemal Pasha hoped that Egyptians would rise to greet him in a holy war against the British.

The expedition was boldly executed under the direct command of Kress von Kressenstein. The British commander in Egypt, General Sir John Maxwell, had been alerted by aerial reconnaissance of the Turkish approach. Outnum-bered by more than three to one and at a striking disadvantage in guns and aircraft, the Turks nonetheless succeeded in paddling several pontoon rafts across the canal before being driven back (2 February). Happily for the Turks, the British did not pursue. Tactically unsuccessful, the assault against the canal was a partial strategic success. British troops earmarked for the Western Front were retained in that theater, and Allied attention was distracted at a time when the Dardanelles might have been forced and when Allied troops might have been landed near Constantinople.

General Sir Archibald Murray assumed command of the newly constituted Egyptian Expeditionary Force (EEF) in March of 1916. Conversely, the Turks were reinforced by a small German group code-named "Pasha 1" and by June had formed the Turkish Expeditionary Force on the Sinai-Palestine frontier.

The middle of 1916 may be seen as a turning point in the campaigns. The Arab Revolt ignited against Ottoman rule in June. The powder keg was Mecca, where Hussein Ibn Ali, Sharif, Amir of Mecca, King of the Hejaz and Keeper of the Holy City, raised the standard of revolt. Medina and other localities in the Hejaz followed. Secondly, the EEF met and halted a Turkish thrust of 15,000 men across the Sinai at Români (3 August), inflicting 5,000 casualties on the attackers; thereafter, the British and their allies held the initiative.

Murray's most important contribution to the Allied cause was logistical. A water pipeline and railway were constructed from Egypt across the Sinai Peninsula to the Palestinian border. Standing camps, aerodromes, and roads were established, for the most part with Egyptian labor. By the end of the year Murray's mounted arm, the Desert Column, had flanked the last of the Turkish strongholds in the Sinai, Magdhaba, and Rafa. The British stood before Gaza on the Mediterranean Sea, the ancient portcullis leading into Palestine.

Murray's undoing proved to be the Turkish line he now faced, which covered twenty-five miles from the coastline through Gaza along natural ridges to Tel-es-Sheria and thence to biblical Beersheba. Gaza commanded the coast road as well as the eastward radiation of roads into Palestine. To the south, Beersheba commanded wells critical to any force attempting to flank the Turkish line through the desert.

Murray cut his teeth twice on this parapet of Palestine and failed. The First Battle of Gaza,

26–27 March 1917, commenced during the night, when the Desert Column penetrated the eastern perimeter of Gaza and nearly encircled the town. Night maneuvers are always tricky, and in the morning the infantry discovered that they had moved into a disadvantageous position; Kressenstein's Turks then forced the EEF to retreat.

Murray misrepresented the results of the battle to the Imperial General Staff and was, consequently, ordered to try again. The Second Battle of Gaza, on 17–19 April, resembled a miniature battle on the Western Front. The war office had even sent out eight Mark 1 heavy tanks. Instead of trenches and barbed wire, however, the British met recently reinforced redoubts and cactus hedges. They were repulsed.

Despite the check, early summer of 1917 saw another turning point in the campaigns. On 29 June General Edmund Allenby was transferred from France as Murray's replacement. The Imperial General Staff had recommended Allenby because of his independent initiative. Prime Minister David Lloyd George informed the new commander of the EEF that he wanted Jerusalem "as a Christmas present for the British people," and two divisions of infantry and more than three squadrons of aircraft followed as a token of commitment. Characteristically, Allenby moved his headquarters near the front line and re-formed the EEF into three corps, the 20th, 21st, and the Desert Mounted, a cavalry detachment.

Over the next weeks the Royal Flying Corps took to the skies and achieved aerial mastery over the Gaza-Beersheba line. Having prevented Turkish reconnaissance, Allenby's intelligence department "leaked" special papers purporting that extensive operations were underway to assault Gaza. Instead, 20th Corps secretly deployed opposite Beersheba, while the Desert Mounted flanked to the southeast from 28–31 October. The 21st Corps pinned Gaza.

On the 31st the Australian Light Horse delivered their famous charge and captured the critical wells of Beersheba. Allenby then rolled up the enemy line, and the Turks were forced to relinquish their stubborn hold on Gaza. The EEF pursued the retreating Turks over the plains of Philistia. At Huj and at El Mughar EEF cavalry demonstrated that mounted shock action was possible and effective, even in the twentieth century. In seventeen days Allenby had reduced his enemy's combat strength by one-third and had pushed the front back fifty miles.

Unfortunately, the bid for the Holy City had to be made as an "end run," a race against time. Heavy seasonal rains had begun, and the hills before Jerusalem were eminently defensible. Furthermore, in an attempt to recoup their flagging fortunes, the Germans and Turks had formed a special army group, code named Yilderim (Lightning). Commanded by the redoubtable Field Marshal Erich von Falkenhayn, it consisted of several elite Turkish units combined with the Asian Korps, a small German group heavily equipped with technical arms. Yilderim had been directed to capture Baghdad, which had fallen to the British earlier in the year; the EEF breakthrough in Palestine, however, necessitated its diversion to Palestine. Allenby had to take Jerusalem before the enemy arrived in force.

Fortunately for the British, their enemy arrived piecemeal. After limited fighting in the foothills, Allenby's initiative succeeded in securing Jerusalem on 9 December, and Falkenhayn's counterattack later that month stalled. Between 28 October and 9 December, the EEF had lost 21,000 men, the Turks 28,000. Thanks to Allenby's strategic pursuit, "Lightning" had never had time to hurl its bolt.

A second windfall had occurred on the right flank of the EEF on 5 July 1917, when Arab forces captured Akaba (Aqaba) on the gulf leading to the Red Sea. The Arabs now had a secure base of operations from which they could receive supplies and be in position to assist Allied operations in Palestine and Syria. The Arab Northern Army, or ANA, was created under command of Sharif Faisal, third son of the King of Hejaz. Assisting in an advisory position was T.E. Lawrence.

After Jerusalem, Allenby settled into a period of consolidation. The supreme war council of the Allies at Versailles decided that victory was not likely to be obtained on the Western Front until 1919, when the Americans were fully mobilized, but that victory over the Ottoman Empire was conceivable in 1918. Subsequently, the British War Cabinet instructed Allenby to get on with the job.

In compliance, Allenby marched on Jericho from 19–21 February 1918 and captured it as a prelude to his Trans-Jordan Operations. While the ANA orchestrated raids along the southeast and eastern shores of the Dead Sea, in March the EEF launched its first abortive attack across the Jordan Valley toward Amman. The second operation, in April, fared no better, but the combined thrusts in the hinterland achieved a very important strategic dividend: Turks were whipped into a state of anxiety over their left flank.

Unfortunately for the EEF, sixty thousand of its troops had to be transferred to the Western Front to help stop the German spring offensives. Consequently, much of spring and summer was lost equipping and training fresh units dispatched from India. The only consolation was that the Turks were experiencing grave difficulties. German-Turkish relations had seldom been smooth, but by the summer of 1918 the alliance was severely strained. General Otto Liman von Sanders had succeeded Falkenhayn; not only was Liman von Sanders quarreling with Enver Pasha, Enver was siphoning troops from Palestine and sending them on madcap schemes into the Caucasus. Short of equipment, the Turkish rank and file began voting with their feet.

Intelligence emboldened Allenby to test his new model in a major offensive. By early September his air force had achieved virtual air supremacy. Having blinded enemy reconnaissance, Allenby conducted a series of deceptions that convinced Liman von Sanders that an assault would strike at Fourth Army across the Jordan. Reinforcing this misconception, the ANA moved toward the communications hub of Dera on 15 September, four days before the EEF began a concentrated attack in the opposite direction against Eighth Army along the coast. The Turkish Seventh Army was pinned by diversionary probes in the center.

The Megiddo Campaign, which commenced on 19 September, was one of the most decisive in military history. The Turkish Eighth Army was overwhelmed the first day and thrown back like an open gate, and the EEF mounted arm dashed through, securing key mountain passes in the rear of Seventh and Eighth Armies. As the Turks retreated, virtually herded into the net, they were interdicted by the newly independent Royal Air Force. Many units of the Turkish Fourth Army, having waited too long to withdraw, found themselves surrounded by the ANA and elements of the EEF. Turkish units that escaped the cauldron fell back on Damascus, where most were taken prisoner by the Australian Light Horse on 30 September.

Throughout October a mobile column of the EEF and ANA pursued the shattered Turk-ish remnants through Syria and Lebanon to Aleppo. Three-quarters of the Turkish strength of 104,000 men had been killed or taken prisoner. Turkey signed an armistice ending the fighting at Mudros on 30 October.

David L. Bullock

References

Bullock, David. *Allenby's War: The Palestine-Arabian Campaigns, 1916–1918*. London: Blandford, 1988.

Djemal Pasha. *Memories of a Turkish Statesman, 1913–1919*. London: Hutchinson, 1922.

Falls, Captain Cyril. *Military Operations, Egypt and Palestine: From June 1917 to the End of the War*. London: HMSO, 1930.

Liman von Sanders, Otto. *Five Years in Turkey*. Annapolis, Md.: Naval Institute Press, 1927.

MacMunn, Sir George Fletcher. *Military Operations, Egypt and Palestine: From the Outbreak of the War with Germany to June 1917*. London: HMSO, 1928.

Wavell, Colonel A.P. *The Palestine Campaigns*. London: Constable, 1928.

See also ALLENBY, EDMUND; LIMAN VON SANDERS, OTTO; MURRAY, SIR ARCHIBALD

Paléologue, Georges Maurice (1859–1944)

French diplomat, born in Paris on 13 January 1859. Paléologue entered the French foreign ministry in 1880. After serving in French embassies abroad, he achieved the rank of minister plenipotentiary in 1901 and served as ambassador to Bulgaria from 1907 to 1912.

In 1912 Paléologue was Premier Raymond Poincaré's unexpected choice as political director of the foreign ministry. Given Paléologue's well-established reputation for self-promotion and intrigue and unpopularity with his colleagues, the decision was interpreted as part of Poincaré's overall effort to further his own control of foreign policy. In January of 1914 Paléologue became ambassador to St. Petersburg and worked diligently to ingratiate himself with the Russian government. When Poincaré, now president, and Premier René Viviani made a state visit in July, they confirmed the terms of the 1894 Franco-Russian Military Convention but generally counseled caution. Following their departure, Paléologue eagerly offered the Russian government full French diplomatic support and deliberately misled his own government about the pace of Russian mobilization. Paléologue's unfounded claims of intimate friendship with the French president gave his personal advice a spuriously official character.

After the war began, Paléologue urged an immediate Russian offensive in East Prussia to relieve pressure on the French armies and negotiated secret treaties that defined Franco-Russian war aims. The March 1917 revolution and Paléologue's close identification with the czarist regime led to his replacement as ambassador. He became secretary general of the foreign ministry in 1920. A prolific writer, he entered the French Academy in 1928, and his memoirs are an important source on the origins of the war. He died in Paris on 23 November 1944.

David L. Longfellow

References

Keiger, John F.V. *France and the Origins of the First World War*. London: Macmillan, 1983.

Paléologue, Maurice. *La Russie des Tsars pendant la grande guerre*. Paris: Plon-Nourrit, 1921–22.

See also OUTBREAK OF THE FIRST WORLD WAR; POINCARÉ, RAYMOND

Paris Gun

Of World War I's many innovations in weaponry, none was more spectacular than the long-range German gun that suddenly appeared in March of 1918 to begin the shelling of Paris from an incredible distance of over 120 kilometers, about seventy-five miles.

Even after nearly eighty years, many of the gun's technical details and history remain uncertain, as authorities continue to disagree over its characteristics and operational history. Even the publication in the 1980s of newly discovered primary records pertaining to the Paris gun's development and employment has done little to resolve the confusion.

At least seven, and possibly as many as ten or eleven, of this type of gun were in fact produced or in production by the end of the war. Two were destroyed by internal explosions, one in early testing, another in actual service. Following the Armistice, all of the weapons appear to have been successfully hidden or destroyed by the Germans, and only parts and near-empty emplacements were found by the Allies.

The most powerful guns in existence at the time of World War I were generally similar in their characteristics. They were of approximately 15-inch caliber and fired projectiles of just under a ton at muzzle velocities of about 2,700 feet per second. This yielded maximum ranges (at ideal firing elevations—45 degrees or slightly higher) of somewhat over twenty miles, near the worldwide expert consensus of about twenty-five to thirty miles as the practical firing limit for artillery weapons.

Theoretical and experimental work had already begun in several countries toward achieving greater gun ranges. Calculations suggested that the most extreme ranges would be attained with projectiles of about 200mm (about 8-inch) caliber, fired at very high velocities. In 1916 the German firm of Krupp undertook to accomplish this goal by designing a radically new weapon with a muzzle velocity of just over 5,000 feet per second. Unlike the then-conventional maximum bore length of about forty-five bore diameters (or "calibers"), the new gun would have nearly four times that length, which would allow the propelling powder to work far longer upon accelerating the projectile in the course of firing.

The final product, comprising a tube with a caliber of 210mm and a total length of thirty-seven meters (about 120 feet), inserted within an existing 15-inch battleship gun, gave the sought-after characteristics but at the price of extremely short useful life. Guns of this design would wear out after only fifty to sixty firings, and employing them with this rapid internal erosion required a remarkable feat of calculation and engineering. Each gun's projectiles were numbered serially for consecutive firings, each round machined slightly larger and heavier than the last. The weight of the initial 210mm projectiles was 120 kg (264 pounds), while that of the final rounds was about twenty-five pounds greater, because of the caliber enlargement from erosion. Once worn out, the guns were to be rebored to a new, larger caliber, 232mm, and each gun was to be provided with a larger second series of graduated projectiles.

The firings against Paris began on the morning of 23 March 1918 and continued nearly daily until 1 May. A second series of firings took place from 27 May to 11 June, and the final series was fired from 15 July through 9 August. The number of rounds fired altogether is unknown but was perhaps of the order of four hundred, probably from seven separate guns. At least one of these had been rebored to the enlarged diameter, with its range lessened because of the reduced caliber length of the gun barrel and corresponding lowering of muzzle velocity.

In statistical terms the effects of the Paris guns were unimpressive. Not much physical damage was done, certainly not with respect to significant military targets. By best data a total of 256 people were killed and another 620 injured during the forty-four days of actual shelling, an average of fewer than six deaths per day. The worst single day occurred in the very first week of the shelling, on Good Friday, 29 March 1918, when only one shell fell on Paris. That projectile, however, happened to strike an arch of the crowded Church of St. Gervais, causing the collapse of much of the roof and part of the nave, killing eighty-eight people and injuring nearly one hundred. This one shot, among the earliest fired by the second of the guns (the first was already worn out from its three days of firing), came from the most distant firing site, near the village of Crépy, about five miles west of Laon and 121 km (seventy-five miles) from its target.

Given the extreme ranges at which the Paris guns operated, their accuracy was far below the normally accepted standards for usable artillery. While authorities again differ over the number of rounds known to have reached the Paris area, the best sources indicate that 183 fell within the city's walls (an area with a diameter of roughly six miles), while 120 fell in its outer environs. Clearly, this degree of dispersion rendered guns of this nature all but useless against specific or military targets; their employment was analogous to the "area" bombing of World War II, where the large majority of victims were usually civilians.

After three-fourths of a century, the purpose of these remarkable weapons remains a matter of speculation and argument. Some believe that they were intended to spur an enormous exodus from the French capital in order to disrupt communications and clog roads. Others have regarded them as simple terror weapons, no more. Still others view them as "stunt" weapons, intended largely to impress other nations with yet one more instance of German technological preeminence. Whatever they were, the Paris guns opened a new era of innovation in ordnance as the direct ancestors

of the HARP (High Altitude Research Program) weapons of the 1960s, as well as Iraq's monster cannon in the late 1980s and early 1990s.

E. Ray Lewis

References

Bull, G.V., and C.H. Murphy. *Paris Kanonen—The Paris Guns (Wilhelmgeschütze) and Project HARP.* Herford and Bonn: Verlag E.S. Mittler und Sohn, 1988.

Miller, Lt. Col. Henry W. "The German Long-Range Gun." *Mechanical Engineering* 42 (February 1920): 89–100.

———. *The Paris Gun.* London: George G. Harrap, 1930.

Paris Peace Conference, 1919

The meeting convened for the purpose of providing an official peace treaty concluding World War I held its first formal session on 18 January 1919 in the Clock Salon (later renamed the Peace Salon) at the French Foreign Ministry in the Quai d'Orsay. It operated until March of 1919 under the title "Preliminary Conference of Peace." In retrospect it is difficult to think of the conference being held anywhere other than Paris, but at the conclusion of the fighting both the British and the Americans would have preferred a quieter, out-of-the-way city like The Hague, Brussels, Basel, Geneva, or Lausanne. The French persisted in pressing for the honor of hosting the conference, and in deference to their gallant stand against Germany for the duration of the war, that point was eventually conceded.

There were other cogent reasons for selecting a large city and prominent capital. Paris could provide the facilities essential for the multitude of meetings that a prolonged and comprehensive conference entailed. In addition to sessions involving heads of state there would be numerous gatherings of foreign ministry secretaries and under-secretaries, economic advisors, military consultants, colonial experts, ethnic group specialists—a list that lengthened as the conference progressed. Paris was blessed with an abundance of accommodations necessary to house the hordes of delegates and staffs, and even the resources of that metropolis were strained. The American delegation, which included more than 1,300 people, alone occupied entirely the massive Hotel Crillon. The British contingent filled five smaller hotels. Twenty-seven Allied and associated powers were represented, in addition to five British dominions and four vanquished nations. Altogether, more than 10,000 people connected with the conference convened in Paris. That would be a burden for any host city and an impossible task for most.

The disadvantages of holding the conference at Paris should be noted. Harold Nicolson, then a young British Third Secretary who worked at the Peace Conference at the commission level, noted that the selection of Paris was unfortunate because "Paris, in any circumstances, is too self-conscious, too insistent, to constitute a favourable site for any Congress of Peace." Parisians helped determine the attitude and atmosphere of the conference, and for them German war guilt was an established fact. The diversions of the city also made it difficult to concentrate on the tasks at hand. Finally, the citizenry, encouraged by intemperate newspaper articles and cartoons and by speeches by government officials such as Clemenceau, turned against the Americans. President Wilson was castigated and ridiculed, and a tapestry of disrespect served as a backdrop for the deliberations.

The conference was originally scheduled to convene on 18 December 1918, and President Wilson arrived in Europe on Friday, 13 December, a bad omen for the suspicious. The intervening time was consumed by Wilson's state visits to France, England, and Italy, by observance of the Christmas holiday season, and by a waiting period during which, it was hoped, volatile situations in Russia and Germany would settle down. Besides, the British had to await the outcome of general elections in December.

The conclusion of the Armistice had been achieved through the agreement, by leaders of the Allied and associated powers and the German government, that Wilson's Fourteen Points would be the basis for drawing up a peace treaty. Yet each of the nations, and especially the French, had war aims that contradicted one or another of the Fourteen Points. Preconference positions were adopted in November and December of 1918, and these issues would be the subject of frequent, long, and sometimes bitter debate at Paris. Also contributing to the difficulties in finding solutions to problems was the necessity to consider the desires and ambitions presented by the delegates and unofficial representatives from the smaller nations. The Fourteen Points would be in for rough sledding during the winter and spring of 1919.

On 12 January 1919, an informal meeting of the Supreme War Council was held at the Quai d'Orsay. France was represented by Georges Clemenceau and S. Pichon, Great Britain by Lloyd George and A.J. Balfour, Italy by Vittorio E. Orlando and Baron Sidney Sonnino, and the United States by Woodrow Wilson and Robert Lansing. It was decided to add only the representatives of Japan to the supreme council and to exclude all others from the major decisions of the peace conference. Thus, the Council of Ten derived from the Supreme War Council. The lesser powers, which had declared war against the Central Powers or had broken diplomatic relations, were allotted seats and votes in the plenary sessions of the conference in accordance with military strength and contribution to the war effort. Each of the five principal powers received five seats and votes; Belgium, Serbia, and Brazil were assigned three; Canada, Australia, South Africa, India, China, Czechoslovakia, Poland, Greece, the Hejaz, Portugal, Rumania, and Siam were each allotted two; and one seat each went to New Zealand, Bolivia, Cuba, Ecuador, Guatemala, Haiti, Honduras, Liberia, Nicaragua, Panama, Peru, and Uruguay.

The plenary assembly of the conference met for the first time on 18 January 1919, and Woodrow Wilson nominated Georges Clemenceau as president of the conference. Thereafter, the plenary assembly proved to be a body that only rubber-stamped actions already determined by the Council of Ten and, later, the Council of Four.

The Council of Ten recognized that the smaller states would resent relegation to secondary status. It therefore assured the delegates from these states that they could put in writing before the council the territorial and other concessions they desired. These delegates were also invited to state orally before the council the justification for their claims. The result was an inflation of claims far above reasonable expectations, numerous needless and repetitious orations, and the waste of time and precious energy for the elderly heads of state on the council.

One question regarding the conference that was not adequately addressed at the beginning and that was eventually resolved by practice and in compliance with circumstances was whether the resultant treaty should be preliminary or final. Related to this issue was the question of whether the treaty would be imposed or negotiated—whether the defeated nations, especially Germany, would be allowed to attend and speak. During the first ten weeks of the conference the heads of state on the Council of Ten were not sure which course they would pursue, which is why until mid-March the official title was "Preliminary Conference of Peace." By that time, however, many of the pertinent clauses had been drafted by committees and approved in a form that required little revision. Also, Wilson had been advised that even a preliminary treaty would have to be ratified by the Senate. Given his problems with that body, Wilson did not want to have to go through the ratification process more than once. Thus, the theory of a preliminary peace was abandoned, almost by chance. Yet, this confusion and indecisiveness had far-reaching and ominous consequences. For the drift toward making the deliberations and the resultant drafts part of a final treaty also led, almost inescapably, to the determination that the treaty would be imposed rather than negotiated. According to Harold Nicolson, "Had it been known from the outset that no negotiations would ever take place with the enemy, it is certain that many of the less reasonable clauses of the Treaty would never have been inserted."

Two matters pertinent to the proceedings and to the forming of public opinion must be addressed. The first had to do with the activities of the press. Hundreds of the best reporters from newspapers and magazines around the world descended on Paris. They, of course, knew that the peace treaty was supposed to be based on the Fourteen Points; they expected, therefore, to witness "open covenants openly arrived at" but were gravely disappointed. It was Wilson himself who insisted upon complete secrecy of all discussions, and it was with difficulty that Clemenceau prevailed upon him to permit plenary sessions of the conference to be made public. Newsmen relied upon leaks for their reports. Some of the better and more adept reporters established their contacts and rendered amazingly accurate reports of secret sessions. In fact, it was the floodlike nature of the leaks that led to the Council of Ten's being superseded by the Council of Four—Clemenceau, Lloyd George, Wilson, and Orlando. The foreign ministers of the five Allied Powers were relegated to a Council of Five entrusted with only minor assignments of a routine nature.

The second issue was the debate over language. Woodrow Wilson and Lloyd George disputed France's claim to the exclusive use of French as the official language of the conference, although French had been the language of international discourse for centuries. Wilson argued that while French had currency as the language of European diplomacy, English was used in the Pacific hemisphere. Eventually, a compromise was reached by which both English and French were recognized as official languages, with French texts taking precedence in case of dispute. While this solution worked satisfactorily, the need for translations did delay the progress of the conference.

The first order of business for the conference, at Wilson's insistence, was consideration of the League of Nations. Wilson had pointedly made the League the keystone of the peace program and wanted it to be an integral part of the peace treaty. While Wilson was reassured by evidences of British understanding and cooperation, the French response was quite different. In face-to-face meetings with Clemenceau, Wilson met with polite skepticism; in other venues the League of Nations was greeted with ridicule. The French were consumed with ensuring "French security" and resisted any notions that, in their eyes, served to diminish their protection. The French were primarily interested in converting the League into a grand alliance of victorious powers to enforce the peace treaty, like the Quadruple Alliance formed to enforce the provisions of the Congress of Vienna in 1815. The plenary session of 25 January 1919 did, however, approve a League of Nations resolution and authorized the drafting of a constitution. Wilson took over as chairman of the League of Nations Commission, which became the center of all conference activity for the next three weeks. Because of Wilson's energy, single-mindedness, and occasional ruthlessness, the covenant of the League was ready for presentation to the plenary session of the conference on 14 February and it received unanimous approval. Having accomplished his major objective, President Wilson left Paris the next day to return to the United States to deal with domestic issues.

While Wilson was away, an anarchist wounded Clemenceau in an assassination attempt. Thereafter, Clemenceau was confined to his home in the Rue Franklin, and meetings were held there with Wilson's stand-in, Colonel House, and with Lloyd George and Orlando. Emerging from those informal sessions was the

Council of Four that from then on decided high policy. Once Wilson returned to Paris, the four heads of state abandoned the Council of Ten and assumed authority as the supreme council of the conference.

In the early weeks of the conference Wilson was meeting nightly with the League of Nations Commission to draft a covenant. During the day the supreme council continued meeting and raised other issues. Lloyd George craftily inserted discussion of the disposal of Germany's former colonial possessions on 23 January, despite the fact that the council had on 13 January accepted Wilson's order of discussion wherein colonies ranked last. The British, the dominions, France, and Japan each had concrete and explicit territorial desires and intentions. Furthermore, in many instances these former German colonies were already held by the claimants through conquest. Wilson's highminded Fifth Point, calling for "free, openminded and absolutely impartial adjustment of all colonial claims, based upon the strict observance of the principle that in determining all such questions of sovereignty, the interests of the population concerned must have equal weight with the equitable claims of the government whose title is to be determined" annoyed those who simply wanted the colonies as spoils of war. The three options for disposing of the colonies were as follows: (1) internationalization or direct administration by the League of Nations; (2) one nation taking trusteeship over a colony on behalf of the League as mandatory; or (3) old-fashioned direct annexation. The third option was the one of choice for almost everyone except Wilson.

The claimants could make a case that their costs and losses in the war, the need for strategic security, and the promises made by secret treaty while the war was in progress justified their demand for colonies. Wilson countered that exposing the intentions of the claimants to world scrutiny would cast them in the light of unreformed nineteenth-century imperialists. The president insisted that Germany's former possessions be made mandataries of the League and not be distributed to supervising powers until after the League was established and the covenant adopted. After numerous discussions, some bitter and threatening to the continuation of the conference, the deadlock was broken through the efforts of Lloyd George and the presentation of the "Smut's Resolution," which formed the basis of a general compromise. Ac-

cordingly, Germany would lose all former colonial territories, Turkey would lose much of its empire in the Middle East, and these lands and peoples would be entrusted to the care and administration of a major power or significant dominion as mandates under the League of Nations. In practice, the colonies and other areas were assigned to those already in possession of them. Left unresolved by the "Smut's Resolution" were Japanese claims to the former German concession in China at Jaiozhou (Kiaochow) and the Shandong (Shantung) Peninsula. That issue would be among the last decided, in April of 1919, and would cause Wilson considerable mental agony. Japan's claims had been promised by Great Britain and France and recognized in treaties with the imperial Chinese government, but they violated Wilson's goals of national self-determination and preservation of the territorial integrity of China. The president's concession to Japan's position was necessary to preserve world order and, thus, was reluctantly made. All Wilson received in return was Japan's oral promises to restore Chinese sovereignty of Shandong "as soon as possible."

The loss of a colonial empire was distressing to the Germans, but closer to home and to the hearts of the German people were the settlements pertaining to Germany's borders. Since the Germans expected the peace treaty to be based on the Fourteen Points, they knew that the Polish regions of the empire would be lost. Exactly how large Poland was to be and what it would include remained to be determined. France wanted a Poland as large as possible to serve as an alliance partner against the possible resurgence of Germany. The Poles wanted virtually every plot of land that had, at any time in history, been part of Poland. Wilson had promised a Poland with "a free and secure access to the sea." Incorporating territory inhabited by a Polish majority awarded Poland the two former German provinces of Posen and West Prussia, but doing so cut off the largely German-populated province of East Prussia from the rest of Germany. The most viable access to the Baltic Sea was by way of the Vistula River and the port city of Danzig. But the east bank of the Vistula was primarily Germanic, and Danzig was definitely a German city. After many disputes a compromise solution was reached extending a corridor from the main body of Poland to the Baltic—thereby separating parts of Germany—and making Danzig a

P

free city under the auspices of the League of Nations. Poland was guaranteed economic control in the city. This settlement failed to please the Germans, the East Prussians, the citizens of Danzig, and the Poles.

The western borders of Germany provoked even stronger feelings and lengthier discussions. The restoration of Alsace-Lorraine to France posed no problem in principle and was stipulated in the Fourteen Points. The details of restoration were more complicated, for France insisted that "restoration" include expropriating all German property, private as well as public. Despite the unprecedented nature of this demand, French persistence prevailed. France also had plans for the detachment of the Saar Basin from Germany and its annexation to France; much more controversial, the French wanted the separation of the entire Rhineland from Germany and the establishment of a buffer state responsive to the needs and will of France. Debates over these subjects occupied weeks in late March and early April, and the entire peace conference almost collapsed when Wilson, whose health had deteriorated under the strain, in utter disgust ordered the *George Washington* readied for his return to the United States. Thereafter, the French proved more inclined to compromise. Ultimately, the treaty stipulated that the French would have ownership of the mines in the Saar; the region would be administered by the League for fifteen years, at which time a plebiscite would determine the future affiliation of the region; and the left bank of the Rhine would be occupied for up to fifteen years and entirely demilitarized, the right bank being demilitarized to a depth of fifty kilometers. The French were displeased but had to accede to the positions taken by the British and Americans.

Reparations! In retrospect the mere word causes consternation because of the consequences of the positions taken and the decisions reached at Paris in 1919. Long before the peace conference convened it had become apparent that major differences existed between the views on reparations held by Wilson and those of the Allies. The French, British, and other participants wanted the Germans to pay for "everything." Meanwhile, Wilson was proclaiming "no annexations, no contribution, no punitive damages" as an American war aim. The Fourteen Points did call for the "restoration of the occupied territories of Belgium, France, Romania, Serbia, and Montenegro," which the American delegation interpreted to mean reparation of damages to civilian populations and property. Once the conference got under way it set up a Committee on the Reparation of Damages (CRD). Its task was to determine how much the enemy countries should pay, how much they could pay, and how they would pay. Weeks of discussions over matters of principle ensued. Claims generic and specific were submitted; amounts suggested varied from $8 billion to $120 billion. In time, the conference abandoned the idea of arriving at a fixed sum and, instead, agreed on an extensive list of categories of damages for which Germany could be held liable. The peace treaty would charge Germany with the payment of $5 billion by 1 May 1921; also, by that date a Reparations Commission would present Germany with the total amount due and a schedule for payment. That was the best they could do at Paris, for the issue had become too laden with emotion to permit a settlement conforming to reason and reality.

Other issues less stressful or important only in comparison to those previously mentioned were part of the proceedings of the peace conference. The French succeeded in obtaining a prohibition against any future merger of Germany and Austria. Italy's northern frontier was expanded at Austrian expense, but denial of Italian claims to Fiume and Dalmatia caused Orlando to walk out of the conference in a huff. All of the terms agreed to at the Paris Peace Conference were contained in the treaties imposed on the defeated Central Powers, including the Treaty of Versailles (Germany), The Treaty of Neuilly (Bulgaria), the Treaty of St. Germain (Austria), the Treaty of Sèvres (Turkey), and the Treaty of Trianon (Hungary).

The Treaty of Versailles was signed amid great pomp and pageantry in the Hall of Mirrors at the Palace of Versailles on 28 June 1919, five years to the day after the firing of the shot in Sarajevo that initiated the conflict. Immediately thereafter, the Big Four broke up and Wilson left that afternoon to return to the United States. Lloyd George departed for England within a few days. Soon only foreign office underlings were left behind to draft the treaties with the other Central Powers and finish the work of the conference. The results of the efforts at Paris have been praised, they have been condemned; indisputably they have had repercussions that have endured.

Edward L. Byrd, Jr.
Ingrid P. Westmoreland

References

Bailey, Thomas A. *Woodrow Wilson and the Lost Peace.* New York: Macmillan, 1944.

Czernin, Ferdinand. *Versailles, 1919.* New York: G.P. Putnam's Sons, 1964.

Dockrill, Michael, and Douglas J. Goold. *Peace without Promise: Britain and the Peace Conferences, 1919–1923.* London: Batsford, 1981.

House, Edward M., and Charles Seymour, eds. *What Really Happened at Paris.* New York: Charles Scribner's Sons, 1921.

Nicolson, Harold. *Peacemaking.* New York: Grosset and Dunlap, 1919.

Watt, Richard M. *The Kings Depart.* New York: Simon and Schuster, 1968.

See also CLEMENCEAU, GEORGES; LLOYD GEORGE, DAVID; NEUILLY, TREATY OF; ORLANDO, VITTORIO; SÈVRES, TREATY OF; ST. GERMAIN, TREATY OF; TRIANON, TREATY OF; VERSAILLES TREATY

Pašić, Nikola (1845–1926)

Serbian political leader and diplomat, born on 31 December 1845, in Zaječar, Serbia. Pašić studied engineering in Zurich and entered politics in opposition to King Milan Obrenović's rule. Upon being elected to parliament in 1878 he worked toward forming a parliamentary democracy, and in 1881 he established the Radical party, which soon dominated the government in Serbia. He served as prime minister of Serbia from 1891 to 1892, 1904 to 1905, 1906 to 1908, 1909 to 1911, and 1912 to 1918, and for the Kingdom of Serbs, Croats, and Slovenes in 1918, 1921–1924, and 1924–1926.

There is controversy over Pašić's role, if any, in the assassination of Archduke Franz Ferdinand at Sarajevo. Pašić personally delivered Belgrade's conciliatory reply to the Austrian ultimatum, but he knew that Austria-Hungary was bent on war. After Serbia's defeat a rival arose to Pašić's leadership, Croatian Ante Trumbić, who sought to unite all the south Slavs in one state. There is controversy on this issue, but Pašić probably wanted only a larger Serb state.

With the international climate increasingly hostile, Pašić met with Trumbić, and the two signed the Declaration of Corfu on 20 July 1917, claiming Serb willingness to cooperate in the formation of a South Slav state with the Croats and Slovenes in which all would be treated equally. Pašić believed that the Serbs should dominate any Yugoslav solution and worked to secure the Serbian position. Pašić led the Yugoslav delegation at the 1919 Paris Peace Conference, gaining approval for the formation of the Kingdom of Serbs, Croats, and Slovenes.

As Premier, Pašić worked to pass a constitution that appeared to offer equality within the kingdom but actually secured Serb hegemony. Increasing difficulty in forming a stable government forced Pašić to resign in March of 1926. He died in Belgrade on 10 December 1926.

Susan N. Carter

References

Banac, Ivo. *The National Question in Yugoslavia: Origins, History, Politics.* Ithaca: Cornell University Press, 1984.

Sugar, Peter F., and Donald Treadgold, eds. *A History of East Central Europe.* 11 vols. Seattle: University of Washington Press, 1977. See Vol. 9: Joseph Rothschild. *East Central Europe between the Two World Wars.*

See also SERBIA; YUGOSLAVIA, CREATION OF

Passchendaele (Ypres, Third Battle of), 31 July to 10 November 1917

The Battle of Passchendaele (Third Ypres) was initiated by Field Marshal Sir Douglas Haig, commander of the British army in France, to relieve pressure on French forces reeling from mutinies after the disastrous Nivelle Offensive. It was also prompted by British cabinet endorsement of Haig's plan to break through the German lines between the North Sea and the River Lys in order to outflank the German Fourth Army's defensive system from the north and cut enemy communications with major bases on the lower Rhine. Haig asserted that this would not only liberate Belgium, but it would also end the U-boat campaign by depriving the Germans use of Belgian bases. Submarines had been inflicting heavy losses on British merchant shipping, in large part because the Royal Navy was reluctant to institute a convoy system. Either unknown or disregarded at the time was the fact that German U-boats sortied from German, not Belgian, ports.

British Prime Minister David Lloyd George had supported a British drive in Flanders to divert German attention from the French army along the Aisne. He was, however, showing renewed interest in sending British forces to Italy, Macedonia, or the Middle East. If Haig failed to capitalize on the considerable forces at hand, he might find them drained off to minor theaters.

British morale was high and effective strength greater than at any time since the 1916 Battle of the Somme, and the British had a prepared plan. Since November of 1916 Haig and chief of the Imperial General Staff General William Robertson had been making plans for an offensive in the vicinity of Ypres.

French army commander General Henri-Philippe Pétain did offer some support to the planned British operation in the form of the small, elite, French First Army (commanded by General François Anthoine). It was transferred north and placed on the British left wing, between the BEF and the Belgians.

The battle was to have three phases: the major breakthrough around Ypres, an amphibious landing by two divisions of General Henry Rawlinson's Fourth Army on the coast at the Yser River mouth behind the German flank in the direction of Ostend, and an exploitation and pursuit toward Ghent, over forty miles northeast of Ypres. The complicated amphibious component was ultimately scrapped and Rawlinson directed simply to protect the sand belt bordering the inundated area on the seaboard.

Terrain factors dictated that the main British effort proceed northeastward from the Ypres salient. South of the sand dune belt along the coast was an impassable flooded area created by Belgian engineers to hold off the Germans during the 1914 Battle of the Yser. Before the Ypres salient could be utilized as a springboard for further action, the Germans had to be cleared from the ridge stretching from Gheluvelt, on the Menin Road, northward through Passchendaele to Staden, on the railway running northeastward from Ypres to Thorout. Preparatory to an assault toward Passchendaele, the southern anchor of the Ypres ridge-line had to be secured by capturing Messines Ridge, a dominating German-held spur thwarting British concentration to the south of Ypres.

In June of 1917, thanks to a lengthy tunneling project, the British Second Army (General Sir Herbert Plumer) detonated a number of massive mines under Messines Ridge and attacked under cover of the devastation brought about by their simultaneous explosion. The ridge was taken at the cost of 17,000 British casualties; German losses were 25,000.

There was, however, a delay of seven weeks between the victory at Messines and exploitation of that success. The holdup was partially caused by Haig's earlier decision to give responsibility for the main thrust, situated in Plumer's long-held and intimately reconnoitered sector, to General Sir Hubert Gough's Fifth Army. Haig felt that Plumer's methodical, exacting temperament was unsuited to this operation, notwithstanding his keen grasp of local conditions. Haig wanted a fellow cavalryman, one with vigor and boldness. But Gough's newly arrived force needed time to prepare. Vacillation by the British cabinet also delayed the start of the operation. Another concern was that such a large-scale offensive required more help from the French, who were in no position to provide it.

On 30 May Gough's army, expanded to seventeen divisions, took over the Ypres salient from Boesinghe (three miles north of Ypres) down to Klein Zillebeke/Mt. Sorel, south of the Menin Road, linking there with the northern fringe of Plumer's Second Army. The latter was reduced to twelve divisions and allotted a secondary role. Rawlinson's Fourth Army, consisting of seven divisions, held the northern sector between Nieuport and the sea, while French and Belgian troops held the flooded marshlands between Boesinghe and Nieuport.

Gough's army consisted of four corps (ten divisions) backed by three thousand guns, over a third of which were heavy pieces. Additionally, Gough was supported by three brigades of the newly established Tank Corps with 136 tanks. Just to the west of Ypres, two cavalry divisions were prepared to optimize any breakthrough. To the left of Fifth Army, two of the six divisions of Anthoine's First Army were to attack simultaneously, while the right flank assault was assigned to Plumer's Second Army, three corps (five divisions) composing the first echelon.

From a tactical standpoint, the area chosen for the attack was very poor. The Germans held the high ground and were able to observe British troops and installations on the Flemish plain below. German artillery could bring converging fire to bear on any point within the salient. Densely packed British artillery was vulnerable to precisely calibrated German counterbattery fire. The Germans also had made other preparations.

Alerted by the Messines Ridge operation, Arnim's Fourth Army prepared countermeasures against the expected follow-on attack. The Germans organized an innovative elastic defensive scheme incorporating four fighting groups, varying in combat strength from two to eight divisions. They replaced the trench lines of the old linear defense system by a zigzag series of strongpoints and concrete pillboxes, tiered in depth, and supported in the rear by abandoned battered farmhouses converted into forts. Ground was to be held more by interlocking machine-gun fields of fire than by men. Forward positions were lightly held, with the bulk of the forces retained as reserve divisions specially trained for prompt counterattack. In fact, outlying posts were to be abandoned after inflicting as many casualties as possible. Original positions would be retaken by counterattack. The Germans also planned to use mustard gas to overwhelm British concentration areas and artillery sites.

The intense British artillery preparation began on 22 July and lasted ten days. On 31 July twelve divisions of infantry advanced on an eleven-mile front in a torrential rainstorm. The heavy preliminary shelling had wrecked the protective dikes that for generations had preserved the delicate drainage system of the otherwise swampy terrain. On the left, northern, wing of the assault substantial progress was made along shallow valleys, overwhelming defenders of Bixschoote, St. Julien, and the Pilckem Ridge, and securing the line of Steenbeck brook, an advance of some two miles that attained the designated third objective.

Across the higher ground in the more critical sector along the Menin Road, however, destruction of the dikes combined with heavy rains and waterfilled shellholes turned the ground into an impassable quicksand that immobilized tanks and swallowed infantry. Most of the fifty-two tanks in the first wave foundered in deep shell craters; only nineteen were able to support the struggling infantry. The attack foundered short of the second objective.

Notwithstanding temporary Allied air superiority, British gains were insignificant for the effort expended. Gough expressed reservations about continuing the attack, but lower commanders were loath to pass along unfavorable reports for fear of repercussions. Haig took his cue from them and concluded that enemy forces were rapidly approaching exhaustion and could be broken in another attempt.

The second stroke, on 16 August, was a smaller version of the first. As before, the left flank made the most progress. Troops crossed the diminutive Steenbeek hollow and moved on to the remnants of Langemarck. On the right, more crucial, axis progress was trifling for immense losses. This time a complaint about haphazard Fifth Army staff work was added to excuses of weather and mud. Buoyed by the favorable situation estimates of his intelligence officer, Brigadier General John Charteris, Haig extended the Second Army's front northward to embrace the Menin Road plateau, previously controlled by Gough. This reassigned to Plumer the main effort toward the ridgeline east of Ypres.

Following Plumer's typically scrupulous planning, a series of limited attacks on narrow fronts began on 20 September; British troops inched forward against determined counterattacks. As at Messines, the attackers applied piecemeal siege-warfare methods. Shallow rushes never out-ranged artillery support. Divisions were closed to 1,000-yard frontages, often with two of three brigades in support and reserve. This allowed the troops to remain fresh enough to withstand the inevitable counterattacks. Plumer employed six divisions, two of them Australian. Tremendous artillery barrages supported three separate thrusts toward the restricted objectives. Of 1,300 British artillery pieces, fully half were heavy guns; this far outstripped the 31 July ratio of guns per yard of frontage.

The Germans used mustard gas for the first time, and they also flew planes in low to strafe British infantry, the first massive use of air support for ground troops. British and French pilots were unable to deal with the tree-skimming German air attacks.

Swift work by Royal engineers laying plank roads and duckboards permitted Plumer to employ his manpower to maximum effect, easing the difficult portage of artillery shells over waterlogged footpaths. The well-organized British inroads into their defensive works prompted the Germans to revert to the outmoded doctrine of concentrating defensive power in the forward areas, and this produced heavy casualties for the attackers.

The Second Army's assault advanced one kilometer on a four-kilometer front astride the Ypres-Menin Road. On Plumer's left, north of the Ypres-Roulers railway, Fifth Army, with five divisions allotted between two corps, attacked in association with Plumer. Two squadrons of the Royal Flying Corps suppressed enemy artillery and observed troop maneuvers. Tanks, however, were virtually useless because of ground conditions and rarely reached their truncated objectives. Gough's forces also advanced about one kilometer.

The bad weather then lifted somewhat. The first two battles under Plumer's command, Menen (Menin) Road Ridge (20–25 September) and Polygon Wood (26 September–3 October), were actually fought in clouds of blinding dust. The second combined attack by the two British armies, again operating under concepts formulated by Plumer, made gains similar to those of the 20th and captured most of the Gheluvelt plateau, including the Polygon Wood, extending north to Zonnebeke. This time, however, German counterattacks produced substantially heavier British casualties.

Encouraged by the relative success of the confined step-by-step approach, Haig had Plumer and Gough (eight and four divisions, respectively) launch an attack across the axis of the Gheluvelt plateau to Broodseinde, whence it was to swing northward to seize Passchendaele Ridge. This assault on 4 October just managed to preempt a major German riposte and coincided with the return of the rain, although the ground was as yet negotiable. The British were forced to concede, however, that bad weather had arrived for good, and the attack was more costly than the first two combined.

As October wore on, the rain continued. Many concluded that further attacks were futile. Haig, however, refused to abandon the offensive until the beginning of November; this was because he wanted to secure favorable positions for the forthcoming winter beyond the flooded marshlands, upon which the British would be visible from enemy observation posts on the high ground.

The last phase of the offensive was from 26 October to 10 November. It involved the taking of Passchendaele Ridge and Passchendaele village, the latter finally secured by two brigades of the Canadian Corps on 6 November. The British had to construct plank roads in order to move their guns through the cratered morass to the assistance of the fatigued infantry that advanced on the formidable German fortified belt. This final British assault gained little ground but resulted in an appalling 100,000 fatalities. Haig then ordered his men to consolidate and go into winter defensive positions. He resolved to keep

pressure on the Germans and did so at Cambrai in November.

The attacks on Passchendaele Ridge and village gave name to the whole offensive. Passchendaele, or the Third Battle of Ypres, became a lasting symbol of the futility and butchery of the war on the Western Front. The poem *In Flanders Fields,* commemorating the unproductive carnage, solidified this image. While the British-held Ypres salient was deepened by about five miles, it came at great cost—some 300,000 British and 8,528 French casualties—and was more difficult to hold. German losses are estimated at 260,000 men.

Losses associated with Third Ypres led to bitter criticism of Haig and an enduring reputation for tactical inflexibility and insensitivity to wasting lives. The dominant historical view seems to be that Haig greatly underestimated the strength of German forces confronting him and that he believed that a breakthrough was imminent long after many of the men on the spot had given up any hope of achieving it. Haig's defenders point to the fact that, during the battle, Lloyd George had siphoned off five valuable divisions to the Italian front following the Austrian victory at Caporetto, thus weakening the offensive. There is also controversy over the British official history's liberal estimate of German casualty losses in the offensive.

Viewed as a campaign in the war of attrition, Passchendaele was a costly failure. Distrust between Prime Minister Lloyd George and Haig and Robertson was deepened, encouraging Lloyd George to seek to divert British forces elsewhere. Heavy British casualties at Passchendaele not only meant that there were no reserves available to exploit success at Cambrai; they also led to the collapse of depleted British forces during the German offensive of March 1918. The Passchendaele Campaign did, however, have the positive value of relieving pressure on the reorganizing French armies.

James J. Bloom

References

Brice, Beatrix. *The Battle Book of Ypres.* London: J. Murray, 1927. Reprint. New York: St. Martin's, 1988.

Edmonds, Brig. General Sir James E. *Military Operations: France and Flanders, 1917.* Vol. 2. London: HMSO, 1948.

Gough, Sir Hubert. *The Fifth Army.* London: Hodder and Stoughton, 1931.

Schurman, Donald. "The Third Battle of Ypres." In *Great Battles of the British Army*, edited by Donald Chandler. London: Arms and Armour, 1991.

Terraine, John. *Douglas Haig: The Educated Soldier*. London: Hutchinson, 1963.

Warner, Philip. *Passchendaele: The Tragic Victory of 1917*. London: Sidgwick and Jackson, 1987.

Winter, Denis. *Haig's Command: A Reassessment*. New York: Viking, 1991.

See also Gough, Hubert; Haig, Douglas; Messines, Battle of; Plumer, Herbert; Rawlinson, Henry; Robertson, William; Tunneling and Mine Warfare

Pau, Paul Marie César Gerald (1848–1932)

French general, born in Montelimar on 29 November 1848. Pau graduated from St. Cyr in 1869 and lost a hand in battle during the Franco-Prussian War. He continued in the military and rose to become general of a division by 1903.

General Joseph Joffre recalled Pau from retirement on 10 August 1914 to command the newly formed Army of Alsace. Tasked with covering the right flank of the First Army's drive to recover that province, Pau's three corps entered action on 14 August, earning victories at Mulhouse and Dornach and reoccupying Thann and Gabweiler. Reversals at the hands of the Germans at Morhange and Saarbourg put an end to the French offensive. Pau's army was subsequently dissolved and his troops secretly transferred to the Sixth Army on 25 August.

Pau later served as a member of the Council of War and as chief of several missions abroad during the war. He died in Paris on 2 January 1932.

Timothy C. Dowling

References

D'Amat, Roman, and R. Limorizin-Lamothe, dirs. *Dictionnaire de la Biographie Française*. Paris: Librairie Letouzey et Ane, 1967.

Keegan, John, and Andrew Wheatcroft. *Who's Who in Military History from 1453 to the Present Day*. London: Hutchinson, 1987.

Peace Overtures during the War

Following the November 1914 defeat at Langemarck in Flanders, German General Erich von Falkenhayn informed Chancellor Theobald von Bethmann Hollweg that victory was impossible unless either France or Russia could be persuaded to leave the war. Falkenhayn suggested that war aims be modified and that Russia be approached concerning a separate peace. Generals Paul von Hindenburg and Erich Ludendorff strenuously objected. Ludendorff argued that total victory was still achievable. Although Falkenhayn countered that the German army was "a broken instrument," Hindenburg and Ludendorff prevailed.

Ironically, the Brusilov Offensive of July 1916 contributed to the possibility of a separate peace with Russia. The offensive and its ultimate failure had completed the exhaustion of Russia. Influential groups in Russia were inclined now to consider peace. In July, Protopopov, the vice president of the Duma, met with Hugo Stinnes in Stockholm to explore the possibilities of a negotiated peace, and Sergei Sazonov, a dedicated supporter of the Entente, was dismissed from his post as foreign minister.

Poland, however, proved to be an obstacle. Bethmann Hollweg was unwilling to restore Russia's Polish territory. On 12 August he reached an agreement with the Austrians concerning the establishment of a kingdom of Poland. The kaiser, anxious to follow up the Russian feelers, insisted that any German plans for Poland be left in abeyance. The military, however, sabotaged the possibility for peace. Although additional talks had taken place between Protopopov and the banker Felix Warburg—and Swedish Foreign Minister Knut Wallenberg informed the Germans that the Russians were indeed serious about peace—Bethmann Hollweg caved in to demands from Hindenburg. On 5 November he announced the formation of an independent Poland and destroyed the opportunity for a separate peace with Russia. Nationalist fervor in the Duma forced Czar Nicholas II to replace the ministers who had been attempting to bring about peace with Germany.

The United States also attempted to mediate a peace between the Allies and Central Powers. Following conferences with European statesmen, Colonel Edward M. House, friend and advisor of President Wilson, issued the House Memorandum on 22 February 1916. It announced that the president was willing, upon

P

the assent of France and Britain, to propose a peace conference. The proposal called for the restoration of Belgium and Serbia, the return of Alsace and Lorraine to France, the cession of Constantinople to Russia and Italian-speaking sections of Austria to Italy. An independent Poland would be established, but Germany would be compensated with additional colonies. It was intimated that if Germany were to refuse, the United States would join the Allied side. The British, however, banked upon a victorious 1916 offensive.

In August of 1916 Bethmann Hollweg informed the United States that Germany desired peace talks and would relinquish Belgium in order to gain American mediation. When Wilson, preoccupied with a presidential campaign, did not respond, the chancellor, with the support of the kaiser, decided to issue a declaration of German war aims and willingness to negotiate. The military, however, intervened. In November of 1916 Hindenburg demanded German retention of the Briey-Longwy basin and Liège, along with control of the Belgian railways and economy, partition of Montenegro between Austria and Albania, border "rectifications" favoring Austria from Italy and Rumania, the cession of parts of Serbia to Austria and Bulgaria, and the acquisition of the Belgian Congo by Germany. Bethmann Hollweg, therefore, had to send his note on 12 December 1916 without any delineation of German war aims. He merely expressed German willingness to discuss peace but also affirmed Germany's determination to continue the struggle if it were ignored.

France and Great Britain, aware of German policy in Belgium, doubted German sincerity. On 18 December Wilson issued his own peace note. He did not propose mediation but called for statements to determine the possibility of peace. The Germans did not disclose their conditions but along with Austria called for direct exchanges between the combatants. The Allies, however, were not moved, and Bethmann Hollweg, undercut by the German military, was unable to take advantage of the situation. On 10 January 1917 Britain and France informed Wilson that they required the restoration of Belgium and Alsace-Lorraine, reparations, the freeing of the Italians, South Slavs, Romanians, Czechs, and Slovaks from Austrian domination,and the elimination of Turkish territory in Europe.

Wilson's response came on 22 January when he appealed before the American Congress for "peace without victory." The turn of phrase was not appreciated by the British, and it did not prevent Germany's fateful decision to reinstitute unrestricted submarine warfare. The kaiser was apparently persuaded to support this step because France and Britain had failed to discuss Germany's December offer. Nevertheless, Austrian Emperor Karl, through the mediation of his brother-in-law, Prince Sixte of Bourbon-Parma, contacted the French and British governments in early 1917 without informing the Germans. Karl was willing to recognize the right of France to Alsace-Lorraine and to grant Serbia access to the sea and Russia Constantinople. Despite French and British interest, the effort foundered because of the generous concessions made to Italy at the expense of Austria in the 1915 Treaty of London and to Austria's powerlessness to effect its concessions.

The toll of the war brought domestic calls for peace in 1917. French Socialists openly advocated a compromise peace, but the government refused passports to delegates who wanted to meet at Stockholm with counterparts from the British and German left. After Georges Clemenceau became premier in November, he silenced the dissidents. Joseph Caillaux was imprisoned, Louis Malvy exiled, and Aristide Briand made temporarily a pariah. In April of 1917 the German Social Democratic party issued a manifesto that demanded immediate negotiations for "a general peace without annexations and indemnities on the basis of the free international development of all peoples." Matthias Erzberger and the Center party joined with the Social Democrats and Progressives to introduce in the Reichstag a peace resolution that called for a "peace of understanding" and "permanent reconciliation of peoples." The resolution condemned "forced territorial acquisitions" and "political, economic, and financial oppressions." Although Bethmann Hollweg, under pressure from the military, fatally compromised himself in April of 1917 by signing the arch-annexationist Kreuznach memorandum on German war aims, his failure to forestall the peace resolution, which was passed on 19 July 1917, led to his dismissal at the insistence of the supreme command. The advent of military dictatorship under Hindenburg and Ludendorff after his resignation on 13 July precluded peace short of a complete defeat of Germany. Bethmann Hollweg's successor, Georg Michaelis, rendered the resolution meaningless by saying that he accepted it "as I interpret it."

On 1 August 1917 Pope Benedict XV sent a seven-point peace note to the leaders of the Allies and Central Powers. He advocated simultaneous reduction of military might, evacuation of all occupied territory, arbitration, renunciation of war indemnities, a conciliatory examination of territorial claims, and freedom of the seas. Segments of the Italian military denounced the pope's reference to the "useless carnage" as treasonous. Austria, however, expressed support, and German Foreign Secretary Richard von Kühlmann proposed secret negotiations with the British government. His initiative, however, was squelched when Ludendorff insisted on demands that an undefeated Britain would never accept.

On 8 November, after the Bolsheviks had seized power, Lenin appealed to the belligerents to accept a peace without annexations. When his call went unheeded, on 21 November he requested an armistice and peace talks from the Central Powers. State Secretary of the Foreign Office Richard von Kühlmann recommended a moderate peace with the Russians, which would accord with the Reichstag's Peace Resolution and serve as a prelude to peace with the West. His position was supported by the Austrians and General Max Hoffmann but was defeated through the strenuous opposition of Ludendorff and Hindenburg. The supreme command ultimately dictated the annexationist peace of Brest-Litovsk.

On 5 January 1918 David Lloyd George announced Great Britain's conditions for peace in an address to the Trade Union Congress. He called for the evacuation of all territory occupied by the Central Powers, that the issue of Alsace and Lorraine be reexamined (which meant that they should be returned to France), that Poland be restored, that self-government be accorded to the nationalities of Austria-Hungary, that the territorial claims of Italy and Romania be satisfied, and that the Ottoman Empire be dismembered. He called for the establishment of an international organization to limit armaments and prevent future wars.

Three days later, on 8 January 1918, Wilson delivered his Fourteen Points to Congress. The German High Command and annexationists, however, placed their trust in military victory until almost the end. When on 24 June 1918 Kühlmann called for a negotiated settlement with the Western Allies, they forced him from his post. It was not until well after "the black day of the German army," on 8 August, that Hindenburg and Ludendorff accepted the inevitable, that Germany could not achieve military victory. They then turned to civilians to salvage what they could.

Bernard A. Cook

References

Crosby, G.R. *Disarmament and Peace in British Politics, 1914–1919*. London: Oxford University Press, 1957.

Fischer, Fritz. *Germany's Aims in the First World War*. New York: Norton, 1967.

Foster, K. *The Failure of Peace: The Search for a Negotiated Peace during the First World War*. Washington: American Council on Public Affairs, 1941.

Gatzke, Hans W. *Germany's Drive to the West: A Study of Germany's Western War Aims during the First World War*. Baltimore: Johns Hopkins University Press, 1950.

Manteyer, G. de. *Austria's Peace Offer, 1916–1917*. London: Constable, 1921.

Van Der Slice, A. *International Labor, Diplomacy and Peace, 1914–1919*. Philadelphia: University of Pennsylvania Press, 1941.

See also BETHMANN HOLLWEG, THEOBALD VON; KARL I, EMPEROR OF AUSTRIA

Persian Front, 1914–1918

Although political rather than military considerations dominated the Persian front during the war, its military significance was substantial, for Persia (Iran) not only formed a potential eastern flank for the Mesopotamian campaign but also contained recently developed British oil fields. During the conflict Russia, Great Britain—with their long-standing interests in the region—Turkey, and Germany, all became involved there in military actions, as well as in diplomatic intrigues to try to gain or maintain control of the area. As usual, Persia was caught in the middle.

After Turkey entered the war on the side of the Central Powers, the Persian government on 1 November 1914 declared its neutrality. Persia was exceedingly vulnerable to foreign intervention, however, since it was under leadership of the weak and vacillating seventeen-year-old Ahmad Shah. His only effective military forces were a Cossack brigade, 8,000 strong, commanded by Russian officers, and a Swedish gendarmerie of 7,000 troops, led by supposedly neutral but by that time corrupt Swedish commanders who actually favored the Germans.

The objectives of the two sides were clear from the beginning. Russia and Britain had settled their differences over Persia in 1907 by dividing it into spheres of influence, with Russia dominating the northern sector, Britain the southeastern portion, and a neutral zone in between. They hoped that Persia would remain quiet and subject to their desires. Turkey and Germany, for their part, hoped to extend their political influence over Persia and open up an additional front that would help spread the forces of the Entente Powers even more around the globe.

Actual fighting broke out in January of 1915, when a Turkish force, as part of its campaign in the Caucasus, took Tabriz on the 7th. The Russians, who already had a considerable presence in the northern region, retook the city on the 30th and then continued to expand control over their zone, while Britain added the neutral zone to its sphere.

In the meantime, the Germans were not idle. Their legation and military mission in Tehran, headed by Prince Henry of Reuss, began to send agents throughout the country. Captain Oskar von Niedermayer in the northeast and Wilhelm Wassmuss and Dr. Erich Zugmayer in the south were particularly effective in providing local leaders with money, weapons, and propaganda for the Central Powers' cause. In Tehran, Prince Henry gained favor with the Shah and Persian nationalists to such an extent that in October the alarmed Russians dispatched troops under General N.N. Baratov toward Tehran. At that point the Germans tried to convince the Shah and others to join them, since they promised to guarantee Persian independence. Many Persian politicians obviously shared these sentiments and left Tehran for nearby Qum, where Prince Henry had established a command post. They expected the shah to follow, but Russian and British diplomats "persuaded" the shah to remain in the capital.

General Baratov's force then proceeded against the rebels' military contingent of 8,000 irregular and 3,000 gendarmerie troops. They received additional supplies from the Turks, but the Russians were able to take Hamadan and Kirmanshah astride the Tehran-to-Baghdad

road as the Persian units fell back toward the Mesopotamian frontier. In January of 1916 the Germans recalled Prince Henry to Berlin, which in effect ended their attempts to dominate the Persian government.

During the rest of the year, the Russians and Turks traded offensives in western Persia. In March and April Baratov's formations, which never numbered more than 38 guns and 20,000 men, countered a Turkish advance and drove the Turks back into Mesopotamia. The British capitulation at Kut on the Tigris in late April, however, allowed the Turks to release a corps of 16,000 soldiers. A Turkish column under Khalil Pasha then forced 12,000 poorly supplied Russians to retreat all the way to the Sultan Bulak mountain range in northern Persia, where, after receiving reinforcements, the Russians held and set up defensive positions. The onset of winter brought a lull in the fighting.

Initial British combat in Persia took place in connection with the Mesopotamian campaign, when Major General Sir George Gorringe's 12th Division of 9,000 troops defeated 5,000 Turks near Ahvaz in April of 1915. The victory assured the British that the enemy would not threaten their pipeline to the Abadan refinery on the Persian Gulf. Britain's presence also ensured continued friendly relations with the local Bakhtiyari and Arab tribes.

In early 1916 the British decided to send a military mission to southern Persia to regain control of the area in view of Germany's diplomatic successes there. They pressured the shah's government, whose disposition had taken on a decidedly pro-British flavor, to go along. In March Brigadier General Sir Percy Sykes and advisers arrived at Bandar Abbas on the Persian Gulf and started organizing what became known as the South Persian Rifles. His troops first marched to Kirman in May and then Yazd in August, gaining recruits along their march. In September they helped the Russians secure the Isfahan region, and in November they took over Shiraz. Although the force never reached more than 8,000 of the proposed 11,000 troops, it had traveled over one thousand miles through the heart of Persia and had cleared the area of German influence. They remained for the rest of the war, conducting policing duties, such as putting down a revolt by the Qashqai tribe.

Although in 1917 the center of fighting shifted back to western Persia, events elsewhere helped determine the outcome. In March a British victory over the Turks at Baghdad forced the Turks to start pulling out of Persia. The Russian revolutions, however, had an even more profound effect on developments in Persia. With Russia in disarray, the Turks, Germans, and British all wanted a say in the Caucasus region—the Turks to establish an enlarged pan-Turkish state, the Germans and British to assist or influence the Georgian and Armenian Christians and to gain access to the Baku oil fields.

In 1918 the British launched two military expeditions. One under Sir Wilfrid Malleson was sent south and east of the Caspian Sea to prevent any German or Turkish penetration of northeastern Persia (and perhaps beyond). The other, commanded by Major General Lionel C. Dunsterville, left Baghdad in January of 1918, but his British and Indian troops became embroiled in the aftermath of the Bolshevik takeover as it related to northwestern Persia. Finally, in August, the "Dunsterforce" of about 1,000 soldiers, assisted by an improvised Caspian naval flotilla under Commodore David T. Norris, landed at Baku. Dunsterville found himself in an untenable position because of superior Turkish and Red Army formations in the region and therefore had to evacuate his troops by sea back to Persia. In September the British ordered Dunsterville back to Britain.

While involvement in the Caucasus did not cease with the general's recall, British military operations in Persia were for the most part over. As for Persia, after the war it remained subject to British dominance, although a coup by a former colonel in the Cossack Brigade, Reza Khan, in February of 1921 began to move the country in new directions.

Alan F. Wilt

References

Avery, Peter, Gavin Hambly, and Charles Melville, eds. *The Cambridge History of Iran.* Vol. 7: *From Nadir Shah to the Islamic Republic.* Cambridge: Cambridge University Press, 1991.

Barker, A.J. *The Neglected War: Mesopotamia, 1914–1918.* London: Faber & Faber, 1967.

Sykes, Christopher. *Wassmuss, "The German Lawrence."* London: Longmans, Green, 1936.

Sykes, Sir Percy. *A History of Persia,* Vol. 2. 3rd ed. New York: Barnes and Noble, 1969.

Pétain, Henri-Philippe (1856–1951)

French general and commander in chief of the army from 1917 to 1931. Born into a family of farmers on 24 April 1856 in Cauchy-à-la Tour, near Arras, Pétain graduated from St. Cyr in 1878. He served as an officer in a line regiment and then on the staff at the Ecole de Guerre. While Pétain had a good record, it was hardly distinguished; without the intervention of the First World War, he would have retired as a colonel.

Pétain's relative obscurity resulted partly from his distant manner and his inability to push himself with others, but primarily from his championing of an unorthodox military doctrine. Pétain believed that new machine weapons gave the defense the advantage over the offense. His idea clashed with the prevailing doctrine, the *offensive-à-outrance,* which stressed the necessity of offensive attacks with the rifle and bayonet. Pétain drew the correct lesson from the Russo-Japanese War—that such offensives could easily be nullified by machine guns and barbed wire.

When the First World War began, Pétain was temporarily commanding a brigade. He saw quickly that the war would be one of attrition, with victory going to the side "which will possess the last man." His pessimism, which often drove French army commander General Joseph Joffre to distraction, was not well known outside senior army circles. Pétain argued for wearing out the Germans along the entire front and only then mounting a "decisive effort." Pétain's outlook is reflected in such statements as "Audacity is the art of knowing how not to be too audacious" and "Cannon conquers, infantry occupies." That was not what Joffre or the French nation wanted to hear.

The war brought Pétain rapid promotion. By September of 1914 he commanded a division; two months later he had an army corps and before the end of the year he was a full general in command of Second Army. The course of events vindicated his unorthodox military views. Because Pétain was one of the leading students of defensive warfare, Joffre turned to him to stem the great German offensive at Verdun, which began in February of 1916. Pétain received the command there on the night of 25–26 February.

Pétain immediately rushed in reinforcements to Verdun and ordered that the remaining French forts be fully manned and held at all costs. He also ordered a defensive scheme be developed, as elastic as possible for the limited terrain. Pétain questioned the strategic value of Verdun as well as the decision to try to hold everywhere. In early March, when President Poincaré and General Joffre visited his headquarters, Pétain suggested the possibility of withdrawal to the left bank of the Meuse, an idea immediately squashed by Poincaré.

The French contained the German attempt to break through at Verdun. Pétain reorganized Verdun's defenses and transformed logistics so that supplies ran smoothly to the front along the single route into the fortress from Bar-le-Duc, and he did what he could to improve the difficult conditions faced by his men. His order that men be rotated in and out of the battle was a key factor in French success.

Pétain's leadership at Verdun raised him to the status of legend. Upon Premier Aristide Briand's suggestion, he was appointed to command the Center Army Group. General Robert Nivelle succeeded him as commander at Verdun on 1 May 1916.

Pétain was called on again in the spring of 1917 to deal with widespread mutinies in the French army following the disastrous Nivelle Offensive. Known for his concern for his men, he was perhaps the best choice at that difficult time. Promoted to commander of the French army in May, he ended the mutinies and restored calm before the Germans could capitalize on the situation. That was probably Pétain's greatest contribution to Allied victory. He visited disaffected units and talked to the men, convincing them that he cared about their welfare. Some of the ringleaders were subjected to summary courtmartial and shot, but Pétain acknowledged the justice of many of the mutineers' complaints. He assured the men that improvements would be made, particularly in food, wine, furloughs, and relief. In eloquent appeals Pétain told them that he would not send them into battle needlessly. As he put it, "I'm waiting for the Americans and the tanks," which he predicted would turn the tide of war in June of 1918.

As commander of the French army, Pétain employed offensive tactics designed to minimize the loss of French manpower while using up that of the enemy, a necessary precondition for the offensives that would one day win the war. When the Germans launched their final offensives in the spring of 1918, Pétain put into effect new defensive tactics aimed at the same result. French troops no longer contested every foot of ground. Advance positions, where major enemy artillery fire would be directed, were to be thinly held. These tactics, unpopular at first with subordinate commanders, helped stem the final German drive. French losses in the initial German attacks were held to a minimum, allowing French troops to hold their second line and counterattack with reserves. Territory meant little to Pétain; to him, the overriding principle was the war of attrition.

In December of 1918 there was general public satisfaction with Pétain's promotion to marshal, and he led the victory parade down the Champs Elysée on 14 July 1919. Pétain remained commander of the French army until 1931. He supported the construction of the Maginot Line and served as war minister in the Doumergue cabinet of 1934. He was appointed ambassador to Spain in 1939. After the 1940 German invasion of France, in June Pétain was chosen as the last premier of the Third Republic, to conclude an armistice with the Germans. He then became chief of state in the unoccupied part of the country, known as Vichy.

Pétain initially enjoyed near-unanimous support as head of the Vichy government. His government was certainly authoritarian, but it is not exactly clear what Pétain had in mind for France. He accepted the principle of French collaboration with Hitler, recognizing that for the indefinite future Germany would dominate Europe.

After the war Pétain was tried as a war criminal, convicted, and sentenced to death. President of the provisional government General Charles De Gaulle commuted Pétain's sentence to life imprisonment because of his contributions in the First World War, and the fact that Vichy had at least kept alive some semblance of French independence. Pétain was removed to the Isle d'Yeu, where he died on 23 June 1951. There have been several attempts to remove his remains and rebury them at Verdun.

Spencer C. Tucker

References

Griffiths, Richard. *Marshal Pétain*. London: Constable, 1970.
Lottman, Herbert R. *Pétain, Hero or Traitor*. New York: William Morrow, 1985.
Ryan, Stephen. *Pétain the Soldier*. New York: A.S. Barnes, 1969.

See also FRANCE, ARMY; FRENCH ARMY MUTINY; VERDUN, BATTLE OF

Peter (I) Karadjordjević, King (1844–1921)

Serbian king, born on 11 July 1844 in Belgrade. Peter was forced into exile after the abdication of his father, Alexander, in 1858. He spent most of his life in Switzerland, France, and Montenegro, and he graduated from St. Cyr before serving in the French Foreign Legion during the Franco-Prussian War. In 1875 Peter supported the Serb uprising in Bosnia and led Serb guerrilla actions against the Turks and local Muslims under the name Petar Mrkonjiç. He married Zorka, the daughter of Prince Nikola of Montenegro, in 1883, cementing an alliance with that state.

When Peter returned to Serbia as king in 1903, he restored the original (Karadjordjević) dynasty to the Serbian throne and created the first constitutional monarchy there. Peter encouraged Serbian expansion into Ottoman lands and increasingly focused on the South Slavic nationalities in the Hapsburg Empire. His belief in a constitutional government made him popular both at home and abroad. On 24 June 1914, suffering from ill health, Peter named Prince Alexander as regent. The Central Powers' defeat of Serbia in 1915 forced him to flee to the Adriatic, where he remained until his return to Belgrade on 1 December 1918. He reigned as king of the Kingdom of Serbs, Croats, and Slovenes until his death on 16 August 1921 in Topčider (near Belgrade).

Susan N. Carter

References

Banac, Ivo. *The National Question in Yugoslavia: Origins, History, Politics*. Ithaca: Cornell University Press, 1984.

Jelavich, Barbara. *History of the Balkans*. Vol. 2: *Twentieth Century*. New York: Cambridge University Press, 1983. Reprint, 1989.

Jelavich, Charles. *Tsarist Russia and Balkan Nationalism: Russian Influence in the Internal Affairs of Bulgaria and Serbia, 1879–1886*. Berkeley: University of California Press, 1958.

See also BALKAN FRONT, 1915; SERBIA; YUGOSLAVIA, CREATION OF

Pflanzer-Baltin, Karl Freiherr von (1855–1925)

Austro-Hungarian general, born on 1 June 1855 in Pécs, Hungary. Pflanzer-Baltin led troops against the Russians in the eastern Carpathians and Bukovina during the first two years of World War I. While his tactics of movement earned him the nickname "Now Here, Now There" among orthodox commanders, they also made him one of the more successful leaders in the Austro-Hungarian army. In June of 1916, however, his Seventh Army was overwhelmed in the Brusilov Offensive. The disaster seems to have resulted from a combination of his concentrating too many troops in the forward trenches of his lines and being ill at the actual moment of the attack. He was relieved of his command in September. His reputation remained such, however, that he received an independent command in Albania in July of 1918. There he not only held his own but actually managed the last successful offensive by the Central Powers before the end of the war. He died in Vienna on 8 April 1925.

Gary W. Shanafelt

References

Kövess, Géza. "Karl Freiherr von Pflanzer-Baltin (1855–1925)." In *Neue Österreichische Biographie ab 1815*. Vol. 16, 119–31. Vienna: Almathea-Verlag, 1965.

Stone, Norman. *The Eastern Front, 1914–1917*. New York: Charles Scribner's Sons, 1975.

See also ALBANIA; BRUSILOV OFFENSIVE

Piłsudski, Jósef Klemens (1867–1935)

Polish soldier and statesman, born in Zulow, Russian Poland, on 5 December 1867. Piłsudski was an ardent nationalist. He became involved in anti-czarist activism while attending Kharkov University, and he was exiled to Siberia from 1887–92. In 1894 he joined the Polish Socialist party and became editor of an underground newspaper that advocated Polish independence.

Convinced that Russia presented the greatest obstacle to Poland's independence, Piłsudski favored limited collaboration with Austria-Hungary; he organized clandestine military units, which received Austrian support in 1910. In early 1914, believing a war between Austria-Hungary and Russia imminent, Piłsudski reasoned that Polish independence would be ensured if Russia were defeated by the Central Powers, who in turn would be defeated by Great Britain, France, and the United States.

After the outbreak of war in 1914, Piłsudski's Union of Riflemen briefly occupied Kielce in Russian Poland and was soon thereafter absorbed into the Austrian-sponsored Polish Legions. Hoping to secure Polish manpower to serve on the Eastern Front, Germany and Austria-Hungary jointly proclaimed Poland's independence on 5 November 1916. Although he was appointed minister of war in the provisional Polish Council of State, Piłsudski soon withdrew his support from the Central Powers because they refused to commit themselves on Poland's political and territorial composition. In July of 1917 he was interned by the Germans for the remainder of the war.

From 1918 to 1922 Piłsudski guided the revived Polish state through particularly turbulent times. Increasingly disillusioned with the inadequacies of parliamentary government in Poland, in 1926 Piłsudski led a successful military coup and ruled Poland until his death in Warsaw on 12 May 1935.

Mark P. Gingerich

References

Jedrzejewicz, Waclaw. *Piłsudski: A Life for Poland*. New York: Hippocrene, 1982.

Machray, Robert. *The Poland of Piłsudski*. New York: E.P. Dutton, 1937.

Piłsudski, Joseph. *Joseph Piłsudski: The Memories of a Polish Revolutionary and Soldier*. Edited and translated by D.R. Gillie. London: Faber and Faber, 1931.

See also POLAND

Pistols

The first commercially successful automatic pistol, designed by Hugo Borchardt, was produced in Germany in 1893. Military men quickly recognized the value of a handgun that could be fired quickly and easily, and European armies began to adopt automatic pistols officially in the first decade of the new century. All of the principal warring nations adopted or issued automatics in the course of the First World War.

France, Britain, and Russia retained revolvers as their primary handguns. Revolver accuracy and reliability were comparable to that of the newer automatic pistols. Officers of many countries were permitted to carry privately purchased pistols.

Pistol marksmanship requires skill and training, especially with the maximum effective range for a pistol usually considered to be less than fifteen yards. Pistols of all types were used effectively in close combat; they were normally issued as weapons of last resort, however, to men whose primary duties were to lead, to operate heavy weapons or vehicles, or to support frontline troops.

Austria-Hungary adopted the 8mm Rast-Gasser revolver in 1898 and continued to issue it throughout the war. In 1907 the 8mm M7 Roth Steyr auto was adopted for the cavalry. The most commonly carried auto pistol, however, was the 9mm Steyr-Hahn adopted in 1912; as many as 300,000 were manufactured in Austria. Other auto pistols included the 7.65mm 1908 Steyr; the 7.65mm Frommer Stop; and the M1896 Mauser.

The German Imperial Navy adopted the 9mm Luger in 1904. The army adopted the Luger in 1908 to replace the M1879 and M1883 Reichs revolvers. Navy Lugers normally had a 6-inch barrel and were issued with detachable shoulder stocks. Army Lugers had 4-inch barrels and stock lugs, but stocks were issued less often. The army also acquired some 205,000 of the P-08 Lange with an 8-inch barrel and detachable stock, for issue to air crews, artillerymen, machine gunners, and others. A 32-shot drum magazine for this weapon appeared in 1917.

Germany augmented its handgun supply with at least 200,000 M1896 Mauser pistols, sometimes known as the "Broomhandle Mauser," in both the original 7.63mm and in the army's standard 9mm. These M1896 pistols were normally issued with detachable stocks. German manufacturers supplied Bulgaria with Lugers before the war in both 7.65mm and 9mm.

Germany purchased at least 300,000 commercial 7.65mm automatic handguns for issue. Among these were the Walther M6 and M4, the 1913 Sauer, the 1907 Dreyse, the FL Selbstlader, the Beholla, the Menta, the Mauser M1914, and the Jaeger. After Germany captured Belgium's arms factories it produced some 100,000 M1908 Bayard pistols and perhaps some Browning models as well.

Turkey received large quantities of arms from Germany during the war. Pistols known to have been acquired before the war include the M1896 Mauser and the 9mm M1903 Browning.

Belgium was a leading pistol exporter before the war. The Belgian army adopted the 7.65mm M1900 and the 9mm M1903 Browning auto pistols. Belgian artillerymen in 1914 were still armed with 9mm service revolvers, including the models of 1878, 1883, and 1878–86. Britain had used .455 caliber Webley revolvers since 1887. The Mark IV Webley entered service in 1899 and, together with the Marks V and VI, was widely issued. The Mark VI was adopted in May of 1915; Webley & Scott made 300,000 of them during the war.

Britain purchased large numbers of Smith and Wesson and Colt revolvers in .455 caliber. The most common types were the Colt New Service Revolver, and the Smith and Wesson Mark II Hand Ejector Revolver. Britain and Canada bought over 73,000 of the latter. Colt also manufactured automatic pistols for Britain, in .32, .38, .45, and .455 calibers. Among these were some 10,000 M1911 Colt automatics in .455 caliber.

The Royal Navy adopted a .455 automatic in May of 1914. This weapon, made by Webley and designated Mark I, was also issued to the Royal Marines and to some airmen.

Canada issued Webley revolvers, but relied more extensively on Smith and Wesson revolvers and on Colt revolvers and automatics.

France produced and issued its 8mm Model 1892 revolver throughout the war. France also accepted as a standard service pistol the 7.65mm M1914 Ruby, a Spanish copy of the Browning M1900 auto pistol. At least 600,000 of these were delivered to France.

In Italy, the 10.35mm M1872 and M1889 Glisenti revolvers remained in service throughout the war. These weapons were made in small workshops and varied in details and quality. In 1910 Italy adopted the 9mm M1910 Glisenti, a blowback automatic, as a standard sidearm. From 1915 to 1919 Beretta produced the M1915, another blowback automatic, in both 9mm Glisenti and 7.65mm. Both types were commonly used. The Italian navy bought 5,000 M1896 Mauser pistols before the war and designated them the Modello 1899.

Japan adopted the 9mm Meiji-26 revolver in 1893. The 8mm Taisho-04 Nambu automatic was not officially adopted, but many officers purchased them after they appeared in 1915.

Montenegro adopted the Austrian-made 11mm Gasser revolver in 1873. Every Montenegrin liable for military service was required to own one. Russia donated 30,000 of its Smith and Wesson .44 revolvers in 1904.

Portugal adopted the Savage M1907 auto pistol, designating it the M1908. Procurement may have been delayed until 1914, however, when imported Lugers became unavailable.

Portuguese soldiers in France were generally equipped with British arms.

Romania adopted the M1912 Steyr-Hahn and purchased at least 56,000 of them before 1916. The Steyr replaced the 8mm Nagant Model 1895 and the 8mm St.-Etienne Model 1896, which resembled the Russian and French service revolvers, respectively.

Russia adopted the unique gas seal 7.62mm Nagant revolver in 1895 and continued it in service throughout the war. Some Russian officers carried the Mauser M1896 and the Browning M1900.

Serbia adopted the 7.5mm Nagant revolver, made in Belgium, in 1891. After the Serbian army was evacuated to Corfu, it was reequipped with French arms, including at least 5,000 Ruby auto pistols.

Clayton Perkins

References

Bogdanovic, Branko, and Ivan Valencak. *Great Century of Guns*. New York: Gallery, 1986.

Cormack, A.J.R., ed. *Famous Pistols and Handguns*. Berkshire, England: Profile, 1977.

Ezell, Edward Clinton. *Small Arms of the World*. 12th ed. Harrisburg, Pa.: Stackpole, 1983.

Hogg, Ian V., and John Weeks. *Military Small Arms of the 20th Century*. London: Arms and Armour, 1977.

Smith, W.H.B., and Joseph E. Smith. *The Book of Pistols and Revolvers*. 7th ed. Harrisburg, Pa.: Stackpole, 1968.

Still, Jan C. *The Pistols of Germany and Its Allies in Two World Wars*. Vol. 1. Douglas, Ala.: Privately published, 1982.

Taylerson, A.W.F. *The Revolver 1889–1914*. New York: Crown, 1971.

Wilson, R.K. *Textbook of Automatic Pistols*. Plantersville, S.C.: Small Arms Technical Publishing, 1943.

See also RIFLES; UNIFORMS

Plumer, Viscount Herbert Charles Onslow (1857–1932)

British general and army commander. Born in the seaside resort of Torquay on 13 March 1857, Plumer was educated at Eaton. In 1876 he was commissioned directly into the army. Plumer made his reputation in South Africa as commander of a mounted rifle unit during the 1896 Matabele Rising, then as commander of the column that relieved Mafeking in 1900 during the Boer War.

Plumer was promoted to major general in 1902. In 1903 he became the quartermaster general and the third military member of the newly formed Army Council. In 1906 he assumed command of the 5th Division in Ireland. In 1908 he was promoted to lieutenant general and two years later was appointed commander in chief at York.

At the start of World War I, Plumer commanded II Corps. In 1915 he commanded the V Corps in Smith-Dorrien's Second Army at Second Ypres and afterward assumed command of the Second Army. Although the Ypres sector remained relatively quiet for the next two years, Plumer was not idle. Second Army trained new troops for other sectors, while Plumer carefully laid plans for an offensive.

After the failure of France's Nivelle Offensive of April 1917, the Allied leaders felt that they had to pressure the Germans somewhere along the line. That May, British commander General Douglas Haig asked Plumer when he could attack. Plumer's immediate response was "the 7th of June." On that day the British exploded nineteen tunnel mines under German positions at Messines Ridge. The British achieved their objective by mid-afternoon on the first day, at one-fifth the expected casualties. Plumer quickly consolidated his position and beat back a counterattack by three German divisions the next day. On 21 July 1917, the British continued the offensive toward Passchendaele (Third Ypres). Initially, the battle was a joint effort between Gough's Fifth Army and Plumer's Second. In fairly short order, however, Haig shifted complete control of the offensive to Plumer.

Passchendaele was finally secured on 10 November, but in the meantime the Allies had suffered serious reverses at Riga and Caporetto. Part of the Second Army was ordered to Italy, where Plumer took over a force of five British and six French divisions, behind which the Italian army was to reorganize.

Plumer and his British divisions returned to Flanders just prior to the start of Ludendorff's 1918 offensives. The St. Quentin Offensive of 21 March, which fell to the south of Second Army, almost completely devoured Gough's Fifth Army. When Haig asked Plumer what he could do to help, he immediately offered to give up twelve of his fourteen divisions "in return for tired ones." Plumer shortly paid the price for his unselfish gesture, because Ludendorff's second great offensive (Lys) fell squarely on Second Army. Although forced to give ground, Plumer's army doggedly held the Ypres salient until the German drive stalled.

In 1919 Plumer was promoted to field marshal, raised to the peerage as a baron, and made commander of the British Army of the Rhine. As occupation commander he put down German riots and strikes ruthlessly, while at the same time securing shipments of food from Britain for the starving Germans. From 1919 to 1925 he was governor of Malta, and during his tenure the first representative government was introduced there. In 1925 he was appointed high commissioner in Palestine. While he brooked no disorder there either, he earned a reputation for dealing evenhandedly with both the Arabs and the Jewish settlers.

Plumer retired in 1928. He was raised to viscount the following year, and he died in London on 16 July 1932. Although history's evaluation of Plumer is overwhelmingly positive, the far more important judgment came from his troops. During a war in which the vast majority of the common soldiers came to hate their generals, the short, dumpy little general with the big white moustache (he was the model for David Lowe's caricature of British officers, Colonel Blimp) was loved by his men, and for good reason—he kept more of them alive.

David T. Zabecki

References
Falls, Cyril. *The Great War*. London: Putnam, 1959.
Harington, Charles. *Plumer of Messines*. London: J. Murray, 1935.
Liddell Hart, Basil H. *The Real War, 1914–1918*. Boston: Little, Brown, 1930.

See also LUDENDORFF OFFENSIVES; MESSINES, BATTLE OF; PASSCHENDAELE; YPRES, SECOND BATTLE OF

Pohl, Hugo von (1855–1916)

German admiral, commander of the High Seas Fleet, 1915–16. Born on 25 August 1855 in Breslau, Pohl joined the Imperial Navy in the 1870s. He gained renown during the Boxer Rebellion when, as commanding officer of the battle cruiser *Hansa*, he led a multinational assault against Fort Taku. Close to Admiral Alfred von Tirpitz but not unsympathetic to "new school" naval doctrine, Pohl subsequently commanded battleship squadrons, earning a reputation as a fine leader of men and a sound tactician.

In 1913 Pohl, a full admiral, was elevated into the Prussian nobility and became chief of the admiralty staff. Once hostilities were under way, he encountered the common German apprehension over risking the fleet in a direct clash with the superior enemy. He favored limited rather than full-scale fleet operations, while pushing for more aggressive U-boat warfare and accelerated building programs. After the Dogger Bank fiasco in early 1915, Pohl succeeded Admiral Friedrich Ingenohl as chief of the High Seas Fleet. His year-long tenure predictably brought no noteworthy operations in the North Sea but some actions in the Baltic against the Russian navy.

Early in 1915 Pohl personally persuaded Kaiser Wilhelm II to step up submarine activities by declaring a war zone around the British Isles. This policy backfired and had to be reversed after the *Lusitania* incident. In January of 1916 Pohl revealed that he was dying from liver cancer and was replaced by Scheer. His posthumously published notes and letters remain a valuable commentary on the early phase of the war at sea. Pohl died in Berlin on 23 February 1916.

Eric C. Rust

References

Görlitz, Walter, ed. *The Kaiser and His Court: The Diaries, Note Books and Letters of Admiral Georg Alexander von Müller, Chief of the Naval Cabinet, 1914–1918.* New York: Harcourt, Brace, World, 1964.

Herwig, Holger. *"Luxury" Fleet.* London: Allen and Unwin, 1980.

Marineministerium (Berlin). *Der Krieg zur See, 1914–1918.* 24 vols. Berlin and Frankfurt: E.S. Mittler und Sohn, 1922–66.

Pohl, Hugo von. *Aus Aufzeichnungen und Briefen wahrend des Kriegszeit.* Berlin: K. Siegismund, 1920.

See also GERMANY, NAVY

Poincaré, Raymond (1860–1934)

French premier and president, born on 20 August 1860 at Bar-le-Duc in Lorraine. Poincaré was elected to the Chamber of Deputies in 1887 and held his first ministerial post in 1893. A moderate republican, Poincaré rode the crest of a nationalist revival as premier and foreign minister in 1912 and president of the republic from 1913 to 1920. Poincaré dominated French foreign policy in the immediate prewar years and predicated it on maintaining the balance of power between the Triple Entente and the Triple Alliance. This meant strengthening France's ties with England and Russia.

In 1912 Poincaré strengthened the Entente by obtaining a Franco-Russian naval agreement and receiving Russia's promise that if war broke out with Germany, Russia would unleash an offensive on the twelfth day of mobilization. At the same time, however, Poincaré prevented a 1912 Russian-Italian alliance for fear that Russia would be emboldened to take the Straits, thereby triggering an Austrian response. Likewise, Poincaré succeeded in persuading Russia to accept an international conference at London to settle the distribution of Turkish lands following the Balkan Wars. Russia's reluctant refusal to support Serbia's claim to the port of Scutari on the Adriatic coast spared Europe a major conflict.

Poincaré also strengthened France's ties with England in the naval agreement of 1912, whereby the Royal Navy assumed responsibility for the Channel and France's northern coast, while the French fleet guarded much of the Mediterranean. Although France and England never had a formal military alliance, this agreement placed a good deal of moral responsibility upon England to protect French territory if war with Germany should occur.

Elected president in 1913, Poincaré actively used his powers to continue his foreign policy. First, Poincaré, who strongly believed in military preparedness, supported the bitterly contested 1913 Military Law, which increased military service from two to three years. The resultant increase in the size of the French army was a response to Germany's aggressive policies and an increase in the size of her own military.

Second, Poincaré and his carefully selected premiers sought to position France for the eventual collapse of the Ottoman Empire. This was done in early 1914 when Turkey and Germany agreed that France should finance a portion of the Berlin-to-Baghdad railway in Anatolia and Syria. The agreement ensured that France would be the major economic power in Syria and showed that Poincaré was prepared to reach a détente with Germany on imperial matters without compromising France's close ties with Russia and England.

Third, in June of 1914, when Austrian Archduke Franz Ferdinand was assassinated, Poincaré and Premier René Viviani initially pursued a cautious policy: France told Russia that Serbia should accept as many of Austria's conditions as honor would allow and that the Triple Entente should attempt to have an international inquest on the assassination rather than an Austrian one. When Austria, supported by Germany, mobilized against Serbia in July, however, Poincaré supported Russia's mobilization against Austria. He believed that the alliance would otherwise collapse and France would be isolated and prey to German blackmail. Poincaré also fully understood that if Austria were allowed to crush Serbia, the balance of power on the continent would have shifted in favor of the Central Powers. Poincaré was thus determined to lead France into war in order to contain German expansion.

During the first three years of the war, Poincaré played an important role in determining key diplomatic and military policies. He sought the use of force against neutralist Greece's pro-German ruler, King Constantine. Prime Minister Aristide Briand believed that Constantine would follow a neutralist policy; his pro-German policies, however, threatened Allied troops in Salonika. Poincaré welcomed Constantine's overthrow in 1917 and warmly greeted Greece's entry into the war as an ally. Poincaré also supported Briand's decision to keep French troops at Salonika even though the original purpose of the French campaign, to save Serbia, had failed. When Joffre refused to support the Balkan campaign fully, Poincaré abandoned his support for him.

Contrary to the wishes of Premier Paul Painlevé, Poincaré supported General Nivelle's ill-fated April 1917 offensive, which resulted in French military mutinies. Poincaré also goaded French premiers into clarifying war aims. He successfully pushed for Russian-British support for a French role in postwar Syria and Lebanon. Likewise, he successfully urged czarist Russia to recognize French claims to Alsace-Lorraine and the Rhineland.

After the war Poincaré unsuccessfully supported Marshal Foch's position at the 1919 Paris Peace Conference that, since the League of Nations could not protect French security, the Rhineland must be detached from Germany or at the very least be occupied by France until

Germany had repaid all of its reparations. Poincaré broke with precedent to return to active politics after his tenure as president. He served twice as premier, from 1922 to 1924 and from 1926 to 1929. His most controversial decision was the French invasion of the Ruhr in 1923. He died on 15 October 1934 at Sampigny.

Jan Karl Tanenbaum

References

Hayne, M.B. *The French Foreign Office and the Origins of the First World War, 1898–1914.* Oxford: Oxford University Press, 1993.

Keiger, John F.V. *France and the Origins of the First World War.* New York: St. Martin's, 1983.

Krumeich, Gerd. *Armaments and Politics in France on the Eve of the First World War.* Translated by Stephen Conn. Dover, N.H.: Berg, 1984.

Miguel, Pierre. *Poincaré.* Paris: Arthème Fayard, 1961.

Poincaré, Raymond. *Au Service de la France.* 11 vols. Paris: Plon, 1926–74.

Wright, Gordon. *Raymond Poincaré and the French Presidency.* Stanford: Stanford University Press, 1942.

See also ALLIANCES, PREWAR; BRIAND, ARISTIDE; FRANCE, HOME FRONT; OUTBREAK OF THE FIRST WORLD WAR; VIVIANI, RENÉ

Poland

History, often said to repeat itself, occasionally reverses itself. This happened with Poland. In the seventeenth century Poland was second only to France in area and population. It suffered from serious weaknesses, however, including the lack of natural frontiers. The country was largely of flat, open terrain without defensible geographical features. It also had a fractious and self-centered nobility. The nobles won repeated concessions, weakening the central government to the point that Poland was easy prey for outside powers. As a result Austria, Prussia, and Russia carried out three partitions of Poland in 1772, 1793, and 1795, causing it to disappear from the map. The cause of Polish independence did not die, however. Napoleon briefly resurrected a Polish state, and there were a number of insurrections by Poles in the nineteenth century.

The First World War offered a unique opportunity for Poles to secure their independence. A number of Polish military formations fought in the war, and there were also "committees" claiming to speak for Poland. Many Poles also fought in the armies of the major powers. According to one historian, this benefited the cause of a united and independent Poland because "the Polish military and political effort was so spread out that some of its forces could not help but be on the winning side."

The most important Polish military force during the war was the Polish Legion organized by Jósef Piłsudski. On 3 August 1914, Piłsudski announced the formation of an insurrectionary People's Government in Warsaw. Three days later, Piłsudski, who claimed to head all "military forces of Poland," "invaded" Russia's Polish provinces with a force of fewer than 200 men. Piłsudski's anticipated insurrection in the Russian area of Poland did not materialize, and his forces were soon in retreat. The Russian army, meanwhile, mobilized all Polish reservists, totaling some 600,000 men; Germany called up 200,000 Polish reservists from its eastern provinces.

Vienna backed Piłsudski's force only reluctantly. Thousands of Poles served in the imperial army and Vienna had no desire to see a powerful separate Polish force. Still, it was obvious that Poles would prefer to serve in their own military formation. As a result, Vienna authorized the formation at Kraków of the *Naczelny Komitet Narodowy* (Supreme National Committee), or NKN. It included representatives of Polish political groups and was to advise the Austrian government on Polish military and political matters. Vienna also saw to it that there was sufficient representation so that Piłsudski could not dominate it. Subsequent negotiations with the NKN led Vienna to authorize the formation of two brigades of the Polish Legion with a strength of about 2,500 men each. Piłsudski received command of 1st Brigade, and Józef Haller the 2nd Brigade. Until 1912 Haller had been a captain in the Austrian army.

Although Austria did not fare well in fighting in 1914, the situation was reversed in 1915 when the Central Powers succeeded in capturing Warsaw and pushing the Russian army almost entirely out of Russian Poland. The Polish Legion recruited Poles from the liberated areas and added a third brigade that year. By the beginning of 1916, the Legion numbered some 12,000 men.

Generally speaking, the Polish Legion was highly motivated and performed well, often as shock troops. Many were intellectuals. The officers, most of them young, were not highly trained and the brigades were ill disciplined. The Legion gave only grudging allegiance to the Austrians, with whom they considered themselves only temporarily allied. All officers and men were selected for allegiance to Piłsudski, whom they addressed as "Commandant."

Piłsudski proved a difficult ally. The Germans and Austrians believed he would switch sides as soon as it suited his purposes. In fact, Germany, Austria, and Russia all half-promised Polish independence, but none of the three expected to concede it.

Russia also sought to rally Poles to its side in the war. On 14 August 1914, Russian army commander Grand Duke Nikolai Nikolaevich had issued a proclamation promising autonomy to Poland. That was a victory for Roman Dmowski and his National Democratic party, which had placed hopes for Polish independence on an Entente victory. In Warsaw there was great enthusiasm for Russia, and the mobilization of Polish reservists in the Russian army went smoothly. Indeed, Piłsudski was criticized in Warsaw for his invasion. Dmowski, meanwhile, began organizing in East Galicia to recruit Poles to fight in the Russian army. This force was known as the Pulawy Legion.

Poles were cynical about Russian promises. Many believed that the Russians intended an autonomous Poland to include only the Polish provinces of Germany and Austria. Dmowski and his Polish National Committee, forced to flee to St. Petersburg ahead of the 1915 Central Powers' invasion, pressed the Russian government for commitments. When it became clear that the Russian government was not acting in good faith, Dmowski sailed for Britain in 1915 to make his case with Russia's Western allies.

The Germans also tried to play the card of Polish independence. General Erich Ludendorff estimated that there were nearly a million Poles of military age in the areas then occupied by Germany and Austria. On 6 November 1916, Berlin and Vienna announced their intention to create a "self-governing" kingdom of Poland. This consisted only of territory taken from Russia, and Germany and Austria planned to retain their Polish provinces. Pending selection of a king, Poland would be ruled by a regency council and a twenty-five-man provisional council of state. Poland's new army (the *Polnische*

P

Wehrmacht) was to be commanded by German officers.

Initial enthusiasm for the Central Powers' offer soon gave way to disillusionment. The council of state, which included Piłsudski, discovered it had no authority. All important decisions were made by the German governor general in Warsaw, General Hans von Beseler. The council of state refused to recruit Poles for military service until the Germans made meaningful political concessions. Beseler then ordered enrollment in the *Polnische Wehrmacht* of all members of the Polish Legion.

This action led Piłsudski to switch sides. In late spring of 1917 the Germans announced that they would require an oath of loyalty by all those officers and men of the Polish Legion from the German area of Poland. Piłsudski ordered his troops not to comply. On 9 July 1917, members of the 1st and 3rd Brigades were paraded in Warsaw to take the oath. More than 5,000 of the 6,000 men assembled refused and were arrested. Piłsudski himself was arrested on 22 July and sent to a German military prison at Magdeburg.

By mid-1917 there were at least five Polish organizations seeking independence. The Supreme National Committee at Kraków favored the Central Powers. There was also the Polish National Committee at Petrograd, which Dmowski had left. Then there was the Polish Information Agency, created in Paris by Dmowski and other leading Poles, later known as the Polish National Committee. The Western Allies recognized this as the authoritative Polish organization. In Warsaw there was a Central National Committee, loyal to Piłsudski. Finally, the Germans also established the Council of State for the Polish Kingdom, later reduced in size and renamed the Regency Council.

Poles serving in the armed forces were also split. In Paris Dmowski's Polish National Committee set about raising a Polish force to serve under the French on the Western Front. The 1st and 3rd Brigades of the Polish Legion had been disbanded, but Haller and several thousand men of his 2nd Brigade, now known as the Polish Auxiliary Corps, continued in the service of the Central Powers. There were also several Polish legions in the Russian army, and within Poland there was a secret organization sponsored by Piłsudski and known as the *Polska Organizacja Wojskowa* (Polish Military Organization), or POW. At the time of Piłsudski's arrest it numbered about 30,000 men. Commanded by Edward Śmigły-Rydz, the POW was conceived by Piłsudski as the nucleus for a future Polish army.

Haller and his forces subsequently defected from the Austrians and went over to the Russian side, where they hoped to be transported to the Western front. Before this could be accomplished the Germans attacked, and Haller's forces were defeated in battle and dispersed. The Bolsheviks regarded Haller's men as counterrevolutionaries. Some of Haller's men made their way back through German lines to Poland. Others, including Haller, sought refuge with British forces at Murmansk. From there they were transported to France, where they joined the forces raised by the National Committee.

The Allied position on the revival of a Polish state was simplified by the Bolshevik Revolution. France was particularly strong in its support, hoping to secure a state that would help contain Germany. The British government was less enthusiastic but went along under American pressure.

The United States had a Polish emigré population of more than a million people, with another three million second- or third-generation Poles. In 1915 acclaimed Polish pianist Ignacy Jan Paderewski had gone to the United States to raise funds for Polish relief and to gain support for Polish independence. Recognized by Dmowski's Polish National Committee as its American representative, Paderewski proved a superb propagandist. He established a recruiting organization in Chicago that ultimately sent 20,000 Polish-Americans to France to join the Polish army being raised there. Most important, Paderewski utilized his close friendship with Colonel Edward House, President Wilson's confidant and adviser. As early as January of 1917, Wilson declared to the Senate his support for a united and independent Poland. Finally, on 8 January 1918, Wilson made "a free and independent Poland with access to the sea" one of his Fourteen Points.

Meanwhile, the war was drawing to a close. On 8 November 1918 Piłsudski was released from prison. He went to Berlin to negotiate with the Germans but a revolution was underway and Piłsudski returned to Warsaw by train, arriving there on 10 November. Most Polish leaders saw Piłsudski, indisputably Poland's greatest military figure, as the only individual capable of bringing national unity. On 7 November 1918 a provisional government had been proclaimed in Lublin. In Warsaw, meanwhile, Prince Zdzilaw Lubomirski, on behalf of the Regency Council, handed over to Piłsudski full civil and military powers, conferring on him the historic title of chief of state. The only proviso was that he transfer power to the Polish parliament after its election. Piłsudski took office the next day. His powers were confirmed by the first freely elected parliament, three months later.

Establishing the boundaries of the new Polish state turned out to be the most controversial and difficult part of the postwar settlement in eastern Europe. Just before the Armistice, Dmowski arrived in the United States and met with President Wilson. When Wilson asked him what boundaries he had in mind, Dmowski pulled out a map showing the 1772 frontiers plus Upper Silesia and all of East Prussia. Wilson later said, "They presented me with a map which claimed half the world."

During the Paris Peace Conference, the Polish delegation won French support for a large Poland. The commission set up to study the matter of Poland's frontiers recommended that Poland be given access to the sea by means of a corridor running across Posen and West Prussia, including the port of Danzig. This proposal was in accord with the Fourteen Points, but it left 1.5 million Germans in East Prussia. Danzig was made a free city, and Germany was given free transit across the area. The issue of Poland's eastern boundary was so vexing that the Big Four left it to a commission, headed by Lord Curzon. In December of 1919 the commission proposed a boundary (the Curzon Line) that was recognized by neither the Soviet Union nor Poland.

Although Poland had been reunited and had a sizable population of twenty million people, it faced staggering problems after the war. Boundary issues remained unresolved until 1923, leading to much fighting and prolonged controversy as Poland pursued an expansionary policy toward her neighbors. Poland's acquisitions of Vilna, Upper Silesia, and eastern Galicia were mostly through the use of force. Poland fought a war with Russia in 1919–20, and in the March 1921 Treaty of Riga, Poland acquired additional territory beyond that assigned by the Curzon Commission. As finally stabilized, Poland constituted a state four-fifths the size of Germany, with nearly 29 million people.

Poland also had major domestic problems. A nation of small, inefficient farms, the country was overwhelmingly poor. With little in the way of financial aid forthcoming from the Western powers, it was left to deal with problems largely on its own. The constitution of 1921 produced a parliamentary republic similar to that of France. There was a president elected for a seven-year term, but the office was weak, and Piłsudski refused to serve as a "fig leaf" for the parties. The new government was soon floundering, with too many political parties and chronic instability. In May of 1926, in order to save a deteriorating situation, Piłsudski seized power in a coup in which some 400 people died.

Piłsudski restored stability in what the regime's defenders called a "controlled democracy," in which he was the final arbiter. Although Piłsudski was well intentioned, there was a clear shift toward a paternalistic form of dictatorship, which continued after his death in 1935. Piłsudski was followed by a succession of inept military leaders.

Another difficult problem was that of minorities. Poland had within her borders the largest population of minorities in Europe outside of Russia. These included Ukrainians, Byelorussians, Jews (10 percent of the population, 2.8 million of whom died in the German Holocaust during the Second World War), and Germans.

The Second World War began on the plains of Poland. Both Germany and the Soviet Union regarded that country as a *saisonstaat,* to be swept aside at the first opportunity. On 23 August 1939, the two powers concluded a secret arrangement to divide Poland and the Baltic states between them. In September of 1939 the Germans invaded Poland. When Britain and France chose to fight, the Second World War began.

Spencer C. Tucker

References

Bonsal, Stephen. *Suitors and Suppliants: The Little Nations at Versailles*. New York: Prentice-Hall, 1946.

Machray, Robert. *Poland 1914–1931*. New York: E.P. Dutton, 1932.

Roos, Hans. *A History of Modern Poland*. New York: Knopf, 1966. Watt, Richard M. *Bitter Glory. Poland and Its Fate, 1918–1939*. New York: Simon and Schuster, 1979.

See also DMOWSKI, ROMAN; HALLER, JÓZEF; PADEREWSKI, IGNACY JAN; PIŁSUDSKI, JÓSEF; VERSAILLES TREATY

Poland: German Offensive of September–November 1914

By mid-September 1914 the demoralized Austrians had been pushed back through Galicia across the San River, leaving 120,000 comrades behind in the besieged Przemsyl fortress. Thanks to a dilatory Russian pursuit, General Viktor Count Dankl von Krasnik's Austrian First Army managed to establish a new line behind the Dunajec River, a mere fifty miles before the pivotal Cracow blocking position. Austrian chief of staff Field Marshal Count Franz Conrad von Hötzendorf felt abandoned by his German ally, so recently triumphant in East Prussia and now worthlessly stationed far off to the north. He also feared that the Russian steamroller was readying another push that would overrun the intact, albeit badly weakened, Austrian ranks. He therefore pressed newly appointed German chief of staff General Erich von Falkenhayn to draw off the Russian forces concentrating before Cracow.

For his part, Falkenhayn was preoccupied with the critical Race to the Sea on the Western Front and would not detach forces from that theater, despite an urgent estimate of the situation by German Eighth Army commander General Paul von Hindenburg and his operations chief General Erich Ludendorff, stationed in Prussia. They held that there was an imminent danger of a Russian attack on Silesia, that further deterioration on the Galician front could collapse the entire Austrian war effort, and that the war could be decided on the Eastern Front because the Russian threat would likely be eradicated if the advance into Silesia were foiled. Falkenhayn advised Hindenburg and Ludendorff that they could prepare any spoiling attack that could be managed exclusively with troops already at hand in the East.

Insulated from the main war effort, Hindenburg and Ludendorff, ably assisted by the brilliant Colonel Max Hoffmann, fashioned a new command, the Ninth Army, by stripping four corps from the Eighth Army and adding about one and a half corps of second-line reserve units arriving piecemeal from Germany. By a marvel of logistics they moved more than 220,000 men, along with horses, equipment, food, artillery, and munitions, by train over 450 miles to the south within a period of eleven days. These units then formed along a northeasterly front, spanning one hundred miles from the south of Lodz to the Nida River just northeast of Cracow, where they aligned with the left flank of the Austrian First Army. Hindenburg and Ludendorff took direct command of the new Ninth Army and retained operational control of the Eighth.

Hindenburg and Ludendorff's objective was a sweeping spoiling attack, essentially a large-scale raid, to seize the crossings of the Vistula River well below Warsaw. The move was a prelude to envelopment of the fortress rings covering the direct east–west approach, and it would also prevent the Russian forces from crossing the river below Warsaw and threatening the German lines of communication. Hindenburg and Ludendorff discerned that the Russians had at most a cavalry corps dispersed over the vast spaces of southwest Poland leading to the Vistula fords.

The Austrian First Army, dissuaded from a more grandiose venture beyond its capacity, would advance in concert on the right wing, while the Germans sought the flanks and rear of any Russian units menacing the Austrians, permitting the latter to proceed unhindered to the relief of besieged Przemsyl and the liberation of Lemburg. Meanwhile, the Russians had been realigning their forces northward in preparation to thrust into Silesia at the urgent behest of the French government, which sought to divert German troops from the drive for the Flanders ports. Some modification was inevitable in any case because of the terribly congested road net in Galicia. At a conference at Kholm on 22 September Grand Duke Nikolai Nikolaevich advised his staff and key field commanders that he would leave behind only the Third and Eighth Russian armies to screen the Austrians, while shifting the Fifth Army to support the southern perimeter of the Second Army sector in Warsaw. The Fourth would span the river line fortress complexes of Koshenice and Ivangorod, with the Ninth covering the Vistula crossings south to the confluence with the San River. By the end of September, as the German Ninth Army began its thrust, the Russians set in motion their laborious, yet dogged, transfer of 1.25 million men northward over mud-rutted tracks.

The German Ninth Army deployed on 100-mile front. On the left, an extemporized corps, predominantly cavalry, commanded by General Frommel, was to advance to the east of Lodz. To the center were XVII Corps (commanded by General August von Mackensen), XX Corps, and Guard Reserve. Their objective was Czestochowa-Ivangorod. On the right, or Galician, flank, Dankl's Austrian First Army, supported by the German XI Corps and reinforced by General Remus von Woyrsch's Landwehr Corps, delayed its march until 4 October. The tentative nature of the German attack was shown by their preparation of demolitions to retard Russian pursuit in case of retreat.

The Russians reacted to the German attack by shifting their Fourth and Ninth armies. These were to push across the Vistula River and attempt to fix Germans along the river line to the south of Warsaw. That would force the Germans to assault their bridgehead defensive perimeters and deny the maneuverable German columns battle on the open plains. While German guns were engaging the Russian Fourth and Ninth armies, the uncommitted Russian reserves of the Fifth Army and elements of the Second near Warsaw would drive from the north into Hindenburg's left flank, pushing his forces into the Austrians.

Characteristically, open Russian wireless communication allowed the Germans to learn Russian plans, but they discovered the full extent of the Russian deployment only on 9 October through a Russian army order taken from a corpse at Grojec.

To this point the Germans had encountered only light resistance from a rearguard Russian cavalry division at Opatow. It was thrown back by the German XI and Guard Reserve Corps. The Austrians broke the siege of Przemsyl but were halted on the San River line, where Russian forces continued to cover Nicholas's massive northward realignment.

The German Ninth Army rotated its axis of advance ever farther to the north, based on information that the Russians had extended their assembly areas to Warsaw's southern approaches. General Frommel subordinated his corps to Mackensen's XVII, which was on his right. This shifted the focus of the German thrust toward the Warsaw perimeter defenses, where the Germans believed that Russian forces were as yet disorganized and relatively weak.

Mackensen had the option of seizing the Vistula crossings and encircling Warsaw. German radio intercepts revealed that, while the Russian 2nd Corps and Fifth Army were still disorganized and vulnerable, at least seven Russian corps would reinforce the Warsaw defenses by 11 October. Mounting Russian strength and aggressiveness was confirmed when Mackensen's two-corps task force encountered and defeated two Russian corps at Grojec, twenty miles south of Warsaw. Newly arriving crack Siberian units strengthened Russian forces and provided offensive options.

Because of the Ninth Army's new northerly movement, XX and Guard Reserve Corps on the German right flank would have to meet any threat from Russian troops lining the banks of the Vistula. XI Corps would be forced to fill the widening gap between the German main drive and the Austrians, under whose nominal command they operated.

Russian forces attempted to ford the Vistula as far as Sandomierz, where they fought the Austrians to a standstill at the San River line. At Koshenice, ten miles north of Ivangorod, the Russian Fourth Army's III Caucasian Corps gained the west bank. In desperate fighting, they withstood all German efforts to dislodge them. Fifth Army, further north, failed to secure the far bank, largely because they had lost their bridging equipment during the approach.

By 12 October Mackensen's four-division group had reached Warsaw's outer defensive ring and was approaching a vital railway junction twelve miles from the city center. At that point, the Russian Second Army had extended around Mackensen's northern flank, threatening his communications, while the Russian Fifth Army also pressured Mackensen's advance.

Austrian forces refused to aid Mackensen by attacking the Russian Ninth Army across the San River. That would have released German forces restraining the Russian Fourth Army's thrust toward the Vistula fords. Dankl refused to subordinate Austrian troops to German command in the Warsaw area and agreed only to extend his front in order to release the German XI Corps. Instead, Dankl attempted a "Cannae" maneuver, hoping to draw Russian troops into the Ivanograd pocket, where they could be attacked on the flank. This was thwarted when the Russians moved more forcefully than expected, and Austrian forces bogged down in a costly and futile slugfest before Ivangorod.

Hindenburg and Ludendorff continued to have faith in the combat superiority of their soldiers and urged Mackensen ahead until 17 October, when a fifteen-to-five-division adverse ratio proved too much to overcome and they decided to extricate Mackensen from the Fifth and Second Russian armies. Remaining German forces followed suit, withdrawing over 100 miles in two weeks and firing their preset explosions behind them, and creating logjams at demolished tracks, defiles, and bridges. The German Ninth Army quartermaster precisely estimated the pace and limits of the Russian pursuit under these conditions and correctly calculated that the hiatus would enable the German Ninth Army to switch north and mount a counterattack.

Hindenburg and Ludendorff sent the Ninth Army by train north to the Posen-Thorn region on 4 November, where it was joined by eight new divisions. Mackensen now assumed command of Ninth Army, reorganized into five infantry and two cavalry corps. General Karl von Bülow commanded Eighth Army, while Hindenburg became commander in chief of the Eastern Front.

Falkenhayn promised to send four more corps from France, but they would not be available until 20 November and a renewed Russian offensive was expected on 14 November. This forced Hindenburg and Ludendorff to plan a southeasterly thrust to exploit a seam between the Russian First and Second armies and roll up the enemy front.

As the Germans repositioned, the Russian armies prepared to drive toward Breslau. The First Army covered the right flank along the lower Vistula, north of Kutno. The Third Army guarded the left flank south of Kielce. Far to the north, the Tenth Army was tying down German forces in East Prussia. On 12 November, Rennenkampf's First Army began a seventy-mile-wide advance, its two corps straddling the Vistula River.

Meanwhile, on 10 November, unknown to Rennenkampf or his fellow commanders to the south, the German Ninth Army once more invaded Poland, along an eighty-five-mile front. Ninth Army consisted of I Corps Reserve, XI, XVII, and XX corps, and the newly arrived XXV Reserve Corps. The Thorn (Torun) and Woyrsch Landwehr Corps, the 35th Reserve Division, and five cavalry divisions (3rd, 6th, 7th, 8th, and 9th) were also attached. The Guard Reserve Corps was left in southern Poland. Falkenhayn promised Hindenburg and Ludendorff four more corps from the Western Front if they would delay operations another ten days, but they decided that any delay could be fatal.

With his attack deadline only one day away, the Russian commander of the northwest front, General Nikolai V. Ruzsky, had taken no steps to launch his armies westward. On 9 November he had ordered the Second Army, which would be directly in the path of

the German advance, to stand in place. Second Army, however, was as poorly disposed to go on the defensive as it was on the offensive. From north to south the army consisted of the II and V Siberian corps and II, IV, and XXIII Russian corps deployed between the Vistula River and Lodz. There was a twenty-mile gap between the northernmost V Siberian Corps at Wroclawek and the II Corps at Kutno. An even larger gap existed between V Siberian and the VI Siberian Corps of the First Army at Plock. The isolation of V Siberian Corps was to seal its fate.

The commanders of the German forces invading Poland had only a vague idea of what lay before them. Cavalry and air reconnaissance revealed large stretches of territory unoccupied by Russian troops, but it was unclear whether there were one or two Russian corps at Kutno, or whether the V Siberian Corps belonged to the First or Second Army. No Russian forces were encountered until 15 November, when the V Siberian Corps was overwhelmed at Wroclawek. The Russian infantry panicked after being abandoned by their artillery, and two-thirds of the corps were taken prisoner. II Corps was also driven from Kutno as the Germans swung to the south in their effort to turn the Russian flank. The German I Reserve Corps was detached to prevent the First Russian Army from coming up in relief.

By 20 November Mackensen believed that he had the Second Army pinned around Lodz and decided to execute a double envelopment in the hopes of achieving another Tannenberg. General Scheffer-Boyadel's XXV Reserve Corps constituted the left wing of this effort. On 21 November it found itself facing west, far in the rear of the Russian Second Army.

On 19 November Ludendorff received reports indicating that the Russian Fifth Army, to the south of the Second, was withdrawing from its positions. He took this as an indication of a Russian withdrawal toward the Vistula and ordered German forces around Lodz to close around Second Army before it too escaped. In fact, the Fifth Army was heading north to the rescue of the Second, while units of the First Army pushed down from the north.

Meanwhile, General Ruzsky was planning his own double envelopment of German forces around Lodz. Ruzsky's armies were unfit to fully envelop the German Ninth Army, but by 21 November it was obvious that a significant success might still be scored in the destruction of the isolated XXV Reserve Corps. The weather had turned very cold, however. Scheffer-Boyadel realized by 22 November that he was surrounded on three sides by elements of the First, Second, and Fifth Russian armies, and he was instructed to retire by "the most feasible route." Scheffer-Boyadel realized that the Russians would easily block him on the west and so decided to break out northeasterly, where they would least expect it. On the morning of 23 November Scheffer-Boyadel's three divisions disengaged, with a cavalry screen to his front, flanks and rear, and a reserve of infantry and artillery ready to deploy at any critical point.

On the same day Scheffer-Boyadel's corps met the 6th Siberian Division, part of the so-called "Lovitch Detachment" that had been ordered south by First Army. The Russians were caught in march column and completely smashed by the Germans. By evening the 6th Siberian Division had been virtually annihilated and barely 1,500 of its original 14,000-man force escaped death or capture. By counter-punching and feinting, Scheffer-Boyadel's force stymied Stavka and its field commanders, thus holding the entire envelopment at bay.

Scheffer-Boyadel's own escape route was now clear, and he continued his march, shifting to the northwest. Throughout the 23rd, Ruzsky had waited for word of the surrender of XXV Reserve Corps. Stavka had been confident enough of the situation to order up trains to haul away the prisoners (instead of much needed supplies). By 24 November it was obvious that the Germans had slipped away and with them any chance for success.

The fighting around Lodz cost the Germans about 35,000 men, perhaps as many as 10,000 from the XXV Reserve Corps. Russian losses are uncertain but probably exceeded 80,000, including the ill-fated 6th Siberian Division. For the Germans, the battle had been another outstanding tactical victory, highlighted by one of the most daring and remarkable fighting withdrawals in history. In a strategic sense, however, the Germans had largely failed. The Russian flank had not been turned, nor had Russian forces been encircled. The Germans, in fact, had narrowly avoided a debacle. They claimed that a Russian invasion of German territory had been averted, but a major westerly push by Ruzsky had been neither imminent nor possible. The Russians had been consistently outmaneuvered and outfought but had held their ground, and the German breakthrough had not produced a rout.

In the end, it was the Russians who held the field, though no longer threatening Germany. The Russians would continue to hold Lodz until 6 December, when they fell back and rearranged their line. Once again a period of quiet—and mutual exhaustion—fell over the Eastern Front.

James J. Bloom

References
Churchill, Winston. *The Unknown War: The Eastern Front.* New York: Charles Scribner's Sons, 1931.

Freund, Gerald. "Eastern Front." In *A Concise History of World War I*, edited by Vincent J. Esposito. London: Pall Mall, 1965.

Macksey, Kenneth. "The First Battle of Warsaw." In *The Marshall Cavendish Illustrated Encyclopedia of World War I*, edited by Brigadier Peter Young, 1:306–16. Freeport, N.Y.: Marshall Cavendish, 1984.

Neame, Lieutenant Colonel Phillip. *German Strategy in the Great War.* London: Edward Arnold, 1930.

Stone, Norman. *The Eastern Front, 1914–1917.* New York: Charles Scribner's Sons, 1975.

_____. "Lodz." In *The Marshall Cavendish Illustrated Encyclopedia of World War I*, edited by Brigadier Peter Young, 2:460–68. Freeport, N.Y.: Marshall Cavendish, 1984.

_____. "The Second Battle of Warsaw." In *The Marshall Cavendish Illustrated Encyclopedia of World War I*, edited by Brigadier Peter Young, 2:454–60. Freeport, N.Y.: Marshall Cavendish, 1984.

See also CONRAD VON HÖTZENDORF, FRANZ; DANKL VON KRASNIK, VIKTOR; HINDENBURG, PAUL VON; HOFFMANN, MAX; LUDENDORFF, ERICH; MACKENSEN, AUGUST VON; RUZSKY, NIKOLAI

Polivanov, Aleksei Andreevich (1855–1920)

Russian general and minister of war. Born into a Russian noble family on 16 March 1855,

Polivanov was one of the most competent Russian general officers of World War I. Having graduated from both the Military Engineering and the General Staff Academies, Polivanov saw action in the Russo-Turkish War of 1877. He then gravitated toward administrative work. Between 1899 and 1904 he edited the Russian military journal, and during the Russo-Japanese War of 1904–5 he served first as quartermaster general and then as army chief of staff. After that war, which was a Russian military disaster, Polivanov became one of the leading advocates of military reform. Consequently he was an avid supporter of the work of A.I. Guchkov's Third Duma (1907–12) Military Reform Commission. Because military and political reform were necessarily linked, Polivanov became associated with the antimonarchist liberals. As assistant minister of war between 1906 and 1915, Polivanov was the chief critic of his superior, the incompetent minister of war Valdimir Sukhomlinov.

Finally, after the Carpathian military disaster in the spring of 1915, Polivanov was asked to replace Sukhomlinov as minister of war, a post he held for less than a year. It was in that capacity that Polivanov did so much in such a short time to solve many of the critical supply problems. Unlike his predecessor, he quickly established a harmonious relationship with the State Duma as well as other governmental and private agencies involved with military supplies.

In August of 1915 the czar told a few selected people that he intended to replace Grand Duke Nikolai Nikolaevich as commander in chief of the army and personally go to the front to direct the war. In a modern nation for the political head of state to leave the capital permanently was not only unheard of but was dangerous for the operation of the government and for national morale. Polivanov, as minister of war, felt duty-bound to inform the other ministers. He, along with twelve other ministers, signed a letter begging the czar to reconsider. The Empress Alexandra and Rasputin, whom Polivanov detested, saw this letter as a personal challenge to the czar's authority, and consequently the empress became determined to see the guilty ministers dismissed. Thus, in November of 1915 Polivanov lost his post, and the Russian army lost one of its most capable administrators.

After the czar's abdication, Polivanov chaired a commission under the provisional government to reform the military code. It came

under the influence of radical members in the Petrograd Soviet, however, and its final report recommended the virtual elimination of military discipline. Because of this, Polivanov came in for much criticism. Subsequently he offered his services to the Bolshevik regime and urged others to do the same. He was serving as military advisor to the Russian delegation in peace talks with Poland when he died of typhus at Riga on 25 September 1920.

John W. Bohon

References

Gurko, Vladimir Iosifovich. *Features and Figures of the Past.* London: Oxford University Press, 1939.

Pares, Sir Bernard. *The Fall of the Russian Monarchy.* New York: Vintage, 1939.

See also ALEXANDRA FEODOROVNA; GUCHKOV, ALEKSANDR; NICHOLAS II; SUKHOMLINOV, VLADIMIR

Portugal

Portugal entered the twentieth century undergoing political, social, and economic turmoil. In 1908 King Carlos I and Prince Luis Felipi were assassinated, and in 1910 Carlos's successor, Manual II, was forced to flee the country after a revolt. Although a republic was declared, it soon fell into disfavor because of its attacks on the Catholic Church. Over the next decade a series of plots, revolts, and counterrevolts took place. During this same period Germany cast covetous eyes on Portugal's African colonies, and there was an implied threat of the use of armed force from adjacent German colonies.

When World War I began, the majority of Portuguese citizens were indifferent to it. The war did provide an economic stimulus for Portugal. Orders from the Allies for food, raw materials, and finished goods brought prosperity to a segment of the population. It also led to social disorder, for wages failed to keep up with inflation.

Certain segments of the Portuguese ruling class wanted their country to join the war on the Allied side. They were afraid that if Portugal did not participate in the peace conference its colonies might be used as bargaining chips. On 23 November 1914 the Portuguese national assembly voted to declare war against Germany, but action was delayed because of a 28 January 1915 insurrection led by General Pimenta de

Castro. For the next four months Castro, who represented the pro-German faction in the Portuguese army, ruled as dictator. On 14 May he was overthrown by a democratic revolt and Bernardino Machado became president.

On 24 February 1916 Portugal seized all ships belonging to the Central Powers that had taken refuge in her ports upon the outbreak of the war. In retaliation, on 9 March Germany, and on 15 March Austria-Hungary, declared war on Portugal.

After entering the war, Portugal declined simply to provide labor battalions for the Allies and insisted on sending an expeditionary force of 54,000 men to France under the command of General Gomes da Costa. Some 50,000 troops were also organized for service in Africa against German colonies there.

Politics in Portugal, where some 65 percent of the peasants were illiterate, continued to be chaotic. There were numerous insurrections, attempted assassinations, and coups. Cabinets on average lasted only about four months. On 5 December 1917 General Sidonio Pães carried out another pro-German coup, arrested and deported the president, and made himself military dictator. Pães, however, was assassinated on 14 December and the democratic regime was reestablished. The financial situation also worsened, the escudo rapidly depreciating. Meanwhile, on 9 April 1918, the Portuguese 2nd Division suffered heavy losses in the Ludendorff Offensives.

In the end, Portugal was able to take a seat at the peace table and preserve her overseas territories—but at the cost of increased social and political turmoil that ultimately led to the 1928 dictatorship of Antonio de Oliveira Salazar.

Charles H. Bogart

References
Gallagher, Tom. *Portugal—A Twentieth Century Interpretation.* Manchester: Manchester University Press, 1983.
Livermore, H.V. *A New History of Portugal.* London: Cambridge University Press, 1966.
Marques, Antonio H. *History of Portugal.* New York: Columbia University Press, 1972.

Potiorek, Oskar (1853–1933)

Austro-Hungarian military governor of Bosnia-Herzegovina, born on 20 November 1853 in Bleiburg, Austria. Potiorek rose rapidly though the Hapsburg military establishment to become military governor of Bosnia-Herzegovina in 1911. It was during his administration that the Archduke Franz Ferdinand was assassinated in Sarajevo in June of 1914.

Potiorek believed that only a heavy hand could maintain Austrian control of Bosnia. He had no interest in reconciling even the more conservative Serb elements to Austrian rule, seeing all Serbs as potential rebels and attempting to play them off against the other ethnic groups. His repressive measures helped foster the very discontent they were designed to stamp out: They often worked at cross purposes with the directives of the civil administration, headed by Leon Biliński in Vienna, which favored a more conciliatory approach. For all his distrust of the native Bosnians, though, Potiorek took no special security precautions at the time of Franz Ferdinand's visit and rebuffed numerous warnings that they might be necessary.

Condemned from all sides after the assassination for negligence, Potiorek was nevertheless put in charge of the 1914 campaign to invade Serbia. His repeated offensives all failed, and he was relieved of his command in December of 1914. He died in Klagenfurt, Austria, on 17 December 1933.

Gary W. Shanafelt

References
Dedijer, Vladimir. *The Road to Sarajevo.* New York: Simon and Schuster, 1966.
Jerabek, Rudolf. *Potiorek: General im Schatten von Sarajevo.* Graz: Verlag Styria, 1991.

See also BALKAN FRONT, 1914; FRANZ FERDINAND

Prezan, Constantine (1861–1943)

Romanian general and army commander, born on 27 January 1861. Prezan received military training in Bucharest and in France and served on the Romanian General Staff and as adjutant to King Ferdinand. When Romania declared war on Austria-Hungary on 27 August 1916, prompted by Brusilov's success, Prezan's Fourth Army crossed the Carpathians into Transylvania but met stiff resistance from General Arthur Baron Arz von Straussenburg's First Army.

Prezan was forced to divert forces from Transylvania after chief of the German General Staff Erich von Falkenhayn ordered Field Marshal August von Mackensen to invade the Dobrudja from Bulgaria in the south. Falkenhayn's Ninth Army then crossed the Red Tower Pass into Wallachia. With the veteran German commanders converging on the capital, Prezan (or French military adviser General Henri Berthelot) planned a bold strike against Mackensen's left flank, but Romanian forces were too weak and by January of 1917 had been driven to the Sereth.

As commander in chief after the war, Prezan occupied Transylvania in 1919. He retired from the army in 1920. The 1930 political crisis surrounding the return of King Carol II led to his temporary return. Promoted to field marshal, he was asked to form a nonparty government. He failed in this and again retired. He died at his Moldavian estate on 27 August 1943.

A. Harding Ganz

References

Herwig, Holger H., and Neil M. Heyman. *Biographical Dictionary of World War I.* Westport, Conn.: Greenwood, 1982.

Kiszling, Lieutenant Colonel Rudolf. "Eastern European Front Campaigns—Rumanian." In *Encyclopedia Britannica,* 12th ed., 1922. 30:914–22.

See also BALKAN FRONT, 1916, 1917; BRUSILOV OFFENSIVE; FERDINAND I; ROMANIA

Princip, Gavrilo (1894–1918)

The Bosnian nationalist who assassinated Archduke Franz Ferdinand, heir to the Austro-Hungarian throne, and his consort, Sophie, duchess of Hohenberg. Born into a Serb peasant family on 13 July 1894 in Obljaj, Bosnia, Princip aspired to a business, literary, or military career, but was frustrated in each attempt. He was expelled from school in 1912 for espousing revolutionary ideas and for his affiliations with Bosnian secret societies. Princip traveled to Belgrade to enlist for service with Serbia in the First Balkan War but was rejected as medically unfit.

Princip was then trained in terrorist methods with other South Slav nationalists by the Serbian secret society, the Black Hand, or Union of Death. Believing that the assassination of a top Austro-Hungarian official or member of the Hapsburg family was the first step toward Slavic unity and national independence, Princip and fellow terrorist Nedjelko Čabrinović made plans to murder Franz Ferdinand during his official visit to Sarajevo announced early in 1914. Trained and armed by Serbian army officers and Black Hand members Major Vojin Tankosić and Col. Dragutin Dimitrijević, Princip and Čabrinović crossed the Bosnian-Serbian border disguised as peasants on 1 June.

In Sarajevo on 28 June 1914, as the archduke's procession moved through town, Čabrinović threw a bomb at Ferdinand's automobile, but it bounced off and exploded under the vehicle following, wounding several onlookers. Four other co-conspirators lost their will and failed to carry out their attacks as the procession rolled by. Later, as the motorcade bearing the archduke was driving to the hospital to visit an officer wounded earlier, Ferdinand's automobile made a wrong turn and halted immediately in front of Princip. As the driver attempted to back up, Princip pulled out his pistol, mounted the automobile's running board, and shot the archduke and duchess at point-blank range. Sophie died instantly, the archduke within half an hour.

Austria held Serbia responsible for the murders and used them as a pretext for war, thus setting in motion the chain of events leading to the outbreak of a Europeanwide conflict in August of 1914.

Princip was brought to trial in Sarajevo on 28 October 1914. He escaped execution because of his age but was sentenced to twenty years' hard labor. He was taken to a prison near Theresienstadt, Austria. Probably already suffering from tuberculosis, Princip lost an arm to the disease and died in a hospital near the prison on 28 April 1918.

Clayton D. Laurie

References

Cassels, L. *The Archduke and the Assassin: Sarajevo, 28 June 1914.* New York: Stein and Day, 1985.

Dedijer, V. *The Road to Sarajevo.* London: MacGibbon and Kee, 1967.

Gilford, H. *The Black Hand at Sarajevo.* Indianapolis, Ind.: Bobbs-Merrill, 1975.

Seton-Watson, R.W. *Sarajevo: A Study in the Origins of the Great War.* London: Hutchinson, 1926.

See also BLACK HAND; BOSNIA-HERZEGOVINA; FRANZ FERDINAND

Prisoners of War

At the beginning of World War I, the major powers were unprepared for and unconcerned about incarcerating prisoners of war, as most believed the war would end quickly. Initially, prisoners experienced conditions that varied with their captors and circumstance of capture. Some were abused and humiliated, while others were treated kindly.

Within six months, the almost 1.5 million prisoners overwhelmed the major powers. The Germans, Russians, French, and British held the most prisoners. Initially, temporary arrangements such as tent camps were established to care for the prisoners, but necessary items like shelter, food, and clothing were lacking. Prisoners of the Allies were the best cared for, while those in the East suffered the worst conditions.

Richard B. Speed counters traditional historical accounts of World War I prisoners that exaggerate depictions of cruel captors and abused prisoners. He contends that, despite the pressures of total war, most captors treated military prisoners humanely. They were assisted by neutral humanitarian groups. He claims that captors whose prisoners suffered were incompetent rather than cruel. Some prison camps were so notorious, however, that they earned names like the "Black Hole of Cologne." Speed blames these deficiencies on administrative failures, political pressures, and the overwhelming aspects of total war.

The only regulations about treatment of prisoners were those outlined in the Hague Conference of 1907, but those guidelines were ambiguous. The Hague Conference required each power to have an enquiry office compile records on each prisoner for their relatives. It also stated that prisoners were not to be used for war work, but that regulation was quickly ignored as the need for laborers increased throughout the war.

The Germans came to hold the most World War I prisoners—2.5 million by war's end—and for the longest time. This burden was a difficult one, but the Germans attempted to provide prisoners some individual rights and to ameliorate conditions. Prisoners collected in Belgium in August of 1914 were kept in temporary barracks in churches at the rear of the troops. One hundred thousand Russian prisoners were taken at Tannenberg. Because the Germans were unprepared for such numbers, many died of starvation and sickness in makeshift camps or suffered on marches to camps in the severe winter of 1914.

The British were not well prepared to hold prisoners, because they gave military expansion priority. Temporary camps were erected in buildings such as castles, ancestral homes, island camps, and in Scotland and Ireland. The Directorate of Prisoners of War in Britain oversaw these camps.

During the Allied offensives of 1916, great influxes of prisoners filled prison camps, causing overcrowding and hardships. Conditions were especially cruel for the Russian prisoners, of whom 29,297 died in German camps during the first two years of the war. In all, seventy thousand Russian prisoners died in Central Powers' prison camps.

The Russians sent most of their German prisoners to Siberia, where they could guard them more easily because the remote location required fewer guards. The severe Siberian climate caused many hardships. The social upheaval during the Russian Civil War also contributed to prisoners' sufferings. The Russians attempted to care for their prisoners, but that proved difficult. For the most part, prisoners in Russia were treated well but endured horrible conditions. They also were confronted with propaganda encouraging them to join the Red Army.

Most prisoners concurred that the Americans treated their captives best. When the Americans declared war, American army headquarters in France published a pamphlet entitled *Prisoners of War: Regulations and Instructions;* the Prisoner of War Division took responsibility for prisoners held by Americans.

Prisoners endured delays in transit, and wounds were sometimes left untreated. Local citizens often gathered around transport vehicles, spit on prisoners, and threw stones at them. At the camps prisoners were searched and stripped of valuables, including tobacco. Some guards interrogated prisoners and kicked and taunted them. Prison workers cut prisoners' hair, inoculated them for contagious diseases, and issued blankets, clothes, and utensils.

Many prisoners were relieved that they no longer had to endure the terrible conditions on the battlefield and were quite agreeable to incarceration. Guards and prisoners formed friendships in which they shared cigarettes and news from the front.

Prison camps, surrounded by barbed wire and guard towers, lacked amenities. Prisoners lived in deep snow, torrential rains, or hot sun depending on the location of their camp. Many camps were unsanitary, with flies, fleas, and vermin sharing the crowded cells. Latrines were often filthy and clean water inadequate. Cramped prison compounds were poorly ventilated.

Prisoners of varying ethnicity were grouped together, and friendships grew from this intermingling within the camp. Prisoners organized an administrative system within their confines, with prisoners separated into companies, each with a captain acting as a liaison between the commandant and prisoners. Prisoners who were senior officers did receive some special privileges.

Prison food often left much to be desired. The standard World War I diet consisted of black bread, a potato, and flour soup, with little meat available. Soldiers supplemented their diet with local flora and fauna, for example collecting snails to eat. U-boat warfare hindered merchant shipping and reduced the flow of food to Britain, and the British blockade kept food from prisoners in Germany. Captors did not feed prisoners better than their own troops, and periods like the "turnip winter" of 1916–17 in Germany produced great suffering. Many men starved to skeletons, while others were able to survive because of Red Cross parcels prepared by wives, mothers, daughters, sisters, or local women. These packages included nourishment as well as luxuries like tobacco, clothing, chocolate, coffee, and soap. Guards carefully examined parcels for contraband. British relief groups sent packages to both British and Russian prisoners because the Russian prisoners had no organized relief group. The French *Bureau de Secours Aux Prisonniers de Guerre* and the British Prisoners of War Help Committee centralized volunteer efforts, including warehouses in Copenhagen, and these outside agencies saved many prisoners from starving to death.

The International Committee of the Red Cross compiled information on each prisoner to relay to his family, as well as distributing letters, parcels, and money, and supervising prison-camp conditions on both sides. Millions of cards listing prisoners were kept in the Red Cross Central Agency index. The Red Cross maintained records on prisoners' health status and accounted for those who died in the camps, forwarding their belongings to relatives.

Military prisoners were required to work on a strictly regulated schedule, thus freeing men of military age to go to the front. Paid in scrip they could use only in camp, prisoners worked at stone quarries, barbed wire factories, and coal and salt mines. They built roads, cut timber, and harvested crops. Prisoners manufactured their own work uniforms.

Private employers hired POW labor, and prisoners befriended local civilians who gave them extra food and clothing. Many prisoners felt they were being exploited and protested. They disliked having to work double shifts and particularly resented being forced to work when they were ill or weak. Many feigned illness by swallowing tobacco. Prisoners succumbed to diseases, especially typhus, tuberculosis, and pneumonia. The lack of sufficient burial room exacerbated the transmission of disease, and the influenza pandemic at the end of the war killed many prisoners. Dysentery, gangrenous wounds, and lice aggravated life in the camps. Camp physicians refused to treat self-inflicted wounds; depression dominated many prisoners, and suicide was not uncommon. Nutritional deficiencies caused beriberi and dental problems.

Boredom was relieved by writing letters, although mail was censored, and writers who complained too much were punished. Photographs could be sent to relatives but not with anything in the background that could be distorted for propaganda purposes. Prisoners kept mentally and physically active by reading newspapers, listening to music, and playing games. They also formed orchestras and choirs. Prisoners formed prison universities in which each man lectured on some field of study, such as history, sculpture, or foreign languages. Some guards allowed the celebration of holidays, such as Christmas. Prisoners were also permitted to attend church services. Morale was bolstered by such activities and entertainment.

Many World War I prisoners devised escape plans to ease their despair, and they hoarded rations and made crude compasses and maps to facilitate their plans. Prisoners did escape from camps, work parties, or transport trains to Switzerland, Holland, and Scandinavia. Escapees dug tunnels; at escape meetings of tunnel excavators, prisoners decided who would divert the guards' attention and who would escape.

Those who were caught were usually interned in stricter camps or placed in solitary confinement. In an effort to prevent escapes, guards regularly searched cells for contraband and black market goods. Prisoners were fined money or given added work, and collective punishments were also imposed, such as shutting off lights and heat. Prisoners who successfully escaped often brought with them valuable intelligence information about the enemy's morale and weaknesses, as well as technological information about U-boats and weaponry.

Reprisals against prisoners were not illegal under international law. Most powers forced prisoners to dig frontline trenches. The frequency of reprisals resulted in a meeting at The Hague in July of 1917 and agreement on a mandatory four-week notice to the government of prisoners who would be punished. According to regulations, escaped prisoners could be shot at but they could not be sentenced to death. Typical punishments included hard labor, solitary confinement, or confinement at special punishment camps.

Diplomats acted as neutral observers, filing reports requisitioning relief supplies, conferring with prisoners, and negotiating problems. American diplomats initiated the American-German Conference in 1918 to establish specific guidelines concerning the treatment and repatriation of prisoners. The Allies and Central Powers shared similar views about prisoners, summarized by Sir Edward Grey: "We would treat them better if we could."

Captors often used propaganda to try to convert prisoners. The Germans especially tried to enlist Irish soldiers, and the Bolsheviks tried to acquire ideological converts among Slavic prisoners, hoping they would return to break up the Austro-Hungarian Empire. Many prisoners worried about their conduct, fearing retribution when they returned home.

World War I ushered in a new class of war prisoners: alien civilians of enemy nationality. Four hundred thousand "alien enemies" were in Europe when the war began, including stranded students, scholars, travelers, and merchant seamen. After a brief period during which they could depart, these individuals were rounded up. Men, women, and children were grouped together in camps. Not required to work, many alien enemies used their internment to improve themselves intellectually. No diplomatic document dealt with noncombatants in war until the 1949 Geneva Conventions.

Before the war ended, invalid prisoners were exchanged and paroled through repatriation camps in Switzerland, where they underwent medical inspections and took educational courses to prepare for postwar civilian life. Repatriation of healthy prisoners was slow and frustrating.

There were 6.5 million prisoners of war in Europe at war's end. The Allies established the Subcommission on Prisoners of War of the Permanent International Armistice Commission in November to help return prisoners more efficiently. Germany was divided into four zones for the repatriation of Allied prisoners, a process completed by 1 February 1919. Prisoners traveled to ports where they were deloused and then shipped home. Prisoners from Britain were reimbursed for personal property confiscated and given money, personal documents, and a letter from the king. Some repatriation trains had grenades and stones thrown at them by angry citizens, and some repatriates shoved off collaborators. Adjustment to civilian life was difficult for many former prisoners, and some others elected to remain in Germany, where they had more employment opportunities than at home.

Lack of transportation slowed repatriation. Some camps kept prisoners to repair war-damaged roads. Prisoners from Germany remained in custody until the peace negotiations were concluded in June. The Treaty of Versailles emphasized that prisoners would be returned as soon as possible, and by autumn German prisoners had been repatriated.

Russian prisoners were neglected during the repatriation period because relations had been broken off between Russia and the Allies. Many of them attempted to walk the thousands of miles home. In Russia they encountered discrimination because their allegiance to the Bolsheviks was questioned. Many prisoners held by the Russians in Siberia were never repatriated and were utilized to fight in the Russian Civil War.

The liberal tradition of World War I prisoner-of-war camps strengthened diplomatic regulations concerning both military and civilian prisoners. Future wars, however, would see prisoners used as pawns for ideological causes, and made victims of atrocities quite different from anything experienced by prisoners of the Great War.

Elizabeth D. Schafer

References

Dennett, Carl P. *Prisoners of the Great War.* Boston: Houghton Mifflin, 1919.

Fischer, Gerhard. *Enemy Aliens: Internment and the Homefront Experience in Aus-*

tralia 1914–1920. St. Lucia: University of Queensland Press, 1989.

Jackson, Robert. *The Prisoners, 1914–18*. London: Routledge, 1989.

Ketchum, J. Davidson. *Ruhleben: A Prison Camp Society*. Toronto: University of Toronto Press, 1965

Speed, Richard B. *Prisoners, Diplomats, and the Great War: A Study in the Diplomacy of Captivity*. New York: Greenwood, 1990.

See also RED CROSS

Prittwitz und Gaffron, Max von (1848–1917)

German army commander. Scion of an old noble family, Prittwitz was born at Bernstadt in Silesia on 27 November 1848. He joined the Prussian Guards on the eve of the Austro-Prussian War but received his commission in a line regiment. After attending the Kriegsakademie, he rose through a broad range of staff and command postings and was made commanding general of XVI Corps at Metz in April of 1906. For almost four years he was assisted in that position by a particularly talented chief of staff, Colonel Erich von Falkenhayn, and Prittwitz's final verdict (that Falkenhayn "can do anything") no doubt contributed to the latter's meteoric rise in subsequent years.

In the spring of 1913 Prittwitz was put in charge of the First Army Inspection at Danzig and soon thereafter was promoted to colonel general. Although chief of the German General Staff Colonel General Helmuth von Moltke and some of his associates doubted Prittwitz's leadership qualities, he was made commander of the Eighth Army in East Prussia at the beginning of the war. To strengthen that army's leadership, Moltke simultaneously appointed his own deputy, Major General Count George von Waldersee, to Prittwitz's headquarters as chief of staff.

Faced with a very difficult task—to hold East Prussia and other German provinces against numerically superior Russian forces during the opening phases of the war—Prittwitz and Waldersee found their work made even harder by the headstrong ways of one of the corps' commanders, General Hermann von François. The latter repeatedly ignored Prittwitz's orders with regard to the proper deployment of his troops and for a while even concealed vital information from his superior. It was partly under François's influence that Prittwitz and Waldersee agreed, on 19 August, to launch a frontal assault against the Russian First Army. In the ensuing battle (Gumbinnen) some elements of the Eighth Army, particularly its XVII Corps, incurred heavy losses, and a general withdrawal was ordered by Prittwitz on the evening of 20 August. During the next twenty-four hours, Prittwitz informed OHL in a series of telegrams and telephone calls that the situation in East Prussia was becoming critical because of the advance of the Russian Second Army from the south, and that it might become necessary to retreat all the way to the Vistula River. In response, on 22 August Moltke replaced both Prittwitz and Waldersee with General Paul von Hindenburg and Major General Erich Ludendorff. Prittwitz received no further postings and died on 29 March 1917 in Berlin.

Ulrich Trumpener

References

Elze, Walter. *Tannenberg: Das deutsche Heer von 1914, seine Grundzüge und deren Auswirkung im Sieg an der Ostfront*. Berlin: F. Hirt, 1928.

Schäfer, Theobald von. *Tannenberg*. Oldenburg and Berlin: Stalling, 1927.

Showalter, Dennis E. *Tannenberg: Clash of Empires*. Hamden, Conn.: Archon, 1991.

Stone, Norman. *The Eastern Front 1914–1917*. New York: Charles Scribner's Sons, 1975.

Reichsarchiv. *Der Weltkrieg 1914 bis 1918: Militärische Operationen zu Lande*. Vol. 2. Berlin: E.S. Mittler und Sohn, 1925.

See also EAST PRUSSIA CAMPAIGN; FRANÇOIS, HERMANN VON

Propaganda, Use in War

World War I witnessed an all-out attempt by the major belligerents to harness the mass film and print media for the purpose of altering the attitudes and behavior of large audiences in the belligerent and neutral nations and at the battlefront.

Great Britain had the most sophisticated wartime propaganda system; prior to 1918 it concentrated on domestic, Allied, and neutral audiences rather than on enemy civilian and military populations. Private citizen groups like the Neutral Press Committee and the Central Committee for National Patriotic Organizations began Britain's propaganda campaign in August of 1914 by giving speeches and preparing the first of hundreds of pamphlets promoting Britain's war effort. The Asquith government joined these activities in September of 1914, when the War Propaganda Bureau, or Wellington House, an official yet secret propaganda office under foreign office control, was created on the suggestion of Edward Grey and David Lloyd George.

Directed by cabinet member Charles F.G. Masterman, Wellington House delivered cleverly written pamphlets intended to create pro-British attitudes in neutral nations, especially the United States. Its most successful effort was the Bryce Committee Report on alleged German atrocities, released in June of 1915, which inflamed American opinion against Imperial Germany. Wellington House sent limited amounts of disguised propaganda materials to Germany via neutral mails but did undertake combat propaganda against enemy troops. Other, smaller propaganda efforts were undertaken by bureaus in the admiralty, war, colonial, and home offices by late 1915. Duplication of effort was rife, and debilitating interagency rivalries abounded even after the creation of a central Department of Information in February of 1917.

The French Foreign Office established a Press and Information Bureau three days after the declaration of war, but, like the British, the French were initially content to leave propaganda matters to private groups. Although two major reorganizations of the official government program took place between 1914 and late 1917, French efforts to neutral, Allied, and enemy nations lagged considerably behind those of the British.

The events of 1917, in particular the stalemate on the Western Front, the Russian Revolution, the American declaration of war, and military setbacks in Italy, heightened Allied interest in propaganda late in the year. It was seen as a tool with which to break the strategic impasse, shorten the war, and effect a peace favoring the Entente. Allied governments shifted their emphasis away from defensive propaganda, as practiced since 1914 toward neutrals and allies, to an offensive campaign directly targeting the soldiers and civilians of the Central Powers. It emphasized news of the shift in the military balance caused by the American intervention, and Woodrow Wilson's Fourteen Points.

On 13 February 1918, Prime Minister David Lloyd George initiated the shift in emphasis by abolishing all existing British propaganda agencies and creating a single, central Ministry of Information (MOI) under Canadian newspaper magnate Max Aiken, Lord Beaverbrook. MOI was divided into domestic and foreign divisions, but for the first time the latter included an Office of Propaganda to Enemy Countries, named Crewe House, under newspaperman Lord Northcliffe. Unlike its predecessors, Crewe House targeted a mass civilian and military audience and sought to disrupt morale, foster distrust of German leaders, and shake German beliefs in the justice of their cause and the certainty of victory. Northcliffe hoped to use truthful propaganda to appeal to the aspirations of specific groups in the enemy camp, including Austria-Hungary's "oppressed nationalities," and Jews, who sought a national homeland in Ottoman-controlled Palestine. Crewe House supplied the Italian government with ready-made propaganda materials and technical expertise for Italy's relatively small-scale propaganda campaigns against Austria-Hungary.

In France Premier Georges Clemenceau quickly followed Britain's lead and in March of 1918 created a central Commission on Propaganda against the Enemy under André Tardieu. By the time of the Armistice, the commission was the largest Allied operation of its kind. Its output was described by American observers as being "ingeniously varied, sensational, sure-footed, very smoothly organized," and "characterized by . . . ingenuity in distribution and by variety and unscrupulousness in content."

Allied propaganda agencies almost totally disregarded combat propaganda prior to 1918. The British army had used leaflets on the Western Front in October of 1914, but enthusiasm was lacking and no further campaigns were attempted until early 1916. The war office often criticized the government for neglecting combat propaganda, but it was not until the Imperial General Staff and the war office were reorganized in February of 1916 that Major General Sir George MacDonough, chief of the War Office Military Intelligence Division, and Brigadier General G.K. Cockerill received permission to establish a twenty-man special propaganda and censorship division within MID. The new organization, M.I.7, began distributing leaflets along the Western Front; by early 1918 it was dispatching nearly one million units monthly by balloon, infantry patrol, and aircraft.

When Northcliffe took charge of all British strategic propaganda behind enemy lines in 1918, he allowed M.I.7 to continue its independent tactical operations. That arrangement was difficult to control, however, and all propaganda was placed under Crewe House supervision in July. Thereafter, M.I.7's output increased dramatically with the aid of civilian leaflet writers and Northcliffe's publication facilities. Batches of 100,000 leaflets could be written, printed, and dispatched to France within forty-eight hours of the original request. M.I.7 delivered 2.1 million leaflets in August of 1918, 3.7 million in September, 5.3 million in October, and 1.4 million in the first ten days of November, eventually delivering 12 million leaflets of ninety-one varieties by the time of the Armistice.

The French military was quicker to grasp the potential of combat propaganda and in 1914 established a ten-member propaganda service in the Military Intelligence Section of general headquarters. It remained the only French agency targeting the enemy for two years and was transferred to the civilian Maison de la Presse in 1916. In 1918 combat propaganda was returned to the ministry of war as the *Service de la Propagande Aérienne*. By late August of 1918 the military propaganda service had distributed 25 million leaflets of seventy-one different types over the Western Front by paper balloon, rifle grenade, aircraft, Stokes mortar, and 75mm artillery leaflet shell. "The whole French Army," U.S. military propagandist Captain Heber Blankenhorn later reported, "believed in its campaign of ideas; company commanders recognized it as part of the day's work."

Sensing the value of propaganda to sway public opinion and undermine enemies, President Wilson, within nine days of the American declaration of war, created the Committee on Public Information under George Creel. CPI was first and foremost a domestic information and patriotic agency overseeing film, speakers, and press bureaus. It had no overseas function until October of 1917, when a Foreign Education Section was started at the suggestion of Colonel Edward House. Even then, CPI limited its foreign activities to distributing motion pictures and pro-American information through the mail and over cable and wireless services to Allies and neutrals. CPI did not develop any sort

of large-scale or comprehensive strategic propaganda campaign targeting enemy civilian populations prior to the Armistice.

Like the Allied military services, the American army did create a small Psychological Subsection within the M.I.2, Positive Branch, Military Intelligence Bureau, in February of 1918. By July of 1918 a twenty-one-member propaganda subsection (G-2-D) was established at AEF headquarters in France. It began full-scale leaflet operations against enemy forces late in August of 1918 from several forward bases behind the American sectors of the front, using British and French balloons. Between mid-August and early November, G-2-D produced 5.1 million leaflets, delivered by balloon, aircraft, and artillery shell in numbers reaching 1.4 million in September; 3.5 million in October; and 136,000 in the first fortnight in November.

Despite Allied rhetoric to the contrary, the Central Powers failed to realize the potential of propaganda until it was too late to respond adequately. Trans-oceanic telegraph cables were controlled by Great Britain and were cut early in the war, thus denying Germany unhindered access to the world media. Stymied in their ability to communicate outside of areas they occupied, the Germans did little to counteract Allied propaganda. According to Ludendorff, "Propaganda was underestimated too long," the organizations dealing with it were poor, "and the material issued was never sufficient." Most German leaders considered propaganda "quack advertising" and were opposed to it "on the ground that it was too blatant and vulgar." It took two years of requests by the Army High Command before a propaganda bureau was created in the Military Department of the German Foreign Office in July of 1916, but, as Ludendorff recounted, it "only kept up with difficulty," and "its achievements in comparison to the magnitude of the task, were inadequate." Germany "produced no real effect on the enemy people," and although Ludendorff urged the establishment of a British-style agency, no such office existed until August of 1918, when the Central Bureau for Propaganda Purposes was created in the foreign office. Ludendorff concluded, however, that it was "an unhappy appendage . . . devoid of real authority."

Although civilian efforts were few, Section IIIb of the German Military Intelligence Service did drop leaflets around Nancy during the Battle of Grande in September of 1914 and produced a newspaper for French troops. The use of combat propaganda remained localized and sporadic, however, right through the end of the war, although leaflets were used against Belgian forces during the spring 1918 offensive and propaganda newspapers were dropped to American soldiers in the Argonne in September. Germany's Austro-Hungarian allies were similarly late to use propaganda, but they were credited with a major propaganda coup by the Italians, who in part attributed their October 1917 defeat at Caporetto to morale-shattering Austrian propaganda leaflets.

Clayton D. Laurie

References

Creel, George. *How We Advertized America.* New York: Harper & Row, 1920.

Bruntz, George G. *Allied Propaganda and the Collapse of the German Empire in 1918.* Stanford: Stanford University, 1938.

Lasswell, Harold D., and James Wechsler. *Propaganda Techniques in the World War.* New York: Knopf, 1927.

Roetter Charles. *Psychological Warfare, 1914–45.* New York: Stein and Day, 1974.

Sanders, M.L. "Wellington House and British Propaganda during the First World War." *Historical Journal* 18 (1975): 122.

Sanders, M.L., and Philip M. Taylor. *British Propaganda during the First World War, 1914–1918.* London: Macmillan, 1982.

Squires, James D. *British Propaganda at Home and in the United States from 1914 to 1917.* Cambridge: Harvard University Press, 1935.

Stuart, Campbell. *Secrets of Crewe House: The Story of a Famous Campaign.* London: Hodder and Stoughton, 1920.

Taylor, Philip M. "The Foreign Office and British Propaganda during the First World War." *Historical Journal* 23 (December 1980): 876–91.

United States Committee on Public Information. *The Creel Report: Complete Report of the Chairman of the Committee on Public Information, 1917–1919.* Washington, D.C.: GPO, 1920. Reprint. New York: Da Capo, 1972.

Wilson, Trevor. "Lord Bryce's Investigation into Alleged German Atrocities in Belgium, 1914–15." *Journal of Contemporary History* 14 (1979): 369.

See also ATROCITIES

Pulkowski, Erich (1877–?)

German army officer. Born in 1877, Pulkowski came from a military family. His father was a colonel in the foot artillery. Pulkowski and two of his brothers were also in foot artillery, and another brother was in the field artillery. All four served in World War I.

In 1917 Erich Pulkowski developed a system of predicting artillery registration corrections without having to fire the guns. This system, which greatly increased the element of surprise in an attack, used correction factors from current weather data combined with previously measured muzzle-velocity errors from individual guns to derive the registration corrections. At the end of 1918 Pulkowski became closely associated with Colonel Georg Bruchmüller and assisted him in the great artillery preparations of 1918. The Pulkowski Method (*Pulkowski Verfahren*), as it was called in the German army, was used in all five of Ludendorff's 1918 offensives. The same basic system is still used by most NATO armies today.

Despite his significant technical contribution, Pulkowski was not retained in the postwar *Reichswehr*. He retired with the rank of major and assumed the management of his family's toy business in Cologne.

David T. Zabecki

References

Zabecki, David T. *Steel Wind: Georg Bruchmueller and the Birth of Modern Artillery.* Westport, Conn.: Praeger, 1994.

See also BRUCHMÜLLER, GEORG; LUDENDORFF OFFENSIVES, 1918

Putnik, Radomir (1847–1917)

Serbian field marshal. Born in Kragujevac, Serbia, on 24 January 1847 into a peasant family, Putnik received his education in Serbia. He chose a military career as an artillery officer and participated in the Serbo-Turkish War of 1876 and in the Serbo-Bulgarian War of 1885. In 1895 he was dismissed as a result of his involvement with the Radical party. The 1903 coup, which assassinated King Alexander Obrenovich and brought King Peter Karadjordjević to the throne, resurrected his fortunes. He was recalled to service, promoted, and made chief of staff. During the next decade Putnik also served three terms as minister of war, during which time he modernized the Serbian army. In the First Balkan War, Putnik was promoted to field marshal after leading Serbian forces to victory at Kumanovo. He commanded Serbian troops in the Second Balkan War against the Bulgarians.

When World War I erupted Putnik was recuperating from illness in Austria-Hungary. The Austro-Hungarian chief of staff, Franz Conrad von Hötzendorf, gallantly allowed him to return home to assume command of the Serbian troops. Putnik conducted the successful Serbian defense against the Austro-Hungarian invasions in 1914. In 1915 he directed the fighting against the combined German, Austro-Hungarian, and Bulgarian invasion. Putnik supervised the epic Serbian retreat across the Albanian mountains, even though he was so ill that four soldiers had to carry him across Albania in a sedan chair. After the surviving Serbian forces reached safety on Corfu in 1916, Putnik was relieved of command, ostensibly because of illness but also because the Serbian army needed a scapegoat after its defeat. He died a bitter man in Nice, France, on 17 May 1917.

Richard C. Hall

References

Djordjevic, Dimitrije. "Vojvoda Putnik, the Serbian High Command, and Strategy in 1914." In *East Central European Society in World War I,* edited by Bela K. Kiraly and Nandor F. Dresziger, 569–89. Boulder, Colo.: Social Science Monographs, 1985.

———. "Vojvoda Radomir Putnik." In *East European War Leaders: Civilian and Military,* edited by Bela K. Kiraly and Albert A. Nofi, 223–48. Boulder, Colo.: Social Science Monographs, 1988.

Skoko, Savo. *Vojvoda Radomir Putnik.* 2 vols. Belgrade: Beogradski izdavaichko-graiichki zavod, 1984.

See also BALKAN FRONT, 1914, 1915; PETER KARADJORDJEVIĆ, KING; SERBIA

Q

Qingdao (Tsingtao), Siege of (23 August–7 November 1914)

The only major land battle of World War I in east Asia. The battle pitted two powers against each other that would become allies twenty-five years later in World War II—Japan and Germany. Qingdao (Tsingtao) was a German fortress city on the tip of China's Shandong (Shantung) Peninsula. Located halfway between Tianjin (Tientsin) and Shanghai, it commanded the entrance to Jaiozhou (Kaiochow) Bay, which was the home base for Germany's fleet in the Pacific.

The Imperial Navy first moved into the region in 1897, the excuse being the murder of two German missionaries. Germany forced the weak Chinese government to grant a ninety-nine-year lease on 214 square miles surrounding the bay. By 1913 the Germans had built a European-style city with extensive port facilities, including a 16,000-ton drydock—one of the largest in the world. The harbor defenses consisted of a series of small sea forts around the lower end of the peninsula with one major fort on the bay side and another on the Yellow Sea side. The forts had 210mm and 240mm guns in revolving turrets.

The Germans assumed that any major threat to Qingdao would come from the land side, from China, and they built the city's main defenses on two ranges of low hills that spanned the peninsula above the city. The inner defensive line, about four miles from the city, was anchored by a fort on each flank, with powerful Fort Bismarck in the center. The flank forts had 105mm and 120mm guns in open batteries. Fort Bismarck had 280mm howitzers and 210mm guns in reinforced concrete casemates. Spread between the three forts the Germans had ninety guns of various sizes, ranging from 37mm to 90mm. The positions looked impressive enough on paper, but most of the guns were older models and ammunition was in short supply.

The outer line of forts was about eight miles from the city, where the peninsula was some twelve miles in width. Since the German garrison was never large enough to man both lines effectively, the outer one was intended more as a warning, or outpost, line. The key terrain on the outer line was 1,200-foot-high Prinz Heinrich Berg, located on the southern flank. For some reason, however, the Germans never adequately fortified it.

Between the two lines of forts the Germans built an intermediate defensive zone in the flat, marshy Hai Po River valley. Each of the five reinforced concrete redoubts in the zone had field artillery, machine guns, searchlights, and a garrison of about two hundred troops. The redoubts were linked by blockhouses in between. A concrete ditch ran in front of the position, from shore to shore. In front of the ditch were minefields and electrified fence.

Germany's Asian aspirations came into conflict with those of Japan, which had entered into an alliance with Great Britain in 1902 and had defeated Russia in the Russo-Japanese War of 1904–5. With the outbreak of World War I, Japan saw an opportunity to eliminate Germany as a major power in Asia, just as it had earlier eliminated Russia. Thus, in solidarity with their British allies, on 15 August 1914 the Japanese issued an unconditional ultimatum to the Germans to surrender and evacuate Qingdao without compensation. The deadline for a response was 23 August. Three days after receiving the message, German governor Captain Alfred Meyer-Waldeck, sent Kaiser Wilhelm II a telegram stating that Qingdao would resist to the last. Even before the Japanese delivered their ultimatum, the Germans anticipated what was coming. Not wishing to repeat the Russian mistake at Port Arthur, Vice Admiral Maximilian Graf von Spee left for the safety of open waters on 4 August with his small cruiser squadron. That left only the obsolete Austrian cruiser *Kaiserin Elizabeth,* torpedo boat *S-90,* and five small gunboats in Qingdao's harbor. Meyer-Waldeck, meanwhile, started evacuating all nonessential civilians.

Qingdao had a total garrison force of only about two thousand marines. In late July Meyer-Waldeck had pulled in the 460-strong legation guard detachments from Beijing (Peking) and Tianjin and issued mobilization orders for all German reservists in Asia. By the middle of August almost 1,500 reservists had reported. That still gave the Germans only about 4,600 troops with which to defend Qingdao. They also had a tiny air force, consisting of an observation balloon and one Rumpler Taube monoplane piloted by Lieutenant Guenther Plueschow.

For political reasons, the British felt that they had to support the Japanese operation. Their key contribution was the *Triumph,* an older predreadnought battleship. They also sent a token land force, consisting of the 2nd Battalion, South Wales Borders, from Tianjin; later they sent a half battalion of the 36th Sikhs. British ground troops came under the command of Brigadier General Nathaniel Barnardiston, who was not at all pleased about being the first British commander to serve in the field under a nonwhite superior commander. Captain Fitzmaurice of the *Triumph* apparently got along very well with the Japanese naval commander, Vice Admiral Sadakichi Kato.

The first shots of the battle took place the day before the surrender deadline, when the *S-90* encountered the *Kennet,* a British gunboat. The *S-90* scored several quick hits and then raced back to port. On 27 August the main Japanese fleet arrived off Qingdao, immediately established a blockade, and started minesweeping operations. The substantial Japanese force consisted of four battleships, two cruisers, fifteen destroyers, numerous torpedo boats, minesweepers, and even some submarines.

On 2 September lead elements of the Japanese ground force started coming ashore at Longkou (Lungkow) Bay, some 100 miles north of Qingdao. Because of bad weather, it took the one infantry brigade and one cavalry regiment nine days to get ashore and get organized. The weather prevented German air reconnaissance, and it was not until 13 September that Lieutenant Plueschow spotted the Japanese.

Once his cavalry force was on the ground, the Japanese commander, Lieutenant General Mitsuomi Kamio, determined that there was no significant German resistance between him and the city's defenses. Thus he decided to land his follow-on forces at Laoshan Bay, only thirty miles from Qingdao. On 18 September another infantry brigade and the 24th Heavy Artillery Brigade starting coming ashore. Heavy artillery was the key to Kamio's plan. The 24th Brigade, under Major General Kishino Watanabe, had more than 100 guns and howitzers larger than 120mm. The Japanese put 23,000 troops ashore in the first two landings. By the time the siege ended, they had a land force of over 50,000 men, with another 10,000 in the fleet. Meyer-Waldeck was outnumbered better than thirteen-to-one.

The Japanese force started moving down the peninsula toward the Prinz Heinrich line in two columns. The forces closest to the shore were continually harassed by the German gunboats. On 25 September the Japanese sent three army aircraft to attack them. Although the Japanese failed to damage the gunboats, it was one of history's first encounters between aircraft and ships.

The Germans also used their own long-range artillery to fire on the steadily advancing Japanese. Artillery spotting was accomplished by the balloon, while Plueschow and his monoplane conducted deeper reconnaissance. The Japanese tried everything possible to neutralize Plueschow. They attempted to destroy his hangar and runway with naval gunfire, and whenever he landed, Japanese aircraft tried to bomb him on the ground. Eventually Plueschow and Japanese pilots started shooting at each other with pistols, one of history's earliest air-to-air combats.

The German defenders never had a chance. The Japanese took Prinz Heinrich Berg on 28 September, and the rest of the thinly held line fell within hours. The Germans retreated to the middle defensive line in the Hai Po valley, and General Watanabe quickly established his artillery observation post on top of Prinz Heinrich Berg. German artillery maintained fairly effective fire on the attackers until 7 October, when the observation balloon broke loose of its moorings and floated out to sea. After that German artillery was blind. Plueschow gamely tried to observe for the guns, but his plane had no radio, and he could not fly and observe at the same time.

It took the Japanese most of October to get their heavy guns and ammunition into position. Most of the actual fighting that month took place at sea or between ships and the shore. The first major Allied bombardment occurred on 6 October but achieved little because the ships were too far out. They tried again on 14 October, coming in closer. In the process, the *Triumph* sustained a hit from a 240mm shell fired by a German shore battery.

Three days later, the *S-90* slipped out of Qingdao under cover of darkness. A few hours later she found the *Takashio,* an older cruiser working as a minelayer. The *S-90* made a broadside run in the dark, firing three torpedoes. They struck their target and set off 120 mines in the *Takashio*'s hold, killing all but three of the cruiser's crew of 253. The concussion from the blast, however, split the *S-90*'s seams. With their vessel leaking badly and unable to regain the harbor, the crew beached the *S-90* on the Chinese coast.

By 28 October Japanese heavy artillery was in position and General Kamio made his final dispositions for the attack on Qingdao's middle defensive line. Kamio called for classic siege techniques of advancing parallels of trenches. All digging was done at night. At 06:10 on 31 October (the emperor's birthday) Watanabe's heavy artillery opened fire, and the bombardment continued unabated until Qingdao finally surrendered.

Knowing that the end was near, on 1 November Meyer-Waldeck ordered his troops to start the systematic destruction of anything that would be of military or economic value to the Japanese. That night the *Kaiserin Elizabeth* fired her remaining shells at the Japanese, and then the crew scuttled her in the harbor.

By the morning of 5 November the last of the German minefields and wire entanglements had been neutralized by the constant Japanese artillery bombardment. The German artillery was almost out of ammunition. Early on 6 November, under Meyer-Waldeck's orders, Lieutenant Plueschow loaded Qingdao's war diaries and other secret papers into his monoplane and headed for neutral Chinese territory. Plueschow did eventually make it back to Germany, where the kaiser decorated him with the Iron Cross.

Shortly after midnight on 7 November the Japanese launched an assault on redoubt three, in the center of the middle defensive zone. It fell after a half hour of fierce hand-to-hand fighting. Three hours later redoubt four fell. Meyer-Waldeck ordered counterattacks, but that only expended the remaining ammunition in the inner line of forts. With the German center gone the flank positions crumbled rapidly. By 05:00 the artillerymen inside Fort Bismarck started blowing up their own guns.

Meyer-Waldeck held a staff meeting at 06:00 hours. The Germans were virtually out of ammunition, and Meyer-Waldeck concluded that further resistance would be futile. As the Japanese started to re-form for the final assault on the now silent inner line of forts, white flags started going up. The last German position, redoubt five in the middle zone, surrendered at 09:30. By the time it finally ended, the siege of Qingdao had cost the Japanese 1,445 killed and 4,200 wounded. British losses were fourteen killed and sixty-one wounded. Despite the massive pounding from both sea- and land-based heavy artillery, the defenders had suffered only two hundred killed and five hundred wounded.

From a tactical standpoint, Qingdao is significant as one of history's last large-scale actions involving coastal artillery. It also was one of the first major battles in which air, land, and sea power all combined to play significant roles. Despite their relatively high casualty rate, the Japanese military demonstrated a mastery of combined operations far beyond the ability of most armies in 1914. The armies of other nations would eventually learn combined-arms concepts, but only after four years of bloody fighting on the European continent.

Strategically, Qingdao was significant because it eliminated Germany as a major power in East Asia. After Qingdao fell, Germany rapidly lost the remainder of its Far Eastern empire (German New Guinea, the Bismarcks, the Solomons, Samoa, the Carolines, the Marshalls, the Marianas, and Palau). The Germans had hoped that their strong presence in the Pacific would split the attention of the Royal Navy, thus giving the German High Seas Fleet a better chance to dominate the English Channel. That hope was not realized.

Qingdao had long-term geopolitical consequences in the context of World War I. With Germany out of the Pacific and the British

Empire severely weakened around the globe, only two powers remained to compete in the Pacific—the United States and Japan.

David T. Zabecki

References

Burdick, Charles B. *The Japanese Siege of Tsingtau.* Hamden, Conn.: Archon, 1976.

Jones, Jefferson. *The Fall of Tsingtau: With a Study of Japan's Ambitions in China.* Boston: Houghton Mifflin, 1915.

See also JAPAN; KAMIO, MITSUOMI

Q-Ships

Q-ships were regular, nonmilitary ships manned by military crews and armed with hidden guns. They were called Q-ships because so many of them sailed from Queenstown. This unofficial designation eventually replaced "decoy" as their official designation.

Submarines had presented the nations fighting the World War with the difficult problem of trying to destroy an enemy that could decide where, when, and how each battle could be fought. Also, submariners could, in most cases, decline battle as long as they remained undetected. Thus the Royal Navy decided upon two courses of action to combat submarines. The first was to arm as many merchant ships as possible. The other was to use Q-ships.

Countries other than Britain—including Germany, the Ottoman Empire, and the United States—used decoys during the war. A Turkish decoy had actually scored the first such victory of the war by sinking a British submarine shortly after war was declared. But Great Britain faced the most significant submarine threat and therefore made the most use of Q-ships.

The British had used decoys at sea in 1902 to catch Arab slave traders, and thus a small group of officers had had some experience with these covert operations. All of the crews for the Special Service were volunteers initially drawn from regular naval ratings, but, as the demand for decoys grew, reservists were accepted.

The use of decoys to combat submarines was based on a presumption that the attacking submarines would follow the "Cruiser Rules" governing the conduct of commerce raiding. Under those rules, a U-boat was required to surface near the target and allow time for the crew to abandon ship. In most of these cases the U-boat commander would then sink the ship with gunfire. Q-ships and their crews, therefore, tried to appear nonthreatening and of so little value that a U-boat commander would not want to waste a torpedo on them. All manner of craft were used as Q-ships, including steamers, sailing ships, yachts, whalers, passenger ships, salvage vessels, and trawlers. Most were in poor condition and only marginally seaworthy.

A proper disguise for the ships and crew was essential. Gun mounts were carefully camouflaged in deck crates that folded down to allow the guns to fire. Other guns were mounted on platforms that rose out of cargo holds. Q-ships were painted in the colors of friendly and neutral shipping lines and frequently sailed under neutral flags.

The crews worked hard to perfect their disguises. One device was to employ facades that changed the silhouette of their upper works and that could be set up or torn down overnight. Crews also had to appear unremarkable. They wore civilian clothes, sometimes disguised themselves as women, and were forbidden to salute, as that would certainly give them away.

Each Q-ship carried two crews. The "panic party" would evacuate the ship in order to lure the U-boat commander to move in closer to the presumably abandoned ship. When the U-boat was within six hundred meters, the second crew would uncover the guns and attempt to sink it. Although the "panic party" was quite exposed during the battle, the Q-ship itself was usually loaded with a buoyant cargo. Lumber, casks, and cork were cheap and often gave decoys enough reserve buoyancy to stay afloat long enough to engage the submarine successfully. In addition, unused areas of the ships were often sealed to limit flooding.

Another tactic was used in the summer of 1915: A Q-ship towed a submerged British submarine. When a U-boat surfaced to attack, the British submarine would release the tow line and torpedo the U-boat. The Q-ship/submarine combination was used twice to engage U-boats and in both cases was successful. The tactic was discontinued, however, because a submerged submarine could be towed only in calm seas, a rarity near the British Isles.

As early as December of 1914, U-boat commanders became suspicious of all targets—based both on their own experiences and on intelligence information. Since any ship, including a passenger liner, could be a Q-ship, all ships were suspect, and the presence of a woman on the deck of a ship was not conclusive. In many cases the U-boat commander would remain submerged and use a torpedo on any suspected Q-ship. Late in 1916 U-boats were equipped with new deck guns that allowed them to engage suspected Q-ships from two to three miles away. In 1916 these tactics allowed German submarines to sink one third of all operational Q-ships.

U-boat commanders considered Q-ships and their crews pirates, because the crews wore civilian clothes and the Q-ships regularly sailed under neutral colors until the moment they attacked. Q-ship crews, in turn, regarded the U-boats with equal animosity. Many reservists in the crews felt a special sense of mission; they had served in peacetime in the merchant ships now so vulnerable to submarine attack.

During the war Great Britain employed 221 Q-ships. From November of 1914 through September of 1917 they fought seventy engagements with U-boats and sank thirteen. That amounted to 9 percent of the 145 U-boats sunk during the war. That was a respectable showing considering the problems they had to overcome and that hazards for Q-ships grew immensely as the war progressed.

Evaluation of Q-boat effectiveness involves more than simply the number of U-boats sunk. Many others were damaged, some heavily, in engagements with Q-ships, forcing them to cut short their patrols and return to Germany for repairs. Whenever a U-boat commander chose to use a torpedo on a Q-ship, that was one less valuable torpedo that could be used against Britain's commercial shipping. In addition, in at least a few instances U-boat commanders declined an opportunity to attack because they suspected the target to be a Q-ship.

Randall J. Metscher

References

Auten, Lieutenant Commander Harold. "Q" *Boat Adventures*. London: H. Jenkins, 1919.

Campbell, Vice Admiral Gordon. *My Mystery Ships*. London: Hodder and Stoughton, 1928.

Chatterton, Lieutenant Commander E. Keble. *Q-Ships and Their Story*. London: Sidgwick and Jackson, 1922.

Ritchie, Carson I.A. *Q-Ships*. Lavenham, Suffolk: Lavenham Press, 1985.

See also SUBMARINE WARFARE, CENTRAL POWERS

R

Race to the Sea, 1914

From mid-September to November of 1914, after the Battle of the Marne, the battle front extended north as the Allies and Germans engaged in a series of attacks and counterattacks in an effort to gain the only remaining open ground, which lay from the Aisne River to the coast, in order to turn the other's flank. This was known as the Race to the Sea. In late August of that year, the French armies had failed in War Plan XVII to drive the Germans from Alsace and Lorraine. The Schlieffen Plan had been no more successful, as the German army ran short of manpower and swept east of Paris: On the Marne, General Joseph Joffre had rallied the retreating Allied armies to launch a great counterattack that had saved Paris and France. The opposing sides both searched desperately for a way to keep the war of movement open in hopes of gaining victory.

General Ferdinand Foch, who had commanded an army corps hardly a month before, was appointed as assistant to Joffre in charge of coordinating the Allied military effort in the north. On the request of the commander of the British Expeditionary Force, General Sir John French, the BEF was moved from Aisne to Flanders in late September to shorten lines of communications with England. On 14 September German minister of war General Erich von Falkenhayn replaced the broken Helmuth von Moltke as commander of German forces. Falkenhayn was charged with salvaging the remnants of the Schlieffen Plan. To bolster his depleted manpower, Falkenhayn called up large numbers of raw recruits with which to fill the ranks of the regrouped German Fourth Army, which was intended to be the spearhead of an effort to gain the coast and victory.

Meanwhile, invaluable help to the Allied cause was provided by the defense of the fortress city of Antwerp by the Belgian army, aided by three ill-equipped British marine brigades sent there by First Lord of the Admiralty Winston Churchill. These forces tied down German artillery and troops that might earlier have entered the fighting in France.

The fall of Antwerp on 10 October freed troops and artillery for Falkenhayn's planned attack to gain the Channel ports. But Belgian forces that had escaped the fall of Antwerp held along the Yser, through a combination of hard fighting and the opening of the sluice gates to flood the countryside. As the front solidified along the coastline and in the south, British and German forces converged on the town of Ypres. Both sides were maneuvering to outflank the other, but, unknown to the Allies, the Germans were to make their main effort around Ypres.

The Germans began their attack on 20 October, just as the first elements of the British army arrived near Ypres. The First Battle of Ypres proved a bitter and confusing affair. Accurate British rifle fire repeatedly decimated the ranks of the advancing German infantry as the BEF deployed on a sixteen-mile front around Ypres. Several German breakthroughs were halted by determined counterattacks, as the sagging British line was stiffened by the arrival of French reinforcements sent by Foch and the commitment of the newly arrived Indian Corps. Allied counterattacks proved equally unsuccessful in winning the day. By the middle of November, as bad weather set in, the battle drew to a close; both sides were exhausted. The British sustained fifty thousand casualties, and the French roughly the same. The Germans suffered 134,000 killed and wounded.

From August to the end of the year, operations on the Western Front cost the Allies nearly a million casualties; the Germans lost nearly that many. Hopes for a quick, decisive victory lay in ruin. Trench lines, not to vary more than ten miles over the next three years, came into existence all along the front from Switzerland to the Channel coast. The war of maneuver had given way to a war of stalemate and attrition. The failure of the war plans and the inability of either side to successfully turn the flank of the other in the Race to the Sea shattered the illusion of a short war and condemned millions of men to the horrors of trench warfare.

Van Michael Leslie

References

Bourne, J.M. *Britain and the Great War 1914–1918*. London: Edward Arnold, 1989.

Cruttwell, C.R.M.F. *A History of the Great War 1914–1918*. Oxford: Clarendon, 1940.

David, Daniel. *The 1914 Campaign*. New York: Military Press, 1987.

Falls, Cyril. *The Great War 1914–1918*. New York: Capricorn, 1959.

Woodward, Sir Llewellyn. *Great Britain and the War of 1914–1918*. London: Methuen, 1967.

See also BELGIUM, INVASION OF; FALKENHAYN, ERICH; MARNE, FIRST BATTLE OF

Radio
See WIRELESS (RADIO) COMMUNICATIONS

Radoslavov, Vasil (1854–1929)

Prime minister of Bulgaria, 1913–18, born on 15 July 1854 in Lovech, in what is now central Bulgaria. Radoslavov received a doctorate of law from the University of Heidelberg. He became a member of the Democratic party and served as Bulgarian minister of justice from 1884 to 1886. He also served in the cabinet of Stefan Stambulov. After Stambulov's assassination in 1895, Radoslavov formed his own Liberal party. He was prime minister of Bulgaria from 1901 to 1903.

In foreign policy Radoslavov was strongly Russophobe. During the Bulgarian catastrophe of 1913 in the Second Balkan War, he again became prime minister, heading an anti-Russian coalition government. With the approval of Czar Ferdinand, he pursued a pro-German and pro-Austro-Hungarian foreign policy. Recognizing Bulgaria's state of exhaustion after the Balkan Wars, he at first avoided participation in the First World War but negotiated with both sides. His goal was to obtain for Bulgaria what the Balkan Wars had denied it, Macedonia.

Although a large segment of the Bulgarian population favored a pro-Entente policy, in August of 1915 Radoslavov signed an agreement that brought Bulgaria into the war on the side of the Central Powers. Under his leadership Bulgaria occupied Macedonia and became closely tied economically to Germany. When the fortunes of the Central Powers declined in the spring of 1918, a government with less pronounced German sympathies replaced that of Radoslavov. Following the Bulgarian defeat he retired to Germany, where he died in Berlin on 21 October 1929.

Richard C. Hall

References

Kymanov, Milen. *Politicheski partii organizatsii i dvizheniya v Bŭlgariya i texnite lideri 1879–1949*. Sofia: Prosveta, 1991.

Radoslavov, V. *Bulgarien und die Weltkrise*. Berlin: Ullstein, 1923.

Silbertein, Gerard E. *The Troubled Alliance, German-Austrian Relations, 1914–1917*. Lexington: University of Kentucky Press, 1970.

See also BULGARIA

Rasputin, Grigorii Effimovich (1872–1916)

Spiritual advisor and confidant to Czar Nicholas II and Empress Alexandra. In the eyes of many Russians, Rasputin, a mysterious peasant monk who gained a strong hold over the Russian royal family, came to symbolize all that was wrong with Imperial Russia. Born in a peasant village in the western foothills of the Ural Mountains (the exact date is unknown and estimates range from 1864 to 1872), Rasputin was a precocious child, having learned to read the Bible at an early age. According to popular legend, Grigorii Effimovich was a spirited lad (the word *rasputnyi* in Russian means "debauched") who possessed strange powers, such as the ability to converse with animals. As a young man he joined the Khlytsy religious sect in western Siberia, one of many deviant religious groups existing in Russia at that time. The Khlytsy believed that anyone could become Christlike and able to perform miracles. Part of the training was to discover evil, especially sexual excess, which was supposed to contain some sort of religious regenerative power.

Among the peasants Rasputin gained a reputation as a miraculous holy man. He wandered into villages, conducted faith healing and participated in orgies. In 1904 a Russian Orthodox priest traveling in the countryside met Rasputin and, being impressed with his Biblical knowledge, brought him to St. Petersburg, where he was soon practicing his strange brand of Christianity. Among Bohemian circles he became a sensation. It was not long before he was introduced to members of the imperial family.

On 14 November 1905 Rasputin was brought to the Winter Palace, where the young czarevich, Alexei, who was afflicted with severe hemophilia, had taken a fall and was bleeding to death. Alexei had been examined by the leading court physicians, who could do nothing, and had been given last rites. As a last resort one of Czarinia Alexandra's cousins suggested that Rasputin be called. There was nothing to lose. That Rasputin stopped the boy's bleeding was attested to by everyone present, including several who became his enemies. How he did it is still open to speculation. The most common theory is hypnotism. From then on Rasputin was virtually a member of the imperial family, referred to by the royal couple as "our friend." Protected by the czar and empress he regularly engaged in the most outrageous scandals, including the seduction of society women and shady financial deals. Curiously, the great mass of the Russian peasantry saw him as their link to the crown.

In July of 1914 Rasputin warned the czar that a war would be a disaster for Russia, most likely bringing on a social upheaval. In late 1915 when the czar left for the front—having assumed personal command of the army—the direction of government was left to the empress, who took Rasputin as her personal confidant and political advisor. She asked him to approve all ministerial appointments as well as dismissals. The empress went with a vengeance after those whom she thought were enemies of the czar. Within a few months virtually all able

ministers were gone and replaced by incompetents.

This "ministerial leapfrog" shocked everyone, even the conservatives. In December of 1916 the Council of United Nobility passed a resolution referring to the "dark forces" within the government. In the State Duma there was open talk of Rasputin, and perhaps the empress, being in the pay of the Germans. Finally, on 16 December 1916, a group of conservatives decided to act. Rasputin was invited to a party at the home of Prince Yusupov, a member of the imperial family. Once there he was given poisoned wine and cakes, and, after these had produced no appreciable effect, he was shot repeatedly and his body thrown into the Neva River, only to be found a short time later. Arguably, Rasputin helped hasten the political breakdown that led to the March Revolution. His murder was a last attempt to save the monarchy before the revolution, but it came too late.

John W. Bohon

References

Fülöp-Miller, René. *Rasputin, the Holy Devil.* Garden City, N.Y.: Garden City Publishing, 1928.
Massie, Robert K. *Nicholas and Alexandra.* New York: Atheneum, 1967.

See also ALEXANDRA FEODOROVNA; NICHOLAS II; RUSSIA, HOME FRONT AND REVOLUTIONS OF 1917

Rathenau, Walther (1867–1922)

German businessman, wartime administrator, and post-war statesman, born in Berlin on 29 September 1867. The son of an industrial entrepreneur, Rathenau earned a Ph.D. in electrochemistry and was a man of wide interests and considerable energy. He wrote widely on social problems and the reorganization of society. He longed to be taken seriously as an intellectual, but his main accomplishments were political and administrative. He served on the boards of at least eighty-six corporations and became a director, and in 1915 president, of AEG *(Allgemeine Elektrizitats-Gesellschaft),* the electrical giant founded by his father.

Shortly after the beginning of World War I, on 8 August 1914, Rathenau was informed by Prussian minister of war General Erich von Falkenhayn that no steps had been taken to prevent the exhaustion of strategic materials. Rathenau convinced Falkenhayn that a survey of stocks was imperative and that a mechanism had to be created for the control of strategic materials. That led on 9 August to the establishment of the War Raw Materials Department (*Kriegsrohstoffabteilung,* or KRA) with Rathenau as its head. He instituted a program that sequestered and regulated the allocation of strategic materials; it also promoted the manufacture of synthetics and the utilization of substitute products. Inefficient plants were closed and prices controlled.

Some large industrial interests, complaining of Rathenau's "state socialism," utilized anti-Semitism in their campaign against him. Although his department had nothing to do with food, he was accused in the press of causing food shortages. On 1 April 1915 he resigned, but KRA continued to operate effectively under his successor, Major Josef Koeth, and it enabled Germany to avoid critical shortages that might have crippled the war effort.

Rathenau, though a staunch supporter of Germany's role in the war, advocated a negotiated peace and opposed both the rabid annexationists and the resumption of unrestricted submarine warfare. Following the war he became a member of the government's Socialization Committee in March of 1920, and he was a technical assistant at the Spa Conference on Disarmament in July of that year. In May of 1921 Chancellor Joseph Wirth appointed him minister of reconstruction. Rathenau hoped that a policy of cooperation would lead to a tempering of Allied demands.

On 31 January 1922 Wirth appointed Rathenau foreign minister. In that position, he became a leading proponent of economic ties between Germany and Russia. He argued that Germany and Russia, despite their different economic systems, shared a common status as defeated and ostracized nations, and that relations with Russia would provide Germany a degree of international independence. Rathenau, however, made a special effort to keep in touch with Prime Minister David Lloyd George of Britain. He sought British support for a less demanding reparations policy and did not want Germany's Russian policy to be completely at odds with that of Britain. He also negotiated a Franco-German agreement to promote cooperation between French and German industry, with the purported purpose of facilitating payment of reparations.

Fearing the further isolation of Germany, Rathenau met with Russian representatives on 16 April at nearby Rapallo and concluded an agreement by which Germany and Russia restored diplomatic and consular relations. Both parties agreed to a mutual renunciation of reparation claims, and Germany consented to waive indemnification for losses sustained by Germans as a result of the abolition of private property in Russia. Rapallo also paved the way for military cooperation between the two states.

Rathenau did not live to see the ramifications of the agreement. While being driven from his residence to his office he was murdered in Berlin on 24 June 1922 by two young anti-Semitic and anti-republican nationalists.

Bernard A. Cook

References

Felix, David. *Walther Rathenau and the Weimar Republic: The Politics of Reparations.* Baltimore: Johns Hopkins University Press, 1971.

Joll, James. *Three Intellectuals in Politics.* New York: Harper and Row, 1965.

Kessler, Harry. *Walter Rathenau: His Life and Work.* Translated by W.D. Robson-Scott. New York: Harcourt, Brace, 1930.

Rathenau, Walter. *Walter Rathenau: Industrialist, Banker, Intellectual, and Politician. Notes and Diaries, 1907–1922.* New York: Oxford University Press, 1965.

See also GERMANY, HOME FRONT

Rawlinson, Sir Henry (1864–1925)

British army commander. Like most of his fellow British commanders in World War I, Rawlinson had seen extensive active service around the world. Born on 20 February 1864 at Trent Manor, Rawlinson attended Eton and Sandhurst and joined the King's Royal Rifle Corps in India in 1884.

Rawlinson saw action as aide-de-camp to Lord Roberts in the Burma Campaign of 1886–87. After transferring to the Coldstream Guards in 1892, he attended staff college in 1893 and served on *Sirdar* (commander in chief) Horatio Kitchener's staff at the battles of Atbara and Omdurman in the Sudan in 1897. In the Boer War he initially held a key staff appointment at the siege of Ladysmith; later, as commander of a mobile column, he proved himself one of the most able and energetic of the younger commanders. As commandant of the staff college from 1903 to 1906, his great experience enabled him to make the instruction more practical. He subsequently commanded 3rd Division at Aldershot.

The start of World War I found Rawlinson as director of recruiting, but he was soon needed in France. By October of 1914 he was commanding 7th Infantry Division, protecting the right flank of the retreating Belgians. Throughout 1915 he commanded IV Corps at the battles of Neuve Chapelle, Aubers Ridge, Festubert, and Loos. At the end of 1915 he was promoted to lieutenant general and given command of Fourth Army, which bore main responsibility for executing the bloody Somme Offensive of 1916. Unlike General Sir Douglas Haig, Rawlinson did not see the offensive as a chance to win the war in 1916.

In 1917 Rawlinson was promoted to general and chosen by Haig to plan a combined naval-military attack on the German-occupied Belgian coast; this ambitious concept was tabled because the Passchendaele Offensive failed to make sufficient progress. In February of 1918, Rawlinson succeeded General Sir Henry Wilson as British military representative on the supreme war council. A month later the Germans broke through the British Fifth Army, and Rawlinson was hastily sent to take over from General Herbert Gough. In three weeks of fighting, British casualties exceeded those of the entire three months of the Passchendaele Campaign the previous autumn. Under Rawlinson's command, however, the remnants of Fifth Army successfully defended the vital railway junction of Amiens—the Germans' immediate objective. Reconstituted as the Fourth Army, Rawlinson's troops then took the key point of Villers-Brettoneux on 25 April.

The last three months of the war were the pinnacle of Rawlinson's career. His small-scale but completely successful attack on Hamel on 4 July 1918, one of the first examples of infantry/tank cooperation, was a prelude to the larger assault of 8 August, which Ludendorff described as "the black day in the history of the German army." In that assault Rawlinson employed 450 tanks. Between 4 August and Armistice Day his Fourth Army of twenty-two Empire and two American divisions advanced sixty miles from the Somme, smashing through the Hindenburg Line and capturing 80,000 prisoners and 1,100 guns in the process. It was a decisive victory and the end of the war on the Western Front. For his efforts during the war, Parliament granted Rawlinson a cash award and created him a baron.

Rawlinson's service was not yet over. At the end of 1919, he spent three months supervising the evacuation of the Allied force from Archangel. In 1920 he became commander-in-chief, India. His achievements laid the foundations for the successful performance of the Indian army in the Second World War and after independence. He improved the relationship between army headquarters and the government, initiated a modernization program, and above all began the process of Indianizing the officer corps.

A fine horseman and brilliant polo player, Rawlinson was also a thoroughly professional soldier with an excellent tactical mind. He died in Delhi on 28 March 1925.

Philip J. Green

References

Edmonds, Sir. J.E. *Military Operations of the British Army in the Western Theatre of War (Official History)*. London: Macmillan, 1933.
Maurice, Sir F. *The Life of Lord Rawlinson of Trent*. London: Cassell, 1928.
Terraine, John. *The Western Front, 1914– 1918*. London: Hutchinson, 1964.

See also ALLIED COUNTEROFFENSIVE; ARTOIS, THIRD BATTLE OF; LUDENDORFF OFFENSIVES; NEUVE CHAPELLE, BATTLE OF; SOMME, BATTLE OF

Red Cross

For many soldiers in many countries, the symbol of the red cross, or crescent, meant comfort, a bit of refreshment, and a sympathetic ear when all three were elusive treasures. The Red Cross, one of a number of humanitarian relief organizations that served the troops in World War I, had its beginnings in Europe. It was the brainchild of Swiss citizen Jean Henri Dunant, who had observed the suffering of soldiers at the Battle of Solferino in June of 1859 during Austria's war with France and Piedmont. Dunant had organized a makeshift battlefield medical corps to tend the thousands of wounded left in the wake of the fighting. Dunant's small book about the battle drew the attention of the Public Welfare Society in Geneva, which formed the International Committee of the Red Cross (ICRC) in the fall of 1863. A conference was scheduled for the following year to codify and implement the initiatives.

The experience of the United States during the Civil War identified the need for civilian relief agencies to augment the work of military medical services strained to the breaking point. Dr. Charles S. Bowles of the U.S. Sanitary Commission—along with the American minister to Switzerland—was designated to observe the meeting in Geneva. Eleven nations signed the Geneva Treaty on 22 August 1864; the United States was not one of them.

Meanwhile, the familiar red cross on a white background was approved as the international symbol of the ICRC. Dr. Louis Appia, one of its five originators, first wore it as an armband during the Prusso-Danish War of 1864.

Several further attempts to institutionalize the Red Cross in the United States also met with failure, until Clara Barton broke the impasse and brought the American Red Cross into the family of international relief organizations in 1881. The next year the U.S. government formally ratified the international treaty relating to the Red Cross.

In 1901, after years of struggling for the rights of the wounded and prisoners of war, Dunant was recognized with the first Nobel Peace Prize, shared with another Swiss, Frédéric Passy. At the outbreak of war in 1914, thirty-eight countries had active national Red Cross or Red Crescent (as the agency was known in Muslim nations) societies.

In 1905 President Theodore Roosevelt rechartered the American Red Cross as a fully public organization that attended the victims of natural disasters at home and abroad. The image of the American volunteer ambulance driver in Italy in World War I was vividly portrayed in Ernest Hemingway's novel *A Farewell To Arms*. Early in 1915 the teams were withdrawn, and the American Red Cross concentrated on providing assistance through other national relief organizations up until the time the United States entered the war.

At that time, former president William Howard Taft was chairman of the central committee of the American Red Cross. A war council existed under the supervision of the central committee, but its guiding hand was Henry P. Davison. As chairman of the war council, Davison set out "to bind up the wounds of a bleeding world." With belligerency in 1917 the American Red Cross lost its political neutrality and became an agency of Allied relief.

The British Red Cross Society (BRCS) was formed in 1905 from several independent Red Cross organizations. The war office arranged for all civilian offers of relief help to be channeled through the BRCS. The army had a well-developed medical corps, which was reluctant to depend on the BRCS, but the territorial reserve organizations formed in 1908 welcomed the assistance. At the outbreak of war in 1914, the BRCS, cooperating with the Order of St. John, contributed to the effort to organize more than two thousand voluntary aid detachments (VAD) to assist with first aid, sanitation, nursing, ambulance service, hospital staffing, cooking, and other related duties. In 1915 VAD ambulance units, with their female drivers, met with such success that the military began organizing them into convoys. During the Great War, BRCS motor ambulances moved ten million patients in France, peripheral theaters, and the British Isles. Canadian, Australian, South African, and Indian Red Cross societies provided workers and supplies in the theaters where their troops were engaged. *The Times* of London organized huge fund-raising efforts to benefit the BRCS, raising 16.5 million pounds sterling and goods worth a million pounds sterling.

Because the need for care exceeded the capability of the army medical service, the BRCS filled the gap by operating more than three thousand home hospitals. More than 7,800 men and women served in the BRCS overseas during the war, some paid and some volunteer. The recognition they received for providing supplies of comfort items to the troops as well as parcels of food and clothing to prisoners of war was well deserved. The BRCS provided follow-up care for disabled soldiers that was subsidized by the government.

All belligerents were well served by their national relief agencies. In 1876 Turkey had adopted the Red Crescent instead of the Red Cross as its symbol, and other Muslim countries followed suit. The French Red Cross was soon overwhelmed with refugees from German-occupied areas, and, in addition, had the burden of staffing field hospitals and ambulance units. The American Red Cross, long before American troops arrived in France, sent money and nurses to work behind Allied lines to support the French Red Cross. In areas where the French would not allow the American Expeditionary Forces (AEF) to establish military hospitals, the American Red Cross was permitted to do so. Military personnel often staffed those facilities. American Red Cross Military Hospital No. 1, located by agreement with the AEF in July of 1917 in the Paris suburb of Neuilly, accepted only French patients until the Second Battle of the Marne in the spring of 1918. Because American divisions were serving in French corps, the French granted Americans access to ARC Military Hospital No. 1.

The French had agreed to serve all American battle casualties, and thus divisional sanitary trains turned over wounded Americans to French ambulance trains and hospitals; they thereby lost control of their patients for months. As a compromise, the ARC was permitted to establish an evacuation hospital near Beauvais to serve the casualties of the U.S. First Division, in action at Cantigny in May-June of 1918. The ARC hospital, the first of its kind in the battle zone, received only American patients but was commanded by a French officer.

While the French had agreed to service American casualties, actions in the Marne salient proved too much for their system. Some evacuation hospitals had been captured by the Germans. Ambulances had to evacuate directly from the battlefield to the Paris hospitals, a round trip of about eighty miles. The American Red Cross established a tent hospital at Juilly, on the Paris-Soissons road, where Mrs. Payne Whitney had been operating a hospital for French patients. As the campaign continued, Militarized Red Cross Hospital No. 114 was established at Jouy-sur-Morin, near Château-Thierry. Four American Red Cross evacuation hospitals, each commanded by a medical corps officer, supplemented the military hospitals from July until the Armistice. Additionally, the American Red Cross established convalescent homes, usually in mountainous or resort areas, thus greatly expanding the army's recuperation capabilities.

The German Red Cross was formed in 1871 from the societies of Prussia and the other German states composing the new empire. Those organizations were among the most experienced in Europe at the outbreak of war in 1914. The Japanese Red Cross Society was formed in 1877 and quickly developed a reputation for superior nursing skills. The Italian Red Cross Society, like that of the French, was established and often led by wealthy women of the nobility.

The Russian Red Cross organization was overwhelmed by the needs of the army and the civilian population in World War I. It had performed useful adjunct service for the army medical corps during the Russo-Japanese War but did not have the resources to cope with the scope of the world war. The American Red Cross arrived in July of 1917 at Vladivostok with ambulances and medical supplies but soon learned that the most pressing problem was distribution of milk and food to the large cities.

In addition to coordinating assistance from the national societies, the ICRC initiated efforts to mitigate the suffering of prisoners of war. On 21 August 1914, the ICRC formed the International Prisoner of War Agency (IPOWA) and notified the belligerent nations. Early on, a lack of detailed agreements and reciprocity among belligerents threatened to paralyze the exchange of information about prisoners. In 1916, the Danish Red Cross Society established an effective conduit of information for Eastern Front belligerent powers. As the battle intensified the numbers of men missing in action increased significantly, and the IPOWA began a system of "regimental searches" whereby a soldier's imprisoned comrades would be queried directly about the fate of missing men. French prisoners of war filed 90,000 reports of soldiers not included on official tallies. At the conclusion of hostilities, the ICRC continued to provide information on missing soldiers and civilians through a tracing service.

On 5 May 1919 members of the newly organized League of Red Cross Societies met in Paris. Delegates from the United States, Great Britain, France, Italy, and Japan composed the board of governors, and the American Henry P. Davison was elected chairman. Sir David Henderson was elected director-general, and Professor William Rappard became secretary-general. The headquarters of the new league was established at Geneva, and many nations were invited to join. Like the ICRC from which the Red Cross organizations received recognition, the League of Red Cross Societies depended on the faith and support of the national societies for long-term prosperity. The ICRC and the league meet every four years at an international conference, but the league is only a loose association, not a governing body.

The history of the Red Cross and Red Crescent societies in World War I is indicative of the way warfare had changed. Nations, not just governments, became deeply involved in both the conduct of war and the amelioration of war's effects. Today, the Red Cross organizations thrive because of a dedicated membership and the support of governments.

John F. Votaw

References

Davison, Henry P. *The American Red Cross in the Great War.* New York: Macmillan, 1920.

Durand, André. *From Sarajevo to Hiroshima: History of the International Committee of the Red Cross.* Geneva: Henry Dunant Institute, 1984.

Epstein, Beryl and Sam. *The Story of the International Red Cross.* New York: Thomas Nelson & Sons, 1963.

Gumpert, Martin. *Dunant: The Story of the Red Cross.* New York: Oxford University Press, 1938.

Hurd, Charles. *The Compact History of the American Red Cross.* New York: Hawthorn, 1959.

International Committee of the Red Cross. *The International Red Cross Committee in Geneva, 1863–1943.* Geneva: ICRC, 1943.

Peacey, Belinda. *The Story of the Red Cross.* London: Frederick Muller, 1969.

See also MEDICINE, MILITARY; PRISONERS OF WAR

Reichstag Peace Resolution of 1917

On 19 July 1917 a committee of deputies, consisting of Social Democrats, the Center party, and the Progressives, introduced a peace resolution to the German Reichstag. It called for a peace of understanding and reconciliation without annexations or indemnities. It also affirmed that, if the war continued, the German people would resist with all their strength. The resolution passed the Reichstag in a vote of 212 to 126, with Conservatives and the National Liberals opposed. The National Liberals, under the leadership of Gustav Stresemann, an ardent annexationist, rejected any expression of war aims that repudiated the desires of heavy industry for territorial acquisitions.

The resolution repudiated the supreme command, which had attempted to block its passage. It also spelled the end to the political truce with which Germany had begun the war. The new Chancellor Dr. Georg Michaelis, who had just replaced Theobald von Bethmann Hollweg, said that he accepted the resolution "as I interpret it." Michaelis smugly assumed that he had thereby nullified it. He affirmed to the Crown Prince that "one can, in fact, make any peace one likes and still be in accord with the resolution." Even Matthias Erzberger, who had called for a peace resolution to counter Germany's increasingly precarious military position, cynically debased its meaning by asserting that the industrialists could still get the Longwy-Briey Line in the west through negotiation.

To counteract the resolution and push for annexations, Admiral Alfred von Tirpitz and the reactionary East Prussian bureaucrat Wolfgang Kapp set up the Fatherland party. On 2 September 1917 the party issued a manifesto seeking popular support for a "Hindenburg Peace" through which Germany could reap material rewards for its effort. The sympathies of the German people, however, increasingly lay with the resolution. The Reichstag did, however, ratify the annexationist treaties of Brest-Litovsk and Bucharest in 1918.

Bernard A. Cook

References

Halperin, S. William. *Germany Tried Democracy: A Political History of the Reich from 1918 to 1933.* New York: Thomas Y. Crowell, 1946.

Kitchen, Martin. *The Silent Dictatorship: The Politics of the German High Command under Hindenburg and Ludendorff, 1916–1918.* New York: Holmes & Meier, 1976.

See also GERMANY, HOME FRONT; MICHAELIS, GEORG

Rennenkampf, Pavel Karlovich (1854–1918)

Russian general, born on 29 April 1854 to a Russian noble family of Austrian extraction. Rennenkampf spent some forty years in the Russian army. He graduated from the Helsingfors Infantry Cadet School in 1873. He was also a graduate of the General Staff Academy in 1882. During the Manchurian campaign of 1905 Rennenkampf commanded a cavalry division, where he gained a reputation as a capable military leader dedicated to the doctrine of the attack. In the political turmoil that followed Russia's defeat in the Russo-Japanese War he was ordered to quell revolutionary activity, which he did ruthlessly. Appointed general of cavalry in 1910, in 1913 Rennenkampf was given charge of the Vilna Military District.

In the summer of 1914, responding to calls for help from France, the Russian General Staff patched together an offensive into East Prussia. Under the overall command of General Yakov Zhilinsky, a large pincer movement was planned. The northern First Army was assigned to Rennenkampf and was to drive to the fortified city of Konigsberg and then veer south to meet Second Army under General Aleksandr Samsonov, who was moving up from the south. After meeting at Allenstein, the combined force was to move the sixty miles to Berlin. Samsonov and Rennenkampf were said to be personal enemies ever since the Manchurian campaign; the reasons behind the animosity are unclear.

On 17 August the lead units of Rennenkampf's First Army crossed the Prussian frontier on a thirty-five mile front. They were immediately engaged by the Germans, who were in the process of conducting an orderly retreat. Rennenkampf's force, however, was badly disorganized and suffered from inadequate supplies. Consequently, on 19 August Rennenkampf halted his advance in order to regroup and to wait for Samsonov's army, which was to begin its advance on the 20th. From that point, Rennenkampf's leadership ability seemed to disappear. There was a total disregard for security, Rennenkampf was never able to establish contact with Samsonov's army to the south, and radio messages went out uncoded and were easily intercepted by the Germans.

Rennenkampf interpreted the repulse of an attack by German General Friedrich von Prittwitz und Graffon's Eighth Army at Gumbinnen (19–20 August) as the end of German strength in East Prussia. Instead of exploiting this brief victory with a counterattack against thin German lines, Rennenkampf did nothing. On the German side several Russian weaknesses were noted, such as the critical shortage of artillery shells. Colonel Max Hoffmann, Prittwitz's staff officer, was, meanwhile, formulating a plan for dealing with the Russians.

When Generals Paul von Hindenburg and Erich Ludendorff arrived to take command in Prussia, they took Hoffmann's plan and put it into execution. After crushing Samsonov's force in the Battle of Tannenberg (26–29 August) when Rennenkampf failed to answer Samsonov's appeals for help, the combined German forces turned northeast against Rennenkampf's army, which was obliged to fall back. On 6–15 September, in the Battle of the Masurian Lakes, the Germans took a heavy toll of Rennenkampf's forces (125,000 casualties) while suffering only 40,000 casualties themselves. Rennenkampf was able, however, to avoid a double envelopment. On 11 November the Germans launched an attack to the southeast from Thorn. This cut between Rennenkampf's First Army facing East Prussia and Second Army advancing west toward Silesia. In the subsequent Battle of Lódź, Rennenkampf was again slow to act.

In a later inquiry Rennenkampf, who had connections at court, was exonerated, but with no command positions in the offing he retired. He was at Taganrog in south Russia in early 1918 when the Bolsheviks offered him command of an army against the Germans. He refused and was executed by a Bolshevik firing squad in early March of 1918.

John W. Bohon

References

Gurko, General Basil. *War and Revolution in Russia, 1914–1917*. New York: Macmillan, 1919.

Showalter, Dennis E. *Tannenberg, Clash of Empires*. Garden City, N.Y.: Anchor, 1991.

See also EAST PRUSSIA CAMPAIGN; SAMSONOV, ALEKSANDR

Reuter, Ludwig von (1869–1943)

German vice admiral and commander of naval forces interned at Scapa Flow, 1918–19. He was born on 9 February 1869 in Guben. Reuter's actions at Scapa Flow have overshadowed his record as a leader of cruisers during the war. Commanding the battle cruiser *Derfflinger*, Reuter shelled Scarborough in 1914 and fought at Dogger Bank in 1915. At Jutland he led a group of light cruisers before being reassigned to operations against the Baltic islands of Dago and Oesel. He returned to North Sea waters in time for the second battle of Heligoland in 1917. When Hipper took over the High Seas Fleet, Reuter succeeded him as leader of Germany's Scouting Forces.

Following the Armistice, Reuter was chosen to deliver the High Seas Fleet into internment at Scapa Flow in Scotland. After quelling residual mutinies among his reduced crews, Reuter prepared clandestine orders to scuttle his ships, to prevent them from falling into Allied hands. A misunderstanding over the deadline of an ultimatum induced Reuter, on 21 June 1919, to execute his scheme. Some sixty-six major warships went down, with the loss of nine German lives. Seen as heroes for having restored the honor of the German navy, Reuter and his men received a triumphant welcome upon their return home in 1920. Reuter died on 18 December 1943 in Potsdam.

Eric C. Rust

References

Herwig, Holger. *"Luxury" Fleet*. London: Allen and Unwin, 1980.

Marineministerium (Berlin). *Der Krieg zur See, 1914–1918*. 24 vols. Berlin, Frankfurt: E.S. Mittler und Sohn, 1922–66.

Reuter, Ludwig von. *Scapa Flow: Das Grab der deutschen Flotte*. Leipzig: K.F. Koehler, 1921.

See also DOGGER BANK, NAVAL BATTLE OF; GERMAN CRUISER RAIDS, 1914; GERMANY, NAVY; SCAPA FLOW, SCUTTLING OF GERMAN FLEET

Ribot, Alexandre (1842–1923)

French premier and foreign minister, born at St. Omer on 6 February 1842. Ribot was a moderate French republican politician. His most significant achievement before 1914 was as foreign minister, 1890–93, during which time he negotiated the 1892 Franco-Russian Military Convention. That alliance, directed against Germany, was the bedrock of France's prewar foreign policy.

From 1914 to 1917, Ribot served as minister of finance in the René Viviani and Aristide Briand cabinets. He worked to meet burgeoning government expenses by borrowing from Great Britain and the United States. He opposed the introduction of new taxes such as an income tax or an excess war profits tax.

In March of 1917 Ribot became premier and foreign minister, following the resignation of the Briand government. He immediately faced a crisis. French army Commander in Chief Robert Nivelle wanted a French-British offensive in April in order to relieve pressure on Russia. Ribot opposed Nivelle's plan, especially when America seemed ready to enter the war. When Nivelle threatened to resign, Ribot capitulated. The April Nivelle Offensive resulted in mass slaughter and widespread mutinies within the French army.

The Ribot government was also attacked by both the political Left and Right, as France's wartime political truce—the *union sacrée*—began to crumble under the strain of a long, stalemated war. Ribot angered the Left on several fronts. First, he denied passports to French Socialists who wanted to attend an international socialist peace conference in Stockholm. Second, he rejected all overtures, such as those from the Prince Sixte de Bourbon-Parma and Baron Lancken, for a separate peace with Germany or Austria. Ribot wanted Alsace-Lorraine returned to France before negotiations began, but Germany had no intention of yielding that territory. Third, Ribot rejected all Leftist demands for a peace with no annexations; he not only reserved the right of France to annex the Rhineland, but at St. Jean de Maurienne he acknowledged Italy's claims to territorial rights in Anatolia.

The Right also attacked the Ribot government. The focus of the attack was Louis Malvy, minister of the interior. Malvy subsidized the Parisian pacifist newspaper, *Le Bonnet Rouge*, and its director, Almereyda; the newspaper also received funds from Germany. The Ribot government was portrayed as defeatist and lax on matters of internal security.

Ribot resigned as prime minister in September of 1917. He continued to serve as foreign minister for a few more weeks in the succeeding government of Paul Painlevé. Ribot died in Paris on 13 January 1923.

Jan Karl Tanenbaum

References

King, Jere Clemens. *General and Politicians: Conflict between France's High Command, Parliament and Government, 1914–1918*. Berkeley: University of California Press, 1951.

Schmidt, Martin E. *Alexandre Ribot: Odyssey of a Liberal in the Third Republic*. The Hague: Martinus Nÿhoff, 1974.

Stevenson, D. *French War Aims against Germany, 1914–1919*. Oxford: Clarendon, 1982.

See also ALLIANCES, PREWAR; FRANCE, HOME FRONT; NIVELLE OFFENSIVE; PAINLEVÉ, PAUL

Richthofen, Manfred Albrecht von (1892–1918)

German war ace. With eighty victories, Richthofen was the highest-scoring fighter pilot of World War I. Born in Breslau, Germany, on 2 May 1892, Richthofen had been sent to cadet school by his father, who intended for him to become an army officer. Although he was an indifferent student, he excelled at gymnastics and horsemanship. When war began Richthofen was a cavalry lieutenant in the First Uhlans, stationed near the Russian border. After his regiment was posted to infantry duties in the trenches, Richthofen transferred to the air service. He originally flew as an observer but soon trained as a pilot, receiving his license on Christmas Day in 1915.

In September of 1916 the famous ace Oswald Boelcke invited Richthofen to join his new fighter squadron, *Jagdstaffel* 2. Under Boelcke's tutelage, Richthofen became a proficient fighter pilot, scoring his first victory two weeks later. In January of 1917 Richthofen took command of his own squadron, *Jagdstaffel* 11. Two days later, he was awarded the *Pour le Mérite*, the "Blue Max," in recognition of sixteen victories. On 1 July he became commander of *Jagdgeschwader* 1, the first large fighter formation (forty aircraft), but he received a severe head wound six days later, alarming the high command, which had come to realize his worth as a propaganda tool. Sent on a long convalescent leave, Richthofen visited striking munitions workers and wrote his memoirs. He worked to procure better aircraft for his men and initiated an aircraft design competition among manufacturers. In the spring of 1918 he completed a treatise on aerial combat, incorporating Boelcke's teachings with his own squadron commander experience. In his red Fokker triplane, the "Red Baron" was easily the most famous ace of the war and one of its most enduring combatants. Richthofen was killed on 21 April 1918 while pursuing an opponent at low altitude over the enemy lines near Vaux-sur-Somme. Either Canadian pilot Roy Brown, who was credited with the victory, or Australian ground gunners may have fired the fatal shot. Richthofen was buried with full military honors in Bertangles, France, but his body now lies in Wiesbaden, Germany.

Suzanne Hayes Fisher

References

Gibbons, Floyd. *The Red Knight of Germany.* Garden City, N.Y.: Doubleday, Page, 1927.

Nowarra, Heinz J., and Kimbrough S. Brown. *Von Richthofen and the Flying Circus.* 3rd ed. Letchworth, Herts, Eng.: Harleyford, 1964.

Richthofen, Manfred Albrecht von. *The Red Baron.* Translated by Peter Kilduff. Garden City, N.Y.: Doubleday, 1969.

See also ACES; AIR WARFARE: FIGHTER TACTICS; AIRCRAFT, FIGHTERS; BOELCKE, OSWALD

Rifles

European armies conducted extensive testing and development of rifles in the decades before the war. In 1914 most European nations used a five-shot bolt-action rifle that could be loaded quickly using a charger or stripper clip. Most nations issued a rifle to their infantrymen and a similar but shorter carbine to engineers, artillerymen and other specialized troops. Foot soldiers normally carried bayonets, whereas cavalry carbines often lacked stacking lugs and bayonets.

Smokeless powder and sharply pointed bullets made infantry rifles accurate at long ranges; most had sights that could be adjusted to ranges beyond 2,000 meters. Soldiers could seldom see or hit individuals more than 300 to 400 meters away, however. Trench warfare usually involved ranges of less than 100 meters.

Sniping weapons were in development at the beginning of the war. In most cases, sniper rifles were standard infantry rifles modified to accept a telescopic sight. Nations refined sniper equipment and increased the use of trained snipers as their value became apparent. Snipers were often able to hit enemy soldiers more than 600 meters away.

Obsolete and captured weapons were often issued to support troops, to reservists, and to units away from the front. Marines and naval infantry generally used standard infantry rifles, sometimes with minor modifications and different model designations. Semiautomatic rifles were developed by some nations, but none were widely used and they had little influence on operations. Accurate rifles, together with machine guns, gave defenders an advantage that led to bloody stalemate and a war of attrition.

In 1886, France adopted the world's first bolt-action rifle to fire a smokeless cartridge. The weapon, the 8mm M1886 Lebel, prompted other European powers to develop a new generation of rifles that would use smokeless powder and smaller caliber bullets. The Lebel rifle incorporated an inefficient tubular magazine beneath the barrel. The M1890 Berthier carbine used a more efficient Mannlicher-style box magazine holding three rounds. A new infantry rifle, the Model 1907/15, was essentially a lengthened version of the Berthier. The Model 1916 Rifle increased the magazine capacity to five rounds. All these weapons were issued in quantity to the French army. France also issued five-shot semiautomatic "St. Etienne" rifles in 1917 and 1918.

The Belgian army adopted the 7.65mm Model 1889 Mauser rifle and carbine. This landmark weapon incorporated a bolt action, which Mauser retained in all subsequent models with modifications. Cartridges were issued attached to five-round stripper clips. To load the weapon, the soldier inserted the clip into a guide above the magazine, then pressed the cartridges down with his thumb. He then discarded the empty clip and closed the bolt.

After the invasion of Belgium, Belgian units in France continued to use the M1889 weapons, some made by Hopkins and Allen in the United States. The M1916 rifle was a slightly modified version of the M1889.

The Austro-Hungarian Empire equipped its troops chiefly with the 8mm Model 1895 rifle, the M1895 short rifle ("Stutzen"), and the M1895 carbine. These Mannlicher weapons featured a bolt handle that was pulled straight to the rear. Ammunition was fixed in a five-round clip, or charger, that was inserted into the box magazine. When the last round was chambered, the charger dropped out. Austrian snipers used the M1895 rifle with a four-power German scope. An earlier rifle, the Model 1888–90, was issued in quantity. The Bulgarian army also utilized the Mannlicher Model 1895 series of weapons.

Romanian forces used the Model 1893 Romanian Mannlicher rifle and carbine. These weapons resembled the Austrian Mannlichers but used a standard turning bolt. Greece armed its soldiers with the Model 1903 Mannlicher-Schoenauer rifle and 1903/14 carbine, both in 6.5mm. These weapons had a turning bolt designed by Mannlicher but a rotary magazine that could be loaded using stripper clips. Obsolete French 1878 Gras 11mm rifles also continued in Greek service.

The basic Italian service rifle was the M1891 6.5mm Mannlicher Carcano. Its bolt action was a modified Mauser design with a Mannlicher-style magazine. Two versions of the M1891 Mannlicher Carcano carbine were issued.

The British army before the war placed great emphasis on marksmanship training. That training would enable the infantry of the BEF to slow German advances in 1914, especially in the Battle of Mons, despite the low number of machine guns to be found at the front. The primary British rifle of the war was the .303 caliber short magazine Lee Enfield No. 1, Mark III, which was adopted in January of 1907. That rifle had the fastest-working turning-bolt action among the rifles of the major powers and featured a ten-round detachable magazine. It had no carbine counterpart. In January of 1916 Britain adopted the SMLE No. 1 Mk III*, a rifle that lacked the magazine cutoff found on the previous model. More than 3.6 million Mk III and Mk III* rifles were produced during the war.

American manufacturers produced .303 caliber Pattern 14 rifles for Britain. They were issued in limited numbers and, when fitted with fine adjustment sights, used by snipers. The P-14 (T) featured a Pattern 1918 telescope, and the P-14 (T)A was equipped with an Aldis telescope.

Commonwealth units carried standard British rifles. Canada entered the war with straight-pull Ross rifles, but switched to Lee-Enfields in 1916 when it was determined that the Ross's action fared poorly in the mud of the trenches. The Ross was retained as a sniper rifle afterward.

The official Portuguese army rifle of 1914–18 was the Mauser Vergueiro M1904 in 6.5mm. Portuguese units serving in the British sector in France carried British arms.

German soldiers carried the 7.9mm Gewehr 98 and Karabiner 98 developed by Mauser. Germany adopted sharply pointed ("s," or *spitzer*) bullets in 1903 and modified existing weapons to fire the new ammunition. The experimental G-98/17 had a sliding bolt cover and twenty-round magazine. Other innovations included incendiary bullets and armor-piercing bullets intended to penetrate Allied tanks. Germany produced fewer than two thousand self-loading Mauser carbines in 1916 and 1917, for use by air crews; a few hundred semiautomatic Mondragon rifles were purchased from Switzerland for the same purpose.

The German army had so few sniper scopes in 1914 that they were obliged to ask civilian hunters to donate theirs. Delivery of military scopes began in the spring of 1915. By August of 1916 Bavarian infantry units had three snipers per company.

The Turkish army adopted the Mauser bolt-action rifle models of 1890, 1893, 1903, and 1905, all in 7.65mm. The 1903 and 1905 rifles were essentially copies of the German G-98. The German government provided Turkey with large quantities of 7.9mm rifles and carbines, including hundreds of thousands of G-88 "Commission" rifles. Large numbers of M1874 Peabody rifles also remained in service.

Russian soldiers carried the 7.62mm Model 1891 Mosin-Nagant rifle. Its distinctive quadrangular bayonet was left fixed at all times. Mounted troops carried the M1891 dragoon rifle and M1910 carbine, when available. Russian production of weapons seldom met requirements. Over 1.5 million M1891 rifles were made in the United States by Westinghouse and Remington for export to Russia from 1915 to 1917. Other examples of imported weapons include the following: 600,000 Type 38 Arisakas from Japan; 294,000 M1895 Winchesters in 7.62 mm; 600,000 M1878 Gras rifles from France; and 400,000 M1871 Vetterlis from Italy. Russia developed the Fedorov Avtomat assault rifle, capable of both automatic and semiautomatic fire. Chambered for the 6.5mm Japanese cartridge and equipped with a twenty-five-round magazine, it never entered general production.

Montenegrin soldiers carried Russian rifles, including the M1891 Mosin-Nagant and the obsolete 10.66mm Berdan.

Serbian soldiers entered the war with M1893 Mauser rifles, as well as single-shot M1881 Mauser-Milanovics. After the evacuation to Corfu, the Serbs were re-armed with French weapons. Japan developed a modified Mauser action for its 6.5mm Type 38 rifle. The designation refers to the thirty-eighth year of the emperor's reign (1905). Japanese forces also used Type 38 and 44 (1911) carbines.

China imported German rifles and carbines in the late nineteenth and early twentieth centuries and manufactured some copies of these weapons.

Clayton Perkins

References

Goetz, Hans Dieter. *German Military Rifles and Machine Pistols, 1871–1945*. West Chester, Pa.: Schiffer, 1990.

Haythornthwaite, Philip J. *The World War One Source Book*. London: Arms and Armour, 1992.

Smith, W.H.B., and Joseph E. *The Book of Rifles*. 3rd ed. Harrisburg, Pa.: Stackpole, 1963.

Tantum, William H., IV. *Sniper Rifles of Two World Wars*. Alexandria Bay, N.Y.: Museum Restoration Service, 1967.

Weller, Jac. *Weapons and Tactics*. London: Nicholas Vane, 1966.

See also PISTOLS; UNIFORMS

Riga, Battle of (1–3 September 1917)

Riga was one of the most significant battles of World War I on all three levels of warfare. Strategically, it was the battle that took Russia out of the war, allowing Germany to shift significant resources to the Western Front in preparation for Ludendorff's 1918 offensives. Operationally, it was the first significant large-scale penetration of the war, on either front. On a tactical level, the Riga attack saw the first large-scale applications of some of the radical new combat methods that characterized fighting on the Western Front in 1918. Also, as military historian J.F.C. Fuller noted, Riga was the "first skillful use of gas to effect a penetration."

Although the Eastern Front never developed into the static opposing network of trenches that characterized the Western Front, the flat terrain and wide-open spaces in the East, combined with the increased firepower yet limited mobility of World War I armies, produced the Eastern Front's own peculiar version of gridlock. During the first three years of the war, neither side could maneuver fast enough nor mass sufficient power to achieve decisive results. That pattern broke at Riga.

The Baltic port of Riga was the extreme right anchor of the Russian line, which in that area ran roughly east and west along the Dvina River. The entire Riga sector was defended by 10.5 divisions of the Russian Twelfth Army under General Vladislav N. Klembovski. Russian defenses on the north side of the river were organized into two parallel positions. The first consisted of three, and in some places four, successive trench lines on the dunes along the river. The second, consisting of two sets of trench lines, was some three kilometers back from the river. Several islands in the river were also heavily fortified.

Facing the Russians opposite Riga and along the south bank of the river the German Eighth Army of General Oskar von Hutier had 7.5 divisions spread over the 130-kilometer front from the coast to Jacobstadt. The Russians expected the Germans to attack Riga directly, but Hutier planned an attack across the Dvina near Uxkull, about thirty kilometers east of the city. Once across the river the Germans could maneuver around to the rear of Riga and cut off the Russian garrison. Hutier's attack plan called for ten divisions to make the river crossing. The German High Command reinforced the Eighth Army with an additional eight infantry and two cavalry divisions to give Hutier sufficient strength to hold the rest of his line and to conduct holding attacks against the city.

At 09:10 on 1 September 1917, three divisions of LI Corps spearheaded the attack on a nine-kilometer front. The 19th Reserve Division on the right and the 2nd Guards Infantry Division on the left crossed the 350-meter-wide Dvina with assault boats. The 14th Bavarian Infantry Division in the center first had to take heavily fortified Borkum Island. Once on the north bank the three divisions quickly overran the first Russian defensive position and then moved against the second. While it was being stormed, German pioneers emplaced pontoon bridges across the river in each of the three division attack sectors. Once these were up, an additional division crossed behind each of the first-echelon divisions and prepared to exploit the breakout from the second defensive positions.

After three hours of the assault, the Russian Twelfth Army began to break. By nightfall on 1 September the Germans had six divisions across the river in a bridgehead thirteen kilometers wide. By the afternoon of 3 September German troops entered Riga, at a cost of only 4,200 casualties to 25,000 for the Russians. Three weeks later, the Eighth Army finished off Russian forces in the area with a 21–22 September attack across the Dvina at Jackobstadt.

At the time, the Riga victory was regarded as a great feat of arms. Recently, however, some historians and analysts have suggested that Riga was not so much taken by a German army using new tactics as it was given away by an already dispirited and broken Russian army. There is evidence to suggest that as early as 20 August the Russians strongly suspected an attack and began pulling out of their positions.

When the Germans did attack, success apparently came so quickly that the Germans were unprepared to exploit it and many Russian troops managed to escape. The Riga attack had broader significance, however. With the fall of Riga and victory at Caporetto two months later, employing similar tactics, the Western Allies took serious notice.

It was these tactics that have excited the most interest. Hutier prepared for the offensive by assembling his ten attack divisions 120 kilometers behind his front lines. There they trained and rehearsed for almost two weeks. The divisions did not move up into their jump-off positions until the night of 31 August. During the assault the German infantry abandoned traditional linear tactics and advanced in a leap-frog fashion, similar to the fire-and-movement technique still employed by most conventional armies. The attackers infiltrated in small groups, probed for weak spots, and bypassed enemy strongpoints, leaving these for heavier follow-on forces to eliminate. Reserves were committed to reinforce success rather than being thrown in where the attack had stalled. Such tactics were radical by World War I standards. When the Allies encountered them on a large scale on the Western Front in 1918, they erroneously dubbed them "Hutier Tactics."

German artillery, under the brilliant Colonel Georg Bruchmüller, also operated by what appeared to be a completely different set of rules. In addition to the ten extra divisions, the German High Command gave Eighth Army massive artillery reinforcements by stripping the Eastern Front of all but the minimum number of guns necessary to hold the line in the other sectors. Some guns were even transferred from the Western Front. With painstaking secrecy the Germans moved 615 guns and 544 trench mortars into the narrow penetration zone prior to the attack, achieving a density of sixty-eight guns and sixty trench mortars per kilometer. They also stockpiled 650,000 rounds of ammunition at the firing positions.

Once in position most of the newly arrived batteries did not give themselves away by firing registrations before the start of the attack. Reinforcing batteries actually fired abbreviated registrations on predesignated registration points during the first two hours of the preparation itself and then quickly shifted fire onto their scheduled targets. While that was not the most accurate way of firing, it served the purpose. German artillery achieved total surprise against the Russians. Stunned Allied analysts wrongly concluded that the Germans had perfected an accurate technique for delivering surprise fire without registration.

One reason that accuracy was not quite so important in this preparation was the high number of chemical rounds fired. Rather than the usual random gas dump along the entire Russian line, Bruchmüller used specific types of chemical munitions on selected targets to achieve specific results. Throughout the entire length of the fire German guns and mortars fired an average of five hundred gas rounds per minute on the key targets in the penetration zone.

Instead of a standard World War I artillery preparation lasting for days or even weeks, Bruchmüller's Riga preparation lasted just five hours and ten minutes. Although the preparation fire was not long, it was incredibly violent. At 04:00 all 615 German guns opened up against the Russian artillery positions firing 75 percent gas and 25 percent high explosive (HE). After two hours of this reinforced coun-terbattery (CB) fire, German firing units with a specific CB mission continued to gas the Russian artillery, while the rest of the German artillery shifted to Russian infantry targets and started firing 20 percent gas to 80 percent HE.

At 09:10, when the German infantry surged forward across the river, artillery forward observers accompanying the assault crossed with the first wave, after first tying off their phone lines to prepositioned stakes at the ferry points. The assault was preceded by a carefully orchestrated creeping barrage. After the first wave of German infantry was firmly established on the far shore, a number of light German guns crossed the river on rafts. The Germans had rehearsed this technique on lakes in Eighth Army's rear.

The effects of the German fire were devastating. During the slightly more than five hours of the preparation alone, German gunners hit Twelfth Army with over 560,000 rounds—an average of more than 480 from each gun. About 27 percent of the total was gas, the highest proportion fired in the war to that time. The weight of HE shells fired totaled approximately 10,500 tons, equivalent to the payload of over 500 B-52 bombers.

The Riga artillery preparation was not really anything new. Bruchmüller had been experimenting with short, intensive fires and other fire-support techniques for the previous two years on the Eastern Front. Riga, however, was the first time the Allies noticed. In a few short months they too would find themselves on the receiving end of Bruchmüller's firestorms.

David T. Zabecki

References

Fuller, John Frederick Charles. *The Conduct of War: 1789–1961*. London: Eyre & Spottiswoode, 1961.

Hoffmann, Max. *Der Krieg der Versaumten Gelegenheiten*. Munich: Verlag fur Kulturpolitik, 1923.

Hogg, Ian V. *Gas*. New York: Ballantine, 1975.

Pitt, Barrie. *1918: The Last Act*. New York: W.W. Norton, 1963.

Zabecki, David T. *Steel Wind: Georg Bruchmueller and the Birth of Modern Artillery*. Westport, Conn.: Praeger, 1994.

Robertson, Sir William "Wully" (1860–1933)

British field marshal and chief of the Imperial General Staff (1915–18), born in Welbourn, Lincolnshire, on 29 January 1860. Robertson enlisted as a private in the 16th Lancers Division in 1877 and was commissioned nine years later, the first British officer to rise from the ranks and pass through the staff college. In 1895 Robertson received the DSO while serving in India. He also served in South Africa on the intelligence staff, where he was promoted to lieutenant colonel. He was made a colonel in 1903 during an assignment with the war office (1901–7). In 1910 then–Major General Robertson became the commandant of the staff college and in 1913 director of military training.

At the onset of World War I, Robertson was quartermaster general of the British Expeditionary Force (BEF). In January of 1915 he was promoted to chief of the general staff and in December he replaced Kitchener as chief of the Imperial General Staff (CIGS).

Robertson was a Social Darwinist who believed that the military was a means of safeguarding social evolution. He also felt, as stated in a memo of 6 November 1915, that, with enough firepower, any enemy defensive system could be overcome. His belief, in exhausting the enemy by forcing the use of reserves followed by a decisive attack to ensure victory, was the policy behind the joint Somme Offensive of 1916.

Robertson was fiercely devoted to the Western Front. Throughout the war, he emphasized the importance of concentrating Allied forces there. He did not trust the dispersion of forces and wanted to give the other fronts only what was absolutely necessary to ensure success. In 1917 he tried to persuade the cabinet that such dispersion endangered the possibility for success in the West.

Robertson also understood the balance of strategy and politics. Realizing that Britain had no vital interest in the Balkans, he opposed campaigns in the region and sought an immediate withdrawal of forces there. In August of 1916 he submitted a paper stating that the current policy turned the Mediterranean into a French-Italian lake and left the Balkans under Slav domination. He felt that no concessions should be made to Balkan nationalism, and he wanted Austro-Hungarian integrity maintained. He felt that Britain should not provide assistance unless she received a tangible reward, beyond the denial of German access to the Aegean. He attended a conference in Rome in January of 1917 to support these views.

Robertson had many rivals, however. On 26 February 1917, he and his ally Field Marshal Sir Douglas Haig met with other European commanders to discuss the situation on the Western Front. The conference resulted in a proposal that reduced the powers of Robertson and Haig and rewarded their rivals, Sir Henry Wilson and General Nivelle. The proposal was amended to be less severe, but disagreement continued. By February of 1918 Robertson was transferred to the East Command in England, and in May he succeeded French as commander in chief of Great Britain.

After the war Robertson received a baronetcy, and he was made a field marshal in 1920. He died in London on 12 February 1933.

Meredith Kulp

References

Bonham-Carter, Victor. *Soldier True: The Life and Times of Field Marshal Sir William Robertson*. London: F. Muller, 1963.

Dictionary of National Biography: 1931–1940. Oxford: Oxford University Press, 1985.

Robertson, William R. *Soldiers and Statesmen, 1914–1918*. 2 vols. London: Cassell, 1926.

See also GREAT BRITAIN, ARMY; SOMME, BATTLE OF

Romania

The Romanian government, under premier Ion Bratianu, declared war on the Dual Monarchy on 27 August 1916. That was despite the fact that Romania had been allied to Germany and Austria-Hungary by the Triple Alliance of 1883 and that its ruling dynasty (Hohenzollern-Sigmaringen) was a branch of the German imperial family. The Germans, shocked by the Romanian action, promptly retaliated on 28 August, followed a few days later by both Turkey and Bulgaria.

Romania's declaration of war was the culmination of a two-year competition between the Entente and the Central Powers for Romania's support. In this competition, Germany's royal family, economic factors, and treaty connections gave it an initial advantage. An avowed and strict neutral at war's start, Romania's geostrategic position gave it a critical importance in the war far beyond the country's actual military or economic capacity. Sitting astride the Danube River, the most important transportation artery in the Balkans, Romania could deny or facilitate the transport of critical materials between Germany and its Balkan allies, Bulgaria and the Ottoman Empire. It also sat opposite the Central Powers' only remaining uncommitted frontiers. The Central Powers, therefore, were content with Romanian neutrality, which it maintained despite its prewar treaty of alliance with Austria-Hungary and Germany. Austria-Hungary was particularly keen for Romania to remain neutral. Its leadership saw Romania's entry into the war as a potentially fatal blow to its survival.

The Allies saw Romania in similar terms, and they exploited Romania's irredentist claims against Austro-Hungarian territory to bring it into the Allied fold. The Allied effort began to pay off by early 1916, as German successes on the battlefield grew fewer and farther between and Austria-Hungary's disasters expanded in number and scope. King Ferdinand I's advisors saw that year's summer campaign as a key opportunity that Romania could not ignore. The Russian Brusilov Offensive was the critical event influencing their decision. Romania would never gain Transylvania if it fell to Russian arms. Hence, Austria-Hungary's difficulties and seemingly imminent collapse overcame Romania's natural distrust of Russia, bringing it over to the Allied side. In the end the Allies signed a secret treaty with Romania, promising the Banat of Temesvar, Transylvania, and Bukovina. Premier Jan Bratianu and Ferdinand I found Allied promises of territory too tempting to resist. In addition, the Allies promised simultaneous assistance from Russian forces in Bukovina and Allied forces at Salonika.

Romania was a predominantly agrarian country. Despite extensive oil and mineral resources, it was nonetheless poor and underdeveloped. Roads and railroads were sparse. Its army numbered some half a million men but was poorly equipped. It lacked artillery, and what it did have was obsolescent. Ammunition and transport were limited. Moreover, Romania's officer corps was poorly trained and indolent, noted more for its regimental parties and for wearing makeup while in full dress than for any martial qualities. Its performance in the Balkan Wars had been less than auspicious, and little had been done to improve things since. The country's leadership was aware of these shortcomings. In fact, the timing of the declaration of war was calculated to ensure that the fighting would be over before the army could be decisively engaged. Austria-Hungary's troop dispositions did much to engender that expectation.

Although Romania's declaration of war was not wholly unexpected, Austria-Hungary had done nothing to defend its frontier. Placing its faith in conciliatory actions, including the withdrawal of military garrisons and fortifications, Austria-Hungary had based its defense of Transylvania on the trust of a nominal ally. As a result, the Romanians found the going easy the first month, with most of their difficulties brought on by the incompetence of their own logistics organization. They left defense of their southern frontier to the Russians in the false hope that Bulgaria would not attack them.

The Central Powers reacted immediately. General Erich von Falkenhayn, removed as German chief of staff as a result of the Romanian declaration of war, counterattacked less than six weeks after the Romanian invasion began. By October the Romanians had been driven back to their frontier, suffering heavy losses in the process. Meanwhile, General August von Mackensen led a mixed German, Bulgarian, and Turkish force against the Romanian

Dobrudja, which controlled the mouth of the Danube River. Russian support was limited to a handful of units consisting of former Austro-Hungarian prisoners of war. Constanza, Romania's primary Black Sea port, fell on 23 October 1916. Halting there to regroup, Mackensen dispatched German units to reinforce Falkenhayn in Transylvania. Romania, which had entered the war with such high hopes just eight weeks earlier, was on the verge of decisive defeat.

Only rapid reinforcement from its allies could save the little country. Unfortunately, Russia was the only country in a geographic position to assist, and it had little matériel of its own to provide. It was even less inclined to do so. The Russians had lost over a million men in the Brusilov Offensive and believed that the Romanians had deliberately waited until the Russian advance was spent before entering the war. More significantly, many Russian leaders felt that Austria-Hungary would have been driven out of the war if Romania had joined the war in time to coordinate with the Brusilov Offensive. This feeling was exacerbated by Romania's poor performance once its armies encountered significant resistance. The Romanian army was abysmally led, and its communications systems were obsolete and inadequate, even by Russian standards. The Russian general staff therefore saw the Romanians as opportunists who aggravated rather than relieved Russia's already serious strategic problems. With Russia's reserves stretched to the breaking point and its domestic situation bordering on anarchy, the Russian general staff suddenly found itself tasked to provide 250,000 troops with which to defend Romania's southern frontier. Fewer than 50,000 were available. Meanwhile, Romania's military disasters continued.

Facing aggressive Romanian counterattacks in Transylvania, Falkenhayn struck at the flanks of the most forward Romanian units. By 11 November he had broken through the main Transylvanian passes ahead of the winter snows and entered the Wallachian Plain of Central Romania. Mackensen then forced his way across the Danube in an effort to trap the Romanians between the pincers of the two German armies. He was not entirely successful, although the capital, Bucharest, did fall on 6 December. Still, the Romanians had held up the German advance long enough for the

Russians to reinforce their southern border and for the British embassy to organize the sabotage of the Romanian oil wells. It would be months before the wells were flowing again. Overall, the Romanian war effort was a total disaster.

The Romanian army had been reduced to fewer than 70,000 men in little over three months. The country was destroyed and occupied by hostile powers. The Romanians did receive French assistance through Russia over the following year, but Russia's collapse in 1917 left Romania standing alone in the face of a bitter German enemy. Romania had little choice but to sign the disadvantageous Treaty of Bucharest in April of 1918, in which she surrendered her rights to Transylvania and granted a ninety-year lease of the country's oil and mineral rights to Germany.

Romanians deeply resented the Treaty of Bucharest, and the country returned to the war against the Central Powers on 10 November 1918, seizing Transylvania from the dismembered Austro-Hungarian Empire. By then the province and Romania were so damaged by the war that the country gained little but an additional burden for rebuilding. Except for a brief period during World War II, however, Romania has retained Transylvania ever since.

Romania's entry into World War I had no significant effect on the war's outcome. It gained little advantage for the Allies who had lobbied so aggressively for Romania's participation. In fact, it added to Russia's strategic burden by lengthening the front by 250 miles without providing any advantage or reinforcement in compensation. Of course, the same could be said for the Central Powers, who had even fewer resources overall. Romania's war effort did pay off in the postwar period, however, giving Romania access to Western aid and military assistance. Unfortunately, the benefits gained from that access were soon lost in the depredations of the next war.

Carl O. Schuster

References

Czernin, Ottokar. *Im Weltkrieg*. Berlin: Ullstein and Company, 1919.

Lupu, Nicholas. *Rumania and the War*. Boston: Gorham, 1919.

Michel, Bernard. *La Chute de L'Empire Austro-Hongrois, 1916–1918*. Paris: Robert Laffont, 1991.

Stone, Norman. *The Eastern Front 1914–1917*. London: Houghton and Stoddard, 1975.

See also BRĂTIANU, ION; BUCHAREST, TREATY OF; FERDINAND I; ROMANIAN CAMPAIGN, 1916

Romanian Campaign, 1916

The Romanian government declared war on Austria-Hungary on 27 August 1916. The Germans, though shocked by Romania's intervention and the resultant additional strain on their tightly stretched military resources, promptly declared their solidarity with Vienna on 28 August. A few days later, both the Ottoman Empire and Bulgaria followed suit.

Romania's entry into the war lengthened the Eastern Front by another three hundred miles and added over 700,000 fresh soldiers to the Allied side. In the Hungarian regions adjacent to Romania, only a handful of brigades, commanded by General Arthur Arz von Straussenberg, were initially available to deal with three Romanian armies that began to invade Transylvania both from the south and the east in the days following the declaration of war. Advancing across the western ridges of the Transylvanian Alps was the Romanian First Army, commanded by General Joan Culcer. Further east, moving into the Kronstadt (Brasov) region, was General Alexandru Averescu's Second Army, while the Fourth (or Northern) Army, under General Constantine Prezan, pushed across the eastern Carpathians.

After seizing the city of Kronstadt early on, the Romanian invaders continued their advance into Transylvania on a broad front and had reached a line about fifty miles inside Hapsburg territory by mid-September. By that time, the Germans had rushed several of their own divisions into southeastern Hungary. These units, among them the elite *Alpenkorps* commanded by Bavarian general Konrad Krafft von Dellmensingen, and a number of Austro-Hungarian formations were placed under command of General Erich von Falkenhayn. The Romanian declaration of war was the final blow in bringing Falkenhayn's dismissal as head of OHL (it came just one day afterward). Falkenhayn's new command was henceforth known as the German Ninth Army.

While German and Austro-Hungarian preparations for a counteroffensive in Transylvania were still in their infancy, a mixed force of Bulgarian, German, Austro-Hungarian, and Ottoman troops, under the command of Field Marshal August von Mackensen, struck at Romania from the southeast. After crossing the border during the night of 1–2 September, Mackensen's composite force rapidly advanced into the Dobrudja, which was defended by the Romanian Third Army under General Mihail Aslan. By 6 September, Bulgarian and German troops had seized the fortified town of Tutrakan. Over 28,000 Romanians were taken prisoner, and four days later the town of Silistria was lost as well. These setbacks led to Aslan's replacement (briefly by General Averescu and then by Gheorghe Valeanu) and also to the appointment of a Russian general, A.M. Zayonchkovsky, as overall commander in the Dobrudja. Against stiffening resistance from newly arrived Russian and Romanian troops, Mackensen's offensive eventually bogged down well south of the strategic Cernavoda-Constanta rail line.

In Transylvania, Falkenhayn's counteroffensive opened on 21 September with a series of local attacks, followed by more massive action five days later. In the Battle of Hermannstadt (Sibiu), parts of Culcer's First Army were smashed. Pushing east, some of Falkenhayn's divisions next pounced on the Romanian Second Army and eventually, on 9 October, retook Kronstadt. Despite the approach of wintry weather, the Ninth Army next pushed southward into the Transylvanian Alps. After weeks of bitter struggle, several German divisions pushed through the western passes and reached Targu Jiu, on the edge of the Wallachian plain, by mid-November. Subsequently, several other routes through the mountains were forced open by German and Austro-Hungarian units, thus allowing Falkenhayn to advance toward Bucharest both from the west and the north.

On 23 November pressure on the Romanians (and their Russian allies) increased further when two German and two Bulgarian divisions as well as one Ottoman division (constituting a newly formed *Donauarmee* under the Prussian general Robert Kosch) began crossing the Danube River near Svishtov. Although the Romanians briefly put this new invading force into a dangerous situation, the combined attacks by Falkenhayn's and Kosch's divisions eventually overcame the resistance facing them. By 6 December the Romanian capital fell into German hands.

With both Falkenhayn's Ninth Army and Kosch's *Donauarmee* placed under Field Marshal von Mackensen's overall command, the Central Powers subsequently pushed the Romanians and their Russian allies out of Wallachia and the northern half of the Dobrudja. By mid-January Mackensen's forces had reached an easily defensible line stretching from the Danube delta to the Siret and Putna rivers and thence to the crest of the Carpathians.

The Romanian Campaign of 1916 was a major triumph for the Central Powers and added significantly to their material resources, particularly in terms of grain and lumber. (The Ploesti oil wells, on the other hand, had been effectively sabotaged before the Romanians were forced to withdraw from that region). From the Allied point of view, the setbacks suffered by the Romanian army were a matter of great disappointment, and the Russians, in particular, were quite unhappy about the additional burdens that had been thrust upon them since September of 1916. It should be noted, though, that Allied criticism of Romania's performance was not really warranted. Despite mediocre leadership and serious deficiencies in their equipment, many Romanian units had fought both bravely and effectively, and about half of the Romanian army survived to fight another day. In fact, after being reequipped and retrained under French auspices, several Romanian divisions were to give a very good account of themselves in subsequent battles along the Moldavian front.

Ulrich Trumpener

References

Glaise-Horstenau, Edmund, ed. *Oesterreich-Ungarns letzter Krieg 1914–1918*. Vol. 5. Vienna: Verlag der Militärwissenschaftlichen Mitteilungen, 1934.

Kabisch, Ernst. *Der Rumänien-Krieg, 1916*. Berlin: Otto Schlegel, 1938.

Király, Béla K., and Nándor F. Dreisziger, eds. *East Central European Society in World War I*. New York: Columbia University Press, 1985.

Kriegsgeschichtliche Forschungsanstalt des Heeres. *Der Weltkrieg 1914 bis 1918: Die militärischen Operationen zu Lände*. Vol. 11. Berlin: E.S. Mittler und Sohn, 1938.

Silberstein, Gerard E. *The Troubled Alliance: German-Austrian Relations 1914 to*

1917. Lexington: University of Kentucky Press, 1970.

See also FALKENHAYN, ERICH VON; FERDINAND I; MACKENSEN, AUGUST VON; ROMANIA

Rommel, Erwin (1891–1944)

German army officer. Erwin Rommel, the legendary German Desert Fox of World War II, first gained fame for his daring exploits in World War I. Born on 15 November 1891 in Heidenheim, Württemberg, Rommel entered the army in 1910 and then attended the Royal Officer Cadet School in Danzig in 1911. In his first action of the war, on 22 August 1914, Rommel's reconnaissance patrol encountered fifteen to twenty French soldiers in fog near Longwy; Rommel ordered an attack and drove back the French. On 24 September, although wounded and with no ammunition, Rommel attacked three French soldiers; for this action he received the Iron Cross Second Class. In January of 1915, after recovering from his wounds, Rommel led his platoon through barbed wire to attack French positions; his unit captured four bunkers and repulsed a French counterattack, all with the loss of twelve men. Rommel received the Iron Cross First Class and promotion to first lieutenant. After recovering from another wound, in April of 1915 Rommel transferred to a mountain unit from his home area (Württembergische Gebirgs) that joined with the *Alpenkorps* and was sent to Romania in December of 1916.

Rommel's aggressiveness soon resurfaced. In January of 1917 he led a patrol that infiltrated enemy positions at night during freezing weather, captured a village, and took four hundred prisoners. In August he was again wounded while leading four companies through the woods to attack and capture Mount Cosna.

Rommel's unit then moved to Italy to help the Austrians against the Isonzo Offensive. His exploits helped turn Caporetto into an Italian disaster and gained him instant fame. During the main attack Rommel infiltrated the Italian flank with two companies and captured an artillery battalion. He left one company behind and continued with the other. When an Italian battalion counterattacked behind him, Rommel struck it in the rear, forced its surrender, and captured a thousand prisoners. Rommel pushed on, seized a supply column, and captured fifty officers and two thousand Bersaglieri troops. With only a few riflemen Rommel entered the main Italian position and called for the garrison to surrender; 1,500 soldiers and forty-three officers complied. Still not finished, he scaled Monte Matajur from the rear and captured the heights. In a little over fifty hours Rommel had captured 150 officers, 9,000 soldiers, and 81 guns. He received his nation's highest award, the *Pour le Mérite,* and was promoted to captain. A few days later, Rommel and six men swam the Piave River at night and captured Congarone.

At the war's end, Rommel was on a leave of absence but soon returned to his old infantry regiment. Having proven his mettle in combat he was retained in the scaled-down postwar army, and in 1921 he became an instructor at the infantry school at Dresden, where he wrote *Infantry Attacks.* In 1938 Rommel served as the director of the war college at Wiener Neustadt and headed Hitler's personal security battalion. During World War II, Rommel gained international fame as the Desert Fox while a field marshal commanding German forces in North Africa. Implicated in the 20 July 1944 plot to kill Hitler, Rommel committed suicide under Gestapo pressure on 14 October 1944.

Laura Matysek Wood

References

Irving, David. *The Trail of the Fox.* New York: E.P. Dutton, 1977.

Lewin, Ronald. *Rommel as Military Commander.* London: Batsford, 1968.

Rommel, Erwin. *Rommel Papers.* Edited by Sir Basil Liddell Hart. London: Collins, 1953.

See also CAPORETTO

Ronarc'h, Pierre (1865–1940)

French vice admiral and naval commander, born on 22 February 1865 at Quimper. Ronarc'h participated in the expedition against the Boxers in 1900 and went on to become a specialist in naval mine warfare. In August of 1914 as commander of a brigade of marines he took part in the defense of Paris during the battle of the Marne. He next helped cover the withdrawal of the Belgian army onto the Yser, where he held the Dixmunde bridgehead and repelled the initial German attempt to capture Dixmunde on 20 October 1914.

As director of antisubmarine warfare from November of 1915 to May of 1916, he redeployed France's small surface warships for that purpose. From May of 1916 Ronarc'h commanded the Naval Zone of the northern armies, in effect being responsible for that French side of the English Channel. With limited resources, he carried out his task of ensuring safe cover and passage of Allied troops between Britain and France with stout resolution. After a short spell as chief of the naval general staff, he retired in 1920. Ronarc'h died in Paris on 31 March 1940.

Andrzej Suchcitz

References

Cammaerts, Emile. *Albert of Belgium.* London: Ivor Nicholson and Watson, 1935.

Herwig, Holger, and Neil Heyman. *Biographical Dictionary of World War I.* Westport, Conn.: Greenwood, 1982.

See also FRANCE, NAVY

Room 40

The cryptographic office of the British Admiralty. Shortly after the introduction of wireless communications in warfare, which were widely used in the Russo-Japanese War, intelligence services of the various powers started analyzing the intercepted encoded radio messages of actual, or potential, enemies.

The Naval Intelligence Division (NID) of the British Admiralty distinguished itself in this kind of secret war. In August of 1914, Sir Alfred Ewing, Director of Naval Education, was appointed as chief of a new cryptological office. The following November his office was transferred to Room 40 of the admiralty's building.

The new cryptological organization started interpreting encoded WT traffic between German ships at sea and broadcasting stations at home, as well as intercepted cables between Berlin and German colonies and embassies. The seizure of three German naval code books (named SKM, HVB, and VB) in the first months of the war helped but did not originate Room 40's work, contrary to what many historians have repeatedly said. In fact, there is substantial evidence that the British Admiralty was able to read German ciphers much earlier. It broke the new German code books—AFB and FFB, which replaced HVB and SKM—in the first months of 1916 and May of 1917.

The successes achieved by this brilliant intelligence operation included the interpretation of German encoded radio messages on the following occasions: the Mediterranean cruise of the *Goeben* and *Breslau* in August of 1914; the naval bombardment of the English coast the following December; Admiral Maximilian von Spee's movements preceding the Battle of the Falkland Islands; oceanic chases after the cruisers *Dresden, Karlsruhe, Konigsberg,* and *Emden;* the sinkings of the *Meteor* and the *Grief;* the Battle of Dogger Bank; the *Lusitania* affair; several raids of the zeppelin airships; the three operations in the North Sea in February and March of 1916; the naval bombardment of Lowestoft in April of 1916; the 1916 Battle of Jutland (Skagerrak) in May of 1916; the cruises of the German High Sea Fleet in August, October, and November of 1916; engagements between light vessels in January, March, April, and October of 1917; several submarine operations; and the Zimmermann telegram episode that pushed the United States into the war.

Nevertheless, the feeble confidence in this kind of information (shown by the very conservative British Admiralty and by British admirals at sea) and the lack of a connecting-office between Room 40 and operational departments (which the Royal Navy rightly provided to the benefit of the Ultra Secret during the Second World War) prevented the Royal Navy from obtaining greater tactical successes at sea in the First World War.

Only toward the end of the war was the German navy sufficiently concerned about the danger of the enemy cryptoanalysis and the better-known radio-detection. What would have happened if the Royal Navy had given to Room 40 more effective intellectual and material support during the war can only be guessed.

Alberto Santoni

References

Beesly, Patrick. *Room 40: British Naval Intelligence 1914–18.* London: Hamish Hamilton, 1982.

Bennett, Geoffrey. *Naval Battles of the First World War.* London: Pan, 1983.

Deacon, Richard. *A History of British Secret Service.* London: Panther Granada, 1984.

Santoni, Alberto. *Il primo Ultra Secret: l'influenza delle decrittazioni britanniche sulle operazioni navali della guerra 1914–1918.* Milan: Mursia, 1985.

See also HALL, WILLIAM REGINALD; *MAGDEBURG*; ZIMMERMANN TELEGRAM

Roques, Pierre Auguste (1856–1920)

French general, born on 23 December 1856 at Marseillon. Roques spent much of his prewar career in the French colonies. When war began in 1914, Roques commanded XII Corps in the Fourth Army. The French High Command had designated Fourth Army to undertake the principal offensive action against Germany. On 22 August it attacked into the Ardennes forest with the mission of taking Neufchâteau. XII Corps was to support the left flank of the main striking force, the Colonial Corps. Much of the Colonial Corps was surrounded and slaughtered at Rossignol, south of the Neufchâteau. Roques immediately stopped his advance, with the result that XVII Corps, just to the left, was exposed to a German attack and resultant heavy casualties, which forced Fourth Army to begin withdrawing on 24 August.

Although Roques received command of First Army in January of 1915, it was as war minister in 1916 that he had his greatest impact on the war by becoming involved, perhaps inadvertently, in the removal of General Joseph Joffre as commander in chief of the French armies. Joffre in 1915 had dismissed General Maurice Sarrail as commander of the Third Army. But Sarrail had strong support from the political Left. Left-wing politicians forced the French government to appoint Sarrail commander of the newly created Balkan Eastern army. Joffre did not want a Balkan campaign nor did he want Sarrail to be the leader of it. In October of 1916 Joffre sent Roques to Salonika to report on Sarrail's army. Joffre had every reason to expect that Roques's report would be unfavorable to Sarrail, for the Balkan army had thus far accomplished little and the Allies wanted Sarrail removed. Instead, Roques reported that Sarrail was doing a fine job and had the support of the Allied commanders. The Left promptly seized upon the Roques report to attack Joffre, claiming that it proved that Joffre and the conservative high command were hostile to the Left-leaning Sarrail and had withheld troops and reinforcements from him. These political attacks, together with the Verdun, Somme, and Romanian disasters, forced Premier Aristide Briand to remove Joffre as commander in chief.

Briand was furious with Roques and dismissed him as war minister in December of 1916. Roques served for a few months as commander of the Fourth Army and then spent the rest of the war in various technical positions with the military administration. He died at St. Cloud on 26 February 1920.

Jan Karl Tanenbaum

References

Ministère de la Guerre, Etat-Major de l'Armée, Service Historique. *Les Armées françaises dans la grande guerre*, Tome 1, Vols. 1–3. Paris: Imprimerie Nationale, 1923–39.

Tanenbaum, Jan Karl. *General Maurice Sarrail 1856–1929; The French Army and Left-Wing Politics.* Chapel Hill: University of North Carolina Press, 1974.

See also JOFFRE, JOSEPH

Rupprecht, Crown Prince of Bavaria (1869–1955)

Bavarian field marshal and army group commander, born in Munich on 18 May 1869. Rupprecht was the son of the future (and last) king of Bavaria, Ludwig III. He attended grammar school and later studied law and other subjects at the universities of Munich and Berlin. Commissioned in the infantry in 1886, he later attended the Bavarian War Academy and thereafter rose swiftly through the ranks. By 1906 he had become a three-star general and commander of the I Bavarian Corps. Seven years later, he was promoted to colonel general and placed in charge of the Fourth Army Inspection.

When the Great War began Rupprecht was given command of the Sixth Army, deploying in Lorraine, initially made up of three Bavarian and one Prussian corps plus one Bavarian reserve corps. With that force Rupprecht was expected to draw a major portion of the French army into the German borderlands in preparation for an eventual counterblow by his own divisions as well as those belonging to the neighboring Fifth and Seventh armies. After retreating for a few days, however, Rupprecht decided that his troops should take a more offensive stance, and he obtained Moltke's tacit agreement for a change of tactics. In a series of costly attacks, Rupprecht's troops pushed into French Lorraine but eventually got stuck at the French fortifications between Nancy and Epinal.

After the Battle of the Marne, OHL ordered the transfer of Rupprecht's Sixth Army to the northern sections of the front, and by early November most of his divisions were deployed in Artois and southern Flanders. Together with the Fourth Army on its right, Rupprecht's force then tried to reopen a war of movement, but all these efforts ended in mud and mire. From then on, until his appointment as an army group commander, Rupprecht presided over the mainly defensive operations of his Sixth Army from his headquarters at Lille and later at Douai. Promoted to field marshal in July of 1916, Rupprecht relinquished command of the Sixth Army to Colonel General Ludwig Baron von Falkenhausen toward the end of the following month and assumed control of a newly formed army group with headquarters at Cambrai. Initially, the group included the Sixth, First, Second, and Seventh armies; in March of 1917 the latter army was withdrawn from his command and the Fourth Army in Flanders was added. As a result, Rupprecht henceforth was responsible for the entire northern portion of the front, from the Belgian coast to the Oise River.

After a number of desperate defensive battles in Flanders and various other places, in March of 1918 Rupprecht's army group resumed offensive operations on a large scale, advancing as far as the Arras-Albert line. In April his Fourth and Sixth armies launched an equally successful offensive farther north, but the hoped-for collapse of the Allied armies did not materialize. Indeed, by July the Germans almost everywhere were pushed onto the defensive, and for the next four months Rupprecht was kept busy supervising the gradual retreat of his army group. In this work, as indeed in all of his endeavors since November of 1915, Rupprecht was ably assisted by longtime chief of staff Lieutenant General Hermann von Kuhl, a Rhenish schoolmaster's son and, like Rupprecht, a staunch Roman Catholic.

Shortly after his father, King Ludwig III, abdicated on 8 November 1918, Rupprecht gave up his command and retired to one of his estates. Father of four children from his first marriage (his wife had died in 1912), Rupprecht remarried in 1921 and had six more children. Although he welcomed the revival of monarchist feelings in Bavaria, he refused to be drawn into wild schemes aimed at the restoration of his dynasty. During the Second World War, he and his family lived mostly in Italy. He returned to Bavaria in 1945 and died at Leutstetten on 2 August 1955.

Ulrich Trumpener

References

Deuringer, Karl (Bayerisches Kriegsarchiv). *Die Schlacht in Lothringen und in den Vogesen 1914: Die Feuertaufe der Bayerischen Armee.* 2 vols. Munich: Max Schlick, 1929.

———. *Der Wettlauf um die Flanke in Nordfrankreich 1914.* 2 vols. Munich: Max Schlick, 1936.

Kronprinz Rupprecht von Bayern. *Mein Kriegstagebuch.* Edited by Eugen von Frauenholz. 3 vols. Berlin: E.S. Mittler und Sohn, 1929.

Kuhl, Hermann von. *Der Weltkrieg 1914–1918: Dem deutschen Volke dargestellt.* 2 vols. Berlin: Vaterländischer Verlag Weller, 1930.

Sendtner, Kurt. *Rupprecht von Wittelsbach, Kronprinz von Bayern.* Munich: Richard Pflaum Verlag, 1954.

See also FRONTIERS, BATTLE OF THE; LUDENDORFF OFFENSIVES; LUDWIG III; PASSCHENDAELE

Russia, Allied Intervention in

The First World War brought a second "Time of Troubles" upon Russia. Its empire had been defeated, its last monarch had abdicated, the army was dissolving, peasants were seizing land, and the economy continued to decline while the economic separation of town and country proceeded apace. Russia's enemies stood solidly on her territory, assisting the peoples of the periphery to break away from the empire. In early November of 1917 the provisional government of Aleksandr Kerensky was overthrown by Lenin's Bolsheviks, who had pledged to take Russia out of an imperialist war, make peace without annexations or indemnities, and bring about social and political revolution.

This calamitous turn of events did not come unexpectedly. The failure of the 1916 Brusilov summer offensive had already dashed Allied hopes about Russia's ability to contribute significantly against the Central Powers. The year 1917 had not been a good year for the Allies: There was a military stalemate on the Western Front despite prodigious losses that drove part of the French army to mutiny. Allied shipping incurred heavy losses from German submarines, and the Italian front collapsed at Caporetto. The good news was that the enemy had suffered too, and that the United States had entered the war on the Allied side. But it would take time before America's power could be mobilized and deployed. Under these circumstances the Allies panicked. Any collapse of the Eastern Front would threaten the precarious military balance on the Western Front by allowing Germany to shift manpower and material westward. Furthermore, Germany would be able to organize the resources of Eastern Europe, overcoming the effectiveness of the Allied economic blockade. The war might last a year longer or more.

The Allies, therefore, sought somehow to reconstitute the Eastern Front. They were willing to cooperate with any political faction, including the Bolsheviks, that was willing to continue fighting against Germany. The Western governments sent emissaries to various parts of Russia with promises of aid in return for a continuation of the war against the Central Powers. In December of 1917, Great Britain and France concluded a secret convention regarding their activities in southern Russia. The United States government was hopeful that a forceful leader would emerge, one capable of rallying Russia's political and military forces, standing up to the Germans, and restoring order. The Bolsheviks stood for disorder. While they could not be recognized, conflict with them was to be avoided.

Allied policy changed when the Bolsheviks finally signed the Treaty of Brest-Litovsk in March of 1918. The treaty was the ultimate betrayal of the Allied cause and sowed the seeds for the Cold War. With Brest-Litovsk the spectre of German domination in Eastern Europe threatened to become reality, and the Allies now began to think seriously about military intervention. A *pax teutonica* had to be prevented at all cost. But neither in aims nor in methods did the Allies ever achieve unanimity regarding Russia.

Besides the Eastern Front and growing hostility toward the Bolsheviks, there were now also other practical considerations at play in Allied policy toward Russia: protection of the vast stock of Allied supplies stored at Murmansk, Archangel, and Vladivostok; support of "orderly" Russian forces; and protection of the Czech Legion, which had taken over

major parts of the Trans-Siberian railroad following a clash with Bolshevik units at Cheliabinsk in May of 1918. The Czech Corps constituted the best and most organized fighting force in Russia at that time. It had been on its way to Vladivostok, from which it hoped to be shipped to Europe's Western Front. The Czech-Soviet clashes also signaled the beginning of full-scale civil war and foreign intervention, especially after the Soviets attempted to disarm the Czechs.

British Major General F.C. Poole had already been sent to Murmansk to prepare for Allied military intervention, and a British expeditionary force landed there on 6 March 1918. It was joined by other Allied troops, including an American contingent on 4 September 1918. When an anti-Bolshevik coup succeeded in Archangel, Allied units entered that port on 1–2 August 1918. On 26 July Japan had accepted a U.S. proposal for joint action in Vladivostok. Allied men-of-war had already arrived there in February of 1918. British troops landed at Vladivostok on 3 August 1918, followed in short order by Japanese and American units. On 5 September 1918, Japanese troops also occupied Khabarovsk. On 14 October 1918 British forces reached Irkutsk, linking up with the Czech Corps. Thus, the major Allied powers now had troops in Russia. These supported anti-Bolshevik governments wherever they appeared.

The Allies also used economic warfare in support of anti-Bolshevik forces and against the Soviet regime. They had already included all of Russia in their economic blockade of the Central Powers as soon as they had learned of the fall of the provisional government. At first this was directed almost exclusively against the Central Powers, with the Bolsheviks a secondary target, but after the collapse of imperial Germany, the entire economic warfare machinery was directed against Soviet Russia, and this continued unabated until January of 1920. Economic intervention against Russia, with all its ramifications, represented, in the long run, the most dangerous weapon at the disposal of the Allies. Initiated without fanfare as a response to the political uncertainties in Russia at the end of 1917, it soon became an integral part of anti-Soviet policies, applied especially vigorously after the peace of Brest-Litovsk. Economic warfare against Soviet Russia was in operation before any of the other forms of intervention were undertaken.

With the outbreak of the Russian Civil War in early 1918, the Allies began to support the Whites with money, goods, war matériel, and military advisers. In the course of defending itself, the policies and practices of Lenin's government became more and more dictatorial and brutal. "War communism" was largely a response to the requirements of having to fight the civil war. Allied intervention encouraged and supported the anti-Soviet movement. But, paradoxically, it also aided Lenin and his party, now able to exploit a traditional theme in Russian history: patriotic defense against foreign invaders and their domestic handmaidens. Intervention also appeared to confirm Bolshevik-held views and biases against Western capitalist-imperialist regimes. After signing Brest-Litovsk Lenin stated his belief that "world capitalism" was now going to come after the Bolsheviks. These regimes would do anything to eliminate the threat coming from a "superior" social system.

The collapse of Germany in November of 1918 changed the nature of Allied intervention in Russia. There was no longer a need for the Eastern Front, and there was only one remaining enemy, the Bolsheviks. The military collapse of the Central Powers had left a vacuum in and around Russia, and the Allies could now more easily surround Soviet Russia. Allied navies now controlled the Baltic, Barents, White, Black, and Caspian seas, just as they had always controlled the Pacific approaches to Russia's Far East. On 18 December 1918 French troops occupied Odessa in Ukraine, but they were forced to leave in April of 1919. British troops occupied Baku and its oil fields and the Baku-Batum railway. When Admiral Aleksandr Kolchak declared himself "Supreme Ruler of Russia" from his headquarters at Omsk on 17 November 1918, the Allies quickly pledged to support him. The Allied governments, freed from their preoccupation with the Central Powers, now concentrated greater resources of money, men, food, and weapons in support of the anti-Bolshevik forces.

But the "Russian problem" became more complex. A "crusade" against Bolshevism was out of the question: There were not enough volunteers, and the United States refused to finance such an enterprise. There was also little public support in the West for such a war. Thus, there remained only tightening the economic noose around Soviet Russia, and providing surplus war material and some discretionary funds to the White forces.

The United States government, especially, began to believe that famine and economic disorganization were the "parents of Bolshevism." The United States would be in a unique position to use its economic power to influence political developments in Central Europe and the former Russian Empire through economic aid, consisting of food, medical supplies, and domestic goods. In Siberia a distribution network through the Russian Railway Service Corps, operating out of Vladivostok, would secure the areas and populations behind the fronts and restore economic well-being. Washington thus began to consider removing its troops and relying on economic means to support the Whites and undermine the Bolshevik regime.

Great Britain was deeply involved in Russia in late 1918, and such anti-Soviet measures were continued. London sought to encourage and support friendly regimes in the border areas. Great Britain largely armed and supported the forces of General Nikolai Yudenich through British naval units.

Militantly anti-Bolshevik, France wanted to maintain pressure on the Soviet government and encircle Russia in a *cordon sanitaire* by relying on neighboring countries such as Poland and Romania. So much the better if economic encirclement also contributed to Bolshevism's collapse.

Allied leaders at the Paris Peace Conference entertained several initiatives to solve the "Russian question." All failed, the result of little coordination or unanimity. Japan, in particular, was seen as not only a danger to Allied policies but inimical to any new Russia.

As the Allies accepted the fact that no new troops could be sent to Russia, direct military intervention came to an end. By the end of 1919 Allied troops had left north Russia and most of Siberia. The Czechs were ordered to leave and their evacuation was completed in November of 1920. American troops withdrew in April of 1920. Intense U.S. pressure finally persuaded Japan to leave in October of 1922.

The conclusion of peace with Germany made even the blockade a problem. There were legal questions surrounding its maintenance. Furthermore, if Germany did not observe the blockade, she would be able to take advantage of carrying on trade with Russia. Yet there were strong objections to abandoning the blockade, and in early October of 1919 the Allies asked all neutral countries to join what amounted to an all-embracing economic warfare against Soviet Russia.

This action came during the height of the military campaign of the White forces against Soviet Russia. Germany's refusal to participate, the doubtful attitude of many neutral countries, and America's reluctance to agree to even those measures dashed this attempt to achieve a common plan. As a result, the Allied governments lifted the blockade in January of 1920, although most industrialized countries maintained restrictions on economic relations with the Soviet Union until its dissolution in 1991. Both sides were suspicious of the other's motives and capabilities.

Yet conflict continued, the result of Poland's invasion of Ukraine in April of 1920. The effects of this war, coming on the heels of revolutions, civil war, military intervention, and the Allied blockade, led to the economic collapse of Soviet Russia in late 1920. Political opposition grew rapidly, climaxing in the Kronstadt naval base mutiny. To prevent a complete political reversal, Lenin succeeded in ending war-communism and ushering in a New Economic Policy, which Western analysts interpreted as moderation, if not overthrow, of the Soviet Regime.

N.H. Gaworek

References

Bradley, John. *Allied Intervention in Russia.* New York: Basic Books, 1968.

Coates, W.P., and K. Zelda. *Armed Intervention in Russia, 1918–1922.* London: Victor Gollancz, 1935.

Graves, William S. *America's Siberian Adventure, 1918–1920.* London: Jonathan Cape, 1931.

Kennan, George F. *Soviet-American Relations, 1917–1921.* Vol. 2: *The Decision to Intervene.* Princeton: Princeton University Press, 1956–58.

Kettle, Michael. *The Road to Intervention, March to November 1918.* Vol. 2: *Russia and the Allies, 1917–1920.* London: Routledge, Croom Helm, 1988.

Swettenham, John. *Allied Intervention in Russia 1917–1919 and the Part Played by Canada.* London: Allen and Unwin, 1967.

Ullman, Richard. *Intervention and the War.* Vol. 2: *Anglo Soviet Relations, 1917–1921.* Princeton: Princeton University Press, 1961–72.

Unterberger, Betty Miller. *America's Siberian Expedition.* Durham, N.C.: Duke University Press, 1956.

Warth, Robert D. *The Allies and the Russian Revolution.* Durham, N.C.: Duke University Press, 1954.

White, John A. *The Siberian Intervention.* New York: Greenwood, 1950.

See also Kolchak, Aleksandr; Russia, Civil War in, Home Front and Revolutions of 1917

Russia, Army

The prewar Russian army had 1.4 million men. Immediate mobilization added another 3.1 million, and during the entire war 12 million men wore the army uniform. Of these 6.7 million were killed or wounded.

Conscription in the pre-1905 army had lasted for twenty-five years. This term was shortened, however, by the subsequent military reforms. By World War I it was three years active service plus twelve in reserve for infantry and cavalry. Also, after the Russo-Japanese War, Russia went to a reserve system under which all healthy men were assigned to army units that were supposed to receive yearly training, but they rarely did. Aside from the reserve units, the regular army consisted of cadres of professional officers and noncommissioned officers. Generally, the officers remained aloof and had little association with the units they commanded. Their attitude was consistent with the status of medieval nobility. Sergeants and corporals, on the other hand, had a well justified reputation for cruelty toward new recruits. The top of the Russian officers corps was overloaded with aged and incompetent men, especially at the general-officer level. They were so bad that within a single year of the war with Japan, 341 generals and 400 colonels were retired. Many were kept on active duty, however, because they had friends at court. Their duties consisted of playing cards, drinking, and attending social functions.

The Russo-Japanese War exposed the weaknesses and insufficiencies of the Russian military establishment. Commissions were created to design and implement reforms of the army and navy, but these floundered in the face of opposition from reactionary traditionalists, most of whom refused to acknowledge the significance of the revolution in military technology. Out of the Russian defeat at the hands of Japan, however, there emerged a new generation of young officers, men of intelligence and ability who really desired to reform the army. Most of these "young Turks" were political liberals, who wanted the monarchy modified or abolished so that the Russian government might satisfy the needs of a modern industrial nation.

Between 1907 and 1912 in the Third Duma these young officers found a platform for their views in the person of the sympathetic conservative legislator A.I. Guchkov, who chaired a Duma committee on national defense. Guchkov held a series of public hearings during which many of these officers testified. Almost to a man they linked military reform to political restructuring. It was their belief that the monarchy, supported by a Russian aristocracy steeped in medieval tradition, was the chief impediment to a modern, technically proficient army and navy. Reaction to this movement came in 1909 when, under the influence of reactionaries at the court, the czar authorized a purge of politically unreliable officers. At the top, the highly competent minister of war A.A. Rediger was replaced by the aged and incompetent V. Sukhomlinov.

The organization of the Imperial Russian Army was based on the infantry division of about 6,000 men. Each division contained sixteen battalions. Although the German division had only twelve battalions, it had twice the firepower of its Russian counterpart. There is little doubt that Russian military planners put their stock in masses of manpower rather than the firepower of modern weaponry. The standard infantry weapon was the Mosin-Nagant Model 1891 rifle. It was a fairly effective weapon but had a difficult safety catch. It used a five-cartridge magazine that held a 7.62mm rimmed shell. Its weight without bayonet was 9.6 pounds and it was accurate to 250 yards. The automatic version of this weapon was the M-4, 7.62mm water-cooled machine gun. It could fire up to 600 rounds per minute and was usually mounted on a wheeled carriage.

Although these weapons (as well as the Russian artillery) were comparable in quality to those of other armies, the big difference was in the severe shortages in the Russian army of all types of weapons and ammunition. In the initial mobilization of 1914 an estimated one-third of the Russian soldiers did not even have rifles and were told to pick up weapons from fallen comrades. There is at least one documented case, early in the war, of Russians charging German machine-gun emplacements with axe handles.

Although Russian mobilization was announced on 29 July 1914, it had actually begun earlier. By the end of November there were in place thirty-seven corps of two divisions each. Contained in this body were seventy line divisions, nineteen independent brigades, twenty-four cavalry and Cossack divisions, and thirty-five reserve divisions. Before the war Russian strategists opted for quantity over quality. Because of its sheer size the Russian army was referred to as the Russian steamroller. The idea was that a million men marching in the same direction could take any objective no matter what weapons they faced. This concept was taken seriously, even in Berlin.

The initial Russian army mobilization went surprisingly well. Although many well-connected people obtained exemptions, nearly all the peasants called up reported for duty. There was looting only by those who were not given money for food while on the way to their reporting stations. Among the several defects in the Russian mobilization plan was that far too many skilled industrial workers, who were needed at home, were sent into the army in the early levies, sometimes for political reasons. More important, since no one on either side thought the war would last very long, a majority of the veteran cadres were in the frontline units and were lost in the early battles, leaving no one to train the new recruits.

Early military defeats in East Prussia in late August of 1914 and in the Carpathian Mountains the following spring cost Russia dearly. Added to 1.8 million casualties in 1914 alone was the blow to morale both in the army and at home. The original commander of the Russian army, the Grand Duke Nikolai Nikolaevich, one of the czar's uncles, presided over these defeats. He remained popular, however, and by mid-1915 was learning how to make war. After the Carpathian disaster, moreover, new, capable officers were being funneled into high positions. By far the most important of these was General Aleksei A. Polivanov, who replaced Sukhomlinov as minister of war. Polivanov did much to solve the critical army supply shortages before he was dismissed later in 1915 for political reasons. The work of Polivanov and the other new military commanders went far to restore the fighting capability of the battered Russian army.

At the very top, the empress, ever jealous of the popular Grand Duke Nikolai, persuaded her husband, Nicholas II, to assume personal command of the army and to go to the Front. Although he left the conduct of the war to his able chief of staff, General Mikhail Vasilevich Alekseev, the departure of the head of state from the capital in time of war had the most serious political consequences for the future of Russia.

Had the Russian army remained on the defensive after 1915 it might have fully recovered. In the spring of 1916, however, the French once again called for a Russian offensive. This time it was to relieve the pressure on Verdun and to aid Italy, which had just suffered a major defeat at the hands of the Austrians. Consequently, in the summer, at the urging of General Aleksei A. Brusilov, a Russian offensive was launched against the Austrians. After some initial Russian successes the Germans and Austrians counterattacked, blunting the Russian drive and inflicting hundreds of thousands of casualties.

By 1917 the Russian army was once more in a state of near total exhaustion. Losses of officers and noncoms were made up by impressment gangs, who searched homes for men who had evaded conscription. Many of these were educated and politically radical. Having been dragooned into an army at the end of its tether, these people found a fertile ground for their radical propaganda. Germany was also near the end of her strength and needed her eastern divisions in the west for one last offensive, which might produce peace negotiations. German troops were encouraged to establish friendly relations with the Russian soldiers, with a view to their further demoralization. By early 1917 there was large-scale fraternization on the Eastern Front. The Russian army was definitely ready to quit the war.

The March Revolution of 1917 that toppled the monarchy brought to power a new regime that, nonetheless, continued to press for successful prosecution of the war against the Central Powers. This decision to continue the war culminated in the Kerensky Offensive in the summer of 1917. Disaffection was already rife in the army, thanks to horrific casualties and Bolshevik agitation, but the failure of the Kerensky Offensive brought the final collapse of the Russian army. Without the support of the army the provisional government was itself doomed, and the Bolsheviks seized upon this weakness to wrest control. Many deserting soldiers supported the Bolshevik cause; part of the army that opposed the Bolsheviks attempted a counterrevolution, but it failed. Many of these counterrevolutionaries later participated in the civil war.

Ineffective leadership, lack of supplies, horrendous casualties, and poor education, (reflected in the lack of modern managerial methods), led to the collapse of the Russian army in the First World War.

John W. Bohon

References

Florinsky, Michael T. *Russia, A History and an Interpretation*. 2 vols. New York: Macmillan, 1953.

Golovin, General N.N. *The Russian Army in the World War*. New Haven: Yale University Press, 1931.

Jukes, Geoffrey. *Carpathian Disaster, Death of an Army*. London: Ballentine, 1971.

See also POLIVANOV, ALEKSEI; RUSSIA, CIVIL WAR IN; SUKHOMLINOV, VLADIMIR

Russia, Civil War in

The civil war in Russia was a direct result of the effects of World War I. In March of 1917 the czar was forced to abdicate; then in October the moderately socialist regime of Aleksandr Kerensky was toppled by Lenin's Bolsheviks. The "Reds" were determined to restructure Russia internally, but first they had to end her participation in the war. They accomplished this by signing the punitive Treaty of Brest-Litovsk in March of 1918.

The Allied governments suspected Bolshevik collusion with the Central Powers and sought to locate and support elements in Russia loyal to their cause. Centers of anti-Bolshevik resistance soon arose. These "Whites" were determined to drive both the Reds and the Central Powers from Russian soil. Civil war resulted in North Russia, Siberia, South Russia, and the Baltic.

North Russia

In June of 1918 the British landed a force at Murmansk, and in August British and French troops landed at Archangel. These troops were to protect large Allied stores of munitions from falling into German hands. The Allies were also concerned that newly independent Finland would attempt, with German assistance, to seize the Kola Peninsula. German submarines based at Murmansk would be a serious threat to northern Allied waters.

In September the Americans also landed troops at Archangel. Other token Allied forces arrived before the end of the year, allowing British General Edmund Ironside to raise White units to counterbalance Red troops sent up by rail from the Soviet heartland. Unhappily for the White cause, the northern regions were only sparsely populated and largely indifferent to the civil war. The local government under Social Revolutionary leader M.N. Chaikovsky was hesitant and irresolute.

Recruitment finally improved in January of 1919 when General Eugene Miller assumed command. Thirteen regiments were raised, comprising 50,000 men. Yet, with notable exceptions, the overall quality of this force was poor. A mutiny in one company of the experimental Slavo-British Legion hurt morale at the very time that the Allied governments were trying to extract their men before winter.

In the spring of 1919 considerable fighting broke out between the Allies and Bolshevik forces in which the latter were defeated. The French favored escalation, but the British and Americans were opposed. Allied troops were then withdrawn. Archangel was abandoned at the end of September and Murmansk in October. That autumn the Whites executed their own temporarily successful offensive, then contained subsequent Red attacks until they were broken on the Northern Dvina and at Lake Onega in February of 1920.

Siberia

The Allies held out most hope for a second front in Siberia. In May of 1918 the 40,000 men of the Czech Legion revolted against Bolshevik rule and seized the Trans-Siberian Railway. With their assistance, local Social Revolutionaries overthrew the Bolshevik regime at Samara, establishing the Committee of Members of the Constituent Assembly, known as KOMUCH. In August the "People's Army" marched on Simbirsk and Kazan, holding them against ragged and undisciplined Red forces until autumn, when Trotsky galvanized life into this front. KOMUCH melted away in October.

Meanwhile, Japanese, American, and British troops landed in the Siberian Far East. The Japanese had arrived at Vladivostok in December of 1917. As rumors of Central Powers' prisoners of war serving in the Red Army spread, the Allies spoke of forming a new front with the Czechs and Whites. One White government seemed promising, the Provisional All-Russian Government (PA-RG), which tried to establish a common anti-Bolshevik front. Unfortunately, PA-RG proved unacceptable to both extremes of the political spectrum. In November, after a bloodless coup, Admiral Aleksandr Kolchak assumed nominal command over the Siberian front with the title of supreme ruler of Russia. Nearly all White movements eventually gave Kolchak their allegiance, and in May of 1919 the Allies recognized his government as the legitimate Russian regime.

Kolchak's opening military move in December of 1918 took the Reds by surprise and hurled them back 200 miles beyond Perm. His main offensive began in March of 1919 when his center Western Army drove toward the Volga, advancing 250 miles over the next two months. Meanwhile, the Siberian Army moved toward Viatka, offering the possibility of a united Allied front in North Russia. The Red Eastern Army Group, however, staged a pincer's move against Kolchak's center in May and June, and broke it. Retreat turned into rout as the overextended Siberian Army was pushed back to the Urals. The fall of Ufa severed the already shaky link between the Ural and Orenburg Cossacks and Kolchak's main forces. Demoralized, the Whites failed to garrison the defensible Ural Mountains. A White counterattack at Cheliabinsk miscarried and confirmed the loss of the Urals. The last White offensive on the Tobol River in October gained only a hundred miles before being halted and then reversed. Kolchak's capital of Omsk capitulated on 14 November, and the Whites began a long, catastrophic winter retreat across Siberia. Kolchak was taken prisoner by the Reds and executed on 7 February 1920.

Both Whites and Reds found recruiting in the trans-Volga and Siberia difficult. Distance and poor communications especially hampered the Whites; supplies landed in the Far East took six weeks to reach Kolchak's front by rail. Japanese-sponsored warlords also played havoc with Kolchak's rear areas, as did Red partisans.

The Americans left Russia in April of 1920, the Czechs in November, and the Japanese in October of 1922. The last of the Whites retreated into Korea and Manchuria.

South Russia

In December of 1917 Lavr G. Kornilov, former Russian army commander in chief, and Anton I. Denikin, former chief of staff, met Mikhail V. Alekseev, also a former chief of staff, in Don

Cossack territory. There they hoped to create a White Volunteer Army dedicated to the destruction of the Bolsheviks and the deliverance of Russian soil from the Germans. Unfortunately, when the Red Army invaded the Don region, the Cossacks were not yet ready, and the volunteers were forced into snowy Kuban in February of 1918.

During the subsequent "Campaign of Ice" the volunteers fought nearly forty successful actions in fifty days. Denikin assumed command when Kornilov was killed in March during the siege of Ekaterinodar. During the second Kuban campaign the volunteers captured Ekaterinodar, capital of the Kuban Cossacks, and established a base.

By autumn the Kuban Cossack and volunteer forces had 40,000 men in the field. They routed the Red Taman Group and by winter had destroyed the 150,000-man Red North Caucasus Army Group. Unfortunately, Alekseev, who had been widely respected by the Allies, died that October. At least the November 1918 Armistice seemed to augur well for the Whites in south Russia. A British military mission arrived and the French promised troops for a 1919 offensive. In reality, British aid was not significant until the second half of 1919 and French assistance not until 1920.

In January of 1919 several White groups came together under Denikin and the unified banner of the Armed Forces of South Russia (AFSR). The Ataman of the Don Cossacks, P.N. Krasnov, had fought the Reds for much of 1918; unfortunately, he had also been receiving arms from the Central Powers. Having compromised himself with the Allies, he was forced to step down.

Unity was well timed, for the Don was threatened by Red offensives in the spring of 1919. The Bolsheviks were particularly anxious to prevent a juncture between White forces in Siberia and South Russia. Consequently, the Volunteer Army had to be transferred into the Donbas, on the left flank of the Cossacks. The AFSR met and repelled three successive Red pushes, then began its own offensive, which shattered the Red southern front. In June Kharkov and Tsaritsyn fell.

On 3 July Denikin issued his "Moscow Directive." White forces were to converge on Moscow from three axes: the volunteers to Kursk-Orel-Tula-Moscow, the Don Army to Voronezh-Riazan-Moscow, and the Caucasus Army from the Volga to Nizhnyi-Novgorod and to Vladimir-Moscow. Eventually, the AFSR would fan out even into the turbulent Ukraine. Denikin gambled on either a Bolshevik collapse or an uprising to support the Whites. Failing these, the AFSR counted on the quality of its arms, even against superior numbers.

After holding Red counterattacks throughout July and August, the Whites again advanced. The volunteers reached Orel in October. There the Reds had prepared a strategic offensive. A special Shock Group struck the left of the overextended volunteers, while S.M. Budenny's recently massed Red cavalry army punched through the Cossacks and threatened the volunteer right. Fighting around Orel lasted a month, but it was the high point of the White offensive.

The Reds then drove the Whites back beyond the Don and into the Kuban. After a fresh round of battles the AFSR was forced to evacuate Novorossiisk for the Crimea, where, in March of 1920, command passed to General Baron P.N. Wrangel. After reorganizing his forces, Wrangel took advantage of the Polish attack against Bolshevik Russia in April to mount his own offensive in June into the Tauride. From June to November he extended White territory in southern Russia. But, with the conclusion of the Russo-Polish War, Bolshevik forces were freed that autumn for action against south Russia. Wrangel was forced back to the Crimea on 1 November and then obliged to evacuate surviving White units and their families by sea to Constantinople on 14 November. Soviet governments were then set up in Georgia and Armenia, and Turkey restored Batum to Russia.

The Baltic

Most of this area was dominated by the German army before and after the Armistice. A small White army was formed in the Baltic area in October of 1918. It had been supported by the Germans in the final weeks of the war and, after the Armistice, by the new state of Estonia. In May of 1919 this 6,000-man Northwestern Army secured a base of operations inside Russia, then held its enclave against Bolshevik counterattacks throughout the summer.

Finnish and Baltic states' support for General Nikolai Yudenich's Northwestern Army might have been forthcoming if the Whites had been willing to accept British diplomatic prodding to unconditionally guarantee their independence, but the Whites delayed. White forces were also divided: A small Russian Western Army cooperated with General Rüdiger von der Goltz's German Baltic Division, chiefly against Latvia.

Yudenich decided to attack Petrograd in late September, in order to help Denikin's forces driving on Moscow. Covered by British naval support on his left flank, Yudenich led his 15,000 troops against two Red Armies (bolstered by Stalin and Trotsky) that outnumbered him fivefold in men and tenfold in artillery. Surprise and speed got the Whites to the suburbs of Petrograd, but, lacking additional support or an anti-Red rising, they were steadily forced back through November into Estonia, where they were interned.

In retrospect, Allied fears that the Bolsheviks were puppets of the Germans were erroneous. Similarly, Allied hopes in 1918 for a White Russian second front against the Central Powers was a chimera; the Whites were struggling for their own existence. In 1919 the value of the Whites to the victorious Allies diminished, even as White strength surged and peaked. The Reds took advantage of interior lines, superior communications, greater access to factories and imperial arms depots, generally more capable political leaders, and a larger population base for recruits. Further, Red propaganda was more effective with the peasants and was backed, when necessary, by systematic terror.

The Whites failed to achieve coherent political and social programs; consequently, their propaganda was ineffective and inconsistent. Relegated to the peripheries of Russia, their movements were usually based on and ended in open conflict with the new nationalist states that had broken away from the former Russian Empire. Defeated at the end of 1919, the Whites were washed away in the Red tide of 1920.

David L. Bullock

References

Footman, David. *Civil War in Russia*. London: Faber and Faber, 1961.

Lincoln, W. Bruce. *Red Victory: A History of the Russian Civil War*. New York: Simon and Schuster, 1989.

Luckett, Richard. *The White Generals: An Account of the White Movement and the Russian Civil War*. London: Longman Group, 1971.

Mawdsley, Evan. *The Russian Civil War*. Boston: Allen and Unwin, 1987.

Stewart, George. *The White Armies of Russia*. New York: Macmillan, 1933.

See also ALEKSEEV, MIKHAIL; CZECH LEGION; DENIKIN, ANTON; KOLCHAK, ALEKSANDR; KORNILOV, LAVR; RUSSIA, ALLIED INTERVENTION IN; TROTSKY, LEON; YUDENICH, NIKOLAI

Russia, Home Front and Revolutions of 1917

During World War I Russia suffered all the strains and dislocations common to all the national combatants. There was no precedent for this sort of war, which saw the large-scale implementation of new, terrible weapons and necessitated the mobilization of whole populations. Moreover, there was little understanding of the economics of modern war, in which new military industries had to be created, regulated, and financed. Yet, most of the major participants—England, France, and Germany—were able to bring together sufficient talent and put together governments of national unity, under strong leaders, in which political differences were put aside in the face of the war effort. Russia was not up to such a task. With one foot in the Middle Ages and the other in the Industrial Revolution, imperial Russia was a crippled giant. The monarchy viewed every attempt to modernize the government to meet the exigencies of the war as a threat to its traditional authority. All things considered, the revolutions of 1917 constituted a failure of political leadership.

In wartime Russia there was, from the beginning, economic disfunction that only worsened as the government proved unable to cope with the problems of a wartime economy. By 1917, 37 percent of working-age men were in the army. In industry, many of the skilled workers had been lost. While women and children were recruited into the factories, there was still a general lowering of productivity. Prior to the war, moreover, Russian leaders had assumed that a war would close off Russia's external markets; therefore, when it started, they cut back production in some industries by 50 percent. Then, when war orders began to pour in, there was economic dislocation as factory managers tried to rectify these initial errors. As a result, there were critical shortages at the front of all types of military supplies. Reaction by the central government, at least in the early phases of the war, was practically nil.

In the absence of a war industrial policy, local and municipal governmental agencies stepped into the breech. In early August of 1914 zemstvo (provincial and district governmental council) leaders met in Moscow and created the All-Russian Union of Zemstvos. Its early work was to maintain the military medical service, including hospitals, transportation of the wounded, and so forth. Later, under the leadership of Prince Georgi E. Lvov, the Zemstvo Union endeavored to establish priorities for Russia's war industry. Likewise, a joint committee for the supply of the army (zemgor) helped in this work. Finally, a Central War Industries Committee, based in Petrograd and headed by the capable Duma politician Aleksandr I. Guch-kov, coordinated these local agencies. Again, it should be noted that none of these groups were sponsored by the central government.

Russian agriculture was unevenly affected by the war. The big private estates that grew grain for export, including food for the cities, lost their labor, and therefore productivity dropped. Peasants, who produced over 70 percent of Russia's cereal crops, refused to sell grain at the artificially low prices set by the government. The main reason for the shortages of food and other goods, however, was the collapse of the railway system, which had barely been adequate in peacetime. Between 1914 and 1917 the number of locomotives in service fell from 20,000 to 9,000. To make matters worse, the Germans had occupied much of Russia's best agricultural land after its victories in 1914 and 1915.

As disconcerting as were the economic shortages, many of which had been solved by late 1915, the fate of the nation still rested with the central government. Throughout the war Russian politics continued to be a struggle between the medieval prerogatives of the monarchy and democratic encroachments represented by the State Duma. In August of 1914 the Council of Ministers (responsible to the czar) was headed by chief minister Ivan Goremykin, who was seventy-five years old at the time and was reported to be in an advanced stage of sclerosis. He presided over a collection of reactionary incompetents. By mid-1915, however, the needs generated by the war had forced the government to replace many of them with more able ministers. Included among the latter were Minister of War Aleksei Polivanov and Interior Minister Prince Nikolai B. Shcherbatov.

At the onset of the war, there was a wave of patriotic support for the monarchy in the Duma, as in all of Russia. On 8 August in a special session a great majority of its members voted war credits to the crown. This early enthusiasm did not last, however. Early Russian military defeats, coupled with the czar's decision to assume personal command of the army, caused consternation in the Duma. As an omen of things to come, in January of 1915 Goremykin and Minister of War Vladimir Sukhomlinov appeared before the Duma to answer questions about the war. The overall impression among the legislators was one of arrogance and incompetence. Thus, in July a number of centrist Duma members formed a progressive bloc to goad the crown into successfully prosecuting the war effort. The crown and the Duma were, by now, on a collision course.

The proverbial last straw was the meddling of Empress Alexandra and her advisor, Grigorii Rasputin, in the government. After her husband left for the front, she was determined to become another Catherine the Great. When ten of the twelve ministers signed a letter begging the czar to reconsider his decision to leave the capital, the empress saw them as enemies of the monarch and went after them with a vengeance. Although Goremykin was not of this group, he was dismissed for senility and replaced as chief minister by Boris V. Sturmer, who was held in contempt by both the Right and Left. His new minister of interior was the mentally unbalanced Aleksandr Protopopov. By the end of 1916 the cabinet had been dismantled. On 1 November of that year the liberal Duma member Pavel Miliukov, in a bitterly impassioned speech, attacked the empress, Rasputin, and Sturmer. After every part of his oration he pointedly asked, "Is it stupidity or treason?" Needless to say, it caused a sensation in the capital. Shortly thereafter, the ultraconservative Duma member Vladimir M. Purishkevich also attacked Rasputin. On 17 December, Rasputin, the influential peasant monk, was murdered. This violent act seemed to represent a climax of the frustration of the Russian people and opened up a floodgate of protest against the crown.

By 1917 there was open talk, at every level of society, of the need to replace Czar Nicholas II. To the small educated public, newspaper accounts of the political breakdown were enough. But for the masses, mostly peasants, the collapse of morale came more slowly. It was a collective result of huge war casualties, economic hardships, administrative chaos, and most of all a general war weariness. At home, there was an increased frequency in draft evasion. At the front, among the soldiers, the collapse was the result of the casualties, incompetent leadership, and a vagueness as to why they were fighting.

Demonstrations, which soon turned into riots, broke out in the working-class section of Petrograd on 8 March 1917. The city was ripe for an explosion. By the 10th the entire city was in turmoil. All the security forces, the police, the Guards, and the Cossacks were called out to quell the disturbances. But unlike the upheaval of 1905, these demonstrations were met by a reluctance by these units to fire on their own people. From the Duma the legislators looked down at the chaos in the streets. The Duma president Rodzianko wired the czar, still at the front, of the situation in the capital. Nicholas II answered with an order to dissolve the Duma, which was ignored. He then set out for Petrograd, but his train was stopped at Pskov by revolutionary workers.

In the Duma events moved rapidly. A group of centrist politicians formed a provisional committee, the avowed aim of which was to act as a temporary government until order was restored in the city. Simultaneously, a small group of socialist deputies announced the creation of the Executive Committee of the Petrograd Soviet of Workers and Soldiers Deputies. Leaflets were immediately distributed to the mob inviting it to send delegates to the new revolutionary government. There were now two sources of political power in Petrograd. On 14 March the Soviet issued its famous "Order Number One" to all military units, inviting them to arrest their officers, elect revolutionary committees, and await instructions from the Soviet.

This was the effective end of the Russian army as a fighting force. While some units remained at the front, hundreds of thousands of Russian soldiers left for home. On the following day, the 15th, the provisional committee sent two of its members to receive the czar's abdication. The imperial era of Russia's history ended.

On 16 March the provisional committee and the Soviet, realizing that Russia could not be governed by two opposing bodies, came to an agreement. A provisional government would be organized from the Duma but with the Soviet holding a veto power over it. Army units that had not already disintegrated would remain at the front for defensive purposes only. After the war the Russian people would be allowed to vote on a real constitution. In summary, the revolution of March 1917, which toppled the monarchy, was a spontaneous event. There is no evidence of any socialist leadership.

The provisional government lasted from mid-March to early November of 1917 through a series of political coalitions, which lurched from crisis to crisis. Its first chief minister was the liberal aristocrat Prince Lvov. The moderate socialist Aleksandr Kerensky was the only person to hold posts in both the Soviet and the provisional government (he started as minister of justice in the latter). The new government began its existence with a cascade of reforms ranging from the restoration of Finnish autonomy to political amnesty. Under the latter provision thousands of exiles streamed out of Siberia. Among their number were the two Bolsheviks Leo Kamenev and Josef Stalin. As the senior Bolshevik in the capital, Stalin was offered a seat on the Soviet, from where he espoused the majority view of support of the provisional government. On 16 April Vladimir I. Lenin, along with other Russian radicals who had been in exile abroad, arrived in Petrograd. Unlike Stalin, Lenin refused a seat in the Soviet. On the following day, in a *Pravda* editorial entitled "The April Theses," he outlined the Bolshevik strategy for seizing political power, by force if necessary. In late May Leon Trotsky arrived from the United States and later joined Lenin at the top of the Bolshevik leadership.

Considering the overall Russian situation, the war, and the disintegrating economy, it now appears that the provisional government was fortunate to last as long as it did. In late April of 1917, after Foreign Minister Miliukov publicly vowed that Russia would continue her war effort, there were demonstrations in Petrograd. The government fell, and in the new coalition Kerensky became minister of war. A gifted orator, he traveled to the front to explain to the troops the need for an offensive operation so that Russia might secure a strong place at a future peace conference. The offensive took place in late June against the Austrians in Galicia. A German counterattack routed the Russians, causing the collapse of the entire southwestern front. The news of this new military disaster coincided with the "July Days," in which Bolsheviks and other radicals attempted to seize control of the government. The provisional government responded by jailing most of the Bolshevik leaders, except for Lenin, who went into hiding in Finland. In the new coalition, Kerensky became head of the provisional government.

In early autumn promonarchist elements attempted to undo the revolution. In August, General Lavr Kornilov, a military hero and darling of the antirevolutionary generals, was appointed commander of the Russian army in order to restore discipline. In early September, after the Germans captured Riga, leaving Petrograd undefended, Kornilov was asked to dispatch a cavalry division to defend the capital. As the troops proceeded toward Petrograd, there was panic within both the government and Soviet at the thought of a Kornilov dictatorship. Trotsky, who was released from jail, was called upon to defend the revolution by arming the Red Guard (soldiers, sailors, and workers sympathetic to the Bolsheviks). At the same time revolutionary workers and Bolshevik propagandists halted the trains well before they reached the capital and persuaded the tired and hungry soldiers to go home. The danger from the Right had evaporated.

The autumn saw a further deterioration of the conditions of life in Russia, especially in the cities. Food shortages and a collapse of the ruble kept Petrograd volatile. In late September the Bolsheviks turned on their propaganda full force with the slogan of "peace, bread, and land" and "all power to the Soviets." In early October Trotsky was elected chairman of the Petrograd Soviet. In the wake of the Kornilov affair the government coalition fell, and it was not until 6 October that Kerensky was able to form a new government with a socialist majority. Moreover, to fend off the growing Bolshevik surge, Kerensky on 27 September declared Russia a republic and started arrangements for a constitutional assembly.

It was far too late for such measures. On 16 October, in a secret meeting, the Bolshevik leadership voted to seize the government. A political bureau (politburo) was set up in which Lenin was to continue as the political leader, while Trotsky was to coordinate the military operation. On 7 November a congress of Soviets (local socialist councils that had sprung up all over Russia) was meeting in Petrograd. On that day Red Guards occupied strategic positions in the city and arrested members of the provisional government. Kerensky escaped and, having failed to gather military support, fled abroad. In the evening, the last remnants of the opposition, having taken up positions in the Winter Palace, surrendered to the Bolsheviks. At 20:00, with Trotsky presiding over the Congress of Soviets, Lenin marched into the hall and announced the new government. The Communist era had begun.

John W. Bohon

References

Florinsky, Michael T. *Russia, A History and an Interpretation*. 2 vols. New York: Macmillan, 1953.

Lincoln, W. Bruce. *Passage through Armageddeon: The Russians at War and in Revolution, 1914–1918*. New York: Simon and Schuster, 1986.

See also ALEXANDRA FEODOROVNA; GOREMYKIN, IVAN; GUCHKOV, ALEKSANDR; KERENSKY, ALEKSANDR; KORNILOV, LAVR; LENIN, VLADIMIR; LVOV, PRINCE GEORGI; MILIUKOV, PAVEL; NICHOLAS II; POLIVANOV, ALEKSEI; RASPUTIN, GRIGORII; RUSSIA, CIVIL WAR IN; STURMER, BORIS; TROTSKY, LEON

Russia, Navy

Despite her vast size modern Russia was not a naval power. Landlocked by ice and surrounded by enemies, whenever Russia did venture into naval warfare it ended in disaster, as it had at the hands of the Japanese in 1905. After that war the Russian navy, like the army, needed restructuring. Under her capable commander, Admiral Nikola von Essen, a new training program was implemented to restore morale. A major construction program was also begun in order to equip the navy with modern dreadnoughts, although that program was still under way in August of 1914.

Since the mid-nineteenth century, when she had expanded into East Asia, Russia had maintained three fleets. One was at Vladivostok on the Pacific, which was ice-bound six months a year. Because the Russian Pacific fleet had been destroyed by the Japanese in 1904–5, and as many of the German ships in that region were interned by the Japanese, naval warfare in East Asia played no part in World War I.

Since the reign of Peter the Great (1682–1725), Russia had been a Baltic power and had kept a fleet at the naval bases of Krondstadt and Sveaborg. The capital of St. Petersburg was

Russia's foremost seaport. Although in 1914 Germany controlled the exit to the North Sea, within the Baltic Sea itself Russia had naval superiority. The Russian fleet was built around four old predreadnought battleships (with three dreadnoughts under construction in Baltic shipyards). Russia also possessed several excellent cruisers, destroyers, and auxiliary ships. Commanded by Admiral A.I. Nepenin, the Russian Baltic fleet engaged in a war of attrition that was by nature defensive. In naval war games shortly before the war, the Russians had concluded that the Germans were fully capable of landing troops on Russian soil and capturing St. Petersburg. Consequently, the Russians, who manufactured the world's best naval mines, laid extensive mine fields off their coast.

War in the Baltic consisted mainly of naval patrols. Occasionally a ship was hit when two opposing squadrons caught sight of each other. Most naval losses were the result of mines, storms, and ships running aground in foggy weather. By the end of the war, submarines had begun to play an important role in the Baltic.

The other major Russian naval presence was in the Black Sea, at the Crimean base at Sevastopol. Although Russia had long enjoyed a naval advantage over the Turks, the balance was shifted with the arrival of the German battle cruiser *Goeben* and light cruiser *Breslau*. In October the *Goeben*, recently purchased by Turkey but still manned by a German crew, shelled Sevastopol, Odessa, and other Russian ports. When Turkey refused to renounce this aggressive act, Russia declared war on the Ottoman Empire on 2 November. The results were immediate. The Straits were closed, effectively isolating Russia from her allies. Moreover, Admiral Souchon was made head of the Turkish navy, which he molded into a credible force.

The Russian Black Sea fleet contained three old battleships (with three dreadnoughts under construction), two excellent cruisers, and nine new destroyers. The two missions of this force were to support Russian armies operating in the Caucasus by interdicting Turkish supply convoys and to help her allies force the Straits. The latter goal resulted in the mismanaged Allied campaign at Gallipoli. The Russians had greater success against the Turkish convoys sailing along the southern Black Sea shore to Tribizond and other ports. These supply ships were absolutely necessary to Turkish operations in the Caucasus because of the lack of roads in that area. As in the Baltic, war in the Black Sea took the form of naval patrols. In January of 1915 the cruiser *Breslau* was seriously damaged, and also in that month fifty Turkish merchant ships were lost. Later that year two Russian dreadnoughts, the *Imparatritsa Mariia* and the *Ekaterina II*, joined the Russian fleet, giving it clear superiority in the Black Sea (on 22 October 1916 the *Imparatritsa Mariia* sank in the port of Sevastopol when an ammunition dump blew up).

Finally, in July of 1916, young Admiral A.V. Kolchak was sent from the Baltic to assume command of the Black Sea fleet. An expert on naval mines, he used them effectively to neutralize the enemy.

Also limiting the scope of Russian naval operations was her dependence on supplies from abroad. With the Straits closed, that left only two other possibilities: Vladivostok on the Pacific, 7,000 miles from the war zone; and the Arctic ports of Murmansk and Archangel, which were of limited use because of ice but were nevertheless developed as supply bases.

Growing disaffection and disillusionment in Russia spread to the navy. Mutinies had broken out as early as 1915 on inactive ships, although these were quickly crushed. The March Revolution of 1917 reignited unrest in the navy base at Kronstadt and the inactive fleet at Helingsfors; some 120 loyal czarist officers were killed. During the period of the provisional government the Russian navy was a hotbed of Bolshevik activity. Radical sailors provided support for Bolshevik activities ashore and some ships even shelled government supporters during the November Revolution. In the Bolshevik consolidation of power the navy was virtually ignored. A naval rebellion in 1921 was brutally crushed, and not until Stalin was in power did the navy undergo resurgence.

John W. Bohon

References

Eller, Rear Admiral Ernest M. *The Soviet Sea Challenge.* Chicago: Henry Regnery, 1972.

Mitchell, Donald W. *A History of Russian and Soviet Sea Power.* New York: Macmillan, 1975.

Pavlovich, N.B., ed. *The Fleet in the First World War.* Tr. New Delhi: Amerind Publishing Co., for the Smithsonian Institution, 1979.

See also ESSEN, NIKOLAI VON; *GOEBEN* AND *BRESLAU*

Ruzsky, Nikolai Vladimirovich (1854–1918)

Russian infantry general. Born into a Russian noble family on 18 March 1854, Ruzsky was a graduate of the Konstantinovsky Military College (1872) and the General Staff Academy (1881). He saw service in the Russo-Turkish War (1877–78), was deputy chief of staff for the Kiev Military District (1896–1902), and served as chief of staff of the Second Manchurian Army during the Russo-Japanese War.

Ruzsky's career is characterized by an erratic style of field command that could be imperceptive and slow, or quick and energetic. Self-centered and politically well connected, Ruzsky was frequently ill. In the 1914 Galician campaign he advanced slowly, ignoring orders of front commander General Nikolai Ivanov to turn north and assist retreating Russian forces battling the Austrians. Instead, Ruzsky marched his men toward Lemberg in hopes of capturing it.

In mid-September 1914 Ruzsky assumed command of the Northwest Front, where he participated in battle near Thorn. In March of 1915 he resigned that post and took over the Sixth Army. In the winter of 1916 he was given command of the northern front.

In March of 1917 Czar Nicholas II was stranded at Ruzsky's headquarters at Pskov, where Ruzsky pressured the czar into abdicating. Ruzsky acted as the spokesman for the army and arbitrated the abdication, something he later said he regretted.

After the March 1917 Revolution Ruzsky was removed from command and subsequently fled to the Caucasus. He was arrested by Bolshevik forces and executed by decapitation at Piatogorsk on 19 October 1918.

Tom Zucconi

References

Golovine, N.N. *The Russian Army in the World War*. New Haven: Yale University Press, 1931.

Herwig, Holger, and Neil M. Heyman. *Biographical Dictionary of World War I*. Westport, Conn.: Greenwood, 1982.

Knox, Major General Sir Alfred. *With the Russian Army, 1914–1917*. 2 vols. London: Hutchinson, 1921.

Stone, Norman. *The Eastern Front 1914–1917*. London: Hodder and Stoughton, 1975.

Wieczynski, Joseph L., ed. *Modern Encyclopedia of Russian and Soviet History*. Vol. 32. Gulf Breeze, Fla.: Academic International Press, 1983.

See also NICHOLAS II; RUSSIA, CIVIL WAR IN

S

Salandra, Antonio (1853–1931)

Italian politician and premier, 1914–16, born at Troia in the southern Italian province of Puglia on 13 August 1853. Salandra began his career as a professor of law at the University of Rome and later headed the ministries of agriculture (1899–1900), foreign affairs, and finance (1906, 1909–10).

An arrogant and difficult character, Salandra believed in a strong state and favored Italy's alliance with Germany and Austria. Although he had no secure majority when he became premier in March of 1914, the interventionist fervor in the country gave him the tool he needed to defeat Giovani Giolitti's efforts to keep Italy out of the war and to consolidate his government in May of 1915. A practitioner of *trasformismo,* which allowed a small elite to rule Italy, he saw secret treaties, not public opinion, as the key to preparing a successful war. He was convinced that he had only to consult his foreign minister, Sidney Sonnino, and the king to decide whether Italy should enter the war. Although indebted to the interventionists, Salandra appointed none to his ministry, except for the irredentist Salvatore Barzilai, after the king promised his support on 16 May.

When he had taken over the foreign ministry on 18 October 1914, following the death of Marchese Antonio di San Giuliano, Salandra had enunciated a policy of *sacro egoismo,* which excluded all actions that did not directly benefit Italy. Although all other powers also pursued their own interests, they clothed their intentions and actions in euphemism, and Salandra's public espousal of such a selfish policy made Italy appear to be more mean-spirited and rapacious than other states.

When he was attacked for his conduct of the war following an Austrian advance in the Trentino in May of 1916, Salandra blamed Luigi Cadorna and the military, as well as left-wing interventionists embittered by his refusal to include them in his government, and neutralists resentful of his defeat of Giolitti in 1915. He claimed that he then forced a vote of confidence because his nerves were frayed, his relations with parliament and Cadorna were strained, and because of the urgent need to broaden the base of his coalition. He lost the vote of confidence, 197 to 158, and was replaced by the seventy-eight-year-old Paolo Boselli. Only five ministers, including Sonnino and Orlando, survived Salandra's fall, while nineteen were replaced. Salandra died in Rome on 9 December 1931. Like Cadorna, he has come to be associated with the more negative aspects of Italy's war effort.

James J. Sadkovich

References

Melograni, Piero. *Storia politica della grande guerra.* Bari: Laterza, 1971.

Salandra, Antonio. *Dal patto di Londra alla pace di Roma.* Turin: Gobetti, 1925.

———. *Memorie Politiche, 1916–1925.* Milan: Garzanti, 1951.

Salvemini, Gaetano. *La politica estera italiana dal 1871 al 1915.* Milan: Feltrinelli, 1970.

Vigezzi, Brunello. *Da Giolitti a Salandra.* Florence: Vallecchi, 1969.

See also CADORNA, LUIGI; ITALY, HOME FRONT

Salonika Campaign, 1915

On 22 September 1915 Czar Ferdinand of Bulgaria, recently allied with Austria and Germany, ordered the mobilization of the Bulgarian army in preparation to attack Serbia. Bulgaria's mobilization directly affected Greece, which was bound to Serbia by a 1913 treaty that stipulated that if either country were attacked by Bulgaria, Greece would supply 90,000 troops and Serbia 150,000. In September of 1915 Greece's Germanophile King Constantine believed that Greece was not obligated to fulfill its terms of the treaty because Serbia, faced with an Austro-German attack in the north, could not supply 150,000 troops needed to fight Bulgaria. But Greece's pro-Entente premier, Eleutherios Venizelos, asked France and England to supply the 150,000 men. Venizelos assured the Allies that if they did so, Greece would honor her commitments to Serbia. England and France immediately ordered one division each currently stationed at the Dardanelles be sent to the Greek port of Salonika. No sooner had the orders been sent, however, than on 1 October Venizelos informed the Allies that he could not authorize an Allied landing at Salonika. Venizelos's pro-Entente policy was meeting resistance from Constantine and the pro-German Greek military.

On 5 October British and French leaders met at Calais to determine the Allies' future Balkan policy. France agreed to commit three divisions to Salonika, while England agreed to send five divisions. British War Minister Lord Horatio Kitchener made it plain that England would send five divisions to Salonika, not to offer immediate military assistance to Serbia, but in response to Venizelos's earlier request that if the Allies supplied 150,000 troops, Greece would honor its prewar treaty with Serbia. Therefore, when the five British divisions arrived at Salonika, they were to remain there until Greece had irrevocably committed herself to the Entente. French War Minister Alexandre Millerand, on the other hand, declared that French troops, once disembarking at Salonika, would immediately strike northward into Serbia without waiting either for English assistance or for Greece to forgo her neutrality.

There was also disagreement in Greece. On 5 October, as the first French and British troops from Gallipoli were disembarking at Salonika and on the very day when the Allies were disagreeing at Calais on the exact role of the Salonika campaign, Venizelos was forced to resign. Constantine and his general staff reaffirmed Greece's intention to remain neutral. Emboldened by Greece's declaration of neutrality, Bulgaria attacked eastern Serbia on 7 October, while Austro-German troops attacked from the north. Serbia faced a hopeless situation.

Despite the sudden turn of events in Greece, the disunity within the Allied camp, and the illegal act of landing troops in a neutral country, the French government was determined to undertake a Balkan campaign: Serbia had to be saved in order to prevent the establishment of communications between Turkey and the Central Powers, and the presence of Allied troops in the Balkans could possibly encourage neutralist Romania to join the Entente camp.

There was another reason why the French government of René Viviani had to undertake a Balkan campaign: the relationship between General Maurice Sarrail and French domestic politics. Sarrail had been removed by commander-in-chief General Joseph Joffre in late July of 1915 as commander of the Third Army in the Argonne. Sarrail was the most politically powerful general in the French army. His support came from the political Left, which made it clear in mid-1915 that if France's wartime domestic political truce—the *union sacrée*—were to be maintained, Sarrail must be given a prominent command, and that he must have the resources necessary for victory. The French government appointed Sarrail commander of the French forces at Salonika and on 6 October ordered him to depart immediately for Salonika with one division. At the same time two French divisions at the Dardanelles were directed to sail for Salonika. These three divisions were all that Joffre, a "Westerner," would commit to the Balkans. If Joffre were hostile to a Balkan campaign, so was England. On 6 October the British cabinet considered it foolhardy to send Allied forces northward into Serbia without the support of Greece, which had a pro-German king and a pro-German government. In an obvious repudiation of its agreement with France, taken twenty-four hours earlier at Calais, Britain decided that no British troops, except the single division that had been dispatched from the Dardanelles, would be sent to Salonika.

The Viviani government was caught in a bind. Domestic political pressure intensified in mid-October as left-wing deputies, who had saved Sarrail in July and had forced the government to give him a new command, now demanded that his army be supplied with adequate forces. Apprised by Viviani of the intense pressure generated by Sarrail's political supporters, Joffre now realized in late October that if these demands were not satisfied the Viviani government would collapse and consequently his position would be at stake. Joffre, who for months had resisted all attempts to undertake large-scale operations in the Dardanelles and in the Balkans, now went to London and pleaded that it send four more divisions to Salonika. Joffre made it known that his retention as commander in chief of the French army, and even the Alliance itself, was at stake. London yielded, and on 30 October Kitchener agreed to send four additional divisions to Salonika with the understanding that, if communications with the Serbian army were not opened and maintained, the Allied forces would be withdrawn.

Joffre had succeeded in his mission. Before he could return to Paris with his victory, Viviani had resigned and Aristide Briand had formed a new government. Both Premier Briand and his war minister, General Joseph Gallieni, were longtime advocates of a massive Balkan campaign, and in the autumn of 1915 only a government headed by Easterners could have preserved the *union sacrée*.

Meanwhile, in the Balkans, Sarrail's attempts to link up with the Serbs failed. On 22 October the Bulgarians advanced across the railway south of Uskub and severed communications between the Serbian army and Salonika. Three weeks later when Sarrail's withdrawal to Salonika was under way and it had become obvious that Serbia could not be saved, the British government, in accordance with the 30 October agreement, recommended that Salonika be evacuated. Briand, however, was determined to remain at Salonika. Not to do so would have led to another domestic political crisis, for Sarrail's political friends would have equated disengagement with defeat. Briand, however, presented his reasons for staying at Salonika in diplomatic and military terms: First, Italy and Russia had aspirations in the region, and if France and England allowed Germany to have a free hand in the region, the Entente's solidarity would be greatly endangered; second, the 150,000 Allied troops would not only protect Salonika but would keep 400,000 Bulgar-German troops pinned down in the Balkans. When London again balked, Briand arranged to have Joffre appointed commander in chief of all French armies. Previously, Sarrail had taken his orders directly from the war ministry; now his Eastern Army was under Joffre's control. With Joffre directly responsible for the fate of Sarrail's army at Salonika, England capitulated. On 9 December Kitchener agreed that the Allies should remain at Salonika. Briand had now emerged with his greatest wartime diplomatic triumph. The French and British high commands were now committed to a campaign that both detested.

Jan Karl Tanenbaum

References

Cassar, George H. *The French and the Dardanelles: A Study in Failure in the Conduct of War*. London: Allen and Unwin, 1971.

Tanenbaum, Jan Karl. *General Maurice Sarrail, 1856–1929; The French Army and Left-Wing Politics*. Chapel Hill: University of North Carolina Press, 1974.

See also BALKAN FRONT, 1915, 1916, 1917; CONSTANTINE I; GREECE; JOFFRE, JOSEPH; SARRAIL, MAURICE; SERBIA; VENIZELOS, ELEUTHERIOS

Samson, Charles Rumney (1883–1931)

British naval aviation pioneer, born on 8 July 1883 at Crumpsall, Manchester. Samson entered the Royal Navy in 1899 and in 1911 became a certified pilot. His prewar pioneering aviation work included seaplane experiments, cross-country night flights, flying from both a stationary and steaming ship, aerial wireless communication, and air bombardment.

During World War I Samson contributed to the development of tactical aviation. In 1914 aircraft under his command flew reconnaissance missions, bombed zeppelin sheds in Cologne and Dusseldorf, and attacked gun emplacements, submarine depots, and seaplane positions along the Belgian coast. In the Gallipoli Campaign they spotted for naval gunfire, hit Turkish communications, flew ground-support missions, and provided air cover for the evacuation from the peninsula. Later, he conducted antisubmarine and reconnaissance patrols in the eastern Mediterranean and Indian Ocean. In 1917 Samson was based in Great Yarmouth and charged with conducting antisubmarine and antizeppelin operations over the North Sea, while continuing experiments with aircraft taking off from vessels.

After the war, in 1919 Samson transferred to the Royal Air Force. Promoted to air commodore in 1922, he retired in 1929. His major postwar achievement was the round-trip flight of a bomber formation from Cairo to Capetown, a precursor to similar commercial aviation on the continent. Samson wrote two books: *Flights and Flight* (1930) and *Flight from Cairo to Capetown and Back* (1931). He died on 5 February 1931 at Cholderton, Wiltshire.

Donald F. Bittner

References

Baddeley, Vincent W. "Samson, Charles Rumney." *Dictionary of National Biography, 1931–1940.*

Marder, Arthur J. *From the Dreadnought to Scapa Flow.* Vols. 1–5. Oxford: Oxford University Press, 1961–70.

The Times (London), 6 and 11 February 1931.

Samsonov, Aleksandr Vasilevich (1859–1914)

Russian general, born on 14 November 1859. Samsonov completed the Nikolaevsky Cavalry College in 1877 at age eighteen and immediately went off to fight the Turks. In 1884 he graduated from the General Staff Academy. He was a general at forty-three and commanded first a brigade and then a division in the Russo-Japanese War. After 1909, in semimilitary retirement, he was employed by the Russian government as governor of Turkestan. When the First World War began Samsonov was on sick leave in the Caucasus.

The Russian General Staff patched together an offensive against East Prussia. General Yakov Zhilinsky, commander of the northern front, was to coordinate a giant pincer movement. The northern army was given to General Pavel Rennenkampf and the southern one to Samsonov, recalled to full active duty. Even at the time Samsonov was described as "a simple, kindly man" who had had difficulty in commanding even a single unit in 1905. He possessed neither the experience nor the capability of leading an army of thirteen divisions. Moreover, having arrived at Second Army Headquarters in Warsaw only on 12 August 1914, he was unfamiliar with both his staff officers and division commanders. Reportedly, he had doubts about the offensive.

On 20 August, three days after Rennenkampf had started his drive to the north, Samsonov entered East Prussia to the south, in the Masurian Lakes region. Terrain in that desolate area was soft sand, making horse transport difficult and offering no opportunity to forage for food, which the Russian troops found essential because of the breakdown of their own supply trains. Although Samsonov's units reached their initial goal before the lakes, his northernmost unit, VI Corps, under General Blagoveshinsky, was unable to establish contact with Rennenkampf's army to the north. As a result, the Germans succeeded in isolating Samsonov at Tannenberg. Early on the morning of 26 August the Germans struck Samsonov's exposed northern flank, and on the following day his southern flank.

Rennenkampf, with his own force of 200,000 men, remained oblivious to Samsonov's plight and never answered Samsonov's urgent pleas for assistance. Finally, on the 28th, Second Army was surrounded. Samsonov quit his own headquarters after having issued orders for his units to try to get back to Russia as best they could. He mounted his horse and, along with his staff, visited his units. As the German pincers closed around Samsonov's army, which was now under constant artillery fire, at approximately 01:00 on 30 August Samsonov committed suicide. While he had failings in higher command, Samsonov was, above all, the victim of incompetence at higher headquarters.

John W. Bohon

References

Gurko, General Basil. *War and Revolution in Russia 1914–1917.* New York: Macmillan, 1919.

Showalter, Dennis E. *Tannenberg, Clash of Empires.* Hamden, Conn.: Archon, 1991.

See also EAST PRUSSIA CAMPAIGN; RENNENKAMPF, PAVEL; ZHILINSKY, YAKOV

Sarrail, Maurice (1856–1929)

French army commander, born in Carcassonne on 6 April 1856. Sarrail graduated from Saint Cyr in 1877. Unlike his fellow officers, who tended to be politically and religiously conservative, Sarrail was a free thinker, an anticlerical Republican, and married to a Protestant. These views did not go unnoticed. When the political Left took power in 1901 in the aftermath of the Dreyfus Affair, Sarrail's military career blossomed: Promotions and prestigious appointments were quickly forthcoming. By 1914 Sarrail was the most politically powerful general in the French army.

As commander of the Third Army, Sarrail played a distinguished role during the First Battle of the Marne. Attacked by the German Crown Prince's army, Sarrail rejected commander in chief General Joseph Joffre's orders to fall back and clung to the Verdun pivot without losing touch with the Fourth Army. By stopping the major German thrust at Revigny, Third Army contributed to the victory of the Marne.

In July of 1915 Sarrail was less fortunate. Joffre dismissed him because of minor setbacks in the Argonne. But Sarrail's left-wing political supporters demanded that he be given a prominent command. The French government, as a means to maintain domestic political harmony, overrode Joffre's decision for the first time during the war: It not only appointed Sarrail commander of the newly created Eastern Army, but decided that France should open a new campaign in the Balkans as well.

Sarrail's major accomplishment in the Balkans was the capture of Monastir in 1916. The failure to advance further led to his recall in 1917. When the Left returned to power in 1924, Sarrail was appointed high commissioner to Syria. He died in Paris on 23 March 1929.

Jan Karl Tanenbaum

References

Cassar, George H. *The French and the Dardanelles: A Study in Failure in the Conduct of War.* London: Allen and Unwin, 1971.

King, Jere Clemens. *Generals and Politicians: Conflict between France's High Command, Parliament and Government, 1914–1918.* Berkeley: University of California Press, 1951.

Tanenbaum, Jan Karl. *General Maurice Sarrail, 1856–1929: The French Army and Left-Wing Politics.* Chapel Hill: University of North Carolina Press, 1974.

See also BALKAN FRONT, 1916, 1917; JOFFRE, JOSEPH; MARNE, FIRST BATTLE OF

Sazonov, Sergei Dmitrievich (1860–1927)

Russian foreign minister (1910–16), born to a noble family in Riazan Province on 29 July 1860. Sazonov entered the Russian foreign service in 1883. He then served in such posts as Paris, Washington, and London. In 1910 Sazonov was appointed foreign minister, replacing the opportunistic A.P. Izvolsky, who had been discredited by his role in the Bosnia-Herzegovina Crisis of 1908. Described as a deeply religious man of simple thought, Sazonov was timid and pliable and understood neither the complexities of the international scene nor the internal conditions of Russia. At his best Sazonov was a conscientious and well-meaning official, but he had neither the vision nor the character to lead Russia through the crisis that arose in 1914.

Sazonov owed his rapid rise to his marriage to a sister of Prime Minister Peter Stolypin's wife. Thus, from a minor post as the Russian representative to the Vatican, Sazonov became assistant foreign minister in 1909 and minister the following year. With the assassination of Stolypin in October of 1911 under unusual circumstances with possible pan-Slav implications, Sazonov, contemplating some sort of Rightist conspiracy, became even more unsure of himself and unable to make hard decisions.

As foreign minister Sazonov was involved in many areas of Russia's international relations, but it was the Balkans that set off the conflagration of 1914. Sazonov was himself opposed to any Balkan adventure that might lead to war; in attempting to preserve the status quo, however, he was undercut by pan-Slav circles in both the army and at court, and especially by Russia's two fervid pronationalist ambassadors to Serbia and Bulgaria, N. Hartwig and A. Neklidov. In 1912 a Serbian-Bulgarian pact was signed that gave Russia the right to mediate any differences between the two nations. Later that same year the Balkan League (Bulgaria, Serbia, Montenegro, Romania, and Greece) went to war against Turkey, driving the Ottoman Empire out of Europe. In 1913 the members of the Balkan League fell out over a division of the spoils, and in the ensuing war Bulgaria was stripped of her newly won territories. Finally, in December of 1913, Sir Edward Grey, the English foreign minister, presided over a Balkan conference in London during which Sazonov and his Austrian counterpart, Leopold von Berchtold, agreed to try to preserve the Balkan status quo.

By early 1914, despite Sazonov's attempts to moderate the Balkan fires, the situation was largely out of his hands. Duma president M.V.

Rodzianko was urging the czar to seize Constantinople, while Hartwig and Neklidov made inflammatory speeches in Belgrade and Sofia. Then, on 28 June Austrian Archduke Franz Ferdinand was assassinated in Sarajevo. Austria saw the assassination as an opportunity to eliminate Serbia, in which she obtained German backing. But even well into July there was little thought in Europe's capitals that this would lead to war. Sazonov's immediate reaction to the Austrian ultimatum to Serbia was that it meant war. Yet, he advised Serbia to accept as many of the demands as possible and remain calm. But by that time the initiative had passed from diplomatic to military hands. Mobilization orders were issued, and by 4 August the major participants were at war.

During the war, relations among the three Allies were occasionally strained. The personal relationships, however, among Maurice Paleologue, the French ambassador to Petersburg, his British counterpart, Sir George Buchanan, and Sazonov kept these rifts from getting out of hand. While Sazonov urged vigorous action against Turkey and an earnest attempt to bring Bulgaria into the war on the side of Russia, his advice went unheeded. Then, in the purge of 1916, the empress and Rasputin had Sazonov dismissed. He was given the post of ambassador to London, but the March Revolution intervened before he could accept. He later represented the anti-Bolshevik Whites at the Paris Peace Conference. Sazonov died on 25 December 1927. Despite his shortcomings he was one of the ablest ministers on the scene.

John W. Bohon

References

Florinsky, Michael. *Russia, A History and an Interpretation.* 2 vols. New York: Macmillan, 1953.

Pares, Sir Bernard. *The Fall of the Russian Monarchy.* New York, 1939.

Sazonov, Sergei D. *The Fateful Years.* London: J. Cape, 1928.

See also OUTBREAK OF THE FIRST WORLD WAR; RUSSIA, HOME FRONT AND REVOLUTIONS OF 1917

Scandinavia: Denmark, Norway, and Sweden

On the outbreak of war in 1914 many European states—including the Netherlands, Switzerland, and Spain—sought to remain neutral. The Scandinavian states were no exception. They had no national aspirations to satisfy through war and could indeed be seriously hurt by participation in it.

In December of 1914, on the Swedish government's invitation, the kings of Denmark, Norway, and Sweden (Christian X, Haakon VII, and Gustavus V, respectively), met at Malmö to discuss ways to maintain their neutrality. The meeting led to improved relations, especially between Sweden and Norway, which had been acrimonious since their 1905 break. Another such meeting occurred in 1917 in Christiania.

The Scandinavian states were able to maintain their neutrality during the war, although they were forced to accept indignities in the form of Allied restrictions on their trade as a result of the British blockade of Germany. One beneficial effect of the war was heightened interest among the Scandinavian states in cooperation and collective security. Ironically, two of the three states gained territory from the war. Domestically, all three states continued democratization and were in the forefront of progressive legislation, such as granting women the right to vote.

Denmark

The outbreak of the First World War caused great anxiety in Denmark. On 1 August the *Rigsdag,* or parliament, mobilized emergency forces of some 70,000 men. On the 5th Germany demanded to know whether Denmark would lay mines in the Skagerrak to block passage from Danish waters into the Baltic Sea. The Germans implied that if the Danes did not do so, they would. Denmark reluctantly decided to lay the mines, and even London recognized the necessity for the action.

In 1915 the *Rigsdag* passed legislation granting universal suffrage; it came into effect in 1918. In 1916 Denmark sold the Danish West Indies (Virgin Islands) to the United States for $25 million. This decision sparked considerable opposition but was confirmed by a plebiscite in December. In November of 1918 Denmark granted full sovereignty to Iceland. Although some affairs were to be handled jointly, the country was united with Denmark only in the person of the monarch, King Christian X.

The war played havoc with an economy that relied heavily on foreign trade. German unrestricted submarine warfare in 1917 and the more stringent British blockade caused serious difficulties and forced the government to introduce relief legislation and attempt to control prices.

Denmark profited from the First World War territorially. A plebiscite in February and March of 1920, provided for by the Treaty of Versailles, resulted in the return to Denmark from Germany of northern Schleswig. It was officially incorporated into the kingdom that July.

Norway

In 1907 Norway had secured a treaty signed by Germany, Britain, and France guaranteeing her neutrality, but Norway also took steps to improve her own defenses by building up her armed forces and starting a navy. On the outbreak of the First World War Norway proclaimed its neutrality. It also announced that it was prepared to fight to maintain that neutrality and mobilized its coastal defense forces and navy. National sentiment was, however, overwhelmingly pro-Entente. This increased after shipping losses to submarine warfare.

The British naval blockade of Germany affected Norway. The British were concerned about Norwegian fish exports to Germany. At first they simply outbid the Germans for them. Later, the British threatened to halt export of coal and oil to Norway unless the trade were halted. Finally a secret agreement was worked out providing for the British to buy Norwegian fish at maximum prices, providing that Norway cut her exports to Germany to a minimum. British economic pressure also caused Norway to halt export of copper ore, which brought German protests.

During the first two years of the war Norway benefited economically from the conflict. That changed in the last two years of the war, with German unrestricted submarine warfare and British determination to hold down expenses. In the first half of 1917 Norway suffered heavy losses of merchant ships and lives to submarine attacks. There was sentiment for arming merchant ships but, in the end, an arrangement was worked out with the British providing for British vessels to carry cargoes between the two nations while a similar number of Norwegian vessels would be chartered by the British and sail under their flag.

By 1918 Norwegian economic conditions had deteriorated to the point that the government imposed rationing. In April of 1918 Norway signed a trading arrangement with the United States whereby it agreed to a big cut in its trade with Germany in return for imports from the United States.

In September of 1919 the Allied Supreme Council awarded Norway sovereignty over the island of Spitsbergen, which Norway annexed in February of 1920.

Sweden

On the outbreak of the war there was widespread belief in Sweden that a treaty bound her to Germany. While that proved erroneous, a small group of activists did urge intervention on the German side. Other Swedes favored the Allies, but the vast majority of the population demanded neutrality. The government issued such a declaration, while at the same time trying to prevent any military operations within Swedish territorial waters.

Sweden's position was made precarious by the Allied naval blockade against Germany. As the blockade intensified, the British detained more Swedish goods. Stockholm did work out arrangements with both sides for compensation for the right to transport goods. Britain wanted to send goods to Russia through Sweden; the Swedish government granted such transport licenses in return for the right to import certain products, including foodstuffs, from the West. In 1915, however, the Swedish government banned the transport of arms and war materials across its frontiers.

Financial demands occasioned by the war led the Swedish government to pass legislation authorizing it to impose price controls for food and other necessities (a maximum price for grain was imposed for the first time in November of 1915). In 1916 the government imposed rationing of sugar, a procedure later extended even to potatoes. Stockholm set up a War Insurance Commission to provide state-aided insurance for shipping losses at sea. During the war the Swedes lost 280 merchant ships, most sunk by submarines but others by mines. Other government commissions oversaw the importation of food, reported on industry, and carried out provisions of the war trade laws.

German naval control of the Baltic ensured the continuous flow of Swedish iron ore and other vital Scandinavian exports to Germany. It also influenced Swedish policy toward Germany. Before the war Sweden had imported more than 90 percent of her coal from England;

by 1916–17 it was about 26 percent, with Germany making up the difference.

By 1916 the British and French refusal to honor the Declaration of London regarding neutral trade, German intensification of the submarine campaign, the closed areas of the North Sea, and the Allied blockade all produced a situation at variance with international law. In the spring of 1916 negotiations between Stockholm and London led to an arrangement whereby the Allies guaranteed Sweden the right to import certain products, including grain, in return for the release of Entente vessels trapped in the Baltic.

The Allies also requisitioned Swedish vessels. Finally, in the spring of 1918, an arrangement was worked out whereby the Entente allowed Sweden to import large amounts of goods. In return, Sweden had to hand over merchant vessels amounting to 400,000 tons dead weight, promise the Entente a certain proportion of her iron-ore export, grant larger credits for goods purchased by the Entente powers in Sweden, and accept stricter regulations on goods exported to Germany.

At the end of the war a number of Swedes (and Danes) volunteered, along with Finns, to fight on the Estonian side against Red Army invaders. The Swedes were particularly sympathetic to Finnish efforts to wrest their independence from Russia. Although Stockholm was fearful of being drawn into the conflict, a brigade of Swedish volunteers, also including Danes and Norwegians, did fight on the Finnish side in the winter of 1918–19. When in December of 1917 the Aaland Islands voted to separate from Russia and join Sweden, the Swedes sent a warship and a small troop contingent. These were withdrawn when the islands became the German base for military support to the Finns. In 1921 the League of Nations assigned the Aaland Islands to Finland, with the proviso that they be demilitarized.

The Swedish Red Cross was also very active during the conflict. It inspected prison camps of both sides, distributed supplies to the prisoners, and arranged for the exchange of invalided prisoners and their safe passage across Sweden.

Spencer C. Tucker

References
Denmark
Jones, W. Glyn. *Denmark: A Modern History.* London: Croom Helm, 1986.

Rying, Bent. *Danish in the South and North; Denmark: A History.* Copenhagen: Royal Danish Ministry of Foreign Affairs, 1981.

Norway
Larsen, Karen. *A History of Norway.* Princeton: Princeton University Press, 1950.
Popperwell, Ronald G. *Norway.* New York: Praeger, 1972.
Riste, Olav. *The Neutral Ally: Norway's Relations with Belligerent Powers in the First World War.* Oslo: Universitetsforlaget, 1965.

Sweden
Abrahamsen, Samuel. *Sweden's Foreign Policy.* Washington, D.C.: Public Affairs Press, 1957.
Anderson, Ingvar. *A History of Sweden.* Translated by Carolyn Hannay. New York: Praeger, 1968.
Svanstrom, Ragnar, and Carl F. Palmstierna. *A Short History of Sweden.* Oxford: Clarendon, 1989.

See also CHRISTIAN X

Scapa Flow, Scuttling of German Fleet (21 June 1919)

As the Allies prepared armistice terms in November of 1918, a chief concern was the German navy. On 4 November the Allied Supreme War Council agreed on the naval terms of the Armistice. It included surrender of all submarines, continuation of the blockade, sweeping of minefields, and disarmament and internment of a certain number of surface ships under Allied surveillance, with only care and maintenance parties on board. The latter would consist of ten battleships, six battle cruisers, eight light cruisers (of which two would be minelayers), and fifty of the most modern destroyers. All other German ships were to be concentrated at German naval bases, where they too were to be disarmed under Allied supervision.

On 13 November the British government decided that the seventy-four specified ships would be interned at Scapa Flow in the Orkney Islands. On 17 November the Germans were informed only that they would sail these designated disarmed ships to the Firth of Forth. The

190 German submarines would all go to British ports for outright surrender.

Since Fleet Admiral Franz von Hipper detested the Sailors' Council established in the aftermath of the Kiel mutinies, he asked Rear Admiral Ludwig von Reuter to command the ships to the Firth. Reuter assumed command on 17 November. With Admiral David Beatty demanding that the German ships be at the Firth only four days later, much had to be done in a short time. Aboard the bigger ships the sailors allowed the officers to control navigation and operation, while they in turn carried out the day-to-day management. Officers on the smaller ships generally had more authority.

On 19 November the bulk of the ships of the High Seas Fleet (with one-third normal crew complements) sailed to meet the Grand Fleet at the Firth of Forth. Not all the ships were ready in time; three warships (a battleship, a battle cruiser, and a light cruiser) were left behind to join the others later. By a ruse, Reuter got agreement to hoist the imperial ensigns in place of the red flags of the Sailors' Council.

The next day, one of the destroyers was lost to a mine. The remainder of the ships arrived at the rendezvous at 09:30 on 21 November, where they were met by 150 British warships of the Grand Fleet. Beatty expected treachery and ordered his crews to prepare for any provocation.

After the German ships had passed a twenty-mile-long gauntlet of British ships, Admiral Beatty signaled Reuter that the German flag was to be hauled down and not hoisted again without permission. Reuter and the German government later protested this to no avail. British crews then searched the German ships to ensure that they were disarmed and carried no weapons. A more thorough search was conducted the next day. Beatty's orders to British sailors not to fraternize with the Germans and to ignore the Sailors' Council did much to restore Reuter's authority.

Over the next five days the Grand Fleet escorted the German ships in small groups to Scapa Flow. Beatty now ordered that German crews be further reduced: 200 men per battle cruiser, 175 per battleship, sixty per light cruiser, and twenty men per destroyer. Many in the fleet, including Reuter, believed that internment at Scapa Flow violated the Armistice, especially inasmuch as the Allies had not tried to find a neutral port. Once the Germans were in Scapa Flow disarmed, however, they had no choice in the matter.

For the Germans, life at Scapa Flow was dreary and boring. The British restricted visiting between ships, although Reuter did have complete freedom of movement. The Allies censored the mail and, because the blockade of Germany continued, issued the Germans short rations. Coal was also given in limited quantities, which meant that ships could not always be heated.

In December Reuter received permission to return to Germany for a visit. He took with him his surplus crews, in six transports. Reuter returned to Scapa Flow at the end of January 1919. With British support he gradually reestablished his authority. Insubordinate sailors were returned to Germany. By 17 June Reuter had shipped home the majority of the radicals, 2,700 men; that left only 1,800 officers and seamen aboard a fleet that at one time had nearly 100,000.

The Germans at Scapa Flow anxiously followed the proceedings of the Paris Peace Conference, where the disposition of their ships would be decided. News was meager, however; German newspapers arrived only once a month by supply ship, and British papers were as much as a week late. The Allies were in sharp disagreement as to whether German ships would be destroyed, surrendered, or distributed among them. Nevertheless, terms given the Germans on 7 May demanded that "all war vessels interned" must be "finally surrendered" and that "108 less important vessels" would also be given up. The navy was reduced to 15,000 officers and men, six small battleships, six light cruisers, twelve destroyers, and twelve torpedo boats. Germany was not allowed submarines or naval aviation.

On 9 May, Admiral Adolf von Trotha, naval chief of staff since 27 December 1918, wrote to Reuter regarding the interned ships and told him that "their surrender to the enemy is out of the question." The message was brought to Reuter in one of the German supply ships that arrived at Scapa Flow on 15 June.

The Allied governments gave the Germans an ultimatum to sign the treaty by 21 June, later changed to 23 June, or hostilities would resume. Admiral Reuter later claimed that he had ordered the scuttling on the basis of information from a 16 June copy of *The Times* of London giving the deadline of 21 June. He maintained he believed that Germany would resume the war once the deadline had expired, and that justified his order to scuttle the fleet.

Admiral Sir Sydney Freemantle was in charge of guarding the German ships at Scapa Flow. Freemantle scheduled torpedo practice for his ships on 20 June, but rough weather led him to cancel it. When he learned that the deadline had been extended for two more days, he rescheduled the exercise for 21 June. Freemantle planned to seize the German ships on his return to Scapa Flow on the 23rd. He left behind at Scapa Flow only one destroyer and seven patrol craft to guard the German ships. Reuter later claimed that the departure of the British ships was proof the war was being resumed.

At 11:20 on 21 June 1919, Admiral Reuter's flagship signaled the order to scuttle. Each ship relayed it to her neighbors, hoisted the ensign of the Imperial Navy, if one was aboard, and scuttled. The crews lowered boats, mounted white flags indicating their new status as prisoners of war, and waited to be picked up. Meanwhile, British seamen at Scapa Flow boarded ships that were afloat and endeavored to beach those already sinking. Although most German lifeboats flew white flags, in their frustration the British opened fire, killing eight Germans that day and wounding seventeen others.

When Freemantle received news of the scuttling he ordered his ships to return to Scapa flow at maximum speed, but they did not arrive until 14:30. That evening Freemantle ordered Reuter aboard his flagship, the *Revenge*, under armed guard, where he informed him of his disgust at his action.

A total of fifty-two vessels were sunk that day: ten battleships, five battle cruisers, five light cruisers, and thirty-two destroyers. Another twenty-two vessels were beached or not scuttled: one battleship, three light cruisers, and eighteen destroyers.

Controversy surrounds the decision to scuttle. In his memoirs Reuter maintained that he ordered the action because he believed that the German government had refused to sign the peace treaty. In his book, Admiral Friedrich Ruge supported Reuter's position.

As Reuter took sole responsibility, the German government could claim innocence. Reuter was under pressure from his own officers and the resurrected German Admiralty to scuttle his ships. He did not wish the British to seize them, and his memoirs suggest that he would have scuttled the ships in any case. As he put it, "There could be no question of the En-glish taking possession of the ships merely on the grounds of the peace treaty being signed." There was also Trotha's order to Reuter never to surrender the ships. Trotha subsequently promoted Reuter to vice admiral, even though the scuttling effectively sabotaged his country's peace agreements.

Regardless, the Allies accused the Germans of treachery and held their government accountable. The British undoubtedly profited from the fact that the bulk of the German navy went to the bottom (much of it was later raised and sold as scrap; three battleships and four light cruisers remain underwater) rather than being divided in the form of reparations among the Allied powers. But the Allies demanded reparation for the scuttling of the warships. Although scuttling losses represented only 300,000 tons, the Allies acted as if the entire fleet of 400,000 tons had been lost. Germany was forced to hand over an additional five light cruisers within sixty days and "such a number of floating docks, floating cranes, tugs, and dredges equivalent to a total displacement of 400,000 tons" within ninety days. She was thus forced to surrender the majority of her port equipment and some of the best ships of the navy. This left Germany with just thirty-one ships: six battleships, one light cruiser, twelve destroyers, and twelve torpedo boats.

Spencer C. Tucker

References

Reuter, Admiral Ludwig von. *Scapa Flow: The Account of the Greatest Scuttling of all Time*. London: Hurst and Blackett, 1940.

Ruge, Vice-Admiral Friedrich. *Scapa Flow 1919: The End of the German Fleet*. London: Ian Allan, 1973.

Shepherd, David N. "Death of a Fleet: The Scuttling of the German High Seas Fleet at Scapa Flow, June 21, 1919." Ph.D. dissertation, Texas Christian University, 1973.

Stumpf, Richard. *War, Mutiny and Revolution in the German Navy: The World War I Diary of Seaman Richard Stumpf*. Translated by Daniel Horn. New Brunswick, N.J.: Rutgers University Press, 1967.

Van der Vat, Dan. *The Grand Scuttle: The Sinking of the German Fleet at Scapa Flow in 1919*. Annapolis, Md.: Naval Institute Press, 1986.

See also GERMANY, NAVY; HIPPER, FRANZ
VON; PARIS PEACE CONFERENCE; REUTER,
LUDWIG VON; TROTHA, ADOLF VON;
VERSAILLES TREATY

Scheer, Reinhard (1863–1928)

German admiral and chief of the High Seas
Fleet, 1916–18. Born on 30 September 1863 in
Obernkirchen, the son of a Hessian pastor and
schoolmaster, Scheer as a youth entertained
romantic notions about life at sea and joined the
Imperial Navy as a cadet in 1872. As a young
officer he served overseas in Africa and the Pacific before gaining recognition in home waters
as a competent captain and leader of torpedo
boats. In subsequent commands he familiarized
himself with battleships, and, in 1909, while
still a captain, he became chief of staff of the
High Seas Fleet. Two years later, with flag rank,
Scheer moved to Berlin to direct the General
Section within Alfred von Tirpitz's naval office.
In 1913 Scheer resumed duty with the fleet as
chief of the Second Battle Squadron, made up
of antiquated predreadnoughts. A strict disciplinarian, Scheer emerged as a thorough trainer of
men and as a good organizer. Nonetheless, he
entered the war as an old-school officer with
only a limited appreciation for the changing
nature of naval warfare and for the need to
imbue the naval officer corps with new ideas,
more flexibility, and greater political and social
toleration.

By 1915 Scheer had taken command of the
Third Battle Squadron, the most modern
dreadnoughts in the German arsenal. When
ailing Admiral Hugo von Pohl retired in January of 1916, Scheer, then fifty-two years old and
full admiral, succeeded him as chief of the High
Seas Fleet. He was not without opponents in
high positions, and many of his views aroused
controversy. Scheer was known to favor an
aggressive use of the fleet in order to reduce the
British Grand Fleet piecemeal, through carefully
prepared surprise raids, and to bring about an
eventual all-out encounter in which the Germans stood a good chance of winning. In such
limited operations, airships were to act as the
eyes of the fleet before battle cruisers, light
cruisers, torpedo boats, and submarines would
make contact with the enemy and direct
Scheer's battleships to the scene of action for the
kill. One such coordinated fleet sortie into the
waters between Holland and England in early
March of 1916 netted no more than two fishing trawlers; during the shelling of Lowestoft
and Yarmouth in April the Germans almost
trapped an inferior British force, but in a confused tactical situation allowed it to escape.

Prompted in part by political pressure not
to remain idle while the kaiser's troops bled at
Verdun, Scheer took the High Seas Fleet out
again on 31 May 1916 on a sweep of the North
Sea, to shell Sunderland in Durham and to lure,
if possible, a part of the British fleet into action.
That operation brought on the historic Battle of
Jutland, when Scheer encountered Admiral
John Jellicoe's Grand Fleet off the Skagerrak.

Outnumbered and somewhat outclassed in
modern capital ships by a ratio of 37:21, the
Germans opened the engagement on a favorable
note when Vice Admiral Franz von Hipper's
scouting forces, without suffering losses of their
own, sank two of Vice Admiral David Beatty's
battle cruisers. Beatty's sacrifice and subsequent
moves, however, denied Hipper and Scheer
immediate knowledge of Jellicoe's whereabouts.
Once the latter's battle fleet appeared on the
scene, a promising overture for the German side
turned into a bloody artillery duel in which the
British came to control the battlefield and were
twice able to head off Scheer by "crossing the
T" and exposing his units to relentless fire.
Scheer lost the initiative and had to react instead
to Jellicoe's tactical moves. Twice prevented
from returning directly to his bases in the Elbe
and Jade estuaries and fearing disastrous losses
if he continued the fight, Scheer finally ordered
diversionary attacks by torpedo boats and
battle cruisers, and used the dark of night to
make good his retreat. In this only major encounter of the battle fleets during the war, the
British Grand Fleet suffered higher casualties
than the High Seas Fleet but could claim a strategic victory, inasmuch as Scheer thereafter
avoided risking his capital ships in an open-
ended showdown.

For Scheer, the Battle of Jutland signaled
the failure of Tirpitz's "risk" theory and demonstrated the need for immediate strategic and
tactical modifications. In August of 1916 he
briefly experimented with joint units containing
both dreadnoughts and fast battle cruisers,
sending them in a mismanaged and ultimately
abortive bombardment operation against the
English east coast. For his major surface units
he demanded future improvements in speed,
ordnance, and armor. By 1917, he enthusiastically supported the renewal of unrestricted submarine warfare as the only promising alterna-

tive to risky fleet action, underestimating, as did so many others, the reaction of the United States and overrating the submarines' destructive potential. Later that year Scheer reacted harshly and probably imprudently when mutinies spread through the fleet. He ordered the execution of two of the ringleaders within forty-eight hours of the court-martial's guilty verdict, thereby denying the possibility of an appeal to civilian authorities and the kaiser, and further increasing the tension between the navy's officer corps and its enlisted personnel.

By 1918, dissatisfaction with continued civilian and political interference in naval command decisions prompted Scheer, along with Vice Admiral Adolf von Trotha and other associates, to try to shake up the navy's complex leadership system and replace it with a unified supreme command under his personal control. Over the kaiser's misgivings and after forcing several senior officers, such as Holtzendorff, Capelle, and Müller, into premature retirement, the new Naval War Command *(Seekriegsleitung)* took charge in August of 1918. Other than to prepare the ill-fated "final sortie" of the High Seas Fleet to save its honor and to draft the fantastic "Scheer Program" that sought to build some 450 additional U-boats by 1920, the Naval War Command was too late to make a decisive difference in World War I. As an institution, it survived the collapse of the Second Reich and would direct Germany's naval operations in World War II. Among the more prominent, and luckier, warships in that effort would be the pocket battleship *Admiral Scheer.* Scheer died on 26 November 1928 in Marktredwitz.

Eric C. Rust

References
Bennett, Geoffrey M. *The Battle of Jutland.* Philadelphia: Dufour, 1964.
Herwig, Holger. *"Luxury" Fleet.* London: Allen and Unwin, 1980.
Macintyre, Donald. *Jutland.* New York: Norton, 1958.
Marineministerium (Berlin). *Der Krieg zur See, 1914–1918.* 24 vols. Berlin, Frankfurt, 1922–66.
Scheer, Reinhard. *Germany's High Seas Fleet in the World War.* London: Cassell, 1920.

See also GERMANY, NAVY; JUTLAND, BATTLE OF

Scheidemann, Philipp (1865–1939)

German politician. Born in Kassel on 26 July 1865, the son of an artisan, Scheidemann made his living as a typesetter and joined the Social Democratic party (SPD) when he was eighteen. Elected to the Reichstag in 1903, Scheidemann initially supported the war effort. He generally opposed German territorial acquisitions but favored the retention of Alsace-Lorraine and wanted to uphold the territorial integrity of Austria-Hungary and Turkey. He opposed the terms imposed on Russia at Brest-Litovsk.

In October of 1918 Scheidemann joined the government of Prince Max as minister without portfolio. After the abdication of the kaiser and without the permission or knowledge of the head of the provisional government, Friedrich Ebert, he proclaimed a republic from the balcony of the Reichstag on 9 November 1918. This was done in order to forestall the establishment of a more radical regime. Scheidemann became the first chancellor of the Weimar Republic on 13 February 1919, but he resigned on 19 June in opposition to the Versailles Treaty, which he was unwilling to sign. He resumed his seat with the Social Democrats in the Reichstag but went into exile in 1933 after Hitler came to power. He died in Copenhagen on 29 November 1939.

Bernard A. Cook

References
Berlau, A. Joseph. *The German Social Democratic Party, 1914–1921.* New York: Columbia, 1949.
Scheidemann, Philipp. *The Making of a New Germany.* Translated by J.E. Mitchell. 2 vols. New York: Appleton, 1929.
Schorske, Carl E. *German Social Democracy, 1905–1917: The Development of the Great Schism.* Cambridge and London: Harvard University Press, 1955.
Watt, Richard M. *The Kings Depart: The Tragedy of Germany: Versailles and the German Revolution.* New York: Simon and Schuster, 1968.

See also GERMANY, HOME FRONT, REVOLUTION OF 1918; MAX OF BADEN, PRINCE; VERSAILLES TREATY

Schlieffen, Count Alfred von (1833–1913)

Chief of the German General Staff, 1891–1905, and originator of the controversial, comprehensive victory plan for a two-front war that bore his name. An aloof individual, noted for his attention to intricate detail, Schlieffen epitomizes the specialized and narrowly technical general staff mentality of the pre-World War I generation. Born in Berlin on 28 February 1833, Schlieffen was the son of a Prussian major general and, on his mother's side, minor Prussian nobility. His days of elementary education in the Hutterite gymnasia reinforced his familial sense of orderliness, duty to God and country, acceptance of dogma, and utilitarian approach to history. The frail, myopic Schlieffen had a reserved and scholarly disposition, which initially suggested a nonmilitary career. After studying law, he decided to take up the soldier's profession in 1854 and joined the 2nd Garde Uhlans as a first lieutenant.

Predisposed toward staff positions, Schlieffen saw action as a corps headquarters adjutant in the Austro-Prussian War of 1866—where he participated in the Königgrätz Campaign—and the Franco-Prussian War of 1870–71. He missed the epic frontier battles of the latter conflict and had to settle for service in the tedious Loire Campaign. From 1876 to 1883 he commanded the 1st Garde Uhlans, which he molded into a model cavalry regiment. In 1883 he began a series of assignments with the general staff, serving in that esteemed body's quartermaster, war-planning, historical, and education sections.

It was while in the historical section that the seed of Schlieffen's exalted battle of encirclement and annihilation was planted, based on his reading of Hans Delbrück's account of Hannibal's victory over Varro at Cannae in 216 B.C. Upon succeeding Alfred von Waldersee as chief of the general staff in 1891, Schlieffen became obsessed with applying the Cannae solution to the looming two-front threat posed by the Franco-Russian alliance.

Schlieffen immersed himself in professional studies. Reputedly, he often sent complex military problems for his most promising subordinates to solve over their Christmas holidays, and his oft-quoted evaluation of a beautiful lake bathed in East-Prussian moonlight—"an unimportant military obstacle!"—completes the image of a monocled martinet narrowly focused on military operations. Schlieffen could not tolerate idle chatter unrelated to military science.

Schlieffen's advancements in the areas of staff rides, army rail net expansion, field communications, mobile siege artillery, and aerial recon-naissance helped to maintain the German combat edge during the opening weeks of the 1914 Marne Campaign. His focus upon operations disregarded diplomatic consequences essential to comprehensive planning in the age of total war.

Schlieffen's lesson plans on historical battles of annihilation were collected in a series of lectures, known as the *Cannae* studies, published posthumously in 1913. It appeared in numerous translations and abridged editions after World War I. Schlieffen's teachings were influential in United States Army officer training in the late 1920s and 1930s. General Dwight Eisenhower's predilection for a war of maneuver may have owed something to the Schlieffen concept. *Cannae* was also studied in Russia's Frunze military academy in the 1920s.

Schlieffen is mentioned prominently in surveys of the military art. His plan, albeit unsuccessfully executed, is regarded as a model of thorough staff work. His envelopment model and metaphorical battle critiques have had a lasting impact on German, Soviet, French, Italian, Polish, Israeli, and American military thought.

Injured in a riding accident in 1904, Schlieffen retired in 1905 yet continued to tinker with and offer counsel on his "quick-win" itinerary through journal articles and memoranda until his death on 4 January 1913.

James J. Bloom

References

Bucholz, Arden. *Moltke, Schlieffen and Prussian War Planning*. New York: Berg, 1991.

Groener, Wilhelm. *The Testament of Count Schlieffen*. Translated by W.P. Papenforth. Carlisle Barracks, Pa.: U.S. Army War College, 1983.

Ritter, Gerhard. *The Schlieffen Plan: Critique of a Myth*. London: Oswald Wolff, 1958.

Schlieffen, Alfred Graf von. *Cannae*. Fort Leaven-worth, Kans.: U.S. Army Command and General Staff School Press, 1931.

Wallach, Jehuda L. *The Dogma of the Battle Of Annihilation*. Westport, Conn.: Greenwood, 1986.

See also SCHLIEFFEN PLAN

Schlieffen Plan

The German plan for war against France and Russia. Named for its author, Alfred von

Schlieffen, chief of the German General Staff, 1891–1905, it called for the bulk of German resources to be directed first against France; once that country was defeated, Germany could then shift forces to defeat Russia. Since it was essential to defeat France quickly, the plan called for a vast wheeling movement by the bulk of the German army through neutral Belgium, letting the last man on the right "brush the Channel with his sleeve" (as Schlieffen allegedly urged), outflanking the French armies, skirting Paris to the south, and driving the French against their own fortress line to encirclement and destruction in a giant battle of annihilation.

Before Schlieffen's tenure as chief of staff, German war plans, in considering the theoretical possibility of a two-front war, had envisioned dividing the German army into two nearly equal parts. One would conduct a holding operation against France, while the other joined Austria-Hungary to defeat Russian forces deployed in central Poland. There was no real expectation of decisive victory; as late as 1888 the Germans intended to take the offensive in the West against France, while waging defensive warfare against armies in the East.

The appointment of Alfred von Schlieffen as chief of the general staff brought about a fundamental change in German plans. During Schlieffen's tenure as chief of staff the specter of a two-front war became reality with the Franco-Russian Entente (1894). What had been to some degree at least a staff exercise now assumed the greatest importance: planning to fight a war simultaneously against France and Russia. Schlieffen worked out a highly original solution to Germany's strategic dilemma. Like most students of war in that period, he had been imbued with the importance of gaining the decisive battle. He was convinced that winning such a battle was dependent on turning the enemy flanks, since frontal assault, always costly, allowed the enemy to retreat along his own line of communications, drawing supplies and reinforcements to the army and enabling it to pick another position from which to continue resistance.

Schlieffen's solution to this two-front dilemma was to use Germany's interior lines and superior railway system in an attempt to hold off one adversary with minimum forces, while the bulk of the German army sought decisive victory in the other theater of operations. Once that victory was secured, German forces would be transferred to deal with the remaining foe.

Schlieffen chose to attack France first because he considered it the greater immediate threat. France's railroad network and smaller geographical size indicated that she would mobilize more quickly than Russia, threatening Germany with invasion. From the German perspective, however, France's ability to mobilize quickly also provided an opportunity. If properly conducted, a German offensive might "bag" most of the French army, driving that country from the war. In Schlieffen's eyes, Russia's backwardness made her a more difficult foe; her massive mobilization would take many weeks to complete, and until the Russian army was mobilized and concentrated, western Russia offered few if any decisive objectives for the German army to attack. Always there remained grave concern about the immense spaces of the Russian interior, and its ability to swallow up an invading army.

Beginning in 1892, Schlieffen initiated planning for quick victory over France. Early versions of his plan called for the bulk of the German armies to stop an anticipated French offensive toward the Rhine, while strong reserves struck the French left wing in the vicinity of Verdun. Yet the chief of the general staff remained fearful that the French might delay their offensive; such a delay could allow the ponderous yet powerful Russian "steamroller" to attack Germany's eastern frontier. Ultimately, Schlieffen decided that Germany simply could not afford to await the French attack. After her humiliating military performance in the Russo-Japanese War (1904–5), Russia had embarked on a crash course to improve her military capabilities. These improvements, particularly in strategic railroad construction, had diminished the German advantage of a quicker, more streamlined mobilization that Schlieffen counted upon to wage a two-front war successfully. Germany, therefore, had to attack in order to ensure a rapid defeat of France and the quick redeployment of the army east. By the end of 1905, about the time he retired, a series of staff rides, war games, and constant study had convinced Schlieffen that Germany's best hope lay in an offensive of breathtaking boldness. Rather than a narrow enveloping counterattack near Verdun, he opted for a massive wheeling movement through central Belgium. Elements of the right wing would violate the neutrality of Luxembourg and, via the "Maastricht appendix," Holland as well.

The allocation of forces further indicated the plan's boldness. Schlieffen proposed leaving only ten divisions, with supporting local troops, to face the Russians, while sixty-eight divisions marched west. Of those committed to the great offensive, fifty-nine would deploy on the right wing; the remaining nine divisions would guard the common frontier between France and Germany, perhaps even retreating before French forces to entice them east, away from the decisive right wing.

This campaign plan was amended by Schlieffen's successor, Helmuth von Moltke (the Younger), and utilized by the German Empire in the opening campaign of the war. Moltke made two key modifications; he weakened the ratio between right-wing and left-wing forces by adding divisions to the left wing. Secondly, while the offensive was in progress, he detached five divisions from the right wing and sent them across Germany to East Prussia because the Russian army had moved faster than anticipated. Ultimately, the plan failed.

Since the war's end, scholars and soldiers have endlessly debated Schlieffen's plan. Two principal threads of criticism have emerged. At the operational level, critics charge that the plan simply was not practical. The German army lacked the forces and, more important, the logistical "tail" to support so vast and rapid a movement. There also seems to be no notion in the plan of the Clausewitzian concept of "friction," the technical military equivalent of "Murphy's Law." In allocating only six weeks in which to defeat France, Schlieffen tacitly expected a campaign that ran like clockwork. Mistakes, breakdowns, bad weather, or just bad luck were not considered in his timetable.

Criticism of the plan at the strategic level focuses on three closely interrelated points. By invading neutral Belgium, Schlieffen virtually ensured Great Britain's entry into the war, since Britain (along with Prussia) was a guarantor of Belgium's neutrality and had shown a long-standing opposition toward any great power's controlling the Low Countries. Perhaps more important, Schlieffen's critics charge that his plan, with its emphasis on speed and on running grave risks to obtain victory, put Germany's soldiers and statesmen under intense and ultimately unbearable pressure once the crisis of 1914 began. The imperatives of time, the absolute requirement to win quickly—these acted as accelerators, pushing Germany's decision-makers to opt for war lest they lose their carefully crafted and crucial advantage in speed of mobilization. Most important, Schlieffen's critics

underscore that in the very homeland of Clausewitz, Schlieffen put together his war plan without any apparent consultation or influence from Germany's government. Rather than policy directing war, the ultimate negation of Clausewitz's famous dictum occurred—war was now driving policy.

Schlieffen's defenders generally claim that, operationally, the plan came very close to success, despite being drastically modified and then haltingly implemented by Schlieffen's successor. Had the old general himself been in charge, they assert, things might well have gone differently. The issue of bringing Britain into the war is answered by the general belief, shared by Schlieffen, that the next European war would be short: A great battle would decide its outcome. In this scenario, Britain's fleet and economic power would not be an important part of the equation. Finally, there is no record that Germany's statesmen ever protested or in any way tried to alter the Schlieffen Plan.

In retirement Schlieffen continued to study and tinker with his great work. He died in 1913 at age eighty. His oft-quoted last words, "It must come to a fight. Keep the right wing strong!" even if apocryphal, fittingly capture his obsession with this plan, which was to have such fateful consequences for Germany and the world.

Gary P. Cox

References

Miller, Steven E., Sean M. Lynn-Jones, and Stephen Van Evera, eds. *Military Strategy and the Origins of the First World War*. Princeton: Princeton University Press, 1991.

Ritter, Gerhard. *The Schlieffen Plan: Critique of a Myth*. New York: Praeger, 1958.

———. *The Sword and the Scepter*. Vols. 2 and 3. Coral Gables, Fla.: University of Miami Press, 1972.

Van Creveld, Martin. *Supplying War: Logistics from Wallenstein to Patton*. London: Cambridge University Press, 1980.

See also FRONTIERS, BATTLE OF THE; MARNE, FIRST BATTLE OF; MOLTKE, HELMUTH VON; SCHLIEFFEN, ALFRED VON

Seeckt, Hans von (1866–1936)

German general and head of the *Reichswehr* from 1920 to 1926. Born on 22 April 1866 in Silesia, the son of a Pomeranian noble, Seeckt joined the German army in 1885 and quickly displayed his leadership and organizational skills. In 1899, at the age of thirty-three and while only a lieutenant, he was transferred to the General Staff Corps, where he remained for the next twenty years. A lieutenant colonel at the beginning of World War I, Seeckt served as chief of staff for the III Corps, where he distinguished himself at the breakthrough at Soissons. His achievements secured him promotion to major general and the position of chief of staff of the new Eleventh Army on the Eastern Front. In May of 1915 he achieved a great victory with the breakthrough at Gorlice, for which he earned the coveted *Pour le Mérite*. Seeckt went on to serve as the exemplary chief of staff for General Mackensen's composite army group in the Balkans during the conquest of Serbia (1915), for Archduke Karl's Twelfth Army in Hungary and Romania (1916), and for the Turkish army (1917–18).

Seeckt returned home at war's end and was promoted to lieutenant general. In January of 1919 Field Marshal Paul von Hindenburg and General Wilhelm Groener sent him to organize the retreat of German armies still in Russia and to protect the eastern frontiers. To that end, Seeckt launched a successful attack in May that recaptured Riga. He was then sent to Paris as part of the German Peace Commission, where he warned of the harshness of the settlement. Having served as the last chief of the general staff, he was appointed chairman of the Preparatory Commission of the Peace Army in recognition of his skills.

A worldly man with a love of the arts, Seeckt clandestinely rebuilt the German army from the ashes of World War I. His small, efficient force was meant to be quickly expandable in time of need. He also encouraged the Russo-German alliance forged at Rapallo in 1922, which allowed him to train his army secretly in Russia. Above all, Seeckt sought to restore the power and prestige of the army, while avoiding political entanglements and dissension.

Seeckt failed to support the government during the Kapp Putsch but remained as head of the *Reichswehr* until forced to resign in 1926 for promising a military post to the crown prince's son. He was a conservative deputy (German People's party) in the Reichstag from 1930 to 1932 and was ambassador to the Chinese Nationalist Army during 1934 and 1935. He died on 29 December 1936 in Berlin.

Laura Matysek Wood

References

Meier-Welcker, Hans. *Seeckt*. Frankfurt: Bernard U. Graefe, 1967.
Seeckt, Hans von. *Thoughts of a Soldier*. London: E. Benn, 1930.

Senussi and Sultan of Darfur Rebellions

In 1914 the Islamic world was at a crossroads. Arabs were not masters of their own house; they were controlled by European and Ottoman imperial administrations. In November of 1914 the Ottoman Empire entered the war on the side of the Central Powers. Moslems had to choose sides.

Traditionally, there had been no distinction in Islam between civil and religious authority. For centuries the "sultan" in Constantinople had been recognized as the "caliph," or head of orthodox Islam. In 1914 Sultan and Caliph Mehmet V had approximately 300 million religious adherents, many of them subjects of the Entente. When he declared *jihad*, or "holy war," in November and called on all Moslems to support the Turks, this presented a serious threat to the Entente, especially Britain.

Fortunately for the British Empire, Islam's second most important leader, Hussein Ibn-Ali, the Keeper of the Holy Places, did not endorse the caliph's call. In June of 1916 he revolted against the Turks and received British aid. The revolt in Arabia, based on emergent Arab nationalism, went far in blunting the caliph's attempt to achieve Islamic unity. From the early months of the war, however, Britain was challenged by those who did respond to the caliph.

The most critical area was Egypt, site of the Suez Canal and the Entente's main base in the Middle East. Mindful of the 70,000 Turkish nationals in Egypt, the British deposed the pro-Ottoman Khedive and imposed press censorship. In January of 1915 a Turkish attempt to capture the canal was beaten back, and there was no popular uprising within Egypt.

Later that year German and Turkish *agents provocateurs*, who had infiltrated by submarine to Libya, convinced the Grand Sheikh of the Senussi, Sayed Ahmed, to commence raiding along the western frontier of Egypt. The Senussi attacked along the coast from Sollum and through the desert from Siwa, threatening to destabilize the population of the Nile Valley. In February of 1916, after numerous engagements, the British Western Frontier Force defeated the Senussi at the decisive battle of Agagiya. Thereafter, fighting was sporadic until British armored cars took Siwa in January of 1917. Sayed Ahmed escaped by Austrian submarine to Constantinople, where he carried on pan-Islamic propaganda until the end of the war.

Egypt was also threatened from the south. The last of the Dervish *grandeés*, Sultan Ali Dinar of Darfur, attempted to assist the Senussi by invading the Sudan. In May of 1916 a British force mounted a preemptive invasion, catching Ali Dinar at his capital at El Fasher. The sultan was pursued into the desert and killed in November.

Egypt and its environs, of course, were not the only areas affected by the call to holy war. In January of 1915 British troops assisted the Sultan of Oman against pro-Turkish locals; Arabs assisted both sides in Mesopotamia; and for the duration of the war Britain defended the besieged port of Aden. India, with its millions of Moslems, was a particular cause for concern.

Although the caliph's exhortation to *jihad* did not result in a massive rising against the British, the call did force Britain to retain a large number of troops in the Middle East, far from the Western Front.

David L. Bullock

References

Antonius, George. *The Arab Awakening: The Story of the Arab National Movement.* New York: Capricorn, 1965.

Falls, Captain Cyril. *Military Operations: Egypt and Palestine. To June 1917.* London: H.M. Stationery Office, c. 1920s.

Shaw, Stanford, and Ezel Kural. *History of the Ottoman Empire and Modern Turkey.* Vol. 2: *Reform, Revolution, and Republic: The Rise of Modern Turkey.* Cambridge: Cambridge University Press, 1977.

See also ARAB REVOLT; EGYPT; MEHMED V

Serbia, Role in the War

The assassination of Archduke Franz Ferdinand by a Bosnian student, Gavrilo Princip, with a Serbian-furnished pistol on 28 June 1914 led the Austro-Hungarian government to declare war on Serbia exactly one month later. This declaration opened the First World War. The Serbian government, together with the aged King Peter Karadjordjević, immediately left Belgrade, right across the Sava River from

Austro-Hungarian positions, for the interior city of Nish.

Within two weeks the Austrians under General Oskar Potiorek began a three-pronged invasion of western Serbia, with one force taking the city of Sabac, a second moving across the Drina River toward the Jadar Valley, and the third advancing across the upper Drina. The Austrian forces of over 250,000 heavily outnumbered the Serbs. On 16–19 August Serbian defenders, led by Vojvoda Radomir Putnik, repulsed the Austrians at the Battle of Cer Mountain, achieving the first Entente victory in the war. Both sides sustained heavy casualties. By 25 August the Austro-Hungarian forces had retreated back across the border.

The Serbs responded with an incursion into Srem and a joint Serbian-Montenegrin invasion of Bosnia. Neither effort achieved any lasting success. Especially disappointing to the Serbs was the failure of the Bosnian population to respond to the prospect of Serbian liberation. Nevertheless, the Serb invasion did help to keep the stronger Austro-Hungarian forces off balance.

In November of 1914 a new Austro-Hungarian offensive crashed into Serbia. By 2 December it had pushed the exhausted and ill-equipped Serbian forces out of Belgrade, as well as the important city of Valjevo. Soon afterwards, the invading forces bogged down in the mud south of Belgrade. With the help of emergency shipments of munitions from France and Greece, Serbian forces counterattacked on the Kolubara River. There the Serbs achieved their greatest victory in World War I, forcing back the invaders. By 15 December Serbian troops had reentered Belgrade and the only Austro-Hungarian soldiers still on Serbian soil were prisoners of war. The Serbs, however, were so weakened by the loss of over 170,000 men in battle and by the ravages of disease in their army that they lacked the strength to pursue their defeated enemy into Austria-Hungary.

The victories of 1914 gave the Serbian government, led by Nikola Pašić, a strong basis for expansive war aims. The Serbian government envisioned the annexation of Bosnia, Dalmatia, southern Hungary, and northern Albania. It was not at all receptive to Entente pleas for the surrender of a portion of Macedonia to Bulgaria in return for Bulgarian neutrality or participation in the war on the Entente side.

Nevertheless, by 1915 Serbia was in a difficult position. Its armies, which had been fighting since 1912, were utterly exhausted. Munitions, food, fuel, medicine, and most other commodities were in short supply. The other Entente states, who were themselves beginning to feel the demands of war, were unable to send the Serbs much material aid.

In the summer of 1915, after successes on both the Western and Eastern fronts, the Central Powers decided to reckon with Serbia. In August and early September German and Austro-Hungarian forces began to concentrate on the Danube River across from Serbia. On 22 September the Bulgarian army mobilized. The British and French discouraged a Serbian preemptory attack on Bulgaria. On 12 October 1915 Bulgaria declared war on Serbia. This initiated a Bulgarian invasion from the east and a joint Austro-German invasion from the north, under the overall command of General August von Mackensen. Serbian forces could not cope with an enemy numbering over 600,000 men. The Bulgarian advance precluded any retreat to the south, so the Serbian army and government, joined by tens of thousands of civilians, conducted an epic retreat over the Albanian Alps, reaching the Adriatic Sea at Durres and San Giovanna di Medua. Also accompanying the Serbs were almost 20,000 Austro-Hungarian prisoners of war. Exposure, hunger, disease, and the attacks of hostile Albanians took a heavy toll of the retreating Serbs. The survivors of this anabasis eventually found shelter on the island of Corfu. Serbian sources estimated that over 140,000 people died on the retreat. The conquest of Serbia established a direct land connection from Berlin to Constantinople and Central Power control of Europe from the Baltic to the Black Sea.

After a period of rest and resupply, the Serbian army reformed at Corfu. By the end of May 1916 over 112,000 Serbs, by now fully recuperated, joined the Entente forces at Salonika. There they participated in the Entente offensive in the autumn of 1916 and on 29 November 1916 reentered Serbian territory with the capture of Bitola.

The international situation worsened for Serbia in 1917. The downfall of czarist Russia deprived Serbia of its major Entente supporter. The subsequent publication of Italy's claims in the eastern Adriatic raised concern in the Serbian government-in-exile on Corfu that an Italo-Serbian rivalry might replace the old Austro-Hungarian-Serbian one. To strengthen its position, the Pašić government met with representatives of Serbian, Croatian, and Slovene groups in exile, known as the Yugoslav Committee. On 20 July 1917 the Serbs and the Yugoslav Committee signed the Declaration of Corfu, which envisioned the creation of a South Slav kingdom under the Karadjordjević dynasty. The Austro-Hungarian and Bulgarian occupation regimes imposed great hardships on the Serbian population. The Serbs suffered from disease and lack of food. In 1917 resistance erupted in the Toplica rebellion, in which over 20,000 Serbian lives were lost. Eventually Austro-Hungarian, Bulgarian, and German troops participated in its suppression.

With the collapse of Bulgaria in September of 1918, Serbian troops reentered Serbia from the south. The country was devastated. As much as one quarter of the population, 1.2 million, including over half of the male population between the ages of fifteen and fifty-five, had lost their lives in the war. Material losses were incalculable. On 1 December 1918, at Belgrade, the representatives from the former Hapsburg South Slavic lands, Serbia, and Montenegro proclaimed the new Kingdom of the Serbs, Croats, and Slovenes.

Richard C. Hall

References

Adams, J.C. *Flight in Winter*. Princeton: Princeton University Press, 1942.

Petrovich, Michael Boro. *A History of Modern Serbia, 1804–1918*. New York: Harcourt, Brace, Jovanovich, 1976.

Zhivojinovich, Dragan. "Serbia and Montenegro: The Home Front, 1914–1918." In *East Central European Society in World War I*. Edited by Bela K. Kiraly and Nandor F. Dreisziger, 239–59. Boulder, Colo.: Social Science Monographs, 1985.

See also BALKAN FRONT, 1914, 1915, 1916, 1917; FRANZ FERDINAND; PAŠIĆ, NIKOLA; PETER KARADJORDJEVIĆ, KING; PRINCIP, GAVRILO; SALONIKA CAMPAIGN

Sèvres, Treaty of (August 10, 1920)

Peace treaty between the Allies and Turkey at the end of World War I. With the end of the war, British Prime Minister David Lloyd George was determined to dismember the Ottoman Empire.

His views were made clear in 1920 when he declared: "The Turks nearly brought about our defeat in the war. . . . You can not trust them and they are a decadent race. . . . We must secure Constantinople and the Dardanelles. You can not do that effectively without crushing Turkish power." As chief architect of the Treaty of Sèvres between the victorious Allies and Turkey following World War I, Lloyd George, therefore, sought to partition the Ottoman Empire and replace it with a collection of allies, mandates, and vassal states, all closely tied to Britain.

Racked by famine, revolution, and economic collapse, Turkey had few options in the fall of 1918. Aware of Bulgaria's imminent collapse, Grand Vizier Ahmed Izzet Pasha agreed to send captured British General Charles Townshend over the lines with an offer of armistice. Townshend's report convinced London that the Turks were about to collapse. Purposely excluding their French allies, the foreign office approved a meeting that resulted in the Mudros Armistice of 30 October 1918.

When Premier Georges Clemenceau argued that the failure to allow France a representative at Mudros violated previous agreements, Lloyd George responded that England had provided the vast majority of troops needed to fight the Turks. He sarcastically referred to the French contribution as "a few nigger policemen sent to see that we did not steal the Holy Sepulchre!" Mudros marks the beginning of a rift between the two allies, one that would significantly affect the final settlement of World War I in the Middle East. In addition, Mudros triggered a diplomatic scramble as various wartime pacts—such as Sykes-Picot, Hussein-MacMahon, and the Balfour Declaration—came due. The basic incongruities of these agreements made an Allied-Ottoman settlement difficult.

To further complicate the negotiations, the Turks quickly split into two rival factions, one in Constantinople and the other in Ankara. The former, under Sultan Mehmed VI Vahdeddin, was recognized as "official" by the Allied Powers. The latter, led by war hero Mustafa Kemal, was diplomatically isolated but more representative of the Turkish people.

The sultan, who dissolved parliament and had been ruling by decree since 21 December 1918, believed that collaboration with Britain could secure his power and preserve the dynasty. Kemal and his Ankara government, already aware of Allied wartime negotiations, had signed the National Pact (Misak-i Milli), which proclaimed Anatolia to be Turkish and opposed any special status for minority groups not reciprocated for Turks elsewhere.

In March of 1920 pressure from the British led the sultan to declare the Ankara nationalists outlaws. He also agreed to send delegates to Versailles. There, despite U.S. General James Harbord's report on conditions in Anatolia, the diplomats were in a mood for blood. Fueled by the masterful negotiating powers of Greek Premier Eleutherios Venizelos and the rabid anti-Muslim prejudices of David Lloyd George, the Allies were ready to partition Turkey.

This was to be accomplished via the Treaty of Sèvres. Forced on the sultan's representatives in August of 1920, it was an extremely harsh settlement. It called for the surrender of all imperial holdings outside of Anatolia and Thrace. Parts of southeastern Anatolia were granted to France and Italy, while oil-rich Mosul was given to Britain via its Iraqi mandate. The Greeks, Turkey's ancient enemies, were presented with most of Thrace, including Adrianople (Edirne), the islands of Imbros and Tendos, and the option to occupy Smyrna (Izmir) along with a nebulous "hinterland" for five years. At the end of that period, a plebiscite could allow for its incorporation into Greece.

Compounding these losses, two states were to be carved from the rest of Anatolia: Armenia and Kurdistan. Both were to become mandates supervised by the League of Nations. Additional supervision came in the form of an International Straits Commission. Dominated by Great Britain, France, Italy, and Japan, its mission was to supervise all commercial and military traffic through the Straits.

Sèvres also included significant financial reparations, Allied control of the Turkish economy, and continuation of extraterritoriality. Complete freedom of transit was granted to the Allies. Turkey's military was limited to 50,000 men with no air units. Other clauses demanded the surrender of war criminals for trial by the League of Nations.

Drawing up a treaty and enforcing it were two very different matters. Lloyd George, the chief proponent of Sèvres, had been advised to ask for less. Britain was short of resources, and her armed forces were rapidly being demobilized. Italy, angry over Britain's decision to grant Smyrna to Greece, was unsupportive, while France, still smarting over the Mudros affair, was suspicious. The Allies were no longer working in tandem, yet Lloyd George pressed onward.

Under the guns of British warships, the sultan and his government signed the treaty. In so doing, they condemned themselves as collaborators, and implementation of the treaty led the vast majority of Turks to support the Ankara government. The clauses that granted ancient Turkish lands to Armenians and Greeks probably aroused more genuine Turkish patriotism than any event of World War I.

A clash was inevitable. It began when the Allies condoned a Greek invasion of the Turkish heartland. For the next two years, Anatolia was the scene of intense fighting. Kemal, the most gifted Turkish military leader during World War I, suffered initial setbacks but marshaled his forces via a "Parthian retreat." Finally, he crushed the exhausted Greek invaders and drove them back to the sea.

Success on the battlefield quickly converted into diplomatic power. On 16 March 1921, Ankara pierced its international isolation by signing the Turkish-Soviet Treaty of Friendship. Among its provisions was a clause announcing the Russian government's refusal to recognize Sèvres. Next, France cut a deal with the Nationalists. In exchange for guarantees on the repayment of pre-1914 bonds, which were mainly in French hands, Special Envoy Henri Franklin-Bouillon agreed to the evacuation of Cilicia in October. Italy quickly followed suit, and, in the words of Kemal, the Treaty of Sèvres was now "merely a rag."

With the Greek invaders routed and Turkish forces poised to strike the small British garrison at Constantinople, Great Britain was in a weak position. On 3 October 1922, a last-minute armistice was signed at Mudania and negotiations were transferred to Lausanne in Switzerland. There, Lord Curzon battled Turkey's representative, Izzet Pasha, along with Premier Raymond Poincaré of France and Italy's new strong man, Benito Mussolini. The end result was a vastly improved settlement for the Turks, who secured full control over both Anatolia and Thrace. Also, financial and military restrictions were eliminated and the powers of the International Straits Commission drastically reduced.

These events were most significant to the postwar world. Sèvres marked the high-water mark of British imperialism. It was also a major factor in the split between France and Britain that ended the Entente Cordiale. Finally, by forcing the Allies to renegotiate at Lausanne, Kemal secured the independence of Turkey and established the power base needed to initiate his remarkable program of westernization.

John P. Dunn

References

Davison, R. "Turkish Diplomacy from Mudros to Lausanne." In *The Diplomats, 1919–1939*, edited by Gordon A. Craig. New York: Atheneum, 1974.

Hemelreich, Paul C. *From Paris to Sèvres: The Partition of the Ottoman Empire at the Peace Conference of 1919–1920.* Columbus: Ohio State University Press, 1974.

Howard, Harry N. *The Partition of Turkey: A Diplomatic History, 1913–1923.* New York: H. Fertig, 1966.

Salahi Ramsdan Sonyel. *Turkish Diplomacy, 1918–1923: Mustafa Kemal and the Turkish Nationalist Movement.* London: Sage, 1975.

Tamkoc, Metin. *The Warrior Diplomats: Guardians of the National Security and Modernization of Turkey.* Salt Lake City: University of Utah Press, 1976.

See also KEMAL, MUSTAFA; LAUSANNE, TREATY OF; MEHMED VI; OTTOMAN EMPIRE

Shcherbachev, Dmitry Grigorevich (1857–1932)

Russian general, born on 6 February 1857. Shcherbachev was a graduate of both the Mikhailovsky Artillery School (1876) and the General Staff Academy (1884). He commanded IX Infantry Corps in the 1914 Galician Campaign. After promotion to general of infantry in late 1914, Shcherbachev received command of the Eleventh Army just before its summer retreat. By October he was in command of the Seventh Army and participated in General Nikolai Ivanov's disastrous Strypa River offensive.

As a commander, Shcherbachev favored attacking narrow fronts while supported by heavy artillery. Considered somewhat limited in command abilities, he performed well under direction from General Aleksei Brusilov.

In June of 1916, during the Brusilov Offensive by the Russian Southwestern Army Group, Shcherbachev's army crossed the Strypa River to cut the lines of communication for the Austro-German South Army commanded by General

Felix von Bothmer. The attack stalled without support from the two other Russian army groups on the front, and German General Alexander von Linsingen's army group counterattacked.

In April of 1917 Shcherbachev received command of Russian forces on the Romanian front and was advisor to Romania's King Ferdinand. In November, Shcherbachev and his loyal soldiers anticipated opening up a new Ukrainian front to fight both the Germans and the Bolsheviks. He created a force composed of Romanian and czarist troops that entered the Russian Civil War, attempting to keep Bessarabia free of Bolshevik control. In early 1918 the Romanians pressured Shcherbachev not to join White forces near the Don River. Instead, he sought French contingents to fight in southern Russia, but French Premier Georges Clemenceau would not support him. In January of 1919 Shcherbachev mediated differences among the various factions on the Don, helping to form the White Army that fought on for two more years. Shcherbachev went into exile later in 1919 and died in Nice, France, on 18 January 1932.

Tom Zucconi

References

Herwig, Holger, and Neil M. Heyman. *Biographical Dictionary of World War I.* Westport, Conn.: Greenwood, 1982.

Stone, Norman. *The Eastern Front 1914–1917.* London: Hodder and Stoughton, 1975.

Wieczynski, Joseph L., ed. *The Modern Encyclopedia of Russian and Soviet History.* Vol. 33. Gulf Breeze, Fla.: Academic International, 1983.

Wrangel, Alexis. *General Wrangel: Russia's White Crusader.* New York: Hippocrene, 1987.

See also BRUSILOV OFFENSIVE; ROMANIAN CAMPAIGN; RUSSIA, CIVIL WAR IN

Ships, Auxiliary

An auxiliary naval vessel is one not equipped or armed to carry out offensive operations. Although often carrying defensive armament, auxiliary ships are not expected to sail in harm's way.

Before World War I, naval strength was determined by the number of dreadnoughts a country possessed. The building, outfitting, and maintenance of these battleships was expensive,

and funds were not available to provide sufficient escort vessels or ships to patrol trade lanes. Although the ability of fighting fleets to operate for sustained periods away from their main bases, or to receive support at permanent bases, depended upon auxiliary vessels, they fared even worse than escort vessels in funding. The need for auxiliary vessels during peacetime was often met by short- or long-term charter of merchant vessels and crews. This was particularly true during fleet exercises.

Auxiliary ships and boats performed numerous services, such as supplying fuel (colliers and tankers), carrying rations (cargo ships for livestock and dry, fresh, and frozen foods), hauling supplies (cargo ships and ammunition ships), and providing maintenance and upkeep services (floating dry docks, submarine rescue, salvage vessels, floating cranes, repair ships, tenders). They also transported men (troopships, ferries and liberty launches), assisted in shipyard availability (tugs, water carriers, garbage scowls, fuel barges, lighters), and helped the sick and wounded (hospital ships, rescue ships, and lifeboats). These vessels were also responsible for maintaining navigational aids (icebreakers, buoy tenders, lightships, survey vessels), providing communications (weather ships and cable ships), guarding the ports (boom tenders, mine planters, inspection vessels, and patrol craft), storing goods at forward bases (store ships, barges, tenders), housing men (hulks, barrack barges and ships), and providing target service (target ships and sleds). In all, they performed hundreds of tasks to keep the fighting fleet at maximum readiness.

During the Great War, auxiliary vessels came in a variety of shapes and sizes. They were both powered and nonpowered vessels, including sailboats. Their area of operations extended from dockyard creeks to the high seas. They were both commissioned and noncommissioned vessels and were wholly, partially, or not at all manned by the navy. Many were civilian contract vessels or were operated by another governmental service. In fact, all armies of the day operated their own fleets of various sizes of seagoing, coastal, river, and harbor craft to support their own operations. While these other government naval auxiliary vessels were not listed by Jane or Brassey or Weyer in naval fleets, navies could not have operated without their support. In fact, many of their noncombat duties would have become navy chores if other agencies had not performed them.

The ratio of auxiliary vessels to fighting ships varied widely from navy to navy. In no case was it less than one to one, but it could run as high as five to one. The German High Seas Fleet and the Austro-Hungarian Fleet based on their home ports were in less need of auxiliary vessels than the Royal Navy, which had deployed its ships to northern Scotland, the Orkney Islands, the Mediterranean, and throughout the Atlantic and Arctic oceans.

After the start of the war all navies discovered that they were sadly lacking in auxiliary vessels. All incorporated merchant marine vessels, which resulted in an instant decrease in ships available to move goods and people. Particularly hard hit were fishing fleets. While most naval leaders had vaguely realized at the start of a war that there would be a loss of shipping available to the civilian community, all were surprised at the number of auxiliary vessels needed to keep the fleet on a war footing. An even greater problem was the demand for naval auxiliaries with which to perform support to nonnaval operations. For example, the German and Austro-Hungarian navies had to support their armies along the rivers and lakes on the Eastern Front.

The failure to appreciate the importance of auxiliary vessels was largely the product of naval writers who emphasized strategic and tactical aspects of fleet action without also discussing the logistic system. Alfred Thayer Mahan, for example, wrote glowingly of the Royal Navy's blockade of the French coast during the Napoleonic Wars, but he never emphasized the stream of auxiliary vessels that provided the supplies, allowing men-of-war to remain on station year-round.

All warring navies eventually developed forces to support their fighting fleets. How well these were organized and managed helped determine the outcome of the war at sea. The importance of auxiliary ships was recognized by most navies by the end of the war, when they were organized into separate commands under flag officers.

Charles H. Bogart

References

Clephane, Lewis P. *History of the Naval Overseas Transportation Service in World War I.* Washington: GPO, 1969.

Jane, Fred T. *Jane's Fighting Ships—1914.* London: Sampson Low Marston, 1914.

———. *Jane's Fighting Ships—1919.* London: Sampson Low Marston, 1919.

Marder, Arthur J. *From the Dreadnought to Scapa Flow.* Vols. 1–5. New York: Oxford University Press, 1970.

Scheer, Admiral Reinhard. *Germany's High Sea Fleet in the World War.* New York: Cassell, 1920.

Shuvaev, Dmitry Savelevich (1854–1937)

Russian general and minister of war. Born in Orenburg Province on 24 October 1854 into a respected but lower-class family, Shuvaev joined the army and graduated from the Aleksandr Military School in 1872 and the General Staff Academy in 1878. Much of his military service was in teaching and staff assignments. In 1905 he was a division commander, and in 1907 he became a corps commander. In 1909 Shuvaev was appointed chief quartermaster and head of the Main Quartermaster Directorate. From December of 1915 to March of 1916 he served as chief field quartermaster for the Russian army.

In March of 1916 the capable and popular General Aleksei Polivanov was dismissed as minister of war on the instigation of Empress Alexandra Feodorovna because of his liberal views and opposition to Rasputin. The empress wanted General Mikhail Beliaev, a reactionary and political toady, but in this rare instance she was overruled by Czar Nicholas II, who appointed General Shuvaev. When he learned of his appointment, according to one of his friends, Shuvaev was reduced to tears because he thought he was not up to the job. Since the most critical problem facing the Russian army was that of supply, Shuvaev seemed a logical choice. Nonetheless, his appointment was criticized by many who thought he lacked experience.

As minister of war, Shuvaev concentrated his attention on supply matters to the detriment of other concerns. No matter the subject of conversation, Shuvaev always ended up on the subject of boots. He once gave a lecture to the Council of Ministers on the manufacture of boots. Another of his traits was that he claimed to be "an old soldier," which meant that he professed loyalty to the czar, did his job, and did not express himself on controversial issues. Certainly, he was an honest and straightforward, if weak, leader. Shuvaev did commit one unforgivable error. He believed that cooperation between the government and the state

Duma was necessary to a successful war effort. Consequently, in November of 1916 he paid a visit to the Duma and was seen shaking the hand of Pavel Miliukov, liberal Duma member and enemy of Rasputin. From that time Shuvaev's days as minister of war were numbered. In January of 1917, in the wake of Rasputin's murder, the empress had him dismissed and replaced by General Beliaev. After the Bolsheviks seized power, Shuvaev taught at Red Army military educational institutions, including the command school of Vystrel. Shuvaev retired in the late 1920s and is said to have died in 1937.

John W. Bohon

References

Florinsky, Michael. *Russia, a History and an Interpretation.* 2 vols. New York: Macmillan, 1953.

Gourko, General Basil. *War and Revolution in Russia, 1914–1917.* New York: Macmillan, 1919.

Pares, Sir Bernard. *The Fall of the Russian Monarchy.* New York: Vintage, 1939.

See also ALEXANDRA FEODOROVNA

Siegfried Line

See ALBERICH, OPERATION OF

Sinai Campaign

When the first World War began, the Ottoman Empire held suzerainty over two choke points threatening Great Britain's control of the seas—the Dardanelles and the Suez Canal. Britain had occupied and effectively ruled Ottoman Egypt since 1882, and the Turks made recovery of Egypt and the canal one of their primary war aims. To this end, Djemal Pasha (one of three pashas in control of the empire) mounted an invasion of the Sinai in 1915.

Djemal and his German advisor, Kress von Kressenstein, took the Ottoman Fourth Army into the Sinai in January of 1915. The Turks brought twenty thousand rifles, nine field batteries, and one 15cm howitzer to Beersheba. The Ottoman Expeditionary Corps faced horrendous logistical problems along the 1,200 miles from Constantinople to Suez. The trip was divided into three stages, beginning with the railway from Constantinople to Aleppo. Two difficult portages, one of which passed close enough to the Mediterranean to be vulnerable to naval bombardment, complicated this stage. The rail link from Aleppo to Beersheba was completely reliant on a small store of coal left at Haifa in 1914. The final two hundred miles across the Sinai were without roads and with scarce and unreliable water supplies. Von Kressenstein, an engineering officer, was remarkably successful at improving cisterns that had been in use since antiquity to alleviate the water problem.

The British, under General Sir John Maxwell, elected to pull back from the Sinai and establish a defensive position along the eastern bank of the canal. They dug eighty miles of trenches in the sand and supplemented them by flooding plains adjoining the waterway's southern end. The British were convinced that no army could cross the Sinai and were more concerned about an invasion up the Nile from Mombasa. Britain's professional army of occupation had been shipped to France, and Maxwell was left with two divisions of Territorials (the 42nd Lancashire and the 52nd Lowlanders), several brigades of yeomanry, units from Australia and New Zealand, and two divisions from India.

On 2 February Djemal launched an attack on the central part of the canal at Qantara. A few Turks managed to cross the canal using German pontoons they had carried across the desert. A combination of British defenses and a fortuitous sandstorm stopped the Turkish attack on 3 February, and Djemal withdrew to Beersheba having lost 1,250 dead, missing, or injured. He lost 7,000 camels in his retreat, but Maxwell failed to pursue and lost a chance to bring the war in the Sinai to a quick end.

After the battle, Djemal was replaced by Kressenstein, and Maxwell by the more aggressive Sir Archibald Murray. Kressenstein began a series of raids and sporadic, ineffective attempts to mine the canal and its approaches. Early in 1916 Murray used British airplanes to bomb Turkish water supplies in one of the earliest uses of strategic air warfare.

In April of 1916 Kressenstein attacked and defeated the British in the coastal outpost of Qataya, and from there he attempted to encircle the British garrison at Romani. In the ensuing battle, which lasted from 19 July to 12 August, Anzac units turned back the Turks. Murray then began a fitful advance up the coastal road toward Gaza, while Kressenstein carried out an organized retreat.

Murray, after suffering defeats at Gaza in March and April of 1917, was replaced by Sir Edmund Allenby. Allenby moved military headquarters from Cairo to Palestine and began a new, aggressively offensive phase of the desert war.

Jack McCallum

References

Elgood, Percival G. *Egypt and the Army.* London: Oxford University Press, 1924.

Massey, William T. *The Desert Campaigns.* London: Constable and Company, Ltd., 1918.

See also ALLENBY, EDMUND; DJEMAL PASHA; EGYPT; MAXWELL, JOHN; MURRAY, ARCHIBALD

Sixte, Prince of Bourbon-Parma (1886–1934)

Noted French historian, explorer, and emissary for peace, born in Castello di Wartegg, Switzerland, on 1 August 1886. Sixte (or Sixtus) Bourbon-Parma, with his brother Xavier, served with great distinction in the Belgian army early in the war.

In 1917 the two brothers, at the suggestion of their sister, Empress Zita of Austria-Hungary, became envoys between Vienna, Paris, and London in the search for a separate peace. After receiving Emperor Karl's terms at Neuchâtel in February, the brothers visited Paris and found Premier Aristide Briand and President Raymond Poincaré receptive. After conveying this information to Emperor Karl in March, the brothers visited Paris again in April. A new French government received them with hostility, however; negotiations were dropped after another visit by the Bourbons to Vienna in May. Contrary to its promises, the French government then published letters Sixtus had delivered in April of 1918. This had great impact on peace proposals discussed that spring and even regarding the Avesnes Conference, for the Austrian denial of the letters bound her more closely to Germany and increased the belief that the Central Powers could mount a strategic offensive.

Sixte's own book on his role in peace negotiations with the French government was published in 1920. He died in Paris on 14 March 1934.

Timothy C. Dowling

References

Esposito, Vincent J., Brig. Gen. (Ret.) *A Concise History of World War I.* New York: Praeger, 1964.

Grey, Ronald, with Christopher Argyle. *Chronicle of the First World War.* 2 vols. New York: Facts on File, 1990.

Sestan, Ernesto, with Giovanni Cherubine. *Dizionarrio Storico Politico Italiano.* Florence: Samsoni, 1971.

See also KARL I; PEACE OVERTURES

Skoropadsky, Pavlo P. (1873–1945)

Czarist general and Ukrainian hetman. Born in Wiesbaden, Germany, in May of 1873, General Pavlo P. Skoropadsky was a russified aristocrat from an old Ukrainian family who quickly accumulated a distinguished combat record after the outbreak of the Great War. Decorated with the Order of St. George for his success in battle, he was subsequently promoted to lieutenant general.

Skoropadsky's transition from the military to politics ended in disaster. When the czarist regime collapsed in March of 1917, he "Ukrainized" the forces under his command and offered to place a 40,000-man Ukrainian corps at the disposal of the Central Rada, the national government that had come to power in the Ukraine in March as the Russian empire began to disintegrate. Suspicious of Skoropadsky's military and social intentions, the popular, socially radical government refused the offer.

Skoropadsky subsequently orchestrated a successful coup against the government on 29 April 1918 in alliance with the German military, which, after concluding the war with Russia in the Treaty of Brest-Litovsk in March of 1918, had became the real authority in Ukraine. Skoropadsky took on the historical Cossack title of hetman in an effort to evoke the quasi-monarchical traditions associated with the Cossack hetmans of the past. His socially conservative dictatorial regime, however, found itself badly compromised by its complete reliance on the Germans, its limited Ukrainian character, and its lack of popular support. When the Germans surrendered in November of 1918, Skoropadsky's government collapsed and the erstwhile general went into exile in Europe. He died at Metten, Bavaria, on 26 April 1945, when the train in which he was riding was destroyed by Allied aircraft.

Sylvia Russell

References

Adams, Arthur E. *Bolsheviks in the Ukraine: The Second Campaign, 1918–1919.* New Haven: Yale University Press, 1963.

Hunczak, Taras, ed. *The Ukraine, 1917–1921: A Study in Revolution.* Cambridge, Mass.: Harvard Ukrainian Research Institute, 1977.

Pipes, Richard. *Formation of the Soviet State.* New York: Atheneum, 1964.

Reshetar, John. *Ukrainian Revolution, 1917–1920: A Study in Nationalism.* Princeton: Princeton University Press, 1952.

Subtelny, Orest. *Ukraine: A History.* Toronto: University of Toronto Press, 1988.

See also UKRAINE

Slovaks

The outcome of the First World War, particularly the dismantling of the old Austro-Hungarian Empire, liberated many in Eastern Europe, including the Slovaks. Closely related to the Czechs, who had undergone a national revival in the nineteenth century, the Slovaks had lived under Magyar rule, and their own language and culture had been suppressed. The *Ausgleich* of 1867 widened this split. Czechs and Slovaks were now each ruled by the two separate, dominant ethnic groups of the empire, the Germans and Magyars, respectively. Before the *Ausgleich* the emperor had occasionally shown favor to the Slovaks in order to gain their support against the Magyars, but, afterwards, the emperor could not intervene on their behalf.

Mostly peasants and country folk, Slovaks were very weak in comparison with the more prosperous and powerful Magyars. Unlike the Romanian and Serb minorities within the Hungarian portion of the empire, the Slovaks had no outside national state to help them. The Magyars consistently blocked possible help from the Czechs, such as discouraging the construction of railroads and roads to the west from Slovakia. Rigid Magyarization squashed most Slovakian nationalism. Not until the end of the 1800s did a few educated, younger Slovaks begin to work for more voice. Those leaders, known as Young Slovakia, soon found a compatriot, the Czech Tomáš Masaryk, who believed that only by working together could the Czechs and Slovaks gain independence.

Because the Slovaks were so few in number, less organized, and so carefully watched by the Hungarian government, their leaders had trouble inspiring the people to participate in any political movement. While contributing all they could, and for many that included their very lives, the Slovaks assented to Czech leadership in the quest for independence during the war.

As with their Czech brethren, many Slovaks deserted the Austro-Hungarian army and fought with the Russians and Serbs against the Central Powers. In 1915 Slovak leader Milan Rastislav Stefánik joined Masaryk in Paris, where Masaryk and other Czech leaders sought help for Czech-Slovak independence. On 14 November 1915 the Paris exiles launched the Czech-Slovak movement for independence: The Czech Foreign Committee, as the group was known, issued a declaration demanding the establishment of an independent Czech state. In 1916 the committee transformed itself into the National Council of the Czech Lands, with its headquarters in Paris; Masaryk served as chairman, with Josef Dürich and Stefánik as vice-chairmen, and Edvard Beneš as secretary-general. Czech-Slovak persistence began to pay off when on 10 January 1917 the Allies issued a statement on their war aims that included the liberation of Czech lands.

Some attempts were made during the war to align Czechs and Slovaks with the future of Russia, but that proved difficult with all of the latter's problems. After Russia signed the Treaty of Brest-Litovsk, Czechs and Slovaks turned to America for help. In the summer of 1918 the Czech National Council received recognition as the de facto government of the Czech nation, for all practical purposes that organization also spoke for the Slovaks.

The few educated Slovak nationalists who were active were working with the council. Magyar repression during the war had made it extremely difficult to organize a grassroots national Slovak organization at home. Only in May of 1918 had a few Slovak Socialists and Social Democrats, led by Dr. Vavro Šrobár, demanded "self-determination for all nations, including also that branch of the Czechoslovak nation which lives in Hungary." Šrobár's actions landed him in jail, but Slovaks were aroused and, though they would have to work mainly underground, they were united with

Czechs in seeking independence. There would be no further public statements in Slovakia until the Slovak National Council was formed in October of 1918 as the empire began to disintegrate.

The Prague National Committee, formed by Karel Kramár in July as preparation for dissolution, issued its first law on 28 October: "The independent Czech state has come into being." On 30 October the Slovak National Committee, assembled at Turčansky Svätý Martin, issued a declaration stating that "the Slovak nation is a part of the Czechoslovak nation, one with it in language and in the history of its civilization. . . . We also claim for this, the Czechoslovak nation, the absolute right of self-determination on a basis of complete independence." Kramár and Beneš met at Geneva on 31 October to iron out the specifics for starting the new Czech state. It would be a democratic, parliamentary system with Masaryk as president, Kramár as premier, Beneš as foreign minister, and Štefánik as minister of war. Two days after the emperor abdicated and one day after the declaration of the German-Austrian Republic, a provisional constitution was issued on 13 November, creating a provisional national assembly; that body elected Masaryk as president. The two brethren peoples, separated for almost one thousand years, were to be joined together again.

Laura Matysek Wood

References
Seton-Watson, R.W. *History of the Czechs and the Slovaks*. London: Hutchinson, 1943.
Thomson, S. Harrison. *Czechoslovakia in European History*. Princeton: Princeton University Press, 1953.

See also AUSTRIA-HUNGARY, HOME FRONT; BENEŠ, EDVARD; CZECHS; MASARYK, TOMÁŠ

Śmigły-Rydz, Edward (1886–1941)

Polish army officer, born on 11 March 1886 at Brzeżany. Śmigły-Rydz was active in Jósef Piłsudski's struggle for Polish independence.

When Jósef Piłsudski organized Polish forces to fight for independence on the German side, Śmigły-Rydz volunteered. He commanded a battalion and then the first infantry regiment of Piłsudski's I Legionary Brigade, distinguishing himself at the battles of Anielin (October of 1914), Konary (May of 1915), and Kostiuchnówka (July of 1916). Following the summer 1917 crisis, when Piłsudski and his men refused to swear an oath of allegiance to the kaiser, Śmigły-Rydz resigned his commission and left for Cracow. There, in the absence of the imprisoned Piłsudski and his chief of staff Colonel Sosnkowski, Śmigły-Rydz took command of the underground Polish Military Organization *(Polska Organizacja Wojskowa)*, moving to Kiev in the spring of 1918. Śmigły-Rydz's aim was to build an organization without whose cooperation Polish political and military activities in the East would be impossible. He also prepared it to assume political leadership following the collapse of the Central Powers.

Śmigły-Rydz was minister of war in Ignacy Daszyński's shortlived Lublin government. He went on to become a marshal of Poland and commander in chief of the Polish armed forces during the 1939 Polish Campaign. He died on 2 December 1941 in Warsaw.

Andrzej Suchcitz

References
Mirowicz, Ryszard. *Edward Rydz-Śmigły*. Warsaw: Instytut Wydawniczy Związku Zawodowych, 1988.
Suchcitz, Andrzej. "Materiały do życiorysu Marszałka Śmigłego-Rydza," in *Przegląd Kawalerii i Broni Pancernej* No. 129 (May-August 1988). London.

See also PIŁSUDSKI, JÓSEF; POLAND

Smith-Dorrien, Sir Horace Lockwood (1858–1930)

British general, born at Haresfoot on 26 May 1858. Smith-Dorrien was educated at Sandhurst and joined the British army in 1877. He fought in the Zulu Wars, Egypt, India, and the Sudan (including the Battle at Omdurman) and served as Kitchener's escort at Fashoda. Promoted to major general during the Boer War, he subsequently had commands in India and became head of Southern Command at Salisbury in 1912.

On Britain's entry into the First World War, Smith-Dorrien received command of II Corps British Expeditionary Force in France. His corps suffered heavy casualties at Mons and was effectively left on its own. Nevertheless, it stood and fought at Le Cateau on 26 August. His three divisions fought the whole of General

Alexander von Kluck's First Army, which tried to carry out a double envelopment. Casualties in the battle were high. Although forced to retreat toward St. Quentin after eleven hours of fighting, Smith-Dorrien's corps had given the BEF time to regroup. The Germans, impressed by British stubborn resistance, failed to press the pursuit.

In December of 1914 Smith-Dorrien took over command of Second Army in the Ypres salient. The German assault of 22 April 1915, and subsequent British counterattacks ordered by General John French, resulted in confusion and mounting British casualties. Smith-Dorrien then ordered a cessation of British attacks and turned to consolidating his positions. His long and bitter letter of 27 April to French asking for a tactical withdrawal to more defensible positions was rejected and resulted in his recall to Britain on 6 May. His successor, General Herbert Plumer, was subsequently forced to carry out this withdrawal.

Smith-Dorrien was assigned command of First Army for the home defense. In December of 1915 he was given command of a British expedition in East Africa, but pneumonia made that or any further military assignment impossible until September of 1918, when he became governor of Gibraltar. He retired from the British army in 1923 and died in an auto accident on 12 August 1930. Smith-Dorrien was arguably one of the best British generals of the war. Unfortunately, he never had a chance to prove himself in higher command, as a result of the vindictiveness of a less capable superior.

Andrzej Suchcitz

References

Clark, Alan. *The Donkeys*. London: Hutchinson, 1961.
Smith-Dorrien, Sir Horace Lockwood. *Memories of Forty-Eight Years Service*. London: Murray, 1925.
Young, John. "The Man who Disobeyed?" *Military Illustrated* 52 (September 1992): 48–50.

See also FRONTIERS, BATTLE OF THE; YPRES, FIRST BATTLE OF

Smuts, Jan Christiaan (1870–1950)

South African military leader, born on 24 May 1870 in Bovenplaats, South Africa. Smuts was a lawyer, politician, and administrator. An anomaly in South Africa, Smuts nevertheless ranks among the top leaders in the country's history: Smuts had solid Afrikaner credentials and enjoyed great success as a guerrilla commander against the British in the Boer War, rising to the rank of general, yet he spent most of his political life cementing his country's fate to that of Great Britain.

Smuts pursued the goal of a union of South Africa, which was attained in 1910. Despite much Afrikaner opposition, he saw South Africa as a loyal member of the British Commonwealth, an organization on which he also left his imprint. When war began in 1914 Smuts was defense minister under Prime Minister Louis Botha and did not hesitate to support the British effort.

Anti-British sentiment among Afrikaners had not subsided, and opposition to the alliance became violent. The Germans had in fact supported the Afrikaner cause in the Boer War, and some South African troops under Colonel S.G. Maritz rebelled and joined the Germans. Smuts and Botha had to use force to restore order. Under Botha's overall command and with British naval support, Smuts headed the southern offensive that took control of South-West Africa from the Germans. German opposition was only modest, and their forces fled northward.

Smuts gained the respect of the British, who made him a general and selected him to command British operations in East Africa. Before the end of the war, Prime Minister David Lloyd George invited Smuts to join the British War Cabinet, a position that allowed him a chance to develop his concept of Commonwealth relations. As minister of air, Smuts helped organize the Royal Air Force. Smuts was also a major architect of the League of Nations. Smuts represented South Africa during the Paris Peace Conference, where he favored reparations and developed the mandate system under which the victors received control of the former German colonies. At the end of the conference, however, Smuts labored extensively, and unsuccessfully, for a more moderate stance toward Germany.

Smuts became prime minister of South Africa on the death of Louis Botha in August of 1919. In 1941 Smuts was made a British field marshal, and in 1945 at San Francisco he was one of the founders of the United Nations. Smuts died on 11 September 1950 at Irene, near Pretoria, South Africa.

Karl P. Magyar

References

Crafford, F.S. *Jan Smuts: A Biography*. London: Allen and Unwin, 1946.

Hancock, W.K. *Smuts: The Fields of Force 1919–1950*. Cambridge: Cambridge University Press, 1968.

———. *Smuts: The Sanguine Years 1870–1919*. Cambridge: Cambridge University Press, 1962.

Smuts, Jan Christian. *Jan Christian Smuts*. London: Cassell, 1952.

Uwechue, R. *Makers of Modern Africa: Profiles in History*. London: Africa Books, 1991.

See also AFRICA; BOTHA, LOUIS; LEAGUE OF NATIONS, COVENANT OF; PARIS PEACE CONFERENCE; SOUTH AFRICA, UNION OF

Somalia, War in

Prior to World War I the British had met repeated resistance from Somali leader Muhammad Abdille Hassan, who once told his British enemies: "I have no cultivated fields, no silver or gold for you to take. All you can get from me is war, nothing else." With Abyssinian, Italian, and local forces the British fought a long struggle against this "Mad Mullah," suffering a string of setbacks that only increased Hassan's prestige. By 1914 he commanded an army of almost 6,000 men that pinned Allied forces to the coast.

With the outbreak of World War I, both Ottoman and German officials saw Hassan as a possible Islamic Cromwell who might draw enemy troops from other theaters. They encouraged Lij Yasu, Abyssinia's pro-Ottoman ruler, to send him arms and consider an alliance. In August of 1916 some weapons arrived at Taleh, Hassan's fortified headquarters, but apart from propaganda and moral encouragement that was the extent of aid from the Central Powers.

At the same time both British and Somali strategies were in flux. Although his previous campaigns featured elusive native columns practicing hit-and-run tactics against slow-moving infantry units, in 1914 Hassan opted for construction of fortifications and static garrisons. British forces, augmented by a powerful Camel Corps, prepared for offensive action. Such changes spelled disaster for the Somalis. In November of 1914 they lost a key fort, Shimber Beris, along with much of its garrison. British forces secured another major victory on 9 Oc-tober 1917 when the Camel Corps smashed through Hassan's entrenched lines at Endow Pass. Somali forces rapidly declined after this, although it took a postwar infusion of motorized troops and RAF bombers to finish off the "Mad Mullah" in 1919.

John P. Dunn

References

de Wiart, Sir Adrian Carton, Lt. Gen. *Memoirs*. London: Macmillan, 1950.

Jardine, Douglas. *The Mad Mullah of Somaliland*. London: Herbert Jenkins, 1923.

Samatar, Said S. *Oral Poetry and Somali Nationalism: The Case of Sayyid Mahammad Abdille Hasan*. New York: Cambridge University Press, 1982.

United Kingdom. War Office, Directorate of Military Operations and Intelligence. *Somaliland 1897–1919, No. 106*. London: HMSO, 1920.

Somme, Battle of (1 July–19 November 1916)

On 6–8 December 1915 the second Inter-Allied Military Conference met at the Chantilly headquarters of French army commander General Joseph Joffre. Military representatives of France, Russia, Great Britain, Italy, and Serbia agreed to Joffre's plan to deliver simultaneous maximum-effort attacks against the Germans and their allies on all fronts. For the Franco-British front, Joffre planned a joint offensive on both sides of the Somme River. The French army would conduct the main attack, which would give the greatly expanded British army the opportunity to gain some experience with its new volunteer units. British army commander General Douglas Haig preferred to conduct his own offensive in the Ypres area but agreed to Joffre's plan. The Somme offensive was tentatively planned for late summer of 1916.

The Germans, meanwhile, had plans of their own. On 21 February they struck the French at Verdun, a battle that would drag on through December. The massive German attack unhinged the previous Allied plans. Verdun tied down the major portion of the French army, making the joint effort on the Somme impossible and therefore shifting the major burden for that offensive to the British. The purpose of the attack also changed. Rather than bringing pressure on the Germans, the purpose of the Somme offensive became relieving the pressure on the French.

The plan called for an attack along a sixteen-mile front north of the Somme River, running from Maricourt to Gommecourt in the north. The central axis of the attack ran roughly along the main road from Albert to Bapaume. The main effort would be conducted by the five corps of General Sir Henry Rawlinson's Fourth Army, with the VII Corps of General Sir Edmund Allenby's Third Army conducting a diversionary attack on either side of the Gommecourt salient on the north flank. South of the Somme the five divisions of the French Sixth Army under General Marie Fayolle would conduct a supporting attack. (The French XX Corps was actually north of the Somme, occupying an eight-mile sector between the river and Montauban.) Once a breakthrough was achieved, Haig envisioned a swing to the northeast, then an exploitation with the three British and two Indian cavalry divisions he held in reserve. Haig formed three of those divisions into the Reserve Army, under Lieutenant General Sir Hubert Gough. Before committing the Reserve Army to any exploitation, Haig planned to augment it with additional infantry divisions to support the cavalry.

On the German side, General Fritz von Below's Second Army had six divisions on line and five more in close reserve. The Germans expected some sort of attempt to relieve pressure at Verdun, but chief of the general staff General Erich von Falkenhayn believed that the blow would come in Alsace. Below was convinced that the attack would come in his sector. The Germans had worked long and hard to develop an impressive defensive complex in depth. They dug their trenches into the hard chalk ground and excavated numerous deep bunkers, impervious to anything but a direct hit from the heaviest of Allied guns. Along the whole line they had three, in some places four, defensive lines, to an average depth of five miles.

The British committed eighteen divisions to the attack—fourteen of which were in the first line. Eleven of those divisions were from Field Marshal Earl Horatio Herbert Kitchener's New Armies. There were very few conscripts in the British ranks at the start of the battle. Most were volunteers who had joined up in large groups, in some cases from whole neighborhoods or villages. What they lacked in training

and experience they more than made up for in spirit—or so they believed. Because of their lack of training, the initial assault was to be conducted with no complicated tactics or fancy movements. Straight linear assault formations were the best these raw troops could be expected to master under their first exposure to combat.

To compensate for the lack of infantry skills, the British planned a massive artillery preparation, which Rawlinson and the other generals believed would eliminate the majority of the first-line German defenders. When the shelling lifted, the British Tommies would simply have to climb out of their trenches, dress up their formations, and walk (not run) across no-man's-land to the German trenches.

The British started their artillery preparation with 1,537 guns on 24 June. Originally scheduled to last five days, the prep continued for two more days when the start of the attack was delayed because of bad weather. By the time the shelling lifted, the Royal Artillery had fired 1,627,824 rounds.

The 1st of July dawned bright and sunny. The attack was scheduled to begin at 07:30. Just prior to that the British detonated three large and seven smaller mines they had dug under the German positions. At 07:20 they blew the northernmost mine, under the German redoubt on Hawthorn Ridge, and at 07:28 they detonated the others. The two largest mines were at La Boisselle, on either side of the Albert-Bapaume Road. With twenty-four tons of explosives each, they were the biggest mines blown on the Western Front. Two minutes later artillery fire lifted from the leading German positions. Almost seventy thousand British troops, eighty-four battalions in all, started moving out across the 500 to 800 yards of no-man's-land. Even though they went forward weighted down with an unbelievable load of ammunition, rations, personal gear, entrenching equipment, and even barbed wire, many of the inexperienced but high-spirited British troops believed it would be a bit of a lark. In the 18th Division area, Captain W.P. Nevill, a company commander in the 8th East Surreys, gave each of his four platoons a football to kick across no-man's-land and even kicked out the first ball himself.

The German *Landser* refused to cooperate with the British plans. As soon as the shelling shifted they swarmed out from beneath the rubble of their deep bunkers, set up their

Maxim machine guns in the protective depressions of newly created shell craters, and proceeded to slaughter the even rows of advancing Tommies. Some British units did not even get out of their own barbed wire before they were mowed down. Others managed to take their initial objectives but at high cost. The 36th (Ulster) Division, just north of Thiepval in the middle of the British line, took the Schwaben Redoubt in the German first line. When the division's 107th Brigade attempted to capture their next objective, in the German second line, they came under heavy shelling from their own artillery. The British gunners were firing on a fixed timetable, but the infantry was attacking ahead of schedule.

As the day progressed Rawlinson continued to feed more forces into the battle. By midday, 129 battalions—100,000 troops—had been committed. At the end of that first day the British losses totaled 57,470, the largest single-day loss in British history. Of that number, 19,240 were killed or died of wounds, including footballer Captain Nevill. Almost 50 percent of the total casualties were suffered in the first hour of the attack. The numbers are almost impossible to visualize. They amounted to something like two casualties for every yard of the sixteen-mile front. The 34th Division alone suffered 6,380 casualties. Thirty-two of the battalions committed suffered over 500 casualties each. Put another way, British losses on that single day added up to more than seventy-five battalions, which is much larger than the entire British army of 1993. It would take twenty days of fighting after the Normandy landing in 1944 to equal what the British lost the first day of the Somme.

As night fell on the first day, hundreds of wounded British soldiers who had been cut off and stranded in no-man's-land started to crawl back into their own lines. Slowly, the senior British commanders in the rear areas came to understand the magnitude of the catastrophe. Almost nowhere along the line did the British come close to achieving their first-day objectives. Not only casualties but ammunition expenditures far exceeded initial estimates. On the extreme right, the French did make considerable gains, but that was not the main attack. Only the British XIII Corps, on the British far right and next to the French, had some success, capturing Montauban and crushing a subsequent German counterattack.

Haig decided to continue the offensive on the right flank where he had some success to exploit. He reorganized his forces and established a new army (later designated the Fifth) under Gough on the left, astride the Ancre River. Meanwhile, the British rushed fresh divisions into the area and started rotating out those that had been badly mauled.

The next major British effort came on 14 July. Despite his postwar reputation for dull and almost mindless generalship, Rawlinson showed imagination and daring in his plan. Attacking abreast, four divisions took a 6,000-meter stretch of the Bazentin Ridge, the forward slope of which was the German second defensive position. The initial approach was conducted over open ground and in the dark—a monumental command and control challenge considering the primitive communications systems of that time. Thanks to effective leadership, it was carried off with minimal losses. The Germans immediately rushed in three divisions to reinforce the sector. Six days later the French XX Corps took a strong German intermediate position between Maurepas and the north bank of the Somme.

On 23 July the British tried to extend their advances farther north along the ridge. This time Rawlinson's troops suffered severe setbacks, fighting over, taking, losing, and retaking scraps of ground. The sole British success came in Gough's sector, when two Australian divisions of the Anzac I Corps took Poziers. The Germans, meanwhile, continued to pour troops and guns into the area. The number of German units became too large for one field army to control, and Below's units south of the Somme were reorganized into another army under General Max von Gallwitz. Both armies were formed into an army group, also under Gallwitz.

On 4 September the French committed their Tenth Army under General Joseph Micheler, which extended the line of fighting to twelve miles south of the Somme. On both sides of the Somme, north to the Ancre River, the Allies continued the bloody push forward. The weather, meanwhile, turned wet, creating muddy conditions. After a short pause to regroup, Haig launched another major assault on 15 September, attacking with twelve divisions along a ten-mile front from Combles to the Ancre. That offensive quickly bogged down in the mud, although the French south of the Somme again achieved some success by advancing five to eight miles. The actions on the extreme flank, however, did little to influence the main battle.

Perhaps the most significant thing about 15 September was the first appearance of tanks on the battlefield. Their debut was not impressive. Plagued by mechanical problems, only eighteen of the forty-nine tanks the British committed managed to even make it to the line of departure. Still, the handful that did get into action had such a psychological impact on friend and foe alike that five days later Haig sent a message back to Britain urgently requesting one thousand more. Six months later, at the battle of Arras, the British still could muster only sixty.

The day following the British tank attack, Field Marshal Paul von Hindenburg arrived on the Western Front to assume command of the German armies. Hindenburg and his quartermaster general, Erich Ludendorff, did little to alter the situation on the Somme. But the same day he arrived, Hindenburg gave the orders to start construction of the rear defensive line, known as the Siegfried (Hindenburg) Line, to which the Germans withdrew in early 1917.

Haig attacked again on 25 September, this time north of the Ancre. After two days of vicious fighting the results were negligible. By this time the fall rains had settled in, and the shell-torn ground of the Somme battlefield became a sea of mud. Haig favored shutting the campaign down for the winter, but Joffre insisted that the British continue to exert pressure on the Germans. The fighting continued on a low but lethal scale. On 13 November the British won their last "victory" in the Somme campaign. A seven-division attack on either side of the Ancre was launched following the detonation of a mine under the German positions. The British advanced three-quarters of a mile and captured the fortified position at Beaumont-Hammel, along with 1,200 German prisoners. From there the British continued to inch along until 19 November. That day a blizzard hit, and that was followed by more rain. The Somme Campaign, which had started with such a terrible bang, ended with a pathetic whimper.

By the time the Somme offensive was over, the British had committed fifty-five divisions (including four Canadian, four Australian, and one New Zealand), the French had committed twenty, and the Germans ninety-five. (German divisions, however, tended to be slightly smaller than their French and British counterparts.) The losses were enormous. In 142 days of fighting, the British suffered a total of 419,654 casualties and the French, 194,451. All they had to show for it was about 125 square kilometers of ground, none of it key terrain. The German defenders had fought the Allies to a standstill, but they too had paid a terrible price. Estimated German casualties ran as high as 650,000. Losses were especially heavy among officers and experienced NCOs.

In the long run the Somme battles did have some influence on the course of the war. The 1916 attrition battles confirmed that an enemy's defensive position could be penetrated if the attacking commander were willing to pay the price. A decisive breakthrough, however, remained illusive. Some tacticians on both sides of the line had been advocating change for some time, but now they were taken more seriously—especially in the German Army. The heavy losses, particularly among their leadership, contributed to the German decision to pull back to the Hindenburg Line, a better-prepared and shorter position that could be held more easily with fewer troops. From that position the Germans perfected their doctrine of the flexible defense-in-depth that would cause the Allies so much heartache in 1917.

Some historians point to the Somme, especially the terrible first day, as a major turning point in British history. Some would even go so far as to say that the empire snapped psychologically when the results of that day became known at home. As noted, the majority of the British troops at that point were patriotic and highly motivated volunteers, who had responded to Kitchener's call to defend the empire. They had signed up by the thousands, from every level of British society, and were the cream of each stratum—and they died together on the Somme. Because of the particular recruiting methods of the New Armies, whole units were created from neighborhoods, trade associations, athletic clubs, and so forth. These units often were designated "Pals Battalions"—the Leeds Pals, the Grimsby Chums, even a Public Schools Battalion whose privates came from Britain's top families. They went into combat in these units and suffered their fate accordingly. Cities like Liverpool and Belfast were hit especially hard. As British historian A.J.P. Taylor later put it, "Idealism perished on the Somme."

David T. Zabecki

References

Farrar-Hockley, Anthony H. *The Somme*. London: Batsford, 1964.
Graves, Robert. *Goodbye to All That*. London: Folio Society, 1929.

Middlebrook, Martin. *The First Day on the Somme: 1 July 1916*. London: Allen Lane, 1971.

Sassoon, Siegfried. *Memoirs of an Infantry Officer*. London: Faber & Faber, 1930.

See also ALLENBY, EDMUND; BELOW, FRITZ VON; GREAT BRITAIN, ARMY; HAIG, DOUGLAS; HINDENBURG, PAUL VON; JOFFRE, JOSEPH; RAWLINSON, HENRY; VERDUN, BATTLE OF

Sonnino, Baron Giorgio Sidney (1847–1922)

Italian foreign minister and premier. Born at Pisa on 11 March 1847. Sonnino was the son of a Jewish father and Scottish mother. As a youth he studied with Leopoldo Franchetti, one of the leading experts on the underdevelopment of southern Italy. Elected to parliament in 1880, he served as minister of finance (1893–94), minister of the treasury (1894–96), and premier (1906 and 1909–10). He became minister of foreign affairs on 4 November 1914, after Marchese Antonio di San Giuliano's unexpected death.

A conservative of great personal integrity, Sonnino was also an introvert, diffident, and stubborn, who enjoyed no popular support even though as owner of the newspaper *Giornale d'Italia* he could shape public opinion. In 1895 he had successfully limited Italian expansion in East Africa, and in 1914 he favored obtaining concessions from Vienna and opposed intervention, a policy also embraced by Antonio Salandra, who saw Sonnino as his friend and political disciple. Dependent on the support of northern industrialists, conservative nationalists, and the southern bourgeoisie to overcome Giolitti's dominant coalition, both men sought to expand Italian influence in the Balkans while consolidating a conservative social order at home.

During early 1915, as interventionist agitation inside Italy mounted and the Central Powers faltered militarily, Sonnino decided that the Entente could win and that Rome could not expect to gain anything from Vienna except by force. Consequently, on 12 February 1915 Sonnino warned that any change in the status quo in the Balkans without consulting Italy would violate the Triple Alliance. In early March, after Austrian landings at Antivari (Bar) in Montenegro, he denounced the treaty, demanded the cession of Italian regions in Austria, and ordered his ambassador in London to open talks with the Entente.

Although Vienna offered to concede Italy some of its territorial demands, including Trieste and part of the Trentino, Sonnino rejected its proposal that all awards be made by a commission guaranteed by Germany. But Russian protection of Serbian interests also hampered his negotiations with the Entente, and Sonnino committed Italy to war with the Treaty of London on 26 April 1915, without obtaining colonial compensation, guarantees of a postwar alliance, outlets for Italian emigration, commercial provisions, or a mechanism to coordinate Italy's war effort with that of its allies. He even conceded the Italian city of Fiume to Hungary in the belief that the Dual Monarchy would remain a bulwark against a Slavic inundation after the war.

Sonnino survived Salandra's fall in 1916, helped to kill Austrian peace overtures in 1917, and obtained the city of Smyrna in the Treaty of San Giovanni di Moriana in April of 1917. Anxious to prevent the creation of a strong south-Slav state, he refused to recognize the July 1917 pact creating the Kingdom of the Serbs, Croats, and Slovenes. He also opposed the formation of eastern European legions to fight on the Italian front and ignored the Congress of Oppressed Peoples held in Rome in April of 1918. A bitter enemy of Leonida Bissolati and the Italian Left, Sonnino only grudgingly approved the independence of Poles, Czechs, and Yugoslavs.

At the Paris Peace Conference in 1919, Sonnino was unable to obtain Italy's demands. The final settlement of Italian claims fell to Tommaso Tittoni, Italy's ambassador to France in 1915, who had urged a more moderate policy toward the south Slavs. Sonnino died at Rome on 24 November 1922. Like his political ally, Salandra, Sonnino has become synonymous with the narrowly nationalist view of diplomacy and warfare contained in the phrase *sacro egoismo*.

James J. Sadkovich

References

Melograni, Piero. *Storia politica della grande guerra*. Bari: Laterza, 1971.

Salvemini, Gaetano. *La politica estera italiana dal 1871 al 1915*. Milan: Feltrinelli, 1970.

Sonnino, Sidney. *Diario, 1866–1922*. Edited by Benjamin F. Brown and Pietro Pastorelli. Bari: Laterza, 1972.

Vigezzi, Brunello. *Da Giolitti a Salandra*. Florence: Vallecchi, 1969.

See also ITALY, HOME FRONT; LONDON, TREATY OF; PARIS PEACE CONFERENCE; SALANDRA, ANTONIO

Souchon, Wilhelm (1864–1946)

German admiral and commander of the *Mittelmeerdivision*, 1913–17, and of the Ottoman Fleet, 1914–17. Born at Leipzig on 2 June 1864, Souchon entered the navy in 1881. He served on the admiralty staff *(Admiralstab)* from 1902 to 1904 and in October of 1913 assumed command of the *Mittelmeerdivision*, which consisted of the new battle cruiser *Goeben* and light cruiser *Breslau*.

At daybreak on 4 August he opened hostilities in the Mediterranean by bombarding the French Algerian ports of Bône and Philippeville. Souchon returned to Messina to coal only to learn that Italy's declaration of neutrality meant that he would not be able to stay in port long enough to fill his bunkers. He had no desire to be bottled up in the Adriatic with the Austrians, and decided to make a break for Constantinople. Souchon might well have been intercepted by British Rear Admiral E.C.T. Troubridge's 1st Cruiser Squadron near the Adriatic, but the admiralty had ordered Troubridge not to engage superior forces except in combination with the French. The admiralty apparently meant the Austrian fleet, but Troubridge took the order to mean the *Goeben*, whose speed and 11-inch guns might have permitted her to sink his four cruisers before they and their 9.5-inch and 7.5-inch guns were in range. The French fleet was far away, primarily concerned with protecting troop transports between North Africa and the mainland. Souchon, therefore, had a clear field to reach the Aegean, coal from a German collier at a prearranged rendezvous, and pass through the Dardanelles. Troubridge was later court-martialed but acquitted.

The German government arranged a fictitious sale of *Goeben* and *Breslau* to the Turkish government, and Souchon subsequently became chief of the Turkish fleet, with German officers in other key positions, although final decisions in theory rested with the Turkish High Command. Frustrated by Turkish neutrality, Souchon soon entered into a conspiracy with pro-war members of the Turkish government. On the morning of 29 October he attacked Odessa and other locations along the Russian coast, thereby earning the distinction of having initiated hostilities in the Black Sea as well as the Mediterranean. Souchon was proud of this action and wrote his wife, "I have thrown the Turks into the powder-keg and kindled war between Russia and Turkey."

The attack caused little harm to the Russians, and Souchon soon found that his two most precious assets, the *Goeben* and *Breslau*, led a precarious existence, dependent on their speed for safety. The entry of Russian dreadnoughts into service in 1915 along with fast, large destroyers further curtailed his freedom of maneuver, while Russian submarines instituted a blockade of the Bosphorus. Souchon found it frustrating to deal with the Turks and never developed a rapport with them. Constantinople lacked adequate repair and docking facilities, and the campaign of Russian destroyers against the colliers carrying coal from Zonguldak to Constantinople caused severe shortages. Souchon was never able to dislodge Russian control of the Black Sea. In early September of 1917 he left Turkey to command the Fourth Battle Squadron of the High Seas Fleet. He and his squadron participated in Operation Albion, the successful operations in the Gulf of Riga in October. In late October of 1918 Souchon became commander of the Baltic Naval Station and governor of the naval base at Kiel. Within a few days the mutiny in the High Seas Fleet spread to Kiel, and Souchon lost control of the situation and virtually abdicated power to the Sailor's Council. Souchon retired in March of 1919 and died in Bremen on 13 January 1946.

Paul G. Halpern

References

Horn, Daniel. *The German Naval Mutinies of World War I*. New Brunswick, N.J.: Rutgers University Press, 1969.

Lorey, Hermann. *Der Krieg in den türkischen Gewässern*. 2 vols. Berlin: E.S. Mittler und Sohn, 1928–38.

Mäkelä, Matti E. *Auf den Spuren der Goeben*. Munich: Bernard & Graefe Verlag, 1979.

———. *Souchon der Goebenadmiral*. Braunschweig: Vieweg, 1936.

See also BLACK SEA, NAVAL WAR IN; *GOEBEN* AND *BRESLAU*

South Africa, Union of

Although the Union of South Africa joined other members of the British Empire in supporting the British war effort in World War I, its participation did not come without substantial controversy. The major problem concerned Prime Minister Louis Botha's underestimation of Afrikaner resistance to fighting on behalf of or alongside Britain. Botha and Defense Minister Jan Smuts managed to involve South Africa in World War I, but they made many enemies among their fellow Afrikaners. Many Afrikaners had developed negative views of capitalism, identifying it with British imperialism and financial control over South Africa at a time when Afrikaners were still farmers and laborers. The memory of devastating British destruction and the harsh concentration camps instituted for Afrikaners during the Boer War also made it unpalatable for many to fight on behalf of the British cause. Many Afrikaners also remembered Germany's support during that war.

Botha and Smuts were motivated not only by expectations of favorable treatment for South Africa politically, but also by prospects of incorporating South West Africa and possibly Southern Rhodesia and Mozambique into the union. In the war, South Africa played a leading role in actions in German South West Africa and German East Africa, and sent some contingents to Europe. Because of South Africa's valuable participation, Smuts was appointed to the British War Cabinet in 1917.

The Campaign in South West Africa

This theater of war was the site of South Africa's greatest commitment; it also produced the greatest controversies. Essentially, two battles were involved. The first was a rebellion in the Afrikaner ranks that included military contingents led by top officers of the Boer War. The second concerned the takeover of South West Africa from the Germans. Of the two, the latter was the easier to accomplish, as it was politically less sensitive.

When the First World War began in Europe, the South African government, sensing the problem of anti-British sentiment, constituted a volunteer force for service in South West Africa. Britain had asked for assistance in dismantling Germany's wireless stations at Luederitz Bay and Swakopmund, and in the administrative town of Windhoek. The first two objectives were to be gained with British naval assistance, and the latter by a land invasion from South African territory.

Before that could take place, however, an Afrikaner rebellion occurred. Its leaders included Generals Beyers, Kemp, and de la Rey, and Colonel Maritz, who, with his military unit, went to Windhoek and for a while joined the Germans. That was a serious development, which apparently included a rebel takeover of the Pretoria government. The rebellion also fed secessionist demands in the Transvaal and Orange Free State. Botha tried persuasion but in the end resorted to force to reestablish order. Thousands of rebels were disarmed; overall, they received surprisingly lenient treatment.

With domestic order restored by February of 1915, Botha, as general, took personal command of the war against the Germans in South West Africa. It was not much of a battle. The Germans, greatly outnumbered, mostly retreated northwards. All told, four South African columns advanced on German targets and objectives, with Smuts commanding the southern and Botha the northern forces. An April battle near Gibeon saw the Afrikaners prevail. By May Botha was in Windhoek, where he refused a German compromise offer. The Germans withdrew in disarray northward again and in July surrendered. One year into the Great War, South West Africa was lost to the Germans, and South Africa gained a problem.

East Africa

As part of her imperial obligation, South Africa was expected to provide assistance wherever in Africa her military services were needed. In 1915 the British government asked for South Africa's help in fighting the Germans in East Africa, ably led by General Paul von Lettow-Vorbeck. South Africa supplied a sizable troop contingent, and Smuts was given command of the entire operation when the British commander took ill. European, African, and even Indian forces were employed in the effort, but Lettow-Vorbeck fought a dogged mobile guerrilla campaign. Although he was chased out of German territory, he survived in neighboring lands and reentered German East Africa, remaining an active combatant until the end of the war.

South Africans in Europe

By the end of 1915, a 6,000-man brigade was in Britain for training. The men in turn transferred to Egypt, where they helped protect the Suez Canal against the Turks. While they met with success in Egypt, they suffered heavy casualties after being transferred to France. The worst disaster occurred at Delville Wood, where only a quarter of a force of 3,000 men survived. South Africans also fought in the battle of the Somme, in Belgium, and Palestine. Whites were also joined by black South Africans overseas—though the whites insisted that blacks not be allowed arms; as a result, blacks served only in support capacities.

At the Paris Peace Conference at war's end, Smuts engineered the mandate system. South Africa, however, got a mandate over only South West Africa—the source of ongoing problems until that colony's independence as Namibia.

Karl P. Magyar

References

Davenport, T.R.H. *South Africa: A Modern History*. Toronto: University of Toronto Press, 1987.

Geen, M.S. *The Making of the Union of South Africa*. London: Longmans, Green, 1947.

Hancock, William K. *Smuts: The Sanguine Years*. Cambridge: Cambridge University Press, 1962.

Walker, Eric A. *A History of South Africa*. London: Longmans, Green, 1935.

See also AFRICA; BOTHA, LOUIS; LETTOW-VORBECK, PAUL; SMUTS, JAN

South Pacific

Although the South Pacific islands played only a minor role in World War I, there were changes resulting from the conflict. During the nineteenth century the leading colonial powers vied to win control over islands in the South Pacific. Great Britain wanted them as a barrier to protect approaches to Australia, but she also sought to profit from them economically by the extraction of indigenous metals. The British regarded Germany as the principal threat to her interests in the South Pacific.

Within days of her declaration of war against Germany, Great Britain issued orders for a South Pacific force to occupy German-controlled islands. German wireless stations were chief targets. New Zealand troops boarded Australian and French cruisers at New Caledonia, and additional troops were taken on at Fiji. After a 1,000-mile journey, on 30 August they landed at German Samoa. The Germans refused to surrender, but a day later the New Zealanders took control, removed German officials to an internment camp, and initiated a peaceful occupation.

After Samoa was secured, an Australian invasion force sailed to New Guinea. Its primary target was a powerful wireless station at Rabaul, where local German reservists trained native troops to reinforce the defenses. Australian troops landed on 11 September and began to move on the wireless station, sparking the only World War I skirmish in the South Pacific. The Australians encountered snipers but by the next morning had successfully secured the station. The capture of Rabaul entailed six Australian casualties, one native German, and thirty New Guinea soldiers. By the 17th, the German governor surrendered the island. British military rule retained German regulations, and the residents, primarily planters and traders, swore oaths of neutrality so that their commercial activity would not be interrupted. In 1916, Great Britain annexed the Gilbert and Ellice islands as colonies.

Japan also seized the opportunity of war in Europe to expand its empire at Germany's expense. In the fall of 1914, Japanese naval units took the German possessions in the northern Marianas, the Carolines, and Marshall Island.

During the remainder of the war the South Pacific theater remained placid, save for some German navy raids against Entente shipping. Allied naval units also sank German ships. Some industries, such as pearling, ceased during the war—enabling shell beds to replenish after decades of heavy harvests. Other commodities, such as copra—dried coconut meat used to derive oil for soap and nitroglycerine—enjoyed wartime booms, boosting the overall economy of the region.

A 1917 secret treaty between Britain and Japan recognized permanent claims to German South Pacific possessions. The Paris Peace Conference, however, assigned these islands as mandates, emphasizing national self-determination. Because many of these former German islands were unable to be independent economically, the Permanent Mandates Commission of the League of Nations supervised their administration by selected nations. When military occupation ceased in 1921, Australia received a mandate over German New Guinea. New Zealand was awarded trust of German Samoa, and Japan was entrusted with German Micronesia. Great Britain, Australia, and New Zealand were given joint trusteeship of Nauru.

In addition to contributions by Australia and New Zealand to the Entente war effort, a Maori battalion fought with British troops in Europe and a Fijian labor unit provided noncombat services.

Elizabeth D. Schafer

References

Campbell, I.C. A *History of the Pacific Islands*. Berkeley: University of California Press, 1989.

Dane, Edmund. *British Campaigns in Africa and the Pacific: 1914–1918*. London: Hodder and Stoughton, 1919.

Grattan, C. Hartley. *The Southwest Pacific since 1900*. Ann Arbor: University of Michigan Press, 1963.

Mackenzie, Seaforth S. *The Australians at Rabaul: The Capture and Administration of the German Possessions in the Southern Pacific*. St. Lucia: University of Queensland Press, 1987.

Oliver, Douglas L. *The Pacific Islands*. 3rd ed. Honolulu: University of Hawaii Press, 1989.

See also JAPAN; PARIS PEACE CONFERENCE; VERSAILLES, TREATY OF

Spain

At the beginning of the twentieth century, Spain was a country in turmoil. The country had just lost most of its overseas colonies in a war with the United States and through sale to Germany. Spain was also involved in an unpopular colonial war in Morocco (1909–26). Spain itself was rife with calls for social and political change of every spectrum. In November of 1912 Premier Jose Canalejas was assassinated, and in April of 1913 an attempt was made to assassinate King Alphonso XIII. The parliament was divided between the Liberal and Conservative parties, which were in turn torn by internal dissent that put ideology before party welfare. As a result, neither party could muster enough votes in parliament to pass its own program.

When war began in Europe in 1914, a consensus soon developed in Spain that the coun-

try should remain neutral. The Spanish people were divided over which side to favor in the war, but there were no major political or economic issues that would cause Spain to intervene.

The war brought prosperity to certain segments of Spain as orders for raw materials, finished goods, and agricultural products were placed by the Allies. The Spanish merchant marine profited from the Allies' need for shipping. There was a price, however. During the war the Spanish merchant marine suffered heavily from German U-boat attacks and lost more than sixty-five ships, totaling approximately 140,000 tons. Shipping interests prevailed on Premier Count Alvaro de Figueroa y Torres de Romanones in January of 1917 to send a strong protest to Germany against these sinkings. There was, however, no strong political will to bring it to confrontation. A German assurance to replace lost tonnage on a one-to-one basis at the end of the war also quieted the shipping industry.

During the war Spanish industry profited from foreign orders, but the resulting inflation created social disorder as wages did not keep up with the increase in the cost of living. Spanish industrialists failed to invest this influx of foreign currency in expanding and modernizing the industrial base, transportation networks, and communication systems. As a result, postwar Spain was unable to compete with other European countries for overseas markets.

Spanish budget deficits and social and economic turmoil led to a succession of gradually worsening parliamentary crises. The forming of new cabinets became a common occurrence. A military coup was just as ineffective in solving problems. Demands for a new constitution foundered on the irreconcilability of the various types of governments advocated and the demand for political autonomy by some regions. In August of 1916 there was violence when the government resorted to force to put down a major industrial strike. Nonetheless, political turmoil and terrorist violence continued to increase throughout the war years and afterward. The Spanish Civil War of 1936–39 was a continuation of the basic fundamental and unreconcilable differences between the Left and the Right.

A major event in Spain was the outbreak of what has been labeled "Spanish Influenza." This flu epidemic supposedly originated at San Sebastian, Spain, but was most probably of Asian origin. Its deadliness, however, was first recognized in Spain. The epidemic swept through Europe and the rest of the world between 1918 and 1919. It was the most deadly disease to hit modern man, claiming an estimated twenty-seven million people worldwide in the two-year period.

Charles H. Bogart

References

Carr, Raymond. *Spain 1808–1939*. London: Oxford University Press, 1966.

De Madariaga, Salvador. *Spain—A Modern History*. New York: Praeger, 1958.

Smith, Rhea. *Spain*. Ann Arbor: University of Michigan Press, 1965.

Spee, Maximilian Johannes Maria Hubert Graf von (1861–1914)

German admiral and commander of the German East Asian Cruiser Squadron at the battles of Coronel and the Falklands. Born on 22 June 1861 at Copenhagen to an imperial count, Spee entered the navy in 1878 and as a junior officer served at Kiel and in foreign service off the African Coast. In 1887–88 Spee commanded the German port in the Cameroons but was invalided home because of a severe fever. During the China War he was on the staff of Rear Admiral Prince Henry of Prussia. Promoted to commander in 1899, Spee served as executive officer aboard the *Brandenburg* for two years and then worked in the weapons department of the German Admiralty for three more years. As captain, Spee commanded the cruiser *Wittelsbach* and in 1908 became chief of staff on the North Sea Command. Spee reached flag rank (rear admiral) in 1910 and raised his flag on the cruiser *Yorck* as second in command of the High Seas Fleet's scouting groups. After a brief period of special duty at Kiel, Spee was given command of the German East Asian Cruiser Squadron in 1912 and promoted to vice admiral the next year.

At the outbreak of World War I in 1914, his squadron consisted of the armored cruisers *Scharnhorst* and *Gneisenau,* as well as the light cruisers *Emden* and *Nürnberg.* The squadron had been at Ponape Island in the Carolines when hostilities began, and Japan's declaration of war against Germany precluded its return to Chinese waters. Spee dispatched the *Emden* to raid shipping in the Indian Ocean and gave orders for the *Dresden* and *Leipzig,* which were off the eastern coast of the United States, to join him. On 22

September Spee's squadron bombarded Tahiti, then headed for the west coast of South America.

On 1 November British Admiral Sir Christopher Cradock's 4th Cruiser Squadron spotted Spee's enlarged squadron off Coronel, Chile, and moved to engage. The Germans held the advantage in speed and guns and used them to inflict serious damage on the British squadron. The armored cruisers *Good Hope,* with Cradock aboard, and *Monmouth* were sunk with a loss of all hands, totaling 1,600 officers and men. This was one of the few big victories for the German navy during the war.

Spee's victory and the fear it instilled in the British are amazing in light of the conditions in which he was forced to operate—half a world away from Germany, without a base, dependent on a tenuous lifeline of supply ships, and hunted by an ever-increasing number of enemy ships. After a brief stop at Valparaiso, Spee decided to head for home through the Atlantic, but, unknown to him, the angry British Admiralty had dispatched a powerful squadron to the South Atlantic. With his aggressive nature, Spee decided to stop at the Falkland Islands on 8 December and destroy the wireless station there. Unfortunately, the British squadron had just put in at Port Stanley in the Falklands. The German squadron was doomed as soon as the faster and more heavily armed British ships gave chase. By nightfall the Germans had lost *Scharnhorst, Gneisenau, Nürnberg,* and *Leipzig,* and a total of 2,200 men, including Admiral Spee and his two sons. Only the *Dresden* managed to escape, at least temporarily. Spee's keen intelligence, aggressiveness, strength of will, and fighting spirit had given the German navy its first victory of the war. In his honor, the German navy in 1934 christened the pocket battleship *Admiral Graf Spee,* which during World War II would be scuttled in Montevideo, not so far from the admiral's resting place.

Laura Matysek Wood

References

Hoyt, Edwin P. *Kreuzerkrieg*. Cleveland, Ohio: World Publishing, 1968.

See also CORONEL, BATTLE OF; *EMDEN;* FALKLANDS, BATTLE OF

Stab-in-the-Back Myth *(Dolchstoss)*

Symptomatic of the internal difficulties faced by the postwar Weimar Republic, the stab-in-the-back (Dolchstoss) myth was propagated after the end of the war by those who wanted to shift responsibility for Germany's defeat away from the military and the wartime government. The myth was that the Second Reich had lost the war not because its army was defeated in the field but because of a treacherous attack behind the army's back by the radical, pacifist, and revolutionary movements inside Germany itself. Typifying the conservative military position, General Heinrich von Scheuch reassured a group of returning soldiers one month after the Armistice, "If ever anybody should affirm that the German army was beaten in this war, history will call it a lie. Let the consciousness of having returned home undefeated never be taken from you!"

The German political Right—Monarchists, Junkers, industrialists, the military—had long felt concern about the weakening of the German nation from within by disparate, often radical, left-wing factions. By pointing to treachery from within, the stab-in-the-back theory identified and left vulnerable to retribution enemies of the German Right, and seriously undermined the credibility of the new republic. Radicals among the Communists and Independent Socialists, like the Sparticists, were already in open combat with counterrevolutionary forces immediately after the war, but even moderates of the Social Democratic party, the labor unions, and the constitutional democrats found themselves implicated in the Dolchstoss myth.

In a nation unified through war and a society that had been educated to look upon the soldier as its highest ideal, the stab-in-the-back myth preserved many Germans' sense of honor and national identity. In an effort to discredit this reactionary nationalist explanation of the war, the liberal Weimar Republic set up after the war a Reichstag Inquiry Commission to examine the Dolchstoss legend. Historian Hans Delbrück argued at the time, "The attempt to explain our defeat by the stab-in-the-back is not only a distortion of the truth . . . but stupid propaganda." These efforts fell far short of dissociating the Republic from culpability for defeat. Instead of enlightening people regarding the responsibility of the imperial leadership for war and defeat, republican leaders vied amongst themselves to make the strongest nationalist denunciations of war guilt and the "chains of Versailles." Not a single school textbook of the interwar period attempted to show the role played by General Erich Ludendorff or the general staff in Germany's collapse.

The stab-in-the-back myth was highly appealing propaganda to people facing hard and threatening times in postwar Germany. Racked by revolution, forced to justify its acceptance of the Versailles Treaty, surrounded by national and ideological enemies, the Weimar government was beset by nationalist groups that associated it with the collapse of 1918. People who expressed nostalgia for an idealized recollection of monarchical paternalism and those who heard increasingly harsh and polarized appeals from the reactionary extreme found comfort in a simple explanation for German defeat and postwar troubles.

Craig Cameron

References

Endres, F.C. *Die Tragödie Deutschlands*. Munich: Duncker and Humbolt, 1922.

Maurice, Frederick. *Armistices of 1918*. London: Oxford University Press, 1943.

Petzold, J. *Die Dolchstosslegende*. 3rd ed. Berlin: Akademie Verlag, 1963.

Rudin, Harry R. *Armistice 1918*. New Haven: Yale University Press, 1944.

See also GERMANY, REVOLUTION OF 1918

Stalin, Joseph (1879–1953)

Prominent Bolshevik leader. Joseph Stalin was born Iosif Vissarionovich Dzhugashvili on 21 December 1879 in the Georgian village of Gori. His father, a former serf, was a shoemaker given to drunkenness and beating his wife and child. His mother, like most peasant women, married young. As the only avenue of escape from peasant poverty, she enrolled Iosif in a Russian Orthodox seminary. He remained there as an average student for two years and was then expelled, possibly for his radical political views.

The two important contributions of the seminary to Stalin's life were that it taught him to view the world dogmatically, and its rigidness forced him into a local Georgian Marxist group, the Mesame Dasi. The latter was not unusual, as clandestine revolutionary groups were widespread in Russia around the turn of the century. What was unusual was that, after the split within the Russian Social Democratic party in 1903, Stalin chose to join Lenin's Bolshevik faction, little more than a fringe group at the time. Perhaps Stalin wished to be a big fish in a small pond. Most of the Marxist intellectuals belonged to the Mensheviks.

In the first decade of the twentieth century Stalin took the name Koba, after an ancient Georgian Robin Hood–type hero. While Lenin and the other Bolshevik leaders were in exile abroad Koba remained in Russia, where he belonged to a fighting squad that raised money for the party. After one daring train robbery he was able to send 250,000 rubles to the Bolshevik leaders. Koba was soon noticed as a man who got things done. In 1912 he wrote an article on the nationalities issue that he signed K. Stalin (the man of steel) and that caught the attention of Lenin. In the same year he was elevated to the Bolshevik Central Committee.

The outbreak of the war in 1914 saw Stalin already in Siberian exile, where he shared a hut with L.M. Sverdlov, future president of the Soviet Republic. The latter described Stalin as rude and irritable, a complaint that became common among those who knew him. In 1915 Stalin appeared before a local draft board but was rejected because of a withered arm. Then, in March of 1917, under a provisional government political amnesty, Stalin returned to Petrograd; there he found himself the senior Bolshevik in the Russian capital. He resurrected the party newspaper, *Pravda,* accepted a seat on the Soviet, and adopted the general line of support for the provisional government. On learning of this, Lenin, still in Switzerland, became angry because Stalin had violated his own strategy for gaining power. Upon Lenin's arrival in Petrograd on 16 April he severely castigated Stalin and others who had adopted the majority political line. Lenin's own strategy was outlined in the editorial "The April Theses," which stated that the Bolsheviks would go underground and seize power at the proper time, by force if necessary. On 7 November, when this actually occurred, Stalin was given the post of Commissar of Nationalities in the new government. Within the Bolshevik party he sat on more committees than any other member. During the Civil War (1918–21) he served as a troubleshooter, being sent to places where serious problems arose. After Lenin's death in 1924, Stalin used his position as general secretary of the Communist party as a springboard to supreme power. From the late 1920s until his death in 1953 he was dictator of Russia.

Although Stalin's role in World War I was minimal, his significance for Soviet Russia and the entire twentieth century was monumental. Stalin and his German counterpart, Adolf Hitler, defined the modern era in political terms. In a larger sense, World War I produced both these men, and they were its legacy. Stalin died in Moscow of a cerebral hemorrhage on 5 March 1953.

John W. Bohon

References

Tucker, Robert C. *Stalin as Revolutionary, 1879–1929.* New York: Norton, 1973.
Ulam, Adam. *Stalin, the Man and His Era.* Boston: Beacon, 1989.

See also LENIN, VLADIMIR; RUSSIA, HOME FRONT AND REVOLUTIONS OF 1917

Stein, Hermann von (1854–1927)

Prussian general and minister of war, 1916–18, born into a middle-class family (his father was a pastor) on 13 September 1854 at Wedderstedt in the Harz region. Stein was commissioned in the field artillery in 1875 and attended the Kriegsakademie in the 1880s. With his keen mind and strong nerves, he was given increasing responsibilities in the Prussian general staff and in 1910 became General Helmuth von Moltke's righthand man as *Oberquartier-meister* I (first deputy chief of staff). In 1913, while commanding a newly created division in East Prussia, Stein received a patent of nobility from the kaiser.

When war began, Stein returned to Moltke's staff as his official deputy. He was removed from the high command (along with Moltke) in mid-September of 1914 and sent to the Western Front as a corps commander. In that capacity he participated in several major battles and received the *Pour le Mérite* medal in September of 1916. Eight weeks later, on 29 October, he was appointed Prussian minister of war. That position caused him to become involved in numerous political and economic issues on the home front. While he usually tried to act in consonance with the wishes of the Third OHL, Stein repeatedly opposed their demands for an extension of military service obligations to all males between the ages of fifteen and sixty. In September of 1918 Stein also played a major role in forcing General Erich Ludendorff to replace his chief of operations, Lieutenant Colonel George Wetzell, with Colonel Wilhelm Heye.

Following Germany's peace overture to President Wilson and the change of government in Berlin, Stein gave up his portfolio and was placed on the standby list. He retired from the army six days after the Armistice came into effect. Stein died at Wedderstedt on 26 May 1927.

Ulrich Trumpener

References

Deist, Wilhelm, ed. *Militär und Innenpolitik im Weltkrieg 1914–1918.* 2 vols. Düsseldorf: Droste, 1970.

Feldman, Gerald D. *Army, Industry, and Labor in Germany, 1914–1918.* Princeton: Princeton University Press, 1966.

Jäschke, Gotthard. "Zum Problem der Marne-Schlacht von 1914." *Historische Zeitschrift* 190 (1960): 311–48.

Priesdorff, Kurt von. Nachlass N556/6, No. 1910/10. Freiburg, Bundesarchiv-Militärarchiv.

Ritter, Gerhard. *The Sword and the Scepter: The Problem of Militarism in Germany.* Vols. 2–4. Coral Gables, Fla.: University of Miami Press, 1970–73.

See also MOLTKE, HELMUTH VON

St. Germain, Treaty of (10 September 1919)

After four months of agonizing over the harsh peace terms drawn up in Paris by the Allied and associated powers, the national assembly of the newly created Republic of Austria voted 97 to 23 to accept the treaty on 6 September 1919. Four days later, the Social Democratic president of Austria, Karl Renner, formally signed the document at the palace of St. Germain-en-Laye, France.

Composed of 381 articles and several annexes, the treaty registered the dissolution of the Hapsburg Empire, awarded much of its territory to the new states of Poland, Czechoslovakia, and Yugoslavia (the "Serb-Croat-Slovene State") as well as to Italy and Romania. The treaty also stipulated (Article 88) that the remaining rump state, Austria, must not compromise its independence (that is, merge with Germany) without the consent of the Council of the League of Nations.

As with the Versailles Treaty imposed on Germany, the Treaty of St. Germain opened with the Covenant of the League of Nations. In Part II, Austria's border with Italy was shifted to the Brenner, thus separating 240,000 German-speaking inhabitants of South Tyrol from their compatriots north of that mountain pass. Similarly, three million German-speaking people in Bohemia and Moravia were assigned to the new "Czecho-Slovak State," despite vehement previous protests from members of that group. As for the bitterly contested frontier with the new "Serb-Croat-Slovene State," Articles 49 and 50 of the treaty prescribed a plebiscite in the Klagenfurt area of Carinthia. (Held in October of 1920, the plebiscite resulted in a majority vote for Austria.) Austria was awarded a small slice of Hungarian territory, the "Burgenland."

Part III of the St. Germain Treaty dealt with a variety of political and financial issues arising from the collapse of the Hapsburg Empire and the concomitant rise of various successor states, while Part IV covered "Austrian Interests Outside Europe."

In Part VI the armed forces of Austria were placed under a multitude of restrictions. The Austrian army was limited to 30,000 men and conscription was banned. As with Germany, the new republic was not allowed to have "armored cars, tanks or any similar machines suitable for use in war," nor a variety of other weapons (Article 135). Moreover, like Germany, Austria could not maintain "any military or naval air forces" (Article 144). Since the deposed Hapsburg Emperor Karl had already "donated" the Austro-Hungarian fleet to Yugoslavia toward the end of his reign (31 October 1918), the naval clauses of the St. Germain Treaty were fairly straightforward: Austria was permitted to keep three patrol boats on the Danube River, and the "construction or acquisition of any submarine, even for commercial purposes," was explicitly forbidden (Article 140). Compliance with these and a host of other disarmament measures was to be supervised by "Inter-Allied Commissions of Control."

In Article 177 the Allied and associated powers made the new republic accept "the responsibility of Austria and her allies for causing the loss and damage to which the Allied and Associated Governments and their nationals have been subjected as a consequence of the war imposed upon them by the Aggression of Austria-Hungary and her allies." Like Article 231 of the Versailles Treaty, this statement was primarily designed to buttress Allied claims for reparations, but many Austrians (as with the Germans before them) regarded it as a "war guilt" clause and were outraged by it. Since Austria's economy and finances remained in a rather feeble state in subsequent years, the Allied reparation demands soon became illusory.

The peace terms imposed upon the Republic of Austria (its original name, *Deutsch-Österreich,* or German-Austria, having been abandoned under Allied pressure) evoked much resentment in that country, even in Leftist circles. Probably the most objectionable aspects of the St. Germain Treaty were the de facto prohibition of a merger with Germany *(Anschluss)* and the blatant disregard of the right of self-determination in the case of the South Tyrolese and the German-speaking millions assigned to Czechoslovakia. Similarly resented was the Allied statement in Article 177, both because it suggested that the Central Powers were exclusively responsible for the outbreak of the Great War and because it held the small republic financially accountable for the deeds of an empire that no longer existed. Duly ratified, except by the United States, the Treaty of St. Germain came into effect in 1920.

Ulrich Trumpener

References

Ackerl, Isabella, and Rudolf Neck, eds. *Saint-Germain 1919.* Munich: Oldenbourg, 1989.

Almond, Nina, and Ralph Haswell Lutz, eds. *The Treaty of St. Germain: A Documentary History of Its Territorial and Political Clauses.* Stanford: Stanford University Press, 1935.

Fellner, Fritz. "Der Vertrag von St. Germain." In *Oesterreich 1918–1938: Geschichte der Ersten Republik,* edited by Erika Weinzierl and Kurt Skalnik. Graz: Styria, 1983.

Mayer, Arno J. *Politics and Diplomacy of Peacemaking.* New York: Knopf, 1967.

Treaties of Peace 1919–1923. Vol. 1. New York: Carnegie Endowment for International Peace, 1924.

See also AUSTRIA-HUNGARY, HOME FRONT; CZECHS; PARIS PEACE CONFERENCE; POLAND; YUGOSLAVIA, CREATION OF

Stockholm Conference

The Stockholm Conference was the abortive 1917 socialist peace conference. Despite the antiwar position of the socialist Second International, the umbrella organization for the socialist parties of Europe, when World War I began all the major parties supported the war efforts of their respective governments. Three years of hostilities led European socialists to reconsider that position. Radicals from the belligerent countries met together at Zimmerwald (1915) and Kienthal (1916) in neutral Switzerland to denounce continuation of the war. In 1917 both moderate socialists and the socialist-dominated Petrograd Soviet called for a socialist conference in Stockholm, Sweden, which would bring together socialists from all the neutral and warring countries to coordinate a common policy toward ending the conflict. In early 1917 delegations from Russia and the Central Powers visited Stockholm, but the British, French, and Italian governments refused permission for their socialists to attend. As a result, the meeting as projected never took place.

In the wake of the aborted conference, the major socialist parties in Europe split down the middle. The moderate wings continued to support their respective governments, attempting to influence them through parliamentary means toward a compromise peace. Radicals and independents, however, argued that only noncooperation—if not outright resistance—toward their nonsocialist rulers would make possible a just peace settlement. Many of the latter joined the new communist parties that appeared on the left of the moderate socialists after the Bolshevik seizure of power in Russia in the fall of 1917.

Gary W. Shanafelt

References

Mayer, Arno J. *Wilson vs. Lenin: Political Origins of the New Diplomacy, 1917–1918.* Cleveland: World, 1964.

Stevenson, David. *The First World War and International Politics.* Oxford: Oxford University Press, 1988.

Stormtroopers

Stormtroopers *(Stoßtruppen)* were élite attack units of the German army created in response to the stalemate of trench warfare on the Western Front. The two sides in fact employed a number of techniques to break through the enemy lines and restore a war of movement, the most obvious being the use of ever larger artillery barrages combined with mass infantry attacks. The general result of these efforts was simply more elaborate defensive works and massive casualty rates. Stormtroopers were organized as an alternative way of overcoming the enemy defenses.

The first assault detachment *(Sturmabteilung)* was authorized in March of 1915 and consisted of two companies of Pioneer troops brought together from the Eighth Army Corps on the Western Front. In August it was put under the command of Captain Willy Rohr. Rohr began experimenting with a number of different weapons and techniques of attack. His basic idea was to create small units of highly motivated soldiers capable of fighting at close quarters in surprise attacks against enemy forces. They were trained to act independently with a minimum of supervision from the higher German command system so that they could maximize the advantages of speed and surprise at the local level. In addition to rifles, they were armed with flamethrowers, light trench mortars, and short-range field guns, to put as much firepower under their immediate control as possible. Grenades proved to be especially effective in securing enemy trenches and became a major staple of stormtrooper attacks.

As the tactics developed, stormtroopers were used to spearhead attacks, smashing holes in weak points of the Allied lines ahead of the main infantry advance. They attempted to avoid enemy strongpoints or to attack them from the flank and rear, reckoning their speed of advance and ability to disrupt the enemy defensive system as more important than maintaining unbroken contact with the units to either side of them. Those pockets of Allied soldiers who did continue to resist would be cut off and mopped up by the regular troops following in the wake of the stormtroopers. German successes in "infiltrating" the enemy lines and rolling them back led Erich Ludendorff, in planning his offensive for the Western Front in 1918, to make stormtrooper tactics the basis of the entire campaign. Whole units—not just élite squads—were trained in the tactics of infiltration and movement.

Stormtrooper aggressiveness and bravery were popularized after the war by writers like Ernst Jünger, a stormtroop officer who was repeatedly wounded and won both the Iron Cross and the *Pour le Mérite*. Those associations led Hitler to choose the name for his brown-shirted paramilitary squads.

Gary W. Shanafelt

References

Gudmundsson, Bruce I. *Stormtroop Tactics: Innovation in the German Army, 1914–1918*. New York: Praeger, 1989.

Jünger, Ernst. *The Storm of Steel, From the Diary of a German Storm-Troop Officer on the Western Front*. New York: Fertig, 1975.

See also GERMANY, ARMY; HUTIER, OSKAR VON; INFANTRY TACTICS; LUDENDORFF OFFENSIVES; RIGA, BATTLE OF

Sturdee, Sir (Frederick) Doverton (1859–1925)

British admiral, born on 9 June 1859 at Charlton. Sturdee entered the Royal Navy in 1871. Achieving flag rank in 1910, he served as commander of the 2nd Cruiser Squadron from 1912 to 1913. At the outbreak of war he was chief of the war staff at the admiralty with responsibility for day-to-day policy. Not a natural delegator, Sturdee shared part of the responsibility for the initial dispositions of the fleet that led to a number of reversals. He was replaced in November of 1914, following the disaster at Coronel. Appointed commander in chief of the South Atlantic Fleet, Sturdee sailed with the battle cruisers *Inflexible* and *Invincible* to destroy Admiral Count Maximilian von Spee's East Asia Squadron and avenge Cradock's defeat. Sturdee proceeded without undue haste, to conserve fuel, and carried out gunnery practice. He arrived at Port Stanley in the Falklands on 7 December. The following morning, Spee's squadron appeared off Port Stanley. Sturdee pursued, engaging the enemy at maximum distances to keep damage to his own ships to a minimum. Sturdee's ships annihilated Spee's squadron; only the light cruiser *Dresden* escaped.

In January of 1915 Sturdee was appointed commander of the 4th Battle Squadron of the Grand Fleet and participated in the Battle of Jutland in 1916. A staunch supporter of divided tactics and in closing with a retreating enemy, Strudee was critical of Admiral John Jellicoe's deployment and use of the fleet at Jutland. In February of 1918 he was appointed commander in chief, the Nore. He was promoted to admiral of the fleet in 1921, when he retired. He died at Camberley on 7 May 1925.

Andrzej Suchcitz

References

Bennett, Geoffrey. *Coronel and the Falklands*. London: Pan, 1967.

Goldrick, James. *The King's Ships Were at Sea*. Annapolis, Md.: Naval Institute Press, 1984.

Hough, Richard. *The Pursuit of Admiral von Spee*. London: Allen and Unwin, 1969.

See also CORONEL, BATTLE OF; FALKLANDS, BATTLE OF; GREAT BRITAIN, NAVY

Stürgkh, Count Karl (1859–1916)

Austrian politician and minister president, born in Graz, Austria, on 30 October 1859. Stürgkh was minister-president of Austria from 1911 until his assassination in 1916. He assumed office after several years in the Austrian parliament, followed by a stint as Austrian minister of education. As minister president, Stürgkh attempted to maintain the status quo by governing as much as possible through administrative fiat. The Austrian parliament, paralyzed by rival nationality demands, was prorogued in March of 1914, shortly before the outbreak of World War I, and remained closed for the duration of his tenure in office.

Like most leading Hapsburg policy makers, Stürgkh favored war with Serbia after the assassination of Franz Ferdinand. During the conflict, Stürgkh allowed much of Austria to be put under military administration, while his immobility and lack of imagination frustrated all groups of the political spectrum. He dealt with the rival demands of Austrian Slavs and Germans by ignoring them both. On 21 October 1916 he was shot and killed by Friedrich Adler, the son of the leader of the Austrian Socialist party, who hoped in that way to protest both the war itself and the shortcomings of the Hapsburg regime.

Gary W. Shanafelt

References

Florence, Ronald. *Fritz: The Story of a Political Assassin*. New York: Dial, 1971.

Redlich, Josef. *Austrian War Government*. New Haven: Yale University Press, 1929.

See also AUSTRIA-HUNGARY, HOME FRONT

Sturmer, Boris Vladimirovich (1848–1917)

Russian chairman of the council of ministers. Born in Tver Province in 1848 to a Russian noble family of Austrian origin, Sturmer was described by those who knew him, ranging from the political Right to the Left, as one of the most contemptible figures to hold power at the end of the Russian monarchy. Sturmer was interested solely in furthering his own career. He graduated from St. Petersburg University and entered the Ministry of Justice in 1875. In 1878 he was in the Department of Heraldry of the senate. From 1892 to 1894 he was chairman of the Tver Zemstvo and from 1894 to 1902 governor of Yaroslavl and Novgorod. Sturmer was a member of the state council from 1902 to 1904; prime minister, January-November 1916; and minister of foreign affairs, November of 1916.

Sturmer was a complete toady who would suffer any humiliation or turn in a colleague if it would advance his career. Minister of Interior V. Plehve, who had Sturmer as a subordinate in 1904, enjoyed insulting him just to see him grovel. People strive for power for many reasons. Sturmer's motive was to satisfy his personal vanity. He loved to wear gold-braided uniforms and kept his meaningless medals (a tradition in the Russian bureaucracy) in a special show case. During World War I, the comments on Sturmer by foreign ambassadors and Russian politicians included "of universal low reputation," "a nonentity," "double faced," and "of doubtful honesty." As the war went from bad to worse and the czar left for the front, Sturmer, taking into account the new source of political power, became close to empress Alexandra and Rasputin. Near the end of 1915 the aged Ivan Goremykin was dismissed as prime minister because of senility. The Russian Orthodox Metropolitan Pitirim, a protégé of Rasputin's, recommended Sturmer for that post because he was both loyal and pliable, and in January of 1916 the empress appointed him prime minister. Members of the Duma were shocked. Shortly thereafter, Alexander Protopopov, who was near insanity, was appointed minister of the interior. With those two posts in safe hands the empress and Rasputin went after those ministers whose loyalty to the czar was suspect, at least in their eyes. In sixteen months Russia had four prime ministers, five ministers of interior, four ministers of agriculture, and three ministers of war. All competent ministers, such as War Minister Aleksei Polivanov and Foreign Minister Sergei Sazonov, were dismissed.

By the end of 1916 there were signs of total collapse in Russia. In November of that year

Pavel Miliukov, a liberal, openly attacked Sturmer and the empress from the floor of the Duma, suggesting that they were German agents. The economic situation was so serious that even the czar hinted to his wife that Sturmer might have to go. On a trip to Kiev for rest, the czar was confronted by his mother, the Dowager Empress Marie, who demanded that Sturmer be dismissed as prime minister and minister of foreign affairs, a post to which he had been recently appointed. On 21 November Sturmer was told to resign. Later, in March of 1917, Sturmer and other czarist ministers were arrested by the provisional government. He died in prison on 2 September 1917, before he could be shot by a Bolshevik firing squad.

John W. Bohon

References

Gurko, Basil, General. *Features and Figures from the Past.* Stanford, Calif.: Stanford University Press, 1939.

Massie, Robert K. *Nicholas and Alexandra.* New York: Atheneum, 1967.

See also ALEXANDRA FEODOROVNA; MILIUKOV, PAVEL; RASPUTIN, GRIGORII; RUSSIA, HOME FRONT AND REVOLUTIONS OF 1917

Submarines

The submarine added a novel element to World War I navies and to naval warfare ever since. Developed from prototypes predating the nineteenth century, its basic design characteristics were in place by 1900 thanks to the availability of steel for hull construction, the self-propelled Whitehead torpedo, and electrical motors for underwater propulsion. Experiments conducted notably both in Europe and the United States resulted in a standard boat of cigar or tubular shape with a single hull or a double hull to maximize resistance to water pressure when submerged.

Pre-World War I submarines ranged in size from approximately 100 to 750 tons. Subsequent models, especially those built for long-range deployment or extended patrols, sometimes displaced upward of two thousand tons. Their flush upper deck was dominated by a conning tower, from which periscopes extended for observation purposes during submerged runs or attacks. The upper deck also featured one or several guns of medium caliber, for engaging the enemy with artillery fire. This saved precious torpedoes for attacks under more dangerous circumstances. Ballast tanks controlled buoyancy during diving and surfacing maneuvers. They could be flooded with sea water and emptied by compressed air. Hydraulic or manually controlled rudders and hydroplanes guided the submarine when diving or running below the surface.

After prolonged trials, diesel engines emerged as the preferred means of surface propulsion because of their reliability and economy, allowing for speeds of up to twenty knots and, at a more moderate pace, a range of several thousand miles. Some early designs used gasoline engines. Others, such as many French boats and Britain's large K-class cruisers, employed a complicated and not entirely trouble-free system of steam engines. Fuel needs ranged from about twenty tons of oil for coastal boats to more than two hundred tons for submarine cruisers on extended patrols. Wireless transmitters allowed the boats to stay in touch with one another and their headquarters ashore.

Underwater movement required electrical motors driven by rechargeable batteries, which limited the boats' speed, range, and maneuverability and made them vulnerable when pursued by antisubmarine chasers. These batteries, moreover, could become a source of unenviable peril for the crews in their cramped quarters when salt water reacted with the batteries' chemicals and produced toxic fumes. Underwater endurance was also limited by the boats' oxygen supply. Whenever conditions permitted, submarines would run on the surface to recharge their batteries, to ventilate the interior, and to search for prey. Diving speeds depended on the size of the craft; maximum diving depths lay generally between 300 and 500 feet.

The submarines' most effective armament consisted of torpedoes fired from bow and stern tubes while running on the surface or at periscope depth. The torpedoes' range, accuracy, sophistication, and destructive power differed from navy to navy and depended much on their speed, size (usually eighteen or twenty-one inches), the warhead and firing mechanism, the weather and sea conditions, and the nature of the target. Attacks could be made from a distance of over ten thousand yards, but most submarine commanders preferred shorter ranges for enhanced accuracy. The torpedoes ran several feet below the surface and, upon impact, the exploding warhead either broke their victim's keel or caused extensive and usually irreversible flooding. Larger boats carried spare torpedoes so that the tubes could be reloaded after or even during an attack. Several navies developed mine-laying submarines, which usually released their deadly cargo from vertical shafts.

Besides submarine traps (innocent-looking but heavily armed so-called Q-ships), artillery fire, and ramming on the surface, no effective antisubmarine technologies existed until 1916. The introduction of hydrophones for detection and depth charges with hydrostatic timers allowed for the destruction of submerged boats. Antisubmarine nets were also used with limited success, especially in the restricted waters of the English Channel. The widespread installation of radio equipment on merchantmen, and, after February of 1917, Allied adoption of a convoy system, forced submarines to take increasingly greater risks.

While most technical problems had been solved prior to the outbreak of hostilities, the practical role of submarines in modern naval warfare remained far from defined and hotly debated well into the war. For the proponents of battle fleets as the core and essence of any navy past or present, submarines constituted mere auxiliary vessels, perhaps useful for coastal defense and scouting but otherwise unproven and disturbingly unconventional. Only the war experience itself revealed the multiple capabilities of submarines on both sides. Characteristically, by August of 1914 not even German naval planners had seriously anticipated the U-boats' deadly and flexible roles, such as raiding commerce, laying mines, providing reconnaissance, running blockades, and attacking enemy warships.

While all major belligerents had submarines in their arsenals by 1914, the Royal Navy led all competitors in numbers built and under construction. Britain entered the war with seventy-four operational boats, about half of them coastal craft of the A, B, and C classes. Her most reliable and effective submarines for regular patrols belonged to the D (begun in 1907), E (1912), G (1915), and H and L (1917) classes. Displacing between 500 and 1,070 tons submerged, they featured three to six torpedo tubes, good speeds of up to seventeen knots on the surface and ten knots submerged, and carried a complement of twenty-two to thirty-six officers and men. They became Britain's "workhorses" during the war,

saw service in Atlantic, North Sea, Baltic, and Mediterranean waters (including the Dardanelles), and collectively suffered the highest losses in action (forty-three out of a total of fifty-four British boats lost).

Some E, H, and L-class boats carried mines. Britain's largest submarines, her steam-driven K-class cruisers of 2,650 tons displacement with surface speeds of up to twenty-four knots, had raised bows for extra buoyancy. They also had a history of engine trouble and diving accidents. The two M-class boats of 1918 were classified as submarine monitors on account of their single, fixed, 12-inch gun mounted before the conning tower; like the K-boats, they cannot be considered a successful design. Altogether, Britain's 203 submarines that saw action in the war sank 274 enemy merchantmen and fifty-four warships, among them fourteen U-boats.

France ranked second among Allied navies with substantial submarine components. By 1918 some seventy-five boats had been constructed or were nearing completion, fifty-five of them of seagoing size. The French, too, experimented extensively, and not altogether conclusively, with steam as a means of surface propulsion. Twelve boats became combat casualties, all but one in the Mediterranean.

The third member of the Triple Entente, Russia, traditionally divided its forces among the Arctic, Baltic, Black Sea, and Far East stations, with virtually all of its submarines assigned to the Baltic and the Black Sea. Fifty-nine boats, including several minelayers, were completed and saw limited service before Russia's withdrawal from the war. Only five appear to have been lost in action, while the majority were either surrendered to the Germans or scuttled to avoid capture by the Bolsheviks. Generally old, small, and technologically backward, Russian submarines had little impact on the war except in the Black Sea.

Italy's submarines, designed primarily for operations in Mediterranean waters, were mostly of the coastal variety; that is, they were small, had limited endurance, and rarely carried more than two torpedo tubes as their primary armament. Italy entered the war with twenty-one operational. Wartime construction added some forty seagoing units, not counting nine midget boats. Their principal opponent was Austria, in the waters of the Adriatic Sea. All Italian submarines used oil motors or diesels for surface propulsion. They suffered comparatively minor losses of ten boats, including two accidentally sunk by British warships.

The last of the major Allied powers, the United States, entered the war in 1917 with forty-seven boats in commission, half of them oceangoing craft of relatively recent design along lines suggested by the Irish-born designer and engineer John P. Holland. Fewer than twenty additional submarines, primarily of the O-class, were completed before the Armistice. Seven L-class boats were stationed in Ireland late in the war. Interestingly, the United States never developed mine-laying boats or chose to experiment with steam as a means of propulsion during the war. No U.S. submarine was lost in action. Other Allied navies with small submarine contingents, almost exclusively of the coastal variety, included Japan (twelve boats), Australia (eight), Portugal (four), Brazil (three), Canada (two), Greece (two), and Peru (two).

Among the Central Powers, Germany played the submarine card more enthusiastically and arguably more successfully than any other belligerent. With her High Seas Fleet tied up in its North Sea bases and the distant Allied blockade effectively preventing access to the open oceans for surface vessels, Germany came to rely reluctantly but increasingly on submarines, or U-boats *(Unterseebots),* to carry the war to the enemy. A psychological turning point was the spectacular feat of U-9, which on 9 September 1914 single-handedly sank three British armored cruisers off the Dutch coast with heavy loss of life. Germany chose to establish a counterblockade of the British Isles. That measure, with its corollary of unrestricted submarine warfare, not only succeeded in sinking some six thousand Allied merchantmen and warships by 1918, but also, through the abandonment of prize warfare regulations *(Lusi-tania, Arabic,* and *Sussex* incidents, among others), pulled the United States into the war in April of 1917. Most U-boats operated from bases along the German North Sea and in Flanders. They also played a conspicuous role in Mediterranean and Black Sea waters, to which they sailed by way of Gibraltar or were transported in sections overland.

While Germany began the war with only twenty-nine ready for action, the inactivity of her battle fleet, the Allied blockade, and the dramatic exploits of individual U-boats even before the end of 1914 resulted in a massive submarine building program and a shift in naval warfare philosophy in favor of a *Kleinkrieg* strategy. By November of 1918 German ship-

yards had delivered no fewer than 372 boats of all types. An additional 162 were begun but never completed. Some 178 boats were lost in action, while others fell victim to accidents or were scrapped or cannibalized because of old age; 138 became Allied booty after the war.

Germany's submarines fell into four distinct categories: 140 coastal boats (U-1 to 8 and all UB-classes); 107 oceangoing boats (numbered intermittently U-9 to 167); seven large merchant cruisers of the *Deutschland* class built to run the economic blockade (capable of carrying up to four hundred tons of cargo and eventually designated U-151 to 157); and 116 minelayers (U-71 to 80 and 117–26 for long-range operations, plus ninety-six smaller boats of the UC classes for more limited missions). With negligible exceptions, notably the poorly armed and unwieldy merchant cruisers, Germany's U-boats demonstrated sound engineering and craftsmanship, fine handling qualities at sea and under water, good endurance, and reliable propulsion and weapons systems. One single boat, U-35, sank no fewer than 226 ships, totaling some half million tons. When Hitler resumed submarine construction in the 1930s, he could build on a solid foundation, both in terms of successful designs and experienced personnel.

Germany's principal ally, Austria-Hungary, likewise maintained submarines for operations in the Mediterranean. Her initial force, based at Pola, Fiume, and Monfalcone in the Adriatic, consisted of seven coastal craft similar to Germany's UB-classes. Austria-Hungary constructed or otherwise acquired twenty additional boats during the war. About half of her boats were lost during the war, the remainder surrendering to Italy in 1918. No submarines served under the Turkish flag, while one former Austrian boat was ceded to Bulgaria.

Neutral navies with submarine components included Denmark (seventeen boats), Sweden (thirteen), Holland (nine), Chile (six), Norway (four), and Spain (four). In all, some 870 submarines served at one time or another in the navies of the belligerents. Approximately 350 of them, or 40 percent, were lost in action or accidents.

Eric C. Rust

References

Compton-Hall, Richard. *Submarine Boats: The Beginnings of Underwater Warfare.* New York: Arco, 1983.

Gray, Edwyn A. *The Killing Time: The U-Boat War, 1914–18.* New York: Charles Scribner's Sons, 1972.

Herwig, Holger H. *"Luxury Fleet": The Imperial German Navy, 1888–1918.* London: Allen and Unwin, 1980.

Jane's Fighting Ships of World War I. New York: Military Press, 1919. Reprint, 1990.

See also AUSTRIA-HUNGARY, NAVY; FRANCE, NAVY; GERMANY, NAVY; GREAT BRITAIN, NAVY; ITALY, NAVY; RUSSIA, NAVY; SUBMARINE WARFARE, ALLIED POWERS, CENTRAL POWERS

Submarine Warfare, Allied Powers

Although submarine warfare in World War I is most associated with Germany, submarines also played an important role in Allied naval operations. In the North Sea the British used their bigger submarines to cover the exits of the German High Seas Fleet *(Hochseeflotte)* in the area of Borkum Reef and Horns Reef, and stationed the older and smaller boats along the east coast to defend against German raids or even an invasion. Another group of smaller submarines was used—to some extent in cooperation with French submarines from Calais—to block the Channel entrance to cover the transfer of the British Expeditionary Force to France.

The British achieved their first success in the German Bight on 12 September 1914, when *E-9* sank the old German cruiser *Hela.* On 6 October the same submarine sank torpedo boat *S-116.* Some E-class boats were even sent into the Kattegat to watch for German ships coming from the Baltic. When German battle cruisers came to shell the British coast, small submarines in the area were sent out. The commander of submarines, Commodore Roger John Brownlow Keyes, established a submarine line with seven E boats and the French steam-driven *Archimède* to intercept German ships, but without result. The *Archimède* developed problems with its funnels when diving. It was taken out of this service and sent to the Mediterranean, where it later sank four merchant ships and became the most successful French submarine.

In 1915 it became increasingly urgent, especially after the Germans sent U-boats to newly established bases on the Belgian coast, to use submarines against the U-boats. One method was to tow some of the old boats of the C class with disguised Q-ships or U-boat traps. This led to the sinking of two U-boats in June and July. When more modern submarines were used to hunt U-boats in the North Sea, the English Channel, and to the west of the British Isles, they had more success. They sank one U-boat in 1915, three in 1916, five in 1917, and five in 1918. In 1918 seven U.S. L-class submarines were sent to Bantry Bay in Ireland to be used against German U-boats, and four K-class boats were sent to the Azores to operate against German U-cruisers, but they had no success.

When in 1916 the Germans again initiated operations with the *Hochseeflotte,* the Royal Navy laid submarine patrol lines out at possible German exit routes between the mine fields. These had no success during the Battle of Jutland, but on 19 August 1916, when the Germans tried to lure the Grand Fleet over their U-boat lines, *E-23* torpedoed the battleship *Westfalen.* During the next operation, on 19 October, torpedoes from *E-38* missed the cruiser *Stettin,* struck the cruiser *München,* and then missed the cruiser *Berlin.* The greatest British success came on 5 November 1916, when *J-1* torpedoed the battleships *Kronprinz* and *Grosser Kurfürst.*

The British effort to use their new large, steam-turbine-driven, K-class submarine cruisers in fleet operations ended in failure when, on 31 January 1918, units of the Grand Fleet departed Rosyth. Running at the high speed of twenty knots in bad visibility at night, collisions between submarines and surface ships led to the loss of *K-4* and *K-17,* damage to *K-6, K-14,* and *K-22,* and heavy loss of life. On 24 April 1918 *E-42* torpedoed a German capital ship, the battle cruiser *Moltke,* almost immobilized by a machinery breakdown.

One special Royal Navy submarine operation was the use of modified E-class submarines as minelayers in inner passages between minefields. The many minefields they laid made extensive German minesweeping operations necessary and led to some minesweeper losses. But minefields laid by both sides also took a heavy toll of British submarines in the North Sea. At least fifteen were lost, some on mines laid by German UC boats. The extensive mining of the North Sea made both surface and subsurface operations increasingly costly for both sides. Two old C-class boats were used as blockships at Zeebrüggen in an effort to block the German U-boat bases in Flanders.

In the Baltic the old Russian submarines at first had no successes. But in October of 1914 two British submarines, *E-1* and *E-9*, forced the Danish narrows and reached Liepaja. They were followed in 1915 by four more E boats and in 1916 by four C boats, transported to Archangel and by waterways to Petrograd. The most successful were *E-9*, which on 23 October 1915 sank the armored cruiser *Prinz Adalbert* and four merchant ships, and *E-19*, which on 7 November 1915 sank the cruiser *Undine* and seven merchant ships. In all, the British submarines sank fifteen merchant ships, while newly commissioned Russian boats of the *Bars* class sank eight in 1916–17. Two of the British and six of the Russian submarines were lost, but with the Bolshevik Revolution the British had to scuttle their remaining boats.

In the Black Sea the bigger Russian submarines interrupted coal and supply traffic off the Bosphorus and the Turkish north coast. Between 1915 and 1917 they sank and captured twenty-five ships and 103 small sailing vessels. The Russian minelayer *Krab* laid some mine barrages off the Bosphorus; and one Russian submarine, the *Morzh*, was lost on a mine.

In the Mediterranean at the beginning of the war one squadron of French submarines was sent to the Ionian Islands to support the blockade of the Adriatic Sea. When Italy entered the war, her small submarines were used for coastal defense from bases at Venice, Ancona, and Brindisi. But they registered no important results. That changed when Allied submarines were used to support the Gallipoli campaign by forcing the Dardanelles. Against a loss of seven of their own boats—two British and five French—Allied submarines sank fifty-three auxiliaries and supply vessels and 188 sailing boats, mostly in the Sea of Marmara. Their biggest successes against warships were the sinking of the old Turkish battleships *Messoudiye*, by *B-11* on 13 December 1914, and *Chaireddin Barbarossa*, on 8 August 1915 by *E-11*.

From 1915 onward, operations against German and Austro-Hungarian U-boats, which had great successes against the Allied surface fleets and played havoc with the merchant traffic in the Mediterranean, became the main object of Allied submarines. But only three German U-boats were sunk, one each by French, British, and Italian submarines. One Austrian submarine was also sunk by an Italian submarine.

Of 203 British submarines commissioned during the war, fifty-four were lost; of seventy-five French, fourteen; of seventy Italian, ten; and of fifty-nine Russian, twenty-six, including those scuttled at the end of the war.

Jürgen Rohwer

References

Conway's All the World's Fighting Ships 1906–1921. Greenwich: Conway Maritime Press, 1985.

Greger, René. *Die russische Flotte in Ersten Weltkrieg 1914–1917*. Munich: Lehmanns, 1970.

Le Masson, Henri. *Du Nautilus (1800) au Rédoutable. Histoire critique du sous-marin dans la marine française*. Paris: Presses de la Cité, 1969.

Lipscomb, F.W. *The British Submarine*. Greenwich: Conway Maritime Press, 1975.

Pollina, Paolo M. *I Sommergibili Italiani 1895–1962*. Rome: Ufficio Storico della Marine Militare, 1963.

Sander, Helmut. *Die Verluste der Kriegsflotten 1914–1918*. Munich: Lehmanns, 1969.

See also FRANCE, NAVY; GREAT BRITAIN, NAVY; ITALY, NAVY; RUSSIA, NAVY; SUBMARINES

Submarine Warfare, Central Powers

Although much of Germany's naval successes in World War I rested on the submarine, that was not according to prewar plans. When the war started in August of 1914, the Germans had intended to use their U-boats as a reconnaissance and support force for the High Seas Fleet. They were to locate British blockade lines in the North Sea, establish contact with British battle squadrons, and attack capital ships in order to bring about a more favorable balance of forces. Tirpitz saw the latter as a prerequisite for a fleet engagement.

On 6 August 1914 the first U-boat flotilla, with ten boats, departed Heligoland to search in a patrol line from east of the Dogger Bank to the north up to the area between the Orkney Islands and Norway. There was no report of British forces, because the two U-boats that had come into contact with the *Grand Fleet*, *U-13* and *U-15*, were rammed and sunk by British ships.

Fear of U-boats led the British big ships to retreat for some weeks to the west of the British Isles. Meanwhile, reports of the transfer of the British Expeditionary Forces to France led to U-boat operations against Channel traffic, while a few U-boats continued to search for the British blockade lines.

On 28 August 1914, when British battle cruisers attacked German reconnaissance lines near Heligoland and sank three light cruisers, there were no U-boats available in the area. In September the U-boats achieved their first sinkings. *U-21,* commanded by Lieutenant Commander Hersing, sank the British light cruiser *Pathfinder,* and Lieutenant Commander Weddigen in *U-9* had the spectacular success of sinking in one day three armored cruisers— *Cressy, Hogue,* and *Aboukir*—while they covered the Channel entrance for the transfer of the British Expeditionary Force to France.

These successes opened the way for more offensive use of the U-boats against units of the Grand Fleet and older blockade vessels. In October of 1914, *U-9* sank the cruiser *Hawke,* and *U-27* sank the submarine *E-3* and the seaplane carrier *Hermes.* In November *U-12* sank the gunboat *Niger,* and on 1 January 1915 *U-23* sank the battleship *Formidable.*

The employment of German U-boats against merchant ships carrying supplies to Great Britain and France began only after the first six months of the war and without the German Naval Command's having a clear strategic concept. At first it was only retaliation against the British blockade. There was no unified U-boat command. The U-boats were subordinate to three independent commanders: the chief of the High Seas Fleet, the leader of submarines-Flanders, and the commander of the Baltic Fleet—and, from May of 1915, the U-boat flotilla at Pola cooperated with the Austro-Hungarian fleet command and its submarines. As a result, the German navy executed strategies directly opposing one another until early 1917.

Up to the end of January 1915, U-boats of the High Seas Fleet had sunk only eleven merchant ships according to prize regulations. The British blockade led Tirpitz to propose retaliation by U-boats against British and Allied merchant ships. After discussions on 4 February 1915, Berlin declared a war zone around the British Isles. On 18 February U-boats were allowed to initiate attacks against enemy merchant ships. If possible, they were to follow prize regulations, but in areas with stronger naval defenses they were authorized to attack submerged.

Only twenty-four U-boats were available when the U-boat war really started. In the North Sea and off the western approaches U-boats of the High Seas Fleet sank thirty-eight ships in February-March, twenty-nine in April, and fifty-two in May.

On 7 May 1915, off the south of Ireland, *U-20* intercepted the large British passenger ship *Lusitania* and sank it with one torpedo. There was a great explosion, probably of munitions the ship was transporting. Of 1,959 people on board, 1,198 lost their lives, including 128 U.S. citizens. An intense exchange of diplomatic notes between Germany and the United States followed, leading to Kaiser Wilhelm II's secret order not to sink any more passenger ships. After the sinking of the steamer *Arabic* on 19 August 1915 by *U-24* (three Americans were among the forty-four victims), new American protests led, on 18 September, to another secret order by the kaiser to halt the U-boat war around the British Isles. Prior to September of 1915, German submarines sank 379 Allied and neutral merchant ships totaling about 669,000 GRT.

In the Baltic there were only a few German U-boats. There, on 11 October 1915, *U-26* sank the Russian armored cruiser *Pallada* and, on 4 June 1915, the minelayer *Enissej.*

The commitment of small torpedo-carrying and mine-laying U-boats of the UB and UC types from bases in Flanders inside the Channel and off the coast of southeast England began in June of 1915. It continued without interruption to the end of the war. Because of hydrographic conditions, with many shallows and strong currents in the Channel, and Allied efforts to block the Dover-Calais narrows, U-boats experienced considerable difficulties. They also achieved great successes against traffic between England and France. U-boats sank 131 transports and merchant ships in 1915, 512 in 1916, 620 in 1917, and 327 in 1918. In addition, many warships became victims of U-boats.

In the Mediterranean Austro-Hungarian U-boats had their first great success when, in December of 1914, *U-12* attacked the French fleet blockading the Adriatic Sea and torpedoed its flagship, the dreadnought *Jean Bart,* forcing the French to retire. German U-boats were first transferred to help in the defense of the

S

Dardanelles, where *U-21* on 25 and 27 May 1915 succeeded in sinking two battleships, the *Triumph* and *Majestic*.

In the meantime, Austro-Hungaria's *U-5* and *U-4*, and *UB-14* (one of the small German U-boats transferred by rail to Pola) had sunk the French armored cruiser *Léon Gambetta* in April and the Italian armored cruisers *Giuseppe Garibaldi* and *Amalfi* in July of 1915. The British cruiser *Dublin* was torpedoed and damaged by an unknown U-boat in June of 1915.

In August of 1915 mercantile warfare according to prize regulations was begun in the Mediterranean by German and Austro-Hungarian U-boats and was continued with increasing success. German U-boats sank 102 merchant ships in 1915, 415 in 1916, 627 in 1917, and 325 in 1918. Over the same period Austro-Hungarian U-boats sank an additional ninety-four ships. The most successful U-boat of World War I, *U-35*, sank most of its 224 victims, of 539,741 GRT, in the Mediterranean. Lieutenant Lothar von Arnauld de la Perière carried out the single most successful sortie of either world war in *U-35* between 26 July and 20 August 1916, when in the Mediterranean he sank twenty-nine steamers and twenty-five sailships of 90,350 tons. Other famous German commanders in the Mediterranean in World War I were Lieutenants Karl Dönitz, Wilhelm Canaris, and Martin Niemöller.

The threat from armed merchantmen and U-boat decoy vessels (Q-ships) led the *Hochseeflotte* to demand that its U-boats engage only in unrestricted submarine warfare. But German political leaders in 1916 did not agree, and this led to Tirpitz's retirement. Thus, for many months the most effective U-boats could be used only in fleet operations, and that meant limited successes.

When battle cruisers of the *Hochseeflotte* renewed their raids to shell British east-coast harbors, U-boats were sent to reconnoiter the approach routes of the Grand Fleet and to cover the German ships. Apart from some contact signals, they made no successful attacks. During the Battle of Jutland U-boats were again sent to British bases but were able to attack only some of the returning British ships damaged in the battle. Torpedoes from *U-51* and *U-46* missed the battleships *Warspite* and *Marlborough*.

During the next big operation of the *Hochseeflotte,* in August of 1916, *U-63* and *U-52* sank the light cruisers *Falmouth* and *Nottingham*. Some big ships were also victims of mines laid by U-boats. On 5 June 1916 the British armored cruiser *Hampshire* sank, with Field Marshal Lord Kitchener on board, off the Orkney Islands after striking a mine laid by *U-75*. On 19 July 1917 the American armored cruiser *San Diego* went down from a mine laid by *U-156*, as did the British armored cruiser *Drake* on 2 October from a mine from *U-79*. The most important reason for the limited German successes was the ability of admiralty Room 40 to decrypt German radio traffic.

In 1916 two voyages of the freight U-boat *Deutschland* to the United States aroused great public interest. In 1915 the *Deutsche Ozean Reederei,* an especially founded firm, ordered eight cargo U-boats of 1,512 tons in order to break the British blockade and transport goods to the United States and return with needed imports. Only the first two of those boats were finished and made such voyages. The *Deutschland* made two successful trips, but the *Bremen* disappeared without a trace on its first outward voyage. To impress the American public, a fleet boat, *U-53*, was sent to make a short visit to an American port and conduct mercantile warfare according to prize regulations outside U.S. territorial waters, but this did not work out as intended. After February of 1917, the *Deutschland* and the other six unfinished freight boats were rebuilt into U-cruisers with two 150mm and two 88mm guns. Later they made long cruises to distant areas and together sank 215 ships. They were followed by specially designed larger UK-cruisers of the *U-139* type of 1930 tons, but only the first three of the vessels actually took part in operations.

Large U-boat building programs were begun in 1916. These focused on the fleet MS or U-type submarines, a few bigger fleet-type U-boats, and a similar minelayer, but mainly the medium UB-III and minelaying UC-III type, of which a considerable number were commissioned in 1917 and 1918. A smaller coastal type UF was also ordered, but these were not completed before the end of the war.

Under the pressure of the military situation at the end of 1916 and early 1917, the naval staff and the high command forced the German government to renew unrestricted submarine warfare against merchant shipping. Operating from statistics prepared by the *Admiralstab*, the navy hoped to force Great Britain to her knees by sinking 600,000 GRT of shipping in each of the next five months before the expected American entry into the war could have an effect. On 9 January 1917 Kaiser Wilhelm II ordered unrestricted U-boat warfare to begin on 1 February. That forced President Wilson to sever diplomatic relations on 3 February. A short time later, the notorious Zimmermann Telegram became public. Combined with German sabotage against American shipping facilities and the sinking of American ships by German U-boats, it finally brought a U.S. declaration of war against Germany on 6 April 1917.

From 1 February 1917 to the end of that year, the five flotillas of the *Hochseeflotte* had sixty fleet U-boats of the U type, twenty-five of the UB type, and twenty of the UC type. To the end of 1917 these U-boats sank—in addition to sinkings registered by U-boats from Flanders or the Mediterranean—more than 1,000 ships. But only in April and June of 1917 did sinkings by all U-boats reach the mark of 600,000 GRT set as the target that would bring the collapse of Britain. In April 458 ships of 841,118 GRT were sunk, and in June 352 ships of 669,218 GRT.

The Allies took a number of measures to overcome the U-boat danger. Destroyers and other escort vessels were equipped with new audio receivers to locate submerged U-boats, and also with new depth charges. Submarines were sent into areas off German bases to intercept U-boats going out or returning. And extensive mine barrages were laid in the North Sea and the Channel to block routes used by the U-boats. Trawlers and small merchant ships were equipped with disguised weapons to act as Q-ships or U-boat traps, such as the notorious *Baralong*.

Improvement of sensors and antisubmarine weapons caused a rise in the losses of U-boats at the same time that mass construction of merchantmen in England, and especially in the United States, helped offset merchant tonnage losses. The British also began to employ aircraft against the U-boats. In the last six months of the war 565 aircraft and airships were used to support convoys. They sighted twenty-eight U-boats and made nineteen attacks on them. Even if the aircraft could not sink any U-boats, among the many hundreds of convoys they supported only six were attacked and those lost only five ships.

To inhibit German U-boat bases in Flanders, the British began a blocking operation there on 22 April 1918 against Zeebrugge and Ostend. It was only partially successful at Zeebrugge and a failure at Ostend, because the blocking ships were not able to reach their positions. A total of 1,200 British sailors and soldiers were killed or wounded in the operations and, after some salvage work, German U-boats continued to use the Flanders ports.

By far the most important and successful Allied response to the German submarine campaign was the convoy system. With the aid of cryptanalysis of German radio messages, which made known to the admiralty attack orders given to individual U-boats, convoys could be detoured around U-boat positions. This drastically reduced sinkings of merchant vessels.

The Allies also laid a thick mine barrage in the Dover-Calais narrows in the winter of 1917–18 and strengthened it over the following months. Finally, in August of 1918, after the loss of twelve U-boats, the Germans stopped using that passage. Based on that success, the British and U.S. navies began laying a large minefield between the Orkney Islands and Norway, to block German U-boat access to the Atlantic from that direction. Probably only one U-boat was lost to the more than 70,000 mines laid there.

As a result of the Allied response, sinkings of merchant ships declined from an average of 451,000 GRT monthly in the third quarter of 1917 to 365,000 GRT monthly in the fourth quarter of 1917, to 333,000 GRT in the first quarter of 1918, to 288,000 GRT in the second quarter of 1918, and to 177,000 GRT in the last five months of 1918. At the same time, U-boat losses mounted. In 1917 61 out of 231 U-boats were lost, and 82 out of 232 were lost in 1918.

During the First World War, German U-boats sank, in addition to many warships, a total of 5,554 Allied and neutral merchant ships of 12,191,996 GRT. A total of 178 U-boats were lost to war-related causes.

Jürgen Rohwer

References

Corbett, Julian Stafford, and Henry Newboldt. *Naval Operations*. Vols. 1–5. London: Longmans Green, 1920–31.

Gröner, Erich. *Die deutschen Kriegsschiffe 1815–1945*. Vol. 3. *U-Boote, Hilfskreuzer, Minenschiffe, Netzleger, Sperrbrecher*. Koblenz: Bernard & Graefe, 1985.

Herzog, Bodo. "Die Erfolge der österreichisch-ungarischen U-Bootwaffe im Ersten Weltkrieg." In *Marine-Rundschau 56* (1959), III: 164–68.

Sieche, Erwin. "Austria-Hungary." In *Conway's All the World's Fighting Ships 1906–1921*, 326–47. Greenwich: Conway Maritime Press, 1985.

Sokol, Hans Hugo. *Österreich-Ungarns Seekrieg 1914–1918*. Vols. 1 and 2. Graz: Akademische Druck- und Verlagsanstalt, 1967.

Spindler, Arno. *Der Handelskrieg mit U-Booten*. Vol. 1: *Vorgeschichte*. Vol. 2: *Februar bis September 1915*. Vol. 3: *Oktober 1915 bis Januar 1917*. Vol. 4: *Februar bis Dezember 1917*. Vol. 5: *Januar bis November 1918*. Berlin/Frankfurt: E.S. Mittler und Sohn, 1932–34, 1941, 1966.

Terraine, John. *Business in Great Waters: The U-Boat Wars, 1916–1945*. London: Leo Cooper, 1989.

See also ARNAULD DE LA PERIÈRE, LOTHAR VON; ASDIC; AUSTRIA-HUNGARY, NAVY; CONVOY SYSTEM, NAVAL; DEPTH CHARGES; GERMANY, NAVY; MINE WARFARE, SEA; OSTEND AND ZEEBRUGGE, RAIDS OF; SUBMARINES

Sueter, Sir Murray Fraser (1872–1960)

British admiral and aviation pioneer, born on 6 September 1872 at Alverstoke, Gosport, Hampshire. Sueter entered the Royal Navy in 1886. Before World War I he specialized in submarines, wireless, and aviation. In 1912 he became director of the new air department at the admiralty.

During World War I Sueter helped develop torpedo-carrying float planes, small nonrigid airships for antisubmarine operations, the combat armored car, and the early tank, although he noted that the latter was "quite outside our legitimate air work." In 1915 he assumed responsibility for aircraft construction. In 1917, however, he was, in his own words, "banished" to southern Italy, to command Royal Naval Air Service units there, for "holding unorthodox views in advocating a separate air service." He further damaged his relations with the admiralty by writing directly to King George V to press development of the tank. Upon his return to Britain in January of 1918 no further employment was offered, and he retired in 1920.

Sueter then became involved in the development of imperial air mail postal services. He also served as a member of the House of Commons from 1921 to 1945. He died on 6 February 1960 at Watlington, Oxfordshire. Sueter wrote three books: *The Evolution of the Submarine Boat, Mine, and Torpedo* (1907), *Airmen or Noahs* (1934), and *The Evolution of the Tank* (1937).

Donald F. Bittner

References

Baddeley, Vincent W. "Sueter, Sir Murray Fraser." In *Dictionary of National Biography, 1951–1960*. London: Oxford University Press, 1971.

Marder, Arthur J. *From the Dreadnought to Scapa Flow*. Vols. 1–5. Oxford: Oxford University Press, 1961–70.

The Times (London), 5 and 9 February 1960.

See also GREAT BRITAIN, NAVY

Sukhomlinov, Vladimir Aleksandrovich (1848–1926)

Russian general and minister of war. Sukhomlinov was one of several incompetent officials who occupied high positions in the Russian government at the beginning of World War I. As a young officer, however, Sukhomlinov had a rather brilliant career. Born near Kovno on 16 July 1848, the son of a retired officer turned official, he graduated from the Nikolaevsky Cavalry School in 1867 and the General Staff Academy in 1874. He served on General Skobelev's staff during the Russo-Turkish War of 1877–78 and was decorated. By 1890 he was a general. Between 1904 and 1908 he held the important post of commander of the Kiev Military District. He did not have field command in the Russo-Japanese War and was promoted to general of cavalry in 1906. By that time Nicholas II consulted with him on a wide range of matters, and in 1908 he became army chief of staff. The next year, as part of a military shakeup aimed at staffing the high military posts with conservative officers loyal to the monarchy, Sukhomlinov was elevated to minister of war. He held that post until 1915, when he was dismissed in disgrace.

Sukhomlinov was an officer who allowed his personal life to influence his military career. Prior to the war he appeared on the surface to be a well-educated, resourceful officer who wrote scholarly articles in military journals. After the death of his wife, however, he fell in love with and married a young widow who was part of Bohemian theatrical society. She purchased expensive clothes, gave lavish parties, and made Sukhomlinov's home the center of the social set in whatever city he happened to be stationed. After her death the general married for a third time, to a Madame Butovich, who also enjoyed the good life, which included frequent trips to fashionable German spas. It was not long before Sukhomlinov's expenses exceeded his income and forced him to borrow money from unsavory characters. One of these was a certain Altschuler, an Austrian by birth, who was in the pay of Austrian military intelligence. Because Sukhomlinov owed him large sums of money that he could not pay, Altschuler was appointed to his staff where he remained, while Sukhomlinov was both chief of staff and minister of war. Another German spy on Sukhomlinov's staff, and also his personal friend, was Colonel Miasoyedov. Sukhomlinov repeatedly chose to ignore warnings about retaining the two spies. It might also be added that neither the czar nor the empress was unduly concerned over this situation. Sukhomlinov, probably not a spy himself, enjoyed the confidence of the Imperial Family to the end of his career.

Sukhomlinov was an officer of the "old school," whose nineteenth-century notion of combat relied excessively on manpower and personal bravery and discounted the significance of military technology. Shortly after his appointment he boasted that he had not read a single book on military technology in twenty-five years. After the outbreak of the war it was immediately apparent that Sukhomlinov was not competent to handle the exigencies of modern warfare. Pleas to him from field commanders begging for more supplies were marked as exaggerated hysteria and ignored. Agencies such as the zemstvo councils and the War Industries Committee saw Sukhomlinov as irrelevant to the war effort and ignored him in conducting their business.

By mid-1915, after the early Russian military disasters, deputies to the state Duma came to see Sukhomlinov as the symbol of the monarchy's ineptitude. He was attacked by Duma liberals, not only for incompetence but as a German spy. Opponents of the government orchestrated a campaign to bring him to trial for treason. The pressure became so great that in June of 1915 Nicholas II was forced to dismiss Sukhomlinov and, in August, army chief of staff General Nikolai Yanushkevich.

Shortly thereafter, in a sensational trial that exposed all the weaknesses of the monarchy in conducting the war, Sukhomlinov was convicted of treason. Because of the intercession of the czar, however, he did not go to prison. Although the provisional government arrested Sukhomlinov and sentenced him to hard labor, through some oversight the Bolsheviks released him and he fled to Finland. He died in Berlin on 2 February 1926.

John W. Bohon

References

Gurko, General Basil. *Features and Figures of the Past*. Stanford: Stanford University Press, 1939.

Pushkarev, Gergei. *The Emergence of Modern Russia 1801–1917*. New York: Holt, Rinehart, and Winston, 1963.

See also NICHOLAS II; RUSSIA, ARMY; RUSSIA, HOME FRONT AND REVOLUTIONS OF 1917

Supreme War Council

The Entente Powers and their associates rejected inter-Allied unity of command until 1917. Disasters of that year, including the failed Nivelle Offensive, the terrible deadlock in Flanders, huge losses of merchant ships to German U-boats, and the Italian debacle at Caporetto, finally forced them to improve coordination of their political ends and strategic means. The Supreme War Council (SWC) was founded at Rapallo, Italy, on 7 November 1917, with the British government taking the initiative.

Prime Minister David Lloyd George, tired of deadlock and long casualty lists, wished to bypass his principal military advisors, including Field Marshal Sir Douglas Haig, commander of the British Expeditionary Force, and General Sir William Robertson, Chief of the Imperial General Staff. Lloyd George hoped to modify the "western strategy" of concentrating on the Western Front. He proposed to attack Germany's allies—Austria-Hungary, Turkey, and Bulgaria. This "eastern strategy" would minimize casualties, preserve communications to British possessions in Asia, and set the stage for eventual triumph in France. He wanted to create a "joint council" that "had knowledge of the resources of all the Allies" and "could prepare a single coordinated plan for utilizing those resources in the most decisive manner, and at the most decisive points." It would view the enemy front as a whole and exploit the enemy's political, economic, and diplomatic weaknesses as well as his military deficiencies.

France preferred a generalissimo to accomplish unity of command but accepted Lloyd George's proposal for unity of control because it might lead to a supreme command. The Rapallo "Scheme of Organization" allocated two political representatives to each of the four principals maintaining armies in Europe—Britain, France, Italy, and the United States. Its task was "to watch over the general conduct of the war," recommend military plans to the member states, and report on their execution. To provide professional expertise, each member would appoint a "Permanent Military Representative" (PMR) who did not represent his country's general staff, a provision that excluded General Robertson. Several lesser bodies under the SWC's umbrella were soon founded to treat specific concerns, such as naval action, land transportation, the blockade, food supplies, munitions, and war finance.

The council usually met at Versailles, eight times in 1918, to consider recommendations known as joint notes approved by unanimous votes of the PMRs. Joint note no. 1 proposed a defensive posture in France until American troops arrived in sufficient force to allow resumption of the offensive. Joint note no. 12 spelled out this general approach. The French and British armies could defend themselves on the Western Front provided American divisions came to France at the rate of two per month. Lloyd George managed to insert a proviso allowing an attack on the Turkish army, but the French and American governments answered with a clause that precluded diversion of resources from the main theater.

To improve inter-Allied cooperation during an expected German offensive, the SWC adopted joint note no. 14, which called for a "General Reserve" of thirty divisions. It would maneuver to threatened sectors and reinforce the defenders. This force did not materialize, because Haig and French commander in chief General Henri-Philippe Pétain refused to contribute divisions, preferring to make bilateral arrangements for mutual support.

The Haig-Pétain scheme failed when the German offensive of 21 March 1918 achieved a remarkable breakthrough and threatened Amiens, a vital communications center. This grave situation forced the SWC to abandon

unity of control in favor of full-fledged unity of command. General (later Marshal) Ferdinand Foch became the inter-Allied generalissimo with authority to direct the armies opposed to Germany from the North Sea to Italy. At first Foch's command seemed to undermine the SWC, but it recovered by shifting its emphasis to strategies for secondary theaters and solutions to specific political-military problems. A long controversy developed over the use of American troops in France. The United States wanted to create a large independent army to fight in its own sector under its own command and staff. Because of the need to develop this force almost from nothing, American troops would not take the field in significant numbers until 1919. The British and French, fearing a German attempt to end the war in 1918, proposed that the United States allow integration of American troops into the British and French armies, a policy that became known as "amalgamation." It was not adopted, because the American army and citizenry desired an independent force, and President Wilson believed that such an army would strengthen his influence on the peace settlement.

Another controversy developed over various proposals for inter-Allied intervention in Russia to reconstitute the Eastern Front. Wilson opposed intervention: It would divert troops from France, violate the principle of national self-determination, and encourage Japanese aggrandizement in East Asia. Pressure from the SWC finally forced Wilson to condone limited interventions in North Russia and Siberia, but American opposition precluded action on the scale contemplated in London and Paris.

The success of Foch's counteroffensives during July–November 1918 reduced activity at the SWC. Its last major contribution was to decide two important matters, the armistice terms to be offered to Germany and the separate question of the guidelines for the peace negotiation. The SWC endorsed armistice terms that were sufficient to prevent resumption of hostilities at a later date. It also accepted the American proposals known as the Fourteen Points and associated pronouncements as the basis for postwar negotiations. The Allies did so reluctantly, embodying their concessions in the Pre-Armistice Agreement of 4 November 1918.

The Supreme War Council continued in modified form at the Paris Peace Conference as the Council of Four. It later influenced inter-Allied agreements made during World War II, and its basic rationale was embodied in the North Atlantic Treaty Organization.

David F. Trask

References

Palmer, Frederick. *Bliss, Peacemaker: The Life and Letters of General Tasker Howard Bliss*. New York: Dodd, Mead, 1934.

Shumate, Thomas Daniel, Jr. "The Allied Supreme War Council, 1917–1918." Unpublished Ph.D. dissertation. University of Virginia, 1952.

Trask, David F. *The United States in the Supreme War Council: American War Aims and Inter-Allied Strategy, 1917–1918*. Middletown, Conn.: Wesleyan University Press, 1961.

See also ARMISTICE; FOCH, FERDINAND; LLOYD GEORGE, DAVID; RUSSIA, ALLIED INTERVENTION IN

Swinton, Sir Ernest Dunlop (1868–1951)

British army officer and proponent of tanks. Born in Bangalore, Mysore, India, on 21 October 1868, son of a judge in the Madras civil service, Swinton was educated in England and attended the Royal Military Academy, Woolwich. In 1888 he was commissioned a lieutenant in the Royal Engineers and spent five years in Indian service before becoming an instructor in a school for military engineering. He participated in the Boer War in military bridging and railway work, and after the war he published two books on tactics and future warfare. Promoted to major in 1906, a year later he was chief instructor in fortification at Woolwich. In 1910 he was posted to the historical section of the Committee of Imperial Defence (where he helped write the British official history of the Russo-Japanese War) and in 1913 became its assistant secretary.

At the beginning of World War I Swinton was appointed deputy director of railway transport, but Field Marshal Lord Horatio Kitchener made him a semiofficial war correspondent for British forces following the public opposition to French General Joseph Joffre's ban on war correspondents in the war zone. Swinton wrote under the pen name Eyewitness.

Swinton was well placed to realize the deadlock of trench warfare. His solution was an armored vehicle "capable of destroying machine-guns, of crossing country and trenches, of breaking through entanglements, and of climbing earthworks." In October of 1914, while he was in London, Swinton went to see Maurice Hankey, secretary of the Committee of Imperial Defence, and suggested the conversion of Holt caterpillar tractors into fighting machines. The idea was rejected by senior military officials but was seized upon by First Lord of the Admiralty Winston Churchill, who had already ordered experiments with a trench-crossing machine.

The failure of the 1915 Allied offensives produced more support for Swinton's ideas, and in June of 1915 he drafted a memorandum that made a favorable impression. Swinton also provided specific details of capabilities for such machines and a clear idea of how these "armoured machine-gun destroyers" should be employed. Churchill's successor at the admiralty, Arthur Balfour, was sympathetic to the project, as was Lloyd George as minister of munitions. As a result, the Landships Committee at the admiralty became a joint army-navy group.

In July of 1915 Swinton returned to London at Hankey's suggestion as secretary to the Dardanelles Committee. Before the end of the month a contract was placed and by September a prototype vehicle had been produced. It was Swinton who provided the generic name "tank" for the new fighting vehicles in order to camouflage their identity. In February of 1916 a demonstration of the tank went well, although Lord Horatio Kitchener characterized it as "a pretty mechanical toy" that would easily be destroyed by enemy artillery. GHQ asked for forty machines, but on Swinton's initiative the total was raised to one hundred.

Swinton was appointed commander of the new unit, but he was allowed only to train the men. In France the tanks would be under local commanders. In February of 1916 Swinton completed "Notes on the Employment of Tanks." Unfortunately, many of its key points were ignored in operational planning until the Battle of Cambrai. In April of 1916 Swinton met with General Sir Douglas Haig in London. Haig asked that some of the new machines be provided for his summer offensive planned for the Somme. Swinton swallowed his own inclination to oppose token employment and premature disclosure of the new weapon, but under further pressure some fifty tanks were sent to France with semitrained crews and employed, with mixed result, along the Somme on

15 September 1916. When Swinton went to France in October of 1916, Haig showed more satisfaction with the results than some of his subordinates. Unfortunately, Swinton was not included in the organization of the new force. On his return to Britain he was "released" to his former duties in the war cabinet secretariat, ending his direct association with the force he had fathered. It was only after World War I that Swinton's services were properly appreciated.

When the United States entered World War I, Swinton was given the temporary rank of major-general and traveled to the United States at the request of the State Department to speak on behalf of war bonds. He retired from the army in 1919. In 1922 he became a director of the Citroen Company, and three years later was named Chichele Professor of Military History at Oxford, a post he held until 1939. In 1934 Swinton was chosen colonel-commandant of the Royal Tank Corps. He died at Oxford on 15 January 1951.

Spencer C. Tucker

References

Dictionary of National Biography, 1951–1960. London: Oxford University Press, 1971.

Liddell Hart, Basil H. *The Tanks.* Vol. 1. London: Cassell, 1959.

Swinton, Major General Sir Ernest D. *Eyewitness; Being Personal Reminiscences of Certain Phases of the Great War, Including the Genesis of the Tank.* Garden City: Doubleday, Doran, 1933.

———. *Over My Shoulder: The Autobiography of Major-General Sir Ernest D. Swinton.* London: Ronald, 1951.

See also CAMBRAI, BATTLE OF; FULLER, J.F.C.; LIDDELL HART, SIR BASIL; SOMME, BATTLE OF; TANKS; TANK WARFARE

Switzerland

On the outbreak of the First World War the Swiss government immediately took steps to preserve the confederation's neutrality. On 1 August the Federal Council mobilized the entire army of 250,000 men to guard the frontiers; and on 4 August, at the behest of the Federal Assembly, the council proclaimed the country's neutrality. The confederation remained on a war footing throughout the conflict, and the Swiss believed that their readiness to defend themselves ensured that both sides would respect their territory. On 3 August 1914, the Federal Assembly granted the council exceptional powers, and during the war the central government gained power at the expense of the cantons, even though this probably violated the constitution.

The war was a difficult period for the confederation, especially economically. Despite treaty provisions, Switzerland found it impossible to maintain strict neutrality. Overpopulated and overindustrialized in relation to its resources, it was not self-sufficient in food. The Allies refused food stuffs unless Switzerland halted its trade with Germany, but the Germans threatened to withhold supplies of coal. Since both sides wanted Swiss factory production, however, in 1915 they opened trade with Switzerland after its government agreed not to re-export imports.

The financial burden of the war was heavy, in large part because the Swiss kept their army mobilized or partially mobilized throughout the war. Deployed troops served an average of six hundred days of border duty, the longest in centuries. The Swiss also imported large numbers of machine guns, introduced hand grenades and steel helmets, began construction of aircraft, and established a military airfield. Total military costs were approximately 1.2 billion Swiss francs. In order to prevent inflation and devaluation of the franc, in 1915 the Swiss passed a federal tax, the first direct levy by the confederation. A similar tax was voted in 1919.

Swiss efforts to maintain neutrality were more difficult because public opinion was bitterly divided along national and linguistic lines. The French-speaking part of the country was pro-Allied and angry that the central government had not protested the 1914 German violation of Belgian neutrality. Although German-speaking portions of the country were less pronounced in their loyalty to Germany, Switzerland was bound to Germany culturally and economically, and many high-placed military and civilian leaders openly sympathized with the German cause.

Two events jeopardized Switzerland's neutral status. The first was the 1916 "Affair of the Colonels," in which two Swiss army colonels shared intelligence information with German and Austro-Hungarian military attachés. The second was the "Hoffmann Affair" of 1917, when the most influential member of the federal government, Federal Councilor Arthur

Hoffmann, attempted to negotiate a peace treaty between Germany and Russia without informing other warring powers. Hoffmann promptly resigned, ending the threat of Entente intervention.

During the war Switzerland gave shelter to some 68,000 internees, and the International Red Cross in Geneva was quite active during the conflict. Switzerland was also the scene for peace talks in late 1917 and early 1918. General Jan Smuts met Count Albert Mensdorff, former Austrian ambassador to Britain. Smuts proposed a separate peace, but Mensdorff made it clear that Vienna was interested only in a general settlement. Austrian businessman Julius Meinl and law professor Heinrich Lammasch held talks with American Protestant minister George Davis Herron, who was in contact with President Wilson.

Economic deprivation in Switzerland during the war and an influx of foreigners during the conflict led to the spread of socialist and radical thought. Heightened social pressures exploded at the end of the conflict in a general strike *(Landesstreik)* on 11 November 1918. The government mobilized the army, expelled the Soviet legation established at Berne, and rejected strikers' demands. The strike then collapsed, although some of the strikers' demands were subsequently met through legislative action.

After the war the new League of Nations established its headquarters at Geneva. This had the support of most of the Swiss people, although it was opposed by the Social Democrats.

Spencer C. Tucker

References

Bonjour, E., H.S. Offler, and G.R. Potter. *A Short History of Switzerland*. Oxford: Clarendon, 1952.

Luck, J. Murray. *Modern Switzerland*. Palo Alto, Calif.: Society for the Promotion of Science and Scholarship, 1985.

Sykes-Picot Agreement

The 1916 Sykes-Picot Agreement between England and France aimed to take control of the Ottoman Empire's Arab territories once the First World War had been victoriously concluded. Named after British and French negotiators Sir Mark Sykes and François Georges Picot, it would have given France direct control of Lebanon and Cilicia and indirect control of Syria. England would have received direct control of Iraq from Baghdad to the Persian Gulf and indirect control of the territory stretching east of Palestine to the Persian border north of Baghdad. Palestine was to be under international control. Czarist Russia and Italy agreed to the Sykes-Picot arrangement but at a price. In 1916 Russia was promised Turkish Armenia, and in 1917 Italy was to receive Turkish territory in western and southern Anatolia.

The Sykes-Picot Agreement revealed Allied imperial intentions. There is controversy, however, as to whether it contradicted several wartime British statements concerning independence for the Arabs. Britain had frequently placed several restrictions on any such promises. For example, on 24 October 1915 British High Commissioner to Egypt Henry McMahon had sent a letter to Sharif Hussein of Mecca stating that in the postwar Middle East, Britain would have direct control of the Baghdad-Basra region, that the area west of Hama, Homa, Aleppo, and Damascus could not be under Arab control, and that any Arab state east of the Hama-Damascus area would have to seek British advice. Lastly, McMahon warned that Britain could make no promises that would injure French interests. Consultation with the French resulted in the Sykes-Picot Agreement.

The Sykes-Picot Agreement also proved to be a source of bitter conflict between France and England at the 1919 Paris Peace Conference. French Premier Georges Clemenceau arrived at the conference expecting to have England's support for French claims to Lebanon, Cilicia, and Syria. His optimism was based on a 2 December 1918 London meeting with British Prime Minister David Lloyd George. In a verbal understanding with no witnesses, Clemenceau agreed to modify the Sykes-Picot Agreement. Recognizing England's military contributions against Turkey and her overwhelming postwar military superiority in the Middle East, Clemenceau agreed that the oil-producing area of Mosul, which in 1916 had been placed in the French zone, would be transferred to the British sphere. Palestine, which in 1916 had been reserved for some form of international control, would also be placed under British control. In return for these concessions, Clemenceau believed that Lloyd George had promised British support for French claims to Syria and Cilicia.

Lloyd George, however, came to the Paris Conference determined to deny France the territory promised her under the terms of the Sykes-Picot Agreement. He saw no reason to share Arab lands when France had very few troops in the area. Appealing to Wilsonian principles of self-determination, he argued that since the Arabs had rebelled against Turkey, they were entitled to self-rule in Lebanon and Syria. Lloyd George wanted Emir Faisal to rule Lebanon and Syria. And for good reason: Faisal was under British control. At the same time that Lloyd George was arguing for Arab independence in Lebanon and Syria, he insisted that Britain would maintain control of Iraq and Palestine. Clemenceau rejected such a plan, arguing that France was entitled to the same fruits of victory as England. The standoff between the two allies ended in April of 1920 at the San Remo Conference, when they agreed that England would rule Palestine and Iraq, and France would rule Lebanon and Syria. England made this concession because she was facing colonial rebellions from Ireland to India. The spread of Arab and Moslem discontent now threatened British security in the Middle East and in India. France was to be an antidote to Arab nationalism. French troops, landing at Beirut, poured into Syria in June of 1920. England and France now ruled as mandates on behalf of the League of Nations much of the territory that the two Allies had agreed to rule in the 1916 Sykes-Picot agreement.

Jan Karl Tanenbaum

References

Andrew, Christopher, and A.F. Kanya-Forstner. *The Climax of French Imperial Expansion, 1914–1924.* Stanford: Stanford University Press, 1981.

Kedourie, Elie. *In the Anglo-Arab Labyrinth: The McMahon-Husayn Correspondence and Its Interpretations.* Cambridge: Cambridge University Press, 1976.

Nevakivi, Jukka. *Britain, France and the Arab Middle East, 1914–1920.* London: Athlone, 1969.

Tanenbaum, Jan Karl. *France and the Arab Middle East, 1914–1920.* Philadelphia: American Philosophical Society, 1978.

See also ARAB REVOLT; CLEMENCEAU, GEORGES; LLOYD GEORGE, DAVID

Talât Pasha, Mehmed (1874–1921)

Turkish government official during the First World War. Born into a poor farming family in Edirne in Ottoman Thrace in 1874, Talât was one of the earliest leaders of the Young Turk revolutionary movement. Talât played a major part in the 1908 Young Turk Revolution, after which he was elected to the parliament. He served as minister of the interior from 1909 to 1911 and from 1913 to 1918. Talât did much to involve his nation in the First World War. He believed that in the event of a general war Turkey should ally itself with Russia to protect the Straits; a proposal of alliance, however, was rejected by Russian Foreign Minister Serge Sazonov. Talât had demanded a guarantee of the territorial integrity and independence of the Ottoman Empire and abolition of the capitulations that impaired her sovereignty as preconditions for such an alliance, but the Russians were unable to secure the approval of France and England and rejected the offer. Unable to bring about an alliance with Russia, Talât became convinced that Germany was the only country willing to ally with Turkey, although for some time he vacillated between pro-Entente and pro-German members of the Ottoman government. On 2 August 1914, Talât was present at the signing of the Turco-German Secret Alliance Treaty.

By the outbreak of the war Talât and Enver Pasha were the two key figures in the Turkish government. Although he was pro-war, Talât wanted to delay Turkey's entry as long as possible. He feared an attack by Bulgaria and traveled to Sofia to secure an alliance with that country. It was not until the end of October that Talât decided on entry on the side of the Central Powers. After the attack of the battle cruiser *Goeben (Yavuz Sultan Selim)* and light cruiser *Breslau (Midilli)* on the Russian Black Sea coast, Turkey formally entered the war on 2 November 1914.

Turkish problems multiplied rapidly. In 1915 anti-Turkish rioting broke out in the eastern Anatolian city of Van, where Armenians, motivated by Russian promises of an independent Armenia, joined the ranks of the Russian army and formed guerrilla units. As he recorded in his memoirs, Talât ordered the deportation of Armenians "in order to stop the destructive activities of the Armenians in the rear of the Turkish army." As a result, a great many Armenians died.

On 4 February 1917 Sultan Mehmed V appointed Talât Grand Vizier (prime minister), in which post he sought concessions from Germany. Talât traveled to Germany several times to request more aid and to resolve the issue of Caucasian territory. He also represented Turkey at negotiations at Brest-Litovsk, where a treaty in March of 1918 arranged for Russia's withdrawal from the war. Aware of German interest in the Baku oil fields, Talât, wanting to secure Transcaucasia for Turkey, threatened the Germans with Turkish withdrawal from the war unless his demands were met. Finally, Germany and Russia agreed to surrender Ardahan, Kars, and Batum to Turkey.

The subsequent deterioration of Turkey's position was too rapid for Talât to control his country's fate. In the late summer of 1918, while returning from a trip to Berlin, Talât witnessed the collapse of the Bulgarian army and realized that the war had been lost. Toward the last months of the war, Talât tried unsuccessfully to conclude an armistice through President Wilson. In October of 1918, after the Turkish defeat, Talât, fearing prosecution, resigned his position and fled to Germany with the rest of the Young Turk government. Talât lived in Berlin until his assassination by an Armenian on 15 March 1921.

Yücel Yanikdağ

References

Bolayir, Enver, ed. *Talât Pasa'nin Hatiralari*. Istanbul: Bolayir, 1958.

Feroz, Ahmad. *The Young Turks: The Committee of Union and Progress in Turkish Politics. 1908–1914*. Oxford: Oxford University Press, 1969.

Morgenthau, Henry. *Secrets of theBosphorus, 1913–1916*. London: Hutchinson, 1921.

Shaw, Stanford J., and Ezel K. Shaw. *History of the Ottoman Empire and Modern Turkey*. 2 vols. Cambridge: Cambridge University Press, 1977.

Talât Pasha. "Posthumous Memoirs of Talât Pasha." *Current History* 15 (1921): 287–95.

See also ARMENIA; OTTOMAN EMPIRE

Tank Warfare

Tactical innovation in warfare usually has involved some new technological advance or discovery, but the critical elements in the application of a new idea on the battlefield are timing and perseverance. Although there is some credible evidence that Colonel (later General) Jean Baptiste E. Estienne of the French artillery was on the verge of developing an armored land fighting machine at about the same time, most sources credit British Lieutenant Colonel of Engineers Ernest D. Swinton as the intellectual originator of the battle tank.

Although British and other officers from Western armies had seen machine guns and quick-firing artillery in action during the Russo-Japanese War in 1904–5, the Europeans and Americans failed to understand the way that those weapons had changed what was possible on the battlefield. The Americans in particular were slow with industrial response to military production requirements for artillery, and were reluctant to adapt foreign developments in weapons and tactics.

Mobility, which characterized the early months of fighting on the Western Front, disappeared as the front extended quickly to the English Channel and the Alps. As the battle lines stalemated into trenches, it soon became clear that maneuver and deep movements against the rear of enemy positions were less likely. Artillery barrages and curtains of machine-gun bullets dominated, while poison gas added to the lethal morass. Lengthy artillery bombardments erased roads, communications, and even the shape of the land in front of the friendly wire. Surprise was nearly impossible. Swinton had observed all this while serving as a war correspondent for the war office press. The breakthrough idea was Swinton's recollection of an American farm machine that a friend had seen in Antwerp—the Holt tractor.

Swinton's early suggestion in July of 1914—that a caterpillar-tracked armored land machine fortified with cannon and machine guns could be built in a way that would be effective—was at first politely filed away in the offices of British government. Crisis and urgency later stimulated the receptiveness of bureaucrats, particularly when the casualty reports from France began to pour into the war office.

The wonderful simplicity of the tank was its melding of armored protection for the crew, the caterpillar-tracked drive system that allowed the machine to "float" over ruined terrain, and automatic firepower in the form of the machine gun and the quick-firing cannon. It was the best of artillery, cavalry, and the armored knight all rolled up into one. But a marvelous machine, even if it worked, did not guarantee a sensible system of tactical employment. The intense problem-solving that gave birth to the tank did not at the same time generate an effective system of employment.

Was this machine simply a mobile, protected machine gun or artillery emplacement? Or was it a cavalry machine in the sense that it combined a steed with a mounted warrior to engage in battle as a medieval knight might? Should these new "tanks" be grouped together to form a mass of moving steel to break through the static defensive lines by momentum as well as by firepower, or should they be parceled out among the attacking infantry divisions to provide forward-moving fire support? Each method of employment had its advocates and its detractors. Each method was tested in battle and neither approach produced decisive results.

The Mark I production model tank, based on the "Big Willie" design, had a radius of action of about twelve miles; its crew could remain effective in a fight for about a half-day at most. Even Swinton, in his earliest thinking about the employment of the tank, judged it to be "primarily a machine gun destroyer" to assist the infantry assault. He correctly assessed that tanks would be used best in mass in a surprise assault without a preliminary artillery barrage. Also, firm ground was essential.

On the Somme in September of 1916, during the third phase of the British offensive begun on 1 July, Lieutenant General Sir Henry S. Rawlinson, commanding the British Fourth Army, distributed his available forty-nine tanks evenly among his attacking divisions. In that way they would have been positioned to attack unexpected strongpoints in the German lines. Rather than having tanks leading the infantry, he acceded to his superior's view that tanks and infantry should boldly advance together. Thirty-two tanks reached the line of departure, but only eighteen were able to continue the attack. The remainder either failed mechanically or were ditched. Captain B.H. Liddell Hart described this plan as "the driblet form," where the tanks were distributed without regard to unit integrity and rushed into action without adequate preparation. Nevertheless, there were occasions where individual tanks had worked splendidly with supporting infantry to clear long sections of enemy trench.

Field Marshal Sir Douglas Haig's staff viewed the experiment as generally disappointing, thus reinforcing their predisposition, but Haig himself was less critical. He saw the potential and favored increased production of tanks with heavier armor and larger guns. Chief of the Imperial General Staff Field Marshal William R. Robertson thought Haig's plans for the September offensive and the aggressive employment of tanks in the offense were a "somewhat desperate innovation."

In the fall of 1916 a reorganization and expansion of the British Tank Corps was initiated, although its final divorce from the Machine Gun Corps was deferred. On 29 September command of British tank units in France was given to Lieutenant Colonel Hugh Elles. Each of the four companies of tanks in France formed the cadre for a new battalion of seventy-two tanks. Early in 1917 the size of each battalion was reduced to thirty-six fighting and twelve training tanks, mostly because of lagging production but also because experience had shown that section leaders could not control more than four tanks in battle. As part of this shuffle, Swinton was replaced in March of 1917

by Brigadier F. Gore Anley, a seasoned infantry commander.

Eight well-worn training tanks were sent to Egypt for use in the Palestine campaigns of early 1917. In most instances the tanks fulfilled their traditional role of attacking enemy outposts and strongpoints. Operations on the Palestine front did not produce any innovation in the use of tanks that had not been revealed in the main event in France.

In January of 1917, without benefit of Swinton's "Notes on the Employment of 'Tanks,'" written a year earlier, the Heavy Branch attempted to standardize tank tactics. The preferred attack formation was four tanks, and never fewer than a pair, so that mutual support in case of a mechanical failure would increase the probability of survival of the machine and its crew. As the tanks penetrated the enemy line and began to role up the flanks, it was essential for infantry to follow closely to deal with the enemy infantrymen. When working with infantry and machine guns in open terrain, it was preferable for tanks and infantry to advance together with the tanks forming mobile forts and the infantry machine-gun sections covering the gaps between them. Coordination with artillery barrages gave greater weight to the tank-infantry attack, which had the greatest potential for success if surprise were achieved. If available, airplanes added another element of combat power to the attack formation.

The next significant employment of tanks by the British Expeditionary Force was at Arras in April of 1917. Despite increased production emphasis, not one of the improved Mark IV tanks had arrived in time for that battle. The tank units were embarrassed by the exaggerated newspaper accounts of their role on the Somme. The newly formed 1st Tank Brigade, still equipped with only sixty late-production Mark I tanks, made the attack. The Mark I's were improved by removing the failure-prone tail section and replacing the French Hotchkiss machine guns with Lewis guns. Soldiers had begun the backbreaking work of moving supplies forward because the often-requested "supply" tanks had not yet joined the force. Inadequate logistics, stemming from a lack of tracked supply vehicles that could operate over broken terrain, most often prevented any exploitation of initial success.

On the night of 8–9 April a small number of tanks making the approach march for the attack became mired in a black mud bog south of Arras but were able to join the main group in time to influence the course of battle as a reserve force in the sleet and driving rain. With sixty tanks spread all along the line when the bursting signal shell started them forward, there was no effective control over them from higher headquarters; it was an affair of individual tanks and their immediate supporting infantry. If a tank became immobilized because of enemy fire or hung up on a tree stump or in a trench, it continued to fight as a pill box as the tide of battle swept around and past it. Despite very heavy losses in tanks, the experience of the battles around Arras was positive and indicated that the pre-battle training conducted at Bermicourt had been worthwhile.

The lessons of Arras were that tanks, skillfully trained and led, should be employed *en masse* with a large reserve to exploit success. Tanks for signaling and supply were badly needed in the organization. By June of 1917 the British High Command was convinced that tanks had significant potential to break the deadlock on the Western Front. They ordered the Heavy Branch expanded to eighteen battalions, organized in six brigades, and officially redesignated it the Tank Corps.

German defensive tactics had been adjusted to provide greater depth to the defensive positions and greater flexibility to local commanders in conducting defensive operations. Tactically it was a familiar story. Tanks working with infantry were able to make substantial penetrations of the initial German defensive lines, but there were insufficient reserves to complete the breakthrough and exploit the success. This was an intellectual as well as a logistical problem for the BEF.

French tanks made their debut on 16 April 1917 during the Champagne offensive. Only 128 Schneiders (CA.1) were available because of serious delays in production. The French units were organized into *batteries* (four tanks), *groupes* (sixteen tanks), and *groupements* (thirty-two or more tanks), the latter corresponding to an American or British battalion. By the time the Schneiders appeared on the French battle line, the Germans, learning from the British tank attacks on the Somme, had widened their trenches. Assisted by aircraft observation, German artillery destroyed many of the Schneiders during the long approach march. As with the British tanks, some significant penetrations of the enemy defenses went unexploited because reserves were not positioned to follow up.

Recent scholarship suggests that British staff officers were not impressed with the performance of their tank brigades in Flanders in July and August of 1917. The wretched, chopped-up terrain erased even the slightest probability of good trafficability. If the tanks could not move forward, they could not accomplish their purpose. Although as a general rule the tanks did not fare well in Flanders, there were instances where small tank units worked extraordinarily well with their supporting infantry in overcoming strongpoints.

Haig had proposed in February of 1917 that massed tanks be used for a surprise attack against the center of the line without any artillery preparation to seize the high ground. Although eliminated in the Passchendaele operation, the idea was used later, in November of 1917, in the Cambrai offensive planned by J.F.C. Fuller. Cambrai marked the tactical transition from destruction by artillery fire to close battle by coordinated fire and movement. On 20 November 1917 three hundred tanks advanced on a six-mile front assigned to five infantry divisions. By noon the tanks had broken through the four belts of trenches to a depth of four miles. The opportunity had been presented, but then it was squandered when the exploitation force of five cavalry divisions once again demonstrated the obsolescence of horse cavalry on the modern battlefield. The campaign in Flanders had ensured that there were not enough tanks to form an adequate exploitation force of tanks and infantry. The Germans had time to close the gap with their reserves, and on 30 November they counterattacked to restore the position.

British tank operations in the spring of 1918 reflected an effective learning and training effort. The training base in England began to produce skillful crews in sufficient numbers to man the new Mark A (Whippet) and the improved Mark V tanks. The flow of the new tanks to France, however, was slow because of insufficient sea transport. When the German drives began on 21 March 1918, the British had only 320 Mark IV and fifty Whippets available for counterattack duty with the reserve infantry units, and only half of those made it into battle. As tanks were lost in action, the remaining machines were consolidated and the dismounted crews fought as machine-gun battalions. Although an expedient, this resulted in the loss of many trained tank crewmen, especially drivers.

On 4 July 1918, at the village of Hamel on the Somme River, the British demonstrated the economy of force that resulted from the skillful employment of tank units tactically integrated with infantry battalions. Hamel marked the combat initiation of sixty Mark V tanks.

During the second Battle of the Marne in July of 1918, 337 French tanks of all types were available, and 70 percent of them saw action. Forty-five percent of engaged tanks were disabled or destroyed, and 25 percent of engaged tank crews were casualties. French light tank units were shifted by motor transport and rail along the nose of the German penetration between Château-Thierry and Reims to provide tanks for local counterattacks. In July the French tank factories were at peak production, with a new battalion of Renault light tanks joining the field armies each week.

At Amiens in August of 1918, the successful tactical integration of tanks, airplanes, and armored cars with infantry nevertheless resulted in substantial tank losses that could not be quickly replaced. Of more than 450 British fighting tanks and more than 100 supply tanks engaged, nearly 70 percent were lost to enemy fire. Nonetheless, the tanks did significantly lessen infantry casualties and contributed to the victory.

The American tank experience in World War I was brief. Four American brigades, equipped with mostly French and some British machines, fought in the St. Mihiel and Meuse-Argonne operations from September through October of 1918. The U.S. 301st Heavy Tank Battalion, equipped with British Mark V and Mark V Star tanks, served in the British sector throughout the war.

Designing and producing tanks for service in France during World War I proved easier than designing and implementing effective tactics to capitalize on the tank's potential. General Swinton was convinced as early as February of 1916 that tanks should be employed in massed formations, in favorable terrain without advanced artillery preparations so as to gain surprise. Because the tank force was subordinated to infantry-dominated leadership and tactics, those conditions were seldom achieved. Advances in wireless communications and the logistical support of fighting tank units in 1918, along with refinements in organization, were focused on achieving victory in 1919. The French experience with tanks paralleled that of the British, and the Americans depended initially on French units for their tank support until their own brigades were ready in September of 1918. The German experience with tanks was mostly reactive and not tactically productive. In its first exposure to battle, the tank did not realize its full potential.

John F. Votaw

References

Fuller, J.F.C., Major General. *Tanks in the Great War, 1914–1918*. London: John Murray, 1920.

Harris, J.P., and F.H. Toase, eds. *Armoured Warfare*. London: B.T. Batsford, 1990.

Jones, Ralph E. *The Fighting Tanks since 1916*. Washington, D.C.: National Service Publishing, 1933.

Liddell Hart, B.H., Captain. *The Tanks: The History of the Royal Tank Regiment and Its Predecessors Heavy Branch Machine-Gun Corps, Tank Corps and Royal Tank Corps 1914–1945*. 2 vols. London: Cassell, 1959.

Swinton, Sir Ernest D., Major-General. *Eyewitness*. Garden City, N.Y.: Doubleday, Doran, 1933.

Travers, Tim. *How the War Was Won: Command and Technology in the British Army on the Western Front, 1917–1918*. London: Routledge, 1992.

Williams-Ellis, Clough. *The Tank Corps*. New York: George H. Doran, 1919.

Wilson, Dale E. *Treat 'Em Rough! The Birth of American Armor, 1917–20*. Novato, Calif.: Presidio, 1989.

See also ALLIED COUNTEROFFENSIVE, 1918; CAMBRAI, BATTLE OF; FULLER, J.F.C.; LIDDELL HART, BASIL; SWINTON, ERNEST; TANKS

Tanks

The tank was one of a handful of mechanical innovations during the First World War. It had enormous potential, but only when employed within an effective tactical system.

While Lieutenant Colonel of Engineers Ernest D. Swinton and his British colleagues receive principal credit for transforming the tank from a theoretical possibility to a battlefield reality in World War I, other belligerents, notably the French and the Germans, were developing their own tank production programs and introduced fighting vehicles during the First World War. Other nations—for example Italy, Russia, Japan, Sweden, Czechoslovakia, Spain, Poland, and the United States—produced tanks either during or immediately after the Great War and during the 1920s. But only Great Britain, France, and Germany produced tanks that actually saw combat service in World War I.

The tank of World War I was a manned fighting machine. Its principal parts were an armored hull, two continuous caterpillar tracks, gasoline engine(s), and cannon or machine guns. Its name, "tank," resulted from British efforts to disguise the machine's true function by shipping them to France in crates marked "tank." In this way the British hoped to surprise the Germans when they were introduced in the Battle of the Somme in September of 1916.

Although the mechanical systems incorporated in the tank were known previously, it took the determined efforts of a team of British officers to bring those systems together in a potentially effective fighting machine. Early in the war, British artillery tractors powered by gasoline engines were used to pull heavy guns across ruined terrain. Armored cars saw limited use in combat situations and were used to recover downed aviators from no-man's-land. The idea of combining those technological realities into a manned fighting machine to help attacking infantry offset the terrible advantages of enemy artillery and machine-gun fire did not emerge until Swinton and his colleagues culminated their work.

In January of 1915 First Lord of the Admiralty Winston Churchill wrote to Prime Minister H.H. Asquith and recommended the development "of special mechanical devices for taking trenches." He proposed that "a committee of engineering officers and other experts" should be in continual session at the war office to examine those matters.

In June of 1915 Swinton described the characteristics of an armored fighting machine to overcome German machine guns: It must be able to climb a five-foot ledge, span a five-foot trench, have a twenty-mile radius of action, weigh about eight tons, and be served by a crew of ten men manning two machine guns and one field gun. In July Swinton completed his assignment as war correspondent for the war office press and returned to Britain to serve as assistant secretary for the Committee of Imperial Defence, known since the beginning of the war as the Dardanelles Committee of the cabinet. The process for converting the idea of a fighting "landship" into a practical machine now began.

British Tanks

The patronage of the British Admiralty in the development of the fighting tank is significant beyond the important assistance of Winston Churchill. The war office had shown both apathy and inability to bring the land fighting machine to reality; the navy was both willing and able to accomplish the task. The naval nomenclature of the tank was no accident.

The first tank, "Little Willie," was pieced together at the factory of William Foster & Co. in Lincoln and made its appearance on 19 September 1915. It failed its test, mainly because of a defective tractor drive system. The follow-on design was already underway. Given the name H.M.S. *Centipede,* it was a larger machine and in production was affectionately known as "Big Willie" and later as "Mother." The "Big Willie" design led to the first production tank, the Mark I, which entered combat in France on the Somme in September of 1916.

The Mark I tanks had notable defects, which were corrected for later production machines. The stabilizer tail proved worthless; the fuel tanks were in a vulnerable position; the exhaust outlet on the top emitted telltale sparks and flame; and there was no way for a "ditched" tank to retrieve itself. At thirty tons with a crew of eight, the Mark I sported two 6-pounder guns and four machine guns in the "male" version, and six machine guns in the "female" version. The Mark I was the mainstay of fighting in 1916 and early 1917. Fifty Mark II and fifty Mark III tanks were manufactured by the Foster Company. These corrected the defects of the Mark I and were employed along with Mark I's in early 1917.

The Mark IV was produced in 1917 by the Foster Company. It added 420 males and 595 females to the tank force. The Mark IV engine was slightly more powerful, but its other characteristics were the same as those of the earlier models. The Mark IV saw service in France from mid-1917 in Flanders through late 1918.

Two hundred Medium "A" tanks ("Whippets") were produced by Foster in 1917. With a crew of three and an armament of four machine guns, it moved its sixteen-ton weight at a speed of 8.3 mph and gained its power from two 45-horsepower engines. The Whippets saw service during the German drives in the spring of 1918 through to the Armistice.

Two hundred each of the male and female Mark V tanks were produced in 1918 by the Foster Company and the Metropolitan Carriage Wagon and Finance Company. The Mark V was equipped with a six-cylinder, 150-horsepower engine capable of moving the thirty-ton tank at 4.6 mph with a range of twenty-five miles. Other features were the same as in the earlier models. Sixty Mark V's were in action at Hamel on 4 July 1918, and 288 saw service at Amiens on 8 August 1918, the "black day" of the German army.

The Mark V Star tank was produced by various manufacturers; 642 were made. It differed from the basic Mark V tank by the addition of another machine gun (male with five, female with seven), and added weight (thirty-six tons). It was six feet longer and could span a fourteen foot trench. It had a range of forty miles. The Mark V Star tank participated in the fall 1918 engagements by the Tank Corps.

The British developed troop carriers and supply tanks modeled on the fighting tank frames. Additional tanks were modified as signal vehicles. A few Mark V's and Whippets were sent to support the Allied forces engaged in Russia in 1919.

French Tanks

The French tank production program began with emphasis on medium tanks in 1916. Colonel (later General) J.E. Estienne, a French artilleryman, provided the necessary stimulus and leadership to guide the French program to productivity. The first tanks, however, did not measure up to expectations.

The first orders for 400 medium tanks went to the Schneider Company in February of 1916, followed by an order for 400 more from the Compagnie des Forges d'Honecourt at St. Chamond. The Schneider Char d'Assaut 1 (CA.1) went into action on the Chemin des Dames on 16 April 1917. The St. Chamond tank first experienced the trial of battle at Laffaux Mill on 5 May 1917.

The Schneider, a "cheese box" with a 75mm gun in a sponson on the right side and two machine guns, one on each side, weighed in at fifteen tons and required a crew of six. It was powered by a seventy-horsepower engine made by the Schneider Company and could move at five mph. It had a range of twenty-five miles and could span only five feet ten inches of trench, a major shortcoming. Three batteries of Schneider tanks supported the American First Division in its attack on the village of Cantigny on 28 May 1918. Following the battle, on 31 May, Lieutenant Colonel George Patton interviewed the French tank leaders to capitalize on the lessons for his Light Tank School at Langres.

The St. Chamond, at twenty-five tons with a crew of nine, was a larger machine with a 75mm gun and four machine guns, giving all-around automatic weapons fire for the tank. It was powered by a ninety-horsepower, water-cooled, four-cylinder engine supplemented by a dynamo, two electric motors, and storage batteries. It could span an eight-foot trench and had a range of thirty-seven miles. Dual controls allowed the tank to be driven from either end, but it had poor cross-country maneuverability. At Laffaux Mill the St. Chamonds performed poorly compared with the Schneiders. Many failed to arrive on the battlefield because of mechanical failures during the long approach march. From the *groupe* of sixteen, twelve made it to the line of departure. Several more were unable to advance and three were destroyed in action.

In late 1916 the French army made the decision to refocus tank production on light, rather than medium, tanks. The Renault seven-ton tank made its appearance at Ploisy-Chazelle on 31 May 1918. Throughout the remainder of the war the tiny Renault became the commonplace image of the World War I tank. By the end of the war nearly five thousand had been produced. The Americans began production of a Renault clone, the 1917 six-ton, in 1918, but none were delivered in time to see action.

The two-man Renault was powered by a four cylinder, (thirty-nine) horsepower gasoline engine and could attain the blinding speed of six mph. Its armor plate varied from a quarter-inch to a half-inch thick, which could be penetrated by a high-powered rifle with armor-piercing ammunition. A single 37mm gun or an 8mm Hotchkiss machine gun was mounted in a fully rotating turret, the first tank thus equipped. The little machine could span a trench 6.5 feet wide and had a cruising range of twenty-four miles. Beginning in the spring of 1918, a new battalion of the Renaults joined the French field forces each week.

German Tanks

The only production tank fielded by the German army in World War I was the A7V, which took its name from the section of the war department responsible for its development and deployment. This giant machine, eleven feet high, twenty-four feet long and ten feet wide, was built by the Daimler Motor Company near Berlin in the spring of 1917. It weighed thirty-three tons and could achieve eight mph on level, firm ground, powered by two Mercedes-Daimler engines of 150 horsepower each. It could span a six-foot trench and climb a vertical wall of eighteen inches. Crewed by eighteen men, the tank was armed with one 57mm gun at the bow and six machine guns to protect the sides and rear. The shape of its hull, which overhung the suspension system and tracks, resulted in poor trench crossing and cross-country capability. Each track could be powered separately, forward or backward, so the tank could almost "neutral steer," a characteristic of short radius turning normally associated with the modern cross-drive transmission found in later tanks.

The A7V first appeared in action at St. Quentin on 21 March 1918. Ten days later, five captured British Mark IV tanks were put in action at the same location. German tank units were organized into sections *(abteilungen)* of five tanks each. General J.F.C. Fuller noted that morale was not high in the German Tank Corps, probably because their tanks were "both vulnerable and ineffective." German tank tactics consisted of "mopping up strong points" and did not show an appreciation of the need to cooperate with other arms. The German Tank Corps consisted of four sections of A7V tanks and five sections of captured British tanks.

Conclusion

Tanks in the Great War sometimes are viewed as a novelty that had little impact on the course of the war. Although British and French tanks never achieved their maximum potential, the possibilities were noted and implemented by the defeated Germans in the interwar period. Tank development in Britain and the United States languished. The French developed large numbers of tanks in the interwar period. These advances were stifled, however, by their view of the tank strictly as an infantry support weapon. The tank had made a spectacular debut in 1916, but its professional repertoire was not developed until World War II.

John F. Votaw

References

Browne, D.G., M.C. *The Tank in Action.* Edinburgh and London: William Blackwood and Sons, 1920.

Doughty, Robert Allan. *The Seeds Of Disaster: The Development of French Army Doctrine, 1919–1939.* Hamden, Conn.: Archon, 1985.

Fuller, J.F.C. *Tanks in the Great War, 1914–1918.* London: John Murray, 1920.

Jones, Ralph E. *The Fighting Tanks since 1916.* Washington, D.C.: National Service Publishing, 1933.

Macksey, Kenneth, and John H. Batchelor. *Tank: A History of the Armoured Fighting Vehicle.* New York: Charles Scribner's Sons, 1970.

Swinton, Sir Ernest D., Major General. *Eyewitness.* Garden City, N.Y.: Doubleday, Doran, 1933.

Wilson, Dale E. *Treat 'Em Rough!: The Birth of American Armor, 1917–20.* Novato, Calif.: Presidio, 1989.

See also Fuller, J.F.C.; Swinton, Ernest; Tank Warfare

Tardieu, André (1876-1945)

French journalist, diplomat, and politician. Born in Paris on 22 September 1876 to a prosperous upper-middle-class family, Tardieu was a brilliant student. He graduated from the Ecole Normale Supérieure at age twenty and entered the French Foreign Service as secretary at the French embassy in Berlin. Tardieu made his mark as a cabinet secretary in the Waldeck-Rousseau government and then as secretary-general to the interior ministry. At the same time, he established a reputation as a respected commentator on foreign affairs in *Le Figaro* and *Le Temps* and received chairs at the *Ecole des sciences politiques* and the war college. Tardieu also developed a working relationship with Georges Clemenceau during the latter's 1906–8 term as premier.

Elected to the Chamber of Deputies in April of 1914, Tardieu left to serve on General Ferdinand Foch's staff but returned in 1916, advocating General Joseph Joffre's replacement and closer parliamentary scrutiny of the army. In 1917, he was named high commissioner for Franco-American cooperation and spent a year in the United States, returning to France to become a member of Clemenceau's inner circle of advisers and one of France's chief negotiators during the Paris Peace Conference. A supporter of Rhineland separation and heavy German reparations, Tardieu remained a vigorous postwar defender of France's treaty demands. In 1919 he entered the cabinet as minister for liberated territories and was one of the organizers of the conservative *Bloc national* in the Chamber of Deputies.

Tardieu served in many interwar cabinets and was three times premier in 1929 and 1932. Poor health forced his retirement in 1936. He died at Menton on 15 September 1945.

David L. Longfellow

References

Binion, Rudolph. *Defeated Leaders*. New York: Columbia University Press, 1960.
Tardieu, André. *The Truth about the Treaty*. Indianapolis, Ind.: Bobbs-Merrill, 1921.

Thaon di Revel, Paolo (1859–1948)

Italian admiral and navy commander, born at Turin on 10 June 1859. Revel entered the naval school in 1873 and commanded the Second Naval Division during the Libyan War in 1911. As chief of the Italian naval general staff from March of 1913 to October of 1915 and February of 1917 to November of 1919, Revel was a conservative brake on the bold plans of the commander in chief of the fleet, the Duke of the Abruzzi. After the painful lessons inflicted by submarines in the early days of Italian operations, Revel determined that the Italian fleet had to be preserved either to face the Austrians in a classic battle, should the Austrian fleet sortie, or as a diplomatic factor in the Mediterranean after the war.

Revel was forced from office in October of 1915 when the minister of marine decided to combine the position of chief of staff with his own office. This ultimately turned out to be an unsuccessful experiment, and Revel returned as chief of staff in February of 1917 with the additional title of head of mobilized naval forces. He proved a vociferous champion of Italian interests and a thorn in the side of Italy's allies. He refused to consider anyone but an Italian to command in the Adriatic and bore much of the responsibility for the failure to achieve a unified naval command in the Mediterranean.

In November of 1918 King Victor Emmanuel III raised Revel from vice admiral to admiral and, a few years later, to grand admiral. Revel was technical advisor to the Italian delegation at the 1919 Paris Peace Conference and minister of marine in Mussolini's first cabinet from October of 1922 to May of 1925. In May of 1924 the King recognized his past services by bestowing upon him the somewhat grandiloquent title "Duke of the Sea" *(Duca del Mare)*. He died at Rome on 24 March 1948.

Paul G. Halpern

References

Ferrante, Ezio. *Il Grande Ammiraglio Paolo Thaon di Revel*. Rome: *Rivista Marittima*, 1989.
Halpern, Paul G. *The Naval War in the Mediterranean, 1914–1918*. Annapolis, Md.: Naval Institute Press, 1987.
Po, Guido. *Il Grande Ammiraglio Paolo Thaon di Revel*. Turin: S. Lattes, 1936.
Ufficio Storico della R. Marina, *La Marina Italiana nella Grande Guerra*. 8 vols. Florence: Vallecchi, 1935–42.

See also ABRUZZI, AMEDEO DI; ITALY, NAVY; MEDITERRANEAN NAVAL OPERATIONS

Tirpitz, Alfred von (1849–1930)

German admiral, state secretary of the navy office, and architect of the German High Seas Fleet. Born on 19 March 1849 in Küstrin, son of a Brandenburg judge, Tirpitz joined the navy in 1865 and was commissioned four years later. He was appointed captain in 1888 and from 1892 to 1896 served as chief of staff of the high command. Promoted to rear admiral in 1895 and admiral in 1903, he became the Imperial Navy's first and only grand admiral in 1911. On 18 June 1897 Kaiser Wilhelm II named Tirpitz state secretary of the navy office, with instructions to build up the navy. He held this post until March of 1916. Wilhelm II enobled Tirpitz in 1900. Patriotic and energetic, Tirpitz was also domineering, ruthless, and overbearing, as well as an adroit politician and manipulator of men.

Wilhelm II wanted Germany to have the world's largest navy. In 1895, while Germany was second in the world in the value of her foreign trade, her navy was fifth. Tirpitz agreed with the kaiser's plans and convinced him that emphasis should be on battleships rather than commerce-raiding cruiser-type vessels. Tirpitz furthermore saw to it that the navy came under Wilhelm II's personal control and that the Reichstag had no power over naval construction or organization. Ships were to be built and maintained, regardless of cost.

In April of 1898, just a year after rejecting the modest building program of Tirpitz's predecessor, the Reichstag passed Tirpitz's much more ambitious program in a vote of two to one. While Tirpitz took advantage of growing support in Germany for the navy, his success resulted in large part from his own extraordinary promotional abilities. He cultivated an alliance with Rhineland industrialists, supported creation of the Navy League, and took advantage of foreign policy crises to push for additional naval construction.

Tirpitz relied on a program of steady expansion *(Etappenplan)*, the "patient laying of brick upon brick." This was designed in part to deceive the Reichstag and German public from his real goals. He said that Germany wanted only a fleet capable of keeping the North Sea and Baltic shipping lanes open in time of war and protecting overseas lines of communication. He called this the "risk theory" *(Risikoge-danke)*. The navy was to be only large enough that another major naval power (that is, Great Britain) would not "risk" battle for fear that its strength might be crippled to the point where it would be vulnerable to another major naval power. Tirpitz said that Germany did not need a fleet as large as that of Great Britain; her warships could be concentrated, whereas the Royal Navy would have to spread its strength worldwide. He also saw the fleet as a useful diplomatic tool, and stated privately that Britain might be willing to surrender half her colonial empire to Germany in return for alliance.

Such arguments were designed to mask Tirpitz's real intent, of building a fleet strong enough to challenge Britain for control of the seas and world mastery. He stated in 1899 that the navy was "a question of survival" for Germany. If Germany could not continue to grow and project her power worldwide, she "would sink back to the status of a poor farming country." Germany had to prepare for a showdown with the Anglo-Saxon powers. This would probably be decided in one great naval battle in the North Sea or Atlantic, a scenario that almost came to pass at Jutland in 1916. Tirpitz believed that after 1920 Germany would stand a good chance of winning such a battle. His greatest worry was that Britain might carry out a preemptive strike.

The 1898 Naval Bill called for the construction of nineteen battleships, eight armored cruisers, and twelve large and thirty small cruisers in six years. Taking advantage of the international situation (the impact of the Spanish-American War, sentiment against Britain aroused by an incident during the Boer War when a British warship intercepted a German merchant vessel, and the Boxer Rebellion in China), Tirpitz introduced a second naval bill, which passed the Reichstag in June of 1900. This bill doubled the size of the projected navy to a total of thirty-eight battleships, twenty armored cruisers, and thirty-eight light cruisers—all to be built within twenty years. This was a direct challenge to the British Home Fleet, then of about thirty-two battleships. Passage of the bill so delighted Wilhelm II that he raised Tirpitz to the hereditary Prussian nobility.

A naval building race between Britain and Germany ensued. Britain answered with two new ship types: the superbattleship, *Dreadnought,* and the battle cruiser. Tirpitz replied in kind. Although the pace of the naval race later slowed, Tirpitz used international crises to secure the passage of supplementary German naval construction laws *(novellen)* in 1906, 1908, and 1912. The 1906 law provided for six dreadnoughts to be built by 1918; it also authorized six large cruisers, as well as funds to expand dock facilities and widen existing canals. The 1908 *novelle* provided for battleship replacement to occur every twenty years instead of twenty-five (four were to be built yearly from 1908 to 1911, and two per year from 1912 to 1917). The *novelle* of 1912 increased the projected size of the fleet to forty-one battleships (in five squadrons), and twenty large and forty light cruisers. This was probably not all Tirpitz intended. He was opposed to any reductions in the naval sphere and helped scuttle British War Minister Richard Haldane's 1912 effort to reduce the naval race between the two countries.

With his attention fixed on battleships, Tirpitz was late to embrace submarines. The first German submarine was not completed until 1906. The budget of 1912 projected a total of seventy-two boats, yet Germany entered the First World War with only twenty-eight (far fewer than the number for France and Great Britain), and there was no plan to employ them against commerce. By 1913 Tirpitz had been won over to the use of naval airships.

Gerhard Ritter has called the Tirpitz plan a "gruesome error" and German naval policy a "monstrous error in judgement." Far from driving Britain to panic, German naval construction drove Britain into alliance with France.

Although facing serious fiscal problems, Britain also outspent Germany in the naval sphere. By 1914 the German navy was second only to that of Britain, but the Royal Navy had widened its advantage over Germany in most classes of ships—the capital ship ratio was approximately thirty-two to eighteen. There were limits to what Germany could do, particularly as she was at the same time maintaining the world's largest standing army. By 1907–8 the army again received priority in armaments expenditure. Had the bulk of assets spent on the navy gone to the army instead, Germany might have achieved a land victory over France in 1914.

Tirpitz was unsuccessful in his efforts to assume operational control over the navy at the beginning of the First World War. He opposed keeping the fleet in port, where it spent most of the war. His advice to employ unrestricted submarine warfare against England in early 1916, in conjunction with General Erich von Falkenhayn's Verdun Offensive, was rejected by Wilhelm II and Chancellor Bethmann Hollweg. He resigned his offices in March of 1916.

After leaving the navy Tirpitz entered politics. He was one of the founders of the *Vaterlandspartei* and from 1924 to 1928 a deputy in the Reichstag. Tirpitz died at Ebenhausen near Munich on 6 March 1930. A German pocket battleship of World War II was named after him.

Spencer C. Tucker

References

Herwig, Holger. *"Luxury" Fleet: The Imperial Germany Navy, 1888–1918*. London: Allen and Unwin, 1980.
Hubatsch, Walter. *Die Ara Tirpitz. Studien zur deutschen Marinepolitik, 1890–1918*. Göttingen: Musterschmidt Verlag, 1955.
Tirpitz, Alfred von. *Einnerungen*. Leipzig: K.F. Koehler, 1919.

See also GERMANY, NAVY; WARSHIPS; WILHELM II

Tisza, Count István (1861–1918)

Prominent Hungarian politician and prime minister. Born in Bihar county on 22 April 1861 to an influential aristocratic family, Tisza followed in the footsteps of his father, Kálmán Tisza, who served as Hungarian prime minister from 1875 to 1890. After studies in Berlin and Heidelberg, Tisza returned to Hungary and was elected to parliament in 1886. Leader of the Liberal party founded by his father, Tisza's political beliefs centered on preserving the 1867 *Ausgleich* (compromise) that created the Dual Monarchy and Magyar domination over other nationalities within Hungary. This put him into opposition to both Magyar nationalists, who wanted to lessen Hungary's ties with Austria, and liberals who advocated greater rights for Hungary's minority nationalities.

In the early years of the twentieth century the touchstone of Austro-Hungarian relations was the unitary Hapsburg army. Kálmán Tisza's last ministry was wrecked in 1890 by his passage of a bill that upheld the integrity of the army; the opposition Party of Independence demanded two separate military establishments. István Tisza, like his father, believed that the common army was an essential prerequisite for the maintenance of Hapsburg power in Europe. In October of 1903 he became prime minister and secured passage of another army bill after threatening the opposition with drastic measures. His party was completely defeated in the January 1905 elections, however, because of widespread opposition to the army bill and also because Tisza refused to resort to the customary electoral corruption.

Tisza remained active in parliament and was the dominating figure in the 1910–13 Khuen-Héderváry ministry. He was convinced of the need to end internecine struggles and strengthen the common army because of the threat of general European war. Tisza reorganized the old Liberal party into the National Party of Work, which won a majority of seats in the 1910 elections. In 1912 Tisza, as president of the Chamber of Deputies, succeeded in pushing through parliament both a further army bill and a modification of parliamentary procedures that made obstructionism more difficult. He was again prime minister from June of 1913 to June of 1917.

At a crucial meeting of the Crown Council on 14 July 1914, Tisza opposed an immediate declaration of war against Serbia and insisted on diplomatic action to avoid a wider European war. He also demanded that the Dual Monarchy not annex Serbian territory because he wanted no additional Slavs in the empire.

Once the war began, however, Tisza became a firm believer in final victory by the Central Powers, meeting all opposition with a show of inflexibility and force. His dictatorial methods created great bitterness in both halves of the monarchy, and even Germany's leaders found themselves often rebuffed by their strong-willed ally in Budapest. When the question arose of ceding territory to Italy and Romania to keep them from entering the war against Austria-Hungary, Tisza blocked any concessions as a sign of weakness. After Hapsburg defeats made this position untenable he did become an advocate of territorial concessions, but only of non-Hungarian parts of the Dual Monarchy.

On the death of Emperor Franz Josef, Tisza secured an early coronation in Budapest of his successor, Karl (King Charles IV in Hungary), committing him to maintenance of the constitutional status quo. Karl, however, disliked Tisza and hoped to liberalize the Hungarian political system. Tisza also quarreled with Count Mihály Károlyi, who demanded universal suffrage, breakup of the large estates, and autonomy for the non-Magyar nationalities. Tisza rebuffed all social reforms proposed in the parliament and ordered partial suspension of civil rights.

On 22 May 1917 Karl ordered Tisza to resign, and he did so the next day. His National Party of Work continued to have a majority of seats in the Hungarian parliament, so that even out of office Tisza remained a major political figure, opposing any substantial changes in the Hungarian constitutional system. Tisza was assassinated in Budapest on 31 October 1918 by mutinous soldiers after publicly declaring that the Central Powers had lost the war.

Spencer C. Tucker

References
Hoensch, Jörg K. *A History of Modern Hungary.* New York: Longman, 1988.
Károlyi, Mihály. *Memoirs. Faith without Illusion.* London: Jonathan Cape, 1956.
Vermes, Gabor. *István Tisza. The Liberal Vision and Conservative Statecraft of a Magyar Nationalist.* New York: East European Monographs, 1985.

See also AUSTRIA-HUNGARY, HOME FRONT; HUNGARY, REVOLUTION IN; KARL I; KÁROLYI, MIHÁLY

Townshend, Sir Charles Vere Ferrers (1861–1924)

British general, born on 21 February 1861. Townshend joined the Royal Marines in 1881. He saw military action in the Sudan, the India/North-West frontier (besieged at Chitral, 1895), and South Africa. When World War I began, Townshend was assigned the Sixth Indian Division for service in Mesopotamia. General Sir John Nixon, the senior commander in Mesopotamia, ordered Townshend to sail up the Tigris and drive northwards. His fleet became known as "Townshend's Regatta."

Seizing Kut al Amara from the Turks, Townshend continued towards Baghdad, urged on by both military and civilian leaders. His Anglo-Indian force of 12,000 men was halted at Ctesiphon, however, and he retreated back to Kut al Amara to await reinforcements. Turkish forces under General Nur-ud-din and Baron von der Goltz pushed Townshend to Kut, where he was besieged on 8 December. The Turks repelled three British relief columns, inflicting heavy losses. T.E. Lawrence took part in negotiations to ransom Townshend's men but failed to win their release. On 29 April 1916, starvation and disease forced Townshend to surrender his remaining 10,000 Anglo-Indian soldiers, the largest British military surrender until Singapore in 1942. Townshend spent the remainder of the war in relative comfort as a POW on Prinkipo Island. He left the army in 1920 and died on 18 May 1924 in Paris.

Jose E. Alvarez

References
Barker, A.J. *The Bastard War—The Mesopotamian Campaign of 1914–1918.* New York: Dial, 1976.
———. *Townshend of Kut—A Biography of Major-General Sir Charles Townshend K.C.B., D.S.O.* London: Cassell, 1967.
Townshend, Sir Charles Vere Ferres, Major General. *My Campaign.* 2 vols. New York: James A. McCann, 1920.

See also GOLTZ, COLMAR VON DER; MESOPOTAMIA; NIXON, SIR JOHN

Transylvania

Transylvania, the easternmost province of Hungary, was a battleground in the struggle for ethnic self-determination and nationalism in World War I. Since the mid-nineteenth century Romania had sought to liberate Transylvania, where three million Romanians encountered cultural and political discrimination by minority Magyar rulers. Although Romania was allied to Austria-Hungary and Germany (Triple Alliance of 1883), the Entente powers offered Transylvania to Romania to entice her to enter the war; but Romania remained neutral from 1914 to 1916 for fear of German retaliation.

Romania's pro-German king, Carol I, resisted popular demands for Transylvania's annexation but agreed to a secret pact with Russia in October of 1914, which offered to protect and support Romanian claims to Transylvania in exchange for neutrality. His successor, King Ferdinand, acquired the throne soon thereafter and continued the neutrality policy. The initial success of the 1916 Brusilov Offensive convinced Ferdinand to enter the war for fear that Austro-Hungary would seek peace and Russia would seize Transylvania. A secret treaty arranged for Romania to receive Transylvania in return for siding with the Entente.

When Romania declared war on Austria-Hungary on 27 August 1916, Austro-Hungarian troops defending Transylvania consisted of only 34,000 border guards. Hostilities were initiated thirty minutes before the declaration of war, when an invasion force of 400,000 men—the Romanian First, Second, and Fourth armies, under the command of Lieutenant General Constantine Prezan—penetrated Transylvania. Although the border fortifications were easily traversed, the Romanian troops were hindered by poor leadership and held southern Transylvania for only a brief time. Some 200,000 troops led by General Erich von Falkenhayn from the north and General August von Mackensen from the south converged on the Romanians and forced them to retreat by the end of September. In November Falkenhayn's troops crossed the Transylvanian Alps, opening Romania itself to invasion. German troops soon overran the country, capturing the Romanian capital of Bucharest on 6 December 1916 and forcing Romania to sign an armistice on 9 December 1917 in which it renounced claims to Transylvania.

As the war shifted against the Central powers, in October of 1918 the Transylvanian Romanian national party demanded self-determination. Shortly before the final armistice, Romania again declared war on Germany and marched troops into Transylvania. A proclamation at Alba Iulia on 1 December 1918 announced the desire for a union between Transylvania and Romania. Although two million Magyars also lived in Transylvania, Hungary was forced to sign the Treaty of Trianon on 4 June 1920, ceding substantial territory, including Transylvania, to Romania. Racial tensions in Transylvania, solidified by World War I diplomacy, ensured strife in that region throughout the twentieth century.

Elizabeth D. Schafer

References

Pascu, Ştefan. *A History of Transylvania.* Translated by D. Robert Ladd. Detroit, Mich.: Wayne State University Press, 1982.

Pastor, Peter. "The Transylvanian Question in War and Revolution." In *Transylvania: The Roots of Ethnic Conflict.* Edited by John F. Cadzow, Andrew Ludanyi, and Louis J. Elteto. Kent, Ohio: Kent State University Press, 1983.

Torrey, Glenn E. "Romania's Entry into the First World War: The Problem of Strategy." *Emporia State Research Studies* 26 (Spring 1978): 5–19.

See also FALKENHAYN, ERICH VON; FERDINAND I; MACKENSEN, AUGUST VON; ROMANIA; ROMANIAN CAMPAIGN; TRIANON, TREATY OF

Trench Warfare

There are no more enduring symbols of World War I than the trench and its ubiquitous first cousin, the barbed-wire entanglement. Trench works were not new to World War I. They had appeared in certain static situations in the American Civil War, and somewhat more prominently in the Russo-Japanese War. But for the most part they were exceptions to the rule, temporary emplacements until the normal flow of warfare could resume. World War I marked the first appearance of the trench line as the dominant feature of the battlefield.

Neither side in the Great War anticipated or planned for static warfare. Prior to 1914 the tactical doctrines of most major armies envisioned combat operations consisting of vast sweeping maneuvers and meeting engagements. By the start of the war, however, the density of forces along the German, French, and Belgian borders was so great that there was little room for maneuver and open flanks rarely existed. Added to that problem was the vastly increased volume, range, and lethality that technology had given to the new generation of weapons that had appeared in the previous forty years. Smokeless powder, the magazine-fed repeating rifle, quick-firing artillery with recoil systems, and above all the machine gun put the soldier in the open at a great disadvantage to one fighting from a protected position. In order to survive, the soldiers of 1914 started digging. Firepower had gained the upper hand over maneuver, and the result was trench warfare.

The earliest trench systems were simple lines of foxholes and slit-trenches. In some areas where the ground water level was high the soldiers put up brims and parapets above ground level. As the tactical situation on the Western Front became more static, the defenses were improved, reinforced, and became more elaborate. In general, Allied commanders pushed their lines as far forward as possible, believing that control of terrain mattered most. The Germans were more careful to place their trenches in the best positions to maximize concealment, fields of fire, and observation. Before the start of the war French and British soldiers had received almost no training in the construction of defensive positions, and their supply trains carried almost none of the required materials. The Germans were better off. Although their prewar doctrine had overwhelmingly stressed the attack as well, they did train a little in defensive techniques—perhaps as a result of the reports from the extensive network of observers they had sent to the Balkan Wars.

By 1917 fully mature trench systems had evolved. Since the Germans spent most of the first three years on the Western Front on the defensive, they developed a significantly more sophisticated concept of defense. After their experiences on the Somme the Germans started holding these positions much more thinly (using as little as 20 percent of their combat power), as they developed their flexible defense-in-depth concept.

On the Allied side, trench systems consisted of three basic sets of lines. The outpost line was a thinly held string of strongpoints and early-warning positions held together in some areas by connecting trenches but usually not forming a continuous line. Several hundred meters to the rear, the main line consisted of three and sometimes more sets of roughly parallel trenches, reinforced with periodic strongpoints. Until the spring of 1918, the Allies kept up to two-thirds of their combat power packed into the main line. The third position was the reserve line, which held the counterattack forces and also provided the final line of defense for the artillery positions.

Trenches did not run in straight lines; rather, they were laid out in a zigzag pattern with sharp angles, with the line as a whole running parallel to the front. There were two reasons for this: It minimized the effects of a shell landing in the trench; also, in the event of a trench raid by the enemy, a straight trench would have allowed a raiding party that gained a foothold to set up a machine gun and effectively clear the entire trench. With the zigzag pattern any raiding party had to fight its way from each straight stretch, called a bay, to the next.

Trenches both within and between zones were connected by perpendicular legs called communications trenches. The whole system was entered from the rear by an access trench that started beyond the enemy's line of sight. By 1917 it was theoretically possible to walk from the Swiss border to the Belgian coast without ever coming up above ground level. In practice, however, some sectors of the line were better constructed than others. The more static the situation in a sector, the more permanent the trench lines became. Generally, they were reinforced with wooden beams and sandbags to prevent them from collapsing during enemy shelling, or under their own weight during the periods of heavy rain so common to that corner of Europe. Trenches were usually slightly deeper than a man's height, with a fire-step built into the forward wall to allow defenders to fire their rifles in the event of an attack. The floors of the better trenches were covered with wooded slats, called duckboards, to keep the soldiers out of the mud and water.

The space between the opposing sets of trench lines (anywhere from 50 to 3,000 meters) was called no-man's-land. Extending out into this area, the front of the trench system was covered by massive entanglements of barbed wire to impede the forward movement of any attacker. The emplacements took two basic forms. "Dannert," or "concertina," wire came in prepackaged coils about a meter in diameter. When spread out (like a concertina) it formed an open cylindrical line about ten meters long and waist high. These lines were connected end to end and even stacked on top of one another. The other form was an apron fence, with regular agricultural barbed wire strung between corkscrew steel poles screwed into the ground. Most wire complexes used both forms in combination and consisted of multiple lines. Wire complexes were designed with carefully concealed paths, to allow friendly patrols in and out. These paths were always covered by observation and fire, usually machine guns. This same system of barbed wire was widely used by United States forces in Vietnam to protect their base camps and isolated fire bases.

Trench warfare also produced its own specialized weapons, some of which are still in use today. The mortar, a small, high-trajectory, short-range artillery weapon, had been around for hundreds of years, but it was almost extinct by the time World War I started. With trench warfare, the mortar came back into its own. Since it fired only at high angles and all of its recoil was directed into the ground, the mortar was an ideal source of heavy firepower for the forward trenches. Throughout the course of the war both sides built up large trench-mortar organizations. In some armies these trench artillery units were part of the artillery; in some they were part of the infantry; and in the German army they were part of the Pioneers (combat engineers). The early World War I mortars bore little resemblance to the mortars of today until the British introduced the Stokes mortar, the forerunner of all modern "stovepipe" mortars.

Flamethrowers and hand grenades were weapons of trench warfare that are still a part of modern arsenals. The Germans were famous for their stick grenade, called the "potato masher" by Allied troops. The British Mills bomb was the forerunner of the modern "egg" or "pineapple" grenades. Most of the World War I grenades had a four- or five-second delay fuse. At first only specially trained soldiers called bombers were allowed to throw grenades. During an offensive every soldier in an attack wave might carry several grenades, but they were to be passed to the unit's bomber for actual use. As the Germans evolved their stormtroop tactics, every soldier in these elite units carried and threw grenades.

The grim hand-to-hand combat that trench fighting sometimes produced also resulted in a grisly assortment of more primitive weapons for quick and silent killing. A wide array of trench knives, blackjacks, and knuckle-dusters were fabricated right in the trenches and carried by most men. A form of mace even appeared, a weapon not seen on the battlefield since medieval times.

Life in the trenches quickly settled into a routine. The day started with "stand to," about a half hour before first light. All soldiers would mount the fire-step, man their positions, and be prepared to repulse any enemy attack that might come (dawn supposedly being the preferred time for such attacks). After stand to, the men washed up as best they could and prepared breakfast over small fires. The food was almost always canned and generally bad. Aside from guards and observers, most of the day was taken up with sleeping. At dusk stand to was usually repeated, and some units tried to send up hot meals at this time.

When night fell the real work of trench warfare began. Under cover of darkness ammunition and supplies were brought up and repairs were made to whatever damage might have been sustained from the daily shelling. Patrols slipped out into no-man's-land. Wiring parties went out to repair damage to the wire entanglements, and stretcher parties went out to look for the wounded and recover the dead. In the sectors where no-man's-land was narrow, opposing parties sometimes ran into each other, resulting in fierce hand-to-hand fighting. Throughout the night both sides randomly shelled and sprayed sections of no-man's-land with machine-gun fire—those sections, of course, where one's own patrols were not supposed to be working. Both sides often fired parachute flares from mortars and artillery and dropped them from aircraft. If caught under the sudden light of a flare the best tactic was to freeze, because it was movement that attracted the enemy's eye. The flares stayed lit and aloft only a short time, and the eyes of any observing machine gunners took a few seconds to get adjusted to the light.

The trench raid was also a favorite nighttime activity of both sides. Trench raids were sent out to locate enemy machine guns and artillery, capture prisoners for interrogation, and just simply to terrorize the enemy. Some soldiers excelled as trench raiders and specialized in that one activity. Some enjoyed working as lone operators, and some, no doubt, came to take a perverse pleasure in the killing.

The size of a raid could be anything from a few men to an entire company, depending on the mission.

Units did not remain in the trenches for months on end. Normally units were rotated in and out of the line on a routine basis. When out of the line, a unit was supposed to relax and re-fit; but most of the time was taken up with intensive training on new weapons and tactical methods. Sometimes a soldier was able to get more rest in the line than out of it, but his living conditions out of the line were generally better.

Trench warfare, like all other forms of combat, consisted of hours and hours of grinding, boring routine, punctuated by brief intervals of sheer terror. During daylight hours anything that exposed itself above ground level drew instant fire from opposing snipers and machine gunners. There was always a danger of random shelling from artillery and mortars. Some soldiers snapped under the strain of the constant shelling, a psychological condition that came to be known as shell shock.

In wet periods the trenches filled with water and mud, making life miserable for the soldiers. The primitive sanitary facilities at the Front, combined with the ever-present (but none-too-clean) water, produced serious health problems: frostbite, trench foot, trench mouth, dysentery, and others. Garbage, waste, and decaying and hastily buried bodies drew fleas and rats, complicating matters. (According to writer Erich Maria Remarque, the Germans called the big fat rats "corpse rats.")

Even during "quiet" periods in the line, a typical battalion might expect to take up to sixty casualties per month from wounds and disease. As in previous wars, the armies of World War I took more casualties through disease and sickness than through combat action. It is almost impossible for a sane person to visualize the horror of World War I trench warfare. Most military historians agree that with the possible exception of the Eastern Front in World War II, the Western Front in World War I was the most horrible period of prolonged combat in human history.

David T. Zabecki

References

Graves, Robert. *Goodbye to All That*. London: Jonathan Cape, 1929.
Middlebrook, Martin. *First Day on the Somme, 1 July 1916*. New York: Norton, 1972.

Rawling, Bill. *Surviving Trench Warfare: Technology and the Canadian Corps, 1914–1918*. Toronto: University of Toronto Press, 1992.
Remarque, Erich Maria. *All Quiet on the Western Front*. London: G.P. Putnam's Sons, 1929.
Sassoon, Siegfried. *Memoirs of an Infantry Officer*. London: Faber and Faber, 1930.
Service, Robert W. *Rhymes of a Red Cross Man*. New York: Barse & Hopkins, 1916.

See also CASUALTIES; INFANTRY TACTICS; STORMTROOPERS

Trenchard, Hugh Montague (1873–1956)

British general and commander of the Royal Flying Corps, born on 3 February 1873 at Taunton. Trenchard entered the militia in 1893 and served in the Boer War (1899–1902) and in Nigeria (1902–4). He earned his pilot's license in 1912 and joined the new Royal Flying Corps. In 1913 Trenchard became commandant of the Central Flying School, training squadrons when World War I began.

By November of 1914 he commanded the 1st Wing in France, installing radio and photographic equipment in planes and experimenting with tactical bombing. In August of 1915 he was appointed commander of the Royal Flying Corps in France. He stressed gaining air superiority by aggressive offensive maneuvers and pushed for an independent air force.

Trenchard became the first chief of staff for the Royal Air Force in January of 1918 but resigned in April because of conflicts with Air Minister Lord Rothermere. In France he led the Inter-Allied Independent Air Force, a strategic bombing group that conducted five hundred raids on German civilian and military targets.

Trenchard was knighted for his service and reappointed air chief of staff after Winston Churchill became air minister in February of 1919. He continued in that position until 1929, becoming the first marshal of the RAF (1927). Known as the "Father of the Royal Air Force," Trenchard demonstrated great administrative skills, creating the staff and support systems of the RAF. After a stint as metropolitan police commissioner (1931–35), he served in the House of Lords. Made a viscount in 1936, Trenchard was chairman of the United Africa

Company, 1936–53. During World War II, he visited RAF squadrons as an advisor. Trenchard died in London on 10 February 1956.

Elizabeth D. Schafer

References

Allen, Hubert R. *The Legacy of Lord Trenchard.* London: Cassell, 1972.

Boyle, Andrew. *Trenchard, Man of Vision.* New York: W.W. Norton, 1962.

Cooper, Malcolm. *The Birth of Independent Air Power: British Air Policy in the First World War.* London: Allen and Unwin, 1986.

Ranson, Harry H. "Lord Trenchard, Architect of Air Power." *Air University Quarterly Review* 8 (Summer 1956): 59–67.

Trenchard, Hugh M. "Bombing Germany: General Trenchard's Report of Operations of British Airmen against German Cities." *Current History* 10 (April 1919): 151–56.

See also AIR WARFARE

Trentino Offensive (15–30 May 1916)

Austrian commander Field Marshal Franz Conrad von Hötzendorf conceived his May 1916 offensive as a *Strafexpedition,* or punitive campaign. He had never been comfortable with the Italian alliance and had even proposed a preventive war against Italy in 1906. His antagonism was increased by Rome's "betrayal" of Vienna in 1915.

Conrad hoped to overcome resistance on the Asiago Plateau in the Trentino, break through to the plains of the Val d'Astico, and drive on Verona, Vicenza, and Padua, thereby cutting off the Second and Third Italian armies on the Isonzo and knocking Italy out of the war. To ensure success, he pulled thirteen divisions from Galicia and the Isonzo front, building up the Austrian Third and Eleventh armies to a total of fourteen divisions supported by a hundred heavy and five hundred medium guns, as well as the German *Kaiserjäger* division, which had replaced the *Alpenkorps.*

Conrad planned to attack on a twenty-five-kilometer front with 144 battalions in two armies supported by 1,193 guns and a reserve of sixty-three battalions. The Italian First Army, which was deployed on the plateau, had 76 battalions in forward positions and 40 to the rear, with 655 guns. Neither Italian line was well prepared, and Conrad's prospects for success were relatively good.

The attack was set for 10 April, but heavy snows and problems in moving troops from Russia and the Isonzo delayed it until 15 May. Italian intelligence, which had cautioned that an attack was possible in December of 1915, warned that one was imminent in March. But Italian army commander General Luigi Cadorna doubted that Conrad would risk a major operation in the Trentino, where he could be supplied by only two rail lines; he was sure that the Austrian commander was preparing to fend off an impending Russian attack. He therefore felt that any attack in the Trentino would be a feint. Even so, in late March and early April Cadorna sent three newly formed infantry brigades, sixteen alpine battalions, eighteen medium batteries, and two divisions—the equivalent of sixty-four battalions, or five divisions—to reinforce First Army. After a visit to the front, he also cashiered First Army commander General Ugo Brusati, who seemed incapable of organizing a viable defense, and named General Guglielmo Pecori-Giraldi as his new commander.

Cadorna ordered that troops in forward positions, which local attacks had pushed four to six kilometers beyond the main Italian line by mid-April, should withdraw if they found themselves hard pressed. These orders were largely ignored by commanders on the spot, however, who tended to fight rather than retreat. Cadorna himself complicated matters by keeping seven reserve divisions on the Tagliamento River near his headquarters rather than deploying them closer to the Trentino. He continued to doubt that an attack would occur in the mountains, where the terrain was not ideal for a major offensive, despite a Czech deserter's warning on 26 April that an offensive was imminent.

When Conrad attacked on 15 May, he encountered three of the First Italian Army's six divisions between the Adige River and the Sette Comuni. In poorly prepared positions with few reserves, forward units still hesitated to withdraw. As a result, between 15 and 19 May the Austrians decimated the 35th division and overwhelmed the Italian front line between Astico and Pasubio, taking Col Santo and the Tonezza Plateau. By 19 May the Austrians' advance had faltered, as Italian units held in the west and those in the Valsugana counterattacked. Whether Pecori-Giraldi could have now contained the offensive by withdrawing to his rear positions is not clear, but it seems that by trying to hold his forward positions the Italian commander precluded a more rational use of his reserves, which were thrown in piecemeal on the 20th. He thus wasted two reserve divisions trying to save the 34th Division, which was overwhelmed and pushed back. Cadorna was now forced to commit two more divisions, as well as fifteen alpine battalions, and to recall a division from Albania. To avoid committing these troops haphazardly, he created a new army, the Fifth, under General Frugoni, who commanded 179,000 men in four corps of two divisions each.

Cadorna could thus commit eight divisions, while Conrad was using up his last reserves and vainly calling for Field Marshal Svetozar Boroević von Bojna, commander of Austrian forces along the Isonzo, and German chief of the general staff General Erich von Falkenhayn to send more troops from the Isonzo and Galicia. Consequently, while Conrad's forces managed to reach the edge of the Asiago Plateau between 25 and 28 May, occupying Monte Cimone, Arsiero, and Asiago, they stalled on the 31st, and Italian resistance stiffened the following day. On 2 June the Italian Supreme Command felt confident enough to announce that the crisis had passed, and, although Monte Cenigo fell, by holding out to 3 June it had worn down Conrad's forces and given Cadorna time to react. After the Italians held the Austrians at Novegno and Lemerle from 12 to 16 June and the Brusilov Offensive drained away four of Conrad's divisions to the Russian front by the 16th, the Italian reserves went over to the counterattack.

Although parts of the Italian First Army had collapsed and the Austrians had advanced as many as twenty kilometers, reached the edge of the Asiago Plateau, and inflicted 148,000 casualties on the Italians, Cadorna and Pecori-Giraldi had denied Conrad entry into the Val d'Astico, and Italian troops had inflicted 100,000 casualties on the Austrians. They had held long enough for Brusilov's offensive to begin to drain Conrad's strength in late June. On 24 and 25 June, Italian troops forced Conrad to withdraw to more defensible positions as they retook Arsiero, Asiago, Franzela, Melette, and Sisemal.

Although Cadorna's use of his reserves and the fighting quality of the Italian soldier denied Conrad his victory, the partial success of the

Strafexpedition inflicted 300,000 Italian casualties, caused Salandra's fall, and raised serious doubts about the army's solidity and Cadorna's leadership. The Italians were unable to regain all of the territory lost. In some ways that was an advantage, because to maintain their salient against Cadorna's counterattack, which continued through 24 July, the Austrians had to garrison the Trentino with twelve divisions, rather than the three previously deployed there. Vienna could therefore send only four divisions to Russia. Conrad's offensive had been a gamble for high stakes, but rather than knocking Italy out of the war the battles on the Asiago Plateau had worn down Austria-Hungary, opening the way for the Italian capture of Gorizia in August and facilitating Brusilov's summer offensive in Galicia.

James J. Sadkovich

References

Caracciolo, Mario. *L'Italia nella guerra mondiale*. Rome: Edizioni Roma, 1935.

Faldella, Emilio. *La grande guerra*. 2 vols. Milan: Longanesi, 1965.

Pieri, Piero. *L'Italia nella prima guerra mondiale (1915–1918)*. Turin: Einaudi, 1968.

Valori, Aldo. *La guerra italo-austriaca, 1915–1918*. Bologna: Nicola Zanichelli, 1920.

See also CADORNA, LUIGI; CONRAD VON HÖTZENDORF, FRANZ; ITALY, ARMY, HOME FRONT

Trianon, Treaty of (4 June 1920)

Peace treaty with Hungary following World War I. On 3 November 1918, the defeated Austro-Hungarians signed an armistice with the Allied Powers that not only ended their involvement in World War I but also marked the end of five centuries of Hapsburg rule in Central Europe.

Following the Armistice, the Allied and associated powers gathered in Paris for a peace conference to construct a settlement with the Central Powers. President Wilson's Fourteen Points provided the basis for the decisions of the Paris Peace Conference, and point 10 had a profound effect on Hungary. It basically guaranteed autonomy to national minorities within the Austro-Hungarian Empire, at least five of which (Slovaks, Romanians, Croats, Serbs, and Germans) lived in the Hungarian half of the

Dual Monarchy. Throughout the peace conference, these groups demanded that they be allowed to form independent states or be united with other states; Slovaks, for example, demanded that they be allowed to join with Czechs in forming the new state of Czechoslovakia, while Romanians in Transylvania demanded union with Romania.

Initially, the Hungarian government, under Mihály Károlyi, placed its trust in the United States, for Károlyi agreed to the right of national self-determination for the minorities. He never expected the Allied Commission to accept all the demands for independence. Even Edvard Beneš, representative of the Czechoslovakian delegation, was surprised that the Allied Commission gave him all that he asked.

On 7 July 1919, after hearing the complaints and demands of those representing Romania, Czechoslovakia, and the Kingdom of Serbs, Croats, and Slovenes (Yugoslavia), the Supreme Council of Principal Allied and Associate Powers completed the terms for the Hungarian peace agreement. Although the Allied Powers invited the Hungarian delegation to Paris following the completion of the decisions, on 1 December 1919 they allowed it to speak only once to the committee, as they had already made their decision.

The delegation requested that the commission hold plebiscites in certain areas, particularly Transylvania—a major contention between the Romanians and the Hungarians—to allow the population to choose whether they preferred union with Romania or to remain part of Hungary. French Foreign Minister Alexandre Millerand rejected this request, for he believed that the plebiscites would coincide with the decision of the peace committee. Under Italian pressure, however, the commission allowed a plebiscite in Sopron, an area in western Hungary on the border of Austria, whereby 65 percent of the population opted for Hungary. This was the only form of leniency that the peacemakers granted to Hungary. Both the United States and Russia refused to sign the final agreement on the Treaty of Trianon, for they both disagreed with some of its stipulations. A few months later, the United States government created a separate peace with Hungary that made no mention of Trianon's territorial adjustments.

The Treaty of Trianon, named after the Trianon Palace located in the outskirts of Paris, imposed the harshest penalty of the postwar peace settlements. The leaders of the Hungarian delegation, Count Pal Teleki and Count Albert Apponyi, signed the final text of the treaty on 4 June 1920. Hungary lost two-thirds of its land and the same percentage of its population. Germany, on the other hand, lost only 13.5 percent of its lands and Bulgaria 8 percent for its involvement in the war. More specifically, Hungary's territory was reduced from 282,876 square kilometers, which it had possessed since the ninth century, to 92,963 square kilometers. Hungary's prewar population of 18.3 million people shrank to 7,615,117 people, for a loss of 10.6 million people. Yugoslavia received the Basca-Banat and Baranya, which equaled 20,956 square kilometers (6.44 percent of the confiscated lands) and a population of 1.5 million.

Czechoslovakia received Slovakia and the Carpatho-Ukraine, which amounted to 62,937 square kilometers (19.34 percent of the land) and 3.25 million people. Romania acquired the most from the treaty, obtaining 102,787 square kilometers of land (31.59 percent of land), including Transylvania and East Banat and 5.26 million people. Other nations that obtained land through the Treaty Of Trianon included Austria, which received Burgenland; Poland, which received 390 square kilometers; and Italy which received the city of Fiume (Rijeka). Although much of the population loss constituted non-Magyars, the treaty placed three million Magyars under the control of foreign nations: 1,063,00 Hungarians in Czechoslovakia, 1,700,000 in Romania, and 558,000 in Yugoslavia. This clearly defied the original intentions of Woodrow Wilson for national self-determination. The Treaty of Trianon created a homogenous Hungarian nation with a 96 percent Magyar population, the remainder including several thousand Slovaks and Germans.

Economically, Hungary suffered under the stipulations of the treaty. The loss of land deprived the nation of 62.2 percent of its railway systems, 73.8 percent of its public roads, 64.6 percent of its canals, 88 percent of its forests, 83 percent of its iron mines, and all of its salt mines. In addition, 350,000 people immigrated into the now small nation from neighboring areas, which created an overload for housing and employment. Hungary lost its economic market without Austria as its partner, and in the face of the hostilities arising with its neighbors over the division of territory. Fortunately, however, the Allies did not impose an indemnity for reparations, which would have had a devastating effect on their already suffering economy, as the Treaty of Versailles did to Germany.

Militarily, the treaty allowed Hungary a small professional army of only 35,000 men and prohibited any sort of heavy artillery, tanks, and air force. The military function entailed the preservation of internal order and defense of the nation. The Supreme Council of Principal Allies and Associate Powers organized an Inter-Allied Commission to oversee the strict supervision of the stipulations of the treaty.

The harsh stipulations in the Treaty of Trianon evoked resentment among Magyars and the government. The common slogan of that time was "Nem Nem Soha" which meant "No, No, Never!" and reflected their disapproval and humiliation over the treaty. While most historians have agreed that some territorial exchanges seemed necessary to redistribute power throughout Central Europe in order to create peace, the controversy of the Treaty of Trianon stemmed from the extreme stipulations and the amount of territory removed from Hungary in accordance with the role of the Hungarians in the war.

During the interwar period, the Hungarians' irredentist aspirations grew. The negative impact of the treaty in conjunction with the Depression and the inability of the Hungarian government to espouse a Western-styled democracy propagated further problems in Hungary. In addition, France sponsored the Little Entente of Czechoslovakia, Romania, and Yugoslavia to check Hungarian desires for a territorial revision to the treaty. For these reasons, Hungary would turn to Fascist Italy and Nazi Germany for support and would join the Second World War on their side.

Judith Podlipnik

References

Bogdan, Henry. *From Warsaw to Sophia.* Santa Fe: Pro Libertate, 1989.

Hoensch, Jörg. *A History of Modern Hungary, 1867–1986.* London: Longman House, 1988.

Horthy, Nicholas. *Memoirs.* London: Hutchinson, 1956.

Macartney, C.A. *October Fifteenth.* Edinburgh: Edinburgh University Press, 1956.

See also AUSTRIA-HUNGARY, ARMY, HOME FRONT, NAVY; HUNGARY, REVOLUTION IN; KÁROLYI, MIHÁLY; PARIS PEACE CONFERENCE

Trotha, Adolf von (1868–1940)

German vice admiral and chief of staff of the High Seas Fleet, 1916–18. Born on 1 March 1868 in Koblenz, the son of an army officer killed in the Franco-Prussian War, Trotha joined the navy in 1886. He served in the torpedo branch, attended the navy academy, and then was attached to the East Asia Cruiser Squadron. From 1901 to 1906 he was in the navy office under Admiral Alfred von Tirpitz. Trotha then returned to fleet duty, but from 1910 to 1913 he was in the navy cabinet. In 1913 he received command of the dreadnought *Kaiser.*

Trotha believed in both the need for a decisive naval battle with the Royal Navy and unrestricted submarine warfare. In January of 1916 he became Admiral Reinhard Scheer's chief of staff. While clamoring for resumption of unrestricted submarine warfare, he also shared Scheer's goal of a unified and independent supreme naval command to replace the traditional, decentralized structure. In August of 1918 Scheer and Trotha succeeded in creating the Naval War Command, forcing opponents like Henning von Holtzendorff, Eduard von Capelle, and Georg von Müller into retirement.

Trotha seriously underestimated the mutinous mood among enlisted men after 1917. When he pushed for a last sortie of the High Seas Fleet in late October of 1918 to end its idleness and rescue the navy's honor, the sailors rebelled and hastened the general collapse of the Second Reich. Such leadership failures notwithstanding, Trotha served as chief of the admiralty in the early Weimar Republic until his resignation in October of 1920. He died in Berlin on 11 October 1940.

Eric C. Rust

References

Herwig, Holger. *"Luxury" Fleet.* London: Allen and Unwin, 1980.

Horn, Daniel. *The German Naval Mutinies of World War I.* New Brunswick, N.J.: Rutgers University Press, 1969.

Marineministerium (Berlin). *Der Krieg zur See, 1914–1918.* 24 vols. Berlin, Frankfurt, 1922–66.

See also GERMANY, NAVY; SCHEER, REINHARD; TIRPITZ, ALFRED VON

Trotsky, Leon (1879–1940)

Russian revolutionary and one of the central figures of the 1917 Bolshevik Revolution. Described at various times as brilliant, logical, overbearing, innovative, and arrogant, it is no exaggeration to say that Trotsky was the Renaissance man of the revolution. He was an orator, polemicist, historian, political scientist, administrator, and military organizer who created and led the Red Army to victory in the Russian Civil War (1918–21). He also represented the Jewish contribution to the Russian revolutionary movement.

Trotsky was born into a Jewish family on 7 November 1879 in Yanovka, Ukraine, under the name Lev Davidovich Bronstein. His father, a farmer, had married the well-educated daughter of a Jewish merchant. Taught to read and write by his mother, Trotsky showed an early interest in literature and became an avid reader of the classics as a young child. After attending elementary school, he used family connections to enter a German-run *realschule* in Odessa, which was known as a center of the radical Left and Right in politics. It was there that he first encountered anti-Semitism and Marxist ideology. After leading a student revolt against an incompetent teacher, he was expelled from the *realschule* and became active in Marxist circles. He was eventually arrested for his political activities and exiled to Siberia. After escaping from Siberia, he made his way to London, where he joined the Russian Social Democratic party under the *nom de plume* of Pero (the pen) because of his polemical talents. Shortly thereafter, he adopted the name Leon Trotsky. When the Social Democrat Congress of 1903 resulted in a split into the moderate Mensheviks and Lenin's radical Bolsheviks, Trotsky took an independent position.

During the Russian general strike of 1905 in the wake of the Russo-Japanese War, Trotsky demonstrated his flair for political activism. He, rather than Lenin, made his way to St. Petersburg. Gathering a few radicals in the capital, Trotsky announced the creation of the Petersburg Soviet of Workers Deputies and flooded the city with leaflets urging the strikers to overthrow the monarchy. Subsequently arrested and brought to trial, Trotsky was exiled a second time to Siberia but once again managed to escape.

In 1907 Trotsky began his political wanderings. He spent three and a half years in Vienna, where he edited the "Vienna Pravda," which advocated reunification of the Russian Social Democratic party. It was also during his stay in Vienna that Trotsky developed the doctrine of "permanent revolution," which was to become the Russian Bolshevik party line. It held that the building of communism must be treated as a global phenomenon, and once Russia became communist she must press for revolutions in other countries. Trotsky then served as a war correspondent in the Balkans, was expelled from Spain, and shortly before the war went to New York City, where he edited a Russian-language radical newspaper.

With the upheaval in Russia in March of 1917, Trotsky attempted to return to his homeland. After some trouble he arrived in Petrograd at the end of May. He immediately began working with Lenin to form one of history's most effective political teams, and in July he formally joined the Bolshevik party. From the time of his arrival Trotsky occupied the center stage of the revolution. During the Kornilov affair he volunteered to defend the revolution and was able to arm the Red Guard.

On 20 October, after the Bolshevik vote to seize power, Trotsky was made chairman of the Military Revolutionary Committee and was entrusted with the military planning while Lenin assumed the political leadership. At about the same time, Trotsky was elected chairman of the Petrograd Soviet. On 7 November the Bolsheviks took over the government. That evening, with Trotsky presiding, Lenin announced the takeover to the Congress of Soviets.

In the new Bolshevik government Trotsky was given the important post of commissar of foreign affairs. When the Germans agreed to an armistice on 21 November, Trotsky headed the Russian delegation that went to Brest-Litovsk to negotiate a peace treaty. Operating on the assumption that Germany was ready for revolution, the Russian delegation put into practice Trotsky's doctrine of "permanent revolution" by throwing out from their train leaflets urging German soldiers to turn against their government. The German delegation was headed by General Max Hoffmann and diplomat Richard von Kühlmann. They were under pressure from Berlin to get a quick peace treaty so that the German divisions in the East could be transferred to the West.

Negotiations dragged on for two months as Trotsky launched a number of tirades against German militarism. Trotsky's position was undermined, however, when the Ukraine declared its independence at the end of January of 1918; its government, the *Rada*, sent a delegation to Brest-Litovsk that negotiated a separate peace. Germany granted the Ukraine immediate recognition and sent German troops into the new state to help protect it. This enabled the Germans to take a much more forceful stance against Trotsky, and on 9 February Kühlmann formally demanded that Russia give up Poland, the Baltic states, and the other territory presently under German occupation. Trotsky's reply was, "We are out of the war, but we refuse to sign the treaty." This "no war, no peace" policy was aimed at allowing the Germans to occupy Russia and infecting them with Bolshevism, which they would then carry back to Germany. On 13 February however, Germany forced the issue by renewing its advance into northern Russia. With the road to Petrograd undefended, Lenin overrode Trotsky's vehement objections and ordered that a peace treaty be signed. Trotsky refused to attend the treaty signing, which occurred on 3 March 1918.

Trotsky resumed an active role in March of 1918 as commissar of war. He helped create the Red Army and subsequently proved to be an extraordinarily talented leader in the Civil War. Following Lenin's death in January of 1924, everyone expected Trotsky to assume leadership of the Soviet Union. Joseph Stalin, however, was able to use his position as general secretary to force Trotsky from his leadership posts and in 1927 strip him of party membership. He went into exile in 1929, ending up in Mexico City, where he was assassinated by a Stalinist agent on 21 August 1940.

John W. Bohon

References

Fischer, Louis. *The Soviets in World Affairs*. New York: Alfred A. Knopf, 1960.

Trotsky, Leon. *My Life*. New York: Grosset and Dunlap, 1960.

Wolfe, Bertram D. *Three Who Made a Revolution*. New York: Stein and Day, 1984.

See also BREST-LITOVSK, TREATY OF; LENIN, VLADIMIR; RUSSIA, HOME FRONT AND REVOLUTIONS OF 1917

Troubridge, Sir Ernest Charles Thomas (1862–1926)

British admiral, born at Hampstead on 15 July 1862. Troubridge entered the navy in 1875 and rose to prominence as a naval attaché in Tokyo during the Russo-Japanese War. He was chief of the Naval War Staff from 1911 to 1912.

Troubridge, commander of the First Cruiser Squadron in the Mediterranean at the beginning of the war, was on patrol with four armored cruisers near the entrance to the Adriatic when the *Goeben* and *Breslau* broke out of Messina. He probably could have intercepted the Germans, and started to do so, but apparently let himself be convinced by his flag captain that this would be a violation of his orders to avoid action with superior forces. The 11-inch guns of the *Goeben* outranged the 9.5-inch and 7.5-inch guns of the British, and the battle cruiser's superior speed probably would have permitted her to sink the British cruisers before they came in range. The admiralty orders were ambiguous, for they meant the Austrian fleet, not *Goeben*. Because of his failure to engage the German ships, a court of inquiry decided Troubridge should be court-martialed. He was acquitted but not employed at sea again.

Troubridge was subsequently appointed head of the British naval mission to Serbia and was in the thick of the fighting around Belgrade in 1915. He joined the epic winter retreat of the Serbian army over the Albanian mountains to the Adriatic and supervised the evacuation at San Giovanni di Medua. For the remainder of the war, he was attached to the personal staff of Crown Prince Alexander of Serbia at Salonika. Troubridge was subsequently admiral commanding on the Danube in 1918–19, and, after leaving active service, was president of the International Commission of the Danube, 1920–24. He died at Biarritz on 28 January 1926.

Paul G. Halpern

References

Fryer, Charles E.J. *The Royal Navy on the Danube*. Boulder, Colo.: East European Monographs, 1988.

Halpern, Paul G., ed. *The Royal Navy in the Mediterranean, 1915–1918*. Publications of the Navy Records Society, 126. Aldershot: Temple Smith for the Navy Records Society, 1987.

Kemp, Paul J. *Die Royal Navy auf der Donau, 1918–1925*. Graz: H. Weishaupt, 1988.

Lumby, E.W.R., ed. *Policy and Operations in the Mediterranean, 1912–1914*. Publications of the Navy Records Society, 125. London: Navy Records Society, 1970.

Marder, Arthur J. *From the Dreadnought to Scapa Flow*. Vol. 2: *The War Years: To the Eve of Jutland*. London: Oxford University Press, 1965.

See also GOEBEN AND BRESLAU; MEDITERRANEAN NAVAL OPERATIONS

Truck Transport

World War I, the first major road test for military trucks, demonstrated the vital importance of motor transport in modern warfare. In 1914 General Joseph Simon Gallieni's "taxi brigade" of 1,200 Paris cabbies rushed reinforcements to the Front during the Battle of the Marne. Two years later, the drivers of some 3,500 trucks braved artillery fire for months while carrying supplies along the thirty-five-mile *Voie Sacrée* to the besieged fortress of Verdun. By war's end, all major powers had come to depend on a combined total of more than 200,000 trucks.

Motor transport fulfilled a number of vital missions. Although railroads carried heavy supplies from the factory to the front, the railhead often ended from five to twenty-five miles behind artillery batteries and forward trenches. Horse carts quickly proved inadequate for the job of supplying troops, and so trucks took much of the work. Motor vehicles were also used for ambulance service, to move artillery, and to support maneuvers in the rare openings from the trench deadlock. For example, a shortage of trucks proved fatal to the 1918 German offensives. Once out of reach of the rail lines, the troops could not be supplied and the advances stalled.

The major combatants produced large numbers of trucks for the war effort. The French, already leaders in the automotive industry, were the most active truck builders; by 1918 they had almost seventy thousand trucks and tractors in military service. Louis Renault built more than nine thousand different types of trucks in addition to shells, tanks, and aircraft. André Citroën expanded production, despite manpower shortages, by employing women. Marius Berliet constructed an integrated automotive factory more ambitious than Henry Ford's River Rouge works. British firms Leyland and Thorneycroft built more

modest numbers of trucks, although by the war's end the British Expeditionary Force operated 56,000 trucks. The Italian company Fiat topped all other firms with production of 45,000 vehicles over the course of the war; a third of these were sold to Britain and France. The Russians, with virtually no automotive industry at the war's outset, relied largely on imported trucks, most from the United States. American manufacturers, including White, Ford, Mack, Packard, and International Harvester, supplied the Allies with large numbers of trucks. Doughboys, seeing the Mack's unusual hood, called it "Bulldog," and the nickname stuck. Daimler, Benz, and Opel built smaller numbers of vehicles, and by the war's end Germany faced a critical shortage, having fewer than thirty thousand trucks in service. Austria-Hungary never exceeded an annual output of two thousand machines.

Organizational difficulties abounded in the use of this new military tool. Allied armies generally operated motor transport corps independently from their railroad corps. Fuel demands were massive: For example, in 1918 the American Expeditionary Force used more than 33 million gallons of gasoline. Maintenance posed even greater problems, in part because teamsters had more experience with horses than motors. More than 60 percent of all German trucks broke down in the first month of the war. The lack of trained mechanics plagued all powers, and thousands of trucks lay idle when only simple repairs were needed. The problem of spare parts was compounded by the multitude of different models in service. The prewar truck industry in Europe and the United States had been fragmented into large numbers of small producers, and although governments eventually demanded standard models, with the needs of combat they used any vehicles they could find. The United States Army alone possessed trucks built by almost three hundred different manufacturers.

The newly developed motor industry had a major impact on World War I—and vice versa. Military demands for huge numbers of standardized vehicles transformed a virtual cottage trade into a mass-production industry. Smaller producers were shaken out, and firms that benefited from military contracts, such as Fiat, Renault, White, and Daimler, became leading manufacturers in the postwar era. In turn, their trucks served an indispensable role supplying troops in combat, so much so that the French government awarded the Military Cross to the White Corporation's A model truck.

Jeffrey M. Pilcher

References
Karolevitz, Robert F. *This Was Trucking*. Seattle: Superior Publishing, 1966.
Laux, James. *The European Automobile Industry*. New York: Twayne, 1992.

Trumbić, Ante (1864–1938)

Croatian nationalist and advocate of South Slav unity, born in 1864 in Spit, Dalmatia (Austria-Hungary). Trumbić played a leading role in local politics as an opponent of Hapsburg supremacy. In 1905 he participated in drafting the South Slav nationalist program called the Resolution of Fiume (Rijeka). With the outbreak of the First World War, Trumbić saw the defeat of Austria-Hungary as an opportunity to achieve South Slav unity. In 1915 he and other leading Croats fled to Rome and then moved to London, where they established the Yugoslav Committee to represent South Slav aspirations and to gather support from the Allies for the Croats. In 1917 he negotiated with Serbian leaders on the Declaration of Corfu, which called for unity among Serbs and Croats and the establishment of a Yugoslav state. He insisted on equality with the Serbs, working for more guarantees for Croats within this proposed state.

In 1918, following the conclusion of World War I, Trumbić became the first foreign minister of the Kingdom of Serbs, Croats, and Slovenes and represented his country at the Paris Peace Conference. He handled disputes with Italy over Fiume and territory on the eastern Adriatic coast, managing to gain most of these lands for the newly formed state. He retired from politics in 1929 and died on 18 November 1938 in Zagreb.

Susan N. Carter

References
Banac, Ivo. *The National Question in Yugoslavia: Origins, History, Politics*. Ithaca: Cornell University Press, 1984.
Grlica, George. "Trumbić's Policy and Croatian National Interests from 1914 to the Beginning of 1918." *Journal of Croatian Studies* 14–15 (1973–4): 74–112.

See also CORFU, DECLARATION OF; YUGOSLAVIA, CREATION OF

Tsingtao, Siege of (23 August–7 November 1914)

See QINGDAO

Tunneling and Mine Warfare

Tunneling and mine warfare grew out of the stalemate on the Western Front. The massive loss of life and lack of success involved in infantry attacks directed against enemy trenches demanded new tactics. Land mines were initially used as an alternative to artillery in preparing for an infantry assault against enemy lines, but they were also important for their psychological impact.

Land mines were created by stacking piles of explosive materials, such as gunpowder, TNT, or ammonal (a mixture of ammonium nitrate, TNT, and flaked aluminum) in galleries at the end of the underground tunnels. Carrying the bags of explosives into the mines was considered very dangerous. A stray bullet or piece of shrapnel could instantly set off charges being carried into the tunnels. The order of the day when carrying explosives was fifty yards between each man.

Once bags of explosives were placed inside the tunnel, the charge was fired by means of a fuse or electric detonator. Wires leading from the land mines through the tunnel and out to the detonator, however, were often cut by artillery fire. In order to check that the wires were intact and secure, lines were tested with low-voltage currents. Despite the efforts of mining engineers, unsuccessful or delayed detonations still occurred as a result of countermining operations, water damage, or bad luck. One instance of the unpredictable nature of land mines occurred on 7 June 1917, when the 8th Battalion, Royal Irish Rifles of the 36th Ulster Division went "over the top" following the detonation of a number of British land mines under the German lines. As the troops crossed no-man's-land one of their mines detonated late, killing many of them.

German military engineers began tunnel operations as soon as the static nature of trench warfare became apparent. On 20 December

1914 they exploded ten mines beneath British trenches near Festubert. Defending Indian troops of the Sirhind Brigade were taken completely unawares. Those who were able made it back to the British rear as German infantry quickly moved up to secure the British defensive positions. General Erich Ludendorff later referred to the effect of the mines as "simply staggering."

It quickly became apparent to both sides that tunneling and mining operations could have a tremendous psychological impact on enemy troops. Artillery shells, mortars, hand grenades, machine guns, gas, and snipers had already done much to de-romanticize the war for many troops; the knowledge that the very ground beneath one's feet might erupt and tear one to pieces, however, was often unbearable.

In February of 1915, following further German successes with mining operations, the British decided that they could no longer ignore tunneling and mine warfare. Field Marshal Horatio Kitchener brought in J. Norton Griffiths, a "flamboyant commercial adventurer," to organize a special mining unit. Before Griffiths's arrival, the Royal Engineers devoted only three days to "sapper" (tunneling) training. Griffiths was far more ambitious. The Germans sought to destroy British trenches by shallow mines, but Griffiths wanted to go much deeper and create larger tunnels and galleries for huge mines. For this Griffiths recruited volunteers with experience as miners and construction workers. In addition, the ranks of the military were scrutinized to locate volunteers from mining towns, such as Durham, or members of Mine Rescue Brigades from all over Britain, including Welsh miners from the Monmouthshire Regiment.

British miners considered themselves elite troops. Their pay reflected this: six shillings a day versus one shilling a day for the average "Tommy." Despite their lack of formal military discipline and training, the newly formed Tunneling Companies of the Royal Engineers quickly proved their worth.

On 17 April 1915 the British exploded their first mines under Hill 60 in the Ypres sector. The hill and its German defenders were virtually obliterated. The British 13th Brigade quickly occupied the former enemy positions.

At Hill 60, the largest mines contained 2,700 lbs. of explosives. In July of 1915 the British exploded even larger mines, totaling almost 5,000 lbs. of powder, a few miles north of

Hill 60 at Hooge. Once again, the British took the former German positions with little or no resistance. The second line of German trenches, however, was invariably even stronger than the first. This fact, and the destruction caused by the mines to dug-outs and trenches, made it nearly impossible for the attackers to find shelter and defend newly acquired positions against inevitable German counterattacks.

War office records show that, despite their psychological impact on the enemy, mining operations were minimally effective in a tactical sense and required more than a thousand well-trained men a month. The war office decided to reorganize the tunneling companies and appointed Brigadier General Robert Napier Harvey, Royal Engineers, as the army's inspector of mines. With nearly 20,000 men in twenty tunneling companies, Harvey began the largest mining operation of the war.

In an attempt to draw German attention away from weakened French forces and remove the enemy from the high ground in the Ypres sector, the British decided to mine Messines Ridge in 1917. Mining there had actually begun early in the spring of 1915 but was not fully organized until it was decided to implement the earlier plan proposed by Griffiths. That plan called for twenty-one mines running much deeper than earlier shafts. The tunnels at Messines were between sixty and ninety feet below the surface. In this way, Griffiths hoped to avoid German countermining efforts, which had intensified. The plan also allowed the miners to work in the relative safety of the more stable blue clay found at deeper depth.

One problem with this plan was the disposal of the blue clay dug out of the huge tunnels, which were up to seven hundred yards long. At one point a German raiding party did come upon some of the lightly colored clay and returned it to their headquarters, but nothing was done with this evidence. The Germans remained unaware of the British work beneath them.

The terror created by the threat of land mines led to extraordinary efforts to locate enemy tunnels before mines could be fired. Soldiers would bury drums of water and stick their ears into the water in hopes of detecting the faint sound of digging. Later the University of Paris developed the geophone. Made from wood, mica, and liquid mercury combined in a little ball about three inches across, it was placed against the ground and an operator would use it to listen through a tube and earplugs for sounds of enemy digging activity.

Suspicions of tunneling on the part of the enemy led to countermining. A smaller tunnel was dug, referred to as a "sap," and men digging them were called "sappers." If an enemy tunnel was located, sappers would set a smaller land mine called a camouflet. It consisted of two to ten 50-lb. bags of gunpowder, TNT, or ammonal. Chambers containing the explosives were tamped with sand bags to direct the force of the explosion to collapse the enemy tunnel. Camouflets were sometimes set off in the hope that the smoke and disruption of a small cave-in could be used to attract enemy artillery fire into the vicinity to collapse the entire enemy tunnel system. Although the Germans increased the use of listening posts, the digging at Messines was too deep to be easily detected.

Occasionally, in shallower systems, opposing tunnels actually met, resulting in subterranean battles. In the Ypres sector, near St. Eloi, subaltern Richard Brisco twice breached Germany tunnels and drove off enemy miners.

The tunnels themselves were dug almost entirely by hand by means of a wide-bladed pick or a small spade. At one point the British imported a 7.5-ton boring machine built by the Stanley Heading Machine Company. It dug at almost three times the speed of a man, but after two hundred feet it became completely caught in the mud. It remains today where it stopped, eighty feet underground.

The most effective method of digging was a technique that also gave its practitioners their name of "clay-kickers." Lying on their backs supported at a 45-degree angle to the face of the shaft by a wooden cross, the men were able to kick and hack away at the clay. As they "worked the cross," the men used a small spade with footrests and kicked the clay behind them for others to remove. Digging went on twenty-four hours a day: eight hours "in the hole" and sixteen hours off. Like other troops, men in the tunneling companies were also regularly rotated from the front lines to their camp at Vlamertinghe in the rear.

Despite countermining efforts by the Germans, including exploding two shallow mines on 4 April near Hill 60 and the use of raiding parties, the work at Messines remained undetected, and by early 1917 the British had completed five miles of tunnels. Over one million pounds of explosive were then placed in the mines. Some of these mines, such as two just south of St. Eloi, contained 95,600 lbs. of explosive ammonal.

On 7 June 1917 at 03:10, as eighty thousand British troops waited to go over the top, the song of nightingales was interrupted by the explosion of nineteen mines beneath the Germans at Messines. One correspondent reported "enormous volumes of scarlet flame and of earth and smoke all lighted by the flame spilling over into fountains of fierce colour." Some of the craters created were eighty feet deep and three hundred feet across. Advancing British troops met little German resistance as enemy soldiers stumbled blindly about, "some weeping uncontrollably—shattered objects invoking the compassion of their enemy." A full accounting of German dead was impossible. Some 10,000 men were simply listed as "missing," their bodies shattered by the force of explosions heard in London.

Messines was the last major use of mines by the Allies. As a psychological weapon mines were quite effective, but tactically and strategically they failed. Both sides found it too easy to counterattack. The war quickly returned to trench stalemate.

William Christian Dughi

References

Barrie, Alexander. *The War Underground.* London: F. Muller, 1962.

Lloyd, Alan. *The War in the Trenches.* New York: David McKay, 1976.

Macdonald, Lynn. *They Called it Passchendaele.* London: Michael Joseph, 1978.

Tyrwhitt, Reginald Yorke (1870–1951)

British admiral, born at Oxford, the son of a vicar, on 10 May 1870. Tyrwhitt entered the navy in 1883. In 1913 he was named commander of destroyer flotillas in the First Fleet, a position he held until 1918. During the war, Tyrwhitt's two destroyer flotillas of thirty-five to forty destroyers and three to seven light cruisers formed a powerful group. It was known as "Harwich Force" for its base. Tyrwhitt's responsibilities included patrolling the southern portion of the North Sea and assisting the Grand Fleet in its sweeps. One of his destroyers, HMS *Lance*, fired the first shot of the war in the North Sea, and Tyrwhitt's force played a major role in the Heligoland action. It also escorted seaplane carriers into the Heligoland Bight for raids on the German coast.

Tyrwhitt was a natural leader, one of the true fighting admirals of the war, and the Harwich Force was known for its *élan*. It lost two cruisers and fourteen destroyers, and Tyrwhitt and his men earned the reputation of having spent more time at sea and having engaged in more actions than any other naval force during the war. Created a baronet in 1919, Tyrwhitt later commanded the 3rd Light Cruiser Squadron in the Mediterranean (1921–22) and served as commander in chief, China Station (1927–29) and the Nore (1930–33). In 1934 he was named principal naval aide-de-camp to the king. He died at Hawkhurst, Kent, on 30 May 1951.

Paul G. Halpern

References

Carr, Lieutenant William G. *Brass Hats and Bell-Bottomed Trousers: Unforgettable and Splendid Feats of the Harwich Patrol*. London: Hutchinson, 1939.

Domvile, Sir Barry, Admiral. *By and Large*. London: Hutchinson, 1936.

Patterson, A. Temple. *Tyrwhitt of the Harwich Force*. London: Macdonald, 1973.

See also GREAT BRITAIN, NAVY; HELIGOLAND BIGHT, BATTLE OF

T

U

Ukraine

In 1914 present-day Ukraine was divided between Austria and Russia. The vast majority of some 30 million Ukrainians lived in southwestern Russia. Fewer than 20 percent lived in East Galicia, controlled by Austria-Hungary. Ukraine's manpower (3.5 million Ukrainians served in the Russian army and 250,000 in the armed forces of the Dual Monarchy) and its important food production and raw materials made it vital to both sides. World War I stirred Ukrainian hopes for autonomy within their respective countries. Independence was only a remote hope, but with the beginning of the war a nationalist movement formed, known as the League for the Liberation of Ukraine. It included Ukrainians under Austrian control as well as those in Russia.

Western Ukraine experienced fighting early in the war when the Russians advanced into Galicia and captured its capital of Lemberg (Lwów or Lvov) in September of 1914. The tide changed in 1915, when forces under General August von Mackensen expelled the Russians from the province. Poland posed another threat because Polish nationalists sought from both sides a promise of an enlarged Polish state at the end of the war, to include East Galicia. Before 1667, the whole Ukraine had been part of the Polish-Lithuanian kingdom.

Ukrainian nationalists hoped that the March 1917 Russian revolution would produce a federated Russia. In March of 1917 Ukrainian leaders, led by Michael Hruschevsky, created a Ukrainian Central Council *(Ukrainska Centralna Rada)*. The *Rada* called for an All-Ukrainian National Congress, which met at Kiev in April of 1917 and included delegates from all Ukrainian provinces, including those controlled by Austria-Hungary. It began negotiations for autonomy with the Russian Provisional Government. Support for autonomy came from numerous Ukrainian organizations but was by no means universal. When Petrograd rejected autonomy on 23 June 1917, the *Rada* declared the Ukraine free to enact its own laws. This was done in the expectation that it would be approved by the All-Russian Constitutional Assembly. The *Rada* also created a cabinet, the General Secretariat, and on 28 June 1917 selected Volodymyr Vynnychenko as premier.

Petrograd, meanwhile, condemned the establishment of an autonomous Ukraine and sent a delegation to Kiev to meet with Vynnychenko. Talks produced a compromise, whereby the *Rada* and secretariat were recognized as legitimate representatives of the Ukraine with autonomy deferred until the meeting of the constitutional assembly. On 16 July the *Rada* issued another declaration, which did not call for separation from Russia and made no territorial claims. Political leaders hoped this declaration would thwart any call for independence from Russia, but it only weakened the *Rada*'s standing among Ukrainians.

On 29 July 1917, however, the Petrograd government rejected autonomy for Ukraine. When the Bolsheviks came to power, this view did not change. Indeed, Lenin sent agitators to Ukraine in an attempt to discredit the *Rada*. In response, on 22 January 1918, the *Rada* proclaimed the Ukrainian National Republic *(Ukrainsha Narodna Republika)* and promised reforms.

The Bolsheviks reacted by calling for the complete surrender of the *Rada* to Moscow's authority. When the *Rada* expelled Bolshevik troops, Moscow established a rival Ukrainian government at Kharkov. This brought civil war in Ukraine, which saw some Ukrainians joining the Bolsheviks.

The situation for Ukraine changed with the military collapse of Russia, however. When the Central Powers and Russia began peace negotiations at Brest-Litovsk, Ukraine sent a delegation. Separate negotiations resulted in an agreement on 9 February 1918, whereby the Central Powers recognized Ukrainian independence. Under an agreement of 12 February Ukraine agreed to supply substantial amounts of food in return for manufactured goods. There are some who contend that Ukrainian grain kept Germany and Austria in the war for an additional six months. The Central Powers also agreed to return all prisoners of war and their arms to Ukraine in order that the new nation might defend itself against the Bolsheviks.

Recognition of its independence by the Central Powers did not prevent Ukraine from undergoing a Bolshevik invasion. Kiev fell on 18 February and the *Rada* was forced to relocate to Zhytomyr. Dissension among the peasantry and within Ukrainian military units further weakened the *Rada*'s authority. The Kiev government appealed to the Germans for help. Austrian and German troops occupied Ukraine, mainly to ensure delivery of the negotiated grain, which had fallen short of expectations. The troops forced a Bolshevik withdrawal from Kiev at the beginning of March and the entire country by April.

A proclamation by German Field Marshal Hermann von Eichhorn calling for cultivation to proceed led to a quarrel with the *Rada*. On 28 April 1918 the Germans dissolved the *Rada* and installed their own puppet ruler, Hetman (monarch) Pavlo Skoropadsky. Violent unrest among the peasants followed; they demanded reestablishment of the republic. On 30 July Eichhorn was assassinated in Kiev. Skoropadsky crushed resistance and also ended many of the *Rada*'s reforms. An armistice had been concluded with Soviet Russia in May but Bolshevik propagandists operated in Kiev, ostensibly to prepare for a peace treaty between the Ukraine and Russia. They were well financed by Moscow, while Skoropadsky had little support from the Germans, who were then involved in their massive spring offensive on the Western Front and understandably reluctant to reopen the Eastern Front.

With the collapse of the Central Powers and an armistice on the Western Front, Skoropadsky was left without support. On 14 December Skoropadsky fled Kiev for Berlin. The month before, General Simon Petliura and Volodymyr Vynnychenko, former president of the republic, had taken charge of a five-man directory to head a new revolutionary government. They proclaimed the union of Ukraine with the West Ukrainian Republic, set up in Lwów (Lemberg) by Galician Ruthenes. This led to war with Poland, which had been assigned East Galicia by the Allied Powers.

Petliura marched to the aid of the new government in Lemberg, threatened by the advance of General Józef Haller's Polish Legion from the Western Front, but he was soundly defeated. Bolshevik forces took Kiev on 3 February 1918, and Petliura was forced to flee with his armed supporters into East Galicia. In 1920 they joined forces with the Poles fighting the Bolsheviks. Bolshevik troops, meanwhile, forced French troops, who had occupied Odessa the previous December, to evacuate that port on 8 April 1919.

Ukraine became a Soviet Republic, but in October and November of 1919 it was occupied by White forces commanded by General Anton Denikin. The Bolsheviks drove the Poles back and in December reconquered Kharkov and Kiev. Odessa fell to them in February of 1920. In May of 1920 the Poles, with Petliura's troops, occupied much of Ukraine, including Kiev, but were forced to withdraw when the Russian Red Army took the offensive. By the Treaty of Riga (19 March 1921), Poland and Russia recognized Ukraine's independence. On 28 December 1920, Russia and Ukraine had signed a treaty regularizing relations between the two states. In July of 1923, Ukraine became a constituent member of the Union of Soviet Socialist Republics.

Corie Delashaw

References

Dushnyck, Walter. "The Russian Provisional Government and the Ukrainian Central Rada." *Ukrainian Quarterly* 3 (1946): 66–71.

Fedyshyn, Oleh. *Germany's Drive to the East and the Ukrainian Revolution, 1917–1918*. New Brunswick, N.J.: Rutgers University Press, 1971.

Hrushevsky, Michael. *A History of Ukraine*. New Haven: Yale University Press, 1941.

Manning, Clarence. *Twentieth-Century Ukraine*. New York: Bookman, 1951.

Reshetar, John, Jr. *The Ukrainian Revolution, 1917–1920. A Study in Nationalism.* Princeton: Princeton University Press, 1952.

Subtelny, Orest. *Ukraine: A History.* Toronto: University of Toronto Press, 1988.

See also EICHHORN, HERMANN VON; HALLER, JÓZEF; SKOROPADSKY, PAVLO

Uniacke, Sir Herbert C.C. (1866–1934)

British general, born on 4 December 1866. Uniacke was commissioned into the Royal Artillery in 1885. Just prior to the start of the First World War he was chief instructor at the School of Gunnery for both horse and field artillery. In August of 1914 he assumed command of the 5th Brigade, Royal Horse Artillery, and took that unit to France.

In July of 1916 Uniacke was given command of the artillery for the newly formed Fifth Army. He pioneered a technique of bringing prolonged and intensive artillery fire on all but one of the approach routes to German forward positions. After intelligence indicated that the Germans were using the unshelled route almost exclusively, Uniacke would quickly shift all his guns there, with disastrous effects for the Germans. In April of 1917 Uniacke urged the use of unregistered, surprise fire in the Arras attack, but Field Marshal Sir Douglas Haig vetoed it because he thought the new technique too risky.

Uniacke was in charge of Fifth Army's artillery planning at Passchendaele and the desperate defensive fighting in the German St. Quentin Offensive. In July of 1918 he became deputy inspector of training for all the British armies in France. After the war he commanded the Indian 1st Division in India and in 1925 was promoted to lieutenant general. Known for his innovative methods and attention to training, he retired from the army in 1932 and died at Marlow on 14 May 1934 after a prolonged illness caused by gas poisoning in France.

David T. Zabecki

References

Bidwell, Shelford, and Dominick Graham. *Fire-Power: British Army Weapons and Theories of War, 1904–1945.* London: Allen and Unwin, 1982.

Farndale, Sir Martin. *History of the Royal Regiment of Artillery: Western Front,* *1914–1918.* London: Royal Artillery Institution, 1986.

Royal Artillery. *The Royal Artillery War Commemoration Book.* London: Published on behalf of the R.A. War Commemoration Fund by G. Bell and Sons, 1920.

See also ARTILLERY; PASSCHENDAELE (YPRES, THIRD BATTLE OF)

Uniforms

Uniforms of World War I reflected the change from nineteenth- to twentieth-century warfare. One of the most obvious changes was from soft caps to steel helmets by most major armies. The "basin," "adrian," and "coal scuttle" helmets were the three basic designs. In some cases they have lasted until today. Another change was from bright colors to those pigments that blended with the terrain and weather.

Items like rank insignia, unit insignia, and specialized badges and patches varied from nation to nation, but all nations had some manner of identifying officers from the other ranks and differentiating units. Weapons and dress also varied with the role of the arm or service. Mounted troops, in particular, required specific types of clothing and equipment, as did artillery personnel.

The uniforms of the French army underwent the most immediate and drastic changes. In 1914 the French were attired in dark blue (black for officers), long tunics with red pants/pantaloons, ankle boots, and black gaiters. Officers wore riding boots and white gloves. A red kepi, or soft cap, bearing either the regimental designation for other ranks (OR) or braid in patterns to identify the officers completed the uniform. Leather belts and strapping were used for load-bearing equipment (LBE). For field service in 1914, the French wore light blue overalls and cap covers. Filled with the "spirit of the offense," the army went off to war in blue and red.

These uniforms made easy targets for German riflemen and machine gunners. The early fighting showed the unsuitability of this attire, and, late in 1914, the French adopted a single-breasted tunic and trousers in light blue, more commonly known as "horizon blue." Steel helmets and side caps replaced the kepi for ORs, but officers' standard headgear remained the kepi. Steel helmets were used in the trenches. All

French colonial troops who served on the Western Front adopted the standard service uniform, but they kept certain distinctive items of clothing and equipment (for example, white kepi for the Foreign Legion, fezes and turbans for certain African troops). French soldiers wore a greatcoat of a similar blue for cold weather, but there are indications that French infantry wore the coat year-round to protect themselves from horrendous conditions in the trenches. The standard infantry weapon was the 8mm Lebel rifle or carbine, and the 8mm Lebel revolver was the standard French sidearm.

The basic German army uniform was first introduced in 1907 and approved for issue in 1910 by the general staff. Prussian blue and the variants of other German states gave way to a grayish green shade of color known as *feldgrau*. The basic uniform was the same for all ranks, arms, and services. Differences were manifested in the cut or style of the tunic and by button patterns that identified specific regiments, arms, and specializations. Germany also adopted a system of identifying ranks and arms by cuff designs and shoulder straps. Certain units had a more green uniform to identify special skills or status (for example, machine-gun units).

Perhaps the most distinctive item of the German uniform was the spiked steel helmet, or *Pickenlaub*. It was first in service in the 1870s and had been adopted by many of the world's armies, usually as a dress hat. The front plate on the helmet had crests of varied designs from the national insignia, state crests, or regimental insignia. For "undress," officers wore a peaked cap, and other ranks wore a similar hat without the visor. Certain types of cavalry wore a shako or busby helmet. Machine-gun troops wore a modified shako or jager helmet. In 1916 the German army issued the "Coal Scuttle," or swept-down helmet, to replace the *Pickenlaub* for front-line service.

The general system for carrying personal items consisted of a leather belt, pouches, and straps to secure the pack, canteen, entrenching tool, and other items as required. The belt buckle or belt plate was gun metal and had either a national, state, or regimental designation. ORs had a square closure, the officers a rounded clasp. As the war went on, officers adopted a "Sam Brown"–type belt and buckle. From the beginning of the war cavalry and artillery drivers and support personnel used an open-faced buckle. As the war progressed, the uniform became more simple and functional,

yielding to the demands of production and active service. High boots completed the basic uniform. In Africa and the Middle East, German troops wore a khaki uniform suitable for tropical and warm climates.

German infantry weapons were the excellent Mauser 7.92mm rifle, with carbine variant issued to mounted troops. Germany utilized many pistols, but the most common was the 9mm Lugar '08. Brownings, Styers, and revolvers of 1870s vintage were also used. Pistols were more widespread in the German army, as they were issued to service troops, mounted troops, and machine gunners.

Perhaps no other country in the world issued as wide a variety of dress and service uniforms as did the United Kingdom. Every regiment had some special modification to the standard uniform. The service uniform at the beginning of the First World War was developed from experiences in colonial warfare, particularly in India and South Africa. In 1914 the British army consisted of the British Expeditionary Force (BEF) and territorial regiments for home defense.

In 1914 the British service uniform was the most practical among those of all European armies at the time. The khaki serge dress, developed from colonial experiences, provided a great degree of warmth and durability. The basic uniform consisted of trousers, a standing-collared tunic for ORs, and a step collar with shirt and tie for officers. Officers wore breeches and high boots, while soldiers wore an ankle boot and leggings or puttees. Standard headgear for all units was a peaked cap. Certain Scottish regiments wore the traditional kilt with aprons for field service; they also wore knee socks and ankle boots. Headgear consisted of either the "Tam-O-Shanter" or side cap, depending on the regiment. Kilts continued in use until after 1914. Scottish tunics were cut differently to accommodate the wearing of the kilt.

The British introduced the all-webbed load-carrying system in 1908. Made of cotton material, the webbing was more flexible and water resistant than leather, and it was longer lasting. It was also easier to mass produce. With it the soldier could carry all required equipment plus 150 rounds of ammunition. Once all the components were assembled, the soldier could put on or remove all his equipment in one piece, much like a coat. The self-fastening belt was the central feature to this system, and there were no cross straps to impede the soldier from using his pockets. Officers utilized the "Sam Brown" system of leather equipment that accommodated side arm, sword, map case, and other equipment.

British small arms consisted of the short magazine Lee-Enfield rifle with long bayonet. The Webley-Scott .38 caliber revolver was the standard issue pistol, although a Webley automatic pistol was also in use.

The diversity of the Austro-Hungarian Empire was reflected in its uniforms. A complex system of badges and other devices delineated Austrian and Hungarian units. In 1908 the empire attempted to standardize service uniforms in a pike gray tunic and trouser. Boots or ankle boots with leggings completed the uniform. A soft kepi-type hat with ear flaps served as standard head gear. A double-breasted greatcoat was issued for winter and mountain use. The cavalry retained its flamboyant uniforms into the first year of war. Hussars, Dragoons, and Uhlans (Lancers) all wore light blue tunics and red pantaloons; distinctive caps and shakos differentiated units and nationalities. Leather belts with a belt plate bearing the imperial coat of arms or Hungarian national crest with straps and pouches completed the uniform. In 1916 the Austrians adopted the German field-gray uniform and issued German steel helmets to their assault troops. The standard infantry arm was the Mannlicher 8mm rifle; officers procured their own side arms, with the Steyr-Hahn 9mm pistol being the most preferred.

Imperial Russia introduced the "slavic" uniform in 1877. This consisted of standing-collar tunic, trousers, and boots. The uniform color was a dun gray. Brown leather belts and pouches with the belt plate bearing the imperial crest completed the basic ensemble. To meet the demands for equipment during mobilization, the Russians used a plain, open-faced buckle on the belt. A peaked cap with the imperial cockade completed the uniform. The soldiers utilized a cross-shoulder blanket roll for carrying ammunition and equipment. A greatcoat was issued for winter use. Cossacks and officers wore the traditional fur cap during cold weather. Certain units at the czar's headquarters wore traditional white or green tunics.

There was much disparity in Russian uniforms, as the comfort and basic needs of the common soldier were never a very high priority at imperial court. Many times individual soldiers had to provide their own items to sustain themselves while on active service.

The standard Russian rifle was the Mosin-Nagent 7.62mm, with bayonet attached. The standard sidearm was the Mosin-Nagent revolver, 1895, 7.62mm (short).

The Italian army introduced a green-gray, single-breasted tunic and trouser in 1909, but the more traditional blue was found in some units in 1915 when Italy entered the war. The Italians used a kepi-type hat, but certain units used the Tyrol fedora, primarily the Alpini mountain troops. As was the case with German, Austrian, and French mountain troops, special uniforms and equipment were issued to the *Alpini,* such as climbing boots and breeches with long gaiters or leggings. Black leather belts, pouches, and straps completed the soldiers' load-carrying equipment. Italy adopted the French "adrien" steel helmet and issued a greatcoat for cold weather. Since Italy fought a mountain campaign against the Austrians, individual clothing and equipment varied to suit the weather conditions. The Carcano 6.5mm rifle and Beretta pistol were the basic infantry arms.

In 1903 the United States Army received new uniforms. While blue remained the traditional dress color, khaki was the official service uniform color. The basic uniform consisted of a four-pocket stand-up collar tunic and trousers or breeches. Boots or ankle boots with leggings were the standard foot wear. An open-collar, pull-over, two-pocket shirt was authorized for field wear or use under the tunic. The army retained the distinctive American "slouch hat" by replacing the 1898 campaign hat with the "Montana" peak hat. Officers wore either the campaign hat in field service or a peaked cap bearing the national coat of arms. Since the campaign hat proved impractical for transport and storage, European-bound units were issued a side cap, or "overseas" cap. For service in the trenches, most American units adopted the British "basin"-pattern steel helmet. A wool overcoat was issued for winter wear. American officers adopted the "Sam Brown" belt upon arrival in Europe, and the American system of load-bearing equipment was similar to that of the British, with web belts, straps, and a backpack.

The standard infantry arms were the 1903 .30 caliber Springfield rifle, perhaps the most accurate infantry rifle ever developed. The robust M1911 pistol, cal .45, was the standard sidearm, but because of the demands of mobilization the .45 revolver was issued in bulk to rear-echelon personnel and to some artillery units. The Americans made wide use of shotguns in trench warfare. The Winchester M1897 pump shotgun was preferred for trench raids.

Julius A. Menzoff

References

Barthrop, Michael. *The Old Contemptibles.* London: Osprey Books, 1989.

Bishop, Chris, and Ian Drury, eds. *Combat Guns.* New Jersey: Chartwell, 1987.

Haythornwhite, Philip J. *The World War I Source Book.* New York: Sterling, 1992.

Katcher, Philip. *The US Army, 1890–1920.* London: Osprey, 1980.

Windrow, Martin, ed. *The German Army, 1914–1918.* London: Osprey, 1978.

See also PISTOLS; RIFLES

V

Van Deventer, General Louis Jacob "Japie" (1874–1922)

South African cavalry officer. General "Japie" Van Deventer was born on 18 July 1874 in Ficksburg, South Africa. He led mounted riflemen against the British in the Boer War. In 1914, as a colonel, he led a South African brigade against the Germans in Southwest Africa. Adept at fast-paced movements, Van Deventer was promoted to brigadier general, and his brigade was transferred to the German East African front in 1915, where he and his men came to be feared by their German opponents.

In the course of the East African campaign, Van Deventer rose to the rank of major general and commanded a division. Early in 1917 he was knighted and took control of the British East African Expeditionary Force, pursuing remnants of Major General Paul von Lettow-Vorbeck's army until the end of the war. In December of 1918 Van Deventer returned to South Africa. He retired the next year and served as a part-time inspecting officer until his death at Johannesburg in 1922.

Donald S. Frazier

References

Brown, James Ambrose. *They Fought for King and Kaiser: South Africans in German East Africa, 1916.* Johannesburg: Ashanti, 1991.

L'Ange, Gerald. *Urgent Imperial Service: South African Forces in German South West Africa, 1914–1915.* Johannesburg: Ashanti, 1989.

Miller, Charles. *Battle for the Bundu: The First World War in East Africa.* New York: Macmillan, 1974.

See also AFRICA; LETTOW-VORBECK, PAUL VON

Venizelos, Eleutherios (1864–1936)

Greek premier, born on 23 August 1864 in Mourniés, Crete. Venizelos gained his early political experience in Crete. He served as premier of Greece in 1910–15, 1917, 1924, 1928–32, and 1933. Born to Kiriakos Venizelos Krivatas, a Cretan revolutionary, Eleutherios joined his family in exile on the island of Siros at age two. He eventually attended Athens University, graduating with a degree in law. He began his career in politics by becoming a member of Crete's National Assembly and the newly formed Liberal party. In 1909, after a coup by the Military League, he went to Athens as the League's political advisor. Following the 1910 elections he became premier, and, with King George's support, began a program of reform to revise the constitution of 1864. Under his direction, during the Balkan Wars of 1912–13 Greece doubled in size and population. He concluded a series of bilateral treaties resulting in the Balkan League.

The onset of World War I brought a flurry of activity from Venizelos as he struggled to preserve the status quo in the Balkans. His greatest fear centered on a Turkish-Bulgarian rapprochement that would weaken the position of Greece. In 1914 he opposed King Constantine's policy of joining the Central Powers. Against the king's wishes, Venizelos promised the Entente that Greece would support an alliance with them. When that failed, Venizelos supported Greek neutrality. He continued to work for a Greco-Serbo-Romanian bloc, opposing any arrangement that would result in territorial losses for Greece.

In October of 1915, Venizelos, without the approval of King Constantine, allowed four Allied divisions to land at Salonika. Constantine, although sympathetic to the Central Powers, supported a policy of neutrality, recognizing Greece's inability to defend itself against an Allied attack. Venizelos resigned in October of 1916 following extensive battles between his government and that of the King and Military League over whom Greece should support in the war. He formed a separate government in Thessaloniki, and, in December, Britain recognized it as the legitimate government of Greece. The presence of British and French warships at Piraeus convinced Constantine to relinquish his throne to his second son, Alexander. In June of 1917 Venizelos returned to Athens as premier, and Greece entered the war against the Central Powers.

The defeat of the Ottoman Empire and Bulgaria in World War I proved beneficial for Greece. Venizelos allowed Greek forces to be landed on Anatolia with British, French, and American assistance. He negotiated skillfully, and Greece gained most of his objectives from the Treaty of Sèvres, including much of Thrace, important Aegean islands, and the right to administer Izmir and its hinterland for five years. Elections in Greece after the conclusion of the treaty in 1920 failed to give Venizelos and his Liberal party a majority. He resigned and left the country, giving King Constantine the opportunity to return.

Venizelos returned as premier for a short time in 1924 and again from 1928–32 and in 1933. After instigating an unsuccessful military and naval revolt in March of 1935, he was forced into exile and died in Paris on 18 March 1936.

Susan N. Carter

References

Alastos, Doros. *Venizelos: Patriot, Statesman, Revolutionary*. London: Lund Humphries, 1942.

Leon, George G. *Greece and the Great Powers 1914–1917*. Thessaloniki: Institute for Balkan Studies, 1974.

Sugar, Peter F., and Donald Treadgold, eds. *A History of East Central Europe*. Vol. 8: *The Establishment of the Balkan National States, 1804–1920*, by Charles and Barbara Jelavich. Seattle: University of Washington Press, 1977.

See also CONSTANTINE I; GREECE; SÈVRES, TREATY OF

Verdun, Battle of (1916)

The 1916 Battle of Verdun was one of the costliest conflicts of World War I, with the highest number of dead: approximately 410,000 men. Alistair Horne has called it "the worst battle in history."

The city of Verdun is located about 160 miles east of Paris and is split by the Meuse River. Overlooking it to the east is the rocky escarpment of the Meuse Heights. Farther eastward is the Woëvre, a flat, clay plain. The original Verdun sat on a steep promontory abutting the Meuse. Settled as early as the third century B.C., it was an important Gallic fort (the word Verdun means "powerful fortress"). In Roman times it controlled transportation between Reims to the west and Metz to the east. The first citadel was built in the sixteenth century. France acquired Verdun at the end of the Thirty Years War. Vauban, Louis XIV's master of fortifications, strengthened Verdun with a bastioned wall around the city.

After the loss of Alsace-Lorraine in the Franco-Prussian War, the fortress complex there became even more crucial to French defense. As the cornerstone of the new French defensive system, a lower citadel was added. French military engineers excavated more than four kilometers of underground passageways, capable of lodging 6,000 men and storing supplies. In the 1916 battle, the lower citadel played a critical role as a logistics center and barracks.

Although in the years immediately preceding the First World War the French High Command played down the importance of fortifications when it adopted the doctrine of *attaque à outrance,* the existence of the fortified Verdun-Belfort line induced General Alfred von Schlieffen to develop the strategy of going around it to the north, through Belgium. Indeed, the series of French forts located both to the east and west of Verdun in 1914 had the reputation as the world's most powerful.

There had been fierce fighting in the Verdun region in 1914 and in 1915. During the Battle of the Marne, in September of 1914, Verdun had anchored the right flank of the French army. From 21 September 1914 onwards the Germans occupied Les Eparges plateau, which dominated the Woëvre plain from the east. This was the scene of bitter fighting from February to April of 1915.

In 1916 both sides planned great offensives to break the deadlock in the West, but the Germans struck first. Chief of the general staff General Erich von Falkenhayn was well aware that the Central Powers could not remain on the defensive. The Allies, with superior resources in men and matériel, were increasing their numbers faster than were the Central Powers. A decisive blow had to be struck in 1916. Austria-Hungary urged an attack against Italy, but the Germans vetoed this, as well as an attack on Russia. The high command believed that internal pressures would soon force both powers out of the war. It therefore selected the Western Front as the theater of attack with Verdun as the objective.

In 1916 Verdun lay in the middle of a narrow salient jutting into German-controlled territory; the southern face of the salient was framed by the counter-salient of St.-Mihiel. Capture of the Verdun salient would enable the Germans to threaten the entire right wing of the French defenses and give them a strongpoint threatening the rich Briey coal basin. In addition, the French lines lay less than twenty kilometers from the main German railway communications south, and an Allied push there might render the whole German front untenable. Victory at Verdun would also boost German morale, shaken recently by failure in the Argonne and by doubts in Germany about final victory raised by the institution of rationing.

Although Verdun was heavily fortified, it was only lightly garrisoned. At the time of the German attack in 1916, the French front lines in the Verdun sector consisted of a single trench line some three miles beyond the outer forts on the Meuse Heights and only one reserve trench line. For the Germans, the Verdun salient lent itself to converging attack and concentrated artillery fire. Its woods and many hills allowed the Germans to screen their troops and artillery, which were easily brought up by nearby railways and from Metz. The Germans reasoned that the French would find it difficult to resupply and reinforce their positions at Verdun, because only one road and one railroad line connected Verdun, via Ste.-Memehould, with the rest of France. The extreme narrowness of the salient would also make it difficult for the French to maneuver, especially on the right flank, where they would be fighting with their backs to the Meuse.

For some time after the battle opened, the French assumed that the Germans had chosen Verdun to effect a breakthrough similar to the attempts of 1915. That was not the case. Falkenhayn believed that France was strained to the breaking point and would throw all remaining manpower into the defense of Verdun, bleeding France white (aufbluting). Even if that was not achieved, the Germans hoped to capture Verdun with disastrous effect on French morale. At the very least, they expected to capture the east bank of the Meuse and hold the shortened front with fewer men.

The Germans planned to catch the French by surprise. Their attack would be on a narrow front from the north. With only a small outlay of forces but with massive amounts of artillery, the Germans expected to bleed the French army to death. Indeed, the code name for the operation was Gericht (execution place). Verdun was to be a battle of annihilation, with massive artillery concentrations not only on points to be attacked but also on all areas that might support them. But battles seldom turn out the way generals envision, and Verdun turned into a disaster for both sides.

The Germans spent several months gathering artillery and other supplies for the offensive, which was entrusted to the Fifth Army, commanded by the kaiser's son and heir, Crown Prince Wilhelm. The preliminary German bombardment opened at 07:15 on 21 February. Between 1,500 and 2,000 guns rained down shells on the French positions on a front of only about twenty-two kilometers at the start of the most intensive artillery bombardment to that date. The German guns then shifted to provide fire behind the French lines, and at about 16:40, elements of three German army corps (seven divisions, five of which were in the first line) launched a ground attack on a front of only ten kilometers, between Brabant and Ornes. The Crown Prince had wanted a simultaneous attack on both flanks, but, to minimize losses, Falkenhayn initially ordered the attack confined to the left bank of the Meuse.

The German attack caught the French by surprise and succeeded in capturing the outlying mobile French defense zone between the Bois des Caures and Herbebois. General Joseph Joffre and the French High Command had discounted indications of an attack at Verdun, believing that the main blow would come elsewhere. In addition, the French High Command had failed to give proper attention to the Verdun sector because it had planned a joint spring offensive with the British along the Somme. Joffre now reluctantly abandoned those plans.

In February of 1916 Verdun was only lightly defended. The French High Command believed that the area had little strategic value, and the opening campaign of 1914 had seemed to prove the ineffectiveness of fortifications. In 1915 many of the men and heavy artillery pieces at Verdun had been sent off to participate in other French offensives. Not knowing whether the German offensive would take place in Champagne or Lorraine, the French High Command had not sent reinforcements to Verdun. At the time of the German attack, the French had only nine infantry divisions and six heavy artillery regiments divided between both sides of the Meuse River (a total of 612 artillery pieces, 244 of which were heavy guns); beginning in early February, however, the French had assembled in reserve in that sector of the front an army of four corps with some heavy artillery.

The seven attacking German divisions met only two French divisions, very much reduced in strength by the German artillery bombardment. In order to reach the main French forts, the Germans had first to capture the Bois des Caures, a small wooded area held by only two battalions of *chasseurs* (light infantrymen). These 1,300 men were commanded by Lieutenant Colonel Emile Driant, a former deputy in the National Assembly and writer, who had vainly warned of the impending attack. The full power of the German thrust was concentrated on the Bois des Caures, but Driant managed to hold for two critical days. His force was annihilated, and he was killed on 22 February, one of the first French heroes of the battle. Most of the nine Meuse villages to the east of Verdun were completely obliterated.

The initial German assault had not gone as smoothly as hoped. The French fought very well; the narrowness of the assault frontage also worked against the Germans, as did the lack of a supporting attack west of the Meuse, which allowed French artillery to enfilade the Germans from across the river.

Fighting on the 23rd was even more intense. Brabant fell that day, and the French counterattack failed at the Bois des Caures. By the 24th the defenders had lost half of their total strength of 20,000 men and the Germans had taken the reserve trench.

Having taken the Bois des Caures, the Germans now faced Fort Douaumont, the most important fortification in the Verdun region. Located on high ground and commanding any German approach, Douaumont was the linchpin of the Verdun defensive system. Reputedly impregnable, Douaumont had been built from 1885 onwards; it was a quarter-mile across and constructed of steel and concrete, designed to be impervious to even the Germans' 420mm "Big Berthas." Its heaviest guns were one 155mm and two 75s in retractable steel turrets. Impregnable vaults could house a whole battalion of infantry, but on 25 February it was manned by just fifty-seven territorials. This was unknown to the Germans and to the French sector commander. That day, Lieutenant Eugen Radtkeaken and a handful of German soldiers captured the fort without loss. Crack French units were available and were to have moved into the fortress, but through a command mix-up they did not receive orders to do so. The failure to provide for the defense of Douaumont proved an almost fatal blunder for the French in the Battle of Verdun. In German hands, the fort dominated the French defensive positions; its loss is estimated to have cost the French 100,000 casualties.

That same night General Noel de Castelnau arrived at Verdun, sent by Joffre to assess the situation. He decided to maintain the defense on the right bank of the Meuse with no withdrawal to the river, a decision that condemned the French army to a costly holding action. De Castelnau also recommended that General Henri-Philippe Pétain be given command of the Verdun front; Joffre had already alerted Pétain, and he was officially appointed the night of 25–26 February.

Pétain set up his headquarters in one room of the *mairie* at Souilly, a village south of Verdun on the Bar-le-Duc road. He immediately rushed in reinforcements and ordered that the remaining forts be fully manned. Pétain developed a defensive scheme, as elastic as possible for the limited terrain, centered on a solid line ("principal line of resistance") based on the remaining forts, to be held at all cost. In front of that extended an "advanced line of resistance," designed to break and canalize German advances. In the rear was a third line of redoubts for reserves and reinforcements. Pétain did question the strategic value of Verdun as well as the decision to try to hold everywhere. In early March, when President Raymond Poincaré and General Joffre visited his headquarters, he suggested the possibility of withdrawal, whereupon Poincaré told him, "Don't think of it, General. It would be parliamentary catastrophe."

The French now faced a critical situation. By the 28th they had contained the German attempt at a breakthrough, although the attacks continued until 5 March. The only communication into Verdun was by means of a single secondary road from Bar-le-Duc (*La voie sacrée*, "the sacred way"). On it, sixty-six French divisions, three-quarters of the entire army, marched into the caldron of battle. Pétain's watchword (also attributed to General Robert Nivelle), "Ils ne passeront pas" (they shall not pass), became the French rallying cry. Verdun became a matter of national honor for the French, and for the same reason kept the Germans from breaking off the attack.

The Germans hoped they could attract large numbers of French troops to the battle and inflict so much damage to the thin line of communications that the defenders could not be relieved and would simply be worn down. As a result, Falkenhayn now expanded the battle by extending it to both banks of the Meuse River. On 6 March the Germans attacked the western face of the salient, broadening the front by an additional twenty kilometers, and extending it as far as the town of Avocourt on the right bank. Pétain had reinforced there, and the Germans gained only two kilometers. Bad weather also grounded German aircraft. On 8 March the Germans attacked on both banks of the Meuse, but the French lines held.

The battle now became a true contest of attrition. For the remainder of March both sides attacked and counterattacked, resulting in mounting casualties. Savage fighting raged back and forth across a ridge commanding the Meuse, already ominously known as Mort-Homme ("dead man"). On 2 April the French lost the village of Vaux, and its fort was threatened.

By rotating units in and out of the battle, the French frustrated the German plan to wear them down. The French also managed to organize an effective supply system along the Sacred Way to sustain their eventual force of 450,000 men and 140,000 animals at Verdun. Despite German artillery fire, a steady stream of trucks (as many as 6,000 a day, or one every fourteen seconds around the clock) made their way to bring in supplies and carry out the wounded. Indochinese and African road gangs filled shell craters as soon as they were made.

On 9 April the Germans launched their third main attack, a general offensive on both sides of the salient. Again the French checked them. Attacks and counterattacks continued (including an unsuccessful French effort to recapture Fort Douaumont on 22 May) until the German offensive ground out on 29 May.

Pétain got help during the battle from two capable lieutenants, Generals Robert Nivelle and Charles Mangin. During the battle Pétain became such a national figure that Premier Aristide Briand suggested his appointment to command an army group. Nivelle succeeded him in command at Verdun on 1 May.

At the beginning of June, the Germans launched another attack against Fort Vaux, the smallest of the Verdun forts and the northeast bastion of Verdun's permanent fortifications, and Thiaumont Farm. After a week of bitter fighting, with its water gone and interior in rubble, Vaux finally fell to the Germans on 7 June. The crown prince personally congratulated its French commander, Major Sylvain-Eugène Raynal, on his defense.

Once in possession of Douaumont and Vaux, the Germans could assault the last ridges on the right bank of the Meuse before Verdun: Froideterre, Thiaumont, and Souville. They assigned nineteen regiments to the attack, of which twelve were on the six-kilometer-long front line. The Germans positioned reserves close behind the front line in order to take advantage of successes and provide continuity of effort. Mangin described it as "the most important and most massive attack" against Verdun. After a two-day artillery preparation (including the use of deadly phosgene gas for the first time), the German attack opened on 23 June. They hoped to enter Verdun two days later.

The bitter fighting centered principally on the Thiaumont-Fleury-Chapelle-Ste. Fine-Souville-Vaux-Douaumont "quadrilateral." Fleury and the fortifications of Thiaumont were captured and retaken again and again. German losses forced them to commit their reserves on 25 June. Even Pétain doubted the French could hold and recommended abandonment of the eastern Meuse line. With a British offensive along the Somme in the offing, Joffre refused. The French High Command had been pressing the British for a diversion to drain off German strength. This speeded up an attack by General Douglas Haig along the Somme on 1 July. While ill-advised, this offensive did draw off

German forces to the north, as did the Russian Brusilov Offensive on the Eastern Front.

On 11 July the crown prince ordered thirteen regiments to attack on virtually the same front as that of 23 June. The Germans reached the superstructure of Fort Souville, within a few kilometers of Verdun, the closest they came to the city. By 20 July French counterattacks pushed the Germans back to their position of departure.

The Somme Offensive forced the Germans to abandon their attack on Verdun and allowed the French army to recapture the initiative there. In the fall, the French, now under the command of General Mangin, went over to the offensive. The Moroccan Colonial Infantry Regiment recaptured Fort Douaumont on 24 October. On 2 November Fort Vaux was retaken. On 15 December another French attack forced the Germans back more than five kilometers from Souville. In August of 1917 the French retook their front positions of February 1916; finally, in September of 1918, the Americans pushed the Germans completely away from Verdun, toward Montfaucon to the north.

The 1916 Battle of Verdun was a victory of sorts for the French. The Germans had not bled France to death, broken through, or even taken Verdun. While they had captured a few square miles of territory, they had paid a terrible price. Estimates on casualties in the Battle of Verdun vary widely. Official French figures (published in 1936) for the ten months of 1916 list 377,231, of which 162,308 were killed or missing. A substantial number of the missing, which included prisoners, were dead. German losses were about 337,000. Contemporary German estimates put the number of dead and missing at over 100,000. Together these total more than 700,000 casualties. Taking into account the fighting at Verdun both before and after the 1916 battle, the total number of casualties reaches 420,000 dead and 800,000 gassed or wounded.

Neither army was quite the same after the battle. The Germans were unable to mount another considerable attack until the spring of 1918, after the collapse of Russia. General Falkenhayn was dismissed (29 August 1916) as commander of German armies and replaced by Field Marshal Paul von Hindenburg with General Erich Ludendorff as his assistant. They shifted the German effort to the East. The battle also had a tremendous effect on France. War weariness gripped the country, and doubts arose

about victory. When Nivelle attempted his Champagne Offensive in the spring of 1917, it brought widespread mutinies in the French army. For France Verdun symbolized heroism, fortitude, and suffering; but there was a much more profound negative influence that lingered on long after the war. As much as three-quarters of the French army in the First World War fought at Verdun, and that awful place was seared into their memories. After Verdun, the French army, perhaps even France, was never the same again.

Almost unique among World War I battlefields, Verdun still looks very much as it did after the 1916 battle. Shell craters, barbed wire, and twisted gun turrets are still in evidence. There are no birds. An ossuary at Douaumont contains the unidentified remains of approximately 130,000 German and French soldiers killed in the battle.

Spencer C. Tucker

References

Hermanns, William. *The Holocaust. From a Survivor of Verdun*. New York: Harper & Row, 1972.

Horne, Alistair. *The Price of Glory. Verdun, 1916*. New York: Macmillan, 1962.

Ryan, Stephen. *Pétain the Soldier*. New York: A.S. Barnes, 1969.

See also BRUSILOV OFFENSIVE; FALKENHAYN, ERICH VON; JOFFRE, JOSEPH; MANGIN, CHARLES; NIVELLE, ROBERT; PÉTAIN, HENRI-PHILIPPE; SOMME, BATTLE OF; WILHELM, CROWN PRINCE

Versailles Treaty (28 June 1919)

The treaty imposed upon the defeated Germans by the Allied and associated powers. Deliberations began in January of 1919 and continued through the winter and spring. The formal signing took place on 28 June 1919 in the Hall of Mirrors at the Palace of Versailles. As a result of this treaty, Germany would face the bitter consequences of defeat, and much of central and eastern Europe would undergo reconstruction.

In agreeing to the armistice that ended fighting on 11 November 1918, the Germans had hoped that the subsequent treaty would be based on the Fourteen Points announced and advocated by American President Wilson. At the peace conference, however, the idealistic

American program was overwhelmed by French realism, British politics, and wartime promises. The European victors had paid for the war "with the blood of their young and the coins of their realms." Now they wanted recompense for their efforts and expenditures. When Wilson refused to consider secret wartime agreements, the Allies withheld support for the point closest to Wilson's heart—the League of Nations. All participants in the deliberations made concessions but often at the expense of good will and prudence.

The negotiators at Paris felt a sense of urgency. Revolutions in Hungary, Russia, and Germany threatened the spread of Bolshevism over central Europe; general demobilization, and war between Russia and Poland, menaced decisions concerning Eastern Europe; and a starving and blockaded Germany plagued by inflation, disease, and the separation of families could not await long-term decisions. Immediate solutions had to be found regardless of their shortcomings. The haste, passions, acquisitiveness, and fears, and the exclusion of German representatives, made the realization of "a just and honorable peace" difficult.

On 25 April 1919 the German delegation was invited to receive the treaty, and, upon the insistence of the Allies, Germany was to send her foremost ambassadors to Versailles. On 28 April two trains with 180 members of the German delegation, led by Foreign Minister Count Ulrich von Brockdorff-Rantzau, left Berlin, rapidly passing through Germany and Belgium, but slowing down to fifteen kph at the sight of the battlefields of France and stopping for extended periods in towns with heavy devastation. Visible to the German entourage were German prisoners of war working to rebuild the destruction. When the delegation threw newspapers and oranges to the prisoners from the train, they were appalled to see French guards clubbing the men back to work. At Versailles the Germans were restricted to the Hotel de Reservoirs, the domicile of the French peace commission in 1871 after the Franco-Prussian War. After their luggage was dumped in the courtyard, the delegates sought their own rooms and found their quarters to be without central heating, and the adjoining park fenced in by barbed wire and patrolled by French sentries. All of this was ostensibly for the protection of the delegation, and there were times when the citizenry pelted them with stones and vegetables. Forewarned in Berlin that their rooms might be bugged, the

delegation conferred to the accompaniment of loudly recorded passages from *Tannhäuser* and refrains of a "Hungarian Rhapsody." After thoroughly searching the premises, the delegation found no listening devices, and the musical cacophony was abandoned.

In the meantime the Allies worked on the last chapters of the treaty and sent the two hundred pages entitled "Conditions of Peace" in its finished English and French versions to the printers on 5 May. Two days later, copies were delivered to senior Allied officials. The top American economic advisor, Herbert Hoover, was awakened at 04:00 to receive his copy. Upon reading it through immediately, he was "horrified by its harshness" and started to walk the streets of Paris, only to run into General Jan Christian Smuts and John Maynard Keynes, who seemed to have similar thoughts.

Germany's confrontation with the Allies had been prepared with great care. Prime Minister David Lloyd George, Wilson, and Premier Georges Clemenceau personally visited the Trianon Palace on 5 May to ensure themselves of its readiness. The meeting was to occur in a room seventy-five feet square. Three sides of the square were occupied by the Allied plenipotentiaries; the fourth side, facing Clemenceau and other major figures, was reserved for the German delegation, referred to as the "*banc des accusés*" by the Parisian press. The German delegation read about the arrangement in the newspapers and received a document entitled "Agenda for a Meeting to be Held on May 7, 1919." Additionally, they learned that the meeting was scheduled for 15:00 and was to last five minutes. Any German hopes that opportunities for compromise, defense, or response were in the offing were quickly dashed.

German Foreign Minister Brockdorff-Rantzau prepared three separate drafts of the German response to the treaty presentation. He would decide which to use depending on the Allies' statements. Dressed in black morning coat, high wing collar, and bowler hat, the count led his entourage to the already-gathered Allies. Entering the "dazzling light of the room" to the announcement of *Messieurs les délégués allemands,"* Brockdorff-Rantzau formally bowed to the assemblage, a gesture returned by the standing delegates, and was led to his seat.

As president of the peace conference, Clemenceau opened the meeting with a brief statement and told the Germans that they had fifteen days to send "written observations"

V

about the treaty. The Allies then would comment on their replies and inform Germany about the date on which to sign the document. When Clemenceau asked, "Does anyone wish to speak?" Brockdorff-Rantzau raised his hand, and Clemenceau called for translators. Remaining seated, the German foreign minister shocked the Allies when he replied:

> We have heard the victors' passionate demand that as vanquished we shall be made to pay and as the guilty we shall be punished. The demand is made that we shall acknowledge that we alone are guilty of having caused the war. Such a confession in my mouth would be a lie.

The curt response left "a most unfortunate impression." Clemenceau's face became "red with anger," Wilson obviously was not favorably impressed, and Lloyd George "feigned boredom." After delivering the caustic reply, the German delegation left, the baron lighting a cigarette while on his way out. The consensus of Allied opinion was that the Germans were unrepentant, brash, and tactless. Even the German delegation felt that Brockdorff-Rantzau had gone too far. By midnight they had translated the whole treaty and found the document "worse than anything they had dreamed possible." The treaty was perceived as a *"Diktat,"* and the Germans felt that Wilson in particular had betrayed them.

The focal part of the treaty, the League of Nations (articles 1–26) excluded Germany from participation. Its covenant united the signatories in a league guaranteeing their independence and territorial integrity (article 10); the League's most important power (article 22) was the supervision of the mandates, consisting of the former German colonies and parts of the former Ottoman Empire. Germany had hoped to write off the loss of the colonies against the reparations obligation.

Territorial dispositions in Europe were perceived as an even greater loss. Germany lost territory in the west, north, and east. The coal mines of the Saar were ceded to France to compensate for French mining losses during the war. The League would administer the Saar basin for fifteen years, after which time the inhabitants would decide by plebiscite whether to become French or German (articles 45–50). Alsace-Lorraine was re-ceded to France "to redress the wrong done by Germany in 1871" (articles 51–

79). Belgium acquired from Germany the districts of Moresnet, Eupen, and Malmédy (articles 32–34) as compensation for German occupation. To the north Germany lost northern Schleswig to Denmark as a result of a plebiscite; Flensburg, the southern zone, opted to become German (articles 109–14). The east bank of the Rhine was to be demilitarized to the extent of 31.25 miles (fifty kilometers) behind the river; fortifications had to be dismantled, and permanent works for maneuvers were prohibited (articles 42–43).

In the east Germany ceded West Prussia to Poland along with the greater part of Poznan, creating the Polish corridor, which separated East Prussia from the rest of Germany. This territorial disposition gave the independent state of Poland access to the sea (article 87). Danzig, a German city, was placed under League jurisdiction (articles 100–108). The East Prussian districts of Allenstein and Marienwerder were to decide by plebiscite whether to belong to Germany or Poland (articles 94–98). Memel and its surroundings were ceded to the principal Allied and associated powers (article 99) and eventually added to Lithuania. Overall, Germany lost 25,000 square miles (13 percent) of her territory, inhabited by six million people. Economically more devastating, however, was the loss of 65 percent of her iron ore in Lorraine and Luxembourg, 45 percent of her coal in the Saar area and Silesia, and 72 percent of her zinc and 57 percent of her lead deposits in Alsace.

Outside Germany, most of the overseas colonies would be administered by the Allied and associated powers as mandates under the League of Nations (article 119). The Cameroons and Togoland were divided between France and Great Britain, East Africa between Great Britain and Belgium, and South-West Africa went to the Union of South Africa, a British dominion. In the Pacific, the Marshall Islands went to Japan, New Guinea to Australia, Western Samoa to New Zealand, and Nauru to Great Britain, Australia, and New Zealand. The province of Shantung became a Japanese sphere of influence (articles 156–58).

The military, navy, and air force restrictions were equally severe. By 31 March 1920 the German army was to be reduced to and not thereafter to exceed the strength of seven infantry and three cavalry divisions (100,000 men); the manufacture of munitions was to be closely restricted; and the importation of munitions of war prohibited (articles 159–70). The existence of a general staff was forbidden (article 160); universal military service was abolished; and the term of enlistment was to be at least twelve years for noncommissioned officers and other ranks and twenty-five years for newly appointed officers (articles 173–79). The German navy would be reduced to six antiquated battleships, six light cruisers, twelve destroyers, and twelve torpedo boats; submarines were forbidden (article 181). All naval and military air forces were prohibited (articles 198–202).

The Allies were to try Wilhelm II "for a supreme offence against international morality and the sanctity of treaties" (article 227). Germans "accused of having committed acts in violation of the laws and customs of war" were to be tried by Allied military tribunals (articles 228–30). The infamous Article 231 forced Germany and her allies to accept responsibility "for causing all the loss and damage to which the Allied and Associated Governments and their nationals have been subjected as a consequence of the war imposed upon them by the aggression of Germany and her allies." Since Germany was unable to compensate the Allies in full, she was to compensate "allied civilians for all damage to property and life, in a manner seen fit by the Inter-Allied Reparation Commissions." Germany was expected to deliver an immediate payment of $5 billion. As a guarantee of German compliance with the terms of the treaty, the Allies could occupy the Rhineland for fifteen years (article 428). Article 80 forbade the merging of Austria with Germany.

To guarantee the settlement of the eastern frontier, Germany had to abrogate the treaties of Brest-Litovsk and Bucharest, and other agreements made with the Bolsheviks, and to withdraw its troops in the east within its new frontiers when the Allies "shall think the moment suitable" (article 433).

By 10 May the German public was fully aware of the provisions of the treaty and particularly angry about the sections concerning reparations and war guilt, which were referred to as the "disgraceful paragraphs" (articles 227–31). The Germans were amazed as well at the demands for reparations, which were far in excess of the total national wealth of the country.

To counter the German notes of observation, the Allies referred each received note to the conference commission or subcommittee responsible for the original draft. Final decision was left to the Council of Four to approve it or to redraft it. Once a typed reply had Clemenceau's signature, it was sent back to the Germans. The Germans were further frustrated by problems of communication. The decisions made at Versailles had to be communicated to the German Cabinet at Weimar, the German Armistice Commission at Spa, and the *Paxkonferenz* in Berlin. Plagued by these organizational difficulties, the Germans requested that their period of "observation" be extended to 29 May.

When the Germans finally turned their counterproposal over to the Allies on 29 May, it amounted to 119 pages and 25,000 words printed by German printers expressly rushed to Versailles. Reminding the Allies that Germany had laid down her arms only after the Allied Powers had promised that the Fourteen Points were to be the basis of peace, they felt that the Allies had broken an "international legal agreement." Nearly every article was contested, conceding virtually nothing. Most harshly attacked were the articles concerning reparations, territorial losses, and the question of war guilt.

The situation deteriorated even more when it became apparent that the Germans were not willing to sign the treaty. British troops mutinied at Calais; most American soldiers had already gone home; John Maynard Keynes attacked the treaty in *The Economic Consequences of the Peace*; and Lloyd George conferred with Wilson about possible revisions of the treaty to appease the Germans. Not willing to drag this ordeal out any further, Wilson refused to consider the British suggestions, and without American support the British gave in to French persistence. Consequently, the treaty was returned to the Germans with very few alterations (only in Upper Silesia and in the Rhineland were concessions granted) added in red ink to the original copy. Upon receipt of the treaty Brockdorff-Rantzau decided to return to Germany. A hostile crowd threw stones at the delegation's cars, injuring diplomats on their way to the train. Securing a two-day extension to accept the treaty, the German government had to reply by 23 June whether to accept the treaty or not.

Arriving in Germany on 18 June, the German delegation drove directly from the station at Weimar to the former Grand Ducal Palace, where President Friedrich Ebert and Chancellor Philipp Scheidemann awaited their report to the cabinet. Urging his fellow ministers to reject the treaty, as the Allies had agreed only to minimal changes, Brockdorff-Rantzau found himself opposed by Matthias Erzberger, leader of the

Catholic Center party. Predicting that the Allies were prepared to invade Germany if she resisted signing the treaty, Erzberger warned the cabinet of the Allied strategies to break up Germany into various states and then force separate peace treaties on them. Erzberger's influence divided the cabinet and set frantic meetings into motion. Threatening to resign, Brockdorff-Rantzau counted on time to force further concessions within the Allied ranks. The German army reported to their government that resistance would be "sporadic and futile on Germany's part" and that, if invaded, Germany could not resist successfully. When the cabinet voted to accept the treaty, Brockdorff-Rantzau and Scheidemann resigned, and four days before the deadline expired Germany had no government.

While contemplating resignation himself, President Ebert concentrated on finding a new chancellor and a cabinet. Then, just one day after the collapse of Germany's government, all hopes for any possible compromise with the Allies were destroyed when crews of the interned German High Seas Fleet opened seacocks of their vessels and sank them at Scapa Flow in the Orkney Islands on 21 June. News of the scuttling of the fleet was received with anger and embarrassment and resulted in the Allies' demand that the German delegates come to "an unequivocal decision as to their purpose to sign and accept as a whole or not to sign. . . ." The note also reminded the representatives that they had but twenty-four hours left to arrive at a reply.

Awaiting the German decision, the Allies readied their forces for the occupation of Germany, despite Marshal Ferdinand Foch's concerns that his forces were insufficient for a march on central Germany. Warned by Clemenceau "not to intervene in political affairs," and questioned by Lloyd George about the strength of the "underarmed and undermanned 550,000-man German army," Foch yielded, and on the morning of 23 June the army of the Western Allies was ready to cross the Rhine. In the East, Czech and Polish troops eagerly anticipated advancing into Germany in "bounds" of 100 kilometers each.

In view of this development the chancellor of the newly formed German government, Gustav Bauer, was utterly defenseless. Ninety minutes before the resumption of war, the German acceptance arrived. It read: "Yielding to overwhelming force, but without on that account abandoning its view in regard to the unheard-of injustice of the conditions of peace, the government of the German Republic declares that it is ready to accept and sign the condition of peace imposed by the Allied and Associated Powers."

Returning to Versailles, without Brockdorff-Rantzau, were the German representatives Drs. Hermann Müller and Johannes Bell. In the *Galerie des Glaces* (Hall of Mirrors), at 15:50 on 28 June 1919, five years to the day after the assassination at Sarajevo, the Germans were ushered in to put their signatures to the treaty. Artillery volleys interrupted the silence of the room to announce to the world the signing of the peace treaty. Lloyd George, Clemenceau, and Wilson gathered on a terrace to watch the fully flowing fountains and cheering crowds—the war was officially over.

Edward L. Byrd, Jr.
Ingrid P. Westmoreland

References

Bailey, Thomas A. *Woodrow Wilson and the Lost Peace*. New York: Macmillan, 1944.

Czernin, Ferdinand. *Versailles, 1919. The Forces, Events and Personalities that Shaped the Treaty*. New York: G.P. Putnam's Sons, 1964.

Dockrill, Michael, and Douglas J. Goold. *Peace without Promise: Britain and the Peace Conferences, 1919–1923*. London: Batsford, 1981.

House, Edward M., and Charles Seymour, eds. *What Really Happened at Paris*. New York: Charles Scribner's Sons, 1921.

Nicolson, Harold. *Peacemaking*. New York: Gorsset & Dunlap, 1919.

Watt, Richard M. *The Kings Depart*. New York: Simon and Schuster, 1968.

See also BROCKDORFF-RANTZAU, ULRICH; CLEMENCEAU, GEORGES; LLOYD GEORGE, DAVID; PARIS PEACE CONFERENCE

Veterinary Medicine

Veterinary services during World War I were crucial for both animals and humans. Cavalry and horse-drawn artillery were still prevalent in military forces that had not yet been mechanized. World War I was the first war in which properly trained veterinarians practiced in an organized manner on the field. In previous wars farriers had performed veterinary services, as had veterinarians who lacked professional credentials from accredited institutions.

Having a veterinary corps that could evacuate sick and wounded animals was essential for successful military campaigns, and the Allies' veterinary corps performed well on all fronts. In 1913 Britain's Army Veterinary Corps attached a mobile veterinary section to every cavalry division and brigade to evacuate sick and wounded animals. A veterinary officer was in every brigade to perform triage duties. Evacuation and treatment of sick and wounded animals in World War I was comparable to medical care for humans. More than 2,562,549 horses and mules were treated in British veterinary hospitals in France, of which 78 percent were healed to return to duty.

Veterinarians also worked to combat animal diseases. Post mortems were conducted routinely; veterinarians also inspected meat animals before and after slaughter and dairy herds to ensure safe food for the troops. Among the animal diseases treated were several transmissible to humans—glanders, influenza, and mange, which was controlled by disinfecting horses and their equipment in sulphur gas chambers.

Armin Anton Leibold, a prominent military veterinarian, was placed in charge of a new bacteriological laboratory at Veterinary Base Hospital No. 6 at Neufchâteau in April of 1918 to investigate the causes and prevention of ulcerative lymphangitis, from which many horses and mules suffered.

Horses also had to be treated for shell wounds, reaction to poison gases, broken bones, shrapnel wounds, smoke inhalation, and other battlefield injuries. Such wounds, however, did not account for the majority of deaths. Exposure to the elements also accounted for many casualties. Of 256,000 horses lost by the British in Europe, exposure was the chief cause of death. When picketed outside in winter and forced to stand in cold mud, horses developed lung and digestive troubles. During the winter of 1916 one veterinary hospital in France lost fifty horses weekly to influenza. Laminitis, anthrax, and founder also caused premature death.

Royal Society for the Prevention of Cruelty to Animals (RSPCA) inspectors joined the veterinary corps and raised funds for veterinary hospital equipment by selling Fortunino Matania's painting of a soldier with his dying horse. The Red Star Animal Relief donated additional money, and the RSPCA Sick and Wounded Horse Fund raised £250,000 to build thirteen hospitals in France. In addition, the RSPCA financed tent hospitals, convalescent depots, ambulances, rugs, and corn crushers. The Blue Cross built kennels attached to the horse hospitals for sick and wounded dogs. These facilities returned nearly two million animals to the front. The RSPCA also purchased horse-drawn horse ambulances for wounded horses unable to walk.

In addition to bogging down in mud and having to be destroyed, horses were casualties of gas attacks. Between 1916 and 1918, 2,220 horses required veterinary attention because of eye and skin irritations resulting from exposure to mustard gas. Veterinarians on both sides innovated "horsepirators," or horse gas masks, that fit over the horse's head, covered its nostrils, and permitted it to breathe pure air. These gas masks, however, did not last long, as horses confused them with feed bags and tore out their bottoms.

Veterinary services, pressured by troops lacking sufficient animals, often released horses from hospitals before they were fully healed, resulting in horses breaking down. Veterinarians also had to remain in trenches during barrages, only to have to run out during brief respites to destroy wounded animals. Because such conditions prevented regular inspection and treatment, one veterinarian complained that the only qualification for a military veterinary surgeon "was to be a good shot."

It is believed that the Germans lost four horses to every Allied horse casualty because of lack of care. The Germans did not attempt to cure or destroy their wounded horses, which were often acquired by Allied troops. Some historians even hypothesize that if the German equine force had been strengthened with professional veterinary services, they might have been able to defeat the British and French.

Allied veterinary services, however, enabled their troops to remain supplied with ample animal power with which to win the war. In 1918 King George V added the prefix "Royal" to the Army Veterinary Corps because of their work "in mitigating animal suffering, in increasing the mobility of the mounted units, and for reducing animal wastage."

World War I exposed weaknesses in veterinary education, and public institutions gained prominence over private schools, becoming more research oriented and promoting preventative care. World War I veterinary services were extended when Dorothy Brooke established the War Horse Fund, for the veterinary care of World War I cavalry horses sold in Egypt that required professional attention. The Old War Horse Memorial Hospital also continued the services of World War I veterinarians beyond the battlefield.

Elizabeth D. Schafer

References

Bemis, H.E. "Veterinary Corps of the American Expeditionary Forces." *Journal of the American Veterinary Medical Association* 10 (April 1920): 61–74.

Blenkinsop, Sir L.J., and J.W. Rainey. *Veterinary Services*. London: HMSO, 1925.

Merillat, Louis A., and Delwin M. Campbell. *Veterinary Military History of the United States*. 2 vols. Chicago: Veterinary Magazine Corp., 1935.

Schafer, Elizabeth D. "Armin Anton Leibold's World War I Trunk," *Trails in History: Official Newsletter of the Lee County Historical Society* 24 (December 1992): 6–7.

"Veterinary Corps Commended by Gen. Pershing." *Journal of the American Veterinary Medical Association* 9 (June 1919): 334.

See also ANIMALS, USE OF

Victor Emmanuel III (1869–1947)

King of Italy. Born in Naples on 11 November 1869, Victor Emmanuel III (Victorio Emanuele III) was the only son of King Umberto I and Queen Margherite. Educated by tutors, Victor Emmanuel entered the army in 1886 as a lieutenant and by age twenty-eight was nominal commander of a corps. Umberto, unpopular because he was a reactionary and supported the Triple Alliance, was assassinated by an anarchist and Victor Emmanuel became king on 19 July 1900.

Shy of the limelight and skeptical by nature, Victor Emmanuel's primary interest was preserving the monarchy by maintaining close ties to the Italian people. During the first decade of his reign this led him in a radical direction. His pro-French sympathies and hostility toward Austria helped bring changes in foreign policy. The Franco-Italian Accords of 1902 and 1904 reconciled Italy with France and weakened her ties with the Triple Alliance.

Victor Emmanuel played a key role in bringing Italy into the war on the Allied side. He helped secure the Treaty of London (26 April 1915), although it is a matter of debate among historians whether he concealed its binding nature from Giovanni Giolitti. On 4 May Italy renounced its alliance with the Central Powers, but Premier Antonio Salandra soon discovered that a majority in both the Chamber of Deputies and Senate were in favor of Giolitti's neutralist stance. On 13 May Salandra chose to resign rather than risk rejection in the chamber of his decision for war. On 16 May, contrary to the majority in parliament and probably the population as a whole, Victor Emmanuel III reappointed Salandra as premier. Italy declared war on 24 May. Perhaps Victor Emmanuel wanted one of Italy's most effective leaders in power at this critical juncture, but his decision to reappoint Salandra may also have sprung from his desire to complete the final steps of Italy's territorial redemption. The king's strong support for war was vital in undermining the neutralists.

As nominal commander in chief of the armed forces Victor Emmanuel gained wide support, spending most of the war years near the front and occasionally exposing himself to danger. He often intervened to resolve disputes between chief of staff General Luigi Cadorna and the government. After Caporetto he helped choose General Armando Diaz to replace Cadorna. His strong public stance that Italian troops would retreat no farther than the Piave helped secure Allied reinforcements. At that point he was also ready to abdicate if this would help secure better peace terms for Italy. By 1918 the king was appearing publicly with left-wing political leaders in an effort to rally the nation.

Victor Emmanuel proved ineffective in dealing with Italy's postwar economic and social unrest. In October of 1922 his refusal to sign Premier Luigi Facta's decree for martial law (the army was still loyal to the king) led to the latter's resignation and probably doomed parliamentary democracy in Italy. His decision to appoint Benito Mussolini premier resulted more from his desire for a return to order after several years of social upheaval than an embrace of fascism.

During the fascist era Victor Emmanuel was increasingly marginalized by Mussolini. In June of 1944 he gave his son Umberto all "royal prerogatives." In May of 1946, tainted by his long association with fascism, Victor Emmanuel abdicated in favor of Umberto II. The move had Allied sanction as a means of preserving the monarchy. The abdication, only a month before a plebiscite on the monarchy, came too late to influence the vote. Although the conservative south heavily supported retention of the monarchy, the populous north was opposed, and the monarchy was abolished by 12.0 to 10.7 million votes. The royal family went into exile in Portugal and then Egypt. Victor Emmanuel died in Alexandria, Egypt, on 28 December 1947.

Spencer C. Tucker

References

Bertoldi, Silvio. *Victorio Emanuele III*. Turin: Unione tipografico-editrice torinese, 1970.

Mack Smith, Dennis. *Italy: A Modern History*. Ann Arbor, Mich.: University of Michigan Press, 1969.

Melograni, Piero. *Storio politica della grande guerra, 1915–1918*. Beri: Laterza, 1969.

Puntoni, Paolo. *Parla Vittorio Emanuele III*. Milan: A. Palazzi, 1958.

Saladino, Salvatore. *Italy from Unification to 1919*. New York: Thomas Crowell, 1970.

Seton-Watson, Christopher. *Italy from Liberation to Fascism, 1870–1925*. London: Methuen, 1967.

See also CADORNA, LUIGI; ITALY, HOME FRONT; SALANDRA, ANTONIO

Vimy Ridge (9 April 1917)

Vimy Ridge is a commanding height north of the River Scarpe and city of Arras, France. From it the whole Douai plain to the east is open to observation. Its importance as a terrain feature made Vimy Ridge the scene of several important World War I battles. The Germans captured the heights at the beginning of the war and turned them into a formidable defensive position. French commander General Joseph Joffre was determined to retake Vimy Ridge and sent French forces against it twice in 1915: The first attempt was during the 9 May to 18 June Second Battle of Artois, and the second came during the 25 September to 16 October Third Battle of Artois.

In 1917 the Allies again tried to take Vimy Ridge. The British were embarrassed by the fact that in May of 1916 the Germans had recaptured ground there won at high cost by the French. The 1917 Vimy Ridge attack was one of the notable feats of arms of the entire war. It occurred during the 9 to 15 April Battle of Arras, the British preliminary operation to the Nivelle Offensive, designed, in part, to draw off German reserves to the north.

In the Battle of Arras, the British sent two armies to attack eastward—the First under General H.S. Horne and the Third under General Sir Edmund Allenby—against positions held by the German Sixth Army (General Baron L. von Falkenhausen). Allenby's Third Army was to advance from Arras. First Army on its left was assigned the capture of Vimy Ridge. Horne gave the task to the four divisions of his Canadian Corps, commanded by General Sir Julian Byng.

A heavy five-day artillery bombardment and gas attack preceded the assault. The British also employed forty-eight tanks in the offensive. The gas shells forced the Germans to keep their gas masks on for prolonged periods and, by killing large numbers of horses, prevented them from transporting shells to the front. The British also had air superiority during the attack, and Byng had planned the assault meticulously.

The Canadian infantry moved out at 05:30 on 9 April, Easter Sunday, covered by a well-timed creeping artillery barrage. In less than an hour they has taken the entire German first-line system. In capturing the ridge the Canadians also took 10,000 German prisoners. One German defender said that the attackers came as "an all-engulfing maelstrom of earth, smoke, and iron." Fortunately for the Canadians, however, General Falkenhausen had not adopted the new German three-tiered defensive system along all of his front, and he kept his reserve divisions farther to the rear than Ludendorff recommended.

The Canadian success, and that of Third Army, produced what Ludendorff recognized as an "extremely critical" situation. Unfortunately for the Allies, the capture of Vimy Ridge was the only major success of the Battle of Arras. Although British troops ultimately penetrated nearly four miles into the German lines, there was no breakthrough. Fifth Army under General Hubert Gough, around Bullecourt to the south, made little progress. Some of its Australian units broke through to the Hindenburg Line on 11 April but withdrew for lack of reinforcements and artillery support. With the arrival of bad weather the British advance slowed.

The Canadian seizure of Vimy Ridge is also notable for tactical changes it brought in deployment of machine guns. Up until that point machine-gun fire had been regarded as primarily defensive. The Vimy Ridge battle demonstrated its offensive potential. The Canadians used numbers of machine guns to lay down offensive barrages both during the Vimy Ridge battle and the later Messines operation. This was facilitated by having a divisional commander of machine-gun operations. At first they were advisory only. By January of 1918, however, divisional machine-gun commanders were given command over all machine guns in their divisions.

Despite the tactical success of the capture of Vimy Ridge, the Battle of Arras failed to achieve a breakthrough. The Germans were able to patch their lines and none of their reserves were drawn away from the Aisne front. Total British casualties in the battle were 84,000, while the Germans sustained about 75,000.

The capture of Vimy Ridge was the high point of Canadian arms in the First World War. One historian has written of it, "Canada became a nation on the slopes of Vimy Ridge." On being ennobled after the war, Byng took the title of Baron Byng of Vimy.

Spencer C. Tucker

References
Falls, Cyril. *The Great War, 1914–1918*. New York: Capricorn, 1961.
Stokesbury, James L. *A Short History of World War I*. New York: William Morrow, 1981.
Travers, Tim. *The Killing Ground: The British Army, the Western Front, and the Emergence of Modern Warfare*. Boston: Allen and Unwin, 1987.
Williams, Jefferey. *Byng of Vimy*. London: Leo Cooper, 1983.

See also ARTOIS, SECOND BATTLE OF; ARTOIS, THIRD BATTLE OF; BYNG, JULIAN; CANADA, ARMY; NIVELLE OFFENSIVE

Vittorio Veneto Campaign, 1918

The last major action on the Italian front and the last battle fought by the Austro-Hungarian army began on 24 October 1918. In a phased offensive across the Piave River and northward into the Alps, fifty-seven divisions (fifty-one Italian, three British, two French, and one Czechoslovak) pounced on the Austro-Hungarian Isonzo, Sixth, Eleventh, and Tenth armies and the so-called Belluno Group. While the two sides were roughly equal in numbers, the Austro-Hungarian troops were under-nourished, under-equipped, and out-gunned. More important, growing political unrest at home and the incipient disintegration of the Dual Monarchy into its constituent ethnic parts seriously affected the morale of many Austro-Hungarian regiments. Indeed, even before the Allies struck, incidents of collective undiscipline and of outright mutiny had erupted in several Austro-Hungarian divisions.

Between 23 and 27 October several Allied divisions, with the British 7th Division in the van, secured a number of bridgeheads across the Piave River and advanced eastward. Farther north, in the Grappa Mountains, the Italian Fourth Army, under General Gaetano Giardino, encountered tenacious resistance and lost almost 35,000 men within three days. The Italian Sixth Army, which included the 24th French and the 48th British Divisions, likewise ran into fierce opposition on the Asiago Plateau.

By 28 October, however, Allied troops in several regions began to make better progress. On the evening of 29 October, Italian advance guards reached Vittorio Veneto and thereafter closely followed Field Marshal Svetozar Boroević von Bojna's army group during its retreat across the Venetian Plain. On 31 October units of the Italian Fourth Army seized the town of Feltre; the next morning the Italian Eighth Army, commanded by General Enrico Caviglia, reached Belluno. During the next two days, more and more units of the Austro-Hungarian army joined the general retreat toward the frontiers of the Hapsburg Empire, though they often fought back if approached by Allied pursuit columns. In some areas, the retreating troops engaged in massive looting or commandeered railway trains to carry them home.

Faced with growing unrest both in the various regions of the empire and in the rear areas of the Italian theater of war, the Austro-Hungarian High Command dispatched an armistice commission to the front. Headed by General Viktor Weber von Webenau, the commission crossed the Italian lines in the Adige (Etsch) Valley on the evening of 30 October and was then taken to Villa Giusti, near Padua and Italian general headquarters at Ábano. On the morning of 1 November the deputy chief of the

Italian general staff, General Pietro Badoglio, presented a preliminary version of the Allied Armistice terms to General Weber, who declared himself unable to accept them without commission motored back to Trent, from where they telegraphed the Allied demands to the Austro-Hungarian High Command at Baden (ten miles south of Vienna).

Like Weber, the chief of the Austro-Hungarian general staff, Colonel General Arthur Baron Arz von Straussenburg, was shocked by the Allied terms, but, during a meeting with Emperor Karl on the morning of 2 November, he nevertheless recommended their acceptance. Since the Allies were demanding the immediate evacuation of certain Alpine and coastal regions of the Dual Monarchy, including all of South Tyrol up to the Brenner Pass, as well as the right to move their own troops through Austria-Hungary (for action against Germany's southern flank), Emperor Karl decided that further consultations, especially with the German High Command and with representatives of the newly formed German-Austrian state council, were required. After much agonizing, and faced with a high-handed decree issued by the war minister of Count Mihály Károlyi's newly formed revolutionary government in Budapest that all Hungarian troops were to lay down their arms, late on 2 November Karl authorized the conclusion of the Armistice. This decision was communicated to Trent (for further transmission to General Weber) at 01:20 on 3 November. About a half hour later the two Austro-Hungarian army group headquarters on the Italian front were informed by telephone that the Allied Armistice terms had been accepted and that "all hostilities on land and in the air are to be terminated immediately."

As a result of these instructions, many Austro-Hungarian units prematurely laid down their arms during the next thirty-six hours; for while the Armistice Agreement was duly signed on the early afternoon (15:00) of 3 November, the Italians insisted that the cease-fire could be implemented only twenty-four hours later. In consequence, a large number of Austro-Hungarian soldiers were rounded up by Allied troops and treated as prisoners of war prior to the afternoon of 4 November.

The total Allied bag, probably over 400,000 enlisted men and officers of the Austro-Hungarian army, including twenty-four generals, marked the end of an era. It also gave rise to lively controversy in subsequent years, with some historians denouncing the Austro-Hungarian military authorities for their alleged incompetence. Others have suggested that the capture of so many Austro-Hungarian soldiers during the last thirty-six hours of the war was a blessing in disguise, as it removed, at least temporarily, the threat of further massive looting and chaos from the rear areas. What is clear is that during the last campaign of the Austro-Hungarian army many of its regiments, including those recruited from the various ethnic minorities of the Dual Monarchy, fought with exceptional bravery until the bitter end.

Ulrich Trumpener

References

Edmonds, Sir James E., and H.R. Davies. *History of the Great War: Military Operations Italy, 1915–1919*. London: HMSO, 1949.

Glaise von Horstenau, Edmund, et al. *Oesterreich-Ungarns letzter Krieg 1914–1918*. Vol. 7. Vienna: Verlag der militärwissenschaftlichen Mitteilungen, 1938.

Hanks, Ronald W. "Vae Victis! The Austro-Hungarian Armeeoberkommando and the Armistice of Villa Giusti." *Austrian History Yearbook* 14 (1978).

Jedlicka, Ludwig. *Vom alten zum neuen Oesterreich*. St. Pölten: Verlag Niederösterreichisches Pressehaus, 1975.

Regele, Oskar. *Gericht über Habsburgs Wehrmacht*. Vienna: Herold, 1968.

See also AUSTRIA-HUNGARY, ARMY, HOME FRONT; BOROEVIĆ VON BOJNA, SVETOZAR; ITALY, ARMY; KARL I; KÁROLYI, MIHÁLY

Viviani, René (1862–1925)

French socialist and premier, born in Sidi-Bel-Abbés, Algeria, on 8 November 1862, the son of an Italian immigrant. Viviani began his career as a Parisian attorney representing labor unions, which brought him into socialist circles. With fellow socialists Jean Jaurès and Alexandre Millerand, he gained a national reputation, editing several Leftist newspapers and playing an active role in the well-publicized strike of the Carmaux glassworkers in 1893. In that same year he won election to the Chamber of Deputies as an independent socialist.

Viviani's socialism was reformist, not revolutionary, and he supported Millerand's controversial 1898 decision to accept a cabinet post in the government of René Waldeck-Rousseau. Although he was one of the founders of the new socialist daily, *L'Humanité*, in 1904, he declined to join the unified socialist party (SFIO) that was created in the same year. Two years later, he accepted Georges Clemenceau's offer of the new cabinet office of minister of labor, a post he continued to hold in the subsequent Briand government.

His appointment as premier by conservative president Raymond Poincaré in June of 1914 reflected both Viviani's political moderation (he was willing to support the new Three Year Law extending military service) and the president's desire to neutralize radical and SFIO opposition in parliament and to guide French foreign policy. Viviani, who lacked experience in foreign affairs, formed his government on the eve of Sarajevo, and he repeatedly looked to Poincaré for guidance as the July crisis deepened.

Initially untroubled by the assassination of Franz Ferdinand and unaware of the diplomatic initiatives being pursued in Berlin and Vienna, Viviani and Poincaré left Paris on 15 July for a state visit to Russia, Sweden, and Denmark. The trip, on the battleship *France,* left them effectively out of contact with their government for days at a time. Viviani played little role in the inconclusive negotiations in St. Petersburg (20–23 July), and the French delegation was back at sea when the Austrian ultimatum to Serbia was delivered (late on 23 July). Only on 27 July did the escalating crisis cause them to cut short their visit to Denmark. In the few days of peace that remained, French policy was shaped largely by Poincaré, who had long been committed to a policy of "firmness" toward Germany, and French ambassador to Russia Michael Paléologue, who independently encouraged Russian mobilization.

Viviani continued as premier, deferring to Poincaré on political matters and leaving General Joffre a free hand in military ones. French defeats forced him to surrender leadership of the government to Briand in October of 1915, though he remained in the cabinet. Viviani carried out diplomatic missions and held postwar cabinet posts, but his failure as a wartime premier marked the real end of his political influence. He died near Paris on 6 September 1925.

David L. Longfellow

References

Keiger, John F.V. *France and the Origins of the First World War*. London: Macmillan, 1983.

King, Jere Clemens. *Generals and Politicians*. Berkeley: University of California Press, 1951.

See also BRIAND, ARISTIDE; FRANCE, HOME FRONT; OUTBREAK OF THE FIRST WORLD WAR; POINCARÉ, RAYMOND

War Aims

Prior to the assassination of Archduke Franz Ferdinand on 28 June 1914 and the subsequent outbreak of war, all of the countries of Europe that became involved had national aspirations, desires for territorial expansion or economic aggrandizement, and concerns of national security. The occurrence of war transformed these wishes into the more formal and specific category of war aims. The fortunes of war brought modifications of these aims, as would the pressing needs to keep allies happy and to attract additional supporters. Still, each of the participants would cling to its original hopes for as long as possible. The war aims of each power are presented in the order of entry into the war.

Austria-Hungary

By the summer of 1914 Austria-Hungary faced a number of difficulties, including rebellious ethnic minorities, internal erosion within the multinational empire, the decline of her position among the great powers, and the annoyance and danger posed by burgeoning Serbian nationalism. The assassination of Archduke Franz Ferdinand afforded the pretext and moral justification for dealing directly with the Serbian issue and indirectly with the other matters causing concern. Austrian Foreign Minister Count Leopold Berchtold and chief of the general staff Franz Conrad von Hötzendorf were convinced that Serbia must be eliminated as a threat to the Dual Monarchy's security. Therefore, the war aims of Austria-Hungary were to impose a military defeat on Serbia that would eliminate that country's appeal to the Serbian and Croatian minorities of the empire, result in the dissolution of the Serbian state, expand the empire southward, and check Russian influence in the Balkans. A speedy victory in a localized war, which was the original intent, would restore the empire's international prestige and serve as an object lesson to recalcitrant minorities within the Dual Monarchy.

Serbia

Once Serbia's response to the Austrian ultimatum was declared unacceptable and war declared, the primary war aim for the Balkan nation was survival against the larger and stronger foe. The nationalistic aspirations that had caused Serbia to be a bothersome pest to Austria-Hungary, however, remained in the hearts of Serbs and on the planning tables of the Serbian government. Specifically, Serbia wanted to annex Bosnia-Herzegovina, Croatia, Slovenia, and the Dalmatian coast of the Adriatic. Those acquisitions, accompanied by a merger with Montenegro, would produce the new nation of Yugoslavia.

Germany

Germany's prewar intentions and responsibility for the outbreak of war have been debated extensively. Regardless of any conclusions reached pertaining to those issues, once the war began, Germany's aims became a matter of record and were very specific. The primary objective was to strengthen the state through annexations and hegemony in central Europe. German Chancellor Theobald von Bethmann Hollweg wanted to strip Russia of its Polish territory along with the Baltic provinces. Those regions would be established as a puppet buffer state or annexed directly to Germany; these gains would safeguard German security and provide opportunities for economic development. In the West, German plans for "security" included the conquest of

Belgium and Holland for use as protective buffers. France would have to cede Belfort, the western slopes of the Vosges, the coastal strip from Dunkirk to Boulogne, and the ore field of Briey. Furthermore, France would be required to pay a significant war indemnity and sign an economic treaty whereby trade with Great Britain would be prohibited.

Germany also planned to create a central European economic association through common customs treaties establishing German dominance over middle Europe *(Mitteleuropa)*. Additional economic benefits would be derived from the acquisition of the French and Belgian Congo regions, thereby ensuring control of central Africa. By enticing Turkey into the war on the side of the Central Powers, Germany sought to secure her economic interests in the Middle East. Despite the fluctuations in the fortunes of war, these German goals remained remarkably constant until defeat became inevitable.

Russia

One of Russia's war aims was manifested in the assurances offered Serbia and the mobilization of Russian forces in July of 1914; that aim was to maintain and even enhance Russian influence in the Balkans. Sensitive to its humiliating defeat in the Russo-Japanese War and the embarrassment of concession in the Bosnian Crisis of 1908, Russian leadership feared that another retreat would permanently undermine her influence in the Balkans and further erode her international standing. Russian support of Serbia was crucial for the continuance of the Pan-Slav Movement and also for the prevention of the spread of Austro-German hegemony in the Balkans and Turkey. Czarist advisors also argued that war would rally Russians behind the monarchy, shaken by the Revolution of 1905.

Russia also hoped to expand her interests in the Balkans with hopes for reaching the Aegean Sea. The longtime quest for free passage through the Bosphorus and Dardanelles was dependent on the preservation of Serbia and Romania as buffer states.

France

Many of the French war aims derived from prewar foreign policy objectives that, in turn, were often generated by the desire to redress the humiliating defeat of the Franco-Prussian War. France perceived an aggressively rising Germany as a threat to the balance of power in Europe, and German success would work to the detriment of French fortunes and status.

When war began, the first priority was to repel the invasion and, ultimately, emerge victorious over the enemies. The prolongation of the war made the formulation of specific war aims a necessity in order to justify the carnage and expense incurred. The most pressing aim was to clear northern France of the invaders and to reunite Alsace-Lorraine with the homeland. A subsequent major aim was to eliminate Germany permanently as a threat to the security of France. To do that France intended to acquire for itself the Saar Basin, make further territorial acquisitions in the Rhineland, create buffer states such as an independent Hanoverian kingdom, return all of Schleswig to Denmark, and establish a large independent Poland. France also desired the dissolution of Germany's colonial empire, with some of the territories becoming French possessions.

Great Britain

When Germany declared war on France and violated Belgian neutrality, Great Britain had the moral justification required to enter the war as a member of the Entente. Immediate goals were to free Belgium and return the Low Countries to their former positions as buffers, and to retain France as a major European power to counteract German aspirations of hegemony. The British also expected that victory would eliminate the German naval challenge to British supremacy. The war provided the opportunity to deprive Germany of coaling stations, bases, and raw materials. Impediments to British control of Africa posed by German Southwest Africa and, especially, German East Africa could be removed by fighting the war to a successful conclusion. These objectives, along with acquiring Germany's Pacific possessions, constituted the war aims of Great Britain.

Japan

Japan had emerged from diplomatic isolation in 1902 with the signing of the Anglo-Japanese Alliance. When warfare began in Europe, Japan eagerly wanted to intervene on the side of its alliance partner. The British prevailed upon the Japanese to show restraint, however—but only for a short time. On 23 August 1914 Japan declared war on Germany so that its war aims could be effected. Very simply, Japan coveted and proceeded to seize the German sphere of influence and holdings on the Shantung Peninsula as well as some of the German Pacific islands.

Turkey

Turkey concluded a secret treaty with Germany, directed against Russia, in July of 1914 and openly joined the Central Powers in the autumn of that year. Turkey's motivations were to thwart Russian expansion into the Balkans, regain some territory and control in that region, recover prestige lost during the Balkan Wars, and get a measure of revenge for British intrusion into Egypt.

Italy

Although Italy had been a member of the Triple Alliance since 1882, by 1914 Italy's ties to the Central Powers had loosened, especially since the interests of Italy and those of Austria-Hungary were often in conflict. After Austria delivered the ultimatum to Serbia without consulting Italy and, after Austria declared war on Serbia, Italy claimed that she was not bound by the alliance to take part in an aggressive war or to fight against the British. Consequently, the government issued a declaration of neutrality on 3 August 1914.

As the war stretched on into 1915, the Allied Powers let it be known that neutrals could expect few gains at the peace table. More important, inducements in the form of territorial concessions were offered to Italy. On 26 April 1915, Italy signed with the Entente powers the Treaty of London whereby, in return for the fulfillment of her territorial ambitions (the Trentino, the Tyrol, Trieste, Gorizia, Istria, and Dalmatia to the Cape Planka), Italy was to join the Entente by declaring war within one month. On 23 May 1915, Italy entered the war as an Allied nation.

Bulgaria

When war began in 1914, Bulgaria was still smarting from its defeat in the Second Balkan War and the terms of the Treaty of Bucharest (10 August 1913). After the government of Vasil Radoslavov was refused a loan by Great Britain, France, and Russia, it turned to the Central Powers and, in July of 1914, obtained a loan from German sources. Thereafter, Bulgaria leaned toward the Central Powers.

Bulgaria's foremost aim was to regain Macedonia and to secure the return of lost territory in the Dobrudja. Neither Serbia nor Greece would cede parts of Macedonia, and thus Bulgaria sought concessions from the Central Powers, which were granted. Consequently, on 6 September 1915, Bulgaria signed an alliance treaty at Pless and declared war on Serbia on 12 October 1915.

Romania

Romania, like Italy, renounced her alliance with the Central Powers, and joined the Entente on 17 August 1916 after signing a treaty guaranteeing the desired territorial acquisitions. Great Britain, France, Russia, and Italy promised Romania the Banat, Transylvania, the Hungarian plain to the Tisza River, and Bukovina as far as the Prut River. Romania declared war on Austria-Hungary on 22 August 1916.

Greece

On 29 June 1917 Greece declared war on the Central Powers. Greek war aims were twofold: protection from Bulgarian and Turkish expansionism, and the acquisition of Bulgaria's Aegean coastline.

Edward L. Byrd, Jr.
Ingrid P. Westmoreland

References

Fay, Sidney B. *The Origins of the World War.* 2 vols. New York: Macmillan, 1966.

Fischer, Fritz. *Germany's Aims in the First World War.* New York: Norton, 1967.

Schmitt, Bernadotte E. *The Coming of the War 1914.* 2 vols. New York: Charles Scribner's Sons, 1930.

Taylor, A.J.P. *The War Aims of the Allies in the First World War.* Essays presented to Sir Lewis Namier. London: Macmillan, 1956.

See also ALLIANCES, PREWAR; ORIGINS OF THE FIRST WORLD WAR; OUTBREAK OF THE FIRST WORLD WAR

Warships: Aircraft Carriers

No true aircraft carrier had emerged by the end of World War I. Nonetheless, carrier operations did take place and what could be termed "proto-carriers" were put into service by the Royal Navy and the Imperial Japanese Navy. These early "carriers" were used for spotting, reconnaissance, and anti-zeppelin duties. None were built as carriers from the keel up but were converted on the stocks or afterwards. In World War I only the Royal Navy used carriers in combat.

The designers of World War I carriers focused on the qualities of high speed and endurance, plus large storage capacity, which have characterized aircraft carriers to the present day. One characteristic not achieved until just before the Armistice of November 1918 was the uninterrupted flight deck for both takeoffs and landings, the final configuration necessary for a true carrier.

Although aircraft had successfully flown off ships before 1914, the problem lay in aircraft retrieval or in their landing. Carrier landings, even at the present time, are difficult and dangerous, and the development of routine, safe procedures took time. All seaplane carrier aircraft of the World War I era required long takeoff space, leaving them little room for landing platforms. (It should be noted, however, that some landplanes were able to take off from platforms [atop gun turrets] little longer than the planes themselves.) Various expedients attempted to circumvent the problem. Landplanes were flown off ships and then landed ashore; but this defeated the long-range advantage of carrier-based aviation. Wheeled aircraft could put down in the sea after their missions and be written off, but this was an expensive and dangerous procedure and one obviously not suitable for sustained operations.

Seaplanes could take off from carriers, land nearby, and then be hoisted back on board. The large floats affixed beneath seaplanes exacted a heavy performance penalty since no seaplane could match a landplane's performance. Seaplanes could be lost almost as easily as landplanes if they put down in rough waters. They were often damaged in landing, and the hoisting process was laborious. Plus, the dangerous situation of seaplanes lined up alongside a carrier awaiting retrieval in combat or during a storm hardly needs emphasizing.

Despite these problems, the Royal Navy persevered, utilizing carrier-based aircraft throughout the war. Seaplanes from the *Ark Royal* bombed Turkish positions and shipping in the Dardanelles and were active over the Western Front. On 7 July 1918 seven Camel aircraft flying from HMS *Furious* struck the zeppelin sheds at Tondern, destroying two sheds and two zeppelins (L54 and L60) inside. One of the most famous exploits of the Royal Naval Air Service (RNAS) involved the shooting down by a carrier-based landplane of a German zeppelin, a feat practically impossible by the lumbering seaplanes of the time. Obviously, some way had to be found to enable landplanes, with their superior performance, to land on carriers.

HMS *Ark Royal* could be considered the first "proto-carrier," as she was converted while still in frame from a bulk cargo ship to a seaplane tender. At roughly the same time, the Japanese similarly converted their *Wakamiya*. *Ark Royal's* conversion was encouraged by First Lord of the Admiralty Winston Churchill who was anxious to secure a zeppelin interceptor.

HMS *Argus* was the first carrier built with a landing deck, but was preceded in service by HMS *Furious* and *Vindictive*. *Furious* was one of a trio of "very large, light cruisers, the other two being *Courageous* and *Glorious*, designed for use against the Germans in the Baltic. (In the fleet these bizarre warships were often facetiously termed HMS "Curious," "Outrageous," and "Uproarious.") All three were converted to carriers, beginning with *Furious* (the latter two were not converted until the mid 1920s). All three carriers featured takeoff and landing platforms for landplanes, but these decks were still separated by a superstructure and pilots found the landing deck too short and funnel gases interfering with their touch-downs.

With her flush landing and takeoff deck, HMS *Argus* was the world's first true aircraft carrier and the answer to the problem of landing wheeled aircraft at sea. The *Argus* had no deck structure at all, machinery gases were diverted by horizontal funnels and the charthouse was poised on a retractable hydraulic piston. Converted from the unfinished Italian liner *Conte Rosso*, the *Argus* did not carry out her sea trials until October 1918. Although the war ended before her air complement could be put to use, *Argus* pointed the way for carrier development in the years to come.

Stanley Sandler

References

Chesneau, R. *Aircraft Carriers of the World, 1914 to the Present: An Illustrated Encyclopedia.* Annapolis, Md.: Naval Institute Press, 1984.

Layman, R.D. *Before the Aircraft Carrier: The Development of Aviation Vessels, 1849–1922.* Annapolis, Md.: Naval Institute Press, 1989.

MacIntyre, Donald. *Aircraft Carrier: The Magnificent Weapon.* New York: Ballantine Books, 1972.

Melhorn, Charles M. *Two-Block Fox: The Rise of the Aircraft Carrier, 1911–1929.*

Annapolis, Md.: Naval Institute Press, 1974.

See also GREAT BRITAIN, NAVY

Warships: Battle Cruisers

The battle cruiser was a hybrid warship—a ship with the speed of a cruiser and the gun power of a battleship. To gain these characteristics, the ship sacrificed armor protection. An outgrowth of the large armored cruiser, the battle cruiser was the creation of Admiral Sir John Fisher. Designed to reconnoiter by pushing through the enemy's cruiser screen to his battleships, the battle cruiser could undertake other missions such as screening for its own battle line and hunting down enemy raiders.

The first battle cruiser was HMS *Invincible,* the lead ship of a class of three. Laid down in 1906 and built in great secrecy, *Invincible* carried an armament of eight 12-inch guns; the turbine machinery of 41,000 hp gave it a maximum speed of twenty-five knots. Armor was skimpy: 6 inches on the belt and 7 inches on the turret faces. For Fisher, the trade-off was merited. More armor would simply "handicap the racehorses," he said. The later British battle cruisers followed this same formula: The three ships of the Indefatigable class were quite similar to the Invincibles, but the three later ships of the Lion class introduced the 13.5-inch weapon. With eight of these guns and speed increased to twenty-eight knots, the "Splendid Cats" (*Lion, Princess Royal,* and half-sister

Queen Mary) enjoyed a great reputation with the press and public. HMS *Tiger,* close to completion when the war began, was similar but with an improved armament distribution. None of these ships had armor protection against 12-inch projectiles; in many vital areas 11-inch shells would penetrate as well.

The first German replies to the British initiatives were belated and seemed unimpressive. *Von der Tann,* their first battle cruiser, carried eight 11-inch guns, and armament increased in number (to ten) but not in caliber in the *Goeben, Moltke,* and *Seydlitz.* In 1912 the Germans finally went to the 12-inch gun, with eight in *Derfflinger* and her two near sisters, *Lützow* and *Hindenburg.* Advertised speeds for these ships generally lagged behind the sometimes inflated British figures. But the German numbers were conservative, and in service their ships proved as fast as their British counterparts. In the less visible aspect of protection the German warships were significantly superior, with thicker armor and better damage-control measures.

Although most other major navies considered constructing battle cruisers, only the Japanese and Russians began ships of this type before the outbreak of the war. The czarist ships of the Borodino class were all laid down in 1913 but were never completed. By 1915 the Japanese commissioned the four ships of the Kongo class, with the lead ship being built in Britain by Vickers. Excellent vessels with a powerful main battery of eight 14-inch guns and a top speed of 27.5 knots, they patrolled in the Pacific dur-

BATTLE CRUISERS OF THE BELLIGERENTS

	Complete as of 1/8/14	Building as of 1/8/14	Begun after 1/8/14	Finished during the War	Lost	On Hand as of 11/11/18
Germany	4	3	5	3	1	5*
Great Britain	9	1	9	6	3	11**
Japan	1	3	—	3	—	4
Russia	—	4	—	—	—	—
Turkey	—	—	—	—	—	1*
Totals	14	11	14	12	4	21

*This disparity in numbers is because of the transfer during the war of SMS *Goeben* to the Turks, who renamed the ship *Yavuz Sultan Selim.*

**By 1918 HMS *Furious* had been stripped of her main gun armament and converted to an aircraft carrier.

ing World War I and gave good service in World War II.

The outbreak of hostilities in 1914 placed the battle cruiser quickly in the spotlight. In the Mediterranean, SMS *Goeben* was the first of her type to fire shots in anger when she shelled Philippeville, Algeria. Instrumental in bringing Turkey into the war on the side of the Central Powers, the battle cruiser remained throughout the conflict a constant irritant to the Allies. She bombarded Russian ports, skirmished with czarist battleships, and sank the British monitors *M28* and *Raglan* in 1918.

In the North Sea battle cruisers were the first capital ships to engage the enemy. On 28 August 1914, at Heligoland Bight, British battle cruisers under Vice Admiral David Beatty easily sank two German light cruisers (SMS *Ariadne* and *Köln*) very close to their bases.

Further validation for Fisher's creation came on 8 December 1914, when Vice Admiral Doveton Sturdee's squadron of *Invincible* and *Inflexible* ran down and destroyed the armored cruisers *Scharnhorst* and *Gneisenau* of Vice Admiral Graf von Spee's squadron off the Falklands. Sturdee used his speed advantage to keep his battle cruisers at a range where their armor was proof against the German fire. In almost five hours of deliberate firing, the British sank both of the German ships without serious damage to themselves.

Events in 1915 cast the first shadows on the reputation of the battle cruiser. On 24 January the clash at Dogger Bank showed again the inferiority of the conventional cruiser to the battle cruiser, when Beatty's force sank the German armored cruiser *Blücher*. This action, however, for the first time pointed to the fragility of the larger warship. HMS *Lion* was damaged and out of action for four months; SMS *Seydlitz* barely avoided a magazine explosion.

Less than two months later, on 18 March, *Inflexible* took part in Vice Admiral Sackville H. Carden's attempt to force the Narrows at Gallipoli. Hit by Turkish artillery fire, the battle cruiser also struck a mine. She limped off with two thousand tons of water aboard and reached Malta only with great difficulty.

These blemishes aside, wartime experience seemed to validate the basic soundness of the battle cruiser concept. Back in office as first sea lord, Fisher managed to win Parliamentary backing for five additional ships: the two Renowns and the three "large light cruisers" of the Courageous type. The first four were armed

with 15-inch guns (six in the *Renown* and *Repulse*; four in *Courageous* and *Glorious*), while the *Furious* was designed to carry two 18-inch pieces. Speed was very high—about thirty-one knots—and armor was correspondingly light, with belts of only three inches on the last ships. Late in 1915 the admiralty also began plans for four much larger ships. The first, HMS *Hood,* was laid down on 31 May 1916.

The Germans, for their part, initiated an ambitious wartime construction program. Following their preference for better protection, the seven ships of the Mackensen type, begun or ordered in 1915, were to be armored with 11.8-inch belts. Their main battery was upgraded to eight heavy guns of almost 14-inch (350mm) caliber.

In 1916 the United States Navy, after years of deliberation, finally followed the British footsteps by seeking Congressional approval for six ships of the Lexington class. To carry ten 14-inch guns at thirty-five knots, the vessels sacrificed protection by mounting thin armor (5-inch belt) and by placing half the boilers above the armored deck.

On the very day that HMS *Hood* was begun, the Battle of Jutland (31 May–1 June 1916) threw all these calculations into limbo. In that clash the German battle cruiser design seemed vindicated. True, *Lützow* sank, but she took tremendous punishment before sinking. *Seydlitz* managed to return to base despite 5,329 tons of water aboard, after having suffered hits from a torpedo and twenty-two large projectiles. *Derfflinger, Moltke,* and *von der Tann* also survived serious damage. The British record was different: three battle cruisers lost to catastrophic magazine explosions *(Invincible, Indefatigable,* and *Queen Mary), *while the *Lion* narrowly escaped a like fate.

Although the British cordite ammunition was largely to blame, this experience cast a pall over the lightly armored battle cruiser. Fisher's five ships were too far along to alter substantially. As they entered the fleet, their lack of armor made them highly suspect. When *Courageous* and *Glorious* saw their only action (on 27 November 1917), they suffered more damage from German light forces than they inflicted.

For those battle cruisers in embryo, Jutland caused both the British and Americans to revise their specifications. The Royal Navy stopped construction of the Hood class and recast the design to incorporate significantly more armor, thereby turning the ships into fast battleships in all but name. American planners also reworked the Lexington drawings to incorporate better protective measures.

In the end, none of these later ships were completed during the war. The Germans, with their naval focus increasingly on the submarine, halted the Mackensens in 1917. Consequently, the British proceeded only with *Hood,* her three sisters being canceled in 1918. During the last year of the war, the entire American battle cruiser program was suspended in favor of the more needed antisubmarine craft. Resurrected after the Armistice, the six Lexingtons were laid down in 1920 and 1921 but the Washington Naval Treaty of 1922 stopped work on them again. Two were ultimately completed as aircraft carriers.

As a type, the battle cruiser saw more action in World War I than did the slower battleships. When pitted against lesser craft, it performed up to expectations. Used against other big-gun ships, its lack of protection proved a severe flaw. The German designs, offering superior defensive measures and thicker armor, better withstood the test of combat; they thereby helped lay the later pattern for a melding of the protection of the battleship with the speed of the battle cruiser into the fast battleship.

Malcolm Muir, Jr.

References

Conway's All the World's Fighting Ships 1906–1921. Annapolis, Md.: Naval Institute Press, 1985.

Parkes, Oscar. *British Battleships, "Warrior" 1860 to "Vanguard" 1950; a History of Design, Construction and Armament.* London: Seeley Service, c. 1957.

Sturton, Ian, ed. *Conway's All the World's Battleships: 1906 to the Present.* Annapolis, Md.: Naval Institute Press, 1987.

Young, Filson. *With the Battle Cruisers.* Annapolis, Md.: Naval Institute Press. Reprint. 1986.

See also DARDANELLES CAMPAIGN; DOGGER BANK, NAVAL BATTLE OF; FALKLANDS, BATTLE OF; FISHER, JOHN; GERMANY, NAVY; GREAT BRITAIN, NAVY; HELIGOLAND BIGHT, BATTLE OF; JUTLAND, BATTLE OF

Warships: Battleships

By definition a battleship was a naval vessel carrying the heaviest guns and protected by the thickest armor. Speed was generally sacrificed for offensive and defensive power, with most new battleships in the World War I era capable of about twenty-one knots. Regarded as the backbone of any significant fleet, the battleship rested its reputation in part on the writings of naval theoreticians such as Alfred Thayer Mahan and Sir Julian Corbett, and in part on historical precedent dating from the Spanish Armada and running through recent experiences in the Russo-Japanese War of 1904–5.

All modern battleships carried a mixed gun battery of heavy (from 10- to 13-inch), medium (from 5- to 9.4-inch), and light pieces. Following the revolution wrought by the *Dreadnought,* every power with significant naval aspirations embarked on a battleship building program. A race ensued, which led to the commissioning of ever larger and more powerful warships. For example, in six years British battleships grew in size from the *Dreadnought,* commissioned in 1906 (21,845 tons at full load, ten 12-inch guns, 11-inch belt armor, 21 knots), to *Orion* of 1912 (25,870 tons, ten 13.5-inch guns, 12-inch belt, 21 knots). Three years later, *Queen Elizabeth* was commissioned at 31,500 tons, eight 15-inch guns, 13-inch belt, and 24 knots.

Battleship growth in other navies was similar. For instance, the first German dreadnoughts of the Nassau class displaced 21,000 tons, were armed with twelve 11-inch guns, and were protected by belt armor twelve inches thick. By 1914 the kaiser's fleet had under construction the Bayern-class of 31,690 tons, carrying eight 15-inch guns and a belt of fourteen inches.

Behind these figures lay large increases in fighting power. The German 11-inch gun fired a shell weighing 666 pounds; the 15-inch, 1653 pounds. Higher gun elevations led to longer ranges, while improved fire control equipment allowed for hits at those distances. Oil fuel, introduced to battleships in the fine Queen Elizabeth class, offered numerous advantages in transportation, in handling, and especially (with its greater thermal efficiency) in higher speeds.

Other notable improvements in battleship design included new schemes for armor protection and better arrangement of the main battery. With the Nevada class, the United States introduced the "all-or-nothing" principal by omitting most armor of medium thickness to secure the maximum protection for the ship's vitals—the magazines and machinery spaces. Italy led the way in economical gun layout by substituting the triple turret for the double in the *Dante Alighieri*.

With virtually all the British battleships of the Grand Fleet concentrated in August of 1914 at Scapa Flow and Rosyth and those of the German High Seas Fleet at the Jade, most observers expected an immediate Armageddon in the North Sea. Instead, battleships saw no action in those waters for almost two years. The commanders of both forces played a generally cautious hand. Because the construction time for the average dreadnought measured about three years, combat losses could probably not be replaced in the course of the struggle. It is instructive to note that before the Armistice only two of the warring powers—Japan and the United States—finished battleships started after August of 1914. Indeed, many navies stopped work altogether on those battleships that were not close to completion.

Dreadnought stalemate reigned elsewhere during most of the war as well. In the Mediterranean French and Italian battleships engaged in convoy duties and watched the four innovative Austro-Hungarian ships of the Tegetthoff class, moored at Pola for most of the war. The Tegetthoffs did bombard the Italian coast in May of 1915 but emerged again only in June of 1918 to attack the Otranto barrage, an operation canceled upon the loss of the *Szent István*.

In the Baltic the four new Russian battleships principally constituted a fleet for defense of the capital. Plans to use them more vigorously in 1915 and again in 1917 were thwarted by mutinous crews. In the Black Sea the Russian vessels of the Imperatritsa Maria class took an active role in bombarding Turkish and Bulgarian positions and in escorting convoys, during which operations they exchanged fire on several occasions with their Turkish/German opponents. As for the Pacific, Japan kept her growing fleet of powerful capital ships in home waters.

Only one major engagement between dreadnought battleships took place, the Battle of Jutland on 31 May–1 June 1916, which demonstrated just how much damage those ships could take from shellfire. For example, HMS *Warspite* was struck by fifteen heavy projectiles and remained in action; on the other side, the German *König* was still battle-worthy after ten hits. It should be pointed out that German los-ses would doubtless have been heavier in this battle had not the British shells been too brittle, often disintegrating on impact with the German armor.

During the course of the war not one dreadnought battleship succumbed to gunfire. Underwater damage posed a greater threat. At Jutland HMS *Marlborough*, after being hit by one torpedo, which tore a hole seventy feet long amidships, kept station in the line for a time, but the damage was severe enough to require three months of repair work. On 27 October 1914, after a twelve-hour struggle, the British lost the new bat-tleship *Audacious* to a single mine. The Austro-Hungarian dreadnought *Szent István* was sunk by an Italian motor torpedo boat on 10 June 1918. On 1 November 1918 her sister, *Viribus Unitis,* just transferred to Yugoslavia, was lost at Pola to a limpet mine attached by Italian divers. In addition to these three, enemy action claimed one more dreadnought: *Leonardo da Vinci,* blown up at Taranto as a result of Austrian sabotage on 2 August 1916.

Four other dreadnoughts were destroyed during the war. The Soviets scuttled the *Svobodnaya Rossiya* (formerly *Imperatritsa Ekaterina Velikaya*) at Novorossisk on 18 June 1918, to keep her from falling into German hands. Inaction also presented hazards, with propellants becoming unstable over time. In three cases, accidental explosions claimed dreadnoughts: the Russian *Imperatritsa Mariya* on 20 October 1916; HMS *Vanguard,* 9 July 1917; and IJN *Kawachi,* 12 July 1918. Thus, of ninety-four dreadnought battleships commissioned by the belligerent powers from 1906 to 1918, only eight were lost, including three to defective ammunition.

The entry of the United States into the war in 1917 reinforced the strategic stalemate in the North Sea. Five American battleships joined the Grand Fleet as the Sixth Battle Squadron, while three others were based in Ireland to counter any German raids into the Atlantic with heavy ships. This preponderance of Allied dreadnought strength virtually ensured that the High Seas Fleet would remain at anchor. And when Admiral Franz von Hipper planned a sortie in October of 1918, his crews mutinied rather than embark on what they saw as a suicidal mission.

If the war for the dreadnoughts of all the belligerents was mostly one of watchful waiting, the older battleships, which now counted for little in the naval balance, saw significantly more action. As the following table shows, casualties for this type were greater than for the newer ships.

	On Hand as of 1/8/14	Lost	On Hand as of 11/11/18
Austria-Hungary	9	—	9
France	27	4	22 (one struck)
Germany	22	1	21
Great Britain	41	11	30
Greece	2	—	2
Italy	14	2	11 (one struck)
Japan	13	—	10 (two returned to Russia); (one struck)
Russia	12	2	12 (two from Japan)
Turkey	2	1	1
United States	23	—	23
Totals	165	21	141 (three struck)

Ironically, then, these predreadnoughts (as they were now called) frequently saw combat service in a variety of roles because they were expendable. At the very beginning of the war, the oldest battleship in the Royal Navy, HMS *Revenge* (renamed in August of 1915 *Redoubtable*), shelled German troops in Belgium, a duty later shared with other predreadnoughts although their deep draft caused them troubles in coastal waters.

Similarly, the Russians used the old battleship *Slava* aggressively and effectively in supporting troops in the Gulf of Riga area in 1915 and 1916. She proved such a thorn in the German side that the Germans went to extraordinary lengths to sink her, attacking her with aircraft on 27 April 1916 (thereby giving her the dubious distinction of being the first capital ship hit by bombs) and finally, in 1917, sending new dreadnoughts of the König class against her. On 17 October *Slava* was so damaged by *König* that the Russians scuttled her.

The largest single operation in which battleships were employed as gunfire support ships was Gallipoli in 1915. Although they succeeded in silencing many of the Turkish batteries, their attempt on 18 March 1915 to force the straits was a failure. Of the twelve British and four French battleships that took part in the attempt, only HMS *Queen Elizabeth* was a dreadnought. Three of the old battleships (HMS *Irresistible* and *Ocean,* and French *Bou-vet*) were sunk by gunfire and mines, with most of the others being damaged.

Predreadnoughts undertook a number of other roles, serving for example as guardships. The six British ships of the Canopus class were used as station ships in places as disparate as the Falklands, Murmansk, and East Africa. Other British predreadnoughts in 1914 provided escort for troop transports carrying Indian troops or the British Expeditionary Force.

A few of the oldest predreadnoughts gave up their big guns for shore batteries or for monitors. When disarmed, some then served as troopships, ammunition store ships, or accommodation ships. HMS *Jupiter* and *Albemarle* were even employed as icebreakers at Archangel.

The newest of the predreadnoughts served as the primary heavy units in secondary theaters. The British Channel Fleet was made up almost entirely of predreadnoughts, some of which eventually went to the Mediterranean and to the Adriatic to help the French and Italians contain Austrian and Turkish forces.

German Admiral Reinhardt Scheer did reluctantly employ six predreadnoughts at Jutland where their slow speed proved a significant handicap to his fleet. And the loss of SMS *Pommern* with her entire crew of 844 men to a single torpedo showed her type to be quite vulnerable to underwater damage.

Experience in other navies reinforced the general validity of this conclusion. For example, at the Dardanelles the French *Bouvet* sank in two minutes taking down 660 of her 710 men. HMS *Formidable,* torpedoed on 1 January 1915 in the Channel, went down with 547 of her 780-man complement. The French *Suffren* sank with her entire crew on 26 November 1916 when torpedoed by *U-52.* On the other hand, HMS *Cornwallis,* hit by three torpedoes from *U-32* on 9 January 1917, remained afloat long enough for all hands to be rescued except those killed by the explosion.

With the vastly increased threat posed by mines and torpedoes, resistance to underwater damage became one of the main concerns of naval architects during the war. New dreadnought plans incorporated greater internal subdivision and bulges. The other major advance in battleship design during the war came with attempts to improve shellfire at long range by increasing gun elevation, by incorporating superior range-finding equipment, and by experimenting with aerial spotting. Defenses against aircraft were only in embryonic stages. The battleship ended World War I with its reputation largely intact, but with challengers in the submarine and in aircraft already visible on the horizon.

As the following table shows, the British and the Germans were in the forefront of dreadnought strength at the beginning of the war, with the United States a close third and the other navies running well behind.

Malcolm Muir, Jr.

References

Burt, R.A. *British Battleships of World War One.* Annapolis, Md.: Naval Institute Press, 1986.

Conway's All the World's Fighting Ships 1860–1905. Annapolis, Md.: Naval Institute Press, 1979.

Friedman, Norman. *Battleship Design and Development, 1905–1945.* New York: Mayflower, 1978.

Parkes, Oscar. *British Battleships, "Warrior" 1860 to "Vanguard" 1950; a History of Design, Construction and Armament.* London: Seeley Service, c. 1957.

Smith, Myron J., Jr. *Battleships and Battle-Cruisers, 1884–1984: A Bibliography and Chronology.* New York: Garland, 1985.

Sturton, Ian, ed. *Conway's All the World's Battleships: 1906 to the Present.* Annapolis, Md.: Naval Institute Press, 1987.

Watts, Anthony J. *The Imperial Russian Navy.* London: Arms and Armour, 1990.

See also DREADNOUGHT; GERMANY, NAVY; GREAT BRITAIN, NAVY; JUTLAND, BATTLE OF

Warships: Cruisers

Like the frigate from which it descended, the cruiser of the World War I era could be characterized as a warship of medium tonnage with

DREADNOUGHTS OF THE BELLIGERENTS

	Complete as of 1/8/14	Building as of 1/8/14	Begun after 1/8/14	Finished during War	Lost	On Hand as of 11/11/18
Austria-Hungary	3	1	—	1	2	2
Brazil	2	—	—	—	—	2
France	4	8	—	3	—	7
Germany	13	7	1	6	—	19
Great Britain	20	12	—	15*	2	33
Greece	—	1	—	—	—	—
Italy	3	3	4	3	1	5
Japan	2	2	4	4	1	5
Russia	—	7	1	7	2	5
Turkey	--	3	—	—*	—	—
United States	10	4	6	6	—	16
Totals	57	48	16	45	8	94

*The Royal Navy took over three dreadnoughts being built in British yards in August of 1914, two Turkish and one Chilean.

decent armament and protection, long range, high speed, and many missions to perform. Inside these broad parameters, cruisers differed widely, however, ranging from sizable armored cruisers almost as big and expensive as battleships to light (or protected) cruisers little larger or more powerful than the biggest destroyers.

Typifying the armored cruiser was HMS *Duke of Edinburgh,* displacing close to 14,000 tons, armed with six 9.2-inch and ten 6-inch guns. Her speed was twenty-three knots; her armor belt, six inches thick. At £1.2 million, the ship, launched in 1904, cost almost exactly as much as a contemporary King Edward VII class battleship. Notwithstanding the expense, navies built large numbers of these ships, with the most powerful representatives of the genre being SMS *Blücher* (17,250 tons, twelve 8.2-inch guns, 7-inch belt, 24 knots) and the Russian *Rurik* (15,190 tons, four 10-inch and eight 8-inch guns, 6-inch belt, 21 knots).

At the other end of the scale was the protected cruiser. Many were as small as HMS *Sentinel* (2,880 tons, ten 12-pounders, 1.5-inch deck armor only, 25 knots). This sort of light cruiser was particularly favored by the Germans.

Cruisers performed several types of missions: warring on and defending trade, scouting and screening for the battle line, serving on colonial station, and leading flotillas of torpedo craft. During the Russo-Japanese War, large armored cruisers also seemed useful as a fast wing of the battle line.

The dreadnought revolution brought the very raison d'etre of the conventional cruiser into question. The armored cruiser metamorphosed into the even larger battle cruiser, with its cruiser speed and battleship armament. Certain navy leaders, such as the first sea lord Admiral Sir John Fisher, assumed that the cruiser would lose its place as scout to large destroyers. Some navies, such as the American and French, stopped building conventional cruisers altogether prior to and during the war. Others constructed the type in small numbers only (from 1906 to 1914, Italy and Japan built four each).

In sharp contrast, the British and Germans quickly concluded that destroyers lacked the military qualities, the seaworthiness, and the range to undertake all of the cruiser's tasks. By 1909 the Royal Navy had started construction of five light cruisers of the Bristol class (5,300 tons) with good speed (25 knots), decent offen-

sive power (two 6-inch and ten 4-inch guns), and some protection. These ships—and the succeeding fourteen of the improved "Town" classes—gave excellent service during the war. To lead the destroyer flotillas the British in 1911 began the high-speed HMS *Arethusa* (4,400 tons, two 6-inch and six 4-inch guns, 28.5 knots), followed by the similar but larger "C" classes, totaling thirty-six ships commissioned during the war.

The Germans built ships like HMS *Arethusa* but stuck with the 4-inch gun long after the British went to the heavier 6-inch. Typical of German cruisers of the late prewar period was SMS *Magdeburg* (4,570 tons, twelve 4.1-inch guns, 27.5 knots).

The wartime cruiser strength of the belligerents is represented in the table on page 738. Note in the table the small number of cruisers completed during the conflict, except by Britain and Germany. Also note the heavy war casualties of the British and especially the Germans, whose losses totaled almost 50 percent of their cruiser strength at the beginning of the conflict.

For their new construction during the war, the British and Germans improved the armaments of their ships in two ways. Eschewing the older broadside positioning of main battery guns, both navies moved to a centerline distribution. Second, both dropped the two-caliber battery and standardized instead on the 6-inch (British) or the 5.9-inch (German). The new light cruisers also featured better protection, partially through the fitting of thin armor belts (which had begun in 1911), and partly through better subdivision, making the ships more resistant to underwater damage.

During World War I cruisers performed every mission for which they were designed—and added some new ones. From the outbreak of the conflict, trade war occupied many cruisers. In the opening weeks, Allied cruisers searched for German merchantmen headed for home or for neutral ports. In a short span the British cruiser HMS *Falmouth* bagged four of them.

The Germans set five cruisers loose on the sea lanes, and these found rich hunting. Two had remarkable success—the *Emden* and the *Karlsruhe.* The latter captured seventeen merchant vessels off the Brazilian coast but was blown up on 14 November 1914 by an accidental explosion as she was preparing to attack the Bahamas. SMS *Dresden* and *Leipzig* took only a few prizes each, as did *Königsberg,* although

CRUISERS OF THE BELLIGERENTS

	Complete as of 1/8/14	Finished during the War	Lost	On Hand as of 11/11/18*
Austria-Hungary	9	3	2	10
Brazil	5	—	—	5
China	3	—	—	3
France	37	—	5	32
Germany	51	14	23	42
Great Britain	125	35	19	141
Greece	2	—	—	2
Italy	22	3	3	22
Japan	20	—	3	16**
Portugal	4	—	—	4
Russia	15	—	2	14**
Turkey	2	—	—	2
United States	38	—	3	35
Totals	333	55	60	328*

* Some of the oldest ships listed in this column were relegated by the end of the war to subsidiary duties.
**Soya returned to Russia as Varyag on 5 April 1916.

that ship caused the British great difficulty by her mere presence on the East African coast. Given how these few ships troubled the Allies, Vice Admiral Maximilian Graf von Spee's squadron should probably have been dispersed as raiders early in the conflict.

On three occasions outside the European theater, German cruisers sank their Allied counterparts. SMS *Königsberg* destroyed HMS *Pegasus* at Zanzibar on 20 September 1914. Little more than a month later, on 28 October, *Emden* shelled and torpedoed the Russian cruiser *Jemtchug* in Penang harbor. At Coronel on 1 November 1914, von Spee's squadron sank HMS *Good Hope* and *Monmouth* by gunfire.

Naturally, the task of chasing down these German marauders fell to Allied cruisers. HMS *Sydney* destroyed SMS *Emden* in the Cocos Islands on 9 November 1914; HMS *Cornwall* and *Glasgow* sank SMS *Leipzig* at the Falklands; and HMS *Kent* and *Glasgow* caught SMS *Dresden* in Chilean waters on 14 March 1915.

In home waters of the North Sea, the Baltic, and the Adriatic, cruisers searched for enemy units, screened their own battleships, and led destroyer flotillas. The provision of radio, which had started with the Russo-Japanese War,

greatly enhanced the cruiser's performance in the scouting mission. Commodore W.E. Goodenough's Second Light Cruiser Squadron at Jutland turned in a particularly fine performance in the reconnaissance role.

During that engagement British cruiser losses totaled three: *Defence, Black Prince,* and *Warrior*. All were obsolescent armored cruisers sunk by German gunfire. Casualties were very heavy, the first two ships blowing up with their entire complements (903 and 857, respectively). The High Seas Fleet lost four light cruisers: *Elbing, Frauenlob, Rostock,* and *Wiesbaden*. The last ship survived remarkable punishment: hits by over twenty heavy and medium projectiles, by an undetermined number of 6-inch shells, and by a torpedo. After having taken most of this damage, the cruiser was still able to fire a torpedo that crippled the British battleship *Marlborough*. All but one of *Wiesbaden*'s company of 590 died with their ship.

Some British light cruisers also survived severe damage: *Castor* was hit by ten shells (of cruiser caliber, that is, 5.9- and 4.1-inch), *Chester* by about seventeen 5.9-inchers; and Goodenough's flagship, *Southampton*, by one 11-inch and approximately twenty lighter shells. Not surprisingly, the latter two ships suffered heavy personnel casualties: eighty-nine in *Southampton* and seventy-eight in *Chester*.

Cruisers showed their usefulness in a wide variety of other roles during the war. Some older cruisers were occasionally used as minelayers— as, for instance, was the Japanese *Takachiho* when she was sunk at Tsingtao on 17 October 1914. The Russians particularly favored this sort of warfare, and they modified their largest armored cruiser, *Rurik,* to carry four hundred mines. This ship undertook sorties into the Baltic during the winter of 1914–15 when ice made operations by thin-hulled destroyers impossible. On one such foray, in February of 1915, *Rurik* grounded on the Swedish island of Gotland and was salvaged only with the greatest difficulty.

The Germans also employed certain of their older cruisers for mining. *Berlin* carried out the most productive mission, laying the mine that sank the new British battleship HMS *Audacious.* In 1915 the Germans began construction of two cruisers, *Brummer* and *Bremse,* specifically designed for minelaying. With a twenty-eight knot speed, they carried a light main battery of four 5.9-inch guns plus four hundred mines. Following their completion, both executed a number of minelaying missions but ironically had their greatest success on 17 October 1917 when they attacked with gunfire a British convoy on the Lerwick-Bergen route. The German cruisers sank first the escorting destroyers, HMS *Strongbow* and *Mary Rose,* and then nine of the twelve merchant ships.

For amphibious and raiding operations the British extensively modified certain of their oldest cruisers. HMS *Endymion,* an obsolete armored cruiser launched in 1891, was rearmed and bulged for the Dardanelles operations. The most noted of such conversions was that of HMS *Vindictive,* which was equipped for the Zeebrugge raid with flamethrowers, howitzers, and mortars. Surviving severe damage in the 23 April 1918 attack, she was then scuttled as a blockship at Ostend on 10 May.

With the increasing importance of aviation toward the end of the war, a number of cruisers were fitted with antiaircraft guns and in certain cases with aircraft and launching platforms. By 1918 twenty British cruisers carried aircraft; others could tow kite balloons. The most extensive conversion in this vein was of HMS *Cavendish*. Renamed *Vindictive* to commemorate the valiant older ship, the new cruiser lost part of her main battery to a box hangar/flight deck and an "alighting" deck. She was commissioned only in September of 1918.

The war certainly proved the usefulness of cruisers in many roles and many guises. Those navies that had earlier neglected cruiser construction initiated sizable building programs as a result of the wartime experience. Just after Jutland the United States Congress authorized ten scout cruisers of the Omaha class, although none were begun before war's end. In 1917 and 1918 the Japanese navy started two new classes of light cruisers—the Tenryus and Kumas— modeled on the British "C"s.

The following tabulations show cruiser losses for the belligerent navies. The very high numbers for the British and Germans are certainly indicative of the hard use to which their ships were put. It is well to note that six of the ten British losses to U-boats came in the first three months of the war, with three (*Aboukir, Cressy,* and *Hogue* to U-9) falling on one day, 22

Cruisers Sunk during World War I

	Surface Ship	Sub	Mine	Scuttled	Internal Explosion	Wrecked	Total
Austria-Hungary	1			1			2
France		4	1				5
Germany	12	2	4	4	1		23
Great Britain	6	10	3	1	1	1	22
Italy		2			1		3
Japan	1					2	3
Russia	1	1					2
United States	1					2	3
Totals	22	19	8	6	3	5	63

September 1914. Of the sixty-three cruisers sunk during the war, none cost more to her navy than did SMS *Magdeburg*. After that German ship ran aground in the Baltic on 26 August 1914 Russian divers recovered her codebooks, which were passed to the British—a gift of inestimable value.

Malcolm Muir, Jr.

References

Campbell, John. *Jutland: An Analysis of the Fighting*. Annapolis, Md.: Naval Institute Press, 1986.

Conway's All the World's Fighting Ships 1860–1905. Annapolis, Md.: Naval Institute Press, 1979.

Conway's All the World's Fighting Ships 1906–1921. Annapolis, Md.: Naval Institute Press, 1985.

Friedman, Norman. *US Cruisers*. Annapolis, Md.: Naval Institute Press, 1984.

Gardiner, Robert, ed. *The Eclipse of the Big Gun: The Warship 1906–45*. Annapolis, Md.: Naval Institute Press, 1992.

See also EMDEN; FISHER, JOHN; GERMAN CRUISER RAIDS; GERMANY, NAVY; GREAT BRITAIN, NAVY; *KÖNIGSBERG; MAGDEBURG;* MINE WARFARE; MINES, SEA; WARSHIPS: BATTLE CRUISERS

Warships: Destroyers

The destroyer originated in the Royal Navy in the early 1890s as a counter to the large flotillas of French and Russian torpedo boats. With quick-firing guns, twenty-seven knot speed, and adequate size for sea-going work (about 300 tons), the earliest destroyers promised to provide the battle line with protection against the smaller coastal torpedo boats (typically of 120 tons, 23 knots, and two torpedo tubes). Inevitably, the destroyers themselves were armed with torpedoes and grew to the 600 ton River type of 1902, robust and reasonable seaworthy vessels with a speed of twenty-five knots. Grouped in flotillas of twenty ships, they were usually led by a light cruiser.

One of the fathers of the destroyer, Admiral Sir Jackie Fisher, by 1904 the first sea lord, proposed that large destroyers could take over the principal missions of the cruiser. He fostered the construction of the experimental destroyer *Swift* (2,390 tons, 35 knots) and the Tribal class (1,000 tons and 33 knots). Their high speeds were widely publicized but in service the ships proved disappointing, especially with their inadequate endurance. Consequently, the admiralty reverted to the more modest Beagle class of the 1908–9 program. Steady development of this basic design culminated in the "L" class of the 1912–13 program (1,200 tons, three 4-inch guns, four 21-inch tubes, 29 knots). These ships proved so successful that their basic characteristics were little altered in the following "M" class. On 1 August 1914 the Royal Navy counted on its lists 207 destroyers, of which seventy-five were modern oil-burners suitable for fleet work. Most of the remainder were fit only for coastal duties.

Prior to World War I, the Germans built smaller ships than their British counterparts. In fact, until 1914 the Germans officially classified their craft as "high seas torpedo-boats." These vessels, with their distinctive turtle-back forecastle and break before the bridge, differed also in emphasizing the torpedo at the expense of gunpower. German destroyers initially were outfitted with three 17.7-inch tubes, an armament that was increased in 1910 to four 19.7-inch tubes. The destroyer *V 25*, launched in 1914, set a new standard by carrying six torpedo tubes and twenty-four mines.

German planners intended for their torpedo craft to offset the British superiority in capital ships. In 1906 Admiral Alfred von Tirpitz received Reichstag approval for his program aiming to achieve a total force of twelve flotillas (that is, 144 destroyers). Built until 1914 by only three firms, the German craft carried alphanumeric designations in place of names, with G meaning a boat built by Krupp's *Germaniawerft* at Kiel; S by Schichau at Elbing; and V by Vulkan Werke at Stettin. By August of 1914 Germany had in commission or on order 168 modern destroyers and torpedo boats with speeds above thirty knots.

Other navies, notably the French and the Austrians, followed the German predilection for small size, with the torpedo stressed over gunpower; Italy, Japan, Russia, and the United States preferred a larger vessel with a heavier gun armament. Late in the prewar period, most navies did increase the size of their designs to get better seakeeping, higher speeds, and stronger armament, both in guns and torpedoes. Another change of great importance was the substitution of fuel oil for coal. All these trends were epitomized by the Russian *Novik* of 1913, which displaced 1,280 tons, mounted four 4-inch guns and eight 18-inch torpedo tubes, and was the fastest ship in the world at a trial speed of thirty-seven knots.

With the outbreak of the war all navies quickly discovered that they needed more destroyers. Losses of the swift craft were heavy; demands on them were prodigious. For example, by 1916 the Grand Fleet required one hundred destroyers (plus ten flotilla leaders) ready for sea at all times to counter the ninety German destroyers estimated available to the High Seas Fleet. About one-quarter of the Grand Fleet's destroyers were away at any time undergoing refit or escorting critical convoys from Scandinavia.

To buttress its flotillas, in August of 1914 the admiralty purchased from British yards twelve foreign destroyers under construction. With the "M" class giving excellent service, the admiralty ordered additional ships of the similar "R" and "S" classes. The later vessels offered engineering advances such as the geared turbines introduced in the "R"s, giving these destroyers a top speed of thirty-six knots. Higher speeds were becoming essential, as wartime experience showed that the older destroyers attached to the scouting forces had frequent difficulty in keeping up with the fast battle cruisers. By March of 1916 the admiralty had ordered 146 destroyers of "M," "R," and "S" classes. So successful was this basic design that construction of the "S" class continued to the end of the war. Some were built very quickly—*Scythe* was constructed by John Brown in twenty-five weeks.

Destroyers took part in every naval engagement except for those in distant waters. At the Battle of Jutland, 31 May–1 June 1916, German destroyers played a pivotal role, despite scoring only two hits with the ninety-seven torpedoes they fired. The very threat that they posed forced the British battle line to turn away, giving the German heavy ships the opportunity to escape a lethal trap. On the other side, British destroyers were more successful tactically, firing seventy-one torpedoes and making six hits (including one by HMS *Onslaught* that sank the predreadnought SMS *Pommern,* the only battleship lost in the engagement). Part of this discrepancy can be explained by defective German torpedoes—eight were observed to run right under British ships without exploding. Also, British destroyers engaged some larger German ships at very short range during the night phase of the battle—the sort ^f opportunity denied the German craft. Indeed, the night

fighting was so close and confused that the destroyer HMS *Spitfire* collided with the German dreadnought *Nassau*. During parts of this swirling action, the British destroyers badly shot up the bridges, searchlights, and upper works of their much larger opponents.

If Jutland showed the potency of the destroyer, the battle also showed the vulnerability of the unarmored craft, especially to shellfire in its large engineering plant. Of the eight British destroyers lost in the battle, five were disabled first by hits in their machinery spaces. Similarly, of the five German destroyers lost, two were hamstrung by one or two 4-inch shells in the engine rooms.

Jutland also showed that destroyers could occasionally survive surprising damage. HMS *Broke* was hit by at least nine shells. In certain unusual cases, lack of armor proved a positive blessing, as when HMS *Marvel* and *Spitfire* were hit by battleship projectiles that passed completely through the craft without exploding.

Aside from major fleet actions, destroyers saw much flotilla fighting, especially at night in the Channel and the Adriatic. In the last two years of the war, the French *Magon* fought four separate actions with German torpedo craft. On 21 April 1917 *Broke* rammed the German destroyer *G 42,* some of whose crew jumped onto the British ship. *Broke*'s captain piped, "Repel boarders." In such combats the British preference for size and gunpower generally showed to advantage, with a particularly good example occurring off Texel in the North Sea on 17 October 1914 when five British destroyers sank, without loss to themselves, four smaller German torpedo boats.

In consequence, the Germans reversed completely their design philosophy and began building large destroyers. The culmination of this trend was the S 113 type of 1918. Displacing over 2,000 tons, S 113 was armed with four 5.9-inch guns and four 23.6-inch torpedo tubes (this torpedo possessed a warhead of 540 pounds and a range of 15,000 yards—about 50 percent greater than the British 21-inch with its 400-pound warhead). Postwar analysis showed that the Germans had gone too far in the other direction: The hundred-pound projectile of the cruiser-size gun proved very difficult to load in any sort of seaway.

Intelligence of the German move to larger dimensions led the admiralty in the last two years of the war to order the "V," "W," and

Modified "W" classes of 1,500 tons, as well as additional flotilla leaders of 2,000 tons. These destroyers featured all their guns on the centerline; the later ships carried 4.7-inch pieces. Staunch and powerful vessels, they set the world's standard for destroyers by 1918. The output of British shipyards during the war was nothing short of phenomenal. During the conflict, the admiralty placed orders for 321 destroyers and thirty-nine leaders, of which 255 destroyers and twenty-eight leaders were completed before the Armistice. On that day the Royal Navy counted twenty-one leaders and 412 destroyers in commission.

The size of this force reflected the wide usefulness of the type; the destroyer had proved itself the "jack-of-all-trades." Some laid mines in waters where slower minelayers dared not venture. The British 20th Flotilla placed over 15,000 mines in the channels around Heligoland between February and August of 1918. Other destroyers, like HMS *Talisman,* served as leaders for submarine flotillas. A few destroyers engaged in aviation experiments—HMS *Stronghold* was fitted with a launching catapult forward.

Of greater importance was the role of the destroyer in antisubmarine warfare. Even the older small destroyers made good antisubmarine craft, with their speed and handiness. Until 1916 destroyers were handicapped by a lack of suitable detection devices and armament, their only effective weapons being gunfire or ramming. Neither, of course, was of value against a submerged submarine. The hydrophone, although invented in 1915, was not standard equipment aboard destroyers until late in 1917. The depth charge, first issued in 1916, was so limited in supply that destroyers frequently put to sea that year with a total of two. Not until 13 December 1916 did a destroyer sink a submarine with a depth charge (HMS *Landrail* sank *UB 29*). As supply caught up to demand in 1918, some destroyers carried as many as fifty depth charges.

With 1917 the crisis year in the U-boat war, other Allied powers made great efforts with their destroyers. The French, desperately short of modern craft, ordered twelve from Japan (the Arabe class). Built in as little as five months, these 685-ton ships performed well in the Mediterranean. To that same theater, the Japanese at British request dispatched twelve destroyers with their two cruiser flagships—the only imperial warships to serve outside

home waters after the opening months of the war.

When the United States entered the conflict in April of the same year, it already had in hand an ambitious program to build destroyers. Under construction or on order were fifty-six ships, the first of the famous "flush deckers." Displacing 1,200 tons, they were armed with four 4-inch guns and twelve 21-inch torpedo tubes. For escort duties they had a good range (of about 5,000 miles) and an ample speed (thirty-five knots).

Under the press of the U-boat menace, some American building yards even beat the best British records, with Mare Island Navy Yard completing destroyer *Ward* in less than two months. Many "flush deckers" bore testimony to the haste of their construction, with leaking seams and loose rivets. Wartime orders brought the total number ultimately completed to 273, although most were finished too late to take an active role in the closing campaigns or after the Armistice.

Recent analysis of the Allied record shows that the destroyer's effectiveness as a submarine killer was second only to that of mines. During the course of the conflict destroyers sank six U-boats by ramming, fourteen by depth charges, and two by explosive sweeps. Thus, Allied destroyers accounted for twenty-two of the 178 U-boats lost during the war.

On the flip side of the coin, British destroyers sustained heavier losses than any other class of warship in the Royal Navy. During the war, sixty-seven British destroyers were sunk: seventeen by surface ships, twenty by mines, eight by U-boats, and one by an unknown cause (probably a mine). Eight were wrecked and thirteen lost to collision. Several had very short lives. HMS *Turbulent,* completed on 12 May 1916, was sunk barely two weeks later at Jutland.

Some destroyer classes suffered few losses; others were especially hard hit. Of the twenty British vessels of the Acasta class, seven were lost during the war. Of the twelve destroyers in the corresponding German 1912 flotilla—the S 13 class—only four survived the conflict. Fifty-two German destroyers were lost to all causes. Following are the figures for the other major belligerents: Austria-Hungary, four; France, nine; Italy, seven; Japan, one; Russia/Soviet Union, twenty-three; United States, two. Destroyers paid a heavy price for their ubiquity.

Malcolm Muir, Jr.

References

Alden, John D. *Flush Decks and Four Pipes.* Annapolis, Md.: Naval Institute Press, 1965.

Campbell, John. *Jutland: An Analysis of the Fighting.* Annapolis, Md.: Naval Institute Press, 1986.

Conway's All the World's Fighting Ships 1906–1921. Annapolis, Md.: Naval Institute Press, 1985.

Gardiner, Robert, ed. *The Eclipse of the Big Gun: The Warship 1906–45.* Annapolis, Md.: Naval Institute Press, 1992.

March, Edgar J. *British Destroyers: A History of Development 1892–1953.* London: Seeley Service, 1966.

See also DEPTH CHARGES; FISHER, JOHN; JUTLAND, BATTLE OF; MINE WARFARE; MINES, SEA

Wemyss, Rosslyn Erskine, Baron Wester (1864–1933)

British admiral of the fleet, born in London on 12 April 1864. "Rosy" Wemyss entered the navy in 1877 with his third cousin, Prince George (later King George V). Blessed with abundant common sense, charm, and tact, Wemyss advanced rapidly. He participated in the Boer War, and in 1903 Admiral John Fisher selected him as the first commander of the new cadet college at Osborne. In 1910 he was appointed naval aide to King George V and in 1912 was promoted to rear admiral.

In August of 1914 Wemyss commanded Twelfth Cruiser Squadron in the English Channel with orders to protect the transit of the British Expeditionary Force to France. In September his vessels escorted the first Canadian troops to England.

In February of 1915 Wemyss had charge of the island of Lemnos and the naval station at Mudros, future base for the naval assault on the Dardanelles. A month later, following Admiral Sackville Carden's sickness, Wemyss unselfishly recommended that a junior officer, Rear Admiral John De Robeck, succeed Carden while he remained at Mudros. A year later, as acting vice admiral, Wemyss commanded the First Naval Squadron during De Robeck's absence. Even then Wemyss supported Commodore Roger Keyes's proposal for another attempt to force the Dardanelles and opposed the evacuation of Gallipoli.

In January of 1916 Wemyss was appointed commander in chief of the East Indies and Egypt Station. He supplied naval support for General Edmund Allenby's advance into Palestine that August.

In 1917 Wemyss was appointed deputy sea lord and given the task of reorganizing and expanding the war staff. When First Sea Lord John Jellicoe was dismissed, Wemyss replaced him. Although criticized by other officers as a "court sailor," Wemyss worked diligently with Sir Eric Geddes to plan the raid on Zeebrugge.

Wemyss represented the Allied navies during armistice negotiations at Compiègne. He also represented England, as admiral, at the Paris Peace Conference.

Deeply offended by calls for his dismissal by Admiral David Beatty and having been overlooked from the list of peerage and money awards, Wemyss resigned in November of 1919. He was subsequently promoted to admiral-of-the-fleet and raised to the peerage as Baron Wester. In 1924 he published *The Navy in the Dardanelles Campaign.* He died at Cannes, France, on 24 May 1933.

Tom Zucconi

References

Concise Dictionary of National Biography: Part II, 1901–1970. Oxford: Oxford University Press, 1982.

Herwig, Holger, and Neil M. Heyman. *Biographical Dictionary of World War I.* Westport, Conn.: Greenwood, 1982.

Wemyss, Lord Wester. *The Navy in the Dardanelles Campaign.* London: Hodder and Stoughton, 1924.

See also DARDANELLES CAMPAIGN; DE ROBECK, JOHN; GREAT BRITAIN, NAVY

Wetzell, Georg (1869–1947)

Prussian staff officer, born in Hesse on 5 March 1869. Wetzell began his career in a Prussian engineers battalion, but he eventually succeeded in getting a transfer to the infantry. After attending the Kriegsakademie, Wetzell held a number of staff positions and was promoted to major in 1912. The following year he became the GSO 1 of III Corps in Berlin, and it was in that capacity that he participated in the opening campaigns of the war. In March of 1915 Wetzell succeeded Colonel Hans von Seeckt as the chief of staff in the same corps, advising his commanding general, Ewald von Lochow, during the ensuing operations on the Western Front and in the Balkans. When Lochow received authority over all German divisions advancing on Verdun from the east *(Angriffsgruppe Ost)* Major Wetzell's responsibilities increased accordingly.

When General Erich von Falkenhayn was replaced at the OHL by Field Marshal Paul von Hindenburg and Quartermaster General Erich Ludendorff on 29 August 1916, the latter dropped the head of the operations branch, Major General Gerhard Tappen, and brought in Wetzell to take his place. Despite his low rank (he was finally made a lieutenant colonel in December of 1917), Wetzell became one of the key figures in the German High Command. Although he often disagreed with Ludendorff on strategic issues, the latter kept Wetzell on his staff until September of 1918—long after various senior commanders and staff officers at the front had raised questions about his capabilities. Under massive pressure from the Prussian war minister and others, Ludendorff finally brought in Colonel Wilhelm Heye to replace Wetzell at the operations branch. Wetzell spent the final months of the war as chief of staff at Fifth Army headquarters.

Wetzell continued in the service after the war and eventually became a two-star general and head of the *Reichswehr's* camouflaged general staff (the *Truppenamt*). After his retirement in October of 1927, he became active as a writer and editor. From 1930 to 1934, he served in China as a general advisor to the Kuomintang regime. He died in 1947.

Ulrich Trumpener

References

Carsten, F.L. *The Reichswehr and Politics, 1918–1933.* Berkeley and Los Angeles: University of California Press, 1973.

Martin, Bernd, ed. *Die deutsche Beraterschaft in China 1927–1938.* Dusseldorf: Droste, 1981.

Moller, Hans. *Geschichte der Ritter des Ordens 'pour le mérite' im Weltkrieg.* 2 vols. Berlin: Bernard & Graefe, 1935.

Reichsarchiv et al. *Der Weltkrieg 1914 bis 1918: Militärische Operationen zu Lande.* Vols. 11-14. Berlin: E.S. Mittler und Sohn, 1938–44.

Wallach, Yehuda L. *The Dogma of the Battle of Annihilation.* Westport, Conn.: Greenwood, 1986.

See also HINDENBURG, PAUL VON; LUDENDORFF, ERICH

Weygand, Maxime (1867–1965)

French army staff officer, born on 21 January 1867 in Brussels, Belgium. Weygand moved to Paris in 1873 and entered St. Cyr as a foreigner. He graduated in 1885, a French citizen. Weygand rose rapidly in the army, distinguishing himself as a cavalry instructor at Saumur and as a student at the Centre des hautes études militaires.

At the beginning of the war Weygand served as a lieutenant colonel of hussars in the Fourth Army. General Joseph Joffre assigned him as chief of staff to General Ferdinand Foch, who was given command of the newly formed Ninth Army on the Marne. Weygand spent the entire war working with Foch. Weygand had a keen understanding of the mental processes of his chief and was able to express Foch's plans quickly and in clear and precise terms. Weygand faithfully served Foch at the battles of Ypres in 1914, Vimy Ridge in 1915, and the Somme in 1916, and continued to do so even after Foch was named supreme Allied commander in 1918. He read the Armistice terms to the Germans at Compiègne. Likewise, when Foch appeared at the Paris Peace Conference to plead that the Rhineland be detached from Germany, Weygand was at his side.

The close association with Foch introduced Weygand to the French and foreign public and did much to advance his military career after the war. He was chief of the general staff (1930–31) and vice president of the Supreme War Council and inspector general of the army (1931–35). Brought back from retirement to replace General Maurice Gamelin as supreme commander in May of 1940, he ultimately advised French capitulation to the Germans. Imprisoned by the Germans in 1942, he was arrested by the French government in 1945. Rehabilitated in 1948, he wrote several books and died in Paris on 28 January 1965.

Jan Karl Tanenbaum

References

Bankwitz, Philip Charles Farwell. *Maxime Weygand and Civil-Military Relations in Modern France.* Cambridge: Harvard University Press, 1967.

Liddell Hart, Basil. *Foch: The Man of Orléans:* London: Eyre & Spottiswoode, 1931.

See also FOCH, FERDINAND

Wilhelm, Crown Prince (1882–1951)

Crown Prince of Prussia and the German Empire. Born on 6 May 1882 in Potsdam. Wilhelm was the eldest son of Kaiser Wilhelm II. He received an excellent education at court and in a school for cadets. From early on, however, he lived in the shadow of his father and was never able to escape his influence.

At the beginning of World War I Wilhelm was commander in chief of Fifth Army, named in his honor "German Crown Prince." On the political front, he sought a speedy peace. But that did not prevent him from following the policy of chief of the general staff General Erich von Falkenhayn in the bloody battles of Verdun, where Friedrich Wilhelm served with his Fifth Army and was equally to blame for the horrible losses on both sides in the bloodbath planned by Falkenhayn.

In 1917 the crown prince became commander in chief of army group "German Crown Prince." In that capacity and because of his background he played an important role in the intrigues of Field Marshal Paul von Hindenburg and Quartermaster General Erich Ludendorff, which forced the resignation of Reich Chancellor Theobald von Bethmann Hollweg.

At the end World War I Crown Prince Wilhelm accompanied his father, Wilhelm II, into Dutch exile. There he remained on Wieringen Island for five years. Upon his return to Germany in 1923, Wilhelm's entry into politics led to connections with Adolf Hitler and the National Socialist party. Wilhelm hoped that this connection and candidacy for the office of the Reich Minister would enable him to return Germany to a monarchical form of government, but his father refused to allow it. The crown prince broke off relations with Hitler in 1934 and retired to private life. After World War II he spent his last years at the Hohenzollern castle in Hechingen-Württemberg and a nearby villa, where he died on 20 July 1951.

Ekkehart P. Guth

References

Eppstein, Georg von. *Der Deutsche Kronprinz.* Leipzig: Max Koch-Verlag, 1926.

Herre, Paul. *Kronprinz Wilhelm.* Munich: Beck-Verlag, 1954.

Ludendorff, Erich. *Meine Kriegserinnerungen, 1914–1918.* Berlin: Mittler-Verlag, 1919.

See also VERDUN, BATTLE OF

Wilhelm II, German Kaiser (1859–1941)

German Kaiser, 1888–1918. Born on 27 January 1859, Kaiser Wilhelm II was the eldest son of Crown Prince Friedrich Wilhelm of Prussia and Princess Victoria, the daughter of Queen Victoria of England. Wilhelm's left arm was damaged by an injury at birth, leading some to attribute his propensity for demonstrative behavior and unrestrained and at times violent language to over-compensation for this physical abnormality. After the ninety-nine-day reign of his dying father, Friedrich III, Wilhelm became kaiser on 15 June 1888. Wishing to plot his own course, he forced the resignation of Chancellor Otto von Bismarck on 18 March 1890.

During the remainder of Wilhelm's reign Germany lacked clear direction and coherent policy. Wilhelm's *Weltpolitik,* with its quest for a "place in the sun" and his enthusiastic support for Admiral Alfred von Tirpitz's High Seas Fleet, helped to alienate Great Britain and contributed to growing tension that led to World War I. His outspoken sympathy for the Boers and his indiscretions in a 1908 interview with the *Daily Telegraph* added to British misgivings. The *Daily Telegraph* incident also led to a domestic crisis in Germany, when the kaiser was censured by the Reichstag. Despite growing opposition, Wilhelm remained committed to the naval program and thwarted the Reichstag through his defense of military arrogance following the 1913 Zabern affair. With Tirpitz, he rejected as totally inadequate concessions offered by British emissary Lord Haldane during his 1912 mission.

Wilhelm, despite his impetuosity, is to be credited with some good judgment and reservation. He had balked before launching the First Moroccan Crisis with his dramatic landing at Tangiers in 1905, had blanched at the Austro-Hungarian annexation of Bosnia-Herzegovina in 1908, and had initially opposed the adventurism of Foreign Secretary Alfred von Kiderlen-Wächter, who launched the Second Moroccan Crisis in 1911.

Wilhelm was shocked by the assassination of Archduke Franz Ferdinand. His initial reaction was that the Serbs must be punished. There was concern among more militant advisors that Wilhelm would go to the brink only to withdraw again. Indeed, the surprising response of the Serbs to Austria's ultimatum and the resolve of the British gave him momentary second thoughts. But he acquiesced to the demands of the military and the pace of events, and he responded to Russian general mobilization with a declaration of war. In view of Germany's sole war plan, he quite illogically hesitated momentarily to declare war on France but quickly bowed to the inevitable consequence of his prior decision.

Once war had commenced Wilhelm supported the military by his frequent presence at military headquarters, but strategic decisions were left to the chief of staff. The kaiser's retreat to the background was particularly apparent after he handed the military command over to Field Marshal Paul von Hindenburg and his assistant, General Erich Ludendorff, on 28 August 1916. Wilhelm, despite the misgivings of Chancellor Theobald von Bethmann Hollweg, gave way on the question of unrestricted submarine warfare in the Pless conference of 9 January 1917. Finally, in July of 1917, the kaiser dismissed Bethmann Hollweg at the behest of the military commanders, who had for all practical purposes assumed the role of military dictators; he replaced Hollweg with their handpicked puppet, Georg Michaelis. Although Wilhelm promised postwar electoral and constitutional reform on 8 April 1917, he ignored the Reichstag's July peace resolution and accepted the draconian peace of Brest-Litovsk on 3 March 1918.

After the successful commencement of the Allied counteroffensive in August of 1918, Wilhelm, and eventually Hindenburg and Ludendorff, recognized that victory was beyond Germany's grasp. In defeat, Wilhelm acceded to the demands of the military leadership for a government that could rapidly win acceptable conditions from the Allies. On 1 October Wilhelm appointed his cousin, the liberal Prince Max von Baden, chancellor. Although Max formed a parliamentary ministry, President Wilson expressed reluctance to make peace with "the military masters and monarchical autocrats" of Germany. Ludendorff, enraged by the terms the Allies sought to impose through the Armistice, called for the fight, which he had earlier declared impossible, to continue. Max demanded his ouster, and, when Hindenburg sought to depart as well, the kaiser successfully appealed to his sense of honor.

In order to placate Wilson and obtain peace, Max finally sought the kaiser's abdication. Enraged by Max's request, Wilhelm, who had gone to the military headquarters at Spa for protection and solace, sought support from the army for a punitive march on Berlin. General Wilhelm Groener, who had replaced Ludendorff, dismissed the kaiser's plea as quixotic. Groener stated, "The Army will march home in good order under its generals, but not under Your Majesty." Hindenburg was compelled to concur with his new adjutant. On 9 November Max announced that the kaiser had abdicated and handed the government over to Friedrich Ebert, the leader of the Majority Social Democrats. After the dismissal of Groener's suggestion that he seek an honorable end on the front, the kaiser had no alternative but to board a train for the Netherlands, whose government granted him asylum. He formally abdicated on 28 November 1918.

Despite calls that Wilhelm be tried as a war criminal, the Dutch government refused to consider his expulsion. Wilhelm's first wife, Augusta Victoria "Dona" of Schleswig-Holstein-Augustenburg, who bore him six sons and a daughter, died on 11 April 1921. On 3 November 1922 he married Hermine (née Reuss), the young widow of the Prince of Schönaich-Carolath. Although Wilhelm admired the nationalist fervor of the Nazis and relished Germany's 1940 victory over France, he remained aloof from the party and Adolf Hitler. Wilhelm's response to the November 1938 *Kristallnacht* was: "For the first time I am ashamed to be a German." Wilhelm resided undisturbed at his estate at Doorn in the Netherlands until his death on 4 June 1941. Buried first at Doorn, his remains were reinterred alongside those of his forbears at Potsdam in 1993.

Bernard A. Cook

References
Balfour, David. *The Kaiser and His Times.* New York: W.W. Norton, 1964.
Kohut, Thomas A. *Wilhelm and the Germans: A Study in Leadership.* New York and Oxford: Oxford University Press, 1991.
Wilhelm II. *The Kaiser's Memoirs.* New York: H. Fertig, 1976.

See also GERMANY, HOME FRONT

Wilson, Sir Henry (1864–1922)

British general, born on 5 May 1864 at Currygrane, Ireland. Educated at Marlborough and Sandhurst, Wilson entered the army through the militia in 1884 and subsequently began a career of rapid promotion. He saw action in Burma, where he was wounded, and later in South Africa during the Boer War, where he served with little distinction. Wilson did, however, cultivate a network of useful friends, such as Lord Roberts. In 1906 he was posted to the command of the staff college at Camberley, and by 1910 he was selected as director of military operations at the war office. Prior to the war, Wilson made frequent trips to France, accompanied by Sir John French, that led to an ever-closer military relationship between Britain and France. He struck up a friendship with Ferdinand Foch, the head of the French Staff College. Convinced of the necessity of giving France maximum support in case of war, Wilson played an important role in preparing the British army for a continental campaign.

The coming of war saw Wilson serving in the capacity of sub-chief of the general staff. In part through his efforts, the mobilization and transport of the British Expeditionary Force to France went smoothly. Wilson's performance, nevertheless, in the retreat after the battle of Mons was far from exemplary. In early 1915 he was appointed chief liaison officer with French field headquarters. Wilson was reassigned by December of 1915 to command an army corps on the Western Front, where he proved temperamentally unsuited for such work. For a brief period, after March of 1917, he returned to the job of liaison officer to French headquarters. But the replacement of Robert Nivelle by Henri-Philippe Pétain led to Wilson's removal in September of 1917 to England to take charge of Eastern Command.

While back home, Wilson caught the attention of British Prime Minister David Lloyd George, who named him British military representative to the Allied Supreme War Council. By February of 1918 he was given the job of chief of the Imperial General Staff. In that capacity he participated in directing the war in its final stages. With the launching of the Ludendorff Offensives, which threatened to break the Allied lines, he supported unity of command through the appointment of Foch as commander of Allied forces. In 1919 he was promoted to field marshal and created a baronet.

After the war Wilson continued in his duties as chief of the Imperial General Staff. He served as the chief British government military advisor at the Versailles Peace Conference but found himself increasingly at odds with Lloyd George's peace policy and stance on Ireland. After Wilson's four years as chief of staff, Lloyd George refused to renew his appointment. This was followed by his retirement from the army and election to Parliament as a conservative member; he voiced strong opposition to the government's Irish policy. On 22 June 1922, outside his house in London, Wilson was assassinated by two members of the Irish Republican Army.

Van Michael Leslie

References

Collier, Basil. *Brasshat: A Biography of Field-Marshal Sir Henry Wilson*. London: Secker and Warburg, 1961.

Wilson, Trevor. *The Myriad Faces of War: Britain and the Great War 1914–1918*. Cambridge: Polity, 1986.

Woodward, Sir Llewellyn. *Great Britain and the War of 1914–1918*. London: Methuen, 1967.

See also LLOYD GEORGE, DAVID

Wireless (Radio) Communications

Wireless telegraphy and telephony improved war communications, increasing the distances over which messages were transmitted and their delivery speed. Both the Allies and Central Powers utilized wireless communications, and each side established interception services vital for their intelligence services.

World War I wireless communications were revolutionized by the replacement of spark transmitters with the Poulsen arc system. This generated continuous waves, making possible long-distance communications. Another important invention was the triode audion amplifier radio tube.

When the war began wireless telegraph stations dotted the Western Front. Gunners used continuous-wave sets to talk to forward observation posts, where artillery officers gave firing directions.

Britain expanded wireless research at Woolwich, and Gustaf-Auguste Ferrié directed French radio research within Radiotélégraphie Militaire. He established the Ecole de T.S.F. to train wireless engineers and telegraphists. A military transmitter was maintained on the Eiffel Tower. French engineers developed a more efficient audion that operated in higher vacuums, improving range reception and transmission. Some 100,000 French audions were manufactured and distributed to the military radio service.

The first decisive effect of military wireless communications occurred in the 1914 Battle of Tannenberg. German radio operators intercepted, translated, and transmitted to their own command several dozen uncoded Russian radio messages detailing attack orders, including time, troop strength, and location. As a result, the Germans inflicted a crushing defeat on the Russians. German decoding of intercepted radiograms was also important in defeating the Russians in the 1915 Battle of the Masurian Lakes.

Tannenburg revealed the immaturity of wireless communications. Operators often transmitted uncoded messages and conveyed personal comments, unintentionally providing information and revealing declining morale. Many of these novices did not realize that enemies as well as allies could hear their transmissions. When this was realized incorrect messages were sometimes relayed for the enemy to intercept and be misled. Although some radio operators did not take intercepted messages seriously, most realized the advantages that could result. Defectors often assisted in cracking codes and translating messages.

The French intercept service quickly understood the operations of the German radio system and followed German movements toward Paris in the late summer of 1914, learning orders and weaknesses on the German front. This aided the French in the Battle of the Marne.

Interception services increased as both sides attempted to capture cipher books and use direction-finding to locate enemy transmitters. British operators averaged two thousand intercepted messages daily. On the Eastern Front the Central Powers had intercept stations every ten kilometers, and the French and British used similar methods in the West.

The Battle of Verdun was the turning point in wireless communications, as earth telegraphy was implemented during static warfare. The French installed ground-telegraphy instruments when artillery fire damaged wires. Currents traveled in the earth, and, unlike radiotelegraphy, interceptors had to decipher Morse code, not oral messages. German engineers captured these devices, improved the design, and used them near enemy trenches to intercept messages. While previously intercepted radio messages were from higher staff officers, these ground interceptions were from troops near the front line.

Ferrié developed the Parleur TM2 to send secure signals, and the Germans built a similar set. British soldiers used the Fullerphone, which hindered enemy interception of signals. Lack of raw materials slowed production of these anti-interception devices.

Wireless communications were most useful for naval warfare, being installed in the British, French, and German navies by 1916. German submarines could transmit and receive signals as far as three hundred miles. Wireless sets for communicating plane-to-plane and plane-to-ground, for reconnaissance purposes, were designed and employed. Normal reception was limited to 180 miles but occasionally signals could reach as far as three hundred miles. By 1917 aircraft wireless-telegraphy tracking systems reported enemy bomber movements to ground stations.

Elizabeth D. Schafer

References

Flicke, Wilhelm F. *War Secrets in the Ether*. 2 vols. Laguna Hills, Calif.: Aegean Park, 1977.

Hartcup, Guy. *The War of Invention: Scientific Developments, 1914–18*. London: Brassey's Defence Publishers, 1988.

Lavine, A. Lincoln. *Circuits of Victory*. Garden City, N.Y.: Doubleday, Page, 1921.

See also ROOM 40

Witos, Wincenty (1874–1945)

Polish politician, born at Wierszchosławice on 21 January 1874. Witos entered politics and from 1916 was leader of the Polish peasant party, Piast, in the Austrian parliament. He spent the early part of the war in Switzerland, endeavoring to secure relief supplies to alleviate Polish suffering in the war.

Witos openly advocated establishment of a unified and sovereign Polish state. He was critical of any arrangement that would lead to only a partial solution of the Polish problem, such as the Kingdom of Poland set up by the

Central Powers in 1916. Witos was one of the architects of the May 1917 resolution in the Austrian parliament that demanded the Polish question be settled in its entirety. This demand encouraged the Polish Parliamentary Circle to withdraw its support of the Austrian government.

With the disintegration of the Austro-Hungarian Empire in 1918, Witos became head of the Polish Liquidation Commission (government for the Austrian partition of Poland), established to terminate Austrian rule and organize all aspects of political administration before the reunification of Polish lands. Witos subsequently served three times as prime minister of independent Poland (1920–21, 1923, and 1926). After 1926 he was in opposition to the government, and from 1933 to March of 1939 he lived in exile in Czechoslovakia. He died at Kraków on 31 October 1945.

Andrzej Suchcitz

References

Witos, Wincenty. *Moje Wspomnienia*. Paris: Instytut Literacki, 1964.
Zakrzewski, Andrzej. *Wincenty Witos*. Warsaw: Ludowa Spółdzielnia Wydawnicza, 1978.

See also POLAND

Woëvre Battle (St. Mihiel Salient), April 1915

In 1914, while trying to outflank Verdun, German forces created a large triangular salient that peaked at a small German bridgehead on the Meuse River's west bank near St. Mihiel. Throughout late 1914 and early 1915, French Marshal Joseph Joffre and General Auguste Dubail, commander of the Eastern Army Group, repeatedly sought to eliminate "the St. Mihiel hernia" in order to straighten French lines, raise morale, divert German attention from more critical areas of the front (Champagne and Artois), and sever the rail lines in the Metz area.

On 5 April 1915 seven corps of the French First Army began the most significant of these offensives by striking nine divisions of the German army on both sides of the salient. Particularly bitter fighting developed at Combres (near the northern end of the salient), in the Forêt d'Ailly (just east of St. Mihiel), and along the salient's southern face at Flirey, Regneville,

and the Bois le Prêtre. By 13 April poor weather, ineffective artillery, ammunition shortages, rugged terrain, strong German defenses, fierce counterattacks, and the arrival of three fresh German divisions had halted the French. Fighting continued for tactical advantages in sectors such as the Combres Heights, but after minor gains and nearly 64,000 casualties (including those taken in the Third Army's supporting attacks west of Verdun), Joffre suspended offensive action in the area on 30 April. Bitter, sporadic fighting dragged on until well into the summer months, after which the St. Mihiel salient became a quiet backwater until the American offensive in September of 1918.

David K. Yelton

References

France. *Ministère de la Guerre. Etat-Major de l'Armée Service Histoirique. Les Armées Française dans la Grande Guerre*, Vol. 2. Paris: Imprimerie Nationale, 1931.
Reichsarchiv. *Der Weltkrieg 1914–1918*, Vol. 7. Berlin: E.S. Mittler und Sohn, 1931.

See also DUBAIL, AUGUSTE; FOCH, FERDINAND

Women in the War

Even the most casual observer of history cannot disregard the role played by women in World War I. Traditional histories maintain that both great wars were watersheds for women. New opportunities arose in high-paying, skilled manufacturing jobs, government service, and education. In the armed forces women served as ambulance drivers, medics, and resistance fighters. They also attained political rights, gaining suffrage in England, the United States, and Germany after the war. Perhaps less obvious but just as significant, feminist movements turned to pacifistic activities during and after the fighting, articulating for many their antipathy to aggressive nationalistic tendencies. The war had both long- and short-term impacts on women, and although some progress was temporary, for the "duration" only, the war initiated a revolution in women's rights that finally saw fruition in recent years.

The status of women in the labor force varied among the belligerents. In 1906 women constituted 38 percent of the workforce in

France, with 20 percent of married women working (the highest percentage in Western Europe). The majority of French women held traditional jobs as domestics or home workers (52 percent), whereas only 25 percent worked in factories. Although statistics are scarce because the government did not conduct the 1916 census, the percentage of working women did not rise as significantly as earlier assumed. Instead, women merely moved from domestic and textile employment into positions held previously by male workers.

In 1913, for example, the French railway industry employed only 6,000 women, with 85 percent of those serving as barrier guards, whereas by 1918 the number had increased to 57,000. In the Ministry of Posts the conscription of 20,000 men opened that number of positions to women, adding to the 18,000 already employed by that government agency. The Ministry of Education added 30,000 positions, mostly secondary, to the 71,000 female workers holding mostly primary teaching jobs. Similarly, banks and businesses placed women in clerical and secretarial tasks previously held by men.

The largest increase in French female employment occurred in chemical, wood, and transport manufacturing, industries directly related to war matériel. In 1914 women made up only one-twentieth of this industry's workforce; this grew to one-fourth by 1918. They held jobs ranging from running presses, cranes, and lathes to loading ships or packing shells. Women also advanced into control and inspection positions requiring elevated skills, but rarely moved into the building-trade occupations of cabinetmaker or toolmaker, thus limiting their participation in postwar industry.

Similar increases occurred in Great Britain. Although not as large a percentage of English women performed paid work, the 1911 census revealed that one-third of women worked, primarily as domestics and in textiles. Women in commerce and industry numbered 3.2 million in 1914 but surged to just under five million by 1918. As the domestic economy tightened, many households eliminated domestic help. Women employed in this area lost their income and moved into 168,000 civil service clerk positions. Government factories employed 220,000 and another 420,000 stepped into the metal trades. By 1917 women held nearly one-half of the jobs in wartime England, including new positions in war textiles and munitions. Female workers welded, built a shipyard, shov-eled coal, and drove trams, but, as in France, few moved into positions that could translate into postwar industries.

The "munitionettes" most eloquently portray the British woman's sacrifices for the war effort. In 1914 the nationalized Woolwich Arsenal employed only men, but two years later half of the 100,000 workers were women. Conditions were barely tolerable with women living in government barracks and working twelve-hour shifts for less than half of men's wages. Life-threatening exposure to high-explosive powder caused pernicious anemia, and unsafe manufacturing processes like the "beater," which packed TNT and amatol into shell cases, blasted several hundred women to their deaths.

On the bottom in employment rights, women took the bulk of the burden as British industry began demobilizing. As the Russian front folded, the Ministry of Munitions discharged nearly a million workers, mostly women. British policy reiterated the prewar thinking that woman's work was "in the home," especially if she was married. Matters of health and child-bearing continued to dominate employment issues, with the government and trade unions recommending exclusion of women from unhealthful or dangerous trades and advocating motherhood. Clearly, although women moved from traditional positions to war-related industries in large numbers, the war experience was ambiguous for most women. The war had brought many into the labor force, but its end found most returned to domestic positions or to the home.

Histories of the Great War claim that an unprecedented level of female employment also changed women's status significantly in Germany, asserting that thousands of former maids kept the war economy moving. Recent historiography refutes this traditional view, for only a small number of women entered the labor force for the first time during the conflict. The most compelling reasons for women remaining at home were the increasing difficulty that the war imposed on maintaining a household and women's preference for performing piecework near the hearth. Women who previously crafted corsets turned to manufacturing tents and gasmasks, and clockmakers produced munitions. As in Britain, women employed in other areas moved into war-related industries. A 1916 trade union survey revealed an increase from 63,000 to 266,000 women in metalworking. Women previously in domestic service and agriculture moved into engineering, chemical, and electrical fields. As with their counterparts among the Allies, German women stepped into positions held by the fighting force and, at war's end, reverted to their prewar status. In a nation where a woman's position was beside her husband and the cradle, professional child care nonexistent, and wages half those of men, women found little motivation to remain in the industrial workforce even if the opportunity were afforded them.

Besides participating in industry, women served their countries in varying degrees in medical organizations. British authorities saw women only as nurses before 1914, as evidenced by the formation of the Voluntary Aid Detachments (VADs) in 1910. Originally intended as a technical reserve, VADs were to provide aid to the sick and wounded in case of invasion under the auspices of the Territorial Force Medical Service. By the end of 1918, 23,000 nurses and 15,000 orderlies had worked in service hospitals, some overseas. Most were from middle- or upper-class families and found war wounds horrifying, but the majority weathered professional nursing's contempt for their lack of training and served twelve-hour shifts in less than ideal conditions.

In addition to voluntary organizations, women sought expression in the Women's Emergency Corps, founded in August of 1914 by feminist leaders. The WEC organized women to deal with national emergencies, and most adopted military-style uniforms symbolic of their willingness to fight alongside the men. One such group, the Women's Emergency League, trained army cadets in signaling at the home base of the British army in Hampshire. The Women's Auxiliary Force, founded in 1915, trained part-time workers in the usual drills, first aid, cooking, and sewing, as well as providing canteens and entertainment, stewards for air-raid shelters, and hospital visitations.

Englishwomen also found outlet in the First Aid Nursing Yeomanry (FANY), which initially trained nurses to render battlefield aid on horseback, moving to motorized transport as the war continued. The FANY also holds the distinction of surviving two world wars, flourishing today as the Women's Transport Service. The Women's Convoy Corps (WCC), which included female physicians, was also founded in 1907. As manpower needs grew more critical, the military involved women on a more active

level, creating the Women's Army Auxiliary Corps (WAAC) and Women's Royal Naval Service (WRNS) in 1917 and the Women's Royal Air Force (WRAF) in 1918. By war's end more than 100,000 British women had worked in kitchens, behind desks, and even as gardeners in war cemeteries, contributing to England's battle with the kaiser.

British women also entered the fray on the continent. Lady Leila Paget, whose husband served as British ambassador to Serbia in 1911, left London society in 1914 to form a medical unit to aid the Serbs. Novelist Sarah Broom Macnaughtan joined the Red Cross Society, treating the wounded in Antwerp and opening a soup kitchen in Flanders. Other daring women volunteered as ambulance drivers in the Munro Corps, roaring onto the battlefields of Belgium. The Women's Hospital Corps, uniformed in grey-green topped by a green-veiled hat, avoided the war office and negotiated directly with the French Red Cross, staffing a surgical unit in Paris in 1914. Chief Surgeon Louisa Garrett Anderson's remarkable surgical skills prompted the French press to question who actually performed the operations. As the war stalemated, the British Army Medical Services turned the administration of a new five-hundred-bed hospital in London over to the hospital corps. Opening in May of 1915, a staff of 159 women with twenty-one men as stretcher bearers and ambulance drivers treated some 26,000 patients by conflict's end.

European women did not serve alone; almost 25,000 American women went overseas beginning in 1914, long before the United States entered the war. American women initially responded on their own to the call for aid, with later participants joining organizations like the Red Cross and eventually working with the government. Early in their involvement, the American women followed Washington's course, remaining neutral and serving both the Allies and the Central Powers with a Red Cross "Mercy Ship" fully prepared to nurse the wounds of Germans, French, and British alike. Hundreds of relief agencies emerged, such as the Woman's Committee of the Commission for Belgian Relief, the Vacation War Relief Committee, the Surgical Dressings Committee, and the National Patriotic Relief Society. National service training camps equipped middle- and upper-class women with such skills as camp cooking, map reading, motorcar driving, and signaling. American women in Europe formed

W

groups like the American Ambulance in Paris and the American Women's War Relief Committee in London.

American women had been serving in auxiliary nurse corps of the army and navy since the turn of the century, eventually numbering more than ten thousand in Europe. The navy and marine corps gave women enlisted rank, recruiting thirteen thousand into their active reserves. Popularly referred to as Yeomanettes but formally as yeomen(F), or USNR(F), these women performed clerical work stateside, with a handful serving in hospitals in France. The marine corps added some 305 women marines, or USMCR(F). Additionally, the Army Signal Corps placed more than two hundred female telephone operators on the continent. Although most American women who participated in the Great War were nurses, some women also worked as physicians, pathologists, administrators, entertainers, decoders, translators, refugee workers, and peace activists.

Many forces contributed to women's more active role in World War I. The turn of the century shift from heavy to light industry produced a corresponding adjustment in class structure, as management and clerical positions challenged the primacy of manufacturing labor. The late eighteenth-century division between owner and worker began to fade, and this was nowhere more evident than in the blurring of women's roles in the home and in industry. Women moved into professional and political areas unforeseen in the nineteenth century, with World War I serving as a catalyst to changes already in motion before 1914. With increasing numbers of women entering law and medicine, women's rights advanced further in the four years of conflict than during the preceding generation of female activism. As Europeans observed these rapid changes in 1919, widespread nostalgia for prewar Europe worked against feminist progress, as many of the old guard advocated a return to the more class- and gender-conscious days. Although state policy in Britain, France, and Germany strongly advocated motherhood and hearth, and many women happily accepted that role, others would continue to agitate for equal opportunity.

Brenda Taylor

References

Higonnet, Margaret Randolph, ed. *Behind the Lines: Gender and the Two World Wars*. New Haven: Yale University Press, 1987.

Hughes, H. Stuart. *Contemporary Europe: A History*. Englewood Cliffs, N.J.: Prentice-Hall, 1991.

Mitchell, David. *Monstrous Regiment: The Story of the Women of the First World War*. New York: Macmillan, 1965.

Schneider, Dorothy and Carl J. *Into the Breach: American Women Overseas in World War I*. New York: Viking, 1991.

Wall, Richard, and Jay Winter, eds. *The Upheaval of War: Family, Work and Welfare in Europe, 1914–1918*. Cambridge: Cambridge University Press, 1988.

Woodward, Sir Llewellyn. *Great Britain and the War of 1914–1918*. Boston: Beacon, 1967.

Writers

See LITERATURE

Y

Yanushkevich, Nikolai Nikolaevich (1868–1918)

Russian general. Yanushkevich was typical of officers in the pre–World War I Russian army who advanced because of political influence. Born in May of 1868, Yanushkevich graduated from the Mikhailovsky Artillery School (1888) and the General Staff Academy (1896). He served as a staff officer in the Ministry of War for over fourteen years. He was then appointed professor of military administration at the General Staff Academy in 1910 and became its commander three years later.

As a result of a purge of politically unreliable military officers in 1909 and 1910 that saw the incompetent Vladimir Sukhomlinov become minister of war, Yanushkevich was appointed head of the General Staff Academy. This appointment surprised the high military circles because his reputation was one of inexperience and at best mediocrity. In 1914 Sukhomlinov recommended Yanushkevich as chief of staff to commander in chief Grand Duke Nikolai Nikolaevich, who had wanted General M.V. Alekseev. When Yanushkevich learned of his appointment, he was honest enough to admit that he was not qualified for the post.

The apex of Yanushkevich's career was his bold decision to supersede the czar's authority and order the early general mobilization of the army on 30 July 1914. Yanushkevich's inadequacies soon became all too apparent. He was adept at blaming others for failures, ranging from shortages of supplies to defeats on the battlefield. In late 1914 in a letter to Minister of Agriculture A.V. Krivoshein, he referred to the Russian peasant soldier as greedy and cowardly. In the same letter he suggested that acts of bravery by common soldiers be rewarded with land, and, conversely, cowardice result in the government's taking away land from the soldier's family. By late 1914 it was apparent to all that Yanushkevich was incompetent. Unable to make competent military decisions, he concentrated his attention on persecuting Russian Jews. His decision to initiate a scorched earth policy during the Russian retreat from Poland in May of 1915, caused serious problems as the displaced inhabitants clogged the retreat routes and overtaxed civil authorities.

In August of 1915 Yanushkevich was relieved as chief of staff and relegated to duty in the Caucasus, where he retired after the March Revolution. While in the Caucasus, Yanushkevich died under mysterious circumstances in 1918.

John W. Bohon
Jeff Kinard

References

Gurko, Basil I., General. *Features and Figures of the Past.* Stanford, Calif.: Stanford University Press, 1939.

Herwig, Holger H., and Neil M. Heyman. *Biographical Dictionary of World War I.* Westport, Conn.: Greenwood, 1982.

Pushkarev, Sergei. *The Emergence of Modern Russia 1801–1917.* New York: Holt, Rinehart and Winston, 1963.

Shukman, Harold, ed. *The Blackwell Encyclopedia of the Russian Revolution.* Oxford: Basil Blackwell, 1988.

See also Russia, Army; Sukhomlinov, Vladimir

Ypres, First Battle of (13 October–22 November 1914)

The First Battle of Ypres resulted from a German drive to seize the English Channel ports of northern France and Belgium at the conclusion of the so-called "Race to the Sea," after the deadlock at the First Battle of the Aisne River. This bloody series of clashes converging on Ypres marked the war's transition from quixotic mobile operations to positional warfare and raiding tactics across a fireswept belt.

At the beginning of October of 1914, after the failure of his first two attempts to turn the Germans' western flank, first on the Somme and then in the Artois sector near Arras, French army commander General Joseph Joffre decided to try farther north. He enlisted the aid of British Field Marshal Sir John French and the British Expeditionary Force (BEF), which was already conveniently moving northward from the Aisne.

The BEF's reshuffling was initially independent of French objectives and plans. Having been awkwardly sandwiched between French forces along the Aisne River, on 2 October the BEF began to redeploy. The move would improve BEF proximity to the Channel ports where resupply could be protected by the Royal Navy's heavy guns, and the move could exploit the British army's flair for maneuver warfare. Also, a hastily improvised British rescue mission to the beleaguered Antwerp garrison demanded a British-held corridor along the most direct route.

At the same time, the French Tenth Army under General Louis de Maud'huy was threatened by a German envelopment on its left. Elements of the reconstituted German Sixth Army had taken Lille and were pressing westward around Armentières to threaten St. Omer and the vital Channel ports. Joffre not only welcomed the BEF extension of the front but also devised a role for it in assisting his own plans. General French was optimistic about using his cavalry to surround and cut off what he believed were scattered German pockets.

Joffre hoped to exploit a presumed weak spot in German deployments between Armentières and Antwerp, through which he could envelop the shifting German front. He planned to extend his left wing so as to hold the line of the Scheldt River from Tournai to Antwerp, aligning the front southwesterly from Tournai through Douai to Arras. Joffre expected Antwerp to hold against the besieging German III

Corps commanded by General Hans Hartwig von Beseler. Joffre's enthusiasm for this perceived opportunity was echoed by General Ferdinand Foch, appointed by Joffre to coordinate French army detachments in Flanders with Belgian and British forces. Joffre correctly sensed that Foch's forceful personality would bring success despite his lack of command authority.

General Maud'huy's Tenth Army held the Arras to Bethune-La Bassée portion of the line. It included the understrength II Cavalry Corps under General M. Henri de Mitry, augmented by the 87th and 89th divisions, two second-rate territorial infantry units. When it became apparent that Antwerp would fall and leave the Flanders coast in jeopardy, De Mitry's command was rushed north to plug a void at the Forest of Houthulst, south of the Belgian army sector along the Yser.

Antwerp fell on 9 October. Under German pressure, some sixty thousand Belgians, a British naval division, and some French marines were subsequently relocated to the Yser. Nonetheless, the fall of Antwerp threatened the loss of the BEF's lifeline. This dictated going on the offensive before the Germans could seize the opportunity.

Chief of the German General Staff General Erich von Falkenhayn saw an opportunity to sweep what he referred to as the "contemptible little [British] army" into the sea. He knew that the front from Ypres to the south was manned only lightly, mostly by British cavalry and the two divisions of French territorials.

Falkenhayn planned to outflank the Allies, cutting them off from the coast before they could fully mobilize or reinforce. Time was essential, for the German numerical superiority on the Western Front was dwindling rapidly. Ignoring Hindenburg's demands that reinforcements be sent East, Falkenhayn determined to break through the thinly held Allied line and seize Dunkirk, Calais, and Boulogne. Falkenhayn had available five fresh corps sent by rail via Bruges, plus heavy siege artillery used against Antwerp. A large proportion of the men in the five corps were volunteer, undertrained university students. These new corps were combined with Beseler's III Corps into the German Fourth Army, commanded by Duke Albrecht of Württemberg. Albrecht also had available the powerful German siege guns from Antwerp.

The Allies were unaware of German strength. Generals French and Foch believed that only two or three German corps were in the area from Bruges and Ghent.

The British 7th Infantry Division and 3rd Cavalry Division under General Sir Henry Rawlinson had disembarked at Ostend and Zeebrugge too late to reinforce Antwerp. After covering the retreat of the Antwerp defenders to the Belgian coast, on 14 October this ad hoc force was redesignated IV Corps, taken under Sir John French's command, and sent to close the gap in the Allied line between de Mitry's cavalry and Ypres.

To the south of Ypres the BEF was gradually coming into line. The III Corps (General Sir William Pulteney) had been shifted to the Bethune-La Bassée corridor shortly after the French Tenth Army had been driven back from its attempted relief of Lille. Stopped short in its efforts to recover the city, the Tenth was hard pressed to contain the German Sixth Army's drive.

General Horace Smith-Dorrien's II Corps entered the line in the Armentières area northwest of Lille (and north of Pulteney's force) on 13 October, with Allenby's Cavalry Corps shifting to its left to link with IV Corps. With the German XIX Infantry Corps and Lieutenant General Georg von der Marwitz's Cavalry Corps already advancing to the important ridgeline centered on Messines southeast of Ypres, III Corps and Allenby's cavalry were engaged before they reached their intended forward base at Armentières and made it to only just east of that position.

The BEF's remaining component, General Sir Douglas Haig's I Corps, did not arrive in position three miles north of Ypres until 20 October, at which point it went immediately into action against the German XXVI Reserve Corps (an element of the heretofore undetected Fourth Army) at Poelkappelle, barely a mile northeast of Haig's forward elements. Additional pressure from the northwest was applied by the German XXIII Reserve Corps, which sliced through the sector patrolled by de Mitry's cavalry.

On 17 October Falkenhayn launched his main attack against Allied positions at Ypres. It was part of a general offensive, including Armentières and the Artois sector to the south and a battle at Yser, to drive through to Calais and other Channel ports.

The first Allied units to grasp the magnitude of the German drive were forward elements of Rawlinson's force, ordered on the night of 17 October simply to "move on Menin." Rawlinson advanced cautiously, concerned that he not push too far ahead of III Corps to his right and worried about reports of German troops converging north of Menin, where they would menace his flank.

Rawlinson's caution exasperated French, who had no inkling of the massive accumulation of German forces to his front. When IV Corps moved out again on the 19th, air reconnaissance confirmed the arrival of the vanguard of the German Fourth and Sixth armies, threatening the slopes and ridges dominating the eastern and southeastern approaches to Ypres, from which all troop movements in the town could be observed. Alarmed, Rawlinson pulled 7th Division back from the outskirts of Menin to Gheluvelt, where it dug in pending the arrival of I Corps.

French acknowledged that the German III Corps was a powerful threat to Belgian forces holding the Flanders coast; nonetheless, he assumed that the main German strength was on the Lys River line, Courtrai-Menin-Armentières, well to the south of Ypres. French believed that there was but one German corps between Menin and Ostend, ignoring even his own intelligence officers' underestimation of three and a half corps.

By the time Haig's I Corps arrived on line on the 20th, British headquarters realized that the Germans had begun a broad advance. Haig, therefore, moved cautiously, consolidating each newly won position before attempting another move. Just a few miles north of Ypres, near Langemarck, I Corps collided with advance elements of the German XXIII and XXVI reserve corps. This inadvertent melee ended in stalemate, but the specter of the German soldiers singing to band music as they marched in close order into the waiting muzzles of the expert British marksmen spawned the term *kindermord bei Ypern* (massacre of the innocents at Ypres).

Until 20 October the Allies had enjoyed limited tactical success. The marshy and obstructed Flemish tableland, densely choked with farms in stretches between large villages, was exceptionally suitable for defense. The Germans, after initial gains, had been pushed back from the insubstantial knolls and wooded ridgelines dominating Ypres. The British had crossed the Lys River and secured Armentières. They now held a line to Givenchy on the tiny Aubers Ridge covering Lille.

By 21 October, however, Falkenhayn had gained the initiative. The Germans had the new reserve corps and considerable heavy artillery, vastly outnumbering expertly handled British batteries and quick-firing French 75mm guns. Falkenhayn has been chided for stretching his attack over so large an area, but he gained superiority at the two critical positions on the perimeter of what was to become the Ypres salient, and his more remote operations tied down enemy troops.

British I Corps was stalled north of Ypres by the flood of fresh German troops, whereupon French at last agreed with Haig and Rawlinson that the intended advance to Bruges would be shelved in favor of trying to hold the newly gained ground. Beginning on 22 October and continuing for the next three weeks, Haig's command was attacked almost daily. The first critical test came on 22 October, when General Sir Julian Byng's 3rd Cavalry Division and a brigade of de Mitry's horse were forced back from the crucial Passchendaele ridge, uncovering Haig's flank.

The true significance of the German movements was just beginning to unfold. The German Fourth Army, advancing southwestward, and Sixth Army, advancing west and northwestward, were compressing the Allies into a salient at Ypres. German forces in that area outnumbered the Allies by three to one.

The arrival of the French IX Corps (General Pierre Dubois) on 23 October permitted Haig to withdraw his exposed 1st Division to Zillebeke in the rear as a reserve strike force, but Foch sent Dubois on a futile three-pronged attack along the northern fringe of Polygon Woods. Massed ranks of the German assaults were shattered by the accurate rifle fire of the "Old Contemptibles." Their fire was so rapid that the Germans mistook them for machine-gun formations. Nevertheless, the Germans had ample reserves.

On 24 October the weight of the German assault switched to Rawlinson's sector on the southeast fringe of the salient, focusing upon the 7th Division at Gheluvelt. The point of the British wedge at Kruiseecke was sliced off through the flanks. The 7th Division was so dissipated from this hammering that on 26 October IV Corps was dismantled. The 7th Division was taken under Haig's command, and 3rd Cavalry absorbed into Allenby's corps at Messines, the seam between the British IV and III corps.

On 24 October Falkenhayn concluded that forces at hand were insufficient to crack the Allies near Ypres. The frustration of Albrecht's Fourth army before Ypres was matched by the inability of Prince Rupprecht's Sixth army to turn the city's southeastern defenses and the Armentières front held by the British III Corps. From inactive sectors of the line near the Aisne Falkenhayn formed Army Group Fabeck (General Max von Fabeck), consisting of the augmented II Bavarian and XV corps, six divisions, and 257 heavy guns and howitzers. It was inserted between Fourth and Sixth armies and positioned to thrust northwestward between Zandvoorde and Messines to capture the dominating Kemmel Heights and isolate Allied troops north of Ypres. News of General Paul von Hindenburg's repulse before Warsaw and an imminent Russian advance through Silesia intensified Falkenhayn's sense of urgency.

The preliminary German assault on 29 October came out of a dense mist at the junction of the British 1st and 7th divisions along the Menin to Ypres road. Hampered by surprise, a shortage of artillery shells, and badly fitting rifle ammunition, two Guard battalions were annihilated in a vain defense of the Gheluvelt crossroads. Haig's counteroffensive succeeded only in retaking high ground to the south of Menin road but not the crossroads just to the east.

On the morning of 30 October the XXIII Reserve Corps of the German Fourth Army moved against Bixschoote and Langemarck on the north, while its XXVII Reserve Corps was directed on Gheluvelt in concert with Army Group Fabeck's attack on the Messines Ridge along the Menin Road. Although the 87th French Territorial Division was driven from Bixschoote, the French 17th Infantry held against repeated German blows at neighboring Langemarck. Farther south, the British 2nd Cavalry Division was forced back on St. Eloi, the 1st Division's efforts at assistance being obstructed by heavy German howitzer fire.

Responding to Haig's appeals for support, Dubois sent his IX Corps reserve from de Mitry's sector on the north to bolster Allenby's battered three cavalry divisions, outnumbered six to one by the German forces pushing toward the Messines ridge and the Kemmel elevation. Allenby's corps had been pressured from Zandvoorde and was being hammered at Hollebeke, dangerously exposing the right flank of the depleted 7th Infantry Division on their north.

The following day, 31 October, was the crisis point. Allenby's reinforced cavalry stood firm, but, farther north at the Gheluvelt position, the British 1st Division caved in, allowing the Germans into the village. Haig issued orders to fall back to cover Ypres. A fragment of 1st Battalion, the South Wales Borderers, retook a vital north flank position at Gheluvelt chalet, however, and held on while a battalion provided by the 2nd Division counterattacked from Polygon Woods to link up with the beleaguered Borderers and push into the disordered German ranks in the village. The recapture of Gheluvelt reestablished the line and prevented the shattering of the Ypres defensive network.

On 1 November persistent German offensives succeeded in penetrating to Messines ridge, but by now French reinforcements were taking over most of Allenby's sector. During the next week, detachments from French General Victor d'Urbal's Eighth Army contained German efforts to expand the narrow wedge at Messines. At that point the British battalions were on the average down to less than half strength, most having a third or less of their starting numbers.

Meanwhile, Falkenhayn had been preparing one last bid for Ypres. As German artillery continued to smash the shallow, sandy Allied trenches and demolish the town, a new German corps of two divisions of the elite Prussian Guard under General Plettenberg arrived and was reorganized with elements of Army Group Fabeck and Fourth Army to form Army Group Linsingen. On 11 November a German diversionary attack near the Yser canal drew off precious French reserves to the north.

The main German blow fell on the debilitated defenses along the southern hinge. Twelve and a half German divisions, including the Guard, attacked in dense formation out of the mist in pouring rain and wind on a front of nine miles from Messines to north of the Menin road. This attack failed, and the Guards were decimated. A scratch force of sappers, cooks, batmen, and transport-drivers of the 52nd Battalion, Oxfordshire Light Infantry, drove the fatigued German troops back through the tangled undergrowth of Nun's Wood.

With the onset of winter weather fighting at Ypres ceased, except for sporadic action. The battle had been very costly. The British regular army, the Old Contemptibles, sustained fifty thousand casualties and for all practical purposes ceased to exist. The French also sustained approximately fifty-thousand casualties, but the Germans suffered one hundred and thirty thousand. The Battle of First Ypres also ended the war of maneuver on the Western Front.

James J. Bloom

References

Brice, Beatrix. *The Battle Book of Ypres.* London: J. Murray, 1927. Reprint. New York: St. Martin's, 1988.

Edmonds, Sir James, Brigadier General. *Military Operations: France and Belgium, 1914.* Vol. 2. London and New York: Macmillan, 1925.

Farrar-Hockley, Anthony, General. *Death of an Army.* New York: William Morrow, 1968.

Foch, Ferdinand. *The Memoirs of Marshal Foch.* Translated by Colonel T. Bentley Mott. New York: Doubleday, 1931.

Poseck, M. von, Lieutenant General. *The German Cavalry in Belgium and France, 1914.* Berlin: E.S. Mittler und Sohn, 1923.

Schwink, Otto. *Die Schlacht an der Yser und bei Ypern im Herbst, 1914.* Oldenburg: G. Stalling, 1918.

See also ALLENBY, EDMUND; FALKENHAYN, ERICH VON; HAIG, DOUGLAS; JOFFRE, JOSEPH; MAUD'HUY, LOUIS; RACE TO THE SEA; RAWLINSON, HENRY; SMITH-DORRIEN, HORACE

Ypres, Second Battle of (22 April–25 May 1915)

Second Ypres saw the first practical employment of poison gas in warfare, although the Germans' low expectations for its success and resulting limited objectives squandered its potential effectiveness.

In late winter of 1915 chief of the German General Staff General Erich von Falkenhayn was preparing to shift a considerable segment of his forces in France and Belgium to the Eastern Front for the Gorlice-Tarnow offensive, while standing fast in the West. Amidst indications that the French were readying their own initiative (they were replacing the British forces in portions of the line preparatory to the Vimy Ridge assault), Falkenhayn determined to mask his realignment of forces by a demonstration along the vulnerable enemy-held Ypres salient.

On a tactical level the Germans were hopeful of flattening the exposed salient. Chemical warfare experts advised Falkenhayn that the designated area was a poorly protected objective, and that for purposes of employing gas the Ypres feature possessed the most suitable combination of trench configuration, terrain composition, and prevailing winds.

Allied forces had gained possession of a rather ragged bulge enclosing the Belgian town during the First Battle of Ypres in October-November of 1914. The northern face of the salient was held by two French divisions under the overall command of General Ferdinand Foch's Northern Army Group. British General Sir Horace Lockwood Smith-Dorrien's Second Army manned the line from that point southward, five divisions strong along the salient itself. Falkenhayn assembled eleven divisions of the Fourth Army under General Sixt von Arnim against Ypres.

Falkenhayn doubted that the employment of chlorine gas would bring significant success. The first experience with asphyxiating agents, against the Russians in Poland on 31 January 1915, had been disappointing; on that occasion, however, the extreme cold did not permit the gas to vaporize sufficiently for dispersal. While there were valid strategic and tactical incentives for the project, it was principally ventured as a technical experiment in the application of gas warfare.

The indifference with which the German High Command viewed the attack was indicated by the lack of special facilities adapted for efficient direction and release of the vapors. Five thousand commercially available cylinders were simply set into a forward trench on the southern face of the salient in batteries of twenty each. This arrangement conformed with the German meteorological service's forecast for southerly winds during the early spring season. When the winds continued to blow from the north throughout February, the cylinders had to be switched to the salient's northern perspective early in April.

The Allies were deplorably negligent in their evaluation and transmittal of intelligence—distinct corroboration—divulging the placement and intended use of the gas cylinders. The removal and replacement of cylinders was noticed by French observers, but the information was not passed on to the British commanders who relieved their French counterparts in the affected sector. This nonchalance was again demonstrated when prisoners taken on the southern perimeter early in March provided their French captors with details of the position and use of the cylinders, as did a German deserter just a week before the attack. This information was lost at lower levels in the French army chain of command. Conclusive evidence was provided when a British trench-raiding party captured gas cylinders. Smith-Dorrien failed to attach any significance to the matter and did not issue any alert. One of the corps commanders did circulate a rather casual advisory on the conceivable use of gas.

Possibly, the Entente commanders were conditioned by their own humane trust in the strictures against a barbarous weapon that had been outlawed by the Hague Convention. Further, British officials had earlier rejected proposals to develop and employ asphyxiating agents because they were considered beyond the pale of civilized behavior. Mirror-imaging attributed similar sentiments to the Germans.

Falkenhayn's lukewarm attitude toward the tactical experiment was demonstrated by his failure to allocate reserves to exploit any possible breakthrough. In fact, this omission worked to German advantage to some extent in the maintenance of surprise. British Royal Flying Corps patrols did not detect the usual troop concentrations that would herald an impending attack.

The attack was preceded on the morning of 22 April 1915 by the usual cannonade. Then, at 17:30, a second brief but intense bombardment was accompanied by a strange greenish yellow cloud observed rolling toward a portion of the line held by a division of French colonial troops from Algeria and another division of territorials, composed of middle-aged second-line troops. The Algerians were the first to experience the choking chlorine gas. They immediately fled their positions in dazed agony, choking and spitting. The scene unnerved the adjacent territorials, who were next to experience the suffocating fumes and the panic, joining their neighbors in an effort to escape the choking fog.

The abandoned trenchworks formed a four-mile gap in the Entente's line, which elements of the German Fourth Division moved up to occupy. Because of the presence of the gas, notwithstanding the rudimentary respirators issued to the first wave, the German pursuit was rather dilatory. Darkness and confusion of the flight left the Germans ignorant of the full extent of the rout. Further, the lack of German reserves to exploit the breach allowed time for the British and French troops just to the rear to reform.

Second Army commander Smith-Dorrien exploited the German caution after the initial thrust in order to plug the hole with the only available troops, the green 1st Canadian Division. The Canadians braced to contain any follow-on attack and even mounted some counterattacks on the 23rd, which convinced Arnim that the enemy line was more secure than it actually was. During the hiatus, Smith-Dorrien had the Canadians construct improvised defense works and issued them crude respiratory protectors—dampened cheesecloth. These improvisations were sufficient to allow the Canadians to stand fast in the face of a second gas attack on 24 April. A reserve brigade displayed exemplary courage on that day, while suffering heavy casualties with both flanks enveloped.

General Foch, oblivious to the dread aroused by the new form of warfare, ordered his French troops to mount a major counterattack. Still attempting to resuscitate their fractured divisions, the French troops ignored the command. The demonstrated effects of the new terror weapon were enough to convince Smith-Dorrien to regard Foch's orders as nonsense. He instead suggested re-forming a more defensible line three miles to the rear, just in front of Ypres. Angered by this proposal, British Expeditionary Force commander Field Marshal Sir John French sacked Smith-Dorrien and replaced him with Sir Herbert Plumer.

The Canadians had shown remarkable aggressiveness in the face of the ghastly effects of the new weapon, but their counterattacks could barely hold back the weight of the German attacks against the poorly situated salient. Additional German assaults accompanied by poison gas on 27 April convinced Plumer to retire to the line originally proposed by the ousted Smith-Dorrien on 1 May. This time French acquiesced. The unjustified stain on Smith-Dorrien's record was never rectified.

The German Fourth Army continued to squeeze the slightly flattened Ypres bulge until 25 May, when all attacks were broken off. The arrival of Indian reinforcements had provided enough solidity by then to contain the German pressure, while the surprise factor underlying the use of gas had been squandered.

James J. Bloom

References

Crutwell, C.R.M.F. *History of the Great War, 1914–1918*. 2nd ed. Oxford: Clarendon, 1936.

Edmonds, Sir James E., and Captain G.C. Wynne. *Military Operations: France and Belgium 1915*. Vol. 2. London: Macmillan, 1928.
Falls, Cyril B. *The Great War*. New York: Putnams, 1959.
Liddell Hart, B.H. *History of the World War*. 2nd ed. London: Faber & Faber, 1934.
McEntee, Girard Lindsley. *Military History of the World War*. New York: Charles Scribner's Sons, 1937.

See also CANADA, ARMY; CHEMICAL WARFARE; FALKENHAYN, ERICH VON; FOCH, FERDINAND; PLUMER, HERBERT; SMITH-DORRIEN, HORACE

Ypres, Third Battle of
See PASSCHENDAELE

Yudenich, Nikolai Nikolaevich (1862–1933)

Russian general, born in Minsk province to a noble family on 30 July 1862. Yudenich graduated from the Aleksandrovsky Military College in 1881. Completing the General Staff Academy in 1887, he served in a variety of staff assignments until 1904. During the Russo-Japanese War Yudenich distinguished himself as a combat commander, first of an infantry regiment, then a brigade. Promoted to major general in 1905, Yudenich was posted to the Caucasus and became deputy chief of staff of the Caucasus Army in 1907. By 1912 he had risen to become chief of staff and was serving in that capacity on the outbreak of the First World War.

While many of the best Caucasus units were being sent to other fronts, the Third Turkish Army invaded. Yudenich resisted suggestions of Caucasus Army commander General Myshlaevsky that he withdraw. Instead he defended Sarikamish and in December won a great victory there. In January of 1915 Yudenich was promoted to lieutenant general and given command of the Caucasus Army. Known as a daring, resourceful general, Yudenich defeated another Turkish advance in the summer of 1915 and in 1916 he mounted a series of spoiling attacks that captured Erzurim, Trebizond, and Erzincan and won him lasting professional acclaim.

In March of 1917 Yudenich replaced Grand Duke Nikolai Nikolaevich as supreme civil and military commander of the Caucasus front. He himself was soon recalled and remained in Petrograd until the November Revolution forced him into hiding. In 1919 he joined anti-Bolshevik forces near Petrograd and was for a time commander of the northwestern front. In October of 1919 his quite small White force reached the outskirts of Petrograd before it was forced to retire into Estonia. Yudenich went into exile in France in 1920 and died at Nice on 5 October 1933, hailed by exile community members as the only undefeated Russian general of the war.

Spencer C. Tucker

References

Allen, W.E.D., and Paul Muratoff. *Caucasian Battlefields: A History of the Wars on the Turco-Caucasian Border, 1828–1921.* Cambridge, 1953.
Herwig, Holger H., and Neil M. Heyman. *Biographical Dictionary of World War I.* Westport, Conn.: Greenwood, 1982.
Rutherford, Ward. *The Russian Army in World War I.* London: Gordon Cremonesi, 1975.

See also CAUCASUS FRONT; RUSSIA, CIVIL WAR IN

Yugoslavia, Creation of

The idea of forming a south-Slav, or Yugoslav, state had its roots in the Slavic national revival of the 1800s and drew its most ardent supporters among the Croatians, Slovenians, and Serbians of the Austro-Hungarian Empire. There were, however, a number of obstacles to creating such a state, including the movement that sought to change the Dual Monarchy into a confederation of Germans, Hungarians, and Slavs. The existence of an aggressive, expansionist Serbian state also augured ill for the creation of a Yugoslav state, since many, including Bishop Strossmayer, an early proponent of the Yugoslav idea, feared that the Serbians would dominate rather than cooperate with their brother Slavs. Many Croats also were intensely loyal to the Hapsburg royal house, and a number of Austria's general staff were Croatian, among them Ivo Perčević, Stjepan Sarkotić, and Svetozar Boroević von Bojna. Finally, Austro-Hungarian Slavs had evolved a cosmopolitan Catholic culture that looked to Rome, Vienna, and Budapest, while the Serbs had developed a narrowly Orthodox culture that identified religion with nationality under an autocratic Turkish rule.

During the war the Serbian government led by Nikola Pašić, pursued a narrowly nationalistic program of expansion, alternately seeking to enlarge Serbia's territory and championing the creation of a Yugoslav state, as the diplomatic and military climate dictated. The Austro-Hungarian Slavs organized a Yugoslav committee under the leadership of Ante Trumbić and Frano Supilo, who sought the support of the Entente for the creation of a federal Yugoslav republic. Such a program was anathema to the Serbian ruling parties, who had no desire to share power with Croatians, Slovenes, and Bosnian Muslims, and whose efforts to "serbianize" Macedonia and Kosovo would have been threatened by the creation of a federal state. Nor was the Serbian monarchy happy with the Yugoslav Committee, since its republican leanings threatened the very survival of the Karađorđević dynasty. By 1916 Supilo had resigned, frustrated by the Yugoslav Committee's inability to obtain support from the Entente and fearful that "Serbian Orthodox exclusivism" would "ruin everything."

Trumbić, who now emerged as the real leader of the Yugoslav Committee, found himself diplomatically isolated and forced to accept an agreement in 1917 that recognized the Serbian royal house as that of a state of "Serbs, Croats, and Slovenes." The agreement was signed on the island of Corfu by members of the Serbian government and the Yugoslav Committee and came to be known as the Corfu Declaration. Its signature lost the émigrés the support of the republican-minded emigrants in the Americas, and it failed to ensure equal treatment for non-Serbs within the new state, which initially would be under a Serbian monarch and a Serbian government.

In late October of 1918, as Austria-Hungary disintegrated, members of the Slovene and Croatian parties met in Zagreb and declared the creation of a new state comprising Croatia, Slovenia, Dalmatia, and Bosnia in order to preclude the possibility of an Italian occupation of the Dalmatian coast and Istria. Members of the newly declared state also found themselves forced to deal with Pašić and the Serbian government, owing to their inability to obtain recognition from the Entente. Isolated diplomatically and fearful that Italy would obtain large areas of Croatian and Slovene territory, the new government concluded an agreement with Pašić in Geneva in November of 1918. It renounced its sovereignty and joined Serbia to form a south-Slav state under the Serbian monarchy in return for promises of a freely elected constituent assembly and equality for all ethnic groups. At the same time, Serbian troops were occupying Montenegro, where they staged a hasty plebiscite that ousted King Nikola and joined Montenegro to Serbia.

Serbian forces had also occupied the rest of the new state, and protests against unification, such as that by Croatian nationalists in early December, were put down by military force. When the Constituent Assembly was finally convened two years later, Serbian police and military forces had effectively crushed all opposition to the creation of a centralized, monarchical state controlled by the Serbian parties of old Serbia, who had formed alliances with the Serbians in Croatia and opportunistic groups in other areas. Those delegates who refused a loyalty oath to the Karađorđević dynasty were simply not seated. The constitution, which consolidated Serbian control of the new state, was appropriately passed on Vidovdan, the anniversary of the Serbian defeat by the Turks on Kosovo Polje in 1389. The result was twenty years of repression and internal unrest as non-Serbs within the new state sought to obtain equal rights, and the Serbian royal house and Serbian politicians tried to maintain their hold on power.

James J. Sadkovich

References

Grlica, George. "Trumbić's Policy and Croatian National Interests from 1914 to the Beginning of 1918." *Journal of Croatian Studies* (1973–74).

Janković, Dragoslav. *Jugoslavensko pitanje i krfska deklaracija 1917. godine.* Belgrade: Savremena Administracija, 1967.

———. "Ženevska konferencija o stvaranju jugoslavenske zajednice." *Istorija xx veka* (1963).

Jugoslavenski odbor u Londonu u povodu 50–godišnjice osnivanja. Zagreb: Jugoslavenska Akademija Znanosti i Umjetnosti, 1966.

Lederer, Ivo. *Yugoslavia and the Paris Peace Settlement. Yugoslav-Italian Relations and the Territorial Settlement, 1918–1920.* Princeton: Princeton University Press, 1957.

Naučni skup u povodu 50–godišnjice raspada Austro-ugarske monarhije i stvaranja jugoslavnekse države. Zagreb: Jugoslavenska Akademija Znanosti i Umjetnosti, 1969.

Paulova, Milada. *Jugoslavenski Odbor. Povijest jugoslavenske emigracije za svjetskog rata od 1914 do 1918.* Zagreb: Prosvjeta, 1925.

Šepić, Dragovan. *Italija, saveznici i jugoslavensko pitanje, 1914–1918.* Zagreb: Školska Knjiga, 1970.

———. "The Question of Yugoslav Union in 1918." *Journal of Contemporary History* (1968).

Živojinović, Dragovan. *America, Italy and the Birth of Yugoslavia.* Boulder, Colo.: East European Quarterly, 1972.

See also ALEXANDER, PRINCE; BOSNIA-HERZEGOVINA; CORFU, DECLARATION OF; MONTENEGRO; PAŠIĆ, NIKOLA; SERBIA; TRUMBIĆ, ANTE

Y

Z

Zaionchkovsky, Andrei Medardovich (1862–1926)

Russian general, born into a noble Russian family in Orel Province on 20 December 1862. Zaionchkovsky graduated from the Nikolaevsky Engineering School in 1883 and the General Staff Academy in 1888. Seeing combat in the Russo-Japanese War, Zaionchkovsky rose from a regimental commander to brigade commander. In 1912 he was assigned the command of the 37th Infantry Division, from which he was promoted to Corps Commander in early 1915.

By 1916 Zaionchkovsky was commanding the Russo-Romanian Dobrudja Detachment defending the Romanian-Bulgarian border. His assignment was unenviable. Russian strategists had correctly concluded that their Romanian ally's borders would be difficult to defend and her troops inferior. The Dobrudja Detachment proved unmanageable at best. Romanian troops repeatedly failed to support the Russians in combat and the Russians tended to pillage the local Romanian farms and villages.

Zaionchkovsky failed to maintain cohesion within his forces when attacked by a smaller force commanded by German Field Marshal August von Mackensen. His troops were pushed out of the strategic port of Constanza in late October of 1916. Zaionchkovsky was relieved of command after his forces collapsed under General Erich von Falkenhayn's Ninth Army.

Despite his failures in Romania, Zaionchkovsky was promoted to general of infantry in 1917 and appointed commander of the XVIII Corps. He was pensioned after the March Revolution but joined the Red Army in 1918. He served as chief of staff of the 13th Red Army during operations against the White forces.

After the revolution Zaionchkovsky distinguished himself as a military scholar. A specialist in Russian operations during the war, he led the Red Army Commission on the study of the war and taught at the Red Army Military Academy. He died in Moscow on 22 March 1926.

Jeff Kinard

References

Herwig, Holger H., and Heyman, Neil M. *Biographical Dictionary of World War I.* Westport, Conn.: Greenwood, 1982.

Stone, Norman. *The Eastern Front, 1914–1917.* New York: Charles Scribner's Sons, 1975.

See also MACKENSEN, AUGUST VON; ROMANIAN CAMPAIGN; RUSSIA, CIVIL WAR IN

Zeebrugge, Raid of, 1918

See OSTEND AND ZEEBRUGGE, RAIDS OF

Zeppelins

Zeppelins were German rigid hydrogen-filled airships employed by the Imperial German Army, most notably by the Imperial German Navy, for reconnaissance, patrol, and bombardment. Zeppelin airships inaugurated the era of sustained strategic bombardment of urban areas.

The zeppelin was the brainchild of Count Ferdinand von Zeppelin (1838–1917), a wealthy retired army officer and inventor. After years of experimentation Zeppelin flew his first airship, the LZ 1, in 1900. The LZ 1 consisted of an aluminum hull structure containing a series of hydrogen-filled gas cells to provide lift;

it was powered by two fifteen-horsepower engines at a speed of only sixteen miles per hour. The early airships were technically unreliable and capable of limited performance. They did, however, fire the imagination of the German public. When one early airship, the LZ 4, was destroyed at its moorings in a freak accident in August of 1908, an apparently spontaneous outpouring of public support provided the financing necessary for Zeppelin to continue his developmental work. By 1914 a commercial airline (*Deutsche Luftschiffahrts Aktien Gesellschaft*, DELAG) was operating scheduled service to a number of German cities and compiled an admirable distance and safety record.

The German military was not slow to see the military possibilities of the count's invention. The navy's Admiral Alfred von Tirpitz and Admiral Paul Behncke expected mass raids by bomb-carrying zeppelin airships to cause panic among an enemy population. Chief of the general staff General Helmuth von Moltke believed that in the zeppelin Germany possessed a weapon of potentially awesome power, given its great range and payload. "England will cease to be an island," one commentator predicted confidently. By 1914 some twenty zeppelins were in service with both the German army and navy airship divisions. It is likely that the emphasis placed upon the airships retarded to a certain extent the development of heavier-than-air flight in Germany during the prewar era.

At war's outbreak, however, the zeppelin force was unleashed not over enemy capital cities but over the battlefield. Army airships attacked French and Belgian garrison towns and reconnoitered over the Front. Losses were extremely heavy (including one airship finished off by German ground fire). This early combat experience caused the army leadership to sour on the zeppelin to some extent; it would abandon rigid airships entirely in June of 1917. The German navy would enthusiastically carry the concept forward.

Kaiser Wilhelm II, mindful of his close familial ties to the British royal family, initially refused to sanction air raids on London but was gradually persuaded to alter his position. On the night of 31 May 1915 army zeppelins bombed London for the first time. On 8 September of that year a naval airship raid under the command of Captain Heinrich Mathy caused extensive damage to the capital. The public outcry was substantial, and British coro-

ners' inquiries turned in verdicts of "willful murder" against Kaiser Wilhelm.

The actual material damage inflicted by the zeppelins on Great Britain was modest. In fifty-one recorded zeppelin attacks on the British Isles, the airships dropped only 196 tons of bombs, killing 557 and wounding 1,358 civilians. British sources estimated that the raids caused £1.5 million in property damage throughout the war (rats, by comparison, destroyed some £70 million worth of property annually).

British defenses and countermeasures, consisting of searchlight batteries, antiaircraft guns, and interceptors firing incendiary bullets, exacted a steady toll of the raiders as the campaign continued. British sources estimate that defense against the zeppelin menace required stationing twelve RFC squadrons, consisting of 110 aircraft and 2,200 men. Antiaircraft units employed an additional 17,341 personnel. While this diversion represented a substantial commitment, British defenses by mid-1916 had definitely gained the upper hand against the zeppelin threat. While raids by the Naval Airship Division, under the energetic leadership of Captain Peter Strasser, continued until the final months of the war, the German airship offensive had passed its peak in autumn of 1916, in a series of raids that claimed, among others, LZ 31 and its ace commander, Mathy.

Zeppelins were used throughout the war for many tasks other than strategic bombardment. The German High Seas Fleet relied on zeppelins to carry out reconnaissance and scouting missions (a role traditionally reserved for light cruisers), but bad weather frequently curtailed their use. At the Battle of Jutland, for example, dense mist prevented the two zeppelins present from making any notable contribution to the naval action. On occasion, the airships were employed in an antisubmarine role, with little success. Finally, in November of 1917, one airship, the L. 59, *Afrikaschiff*, carried out an epic long-distance flight intended to reach German East Africa with a cargo of provisions for the German garrison there. It got as far as Khartoum, only to be recalled by a radio message that German troops under General von Lettow-Vorbeck had been defeated at Makonde Heights.

Although the operational effectiveness of the zeppelins slumped as the war progressed, technical improvements in German airship design continued apace. A refined late-war zeppelin, the L. 70, commissioned in July of 1918, was 694 feet long, powered by seven Maybach engines (1,715 total horsepower) and attained a trial speed of eighty-one miles per hour. It carried a "useful lift" of 97,100 pounds. By way of comparison, LZ 1 had been only 420 feet long and was virtually incapable of making any headway against a light breeze.

On balance, the zeppelin was simply not a cost-effective weapon. During the series of airship operations, the navy lost fifty-three of seventy-three airships, while the army lost half of its fleet of fifty-two. Bad weather, accidents, air raids on zeppelin sheds, and improved British defenses combined to make zeppelin service even more hazardous than was duty in the navy's U-boat arm. Although the Zeppelin campaign played a role in diverting British air defense resources from the Western Front, the actual effect of the raids was minimal, once the British population overcame the initial shock of the new mode of warfare. The German official air historian, assessing the campaign a few years after the war, concluded that "the vast waste of material and personnel" stood "in no relation to the success that could have been achieved." The zeppelin ushered in the era of strategic air warfare, but it was an inauspicious debut.

Richard R. Muller

References
Kennett, Lee. *A History of Strategic Bombing.* New York: Charles Scribner's Sons, 1982.
Morrow, John H., Jr. *The Great War in the Air: Military Aviation from 1909 to 1921.* Washington: Smithsonian Institution Press, 1993.
Norman, Aaron. *The Great Air War.* New York: Macmillan, 1968.
Robinson, Douglas H. *The Zeppelin in Combat: A History of the German Naval Airship Division, 1912–1918.* Sun Valley, Calif.: John W. Caler, 1966.

See also AIR WARFARE: STRATEGIC BOMBING

Zhekov, Nikola Todorov (1864–1949)

Bulgarian general, born in Sliven on 25 December 1864. Zhekov graduated from the military academy in Sophia and fought in Bulgaria's war with Serbia in 1885. During the Balkan Wars of 1912–13 Zhekov rose from regimental commander to chief of staff of the Second Army. Having risen to war minister in the cabinet of Premier Vasil Radoslavov, Zhekov readied the Bulgarian army in anticipation of Bulgaria's alliance with Germany and Austria (August-October 1915). He assumed direct command of the army on 11 October 1915.

The Germans proved difficult allies. Showing little concern for Bulgaria's own military interests, the larger German army brought incorporated Bulgarian units under its command to achieve German objectives. As an element of Army Group Mackensen, Bulgaria's First Army helped the Germans shatter Serbia's defenses in 1915. Bulgarian troops took the Aegean port of Kavalla as part of the successful offensive of August-September 1916. In the fall of 1916 Zhekov was again pressed to detach more troops to Field Marshal August von Mackensen for an offensive against Romania. All the while, the Germans offered little aid to Bulgaria for defense of its extensive Macedonian front against threats from eastern Greece and Salonika.

In addition to the friction with his German allies, Zhekov found himself caught up in the secret movement to oust premier Radoslavov. In the fall of 1917, aware of the severe conflicts between Zhekov and the government over army supply problems, an opposition group attempted to enlist Zhekov. Zhekov declined and reported the plotters. External as well as internal conflicts became so extreme, however, that Zhekov finally joined the anti-Rudoslavov movement, which ousted the premier in June of 1918.

With Bulgaria losing the war and the army close to mutiny, Zhekov entered exile in Germany. Returning to Bulgaria after the war to defend his reputation, he was sentenced to a lengthy prison term. After three years Zhekov was granted amnesty and returned to Germany. A pro-fascist, Zhekov supported Hitler and the Nazi movement. He died in Germany on 6 October 1949.

Jeff Kinard

References
Bell, John D. *Peasants in Power.* Princeton: Princeton University Press, 1977.
Herwig, Holger H., and Heyman, Neil M. *Biographical Dictionary of World War I.* Westport, Conn.: Greenwood, 1982.

See also BULGARIA; RADOSLAVOV, VASIL

Zhilinsky, Yakov Grigorevich (1853–c. 1920)

Russian general, born on 27 March 1853 in Mikhailov, Riazan Province. Zhilinsky was commissioned in the Russian army after graduation from the Nikolaevsky Cavalry School in 1876. After graduating from the General Staff Academy in 1883, he held a variety of staff positions. Promoted to major general in 1900, he served on the staff of commander in chief General Aleksei Nikolaevich Kuropatkin during the Russo-Japanese War. Although Zhilinsky left no appreciable military record, there is indication that he was an opportunist who avidly pursued the advancement of his military career. Chosen by Minister of War Vladimir Sukhomlinov in 1911 as chief of staff of the Russian army, in 1912 he visited France, where he became an admirer of General Ferdinand Foch. In 1913 he was commander of the Warsaw Military District. With the outbreak of the war Zhilinsky openly campaigned to be commander in chief, but that post went to Grand Duke Nikolai Nikolaevich; Zhilinsky received command of the Northern front.

General Zhilinsky supported General Gregorii Danilov's argument that the key to Russian victory lay in defeating Germany first, instead of Austria-Hungary. Consequently, he played a major role in planning the Russian offensive into East Prussia in late August of 1914. As commander of the entire front, it was his task to coordinate the movement of the two pincers commanded by Generals Pavel Karlovich Rennenkampf and Aleksandr Vasilevich Samsonov. In this he failed miserably. The southern army under Samsonov started two days late and then encountered inhospitable terrain. What was even worse was that the two armies never established communication with each other and their uncoded radio messages were intercepted by the Germans. Finally, when the Germans attacked Samsonov's exposed flank, Zhilinsky, at headquarters, remained oblivious to the danger and failed to urge Rennenkampf to attack from the north until it was too late. The Tannenberg Campaign cost Russia 90,000 soldiers and was her first major military disaster of the war. During the subsequent investigation Rennenkampf and Zhilinsky blamed each other for the defeat (Samsonov had committed suicide). Rennenkampf, however, had powerful friends at court and remained unscathed, while Zhilinsky was relieved of his command. Appointed in 1915 as Russian military representative to the French High Command, Zhilinsky was a failure as a diplomat as well; Joffre secured his recall at the end of the next year. Zhilinsky returned to Russia and retired following the February Revolution. With the outbreak of the Russian Civil War, he joined the Whites and died somewhere in south Russia between 1918 and 1920.

John W. Bohon

References

Gurko, Basil, General. *Features and Figures of the Past*. Stanford: Stanford University Press, 1939.
Showalter, Dennis E. *Tannenberg, Clash of Empires*. Hamden, Conn.: Archon, 1991.

See also RENNENKAMPF, PAVEL

Zimmermann, Arthur (1864–1940)

German diplomat and foreign minister from November of 1916 to August of 1917; born on 5 October 1864 in Treuburg, East Prussia. Zimmermann joined the foreign service and served as consular agent in Shanghai, Canton, and Tientsin. His reputation for hard work allowed him to rise above his middle-class origins and become foreign office under-secretary in 1911. When a split developed in 1916 between the German civil government and the Army High Command over unrestricted submarine warfare, Zimmermann sided with the generals. He was promoted to foreign secretary on 25 November.

While the hardliners recognized that a U-boat campaign would provoke American belligerency, they calculated that the submarines would strangle Allied resistance before the United States Army could mobilize. To hedge the bet, in January of 1917 Zimmermann invited Mexican President Venustiano Carranza to enter a military alliance. Germany would supply Mexico with enough arms to reconquer the lands lost to the United States in the Mexican War. This absurd proposal was sent by coded telegram, but the British deciphered its contents and passed them along to President Wilson. When the note was released to the press, many denounced it as a fraud. On 3 March 1917 Zimmermann stupidly confirmed its authenticity, perhaps not realizing the effect on American public opinion.

Despite vehement attacks from the Reichstag, Zimmermann retained Kaiser Wilhelm II's favor and continued to pursue the alliance with Mexico. Carranza, already fearing a war with the United States, refused to take offensive action. Zimmermann was removed from office on 5 August 1917, and died in obscurity in Berlin on 7 June 1940.

Jeffrey M. Pilcher

References

Bosl, Karl, et al. *Biographisches Worterbuch zur Deutschen Geschichte*. Munich: Francke Verlag, 1975.

Katz, Friedrich. *The Secret War in Mexico: Europe, the United States, and the Mexican Revolution*. Chicago: University of Chicago Press, 1981.

Tuchman, Barbara W. *The Zimmermann Telegram*. Toronto: Macmillan, 1970.

See also ZIMMERMANN TELEGRAM

Zimmermann Telegram

The Zimmermann Telegram played a decisive role in the decision by the United States to declare war against Germany. Prior to receiving it from the British, President Wilson had believed that the United States must remain neutral if he were to be able to negotiate peace in Europe. By revealing Germany's offer of American territory as an enticement to bring Mexico and Japan in on her side in the event of war with the United States, the Zimmermann Telegram, combined with Germany's resumption of unrestricted submarine warfare, outraged Americans and forced Wilson to revise his foreign policy.

When, on 9 January 1917, the German High Command gambled to risk American intervention by renewing unrestricted submarine warfare, Foreign Minister Alfred Zimmermann assured his superiors that he could embroil the United States in a war with Mexico and Japan, thereby preventing it from playing a role in Europe. His confidence was based on Wilson's already strong involvement in Mexican affairs. General Victoriano Huerta's coup d'état and the assassination of President Francisco Madero in 1913 had led Wilson to support Huerta's chief rival, General Venustiano Carranza. Indeed, it had been German efforts to supply Huerta with arms that had led to the American occupation of Veracruz on 21 April 1914. With the outbreak of World War I, Germany had continued to support Huerta and then Pancho Villa in hopes of diverting American attention from Europe. Villa's raid on Columbus, New Mexico, on 9 March 1916 produced the desired results when Wilson sent 12,000 troops into Mexico. Although Carranza, by then president of Mexico, originally consented to the American expedition, he eventually demanded its withdrawal. It was this situation that made Zimmermann so confident of success.

On 12 November 1916, Zimmermann had cabled German ambassador von Eckhardt in Mexico with instructions to broach the possibility of an alliance with Mexico in exchange for U-boat bases. Carranza proved receptive to the overtures and sought closer economic, political, and military ties to Germany. Eckhardt, meanwhile, informed Zimmermann that Japan had established closer relations with Mexico and might be drawn into an alliance with Mexico. Zimmermann jumped at this "opportunity," hoping to entice Japan away from the Allies and into an alliance with Germany via Mexico. If he succeeded, he would not only sever the flow of American arms to the Allies by embroiling the United States in a war with Mexico and Japan, but also force Russia to fight a two-front war against Germany and Japan.

The German decision to resume unrestricted submarine warfare put Zimmermann's plans in motion. Zimmermann informed Eckhardt that the U-boat campaign would begin on 1 February 1917. If this resulted in war with the United States, Eckhardt was to propose that Mexico declare war on the United States in return for German financial support and, most important, the recovery of Texas, New Mexico, and Arizona. Eckhardt was also to urge Mexico to invite Japan into the alliance. On 16 January 1917, Zimmermann cabled the instructions to German ambassador to the United States Count Johann von Bernstorff. As senior German diplomat in the Western Hemisphere, he was responsible for conveying messages and overseeing German policy in the region. Zimmermann sent the telegram simultaneously by three different routes: first, over the powerful wireless station at Nauen (outside Berlin); second, through the Swedish Foreign Office; and third, through the American embassy in Berlin. The last route had been arranged by Colonel Edward M. House for the German government to communicate with Bernstorff in order to facilitate peace negotiations. Zimmermann enjoyed the irony of using American diplomatic cables to plot war against the United States.

Had Zimmermann acted sooner, he might have found Carranza more receptive. Instead, Mexican relations with the United States had improved after Wilson's decision on 25 January to withdraw American troops from Mexico. Although on 5 February Zimmermann instructed Eckhardt to propose the alliance without further delay, it was already too late because the American withdrawal was completed on the same day.

Ironically, Great Britain profited from the Zimmermann Telegram by one of the greatest intelligence coups of the war. Since the British had severed German transcontinental cables in the first weeks of the war, Germany had to rely primarily on the Nauen wireless station to send overseas messages. These were easily intercepted by Room 40, a special office within British Naval Intelligence under the leadership of Admiral Sir William Reginald Hall. Although German messages were coded, Room 40 possessed several German code books that had been recovered from sunken ships during the war. Since the Germans foolishly used the same code throughout the war, when Room 40 intercepted the Zimmermann Telegram along all three routes, cryptographers William Montgomery and Nigel de Grey had it deciphered before it reached Eckhardt.

Admiral Hall realized immediately that he might hold the key to bringing the United States into war. Before releasing the Zimmermann Telegram to the American government, however, Hall had to take precautions to keep the Germans from discovering that the British had obtained it. Hall also did not want the Americans to know that the British had tapped their diplomatic cable lines. British agents in Mexico, therefore, bribed a telegraph official and obtained a copy of the telegram as sent by Bernstorff to Eckhardt via Western Union. This led the Germans to believe that the United States had intercepted the message in America. On 23 February Foreign Minister Arthur Balfour formally presented the telegram to Ambassador Walter Page, who had long urged Wilson to intervene on the Allied side. Page promptly forwarded the telegram to Wilson, who did not question its authenticity.

The telegram had the desired effect in the United States. Wilson called upon Congress to pass legislation authorizing the arming of merchant ships. When ten senators led by Robert La Follette attempted a filibuster, Wilson released the telegram to the press on 28 February. Although a few Americans, including some senators, denounced it as a hoax, all doubts were removed when Zimmermann foolishly admitted it was authentic.

More than any single event, the Zimmermann Telegram prepared the vast majority of Americans for war because American territory was directly threatened. Its revelation was followed by the sinking of three American ships in the next three weeks. This brought home the German threat and led Wilson to ask Congress for a declaration of war, which came on 6 April 1917.

Justin D. Murphy

References

Bemis, Samuel Flagg. *Diplomatic History of the United States*. Rev ed. New York: Henry Holt, 1942.

Link, Arthur S. *Woodrow Wilson and the Progressive Era. 1910–1917*. New American Nation Series. New York: Harper & Row, 1954.

Tuchman, Barbara W. *The Zimmermann Telegram*. New York: Viking, 1958.

See also HALL, WILLIAM; ROOM 40; ZIMMERMANN, ARTHUR

Zionism

Zionism was the effort to establish a Jewish national state in Palestine. It emerged during the 1890s as a potent force in central and eastern Europe. The term Zionism was first used publicly on 23 January 1882 when Nathan Birnbaum, founder of a Zionist journal and originator of a plan for a Jewish state in Palestine, spoke to a group in Vienna. Zionism became a political force only with the 1896 publication of Theodor Herzl's *The Jewish State: An Attempt at a Modern Solution of the Jewish Question*, a powerful call for a Jewish homeland. Herzl, a journalist, was politicized as a result of the Dreyfus trial in France.

The French Revolution and the political changes it ushered in had given Jews in Western Europe fundamental civil rights. In Eastern Europe, however, restrictions persisted. During the nineteenth century the rise of nationalism affected the Jews as well as other Europeans, particularly in Central and Eastern Europe, where their ethnic cohesion and exclusion from political life led many Jews to view themselves as a distinct and separate nation. Nationalism led to animosity toward national groups and ethnic minorities, including Jews. Beginning in the 1880s a tide of anti-Semitism moved across Germany and Austria, while a series of pogroms were launched in Russia.

In response to organized violence against Jews came the first clear appeal for a Jewish state as the answer to the terror. Dr. Leon Pinsker's pamphlet *Self-Emancipation* appeared in 1892, and it provided a well-thought-out basis for a

Jewish homeland. Pinsker maintained that enlightenment and assimilation would not work and that a physical homeland was essential for the liberation of Jews. Others had already looked to Palestine, and in the 1880s emigration societies had been established in Russia. A number of individuals, encouraged by the Lovers of Zion and other such groups, went to Palestine.

It was the call of Herzl for a "congress of Jewish notables to discuss migration to a sovereign Jewish state" and his writings that turned Zionism into a mass movement and potent political force. A Zionist congress met in Basel, Switzerland, beginning on 29 August 1897. In the face of mounting Europeanwide violence against Jews, it announced that the only answer to the Jewish question was the reestablishment of a homeland in Palestine. A World Zionist Organization, led by Herzl, was established, and it began diplomatic negotiations for Jewish settlement. To Zionists, life in the diaspora was physically insecure and morally degrading. Herzl worked tirelessly toward the goal of a Jewish homeland until his early death at age forty-four in 1904. Increasingly, leadership of the Zionist movement shifted from the German Jews to the *Ostjuden,* Eastern European Jews.

Emigration to Palestine continued, and by 1907 about 70,000 Jews were living there. By 1917, just prior to the Balfour Declaration, these settlers had grown to about 90,000, and their educational, cultural, and economic efforts made the offer of a Jewish homeland reasonable and attractive. The historic opportunity for a true homeland came only after the First World War.

Robert G. Waite

References

Eloni, Yehuda. *Zionismus in Deutschland von den Anfängen bis 1914.* Gerlingen: Bleicher, 1987.

Laqueur, Walter. *A History of Zionism.* New York: Schocken, 1972.

Wistrich, Robert S. "The Clash of Ideologies in Jewish Vienna (1880–1918): The Strange Odyssey of Nathan Birnbaum." In *Leo Baeck Institute Year Book* 33. London: Secker & Warburg, 1988, 201–32.

See also BALFOUR DECLARATION

Index

Boldface indicates encyclopedia entry.

Pétain, Henri-Philippe, 27, 76–77, 222–223, 247, 257, 261, 274, 358, 443, 446, 511–512, 535, **553–554**, 716–718

Peter I. Karadjordjević, King of Serbia, 36, 101, **555**, 578, 637

Pflanzer-Baltin, Karl Freiherr von, **555**

phosgene. *See* chemical warfare

Picardy, battle of. *See* Race to the Sea

Piłsudski, Jósef Klemens, 213, **555–556**, 561–563, 646

pistols, **556–557**, 710. *See also* rifles; uniforms

Plehve, Paval, 227, 233

Plessen, Hans von, 95

Plumer, Viscount Herbert Charles Onslow, 478–479, 546–548, **557–558**, 761

Pohl, Hugo von, 302, **558–559**, 631

Poincaré, Raymond, 191, 222, 263, **559–560**, 728

Poland, 213, 219, 223, 333, 535, 543, 555–556, **560–563**, 720

    German offensive, **564–567**, 750–751

Polivanov, Aleksei Andreevich, 35, 37, **567–568**, 611

Portugal, **568–569**

Potiorek, Oskar, **569**, 637

Prezan, Constantine, **569–570**

Princip, Gavrilo, 128, 137, 269, **570–571**. *See also* Black Hand

prisoners of war, **571–574**, 589–592

Prittwitz und Gaffron, Max von, 230–232, **574**

propaganda, 498–499, **574–577**

Protopopov, Aleksander, 37

Przemysl. *See* East Galicia campaign; Eastern Front

Pulkowski, Erich, 75, **577**

Putnik, Radomir, 100, **577–578**, 637–638

Q

Qingdao (Tsingtao), siege of, 385, 395, **579–582**

Q-ships, 161, 449, **582–583**

R

Rabaul. *See* South Pacific

Race to the Sea, 115, **585–586**, 756–759

radio. *See* wireless communication

Radoslavov, Vasil, 149–151, 248, **586**

Rasputin, Grigorii Effimovich, 37, 507–508, **586–587**, 616, 664–665

Rathenau, Walther, 60, **587–588**

Rava Ruska, battle of. *See* East Galicia campaign

Rawlinson, Sir Henry, 43, **588–589**, 648–651, 681, 757–758

Red Cross, 571–574, **589–592**

Reichstag Peace Resolution of 1917, **592**

Rennenkampf, Pavel Karlovich, 228, 230–232, **592–593**, 624

Reuter, Ludwig von, **593–594**, 628–630

Ribot, Alexandre, 535, **594**

Richthofen, Manfred Albrecht von, 4, 9, 10, 22–23, 133, **595**

Rickenbacker, Edward Vernon, 4

rifles, **595–597**, 710, 711

Riga, battle of, 112, 346, 351–352, 358, **597–599**

Robertson, Sir William, 156–157, **599–600**

Romania, 39, 140, 147–149, 150, 249, 557, 569–570, 596, **600–602**, 691, 731. *See also* Balkan Front; Romanian campaign

Romanian campaign, 246, 601, **602–604**, 641, 691, 765

Rommel, Erwin, **604**

Ronarc'h, Pierre, **604–605**

Room 40, 193, 198, 332, 363, 458, **605–606**, 770. *See also* codebreaking

Roques, Pierre Auguste, **606**

Royal Air Force, 15, 313, 647, 694

Royal Flying Corps, 12, 15, 28, 313, 694

Royal Naval Air Service (RNAS), 13, 15, 17, 28

Rupprecht, Crown Prince of Bavaria, 33, 76–77, 78–79, 118, 410, 448, **606–607**. *See also* Artois, second battle of; Artois, third battle of; Belgium, invasion of

Russia, 730

    alliances, prewar, 38–41

    allied intervention in, 202–203, 385, **607–610**, 612–615

    army, 510, 557, 597, **610–612**, 711. *See also* Balkan Front; Brusilov offensive; Caucasus front; East Galicia campaign; East Galicia, counteroffensive; East Prussia campaign; Eastern Front; Kerensky offensive; Naroch, Lake, battle of; Persian front; Poland, German offensive; Riga, battle of

    civil war in, 202–203, 214–215, 406–408, 609–610, **612–615**, 617–618, 641, 699–700

    home front and revolutions of, 59, 131, 399, 408–409, 427, 452, 481, 483–484, 507–509, 587, 608–612, **615–618**, 659, 664, 672–673, 699–700

    navy, 129–132, **618–619**, 665, 667, 733–734, 736–738. *See also* Baltic naval operations; Black Sea, naval war in

    See also Baltic states; Black Sea, naval war in; Caucasus front

Ruzsky, Nikolai Vladimirovich, 207, **620**

S

Sablin, M.P., 131

Saint-Mihiel offensive, 44. *See also* Allied counteroffensive

Saint Quentin offensive, 443–444. *See also* Ludendorff offensives

Salandra, Antonio, 439, **621**, 652, 724

Salonika campaign, 196, 267, 320, 415, 486, **622–623**

Sambre, battle of. *See* Frontiers, battle of the

Samoa. *See* South Pacific

Samson, Charles Rumney, **623–624**

Samsonov, Aleksandr Vasilevich, 230–232, 593, **624**

Sarrail, Maurice, 103, 484, 622–623, **624–625**

Sayyid Muhammad 'Abdille Hassan, 3

Sazonov, Sergei Dmitrievich, 430, 532, **625–626**